PATTERNS IN PREHISTORY
HUMANKIND'S FIRST THREE MILLION YEARS

Fourth Edition

ROBERT J. WENKE
University of Washington

New York   Oxford
OXFORD UNIVERSITY PRESS
1999

For Ann and Chris Wenke

Oxford University Press

Oxford   New York
Athens   Auckland   Bangkok   Bogotá   Buenos Aires   Calcutta
Cape Town   Chennai   Dar es Salaam   Delhi   Florence   Hong Kong   Istanbul
Karachi   Kuala Lumpur   Madrid   Melbourne   Mexico City   Mumbai
Nairobi   Paris   São Paulo   Singapore   Taipei   Tokyo   Toronto   Warsaw

and associated companies in
Berlin   Ibadan

Copyright © 1980, 1984, 1990, 1999 by Oxford University Press

Published by Oxford University Press, Inc.,
198 Madison Avenue, New York, New York 10016
http://www.oup-usa.org

Oxford is a registered trademark of Oxford University Press

Library of Congress-in-Publication Data

Wenke, Robert J.
    Patterns in prehistory : humankind's first three million years /
Robert J. Wenke. — 4th ed.
        p.   cm.
    Includes bibliographical references and index.
    ISBN 0-19-508572-8 (paper)
    1. Man, Prehistoric.   2. Archaeology.   I. Title.
GN740.W46   1996
573.3—dc20   95-43456
                                                CIP

9 8 7 6 5 4 3 2 1

Printed in the United States of America
on acid-free paper

CONTENTS

PREFACE

"Anyone informed that the universe is expanding and contracting in pulsations of eight billion years has a right to ask, 'What's in it for me?'"

Peter De Vries[1]

In this book the reader is invited to stroll through three million years of human history while considering various questions, including some much like that posed above by novelist Peter De Vries: Specifically, what can anyone possibly learn from an extended contemplation of three million years' accumulation of our ancestors' stone tools, broken pots, and other garbage (and the bits and pieces of the bones of our ancestors themselves), and what can one do with that knowledge?

Or, to express this question in more general terms, our human ancestors have been living and dying on this planet for millions of years, generation after countless generation, creating an amazing diversity of societies, technologies, and cultures: What, if any, relevance, do the remains of these past cultures have for any or all of us, and what does this long history *mean*?

Such cosmic questions about the nature and meaning of the human past have a long history, but they have elicited few compelling answers. The great British biologist J. B. S. Haldane addressed a similar question when he was asked by a group of theologians what his many years of studying the biological world had taught him about the attributes of God: he sardonically replied that God must have "an inordinate fondness for beetles"—given the vast numbers of species of beetles Haldane had encountered in his research.

Even if we limit ourselves to the non-theological implications of our past, the lessons and meaning of our long history involve many difficult questions. This book is about these questions and the evidence relevant to them. Why, for example, did our ancestors of several million years ago make that first critical break with our primate relatives by habitually walking upright? Why did our ancestors then begin evolving ever greater brain size while our primate relatives, such as the chimpanzee, and all other animals seem to have retained relatively tiny brain-to-body size ratios? Which of all the many species of primates who have lived in the past three million years are our genetic ancestors? Why, after humans had lived for more than two million years as simple hunter-foragers, did some of our ancestors "suddenly" become farmers about

iv

10,000 years ago, and not just in the Old World but "independently" in the New World as well and at about the same time? Why were all ancient civilizations strictly organized in terms of social classes based on inherited privilege and exploitation of the many by the few, instead of according to the democratic ideals espoused by many philosophers over the millennia? Why does warfare seem to have been so common in history when there are such apparent advantages to cooperation and peace? Why did large cities appear in ancient civilizations in Mexico, China, Pakistan, Mesopotamia, and elsewhere but not at the same time in aboriginal Australia, northwestern Europe, western North America, Hawaii and many other places? Why did people all over the ancient world devote so much of their time and energy to building huge pyramids and other "wasteful" monuments and, in general, passively accept their gross exploitation by elites? Do economic forces really "drive" history, as some Marxists have argued, so that forms of religions and governments are merely by-products of these basic economic dynamics, or do great ideas and powerful individuals determine the course of history? Does "the past" really exist in some analyzable form and sense, or is what we call the past just our personal, evanescent, and unanalyzable imaginings about something that does not exist? Does the past tell us anything of interest about where we are going, about our future, and do we have any control over our future, or are we just "leaves on the stream" of time and circumstance?

This edition of *Patterns in Prehistory*, like its three predecessors, is an attempt to address these and many other questions by reducing the human past to quintessential themes and patterns. The focus of this book is the four great transformations in the history of our genus: (1) the evolution of "culture" itself, in the form of the initial use of human social behaviors, cognitive abilities, and tools of our ape-like ancestors, as they evolved in the bloody struggle of life on the African savannas; (2) the first appearance of "us," *Homo sapiens*, out of the intrepid Ice Age human hunter-foragers who penetrated the world's frontiers, from Australia to the Arctic; (3) the evolution of agriculture, in the form of the small-time farmers of a few thousand years ago, who brought farming and the village way of life to most of the world; and (4) the first appearances of cultural and social "complexity," in the form of the great civilizations of antiquity.

The reader is forewarned that the many questions asked here about the nature of these four great transformations and about the meaning of our past and the nature of human existence cannot be definitively answered with the available evidence and ideas reviewed in this book. The only solid data we have with which to address many of them are the countless stone tools, bones, potsherds, ruined hovels, and other pitiful remnants of three million years of human life on this planet, and our ideas about the nature of the dynamics of history are all rather primitive. But it is the nature of science and philosophy to ask seemingly difficult questions whose answers are uncertain, and many important questions about our past are not entirely beyond empirical analysis.

Perhaps the most difficult thing in analyzing these transformations in our past and in answering these questions is to devise a coherent *theory* of archaeology and the study of world prehistory. Some contemporary archaeologists, for example, reject the "scientific" perspective adopted in this book. As is discussed in the first chapter, these archaeologists argue that archaeology is not the science of what happened in the past so much as it is the study of a past we ourselves create, in that we necessarily see reflections of our own beliefs and values in the bones and stones of our past. Many of these archaeologists also argue that Western "science" is fundamentally inappropriate for interpreting the human past. I have tried to characterize and illustrate this theoretical perspective fairly in this book, and I explore the reasons why some archaeologists reject the kinds of analyses that constitute most of *Patterns in Prehistory*.

I remain convinced, however, that there is much we can know about our past through the application of traditional scientific methods and logic, and this book reflects that belief in empiricism and positivism. There is reason to believe that these great transformations of our past—from bipedalism, to worldwide radiation, to agriculture, to civilization—*were* the result of real, knowable factors and forces. Our efforts to learn what those forces and factors were may be tainted by our biases, corrupted by our personal sociopolitical contexts, but I think there are aspects of these kinds of analyses that are interesting and useful, and that get beyond the limitations of personal biases and idiosyncrasies.

In addition to presenting a coherent perspective on world prehistory, my objective in this book is to present a picture of contemporary archaeology: how it is done, who does it, and what professional archaeologists think about their discipline. As a result, this book includes excursions into the semantic thickets of contemporary debates in archaeological theory that may strike some undergraduate readers as obscure. Sixteen years ago, when I committed the first edition of this book to the printers, archaeology was "political" only in a minor sense. Today, however, many archaeologists see archaeology as inextricably linked to imperialism, colonialism, racism, sexism, and other perceived evils in our highly politicized culture. I address some of these issues, but the focus of this book is on analyses of cultural change, not the sociopolitical context of these analyses. Here, too, some contemporary archaeologists believe that one cannot extricate any analysis of culture change from the sociopolitical context of the archaeological evidence and of the archaeologist himself. I disagree.

The earlier editions of this book have been read by a gratifying number of people outside universities, but *Patterns in Prehistory* is designed primarily as a text for colleges courses. To make this book appropriate for a university class, I have had to jettison some of the "romance of archaeology" one might find in more general books. Most non-archaeologists—students included—are more interested, for example, in the many wonderful things found in King Tutankhamun's tomb than in a long social-science analysis of the evolution of the bureaucratic apparatus and other features of the state that Tutankhamun briefly ruled. To analyze the past, however, one must look beyond the *things*, the material remains of the past, and consider the kinds of difficult questions posed above about the dynamics and meaning of the past—and much of this book is about these difficult questions and these dynamics and meanings.

Patterns in Prehistory contains various excursions into Western intellectual history, literature, aesthetics, philosophy, and other subjects, on the premise that this book should help make a contribution to the undergraduate student's liberal education. I remain convinced that to see oneself in relation to the great antiquity of humankind is an indispensable part of any liberal education, especially for college students, whether they be potential engineers, venture capitalists, mortuary scientists, theologians, etc. Perhaps, especially if they are engineers or theologians. All academicians feel this way about their subjects, of course, and I have no illusions that the study of world prehistory will eradicate poverty or lead to world peace. Nonetheless, I think that the dynamics of the human past, which have shaped us and our cultures, should be topics of interest and be known to everyone. That they are not is indicated by much evidence: a 1982 Gallup Poll, for example, found that 44 percent of the population of the United States rejected the idea of an evolutionary origin for the human species.[2] This book is an attempt to provide an evolutionary perspective on our past and to relate that perspective to the broad spectrum of human knowledge. Long after most students have forgotten the discussions of the minutiae of bones and stones that constitute most of this book, I hope they retain an interest in the general processes of evolution that explain so much about our biological origins, and in the processes that have determined our cultures. Historian G. R. Elton said, "An individual experience . . . is always limited and commonly distorted by prejudice and self-interest: what men and women need is an enlarged experience against which to measure the effects of those disadvantages. . . . History provides the laboratory in which human experience is analyzed, distilled, and bottled for use."[3] This book is an attempt to provide such a context, in which the whole span of the human past can be examined.

The focus of this book is primarily the *origins* of culture, agriculture, and civilizations, and thus some subjects, time periods, and geographical areas are given much more consideration than others. The topic of the origins of complex societies takes up fully two-thirds of this book, in part because I have spent twenty-five years contemplating this problem and pursuing the archaeological evidence relevant to it in Iran, Egypt, Mexico, Turkey, Italy, and elsewhere. And, also, because I believe that the problem of the origins of complex societies is one of the most important topics of historical analysis. As a result, not all areas and cultures of the world are given equal coverage (for a broader survey of world prehistory, the reader is referred to Brian Fagan's comprehensive *People of the Earth, Eighth Edition*[4]). Instead, this book is basically a set of essays on selected cultural developments, and only the archaeological evidence most directly relevant to them is reviewed in detail. This has meant that the culture history of many important and interesting areas of the world, including pre-Roman Europe, Australia, Polynesia, sub-Saharan Africa, and various other places, is unfortunately, reviewed only briefly here.

Many people have helped me with this edition of *Patterns*. Professors David Grove, Richard Pearson, Gregory Possehl, Stevan Harrell, and Bernard Knapp gave me much good advice—not all of which I took. It is formulaic to say that none of these people can in any way be held responsible for errors in this book, but in this case it is certainly true, as I know that each of these people would disagree with some elements in this book.

I am particularly grateful to Gioia Stevens, Karen Shapiro, Philip Laughlin, and Layla Voll, my editors at Oxford University Press, for their patience, assistance, and encouragement. Stacey Caminos of Oxford was very helpful in final editing and production of this book.

For twenty years, students in a variety of courses at the University of Washington have listened to me lecture on the topics in this book, and I appreciate not only their patience and interest but also their many questions and comments that have helped shape *Patterns*.

To many non-archaeologists, archaeology sounds as if it is the most exciting work one could do, and sometimes it is. But it's usually a lot of bloody hard labor as well, and I've tried to acknowledge as many as I could of the thousands of archaeologists who have gone out and done the fieldwork on which surveys such as this are based. I've also tried to give them a chance to speak for themselves, by quoting them at length.

I would also like to thank Maurice and Lois Schwartz for their gracious help in supporting my initial fieldwork in Egypt, the National Science Foundation, the National Endowment for the Humanities, Roxie Walker and the Bioanthropology Foundation, the University of Washington Graduate School Research Fund, and the National Geographic Society for funding my own research on various topics considered in this book. My discussions of matters archaeological and other with many different people have helped shape this edition, and although I cannot thank them all, I would like to mention Kathleen Pyne, Paul Johnson, Nicholas Pyne Johnson, Douglas Brewer, Mary Ellen Lane, Colin Davies, Julia Lane Davies, Emily Teeter, Maria Casini, Kim Honor, Joy McCorriston, and Kevin Johnston. Shireen al-Fostati generously assisted in the preparation of all previous editions of this book, and her contributions to the first three chapters of this edition were crucial. Alas, she did not live to see her assistance realized in the publication of this edition.

Most of all I thank Dr. Nanette M. Pyne, for helping me write and edit all four editions of this book, and for everything else. Because of her, *Albo lapillo notare diem*, indeed.

NOTES

1. In his amusing novel, *The Glory of the Hummingbird, 1976.* New York: Popular Library.

2. Cited in Spuhler, 1985. "Anthropology, Evolution, and 'Scientific Creationism.'" *Annual Review of Anthropology* 14:103–33.

3. From his Cook lectures, delivered at the Law School of the University of Michigan at Ann Arbor, April 1990. Also see his *Return to Essentials: Some Reflections on the Present State of Historical Study.* New York: Cambridge University Press, 1991.

4. *People of the Earth*, 8th ed. New York: HarperCollins, 1995

1

PREHISTORY, HISTORY, AND ARCHAEOLOGY

History is philosophy teaching by examples.
Dionysius of Halicarnassus (c. 40 B.C.)

History is bunk.
Henry Ford

The archaeologist-adventurers of film and fiction never seem to have any doubts about what they are looking for or why they want it. "It" is usually something like a curse-protected pharaoh's tomb treasures, or the Golden City of the Inkas, or the biblical Ark of the Covenant, but whatever the object, it is always something intrinsically interesting and protected by enough snakes, traps, or villains to require a romantic hero for its discovery.

In this prosaic age it will come as no surprise to the reader that contemporary archaeology differs considerably from these fictional notions about it. But the origins of archaeology and the study of world prehistory are partly in the exploits of people who were not entirely unlike their fictional image. In the early 1800s, for example, the Italian adventurer Giovanni Belzoni looted dozens of ancient Egyptian tombs in Thebes (near modern Luxor) and sold their riches to European museums. Belzoni crept and crawled through miles of tunnels in the stinking, dusty air of these crypts, smashing hundreds of mummies into powder as he went:

> [Al]though, fortunately I am destitute of the sense of smelling, I could taste that the mummies were rather unpleasant to swallow. After the exertion of entering into such a place, through a passage of . . . perhaps six hundred yards, nearly overcome, I sought a resting place . . . but when my weight bore on the body of an Egyptian, it crushed like a band-box. . . . I sank altogether among the broken mummies, with a crash of bones, rags, and wooden cases . . . every step I took I crushed a mummy . . . I could not pass without putting my face in contact with that of some decayed Egyptian; but as the passage inclined downwards, my own weight helped me on: however, I could not avoid being covered with bones, legs, arms, and heads roiling from above. . . . The purpose of my researches was to rob the Egyptians of their papyri.[1]

Even the more scholarly of the early archaeologists, if not so candid as Belzoni about their larcenous intent, at least had a clear simple vision of what it was they were after and a rather romantic reason for their quest. In 1876, for example, the German aristocrat Heinrich Schliemann, his imagination fired by his schoolboy readings of Homer (in the original Greek), ravaged the archaeological site of Hissarlik, in western Turkey, looking for the home of the heroes of the Trojan War, as chronicled in *The Iliad*. Schliemann's notebooks show that he made careful records of his finds and that he even had a primitive sense of the importance of proper methods of archaeological excavations. He found gold masks affixed to decayed bodies in one area of the great mound at Hissarlik and concluded that these were the Trojan warriors. When he died, many years later, he was still happily ignorant of the fact that what he had thought were the remains of Troy were actually of an altogether different era, and that he had hacked right through the settlement occupied during the presumed period of the Trojan War.

The archaeology of today is significantly different from that of these nineteenth-century practitioners. If a professional archaeologist today were to excavate, for example, the parts of Troy that Schliemann left, she or he would be expected to use a lot of complicated high-technology equipment (discussed in chapter 2) for both excavations and analyses; a complete map would be made of the areas to be excavated, so that everything found could be located to exact three-dimensional coordinates; and the actual excavations would require many more years than Schliemann spent, so that technical specialists could analyze pottery, animal and plant remains, architecture, and every other kind of find.

But the most profound difference between the archaeology of Belzoni's and Schliemann's times and that of the present is in the *objectives* of the research: almost all early archaeologists were looking for specific *things* (Figure 1.1) and had little sense of the importance of their finds except as curious and valuable relics of bygone ages; most contemporary archaeologists, on the other hand, try to look beyond the objects they find to seek a more profound understanding of the past—and of ourselves in relation to the past.

WHAT ARE ARCHAEOLOGISTS LOOKING FOR? (THE MEANING OF THE PAST)

> *Archaeology is about Facts; if you want the Truth,*
> *go next-door to the Philosophy Department!*
>
> Professor Indiana Jones (dialogue from the film *Indiana Jones*)[2]

Most archaeologists spend years gathering small bits of stone, bone, and pottery that would not arrest the attention of a museum-goer for more than a few seconds; they then spend much of the rest of their lives in Hamlet-like reflection, asking themselves an endless and largely unanswered series of questions, such as: "What does all this stuff mean?" "What do these things tell me about what happened in the past and why it happened?" "What is the point of investigating the past?" "What can I hope to

FIGURE 1.1   In the eighteenth and nineteenth centuries, archaeology was often more like organized looting of antiquities than scientific research. Here, workmen at a site near Les Eyzies, France, destroy a Paleolithic site while looking for nicely fashioned stone tools.

know about the people who made these things?" "Are there causal factors that we can identify that explain the course and nature of human history?" "Does the past have any relevance for our own lives?" "What does the past *mean?*"

This concern with the meaning of the past is one of the most difficult concepts for the non-archaeologist to understand about the discipline—and for many people it shatters an illusion that archaeology is just the happy pursuit of interesting relics in exotic locales. Experience has taught most archaeologists that the non-archaeologist has little patience for the convoluted intricate analyses archaeologists go through when arguing with each other about what the past means. Most non-archaeologists, unsurprisingly, would be much more interested in, for example, viewing the gold masks that Schliemann found at Troy than in listening to professional archaeologists debate the inferred socioeconomic and political organization of the first millennium B.C. town at Tepe Hissarlik, where these masks were found.

Yet one cannot comprehend what contemporary archaeology—or this book—is all about until one understands this search, beyond the artifacts, for patterns and meaning in the past. Most archaeologists are not just trying to answer specific questions, such as what our hominid ancestors first used stone tools for, or why the Neanderthals disappeared, or how the ancient Egyptians built pyramids. In every archaeological excavation or research project many specific questions such as these are at issue, but the context of this research often involves the more abstract goals of trying to understand the factors that have determined the course of human history and the nature of our cultures, and thus not only to see patterns in the past but to understand why those patterns appeared—and to explain in some sense the great variability in the world's long history of cultures.

It may seem odd that archaeologists even consider the possibility that something apparently so chaotic as human history may have some underlying pattern or meaning or explanation, but scholars throughout the ages have sought just such an explanation. The questions they have asked in this regard are many, difficult, and important for understanding ourselves and humanity: Is there some factor, for example, that explains why we seem to have evolved in the direction of ever greater brain size while our primate relatives, such as the chimpanzee, and all other animals seem to have retained relatively tiny brain-to-body size ratios? Why, after humans had lived for about two million years as simple hunter-foragers, did some of our ancestors "suddenly" become farmers about 10,000 years ago, and not just in the Old World but "independently" in the New World as well and at about the same time? Why were all ancient civilizations strictly organized in terms of social classes instead of according to the democratic ideals espoused by many philosophers over the millennia? Why does warfare seem to have been so common in history when there are such apparent advantages to cooperation and peace? Why did large cities appear in ancient civilizations in Mexico, China, Pakistan, Mesopotamia, and elsewhere but not in aboriginal Australia, North America, or Hawaii? Does the archaeological record of the world indicate that human "races" differ in innate abilities and that cultures vary in their "accomplishments"? Do economic forces really "drive" history, as Karl Marx argued,[3] so that forms of religions and governments are merely by-products of these basic economic dynamics, or do great ideas and powerful individuals *decide* the course of history? Does "the past" really exist in some analyzable form and sense, or is what we call the past just our evanescent and unanalyzable imaginings about something that does not exist? Does the past tell us anything of interest about where we are going, about our future, and do we have any control over our future, or are we just "leaves on the stream" of time and circumstance?

Libraries around the world are filled with books that represent several millennia of attempts to answer these and related questions. There are many theories of history, but none has been shown to be a powerful explanation of all of the complexity of the human past. Reasonable people might suspect that, if these questions about the meaning and explanation of the past have not yielded powerful answers in all these millennia of study, then perhaps we are asking the wrong questions or that the questions we are asking have no real answers. But many archaeologists have never been convinced by this apparent futility. This book, in fact, is largely an attempt to chronicle part of the world's past and then review attempts to answer these many questions about the meaning of the past.

The very idea that we can aspire to understand and explain why history has turned out the way it has is one of the most hotly debated and complex issues in contemporary archaeology. British archaeologists Michael Shanks and Christopher Tilley, for example, argue that the human past can never be analyzed in terms of an empirical science that "explains" history, in the sense of answering in a scientific fashion the kinds of questions posed above about *why* history has turned out the way it has.[4] They argue that the material remains of the past are just another "text," and thus, like any novel, the past can be understood differently by different people; and that every "reader" of every text, including the archaeologist who reads the archaeological record, is so bound by his or her own cultural biases and forms that there can be no such thing as an objective or definitive understanding of the past (Figure 1.2).

Other scholars argue that the past can be analyzed scientifically and that with the future development of powerful theories, archaeology can be as much a science as geology, paleontology, or biology.[5]

Although we shall return to these issues with numbing frequency in this book (and find few conclusive answers), one thing seems clear—the primary problem in answering questions about the meaning of the past is not a lack of evidence. All over the world, museum shelves groan under the weight of ceramic pots, stone tools, and the broken skulls of our ancestors. Archaeologists have excavated everything from the first known human camps of two million years ago to 1920s-era Manhattan; and every year, archaeologists in their thousands spread out across the globe to excavate more remains of the past and then inflict the results of their research on their colleagues and the world in the form of hundreds of thousands of books, articles, and lectures.

In the rest of this book, I will review thousands of these studies, testing the reader's patience with seemingly innumerable names for archaeological objects, methods, and chronologies, but before wading into this sea of facts and figures, the reader should

FIGURE 1.2   This sixteenth-century engraving of Florida Indians exemplifies ethnocentrism, or interpreting other cultures in one's own terms. The four women on the right are highly reminiscent of Italian Renaissance renderings of Venus and the Three Muses. Many European scholars of the last three centuries were ethnocentric in their analyses of ancient and non-European cultures—most of which they assumed had incompletely evolved to the high level of European civilization.

join archaeologists in musing on the point of all this sifting through the garbage of the past. These are complex issues, and to begin to analyze them it is necessary to consider the basic logical structure of archaeology as it traditionally has been practiced and some examples of archaeological analyses.

THE GOALS AND OBJECTIVES OF ARCHAEOLOGY I: ARCHAEOLOGY AS THE RECONSTRUCTION OF EXTINCT CULTURES AND THEIR HISTORIES

The past is a different country.
They do things differently there.

L. P. Hartley[6]

Whether one views the past and the world's archaeological record as the product of a meaningless jumble of accidental events and concatenations of unrelated human decisions, or as an explainable, even predictable developmental pattern, to understand the past most scholars begin by trying to reconstruct and describe it.

Reconstructions of the past are usually based on the principle known to the Romans as *ex ungue leonem*, literally, "from the claw, the lion," or the notion that from a part we can know the whole through the processes of analogy and inference. If one looks closely, for example, at the dinosaurs on display in various museums one can see that some of them comprise a very small amount of fossilized bone and a very much greater amount of plastic that has been hopefully inserted in place of the missing parts. And as scholars find new fossils, it is quite common, even today after centuries of research, for them to change the dinosaur reconstructions on exhibit to reflect new ideas about the arrangements of bones.

When we look at attempts to reconstruct entire cultures, not just bones, the principles are the same as in dinosaur reconstructions: we use the preserved parts to infer some of the missing elements based on our knowledge or speculations about the whole. In some situations the inferences one must make seem so obviously accurate and the evidence available seems so comprehensive that our interpretations seem particularly compelling. Archaeologists, for example, have carefully studied the remains found in the tomb of Egypt's Tutankhamun (Figures 1.3 and 1.4), and through a process of scientific analysis and inference we seemingly can know a lot about this pharaoh and his culture. Studies of his teeth,[7] for example, indicate his genetic relationship to his relatives, some of whose mummified bodies have also been found; analyses of the food and wine with which his tomb was supplied appear to reflect both what he ate in this life and apparently hoped to eat in the next; analyses of the chariots, furniture, and jewelry reflect the arts and crafts of his age; and studies of the inscriptions on his tomb's walls and in contemporary documents offer descriptions of his religious beliefs and life-history.

What makes reconstructions such as that of Tutankhamun's life and times so vivid is not just the impressive preservation of objects, it is that by analogy with our own lives we seem to understand so much about him. Most people of our own era,

FIGURE 1.3   The contents of Tutankhamun's tomb provided a vivid picture of many aspects of ancient Egyptian
life.

for example, still commit their dead to the earth with religious invocations offered in
hope of some future resurrection. Even the thoughtful selection, in Tut's tomb, of
dry and sweet wines from an impressive diversity of vineyards and vintages, all carefully labeled by estate, year, and chief vintner, seems so utterly human and part of
the same fabric as our own lives.[8]

Reconstructions such as these, by means of analogy and inference based on our
own lives and knowledge of history, offer satisfying accounts of the past in terms of
our own experiences, and for many people they constitute all or most of what we can
hope to learn about the past. And for many people the "pleasures of ruins" they experience when they read about these reconstructions and interpretations require no
great theoretical justification. Dull, indeed, would be the person insensitive to such
pleasures. We do not know, and can never know, what really went on in Tutankhamun's mind, but by considering his tomb contents most of us think we can
know a lot about his diet, the technology of his times, his place in the royal bureaucracy, etc.

FIGURE 1.4   The entrance to the "Treasury" of Pharaoh Tutankhamun's tomb. The cloaked statue is a representation of Anubis, Lord of the West.

But are our analyses necessarily limited to these speculative reconstructions of Tutankhamun's life and times, or can we go further in attempting to understand Tutankhamun? We might, for example, consider him to have been just one expression of the class-based state societies that existed all over the ancient world. Rich ancient tombs like Tutankhamun's have been found in China, Peru, Mexico, Iraq, and many other places. Thus Tutankhamun is part of a historical pattern in which all of the more complex "civilizations" of antiquity and today have been and continue to be organized on the basis of wealth and social classes. And thus, Tutankhamun brings us back to the most basic and important questions of historical analysis, such as, for example: Why did these societies, Old and New World alike, all evolve social systems based on inherited privilege and wealth, in which the great mass of humanity labored mainly for the benefit of a small elite class?

We shall consider that question at length in chapter 7. It is sufficient here simply to note that once one has "reconstructed" the past of an individual like Tutankhamun, one can lift one's view to larger and more abstract questions.

And these questions apply to all of our past, not just to the comparatively newly dead, such as Tutankhamun. Henri de Lumley's analysis of the 300,000-year-old remains of human occupation in Lazaret Cave in France, for example, manages to link us to these very ancient ancestors through persuasive inferences. By measuring the location of every artifact and bit of bone, de Lumley was able to argue quite convincingly that the cave's occupants had piled up kelp (inferred from the remains of snails that live only on kelp) and covered it over with bear skins (inferred from the position of the claws) to form a comfortable bed in a shelter in this cave. By studying the stone tools and other debris, de Lumley could estimate the number of people in the cave, their diet, the seasons of the year in which they visited the cave, and so on.

But, as we shall see in chapter 4, this analysis of Lazaret raises as many questions as it answers. Were these ancient French our ancestors, or were they, as many scholars now believe, a form of human driven into extinction by our own ancestors as they migrated from Africa a hundred thousand years later? And why did some human groups become extinct and others "carry the torch" of the human line, to eventuate in ourselves?

By asking these grand questions about the past we need not sacrifice the pleasures and rewards of simply trying to reconstruct past times and cultures and their peoples' lives—people for whom we can feel a great deal of kinship and even sympathy. But even reconstructions of cultures that we know a great deal about raise important questions about archaeological inferences and about the "point" of such reconstructions. On about August 24, A.D. 79, for example, a group of people in an Italian coastal town concluded a funeral service for a friend by sitting down to a banquet. We can only wonder about what was said at the meal, but we know what food they ate, how they were dressed, and where they sat, because this town was Pompeii, and at some point in the banquet, poison gases from the eruption of the volcano of Vesuvius killed them all. They and their fellow citizens, and their neighbors in Herculaneum, were preserved in the midst of their daily activities. A half-cooked suckling pig, bread, and other foods were found in ovens; money was left near half-eaten meals in restaurants; wax tablets and papyri lay on library tables; bodies of townspeople were found curled over the children they were trying to protect; and in one case a woman's skeleton was found scattered over the floor of a room filled with volcanic ash, near the intact skeleton of a dog chained to a stake—suggesting that the dog slowly starved and eventually ate the body of its mistress.[9]

Written language aids greatly in "fleshing out" cultural reconstructions. Pompeii's and Herculaneum's daily life were described in great detail in surviving documents; we even have graffiti on toilet walls describing the charms of particular prostitutes and other comments common to such venues. In fact, Pompeii's and Herculaneum's destruction were recorded by people who took boats out to sea to watch it.

Whether an archaeologist is trying to reconstruct Pompeii or a two-million-year-old base camp of early hominids in Africa, the intention is the same: just as an ethnographer describes the daily life of the people he or she lives with and is studying, an archaeologist, substituting analogy and inference for direct observation, uses ancient objects to reconstruct as much as possible about the diet, technology, residences, burial practices, beliefs—in short, the lifeways and cultures—of ancient peoples.

Compared to the riot of full life evident to the ethnographer, even analyses of towns like Pompeii may seem a pale and cold investigation into the dry stalks and stems of dead cultures. But the last several decades have seen major advances in the techniques of cultural reconstructionism (reviewed in chapter 2). An impressive array of electron microscopes, satellite imagery, chemical analyses, elaborate mathematical models, sophisticated computers, and other techniques are available to help the archaeologist make ever more plausible inferences about the past.

But despite these many improvements, cultural reconstructions often include a large measure of speculation, particularly when dealing with extremely ancient societies, whose artifacts and lifeways may have no historical analogs and thus may require even more than the liberal amounts of imagination that inferences about more recent societies involve. And the possibilities for cultural reconstructions are essentially infinite: one can always excavate another site and fill in one more tiny bit of knowledge. Once the thrill of discovery has worn off, most archaeologists begin to wonder just how important it is to know, for example, whether this or that group ate more salmon than reindeer, or vice versa.

And of course there is really no way ever to confirm—to be certain—about one's reconstructions. The reconstruction of the dog at Herculaneum eating the body of his mistress may seem compelling, but one can imagine alternative interpretations; and reconstructions of less well-preserved and earlier sites are much less persuasive than those concocted about the living dead of Pompeii and Herculaneum. In short, one can make up extremely convincing stories about what happened at some ancient place, or what some ancient artifacts were used for, but we'll never be able to confirm such inferences conclusively—at least not in the way an astronomer's understanding of celestial mechanics is confirmed by exact prediction of eclipses.

In this same context consider, for example, the remains of crocodiles we found while excavating in Egypt in 1981.[10] We discovered that one area that had been a few hundred meters from the shoreline of a lake in the late fifth millennium B.C. contained many crocodile bones but no crocodile skulls or teeth. Evidence indicated that this area was probably the site of a temporary camp, occupied in spring and fall, where people came to fish and hunt migratory birds. One evening, after a long day's field work, and inspired by one, perhaps two, "Stella" beers, we evolved the plausible notion that the ancient Egyptians were hunting these crocodiles for some unspeakable culinary purpose and, to aid in transporting the "edible" parts of their kills back to camp, they gutted the animals, cut off their heads and discarded them to rot on the shore, and then brought the rest of the carcass back to the site. Therefore, we conjectured, we had found no head bones in our excavations, just cut-up body bones.

Now, we could go back and "test" this hypothesis by excavating other sites to see if the same pattern is found elsewhere on the lake shore, or by checking the crocodile body bones carefully for cut marks, or in any number of other plausible ways. We could also generalize this specific idea and test some hypotheses about general cultural processes, such as the notion that hunters and gatherers tended to transport the shortest distance those animal parts with the least meat on them. Or we could generalize still further and test the notion that people tend to avoid work as much as possible. But what exactly would we have accomplished?

A crucial problem with cultural reconstructions such as these is *equifinality:* one can imagine many different alternative explanations for our finding few crocodile head parts at this site, and very different factors and combinations of factors could produce extremely similar archaeological records; and in the end all that one could hope to do is show that one hypothesis is more probable than the others. And such hypotheses would really only be particularly interesting in the context of some theory about ancient cultures—some set of generalized principles, which at present we do not have, about the factors that determine the course of cultures in general, including our rag-tag bunch of ancient Egyptian crocodile hunters.

In sum, the archaeological reconstruction of ancient cultures is much like what any perceptive person does while walking through an archaeological museum: one looks at ancient pots, stone tools, etc., and is irresistibly drawn into musing on how they were used and the nature of the people who used them. Most museums help the viewer in these cultural reconstructions by displaying dioramas, scale replicas of Native American villages, for example, and other reconstructions of scenes of daily life in extinct societies.

Thus, archaeological reconstructions of ancient cultures are probably as close to that staple of science fiction, "time-travel," as humans are likely to achieve, and it is the powerful impulse to travel in time, at least cerebrally, that motivates many archaeologists. An archaeologist, given *one and only one* such time-travel opportunity, would probably have a difficult time choosing among so many interesting times and places. One could go, for example, to Africa's Olduvai Gorge about 1.7 million years ago to see how our early hominid ancestors made a living (a problem to which much of chapter 3 is devoted); or to Palestine about 90,000 years ago, to see if Neanderthals and people physically like ourselves really did live at the same time (see chapter 4); or to Egypt to determine once and for all how the pyramids were built (chapter 9); or to Pakistan's Indus Valley 4,000 years ago to learn what is contained in the thousands of Harappan written documents—one of the world's undeciphered languages (chapter 10); or perhaps to London of the later nineteenth century, just to chat with Charles Darwin or Karl Marx or another of the founding fathers of modern historical sciences.

But the important point here is that even if one could go back in time and study an extinct culture as its people lived it, one is still faced with the limits of cultural reconstruction and left with great questions of *why*—why was that culture of that form, and how did it evolve from previous human adaptations?

TIME, CAUSALITY, AND CULTURE HISTORY

> *Very few things happen at the right time and the rest do not happen at all. The conscientious historian will correct these defects.*
>
> (attributed to Mark Twain, Herodotus, and others)

Attempts to reconstruct the past may be "static" in the sense that in studying the long-dead citizens of Pompeii we may be interested only in how they lived on the day they were all killed. But most attempts to analyze the past involve some sense of *sequence*, usually in the form of cultural changes over time. Reconstructing ancient cultures and putting them into chronological sequences are usually complementary parts of any archaeological research project.

For many years archaeology was regarded—and still is in some academic circles, in Europe especially—as a method for reconstructing the histories of cultures, particularly extinct cultures that left no, or only fragmentary, written records. People who view archaeology primarily in this light see no essential difference between an archaeologist and a traditional historiographer, except in the materials each works with. Just as a historian may chronicle the cultural succession from, for example, the Aegean world from fifth-century B.C. Athens to the end of the Roman Republic based on written sources, an archaeologist can reconstruct and describe, for example, the different and successive cultures that existed in northern Europe in the periods before written languages were used there on the basis of their tools and other artifacts.

Like most people, archaeologists are fascinated with historical "firsts." Some of the most intense debates now going on in the profession concern problems of time, such as when the first *Homo sapiens* appeared, when the first people arrived in the New World, and when agriculture was first practiced. But usually these events are seen as outcomes of prior events and determinants. This sense of time as infinitely stretching behind and ahead of us, and ourselves in its stream, is very ancient, but a true recognition of the scale of the past is relatively recent. Today nearly every educated person knows and accepts that our human ancestry extends back millions of years and that our civilizations have slowly evolved over thousands of years. But this sense of our place in time is really quite new. The recognition—or at least the widespread acceptance—of the idea that we and our world have been here for millions of years is only about a century old. Until the nineteenth century, most Western people accepted the biblical implication that the world was about 6,000 years old and that almost from the very beginning our ancestors had lived in towns, engaged in agriculture, and organized themselves in great states and empires. Many scholars searched the Scriptures for clues to the date of Creation. James Ussher (A.D. 1581–1656) computed the ages of Old Testament figures and their children to date the Great Flood to 2349 B.C. and the creation of the world to precisely 4004 B.C. Dr.

John Lightfoot (A.D. 1828–1889), vice chancellor of Cambridge University, pored over the Old Testament and concluded that the universe was created in 3928 B.C., on September 12, at the civilized hour of nine o'clock in the morning, and that God had rested the following Saturday (Sabbath) morning.

But even by Dr. Lightfoot's day, many people had concluded that the world must be hundreds of thousands of years old or older. Nineteenth-century excavations deep below the ground levels of many European cities had revealed the bones of animals long extinct, such as mammoths and cave bears—and amidst many of these bones were stone tools. By the early twentieth century the great antiquity of humankind was evident, and today almost all knowledgeable scientists accept that our hominid, tool-using ancestors go back millions of years.

But specifically where and when did our ancestors live? Eventually these questions coalesced into the goal of locating every prehistoric culture in time and space and arranging all of them, as Lewis Binford expressed it, "in a way which accurately reveals their generic affinities."[11]

Culture histories are fairly easy and accurate when one deals with, say, the Roman Empire, where there are written records and the evidence of thousands of cities. But how do you write culture histories of prehistoric people who left no written records and of whom we have little more than the occasional skeleton and crude flint tools?

The main method of culture history is to make large collections of artifacts (the stone tools, pots, and everything else made or deposited by people) from each site (their houses, graves, or workplaces) and then make a lot of brave inferences about the cultural relationships among the people who made these pots, stone tools, or whatever.

Modern chemical dating techniques (reviewed in chapter 2) have helped arrange collections of artifacts in time, but much culture history has been done on simple comparisons of artifacts. My associates and I, for example, once walked the plains of southwestern Iran for five months, collecting bags of broken pottery from the thousands of ancient villages and towns to be found there. Most of these old settlements are now just mounds of decomposed mud bricks and garbage and are littered with thousands of scraps of broken pottery and stone. Through dating methods, we knew the styles of pottery that were in use in different ancient periods in this part of the world—to the experienced analyst a fragment of a Sasanian (c. A.D. 225–640) clay pot is utterly different from a Late Uruk (c. 3200 B.C.) sherd (though both are impressively ugly). Each day when we finished collecting our pottery samples, we emptied out every bag of ceramics and counted up the numbers of different types of pottery styles from each site. Sites that had very similar kinds of pottery were assumed to have been occupied at about the same time and to have interacted socially or economically; those with markedly different pottery styles were assumed to have been occupied at different times. On this basis, settlement maps for several successive periods of occupation in this area were inferred and a 3,000-year culture history reconstructed, complete with estimates of changes in population density, irrigation systems, possible wars, probable economic collapses—in other words, a rich, even emotionally moving, history of people known almost exclusively from 4134 bags of pottery bits.

Such culture history "works" in the sense that through using these methods, we now know roughly what kinds of cultures inhabited most of the world during most of the past. Although when we are dealing with the relatively slow change of styles in early stone tools, even with the help of modern chemical dating techniques we usually can form only rough categorizations of time into periods hundreds of thousands of years long; nonetheless, most of the world's past cultures have been arranged in an approximate temporal sequence.

It is unfortunate but probably inescapable that culture histories were often done in such a way that all the world's cultures were arranged like a giant ladder, leading to the pinnacle of Western societies. Because American and western European cultures of the nineteenth and early twentieth centuries were technologically the most "advanced," the archaeological record has often been viewed in terms of the way in which modern Western humans evolved from the first culture-bearing animals. Thus, cultural historical "explanations" of, for example, the appearance of agriculture and urban communities have tended to assume that these developments were the "natural" and inevitable products of prehistoric peoples who, like many Westerners, were constantly trying to improve their standard of living.

No histories are purely descriptive, entirely atheoretical. There cannot be an absolutely neutral and value-free history, particularly an archaeological "history," where interpretations frequently soar far beyond the evidence. But there remains in archaeology, when practiced as a method for describing ancient histories, a sense that one is simply trying to reconstruct what happened in the past. Whatever one's political beliefs, for example, the first humans must be assumed to have first set foot on North America at a particular time and place, and one can reasonably try to determine what that time and place was. The Pharaoh Tutankhamun must be assumed to have reigned for a particular span, and one can reasonably hope to determine that span. True, the reasons one might select those questions to answer and the uses to which one might put such answers can be intrinsically political and subjective, but for most people there is a hard core of common sense in trying to use archaeology to infer and describe the major events and cultures of the prehistoric past.

THE GOALS AND OBJECTIVES OF ARCHAEOLOGY II: ARCHAEOLOGY AS A BODY OF THEORIES AND METHODS FOR EXPLAINING THE PAST

> *[Science] is a complex and heterogeneous historical process*
> *[that] contains vague and incoherent anticipations of future*
> *ideologies side by side with highly sophisticated theoretical*
> *systems and ancient and petrified forms of thought. Some of its*
> *elements are available in the form of neatly written statements*
> *while others are submerged and become known only by*
> *contrast, by comparison with new and unusual views.*
>
> Paul Feyerabend

Simply arranging archaeological sites in time and making inferences about the extinct societies that created them does not "explain" the past. But *can* we explain the past? What would we be trying to explain, and how? Take, for example, something as apparently simple as the origins of agriculture—a topic discussed in detail in chapter 6. After three million years as hunter-foragers, about 10,000 years ago our ancestors began to domesticate plants and cultivate them. Farming did not appear in one place and then spread to the rest of the world; it developed in many different places at about the same time, in both the Old World and the New, and involved thousands of species, from yaks to cats, wheat to beets. Surely, one would think, with patient archaeological research one should be able to find the *causes* of agricultural origins— perhaps a combination of, for example, increasing human population densities, climate changes after the end of the last Ice Age, and improvements in technology. Evidence of such changes might be sought to show that they caused agriculture to occur—that they explain in effect why agriculture appeared in Southwest Asia about 10,000 years ago, and not 20,000 or 5,000 years ago, and why it was practiced first in Southwest Asia, and only much later in southwestern North America. And if we could explain agricultural origins in this fashion, it seems plausible that we might formulate similar explanations for the origins of writing, cities, warfare, state religions, etc. And having constructed such explanations, one would think, we might be able to bring them together in a set of general propositions about people and history.

For centuries some scholars have worked on the premise that we can do more than just describe the past: we can understand it in terms of general principles—general principles to be formulated by some future Darwin of the historical sciences. After all, unlike ethnographers, who are limited to the study of societies as they exist today or existed in the recent past, archaeologists can study change over the long term, over the three million years of our history as a genus. It is this great time depth that is the primary resource and data base of archaeology, for if it is ever possible to see the patterns in human history, and to define the determinants, it will likely require that we study the whole sweep of the human past in all its variety. When asked in the 1960s for his opinion about the overall historical impact of the French Revolution almost 200 years earlier, Mao Zedong is reported to have said, "It's too early to tell." We expect major cultural dynamics to be long term. But we now have a vast and detailed knowledge about millions of years of the human past, and surely, one might assume, some major changes should be explainable.

In fact, however, as we will see in detail, there is nothing simple, nothing obvious about such attempts to explain the past, and archaeology is currently in the midst of a great identity crisis concerning such issues as whether or not we will ever be able to explain the past in these terms, what cultural processes, in fact, are in essence, and what "explanation" is. The philosophical origins of these questions go back thousands of years.

A SHORT HISTORY OF ATTEMPTS TO UNDERSTAND THE PAST

> *It's about love, death, torture, infinity. It's a comedy.*
>
> Woody Allen
>
> *A hundred thousand lemmings can't be wrong.*
>
> Anonymous

The reader anxious to get to the blood, sex, and pyramids of prehistory may at this point recoil from a plunge into the philosophy of science and history, but it is simply impossible to understand what contemporary archaeologists are doing and why without a brief excursion into Western intellectual history. What contemporary archaeologists think about world history and how they go about interpreting it are inextricably linked to epistemological (i.e., studies of how we know and the nature and limits of our knowledge) traditions many centuries old. And beyond the relevance of these ideas to archaeology, the student will find that the ideas reviewed below permeate all of the humanities and social sciences in Western intellectual traditions.

The world's literature is littered with attempts to understand our place in the cosmos and make sense of our past. Ancient Middle Eastern literature, especially as reflected in the comparatively late and derivative form of the Old Testament, envisioned a static, created world in which great changes came about through divine intercession, and where the ultimate explanation of events was in terms of God's will—which we see only "as in a glass, darkly." For the devout Christian, Muslim, and many others as well, even if we could see the divine design of history more clearly, we would see that it is predestined, beyond the realm of human initiative. M. E. Hare, as a student at Oxford, whimsically expressed his reaction to this possibility as follows:

> There once was a man who said, "Damn!
> It is borne in upon me I am
> An engine that moves
> In predestinate grooves,
> I'm not even a bus I'm a tram."

If one truly believes that the course of the world's events and history are unintelligible expressions of Divine Will, then history becomes simple *post hoc* description, not analysis—for analysis implies the search for knowable causes.

As far as we know, the ancient Greeks were the first people to think profoundly (or perhaps they were simply the first to record their thoughts) about the problem of cause and effect in a supposedly divinely directed world. "We are all Greeks," it has been said, because so much of modern Western thought is ultimately traceable to ancient Greece. Some scholars feel that the Greeks were more deeply in debt to other cultures than we commonly suppose,[12] but in many ways it seems as if the Greeks simply thought about the world differently from their predecessors. Thucydides and Herodotus, for example, were the first, as far as we know, to travel widely and compile extensive descriptions of the people, cultures, and places of their world in a way that was *analytical*. In the fifth century B.C., for example, Herodotus visited Egypt and became intrigued by the question of why the Nile flooded each and every spring. He asked Egyptian scholars everywhere he went and found that no one had any idea at all. Herodotus then proceeded to analyze several reasonable possibilities—all of them wrong—but all expressed mainly in terms of wind, rain, sun, and oceanic patterns, in other words, in terms of natural causes. In short, Herodotus analyzed, he did not just ascribe the Nile's flood to the inscrutable will of the gods. Similarly, in his late fourth-century B.C. history of the Peloponnesian War, Thucydides tried to explain how the struggle began. He described the personalities involved, the strategies of the warring powers, and the economic realities of the time. In short, by arranging the events and circumstances preceding the war in what he thought was a causal chain, he did what any modern historian would do in trying to explain the events of the past. Archaeologically based culture histories are founded precisely on this logic. Egyptians, Sumerians, and many others recorded aspects of their histories, but their surviving records do not treat the world or history in the same analytical fashion that the Greeks did. It is a mark of how culturally Greek most of us are that what Thucydides did seems so normal and natural to us as hardly to deserve comment. But in truth this sort of real-world explanation of the course of history seems to have been first widely used by the Greeks and became common in many other cultures only recently.[13]

Another central tenet of modern archaeology with Greek roots is evolution. Evolutionary theory was first clearly stated by Charles Darwin, and the ancient Greeks had only a vague sense of this idea. But already by the fifth century B.C. the Athenian scholar Empedocles had formulated a version of the principle of natural selection. And other Greek scholars developed rudimentary sciences of geomorphology and biology that contained glimpses of the fact that the world is very ancient and that plants and animals have changed over time.

But these ideas of evolution and scientific analysis were in some contrast to a concept much more central to the ancient Greek view of the world, the notion of the "Great Chain of Being" or the *Scala Naturae*, which is founded on Greek ideas about the nature of God and "perfection." Greek philosophers found it inconceivable that the world they knew could have arisen by chance, because there seemed to be such a precise design in its every part. The intricate interdependence among plants and animals, the regularity of the seasons—the whole natural world—exhibited to them proof of the existence of a Supreme Intelligence; they therefore defined God as the perfect being who created and controls the world. The Greeks' conception of perfection, however, had a somewhat different connotation than it does for us, for they understood it to be in essence wholeness, or completeness (a concept vividly evident, for example, in classical Greek statues) (Figure 1.5).

Aristotle, in particular, formulated the idea of the world as a *Great Chain of Being*, perfect in its completeness. He concluded that the natural world was rationally ordered according to what he charmingly called "powers of soul," representing different levels within the perfectly whole universe. Thus, a horse is higher than a sunflower because a horse can think, after a fashion, and a man is higher than a horse because he can reason and apprehend God. Early European scholars were greatly influenced by the concept of the Great Chain of Being. They thought it impossible that there should be any "missing links" in the chain, or that any parts of the chain should cease to exist. God, being perfect, could not create an imperfect, that is, incomplete, universe; nor could His sustaining powers allow a whole level of this perfection to vanish. This notion was still at the very core of European culture when the English poet Alexander Pope (A.D. 1688–1744) wrote:

> Vast chain of being! which from God began
> Nature's aethereal, human, angel, man,
> Beast, bird, fish, insect, what no eye can see,
> No glass can reach; from Infinite to thee,
> From thee to nothing.—On superior pow'rs

FIGURE 1.5 The ancient Greek view of the world was that it reflected the "perfection" of the gods in its symmetry and wholeness—attributes reflected in their art, as in this bronze figure from a Greek shipwreck of about 460 B.C.

> Were we to press, inferior might on ours;
> Or in the full creation leave a void,
> Where, one step broken, the great scale's destroy'd—
> From Nature's chain whatever link you strike,
> Tenth, or ten thousandth, breaks the chain alike.

The idea of this Great Chain of Being pervades all Western literature and science and continues well into our own time. It remains, for example, a major element in arguments by those who lead the repeated crusades to have the biblical story of Creation installed in American elementary education as a worthy alternative to evolution.

The concept of the Great Chain of Being is difficult to reconcile with evolutionary theories and the discoveries of modern archaeology. And it is not simply a matter of the great antiquity of the human past, which has been revealed in the past century. For if God had created and sustained every bacterium, every sparrow, every Neanderthal, how could it happen, many people in effect asked, that thousands of species had come into existence, flourished, and vanished? How could humans possibly have evolved from lower primate species and lived for millions of years as "subhuman" races now long since extinct? Thus, it is easy to understand the attractiveness of the Great Chain. It placed humanity, the masterwork of the Creator, "but little lower than the angels." Furthermore, it explained why we were here and why the world seems so marvelously intricate and designed: God designed the world in every detail for His purposes and placed humankind in a position of stewardship over His creation.

In many ways, the last two hundred years of Western philosophy have been a long struggle to come to terms with a gradual and profound loss of faith in the validity of the notion of the Great Chain of Being as evidence for the "Argument from Design," as it came to be known in the West in modern times. This Argument from Design is the conviction that the intricacies and perfections of the world *prove* that humanity and history are under divine control—that such a perfectly ordered and operating universe necessarily implies the existence of a creator and sustainer. The Argument from Design still has great power in the world, in both the Christian West and the Islamic East, for example, but it has been under assault for centuries.

THE ENLIGHTENMENT

Not until the "Enlightenment" of the seventeenth and eighteenth centuries were the intellectual foundations of modern archaeology securely established. Then, primarily in the eighteenth and nineteenth centuries, the *scientific method* was combined with *determinism, materialism,* and *evolutionism* to try to explain the world and history.

There can be no absolute definition of the scientific method, for rather than a method it is a state of mind along with a few assumptions. The key ideas are that most, if not all, things and events can be understood in terms of identifiable, measurable, physical forces, and that the best way to identify and measure these forces is to conceive ideas and then expose them to rejection through scientific experimentation or data analysis.

Although this sounds to most people like nothing more than common sense, history shows that it is a rather late and rare perception of the world. For most ancients and for many moderns, the world swarms with phenomena and forces that can never be understood by science; to them, in fact, precisely those aspects of human existence that cannot be scientifically understood or explained, such as why we are here and the nature and destination of the human soul, are the most important.

But, building on Greek ideas, seventeenth- and eighteenth-century scholars observed natural, social, and historical phenomena, devised hypotheses about their causes, and then tested these ideas by dropping balls from the tops of buildings (Galileo), flying kites in lightning storms (Franklin), and so on. What was scientifically essential in these analyses was that the ideas be exposed to falsification or contradiction by some sort of experimentation or alternative interpretation; that, above all, the explanation of something be considered not absolute, eternal truth, but just the best current hypothesis, subject to correction in the light of new research.

The materialist and determinist elements in this kind of science were the assumptions that the phenomena of this world—including historical and cultural phenomena—had some ultimate causation (that is, were in some way determined by) knowable, measurable, material factors such as population growth, genetic mutation, infections, or gravity. If one accepted this view of the world, then one should look for explanations in the causal relationships and processes governing the attributes of phenomena, not in human decisions or divine agency. The evolutionary component was the notion that over time there had been and would continue to be an increase in complexity in the biological, historical, and political world—an ancient notion.

There is no necessary conflict between these ideas of Western science and religion. Few of the scholars of the Enlightenment were avowed atheists. Benjamin Franklin did important scientific research in the eighteenth century, but he was largely serious when he said that "wine is a continuing proof that God loves us very much and wants us to be happy." Thomas Jefferson, one of the most versatile intellects of the eighteenth and early nineteenth centuries, believed in God—as did many of his contemporaries—as a kind of Great Clock-Maker, who set the universe in motion but does not often intrude upon its operation. Jefferson in fact "scientifically" edited the Bible to what he considered its essential and useful message, deleting everything he considered mythical and obscure, and produced *The Jefferson Bible*, a pamphlet of about forty-eight pages.

The Enlightenment scholars made brilliant advances in determining the physical mechanics of the universe and they avidly looked for the mechanics of human history, but most found no conflict between their science and their belief that God created these mechanics and set them into operation.

The Enlightenment was more than the crucible of modern science; it was in many ways the period in which the social perspective of the West first formed, particularly with regard to the notion of progress and conceptions of material culture. By the end of the eighteenth century, science had shown that the natural world was understandable in terms of the elegant (i.e., comprehensive yet reduced to the simplest possible terms) ideas of mathematics and physics. One result was that scholars everywhere began to apply the scientific method to the understanding of human history and the problem of cultural origins. For example, the Marquis de Condorcet (1743–1794), a French philosopher, proposed a series of universal laws he thought governed the history of human social organizations, and he went so far as to use his analysis to try to predict the future of the world.

Such direct applications of the physical science model to history might seem strange, but one must understand the eighteenth-century mind. "Common sense" tells us that history and culture are far too complex to explain in terms of simple mathematical laws, but common sense also tells us that we walk about on a flat earth, around which revolves the sun. The scholars of the Enlightenment had only recently been shown how treacherous common sense was and how the mysteries of the universe were being reduced to the commonplaces of science. Meanwhile, all around them great advances in the biological and historical sciences were being made.

In France, Georges Cuvier (1769–1832) undertook an extensive analysis of fossilized bones and concluded that hundreds of animal species had become extinct and that there seemed to be an evolutionary trajectory to the biological world. The French naturalist Jean Lamarck (1744–1829) published various arguments that the world was much older than the 6,000 years described in the Bible, and he arranged the biological world in a sequence, from human beings to the smallest invertebrates, in a way similar to later evolutionary schemes.

Scientific archaeology based on evolutionary and materialist assumptions was also emerging in the late eighteenth century, when P. F. Suhm published in 1776 a *His-*

tory of Denmark, Norway, and Holstein, based on the recognition that in many parts of Europe ancient people first made tools of stone, then of bronze, and finally of iron. This Three-Age System was first clearly stated and then developed by the Danish archaeologist Christian Thomsen in 1836 and by J. Worsae (1821–1885).[14] But its origins are much earlier. Lucretius (c. 98–55 B.C.), the great Roman scholar, wrote that "The earliest weapons were the hands, nails, and teeth; then came stones, and clubs. These were followed by iron and bronze, but bronze came first, the use of iron not being known until later." And as K. C. Chang has noted,[15] a near-contemporary of Lucretius, the Chinese scholar Yuan K'ang, stated essentially the same idea.[16]

NINETEENTH-CENTURY EVOLUTIONISM, MATERIALISM, AND DETERMINISM

Excavations for the London Underground Railroad in the mid-1800s produced many curious finds, among them the bones of animals that sorely troubled the scientists of the time. Great elephant-like animals, standing thirteen feet high at the shoulder, had left their skeletons amidst those of gigantic cave bears and many other animals that no longer lived in Britain—or anywhere else in the world. "Animals dead before the Noachian deluge," some concluded. But others sought scientific explanations. In England in the 1830s, William "Strata" Smith and Charles Lyell, among others, attempted to show that the earth was formed through the action of slow geological processes— processes still in effect. Lyell's contributions were particularly important because the dawning realization of the earth's great age had led some scientists and clergy to a belief in a series of "catastrophes," the last of which was Noah's Flood. Adherents of this position saw the fossil animal bones deep in the earth's strata as evidence that God had "destroyed" the world at various times with floods.

In 1848 John Stuart Mill published an evolutionary analysis of history that postulated a sequence of six stages: (1) hunting; (2) pastoralism; (3) Asiatic (by which he meant the great irrigation civilizations of China and the Middle East); (4) Greco-Roman; (5) feudal; and (6) capitalist. He complemented this classification with an extensive analysis of the economic factors determining these stages.

At about the same time Mill was writing, another Englishman, Herbert Spencer, applied the concepts of "natural selection" to human societies some years before Darwin applied them to the biological world, though his constructs were quite different from those eventually arising out of Darwinian thought.

Spencer was much influenced by Thomas Malthus, who in 1798 had noted that human societies—and indeed all biological species—tended to reproduce in numbers far faster than they increased the available food supply. For human groups, he postulated, this meant a life of struggle in which many were on the edge of starvation and more "primitive" societies lost out in the struggle for survival to the more "advanced" cultures. Spencer believed that eventually natural selection would produce a perfect society:

> Progress therefore, is not an accident, but a necessity. Instead of civilization being artifact, it is part of nature; all of a piece with the development of the embryo or the un-

folding of a flower. The modifications mankind have undergone, and are still undergoing, result from a law underlying the whole organic creation; and provided the human race continues, and the constitution of things remains the same, those modifications must end in completeness. . . . So surely must the things we call evil and immorality
disappear; so surely must man become perfect.[17]

Spencer's ideas permeated archaeological analyses of early civilizations and social forms, but they are now largely abandoned, for various reasons (see chapter 7).
Some scholars consider Spencer to have been a racist whose notions of progress have
misled a century of social science. But Spencer was a brilliant analyst, and he was operating on assumptions that seemed eminently reasonable in the nineteenth century:
that history is subject to natural laws, that we can know these laws, and that—as
Spencer's whole life experience showed him—applications of science to human affairs could only lead to progress. Thomas Huxley read a draft of Spencer's *Principles
of Biology* (1864), and he and others convinced Spencer that "progress" was the wrong
concept to apply to biological evolution, so Spencer used "persistence"; but in his
ideas about human history he simply could not escape the notion that what history
principally showed was "progress."[18]

Charles Darwin

How very stupid not to have thought of that.

T. H. Huxley (referring to Darwin's ideas about evolution)[19]

On a warm Saturday afternoon in June 1860, about a thousand people gathered in
Oxford, England, to witness a debate on Charles Darwin's (Figure 1.6) theory of bi-

FIGURE 1.6 Charles Darwin
(1809–1882) altered forever human
conceptions of the dynamics of the
physical world and the nature of history.

ological evolution. For years Darwin had studied the animals and plants of South America, and he had formulated ideas about "descent with modification." But for various reasons he was reluctant to publish his views. Only when he knew that others were about to publish similar evolutionary analyses did he advance his opinion that for centuries the biological sciences had been in error concerning the origins and nature of biological species. Before Darwin, most scholars had assumed that all varieties of plants and animals were the direct product of God's creative might; and humankind itself was viewed as a special act of creation. In fact, as noted earlier, long before Darwin and continuing through his age and into our own, the "Argument from Design," the idea that the intricacy, complexity, and interdependency of the universe point unmistakably to the existence of a Divine Creator, has been one of the major intellectual currents in Western civilization—and in other cultures as well.

But Darwin's research all but eliminated from educated Western thought the Argument from Design, for Darwin's work revealed a world of apparently blind and cruel competition at all levels.

On his travels through South America, Darwin had been particularly impressed by the great diversity of plant and animal life in the Galapagos Archipelago, near Ecuador. There he found islands geologically similar and within sight of one another, but nevertheless inhabited by significantly different species of plants and animals. Why should there be such diversity in such a small area?

> It was evident (after some reflection) that such facts as these could only be explained on the supposition that species gradually become modified; and the subject haunted me. But it was equally evident that neither the action of the surrounding conditions, nor the will of the organism . . . could account for the innumerable cases in which organisms of every kind are beautifully adapted to their habits of life—for instance . . . a tree-frog to climb trees, or a seed for dispersal by hooks or plumes. I had always been much struck by such adaptations, and until these could be explained it seemed to me almost useless to endeavor to prove by indirect evidence that species had been modified.[20]

Darwin knew of course that for millennia farmers had used selective breeding to improve their animals in specific ways, such as increased milk production in cows. But these changes were the result of purposeful intervention in these animals' breeding patterns. How could such selection come about in the natural world?

Darwin was influenced by Malthus's idea of population "pressure" and Adam Smith's concepts of economic competition, and he was much impressed with the importance of competition in all spheres of life:

> Being well prepared to appreciate the struggle for existence which everywhere goes on from long-continued observation of the habits of animals and plants, it at once struck me that under these circumstances favorable variations would tend to be preserved and unfavorable ones to be destroyed.[21]

With these observations and simple conclusions, Darwin provided the world with answers to a whole range of perplexing questions. Why was there such variety in the biological world? Because so many different environments were inhabited for so many millions of years, which allowed natural selection to shape biological populations to these varied environments. Why did animals and plants change over time? Because their environments had changed and some individuals were better equipped to survive and pass on their personal characteristics.

Darwin knew nothing about the genetic mechanisms we now recognize as the agencies through which biological diversity arises and on which natural selection operates, and he believed that characteristics acquired by an organism in its lifetime could be passed on to its offspring. We now know this to be a misconception. We also know that Darwin was intellectually deeply in debt to other scientists.[22] Moreover, there are great debates currently in theoretical biology about the mechanisms of evolution. Some scholars believe, for example, that existing biological systems, whether they be organisms, populations, or species, "constrain" the possible directions of evolutionary change in a way that cannot be accounted for in classical Darwinian ideas about natural selection (see, for example, *Evolution as Entropy*, by Brooks and Wiley). But all this does not detract from his great contribution.

Darwin put in motion an intellectual revolution that has continued to the present and has battered the very foundations of Western ideas about the nature of God, humanity, and history. Through logic and evidence, Darwin and his contemporaries showed there had been millions of years in which the world had been dominated by reptiles, eons in which there were no people. Thus he forced people to wonder how God could be glorified by countless generations of snakes and lizards and dinosaurs breeding, fighting, and dying in primeval swamps, and why they should consider humanity a special act of creation if people, too, developed from earlier, simpler forms, from ancestors who were no more imaginative, intelligent, creative, or religious than any other animal.

As noted earlier, it is important to recognize that there is no *necessary* conflict of these ideas with Christianity or other religions; indeed, many founders of Western science remained true believers until their deaths. They simply assumed that God used the natural processes of the world to work out His Divine and Unknowable Plan. Thus the Austrian monk Gregor Mendel (A.D. 1822–1884) could serenely work out the genetic basis of biological evolution and still die untroubled in his faith. And Darwin thought that through evolutionary processes people would eventually become altruistic and profoundly civilized, and he himself said that he had "never been an atheist in the sense of denying the existence of God" (although he professed a rather muddled agnosticism).[23]

But the great mass of people were shocked and troubled by the implications of evolutionary theory. Evolutionary biology is now the only generally accepted theory of biology, and few scientists doubt its essential validity. But in that room at Oxford in 1860, Darwin and his advocate, Thomas Huxley, were reviled and ridiculed (Figure 1.7). This hostility characterized reaction to Darwinian ideas well into our own times, and it is not at all surprising that this should be so, for as the Marxist Friedrich Engels observed:

> Until Darwin, what was stressed . . . was precisely the harmonious cooperative working of organic nature, how the plant kingdom supplies animals with nourishment and oxygen, and the animals supply plants with manure, ammonia, and carbonic acid.

FIGURE 1.7 Many nineteenth-century cartoonists were amused by the idea of biological evolution.

Hardly was Darwin recognized before these same people saw everywhere nothing but struggle.[24]

In a sense, Darwin completed Galileo's revolution. A critic of Galileo "proved" finally and utterly that Galileo was wrong because Galileo said there were moons orbiting Jupiter. As this critic pointed out, if these moons were too small to be seen, they were too small to affect the earth, and since God designed the earth as the focal point of the whole universe, Jupiter could, therefore, have no moons. Galileo showed that the earth was just one among an inconceivable number of celestial bodies, without apparent special claim to centrality; Darwin showed that today's human being is one of many related life forms and is always a "transitional form," constantly changing, with no apparent claim to centrality in the universe.

The profound effects of Darwin's ideas permeated all of Western arts[25] and sciences. In his poem "Dover Beach," Matthew Arnold, a contemporary of Darwin, likened the Christian faith and view of the world to a comforting tide that surrounded the world as a shining sea, but which was withdrawing under the onslaught of nineteenth-century revolutionary ideas, including Darwinism:

> The Sea of Faith
> Was once, too, at the full, and round earth's shore
> Lay like the folds of a bright girdle furl'd.
> But now I only hear
> Its melancholy, long, withdrawing roar,
> Retreating, to the breadth
> Of the night-wind, down the vast edges drear
> And naked shingles of the world.
> Ah, love, let us be true
> To one another! for the world, which seems
> To lie before us like a land of dreams,
> So various, so beautiful, so new,
> Hath really neither joy, nor love, nor light,
> Nor certitude, nor peace, nor help for pain;
> And we are here as on a darkling plain
> Swept with confused alarms of struggle and flight,
> Where ignorant armies clash by night.

Similarly, Leo Tolstoy, in a letter written in 1910 on his deathbed to his son and daughter, advised them:

> The views you have acquired about Darwinism, evolution, and struggle for existence won't explain to you the meaning of your life and won't give you guidance in your actions, and a life without an explanation of its meaning and importance, and without the unfailing guidance that stems from it, is a pitiful existence. Think about it. I say it, probably on the eve of my death, because I love you.[26]

As Stephen Jay Gould points out, Tolstoy's lament is somewhat unfair. Evolutionary theory makes no pretense of explaining the ultimate nature or purpose of human existence—if it is humanly possible, at all, ever to answer such questions. Evolutionary theory simply supplies powerful explanations of change over time in human biology and society—leaving the problem of ultimate causation to some other forms of inquiry or to faith.

But to understand the vehemence and loathing in the initial reaction to evolutionary theory and its persistent controversial status, one must recognize that evolutionary theory goes beyond simply calling into question the argument that the design of the universe necessarily proves the existence of a divine creator and sustainer. Evolutionary theory calls into question many other cherished ideas, as well. Recent research,[27] for example, on the chemistry of the blood exchanged during pregnancy between a woman and her fetus, suggests that there is an evolutionary contest of sorts going on between the mother and her baby. It is to the woman's genetic advantage to give the fetus enough nourishment and oxygen so that the fetus develops properly, but it would be to her genetic disadvantage to provide the fetus with nourishment at the expense of her own long-term health—since that would thereby decrease her chances of having other children and, therefore, reduce her own genetic representation in future generations. It is to the fetus's advantage, however, to drain as much nourishment as it can possibly use from the mother without regard to her ability to have other children, provided her health—and thereby her ability to care for the fetus once it is born—is not compromised. Scientists working on the premise that this kind of Darwinian contest is taking place have been able to predict fluctuations in blood gasses and chemistry in the mother-fetus relationship: the fetus signals the mother to supply certain levels of oxygen and nourishment, but the mother's body supplies these in a way that balances the welfare of the fetus against the mother's health and long-term reproductive abilities.

Such apparently coldly unemotional mechanisms at the heart of some of humanity's most sacred relationships appall some people; others see such things as elegant demonstrations of the power of Darwinian evolutionary theory to explain natural processes. Also, variant forms of evolutionary theory have been and continue to be used to address questions that are repugnant to many contemporary people. Some scientists, for example, have recently invoked evolutionary theory to argue that human "races" differ in their innate genetic potential for certain kinds of intelligence, and that men and women differ as well. Other evolutionists have suggested that the apparent willingness of mothers to sacrifice their lives for their children may appear to be based on "love," but that it may also be a genetically imprinted behavior that was selected for because it protects one's chances of genetic representation in future generations.

These issues are discussed at greater length in chapter 3. The important point here is that the impact of evolutionary theory on how we view our universe and our past, present, and future has been profound and continues to reverberate through science and culture, and it calls into question some of the most cherished and ancient notions about human morality and worth.

It is important to note in this context, however, that evolutionary theory cannot *prove* that the "Argument from Design" is wrong. It simply provides an alternative explanation of how the biological and cultural history of earth might have happened. And as powerful as evolutionary, materialist, and determinist theories have been in shaping our world, they will probably never eradicate non-scientific "knowledge." One of novelist G. García Márquez's characters says, "I don't believe in God but I'm afraid of Him," and one finds vestiges of the same thought throughout modern cultures.

One reason for this is that from some perspectives the evolution of life is so extraordinarily improbable. If the earth's orbit had been 5 percent closer to the sun, for example, the earth would have been far too hot for life to evolve; if the earth were 1 percent farther out, all the water on the planet would be locked in glacial ice. It is easy to understand why many people through the ages have concluded that the earth was designed for humans. Some scientists accept that the complex chemicals constituting the self-replicating compounds necessary for biological life *could* have evolved by random processes but consider the few-billion-year history of organic earth life to be too short for this to be a probable occurrence. Hence, some hypothesize that the earth passed through a space cloud of organic molecules, from which we are all descended.

But such subtle points were unknown to people of Darwin's age. Darwin and other evolutionists had posed cosmic questions and had provided compelling answers. Their arguments and research showed that not just biological species, but cities, ships, pyramids, farms, religions, parliaments—all things cultural—had evolved out of earlier, simpler forms; they implied that we have no special claim to centrality or exemption from the processes of the universe. And, perhaps most important, Darwin's ideas made it reasonable to ask whether or not there were principles with which to understand our cultural as well as our physical evolution.

It is important to recognize that Darwinian theory is more than just an abstraction about how the biological universe acquired its present form. In its application to cultures and history, Darwinian theory is profoundly political. When it was first widely accepted, in the late nineteenth century, some people justified rampant Western colonialism and exploitation in terms of the "survival of the fittest," implying that it was somehow natural and right that "higher" social systems control, coerce, and replace "primitive" ones.

Darwin was in some senses a "gradualist," who saw evolution operating at a constant rate, finely sifting through variations, perpetuating some, extirpating others. Biologist Stephen J. Gould and others have countered the gradualist vision of evolutionary processes with a concept of "punctuated equilibrium," or periods of rapid change interspersed with long periods of much slower change. Here, too, the possible applications of these ideas are not just to biology. Evolutionists such as Gould, for example, have argued that gradualism has been used implicitly by some to justify a slow, gradual pace of social reform.

In summary, few other ideas have had as profound an impact as evolutionary theory on how people view their place in history and in the cosmos. Evolutionary theory is the basis for much of what we will consider in this book, from the origins of modern *Homo sapiens sapiens* to the rise of "civilization." At a simple level, cultural evolution is undeniable: Durham, for example, defines it simply as "the proposition that all human cultural systems are related by descent to a common ancestral culture."[28] But the larger issue is, how do (and have) cultures changed over time and space?

Historical Materialism

> *[The purpose of critical materialism is] to help men out of their self-made prison of uncomprehending economic determinism.*
>
> Alfred Schmidt[29]

Schmidt's comment is, if true, perhaps the most powerful justification one could make of the contemporary importance of archaeology and historical analysis. Marxists and other determinists conclude that slavery, poverty, violence, and other ills of the world through history have been the result of economic determinants that have never been fully understood. They suggest that if these determinants can be analyzed and applied, then these ills will eventually disappear.

Archaeological analyses of the past have been greatly influenced by various notions about "determinism." Determinism, as applied to human history and culture, is the imprecise collective term for the idea that what happened in history was (partly, or largely, or entirely) the result of determining factors that are outside human "free will" or the influences of divinities.

Although statues of Lenin and Marx are currently and literally being consigned to the "dustbin of history" in eastern Europe, along with the sociopolitical systems purportedly based on their philosophies, it does not necessarily follow that Marxist methods of historical analysis should accompany them. Even archaeologists who consider Marxism a bankrupt political ideology are in debt to Marxian thought in many of its elements of materialist determinism. Marxism, or at least materialist notions, are a "natural" for archaeology, because archaeologists spend their lives amidst heaps of materials—the houses, stone tools, storage bins, pots, weapons, irrigation canals, and other items that constitute the technology of a central Marxian concept, the "means of production."

An early anthropological expression of evolutionary and materialist ideas that had considerable impact on studies of the past was the work of Lewis Henry Morgan (1818–1881), who divided history into a series of stages on the basis of initial uses of fire, bow and arrow, pottery, domesticated animals, writing, etc. Karl Marx (1818–1883) (Figure 1.8) was influenced by Morgan and other earlier evolutionists, and the full impact of nineteenth-century evolutionism was achieved only when it was combined with Marx's ideas about materialist determinism.

Certainly one of the most diverse—not to say solipsistic—associations of all time is that group of individuals who have tried to explain what Marx meant. People have killed each other in disputes over Marxian interpretations, and neo-Marxist variants on the basic Marxian ideology are so diverse as to defy summarization. The student with a sense of humor and a good German dictionary is invited to read Marx's original description of the all-important "modes of production" and "relations of production," then to follow the exegesis of these terms into the contemporary era. Scholars with every inclination of Platonic Idealists have claimed inspiration from Marxist theory on the strength of their interpretation of these ideas. Little wonder that some scholars see more of Groucho than Karl in Marxist anthropology.

But what has all this got to do with archaeology? Precisely this: Some of the most influential archaeologists of this century, up to this day, have used Marxian ideas in their analyses.[30] Often these forms of Marxism are quite different from what Karl Marx himself professed, but they are derived from nineteenth-century ideas about historical materialism and determinism.

As we will see in chapter 7, Marx argued that much of human history can be understood on the basis of an analysis of how a society produces and distributes its wealth. He attempted to show that everything—wars, social classes, poverty, parliaments, religion, art—could be explained if one examined the technology, economy, and environment of a given society, and the social relations people establish in rela-

FIGURE 1.8 Karl Marx (1818–1883) profoundly influenced anthropology and archaeology by revealing the links between the economic basis of societies and their political institutions, social structures, and other cultural characteristics.

tion to these economic and environmental factors. In recent years there have been numerous reworkings of Marxian theory, and the most recent archaeological expressions of these ideas stress the social relations that people enter into in producing and consuming goods. These, rather than just the blunt forces of climate, crops, and technology, are seen by Marxist archaeologists as the determinant factors of history. An important point of departure for some, more traditional, Marxists is that historical analyses must be *comparative*. They "contend that a comprehensive view of all ancient societies, seen in relation to each other, will reveal general outlines of a regularity in the historical development of humanity"[31]; they assume that ancient human societies practiced an initial primitive communism, followed by the inevitable appropriation of surpluses in early agricultural communities, and the subsequent formation of "class society [by] strictly logical laws." They conclude that analysis of the forces that resulted "in the stratification of society into antagonistic classes" provides "the key for our understanding of the course of the subsequent history of ancient society," and that "all Marxist historians adhere to the concept that, in the final analysis, the relations of production are determined by the level of development of the means of production."

In contemporary Marxist archaeology[32] many of these assumptions and ideas are being debated. Contemporary Marxist archaeologists differ greatly in their perspectives, but many of them consider social conflict as major determinants of cultural change; they also are trying to create a "human-centered" view of the past, in which people are not just passive, reacting elements whose actions and beliefs are not simple products of external economic and environmental forces, but instead are themselves the agents of social dynamics and cultural changes.[33]

We will consider contemporary expressions of Marxist ideas in archaeology more fully in chapter 7. It is sufficient here to note that materialist determinism in various forms and philosophies has had a long and profound influence on archaeology.

Early Twentieth-Century Archaeology   From the mid-nineteenth century to the beginnings of the twentieth, archaeology entered a remarkable era of "Discovery and Decipherment"[34]; this was the period in which Egyptian hieroglyphs and Mesopotamian cuneiform were first deciphered and major archaeological excavations were undertaken everywhere. In 1922 Lord Carnarvon and Howard Carter opened the tomb of Pharaoh Tutankhamun in Egypt and in the same year Sir John Marshall began excavating the great Harappan civilization in the Indus Valley; in 1926 Sir Leonard Woolley discovered the Royal Tombs of Ur in Mesopotamia. All over the world at this time other marvelous archaeological discoveries were being made.

Archaeology made great progress in this era, but it was also a time in which archaeology was dominated by Europeans and Americans in an ethnocentric and imperialist way that even today gives the discipline a negative image in many parts of the world. The French and British in particular, but all Western nations to some extent, looted the antiquities of other lands, especially Greece, Turkey, Egypt, Iraq, and Iran. European governments collaborated with archaeologists to extract antiquities concessions from weak governments. When the British and French controlled Egypt, they always made one of their own citizens the director of the Egyptian antiquities service. Archaeologists, in turn, sometimes acted as spies for their governments.[35]

World War I, with its horrible carnage, the Depression of the 1930s, and the other dismal events of this era disillusioned many intellectuals and caused them to doubt any notion of human social evolution—at least in the sense of a world growing more rational and moral, of *progress* in any sense. The first half of the twentieth century saw an age of existentialism and in many senses a rejection of rationalism. Darwinian notions of struggle and godlessness, the irrationality of world wars, all these destroyed for many people the last vestiges of the "Argument from Design," and resulted in a profound sense of cosmic isolation. In this spirit one of America's greatest poets, Wallace Stevens, wrote:

For the listener, who listens in the snow,
And, nothing himself, beholds,
Nothing that is not there and the Nothing that is.[36]

The philosophical currents of the early twentieth century produced in archaeology a largely non-theoretical discipline in which most scholars contented themselves with patient accumulation of artifacts and a minimum of interpretation. This period was the "Golden Age" of cultural reconstruction and culture history. In the United States the federal government invested considerable sums in archaeological investigations, in part as a way to employ people during the Depression. It was widely assumed that progress in explaining prehistoric cultural developments would be made only when much more archaeological evidence had been accumulated and the "facts be allowed to speak for themselves." Even by the 1930s, however, there was a growing frustration with the idea of an archaeology limited just to an endless series of inferences about how ancient people lived and how they were related culturally. And many scholars, such as the Marxist archaeologist V. Gordon Childe, continued to work on a science of history.[37]

One of the earliest and most influential attempts to move archaeology beyond simple data collection and description was Julian Steward's 1949 classic article, "Cultural Causality and Law: A Trial Formulation of Early Civilization."[38] Steward tried to relate worldwide similarities in the evolution of cities, writing, warfare, urbanism, etc., to basic determinants of ecology, technology, and demography.

Archaeology 1960–1996

Every decoding is another encoding.[39]

The New Archaeology   After about 1960 there was a major revival of the idea of archaeology as a historical "science." In the 1960s some archaeologists tried to introduce into archaeology the logical methods they saw in physics and chemistry, on the premise that even if archaeology could not be entirely the same kind of science as these "natural sciences," they could at least use the same kinds of logic for analysis.[40]

Why would physics and these other sciences be so attractive as models for archaeologists, to the extent that archaeologists were accused of "physics envy"? Primarily because physics and the other natural sciences offer powerful *explanations.* Natural scientists use a limited number of principles, such as the principles of relativity, thermodynamics, etc., and powerful mathematical formulations to explain much of the workings of the physical universe. We *know* what causes eclipses, thermonuclear explosions, malaria, and other natural processes to the extent that we can control these forces and make televisions, nuclear reactors, and genetically engineered plants and animals.

Attempts to understand the human past in terms of principles like those of physics have a long history in Western culture. Archaeologists have wanted to know what *caused* the first vaguely human animals to use stone tools, what factors drove these early hominids into the northern temperate latitudes, why people changed from hunting-gathering to agriculture, what forces impelled people to establish cities, develop written languages, wage international wars—in short, why history has turned out the way it has.

One of the most influential scholars in the attempt to make archaeology a powerful science has been Lewis Binford. While a student at the University of Michigan,

Binford was impressed by anthropologist Leslie White's evolutionary, materialistic vision of anthropology.[41] In an influential and programmatic series of papers Binford argued that archaeologists should turn their attention from endless excavations and attempts to reconstruct ancient cultures and culture histories, and concentrate instead on the study of general cultural processes. Binford particularly stressed the importance of problem orientation and testing hypotheses. He argued, for example, that the initial appearance of agricultural economies independently in different areas of the world was the result of climate changes, population growth, and various cultural adaptations of peoples in certain environments. He then related a wide range of archaeological data to his hypothesis in an effort to explain why agriculture appeared when and where it did.

Binford and many others sought to make archaeology an objective, empirical science in which hypotheses about all forms of cultural variability could be tested. This "New Archaeology" (also called "processual archaeology") includes many diverse perspectives, methods, and ideas, but there are some common elements.[42] First, many archaeologists believe that *mathematics* can play a powerful role in archaeological analyses. Mathematical analyses of many different types have been applied to archaeological data, and some of these will be reviewed in later chapters. Second, almost all attempts to make archaeology a science have assumed that this would be an *evolutionary* science—at least in the simple sense that Bruce Trigger described as the assumption that "all significant differences among cultures can be regarded as differing states of development from simple to complex." The application of Darwinian ideas of evolution to human societies has in many ways just begun, and some archaeologists see great potential in this approach. Third, the New Archaeology also has stressed *cultural ecology*, in the sense that they looked for the causes of major cultural changes primarily in factors like climate changes, variability in the agricultural productivity of different environments, technological changes, and demographic factors. But most of the archaeologists of this era assumed that ancient cultures were complex *systems*—that is, the patterns of cause and effect are complexly interrelated, and are rarely unidirectional. Thus, if one were to consider why people in ancient Iraq first began cultivating plants, one would expect that the answer would involve many different factors, such as changes in population densities, climate fluctuations, evolving technologies, the genetic properties of certain plant genera, etc. Human societies are assumed to have regulating mechanisms that promote the group's adaptation. Most human societies, for example, have developed means of birth control to regulate their population-to-resources balance; the intensity with which birth control is practiced can change as the resources change. To some extent then, the systems-view of culture is that they are self-regulating entities, open to influences from their environments. Explanations based on this model are often *functional* explanations: just as a biologist might account for the evolution of the mammalian heart as a way to circulate blood, an archaeologist might account for the rise of state religions in all early civilizations by the functional benefits of a low-cost, ideological mechanism like religion to organize and control the mass of the population for military and economic purposes.

The goal of reformulating archaeology as a mathematical, evolutionary, ecological science for analyzing extinct complex cultural systems remains a strong theme in contemporary archaeology, but there has been a widespread loss of faith in the possibility of a "physics of history." Most archaeologists recognize that human history is in some ways fundamentally different from some of the material phenomena of the world, such as atoms. For one thing, human history is the product of *natural selection* in a way that does not seem true of the history of galaxies and sub-atomic particles (this point is discussed in later chapters). The human past by definition is a specific sequence in time and through a particular space—the planet earth—while the principles of physics and chemistry are applicable (at least theoretically) to all times and places. That the volume of a gas is determined by its pressure and temperature is assumed to be true now and forever, here and in the farthest reaches of the universe.

But biology, population genetics, ecology—these and other life sciences deal with a historical sequence of life-forms in a particular place, earth. Yet these are powerful mathematical explanatory disciplines, and some archaeologists continue the quest to formulate a science of archaeology that is similar to these disciplines. Unlike the natural sciences, however, there is no "theory" that unites and focuses the research of the many practitioners of archaeology in the same way that evolutionary theory and population genetics unite biologists, and thermodynamics unites physicists. Some scholars, nonetheless, see the potential for a unifying theory for archaeology in Darwinian evolutionary theory, and we will consider this approach in more detail in chapter 7.

Archaeology as an Eclectic Social and Historical Science   Various scholars criticized the New Archaeology as being too "functionalist." Functionalism often involves trying to explain the origins of and evolution of something in terms of the function it serves. The classic example here is the explanation of the mammalian heart in terms of its function—to circulate blood. Archaeologists have often used functionalist arguments to explain cultural elements and cultural changes. As we shall see in chapter 7, for example, earlier scholars attributed almost every aspect of ancient Egyptian society to the fact that the whole civilization was dependent on a single river and irrigation agriculture. They suggested, for example, that a powerful state government evolved because it built, maintained and administered a complex irrigation system that was essential to providing the food to sustain a large population. Similarly, the development of writing in various early states has been attributed to the need to keep records of flood levels and crop production.

In the last decade, however, these kinds of easy functional equations between the requirements of living in certain environments in specific forms of cultures have been questioned, and in contemporary archaeology there is a growing emphasis on analyses of the social relations and ideologies of ancient cultures and how these *ideas* shaped these cultures.

One of the major tenets of contemporary archaeology, for example, is that in its effort to become more scientific in the 1960s and 1970s, most archaeologists neglected the ideological aspects of ancient societies and under-rated the power of ideological systems to construct cultures. In some forms of Marxism, ideologies—such as peoples' perceptions of social status hierarchies and their position in those hierarchies—are "false consciousness," and these ideologies are determined by, and are mere reflections of, historical and economic factors that are the true driving forces of cultural change.

But many contemporary archaeologists no longer accept the usefulness or validity of that perception. Timothy Pauketat and Thomas Emerson, for example, in an effort to show that people living in the North American Middle West at about A.D. 900 incised particular designs on their pots in order to communicate an ideology that legitimized the authority of chiefs, argued that:

> Ideology is neither "false consciousness" nor a unitary entity. Ideologies are seen as systems of discursive knowledge, beliefs, and values—cognized models— which legitimize the social status quo through an appropriation of traditional and cosmological referents. . . . These systems of knowledge, beliefs, and values are the means by which individuals within interest groups acquire consciousness of their social position. . . . Ideologies articulate the cultural tradition with the consciousness of individuals.[43]

Some archaeologists would question the extent to which we can analyze ancient ideologies in a systematic and "scientific" manner, but many would agree that attempts at such interpretations are a legitimate part of archaeology.

Many contemporary archaeologists now view archaeology as an eclectic social and historical science. From this perspective, archaeologists can use theories and methods from a wide range of social and natural sciences to formulate an analytical, partly explanatory, science of the past that focuses on the ideologies and behavior. "Behavior" in this sense is, of course, inferred behavior, based on archaeological evidence. The objective in this synthetic approach to knowing about the past is to use any method, technique, or theory that seems to add to our knowledge and understanding of the past.[44]

Consider, for example, the archaeology of the ancient Maya, who lived in what is now southern Mexico, Belize, Guatemala, and adjacent areas. Archaeologists have been analyzing the Maya for almost a century, and we know a lot about them—as is reviewed in detail in chapter 13. One of the most intriguing problems of the Maya is that they seem to have "disappeared" as a distinctive culture sometime after about A.D. 900. To try to explain this, archaeologists have used ideas and data from demography, epidemiology, agronomy, and many other sciences. Dorothy Hosler, Jeremy Sabloff, and Dale Runge,[45] for example, devised a computer model that simulated Maya population growth, labor investments in monumental temples and other buildings, and agricultural productivity. This model suggests that the Maya began to suffer food shortages as an imbalance grew between the population size and the food supply, but that the Maya tried to solve this problem by building more monuments, in order to placate the gods, which in the end made the population decline even more rapidly. As we shall see in chapter 13, there is evidence the Maya "collapse" was actually more of a shift in population densities and other cultural changes than an actual collapse and disappearance of this culture, but the point here is that archaeological analyses of Maya history can draw on a variety of evidence and techniques. Satellite images and aerial photography, for example, have been used to penetrate the jungle cover of much of the Maya homeland to reveal the traces of ancient fields, canals, and roads. Ethnologists have studied the contemporary descendants of the

Maya and found survivals of ancient culture. Because the Maya developed a written language, textual scholars have been able to identify specific rulers and events in Maya history. Art historians have evaluated the motifs in Maya art and architecture and related them to the social and political organization of the Maya. The Maya have also been analyzed at highly abstract levels: Colin Renfrew,[46] for example, analyzed the collapse of the Maya in terms of modern "catastrophe theory"—an advanced, highly mathematical discipline that attempts to explain sudden shifts in the state of systems, whether the system is a weather pattern, degree of turbulence in water flow through pipes, or the collapse of ancient political systems.

In sum, archaeologists have used the analytical methods of many different fields in combination with excavations and archaeological analyses to compile a history and analysis of the Maya. This eclectic social science and historical perspective on the Maya would seem to provide us with a persuasive and detailed picture of their economy, society, politics, religion, science, and some of the major events of their history.

Perhaps the best defense of an eclectic theoretical approach to archaeology is that offered by Bruce Trigger, in his recent calls for a "holistic" archaeology. Trigger notes:

> I have argued that the future of archaeology lies not in replacing the ecological determinism of processual archaeology with the historical particularism that currently appears to be attracting many postprocessual archaeologists, but rather in effecting a synthesis of these seemingly opposed positions. The synthesis I have proposed involves trying to investigate as many of the factors that constrain human behavior as possible. These include not only the external factors championed by the processualists but also the cultural traditions without which human existence would be impossible.[47]

But for many archaeologists this kind of eclectic and empiricist approach to the past has more vices than virtues. Numerous scholars reject the utility of any ideas about cultural evolution and any claim that there can be even a kernel of objectivism in analyzing the past. The collective term applied to this perspective is "postprocessualism," which has much in common with the "post-modernism" that has expressions in fields as diverse as literature and architecture.

Post-Processual Archaeology: Archaeology as a Post-Modernist Discourse

> *For the subjective idealism of scientistic archaeology we*
> *substitute a view of the discipline [of archaeology] as an*
> *hermeneutically informed dialectical science of past and present*
> *unremittingly embracing and attempting to understand the*
> *polyvalent qualities of the socially constructed world of*
> *the past and the world in which we live.*
>
> Michael Shanks and Christopher Tilley[48]

As the above citation illustrates, post-processual approaches to archaeology can be difficult to describe and understand. Indeed, it is one of the tenets of post-processualism that any attempt to summarize and capture the essence of their approach is doomed, because there is no single approach, no unified perspective.

The reader is forwarned that the following discussion of post-processual archaeology will be difficult to understand fully if the reader has not read deeply in the works of such scholars as Jacques Derrida and Michael Foucault—and perhaps even if he or she has read this literature. The reader might also wonder what all this theorizing has to do with the bones and stones of our ancient past: the point here is that many archaeologists say this theorizing has nothing to do with the study of our past, while, conversely, many post-processual archaeologists think it has everything to do with the study of the past.

The name post-processual is a bit propagandistic in that it implies that it is the kind of archaeology that will be done after positivistic processual archaeology is abandoned. As we shall see in this book, for many archaeologists this abandonment is by no means imminent or inevitable.

As the quotation from Shanks and Tilley indicates, it is difficult to explain just exactly what vision of archaeology the post-processualists have. In fact, one of the few things that most post-processualists agree on is that there can be *no* single perspective on the past.

The origins of post-processualism were described by Ian Hodder as follows:

> Within the empiricist and positivist framework, we climbed Hawkes's "ladder of inference."[49] As we began climbing the ladder, making inferences about environment, technology, and economy, everything seemed fine. We thought we had something hard to hold on to: universal generalizations, noncultural processes, objective data, and independent measuring devices. The sides of the ladder felt hard and reassuring. So we kept climbing the same ladder with confidence. We passed the rung of social archaeology. All seemed well. We moved on to ideology, ritual, symbolism, and the archaeology of mind. We reached the top of the ladder, stood on the top rung, looked around, and realized there was nothing to hold on to anymore.
>
> Archaeologists then had two options apart from the solution of falling off. They could quickly climb down. And some would indeed wish to retreat into processual archaeology and remain climbing up and down the first few rungs forever. Alternatively they could jump to another ladder with a different inferential structure.[50]

The post-processualists have found many different ladders, but none that are "scientific" in the classical Western sense of that term. Most post-processualists believe that the search for an empirical science of artifacts is in essence a search for a unicorn; that archaeology can use a few scientific methods, such as radiocarbon dating, but that it will always be a humanistic enterprise and a fundamentally interpretive exercise, not an observational one.

The major flaw the post-processualists discern in the processualists is the assumption that archaeology can be a neutral, value-free, empirical science of artifacts. Young, for example, expresses this difference of opinion as, on the one hand, those who think that "history is what *happened* in the past," as opposed to the post-processualist notion that history "is what a living society *does* with the past."

Bruce Trigger,[51] drawing on the works of philosopher Larry Lauden, has identified and analyzed four main tenets of post-processualism in American and British archaeology. The first is the proposition that "no one perceives the world objectively:

what we perceive, and even more what we interpret what we perceive, is influenced, either to some degree or entirely, by what we believe." A second related premise is what Trigger calls the "underdetermination of theory by evidence." He characterizes this as the assumption that "sensory data or observational evidence is rarely capable of refuting strongly held beliefs." A third premise involves "holism"—the idea that "in order to understand any part of a system or issue we must first understand the whole." The fourth premise is the principle that "science is a social activity. This implies that science is only one source of knowledge among many, including common sense, religious beliefs, and perhaps even delusions."

As Trigger notes in his analysis, all of these premises are at least somewhat true, and few archaeologists would reject them totally. Contemporary disputes in archaeology revolve around the extent to which these premises are true and their implications for archaeological method and theory.

The abstract philosophical points that Trigger discusses are perhaps best illustrated by the work of British archaeologists Michael Shanks and Christopher Tilley.[52] Shanks and Tilley, drawing on the ideas of Derrida, Foucault,[53] and others, have argued that, just as one cannot assign a definitive single meaning to a text, one cannot make an empirically verifiable and definitive interpretation of the archaeological record. We create the past, they argue, and our interpretations of the past are limited by, and arise out of, our own cultural context.

This may seem an obvious point, that archaeologists' interpretations of the past are in part a function of their own sociocultural context. Archaeologists regularly report temples, social stratification, intensified storage, social class, warfare, states, and other "things" that do not, technically, exist. Our own culture determines to some extent what we make of the past. We can dig up people, sort through their feces, measure their bodies, sift their garbage for their food remains, translate their writings, measure their buildings, and do all kinds of scientific things to them, but in the end what we make of them will have a lot to do with our own lives and personalities.

Indeed, just as some ethnographers have concluded that human life and society have "only meanings rather than causes," some archaeologists think that the emphasis of archaeology should be on assessing the meaning of the past for ourselves, rather than on futile attempts to understand the causes of the patterns and trajectory of the human past. The flavor of this form of analysis can be detected in the title of a recent study, "Social Values, Social Constraints and Material Culture: The Design of Contemporary Beer Cans."[54] In this study, Shanks and Tilley attempt to show that if one ignores the meaning that ancient peoples invested their materials with and concentrates only on the materials, the meaning of the past can never be comprehended, and that comparative studies that do not take account of such differences are bound to fail. Shanks and Tilley consider beer cans one of the most ordinary objects of British and Swedish life. They assume that there is a contradiction in both of these countries in the sense that alcohol is viewed in each as both a commercial product and as a drug. They note that these two countries have different ideas about beer that may be presumed to be important in explaining the cans' style and distribution: whereas in Britain alcohol is not generally considered an item of key public or individual concern, in Sweden alcohol consumption is regarded as one of the most pressing social pathologies, at least in governmental circles.

In an extended quantitative analysis of beer bottles and cans, they found that British beer cans tend to be colorful and often incorporate animals and naturalistic themes, whereas Swedish cans are more often decorated with simple geometric symbols. Using multivariate statistics, they distinguished groups within and between British and Swedish beers, and they related these differences to differences in advertising, industrialization, attitudes toward women, social attitudes toward public drinking, and many other factors.

This may seem a trivial study, but Shanks and Tilley's point is that we cannot understand some aspects of the past unless we know the meanings with which people invested the objects they made.

These "post-processual" forms of archaeological theory have had less influence in the United States than in Britain and Scandinavia, but the issues they raise have become prominent in theoretical circles everywhere. Indeed, some elements of post-processual archaeology derive from the "post-modernist" perspective that can now be found in many academic disciplines, such as literary criticism, architecture, and sociology. Exactly what "post-modernism" is in anthropology and archaeology is difficult to define.[55] As archaeologist Ian Hodder wrote:

> It is thoroughly engrossing for an archaeologist, a student of cultural change, to be living through the apparent "birth" of a new cultural style. Yet it is surprising how difficult it is to define and understand what is happening. The more I try to tie down postmodernism, the less coherent it seems . . . the growth of the style seems bigger than any individual's attempt to characterize it. Ultimately it engulfs any attempt to fix it.[56]

Whatever else they have in common, post-processual archaeologists view archaeology as profoundly *political*. Archaeologist Mark Leone, for example, in his archaeological interpretations of the early history of Annapolis, Maryland, discusses how his archaeological work there has involved contemporary African Americans, and how his interpretations of the archaeological data from that city do not necessarily match those of the African Americans. Of this experience he writes:

> American archaeologists have only just begun to accept the constructivist view of knowledge, which implies that data are not neutral. . . . We are not at all accustomed to negotiating truth values with nonarchaeologists who are affected by our work. However, such negotiating does not debase archaeology. . . . The eventual result will be a much richer archaeology. It will produce not a single interpretation of data, but many interpretations; not one uniformly useful literature, but many incommensurable literatures.[57]

The post-processual perspective raises many important issues and poses some significant problems. For example, if "science" cannot be applied to the archaeological record to evaluate competing claims to the truth, and if there can be many equally "true" readings of any text, then it would seem that one would have to accept that Native Americans who believe that the New World archaeological record shows that they originated in North America, not Asia, have a claim to the truth equal to that of the majority of archaeologists who believe that Native Americans first came to the New World between 10,000 and 20,000 years ago. Many archaeologists have had encounters with non-archaeologists who believe that the remains of the great civilization of Atlantis lie flooded on the ocean floor, or that there is a huge undiscovered library in a chamber carved in the rock under the Sphinx, or that ancient astronauts transmitted precious scientific knowledge to our ancestors, or that ancient Mesopotamians sailed from the Tigris-Euphrates Delta to colonize Mexico, or a thousand other improbabilities.

Are these all equally valid ideas? Some post-modernists and post-processualists reject this absolute relativism, but if "positivist" ideas about scientific evaluation are inapplicable to archaeology, as some of these scholars believe, there can be no "correct" or most probably accurate reading of the past.

What archaeologists do may not be "science" in the classical sense of that term, but many archaeologists reject the idea that all readings of the past are equally valid in terms of their accuracy with regard to what actually happened in the past. All of the terms in the previous sentence are "loaded" in a sense; "correct" does not necessarily have to be in relation to whether ancient Mesopotamians did or did not reach Mesoamerica; correctness, validity, and accuracy can be understood here to mean that they are culturally constructed beliefs about the past.

In general, there seems little post-modernists and post-processualists agree on except, perhaps, their belief that archaeologists who think they are doing "science" are mistaken.

One of the most evident impacts of post-processualism in contemporary archaeology is the growing interest in gender and in what some have called "feminist archaeology." Concepts and discussions of gender and sex long predate the current interest in these subjects, of course, and not all discussions of this topic are part of post-processualism. As we shall see in chapter 3, for example, a pivotal concept in most hypotheses about how the first hominids evolved involves the relationship of males and females in economic and other behavior; and in later prehistory scholars have studied everything from the "goddess" female figurines of Neolithic Europe to the status of women in ancient Egypt. But contemporary feminist archaeological studies from the postprocessual perspective diverge from these traditional studies in several ways. Biological sex is a relatively simple and useful dichotomy (although there are, of course, ambiguities), and a trained archaeologist can determine the sex of a well-preserved skeleton with considerable reliability. The exaggerated sexual characteristics of Pleistocene female figurines leave no doubt as to the sexual and reproductive capabilities of the person or idea represented. But gender is a cultural construct and not so easily defined. The terms "lesbian," "homosexual," and "bisexual" roughly fit sexual practices, but perceptions of these genders differ radically in different societies. Even more abstract are the long-term historical dynamics that have shaped perceptions of gender and the processes of interactions of different genders and sexes.

Perhaps the most important element in post-processualist expressions of feminist archaeology involves the rejection of some forms of empiricism. Traditional archaeology long neglected many aspects of sex and gender because they found it difficult to relate the bones and stone of the archaeological record to gender or sex. In excavating an Egyptian archaeological site, for example, one finds what looks like the remains of villages. There are mudbrick walls, floors of compacted sand filled with the bits and pieces of daily life, such as fragments of burnt bone and wheat, small bits of pottery, etc., and there are also things that look like hearths, latrines, animal pens,

and a thousand other remnants of a 5,000-year-old residence. Reasonable archaeological analyses can estimate when people lived here, what foods they ate, what tools
they used, whom they traded products with, how big the community was, how they
buried their dead, and many other aspects of the culture of which these people were
a part. But any attempt to infer the gender of the people who used particular artifacts and the relationship of males and females in this extinct community would seem
to be mere speculation. One might generalize from the many ancient Egyptian paintings and texts and speculate that men and women did very different kinds of work,
but this speculation would seem to be on a lot less secure ground than estimates of
diet based on recovered archaeological materials.[58]

Whatever the evidentiary basis of gender in the archaeological record, this topic
carries with it some complex political and social implications. An enormous amount
of evidence from archaeology, ethnography, and history shows that throughout the
past women have been primary producers of much of the goods and services of all
societies. Even in societies such as the Eskimo, where hunting is the primary source
of food, women provide labor in the form of child care, food preparation, hide-
processing, and many other activities. In agricultural societies throughout history
women have also provided much of the material wealth and available services in these
societies, in the form of the toil of farming, the production of pottery, textile, and
other craft goods, child care, and a thousand other activities.[59] Yet it also seems undeniable that throughout history these goods and services have often been appropriated by men outside the basic family unit, men who had the power to consume and
redistribute this wealth. How does one explain this asymmetry, and is an attempt to
explain it in terms of societal efficiency or biological factors necessarily an attempt
to justify it? And if we write a world prehistory and history that concentrates on the
people of power, the pharaohs, priests, and other male potentates, do we necessarily
ignore and devalue the contribution of women?

These are important issues in contemporary archaeology, and whatever the ultimate long-term impact of post-processual ideas about archaeology as a political act
and statement, considerations of gender have raised topics well worth contemplation.

Who Owns the Past?   In contemporary archaeology the vast majority of fieldwork
and publication is done by Western European and American archaeologists. Some of
these scholars have begun to question their "right" to interpret the pasts of so many
different cultures and peoples around the world.

If one takes the view that archaeology is a science, then one could at least argue
that, like biology, chemistry, demography, and any other science, what matters is the
quality of the science, not the ethnic or cultural identity of the person doing the analyses. Given the various intellectual trends in post-processual archaeology (as reviewed
above), however, the reader will not be surprised to know that many archaeologists
think that it is unethical to "appropriate" the pasts of others. Randall McGuire, for
example, in reviewing the archaeology of North America, suggests:

> The time has come for archaeologists to reunite their object of study, the Indian past,
> with its descendants, and to ask about the needs of Indian people and address those

needs. . . . [This will require] that all archaeologists initiate a process of dialogue with Indian peoples that will alter our perceptions of the past, how we deal with living Native Americans, . . . and how we present our results to each other and the general public. . . . Most fundamentally, archaeologists need to recognize the contradictions between inclusion and exclusion and uniformity and diversity that are at the core of our national heritage. . . . Social evolutionists and material-culture analysts have failed to address these contradictions, the former by relegating Indian people to lower stages of evolution and the latter by refusing to acknowledge that artifacts from the past have power in the present because they present the image of a known past while their interpretation remains infinitely malleable.[60]

Such calls to political action and socially constructed interpretations will probably have little impact on the many archaeologists who are trying to study topics such as the date, routes, and adaptations of the first human occupations of the New World, the possible role of people in the extinction of mammoths and other large animals in the New World, the processes by which maize agriculture was established in North America, and the hundreds of other research topics that dominate professional North American archaeology today (reviewed in chapter 6). McGuire and like-minded archaeologists, however, question the ethics and validity of such "scientific" studies of the past.

THE GOALS OF ARCHAEOLOGY: WHAT DO ARCHAEOLOGISTS WANT? CONCLUSIONS AND SUMMARY

> *I was gratified to be able to answer promptly.*
> *I said I didn't know.*
>
> Mark Twain (1835–1910)

So, where do we—and archaeology and world prehistory—go from here, in the midst of these contrasting ideas about the nature of inquiries into the past? What can we know about the past and how should we go about knowing it?

As we have seen, answers have ranged from the notion that history is God's plan and ultimately unknowable, to the idea that history can be the subject of scientific methods of analysis and can ultimately be explained in terms of general principles. Contemporary archaeologists include those who are working on complex computer models designed to extract historical processes, others who are trying to produce humanistic interpretations of ancient cultures, others who believe they can't really scientifically "know" any thing about the past but are using it for contemporary political purposes, and still others who have no pretense of doing anything other than finding interesting items (the "gold-bowls-and-mummies" or "stamp-collecting" school of archaeology).

The approach taken in this book is a "holistic" one, in the sense described by Trigger (see earlier discussion): that is, many different kinds of evidence and theoretical perspectives are illustrated and examined, in hopes that this will both provide a complex view of the past and stimulate the reader to adopt a critical approach to various perspectives on the past. But the underlying assumption and premise of this book is that an archaeological inquiry into the past can be usefully and productively done in the form of "science," and that all interpretations of the past are not necessarily equally valid.[61]

Archaeology in the holistic sense that is presented in this book is, thus, a blend of many different perspectives and analyses. It must be remembered, however, that the various kinds of "knowledge" that are provided are not all fundamentally the same. A statistical comparison of stone tools from European sites of 20,000 years ago can produce a different kind of knowledge by different methods from that of an interpretation of the symbols these people painted on cave walls and engraved on stones and bones (although post-processualists might see these as fundamentally similar at some levels). Yet each can give us at least a sense that we understand the past better, in a way, and each can be an interesting and instructive exercise.

BIBLIOGRAPHY

Adams, A. B. 1969. *Eternal Quest.* New York: Putnam.

Alexander, R. D. 1987. *The Biology of Moral Systems.* Hawthorne, NY: Aldine de Gruyter.

Ayer, A. J. 1946. *Language, Truth, and Logic.* New York: Dover.

Bernal, M. 1987. *Black Athena: The Afroasiatic Roots of Classical Civilization, Vol 1: The Fabrication of Ancient Greece.* New Brunswick, NJ: Rutgers University Press.

Betzig, L. L. 1986. *Despotism and Differential Reproduction: A Darwinian View of History.* Hawthorne, NY: Aldine de Gruyter.

Binford, L. R. 1968. "Archaeological Perspectives." In *New Perspectives in Archaeology*, eds. Sally R. Binford and L. R. Binford. Chicago: Aldine.

———. 1981. *Bones: Ancient Men and Modern Myths.* New York: Academic Press.

———. 1986. "Reply to J. F. Thackeray Further Comment on Fauna from Klasies River Mouth.'" *Current Anthropology* 27(1):57–62.

Bintliff, J. 1986. "Archaeology at the Interface: An Historical Perspective."In *Archaeology at the Interface*, eds. J. L. Bintliff and C. F. Gaffney. Oxford: BAR International Series 300.

———. 1993. "Why Indiana Jones Is Smarter than the Post-Processualists." *Norwegian Archaeological Review* 26(2):91–100.

Brown, M., and J. Cave. 1989. *A Touch of Genius: The Life of T.E. Lawrence.* New York: Paragon House.

Brumfiel, E. M. 1991. "Weaving and Cooking. Women's Production in Aztec Mexico." In *Engendering Archaeology*, eds. J. M. Gero and M. W. Conkey. Oxford: Blackwell.

———. 1994a. "Distinguished Lecture in Archaeology: Breaking and Entering the Ecosystem." *American Anthropologist* 94(3):551–67.

———. 1994b. "A Review of *Prehistory of the Americas* (by S. J. Fiedel, 1992, Cambridge: Cambridge University Press)." *Norwegian Archaeological Review* 27(2):132–34.

Butzer, K. W. 1975. "Geological and Ecological Perspectives on the Middle Pleistocene." In *After the Australopithecines*, eds. K. W. Butzer and G. Isaac. The Hague: Mouton.

———. 1982. *Archaeology as Human Ecology.* Cambridge: Cambridge University Press.

Ceram, C. W. 1967. *Gods, Graves, and Scholars.* New York: Knopf.

Chang, K. C. 1988. *The Archaeology of Ancient China.* New Haven, CT: Yale University Press.

Childe, V. G. 1936. *Man Makes Himself.* London: Watts.

Claassen, C. P. 1991. "Gender, Shellfishing, and the Shell Mound Archaic." In *Engendering Archaeology*, eds. J. M. Gero and M. W. Conkey. Oxford: Blackwell.

Clifford, J., and G. Marcus, eds. 1986. *Writing Culture.* Berkeley: University of California Press.

Cohen, G. A. 1978. *Karl Marx's Theory of History. A Defense.* Princeton, NJ: Princeton University Press.

Coles, B., & J. Coles. 1986. *Sweet Track to Glastonbury: The Somerset Levels in Prehistory.* London and New York: Thames and Hudson.

Conkey, M. W. 1991. "Contexts of Action, Contexts for Power: Material Culture and Gender in the Magdalenian." In *Engendering Archaeology*, eds. J. M. Gero and M. W. Conkey. Oxford: Blackwell.

Conkey, M. W., and J. M. Gero. 1991. "Tensions, Pluralities, and Engendering Archaeology: An Introduction to Women and Prehistory." In *Engendering Archaeology*, eds. J. M. Gero and M. W. Conkey. Oxford: Blackwell.

Daniel, G. 1967. *The Origins and Growth of Archaeology.* Baltimore: Penguin.

Daniel, G. E., and C. Chippendale, eds. 1989. *The Pastmasters.* London and New York: Thames and Hudson.

Derrida, J. 1978. *Writing and Difference* (trans. A. Bass). London: Routledge & Kegan Paul.

Desmond, A. 1982. *Archetypes and Ancestors.* Chicago: University of Chicago Press.

Desmond, A., and J. Moore. 1991. *Darwin.* New York: Warner.

Diakonov, I., ed. 1969. *Ancient Mesopotamia.* Moscow: Nauka.

———., ed. 1991. *Early Antiquity.* Chicago: University of Chicago Press.

Dunnell, R. C. 1980. "Evolution Theory and Archaeology." In *Advances in Archaeological Method and Theory*, Vol. 3, ed. M. B. Schiffer. New York: Academic Press.

———. 1982. "Science, Social Science, and Common Sense: The Agonizing Dilemma of Modern Archaeology." *Journal of Anthropological Research* 38:1–25.

———. 1986. "Methodological Issues in Americanist Artifact Classification." *Advances in Archaeological Method and Theory* 9:147–207.

Durham, W. H. 1990. "Advances in Evolutionary Culture Theory." *Annual Review of Anthropology* 19:187–242.

Earle, T. K., and R. W. Preucel. 1987. "Processual Archaeology and the Radical Critique." *Current Anthropology* 28(4):501–38.

Easterbrook, G. 1988. "Are We Alone?" *Atlantic*, August 1988, pp. 25–38.

Eiseley, L. 1946. *The Immense Journey.* New York: Time, Inc.

———. 1979. *Darwin and the Mysterious Mr. X.* New York: Harcourt Brace Jovanovich.

Faubion, J. D. 1993. "History in Anthropology." *Annual Review of Anthropology* 22:35–54.

Feder, K. L. 1990. *Frauds, Myths, and Mysteries: Science and Pseudo-Science in Archaeology* Mountain View, CA: Mayfield.

Feyerabend, P. 1993. *Against Method*, 3rd ed. New York: Verso.

Fildes, V. A. 1987. *Breasts, Bodies, and Babies: A History of Infant Feeding.* Edinburgh: Edinburgh University Press.

Flannery, K. V. 1973. "Archaeology with a Capital S.'" In *Research and Theory in Current Archaeology*, ed. C. L. Redman. New York: Wiley.

Foley, D. 1990. *Learning from Capitalist Culture.* Philadelphia: University of Pennsylvania Press.

Foucault, M. 1979. *Discipline and Punish: The Birth of the Prison.* New York: Random House.

———. 1986. *The Foucault Reader.* Ed. by P. Rabinow. Harmondsworth, England: Penguin.

Frayer, D. W., M. Wolpoff, A. G. Thorne, F. H. Smith, and G. G. Pope. 1993. "Theories of Modern Human Origins: The Paleontological Test." *American Anthropologist* 95:14–50.

Friedman, J. 1992. "The Past in the Future: History and the Politics of Identity." *American Anthropologist* 95(4):837–59.

Friedman, J., and M. J. Rowlands. 1977. *The Evolution of Social Systems.* Pittsburgh: University of Pittsburgh Press.

Gamble, C. 1994. *Timewalkers: The Prehistory of Global Colonization.* Cambridge, MA: Harvard University Press.

Gathercole, P., and D. Lowenthal, eds. 1994. *The Politics of the Past.* New York: Routledge.

Gellner, E. 1992. *Post-Modernism, Reason, and Religion.* New York: Routledge.

Gero, J. M. 1991. "Genderlithics: Women's Roles in Stone Tool Production." In *Engendering Archaeology*, eds. J. M. Gero and M. W. Conkey. Oxford: Blackwell.

Gero, J. M., and M. W. Conkey. 1991. *Engendering Archaeology.* Oxford: Blackwell.

Gosden, C. 1994. *Social Being and Time.* Oxford: Blackwell.

Gould, R.A. 1995. *Recovering the Past*. Albuquerque: University of New Mexico Press.

Gould, R. A., ed. 1978. *Explorations in Ethno-Archaeology*. Albuquerque: University of New Mexico Press.

Gould, R. A., and P. J. Watson. 1982. "A Dialogue on the Meaning and Use of Analogy in Ethnoarchaeological Reasoning." *Journal of Anthropological Archaeology* 1:355–81.

Gould, S. J. 1977. *Ever Since Darwin*. New York: Norton.

———. 1988. "Kropotkin Was No Crackpot." *Natural History* 97(7):12–21.

———. 1989. *Wonderful Life*. New York: W. W. Norton.

Graber, R. B. 1994. *A Scientific Model of Social and Cultural Evolution*. Lanham, MD: University Press of America.

Graslund, B. 1987. *The Birth of Prehistoric Chronology*. Cambridge: Cambridge University Press.

Grayson, D. K. 1983. *The Establishment of Human Antiquity*. New York: Academic Press.

Gregg, S. A. 1988. *Foragers and Farmers*. Chicago: University of Chicago Press.

Haberman, J. 1970. "Toward a Theory of Communicative Competence." *Inquiry* 13(4):360–76.

———. 1979. *Communication and the Evolution of Society*. Boston: Beacon Press.

———. 1985. "The Theory of Communicative Action." *Reason and the Rationalization of Society, Volume 1*. Boston: Beacon Press.

Handsman, R. G. 1991. "Whose Art Was Found at Lepenski Vir? Gender Relations and Power in Archaeology." In *Engendering Archaeology*, eds. J. M. Gero and M. W. Conkey. Oxford: Blackwell.

Harris, J. E., and K. R. Weeks. 1973. *X-Raying the Pharaohs*. New York: Scribner's.

Harris, M. 1968. *The Rise of Anthropological Theory*. New York: Crowell.

———. 1979. *Cultural Materialism*. New York: Random House.

Harrold, F. B., and R. A. Eve. 1988. *Cult Archaeology and Creationism*. Iowa City: University of Iowa Press.

Hastorf, C. A. 1991. "Gender, Space, and Food in Prehistory." In *Engendering Archaeology*, eds. J. M. Gero and M. W. Conkey, eds. *Engendering Archaeology*. Oxford: Blackwell.

Hawkes, C. 1954. "Archaeological Theory and Method: Some Suggestions from the Old World." *American Anthropologist* 55:55–68

Hempel, C. B. 1966. *Philosophy of Natural Science*. Englewood Cliffs, NJ: Prentice-Hall.

Herrnstein, R. J. and C. Murray. 1996. *The Bell Curve. Intelligence and Class Structure in American Life*. New York: Simon and Schuster.

Hodder, I. 1989. *The Meanings of Things*. London: Unwin Hyman.

———. 1991. "Postprocessual Archaeology and the Current Debate." In *Processual and Postprocessual Archaeologies*, Multiple Ways of Knowing the Past. ed. R. W. Preceul. Carbondale, IL: Center for Archaeological Investigations.

Hodder, I., Shanks, M., Alexandri, A., Buchli, V., Carman, J., Last, J. and Lucas, G. 1995. *Interpreting Archaeology: Finding Meaning in the Past*. London: Routledge.

Hosler, D., J. Sabloff, J. A., and D. Runge. 1977. "Simulation Model Development: A Case Study of the Classic Maya Collapse." In *Social Processes in Maya Prehistory*, ed. N. Hammond. New York: Academic Press.

Itzkoff, S. 1987. *Why Humans Vary in Intelligence*. Ashfield, MA: Paideia.

Jackson, T. L. 1991. "Pounding Acorn: Women's Production as Social and Economic Focus." In *Engendering Archaeology*, eds. J. M. Gero and M. W. Conkey. Oxford: Blackwell.

Johnson, G. A. 1987. "Comment on T. K. Earle and R. W. Preucel. 1987. Processual Archaeology and the Radical Critique." *Current Anthropology* 28(4):517–18.

Jones, D. 1995. "Sexual Selection, Physical Attractiveness, and Facial Neoteny: Cross-cultural Evidence and Implications." *Current Anthropology* 36(5):723–48.

Kaplan, A. 1984. "Philosophy of Science in Anthropology." *Annual Review of Anthropology* 13:25–39.

Keene, A. S. 1981. *Prehistoric Foraging in a Temperate Forest*. New York: Academic Press.

Kirch, P. V., and R. C. Green. 1987. "History, Phylogeny, and Evolution in Polynesia." *Current Anthropology* 28(4):431–56.

Kirk, G. S., and J. E. Raven. 1966. *The Presocratic Philosophers*. Cambridge: Cambridge University Press.

Kitto, H. D. F. 1951. *The Greeks*. Edinburgh: Penguin.

Kohl, P. L. 1981. "Materialist Approaches in Prehistory." *Annual Review of Anthropology* 10:89–118.

Krebs, J., and N. B. Davies. 1981. *Introduction to Behavioral Ecology*. Oxford: Blackwell.

Langer, W. L. (Gen. Ed.), P. MacKendrick, D. Geanakoplos, J. H. Hexter, and R. Pipes. 1968. *Western Civilization*. New York: Harper & Row.

Leach, E. R. 1984. "Glimpses of the Unmentionable in the History of British Social Anthropology." *Annual Review of Anthropology* 13:1–23.

Leone, M. 1995. "A Historical Archaeology of Capitalism." *American Anthropologist* 97(2):251–268.

Leone, M., P. B. Potter, Jr., and P. A. Schackel. 1987. "Toward a Critical Archaeology." *Current Anthropology* 28(3):283–302.

Ling, R. 1987. "A New Look at Pompeii." In *Origins*, ed. B. Cunliffe. London: BBC Books.

Lodge, D. 1984. *Small World*. London: Penguin.

Lovejoy, A. O. 1960. *The Great Chain of Being: A Study of the History of an Idea*. New York: Harper & Row.

Lumley, H. de. 1969. *Le paleolithique inferieur et moyen du Midi Mediterranean dans son cadre geologique: Vol. 1: Ligurie Provence*. Paris: Editions du Centre National de la Recherche Scientifique.

McGuire, R. H. 1992a. *A Marxist Archaeology*. San Diego: Academic Press.

———. 1992b. "Archeology and the First Americans." *American Anthropologist* 94(4):816–36.

Marx, K. 1904. *The Critique of Political Economy*, trans. I. N. Stone. Chicago: International Library Publication Co.

Meek, R. L. 1953. *Marx and Engels on Malthus*. London: Lawrence and Wishart.

Meltzer, D. J., D. D. Fowler, & J. A. Sabloff, eds. 1986. *American Archaeology Past and Future*. Washington, DC: Smithsonian Institution Press.

Miller, D. 1987. *Material Culture and Mass Consumption*. Oxford: Basil Blackwell.

Morgan, L. H. 1877. *Ancient Society*. Reprinted. 1964, ed. and with an introduction by L. A. White. Cambridge, MA: Harvard University Press.

Neiman, F. D. 1995. "Stylistic Variation in Evolutionary Perspective: Inferences from Decorative Diversity and Interassemblage Distance in Illinois Woodland Ceramic Assemblages." *American Antiquity* 60(1): 7–36.

Nisbet, R. J. 1980. *History of the Idea of Progress*. New York: Basic Books.

Nordbladh, J., and T. Yates. 1990. "This Perfect Body, This Virgin Text: Between Sex and Gender in Archaeology." In *Archaeology After Structuralism*, eds. I. Bapty and T. Yates. London: Routledge.

O'Meara, J. T. 1989. "Anthropology as Empirical Science." *American Anthropologist* 91(2):354–69.

Orton, C. 1980. *Mathematics in Archaeology*. London: Collins.

Paddayya, K. 1985. "Theoretical Archaeology—A Review." In *Recent Advances in Indian Archaeology*, eds. S. B. Deo and K. Paddayya. Poona, India: Deccan College of Post-Graduate and Research Institute.

Patterson, T. C., and C. W. Gailey, eds. 1987. *Power Relations and State Formation*. Washington, DC: American Anthropological Association.

Pauketat, T., and T. Emerson. 1991. "The Ideology of Authority and the Power of the Pot." *American Anthropologist* 93(4):919–41.

Pinsky, V., and A. Wylie, eds. 1995. *Critical Traditions in Contemporary Archaeology*. Albuquerque: University of New Mexico Press.

Pollock, S. 1991. "Women in a Men's World: Images of Sumerian Women." In *Engendering Archaeology*, eds. J. M. Gero and M. W. Conkey. Oxford: Blackwell.

Pyne, K. A. 1996. *Art and the Higher Life: Painting and Evolutionary Thought in Late Nineteenth Century America*. Austin: University of Texas Press.

Read, D. 1996. Personal communication.

Reeves, N. 1990. *The Complete Tutankhamun*. New York: Thames and Hudson.

Renfrew, C. 1978. "Trajectory, Discontinuity and Morphogenesis: the Implications of Catastrophe Theory for Archaeology." *American Antiquity* 43:202–22.

Richards, R. J. 1987. *Darwin and the Emergence of Evolutionary Theories of Mind and Behavior.* Chicago: University of Chicago Press.

Rindos, D. 1984. *The Origins of Agriculture.* New York: Academic Press.

Robertshaw, P., ed. 1990. *A History of African Archaeology.* Portsmouth, NH: Heinemann.

Rogers, J. D., ed. 1995. *Ethnohistory and Archaeology: Approaches to Postcontact Change in the Americas.* New York: Plenum Press.

Ross, E. B., ed. 1980. *Beyond the Myths of Culture: Essays on Cultural Materialism.* New York: Academic Press.

Rowlands, M., and K. Kristansen, eds. 1995. *Social Transformation in Archaeology.* New York: Routledge.

Sahlins, M. D., and E. R. Service, eds. 1960. *Evolution and Culture.* Ann Arbor: University of Michigan Press.

Salmon, M. H. 1982. *Philosophy and Archaeology.* New York: Academic Press.

Salmon, M. H., and W. C. Salmon. 1979. "Alternative Models of Scientific Explanation." *American Anthropologist* 81:61–74.

Salt, G. W., ed. 1984. *Ecology and Evolutionary Biology.* Chicago: University of Chicago Press.

Schiffer, M. B. 1981. "Some Issues in the Philosophy of Archaeology." *American Antiquity* 46:899–908.

———. 1976. *Behavioral Archaeology.* New York: Academic Press.

———. 1987. *Formation Processes of the Archaeological Record.* Albuquerque: University of New Mexico.

Schmidt, A. 1971. *The Concept of Nature in Marx.* London: NLB.

Shanks, M., and C. Tilley. 1987. *Re-Constructing Archaeology.* Cambridge: Cambridge University Press.

Shanks, M., and C. Tilley. 1987. *Social Theory and Archaeology.* Oxford: Polity Press.

Skibo, J. M., W. H. Walker, and A. E. Nielsen, eds. 1995. *Expanding Archaeology.* Salt Lake City: University of Utah Press.

Spaulding, A. C. 1973. "Archeology in the Active Voice: The New Anthropology." In *Research and Theory in Current Archaeology*, ed. C. L. Redman. New York: Wiley.

Spector, J. D. 1991. "What This Awl Means: Toward a Feminist Archaeology." In *Engendering Archaeology*, eds. J. M. Gero and M. W. Conkey. Oxford: Blackwell.

Spencer, H. 1883. *Social Statics.* New York: Appleton.

Spriggs, M., ed. 1984. *Marxist Perspectives in Archaeology.* Cambridge: Cambridge University Press.

Spuhler, J. N. 1985. "Anthropology, Evolution, and Scientific Creationism." *Annual Review of Anthropology* 14:103–33.

Steward, J. 1949. "Cultural Causality and Law: A Trial Formulation of the Development of Early Civilizations." *American Anthropologist* 51:1–27.

Stone, P., and R. MacKenzie, eds. 1995. *The Excluded Past: Archaeology in Education.* New York: Routledge.

Strong, D. E., ed. 1973. *Archaeological Theory and Practice.* London: Seminar Press.

Toth, N., and K. D. Schick. 1986. "The First Million Years: The Archaeology of Protohuman Culture." *Advances in Archaeological Method and Theory* 9:1–96.

Trigger, B. G. 1984. "Archaeology at the Crossroads: What's New?" *Annual Review of Anthropology* 13:275–300.

———. 1989. *History of Archaeological Thought.* Cambridge: Cambridge University Press.

———. 1991. "Distinguished Lecture in Archaeology: Constraint and Freedom." *American Anthropologist* 93(3): 551–69.

———. 1993. *Early Civilizations: Ancient Egypt in Context.* Cairo: American University in Cairo Press.

Tringham, R. E. 1991. "Households with Faces: The Challenge of Gender in Prehistoric Architectural Remains." In *Engendering Archaeology*, eds. J. M. Gero and M. W. Conkey. Oxford: Blackwell.

Turner, H. 1985. *Herbert Spencer: A Renewed Appreciation*. Beverly Hills: Sage.

UNESCO and S. J. de Laet, eds. 1994. *History of Humanity: Vol. 1, Prehistory and the Beginnings of Civilization*. New York: Routledge.

Vasicek, Z., and J. Malina, eds. 1990. *Archaeology Yesterday and Today*. Cambridge: Cambridge University Press.

Watson, P. J., S. A. LeBlanc, and C. L. Redman. 1971. *Explanation in Archeology*. New York: Columbia University Press.

———. 1984. *Archeological Explanation*. New York: Columbia University Press.

Watson, P. J., and M. C. Kennedy. 1991. "The Development of Horticulture in the Eastern Woodlands of North America: Women's Role." In *Engendering Archaeology*, eds. J. M. Gero and M. W. Conkey. Oxford: Blackwell.

Wells, P. S. 1980. *Culture Contact and Culture Change*. Cambridge: Cambridge University Press.

Wenke, R. J. 1975–1976. "Imperial Investments and Agricultural Developments in Parthian and Sasanian Khuzestan: 150 B.C. to A.D. 640." *Mesopotamia* 10– 11:31–217.

———. 1981. "Explaining the Evolution of Cultural Complexity: A Review." In *Advances in Archaeological Method and Theory*, Vol. 4, ed. M. B. Schiffer. New York: Academic Press.

———. 1987. "Western Iran in the Partho-Sasanian Period: The Imperial Transformation." In *The Archaeology of Western Iran*, ed. F. Hole. Washington, DC: Smithsonian Institution Press.

Wenke, R., J. Long, and P. Buck. 1988. "Epipaleolithic and Neolithic Subsistence and Settlement in the Fayyum Oasis of Egypt." *Journal of Field Archaeology* 15(1):29–51.

White, L. A. 1949. *The Science of Culture*. New York: Grove Press.

———. 1959. "The Concept of Culture." *American Anthropologist* 61:227–51.

Willey, G. R., and P. Phillips. 1958. *Method and Theory in American Archaeology*. Chicago: University of Chicago Press.

Wobst, H. M. 1974. "Boundary Conditions for Paleolithic Social Systems: A Simulation Approach." *American Antiquity* 39(2):147–79.

Wright, R. P. 1991. "Women's Labor and Pottery Production in Prehistory." In *Engendering Archaeology*, eds. J. M. Gero and M. W. Conkey. Oxford: Blackwell.

Wylie, A. 1982. "An Analogy by Any Other Name Is Just as Analogical." *Journal of Anthropological Archaeology* 1:382–401.

———. 1989. "Matters of Face and Matters of Interest." In *Archaeological Approaches to Cultural Identity: One World Archaeology, No. 10*, ed. S. Shannen. London: Unwin-Hyman.

———. 1991. "Gender Theory and the Archaeological Record: Why Is There No Archaeology of Gender?" In *Engendering Archaeology*, eds. J. M. Gero and M. W. Conkey. Oxford: Blackwell.

Young, T. C., Jr. 1988. ""Since Herodotus, Has History Been a Valid Concept?" *American Antiquity* 53(1):7–12.

Yoffee, N., and A. Sherratt, eds. 1993. *Archaeological Theory: Who Sets the Agenda?* Cambridge: Cambridge University Press.

NOTES

1. Quoted in Daniel, *The Origins and Growth of Archaeology*, p. 49

2. From the film *Indiana Jones*, quoted in Bintliff, "Why Indiana Jones Is Smarter than the Post-Processualists," p. 100.

3. See chapter 7 for a detailed discussion of this premise.

4. See, for example, Shanks and Tilley, *Social Theory and Archaeology*.

5. See, for example, Rindos, *The Origins of Agriculture*; Dunnell, "Evolution Theory and Archaeology."

6. The *Go-Between*.

7. Harris and Weeks, *X-Raying the Pharaohs*.

8. Reeves, *The Complete Tutankhamun*, p. 203.

9. Ceram, *Gods, Graves, and Scholars*, pp. 8–9.

10. Wenke et al., "Epipaleolithic and Neolithic Subsistence and Settlement in the Fayyum Oasis of Egypt."

11. Binford, "Archaeological Perspectives," p. 8.

12. Greek science and philosophy incorporated elements from other cultures. Metallurgy, geometry, mathematics, and many other arts and sciences all have long histories that predate classical Greek culture by millennia. Martin Bernal (*Black Athena*) and some other scholars have recently argued that Greek intellectual accomplishments were deeply and strongly rooted in Egyptian and Syro-Palestinian achievements, but few scholars agree with his conclusions. There simply is very little in ancient non-Greek cultures that seems to presage the political brilliance of Pericles, the dramas of Aeschylus, Sophocles, and Aristophanes, the oratory of Demosthenes, the architecture of Mnesicles and Ictinus (designers of the Acropolis), the histories of Thucydides and Herodotus, and the philosophy of Socrates and Plato—among many other arts and sciences.

13. H. D. F. Kitto's *The Greeks* is a brilliant and literate summary of the ancient Greek contribution to Western thought.

14. Daniel, *The Origins and Growth of Archaeology*, p. 90.

15. Chang, *The Archaeology of Ancient China*, p. 5.

16. Reviewed in Graslund, *The Birth of Prehistoric Chronology*, p. 18.

17. Spencer, *Social Statics*, p. 80.

18. Desmond, *Archetypes and Ancestors* pp. 100–101.

19. Attributed.

20. Darwin, quoted in Adams, *Eternal Quest*, p. 334.

21. Darwin, quoted in Adams, *Eternal Quest*, p. 335.

22. Eiseley, *Darwin and the Mysterious Mr. X*.

23. Quoted in Desmond and Moore, *Darwin*, p. 636.

24. Friedrich Engels, quoted in Meek, *Marx and Engels on Malthus*, p. 186.

25. See, for example, K. A. Pyne, *Art and the Higher Life: Painting and Evolutionary Thought in Late Nineteenth Century America*, for an analysis of the influence of evolutionary ideas on American painting.

26. Quoted in Gould, "Kropotkin Was No Crackpot," p. 12.

27. Genetic Tug-of-War May Explain Many of the Troubles of Pregnancy," *New York Times* Tuesday, July 20, 1993.

28. Durham, "Advances in Evolutionary Culture Theory," p. 188.

29. Schmidt, *The Concept of Nature in Marx*, p. 41.

30. E.g., V. G. Childe.

31. These and other quotes in this paragraph are from I. M. Diakonoff, *Early Antiquity*, pp. 1–27.

32. See, for example, R. McGuire, *A Marxist Archaeology*.

33. See B. Trigger's perceptive analysis, "Marxism in Archaeology: Real or Spurious?" Also see R. McGuire, *A Marxist Archaeology*, M. Spriggs, ed., *Marxist Perspectives in Archaeology*.

34. Daniel, *The Origins and Growth of Archaeology*.

35. T. E. Lawrence (Lawrence of Arabia), for example, has often been accused of spying for the British while working with Woolley in Mesopotamia (see Brown and Cave, *A Touch of Genius*).

36. Wallace Stevens, *The Snow Man*.

37. G. Childe, *Man Makes Himself*.

38. *American Anthropologist* 51:1–27.

39. Variants of this postmodernist aphorism have been used by various scholars; see David Lodge's entertaining novel *Small World*, p. 328 and elsewhere.

40. See Watson, LeBlanc, and Redman, *Explanation in Archeology*; also see Watson, et al. *Archeological Explanation*; Bamforth and Spaulding, "Human Behavior, Explanation, Archaeology, History, and Science"; Schiffer, "Some Issues in the Philosophy of Archaeology."

41. White, *The Science of Culture*.

42. Trigger, "Archaeology at the Crossroads: What's New?"; also see Bamforth and Spaulding, "Human Behavior, Explanation, Archaeology, History, and Science" and Salmon, *Philosophy and Archaeology*.

43. Pauketat and Emerson, "The Ideology of Authority and the Power of the Pot," p. 920.

44. See, for example, Gould, R. A., *Recovering the Past*; also see Schiffer, *Behavioral Archaeology*.

45. Hosler et al., "Simulation Model Development: A Case Study of the Classic Maya Collapse."

46. Renfrew, "Trajectory, Discontinuity and Morphogenesis: the Implications of Catastrophe Theory for Archaeology."

47. Trigger, "Distinguished Lecture in Archaeology: Constraint and Freedom," pp. 562–63.

48. Shanks and Tilley, *Re-Constructing Archaeology*, p. 243.

49. Hawkes, "Archaeological Theory and Method: Some Suggestions from the Old World."

50. Hodder, "Postprocessual Archaeology and the Current Debate," citing C. Hawkes, "Archaeological Theory and Method: Some Suggestions from the Old World."

51. See Trigger's "Post-Processual Developments in Anglo-American Archaeology," pp. 65–69.

52. See, for example, their *Social Theory and Archaeology*.

53. See, for example, Derrida, *Writing and Difference*, or Foucault, *The Foucault Reader*.

54. Shanks and Tilley, *Re-Constructing Archaeology*, p. 172.

55. Ernst Gellner found it difficult to define post-modernism, but he leaves no doubt about his opinion of it, as seen in his *Post-Modernism, Reason, and Religion*, pp. 22–23: "Post-modernism is a contemporary movement. It is strong and fashionable. Over and above this, it is not altogether clear what the devil it is. In fact, clarity is not conspicuous amongst its marked attributes. It not only generally fails to practise it, but also on occasion actually repudiates it. But anyway, there appear to be no 39 post-modernist Articles of Faith, no post-modernist manifesto, which one could consult so as to assure oneself that one has identified its ideas properly. . . . The movement and its ideas are . . . a little too ethereal and volatile to be captured and seized with precision: perhaps the acute awareness of the movement that all meanings are to be deconstructed in a way which also brings in their opposites, and highlights the contradictions contained in them . . . actually precludes a crisp and unambiguous formulation of the position."

56. Hodder, *The Meanings of Things*, p. 65.

57. Leone, "A Historical Archaeology of Capitalism," p. 263; also see Wylie, "Matters of Face and Matters of Interest."

58. As Dwight Read has observed, "Gender, as a cultural construct . . . is not observable; what is observable are its implications for how gender is embedded in the cultural system which leads, through the actions of individuals, to patterning in the observable world of material objects. The constant problem that archaeology faces is that the mapping from culture to patterning of material objects is never an isomorphism, is sometimes a homomorphism, and most often is a mapping which confounds multitudinous structuring processes. But this is a constant problem, not one peculiar to gender constructs."

59. Brumfiel, "A Review of *Prehistory of the Americas* (by S. J. Fiedel)."

60. McGuire, "Archaeology and the First Americans," p. 828.

61. A similar position has been advocated by John Bintliff, who recently predicted the demise of most forms of post-processual archaeology, suggesting that "[t]he Theoretical Archaeology of the 1990s is undeniably going to be 'Cognitive Processualism,' " ("Why Indiana Jones Is Smarter than the Post-Processualists," p. 100). The sense of Cognitive Processualism as used by Renfrew and Bintliff is close to that of the holistic archaeology advocated by Bruce Trigger (see above) in that all useful methods of analysis are applied to the past, but in the context of an analytical science based on materialist perspectives.

2

FUNDAMENTALS OF ARCHAEOLOGY

Though nothing can bring back the hour
Of splendour in the grass, of glory in the flower;
We will grieve not, rather find
Strength in what remains behind. . . .

William Wordsworth (1770-1850)

In this verse from *Intimations of Immortality*, Wordsworth expressed his recognition that humanity's hopes of immortality must lie elsewhere than in our physical selves, or in our works, or in our world, for these are all transitory; in a process of decay from the moment of birth or construction. "Shades of the prison house begin to close upon the growing boy," he wrote, meaning Death's grip is always there, always tightening.

Philosopher Bertrand Russell shared none of Wordsworth's hopes about our prospects of immortality, but he had the same sense of inevitable decay. When asked what he thought would happen to him after death, he cheerfully said, "When I die, I rot."

Perhaps the only people in the world who view the long record of the world's rot and decay with hope and optimism are archaeologists. In chapter 1 we reviewed some of the great theories of history and the past—the influential ideas about why history has turned out the way it has. Whatever one thinks of these theories, whatever one's view of the past, one must link these ideas to the physical material remains of the past. And in this chapter we shall consider the methods that have been developed to apply these great ideas to the material record of the past.

ARCHAEOLOGISTS AND THE PRACTICE OF ARCHAEOLOGY

Before considering in more detail how archaeology is done, let us consider who actually does it. When trapped in airplanes or up against the wall at a party, archaeologists who reveal their occupation often are told, "When I was growing up I wanted to be an archaeologist," or "It must be exciting to be an archaeologist!"

Not all non-archaeologists realize, however, that most archaeologists have to spend ten years or more in college and graduate school in preparation for their profession, or that for every hour an archaeologist spends excavating, he or she spends thousands of hours teaching university classes, raising money for research, and writing reports on research already completed.

Most professional archaeologists in the United States have a "Ph.D.," a Doctor of Philosophy degree, the dubious prize for an average of six years of post-graduate study. "Those who can, do; those who can't, teach" does not apply to archaeology, where almost every major professional holds a teaching position. Competition for university teaching positions has been ferocious since the early 1970s. Most beginning professorships pay less than $40,000 a year, and literally hundreds of scholars compete for every job. Many people spend six years or more in graduate school preparing for a professional life in archaeology, only to discover that they cannot find an academic position.

The majority of North American archaeologists have been trained as anthropologists; a minority are language scholars, such as Egyptologists, Assyriologists, Classicists (e.g., specialists in ancient Greek and Roman cultures), art historians, and biblical scholars. This division raises the issue of the relationship of the social sciences and the humanities. Some anthropological archaeologists consider their discipline a social science, whereas language scholars often view their work as part of the humanities. Language scholars tend to be particularly interested in relating archaeological remains to ancient written documents, such as the Bible, Greek and Roman texts, Egyptian hieroglyphic inscriptions, etc. These different perspectives are not strictly separate, and anthropological concepts are beginning to be incorporated in the humanities, while some anthropologists also have mastered ancient languages. But, as in most academic disciplines, specialization is a necessary part of training. To be well-trained in both anthropology and Egyptology, for example, requires at least eight to ten years of graduate study for those hardy few who attempt such extensive preparation.

The majority of North American archaeologists who are anthropologists are generally considered "social scientists," but both this term and "anthropology" are increasingly ambiguous. Anthropology literally means "the science (or study) of man," but that leaves rather a lot to be defined. Anthropology today continues to be divided among several specializations, each of which is at least marginally relevant to the study of world prehistory. *Physical anthropologists* are concerned mainly with variations in the physical attributes of humans and primates, and include people who search for the fossils of extinct forms of early humans, others who study the genetics of existing human groups, primatologists who analyze the behavior and other characteristics of non-human primates, specialists in the adaptation of human groups to different environments (especially extreme environments, such as the high Andes Mountains), and scholars engaged in many other kinds of research. *Sociocultural anthropologists* focus on studies of living or recent human societies and include an extremely diverse range of specialists, such as those who study the languages of non-literate peoples, and others who do the traditional ethnological studies of human societies, analyzing the lifeways of selected groups, from the hunter-gatherers of the rain forests of the Amazon to the patrons of the bars of south Texas.[1] *Archaeologists* represent a third major specialization within anthropology. Most anthropological archaeologists have some graduate training in the other fields of anthropology, in addition to their concentrations in archaeological methods and theories. Most archaeologists also take advanced courses in mathematics, geology, demography, and related disciplines.

The lines that used to separate anthropology, sociology, psychology, and other social sciences have blurred greatly in recent times. The concept of "culture"—the uniquely human intellectual and behavioral capacities (see chapter 3)—has been, and remains, for many anthropologists the connective tissue that incorporates them all in a single discipline, but for many anthropologists there is no strong theoretical structure that unites the discipline.

In Europe, Asia, and Africa, archaeology is often a separate university department—not connected with sociocultural anthropology or physical anthropology, as it is in the United States. In those countries archaeology is often viewed as a form of history, or, in some cases, as a natural science like paleontology. But contemporary archaeology in the United Kingdom and in some other European countries has become increasingly viewed as a sociological discipline, and conversely, in North America, some centers of archaeology have separated and allied themselves more closely with the biological and geological sciences.

Archaeology as a discipline has long been dominated by North American and European scholars,[2] but India, Japan, China, Egypt, Argentina, and many other countries have long and productive traditions of archaeological research, and there is a growing internationalism to archaeology.

THE ARCHAEOLOGICAL RECORD: THE BASIC DATA OF ANALYSES OF THE PAST

People are messy animals. More than two million years ago, our ancestors began littering Africa with stone tools and smashed animal bones, and ever since we have been carpeting the world with layer upon layer of our own garbage. Strictly speaking, all this junk, from two-million-year-old stone tools to today's eternal aluminum beer cans, as well as the bones of our human ancestors and the remains of the plants and animals they ate, constitute the *archaeological record.*

Archaeologists see cosmic significance in the archaeological record: the major premise of many archaeologists, in fact, is that much of what we will ever know about our origins, our nature, and even our destiny must be read in the patterns inherent in these layers of debris; archaeologists assume that they can see in the contents, spatial arrangements, and depositional sequence of the world's garbage the reflections of the factors that have shaped our physical and cultural evolution. This material archaeological record is *all* we have to understand more than 99 percent of our past—the period before written languages appeared. And even for the periods when we have written records of our past, the archaeological record is important; whereas historical documents may be full of the usual human lies, propaganda, and misconceptions, the material remains are a physical record of what *did* happen, not what someone said happened or thought happened or even wanted to have happened. Whether or not we can scientifically and objectively analyze this material record is open to question, as we shall see.

ARTIFACTS, FEATURES, AND SITES

All academic disciplines have their own jargon, and archaeology is no exception. Archaeologists analyze the archaeological record primarily in terms of *artifacts*, which can be defined as things that owe any of their physical characteristics or their place in space to human activity. Thus, a beautifully shaped stone spear-point from a 20,000-year-old campsite in France is an artifact, but so is an undistinguished and unaltered rock that some weary Native American pitched out of a Mississippi corn field a thousand years ago. Even the faintest traces of human activity can be considered artifacts, such as the footprints left several million years ago when a few of our earliest bipedal ancestors strolled across a volcanic plain at Laetoli, in Tanzania (Figure 2.1)—or the footprints left on the moon by astronauts.

Nor do things cease to be artifacts because of their recent origins. Since the early 1970s, archaeologist William Rathje and numerous archaeology students at the University of Arizona have been sorting through the artifacts added each day to the Tucson municipal dump and littered along city roads, trying to discern how things are thrown away and what they say about the community that created the trash—and the implications of today's disposal behavior in understanding the past (they learned, among other things, that the average Tucson resident wastes astounding amounts of food; that in rural road litter, unsurprisingly, beer cans and contraceptives are often found together; and that food, newspapers, and other debris preserve extraordinarily well for years in municipal dumps).

Another common archaeological term is *feature*, used to refer to non-portable clusters of artifacts, such as the remains of hearths, walls, latrines, and burials, which are presumed to reflect specific, sometimes repeated, activities.[3]

Perhaps the most common archaeological term is *site*, an imprecise term generally used to refer to relatively dense concentrations of artifacts and features. The ancient city of Babylon, in Iraq, which today comprises a huge mound of slowly dissolving mudbrick buildings, millions of pottery fragments (known as "sherds" to archaeologists), and all the other debris of an ancient city, but which 4,000 years ago was the capital of a great empire, is a site, but so is any one of the many areas in Olduvai Gorge, Tanzania, where a few score stone tools and animal bones mark the spot where 1.7 million years ago a few of our ancestors hungrily disassembled a killed or scavenged gazelle.

Ancient village and town sites are often hard to miss because they are usually marked by walls and massive quantities of pottery and other debris. It is convenient to think of the archaeological record in this case as composed of many discrete sites representing different settlements, but, in truth, the whole world is littered with artifacts and features.

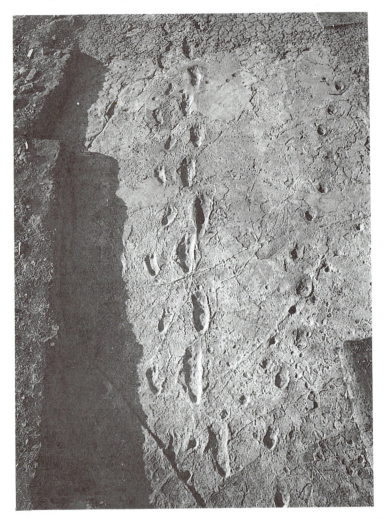

FIGURE 2.1 Hominid footprints at Laetoli. A trail of hominid footprints was found preserved in volcanic ash at Laetoli, Tanzania. These prints demonstrate that hominids were fully bipedal by 3.6 million years ago.

The world's archaeological record is the raw material for the analysis of the past, but to find meaning in it we must bring to bear a wide range of analytical techniques and a body of theories, hypotheses, and ideas of many different kinds.

THE FORMATION OF THE ARCHAEOLOGICAL RECORD

Before we can understand how to analyze the past, we must understand how the past was formed. The "past" in this sense is simply the present archaeological record—although this may sound like a Zen *koan* (a riddle without a solution whose purpose is to demonstrate the inadequacy of logical reasoning and provide enlightenment). But, in fact, the past *is* the present, in that we can only see the past in the present archaeological record.

The artifacts, features, and sites constituting the archaeological record vary widely in their contents and ages, but all must be understood to have been formed by a complex interplay not only of the activities of the people who created them but also of natural forces.[4]

Much archaeological effort and ingenuity has been devoted to trying to untangle the complex interaction of cultural and natural factors—"C-Transforms" and "N-Transforms," to use Michael Schiffer's terms[5]—in the formation of the archaeological record, because any hopes we may have of explaining the past are necessarily linked to our ability to understand how the past—in the sense of the archaeological record—was created.

Consider as an example the problem of understanding the origins of modern humans—that is, of us, *Homo sapiens sapiens*. Many "models" (i.e., sets of linked hypotheses about the causes of a particular development) of modern human origins have been formulated, but two of them are particularly influential in current research on this problem: one, described variously as the "African Origins," "Total Replacement," or "Eve" model,[6] is that modern humans evolved first and only in Africa, just a few hundred thousand years ago or less, and then migrated to the rest of the world, displacing all other hominid forms, and with little or no genetic interchange with them; an alternative model, commonly known as the "Multiregional Evolution" model,[7] holds that North Africa was a conduit for hominid migrations for millions of years and contends that modern humans arose out of gene flow among some or all of the many different human populations that had colonized Africa, Europe, and Asia many hundreds of thousands, perhaps millions, of years ago.

The evidence relevant to these "models" of human origins is discussed at length in chapter 4. The important points here are that they are of considerable interest and even of some contemporary sociopolitical importance (e.g., some scholars see one or the other of these models as "racist" [see chapter 4]), and that the only way in which we can ever test these models is to analyze the archaeological record (although genetic evidence is also relevant). And to analyze this archaeological record we have to sort out a bewildering array of cultural and natural factors that produced the archaeological record of relevance here. Early *Homo sapiens sapiens* in Africa, for example, may have developed a simple advantage in tool-making that made them slightly better than other forms of humans at making a living as hunter-foragers, with the long-term result that this slight advantage allowed them to supplant other groups. If so, then we should be able to see reflections of this supposed advantage in the stone tools, food remains, and other data of the archaeological record. We might look at the animal bones found in sites associated with early *Homo sapiens sapiens* in Africa, for example, and see if they show different, perhaps more efficient hunting techniques, compared to those of Europe and Asia. The problem, however, is to sort out the natural and cultural factors that created these sites. At various South African sites, for example, human skeletal remains and tools have been found in caves along with animal bones. But we know that leopards and other "natural" predators regularly killed animals and brought them back to these cave dens. So how can we tell which animals were killed by people and which by other animals? One can use a microscope to look at marks on some bones and see evidence that they were butchered with stone tools, but what if a leopard killed this animal and humans simply scavenged it? And it is not always easy to differentiate marks left on bones by animal teeth from those made by humans with stone or bone tools.

There are many other ambiguities in the archaeological record pertaining to modern human origins, and this complexity of disentangling cultural from natural factors is found in almost every archaeological project, whether the site is two million or 200 years old. And to the extent that there is brilliance and great creativity in the practice of archaeology, it is usually expressed in formulating some major problems in terms that can be "tested" effectively with archaeological data, whether from new excavations or from laboratory analyses.

The archaeological record is often viewed as "incomplete" because decay and other factors have changed it. But in a sense, the archaeological record is only incomplete if one looks at it as potentially a perfect reflection of the complete history of actions by the human societies that created it. The archaeological record can never be that perfect reflection; instead, it is itself a product of cultural and natural forces, and in that sense it is not really "incomplete"—even though our knowledge of these forces must always be incomplete.[8]

ARTIFACT PRODUCTION AND PRESERVATION

The basic sequence of events that has produced the world's archaeological record is the same for stone tools as it is for today's best DataWhacker computer. In each case, people: (1) acquire the raw materials; (2) make these materials into artifacts by changing them (or simply their location) in some way; (3) use the artifacts; and (4) then discard them.

At each stage of this sequence, a variety of cultural and/or natural factors comes into play. In ancient Mesopotamia, for example, people lived primarily in houses made of mudbricks—made simply by mixing mud with straw and forming bricks by hand or in simple wood molds and leaving them to dry. Mesopotamia's intense sun, occasional rain, strong winds, and ground water seepage then began to degrade these bricks and the buildings created from them. Eventually the buildings were abandoned and a variety of cultural and natural factors continued to operate on them. Wooden roof beams, stone thresholds, and even some mudbricks, for example, were regularly carried away for a variety of re-uses.

This process, of making and using—and reusing—things and then discarding them, is really no different today. For example, landfills around the world are currently filling up with the carcasses of typewriters and early generations of computers, many of which have been scavenged for spare parts. Although these machines may last longer than most of the remains of antiquity, all are subject to eventual obliteration through a combination of cultural and natural forces.

How quickly these materials are returned to their elemental chemical state is simply a matter of their composition and the conditions of preservation. The laws of thermodynamics assert that matter is never destroyed nor lost in the universe, but this is little consolation to the archaeologist looking, for example, at the smear of calcium that is all that is left of a corpse buried many millennia ago in the warm, wet soils of the Egyptian Delta. Even in drier, better-preserved contexts, a depressing number of things can destroy archaeological remains. Floods wash them away, glacial ice sheets grind them to bits, rodents go out of their way to burrow through them, earthworms move them, and rivers and winds bury them under thick layers of silt and sand.

The greatest destruction, however, is caused by people—and not just in our own industrial age. The gleaming limestone sheaths that originally enclosed each of the Egyptian pyramids were looted in medieval times and used as building materials. All over the ancient world, in fact, successive settlements were built on—and of—the remnants of earlier occupations. Still, our own generation is perhaps the worst despoiler of antiquities. In some areas, almost any new construction destroys antiquities: in London, for example, the foundations dug for new buildings often destroy remnants of Roman Londinium.

Industrialization at least has some possible benefits, but the same cannot be said for the other great destroyer of the past, looting. Illegal antiquities from around the world are openly on sale in New York, Tokyo, London, and many other cities. It is sad to relate, but even the mild fines and other penalties currently in force in some countries are only occasionally applied to people convicted of looting, and in many countries the primary looters are impoverished peasants who are simply trying to make a minimal living.

Looting destroys the only hope we have of analyzing cultural processes in the archaeological record because it obliterates the *context* of artifacts and features. Thus, for example, to study the origins of the first civilizations of Mexico, it is crucial to excavate sites in such a way that the goods people were buried with and the contents of their houses are meticulously recorded, so that the distribution of wealth in the community can be estimated. But once a looter has ripped through house floors to loot graves of their contents, the anthropological significance of the site is forever lost.

Natural decay processes affect sites too, but if a site is not looted the effects of these natural processes can be discerned and taken into account in interpretations. Stone tools are almost indestructible, but bones, hides, wood, plants, and people rot. Organic decay is a chemical reaction, and the best preservation of organic remains occurs where there is not enough water, heat, pH balance, or oxygen for the chemistry of decay to occur, such as in dry caves, under thick layers of volcanic ash, or in peat bogs, permafrost, or deep, dark, cold water. Entire mammoths have been retrieved from frozen pits in Siberia, and well-preserved human corpses thousands of years old have been recovered from peat bogs (Figure 2.2), swamps, and in one case, a glacier, in Europe. Eight-thousand-year-old corpses found in waterlogged levels of the Windover site in Florida still had enough brain tissue preserved that it may be possible to compare their genes to those of present-day Native Americans and even estimate what language family they belonged to and how long their ancestors had been in North America.

No one knows how powerful the analytical equipment of the future will be, so it is important that archaeologists preserve as much as possible—even if that means de-

FIGURE 2.2 "Tollund man," a 2,000-year-old hanging victim from the peat bogs of Denmark, illustrates the "pickling" properties of weakly acidic environments.

ciding not to dig some fraction of extremely important sites in the hope that someday we will have equipment and techniques of vastly greater sophistication.

ARCHAEOLOGICAL RESEARCH DESIGN

No matter what an archaeologist's academic orientation, anyone who symbolically dons the pith helmet and examines directly the remains of the past has to do at least two things: choose where to excavate or survey and then interpret what is found. Choosing the place to dig, for example, is usually not so unstructured and speculative a procedure as imagined by non-archaeologists, who frequently ask "How do you know where to look?" In modern archaeology, one rarely sets out on expeditions to remote places on the Micawberish assumption that something interesting will turn up—although many ancient remains are still found by accident or unsystematic exploration. The construction of a subway system in Mexico City in the 1960s, for example, revealed parts of Aztec temples and other buildings. But increasingly, archaeological remains are identified through a process of systematic survey. It does not take a trained archaeologist to find the pyramids of Egypt or Mexico, but most archaeological remains are less evident and accessible, such as those covered by drifting sand or alluvial soils, buried beneath contemporary settlements, or located in remote, unsurveyed areas.

Many archaeological surveys and excavations are done within the context of a specific intellectual question or problem. If one were interested in the origin of maize agriculture in ancient Mexico, for example, one would read the many reports written on this subject, and then examine maps of where early varieties of maize have been found. One might then hypothesize some possible causes of the transition to maize agriculture—and this process of hypothesis formation is one of the more creative aspects of the discipline. The goal for the archaeologist is to develop some novel ideas or ways of looking at a problem that lead him or her to look for certain kinds of data. One might, then, hypothesize that for various reasons maize was domesticated in lowland coastal areas and in the context of certain kinds of communities. One could then identify where relevant remains might be found and then design a program of surveys and/or excavations to study this problem in this area.

Not all research is in this *problem-oriented* format. Often research is exploratory. One might select an area and do surveys to see if any important remains can be found there. Also, in recent years "problem-oriented" archaeological research has been complemented by rapid growth in "public" archaeology, or "CRM"—that is, Cultural Resource Management. In many countries, governments stipulate that new construction must be preceded by an analysis of its impact on the historical and archaeological record, and then research is undertaken if significant remains are found. Hundreds, perhaps thousands, of archaeologists now are employed around the world as "public archaeologists" to do this kind of work.

"Public archaeology" is usually well-funded by the relevant government, but traditional "problem-oriented" archaeology is a different matter. Interesting ideas about the past are in no short supply in archaeology, but money to do the relevant research certainly is. In the United States, for example, an archaeologist can submit a written proposal for research funds to the U.S. National Science Foundation or the National Endowment for the Humanities, explaining precisely what kinds of archaeological evidence he or she hopes to find and why it is important. This proposal will be judged by a group of one's peers, and if it is successful (in recent years only about 15 percent of National Science Foundation archaeology proposals were funded), one then would receive the money and conduct the field research.[9] Most archaeologists who direct long-term research projects must spend months of each year trying to obtain funds to continue the project by writing proposals, administering grants received, requesting funds from corporations and private donors, etc.

Locating and Excavating Sites   Actually locating sites might involve walking surveys, where five or ten archaeologists, working from maps or aerial photographs, simply line up and walk over a selected area, recording sites as they are found. Aerial photographs and other photogrammetric techniques can often be used to reveal ancient agricultural fields, roads, and other features not visible from the ground (Figure 2.3). However they are located, archaeological sites can either be simply mapped and recorded, or they can be excavated—depending on the project's resources and objectives. The methods used to excavate archaeological sites depend on the kind of

FIGURE 2.3 Aerial photographs often reveal archaeological remains that are not directly visible from ground level, as in the outline of this Roman Temple on Hayling Island, Hampshire, England. Stone walls just below ground surface caused parching of grain just above them during the 1976 drought, revealing the outline of the temple walls.

remains involved and the objectives of the archaeologist. Normally the first step is to make a careful map of the site so that objects and features found can be given precise three-dimensional coordinates, the "provenience." Then the site is gridded into, say, 5 × 5 meter blocks, and a sample of these blocks is selected for excavation. Actual digging is done with dental tools, paint brushes, trowels, shovels, bulldozers, or dynamite—depending, again, on the objectives and context.

Like every other profession, archaeology has its variants of Murphy's Law: Veteran field workers know that the most important find will likely be made on the last day of the season, when there is no time or money to continue the excavations, and that particularly important finds are usually located in the most inaccessible places. Archaeology is also a lot of hard work, usually, and much of it takes place at uncongenial hours of the day and seasons of the year. Anyone who has dug a backyard trench for a sewer pipe on a hot August day has already experienced many of the thrills of field archaeology.

The simple mechanics of excavation are within the range of abilities of almost any healthy adult. The best field archaeologists tend to be those who have a good sense of spatial relationships and enormous patience. "God is in the details," said a great architect,[10] and the same is true of archaeology. One usually tries to excavate according to the *stratigraphy* (Figures 2.4 and 2.5) of the site, so that the different layers of debris are removed in the reverse sequence in which they were deposited—as opposed to simply digging the site by arbitrary levels and removing successive layers, each, say, twenty-five centimeters thick.

Thomas Jefferson is often credited for having conducted the first scientific stratigraphic archaeological excavation in history.[11] In 1784 he excavated a trench through a Native American burial mound near his home in Virginia and recognized that it had been built up over time by many burials and reburials. Jefferson was able to read a time sequence in the stratigraphy of the site, and he related the differences in preservation of the human bones to the relative time these people had been buried. Jefferson also applied his research to a specific problem: in Jefferson's time many people thought that the "mound-builders" were ancient Europeans, not Native Americans; Jefferson concluded that Native Americans may have been the builders of these mounds.

Modern stratigraphic excavation techniques are based on the same logic as Jefferson's. In Tabun Cave in Palestine, for example, Neanderthals came each year for a few months and built fires, made tools, butchered animals, and generally lived their unremarkable lives. Rocks falling from the ceiling and animals bringing their prey

FIGURE 2.4 This aerial photograph of the archaeological remains of an ancient city, Tell Leilan, in Syria illustrates the complexity of architecture in early cities as well as the grid-system of archaeological excavation.

FIGURE 2.5   This profile drawing shows the depositional history of a community at Tepe Sabz, near Deh Luran, Iran, from about 5500 to 3500 B.C. Skill in field archaeology is largely the ability to discern and interpret such cultural layers in the confusing jumble of mud-brick, stones, ash, and other debris.

back to the cave when people were not there added to the layers of debris. Thus the excavators,[12] who were interested in subtle changes in diet and tool manufacture over the whole history of the cave's occupation because they were looking for evidence regarding the relationship of the Neanderthals to ourselves, had to tease apart layer after layer of debris, trying to separate layers that were the result of short time intervals and single events. The excavators were, in effect, trying to see *change* in the way the Neanderthals lived over thousands of years.

Aaron Copland described listening to one of Ralph Vaughn Williams's symphonies as like staring at a cow for forty-five minutes, and although studying archaeological strata is even less eventful, it is one of the most important activities in archaeology. Stratigraphic analyses require that the analyst reconstruct the many different processes that produced the sequence of deposits, and this can require considerable skill, patience, and experience. In cave sediments, for example, one must try to discern faint traces of burrowing animals that may have tunneled in from the surface and whose burrows were subsequently filled with charcoal, ash, and artifacts that date to periods long after their stratigraphic position would suggest. Some of the most complex stratigraphy is found in the remains of early villages and towns in the Middle East, where mudbrick buildings were built and rebuilt and replaced in the same area over many centuries, so that the last, most recent community sat (or sits) atop ten or more meters of compacted debris representing the remains of thousands of years of building and then abandoning houses, walls, streets, latrines, hearths, and the other facilities of ancient daily life.

Excavation techniques and stratigraphic analyses in such sites reward patience, work, and imagination. British archaeologist Sir Leonard Woolley, for example, while excavating Ur, in Mesopotamia, removed some debris and saw two holes in the ground where something had apparently rotted away. He poured them full of plaster and when the plaster had hardened Woolley unearthed an almost complete cast of an ancient wooden musical instrument that had long since disintegrated. One of the pioneers in devising the techniques of excavating ancient cities was Sir Mortimer Wheeler, a British archaeologist whose excavations at sites in the Indus Valley (modern Pakistan) were done with great care to reveal a stratigraphic record that would allow him to understand how these cities grew and changed over time.[13]

Stratigraphic analyses are a fundamental part of field archaeology because they provide the primary data for looking at change over time in all aspects of cultures. The archaeologist knows that if he or she can detect disturbances and read the strata correctly, the lowest strata can be assumed to be earlier than the ones above it, and thus a form of "time" can be read in a stratigraphic sequence. Understanding the nature of these changes, however, requires analyses of the materials and artifacts found in these strata.

ARCHAEOLOGICAL METHODS OF ANALYSIS

A century ago, most archaeologists were "generalists" in that they were all broadly trained academically and could do most of the analyses their research required, including the excavations and laboratory analyses. The extreme specialization of modern culture, however, has had its impact on archaeology too, and today almost every professional has some kind of technical specialization or area of research in which she or he is particularly qualified. Every archaeological site is unique and non-renewable, and many technical specialists are required to make the most of the evidence unearthed. Most excavation staffs today include geologists, botanists, palynologists (experts on plant pollen), architectural draftsmen, faunal experts (specialists in analyzing animal remains), artifact illustrators, and other specialists. Conserving finds once they are discovered has also become a highly technical specialty, requiring advanced training in chemistry and other sciences.[14] A few of these specializations are discussed below; others are considered in the context of specific archaeological problems in later chapters.

RECONSTRUCTING ANCIENT ENVIRONMENTS AND CULTURAL ECOLOGIES

A primary step in any archaeological analysis is the reconstruction of the physical environments in which a particular segment of the archaeological record was formed.

Climates and the world's geomorphology—the shape and constituents of land surfaces—have changed greatly over the several million years our genus has existed, and each archaeological analysis begins with an effort to reconstruct the physical world of the culture being analyzed.

Ancient climates can often be reconstructed from floral and faunal remains. The study of animal remains, or *faunal analysis,* is a complex discipline in which in most cases the archaeologist is trying to reconstruct human diet and local environments. Faunal analysts usually tally the numbers and kinds of animals represented by the remains they find, and then use statistical methods to estimate food values, the ages and sexes of the animals involved, and changes in diets and the physical characteristics of the animals being exploited.[15] One of the most prolonged and heated arguments in contemporary archaeology now involves analyses of marks left by humans cutting up animals with stone tools: for reasons discussed in chapters 3 and 4, it is important in understanding the origins of our genus to study butchered animal bones to try to distinguish between cases in which people butchered animals they had killed themselves and those in which they butchered animals they scavenged from kills of other animals, such as lions and hyenas.[16]

Throughout the history of our genus, plants have been the main source of food for most humans, and so *floral analyses*—studies of the remains of plants—are an extremely important part of archaeology, particularly in studies of how domesticated plants and animals and agricultural economies evolved.[17] Carbon is chemically quite stable, so charred plants and seeds preserve well. Carbonized plant remains can be retrieved by *flotation:* excavated sediments are mixed with water or some other fluid and the charred plant fragments rise to the surface, where they can be skimmed off and identified.

The importance of such analyses lies in the fact that these plants indicate much about the climates and vegetation of the periods in which these animals lived. We shall see, for example, that there are debates about when and where various animals were domesticated (chapter 6). If phytoliths of domesticated grains are found on the teeth of these animals, the probability is high that they were part of an agricultural economy.

Human bodies are treasure troves of information for archaeologists, particularly if they are mummified. For example, eleven naturally mummified bodies found in beach sand in northern Chile that date to about 1000 B.C., when analyzed indicate that, among other things, one of them is the earliest known coca leaf chewer, while other bodies showed the changes of the bones of the inner ear that are typical of people who spend a lot of time diving in cold water. In addition, they had the kinds of dental caries and missing teeth associated with the sticky starches of an agricultural diet—although about 40 percent of their diet came from marine resources.[18]

Studies of human *paleopathology,* in general, can tell us much about the demography and health of ancient peoples.[19]

A rapidly growing technical specialty within archaeology is *geoarchaeology,* the combination of archaeological and geological analyses.[20] Geology and archaeology form a "natural" marriage in many obvious ways, for both disciplines are concerned with the alterations of natural landscapes. Glaciers, changing rainfall patterns, and many other natural forces alter landscapes, and so, of course, do people. Geologists are broadly concerned with ancient physical environments, and archaeologists require knowledge of these environments to interpret their finds.

Geoarchaeological analyses involve many different kinds of questions and techniques. In the Egyptian Delta, for example, many of the earliest communities were built on large sand-and-gravel mounds created by the Nile as it deposited the sediments it carried. But many of these communities have been buried under many meters of sediments from all of the annual floods since that time, and by other factors as well. Moreover, the Nile tributaries in the Delta have changed course many times, leaving a maze of criss-crossed buried river channels. To find these buried sand-gravel mounds and the archaeological sites on them thus often requires complex geological analyses involving augering, satellite image analysis, and many other techniques.

Geoarchaeological analyses are sometimes required simply to determine if some alteration to the landscape or objects are of natural or human origin. Other geoarchaeologists deal with dating strata, reconstructing ancient temperature and rainfall patterns, and related problems.

Reconstructing the physical environment and cultural ecology of any particular site usually involves the coordinated efforts of many specialists. In some ancient sites, for example, such as the floors of caves, the archaeological record is principally one in which repeated seasonal occupations of an area have left strata containing small particles of bones, burned seeds and other plant remains, debris from making stone tools, and other remnants. Spilled food, human waste, the manure of domestic animals—all these and many other factors associated with human life change the chemistry, texture, and contents of the surfaces people live on. A geoarchaeologist might, for example, measure the chemical composition of a large sample of sediments taken from different areas of such a site and look for areas relatively high in nitrogen and the other by-products of organic decay. Other specialists would identify the plants and animals that lived or were consumed in the adjacent areas.

ARTIFACT ANALYSES

Aside from ancient buildings, in sheer bulk the largest part of the archaeological record is made up of stone tools and pottery fragments (sherds). Stone tools are the earliest known artifacts, having been first used more than two million years ago, and they have remained in use to the present day. When a chunk of fine-grain stone is struck with sufficient force at the proper angle with another rock or with a wood or bone baton, a shock wave will pass through the stone and detach a flake of the desired size and shape. Classrooms all over the world are bloodied each year as instructors attempt to demonstrate this process, but with a little experience most become quite skilled. In analyzing ancient stone tools, many archaeologists have mastered the skills needed to make stone tools themselves. Few things are sharper than a fragment struck from fine-grain flint or from obsidian (volcanic glass). Obsidian is so fine-grained that flakes of it can have edges only about twenty molecules thick—hundreds of times thinner than steel tools. One archaeologist (Richard Daughtery, of Washington State University) convinced his doctor to use obsidian tools as well as standard surgical scalpels during his own heart surgery and claimed that the incisions made with obsidian healed faster.

Through experimentation, some archaeologists are able to produce copies of almost every stone tool type used in antiquity. A common research strategy is to make flint tools, use them to cut up animals, saw wood, clean hides, bore holes, etc., and then to compare the resulting wear traces with the marks found on ancient artifacts. Sometimes electron-scanning microscopes are used to study minute variations in these use-marks. Some rough correspondence can be found between the types of lithic uses and the characteristics of wear marks, but there are many ambiguities. Patrick Vaughn, Lawrence Keeley, and other archaeologists have shown how subtle and ambiguous the marks produced on stone tools by different uses can be.[21]

Ethnographic data from people who still use lithics, like Brian Hayden's study of stone use in the Mexican highlands, and Polly Weisner's study of how the !Kung hunter-gatherers use styles of stone spear-points to identify their social groupings,[22] indicate that even crude-looking stone tools may reflect a great amount of social life and economic forces.[23]

Ceramics were in use much later than the first stone tools (appearing in quantity in many places about 10,000 years ago), but they were used in such massive quantities in antiquity that, for many archaeologists, life consists mainly of the slow sorting and analyzing of potsherds. Ceramic pots were first made by hand and dried in the sun or low-temperature kilns, but in many areas of the Old World, the invention of the potter's wheel and high-temperature kilns produced pottery that is nearly a form of glass and therefore all but indestructible (Figure 2.6).

Ceramics form such a large part of archaeologists' lives because ceramics express so much about the people who made them.[24] Pots are direct indicators of function, in that they show how diets and economies changed over time. David Braun, for example, has documented how pottery in the American Southeast changed in prehistoric times as a form of agriculture developed in which people boiled seeds of various native plants, and pottery was developed to withstand the heat and mechanical stresses of this kind of food preparation.[25]

Ceramics are almost always analyzed on the basis of their *style*. This idea of style is hard to define, but—as discussed below—changing styles are the basis on which archaeologists date much of the archaeological record. But for many archaeologists, ceramics styles are more than just convenient devices for dating. For many archaeologists, stylistic decoration of artifacts is the primary means by which one can enter the cognitive world of the ancients. Societies throughout history have invested their objects with styles that have profound and complex meanings and effects. As we will see in the case of the Maya (chapter 13) and every other early civilization, rulers used particular symbols and styles, such as in styles of dress, personal ornamentation, and inscriptions, as mechanisms through which they portrayed, communicated, and implemented their power. In all societies, styles fix social meaning and are powerful ways in which these groups define and construct their culture. Styles of objects, language, and personal behavior identify people in terms of gender, age group, ethnic group, socioeconomic class, and in many other important ways.[26] Timothy Pauketat and Thomas Emerson, for example, have argued that a particular kind of pottery, called Ramey Incised (which is incised with figures of eyes, fish, arrows, and abstract

FIGURE 2.6 This "Susa A" style jar, from early fourth millennium B.C. Iran, exemplifies the hand-painted, highly decorated pottery styles that were widely distributed in Southwest Asia just before initial cultural complexity.

objects and was used by the people in the area of present-day Missouri and Illinois at about A.D. 900), was primarily a device to redistribute comestibles, but was also used to communicate elite ideas; these pots may have provided a living metaphor of the role of elites—the source of the pots—as mediators of cosmic forces.[27]

Although stone tools and ceramics make up much of the archaeological record, artifacts of wood, animal hides, metals, minerals, and almost everything else have been in use for thousands, even millions of years (Figure 2.7).

Arranging Artifacts   The novelist Luis Borges imagined an ancient Chinese classification of animals that included the following categories:

(a) those that belong to the Emperor, (b) embalmed ones, (c) those that are trained, (d) suckling pigs, (e) mermaids, (f) fabulous ones, (g) stray dogs, (h) those that are included in this classification, (i) those that tremble as if they were mad, (j) innumerable

FIGURE 2.7 A great part of the world's archaeological record is composed of stone, wood, and clay artifacts. The flint knife depicted here dates from about 4000 B.C., from Egypt. Its ivory handle is carved with scores of delicate animal figures. The ceramic pot and figurine are also from Egypt, from about 3100 B.C.

ones, (k) those drawn with a very fine camel's hair brush, (l) others, (m) those that have just broken a flower vase, and (n) those that resemble flies from a distance.[28]

A zoologist working with the above classification of animals might develop exquisite sensibilities, but he or she would have a difficult time using this system to study comparative anatomy. A fundamental procedure of science, or any form of analysis, is to construct classifications that facilitate certain kinds of research objectives. To understand how the world operates, we have to categorize it into groups of similar things and discover the relationships among these groups. Modern chemistry or physics, for example, would be inconceivable were it not for classes such as electrons, atoms, and molecules, and the laws of thermodynamics. In the same way, evolutionary biology is possible only because of concepts of chromosomes, cells, and species, and the principles of population genetics. These notions about classification and analysis are quite straightforward and simple, but when we consider the kinds of data archaeologists work with, we find that archaeological classifications and analyses have differed somewhat from those of other disciplines. The archaeologists' broken pottery, house foundations, and stone tools have not been organized in classifications in the same ways as the atom and the cell. A potassium atom is exactly the same thing to a Japanese chemist and an American chemist, but when a French archaeologist describes stone tools from southern France as "hand-axes," those artifacts differ in many respects from North Chinese "hand-axes" as described by a Chinese archaeologist. Archaeological classifications have generally been constructed with much more limited purposes than the units of the natural sciences. It is theory, whether biological, quantum, or Marxian, that tells the researcher how to break up the world for analysis, and in archaeology the only theories are relatively weak behavioral generalizations.

Most current archaeological classifications and typologies are inward-looking and descriptive, and they make it difficult to compare artifacts from one site to those from another with precision; in fact, they remind one of Antony's efforts to describe a crocodile to Lepidus in Shakespeare's *Antony and Cleopatra*:

L: What manner o' thing is your crocodile?

A: It is shaped, sir, like itself; and it is as broad as it hath breadth; it is just so high as it is, and moves with its own organs: it lives by that which nourisheth it; and, the elements once out of it, it transmigrates.

L: What colour is it of?

A: Of its own colour too.

L: 'Tis a strange serpent.

A: 'Tis so. And the tears of it are wet.

L: Will this description satisfy him?

One of the most common classifications in archaeology has been in terms of *functional* types. Archaeologists, for example, frequently categorize the 1.75-million-year-old tools from Olduvai Gorge as "cleavers," "scrapers," and "hand-axes." Such a classificatory system is based in part on ideas about how our earliest ancestors actually used these tools. Obviously, imagination plays a role in creating functional types, particularly when archaeologists are dealing with extremely old remains left by people very unlike known or existing cultures. The use of high-powered microscopes to study wear patterns on stone tools and other technical advances have given archaeologists more confidence in their ability to infer the functions of artifacts, but there will always be an element of speculation, inference, and error in these typologies.

Another widely-used archaeological classificatory approach employs *chronological* types. Chronological (or "historical") types are artifacts whose combination of attributes is known to be limited to particular time periods. We have already noted that stylistic elements such as pottery decorations and house architecture have limited distribution in time, and by sorting artifacts into groups based on their similarity of stylistic elements we can often devise relative chronologies of archaeological remains.

While depending on chronological and functional types in most analyses, archaeologists continue to search for more powerful systems of arrangement. In contemporary archaeology, debates about the logic and mechanics of arranging and classifying artifacts into analytical units continue, with some stressing a statistical approach, others more formal methods.[29]

QUANTITATIVE METHODS IN ARCHAEOLOGY

Once archaeologists have grouped the artifacts of the archaeological record into classes or types, they analyze the distribution of these classes and types through time and space. In a film scene, W. C. Fields, while dealing cards, was asked by a prospective player, "Is this a game of chance?" Fields—felonious eyes agleam—replied, "Not the way I play it!" Modern archaeology, on the other hand, is in many crucial ways a game of chance in the sense that we must use probability theory and statistics to interpret what we find. Chance in this sense enters directly into the formation of what archaeologists have to work with—the archaeological record. Some 1.7 million years ago, for example, an individual who from the neck down looked very much like ourselves made a light lunch of a cow-like animal (probably killed and partially eaten by some other animal) and tossed some of its bones into some lakeside sediments, where the bones were preserved—cut marks intact—until Louis Leakey dug them out in the 1950s. Doubtless this same individual of 1.7 million years ago munched on other bones that were thrown away in areas where they rotted or were totally fragmented by hyenas, and have thus disappeared. And chance enters into not only the preservation of objects but also their discovery. Most of the major archaeological sites in European countries, for example, are within a short distance of major roads—a sign that there are probably many other sites that have not yet been discovered because no one has happened on them. Chance—or, more precisely, probability statistics—is also part of the analytical methods of modern archaeology. The costs in time and money of archaeology are such that even well-known sites, like the ancient Iranian city of Susa, where the biblical Esther lived 3,000 years after the city's founding, are so large that even a century of excavation has removed only a small fraction of the site. Even in

Egypt, where centuries of excavations and reoccupation have destroyed many sites, hundreds of huge sites have been only partly excavated.

The only reasonable archaeological strategy in the face of such a massive archaeological record is to *sample:* to excavate some parts of some sites in the hope that these samples will accurately reflect the whole.

The essentials of statistical sampling are familiar to most people. Polling organizations regularly ask a few thousand people how they are going to vote in an election and use this information to make very reliable predictions about the voting behavior of the larger population (all the people who actually vote). Defining the target population—that is, what it is one is trying to estimate—is the key to valid statistical analyses. Introductory statistics professors are fond of citing the fact that the average adult human has one testicle and one breast. One of the reasons sampling works in elections is that pollsters *stratify* samples: they know from previous elections that people in the North vote differently from those in the South, and that certain occupational groups are far more likely to vote than others. Thus, they break up, or stratify, their samples so that these and other sub-populations are proportionately represented. Then, by using procedures of statistical inference, they are often able to estimate election results quite precisely.

Archaeologists also use sampling theory and procedures. If they wish to know relatively straightforward information, such as the number and kinds of sites in a large region, they can divide the area up into sub-areas—perhaps stratifying it according to ecological zones—and then go out and record the number of sites in perhaps 10 percent of all the sub-areas. Excellent results are usually obtained from such procedures, if the objective is simply an estimate of site densities. One critical sampling problem derives from the great size and complexity of the archaeological record. Suppose, for example, that you have the idea that trade in items such as flint and obsidian was a key element in the rise of the first states of ancient Mexico. The only way to test your idea would be to determine if there had been a significant increase in the amount or kinds of these commodities at sites occupied just prior to or during the period when the first states appeared. To do this with statistical precision, you would have to excavate at least portions of a statistically valid sample of at least thirty or forty sites—something just not feasible in today's archaeology. The result is that archaeologists are not purists when it comes to using statistics and probability models. Because so much of the residue of the past has decayed, and because of the high cost of gathering and analyzing archaeological data, archaeologists tend to misuse statistics and probability theory by making sweeping inferences on the basis of inadequate data. No Wall Street trader (or even drunk riverboat gambler) would bet on the odds that archaeologists do when testing their hypotheses; but archaeologists deal only in history and science, whereas gamblers and stockbrokers deal in money.

Archaeologists have opted for the only realistic compromise: they use statistical sampling techniques, knowing that they often don't meet the theoretical requirements of optimal statistical inference, but believing that useful—if not perfect—results can be obtained. Fortunately, most statistical sampling techniques are very "robust" in that one can strain their assumptions badly and still get quite reasonable results.

To a large extent, archaeological interest in sampling and many other aspects of modern archaeology are side effects of the invention and improvement of the modern computer. Applying even the simplest statistical description and inference to archaeology would be impossibly time-consuming without computers. Quantification in archaeology is not just a matter of sampling: it underlies most other methodological advances. The archaeological record is so complex that in most cases the archaeologist cannot see patterns in the welter of data without the aid of numerical summaries or quantitative presentation.

ARCHAEOMETRY

Computers are useless. They can only give you answers.

Pablo Picasso (1881–1973)

The basics of excavating artifacts and features, classifying them, and counting them are relatively straightforward problems common to many sciences. But like other disciplines, archaeology involves many specialized forms of *measuring* artifacts and the rest of the archaeological record. This field is generically referred to as *archaeometry*.

Dating Methods in Archaeology   The primary importance of dating methods in archaeology is in analyzing cultural changes. To take an example, some have argued (chapter 6) that people first domesticated sheep and goats and began farming wheat and barley in the Middle East because human population densities had risen to the point that people could no longer survive on hunting and gathering alone. Other people suggest that rising population densities had little to do directly with the origins of agriculture in this area.

Our only hope of resolving such disputes—of testing hypotheses—about the mechanics of major cultural transformations is to look at the archaeological record. If we conduct archaeological surveys in the area of the Middle East where agriculture first appeared and determine what sites were occupied during what periods and how large they were, we can estimate population densities before, during, and after the period when agriculture first appeared—about 10,000 years ago. If we discover that there is no significant rise in population densities just before and during the period when we find the first domesticated plants and animals and agricultural implements, we might reject the idea that rising population densities were the important direct cause of this change. In short, our only hope of determining cause and effect in ancient cultures is to show correlations in time and space.

But how are we to date artifacts in order to show such correlations?

Archaeologists rely on two different kinds of dating methods. In some situations the objective is to obtain a *chronometric* date: that is, an age expressed in years, such as "that house was built 7,200 years ago." In many situations, chronometric dates may be difficult to obtain or simply unnecessary for the problem at issue, and for these situations archaeologists have devised several methods of *relative* dating, in which the objective is to arrange sites or artifacts in a sequence that reflects the order in which they were created—even though we may not know for certain the actual age of any of them.

Chronometric Dating Many archaeologists dream of a small pocket-sized device, stuffed with microchips and Star Trekian "dilithium oxide" crystals, which, when pointed at an artifact, will read out the object's exact date of manufacture. Fanciful as this may sound, modern physiochemical dating methods have been greatly improved in the last decade, and age estimates are becoming increasingly reliable.[30]

Perhaps the most precise and yet technologically simple form of chronometric dating is *dendrochronology*—the use of sequences of tree rings to infer time.[31] Most trees add a single "ring" each year to their circumference; thus, if we count the number of rings, the age of a tree can be precisely established. Normally the tree grows faster in wet years than in dry ones; therefore, over the centuries there is a unique series of changes in ring widths, and precise dates can be inferred by comparing cross sections of trees that overlapped in time (Figure 2.8). By comparing beams, posts, and other artifacts to cross sections taken from trees that live for long periods, it is often possible to determine the exact year in which the tree used to make the artifact was cut. But here's the rub: in dry climates tree trunks tend to be used and reused for very long times, so that the date that the tree actually was cut may be centuries earlier than the period it was used as a rafter in some house. Also, since local climates vary, dendrochronological records must be built up for each region, and at present detailed records are available only for the North American West and a few other places.

The most widely used chronometric technique is ^{14}C, or carbon-14 dating, a theory first outlined in the 1940s by Nobel laureate Willard Libby.[32] When solar radi-

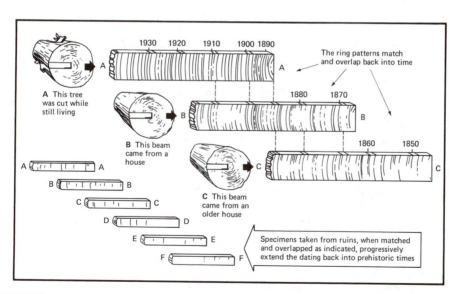

FIGURE 2.8 The most precise dates in archaeology are derived through dendrochronology. In many important areas of the world, however, a dendrochronological sequence has not been established, and in other areas, such as Mesopotamia, there are no native, long-lived species of trees.

ation strikes the upper atmosphere, it converts a small amount of atmospheric nitrogen into the radioactive isotope ^{14}C. Wind and other factors spread this ^{14}C throughout the atmosphere, and because all living organisms exchange gases with the atmosphere, the ratio of ^{14}C in their cells is equal to that in the atmosphere. When the organism dies, the ^{14}C trapped in its cells begins to revert to nitrogen. Because we know that approximately half of any given quantity of ^{14}C will disintegrate in about 5,730 years, we can estimate the time an organism has been dead by measuring the amount of ^{14}C remaining in its cells. After about 50,000 years, too little persists to be measurable with standard laboratory methods, although with large samples and the most powerful equipment, reliable dates up to 100,000 years ago are theoretically possible.

Radiocarbon dating works best on wood and charcoal, but paper, leather, bone, skin, peat, and many other organic materials can also be dated by this method. Grains and grasses make excellent archaeological samples when charred by fire, because they preserve well and are short-lived compared to trees.

The ratio of ^{14}C in the atmosphere has not been constant over the last 50,000 years, and thus ^{14}C dates have had to be "corrected" by measuring the ratio of ^{14}C in tree rings dated through dendrochronology. Fortunately, some trees, such as the bristlecone pine of northern California, live thousands of years; cores from their trunks can be dated through dendrochronology, and then each ring can be radiocarbon-dated to construct a "correction curve."[33] Logs found submerged in northern European bogs, where they have been preserved for thousands of years, have recently allowed the calculation of a radiocarbon correction curve extending back more than 7,000 years for that area. But samples dated by the ^{14}C method can still be contaminated with younger or older carbon sources, such as ground water or petroleum deposits.

A major advance in radiocarbon dating was made in the 1970s when various researchers used particle accelerators (the AMS method, or accelerator mass spectrometry) to date samples. This method allows reliable dates to be obtained from samples the size of a match-head, whereas older methods require about a handful of carbon. Accelerator dating has other advantages: samples can be more easily purified of contaminants, individual samples can be subdivided into very small amounts and tested for internal consistency, and older samples can be dated because problems involving background radiation have been obviated. Because accelerator dating can be done on such small samples, reliable dates can be obtained from the cooking soot on pots, dung, and other organic temper in pottery, slag, textiles, and many other materials.

In February 1989 an international team of twenty-one scientists reported the results of radiometric dating of the Shroud of Turin, a cloth that appears to bear the image of a man who has been whipped and crucified. For centuries, many people have believed that the Shroud was used to wrap the body of Jesus Christ. The scientists took three samples of cloth, each about fifty milligrams (about the size of a postage stamp), and sent them to three different laboratories, in England, Switzerland, and the United States. Using accelerator mass spectrometers, scientists at the three laboratories all concluded independently that the linen used for the Shroud was made about A.D. 1260–1390.

Interpretations of radiocarbon dates are rarely simple. The radiocarbon method was first applied by Libby to wood from the Pyramid of Djoser in Egypt, and over the years thousands of radiocarbon analyses of Egyptian materials have been made. In a recent attempt to refine the radiocarbon chronology of Egypt, I was part of a group of scholars[34] that retrieved hundreds of samples from the twenty-two major Egyptian pyramids and scores of temples and tombs. Because we were engaged in a decade-long project to try to define the basic mechanics of ancient Egyptian cultural change, one of the aims of this study was to determine when the Egyptian pyramids were built. Construction of the enormous pyramids and other monuments in the Nile Valley was obviously a critical part of this cultural change, since they must have required astounding investments of time and energy. But how do we know when they were built, and what their relation in time was to fluctuations in the Nile floods, political developments in neighboring areas, and other important events?

Not a single ancient text from the age when the pyramids were built has ever been found that describes their construction, or even refers to them. Egyptologists have dated the pyramids primarily on the basis of names on inscriptions in temples and tombs in areas near the pyramids. Ancient king-lists have been found, and the length of reigns of specific kings are often given in inscriptions, so Egyptologists have been able to estimate the sequence of pharaohs and how long each ruled. Occasionally, a text would record a specific astronomical event in the reign of a specific king, such as the rising of the star Sirius at a particular time and place on the horizon. Such events can be precisely dated, so we know the dates of some rulers with great accuracy. Unfortunately, such astronomical observations have not been found for the period when the pyramids appear to have been built.

Most of the mortar used to bind the blocks of stone making up the pyramids appears to have been produced by burning gypsum to create a powder that was combined with water and other materials. Thus pieces of carbon from the fires can be found throughout this mortar. We thought that if these charcoal fragments could be dated, then we could estimate when the brush, trees, etc., had been cut to get the fuel to burn the gypsum, and from this we could estimate the age of the pyramids. We also hoped that if we took a lot of samples in sequence, from the base to the top of each pyramid, we might arrive at some estimate of how long it took to construct them and the sequence in which they were constructed.

After having obtained the necessary research funds and permissions, we started at the first course of the Great Pyramid of Khufu and began extracting bits of carbon out of the mortar. Six months later we had just over a hundred samples from seventeen of the largest pyramids. Some samples were about the size of a pea, others constituted roughly a handful of carbon. We sent the larger samples to the Radiocarbon Laboratory at Southern Methodist University for conventional radiocarbon dating, and we sent the smaller samples to a laboratory in Switzerland, to be dated with the recently developed accelerator (AMS) methods (see above). The majority of our dates came out almost four hundred years older than most Egyptologists would estimate as the ages for these various pyramids. We presented a paper on our results at a scientific conference and were informed by most Egyptologists and virtually everyone else that our radiocarbon dates had little or nothing to do with the ages of the pyramids. It was suggested that our dates came out too old because (1) the ancient Egyptians used old wood in the fires to produce the mortar, or (2) the carbon came from plants that naturally absorb relatively large amounts of radioactive carbon, or (3) the mortar itself had contaminated the carbon, or (4) the correlation curves we used were wrong. Because of "wiggles" in the correction curve, for example, for any particular sample one might be able to read three or more different dates from the graph, none of which is more likely than the other dates.

All these factors may, in fact, have played a role in producing our dates, and even though we tried to control for as many of them as we could, we still are in no position to conclude that the traditional Old Kingdom chronology is wrong. In 1994–95 we returned to Egypt and collected hundreds of additional samples, and this time we hope, with botanical identifications of the materials being analyzed and a more comprehensive sampling design, to refine the radiocarbon chronology of Egypt.

In any case, as the above indicates, radiocarbon dating can be very useful, but interpretations of radiocarbon dates are usually difficult: dates that agree with one's suppositions tend to find a ready audience, while dates that do not are often labeled "intrusive."

Another important form of archaeological dating is the potassium-argon method. Potassium-argon dating is based on the fact that a radioactive isotope of potassium (^{40}K), present in minute quantities in rocks and volcanic ash, decays into the gas argon (^{40}Ar) at a known rate (half of a given amount of ^{40}K will change into ^{40}Ar in about 1.3 billion years). Because ^{40}Ar is a gas, it escapes when rock is molten (as in lava), but when the rock cools, the ^{40}AR is trapped inside. By using sensitive instruments to measure the ratio of ^{40}K to ^{40}Ar, it is possible to estimate the time since the rock or ash cooled and solidified.

Because of the long half-life of ^{40}K (1.3 billion years), potassium-argon dating can be used to estimate dates of materials many millions of years old. The remains of our ancestors at Olduvai Gorge and other sites more than a million years old have been dated with the potassium-argon method.

Carbon-14 and potassium-argon dating remain the mainstays of chronometric dating, but archaeologists can now use many other techniques involving chemical changes, although most of these are subject to considerable error and many qualifications.[35]

Paleomagnetic dating is based on the fact that the north and south pole have "reversed" their magnetism many times. Today the north pole is positive and the south pole is negative, but these were reversed in some periods, such as for most of the period between about 700,000 and 1.6 million years ago. Magnetic rocks preserve a record of these changes in polarity. As a result, finds that are, for example, between two layers of magnetic rock can often be dated.

Thermoluminescence dating ("TL") also has considerable potential. Its basis is that clays, silts, and other sediments contain naturally radioactive elements, so that when pottery is fired, or glass is melted—in general, when substances are heated to a certain point—the products of natural radiation are driven out of these materials, setting their radiological "clocks" at zero. Once these materials cool, their constituents continue the natural process of radioactive decay, but the pottery, glass, etc., now trap the electrons released by the natural radiation process. In theory, if one reheats these materials and measures very precisely how much of certain kinds of energy are given off in the process, one can estimate how long it has been since the material was last fired. This has the great advantage of dating the actual construction of the artifact, in contrast to the radiocarbon method, which dates the death of the organism from which an artifact was made and used—events that may be very far apart. Refinements of the TL method raise the possibility that campfires and even sun-baked surfaces can be dated with this method. TL dating was recently used, for example, to date the remains of a fire in Qafzeh Cave in Palestine to about 92,000 years ago, and because an anatomically modern human had been buried in association with the fire, this analysis provided strong evidence that modern humans had lived in the area long before the Neanderthals did. This has great importance for discussions of the origins of modern humans, as we will see in chapter 4.

"Electron Spin Resonance" dating (ESR) is similar to TL dating in that the scientist measures the electrons trapped in ancient bones or other materials. But ESR does not require that the materials be heated—they are placed in a variable magnetic field and the energy interactions between the object and the magnetic field are measured. ESR does not require destroying an object and can be applied to tiny samples (less than 1 g).

Other methods of physical dating have been developed and applied to archaeological problems, and refinements of these methods continue. All of these techniques have inherent expected margins of error and all are still somewhat experimental. Thus, archaeologists tend, where possible, to use as many different techniques on as many samples as possible, in hopes that a clear pattern will be observed with all of the methods converging on approximately the same age estimates. In a recent analysis of Egypt in the period between about 170,000 and 70,000 years ago, scientists on a project directed by Fred Wendorf, Romuald Schild, and Angela Close applied an impressive array of different dating techniques, including uranium series dating of carbonates and tooth enamel; thermoluminescence dating of deposits, both with traditional techniques and the newer optical methods; electron spin resonance dating of tooth enamel and other materials; and amino-acid analyses of eggshells.[36]

Relative Dating   To the novice, perhaps one of the most impressive things archaeologists can do is to be able to tell the approximate date, place of manufacture, and place of origin of a tiny sherd of pottery simply by looking at it.

This kind of relative dating involves the concept of "style." Artisans throughout history have invested their artifacts with characteristics that vary predictably over time and space, and the distribution of these stylistic elements tends to follow certain patterns, whether the objects involved are skirt lengths, musical forms, or stone tools. Styles originate in some small area, spread to adjacent ones, reach a peak in popularity, and then die out (Figure 2.9). To some extent, styles reflect rates of interaction and shared aesthetic preferences, and these are not always exact functions of time and distance. Dress styles in midtown Manhattan, for example, may be more similar to those on Rome's Via Veneto than to those in a small town in rural New Jersey, even though this pattern of stylistic similarity "reverses" their relative distances. And often a style dies out at its point of origin long before it reaches its ultimate dispersal.

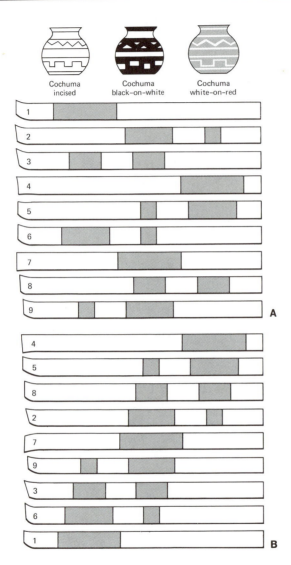

FIGURE 2.9 Relative seriation of nine archaeological sites on the basis of three pottery styles from the American Southwest. The percentage that each pottery style represents of the total pottery found at each site is represented by the width of the colored area on the strip of paper (**A**). Since most styles tend gradually to grow in popularity and then slowly die out, a seriation can be produced by arranging the paper strips in such a way that the three pottery styles have this "battleship shape" distribution through time. The inferred order of the nine sites is shown in **B**. Mathematical models and computer programs have been developed to sort scores of sites and pottery styles into these kinds of graphs. Such mathematical aids are often needed, because the number of possible unique orderings of 9 sites is 9!, or 362,880.

Relative dating, or seriation as it is usually called, is often used where many surface collections of artifacts have been made. Jeffrey Parsons and his students, for example, have surveyed most of the area around Mexico City, identifying thousands of settlements dating from 12,000 years ago up to the Spanish Conquest. Most of these sites are small mounds whose surfaces were littered with pottery sherds and obsidian tools. The differences in style between a Late Aztec Black-on-Orange dish (c. A.D. 900) and Middle Formative plainware jar (c. 550 B.C.) are so obvious that anyone can learn to date sites of these periods in a few days of study. On this basis, Parsons and his students dated thousands of sites without excavating them, simply by grouping them into a relative seriation of four or five major periods. Carbon-14 dating can be used to provide a few absolute dates to anchor this sequence, and most chronologies based on changes in artifact styles are derived from excavations, in which the archaeologist can order the found pottery in time on the basis of stratigraphy. But pottery styles alone are not all that is necessary to construct a seriation. Accurate relative seriations usually require massive quantities of data from artifacts of a highly decorated nature (like pottery) from a relatively small area, and they tend to be least precise when extended to largely undecorated objects such as early stone tools (Figure 2.10).

ARCHAEOLOGICAL RESEARCH DESIGN AND FIELD WORK: AN EXAMPLE

Having considered various elements of modern archaeological methods and theory, it is, perhaps, useful to consider an example of a specific archaeological project. As one such example, I offer the Fayyum Archaeological Project, which I co-directed in Egypt in 1981. I offer this example not as a model of its kind, but simply as an illustration of the kind of archaeology that was in some ways typical of its time.

FIGURE 2.10 Early stone tools.

The proximate cause of the Fayyum Archaeological Project, which was wholly conducted in Egypt, was in fact the Iranian Revolution. I had done archaeological research in Iran on several occasions in the early 1970s and was due to resume work there in 1979, on a day almost exactly between the Shah's departure from Iran and the first seizure of the American Embassy by Islamic militants. I had received my first National Science Foundation grant and would probably have gone to Teheran despite the revolution, had the Iranians permitted—which they most certainly did not. Through a series of events too baroque to recount here, I had the good fortune to be able to go instead to Egypt, where in 1980 I excavated at el-Hibeh, a site on the Nile that was a major town during most of the first millennium B.C.[37]

I had long been interested in the origins of agricultural economies, and I was much impressed by some new ideas about agricultural origins in Egypt. Simply put, I was curious why wheat and barley farming appeared in Egypt so long—about 2,000 years—after it did in Southwest Asia. So while in Egypt I started searching for an area in which to investigate the origins of Egyptian agriculture.

Many of the most important sites in Egypt have been excavated for decades and are already being studied by other archaeologists; one cannot just decide to excavate this or that site. The late Professor Michael Hoffman suggested that I look at unsurveyed parts of the Fayyum Oasis, in central Egypt. Years of work by other archaeologists had shown evidence of early agriculture at the site, but it was not being explored at that time.

Although my main interest was the origins of agriculture, I wanted to do a complete regional survey, to locate sites of all periods in this area. The remains of large towns of the last few centuries B.C., for example, can be found at many places in the research area. Archaeological projects in Egypt usually have on their staffs an Egyptologist—someone who reads ancient Egyptian writing—and I was fortunate enough to recruit a recent graduate from the Sorbonne (the University of Paris), Dr. Mary Ellen Lane, as co-director. With a representative of the Egyptian Antiquities Organization, we made several trips into the deserts of the southern Fayyum without finding much except a restaurant in the provincial capital, where I got deathly ill for only ninety piastres.

In the 1920s, the intrepid British archaeologist Gertrude Caton-Thompson had surveyed the southern edge of the Fayyum Lake, noting here and there scatters of Neolithic-style stone tools. One day, hiking through an area near where she had surveyed, we saw a large pile of bones. On inspection it proved to be the remains of a hippopotamus, and we were delighted to see that near it were stone projectile points ("arrowheads") of a Neolithic type. Within a few hours of surveying, it was evident that we had found a dense scatter of hearths, pottery, stone tools, and animal bones, and that the styles of artifacts suggested two periods of occupation: an "epipaleolithic" period of occupation by hunter-foragers at about 7000 B.C., followed by an occupation by some of Egypt's earliest known farmers, at about 5500 B.C. Thus, we had the opportunity to study one of the most important cultural changes in Egypt, the transition from hunting-foraging to agriculture. Other archaeologists had worked in the Fayyum on this problem, but we had found a well-preserved part of the archaeological record there that we thought would give us new and important data to analyze this transition.

Back in Cairo, several weeks of library research convinced us that what we had was significant, and that we should try for our first field season in the summer of 1981—a year later. All we needed was $200,000, a staff of at least twenty trained archaeologists, and permission from the Egyptian government.

Famed felon Willie Sutton, when asked why he robbed banks, patiently explained, "that's where the money is." Archaeologists, too, must go where the money is, and in this era it is mainly in the hands of the government—although as this is being written, the United States government is considering almost total cancellation of funds for archaeological research. After months of writing proposals, we received about $200,000 from the U.S. Agency for International Development and the U.S. National Science Foundation. We then recruited our staff of specialists in ancient plant remains, animal bones, and geology, and conscripted eight graduate students to assist with the demanding field work.

On June 4, 1981, we left Cairo in several jeeps and trucks to make the four-hour trip to the research area. We lived that summer and autumn in a large gray house that looked across a green palm grove and the blue of the Fayyum Lake to the white limestone cliffs on the northern edge of the Fayyum Oasis. Our villa—the country home of a wealthy Cairo family—was a lovely International Style building with every convenience except three: water, electricity, and a sewage system. But we bought a generator, the provincial governor graciously arranged for a water truck to visit us every three days, and we devised an entertaining method of periodically napalming our open cesspool.

"Tell me what you eat, and I will tell you what you are," said the French gastronome Brilliant-Savarin, but archaeological field projects usually do not offer much scope to express one's self in terms of the food one chooses to eat. Our meager budget and the remoteness of our field quarters meant that our diet was almost wholly composed of canned tuna fish, a vile processed cheese by-product, rice, tomatoes, and several hundred chickens, who were executed on our kitchen steps and then converted into indescribable meals. "Fire-Cracked Veal" and "Dreaded Veal Cutlet" were occasional holiday treats. We bored each other constantly with food fantasies. The morbidity rates—physical and psychological—on archaeological projects are often high, especially when, as in our case, water for washing was scarce and the cook had nothing but contempt for the germ theory of disease. We totaled at least five different strains of parasitical and bacterial infections among our crew, and we lost many days to illness. There was also one emergency appendectomy (mine), performed in Cairo after a thought-provoking four-hour truck ride from the desert, greatly assisted by our geologist, Prof. Fekri Hassan, then of Washington State University, whose truck and driver got me to a Cairo hospital in record time.

When we began our six months of fieldwork, we geared most of our efforts to reconstructing as precisely as possible the ways of life of the people who had lived in the Fayyum in the Qarunian period (c. 6500 B.C.), just before the appearance of domesticated plants and animals in this region, and in the succeeding Neolithic Fayyum A period (c. 5000 B.C.), when the first agriculturalists appeared. We hoped to reconstruct the pattern of human settlement in the Fayyum between 7000 B.C. and A.D. 1500 and explain the changes in these settlement patterns over this long period.

We began by making a topographic map of the area we intended to work in. We then devised a sampling program and collected every artifact in the sampling units defined, that is, in the hundreds of 5 × 5 meter squares in our study area. The Fayyum is surrounded by the Sahara Desert, and the average temperature during most of this work was over 40°C (104°F); by midday the stone tools were often so hot we would have to juggle them as we bagged them. Afternoons were spent back at the field camp, sorting, drawing, and photographing artifacts, drinking warm water, and drawing each other's attention to the heat. In some cases, "It's not the heat, it's the humidity" is not at all true. In September we began excavations, mainly of the hearths and pits that were the dominant feature of both the Qarunian and Fayyum A occupations. In most we found charred animal bones, some carbonized plant remains, and other debris.

To evaluate our "model" of how agriculture appeared in the Fayyum and why, we had to collect sufficient evidence to make statistical arguments about certain kinds of conditions and events in Fayyum prehistory. The details of these arguments are not relevant here, but it should be stressed that as in most archaeological projects, not all the information we had hoped would be there was actually found. But most of it was, and the preliminary analysis of this information was published in several journals and presented at various conferences.[38] We have since made occasional returns to the Fayyum to collect more information, in hopes that eventually we will produce a more complete analysis of this part of the world's archaeological record.

In Cairo, after the season was over, we delivered the artifacts to the Egyptian Museum and made preparations to leave. It is traditional, after the privations of the field, to treat oneself to some rest and relaxation, and some project members agonized between such choices as the Club Med's Red Sea beaches or the delights of Rome. Most of the crew just went home and enjoyed the luxury of sleeping past 4:00 am.

BIBLIOGRAPHY

Adams, W. Y. 1988. "Archaeological Classification: Theory Versus Practice." *Antiquity* 61:40–56.

Aitken, M. J. 1990. *Science-Based Dating in Archaeology*. London and New York: Longman.

Aldenderfer, M. S., ed. 1987. *Quantitative Research in Archaeology*. Newbury Park, CA: Sage.

Aldenderfer, M. S., and R. K. Blashfield. 1984. *Cluster Analysis*. Beverly Hills: Sage.

Ambrose, S. H., and M. J. DeNiro. 1986. "Reconstruction of African Human Diet Using Bone Collagen Carbon and Nitrogen Isotope Ratios." *Nature* 319:321–4.

van Andel, T. H. 1989. "Late Quaternary Sea Level and Archaeology." *Antiquity* 63(241):733–45.

van Andel, T. H., C. N. Runnels, and K. O. Pope. 1986. "Five Thousand Years of Land Use and Abuse in the Southern Argolid, Greece." *Hesperia: Journal of the American School of Classical Studies at Athens* 55(1):103–28.

Anderson, A., ed. 1989. *Prodigious Birds: Moas and Moa-hunting in New Zealand*. Cambridge: Cambridge University Press.

Andersen, S. H. 1986. "Mesolithic Dugouts and Paddles from Tybrind Vig, Denmark." *Acta Archaeologica* 57:87–106.

———. 1987. "Tybrind Vig: A Submerged Ertebolle Settlement in Denmark." In *European Wetlands in Prehistory*, eds. J. M. Coles and A. J. Lawson. Oxford: Clarendon Press.

Antiquity. 1987. "Special Radiocarbon Section: Six articles." *Antiquity* 61:97–138.

Atkinson, T.C., K. R. Briffa, and G. R. Coope. 1987. "Seasonal Temperatures in Britain during the Past 22,000 Years, Reconstructed using Beetle Remains." *Nature* 325:587–92.

Badekas, J., ed. 1975. *Photogrammetric Surveys of Monuments and Sites.* New York: Elsevier.

Bahn, P. G., and J. Vertut. 1988. *Images of the Ice Age.* New York: Facts on File.

Bahn, P. G., and R. W. K. Paterson. 1986. "The Last Rights: More on Archaeology and the Dead." *Oxford Journal of Archaeology* 3:127–39.

Bailey, R. N., E. Cambridge, and H. D. Briggs. 1988. *Dowsing and Church Archaeology.* Wimborne, Dorset: Intercept.

Baillie, M. G. L. 1982. *Tree-Ring Dating.* Chicago: University of Chicago Press.

Baillie, M. G. L., and M. A. R. Munro. 1988. "Irish Tree Rings, Santorini and Volcanic Dust Veils." *Nature* 332:344–46.

Bard, E., B. Hamelin, R. G. Fairbanks, and A. Zindler. 1990. "Calibration of the ^{14}C Timescale over the Past 30,000 Years using Mass Spectrometric U-Th Ages from Barbados Corals." *Nature* 345:405–10.

Barisano, E., E. Bartholome, and B. Marcolongo. 1986. *Télédétection et Archéologie.* Paris: CNRS.

Barker, P. 1986. *Understanding Archaeological Excavation.* London: Batsford.

Bass, G. F., ed. 1988. *Ships and Shipwrecks of the Americas: A History Based on Underwater Archaeology.* New York: Thames & Hudson.

Basset, C. A. 1987. "The Culture Thieves." *Science* 86, July/Aug: 22–29.

Battarbee, R. W. 1986. "Diatom Analysis." In *Handbook of Holocene Palaeoecology and Palaeohydrology,* ed. B. E. Berglund. London: Wiley, pp. 527–70.

Beattie, O., & Geiger, J. 1987. *Frozen in Time.* London: Bloomsbury.

de Beaune, S. 1987a. *Lampes et Godets au Paléolithique.* Supplément à Gallia Préhistoire.

———. 1987b. "Paleolithic Lamps and Their Specialization: A Hypothesis." *Current Anthropology* 28:569–77.

Beck, C., ed. 1995. *Dating in Exposed and Surface Contexts.* Albuquerque: University of New Mexico Press.

Beck, C., and G. T. Jones. 1989. "Bias and Archaeological Classification." *American Antiquity* 54(2):244–62.

Behre, K-E., ed. 1986. *Anthropogenic Indicators in Pollen Diagrams.* Rotterdam and Boston: Balkema.

Behrensmeyer, A. K., and A. P. Hill, eds. 1980. *Fossils in the Making: Vertebrate Taphonomy and Paleoecology.* Chicago: University of Chicago Press.

Behrensmeyer, A. K., K. D. Gordon, and Yanagi, G. T. 1986. "Trampling as a Cause of Bone Surface Damage and Pseudo-Cutmarks." *Nature* 319:768–71.

Bimson, M., and J. C. Freestone, eds. 1987. *Early Vitreous Materials.* London: British Museum Occasional Paper 56.

Binford, L. R. 1964. "A Consideration of Archaeological Research Design." *American Antiquity* 29:425–41.

———. 1985. "Human Ancestors: Changing Views of Their Behavior." *Journal of Anthropological Archaeology* 4:292–327.

Binneman, J., and J. Deacon. 1986. "Experimental Determination of Use Wear on Stone Adzes from Boomplaas Cave, South Africa." *Journal of Archaeological Science* 13:219–28.

Blumenschine, R. J. 1986. *Early Hominid Scavenging Opportunities.* Oxford: British Arch. Reports, Int. Series 283.

Boddington, A., A. N. Garland, and R. C. Janaway, eds. 1987. *Death, Decay and Reconstruction: Approaches to Archaeology and Forensic Science.* Manchester: Manchester University Press.

Bodner, C., and R. M. Rowlett. 1980. "Separation of Bone, Charcoal, and Seeds by Chemical Flotation." *American Antiquity* 45:110–16.

Bogucki, P. 1986. "The Antiquity of Dairying in Temperate Europe." *Expedition* 28(2):51–58.

Bower, J. 1986. "A Survey of Surveys: Aspects of Surface Archaeology in Sub-Saharan Africa." *The African Arch. Review* 4:21–40.

Brain, C. K., and A. Sillen. 1988. "Evidence from the Swartkrans Cave for the Earliest Use of Fire." *Nature* 336:464–66.

Brassell, S. C. et al. 1986. "Molecular Stratigraphy: A New Tool for Climatic Assessment." *Nature* 320:129–33.

Braun, D. P. 1983. "Pots as Tools." In *Archaeological Hammers and Theories,* eds., A. Keene and J. Moore. New York: Academic Press.

Brewer, D. J. 1987. "Seasonality in the Prehistoric Faiyum Based on the Incremental Growth Structures of the Nile Catfish (Pisces: *Clarias*)." *Journal of Archaeological Science* 14:459–72.

Brinkhuizen, D. C., and A. T. Clason, eds. 1986. *Fish and Archaeology: Studies in Osteometry, Taphonomy, Seasonality and Fishing.* Oxford: British Arch. Reports, Int. Series No. 294.

Bronitsky, G. 1986. "The Use of Materials Science Techniques in the Study of Pottery Construction and Use." In *Advances in Archaeological Method and Theory* 9, ed. M. B. Schiffer. New York: Academic Press.

Bronitsky, G., and R. Hamer. 1986. "Experiments in Ceramic Technology: The Effects of Various Tempering Materials on Impact and Thermal-Shock Resistance." *American Antiquity* 51:89–101.

Brothwell, D. 1986. *The Bog Man and the Archaeology of People.* London: British Museum Publications.

Browman, D. L. 1981. "Isotopic Discrimination and Correction Factors in Radiocarbon Dating." In *Advances in Archaeological Method and Theory, Vol. 4,* ed. M. B. Schiffer. New York: Academic Press.

Buchanan, W. F. 1988. *Shellfish in Prehistoric Diet: Elands Bay, S.W. Cape Coast, South Africa.* Oxford: British Arch. Reports. Int. Series 455.

Bunn, H. T. 1981. "Archaeological Evidence for Meat-eating by Plio-Pleistocene Hominids from Koobi Fora and Olduvai Gorge." *Nature* 291:574–77.

Bunn, H. T., and E. M. Kroll. 1986. "Systematic Butchery by Plio-Pleistocene Hominids at Olduvai Gorge, Tanzania." *Current Anthropology* 27(5):431–52.

Carr, C., ed. 1989. *For Concordance in Archaeological Analysis.* Prospect Heights, IL: Waveland Press.

Carver, M. 1987. *Underneath English Towns: Interpreting Urban Archaeology.* London: Batsford.

Chappell, J., and N. J. Shackleton. 1986. "Oxygen Isotopes and Sea Level." *Nature* 324:137–40.

Claassen, C., ed. 1994. *Women in Archaeology.* Philadelphia: University of Pennsylvania Press.

Clark, A. 1990. *Seeing Beneath the Soil: Prospecting Methods in Archaeology.* London: Batsford.

Coe, M. D. 1987. *The Maya,* 4th ed. New York: Thames & Hudson.

Coles, B., & J. Coles. 1986. *Sweet Track to Glastonbury: The Somerset Levels in Prehistory.* London and New York: Thames & Hudson.

———. 1989. *People of the Wetlands.* London and New York: Thames & Hudson.

Coles, J. 1986. "Precision, Purpose, and Priorities in Wetland Archaeology." *The Antiquaries Journal* 66: 227–47.

Coles, J., and A. J. Lawson, eds. 1987. *European Wetlands in Prehistory.* Oxford: Clarendon Press.

Conkey, M. and C. Hastorf, eds. 1990. *The Uses of Style in Archaeology.* Cambridge: Cambridge University Press.

Cooke, W. D., and B. Lomas. 1987. "Ancient Textiles - Modern Technology." *Archaeology Today* 8(2):21–25.

Cotterel, B., and J. Kamminga. 1990. *Mechanics of Pre-Industrial Technology.* Cambridge: Cambridge University Press.

Courty, M-A., P. Goldberg, and R. MacPhail. 1990. *Soils and Micromorphology in Archaeology.* Cambridge: Cambridge University Press.

Crabtree, D. 1972. *An Introduction to Flintworking.* Occasional Papers of the Idaho State University Museum, no. 28. Pocatello.

Crabtree, P. J., and K. Ryan, eds. 1991. *Animal Use and Culture Change.* MASCA Research Papers in Science and Archaeology, supplements to Vol. 8. Museum of Applied Science, Center for Archaeology. Philadelphia: University of Pennsylvania Press.

Dahl-Jensen, D., and S. J. Johnsen. 1986. "Palaeotemperatures Still Exist in the Greenland Ice Sheet." *Nature* 320:250–52.

David, N., J. Sterner, and K. Gavua. 1988. "Why Pots Are Decorated." *Current Anthropology* 29(3):365–89.

Davis, S. J. M. 1987. *The Archaeology of Animals*. London: Batsford.

Deetz, J. 1967. *Invitation to Archaeology*. Garden City, NY: Natural History Press.

Dekin, A. A. 1987. "Sealed in Time: Ice Entombs an Eskimo Family for Five Centuries." *National Geographic* 171(6):824–36.

Diamond, J. M. 1986. "The Environmental Myth." *Nature* 324:19–20.

Dimbleby, G. W. 1985. *The Palynology of Archaeological Sites*. London: Academic Press.

Doran, J., and F. Hodson. 1975. *Mathematics and Computers in Archaeology*. Cambridge, MA: Harvard University Press.

Dormion, G., and J-P. Goidin. 1987. *Les Nouveaux Mystères de la Grande Pyramide*. Paris: Albin Michel.

Dorn, R. I., et al. 1986. "Carbon-ratio and Accelerator Radiocarbon Dating of Rock Varnish on Mojave Artifacts and Landforms." *Science* 231:830–33.

Drennan, R. D. 1976. "A Refinement of Chronological Seriation Using Nonmetric Multidimensional Scaling." *American Antiquity* 41:290–320.

Dunnell, R. C. 1970. "Seriation Method and Its Evaluation." *American Antiquity* 35:305–19.

———. 1971. *Systematics in Prehistory*. New York: Free Press.

———. 1986. "Methodological Issues in Americanist Artifact Classification." *Advances in Archaeological Method and Theory* 9:149–207.

Dunnell, R. C. n.a. "Science, Social Science, and Common Sense: The Agonizing Dilemma of Modern Archaeology."

d'Errico, F. 1987. "Nouveaux Indices et Nouvelles Techniques Microscopiques pour la Lecture de l'Art Gravé Mobilier." *Comptes rendus de 'Acad. Sciences Paris* 304, série II:761–64.

Faegri, K., P. Ekaland, and K. Krzywinski, eds. 1989. *Textbook of Pollen Analysis*, 4th ed. London: Wiley.

Fagan, B. M. 1989. *People of the Earth: An Introduction to World Prehistory*, 6th ed. Glenview, IL: Scott, Foresman.

———. 1990. *The Journey from Eden: The Peopling of Our World*. New York: Thames & Hudson.

Fowler, P. J. 1988/89. "The Experimental Earthworks 1958–88." *Annual Report of the Council for British Archaeology* 39:83–98.

Fox, A. In press. *Out of the Country: Language, Music, Emotion, and Sociability in a Texas Rural, Working-Class Community*. Durham, NC: Duke University Press.

Frayer, D. W., M. Wolpoff, A. G. Thorne, F. H. Smith, and G. G. Pope. 1993. "Theories of Modern Human Origins: The Paleontological Test." *American Anthropologist* 95(1):14–50.

Garnsey, P. 1988. *Famine and Food Supply in the Graeco-Roman World*. Cambridge: Cambridge University Press.

Gifford, D. P. 1981. "Taphonomy and Paleoecology: A Critical Review of Archaeology's Sister Discipline." In *Advances in Archaeological Method and Theory*, Vol. 4, ed. M. B. Schiffer. New York: Academic Press.

Gilbert, R. I., Jr., and J. H. Mielke, eds. 1985. *The Analysis of Prehistoric Diets*. New York: Academic Press.

Gould, R.A. 1995. *Recovering the Past*. Albuquerque: University of New Mexico Press.

Gould, R. A., and P. J. Watson. 1982. "A Dialogue on the Meaning and Use of Analogy in Ethnoarchaeological Reasoning." *Journal of Anthropological Archaeology* 1:355–81.

Gowlett, J. A. J. 1987. "The Archaeology of Radiocarbon Accelerator Dating." *Journal of World Prehistory* 1(2):127–70.

Grayson, D. K. 1984. *Quantitative Zooarchaeology: Topics in the Analysis or Archaeological Faunas*. New York: Academic Press.

Green, L. R., and F. A. Hart. 1987. "Colour and Chemical Composition in Ancient Glass: An Examination of some Roman and Wealden Glass by Means of Ultaviolet-Visible-Infra-red Spectrometry and Electron Microprobe Analysis." *Journal of Archaeological Science* 14:271–82.

Grenier, R. 1988. "Basque Whalers in the New World: The Red Bay Wreck." In *Ships and Shipwrecks of the Americas*, ed. G. Bass. New York: Thames & Hudson, pp. 69–84.

Grün, R. 1989. *Die ESR-Alterbestimmungsmethode.* Heidelberg: Springer.

Guthrie, R. D. 1990. *Frozen Fauna of the Mammoth Step.* Chicago: University of Chicago Press.

Haas, H., J. Devine, R. J. Wenke, M. E. Lehner, W. Wolfli, and G. Bonani. 1987. "Radio-carbon Chronology and the Historical Calendar in Egypt." In *Chronologies in the Near East,* eds. O. Avrenche, J. Evin, and P. Hours. *British Archaeological Reports* 379:585–606.

Hall, A. 1986. "The Fossil Evidence for Plants in Mediaeval Towns." *Biologist* 33(5):262–67.

Hammer, C. U., H. B. Clausen, W. L. Friedrich, and H. Tauber. 1987. "The Minoan Eruption of Santorini in Greece Dated to 1645 B.C.?" *Nature* 328:517–19.

Hardy, D., and C. Renfrew, eds. 1991. *Thera and the Aegean World III, Vol. 3. Chronology.* London: Thera Foundation.

Harris, E. C. 1989. *Principles of Archaeological Stratigraphy,* 2nd ed. Orlando, FL: Academic Press.

Hastorf, C. A., and V. S. Popper, eds. 1989. *Current Palaeoethnobotany: Analytical Methods and Cultural Interpretations of Archaeological Plant Remains.* Chicago: University of Chicago Press.

Hayden, B., ed. 1987. *Lithic Studies Among the Contemporary Highland Maya.* Tucson: University of Arizona Press.

Heaton, T. H. E., et al. 1986. "Climatic Influence on the Isotopic Composition of Bone Nitrogen." *Nature* 322:822–23.

Hester, T.N., H. J. Shafer, and R. F. Heizer. 1987. *Field Methods in Archaeology,* 7th ed. Palo Alto: Mayfield.

Hill, H. E., and J. Evans. 1987. "The Identification of Plants Used in Prehistory from Organic Residues." In *Archaeometry: Further Australasian Studies,* eds. W. R. Ambrose and J. M. J. Mummery. Canberra: Australian National University.

Hillman, G. C. 1986. "Plant Foods in Ancient Diet: The Archaeological Role of Paleofaeces in General and Lindow Man's Gut Contents in Particular." In *Lindow Man: The Body in the Bog,* eds. I. M. Stead et al. London: British Museum Publications.

Hillman, G. C., S. M. Colledge, and D. R. Harris. 1990. "Plant-food Economy during the Epi-Palaeolithic Period at Tell Abu Hureyra, Syria: Dietary Diversity, Seasonality and Modes of Exploitation." In *Foraging and Farming,* eds. D. R. Harris and G. C. Hillman. London: Unwin Hyman.

Hillman, G. C., E. Madeyska, and J. Hather. 1988. "Wild Plant Foods and Diet at Late Palaeolithic Wadi Kubbaniya: Evidence from Charred Remains." In *The Prehistory of Wadi Kubbaniya, Vol. 2: Studies in Late Palaeolithic Subsistence,* eds. F. Wendorf et al. Dallas: Southern Methodist University Press.

Hillson, S. 1986. *Teeth.* Cambridge: Cambridge University Press.

Holden, C. 1987. "A Quest for Ancient Egyptian Air." *Science* 236:1419–20.

Hole, F., and R. F. Heizer. 1973. *An Introduction to Prehistoric Archaeology,* 3rd ed. New York: Holt.

Holliday, V. T., ed. 1991. *Soils in Archaelogy: Landscape Evolution and Human Occupation.* Washington, DC: Smithsonian Institution Press.

Jelinek, A. 1982. "The Tabun Cave and Paleolithic Man in the Levant." *Science* 216:1369–75.

Jensen, H. J. 1988. "Functional Analysis of Prehistoric Flint Tools by High-Power Microscopy: A Review of West European Research." *Journal of World Prehistory* 2(1):53–88.

Jett, S. C., and P. B. Moyle. 1986. "The Exotic Origins of Fishes Depicted on Prehistoric Mimbres Pottery from New Mexico." *American Antiquity* 51:688–720.

Jones, G., et al. 1986. "Crop Storage at Assiros." *Scientific American* 254:84–91.

Joukowsky, M. 1980. *A Complete Manual of Field Archaeology.* Englewood Cliffs, NJ: Prentice-Hall.

Jouzel, J., et al. 1987. "Vostok Ice Core: A Continuous Isotope Temperature Record over the Last Climate Cycle (160,000 Years)." *Nature* 329:403–8.

Keeley, L. H. 1980. *Experimental Determination of Stone Tool Use: A Microwear Analysis.* Chicago and London: University of Chicago Press.

Kerisel, J. 1988. "Le Dossier Scientifique sur la Pyramide de Khéops." *Archéologia* 232, Feb.:46–54.

Kimes, T., C. Haselgrove, and I. Hodder. 1982. "A Method for the Identification of the Location of Regional Cultural Boundaries." *Journal of Anthropological Archaeology* 1:113–31.

Klein, R. G. 1989. *The Human Career*. Chicago: University of Chicago Press.

Koike, H. 1986a. "Jomon Shell Mounds and Growth-Line Analysis of Molluscan Shells." In *Windows on the Japanese Past: Studies in Archaeology and Prehistory*, eds. R. J. Pearson et al. Center for Japanese Studies, University of Michigan, pp. 267–78.

———. 1986b. "Prehistoric Hunting Pressure and Paleobiomass: An Environmental Reconstruction and Archaeozoological Analysis of a Jomon Shellmound Area." In *Prehistoric Hunter-Gatherers in Japan*, eds. T. Akazawa and C. M. Aikens. Tokyo: University Museum Bulletin 27, University of Tokyo.

Koike, H., and N. Ohtaishi. 1987. "Estimation of Prehistoric Hunting Rates Based on the Age Composition of Sika Deer (*Cervus nippon*)." *Journal of Archaeological Science* 14:251–69.

Körber-Grohne, V. 1987. "Les Restes de Plantes et d'Animaux de la Tombe Princière d'Hochdorf. In *Trésors des Princes Celtes*. Paris: Exhibition catalog, Min. de la Culture.

———. 1988. "Microscopic Methods for Identification of Plant Fibres and Animal Hairs from the Prince's Tomb of Hochdorf, Southwest Germany." *Journal of Archaeological Science* 15:73–82.

Kukla, G. J. 1987. "Loess Stratigraphy in Central China." *Quaternary Science Reviews* 6:191–219.

Langford, M., G. Taylor, and J. R. Flenley. 1986. "The Application of Texture Analysis for Automated Pollen Identification." In *Proceedings of the Conference on Identification and Pattern Recognition*, Toulouse, June 1986, Vol. 2: 729–39. Toulouse: Université Paul Sabatier.

Leakey, M. 1987. "Animal Prints and Trails." In *Laetoli, a Pliocene Site in Northern Tanzania*, eds. M. Leakey and J. M. Harris. Oxford: Clarendon Press.

LeBlanc, S. A. 1975. "Microseriation. A Method for Fine Chronological Differentiation." *American Antiquity* 40:22–38.

Legge, A. J., and P. A. Rowley-Conwy. 1987. "Gazelle Killing in Stone Age Syria." *Scientific American* 257(2):76–83.

Lehner, M. 1983. "Some Observations on the Layout of the Khufu and Khafre Pyramids." *Journal of the American Research Center in Egypt* 20:7–29.

———. 1985. *The Pyramid Tomb of Hetep-heres and the Satellite Pyramid of Khufu*. Mainz am Rhein: Philipp von Zabern.

Leonard, R. D., and G. T. Jones., eds. 1988. *Quantifying Diversity in Archaeology*. Cambridge: Cambridge University Press.

Leute, U. 1988. *Archaeometry*. New York: VCH Publishers.

Lewenstein, S. 1987. *Stone Tool Use at Cerros. The Ethnoarchaeological and Use-wear Evidence*. Austin: University of Texas Press.

Lewin, R. 1987. *Bones of Contention: Controversies in the Search for Human Origins*. New York: Simon & Schuster.

———. 1989. *Human Evolution*, 2d ed. Oxford: Blackwell Scientific Publications.

Libby, W. F. 1955. *Radiocarbon Dating*. Chicago: University of Chicago Press.

Longacre, W. A., ed. 1991. *Ceramic Ethnoarchaeology*. Tucson: University of Arizona Press.

Loy, T. H. 1987. "Recent Advances in Blood Residue Analysis." In *Archaeometry: Further Australasian Studies*, eds. W. R. Ambrose and J. M. J. Mummery. Canberra: Australian National University.

Loy, T. H., and A. R. Wood. 1989. "Blood Residue Analysis at Çayönü Tepesi, Turkey." *Journal of Field Archaeology* 16:451–460.

McIntosh, J. 1986. *The Practical Archaeologist*. New York: Facts on File.

Mannion, A. M. 1987. "Fossil Diatoms and Their Significance in Archaeological Research." *Oxford Journal of Archaeology* 6:131–47.

Marquardt, W. H. 1979. "Advances in Archaeological Seriation." In *Advances in Archaeological Method and Theory*, vol. 1, ed. M. B. Schiffer. New York: Academic Press.

Mead, J. I., et al. 1986. "Dung of *Mammuthus* in the Arid Southwest, North America." *Quarternary Research* 25:121–27.

Merkel, J., and I. Shimada. 1988. "Arsenical Copper Smelting at Batán Grande, Peru. *IAMS* (Institute for ArchaeoMetallurgical Studies) No. 12, June, 4–7.

Michels, J. W. 1973. *Dating Methods in Archaeology*. New York: Seminar Press.

Minnis, P. E. 1987. "Identification of Wood from Archaeological Sites in the American Southwest." *Journal of Archaeological Science* 14:121–32.

Montluçon, J. 1986. "L'électricité pour mettre à nu les objets archéologiques. *La Recherche* 17: 252–55.

Mueller, J., ed. 1975. *Sampling in Archaeology*. Tucson: University of Arizona Press.

Nash, D. T., and M. D. Petraglia, eds. 1987. *Natural Formation Processes and the Archaeological Record*. Oxford: British Arch. Reports, Int. Series 352.

Noe-Nygaard, N. 1987. "Taphonomy in Archaology." *Journal of Danish Archaeology* 6:7–62.

Noel, M., and A. Bocquet. 1987. *Les Hommes et le Bois: Histoire et Technologie du Bois de la Préhistoire à Nos Jours*. Paris: Hachette.

van Noten, F., and J. Raymaekers. 1988. "Early Iron Smelting in Central Africa." *Scientific American* 258(6):84–91.

Olive, M. 1988. *Une Habitation Magadalénienne d'Etiolles, l'Unité P15*. Mémoire 20 de la Soc. Préhist. francise.

Ortner, D. J., and A. C. Aufderheide, eds. 1991. *Human Paleopathology: Current Syntheses and Future Options*. Washington, DC: Smithsonian Institution Press.

Owen-Smith, N. 1987. "Pleistocene Extinctions: The Pivotal Role of Megaherbivores." *Paleobiology* 13:351–62.

Parsons, J. R. 1971. *Prehistoric Settlement Patterns in the Texcoco Region, Mexico*. Ann Arbor: Memoir of the Museum of Anthropology, University of Michigan, N. 3.

Parton, J. 1874. *Life of Thomas Jefferson*. Boston: Houghton, Mifflin, and Co.

Patterson, L. W., et al. 1987. "Analysis of Lithic Flakes at the Calico Site, California." *Journal of Field Archaeology* 14:91–106.

Pauketat, T., and T. Emerson. 1991. "The Ideology of Authority and the Power of the Pot." *American Anthropologist* 93(4):919–41.

Pearsall, D.M. 1989. *Paleoethnobotany*. New York: Academic Press.

Pearson, G. W. 1987. "How to Cope with Calibration." *Antiquity* 60:98–104.

Petrie, W. M. F. 1900. "Sequences in Prehistoric Remains." *Journal of the Anthropological Institute* 29:295–301.

Phillips, P. 1988. "Traceology (Microwear) Studies in the USSR." *World Archaeology* 19(3):349–56.

Pickering, M. P. 1989. "Food for Thought: An Alternative to Cannibalism in the Neolithic." *Australian Archaeology* 28:35–39.

Pigeot, N. 1988. *Magdaléniens d'Etiolles: Economie de Débitage et Organisation Sociale*. Paris: Centre National de la Recherche Scientifique.

Piperno, D. R. 1987. *Phytolith Analysis*. Orlando, FL: Academic Press.

Plog, F., and D. L. Carlson. 1989. "Computer Applications for the All American Pipeline Project." *Antiquity* 63:258–67.

Postgate, N. 1987. "Excavations at Abu Salabikh 1985–86." *Iraq* XLIX:91–119.

Potts, R. 1988. *Early Hominid Activities at Olduvai*. New York: Aldine de Gruyter.

Price, T. D., ed. 1989. *The Chemistry of Prehistoric Human Bone*. Cambridge: Cambridge University Press.

Pritchard, J. B., ed. 1987. *The Times Atlas of the Bible*. London: Times Books.

Protzen, J-P. 1986. "Inca Stonemasonry." *Scientific American* 254:80–88.

Rathje, W. 1981. "A Manifesto for Modern Material Culture Studies." In *Modern Material Culture: The Archaeology of Us*, ed., R. Gould. New York: Academic Press.

Read, D. 1989. "The Substance of Archaeological Analysis and the Mold of Statistical Method:

Enlightenment Out of Discordance?" In *For Concordance in Archaeological Analysis*, ed. C. Carr. Prospect Heights, IL: Waveland.

Reeves, N. 1990. *The Complete Tutankhamun*. New York: Thames & Hudson.

Reidhead, V. A. 1979. "Linear Programming Models in Archaeology." *Annual Review of Anthropology* 8:543–78.

Renfrew, C., and P. Bahn. 1991. *Archaeology: A Handbook of Ideas and Methods*. New York: Thames and Hudson.

Renfrew, J. M. 1973. *Palaeoethnobotany*. New York: Columbia University Press.

Rice, P. M. 1987. *Pottery Analysis*. Chicago: University of Chicago Press.

Riley, D. N. 1987. *Air Photography and Archaeology*. London: Duckworth.

Rottländer, R. C. A. 1986. "Chemical Investigation of Potsherds of the Heuneberg, Upper Danube." *Proceedings of the 24th International Archaeometry Symposium*, eds. J. S. Olin and M. J. Blackman. Washington, DC: Smithsonian Institution, pp. 403–5.

Royle, C. 1986. "Summary of Prospection Methods at Sutton Hoo." *Current Arch.* IX(6) 101:171.

Rowley-Conwy, P. 1987. "The Interpretation of Ard Marks." *Antiquity* 61:263–6.

Russell, M. 1987. "Mortuary Practices at the Krapina Neandertal Site." *American Journal of Physical Anthropology* 72:381–97.

Sabloff, J. A., ed. 1981. *Simulations in Archaeology*. Albuquerque: University of New Mexico Press.

Sackett, J. R. 1982. "Approaches to Style in Lithic Archaeology." *Journal of Anthropological Archaeology* 1(1):59–112.

Scarre, C., ed. 1988. *Past Worlds: The Times Atlas of Archaeology*. London: Times Books.

Schiffer, M. B. 1987. *Formation Processes of the Archaeological Record*. Albuquerque: University of New Mexico Press.

Schwarcz, H. P. 1994. "Chronology of Modern Humans in the Levant." In *Late Quaternary and Paleoclimates of the Eastern Mediterranean*, eds. O. Bar-Yosef and R. S. Kra, pp. 21–31. Tucson: Radiocarbon.

Sealy, J. C. 1986. *Stable Carbon Isotopes and Prehistoric Diets in the South-Western Cape Province, South Africa*. Oxford: British Arch. Reports, Int. Series No. 293.

Sealy, J. C., and N. J. van der Merwe. 1986. "Isotope Assessment and the Seasonal Mobility Hpothesis in the Southwestern Cape of South Africa." *Current Anthropology* 27:135–50.

Sease, C. 1988. *A Conservation Manual for the Field Archaeologist*. Archaeological Research Tools 4. Los Angeles: UCLA Institute of Archaeology.

Semenov, S. 1964. *Prehistoric Technology*. Trans. M. W. Thompson. London: Cory, Adams & Mackay.

Shackleton, J. C. 1986. "Prehistoric Shore Environments, Shellfish Availability, and Shellfish Gathering at Franchthi, Greece." *Geoarchaeology: An International Journal* 1(2):127–43.

Shackleton, N. J. 1987. "Oxygen Isotope, Ice Volume and Sea Level." *Quarternary Science Reviews* 6:183–90.

Sharer, R., and W. Ashmore. 1992. *Archaeology: Discovering the Past*, 2nd ed. Palo Alto, CA: Mayfield.

Shennan, S. 1988. *Quantifying Archaeology*. Orlando, FL: Academic Press.

Shipman, P. 1983. "Early Hominid Lifestyle: Hunting and Gathering or Foraging and Scavenging?" in *Animals and Archaeology*, Vol. 1 of *Hunters and Their Prey*, eds. J. Glutton-Brock and C. Grigson. British Archaeological Reports International Series, 163. Oxford, England.

Sieveking, G., and M. H. Newcomer, eds. 1987. *The Human Uses of Flint and Chert*. Cambridge: Cambridge University Press.

Smith, A. B., and C. Poggenpoel. 1988. "The Technology of Bone Tool Fabrication in the Southwestern Cape of South Africa." *World Archaeology* 20(1):103–15.

Spence, C., ed. 1990. *Archaeological Site Manual*, 2d ed. London: Museum of London.

Stead, I. M., J. B. Bourke, and D. Brothwell, eds. 1986. *Lindow Man: The Body in the Bog*. London: British Museum Publications.

Stein, J. K. 1983. "Earthworm Activity: A Source of Potential Disturbance of Archaeological Sediments." *American Antiquity* 48:227–89.

———. 1986. "Coring Archaeological Sites." *American Antiquity* 51:505–27.

Street, M. 1986. "Un Pompéi de L'Ége Glaciaire." *La Recherche* 17:534–35.

Stuiver, M., and G. W. Pearson. 1986. "High-precision Calibration of the Radiocarbon Time Scale, AD 1950–500 B.C." *Radiocarbon 28 (2B), Calibration Issue: Proceedings of the Twelfth International Radiocarbon Conference, 1985.* Trondheim, Norway.

Taylor, R. E. 1987. *Radiocarbon Dating: An Archaeological Perspective.* Orlando, FL: Academic Press.

Thomas, D. H. 1974. *Predicting the Past: An Introduction to Anthropological Archaeology.* New York: Holt.

———. 1988. *St. Catherine's Island: An Island in Time.* Atlanta: Georgia Endowment for the Humanities.

Throckmorton, P., ed. 1987. *The Sea Remembers: Shipwrecks and Archaeology.* New York: Weidenfeld.

Tite, M. S. 1972. *Methods of Physical Examination in Archaeology.* London and New York: Seminar Press.

Toth, N. 1987. "The First Technology." *Scientific American* 256(4):104–13.

Traverse, A. 1988. *Paleopalynology.* Boston: Unwin Hyman.

Tsukuda, M., S. Sugita, and Y. Tsukuda. 1986. "Oldest Primitive Agriculture and Vegetational Environments in Japan." *Nature* 322:632–64.

Tylecote, R. F. 1987. *The Early History of Metallurgy in Europe.* London and New York: Longman.

Valladas, H., J-P. Chadelle, J-M. Geneste, J-L. Joron, L. Meignen, and P-J. Texier. 1987. "Datations par la Theremoluminescence de Gisement Moustériens du Sud de la France." *L'Anthropologie* 91:211–26.

Vance, E. D. 1987. "Microdebitage and Archaeological Activity Analysis." *Archaeology* July/Aug.:58–59.

Vandiver, P. B., O. Soffer, B. Klima, and J. Svoboda. 1989. "The Origins of Ceramic Technology at Dolni Vestonice, Czechoslavakia." *Science* 246:1002–8.

Vaughn, P. 1985. *Use-wear Analysis of Flaked Stone Tools.* Tucson: University of Arizona Press.

Verano, J. W. and D. H. Ubelaker, eds. 1992. *Disease and Demography in the Americas.* Washington, DC: Smithsonian Institution Press.

Villa, P., et al. 1986. "Cannibalism in the Neolithic." *Science* 233:431–37.

Waters, M. R. 1992. *Principles of Geoarchaeology: A North American Perspective.* Tucson: University of Arizona Press.

Weigelt, J. 1989. *Recent Vertebrate Carcasses and their Palaeobiological Implications.* Chicago: University of Chicago Press.

Weisner, P. 1983. "Style and Social Information in Kalahari San Projectile Points." *American Antiquity* 48(2):253–77.

Welsh, F. 1988. *Building the Trireme.* London: Constable.

Wendorf, F., and R. Schild, eds. 1980. *Prehistory of the Eastern Sahara.* New York: Academic Press.

Wendorf, F., R. Schild, A. E. Close, and Associates. 1993. *The Middle Paleolithic of Bir Tarfawi and Bir Sahara East.* New York: Plenum Press.

Wenke, R. J. 1987. "Western Iran in the Partho-Sasanian Period: The Imperial Transformation." In *The Archaeology of Western Iran,* ed. F. Hole. Washington, DC: Smithsonian Institution Press.

Wenke, R. J., J. E. Long, and P. E. Buck. 1988. "Epipaleolithic and Neolithic Subsistence and Settlement in the Fayyum Oasis of Egypt." *Journal of Field Archaeology* 15(1):29–51.

Wenke, R. J., and M. E. Lane, eds. In preparation. *Land of the Lake: 8000 Years of Human Settlement in Egypt's Fayyum Oasis.* Winona Lake, IL: Eisenbrauns.

Weymouth, J. W. 1986. "Geophysical Methods of Archaeological Site Surveying." In *Advances in Archaeological Method and Theory,* ed. M. B. Schiffer. New York: Academic Press.

Whallon, R., and J. A. Brown, eds. 1982. *Essays on Archaeological Typology*. Evanston: Center for American Archaeology Press.

Wheeler, M. 1954. *Archaeology from the Earth*. Baltimore: Penguin.

Wheeler, A., and A. K. G. Jones. 1989. *Fishes*. Cambridge: Cambridge University Press.

Whitley, D. S., and R. I. Dorn. 1987. "Rock Art Chronology in Eastern California." *World Archaeology* 19:150–64.

Wright, R. 1986. "How Old is Zone F at Lake George?" *Archaeology in Oceania* 21:138–39.

Wylie, A. 1982. "An Analogy By Any Other Name Is Just as Analogical." *Journal of Anthropological Archaeology* 1:382–401.

———. 1992. "The Interplay of Evidential Constraints and Political Interests: Recent Archaeological Research on Gender." *American Antiquity* 57(1):15–35.

Yellen, J. 1977a. *Archaeological Approaches to the Present*. New York: Academic Press.

———. 1977b. "Cultural Patterning in Faunal Remains: Evidence from the !Kung Bushmen." In *Experimental Archaeology*, eds. D. D. Ingersoll, J. Yellen, and W. MacDonald. New York: Columbia University Press.

———. 1991. "Small Mammals: !Kung San Utilization and the Production of Faunal Assemblages." *Journal of Anthropological Archaeology* 10:1–26.

Zegura, S. L. 1987. "Blood Test." *Natural History* 96(7):8–11.

NOTES

1. Urban anthropology is becoming an increasingly important area of study. See, for example, Aaron Fox, *Out of the Country: Language, Music, Emotion, and Sociability in a Texas Rural, Working-Class Community*.

2. Including many scholars who teach at universities in Australia, New Zealand, and elsewhere.

3. The idea of "feature," although still common in archaeology, has been discarded by some archaeologists in favor of a terminology based on depositional stratigraphy; see, for example, Harris, *Principles of Archaeological Stratigraphy*, 2nd ed.

4. Schiffer, *Formation Processes of the Archaeological Record*.

5. Ibid.

6. See, for example, Frayer et al., "Theories of Modern Human Origins: The Paleontological Test," p. 17.

7. Ibid., p. 16.

8. Dunnell, "Science, Social Science, and Common Sense: The Agonizing Dilemma of Modern Archaeology."

9. Currently the archaeology programs of the U.S. National Science Foundation and the U.S. National Endowment for the Humanities are threatened with extinction through congressional action.

10. This has been attributed to Mies van der Rohe and others.

11. Jefferson was once described as "a gentleman of 32 who could calculate an eclipse, survey an estate, tie an artery, plan an edifice, try a cause, dance a minuet, and play the violin." James Parton, *Life of Thomas Jefferson*.

12. Jelinek, "The Tabun Cave and Paleolithic Man in the Levant."

13. Wheeler, *Archaeology from the Earth*.

14. Sease, *A Conservation Manual for the Field Archaeologist.*

15. Grayson, *Quantitative Zooarchaeology.*

16. Binford, "Human Ancestors: Changing Views of Their Behavior"; Bunn, "Archaeological Evidence for Meat-Eating by Plio-Pleistocene Hominids from Koobi Fora and Olduvai Gorge"; and Shipman, "Early Hominid Lifestyle: Hunting and Gathering or Foraging and Scavenging?"

17. Dimbleby, *The Palynology of Archaeological Sites; Piperno, Phytolith Analysis;* Renfrew, *Palaeoethnobotany;* Gilbert and Mielke, eds., *The Analysis of Prehistoric Diets;* and Bodner and Rowlett, "Separation of Bone, Charcoal, and Seeds by Chemical Flotation."

18. Ortner and Aufderheide, eds. *Human Paleopathology: Current Syntheses and Future Options.*

19. See, for example, Ortner and Aufderheide, eds., *Human Paleopathology: Current Syntheses and Future Options.*

20. See, for example, Holliday, ed., *Soils in Archaelogy: Landscape Evolution and Human Occupation.*

21. Vaughn, *Use-wear Analysis of Flaked Stone Tools;* Keeley, *Experimental Determination of Stone Tool Use: A Microwear Analysis.*

22. Hayden, *Lithic Studies Among the Contemporary Highland Maya;* Weisner, "Style and Social Information in Kalahari Sun Projectile Points."

23. See also, for example, Gould, *Recovering the Past.*

24. For an excellent review of the role of ceramics in archaeological analysis, see Rice, *Pottery Analysis.*

25. Braun, "Pots as Tools."

26. See, for example, papers by Hodder, Plog, Wiesner and others in Conkey and Hasdorf eds., *The Uses of Style in Archaeology.*

27. Pauketat and Emerson, "The Ideology of Authority and the Power of the Pot," p. 935.

28. Jorge Luis Borges, *Other Inquisitions: 1937–1952,* quoted in Aldenderfer and Blashfield, *Cluster Analysis,* p. 7.

29. See, for example, Whallon and Brown, *Essays on Archaeological Typology;* Read, "The Substance of Archaeological Analysis and the Mold of Statistical Method: Enlightenment Out of Discordance?" pp. 45–86; Dunnell, "Methodological Issues in Americanist Artifact Classification"; Adams, "Archaeological Classification: Theory Versus Practice"; Deetz, *Invitation to Archaeology;* and Beck and Jones, "Bias and Archaeological Classification."

30. Beck, ed., *Dating in Exposed and Surface Contexts.*

31. Baillie, *Tree-Ring Dating.*

32. Libby, *Radiocarbon Dating.*

33. Taylor, *Radiocarbon Dating: An Archaeological Perspective;* Browman, "Isotopic Discrimination and Correction Factors in Radiocarbon Dating." Until recently, radiocarbon dates were often published as a certain number of years before A.D. 1950, the benchmark year in which the method was first established. "BP" was often used for corrected radiocarbon dates, "bp" for uncorrected dates (the "bp" first referred to "before present" or even "before physics"; see Taylor, *Radiocarbon Dating: An Archaeological Perspective,* p. 5). Today there are still no universal standards for reporting radiocarbon dates. Also see Gowlett, "The Archaeology of Radiocarbon Accelerator Dating."

34. Mark Lehner, Herbert Haas, Wille Wölfli and I; we thank David Koch for his support of our research.

35. Michels, *Dating Methods in Archaeology;* and Tite, *Methods of Physical Examination in Archaeology.*

36. Wendorf, Schild, Close, et al., *The Middle Paleolithic of Bir Tarfawi and Bir Sahara East.*

37. I thank Maurice and Lois Schwartz, the National Science Foundation, and the U.S. Agency for International Development for their support of this research.

38. See, for example, Wenke et al., "Epipaleolithic and Neolithic Subsistence and Settlement in the Fayyum Oasis of Egypt."

3

THE ORIGINS OF CULTURE

What a book a Devil's Chaplain might write on the clumsy,
wasteful, blundering low & horridly cruel works of nature!

Charles Darwin

In making the above statement, Darwin was expressing his conclusion that a close study of nature and evolution could be used to argue powerfully for the non-existence, or at least non-involvement in human affairs, of a supreme deity. As discussed in chapter 2, Darwin's analysis had convinced him that the origins of the human species, like that of all other species, are to be found in blind and cruel competition at all levels—that is, in countless millennia of nature "red in tooth and claw" (a phrase coined by Alfred Lord Tennyson, not Darwin).

In this chapter we consider our origins in the competitive world of Pleistocene Africa—how our genus, *Homo*, evolved out of many varieties of other apes in a complex mosaic of environments.

THE PROBLEM OF CULTURAL ORIGINS

The film *2001: A Space Odyssey* includes a vivid scene in which our chimpanzee-like African ancestors of some millions of years ago awake one morning to find themselves at the foot of a huge, black, perfectly smooth, rectangular object—a "monolith." Jabbering in fright and wonder, they are unable to understand where it came from or what it means. In a later scene, a descendant of these creatures, but still an ape-like primate, "discovers" tools by using an animal leg bone to smash the skull of another ape; in bloody triumph, he throws the bone skyward, where, spinning, it is transformed into a rotating twenty-first century space station—carrying a man on his way to examine another—or perhaps the same—monolith, which has been found in an excavation on the moon.

Stanley Kubrick's film of this classic Arthur Clarke story effectively uses the monolith as a symbol, perhaps of human evolution and enlightenment, or of some cosmic intelligence, and it leaves the viewer to muse on the nature of the possible driving force of human evolution: natural processes, God, extraterrestrial beings, or something else.

Anthropological analyses of the beginnings of tool use and the nature and significance of our past and future have, perhaps, much less mythic power than *2001*, but the fundamental questions addressed are similar: What factors transformed us from just one kind of wild African ape into space travelers, and what, if anything, does it all "mean"?

These are, of course, the questions of the ages. Long ago a Greek philosopher suggested we are the progeny of spores blown here millions of years ago through the illimitable reaches of space, and that the answers to our questions of origins are, thus, truly, in the stars. Even today some scientists, impressed by the relatively short time between the formation of the earth and the complexity of contemporary human civilizations, consider it possible that life on earth derives from life elsewhere in the universe, perhaps from the accidental intersection of the earth's orbit with a cloud of complex chemicals brewed in some mighty stellar explosion.

Alternatively, people in every age have found great comfort in their sure and certain knowledge that we and the world are the result of Divine Creation.

Whatever the value of these and other speculations, the fundamental premise of anthropology is that any inquiry into our origins, history, and destiny should begin with a consideration of real-world factors of climate, genetics, culture, etc., on the assumption that with the careful sifting and analysis of the shattered fragments of our ancestors, their tools, and other material evidence, we can "know," in a scientific sense, at least something about our nature and our past. Indeed, in their search for human origins, anthropologists have concentrated on such embarrassingly ordinary subjects as chimpanzee sexual behavior and the cuisine of African hunter-gatherers.

THE NATURE OF CULTURE

> *Intelligence . . . is the faculty of making artificial
> objects, especially tools to make tools.*
>
> Henri Bergson[1]

If we take Bergson's definition literally, we might conclude that the earliest evidence for human "intelligence" dates to some time before 2.6 million years ago, in Ethiopia, where stone tools have been found under volcanic ash layers dated to that time.[2] But what are we trying to explain when we speak of the origins of culture? Anthropologists restrict the term "cultural" to human beings (although chimpanzees are sometimes called "protocultural"), thus the origins of culture are essentially the origins of those human qualities that make us a unique animal. But it is more difficult than it might seem to reduce humanity to a particular constellation of attributes or to capture the essence of being human. For the Roman Catholic theologian, for example, a human fetus, whether six seconds or six months after conception, is human in the only way that really matters, being imbued with an immortal soul. But what observable, *measurable* qualities can we use to distinguish ourselves from other life forms?

Most who address this question turn instinctively, as it were, to attributes of the human mind, and particularly to the unique qualities of human thought. Descartes's famous phrase *Cogito, ergo sum* ("I think, therefore I am") is a classic expression of this idea.

A traditional view is that humans are unique in their ability to manipulate symbols, and that the evolution of this ability underlies all human achievements. Anyone who has seriously studied chimpanzees at play can feel a sense of kinship with these primates; the term *protocultural* seems hardly an exaggeration. But in analyzing the origins of culture, it is how we are *different* from other primates that is important, and in large part this difference resides in our mentality—our creativity, intuition, logic, and aesthetics—all powers of the human mind. Anthropologist Leslie White argued,[3] for example, that although chimpanzees are clever animals who can use tools and can be taught to use plastic counters, computers, and sign languages to express emotions and desires, they are fundamentally different from us in two ways: first, they can never use symbols at an abstract level, for example, understanding concepts such as "holy water" or the casting of a vote; second, even the smartest nonhuman animals seem to pass relatively little new, learned knowledge from generation to generation in such a way that there is an observable long-term net increase.

For White these differences between ourselves and all other animals are qualitative, although one can also view them as quantitative. We simply do not know what a chimpanzee sees or what he or she "thinks," and White's distinction may be less accurate than it appears. Nonetheless, chimpanzees can smear canvasses with paint in an excellent imitation of "modern art," but they seem utterly untalented at more representational painting; and it seems highly unlikely that even chimpanzees can *respond* in great depth to aesthetics—can savor, for example, the vibrancy of a Van Gogh landscape or the sublime delicacy of a Ming porcelain jar. Their ability to pass new learned knowledge from generation to generation is a more complex problem. Japanese monkeys, for example, have been reported to have learned how to wash sand from handfuls of grain and then instruct younger members of each generation how to do this, but there is evidence that even such simple food-related behavior is in part determined genetically.[4] And even if it were not, such behavior is at a sufficiently low scale that it remains true that "the most characteristic part of being human is the ability to profit from the accumulated and transmitted experience of other human beings."[5]

Tooby and DeVore have expressed this sense of the distinctiveness of human intelligence and behavior as a set of two kinds of primate characteristics, those that are unique to humans and those that we share with other primates but to a much different degree. In Table 3.1 (pg. 116), the first fifteen features basically relate to a generalized sense of "intelligence" in combination with some emotional capacities. We know that modern humans are *different* from other primates, but presumably as one goes back in time our earlier ancestors and other primates were increasingly *similar*. We must also recognize that we can never directly ascertain the symbolic capacities of our earliest ancestors: for the first three million years of our genus we must gauge "intelligence" by measuring changes in the size and shape of hominid skulls and bodies and by finding stone tools and the remains of other objects used by our ancestors. These indirect reflections of evolving symbolic ability constitute "culture" for the anthropologist in an analytical sense.

One might question why a "moral" sense is not listed as a defining attribute of human mentality, as morality has been the focus of theological definitions of humanity. Even Mark Twain, no moralist, said, "Man is the only animal that blushes—or needs to." But many scientists[6] have considered human moral systems as learned rather than innate, and to have evolved as extensions of the same ability to symbolize that allows us to categorize "friend" and "foe."[7]

The paradox that we have only one tool with which to try to understand the origins of the human mind, namely, the human mind, is a bit of cosmic whimsy appreciated by philosophers of all ages. There is an embedded circularity to this form of analysis that has led some to kick stones, wondering if they are really "there." Someone observed that "a fish would be the last creature to discover water,"[8] and we may be in similar circumstances—unable to see the reality in which we live because we can imagine no other reality. Readers interested in such topics and with much time to indulge their interest are referred to volumes 2 through 9 of Father Frederick Copleston's rewarding *History of Philosophy*.

What we do know, however, is that our ancestors of about five million years ago were not much different from the chimpanzees of today, and, yet, today *we* are very different from all other apes. This knowledge of our deep antiquity and the nature of our physical and cultural evolution—and the search for an explanation for them—is relatively recent.

EARLY STUDIES OF HUMAN ORIGINS

As discussed in chapter 1, the impact of the discovery of human antiquity was profound.[9] Many scholars lost their comforting faith in a recently created human-centered world and were forced to peer instead into an abyss of millions of years, during which we slowly evolved from rodents, reptiles, worms, and, ultimately, from the same lifeless chemicals that appear to make up the rest of the universe.

By the end of the nineteenth century both Darwin's ideas (see chapter 1) about the biological evolution of the human species and the discovery of stone tools in association with the bones of extinct animals in extremely ancient geological strata had convinced many scholars of the great antiquity of the human race. Nevertheless, so long as no bones were found of an ancestor intermediate between humans and other primates in physical form, it was still possible to believe that humans were an exception: we were an extremely old species, older than had previously been suspected, but a species that had not evolved as other species had.

Those who had studied Darwin and Lyell closely, however, knew it was just a matter of time before the first fossil "missing link" was found—or recognized in the bones that had already been found. The French scholar (and full-time customs inspector) Boucher de Perthes, old and tired of waiting, offered a 200-franc reward to the discoverer of the first "antediluvian" (meaning "before the flood") human in France. His enterprising workers were soon "finding" a number of such remains—all of which they had planted in hopes, of course, of collecting the reward.

Boucher de Perthes did not know that premodern hominids had already been discovered some years before but simply had not been recognized. A fragmentary Neanderthal child's skull was found near Liege, Belgium, in 1829–30, and in 1848 work at a quarry on Gibraltar revealed a skull whose receding chin, heavy brow ridges, and thick bones we now recognize as that of a Neanderthal. Neither the Belgium nor the Gibraltar finds excited much interest at the time. In 1856, however, a skullcap and some limb bones were found in a cave in the Neander Valley near Dusseldorf, Germany (Figure 3.1). Although these remains were dismissed by the great German anatomist Rudolf Virchow as those of a deformed human, Johann Karl Fuhlrott, their discoverer, argued from the beginning that the remains were of an early human form. But Virchow's opinion, and those of others who variously labeled it an ancient Celt, a victim of rickets, an idiot, or a Cossack, conspired to deny these bones their proper significance for many years. One French savant even suggested that the huge brow ridges of the Neanderthal came about because his deformed arm caused him such pain that he continually furrowed his brow, and the expression became ossified.

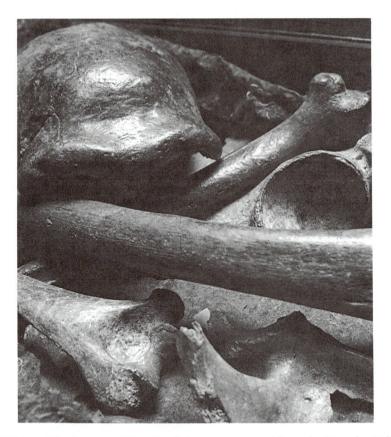

FIGURE 3.1 The remains of Neanderthals were recovered from the Neander Valley, near Dusseldorf, Germany, in 1857. This evidence that ancient people were different from modern humankind was part of the assault by evolutionary ideas and evidence on traditional ideas about our place in the universe.

In 1886 two partial skeletons similar to the Neanderthal specimen were recovered in a cave in Spy, Belgium, in direct association with stone tools and the bones of rhinoceroses, mammoths, and other animal species known to have been long extinct. Although Virchow also refused to accept these as ancient men, the tide of opinion had turned and scientists everywhere were soon looking eagerly for additional specimens of early hominids.

One of these scientists was a young Dutch physician, Eugene Dubois, who spent years wandering the wilds of Sumatra without finding much of interest; only when he arranged a transfer to Java did he make his great discovery. In 1890 he unearthed a fragment of a lower jaw, and over the next few years he recovered a skullcap and a femur (thigh bone).

For the next thirty years, controversy raged over Dubois's find, with some authorities again claiming it to be a deformed freak or a giant chimpanzee, and others recognizing it as an early form of our genus and a direct ancestor of modern humans. Dubois's fossil had an approximate brain volume of 1,040 cubic centimeters, about a third less than modern people but far more than any living primate. Scholars of the time recognized that if this animal were in fact a human ancestor, it was an ancestor considerably different from ourselves and from "Neanderthal man" (whose cranial capacity was slightly larger than that of most modern humans).

In 1906 the German anatomist Gustav Schwalbe proposed three successive stages of hominid evolution: pithecanthropine (as represented by Dubois's fossils), Neanderthal, and modern. It was apparent, however, that if this were the correct succession of hominid forms, there would have been many intermediate types not yet found (Figure 3.2).

The recognition of an earlier stage of hominid evolution did not come until the 1920s, when Raymond Dart discovered a nearly complete skull of a strange-looking child. It was encased in stone quarried from a mine at Taung, some 300 kilometers from Johannesburg, South Africa. The skull's shape, small volume, and primitive teeth convinced Dart he had found one of humankind's earliest, most primitive ancestors, which he labeled Australopithecus africanus ("Southern ape of Africa"). While Dart's conclusions were being challenged by some of the most influential scientists in Europe, another important find was made, this time in northeastern China, near Beijing, at a mining installation called Zhoukoudian (formerly rendered in English as "Choukoutien") (Figure 3.3). For centuries, fossilized bones from the area had been ground into powder and used as aphrodisiacs and medical potions.[10]

A somewhat more scientific interest in these fossils was stimulated in 1921 when a single human-looking tooth from Zhoukoudian was given to the English anatomist Henry Black. He recognized it as belonging to an ancient form of hominid, and as a consequence, excavations at Zhoukoudian were begun. Altogether, the remains of about forty individuals were found, including many skull fragments, and it was obvious that these individuals were similar in brain size, facial structure, and other characteristics to the hominid found by Dubois on Java. This supported Schwalbe's proposed pithecanthropine stage, and fossils of this type were accorded the name *Sinanthropus* or *Homo erectus* ("erect man").

Thus, by the 1930s at least some of the scientific community recognized four categories of early hominids: australopithecines, *Homo erectus*, Neanderthals, and mod-

A Hypothesis of Climate and Evolution

OSCILLATING CYCLES: Cold spells, warm spells.
After a major cooling five to six million years ago, when changes in Earth's orbit affected global climate, subtropical Africa's warm, moist environment was subject to oscillating cycles of cool, dry and warm, wet weather.

The hypothesis linking climate change with stages in prehuman evolution suggests that five million to six million years ago, as its forested habitat shrank, a tree-dwelling quadruped learned to forage as a biped on the savanna.

SUBTROPICAL FOREST

SAVANNA GRASSLANDS

The cycles were relatively brief and mild, and had little effect on the evolution of animal species, until . . .

Forested areas, which proliferated in warm cycles, receded in cool cycles, allowing grasslands to take over until the climate shifted and woodlands returned.

A "PULSE" OF SEVERE COLD: Forests disappeared; creatures adapted or died.
2.8 million years ago, large ice sheets over North America and Europe sent cold, dry air into subtropical Africa. The result was a longer and more severe cold cycle, which so depleted the forests that grasslands took hold permanently. Species that could adapt to open environments and changing food sources prospered; those that could not adapt became extinct.

Around the cold spell about 2.8 million years ago, when there was a permanent shift to grasslands, prehumans apparently split into at least two branches. Australopithecus robustus, a specialist vegetarian eventually became extinct. The genus Homo, which evolved into modern humans was adapted to many habitats and foods.

A SECOND COLD WAVE: Human ancestors migrated.
Cooling and drying intensified in a second major cold "pulse" one million years ago, as ice sheets expanded, diverting cold air from Europe toward Africa and Asia. This set the stage for a second major wave of extinctions and evolution, and led to the migration out of Africa of the ancestors of modern humans.

The second major cold spell, about a million years ago, coincided with the emergence of Homo erectus, the immediate ancestor of Homo sapiens, as the sole survivor of the hominid line. This species migrated out of Africa to colonize the world. Layers of dust buried in ocean sediments link the timing of these events more tightly than ever before.

6 MILLION YEARS AGO   5 MILLION   4 MILLION   3 MILLION   2 MILLION   1 MILLION   PRESENT

Laurentide ice sheet

Sea ice

Fennoscandian ice sheet

Cold sea surface temperatures

The ocean dust layers were thickest when the African climate was driest. The sediment record suggests that about a million years ago, a Northern Hemisphere ice age paved the way for migration of Homo erectus. Ice masses locked up water and sea levels fell, opening up better land connections between Africa and central Asia.

Sources: Dr. Elisabeth S. Vrba; Dr. Peter deMenocal

The New York Times; Illustrations by Megan Jaegerman (time line) and Patricia J. Wynne (hominids and globe)

FIGURE 3.2 Some new hypotheses of human evolution are based on climate and evolution.

102

FIGURE 3.3 Excavations at Zhoukoudian, China. The rope enclosures on the right mark areas where hominid skulls were found.

ern humans. Since that time the arguments have focused not on *whether* humankind evolved from some sort of nonhuman ancestor, but on what these various ancestral forms are, how they were related genetically during their evolutionary histories, and what evolutionary mechanisms produced *Homo sapiens sapiens* from prehuman primates. It is somewhat ironic that many scholars today consider the Javanese *Homo erectus*, the Neanderthals, and most of the australopithecines to have been unrelated or only distantly related to our own ancestors (discussed in chapter 4), but the importance of these early finds is that they demonstrated that we had evolved from nonhuman primates.

We have many sources of evidence about our origins, including the study of our primate relatives, the fossil bones of our ancestors, and the early stone tools and other physical traces our forebears left. But before we look at the collected evidence, we must consider the analytical principles we must use to interpret them—specifically, evolutionary theory. The basic premise underlying the study of human origins is that about five million years ago our ancestors were animals something like chimpanzees, and that the forces of evolution changed us into what we are today. But what were these forces?

EVOLUTIONARY THEORY

The origins of evolutionary theory in the writings of Darwin and others were reviewed in chapter 1, but a more detailed description of evolutionary principles and processes is required here to understand how they can be applied to the human past—and to the entire span of biological life on this planet.[11]

Evolutionary theory is a complex, often mathematically expressed discipline, and its major elements can only briefly be summarized here.[12]

Much of this book is concerned with Darwinian evolution as applied to the biology of people, plants, and animals. As we shall see in later chapters, however, many scholars have investigated applications of evolutionary theory to *cultures*, not just biological species.

As noted in chapter 1, Charles Darwin made the fundamental observations that still serve as the basic paradigm for evolutionary theory. He noted that many more animals and plants were bred than actually lived to reproduce themselves; further, he noted that there was much variation in the form and physical qualities of individuals in any species. He further inferred that there was some connection between these variations and the differing rates of success of individuals in living and reproducing. Finally, he concluded that "natural selection" was the process in which nature—in the form of different environments—selected some individuals to live and reproduce based on the relative "fitness" of individuals in these environments. Darwin then attempted to show how this general process had worked on innumerable generations to produce the awesome visible biological diversity of the world.

What Darwin did not know, however, was how variations in individuals arose and how they were passed on from generation to generation. The answers to these problems were supplied by geneticists, beginning primarily with Gregor Mendel (1822–1884). Mendel studied the inheritance of color and shape in peas, and in a series of convincing experiments showed that there were predictable patterns to the results of breeding plants of different characteristics.[13] Mendel and later scholars formulated what we now call the *particulate theory of inheritance*, which says that physical characteristics of individual organisms are passed from one generation to the next in the form of discrete particles (informally known as "genes") and that these particles retain their ability to express themselves even when they do not express themselves in every generation. The *law of segregation* stipulates that these particles are inherited in pairs, one of each from each of the parents.

The elixir of life, in the sense of evolutionary theory, is the substance known as DNA. Within the nucleus of every animal cell are chromosomes, thread-like structures composed of deoxyribonucleic acid, or DNA. DNA in turn is composed of four *nucleotides*: guanine, cytosine, adenine, and thymine (Figure 3.4). These nucleotides

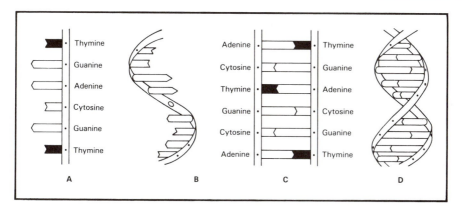

FIGURE 3.4   The genetic code determining the biological characteristics of species lies in the sequence of bases (thymine, guanine, adenine, cytosine) that links two strands of nucleotides to form the double helix that is DNA. (**A**) Bases in part of one strand of nucleotides. (**B**) Part of one strand twisted. (**C**) Complementary bases joined. (**D**) Two strands joined and twisted.

combine in groups of three to form twenty amino acids, which are the building blocks for all protein formation. The arrangement, or sequence, of these bases determines the physical structure of all living things, from AIDS viruses to elephants (Figure 3.5). Except for the sperm or ova, every human cell contains the complete genetic code for that individual. If the DNA strand representing the entire code for a particular person were removed from a single cell and straightened, it would be about six feet

FIGURE 3.5   Amino acid sequences. Organisms (human, Rhesus monkey, rabbit, duck, rattlesnake, tuna, moth, yeast) differ in the sequence of amino acids in protein cytochrome *c*, an enzyme used in energy production. The higher the number shown, the greater the difference between any two.

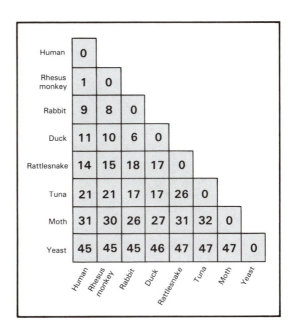

	Human	Rhesus monkey	Rabbit	Duck	Rattlesnake	Tuna	Moth	Yeast
Human	0							
Rhesus monkey	1	0						
Rabbit	9	8	0					
Duck	11	10	6	0				
Rattlesnake	14	15	18	17	0			
Tuna	21	21	17	17	26	0		
Moth	31	30	26	27	31	32	0	
Yeast	45	45	45	46	47	47	47	0

long. The specific sequence of the DNA for any individual reader of this book would be unique and would fill about 125 books the size of the Manhattan telephone directory. DNA contains all the information required to direct the operation of a cell, in combination with another nucleic acid, RNA (ribonucleic acid). DNA has the ability to reproduce itself, and it also offers the potential for the main stuff of evolution, genetic change.

The two main sources of genetic variety are *genetic recombination* and *mutation*. Animal cells are constantly splitting (*mitosis*) and producing genetically identical copies of themselves, and thus growth and maintenance are accomplished. But in *meiosis*, egg and sperm cells are produced that carry only half the genetic code of the parent—in the case of humans, our twenty-three pairs of chromosomes total forty-six total chromosomes in each body cell, but each egg and sperm cell carries only half the total, so each new person receives twenty-three chromosomes each from his or her father and mother. These genes are shuffled and then recombined in sexual reproduction, and thus the number of genetically unique offspring possible for any human couple is determined by the equation $2^{23} \times 2^{23} = 2^{46}$, or about 70,000,000,000,000.[14]

Genetic variability is also produced by *mutations* in chromosomes—errors made by DNA in copying itself. The origins of mutations are not completely known, but some probably arise through the cosmic ray bombardment to which all living organisms are subjected. Early work on DNA involved exposing hapless populations of fruit-flies to radiation, producing monstrous combinations of eye colors, wing size, and other features. And there is reason to believe that industrial pollution, loss of ozone in the atmosphere, and other factors in the modern environment will lead to greater rates of mutation in all living things.

A classic illustration of the elements of evolutionary theory and its power to explain change in the natural world involves a rather unprepossessing insect. Until the early nineteenth century, a native English species of moth (*Biston betularia*) had a mottled gray and white pattern that effectively camouflaged it when it rested on the lichen-covered bark of the trees of the English Midlands, which gave it some protection from birds, its main predator. But the Industrial Revolution produced so much soot that trees all over the range of these moths were blackened, reducing the effectiveness of the moths' camouflage. In 1840, however, a nearly black *Biston betularia*—the result of a slight genetic mutation—was found near Manchester, and by 1895 it was discovered that 98 percent of the *Biston betularia* population in this region was black.[15] The protective advantage of a black wing color on soot-covered trees was subsequently demonstrated by releasing moths of various colors and recapturing them, to see what proportion survived.

This example, seemingly trivial, demonstrates all of the major elements of evolutionary theory. It explains biological changes in life forms over time and space in terms of *natural selection*, at least in the simplistic sense of differential survival over time in organisms on the basis of their genetically determined characteristics. For natural selection to operate there must be *variability*, that is, differences between individuals in their physical form and the specific and unique genetic combinations each individual represents, so that over time there can be selection of characteristics, such as changes in color-camouflage, brain size, instinctive migration, etc.

It is important to recognize that evolution is not goal-directed: these English moths could not intentionally produce black coloration to solve their problem; evolutionary processes simply and blindly sorted the genetic potential for these different colorations on the basis of the advantage of individual moths in reproduction and survival. The biological history of life on this planet is one of uncountable extinctions of species—which makes it clear that evolution does not "solve" all problems of adaptation as neatly as it appears to have done in the case of *Biston betularia*.

But the reader should be aware that currently intense debates are continuing about the status of Darwinism and what is often called "neo-Darwinism." In general, biologists do not doubt the essential validity of Darwin's ideas, but they dispute heatedly the mechanisms involved. For example, a major recent book, *Evolution as Entropy*, by Brooks and Wiley, argues that natural selection is not the most important factor in directional change. Instead, they suggest that existing systems—whether these be organisms, populations, or species—present a configuration that constrains the possible "spaces" or directions in which evolution may take place. These are highly abstract and fundamentally mathematical arguments that are beyond the scope of this book.

Applications of Evolutionary Theory to the Problem of Human Origins   Most genetic mutations seem to be "bad," in the sense that they reduce the chances of the individual carrying them to reproduce successfully. Other mutations are "good," in that they increase reproductive potential, or "fitness." But what is good or bad in evolution is measured entirely by reproductive success—and can be good or bad in different environments. For example, sickle-cell anemia—a genetic condition in which red blood cells are misshapen—is a common disease in Africa and a few other places. People who are born with a certain combination of the genes for this condition often die in childhood; but those with another genetic combination involving this mutation appear to have some protection against malaria—and thus the gene for sickle-cell anemia has persisted, because its presence in a population—although it results in the death of some people—helps others to live to reproductive age in zones of the world where malaria has long been a ferocious killer. Similarly, the gene for cystic fibrosis,[16] which results in thickened mucus and great difficulties in breathing, may have been perpetuated despite the deaths and debilitation it exacts because some genetic expressions of this gene may mitigate the effects of some other diseases. Death from cholera and other plagues, for example, often results from dehydration as mucus membranes are infected and people lose fatal amounts of bodily fluids, and so a resistance to this loss could prove advantageous in some situations. "Natural selection," in this sense, is obviously no master or beneficent craftsman.

The spread and perpetuation of genetic mutations through biological populations are accomplished by various mechanisms. The variations in skin color in contemporary peoples, for example, seem to be the result of *migration* into different environments and subsequent adaptation. Dark skin offers a defense against skin cancers and other maladies that exposure to direct sunlight on human skin can produce, and so we see dark skin tones not just in Africa, but in the Indian subcontinent and far out into the Pacific Ocean island chains. But in humans the critical nutrient vitamin D is synthesized in the skin through the action of sunlight, and in relatively dark and cloudy climates a dark-skinned person will be at a disadvantage in times of scarcity of dietary sources of vitamin D—in winter months, for example. Early humans from Africa, whom we assume to have been dark skinned, invaded environments where heavy pigmentation interfered with the synthesis of Vitamin D, and eventually natural selection produced the blond, fair-skinned, blue-eyed human physical type typical of northern Europe: we must assume that small variations in skin pigmentation over hundreds of thousands or millions of years allowed those with lighter pigmentation to have a slightly greater reproductive "fitness" for living in more temperate environments.

In this way, the world's "races" were formed, with natural selection acting on mutations in hundreds of genetically determined features. Geographical barriers have been a factor in channeling and constraining these migratory patterns: the Sahara, the Himalayas, and other natural barriers have restricted the matings between people in different areas to the point that modern "races" evolved. Most biological scientists reject the term "race" as imprecise and misleading. Patterns of evolutionary variability in people seem best understood in terms of *clines*, or gradients of variation through time and space that are not easily and discretely compartmentalized. Skin color, for example, varies greatly between people on a cline from Sweden and those from South Africa, and these variations are described only crudely as "black" and "white." Also, some of the traits commonly used to identify "race," such as skin tone, eyelid shape, and nose and lip shape, also show immense—and often independent— variation along gradients through time and space: that is, southern Indians, West Africans, some Pacific Islanders, and others share a relatively dark skin pigmentation but differ greatly in nose and lip shape, hair texture, etc.[17]

Changes in physical form can also result from *sexual selection*: once individuals choose mates nonrandomly with regard to some characteristics, evolutionary change can result. Gaudy colors and exaggerated features, such as represented by the male peacock, are probably the result of sexual selection, in which females choose mates partly on the basis of elaborateness of the display. Nor are these displays necessarily irrelevant to genetic "fitness," for they often correlate with superior health and genetic potential of some kinds. Some scientists believe that sexual selection was responsible for features such as the "exaggerated" size (by comparison to other primates) of human penises and female breasts.[18]

Modern population genetics is a complex mathematical discipline and is largely beyond the scope of this book. And many complex debates continue about the application of evolutionary theory to human evolution.[19] But for the study of cultural origins and the other physical changes we will consider here, including plant and animal domestication (chapter 6), the important points to remember are (1) genetic variability is constantly arising through various mechanisms and (2) changing environments, sexual selection, and other factors "select" or act on this variability and differing reproductive success through time and space to produce evolutionary change.

Although modern cultures have erected some barriers to "natural selection" (few people in industrialized countries now die of appendicitis, for example), through our long evolutionary history we have been no less a product of evolutionary forces than any other life form. Most modern human physical characteristics are the result of complex genetic interactions that involve a subtle, long-term balancing of the costs and benefits of genetic changes. Consider, for example, the average height of human beings. As professional basketball teams and the pygmies of central Africa demonstrate, humans can live perfectly normal lives as individuals seven feet or three feet tall. So why, on the average, are people around the world between five and six feet tall? And why do they vary sharply in average height by sex and geographical location? Why are we not all about four feet tall or seven feet tall? As it is with almost all human characteristics, the "environment"—nutrition, for example—is a factor in human height. The high-calorie diets of North America, for example, have produced generations of Asian-Americans who are significantly taller, on average, than their parents. But height is also partially genetically controlled. And we must assume that we average between five and six feet and not between seven and eight feet or three and four feet because our average size made sense in complex evolutionary equations. With selective breeding and adequate nutrition, a group of people could probably have been bred to an average height of seven feet or more, but the costs of maintaining that body mass obviously did not make evolutionary "sense"—given the advantages in reproductive success of larger size, or of being able to see over large bushes, or of winning an infrequent match with a cave bear. The pygmies of the African rain forests appear to have evolved in response to the very low food resources available in a tropical rain forest, where most of the energy is locked in forms of cellulose that is of no use to humans.

Consider another aspect of the human diet. There is overwhelming evidence that contemporary death rates from cancer and other diseases are directly related to the fact that most of us savage our evolutionary heritage with diets that simply do not meet the needs of the omnivorous hunter-gatherers that natural selection fashioned us to be. Every one of us is the direct descendant of tens of thousands of generations of people who were naturally selected to thrive on the omnivorous diets available to hunter-foragers as they radiated from Africa across the world. In many areas these diets would have been high in fiber and fruit, low in fat and salt—diets that involved eating many different species of animals and plants. Although our ancestors' diets varied greatly in different times and places, in most cases they would have been very different from the diets of most of us. In their book *The Paleolithic Prescription*, Eaton et al. suggest, for example, that "Paleolithic humans generally consumed over seven times the currently recommended amount of vitamin C, and much of this might have been in the form of common 'weeds,' such as dandelions, along with fruit."

Since our brief 7000 years as farmers have had little effect on our basic physiology and metabolism, logic might tell us that we should eat as wide-ranging a diet as our hunting-foraging ancestors did. But, alas, evolutionary equations are complex. People might, for example, vastly increase their vitamin C consumption on the grounds that ancient hunter-foragers had high concentrations of this vitamin in their diets, but the factors that improve an individual's chances of becoming a successful mother or father many times before age forty—an all-important accomplishment in evolutionary terms—may not be the same as those that produce fit and happy seventy and eighty year olds. Until about 10,000 years ago—or just yesterday in evolutionary terms—few people lived past fifty. In terms of an individual's success in passing on his or her genes, what probably mattered most was to have children and successfully raise them on a diet of some meat, a lot of plant foods, and an exercise regime that modern medical science would consider dangerous.

In general, human physiology appears to have been selected over millions of years to operate on a diet of almost anything, particularly if there is some variety and moderation. Even Irish coffee, that perfect end to a field archaeologist's day, containing four basic food groups—fat, sugar, alcohol, and caffeine—can be tolerated as long as one scavenges widely among the other food groups the rest of the day. Yet Eskimos are reported to eat, during the long winter months, a diet consisting mainly of meat, augmented only with a few scraps of vegetation they find in the stomachs of seals and other animals they kill. And poor Hindu peasants have produced a population explosion on a meatless diet consisting mainly of vegetables, rice, oils, and sugar.

Whatever the diet of our ancestors, we must assume that we are walking, talking genetic packages that reflect what "worked" for hunters and gatherers, plus an unknown amount of "random" genetic change. So although every characteristic of every person cannot be accounted for in terms of its competitive value in passing on one's genes, much of what we are must be explained in exactly these terms. Thus, for example, our brain size averages about 1,300 cubic centimeters because that size is a good balance between the advantages of greater intelligence and general cerebration and the high costs of large brains in terms of blood supply and the reduced mobility of the broadened female pelvis, which is needed for successful live birth of the cerebral monstrosities that we are.

There are very real problems with the "adaptationist" views of human evolution—the idea that most or all of what we are is the product of selected accumulated successful mutations. Much of what we are, in fact, may be the result of random genetic variation, not the direct product of selection for a particular quality or trait. And it is almost impossible to find some trait or behavior that *cannot* be explained as the solution to some kind of imagined evolutionary problem or opportunity.[20] It is also often difficult to identify exactly what the *focus* of selection was for complex physiological or anatomical evolution. Hamilton, for example, suggests that many of the sex differences between men and women and between humans and other apes are the result of long-term selection for high levels of sex hormones—not to exaggerate our sexuality but to give us the stamina we needed as foragers to walk long and often to find food.[21]

Yet, as Tooby and DeVore note, much of what we are as humans, from our large brains and bipedal locomotion to our tool use and symbolic capacities, involves the kinds of genetically based features that are complex and biologically "costly"—suggesting that they are, in fact, adaptations and the direct result of complex patterns of natural selection.[22]

With this simple introduction to evolution, it is easy to see why "argument from design"—the theory that the universe *had* to have been created by a Divine Being because everything worked together in such harmony—was almost universally rejected by scientists from the late nineteenth century on, and why few professional research biologists and geneticists doubt that humans have evolved from single-cell animals and are genetically related to all other life forms on this planet. Science has shown that (1) the chemistry of human genetics operates identically to that of other life forms and (2) the differences between humans and other animals in the "spelling" of their DNA sequence is slight—there is only about a 1 percent difference between a person and a chimp, for example, and only a 2 percent difference between a person and a mouse. In fact, the human DNA sequence contains bits of the same genetic code that produces or once produced mice, plants, ants, dinosaurs, etc.—a situation that is exactly what would be expected based on evolutionary theory.

And yet it is also easy to see why the "argument from design" was so difficult to give up: looking back from the perspective of the present, evolution seems to be directed toward a goal, such as larger human brain size. But evolution is simply a matter of random variation, plus what worked from individual to individual: it is the individual, and his or her genetic material, that either reproduces successfully or does not.

Biological evolution can shape a world of great complexity and, in a sense, of great beauty. And although it is tempting to see "natural selection" as an active, quasi-intelligent force, shaping plants and animals for certain purposes and to meet certain requirements, this is a fundamentally flawed perspective. Natural selection does not "know" what will be required at some later date. Natural selection in this sense is simply differential rates of reproduction and survival.

If this is so, what is the key to long-term evolutionary success in a lineage? One important element seems to be the maintenance of genetic variability. A classic example of this is the problem caused by the introduction of rabbits into Australia. Without a natural predator, the rabbits multiplied to the point of becoming a major crop pest. Efforts to control them by introducing a rabbit disease killed millions of them, but because of genetic variability a few individuals were naturally immune. They survived and quickly reestablished a population that was more resistant to this disease.

As the AIDS epidemic demonstrates, life is a constant struggle between life forms for survival. The AIDS virus's "strategy" involves rapidly changing forms and a late onset—afflicting many people long after they have already spread the virus to others. But almost certainly some people will be naturally resistant to the virus, and even if the epidemic sweeps the world, these resistant individuals would be able to reestablish human populations. There is no reason to suspect that the AIDS virus will be the last one to sweep the world; in fact, it seems simply another of a long line of human afflictions, and there are likely much worse ones to come.

Human reproduction assures the generation of great genetic variability, as long as inbreeding is not a problem. In a classic study of the problems that inbreeding can produce, a Czech researcher compared two sets of children produced by the same Czech women. One set of these children consisted of 161 individuals who had been fathered by the women's fathers, brothers, or sons. The other set consisted of 95 children who were fathered by men who had no known family relationship to the mothers. The inbred children were about three times more likely to die at birth or before one year of age, and about twelve times as likely to suffer mental retardation, deafness, heart abnormalities, and other maladies. Other researchers[23] have shown that the children of first cousins have an infant mortality rate that is about twice that of children of unrelated couples.

Scholars have long debated whether the "incest taboo" found in many cultures is biologically based or just a culturally based psychological construct.[24] It is clear that today people in many cultures practice incest, and we suspect they did so in the past as well, but there seem to be clear biological advantages to the maintenance of genetic diversity by migration, marriage between unrelated people, and other factors.

This discussion of evolutionary theory as applied to us and our ancestors seems to lead inevitably to a consideration of eugenics—attempts to produce individuals with selected genetic characteristics, either through selective mating, abortion, or—now—direct manipulation of a person's genes.

People are understandably ambivalent about the idea of genetically selected traits. Based on what we know about genetically determined aspects of anatomy and physiology, for example, it seems manifestly evident that not even a lifetime of practice can make one another Mozart and that no amount of education will enable many of us to extend the insights of a Newton. This notion that the potential for various kinds of "accomplishments" is genetically predetermined is especially difficult for social reformers, for it calls into question the ultimate value of much social engineering.

But eugenics, of a sort, is already here. Every year hundreds of thousands of human fetuses are aborted because genetic testing has shown that they would be born afflicted with Down's syndrome, cystic fibrosis, Huntington's disease, or some other malady. In China and India, untold thousands of fetuses are aborted because they are female. And there is every indication that these forms of "eugenics" will expand greatly. From a fetus's genetic structure, scientists can now, or soon will be able to, predict accurately many other conditions an individual is likely to have in later life, such as Alzheimer's disease, manic depression, breast cancer, some forms of bowel cancer, and obesity. Also, current attempts to map the entire human genome probably will make it possible to predict occurrences of alcoholism, homosexuality, and many other conditions previously thought to be mainly consequences of choice.

If so, simple analysis of an individual's genetic pattern—which is possible by examining any given cell of that individual, a hair, a fingernail clipping, etc., none of which is now a legally protected aspect of "privacy"—could be an important consideration in whom one marries, whom one votes for in elections, the amount invested in an individual's education, and many other choices.

Simply put, is such knowledge about genetics good or bad? Every reader of this book can expect to hear increasing debates on this point, for the answer is complex and ultimately a matter of values. One might argue, for example, that our best "strategy" in long-term evolutionary equations is to maintain as much genetic diversity as possible—the antithesis of "eugenics" programs, in effect. For no one can predict what new genetic horrors will arise in AIDS-like viruses or some other disease, and it may well be that only a few individuals have natural genetic immunity to them. And it may be that some yet-to-be mutated natural resistance to skin cancer, to exposure to asbestos and organic pollutants, or to some newly mutated disease will be the key to our long-term survival as a species.

Evolution is in no sense "over" for us just because we currently are doing rather well.

THE ECOLOGICAL CONTEXT OF CULTURAL ORIGINS

> In the bleak mid-winter
> Frosty wind made moan,
> Earth stood hard as iron,
> Water like a stone;
> Snow had fallen, snow on snow,
> Snow on snow,
> In the bleak mid-winter
> Long ago.
> *Christina Rossetti (1830–1894)*[25]

One of the central facts of human physical and cultural evolution is that many of the crucial developments of our species occurred in Africa and southern Eurasia between about five million and ten thousand years ago, a period in which world climates fluctuated greatly but were, on average, cooler than today. About 3.2 million years ago, when some of our first bipedal (i.e., walking upright) ancestors appeared, massive glaciers had spread over northern lands. These glaciers had grown even larger by 2.5 million years ago, and about 1.6 million years ago, when our earliest ancestors were radiating from Africa, climates began fluctuating, with long periods of intense cold followed by periods that were nearly as warm as climates of today. This period of climatic fluctuation during the past 1.6 million years is known as the *Pleistocene* epoch, or the *Quaternary* period. The correspondence between this period of climatic change and our own development has led scholars for many years to suspect that somehow Pleistocene climatic changes directly shaped human evolution, perhaps by creating difficult and demanding environments that "selected" larger and more intelligent hominids. But the relationship between climatic changes and human changes seems to have been very complex.

For the modern individual, sheltered from climate by cities and central heating, the effects of winter are reduced to minor inconveniences, but for our Pleistocene ancestors, the brutal winters of hundreds of thousands of years ago made southern France, Italy, China, and other currently hospitable regions a challenge to human resourcefulness and tenacity. Advancing and retreating glaciers and the weather systems that drove them operated in slow but powerful pulses, alternately drawing human populations into some areas and evicting them from others, all the while mixing genes, eliciting adaptations, and shaping our cultural and physical evolution. In Africa, too, the great climatic changes of the Pleistocene occasionally changed large areas of formerly habitable land into vast deserts, and then later changed them back to forests and grassland.

Average worldwide temperatures have fluctuated more rapidly in the last 14 million years than ever before, and a world as warm as our own has been a rarity during the last 2.5 million years. There have been, however, occasional interglacials, periods often of about 10,000 years, when temperatures rose almost to present-day levels. Even during the main glacial periods, there were interstadials, short warming phases when the temperature rose but did not reach today's levels. Archaeologists use the term *Holocene* to refer to the last 10,000 years, but only time will tell if our age is a short interglacial or a long-term warming trend.

During the glacial periods, ice sheets spread from the poles and from higher elevations to cover much of the higher latitudes. So much of the seas were locked in ice during the coldest periods that the sea level dropped by as much as forty meters, making dry land of coastal areas that today are many meters below the sea. Land bridges that facilitated the spread of peoples throughout the world formed between North America and Asia, Europe and Britain, and Southeast Asia and what are now offshore islands. Unfortunately, Pleistocene ice sheets have ground many critical archaeological sites to powder, and the rising seas of the postglacial periods have covered thousands of others.

During glacial periods many areas that are now quite temperate were either under ice or in permafrost conditions. Other areas, such as parts of China, were much drier than they are today. In still other areas—North America, for example—melting water from glaciers created a lush lake-forest environment.

The great climatic shifts of the Pleistocene seem to have been caused by a combination of factors, including fluctuations in solar radiation, mountain-building activity, and changes in the earth's atmosphere.[26] But in the next several decades the world may see the invalidation of the cliché, "everyone talks about the weather, but nobody does anything about it." We seem to have been doing something to it since the Industrial Revolution. Various scientists have suggested that we are already seeing the results of the "Greenhouse Effect"—a dramatic warming of average world climates as a result of industrial pollution. Some meteorologists predict that by the mid-twenty-first century, and thus within the life span of some readers of this book, coastal cities such as New York will be partially flooded by rising sea levels.

The first million years or more of the history of our genus were spent in the tropics of Africa and perhaps Asia, and we were probably all Africans until just a million years ago, and perhaps much later—late, in any event, in our evolutionary story. Even if evidence (reviewed below) for our ancestors' invasion of Asia before a million years ago is confirmed, we must still look to the grasslands and forests of Africa for the environments of our origins.

In many ways the history of our genus seems tied to *savanna* environments. Savannas are relatively flat, arid expanses with scattered trees and occasional water holes, and their mixed grasses, shrubs, and other plants usually support large herds of grazing animals such as zebras, buffaloes, and gazelles. As we will see, the earliest fossil humans and their stone tools have been found near the lakes and streams that cut through these savannas. The importance of savannas in our past may be overstated, though, because of the difficulties of finding preserved remains in wetter, more forested areas. Also, it is interesting that forest-dwelling chimpanzees seem to show more and more varied tool use, more cooperative group hunting, and more cooperation and food sharing than chimpanzees who live in more open environments.[27] So the central role of savannas in the initial origins of the human genus may be more apparent than real.

THE EVIDENCE OF CULTURAL ORIGINS

We have four basic categories of evidence for analyzing human origins: (1) *paleontology*, the study of ancient forms of animal life, including the ancestors of humankind; (2) *archaeology*, the analysis of the archaeological record—the stones and bones and other tools used by our ancestors; (3) *primatology*, the study of our contemporary non-human relatives, the other primates, whose behavior patterns may give us clues to the behavior of our own ancestors, and whose genetic composition can be compared through molecular biology with our own to address questions of our common descent; and (4) *ethnology*, particularly the study of contemporary or recent hunting-and-gathering peoples, whom we assume to be living in environments and patterns similar to those of our Paleolithic ancestors (although any contemporary human societies must be regarded as fundamentally different from those of our earliest ancestors).

Anthropologists use these four kinds of evidence to produce "models of cultural origins"—sets of related hypotheses about the factors that combined to change our ancestors from unremarkable primates to human beings.

Paleontological Evidence of Human Origins

> *A brain weight of nine hundred grams is adequate as an optimum for human behavior. Anything more is employed in the commission of misdeeds.*
>
> Earnest Hooten

One of the most difficult things for the people of the nineteenth century to accept was the idea that as a species we are the progeny of nonhuman primates. It is perhaps fortunate that they did not know then that an even earlier ancestor seems to have been a small, pink-nosed, libidinous, insect-eating animal whose modern form, the shrew, is on a pound-for-pound basis among the most ferociously effective predators known.

Taken as an overall sequence, from dinosaurs to tree shrews to ourselves, is there any trend in the evolution of animal life on this planet that would help us understand the appearance of culture and our own physical type? One possible answer is suggested by the comparison of the ratio of brain size to body size in successive animal forms during the many millions of years before the first culture-bearing animals appeared. The anatomist Harry Jerison has devised an encephalization index by dividing the total brain volume of each animal by the two-thirds power of its body size. This simple index thus represents a scaled ratio of brain volume to overall size. Jerison's results give us an answer of sorts to our questions. The increase in average human brain size—from about 500 to about 1,450 cubic centimeters in only a few million years—has been extraordinarily rapid, but, overall, we seem to be a continuation of a process that began at least 600 million years ago, a process involving, in some animal forms, long-term natural selection for increased brain-to-body ratios, and, presumably, mental capacity.

But we represent something more than just another species in this long-term evolutionary process, for we are truly monstrosities in terms of brain size. Jerison lists the "encephalization quotients" (which take account of the relationship and brain size across invertebrates) for a variety of primate individuals, including ourselves (see Table 3.1). and it is clear that we are a radical departure from our nearest primate relatives.

Why should there be this long-term evolution of larger brain-body ratios? We assume that it must be because of the reproductive advantages conferred by this development. But with regard to human brain size, Jerison stresses that the important point to remember is that very advanced behavior can be governed by very small amounts of brain tissue. The behavioral adaptations of the lower vertebrates are as remarkable as those of mammals in many ways. Encephalization in mammals, in primates, and in the human species is not easy to explain as a correlate of the refinement of behavior. Information-processing of a kind that could be done only by very large amounts of neural tissue must have been evolving in the mammals. But the exact nature of that processing is difficult to demonstrate. Moreover, "rewiring" of brain tissue through evolutionary processes may result in behavioral changes without an increase in total size of brain.

Most general explanations of why average human cranial capacities increased so drastically are linked to competition. A somewhat reductionist view of this is taken by Richard Alexander, who argues that the human psyche evolved as a vehicle serving the genetic or reproductive interests of its possessors.[28] From this perspective, our huge brains evolved as a way to facilitate our ability to compete and pass on our genes: the only plausible way to account for the striking departure of humans from their predecessors and all other species with respect to mental and social attributes is to assume that humans uniquely became their own principal hostile forces of nature—in the sense that they competed directly against each other. According to Alexander, competition among humans is what produced increased brain size. Alexander argues that if humans become extinct, it is possible that chimpanzees would become more human-like in their habits—that we have essentially driven them by competition into a specialization that they could evolve from were we not here.

In many fictional treatments of the future, people are portrayed with enormous heads and correspondingly impoverished physiques. Is this likely, given Jerison's data? Among the grimmer medical implements that was found in many delivery rooms in

Table 3.1 Encephalization Quotients or Body-to-Brain Ratios

Primate		Body-to-Brain Ratio
Gorilla (male)	1.53	(172.4 kg body weight, 570 g brain weight)
Gorilla (female)	1.76	(90.7 kg body weight, 426 g brain weight)
Chimp (male)	2.48	(56.7 kg body weight, 440 g brain weight)
Chimp (female)	2.17	(44.0 kg body weight, 325 g brain weight)
Human (male)	7.79	(55.5 kg body weight, 1,361 g brain weight)
Human (female)	7.39	(51.5 kg body weight, 1,228 g brain weight)

the last century was a device for crushing the head of the fetus if it was too large to deliver without killing the mother—a situation that, in the absence of medical intervention, may occur as frequently as a few times out of every 100 live births, according to some ethnographic accounts. Even experienced obstetricians[29] dreaded performing this procedure—now no longer necessary if the surgical skills to perform a Cesarean section are available. Mismatched fetal head size and maternal pelvic dimensions are expressions of the trend Jerison has identified, but human brain size, in fact, seems to have stabilized at about 1,300 cubic centimeters over the last 100,000 years. Yet 100,000 years is insignificant in the span of animal life on our planet, and encephalization ratios may well continue to increase—or decrease—during the next millions of years. The size of the human female pelvis puts a limit on the size of the head at birth, but perhaps natural selection will produce people whose heads grow faster and larger during infancy. On the other hand, there is no evidence that the size of an individual's head—or any possible correspondence between skull size and skull contents—is in any direct way a determinant of how many viable and reproductively successful children a person will have in the contemporary world —the ultimate criterion in our evolutionary situation.

The cliché "time will tell" still has some cogency in evolutionary studies. We too, no doubt, are in a sense "missing links" in the ancient evolutionary experiment that is the history of animal life on this planet.

One question must be addressed: Why are people so much smarter than they apparently need to be just to survive and reproduce? As discussed in the next section, we have conclusive evidence that our ancestors, who had brains two-thirds of our size, successfully made stone tools and other implements, competed with a formidable array of other animals, and managed to colonize an area from Java to Spain. In the world of a half million years ago, or even 100,000 years ago, one needed a brain only a few hundred cubic centimeters larger than that of a chimp to do very well indeed. Why then did we evolve the capacities for quantum mechanics, Arabic verb forms, Puccini arias, and the poetry of Ezra Pound?

Once again it must be stressed that when we ask such questions we must look almost exclusively at our lives as hunter-gatherers, that is, before 10,000 years ago. The agriculture and urbanization that appeared in the past 10,000 years is far too short a span to have produced significant differences in our genetically based mentalities, compared to our Pleistocene forebears.

Early Primates and the Australopithecines

> *I don't know, but we call him 'Bob.'*
>
> Sam Erwin, former U.S. Congressman (when asked
> what the name of his horse was)[30]

To return to the paleontological evidence, bits and pieces of various animals have been placed into our family tree as far back as twenty million years ago (Figure 3.6), but there are huge gaps and many questions as to what particular primates are on our ancestral line. Classifying extinct animals is even more contentious than classifying living ones, but in the traditional classification, we are members of the primate or-

FIGURE 3.6 This species of Southeast Asia tree shrew resembles closely the small insectivorous ratlike animals believed to be ancestral to all primates, including ourselves.

der and the anthropoid suborder, which includes humans, apes, and monkeys; the other primate suborder is the prosimians, which includes lemurs, tarsiers, and other similar animals. We are in the superfamily *Hominoidea* and the family *hominidae*, which includes people and our ancestors going back at least several million years. The *Hominidae* separated from the *Pongidae* family (chimpanzees, orangutans, and gorillas) at some point in the distant past of the Miocene era (about 25 to 5 million years ago), when primates included at least sixteen genera of hominoids, some of which were forest-dwelling, quadrupedal animals who may have been on our genetic line. Elwyn Simons recently found a 36-million-year-old primate (classified as *Catopithecus*) in Egypt, and he has claimed that it is "at the bottom of the human family tree, near the roots."[31] This squirrel-sized animal has some higher primate characteristics, such as a flattened face and a fused forehead bone, which is separated in lower primates, like lemurs.

To determine when the human line split from that of other primates, we can combine the fossil evidence with evidence from molecular biology. Based on DNA evidence, Conroy[32] estimates that gibbons separated from our line and that of the other apes and monkeys about 12 million years ago, with the orangutans separating from the line of gorillas, chimpanzees, and humans about 10 million years ago, and humans separating from the chimpanzee and gorilla line about 5 million years ago.

These age estimates and sequences are based on estimates of rates of change in nuclear genetic materials and are known to vary widely in the animal kingdom (rates of change are much faster in rodents than in humans, for example). But several analytical techniques have produced similar estimates for the human/chimpanzee split. This poses a problem since some evidence indicates that not long after 5 million years ago our ancestors were bipedal, so the molecular clock may need to be recalibrated in some way.

In any case, a crucial period in the evolution of culture was between 5 million years ago, when the first australopithecines appeared, and a half-million years ago, by which time all the world's hominids belonged to a single genus, *Homo*, our direct ancestors.

Paleoanthropologists recognize various species of early hominids in the period between about 4.0 and 1.0 million years ago. A substantial number of scholars accept at least four of these species: *Australopithecus afarensis, Australopithecus africanus, Australopithecus robustus,* and *Australopithecus boissei.* These species seem to have differed in various anatomical details and the periods in which they existed, and they may have been arranged in terms of lineage and descent as illustrated in the various schemes in Figure 3.7.

Several factors identify them as probable members of the same genus: (1) they all were bipedal, walking upright on two legs all or most of the time—although they were perhaps not quite as well suited anatomically for this means of locomotion as ourselves; (2) they all appeared to have brains only slightly larger, if at all, than modern gorillas and chimps; (3) they all lived in Africa; and (4) they all had teeth that looked somewhat like ours and differed from those of gorillas and chimps in various details, such as flattened surface of molars—probably to facilitate grinding of foods. Scholars dispute whether any of the australopithecines used stone tools. Their remains have been found with such tools but the association is ambiguous.

EARLY AUSTRALOPITHECINES   Much of the story of cultural origins may have been "over" by 3.8 million years ago. Mary Leakey found human footprints of this age at Laetoli, Kenya, indicating that our ancestors were walking upright by that time. These tracks of two *Australopithecus afarensis* indicate that they may not have had quite the same smooth gait as do modern humans, as they seem to have a somewhat rolling walk in which the hips swiveled side to side more than they do when we walk. But

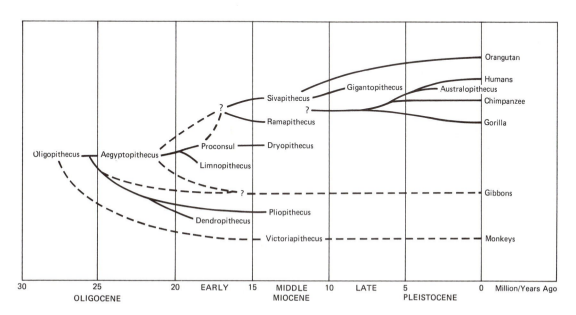

FIGURE 3.7 A simplified hypothetical reconstruction of the genetic relationships of our probable ancestors.

they clearly show two bipedal creatures, both between about 1.4 and 1.5 meters tall, who apparently walked across this stream bed at different times.

There is a sort of destiny in bipedalism: the hands are free to manipulate tools, the field of vision provides them a slice of time and distance that rewards planning, and the arrangement of the limbs and cranium seems to require only additional brain tissue to "convert" a primate into something human.

But upright posture in the absence of tools—and there is no evidence for stone tool use until about a million years after the Laetoli footprints—means something else. It means that an animal with roughly our body shape (but about two-thirds our size) and with our approximate powers of vision, smell, locomotion, etc., could compete in a world teeming with awesome predators. Without speed, claws, significant teeth, night vision, or protective coloration, these primates of 3.7 million years ago flourished. Walking across the same lake bed as the *Australopithecus afarensis* at Laetoli were tigers, rhinoceroses, elephants, and other animals that competed with the australopithecines on these African plains, and one wonders how such an unprepossessing animal could survive in this environment. Perhaps they already possessed embryonic forms of the critical elements of cultural behavior: intelligence, protective human family relationships, and tool-use capabilities that were slightly better than that of the chimpanzees (who use sticks and unmodified stones).

If our ancestors of this era did indeed have these inchoate human capacities, then our answer to the question of why culture appeared may be lost in undetectable changes in climate that encouraged bipedalism and life in savanna environments. As long as our ancestors were forest dwellers, there would have been continuing selection for strong shoulder and arm musculature and dexterity, and once they began moving out to the savannas they might have evolved to a point where natural selection could not easily have converted them back to full quadrupedal locomotion.

If we had only the tracks at Laetoli as evidence of early australopithecines, we would know little about this crucial stage in human evolution, but recent finds have produced the skeletal remains of a growing sample of these individuals—and possibly some of their ancestors. The earliest australopithecines are a likely candidate as one of the founding species of the human line; they are represented by fossils that date to between 4.1 and 3.0 million years ago from several areas east Africa.

In the Hadar region of Ethiopia we find the most substantial early remains, including "Lucy" (named after a Beatles song), a female 25- to 35-year-old hominid. About 3.18 million years ago Lucy strode upright through the river valleys of Ethiopia, as part of a group of primates who were around 1.2 to 1.5 meters tall, but who varied greatly in size and morphological characteristics. No tools have been found to be associated with Lucy and her kin, and without tools, we cannot really know much about Lucy and her group—the "First Family," to use the name Donald Johanson, one of her discoverers, gave them. By counting the number of different bones, we know that there were at least thirteen people in Lucy's group, four of them children. A few bits of geological evidence and the absence of other animal bones near the hominids raise the possibility that the First Family was trapped in a ravine by a flash flood, but we will never really know.

But if "Lucy" and her group were bipedal, how far back in time does bipedalism go? Several recent finds have begun to illuminate this great transformation in the human past. Between 1990 and 1994, however, parts of fifty-three other early hominids were found in the Hadar region, including a particularly well-preserved skull that seems to confirm some of the interpretations of Lucy but raises other questions. Anthropologists William Kimbel, Donald Johanson, and Yoel Rak found what appears to be the first known nearly complete skeleton of an ancient ancestor who lived about one million years before Lucy.[33] The age of the skull was determined by its location between two layers of volcanic rock. Because the rock contains potassium, the rate at which potassium radioactively decays could be used to date each layer accurately (see chapter 2). The skull of this individual has an ape-like jutting jaw, small braincase, and thick protruding ridges above the eyes—a skull, in other words, that was much more ape-like than human-like.

Tim White has identified some of the earliest Hadar fossils as a new genus, *Ardipithecus ramidus*, on the premise that they are different from the early australopithecines. This Hadar fossil suggests that this small-brained, upright-walking, prehuman species with an ape-like body existed for nearly one million years (from four to three million years ago, at least to Lucy's time) without significant anatomical change. Whatever the evolutionary forces were that converted australopithecines into us, at least as far as mentality is concerned, they appear to have been either slow processes or not in force at this time. Despite their human-like posture, the brain-to-body ratios of Lucy and her friends were low enough probably to preclude any full mental or spiritual life: Lucy's brain was probably only slightly larger than a softball, and there is no evidence that she or her colleagues used tools or were cultural in significant ways. But the fact that these australopithecines had brains insignificantly larger than apes is not conclusive evidence on this point. The human brain probably evolved both by increases in size and by internal "rewiring," and we know little about how the latter might have come about.

As always in paleoanthropology, we also have to be careful about sample biases. Our sample of *Australopithecus afarensis* is growing, but given the great time depth and geographic extent that we have "sampled," all conclusions must be considered tentative. Kimbel, Johanson, and Rak maintain, for example, that these primitive upright-walking creatures did not diversify into distinct lineages until sometime after three million years ago. They say their discovery supports their view that all prehuman specimens found in the region represent the same species, a species in which males were considerably larger than females. But other scholars dispute that view. They believe that the variations in fossil size and other features are too great to have come from a single species. According to this latter view, there was a more "robust" species of larger-boned creatures, whose lineage is now extinct but who lived at the same time as the smaller species, which evolved into humans. In their view, the two distinct lines had already diverged before the time of Lucy, more than three million years ago.

Another recent discovery of fossils in Kenya supports the idea that by 4.0 million years ago, our ancestors already walked upright, on two legs. In August of 1995, anthropologist Meave Leakey[34] reported the discovery in northwestern Kenya's Lake Turkana area of fossil hominid jaws, teeth, a piece of skull including the ear region, and a lower leg bone, all of which date to between 3.9 and 4.1 million years ago. The hominid species from which the fossils came has been named *Australopithecus ana-*

mensis. Leakey said primitive features distinguishing the species from other known early human ancestors were in the crania and dentition and included almost parallel mandibular tooth rows set close together, large canines with long strong roots, wide flaring molar teeth, and a small elliptical external opening of the ear.

But she notes that in "contrast, the leg and arm bones have relatively modern morphology and the shape of the former indicates that at this early date, human ancestors were walking bipedally." Leakey said the newly found fossils had features consistent with their being a cross between "Lucy" and the earliest Hadar fossils that have been identified by Tim White as *Ardipithecus ramidus.*

Still another recent find provides cogent evidence about early human bipedalism. Few things are more pedestrian, literally or figuratively, than the human foot, but the archaeological record contains only one reasonably well-preserved set of four articulated hominid foot bones for the critical period when people were becoming (or already were) bipedal. These bones, from South Africa's Sterkfontein Cave, may date to 3.5 million years ago,[35] and they have set off another debate about the origins of human bipedalism (Figure 3.8). They appear to be those of an australopithecine, and they suggest that these hominids may have retained tree-climbing abilities far beyond what later humans had. One of the preserved bones is the beginning of the big toe, and it suggests that this individual had both ape-like and human-like locomotion abilities. There is no question that the basic anatomy is that of an upright-walking individual, but the big toe diverged sharply to the side, in the manner of apes, providing a highly flexible, opposable-toed foot that would allow the hominid to climb trees.

But evidence from elsewhere in Africa suggests that bipedalism was well-established by at least 3.5 million years ago—although some authorities argue that fully normal bipedalism equal to that of modern humans did not emerge until much later.

Summarizing these recent finds, human bipedalism probably extends back to 4.0 million years ago and some unknown time earlier than that, but we still have only vague ideas about why this transformation occurred. Perhaps the primary factor was simply a change in climate that encouraged these animals to invade the savannas. In any case, the most important point about these australopithecines is that they were *bipedal,* and whether or not bipedalism is the stimulus for all later evolution of "culture," our ancestors appeared soon after bipedalism, and there is reason to assume that this was not an accidental correlation.

THE APPEARANCE OF *HOMO*

> *Monkeys are superior to men in this: when a monkey*
> *looks into a mirror, he sees a monkey.*
>
> Malcolm de Chazal

As in the case of most biological classifications, cutting the continuum of hominids into two groups and naming them differently, as in the case of *Australopithecus* and *Homo,* necessarily involves some degree of arbitrariness. Unless we have been badly misled by the data, what we call the first *Homo* arose out of the mix of australop-

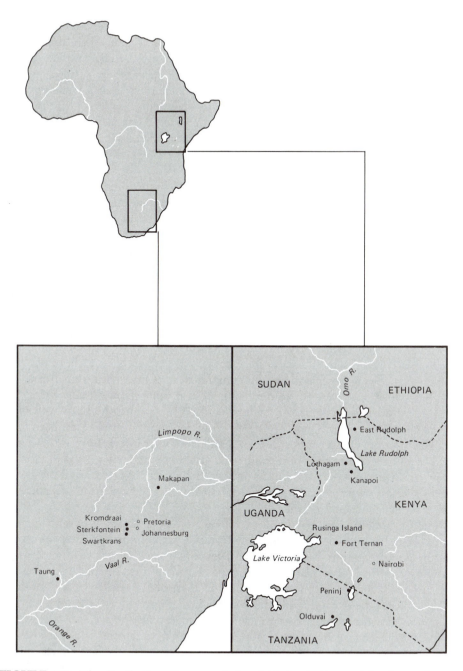

FIGURE 3.8 The distribution of some early hominid sites in East and Southern Africa.

ithecine species and subspecies, and thus these two different genera names are mainly collective descriptions of gradually accumulating anatomical differences.

That *Homo* did succeed the australopithecines now seems clear. Major disputes remain about the relationship of the australopithecines and early *Homo*, but the evidence generally supports the notion that, whatever the genetic relationship between the australopithecines and early *Homo*, early *Homo* (1) appeared after about 2.5 million years ago—long after Lucy and her colleagues; (2) had a brain somewhat larger than the australopithecines (i.e., about 600 cubic centimeters or larger); (3) made stone tools—or at least some groups of them did; and (4) was the first hominid to leave Africa. Early *Homo* is usually assigned to one of two species, *Homo habilis* or *Homo erectus*.

The earliest stone tools known are only between two and three million years old, and we might suspect that they are important markers of the transition to *Homo*. Primates of all kinds, including Lucy, no doubt, used sticks and unmodified stones for a variety of purposes, but making a stone tool requires envisioning the finished artifact in the unworked lump of stone. Evidence suggests that the manufacture of stone tools was a rather late part of the whole transition to humanity, since bipedalism and even increasing brain size were well underway by the time the first stone tools apparently were made. Toth has suggested that "tool use in apes was not directly selected for in evolution but rather was a by-product of a general increase in problem-solving abilities through time."[36] But once humans could make stone tools, that ability became an important factor in the rate at which they evolved and spread throughout the world. The importance of tools to our ancestors can perhaps best be appreciated by imagining oneself standing about four feet tall on the Serengeti Plain of two million years ago, trying to separate into its component nutritious parts a small antelope either just killed or scavenged from a temporarily napping lion. Already harried by vultures and other scavengers, an attempt is made to rip into the body with one's teeth and nails. Even with Lucy's relatively stout dentition, it would have been difficult. The most nutritious parts—the liver, brain, and other internal organs—are protected by thick layers of skin, flesh, and bone that resist the puny tearing motions to which our ancestors would have been limited. But just a chip off one of the quartz pebbles abundantly scattered over this area would instantly have made available life-saving rations for several individuals.

The first hominid to make and use stone tools was probably one of the australopithecine species (simple stone tools made by hitting one lava chunk with another have been found in Ethiopia under layers of volcanic ash that date to 2.5 million years ago[37]) or early *Homo*, but the species of the first toolmakers remains a matter of doubt and dispute. Some of these disputes could be resolved if we had many full skeletons of the earliest *Homo*, but we may never have adequate samples of this hominid. Most anthropologists have used the category *Homo habilis* to refer to the species from which *Homo erectus* and thereby ourselves have descended, and the KNM-ER 1470 skull, dated to about 1.88 million years ago, is perhaps the best example of this. *Homo habilis* is generally thought to have had a cranial capacity of about 660 cubic centimeters, halfway between some of the smaller australopithecines and *Homo erectus*, and specimens have been identified from South Africa and Ethiopia, but its taxonomic position will likely change on the basis of future finds.[38] A skull and some limb bones of *Homo habilis* recently discovered at Olduvai (a specimen known as OH

62) have been dated to about 1.8 million years ago, and raise some interesting questions about *Homo habilis* in general. First, this apparently female adult was only about one meter tall (three feet, four inches). Thus, she was up to a foot shorter than "Lucy," an australopithecine who lived about 1.3 million years before her, and whose height appears to have been somewhere between 3.5 and 4.0 feet. We might expect that human height had been increasing gradually but continuously under the strong selective pressures of the savanna, as we know that the general trend in hominids was certainly toward greater height. But OH 62 suggests this trend may not have been constant. Here, too, possible sample biases intrude. OH 62 may simply have been an exceptionally short person. But OH 62's skeletal anatomy looks very much like Lucy's, and in general she suggests that the australopithecines and early *Homo* were only slightly different until after 1.8 million years ago.

In 1984 a group headed by Richard Leakey found a *Homo erectus* (known as KNM-WT 15000) near Lake Turkana,[39] Kenya, that seems well-dated to about 1.6 million years ago and is virtually complete. Such a modern and "brainy" hominid at this time is somewhat surprising, given the other known fossils (this find is discussed in more detail in chapter 4).

These many arguments about human lineage will doubtless continue for many more years (Figure 3.9), and all that really seems clear at this point is that from 3.0 to 1.5 million years ago bipedal primates of about 1.25 to 1.75 meters in height roamed the grasslands and forests of Africa, the Middle East, and probably as far east as China, and that at least some of these animals made tools.

Archaeological Evidence of the Origins of Culture   If we assume that one of the phylogenies in Figure 3.9 is correct, we can begin to look at the *archaeological record* to determine how our ancestors actually lived and changed over time. As always, the problem is one of poor evidence. Perhaps the only way in which we will understand the details of our origins would be if we found several Pompeii-like sites where volcanic eruptions had trapped early humans some two to three million years ago, toward evening, say, around a water hole on the East African savanna. Such a volcanic event would be most scientifically useful if it happened just after these hominids had scavenged or hunted their food, butchered it with stone tools, and then dispersed into social groups to sleep off the meal.

Although no early hominid sites like this have been found, they may exist. In 1902 on Martinique about 28,000 people were killed within minutes when a volcanic eruption sent a landslide of ash, lava, and debris cascading over part of the island, and we have seen the startling archaeological evidence left at Pompeii. At present, however, our direct archaeological evidence about the initial period of the evolution of culture is extremely meager; we have only a few small sites, almost all of which are in southern and eastern Africa.

About five million years ago, a large lake covered about 130 square kilometers of what today is the Serengeti Plain, in central East Africa. Countless generations of animals, including, no doubt, our hominid ancestors, lived near this lake, and today their fossilized bones are thickly distributed through the black clay of the ancient shoreline and lake bed. About a half-million years before the appearance of culture-

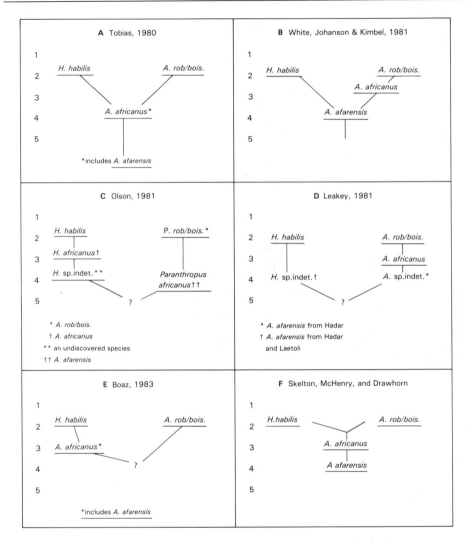

FIGURE 3.9   Six hypothetical reconstructions of the phylogenetic relationships among early hominids.

bearing animals in this part of the world, the lake and the adjacent areas were the scene of dramatic geological activity. Volcanoes near the lake had been erupting for millions of years, and in a particularly violent episode about a million and a half years ago, a volcano to the south of the lake covered it with a layer of ash and molten rock some five meters thick. Similar eruptions occurred in succeeding millennia, and today we can measure the intensity of each volcanic episode by gauging the thickness of each superimposed ash level. Sometime during and after these volcanic eruptions, the climate of the area began a cycle of alternating dry and wet periods. These millions of years of volcanic activity and climatic change eventually covered the original lake and adjacent lands with a 100-meter-thick deposit of sand, ash, and lake sediments, the surface of which is the present Serengeti Plain. Ancient floods cut down through this plain at several points, creating Olduvai Gorge and revealing in its cliffs and floor many concentrations of stone tools and animal bones. These sites represent by far our best archaeological record of human activities at the time of the emergence of the genus *Homo*.[40]

One such concentration, Site DK I, has been radiometrically dated to about 1.75 million years ago, making it one of the oldest in Olduvai Gorge. The site is composed of a layer several meters thick of bones, worked and unworked stone, and other debris. Because of the complex stratigraphy, it is difficult to separate this accumulation into different levels with any assurance that the divisions represent discrete hominid occupations.

The most prominent archaeological feature at DK I is a semicircle of stones (Figure 3.10) lying within a concentration of stone and animal bones. Measuring ap-

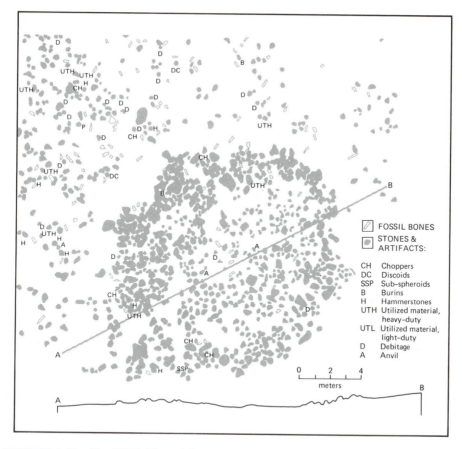

FIGURE 3.10 Site DK I. Plan of the stone circle and the remains on the occupation surface. Stones, including artifacts, are shown in gray. Fossil bones are shown in outline. This may have been a home base or a windbreak built by hominids about 1.75 million years ago, but the evidence for this is ambiguous.

proximately three meters in diameter and made of chunks of vesicular basalt, this feature is interpreted by some as a foundation for a windbreak or some other temporary structure, but the evidence is inconclusive. The tools found here are similar to the other materials from Beds I and II at Olduvai: hundreds of crudely flaked stones, some of them showing evidence of use, others simply by-products of the manufacturing process. Site DK I may have been a "home-base" for hominids, since it seems to have many different stone tools and animal bones. But the evidence is far from clear.[41]

Another Olduvai site, FLK I, is particularly important because several hominid bone fragments were found in its various levels, including the remains of an early hominid that Louis Leakey named *Zinjanthropus*, probably an *Australopithecus boisei* and presumed by many anthropologists not to be a maker of stone tools. This "*Zinjanthropus* floor" covers an area of more than 1036 square meters and contains several thousand pieces of worked stone and about 3500 identifiable mammal bones. Many stone artifacts and pieces of shattered bone are concentrated in a "working area" some five meters in diameter, and a relatively clear arc-shaped area in the midst of all this debris suggests to some the remains of a temporary shelter.

A few other sites in Africa have been shown to have stone tools that date to about two million years ago, including Koobi Fora, where crude stone tools appear to be at least 2.3 million years old.

These early stone tools from Olduvai, Koobi Fora, and a few other sites provide some indications about the nature of our ancestors. Studies of the Olduwan tools by Nicholas Toth indicate that by 1.7 million years ago our ancestors at Olduvai had developed a preference for righthandedness.[42] Based on the marks left that indicate how they held the stone cores when they hit them to produce stone flakes, the Olduvai hominids seem to have had the same proportions of right-handed people—90 percent—as do modern populations. Toth also suggests that archaeologists may have been fundamentally wrong in their assumption that the big Olduvai "core-tools" were the object of the tool making: he studied wear patterns on the putative "hand-axes" from Olduvai and concluded that they rarely show any wear indicative of use—rather it was the *flakes* that were the point of the tool making, and the hand-axes and the core-tools were in many cases the by-products of tool manufacture.

The question of what these tools were used for is a central element in debates about the nature of our early evolution.

Comparative Primatology and the Origins of Culture

Many researchers view human evolution as a long corridor,
where chimpanzees enter at one end and modern
hunter-gatherers exit at the other.

J. Tooby and I. DeVore[43]

To use primate studies to investigate our origins, we must define clearly the ways in which we are different from them. Tooby and DeVore list six major areas in which we differ fundamentally from other contemporary primates: (1) bipedalism; (2) situation-appropriate, intensive male parental investment and an increase in female parental investment; (3) an unparalleled degree of hunting and meat consumption; (4) a change in life history correlates: an extension of life span, an increase in the period of investment in offspring, a marked increase in the altriciality (i.e., the length of time the young remain in the direct care of and physically with the parents) of human young; (5) an expansion of ecozones occupied, from tropical woodland and forest into savanna areas, but eventually including every other terrestrial ecozone; and (6) concealed ovulation with continuous sexual receptivity.

Given that chimpanzees and ourselves share a common ancestor, perhaps as recently as five million years ago, how did these differences arise?

While some scholars think studying contemporary primates will tell us little about our origins, others see in them prototypical behavior for everything that is human. Teleki, for example, argues that nonhuman primates do virtually everything that people do, such as hunting game, sharing food, cooperating, carrying objects, having lifelong kinship ties, practicing labor division by sex, having incest prohibitions, making tools, exhibiting linguistic capacities, possessing long-term memory, and so on.[44]

A major problem in applying primatological studies to the question of human origins, aside from the fact that poachers are killing off the last remaining wild groups of these animals, is that observing them is not a purely scientific procedure. Observers see aggression, dominance, etc., partly as a projection of their own personalities, and thus models of cultural origins based on primate studies are inherently suspect.

To begin with the basic physical changes, to make a human out of a chimpanzee-like ancestor, the legs had to be lengthened greatly in relation to body size, the hip and knee joints had to be repositioned to allow bipedalism, and the spine had to develop an S-shaped curvature to cushion the brain against the shocks of bipedal locomotion. The face, jaw, and teeth had to be changed from the straight-row, prominent canines-and-incisors configuration of early primates to the curved human dental arch with reduced canines and incisors, and adapted to grinding rather than puncturing (Figure 3.11). In the long course of our evolution from apes, we lost most of our body hair, our sexual organs and behavior changed greatly, and our brains were greatly expanded and probably "rewired."

Consider first the simple matter of body size. A survey of numerous primate species indicates that a pronounced size difference between the sexes is relatively uncommon,[45] and thus "marked morphological and behavioral dimorphism is not a primitive characteristic of primates but has evolved in certain genera in relation to particular patterns of living."[46] One clue as to what patterns of living these might have been can be seen in the size differences of the sexes in living nonhuman primates. Male and female gibbons, who spend most of their lives in trees, are almost identical in size; among chimpanzees, who spend some of their time on the ground, males are usually larger than females; and among gorillas, who are almost completely terrestrial, males average almost twice the size of females. Why should the physical size of the sexes show this association with terrain?

A probable factor in the evolution of both sexual dimorphisms and the overall increase in size of *Homo sapiens sapiens* of both sexes was the need for defense against predators. Our ancestors apparently evolved in open savanna-type environments where competition and predation by large cats and other carnivores would have been significant, and thus it is not at all surprising that part of our evolution in these en-

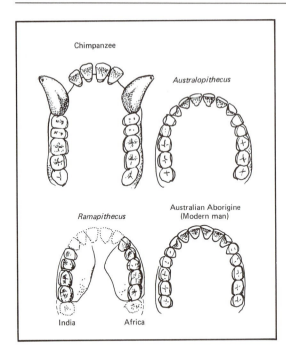

Chimpanzee

Australopithecus

Ramapithecus

Australian Aborigine
(Modern man)

India   Africa

FIGURE 3.11 Teeth preserve best of all body parts and are useful indicators of the diet and adaptation of primates.

vironments would have been in the direction of greater physical size. A human with a rifle, or even a crude spear, would have some reasonable defenses, but until tool use reached this point there would no doubt have been strong direct selection for increasing physical size. Our earliest tool-using ancestors were only about three or four feet tall, weighing perhaps sixty or seventy pounds—not really a formidable competitor, given the other animals in its range. Today, on the African savannas, baboon populations are able to survive, despite occasional predation by leopards and lions, partly because they have retained impressive canine and incisor teeth and great physical strength. By ten million years ago, however, our ancestors had probably lost these dental defenses. Another factor may have been females' preference for mating with larger individuals—who may have had greater ability to provide food and protection and to produce offspring with these same qualities.

But drawing conclusions about a primate's physical characteristics and, especially, social behavior on the basis of the characteristics of its physical environment is plagued with ambiguities and difficulties. In some animal species, sexual dimorphisms seem to be linked to differences in feeding strategies of males and females. While this may have been of some importance to our early primate ancestors, the kinds of food eaten by males and females probably overlapped considerably soon after tool use began and embryonic human social organizations formed.[47] Nonetheless, early hominid males and females would probably have been under increasingly different selective pressures as soon as males began specializing in hunting and females in gathering—specializations that may have appeared only comparatively late and sporadically.

Crook points out one sexual dimorphism in humans that may be tied to differential mortality rates: for every 100 female children conceived in modern human populations, 120 males are conceived, although of these only 105 survive to birth.[48] (Also, mortality is 25 percent higher for males in the first year of life.) In addition, males have a stronger heart than females and more red blood cells per unit volume of blood. Again, these factors could be interpreted in terms of defense, female mating choices, and competition among males for mates.

Another aspect of sexual dimorphism among humans is particularly intriguing when seen in comparison with nonhuman primates: namely, the secondary sexual characteristics that differentiate human males and females. Among human females, breasts are significantly larger than among males — in fact, the size, shape, and other differences distinguishing male and female breasts are much more pronounced than in any other mammal species, and only in humans do breasts first enlarge at puberty rather than at the first pregnancy.[49] Selection for increased breast size appears to have involved a complex set of factors, including the erotic role; Rose Frisch has even suggested that the disproportionate size of the human female breast may have evolved because of its role "as a cooling fin to get rid of body heat."[50] Breast size cannot be explained simply in terms of milk production, since size seems to have almost no relationship to effective functioning in human beings. Similarly, the human penis is far larger, relatively and absolutely, than that of any other primate, including the gorilla. In addition, human females have softer skin and higher voices than males and have lost more of their body hair—although compared to the other species of primates, males also have remarkably little body hair.

Many explanations have been offered for the origins of these characteristics. A primary difference, for example, between humans and other primates, and one that many people link directly to human origins, is that human females do not exhibit estrus; that is, women's receptivity to sexual intercourse does not seem to increase to any large extent with the rise in estrogen levels that precedes ovulation. How can we account for this? One suggestion is that "in all probability the evolutionary development of hair reduction, increased skin sensitivity and tactile changes involving skin tension were [sic] all associated with increasing the tactile sensations of coital body contact, especially in the frontal presentation. Likewise the breasts of young women taken together with other features (limb contour, complexion, and the like) seem to represent the main visual sexual releasers for the male. While the latter features may have been due to straight-forward intersexual selection by ancient males the former features have probably been selected in both sexes for their effect in improving sexual rewards, in inducing sexual love, and in maintaining pair bonds. The same is also likely to be true for the presence of orgasm in women and the absence of the more typical mammalian estrus. The functional significance of all these correlated changes is most plausibly seen within the context of the adaptations of seed-eating and of later partially carnivorous protohominids to open country life with associated shifts in social organization."[51]

Some scholars have emphasized female choice and selection in primate sexuality. As Small notes, "most female primates exhibit a pattern of sexual behavior that is excessive in terms of achieving a pregnancy and . . . are sexually assertive and often 'promiscuous'."[52] "Excessive" sexuality is difficult to define, however, given the short time the primate egg is fertile, the percentage of sperm that are ineffective, and other factors, including the possibility that even in australopithecine times, sex may not have been exclusively a reproductive exercise. And as Small notes, there is no reason to expect that evolution will have produced a fine-tuned sexuality in humans, when a sloppier system works reasonably well.

Our loss of the body hair that our primate relatives retained is a more radical development than it might seem. Naked skins may increase sexual sensitivity, and hair loss even seems to have helped, paradoxically, in water conservation; but naked skins increase the risks of skin cancers and other diseases, and they also open the body to vermin in a way that no chimpanzee must live with.

Other basic differences between ourselves and other primates, and possible reasons for them, are evident if we compare baboons and chimpanzees. Baboons inhabit a diversity of environments, but our most reliable and complete information comes from savanna-adapted populations in central and east Africa. Within the baboon troop, the eldest males have almost unimpeded access to food and sex, and they protect their privileges with aggressive behavior. Younger males are allowed access to females only on the sufferance of more dominant males, although they are constantly testing this dominance by attempting to strike up meaningful relationships with concupiscent females. Often this will incite a dominant male to charge and make threatening gestures and rude remarks. Similarly, when desirable but limited food is available, such as fruit or a clutch of eggs, the dominant males and females take what they want first. A mother and child may share food, but there is no systematic food sharing between adult members of the group.

When baboon troops move across savanna or open environments, they typically position members according to age and sex. Adolescent males are on the periphery, dominant adult males are in the front-center, adult females are behind the adult males, and dependent young are stationed near the adult females. This is of course an excellent defensive formation, offering the best protection to the young and females, on whom the perpetuation of the group depends. There are many more adolescent males than necessary for reproduction, so although they would endure the most losses to predators, the stability of the group would not suffer much. Significantly, when the baboon troop moves into more forested areas, the positioning becomes much more fluid and dispersed, indicating, not too surprisingly, that terrain is an important determinant of behavior for baboons, and that savanna environments seem to put a premium on group cohesiveness and dominance hierarchies—although forest-dwelling chimpanzees, counterintuitively, perhaps, seem to exhibit *more* group hunting, tool use, and forms of cooperation than savanna-dwelling chimpanzees.[53]

Some baboon groups seem to construct dominance hierarchies on the basis of length of residence in the troop, and in general baboons seem somewhat more variable and adaptable in dominance hierarchies and aggression than previously thought.

Thus, in trying to explain how culture-bearing individuals developed from our primate ancestors, we must look for factors or conditions that would work against these dominance hierarchies and promote the distinctive human family structure, with its food sharing, division of labor, and pair bonding.

The relevance of baboons to our own ancestry may be somewhat limited because we are much more closely related to chimpanzees, and our primate ancestors were probably much more adapted to forested environments than savannas.

Chimpanzees also inhabit diverse environments, and generalizations about their behavior are as dangerous as in the case of baboons. The most studied chimpanzees are those of the Tanzanian forests, especially those of the Gombe Stream area.[54] Many of these chimpanzee groups have been regularly fed by the people observing them, and since most groups are cut off by modern development from their complete range and interactions with more distant groups, we cannot expect these primates to be perfect reflections of chimpanzee behavior in the true natural state. But it is striking that the chimpanzees of this area behave very differently from the savanna-dwelling baboons. Access to food and sex is much less rigidly controlled, and the entire dominance hierarchy seems to be less in evidence. In one instance where a female was sexually receptive for a record twenty-one days, the males of the chimpanzee group, young and old alike, stood in line for her favors with only minor apparent bickering.[55] This is not always typical behavior, and the adolescents were effectively barred from mating with some females in many cases, but compared to baboons, chimpanzees are absolute libertines in sexual matters. Strictly speaking, chimpanzees do not have true estrus cycles, but they do have periods of greater and lesser sexual receptivity.

Similarly, there is also a diminution of territoriality. Chimpanzees run for kilometers along trails through the forests, often alone or with one or two others, and individuals frequently leave one small group to go live with another. So relaxed are chimpanzees, in fact, about sex and territoriality that they have aroused envious feelings in some human observers. "Chimpanzees, it seems, successfully achieve what *Homo sapiens* radicals only dream of: peaceful, non-competitive, non-coercive, non-possessive, egalitarian, jealousy-free, promiscuous, non-tyrannical communes."[56]

This may be a somewhat idealized picture. Chimpanzees have elaborate threat rituals and do menace each other according to a well-developed hierarchy. In addition, chimpanzees are the only animals besides ourselves who regularly use objects as weapons—usually wooden clubs or thrown rocks and debris.[57] They fight over food and females, and sometimes over rank, and they are the only other primates known to practice cannibalism, having been observed on several occasions eating young chimps alive.[58] There is some evidence that chimpanzee males murder offspring who are not their own—a highly effective method of perpetuating one's own genes at the expense of others—but a review of the evidence casts doubt on this idea.[59]

Tanner notes that wild chimpanzees place nuts on flat roots or stones and then break them open by hitting them with sticks or rocks, suggesting that "a fairly intelligent ancestral ape could have taken the step from such opportunistic tool use during foraging, to tool-making and more regular use of tools in plant gathering."[60] She also notes that female chimpanzees use tools more often than males in nut-cracking. Moreover, they generally use tools in more complex ways than males, and they teach their daughters to use tools and even supply them with tools.[61]

Books such as *African Genesis* by Robert Ardrey and *The Naked Ape* by Desmond Morris present arguments to the effect that much of our mentality, anatomy, and physiology is a result of millions of years of bloody, relentless hunting and killing.

Indeed, if we look at chimpanzee predatory behavior, we see that in its emotional content and its implications, hunting and meat eating may not be just another way of getting food. Primatologist G. Teleki has observed the hunting behavior of chimpanzees, and he found that hunting, loss of estrus, economic reciprocity, and human family structure may be intimately interrelated.[62] He notes that adult male chimpanzees often cooperate in hunting small mammals and that there is a partial suspension of the dominance hierarchy during these times, as demonstrated by the fact that a low-dominance male sometimes leads the hunt. Significantly, although females and juveniles participate in hunting only rarely, they are often given meat by the males who make the kills, and females who are sexually receptive are more likely to get and eat meat.[63] Symons suggests that there may have been a pattern in early human evolution in which the amount of meat a female received from males was directly proportional to the length of time she was in estrus, and selection might have favored males who used surplus meat to increase their reproductive success at the expense of other males.[64]

But we must be cautious about reading our whole evolutionary history in these few observations; a great deal more research must be done before we can assume these important links between loss of estrus, hunting, and food sharing.[65]

In reviewing recent studies of hunting by chimpanzees, Teleki notes that cooperative behavior among chimpanzees while hunting has not been shown to produce more kills, and he suggests that difficulties in defining what is cooperative and in measuring effectiveness leave this point moot.[66] He concludes that sexual receptivity, kinship ties, and social status all determine how meat is distributed after a kill is made. Teleki suggests that there is sexual division of labor among chimpanzees that is not dependent solely on hunting behavior. He reviews various studies showing that female chimpanzees spend a much greater proportion of their time collecting termites and other invertebrates than males—a prelude, he argues, to the sharp division of labor in human hunting and gathering groups.

In a large number of anthropoid primates (e.g., rhesus monkeys), virtually all the males leave the group they were born into and join other groups to mate, and all the females remain in their natal groups throughout their lives.[67] Melnick and Hoelzer point out[68] that if this is the mating pattern for a species, genetic changes resulting from mutations affecting nuclear DNA would be rapidly dispersed through the whole population, but other genetic changes, such as in mtDNA, which is transmitted solely by the female, would be much more restricted and exhibit large differences among groups in different localities.

Ethnology and the Study of Early Hominid Economies   With the evidence from Olduvai Gorge and the few other sites of this time period (about 2.5 to 1.0 million years ago), we must account for, among other developments: (1) the evolution of stone tool-use; (2) the approximate doubling of human brain size; (3) increased stature and changes in facial architecture and other physical features; and (4) the migrations of hominids throughout the warmer regions of the Old World.

Great controversies have erupted over the explanation of these changes, particularly about the *economic* basis of these transitions. What is at issue here is the very basis of almost all human evolution, since we must assume that we are mainly the physical products of the roughly two million years of natural selection on all the generations that connect us to the hominids of Olduvai Gorge. Arguments on these issues have centered on whether or not early *Homo* did no, some, or a lot of hunting, and how much like modern peoples they were in their social relationships.[69] It is not surprising, perhaps, that in trying to understand what those selective forces and environments were, anthropologists have depended heavily on ethnographic studies of people who until recently lived as hunter-foragers in the savannas of southern and eastern Africa, particularly the Kalahari Bushmen. Some feel that the *behavior* of these modern hunter-gatherers may have almost nothing to tell us about our hominid ancestors.[70] Edwin Wilmsen suggests[71] that almost everything we know about these people is contaminated by Western misperceptions. But the Kalahari hunter-gatherers and others at least illustrate some of the possibilities open to our ancestors in this kind of environment.

Studies of African savanna ecology suggest that *scavenging* could have been a significant part of early hominid repertoires. African savannas would seem to reward animals who are opportunists and generalists when it comes to food: an early hominid might well have adopted the principle of "eat it if it moves, or has reasonably recently moved." Schaller and Lowther spent a few days during the dry season on the Serengeti Plain and found a lot of edible meat in the form of a dead buffalo (which did not appear to have been killed by a predator), some lion kills, and a few incapacitated animals that could have been killed.[72] Blumenschine found that scavenging would have been possible and even rewarding, presuming that our ancestors went for the brains and marrow of lion kills and other casualties.[73] He found that small animals, such as juvenile Thompson's gazelles, persisted as carcasses for only about a day before some scavenger totally consumed them, but larger animals, such as adult buffalo, remained as significant food sources for about four days, after which even if they were not eaten by lions, hyenas, vultures, etc., they were putrid to the point that their "market value" had plummeted.

Even without scavenging, our ancestors may have developed a way to subcontract some of the effort and risk of hunting to lions in a way that is in line with our later history as one of the most selfish, exploitative, rapacious members of the animal family. O'Connell and his colleagues have shown that the Hadza, hunter-gatherers who live in northern Tanzania, sometimes scavenge simply by scaring lions away from kills by making a lot of noise.[74]

The Kalahari hunter-gatherers keep their population densities low and thinly distributed. The low level of productivity of their hot, arid environment, as manipulated by their simple technology (bows, arrows, digging sticks, and so forth), requires that they spend most of the year in groups of twenty-five people or less, often on the move from one camp to another. Most of their diet is made up of vegetable products, tortoises, and other small game, but occasionally giraffes and other large animals are killed, usually through cooperative hunting by several males. Although females provide the bulk of the group's food by gathering and processing plants and eggs, nestlings, turtles, and other small animals, men do all the hunting of large animals among most known hunting-gathering societies, including the Bushmen and Australian Aborigines.

Kalahari Bushmen also illustrate the value of division of labor. We all know that it is better, in complicated tasks, to work as an integrated group doing different things than for everyone to do every task, whether the task involves getting a football downfield or building a supercomputer. The Kalahari split tasks into those that men do, those that women do, and those that everyone does, children included.

Hunter-gatherer economic life is also dominated by the principle of reciprocity: food and other resources are exchanged among kinsmen, balancing out the periodic shortages that may afflict any member or nuclear family in the band.

Like most hunting and gathering societies, the Bushmen are at least somewhat territorial. They move often but always within a relatively restricted region, usually twenty-five to thirty kilometers in all directions from a central water hole or home base. Clearly, some degree of territoriality is an advantage if resources are not uniformly distributed; it is efficient to know where reliable sources of flint, vegetables, game animals, and water are within one's territory, and the group forced out of its territory is faced with unpredictable supplies and, perhaps, the hostility of the group on whose territory it is trespassing. Thus, any models or reconstructions we make regarding our early hominid ancestors should incorporate the assumption that they were probably at least loosely territorial.

Hunter-gatherer population densities are directly determined by resource availability and are maintained by methods of population control that seem harsh to us. The aboriginal population density of most of Australia (or at least these populations as they existed until recent decades), for example, can be predicted with a high degree of accuracy simply from the amount of average rainfall in the various areas. This balance between population and resources is maintained mainly by marriage rules and female infanticide. Birdsell reports that 15 to 30 percent of all babies are killed, usually by the grandmother, who places her hand over the infant's mouth and nose as it is born so that it never draws its first breath.[75] She acts out a group's unstated decision that a mother should not be carrying more than one infant while she works.

Studies of !Kung infant breast-feeding may reveal the powerful controls on fertility rates that are available to a group simply through natural mechanisms. !Kung women breast-feed their babies as often as sixty times every twenty-four hours, including during the night when the mother is asleep, and there is some evidence that this frequency is necessary to produce and maintain the hormonal levels that suppress ovulation; a study of women in Scotland shows that they usually nurse their babies only six times in twenty-four hours and that this has less effect in suppressing ovulation.[76]

In her study of hunters and gatherers in New Guinea, Patricia Townsend observed that although women produce over 90 percent of one group's food, this society is strongly patriarchal.[77] Townsend found that the women in this group usually marry soon after puberty and have about six children. Malaria and other diseases kill off about 43 percent of the children early in life, but girls die from diseases at a much greater rate than boys, probably from malign neglect. If thought necessary, unwanted girls are killed by strangulation with a vine soon after birth.

Most hunter-gatherers keep their numbers at a level far below what could be supported in any average year, and it is the older people who remember the worst winters and the longest droughts that must be accommodated by the group's sizes. Someone said that when an old person dies it is like a library burning down, and this is true also among hunter-gatherers.

In summary, the Kalahari Bushmen and other contemporary hunter-gatherers may offer some general guidelines for interpreting the archaeological remains of our ancestors in these areas of Africa—even though we know that in mentality and many other ways they are profoundly different from early *Homo*.

MODELS OF CULTURAL ORIGINS

The distance is nothing; it is only the first step that is difficult.

Marquise de Deffand (remarking on the legend that St. Denis
walked two leagues carrying his head in his hands)

Having compared nonhuman primates to ourselves, let us look at several attempts to formulate general explanations for the first stages of the evolution of culture. Many people have considered this problem, and it is a subject fraught with political implications, for it involves the basic nature of humanity and the forces that produce cultural change. No explanation for cultural origins is complete or conclusive, but many have points of interest.

A great difficulty in explaining the factors that produced humans out of a chimpanzee-like animal is that it is necessary to try to reconstruct the patterns of natural selection that existed millions of years ago in ecosystems that no longer exist.

Owen Lovejoy has recently argued that bipedalism as an evolutionary product is essentially a matter of sex and the economics of foraging.[78] As he notes, in some ways bipedalism seems an unlikely development; it is a slow method of movement, and an animal expends great amounts of energy just holding itself up. Also, because we evolved as a quadrupedal and semierect animal, bipedalism is in a sense an unnatural form of locomotion. Our spines evolved to serve as a cantilevered bridge-like structure, and even though this structure was successfully modified into a bipedal erect form, we are heirs to many problems, including slipped disks and other back problems, bunions, hernias, poor blood circulation in our legs and feet, and a shortened birth canal that means difficult births for many mothers. If bipedalism is so bad, why should it appear? Lovejoy argues that all apes are potentially semierect animals by virtue of natural selection for "handedness"—the constant use of the hand to forage for food. And if one's evolutionary niche does not reward great bursts of speed over the short run, bipedalism is quite effective for long periods of methodical hunting and gathering.

Lovejoy notes that through the later history of the primates, there has been an evolution in the reproductive strategy. The trend has been toward decreasing the number of offspring a female has but increasing the parental investment in each one, so that they have a better chance to survive and in turn reproduce. (Ecologists call this a "k-strategy," as opposed to the "r-strategy" of an animal like the housefly, which has thousands of offspring, only a few of which survive.)

The heart of Lovejoy's argument is that bipedalism was selected over quadrupedalism in our ancestors because it was a way to increase reproductive success. It allowed our ancestors to have more offspring while maintaining a high level of parental investment in the form of food provision, protection, and training. This was accomplished by evolving an economic adaptation and social organization that allowed the mother to expend less energy getting her own food and more time and energy taking care of offspring. Lovejoy argues that one way females could successfully raise several children born within a short time interval would be to induce the male to provide the female with food on a regular basis, to take part in other tasks of raising many children, and to do it all without competing with other males to the point that the group would break up into murderous, insanely jealous individuals. This meant that the dominance hierarchy and competition common in other primate groups had to be suppressed. One way in which this might occur is if individuals began to differ in perceived "attractiveness," so that qualities of physical appearance and personality played a role in sexual desirability and feelings of "love." The advantages of suppressed conflict in the human group might also be related to the fact that humans developed concealed ovulation and sexual receptivity.

But if one argues, as various scholars have, that the negative aspects of bipedalism are compensated for by the increased intelligence and better toolmaking abilities of our ancestors, how was it possible for bipedalism to appear before any significant increase in brain size and—presumably—intelligence took place? Devine notes that people not living in industrial societies frequently walk many miles each day; he cites the Tarahumara of Mexico, who hunted deer by chasing them until the deer dropped from exhaustion—frequently after a 283–kilometer (176-mile) chase— and he notes that the record run over a twenty-four-hour period by a human is 169 kilometers (105 miles)![79] In sum, by being bipedal humans have sacrificed some of the speed and power a quadrupedal animal has, but even our early bipedal ancestors probably could outrun, both in speed and distance, many of their prey, so bipedalism does have its advantages.

If all this is true, bipedalism probably came before levels of tool use superior to that of chimpanzees were developed. Food sharing, with or without tool use and hunting, would tend to lengthen the period during which a female was sexually responsive, if sex served as an inducement to food sharing. And this was an important evolutionary change in more ways than one. Human females are fertile for only a relatively unpredictable three days a month, so intercourse at least a few times a week would be necessary for successful fertility rates. As Figure 3.12 illustrates, Lovejoy ties all these developments together in an evolutionary progression toward "culture."

Many people have criticized Lovejoy's model. As Kinzey notes, studies of chimpanzees show that it is the females, not the males, who most frequently share food with young chimps.[80] Another problem is that substantial differences in size between male and female primates seem to be associated with competition between males in polygamous mating patterns, whereas Lovejoy proposes monogamous patterns for early hominids. Lovejoy's model is problematic, but the relationships on which he focuses are probably central to any explanation of cultural origins. Bipedalism, intelligence, human family structure, and sexuality seem intimately interconnected in their evolution.[81] In some ways, human sexual differences seem the most radical contrasts between ourselves and other apes, and these differences seem to suggest slightly different evolutionary patterns for males and females.

In an analysis of these arguments about the link between sexual behavior and other aspects of culture, Donald Symons has addressed the problem of human origins on the basis of a sustained comparison of sexuality in men and women.[82] Symons summarizes the major differences between men and women in this regard as follows: (1) Intrasexual competition generally is much more intense among males than among females, and in preliterate societies competition over women probably is the single most important cause of violence. (2) Men incline to polygyny, whereas women are more malleable in this respect and, depending on the circumstances, may be equally satisfied in polygamous, monogamous, or polyandrous marriages. (3) Almost universally, men experience sexual jealousy of their mates. Women are more malleable in this respect, but in certain circumstances women's experience of sexual jealousy may be characteristically as intense as men's. (4) Men are much more likely to be sexually aroused by the sight of women and the female genitals than women are by the sight of men and the male genitals. (5) For men, physical characteristics, especially those associated with youth, are by far the most important determinants of women's sexual attractiveness. For females, physical characteristics are somewhat less important determinants of men's sexual attractiveness; political and economic prowess are more important, and youth is relatively unimportant. (6) Much more than women, men are predisposed to desire numerous sex partners for the sake of variety (although one is reminded here of Cornelia Otis Skinner's remark that "Women's virtue is man's greatest invention"). (7) Among all cultures, copulation is considered to be essentially a service or favor that women render to men, and not vice versa, regardless of which sex derives or is thought to derive greater pleasure from sexual intercourse.[83]

Various scholars have suggested that these apparent sexual differences between men and women also involve aspects of intelligence, but the evidence on this point is far from clear.[84]

In the absence of evidence for a genetic basis for these supposed traits, however, and given the fact that patriarchal societies have dominated human history, we cannot tell if any of these traits are biologically based or are, instead, cultural constructions. Opinions on this point vary. Admitting the great plasticity and potential for variability of human sexual behavior, Symons thinks that there is a strong biological, genetic, profoundly evolutionary basis to these apparent behavioral differences between males and females and these cultural aspects of sexuality. And this is what one would expect, given our evolutionary origins. For millions of years the evolutionary advantage has been with men who have had intercourse with as many young women as they could—provided that the resulting progeny could be raised to reproductive age. Lovejoy's model was based on initial monogamous pairings, but ethnographic evidence suggests that human mating patterns have been primarily polygamous for millions of years. In evolutionary terms, the true loser is the male who provides for another male's offspring, giving rise to the observation that much of the social organization of human hunting-and-gathering societies is designed to allow a man to go on long hunting trips without returning and finding himself the provider for some other man's children.

FIGURE 3.12 These four diagrams illustrate aspects of Owen Lovejoy's model of human origins. These diagrams, reading from left to right, reflect a sequence through time. Section 1 of each diagram traces the the evolution of erectness itself. Section 2 reflects growing epigamic differentiation, the symbols indicating the growing distinctiveness of individuals, which led to growing selectivity in sexual pairing. This is reflected in the mating patterns shown in section 3, where males at first mate indiscriminately with different females but later become mated partners of specific females. Section 4 depicts the changing patterns of birth spacing of infants. In **A** there is no overlap, reflecting the year or two spacing between infants. **B, C,** and **D** show the progression to the human family of several young children. Section 5 indicates how these other changes were accompanied by changes in sexual activity. In each diagram the female menstrual cycle is represented by a long bar with the period of sexual receptivity indicated by the middle figure. In **A** virtually all sexual activity takes place in the female's period of estrus, but this changed until, in **D**, sexual receptivity is largely independent of the estrus cycle, with essentially continuous receptivity. Section 6 shows how kinship relationships changed in concert with these other changes. In **A** the only kinship bonds are between mother and child. In **B** there is the beginning of a male-female relationship but no true bonding. In **D** there are

Marshall Sahlins summarized some aspects of this intertwining of sex, food, and human society as follows:

> Sexual attraction remains a determinant of human sociability. But it has become subordinated to the search for food, to economics. A most significant advance of early cultural society was the strict repression and canalization of sex, through the incest tabu, in favor of kinship, and thus mutual aid relations. Primate sexuality is utilized in human society to reinforce bonds of economic, and to a lesser extent, defensive alliance. All marriage schemes are largely devices to check and regulate promiscuous behavior in the interest of the human economic scheme.[85]

John Tooby and Irven DeVore have recently suggested that the various models of cultural origins and subsequent human evolution seem most plausible if we assume that our ancestors of several million years ago began to increase the time they spent hunting or scavenging other animals: "If hunting were a major part of hominid foraging, it would elegantly and economically explain a large number of the unusual aspects of hominid evolution."[86]

They begin with *male parental investment*. As noted previously, it is highly unusual among primates for males to invest significant energy in providing their offspring with food, yet humans do. Tooby and DeVore note that, whereas it is not economically efficient to carry low-calorie vegetable foods long distances back to one's mate and offspring, meat is a concentrated form of high-calorie nutrition, and thus would be more advantageous to transport. Tooby and DeVore also point out that "male coalitions" may have developed because of the advantages of group hunting. Reciprocity, sharing, and exchange, too, may be linked to hunting. Tooby and DeVore argue that vegetable foods offer few evident rewards to the kinds of exchange, sharing, and reciprocity typical of all human groups. Vegetable foods come in many different forms and sizes, and animals tend to gather them on the basis of energy costs and immediate needs. But meat, "unlike vegetable foods, comes in discrete quantities: an entire animal is either captured or lost. . . . variability in hunting success, and the fact that meat comes in chunked quantities often in excess of what the cap-

---

several such male-female pair bonds. All of these changes take place in the context of changing physical environments, illustrated in Section 7. The tropical forests of our prehuman ancestors gradually changed to the drier, more open savannas and woodlands. The circles in the centers of the four diagrams have to do with foraging and movement. The inner circle delimits the core area of the group, where females and dependent young spend their time. The outer circle represents the outer limits of the group, the farthest distance adult males forage away from the group. In **A** the two circles are nearly the same size because the female is not being given any food by the males and must do her own foraging. In **B** the male ranges more widely to remove himself from the core area and leave more food for the female, which she must have because she is beginning to have more dependent young to feed. In **C** this behavior intensifies. The male is now bringing back food for his mate, which requires him to forage more widely. She must stay closer to the core of the group because she has more dependent young. **D** shows the establishment of a true home base where the mother may leave her children in the care of relatives and forage more widely herself.

turers can readily consume, provides a ready explanation for food sharing, food exchange and risk sharing through deferred reciprocation among the larger social group."[87]

Regarding the pronounced sexual division of labor among humans, Tooby and DeVore suggest that extreme differentiation in the kinds of foods males and females gather is not feasible without food exchange between males and females. "If males changed from occasional to intensive hunting, one consequence would be the extreme sexual division of labor found among humans, with females exploiting the more [fixed, vegetable] food sources. . . . The evolution of this behavior requires no qualitative leaps from other primates: in chimpanzees . . . estrous females receive disproportionate shares of meat from hunts made by males."[88]

Tooby and DeVore also associate the apparent early emergence of the "home base" form of settlement in human groups with the consequences of a hunting adaptation. They suggest that a home base would be of little advantage to primates subsisting mainly on foraging for vegetable foods. But for hunters, the sporadic, irregular, unpredictable nature of success at hunting would make a home base an advantage, in that it would be a place to which everyone knew to return and at which meat could be shared. Similarly, they see stone tool use as probably an adjunct to the requirements of animal butchering and hunting.[89]

Concerning the exaggerated size of the human brain, they note that the human brain is an extremely metabolically costly organ. "It may well be that this cost can only be justified if this expanding hominid brain, in turn, also makes rich new sources of food possible. We know that all carnivores have significantly higher encephalization quotients than do non-predators . . . that some nutrients found in meat are particularly important to brain tissues, and that these are hard to obtain and metabolically process from plant foods."[90] They also note that hunting may be linked to the "pongid-hominid" split, in that "the largest open country primates, savanna baboons, have been reported to have the highest rates of hunting for any non-human primate." This is a controversial point, however, because our closest relative, the chimpanzee, seems to show the most tool use, varieties of tools, group hunting, and food sharing in forested, not savanna, environments.[91] Finally they note that the wide geographic distribution of humans is possible only because of meat-eating and hunting—that, in fact, it is impossible for "modern humans to live exclusively on uncooked plant foods" because of various nutritional deficiencies that such a diet would usually engender.[92]

These forms of small-game hunting and scavenging would have rewarded group cooperation, reduced dominance hierarchies, improved communication systems, and encouraged the development of stone tools for processing meat and vegetable foods.

Summarizing these models, we have seen that bipedalism, human sexuality, social networks, enlarged brains, terrain, hunting, and various other factors may all be related in complex patterns of interaction, resulting in the kinds of animals represented by "Lucy" and the other Hadar fossils. These hominids need not have been major tool users to have been "cultural" in fundamental ways. Hunting and meat eating may have been important for them, but we have no direct evidence with which to test this.

ANALYZING THE EVIDENCE

How can we go about integrating all this ethnographic, archaeological, primatological, and paleontological evidence and use it to understand our origins? To begin with, in an evolutionary analysis we must concentrate on those factors that might have allowed some individuals and not others to have survived to pass on their genes, so that over time our brain size increased and all the other dimensions of the human animal were formed. And once we start examining differential reproduction, we must look directly at how food was procured, shared, and consumed.

Currently, a particularly heated debate is underway in archaeology between people who look at the same bones and stones and see, alternatively, conclusive evidence of hunting, conclusive evidence of scavenging, and no conclusive evidence at all.[93] One might think that the simple conjunction of stone tools amidst piles of animal bones, some of which show obvious cut marks from being hacked at with stone tools, would lead to the inevitable conclusion that our ancestors butchered and ate these animals. But one archaeologist's stone-tool-cutting mark is another archaeologist's hyena-bite mark, and when it comes to statistics on the extent and significance of different kinds of bone alteration, entirely different interpretations arise.

Why is it so important to know if these animals were hunted or scavenged? Here again we are dealing directly with the factors that shaped us physically and to some extent mentally. When anthropologists argue about the economy of early humans they are arguing about one of the driving forces of human evolution.

Early hominid hunting would have been very different from hunting today. Modern rifles kill partially by shock: a deer hit almost anywhere with a high-powered bullet dies instantly. It is rather a different undertaking to stick an elephant in the stomach with a spear and then wait hungrily until it bleeds to death. We know from studies of African pygmy groups, the Kalahari Bushmen, and others that people can hunt and kill large animals regularly with very crude spears and other tools, but the question is, when did our hominid ancestors begin systematic hunting as a major source of food?

Concerning the evidence from Olduvai Gorge—our only sample of the spatial distribution of stone tools and animal bones for the period of about 2.0 to 1.5 million years ago—opinions vary sharply. For example, Binford concluded that with regard to the *Zinjanthropus* floor, "both the skeletal-part frequency data and the cut-mark data are most consistent with and indicative of the scavenging of marginal foods from previously ravaged carcasses."[94] Bunn and Kroll, on the other hand, argue that the site may reflect substantial hunting, in combination with scavenging, perhaps, and that there is some evidence of food sharing reflected in the distribution of animal parts.[95]

Even with high-powered magnification and careful laboratory experiments in cutting bones with stone tools, it would seem difficult to distinguish between human and animal activities. Hominids may have killed and butchered animals, and then, perhaps because their tools and butchering skills were not all that efficient, they may have left fairly meaty bones to be scavenged by hyenas and others.[96] Alternatively, lions or hyenas may have killed many animals and eaten them partially, after which people scavenged these carcasses.

Tooby notes that rewards for an early hominid scavenger may have been quite limited, consisting mainly of the marrow, brain, and heads of medium-size animals left by lions near water courses during the dry season.[97] He concludes that

> The recent surge of interest in scavenging is tacitly predicated on the assumption that hunting is an advanced, difficult, and dangerous attainment, dependent on sophisticated abilities unlikely to appear until late in hominid evolution. Scavenging appears to be viewed as "easy" compared to hunting and putatively therefore a natural first step on the road to meat eating for inept early hominids. However, almost nothing about the ecology of scavenging supports this view.
>
> Although the role of scavenging in human evolution appears likely to have been selectively minor (i.e., a supplementary adjunct to hunting), its role in the creation of faunal assemblages may have been substantial because of the differential preservation bias of larger animal remains—those, according to Blumenschine's research,[98] most likely to have been worth scavenging and also, because of their large size, least likely to have been acquired through hunting by Plio/Pleistocene hominids.[99]

Debates about the factors and circumstances that created the concentrations of stone tools and animal bones at Olduvai and other sites will doubtless continue for many years. There simply is no definitive way, at this point, to differentiate marks made on bones by humans from those made by animals, or to determine in what condition (alive or dead) the animals were when they were butchered by humans.

The tools themselves include quite a diversity of forms. They certainly are adequate for butchering animals, whether hunted or scavenged. The absence of "spear-points" or anything resembling them may suggest that these early humans had no means of killing large animals, but some of the tools may have been used as spear heads, or they could have used wooden spears—or, as noted above, they may not have hunted.

Could Early Pleistocene Humans Speak?   Maybe. Academics are notorious for their maddening penchant for qualifying everything to the point of utter irresolution, but that's the nature of human analysis, and when we ask a question such as the one above, the correct answer has to be that it depends in part on how one defines "speech." Do chimpanzees, for example, speak? Clearly they communicate vast amounts of information to each other through noises they make, and they may well communicate far more than we think they do. If we take the reasonable position that human abilities to convey meaning through speech can all be placed on a continuum between the abilities of a chimpanzee and Winston Churchill, then we can ask when abilities equal to our own first evolved, and why?

Various scholars[100] believe that our contemporary fluency of speech appeared only after about 50,000 years ago and in only a limited number of hominid species (perhaps only one); others believe that even the toolmakers of Olduvai Gorge could communicate vocally with much greater fluency than chimpanzees. We'll probably never know much more about this issue than we do now. The areas of the human brain most associated with speech, Broca's and Wernicke's areas, both of which are located on the left side of the brain, were almost certainly not as developed in early hominids, given that their brains were much smaller than ours. But speech is not simply a matter of brain size. Unlike the anatomy of other animals, the human larynx (air passageway in the throat) and the pharynx (food passageway in the throat) converge low in the throat, so that we cannot breath and swallow at the same time—something most of us occasionally prove by choking on food swallowed "the wrong way." The advantage to this odd configuration is that it provides a relatively large chamber over the vocal cords, permitting sound production of great variety. Some estimates of the extent to which early hominids were evolving this human sound apparatus have been made on the basis of computer models, but we simply do not have adequate samples of the relevant anatomy of early hominids to be sure of their resemblance to us in this regard.

Why would people have a better or worse chance of living and reproducing successfully based on their language abilities? Many possible reasons could be suggested. Just the knowledge conveyed from one person to another, or from one group to another about resource availability in distant areas, conflict resolution, technological methods, or any number of other matters could improve the chances of survival and reproduction. If the !Kung Bushmen are any guide in this matter, language would be an extremely important adaptive tool even in this low-tech era—and it would greatly mitigate the crushing boredom of this way of life as well.

The Initial Radiation of Hominids from Africa   By 1.5 million years ago, "culture" by any definition was present. Hominids with brain sizes on the low end of our own range lived in Africa, and their stone tool repertoire indicates that these hominids could produce different forms for different purposes—often out of materials that had to be brought many kilometers to the place where the tools were made or used.

One of the more important questions about these hominids, however, is, had they already left Africa?

Finds from Pakistan, China, Java, and elsewhere raise the possibility that hominids were distributed across the warmer regions of the world by at least 1.5 million years ago. The lowered seas of the Pleistocene would have facilitated this, opening rich coastal niches far out into the Southeast Asian archipelagos.

Perhaps the best evidence for early hominids outside of Africa are the *Homo erectus* remains found in Java by Dubois. After redating the sediments where the finds were supposedly made, plus some sediments that had adhered to the fossils themselves, de Vos et al. are now confident that these remains date to about 1.7 million years ago.[101]

But there will always be questions about these dates because the exact location these finds were made is not known with absolute certainty, and even sediments adhering to fossils might have come from older formations that had nothing to do with the fossils themselves. One of the most frustrating things about the record of *Homo erectus* in Java is that not a single fossil of this hominid has been found there in good association with stone tools.

Discoveries[102] in Pakistan of what appear to be stone tools in strata that may be two million years old would fit the Java data well, because it must have taken many millennia for hominids to reach far into Asia from Africa, and we should find evidence of their passage along the way. The tools are exceptionally crude quartzite cobbles, but the discoverers of these objects consider the evidence "irrefutable" that they are tools, and they conclude that among the possible explanations of their find are that "(a) *Homo habilis* was distributed as far east as Pakistan, (b) *H. erectus* is an Asian lineage at least as old as *H. habilis*, or another, as yet unidentified tool maker was responsible. One clear implication of this discovery, however, is that early tool making has an Asian as well as [sic] African dimension."[103]

Even if these Pakistani dates are not accurate, it is clear that early hominids were able to inhabit a great diversity of environments—they were a successful genus, expanding into new niches. The most conservative view and probably the most accurate is that hominids evolved bipedalism, then tool using and other cultural behavior in Africa, and then spread out along the warmer margins of the Old World in a long slow process of population growth and very gradual movements, as groups split and moved short distances away from one another, until hominids could be found from southern Africa to Java.

SUMMARY AND CONCLUSIONS

We are but "pulvis et umbra," Horace said, "dust and shadow," and certainly this is true for the long line of fossils that connect us to our beginnings. Nor are the factors that have shaped our evolution entirely clear. Changes in climate, savanna adaptations, scavenging, hunting, reconfiguration of sexual impulses, tool use—all these and many other factors seem to have been ingredients in our evolutionary experiment, but the evidence is far too slight to identify the most important forces and circumstances in our past.

Even if we fight through all these issues of causation and taxonomy and eventually reach a consensus, we will be left with an equally important and profound question—the nature of the mode and tempo of human physical and cultural evolution. The question is this: Does evolution in things such as human cranial capacity (Figure 3.13), technological efficiency, administrative centralization, and urbanization proceed gradually, with approximately the same rate of change, or are there long periods of stability punctuated by periods of rapid change? As Robert McC. Adams phrased it in the context of early states, does the simile of a "ramp" or of a series of "steps" best describe our evolutionary history?[104]

This simple question involves some fairly murky political issues. Some fear that to consider human behavior as largely an adaptation and the result of natural selection means that human behavior is beyond social change, that aggression, racism, etc. may be genetically inherent. Some people think the Marxian concept of dialectical development means that even in matters such as the physical changes from the australopithecines to ourselves, we should look for a developmental pattern showing long periods of stability punctuated by periods in which physical characteristics changed relatively rapidly. Thus, Gould and Eldredge say that "no gradualism has been detected within any hominid taxon."[105] But J. E. Cronin and others who have analyzed the measurements on fossil hominids from four million years ago to ourselves found no evidence of "stasis" or "punctuation," and believe that the record of human evolution is best seen as an example of gradual change with some periods of varying rates

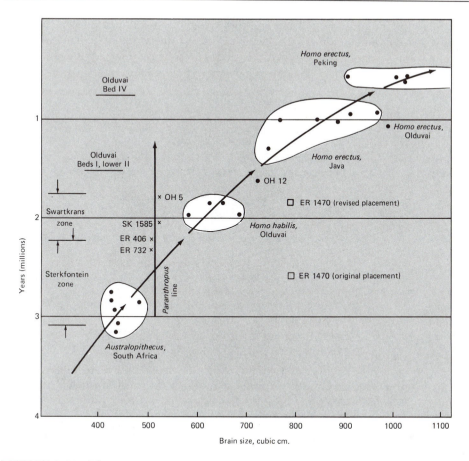

FIGURE 3.13   The increase in cranial capacity over time in our ancestors was enormous and rapid by evolutionary standards, but the rate of increase has slowed in the last 100,000 years, and we may have reached the limits allowed by the mechanics of human birth and locomotion.

of evolution.[106] To have any kind of conclusive test of these competing ideas, we need the remains of hundreds of early hominids, at least some of which fall in the time "gaps" for which we now have no information.

M. Henneberg has taken an interesting and novel approach to the lack of precise dates and the problem of the rate at which human cranial capacities increased. He plotted the estimated dates for a large group of human fossils from the past 3.5 million years against the date for each of these fossils that would be predicted based on the assumption that the increase in cranial capacity over time was gradual, at about the same rate—a rate estimated by a standard mathematical technique called regression.[107] The results suggest that the increase over time in human cranial capacities was in fact gradual and at about the same rate—if one assumes that some fossils are incorrectly dated.

As important as all these issues are, they are in a sense all just refinements on a basic advance in human intellectual history: whatever the tempo of human evolution, we now know its modes, its mechanisms, and its results more clearly than a person of a century and a half ago would ever have thought possible.

BIBLIOGRAPHY

Adams, R. McC. 1966. *The Evolution of Urban Society.* Chicago: Aldine.

Alexander, R. D. 1975. "The Search for a General Theory of Behavior." *Behavioral Science* 20:77–100.

———. 1979. "Evolution and Culture." In *Evolutionary Biology and Human Social Behavior. An Anthropological Perspective*, eds. N. Chagnon and W. Irons. North Scituate, MA: Duxbury Press.

Anati, E., and N. Haas. 1967. "The Hazorea Pleistocene Site: A Preliminary Report." *Man* 2:454–56.

Anderes, P. J. 1984. "The Descent of Man." *New Scientist* 1408:24–25.

Anderson, P. 1983. "The Reproductive Role of the Human Breast." *Current Anthropology* 24(1:)25–45.

Arambourg, C. 1967. "Le deuxieme mission scientifique de l'Omo." *L'Anthropoligie* 71:562–66.

Ardret, R. 1961. *African Genesis.* New York: Atheneum.

Arens, W. 1979. *The Man-Eating Myth.* New York: Oxford University Press.

Barnard, A. 1983. "Contemporary Hunter-Gatherers: Current Theoretical Issues in Ecology and Social Organization." *Annual Review of Anthropology* 12:93–214.

Bartlett, T. Q., R. W. Sussman, and J. M. Cheverud. 1993. "Infant Killing in Primates: A Review of Observed Cases with Specific Reference to the Sexual Selection Hypothesis." *American Anthropologist* 95(4):958–90.

Bar-Yosef, O. 1975. "Archeological Occurrences in the Middle Pleistocene of Israel." In *After the Australopithecines*, eds. K. W. Butzer and G. Isaac. The Hague: Mouton.

Bellwood, P. 1986. *The Prehistory of the Indo-Malaysian Archipelago.* Orlando, FL: Academic Press.

———. 1987. "The Prehistory of Island Southeast Asia: A Multidisciplinary Review of Recent Research." *Journal of World Prehistory* 1(2):171–224.

Bergson, H. L. n.a. *Creative Evolution.* Dover Publications.

Bertram, B. C. R. 1979. "Serengeti Predators and Their Social Systems." In *Serengeti: Dynamics of an Ecosystem*, eds, A. R. E. Sinclair and M. Norton-Griffiths. Chicago: University of Chicago Press.

Binford, L. R. 1977. "A Review of Olorgeesailie: Archaeological Studies of a Middle Pleistocene Lake Basin in Kenya, by G. L. Isaac." *Journal of Anthropological Research* 33(4):493–502.

———. 1981. *Bones: Ancient Men and Modern Myth.* New York: Academic Press.

———. 1985. "Human Ancestors: Changing Views of Their Behavior." *Journal of Anthropological Archaeology* 4(4):292–327.

———. 1988. "Fact and Fiction about the Zinjanthropus Floor: Data, Arguments, and Interpretations." *Current Anthropology* 19(1):123–35.

Birdsell, J. B. 1972. *Human Evolution.* Chicago: Rand McNally.

———. 1987. "Characteristics of the Early Hominid Scavenging Niche." *Current Anthropology* 28(4):383–407.

———. 1993. *Microevolutionary Patterns in Aboriginal Australia: A Gradient Analysis of Clines.*

Boaz, N. T. 1979. "Hominid Evolution in Eastern Africa during the Pleistocene and Early Pleistocene." *Annual Review of Anthropolyogy* 8:71–85.

Boesch, C., and H. Boesch. 1981. "Sex Differences in the Use of Natural Hammers by Wild Chimpanzees: A Preliminary Report." *Journal of Human Evolution* 10:565–83.

———. 1984. "Possible Causes of Sex Differences in the Use of Natural Hammers by Wild

Chimpanzees. *Journal of Human Evolution* 13:415–40.

Boesch-Achermann, J., and C. Boesch. 1994. "Hominization in the Rainforest: The Chimpanzee's Piece of the Puzzle." *Evolutionary Anthropology* 3(1):9–16.

Bowen, D. Q. 1978. *Quaternary Geology*. Oxford: Oxford University Press.

Bower, B. 1988. "Retooled Ancestors." *Science News* 133:345.

Brace, C. L. 1967. "Biological Parameters and Pleistocene Hominid Life-ways." In *Primate Ecology and Human Origins: Ecological Influences and Social Organization*, eds. I. S. Bernstein and E. O. Smith. New York: Garland.

———. *The Stages of Human Evolution: Human and Cultural Origins*. Englewood Cliffs, NJ: Prentice-Hall.

———. 1981. "Tales of the Phylogenic Woods: The Evolution and Significance of Evolutionary Trees." *American Journal of Physical Anthropology* 56:411–29.

Brace, C.L., D. P. Tracer, L. Allen Yaroch, J. Robb, K. Brandt, and A. Russel Nelson. 1993. "Clines and Clusters Versus 'Race': A Test in Ancient Egypt and of a Death on the Nile." *Yearbook of Physical Anthropology* 36:1–31.

Brain, C. K. 1981. *The Hunters or the Hunted?* Chicago: University of Chicago Press.

Bromage, T. G., and M. C. Dean. 1985. "Re-evaluation of the Age at Death of Immature Fossil Hominids." *Nature* 317:525.

Brooks, D. R., and E. O. Wiley. 1986. *Evolution as Entropy: Toward a Unified Theory of Biology*. Chicago: University of Chicago Press.

Brown, F., J. Harris, and A. Walker. 1985. "Early *Homo erectus* Skeleton from West Lake Turkana, Kenya." *Nature* 316:788–92.

Bunn, H. T. 1981. "Archaeological Evidence for Meat-Eating by Plio-Pleistocene Hominids from Koobi Fora and Olduvai Gorge." *Nature* 291:574–77.

Bunn, H. T., L. E. Bartram, and E. M. Kroll. 1988. "Variability in Bone Assemblage Formation from Hadza Hunting, Scavenging, and Carcass Processing." *Journal of Anthropological Archaeology* 7:412–57.

Bunn, H. T., and E. M. Kroll. 1988. "Reply to L. Binford 'Fact and Fiction about the Zinjanthropus Floor: Data, Arguments, and Interpretations.'" *Current Anthropology* 29(1):135–49.

Butzer, K. W. 1975. "Geological and Ecological Perspectives on the Middle Pleistocene." In *After the Australopithecines*, eds. K. W. Butzer and G. Isaac. The Hague: Mouton.

———. 1982. "The Paleo-ecology of the African Continent: The Physical Environments of Africa from the Earliest Geological to Later Stone Age Times." In *The Cambridge History of Africa*, Vol. 1, ed. J. D. Clark. Cambridge: Cambridge University Press.

Cachel, S. 1975. "A new View of Speciation." In *Australopithecus Paleoanthropology: Morphology and Paleoecology*, ed. R. H. Tittle. The Hague: Mouton.

Campbell, B. 1985. *Human Evolution: An Introduction to Man's Adaptations*, 3rd ed. Hawthorne, NY: Aldine de Gruyter.

Cashdan, E. 1983. "Territoriality among Hunter Foragers: Ecological Models and an Application to Four Bushman Groups." *Current Anthropology* 24(1):47–66.

Clark, G. A. 1988. "Some Thoughts on the Black Skull: An Archaeologist's Assessment of WT-17000 (*A. boisei*) and Systematics in Human Paleontology." *American Anthropologist* 90(2):357–71.

Clutton-Brock, T. H. 1989. "Female Transfer and Inbreeding Avoidance in Social Mammals." *Nature* 337:70–72.

Cohen, L. A. 1987. "Diet and Cancer." *Scientific American* 257(5):42–48.

Conroy, G. C. 1990. *Primate Evolution*. New York: W. W. Norton.

Cook-Deegan, R. M. 1994. *The Gene Wars: Science, Politics, and the Human Genome*. New York: W.W. Norton.

Cronin, J. E., N. T. Boaz, C. B. Stringer, and Y. Rak. 1981. "Tempo and Mode in Hominid Evolution." *Nature* 292:113–22.

Crook, J. H. 1972. "Sexual Selection, Dimorphism, and Social Organization in Primates." In *Sexual Selection and the Descent of Man 1871–1971*, ed. B. Campbell. Chicago: Aldine.

Deacon, H. J. 1975. "Demography, Subsistence, and Culture During the Acheulian in Southern Africa." In *After the Australopithecines*, eds. K. W. Butzer and G. Isaac. The Hague: Mouton.

Delson, E., ed. 1985. *Ancestors: The Hard Evidence*. New York: A. R. Liss.

Dennell, H. M., H. M. Rendell, and A. E. Hailwood. 1988a. "Late Pliocene Artefacts from Northern Pakistan." *Current Anthropology* 29(3):495–98.

———. 1988b. "Early Tool-Making in Asia: Two Million Year Old Artefacts in Pakistan." *Antiquity* 62:98–106.

Devine, J. 1985. "The Versatility of Human Locomotion." *American Anthropologist* 87:550–70.

de Vos, J., P. Sondaar, and C. Swisher. 1994. "Dating Hominid Sites in Indonesia." *Science* 266:1726–27.

Diamond, J. M. 1988. "DNA-based Phylogenies of the Three Chimpanzees." *Nature* 332:685–86.

Dunbaar, R. I. 1988. *Primate Social Systems*. Ithaca, NY: Cornell University Press.

Dupre, J. 1987. *The Latest on the Best: Essays on Evolution and Optimality*. Cambridge, MA: MIT Press.

Eckhardt, R. B. 1988. "On Early Hominid Adaptation and Heat Stress." *Current Anthropology* 29(3):493.

Eckhardt, R. B., and A. L. Piermarini. 1988. "More on Phylogenic Analysis of Early Hominids." *Current Anthropology* 29(3):493–94.

Farraro, G., Trevathan, W., and J. Levy. 1994. *Anthropology. An Applied Perspective*. New York: West Publishing.

Ferris, T. 1988. *Coming of Age in the Milky Way*. New York: William Morrow.

Fialkowski, K. 1986. "A Mechanism for the Origin of the Human Brain: A Hypothesis." *Current Anthropology* 27(3):288–90.

Finkel, D. J. 1981. "An Analysis of Australopithecine Dentition." *American Journal of Physical Anthropology* 55:69–80.

Fisher, E. 1979. *Woman's Creation*. New York: McGraw-Hill.

Flint, R. F. 1971. *Glacial and Quaternary Geology*. New York: Wiley.

Foley, R. 1987a. "Hominic Species and Stone-tool Assemblages: How Are They Related?" *Antiquity* 61:380–92.

———. 1987b. *Another Unique Species: Patterns in Human Evolutionary Ecology*. London: Longmeadow.

Freeman, L. G. 1975. "Acheulian Sites and Stratigraphy in Iberia and the Meghreb." In *After the Australopithecines*, eds. K. W. Butzer and G. Isaac. The Hague: Mouton.

Frisch, R. E. 1983. "Comment on P. Anderson, 'The Reproductive Role of the Human Breast.'" *Current Anthropology* 24(1):25–45.

Futuyma, D. J. 1992. "History and Evolutionary Processes." In *History and Evolution*, eds. M. H. Nitecki and D. V. Nitecki. Albany, NY: State University of New York Press.

Garn, S., and W. Block. 1970. "The Limited Nutritional Value of Cannibalism." *American Anthropologist* 72:106.

Goodall, J. 1986. *The Chimpanzees of Gombe*. Cambridge, MA: Belknap (Harvard University Press).

Gould, S. J. 1977. *Ever Since Darwin*. New York: Norton.

Gould, S. J., and N. Eldredge. 1977. "Punctuated Equilibria: The Tempo and Mode of Evolution Reconsidered." *Paleobiology* 3:115–51.

Gould, S. J., and R. C. Lewontin. 1979. "The Spandrels of San Marco and the Panglossian Paradigm: A Critique of the Adaptationist Programme." *Proceedings of the Royal Society of London* B205:581–98.

Grayson, D. K. 1983. *The Establishment of Human Antiquity*. New York: Academic Press.

Grimaud, D. 1980. "Les Paritaux de l'Homo erectus comparison avec ceux de Pithecanthropes de Java." *Bulletins et Memoires de la Societe XIIIe Serie no 3.*

Hamilton, M. E. 1984. "Revising Evolutionary Narratives: A Consideration of Alternative Assumptions about Sexual Selection and Competition for Mates." *American Anthropologist* 86(3):651–62.

Harding, R. S., and G. Teleki, eds. 1981. *Omnivorous Primates.* New York: Columbia University Press.

Harris, D. R., ed. 1980. *Human Ecology and Savanna Environments.* New York: Academic Press.

Harrison, T. 1978. "Present Status and Problems for Paleolithic Studies in Borneo and Adjacent Islands." In *Early Paleolithic in South and East Asia,* ed. F. Ikawa-Smith. The Hague: Mouton.

Henneberg, M. 1989. "Morphological and Geological Dating of Early Hominid Fossils Compared." *Current Anthropology* 30(4):527– 28.

Hill, J. H. 1978. "Apes and Language." *Annual Review of Anthropology* 7:890–112.

Hinterberger, J. 1988. "Crude Food." *Seattle Times/Seattle Post-Intelligencer,* February 28, 1988, "Pacific section," p. 4.

Howell, F. C. 1982. "Origins and Evolution of the African Hominidae." In *The Cambridge History of Africa,* Vol. 1, ed. J. D. Clark. Cambridge: Cambridge University Press.

Howells, W. 1973. *Evolution of the Genus Homo.* Reading, MA: Addison-Wesley.

Hughes, A. R., and P. V. Tobial. 1977. "A Fossil Skull Probably of the Genus Homo from Sterkfontein, Transvaal." *Nature* 65:310–12.

Ikawa-Smith, F., ed. 1978. *Early Paleolithic in South and East Asia.* The Hague: Mouton.

Ingold, T. 1988. *The Appropriation of Nature.* Iowa City: University of Iowa Press.

Isaac, G. 1975. "Sorting Out the Muddle in the Middle: An Anthropologist's Post-Conference Appraisal." In *After the Australopithecines,* eds. K. W. Butzer and G. Isaac. The Hague: Mouton.

———. 1977. *Olorgesailie; Archaeological Studies of a Middle Pleistocene Lake Basin in Kenya.* Chicago: University of Chicago Press.

———. 1978. "Food-Sharing and Human Evolution: Archaeological Evidence from the Pre-Pleistocene of East Africa." *Journal of Anthropological Research* 34:311–25.

———. 1982. "The Earliest Archaeological Traces." In *The Cambridge History of Africa,* Vol. 1, ed. J. D. Clark. Cambridge: Cambridge University Press.

———. 1984. "The Archaeology of Human Origins: Studies of the Lower Pleistocene in East Africa 1971–1981." *Advances in World Archaeology* 3:1–87.

Itzkoff, S. 1987. *Why Humans Vary in Intelligence.* Ashfield, MA: Paideia.

Jantzen, D. 1976. "Why Bamboos Wait So Long to Flower." *Annual Review of Ecology and Systematics* 7:347–91.

Jelinek, A. J. 1977. "The Lower Paleolithic: Current Evidence and Interpretations." *Annual Review of Anthropology* 6:11–32.

Jerison, H. J. 1973. *Evolution of the Brain and Intelligence.* New York: Academic Press.

———. 1983. "The Evolution of the Mammalian Brain as an Information-Processing System." *Advances in the Study of Mammalian Behavior,* eds. J. F. Eisenberg and D. G. Kleinman, Special Publication No. 7. The American Society of Mammologists.

Johanson, D. C., and M. A. Edey. 1981. *Lucy: The Beginnings of Humankind.* New York: Simon and Schuster.

Johanson, D. C., and T. D. White. 1979. "A Systematic Assessment of Early African Hominids." *Science* 203:321–29.

Jolley, C. J. 1970. "The Seed-Eaters: A New Model of Hominid Differentiation Based on a Baboon Analogy." *Man* 5:6–26.

Kauffman, S. 1983. "Developmental Constraints: Internal Factors in Evolution." In *Development and Evolution,* eds. B. Goodwin, N. Holder, and C. C. Wylie. Cambridge: Cambridge University Press.

———. 1993. *Origins of Order.* Oxford: Oxford University Press.

Kinzey, W. G., ed. 1987. *The Evolution of Human Behavior: Primate Models.* Albany, NY: State University of New York Press.

Klein, R. G. 1977. "The Ecology of Early Man in Southern Africa." *Science* 197:115–26.

———. 1989. *The Human Career.* Chicago: University of Chicago Press.

Kranz, G. 1975. "The Double Descent of Man." In *Australopithecus Paleoanthropology: Morphology and Paleoecology,* ed. R. H. Tuttle. The Hague: Mouton.

Krebs, J., and N. B. Davies. 1981. *Introduction to Behavioral Ecology.* Oxford: Blackwell.

Kurland, J. A., and S. J. Beckerman. 1985. "Optimal Foraging and Hominid Evolution: Labor and Reciprocity." *American Anthropologist* 87(1):73–93.

Larichev, V., U. Khol'ushkin, and I. Laricheva. 1987. "Lower and Middle Paleolithic of Northern Asia: Achievements, Problems, and Perspectives." *Journal of World Prehistory* 1(4):415–64.

Leakey, M. G., and R. E. Leakey, eds. 1978. *Koobi Fora Research Project: Vol. 1, The Fossil Hominids and an Introduction to Their Context, 1968–1974.* Oxford: Clarendon Press.

Leakey, R. E., and R. Lewin. 1977. *Origins.* New York: Dutton.

Lee, R. B. 1979. *The !Kung San.* Cambridge: Cambridge University Press.

Lewin, R. 1987. "Debate over Emergence of Human Tooth Pattern." *Nature* 235:748–50.

Lewontin, R. C. 1979. "Sociobiology as an Adaptationist Program." *Behavioral Science* 24:5–14.

Lieberman, P. E. 1991. *Uniquely Human: The Evolution of Speech, Thought, and Selfless Behavior.* Cambridge, MA: Harvard University Press.

Lieberman, P. E., and E. S. Crelin. 1971. "On the Speech of Neanderthals." *Linguistic Inquiry* 2:203–22.

Lieberman, P. E., E. S. Crelin, and D. H. Klatt. 1972. "Phonetic Ability and Related Anatomy of the Newborn and Adult Human, Neanderthal Man, and the Chimpanzee." *American Anthropologist* 74:287.

Lieberman, L., and F. L. C. Jackson. 1995. "Race and Three Models of Human Origin." *American Anthropologist* 97(2):231–42.

Lovejoy, O. 1980. "Hominid Origins: The Role of Bipedalism." *American Journal of Physical Anthropology* 52:50.

———. 1982. "Models of Human Evolution." *Science* 217:304–5.

Lumley, J. de. 1969. "A Paleolithic Camp at Nice." *Scientific American* 225:422–59.

———. 1975. "Cultural Evolution in France in its Paleoecological Setting During the Middle Pleistocene." In *After the Australopithecines*, eds. K. W. Butzer and G. Isaac. The Hague: Mouton.

McArthur, A. J., and J. A. Clark. 1987. "Body Temperature and Heat and Water Balance." *Nature* 326:647–48.

McGrew, W. 1992. *Chimpanzee Material Culture: Implications for Human Evolution.* Cambridge: Cambridge University Press.

Maddison, W. P., and D. R. Maddison. 1992. *MacClade, Version 3, Analysis of Phylogeny and Character Evolution.* Sunderland, MA: Sinauer Associates, Inc.

Martin, K., and B. Voorhies. 1975. *The Female of the Species.* New York: Columbia University Press.

Melnick, D. J. and G. A. Hoelzer. 1993. "What is mtDNA Good for in the Study of Primate Evolution?" *Evolutionary Anthropology* 2(1):2–10

Morris, D. 1967. *The Naked Ape.* London: Jonathan Cape.

Napier, J. R., and P. H. Napier. 1967. *A Handbook of Living Primates.* London: Academic Press.

Newsweek, "Tracking the Sasquatch," September 21, 1987, pp. 71–73.

O'Connell, J. F., K. Hawkes, and N. B. Jones. 1988. "Hadza Scavenging: Implications for Plio/Pleistocene Hominid Subsistence." *Current Anthropology* 29(2):356–63.

Okladnikov, A. P., and G. A. Pospelova. 1982. "Ulalinka, the Oldest Paleolithic Site in Siberia." *Current Anthropology* 23(6):710–12.

Orchiston, D. W., and W. G. Siesser. 1982. "Chronostratigraphy of the Pleistocene Fossil Hominids of Java." *Modern Quaternary Research in Southeast Asia* 1:131–50.

Parker, S. T., R. W. Mitchell, and M. L. Boccia, eds. 1994. *Self-Awareness in Animals and Humans: Developmental Perspectives.* New York: Cambridge University Press.

Pearl, M. C. 1982. Networks of Social Relations Among Humalayan Rhesus Monkeys (*Macaca mulatta*). Ph.D. Dissertation, Yale University.

Penny, D., L. R. Foulds, and M. D. Hendy. 1982. "Testing the Theory of Evolution by Comparing Phylogenic Trees Constructed from Five Different Protein Sequences." *Nature* 297:197–200.

Pfeiffer, J. E. 1978. *The Emergence of Man*, 3rd ed. New York: Harper & Row.

Pianka, E. 1974. *Evolutionary Ecology*. New York: Harper & Row.

Pilbeam, D. 1975. "Middle Pleistocene Hominids." In *After the Australopithecines*, eds. K. W. Butzer and G. Isaac. The Hague: Mouton.

———. 1982. "New Hominid Skull Material from the Miocene of Pakistan." *Nature* 295:232–34.

Pilbeam, D., and S. J. Gould. 1974. "Size and Scaling in Human Evolution." *Science* 186:892–901.

Poirier, F. 1973. *Fossil Man: An Evolutionary Journey*. St. Louis: Mosby.

Pope, G. G. 1983. "Evidence on the Age of the Asian Hominidae." *Proceedings of the National Academy of Sciences USA* 80:4988–92.

Pope, G. G., S. Barr, A. Macdonald, and S. Nakabanlang. 1986. "Earliest Radiometrically Dated Artifacts from Southeast Asia." *Current Anthropology* 27(3):275–79.

Potts, R. 1987. "On Butchery by Olduvai Hominids." *Current Anthropology* 28(1):95–96.

———. 1988. *Early Hominid Activities at Olduvai*. Hawthorne, NY: Aldine de Gruyter.

Quiatt, D. D. 1972, ed. *Primates on Primates; Approaches to the Analysis of Nonhuman Primate Social Behavior*. Minnneapolis: Burgess.

Quiatt, D. D., and V. Reynolds. 1993. *Primate Behaviour: Information, Social Knowledge, and the Evolution of Culture*. New York: Cambridge University Press.

Quiatt, D. D., and J. Itani, eds. 1994. *Hominid Culture in Primate Perspective*. Niwot, CO: University Press of Colorado.

Rightmire, G. P. 1980. "*Homo erectus* and Human Evolution in the African Middle Pleistocene." In *Current Argument on Early Man*, ed. L. K. Konigsson. Oxford: Pergamon.

Rose, K. D. 1994. "The Earlist Primates." *Evolutionary Anthropology* 3(5):159–72.

Sagan, C. 1977. *The Dragons of Eden: Speculations on the Evolution of Human Intelligence*. New York: Ballantine Books.

Salt, G. W., ed. 1984. *Ecology and Evolutionary Biology*. Chicago: University of Chicago Press.

Sahlins, M. 1972. *Stone Age Economics*. Chicago: Aldine.

Sarich, V. 1982. "Comment on M. Wolpoff, '*Ramapithecus* and Hominid Origins.'" *Current Anthropology* 23(5):501–22.

Schaller, G. B., and G. R. Lowther. 1969. "The Relevance of Carnivore Behavior to the Study of Early Hominids." *Southwestern Journal of Anthropology* 25:307–41

Schick, K. D., and C. Zhuan. 1993. "Early Paleolithic of China and Eastern Asia." *Evolutionary Anthropology* 2(1):22–35.

Schrire, C., ed. 1984. *Past and Present in Hunter-Gatherer Studies*. New York: Academic Press.

Schwalbe, G. 1906. *Studien zur Vorgeschichte des Menschen*. Stuttgart: Scheizerbart.

Seabook, J. 1994. "Building a Better Human." *The New Yorker*, March 18, pp. 109–14.

Sevink, J., E. H. Hebeds, N. Priem, and R. H. Verschure. 1981. "A Note on the Approximately 730,000–Year-Old Mammal Fauna and Associated Human Activity Sites Near Isernia, Central Italy." *Journal of Archaeological Science* 8:105–6.

Shapiro, H. L. 1974. *Peking Man*. New York: Simon and Schuster.

Shepher, J. 1983. *Incest, a Biosocial View*. New York: Academic Press.

Simons, E. B., and D. R. Philbeam. 1965. "Preliminary Revision of the Dryopithecinae (Pongidae, Anthropoidea)." *Folia Primatologica* 3:81–152.

Skelton, R. R., J. M. McHenry, and G. M. Drawhorn. 1986. "Phylogenetic Analysis of Early Hominids." *Current Anthropology* 27(1):21–43.

Small, M. F. ed. 1984. *Female Primates: Studies by Women Primatologists*. New York: A. R. Liss.

Small, M. F. 1988. "Female Primate Sexual Behavior and Conception." *Current Anthropology* 29(1):81–100.

Smith, E. A. 1991. *Inujjuamiut Foraging Strategies: Evolutionary Ecology of an Arctic Hunting Economy*. Hawthorne, NY: Aldine de Gruyter.

Smith, F. H., and G. C. Ranyard. 1981. "Evolution of the Supraorbital Region in Upper Pleistocene Fossil Hominids from South-central Europe." *American Journal of Physical Anthropology* 53:589–610.

Smith, F. H., and F. Spencer, eds. 1984. *The Origins of Modern Humans*. New York: A. R. Liss.

Smith, K. C. 1992. "Neo-Rationalism versus Neo-Darwinism: Integrating Development and Evolution." *Biology and Philosophy* 7:431–51.

Smith, P. E. L. 1982. "The Late Paleolithic and Epi-Paleolithic of Northern Africa." In *The Cambridge History of Africa*, Vol. 1, ed. J. D. Clark. Cambridge: Cambridge University Press.

Stringer, C. B. 1985. "Middle Pleistocene Hominid Variability and the Origin of Late Pleistocene Humans." In *Ancestors: The Hard Evidence*, ed. E. Delson. New York: A. R. Liss.

Strum, S. C., and W. Mitchell. 1987. "Baboon Models and Muddles." In *The Evolution of Human Behavior: Primate Models*, ed. W. G. Kinzey. Albany, NY: State University of New York Press.

Speth, J., and D. Davis. 1976. "Seasonal Variability in Early Hominid Predation." *Science* 192:441–45.

Swedlund, A. 1974. "The Use of Ecological Hypotheses in Australopithecine Taxonomy." *American Anthropologist* 76:515–29.

Symons, D. 1979. *The Evolution of Human Sexuality*. New York: Oxford University Press.

Tanner, N. M. 1981. *On Becoming Human: A Model of the Transition from Ape into Human and the Reconstruction of Early Human Social Life*. Cambridge: Cambridge University Press.

———. 1987. "The Chimpanzee Model Revisited and the Gathering Hypothesis." In *The Evolution of Human Behavior: Primate Models*, ed. W. G. Kinzey. Albany, NY: State University of New York Press.

Tattersall, I. 1992. "Species Concepts and Species Identification in Human Evolution." *Journal of Human Evolution* 22:341–50.

———. 1994. "How Does Evolution Work?" *Evolutionary Anthropology* 3(1):2–3.

Teleki, G. 1973. "The Omnivorous Chimpanzee." *Scientific American* 228:32–47.

———. 1981. "The Omnivorous Diet and Eclectic Feeding Habits of Chimpanzees in Gombe National Park, Tanzania." In *Omnivorous Primates*, eds. R. S. Harding and G. Teleki. New York: Columbia University Press.

Testart, A. 1982. "The Significance of Food Storage among Hunter-gatherers: Residence Patterns, Population Densities, and Social Inequalities." *Current Anthropology* 23(5):523–337.

Thomas, D. H. 1986. *Refiguring Anthropology*. Prospect Heights, IL: Waveland Press.

Thorne, A. G., and M. Wolpoff. 1981. "Regional Continuity and Australasian Pleistocene Hominid Evolution." *American Journal of Physical Anthropology* 55:337–49.

Tobias, P. 1980. "A Study and Synthesis of the African Hominids of the Later Tertiary and Early Quaternary Periods." In *Current Arguments on Early Man*, ed. L. K. Konigsson. Oxford: Pergamon Press.

Tooby, J. 1987. "Comment on 'Characteristics of the Early Hominid Scavenging Niche', by R. J. Blumenschine." *Current Anthropology* 28(4):383–407.

Tooby, J., and I. DeVore. 1987. "The Reconstruction of Hominid Behavioral Evolution through Strategic Modeling." In *The Evolution of Human Behavior: Primate Models*, ed. W. G. Kinzey. Albany, NY: State University of New York Press.

Toth, N. 1985. "The Oldowan Reconsidered: A Close Look at Early Stone Artifacts." *Journal of Archaeological Science* 12:101–20.

———. 1993. "Review of W. McGrew. 1992. *Chimpanzee Material Culture: Implications for Human Evolution*." *Current Anthropology* 34(5):791–92.

Townsend, P. K. 1971. "New Guinea Sago Gatherers: A Study of Demography in Relation to Subsistence." *Ecology of Food and Nutrition* 1:19–24.

Van den Berghe, P. L. 1972. "Sex Differentiation and Infant Care: A Rejoinder to Sharlotte Neely Williams." *American Anthropologist* 74:770–72.

van Lawick-Goodall, J. 1968. "The Behavior of Free-living Chimpanzees in the Gombe Stream Area." *Animal Behavior Monographs* 1:161–311.

———. "Some Aspects of Aggressive Behavior in a Group of Free-living Chimpanzees." *International Social Science Journal* 23:89–97.

———. 1973. "The Behavior of Chimpanzees in Their Natural Habitat." *American Journal of Psychiatry* 130:1–12.

Vertes, L. 1965. "Typology of the Buda Industry: A Pebble-tool Industry from the Hungarian Lower Paleolithic." *Quaternaria* 7:185–95.

Von Koenigswald, G. H. R. 1975. "Early Man in Java: Catalogue and Problems." In *Australopithecus Paleoanthropology: Morphology and Paleoecology*, ed. R. H. Tuttle. The Hague: Mouton.

Vrba, E. S., and N. Eldredge. 1984. "Individuals, Hierarchies, and Process: Towards a More Complete Evolutionary Theory." In *Paleobiology* 10:146–71.

Washhburn, S. L. 1968. "Discussion." In *Man the Hunter*, eds. R. Lee and I. DeVore. Chicago: Aldine.

Washburn, S. L., and R. L. Ciochon. 1974. "Canine Teeth: Notes on Controversies in the Study of Human Evolution." *American Anthropologist* 76:765–84.

Wheatley, B. P. 1988. "Cultural Behavior and Extractive Foraging in *Macaca fascicularis*." *Current Anthropology* 29(3):516–19.

White, L. 1949. *The Science of Culture*. New York: Grove Press.

White, T., D. Johanson, and W. Kimbell. 1981. "*Australopithecus africanus*: Its Phyletic Position Reconsidered." *South African Journal of Science* 77:445–70.

Wilmsen, E. 1989. *Land Filled with Flies: A Political Economy of the Kalahari*. Chicago: University of Chicago Press.

Wolpoff, M. 1971. "Vertesszollos and the Prespiens Theory." *American Journal of Physical Anthropology* 35:209–16.

———. 1982. "*Ramapithecus* and Hominid Origins." *Current Anthropology* 23(5):501–22.

———. 1994. "How Does Evolution Work?" *Evolutionary Anthropology* 3(1):4–5.

Wolpoff, M., Xinzhi Wu, and A. G. Thorne. 1984. "Modern *Homo sapiens* Origins: A General Theory of Hominid Evolution Involving the Fossil Evidence from East Asia." In *The Origins of Modern Humans: A World Survey of the Fossil Evidence*, eds. F. H. Smith and F. Spencer. New York: A. R. Liss.

Wood, B. 1987. "Who Is the 'Real' *Homo habilis*?" *Nature* 327:187–88.

Woodburn, J. 1982. "Egalitarian Societies." *Man* (NS)17:431– 51.

Yellen, J. E. 1976. "Settlement Patterns of the !Kung: An Archeological Perspective." In *Kalahari Hunter-Gatherers: Studies of the !Kung San and Their Neighbors*, eds. R. Lee and I. Devore. Cambridge, MA: Harvard University Press.

Zeleznik. S., A. W. Grele, J. Pollack, and I. Aloni. 1989. "On Systematic Butchery by Plio/Pleistocene Hominids." *Current Anthropology* 29(1):151–53.

Zihlman, A., and J. Lowenstein. 1982. "Comment on M. Wolpoff, '*Ramapithecus* and Hominid Origins.' " *Current Anthropology* 23(5):502–22.

NOTES

1. Bergson, *L'Evolution Creatrice*.

2. This report was taken from a *New York Times* report of a paper given at the Annual Meetings of the American Association of Physical Anthropology by Sileshi Semaw. Scientific publication of this article was unavailable at the time this book was written.

3. White, *The Science of Culture*.

4. Wheatley, "Cultural Behavior and Extractive Foraging in *Macaca fascicularis*."

5. Brace, *The Stages of Human Evolution*, p. 51.

6. See, for example, Alexander "The Search for a General Theory of Behavior."

7. Alexander, "Evolution and Culture."

8. Variously attributed.

9. Grayson, *The Establishment of Human Antiquity*.

10. Von Koenigswald, "Early Man in Java." See also Harrison, "Present Status and Problems for Paleolithic Studies in Borneo and Adjacent Islands," pp. 54–55.

11. Campbell, *Human Evolution: An Introduction to Man's Adaptations*, is an excellent introduction to evolutionary theory as applied to people.

12. For the introductory student a good and well-illustrated introduction to evolutionary theory in anthropological applications is in Farraro et al., *Anthropology: An Applied Perspective*, esp. pp. 59–71.

13. There's good reason to believe that Mendel falsified his data because his results are far too "perfect" mathematically and do not show the expected levels of "chance" variation, but this does not detract from his overall contribution. See Thomas, *Refiguring Anthropology*, p. 288–91.

14. Birdsell, *Human Evolution*.

15. Ibid.

16. Based on various newspaper sources reporting research not yet published at the time this book was written.

17. Brace et al., "Clines and Clusters Versus 'Race': A Test in Ancient Egypt and of a Death on the Nile."

18. Crook, "Sexual Selection, Dimorphism, and Social Organization in Primates."

19. See, for example, the exchange between Tatterssall and Wolpoff, in *Evolutionary Anthropology*, 3(1), 1994.

20. Lewontin, "Sociobiology as an Adaptationist Program."

21. Hamilton, "Revising Evolutionary Narratives: A Consideration of Alternative Assumptions about Sexual Selection and Competition for Mates."

22. Tooby and DeVore, "The Reconstruction of Hominid Behavioral Evolution," pp. 215–17.

23. Van den Berghe, "Sex Differentiation and Infant Care: A Rejoinder to Sharlotte Neely Williams."

24. Reviewed in, for example, Shepher, *Incest, a Biosocial View*.

25. Rossetti was describing the day of Christ's birth here in *A Christmas Carol*, not the Pleistocene.

26. Bowen, *Quaternary Geology*; Flint, *Glacial and Quaternary Geology*.

27. Boesch-Achermann and Boesch, "Hominization in the Rainforest: The Chimpanzee's Piece of the Puzzle."

28. Alexander, "Evolution and Culture."

29. I am indebted to Dr. Thomas Morgan for some anecdotes on this point.

30. Attributed.

31. This report was taken from news reports that were not available as published scientific papers when this book was written.

32. Conroy, *Primate Evolution.*

33. This account was taken from news reports that were not available as scientific papers when this book was written.

34. This account taken from C-reuters@clarinet.com, Wednesday, August 16, 1995, 12:37:22.

35. *Science,* July 28, 1995.

36. Toth, "The Oldowan Reconsidered: A Close Look at Early Stone Artifacts."

37. This report was taken from a *New York Times* report (April 25, 1995, B7, B9) of a paper given at the Annual Meeting of the American Association of Physical Anthropology by Sileshi Semaw. Completion of the manuscript for this book did not allow time to consult the original source, but the dating appears to be secure. The dates were done with the argon-argon single crystal laser fusion technique.

38. Stringer, "Middle Pleistocene Hominid Variability"; see also Clark, "Some Thoughts on the Black Skull."

39. Brown, Harris, and Walker, "Early *Homo erectus* Skeleton."

40. Potts, *Early Hominid Activities at Olduvai.*

41. Reviewed in Isaac, "The Archaeology of Human Origins: Studies of the Lower Pleistocene in East Africa 1971– 1981."

42. Toth, "The Oldowan Reconsidered."

43. Tooby and DeVore, "The Reconstruction of Hominid Behavioral Evolution," pp. 215–17.

44. Teleki, "The Omnivorous Diet."

45. Crook, "Sexual Selection, Dimorphism, and Social Organization in Primates," p. 235.

46. Ibid.

47. Pianka, *Evolutionary Ecology.*

48. Crook, "Sexual Selection, Dimorphism, and Social Organization in Primates."

49. Anderson, "The Reproductive Role of the Human Breast."

50. Frisch, "Comment on P. Anderson, 'The Reproductive Role of the Human Breast.' "

51. Crook, "Sexual Selection, Dimorphism, and Social Organization in Primates," p. 254.

52. Small, "Female Primate Sexual Behavior and Conception," p. 81; idem., *Female Primates: Studies by Women Primatologists.*

53. Boesch-Achermann and Boesch, "Hominization in the Rainforest: The Chimpanzee's Piece of the Puzzle."

54. Goodall, *The Chimpanzees of Gombe.*

55. van Lawick-Goodall, "Some Aspects of Aggressive Behavior in a Group of Free-living Chimpanzees."

56. Van den Berghe, "Sex Differentiation and Infant Care: A Rejoinder to Sharlotte Neely Williams," p. 772.

57. van Lawick-Goodall, "Some Aspects of Aggressive Behavior in a Group of Free-living Chimpanzees."

58. van Lawick-Goodall, "The Behavior of Free-living Chimpanzees in the Gombe Stream Area"; idem., "Some Aspects of Aggressive Behavior in a Group of Free-living Chimpanzees"; idem., "The Behavior of Chimpanzees in Their Natural Habitat."

59. Bartlett, Sussman, and Cheverud, "Infant Killing in Primates: A Review of Observed Cases with Specific Reference to the Sexual Selection Hypothesis."

60. Tanner, "The Chimpanzee Model Revisited and the Gathering Hypothesis," p. 20.

61. Ibid., citing Boesch and Boesch, "Sex Differences in the Use of Natural Hammers," and Boesch and Boesch, "Possible Causes of Sex Differences in the Use of Natural Hammers by Wild Chimpanzees."

62. Teleki, "The Omnivorous Chimpanzee."

63. Ibid.

64. Symons, *The Evolution of Human Sexuality*, pp. 96–141.

65. For a somewhat different perspective, see Martin and Voorhies, *The Female of the Species*.

66. Teleki, "The Omnivorous Diet and Eclectic Feeding Habits of Chimpanzees in Gombe National Park, Tanzania."

67. Melnick and Hoelzer, "What is mtDNA Good for in the Study of Primate Evolution?" p. 2; Clutton-Brock, "Female Transfer and Inbreeding Avoidance in Social Mammals."

68. Melnick and Hoelzer, "What is mtDNA Good for in the Study of Primate Evolution?"

69. Binford, "Human Ancestors."

70. Lovejoy, "Models of Human Evolution."

71. Wilmsen, *Land Filled with Flies: A Political Economy of the Kalahari*.

72. Schaller and Lowther, "The Relevance of Carnivore Behavior to the Study of Early Hominids."

73. Birdsell, "Characteristics of the Early Hominid Scavenging Niche."

74. O'Connell et al., "Hadza Scavenging: Implications for Plio/Pleistocene Hominid Subsistence."

75. Birdsell, "Ecological Influences on Australian Aboriginal Social Organization."

76. Anderson, "The Reproductive Role of the Human Breast," p. 31.

77. Townsend, "New Guinea Sago Gatherers: A Study of Demography in Relation to Subsistence."

78. Lovejoy, "Hominid Origins: The Role of Bipedalism."

79. Devine, "The Versatility of Human Locomotion."

80. Kinzey, *The Evolution of Human Behavior: Primate Models*, p. x.

81. Tooby and DeVore, "The Reconstruction of Hominid Behavioral Evolution," pp. 215–17.

82. Symons, *The Evolution of Human Sexuality*.

83. Ibid., pp. 27–28.

84. Itzkoff, *Why Humans Vary in Intelligence*. Some scholars have even proposed genetically and metabolically linked differences between men and women. Seymour Itzkoff, for example, notes that men and women in the United States consistently show simi-

lar mean scores on intelligence tests but that women's scores are less variable. The distribution of IQ scores, he suggests, is one in which men and women both have normal bell-shape curves with the same approximate average, but fewer women are at the extreme high and low ends of these curves. He links this to the extra X chromosome women have—a source of relatively greater female biological stability in other aspects of physiology.

85. Sahlins, *Stone Age Economics*, p. xxx.

86. Tooby and DeVore, "The Reconstruction of Hominid Behavioral Evolution," p. 223.

87. Ibid., pp. 223–24.

88. Ibid., p. 224.

89. Ibid.

90. Ibid., p. 225.

91. Boesch-Achermann and Boesch, "Hominization in the Rainforest: The Chimpanzee's Piece of the Puzzle."

92. Tooby and DeVore, "The Reconstruction of Hominid Behavioral Evolution," p. 226.

93. Binford, "Fact and Fiction about the Zinjanthropus Floor: Data, Arguments, and Interpretations"; Bunn and Kroll, "Reply to L. Binford 'Fact and Fiction about the Zinjanthropus Floor: Data, Arguments, and Interpretations' "; Zeleznik et al, "On Systematic Butchery by Plio/Pleistocene Hominids."

94. Binford, "Fact and Fiction about the Zinjanthropus Floor: Data, Arguments, and Interpretations," p. 135.

95. Bunn and Kroll, "Reply to L. Binford 'Fact and Fiction about the Zinjanthropus Floor: Data, Arguments, and Interpretations.' "

96. Potts, "On Butchery by Olduvai Hominids."

97. Tooby, "Comment on Characteristics of the Early Hominid Scavenging Niche, by R. J. Blumenschine."

98. Blumenschine, "Characteristics of the Early Hominid Scavenging Niche."

99. Tooby, "Comment on 'Characteristics of the Early Hominid Scavenging Niche', by R. J. Blumenschine," pp. 399–400.

100. Reviewed in Lieberman, *Uniquely Human: The Evolution of Speech, Thought, and Selfless Behavior*.

101. de Vos et al., "Dating Hominid Sites in Indonesia."

102. Dennell et al., "Late Pliocene Artefacts from Northern Pakistan"; idem., "Early Tool-Making in Asia: Two Million Year Old Artefacts in Pakisan."

103. Dennell et al., "Late Pliocene Artefacts from Northern Pakistan." p. 498.

104. Adams, *The Evolution of Urban Society*.

105. Gould and Eldredge, "Punctuated Equilibria: The Tempo and Mode of Evolution Reconsidered."

106. Cronin et al., "Tempo and Mode in Hominid Evolution."

107. Henneberg, "Morphological and Geological Dating of Early Hominid Fossils Compared."

4

THE ORIGINS OF *HOMO SAPIENS SAPIENS*

Man is the missing link between anthropoid apes and human beings.

Anonymous

Viewed from space, earth's green and blue beauty is framed by the cold black infinity of the universe. This perspective has compelled many astronauts to reflect (surprisingly poetically for technologists) on our common humanity and fate. A similar contemplation of community should arise when we look back through the millions of years of our common human ancestry and meditate on the embryonic humanity evident in the fragmented bones of our primate ancestors. It is tempting to lapse into a sentimental vision of our ancestors pluckily fighting their way up a long dangerous road, and finally to "succeed"—to become "us." But human evolution was not like this. As in most evolutionary equations, the most intense competition was between individuals of the same species —we are the progeny of people who "won," in the sense that their genes made it through all the accidents of time and circumstance and the sieves of differing competitive abilities to become embodied in us. But chance, randomness, seems to have affected the biological universe in profoundly incalculable ways since the beginnings of our planet, and we seem to be here by virtue of a chain of improbable accidental events.[1]

We can see traces of our origins in all of the earth's ancient life forms, from the earliest marine creatures through the tree-shrews that lived tens of millions of years ago to our last primate ancestors—but only in the crucial interval of two to one million years ago did our genus, *Homo*, become the dominant primate in the world, and not until just a few hundred thousand years ago did humans appear whom we can relate to ourselves by calling them, too, *Homo sapiens*. We reserve the ultimate accolade of "people like us," *Homo sapiens sapiens*, for only some of the humans who lived after about 150,000 years ago, and it was not until about 30,000 years ago that we alone came to constitute humanity.

If we truly want to follow the Socratic dictum to know ourselves, then we must ask, what were the forces and circumstances that produced us, modern humanity, from the pre-human forms of our ancestors, and what does this knowledge tell us about ourselves and our future?

HOMO SAPIENS: **MODELS OF ORIGINS**

> *"I can't believe that!" said Alice. "Can't you?" the Queen said . . . "Try again: draw a long breath, and shut your eyes." Alice laughed. "There's no use trying," she said: "one can't believe impossible things." "I daresay you haven't had much practice," said the Queen. "When I was your age, I always did it for half-an-hour a day. Why, sometimes I've believed as many as six impossible things before breakfast."*
>
> Lewis Carroll, *Through the Looking-Glass*

The major contemporary "models" (that is, sets of linked assumptions, hypotheses, and interpretations of data) about how we changed from early African hominids into us, *Homo sapiens sapiens*, all require one to believe scenarios that, if not exactly impossible to believe, do require some dramatic leaps of faith.

Most models of modern human origins are variants of two basic contrasting hypotheses. One of these, which may soon be the majority view, is described[2] variously as the "African Origins," "Total Replacement," "Noah's Ark," or "Eve" model. It stipulates that modern humans evolved first and only in Africa and only a few hundred thousand years ago or less, and then migrated to the rest of the world, replacing all other hominid forms, and with little or no genetic interchange with these other forms (Figure 4.1).

An alternative model, commonly known[3] as the "Continuity," "Multiregional Evolution," or "Candelabra" model "traces all modern populations back to what was ultimately an African source (but to a time when people lived only there), through a web whose genetic contributions to the present varied from region to region and from time to time."[4] Thus, this model denies that modern human origins occurred only in Africa. The basic idea of this hypothesis is that sometime between about 1.0 and 2.0 million years ago a generic *Homo* ancestor of ours spread out across the warmer latitudes of Africa, the Middle East, Asia, and possibly the southernmost fringe of Europe. With the passage of the millennia these groups began to diverge somewhat as they adapted to local and different environments, but across the whole range of *Homo* they were evolving toward *Homo sapiens* as a result of "genic exchange" (i.e., gene flow through mating and migrations) that connected all human groups to some extent; and because they were under similar evolutionary selective forces, as generalized hunter-foragers, they all emerged in the last 30,000 years as one species, *Homo sapiens sapiens*—but with some of the physical differences that distinguish many modern Europeans, Africans, and Asians from each other.

Leslie Aiello has defined two variants of these models: (1) The "(African) hybridization and replacement model" is similar to the "Total Replacement" model in that it sees modern human origins in Africa, but allows for significant hybridization

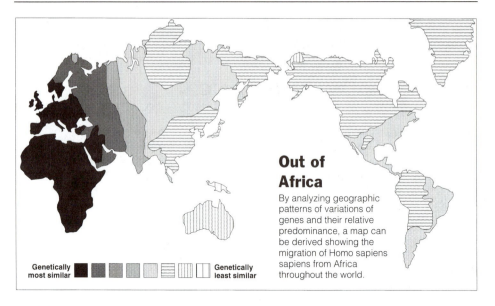

Out of Africa

By analyzing geographic patterns of variations of genes and their relative predominance, a map can be derived showing the migration of Homo sapiens sapiens from Africa throughout the world.

Genetically most similar   Genetically least similar

FIGURE 4.1 The "African Origins" or "Eve" model stipulates that modern humans evolved first in Africa a few hundred thousand years ago or less, and then migrated to the rest of the world, replacing all other hominid forms, with little or no genetic interchange with these other forms.

between the migrating Africans and indigenous populations outside of Africa.[5] (2) The "assimilation" model also accepts an African origin for modern humans, but it rejects replacement and migrations by Africans as mechanisms; instead it suggests that gene flow, admixture, and regional patterns of evolution were factors. Thus, modern humans in some places, such as Asia, could be largely genetically "African" but show some regional genetic continuity over the past million years.

These different views of the origins of modern humans have long histories. Louis Leakey, for example, argued[6] an African origins hypothesis in the 1960s against the then-predominate multiregional view, such as that advanced in the 1930s by Franz Weidenreich.[7] Weidenreich suggested that modern humans exhibit physical features that reflect continued gene flow throughout the world, but from at least four centers where the genetic continuity was sufficient to produce the differences observable in today's major "races."[8]

F. C. Howells challenged this idea: "Weidenreich has at least four different evolving human varieties, living far apart, moving ahead by fits and starts, producing their own peculiarities of form. . . . Yet these four careers at last converged to produce the same kind of man everywhere. And all, miraculously enough, breasted the tape at the same time."[9]

As Frayer, Wolpoff, Thorne, Smith, and Pope[10] point out, however, Howells (and some contemporary scholars) misunderstood Weidenreich to some extent: Weidenreich and most of his like-minded successors assumed continual genic exchange through gene flow and some migration throughout the Old World in the later Pleistocene.

Several versions of these competing models are illustrated in Figure 4.1. All require some difficult assumptions. Since relatively few non-human species have evolved from one species into another over a wide range in a "convergent" fashion, for example, why would we expect humans to be different? One answer might be that if humans actually did evolve in the convergent world-wide pattern imagined by Weidenreich it was because they all shared a similar ecological niche—i.e., "culture." If we ask how many migrants per generation would be required to sustain the gene flow to keep regional evolution convergent, estimates range as low as just one migrant per generation, but many scholars doubt that migrations and matings and convergent evolution were enough to produce *Homo sapiens sapiens* at about the same time and in about the same form in such widely separated areas as, for example, northern China and southern Africa.

This presumed pattern of convergent human evolution over a wide area and through great spans of time remains a problem for the Multiregional Evolution model, but, as we shall see, the African Origins model also requires some dubious assumptions.

Whatever the ultimate accuracy of any of these models, different scholars using the same data have come to very different conclusions about which of these models best fits the data. In fact, most scholars regard the currently available data to be insufficient to resolve these disputes. But it is not necessarily pointless to review the evidence and arguments in such unresolved debates. Resolution of intellectual debates sometimes comes as much from a change in perspective (e.g., Darwin) as from additional data. Fundamental research continues on the nature of evolutionary processes, and this research, along with discoveries of new fossils and tools, will probably resolve these debates.

SOCIOPOLITICAL IMPLICATIONS OF MODELS OF MODERN HUMAN ORIGINS

Before launching into the detailed evidence for and against the ideas illustrated in Figure 4.1, we can ask, why are such disputes important? Why would it be of much significance if one or the other of these two hypotheses were more accurate?

In our politicized era it is probably no surprise that, in addition to the intriguing questions these competing hypotheses pose about the specific facts of human origins, they have also been encumbered with racialist arguments and other sociopolitical disputes.[11] Some versions of the Multiregional Evolution model, for example, stipulate the degree of genetic separation in space and time of different human groups that would be necessary to produce significant group differences in innate human cognitive abilities (although most scholars, including those who believe that the Multiregional Evolution model is most accurate, see no evidence that modern human "races" differ significantly in cognitive abilities—indeed most scholars reject the concept of "race" itself [12]). Most versions of the African Origins model, in contrast, stipulate that all humans are relatively closely and recently related genetically, and that the physical traits used to define "races" involve recently evolved and superficial differences.

But some versions of the Total Replacement version of the African Origins model also assume that at some point in the not very distant past there was a genetic mutation in one small group or just an individual, and that this mutation conferred such a great advantage in mentality, or some other characteristic, that this group's or individual's genes were able to displace all other, "less-fit" genes. If so, such an event is not irrelevant to contemporary debates about genetically based mental abilities as related to different human groups. Many people of our age are uncomfortable with the idea that people and groups have differed in abilities, and also with the idea that such differences might occur again. Genetic mutations are, after all, a continuous fact of life. Contemporary research on human genetics continues to reveal differences among ethnic groups in their susceptibility to a wide variety of diseases and biological conditions (e.g., breast cancer, hypertension, blood types), and although there is no necessary reason why these group differences should correlate with differences in the biology of human mentality, some scholars have argued that differing degrees of cultural "accomplishments" some see in today's "races" result from different evolutionary histories in a wide variety of environments.[13] They assume that the kinds of genetically embedded characteristics and behaviors that made people more "fit" in Ice Age Europe were different from those that did so on the warm plains of East Africa, and that we can see these differences in human populations today.[14] Most scholars are extremely uncomfortable with even the suggestion that such a scenario might be true, and—more important—few see any evidence that it is.[15] Most scientists reject the concept of "race" to begin with, seeing instead just broad patterns of group differences in different superficial—and often uncorrelated—traits (e.g., degree of skin pigmentation and hair texture); also, no "races" in the traditional sense can be distinguished on the basis of differences in cell structure, genetics, or physiology.

Beyond these sociopolitical concerns, as we shall see, the contrasting models of the origins of *Homo sapiens sapiens* raise many interesting scientific questions involving genetics, evolutionary ecology, and anthropology.

To begin to understand and to evaluate these hypotheses about modern human origins, however, we must review human evolution in the many millennia after the first *Homo* appeared but before the first appearance of *Homo sapiens*.

HUMAN EVOLUTION AND RADIATION: 1.8? MILLION TO C. 300,000 YEARS AGO

When we left our African ancestors in chapter 3, at about 1.5 million years ago, some of them had cranial capacities approaching the low end of the normal modern range, they could make and use a variety of efficient stone tools, and some of them may have already been living far outside of Africa. Debates about the evidence for hominids outside of Africa before 1.5 million years ago will doubtless continue, but there is good evidence that by shortly after a million years ago, our ancestors had colonized most of the southern edge of the Old World, from Africa to Indonesia. These were the habitats—rich in flora and fauna and with few seasonal differences in the availability of food—to which we, as tropical animals, were best adapted. But while our hominid ancestors were extending their range in the hot savannas of Africa and the warm margins of Europe and Asia, great fertile tracts of the world lay unknown and untouched by humans.

At some time between about 1.0 and 0.5 million years ago, however, humans were beginning to colonize more temperate northern environments. If there is any answer as to why they would begin to move out of the tropical environments they had evolved in, it probably lies in the nature of the hunting-gathering band. Ethnographic studies suggest that human hunting-gathering bands with primitive technologies need large areas to support themselves, and also that one response to growing populations is for bands to split and for "daughter" groups to establish themselves in open territories on the original group's boundary.

As we noted in chapter 3, there seem to be long-term health advantages to reducing inbreeding to the extent that spouses are only distantly related—second cousins or less. We will never know when the "incest taboo" first was recognized as beneficial, but the colonization of ever greater areas of the world throughout human history would have had the effect of suppressing inbreeding.

In any case, hundreds of thousands of years of this process of band division, coupled with slow evolution in the efficiencies of tools, would have populated the warmer ranges of the Old World and positioned human groups for colonization of more temperate latitudes (Figure 4.2).

Let us begin with the problem of which hominid actually did make the first forays into the Middle East and Asia, and then into the north. The most likely candidate would seem to be the hominid that, until recently, was commonly known as *Homo erectus*. Individuals generally classed as *Homo erectus* averaged just less than four and a half feet feet tall (about 1.3 meters, although one African example may have been 1.6 meters, or 5 feet, 4 inches tall), walked fully erect (though its body and legs differed in various proportions and shapes from ours), and had a cranial capacity that ranged between about 700 and 1,225 cubic centimeters.[16] Compared to us, these hominids had flat skulls, large brow ridges, thick cranial bones, and almost no chins (Figure 4.3).

Alas, physical anthropologists have had a great crisis of faith with regard to the species designation of "*Homo erectus*":

> Does *Homo erectus* exist as a true taxon or should it be sunk into *Homo sapiens?* Is it a palaeospecies that exists . . . as a segment of the line that emerged from *Homo habilis* and gave rise to *Homo sapiens?* Is *Homo erectus* an extinct form that had no part to play in the evolution of *Homo sapiens?* Is *Homo erectus* a good example of a "statis event" . . . with little or no change in its form during its existence? Is there a clear cut example of *Homo erectus* in the European fossil record of man? Finally, are the Asian forms so far removed from the evolution of *Homo sapiens* in Africa to call into question the existence of *Homo erectus sensu stricto* in Africa at all?[17]

In view of these and other problems, some anthropologists have hypothesized that *Homo erectus* consisted of only the east Asian hominids who branched off from the main *Homo* line in Africa at about 1.5 million years ago, and that the African humans of this period should be called *Homo ergaster.*[18] Others classify almost all Asian,

FIGURE 4.2 Distribution of *Homo erectus* sites. *Homo erectus* was the first hominid to invade temperate climates and may have been more widely distributed than is represented here. Land bridges, now submerged, facilitated *Homo erectus* movements.

African, and European hominids of between about 1.5 and 0.5 million years ago as *Homo erectus.*

In what follows here, all of the humans who lived between about 1.5 and 0.5 million years ago are called *Homo erectus,* but this designation is likely to change as these taxonomies are refined.

EARLY RADIATION AND MIGRATIONS OF *HOMO*

If the dates for *Homo erectus* remains from Mojokerto and Sanigran in Java (Indonesia) are accurate, these hominids had reached this area by 1.8 to 1.6 million years ago, and thus must have been in Africa hundreds of thousands of years earlier. But the earliest *Homo erectus* remains known in Africa date to about 1.6 to 1.4 million years ago. The eleven-year-old boy who died on the western shore of Lake Turkana in northern Kenya about 1.6 million years ago, and whose skull (known as KNM-ER

3733) and nearly intact skeleton represent one of the best preserved and earliest *Homo erectus* individuals, seems to tell us much about our ancestors of this age. He was 1.6 meters (5 feet, 4 inches) tall—taller than many modern eleven-year-olds. His cranial capacity, however, was no more than 800 cc, about half our size, and his brow ridges very thick. His skeleton appears very similar to ours, though, and this suggests that our ancestors developed a body much like ours long before their mentalities equaled ours.

No stone tools were found with this individual, but Acheulian-style (named after the French site at Acheul) stone tools associated with *Homo erectus* in Europe at

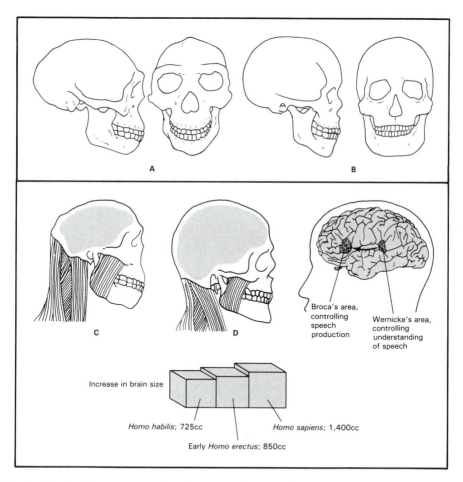

FIGURE 4.3 The *Homo erectus* skull (**A**) was long and low, compared to modern humans (**B**), with heavy brow ridges, no chin, and protruding jaws. In the transition from *Homo erectus* (**C**) to modern humans (**D**) the brain enlarged and the muscles controlling the head and neck were changed. Presumably there were also changes in the internal structure of the brain, such as in the development of speech centers.

a much later date (c. 600,000 years ago at the earliest) were apparently already present in many other East African sites more than a million years ago.[19] For example, at Koobi Fora, on Lake Turkana in Kenya, *Homo* remains and animal bones with what seem to be butchering marks have been found in substantial numbers, and there are small clusters of stone tools, some in concentrations about 5 to 10 meters in diameter with from about ten to one hundred artifacts.[20]

The hand-axes and other stone tools associated with the early African *Homo erectus* are a major improvement on the tools associated with the australopithecines of the previous million years, and this developing technology may have enabled hominids to radiate from warmer latitudes into colder, more demanding climates. The "Acheulian hand-ax" may not seem like a marvelous bit of technological advance, but it has several features that seem to reflect human intellectual evolution. First, it requires more processing—more actual steps of manufacture—than did the Olduvai-style tools. Again, this might not seem like some major technological breakthrough, but in a rather abstract sense the Acheulian hand-ax requires that the maker "see" something in the raw unworked cobble—that is, to envision something that when finished looks significantly different than the raw materials did. Also, in many cases, Acheulian hand-axes seem more standardized in proportions than earlier tools did, and they came in a variety of sizes and shapes. As we shall see, in some cases the best use of flint and hard stones is to knock off a series of flakes, use them until the edges dull, and then strike off more flakes. But Acheulian tools were often fist-size or larger. In such a substantial tool it may have been functionally efficient and effective to get the proportions as close to the ideal size as possible. "Stylistic" aspects of tools often vary widely in any given measurement, but "functional" aspects often converge very tightly on an optimal value—optimal both from the point of view of the functions of the tool and the cost of making it. If one is simply going to smash open a cow femur for marrow, any rock not too heavy to lift or too small to transmit much force would be adequate, but the standardization of Acheulian hand-axes suggests that they were beginning to converge on functionally optimal proportions and overall size.

What these functions were, however, remains unclear. Possibly these tools were used for a great variety of tasks, but they do seem specialized. Many are too heavy to have been hafted (attached to a spear, or other piece of wood) easily, yet they are often found in association with animal bones. It is barely possible that this association with animal bones is accidental, but it seems more likely that one of the main functions of this tool was as a primary butchering tool.

Acheulian hand-axes are usually found with other types of stone tools (and were presumably used with a wide variety of wood and bone tools that did not preserve), and although they may not have been the "Swiss Army" knives of their generation, they were certainly an important tool. Their distribution is particularly impressive. They have been found (Figure 4.4) over most of western Europe and Africa and as far southeast as India. They have not been found in significant numbers and in the same form, however, in southeast and east Asia, where "choppers" appear to be the main stone tool. The reasons for this earliest and relatively sharp technological divide are obscure. Is this simply a stylistic difference, with the divide representing different cultures of early *Homo?* Is this a functional difference, reflecting, perhaps, a

FIGURE 4.4 A cladogram of human evolution. The lines reflect degrees of genetic and cultural relationships and the styles of stone tools found with different hominids.

greater concentration on plant foods, rather than hunting, in these warmer and more vegetated Asian zones? Pope has argued[21] that the chopper tool tradition overlaps the natural distribution of bamboo, suggesting that the tool was used to process that material or other plants or animals distributed throughout this area.

But perhaps the simplicity of the Asian chopper tool tradition has been over-estimated. At the Chinese site of Zhoukoudian (discussed below), for example, evidence suggests a significant improvement in stone tool-making between 700,000 and 230,000 years ago, so that toward the end of that period there were drills, gravers, points, choppers, and other tools that appear to be as efficient and "sophisticated" as the hand-ax complex in the west.

These and many other questions remain largely unanswered. In fact the economy of all humans of this time period remains more a matter of speculation than hard evidence and continues to be the source of sharply different interpretations. Some think *Homo erectus* was primarily a hunter and that the demands of the hunting way of life partially "drove" human evolution toward ourselves; others doubt *Homo erectus* did much more than scavenging and opportunistic hunting.

An interesting site in this dispute is Olorgesailie, near Nairobi, Kenya (Figure 4.5). Here many small concentrations of stone tools and bones are spread out along a peninsula in an extinct lake. Most of the tools are cleavers and hand-axes, and some show considerable chipping and blunting wear. Mixed in with them are bones from several species of large mammals, including a hippopotamus and, curiously, sixty-three individuals of an extinct species of baboon (but no hominids). There are no

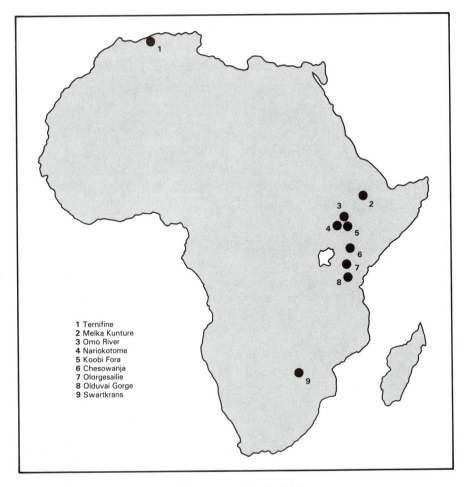

FIGURE 4.5   Some important *Homo erectus* sites in Africa.

hearths or burned bones, but microscopic pieces of charcoal have been found all over the site. Whether these were the result of human or natural activity remains unclear. Potassium-argon dating of the Olorgesailie formation yields an age of about 480,000 years.[22]

Glyn Isaac suggested that ancient hominids—presumably *Homo erectus*—encircled a troop of baboons here, perhaps at night, spooked them by making a lot of noise, and then systematically clubbed them to death as they tried to escape. Pat Shipman, too, has interpreted this site as the result of a hunting episode.[23] If Olorgesailie is a case of hominids hunting baboons, as some suggest, we may have been underestimating the linguistic and physical prowess of *Homo erectus*. It is instructive to try to imagine oneself about two-thirds our size, going out at night with stones and clubs to kill sixty-three baboons.

But Lewis Binford has questioned whether Olorgesailie—and most other early hominid sites—were places where hominids killed and butchered animals. In general he argues that with present techniques we cannot reliably distinguish between human hunting/butchering and other kinds of natural and cultural forces and circumstances. And he specifically suggests that the evidence from Olduvai and Olorgesailie may well be remains left by hominids who scavenged the kills of other animals, mainly for bone marrow, which they obtained by smashing bones with stone tools. He sees no evidence that early hominids shared food in complex patterns like humans, or that they foraged from home bases.[24]

Again, the non-anthropologist might wonder why anthropologists take so seriously these debates about how people made a living in Africa half a million years ago, but from a certain perspective, we really *are* what we eat, and not only that, as modern humans we are very much a product of the natural selective forces that applied over the millions of years of our past and especially to such basic matters as to how we and our ancestors got our food.

THE INVASION OF TEMPERATE ECOZONES

At various times in the past million years the climate of northern Europe and Asia was much warmer than it is at present. So warm were areas of Germany and France about 800,000 or 900,000 years ago that monkeys swarmed through dense forests there. But at other times the icy fingers of glaciers drew down out of the Alps and other mountain ranges, and great expanses of northern Europe were tundra.

One can imagine human groups probing northward during warmer periods—some of which lasted tens of thousands of years—and then their descendants being faced with equally long-term cooling trends. Probably no individual was conscious of the change, since it was so gradual, but kilometer by kilometer, year by year, they would have had to retreat or adapt. For our ancestors to invade the more northern climates, and to survive there during periods of expanding glaciers, would have required control of fire, clothing, and seasonal hunting. Fire would have been vital, not just for keeping warm, but for cooking food and evicting bears and other carnivores from caves and rock shelters—the safest and warmest places to live in northern latitudes.

Climate has had a strong impact on people physically and culturally until very recently, when modern technology began to moderate its direct effects. In the Pleistocene, moving into northern climates depended on people becoming whiter and fatter over many tens of millennia, through natural selection: up to 80 percent of the energy value of food goes simply to maintain body temperatures, and it is an inescapable fact of physics that spheres lose heat more slowly than any other shape of equal volume. Even with the pervasive migrations of people during the last century, the relationship between body shape and mean temperature—as epitomized by the East African Watusi and the Arctic Inuit ("Eskimo")—is strong.[25]

The white skins of northern peoples have to do most directly with their dependency on vitamin D, which is present in some foods but can also be synthesized in humans by the action of sunlight on skin. But whiter shades of skin are also more susceptible to cancer, acne, and psoriasis than darker tones, so for northern Europeans the selection for whiter skins—necessary to maintain vitamin D production in the long dark northern winters—was not an unmixed blessing. It is also probable that these later invasions of cold climates gave rise to many subtle genetic changes, such as—perhaps—resistance to long-term living in smoky environments, such as caves. Even such apparently minor matters as the different blood types may have been developing at this time in response to factors we cannot isolate. Blood type O, for example, seems to be more resistant to various diseases and even certain kinds of bone fractures,[26] but we don't know how or when the different blood types evolved.

Perhaps the best evidence for the early use of fire, however, comes not from Europe but from temperate Africa, at Swartkrans in South Africa, in association with *Homo erectus* and dated to 1.0 million years ago, perhaps as early as 1.6 million years ago.[27] Other possible evidence of fire comes from Chesowanya in Kenya, at about 1.0 million years ago. At sites of such great antiquity it is always difficult to show conclusively that people controlled the fire that is evident in the archaeological record, because fires from natural causes were common in most areas of the pre-industrial world.

The problems of living in northern climates go beyond simply keeping warm. In winter most of the plants suitable for human consumption die, and an animal like ourselves has only two ways to get food: store it—or hunt, fish, or scavenge other animals. On the African savannas and in other warm environments, women supply most of the food in hunting and gathering cultures, and even pregnant women, children, and the aged can gather much of their own food all year long. But such self-reliance would not have been possible in northern latitudes, where snow covered the ground for five to six months of the year. Clearly, strong social systems in which food-sharing and cooperative efforts were common would be important in adapting to these demanding temperate environments.[28]

But it is unlikely that simply the demands of these temperate environments directly caused the changes we associate with the evolution of modern humans, because the increased cranial capacities, use of stone tools and fire, and other signs of effective cultural adaptation seem to have existed in Africa long before they appeared elsewhere. Control of fire was probably an invention made independently by many groups, from southern Africa to the farthest reaches of east Asia.

When we consider the routes out of Africa and into Europe and Asia that early humans took, the dates for *Homo erectus* remains from Mojokerto and Sanigran in Java (Indonesia) of 1.8 to 1.6 million years ago raise many questions. They may be accurate, in which case we have to explain why we have so little evidence for people living in the region between Africa and Indonesia; or they may be wrong, which would fit present evidence, since almost all of the earliest known sites close to the land bridge between Africa and the rest of the world are all younger than 1.0 million years ago.

'Ubeidiya, three kilometers south of the Sea of Galilee in what is now Israel, comprised about fourteen distinct archaeological assemblages, all probably dating to no later than 640,000 years ago, and perhaps much earlier, before 1.0 million years ago (and some dates on animal remains are as high as 2.0 million years).[29] The tools found here seem very similar to those from Middle and Upper Bed II at Olduvai Gorge, being mainly choppers, spheroids (rounded stones), hand-axes, and used flakes. Richard Klein notes that at different times in the Pleistocene, the eastern Mediterranean can be considered part of Africa—in the sense that the climate and animals there very closely resembled nearby areas of Africa.[30] It is no surprise, thus, that some of the earliest dates outside of Africa would be found in the eastern Mediterranean, but it is interesting that so few traces of early *Homo* have been found in Europe. If *Homo* had reached northern China shortly after a million years ago, there seems to be no obvious environmental reason why they could not have invaded southern temperate Europe as well. Klein notes that some scholars believe that humans colonized most of temperate Europe only after 500,000 years ago, but that recent human fossils found in Spain, at Cueva Victoria and Gran Dolina, "suggest that humans in fact arrived in Europe nearer to 1 million years ago."[31] At Gran Dolina (a cave site at a place called Atapuerca), for example, Eudald Carbonell and other Spanish scholars found what could be the oldest known European humans.[32] About thirty-six human bones, including cranial fragments, teeth, jaw, hand, and foot bones were recovered, representing at least four individuals, including an adolescent and a child. These fossils' ages were estimated using a technique known as paleomagnetic dating (see chapter 2), which measures the magnetic fields of strata of rocks. The earth's magnetic field is known to have reversed polarity several times and the irregular timing of these events is well established. The Atapuerca fossils were found just below a reversal that is known to have happened 780,000 years ago.

If this date is accurate—and many scholars consider it to be—these fossils raise many questions. The bones do not seem to be very similar to *Homo erectus.* The Spanish researchers who found the fossils say they do not closely resemble any known form of human but could represent ancestors of the Neanderthals (see below). The stone tools seem even more primitive than those of African *Homo erectus.*

The Atapuerca fossils may represent one of many unsuccessful attempts to colonize Europe, as time after time people migrated into the area but did not persist, in the face of the severe winters and other challenges of Pleistocene Europe.

Another well-dated early European site is Isernia La Pineta, in central Italy, where volcanic deposits overlie deposits of stone tools associated with animal bones. Stone choppers, flakes, and scrapers were found here amidst bones from elephants, bison, and other animals, and the animals and volcanic deposits indicate a date of about more than 500,000 years ago and possibly much earlier.[33] A human thigh bone from Boxgrove in southern England has also been dated to about 500,000 years ago, and various other sites in Europe date to this age. For people to have colonized this far north, into England by 500,000 years ago, we might expect that they began to move out of the Mediterranean area by 600,000 years ago or earlier, and it is certainly possible, given the vagaries of preservation, that people were in northern Europe in substantial numbers by 700,000 years ago, or earlier. But based on the available evidence it seems likely people did not regularly and significantly inhabit northern temperate Europe until about 500,000 years ago.

If people were in Java 1.7 million years ago, however, we might expect dense concentrations along the routes out of Africa and along the southern coasts of Asia that date to this same period, but there is little evidence of this. A few stone tools found at Ban Mae Tha, Thailand, appear to date to 700,000 years ago, and the Lan-t'ien and Q'en-Xia-wo sites in central China contained fragments of *Homo erectus* that date to about 600,000 years ago, but there simply is little other credible evidence of human occupation of these more southern areas before about 900,000 years ago. It is possible that such factors as the sea level rise at the end of the Pleistocene drowned most of the pre-1.0 million-year-old sites along the southern approaches to Java, but it is also possible that the 1.7 million-year-old dates for the Indonesian *Homo erectus* hominids are wrong.

In any case, we have very strong evidence that humans were far into east Asia by 1.0 million years ago at the latest, and thus, if *Homo* did not reach mainland Europe until after 500,000 years ago, we must look for some explanation of this disparity. The more seasonal and demanding climates of Europe may explain this in part, but it remains something of a mystery.

An important site for analyzing human colonization of temperate environments is Zhoukoudian (literally "Dragon Bone Hill"), a cave located forty-three kilometers southwest of Beijing. Using explosives, excavators managed to blast out and examine thousands of cubic meters of collapsed cave debris at the site between 1927 and 1937, and these excavations and later research revealed the remains of more than forty hominids, as well as over 100,000 stone tools, countless animal bones, and many hearths and ash layers, all well stratified in a deposit that is an astonishing fifty meters deep. Not all this was cultural debris—cave bears and other animals alternated with hominids in occupying the cave and they probably brought in many of the animals. But Zhoukoudian has more superimposed occupational layers than any other known *Homo erectus* site. Analysis of the fauna and hominids and various forms of dating (including fission track, uranium-thorium, paleomagnetism, and thermoluminescence) have produced conflicting age estimates. In a recent summary[34] of these dates, Wu Rukang and Jia Lampo conclude that the uppermost layers date to 230,000 years ago and the earliest levels to about 700,000 years ago.

The 14 skullcaps, 6 skull bones, 10 jaw fragments, 147 teeth, and assorted arm, leg, and hand bones found at Zhoukoudian all appear to have come from *Homo erectus*. Brain volumes average about 1040 cubic centimeters and range between about 775 and 1300 cubic centimeters—somewhat larger than the *Homo erectus* from Java—and teeth sizes fall between ourselves and australopithecines (actually, they are only slightly larger than contemporary native Australian populations). Based on the few leg-bone fragments recovered, it is estimated that the Zhoukoudian hominids averaged about 5 feet, 1 inch in height—which may seem short, but is only an inch or two less than the average height of most people of just a few hundred years ago.

Wu and Lampo note that every *Homo erectus* upper incisor found in China, including those from Zhoukoudian, Yuanmou, Yunxian, and Hexian, is "shovel-shaped"—that is, in cross section the tooth is curved like a shovel. They note that this feature is found in nearly as high frequencies in living Mongoloid populations, whereas it is at much lower frequencies elsewhere, and thus they conclude that the Chinese *Homo erectus* are the genetic ancestors of contemporary Chinese. This point is discussed at greater length below.

About 100,000 stone tools were retrieved from Zhoukoudian, most of them simple flakes and choppers made from quartz, but with some more specialized tools, as well, including flakes, drills, and augers that may have been used as spear points. Over the course of the site's occupation, the simple chopper tools of the 700,000-year-old initial occupation were replaced by a sophisticated variety of tools that included re-touch and prepared core flaking.[35]

Zhoukoudian may have been a base camp from which hominids hunted and to which they brought back their kills to be cooked and eaten. The site includes hundreds of thousands of animal bones, mainly from deer, but also from elephants, rhinoceroses, beavers, bison, boars, and horses. The large quantities of charred hackberry seeds found at Zhoukoudian suggest that they were a dietary staple, and pollen analysis indicates that nuts from walnut, hazelnut, and pine would have been available. Such finds remind us that we see only a distorted picture of early hominid diets: they probably ate vastly greater quantities of plant foods than meat, but only when they used fire to cook plants do we find the traces of vegetable foods, and although pollen can show that some plants were available, many plant foods simply were not preserved in archaeologically recognizable forms.

But the issue of fire at Zhoukoudian is somewhat problematic. Binford and Stone argue that most of the bones at the site were deposited by animals who lived in dens there (e.g., bears), that people scavenged but did not hunt the animals represented by the other bones found there, and that much of the presumed evidence for fires may in fact be bat dung.[36]

Many other scholars, however, believe that this site represents unmistakable evidence that these hominids were accomplished hunters.

Not a single skull from this site had an attached face, and the base of each skull was broken, perhaps to get at the brains. But numerous scholars have questioned the idea that these bone alterations indicate cannibalism. Arens, for example, also rejects the notion that cannibalism was a common practice for very long in any culture, ancient or recent.[37] He may well be right, because ecologically, systematic cannibalism is a poor food-procurement strategy.[38] Compared to almost any other animals, people are hard to catch in relation to the amount of food they represent, and one risks depleting the stock extremely quickly if cannibalism is at all frequent. Still, we must consider at least the possibility that *Homo erectus* practiced ritual cannibalism, as did many other human groups, even though there is little about the rest of the artifacts and remains of *Homo erectus* to suggest a rich ritual life.

Some of these questions about the Zhoukoudian humans could be answered if we still had their bones, but all the hominid remains disappeared while being transferred from Beijing to an American ship during the Japanese invasion of China prior to World War II. Although there are some mysterious indications that they have survived, to date no progress has been made in locating any of the fossils.[39] Fortunately, at the time of their discovery the great German anatomist Franz Weidenreich made excellent plaster casts of them all and described them in superlative detail.

Zhoukoudian may offer evidence that our ancestors had mastered the use of fire and clothing to adapt to northern climates, and data from Europe of this same period shows that hominids were penetrating temperate latitudes all across the Old World. Perhaps our best evidence of European adaptations hundreds of thousands of years ago comes from Torralba and Ambrona, located about 1.5 kilometers apart in a deep valley 150 kilometers northeast of Madrid (Figure 4.6). Given the many difficulties of discriminating between human scavenging and hunting, no single site can be taken as convincing evidence of the general nature of early human life in Europe. But many regard Torralba and Ambrona as evidence that at least some groups in Middle Pleistocene Europe engaged in big-game hunting. Excavations at Torralba in the early 1960s by F. Clark Howell exposed about 300 square meters of stratified archaeological deposits, from which were collected hundreds of pollen samples, several thousand stone tools, and countless animal bones (but no human remains). The kinds of pollen found in these remains have convinced some scholars that Torralba

FIGURE 4.6 Some important *Homo erectus* sites in Europe.

dates to about 400,000 years ago, but some think it is only about 200,000 years old. Pollen analysis indicates the area was a cool, swampy valley when the site was inhabited.[40]

The remains of at least thirty elephants were found at Torralba, as well as about twenty-five deer, twenty-five horses, ten wild oxen, and several rhinoceroses. Almost all the skeletons were disarticulated, and many bones were smashed and split, perhaps in an effort to get at the marrow. Nearly all the elephant skulls are missing, as are many of the other bones bearing the most edible cuts of meat—suggesting they were moved some distance to be butchered, and perhaps indicating the efforts of a large, cooperating work force.

Bits of charcoal were found mixed with the bones and stones at Torralba, raising the possibility that these people had driven the animals into the swampy areas of the site by lighting fires. Scattered among the charcoal and other debris were preserved bits of wood, and some have speculated that wood may have been brought to the site to cook the butchered meat. Not a single hearth, ash concentration, or depression has been found, however.

The process of driving animals into the swamps and killing and butchering them would have been quite a spectacle, with great clouds of smoke, shrieking, demented animals, and running, shouting hominids. But how could these tiny, stupid, ill-equipped people have killed these huge animals? Not a single obvious stone spearpoint was found at the site, but Freeman suggests that the animals were either stoned to death with the many fragments of rock found amid the bone or dispatched with wooden spears.[41] It is a bit difficult to envisage any human, let alone *Homo erectus,* about to stone three or four large elephants to death, or to kill them with long-since-rotted wooden stabbing spears, but if they did, it would have been a fantastic Hitchcockian scene played out in this Spanish valley hundreds of thousands of years ago.

The stratigraphy at Torralba is complex, and the site may represent not one, but many different hunting episodes. In fact, various archaeologists have suggested that many of the animals at Torralba and Ambrona show no signs of butchering, that the evidence for the intentional use of fire is slight, and that small groups of humans scavenging some of the animals could have created the site.[42]

In 1965 a bulldozer operation in an alley named Terra Amata[43] in Nice, on the Mediterranean coast of France, uncovered twenty-one discrete sites dating to about 300,000 B.P., when the level of the Mediterranean was 25 meters higher than it is today, and the climate somewhat cooler and more humid. Henry de Lumley, the excavator of the site, found what he interpreted as evidence that the inhabitants of Terra Amata constructed large huts, ranging from 8 to 15 meters in length and from 4 to nearly 6 meters in width, most of them oval-shaped and estimated to have sheltered ten to twenty people. Nothing remains of the huts themselves, but de Lumley found what he thought was a long line of postholes where supporting logs were driven into the sand, as well as rows of stones evidently used to brace the walls. There were many hearths and floors covered with ash and the residue of organic debris, except for some areas close to the fire that were relatively free of debris, perhaps indicating places where people slept.[44]

Archaeologist Paola Villa has questioned[45] de Lumley's interpretation of the hut-building at this site, on the basis of evidence that different occupational strata may have been mixed by natural factors. This is an important point, because until about 30,000 years ago we have few other traces of the kind of organized camp layout de Lumley saw in the Terra Amata remains, and some scholars associate the building of permanent structures only with *Homo sapiens*.[46]

Analysis of fossilized human feces from Terra Amata revealed pollen from plants that bloom in the spring and early summer, suggesting a temporary occupation each year at this time. Most of the animal bones found at the site were from stags, elephants, boars, ibex, and rhinoceroses, but there were also bones of birds, turtles, rabbits, rodents, and a few fish and shellfish.

The tools from the site are mainly the large bifacially worked Acheulian stone tools like those found elsewhere in Africa and Europe at this time, and there are also a few bone tools. Unfortunately, not a single human remain has been found at Terra Amata, but it is likely that we see here the work of *Homo erectus*. A single footprint was uncovered during excavations, and its modern shape and length indicate a person about 5 feet, 1 inch in height.

Terra Amata's occupants were probably hunters and gatherers who ranged widely with the changing seasons, collecting berries, nuts, and other foods, foraging for eggs, small game, and shellfish, and hunting and scavenging mid-size and even large game.

Another important northern European site is Vértesszöllös, a rock quarry west of Budapest, Hungary. A recent series of uranium dates put the site at about 185,000 years B.P.,[47] but it could be as old as 350,000. When the site was first occupied, it was on the banks of some hot springs, and several layers of human occupational debris have been found near these springs. Excavations in the 1960s uncovered about 3,000 stone tools, many smashed and burned animal bones, and the occipital bone from one hominid and a few teeth from another.[48] The estimated cranial capacity of between 1,115 and 1,437 cubic centimeters is large for a *Homo erectus*, and some consider this fossil to be an archaic form of *Homo sapiens*. No hearths have been found at the site, but burned bones here indicate the use of fire.

Various other sites have been found in Europe and Asia that date to the period of several hundred thousand years ago, and, in summary, it seems clear that by 300,000 years ago humans lived across much of the Old World, from England to northern China, from South Africa to Indonesia. Some of this area, particularly Africa, had been occupied by humans for more than a million years, and people had probably lived even on the extreme periphery for many hundreds of thousands of years.

Nearly all the evidence reviewed to this point can be accommodated within each of the four competing hypotheses about human origins with which we began this chapter. It seems clear that some form of early *Homo* left Africa and colonized Europe and Asia between 1.0 and 0.5 million years ago; and most scholars see patterns of regional evolution, with some commonalities but also some differences appearing in human groups as they made their living in highly varied ways, exploiting small areas in a complex mosaic of adaptations that reached from England to southern Africa to Indonesia.

This consensus of scholarly opinion on our ancestors up to about 300,000 years ago evaporates, however, when the question of "what happened next?" is considered.

THE MIDDLE/UPPER PALEOLITHIC TRANSITION
(C. 300,000 - 35,000 B.P.)

I held it truth, with him who sings
To one clear harp in divers tones,
That men may rise on stepping-stones
Of their dead selves to higher things.[49]
Alfred, Lord Tennyson,
from In Memoriam

In their tool use, social systems, and economies, *Homo* of several hundred thousand years ago, as we know them from Zhoukoudian, Torralba-Ambrona, and the other sites described above, seem to have been similar to modern hunters and gatherers in many ways, yet there is something alien about these creatures. We look for artifacts expressing ritual or complex symbolism, but not a single figurine, wall painting, rock carving, or even an elaborately made stone tool can be securely attributed to *Homo erectus.* Later, beginning at least 30,000 years ago, people made exquisitely crafted stone tools, some so delicately worked that even moderate use would ruin them— tools that must have been made in part simply for the pleasure of creating something beautiful. But the tools of *Homo erectus* are undeviatingly simple, efficient, utilitarian objects.

Perhaps even more revealing, there are no known *Homo erectus* burials or ritual dispositions of corpses. For at least the last 30,000 years, death has almost everywhere been an occasion for the outpouring of human emotion, and even the simplest hunters and gatherers during this span usually disposed of their dead by digging a hole and placing a few stone tools or bits of shell in with the body; but not a single *Homo erectus* anywhere in the world appears to have been even intentionally buried, let alone sent off to the next world with a few provisions and expressions of goodwill.

These various absences of stylistic behavior among *Homo erectus* can be interpreted in several different ways. *Homo erectus,* with his brain about two-thirds the size of our own, may simply have lacked the mental equipment to generalize and symbolize his experiences as we do. *Homo erectus*'s language skills, in particular, may have been quite limited.[50] On the other hand, *Homo erectus* may have had the potential for stylistic, religious, and social impulses but lived in circumstances that did not elicit such expressions. As Randall White has observed, the ethnographic record of material forms of representation like that of Pleistocene "art" suggests that these aesthetic expressions are about political authority and social distinctions,[51] and it may be that the social conditions in which such distinctions are important were just beginning to appear in the Middle and Late Pleistocene.

It is difficult to overstate the importance of the evolution of the capacity for aesthetic, ritual, and social feelings, for as we will see, it was precisely these mental characteristics that made possible the rise of great civilizations. Thus, we are particularly concerned in this chapter with the conditions under which these feelings first appeared (as reflected in the archaeological record) and with their concurrent important cultural developments. Richard Klein,[52] for example, suggests that the "explosion" of art about

30,000 years ago, in the form of figurines and highly stylized stone tools, as well as other evident cultural change, reflects the migrations of anatomically modern peoples throughout the world—the first people, he suggests, to have these mental powers.

The multiple ways in which *Homo sapiens* diverged physically and behaviorally from pre-sapiens forms of *Homo* in the period between about 300,000 to 30,000 years ago are collectively referred to as the "Middle/Upper Paleolithic transition."[53] This "transition" is visible in many radical changes in human physical characteristics and material culture, including: (1) an increase of average human brain size from about 1,100 to about 1,400 cubic centimeters (although local variability was high, and the modern range of normal brain functioning is at least 1,000 to 2,000 cubic centimeters); (2) changes in physical form such that modern *Homo sapiens sapiens* have less robust skeletons, a more prominent chin, smaller or absent brow ridges, smaller teeth, a higher rounded skull, and other physical characteristics;[54] (3) increased human population numbers and densities—again with considerable local variation; (4) many technological innovations, including the bow and arrow, atlatl (throwing stick), bone and wood tools of diverse types, and techniques for extracting a relatively great amount of cutting edge from a given amount of stone; (5) increased aesthetic expression in figurines, usually of bone or stone, beautiful wall paintings and rock carvings, burial techniques, and objects used for personal adornment; (6) a shift from generalized hunting patterns to concentrations in some areas on gregarious herd mammals like deer, reindeer, and horses; and (7) the appearance of artifact styles and trade in exotic items that bespeak the first manifestation of some sort of regional "ethnic" identity[55] that exceeds by a wide margin the local band society—in short, changes that may reflect the "total restructuring" of social relationships during the Middle/Upper Paleolithic transition.[56]

The obvious question is: How were our ancestors changed by time and circumstance in these highly significant ways? To consider this question, we must return to the contrasting hypotheses (as seen in Figure 4.1) about modern human origins with which we began this chapter.

As noted above, the "Total Replacement," "African Origins," or "Eve" model contends that modern humans evolved first and only in Africa and only a few hundred thousand years ago or less, and then migrated to the rest of the world, displacing all other hominid forms, and with little or no genetic interchange with them. If this is true, then, as interesting as these many European and Asian fossils and sites of hundreds of thousands of years ago are, the people who left these remains had almost nothing to do with us in terms of our physical or cultural heritage.

This is a difficult premise for many anthropologists to accept, because so much of what we think we know about human evolution has been based on sites such as Zhoukoudian, in China, Toralba-Ambrona, in Spain, etc. If the "African Origins" model is correct, however, these sites were created by a form of human that has virtually nothing to do with us genetically, and probably little to do with us culturally.

Alternatively, the "Multiregional Evolution," "Continuity," or "Candelabra" models propose that: sometime between about 1.0 and 2.0 million years ago a generic *Homo* ancestor of ours spread out across the warmer latitudes of Africa, the Middle East, Asia, and possibly the southernmost fringe of Europe; then, with the passage of the millennia, although these groups began to diverge somewhat as they adapted to local and different environments, across the whole range of *Homo* they were evolving toward *Homo sapiens* as a result of gene flow that connected all human groups to some extent and because they were all under similar evolutionary selective forces as generalized hunter-foragers; so that they all converged at about 30,000 years ago as one species, *Homo sapiens*—but with the physical differences that distinguish modern Europeans from, for example, modern Chinese.

Two variants of these basic models are also illustrated in Figure 4.1, and we can ask: Which of these models is best supported by the evidence?

MOLECULAR BIOLOGICAL EVIDENCE OF MODERN HUMAN ORIGINS

The skulls and skeletons of our ancestors may seem the most direct evidence to assess hypotheses about human origins, but these bones are usually just mineral casts of formerly living individuals, and arguments about the meaning of subtle differences in size and shape of their features are endless and largely irresolvable. An alternative approach is to work backwards—in effect, to look at today's people and see how their degree of biological relatedness fits various ideas about our origins.

Figure 4.7 presents one such form of analysis: it expresses the degree of biological similarity among contemporary peoples of the world. How did such different degrees of relatedness appear, and when, and what do these differences "mean"?

It is an inescapable fact of genetics that all the people alive in the world are genetically related, and that at some point an individual existed whom we can all claim as an ancestor. The only points of debate are how long ago that ancestor lived, and where. Some scholars have argued on the basis of genetic evidence that all of us alive

FIGURE 4.7 **(A)** Analyses of DNA have been used to suggest genetic distances among contemporary groups of people. In this figure the genetic distances between groups is based on a sample of 600 individuals from 8 groups. Between any two groups, the fewer the symbols the shorter the genetic distance and the closer the presumed relationship. In **(B)** these data are arranged in a family tree. These data suggest all modern humans are genetic descendants of one small inbred group of prehistoric Africans.

today have a common female ancestor who lived less than about 200,000 years ago. This "African Eve Hypothesis" is based on the study of DNA taken from the mitochondria, which are features in human cells where energy to keep the cell functioning is produced. The term "mtDNA" stands for mitochondrial DNA; mtDNA is different from nuclear DNA in that it is all in the mitochondria of the mother's egg and therefore is not affected by the sperm's contribution to genetic inheritance as implanted during fertilization. Thus, mtDNA is inherited only through the mother. MtDNA is subject to random mutations at a higher rate than nuclear DNA, and these are expressed as minor mistakes in copying the genetic code that are then passed on to the next generation. Thus, we would not even expect two people from, for example, the same small isolated group of hunter-foragers in highland New Guinea to have identical mtDNA. And we would expect that differences in mitochondrial DNA would increase the longer any two people are separated in terms of a common ancestor, since the minor genetic mutations in mtDNA accumulate over time.

An analogy to accumulation of changes in mtDNA is the fate of last names in many Western cultures, where a child's last name usually comes only from the father. If a man does not have children or has only female children, his individual perpetuation of that last name is "lost" (although, of course, there are usually many others with that last name). Similarly, mtDNA is "lost" if a woman has no children or has only sons.[57]

In an early study to test the relatedness of contemporary human groups, Cann, Stoneking, and Wilson collected the placentas of 147 women in the United States, Asia, Europe, the Middle East, New Guinea, and Australia, and then separated the mtDNA from these samples and compared them. They concluded that everyone living today is descended from an African woman, a "mitochondrial Eve," who lived between 140,000 and 290,000 years ago—probably about 200,000 years ago. They identified Africa as the home of this woman because mtDNA is most variable in today's Africa, and thus these mtDNA differences are assumed to be accumulating longest in Africa. If the estimate of about 200,000 years ago for a common maternal ancestor is correct, it is highly unlikely that the people who lived in Europe and Asia before about 200,000 years had anything to do with us, in terms of our biological and cultural ancestry. Since this study, other researchers have increased the sample of people studied and used various other methods of calculating genetic similarity (reviewed by Aiello[58]), and some have concluded that, indeed, the evidence shows that everyone in the world today is descended from a few Africans who lived a few hundred thousand years ago.

But many scholars question these mtDNA and related studies. For these estimates to be accurate, at least three things must be true: (1) the generation time (i.e., the average number of years between mother and daughter's ages) must be accurately estimated; (2) the molecular "clock," in the sense of the rate at which genetic differences accumulate, must run equally as fast for us, the *Hominidae*, as for other mammals; and (3) nucleotide substitutions must be constant over time. Each of these assumptions has been attacked by recent scholars, and, in any case, Don Melnick and Guy Hoelzer strongly caution about the use of the mtDNA clock, suggesting that various problems with it "render mtDNA unreliable for dating past evolutionary events."[59] Frayer and others[60] strongly criticize assumptions about the mutation rate of mtDNA, and they argue that if the starting date of the "clock" is pushed back to 800,000 years ago for the origins of the mtDNA we now all share, then there would be a better fit between the molecular evidence and the fossil and archaeological records.

The details of these debates about the interpretation of graphs of genetic relatedness based on mtDNA are beyond the scope of this book—and beyond the grasp of those without specific kinds of mathematical expertise. Various mathematical techniques are required to measure similarity and to arrange these patterns of similarity in patterns that show descent and genetic relatedness, and disputes about the appropriateness of these techniques continue. Frayer and his colleagues[61] conclude, for example, that "There is no statistically reliable mtDNA evidence for an African, or any other single, geographically centered origin for Eve."

To evaluate these opposing models of human origins and interpretations of the genetic evidence, we can at least consider the ambiguous and fragmentary record of their bones and stone tools.

FOSSIL AND ARCHAEOLOGICAL EVIDENCE OF MODERN HUMAN ORIGINS: TESTING THE TOTAL REPLACEMENT MODEL

Let us consider the Total Replacement model to be a "null hypothesis," in the sense that we can attempt to demonstrate that it is *not* true. Although some of the most vocal proponents of the Total Replacement model have recently questioned aspects of their model,[62] it at least has the virtue of clearly testable implications. If, for example, the Total Replacement model is accurate, we would expect to see various kinds of specific evidence.[63]

First, the earliest known *Homo sapiens sapiens* should be found in Africa, and there should be evidence that "modern" humans lived only in Africa prior to their appearance in the rest of the world.

A second testable implication of the Total Replacement model is that there should be no anatomical evidence of genetic mixing between the early modern Africans and the people they replaced. That is, except in Africa, there should be an absence of "intermediate" forms of humans—those whose physical forms appear as a blend of early *Homo* and *Homo sapiens sapiens*—in the period between about 400,000 and 30,000 years ago.

Third, everywhere outside of Africa the earliest modern humans should resemble these African ancestors and not the local people who had lived there first. Also, there should be evidence of a "rapid" change from early *Homo* to *Homo sapiens sapiens* in both the fossil and archaeological records as the replacement took place, and in a geographical pattern that reflects the routes they took out of Africa.

Fourth, in areas outside of Africa there should be no evidence of anatomical continuity spanning the time period before and after the replacement occurred: that is, we should not expect to see a pattern of continuous similarity in the physical types who lived, for example, in China at Zhoukoudian 300,000 years ago, 50,000 years ago, and today.

Fifth, we should look for some evidence as to why Africans were able to displace well-adapted hominids all over the Old World. We would expect some evidence in technology, skull size and shape, animal exploitation patterns, site densities and placement, or in some other attribute of the archaeological record that would explain why this replacement was both rapid and complete. As Frayer and his colleagues note,[64] even the European conquest of the Americas, involving as it did far superior technology and the introduction of numerous lethal diseases, left many indigenous Native American hunter-foragers, from Alaska to Tierra del Fuego, and some have persisted even into the present day. So, what evidence is there that the early African *Homo sapiens sapiens* possessed some advantage that allowed them to drive into extinction all other humans?

It is important to note that all of these five categories of evidence are to some degree equivocal: What, for example, would an "intermediate" skull be, and what would "rapid" change look like in the archaeological record? Different scholars have different ideas about what these kinds of terms mean. Also, given the vagaries of preservation and differences in the intensity of archaeological research (much more work has been done in western Europe, for example, than, say, Pakistan), we could be easily misled by sample biases. Moreover, whatever advantages the early African *Homo sapiens sapiens* had that allowed them to replace other hominid forms, if in fact that is what happened, these advantages may not be visible in the archaeological record, given our current knowledge of that record. If early Africans, for example, simply had a slightly greater fertility rate, perhaps because of some genetic mutation and minor cultural adaptation to this mutation, and no other advantages, it is possible that they could have supplanted all other hominids in a few hundred thousand years—although we would still have to explain why no interbreeding by adjacent groups took place, since such gene flow is the common pattern during the recent past. Finally, the basic logic of science stipulates that hypotheses cannot be "proven." One attempts to disprove them and in the end all that science can aspire to is pointing us towards the current "best" model—"best" being defined in terms of "fit" to the data and parsimony.

To "test" these five implications of the Total Replacement model requires that we examine a complex array of evidence, and the reader is forewarned that this review ends inconclusively: reasonable scientists differ on interpretations of this evidence.

The Evidence from Africa One implication of the Total Replacement model is that the earliest modern humans should appear in Africa. Does this appear to be true? Perhaps the best candidate for the earliest known *Homo sapiens sapiens* is the fragmentary human remains from the Klasies River Mouth caves in South Africa, found in association with many stone tools, animal bones, and other evidence of repeated occupation.

Uranium series dates and correlations with dates from marine cores seem to place these remains between 125,000 and 95,000 years ago. Only some elements of the crucially important facial morphology are preserved on just four of the individuals represented by these bones. The scholars who have analyzed the Klasies human remains come to startlingly different conclusions. Some scholars see archaic features in many elements of these bones and little evidence for the "modern" features they would expect if these individuals were part of the population that, according to the Total Replacement model, preceded the appearance of modern *Homo sapiens sapiens* elsewhere in the world. The excavators of this site, R. Singer and J. Wymer, concluded that the *Homo sapiens sapiens* mandible found here is "the earliest date for modern man so far from any site in the world," and they add that the many stone points found at the site indicate substantial hunting with hafted spears.[65]

Early hominid fossils of *Homo sapiens* have been found at Bodo and Omo (Ethiopia), Laetoli (Tanzania), Kanjera (Kenya),[66] Kabwe, or Broken Hill (Zambia), Border Cave (South Africa), and several other sites, but in every case at least some scholars consider the dating unreliable or disagree on the degree of modernity evident in these highly fragmented finds.[67] Frayer and his colleagues, for example, conclude "the African fossil record offers little in support of the Eve hypothesis."[68] Other scholars,[69] however, see a pronounced modern appearance in the African human fossils that span the period between about 200,000 and 100,000 years ago and conclude that the evolution of *Homo sapiens sapiens* had been slow and continuous, and had nearly run its course in Africa by the end of this period, and certainly by 70,000 years ago.

But the Total Replacement model does not require that *Homo sapiens sapiens* appeared in East Africa as early as 100,000 years ago. Richard Klein has suggested that the *Homo sapiens sapiens* who actually replaced all other humans only appeared in Africa after 50,000 years ago, and perhaps only shortly before 30,000 years ago, when we see the spread across the Middle East and Europe of "art," in the sense of wall paintings, figurines, shell and bone ornaments, and beautifully crafted tools (see below), and when we also see standardized tool shapes and highly organized activity areas in the remains of archaeological sites. Klein concludes that

> an abrupt change in the archaeological record about 50,000-40,000 years ago registers the onset of fully modern human behavior. Prior to this time, human morphology and behavior evolved slowly, hand-in-hand. Afterward, fundamental morphological evolution all but ceased, while behavioral (cultural) evolution accelerated rapidly. Preliminary evidence suggests that key archaeological markers of fully modern behavior appeared first in Africa . . . between 150,000 and 50,000 years ago. During this same interval, the sole inhabitants of Eurasia were the Neanderthals and other comparably archaic humans. The novel archaeological traits [i.e., the appearance of "art," complex sites, etc.] effectively signal the development of the fully modern capacity for Culture, and it was almost certainly this capacity, or more broadly, the cognitive and communicative abilities behind it, that explains why anatomically modern Africans largely or wholly replaced archaic Eurasians, beginning 50,000 years ago.[70]

One interesting implication of Klein's hypothesis is that these *Homo sapiens sapiens* could also have replaced the supposedly modern-looking but much more ancient *Homo sapiens*, like those who lived at Klasies, Omo, and elsewhere in Africa about 100,000 years ago (Figure 4.8). Klein suggests that the mutation that accounted for the ability of these *Homo sapiens sapiens* to replace all other forms after 50,000 years ago may have been just an increased ability to conceptualize and communicate—as perhaps is

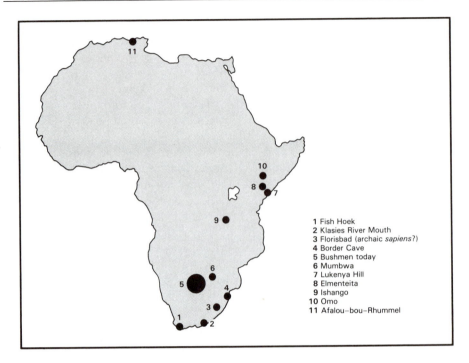

FIGURE 4.8   Early *Homo sapiens* sites in Africa. The dates of some sites are controversial. Most are thought to be between 120,000 and 60,000 B.P. 1, Fish Hoek; 2, Klasies River Mouth; 3, Florisbad (archaic *sapiens?*); 4, Border Cave; 5, Bushmen today; 6, Mumbwa; 7, Lukenya Hill; 8, Elmenteita; 9, Ishango; 10, Omo; 11, Afalou-bou-Rhummel.

evident in "art" and the standardized tools they used and the way they organized their daily activities. Such changes may have had no reflections in the shape or size of human skulls and only very subtle reflections in the ways tools were made, used, and discarded.

Is there any artifactual evidence in African sites after 100,000 or between 50,000 and 30,000, as Klein suggests, for "art" and other improved conceptual skills? Tantalizing bits of evidence have been produced, but the evidence, as always, is ambiguous. Allison Brooks and her group report that they have found sophisticated bone tools, including barbed points that may have been used to spear catfish in rivers in Zaire as early as 90,000 years ago.[71] Fishing in this way seems to have been a very late development in Europe, so one might consider this as some evidence in support of the idea that *Homo sapiens sapiens* evolved in Africa, and only in Africa. Perforated ostrich eggshell ornaments, bones, tools, and some forms of lithic artifacts have been found, but it is difficult to argue on the basis of this evidence that there is a clear reflection of greater cognitive powers than other humans outside of Africa at this time possessed.

Thus, the African evidence, in summary, is ambiguous. There are suggestions of a transition from archaic *Homo* to *Homo sapiens* at 100,000 years ago, but it is not certain that Africa is the *only* place this morphological change occurred, nor is there material evidence of some advantage that explains why Africans might have been able to drive into extinction all other hominids.

The Evidence from East Asia and Australia If the Total Replacement model is correct, at some point we should see a radical change in the human physical types who lived on this far periphery of early human adaptations. That is, the people who almost certainly were in Indonesia and adjacent regions by about 900,000 years ago, for example, would have been abruptly replaced by *Homo sapiens sapiens* of the African type after about 100,000 years ago (and possibly much later). Moreover, there should be no evidence here of hybridization of Africans and Asians, nor any patterns of continuity in the physical evolution of indigenous Asian humans towards modern *Homo sapiens sapiens*. We might also expect some evidence of replacement in the tools and other aspects of the archaeological record.

Consider first the farthest periphery of the Late Pleistocene Old World—Australia. There is now persuasive evidence that people arrived there at least by 50,000 years ago, and possibly by 60,000 years ago.[72] If the "total replacement" occurred at about 200,000 years ago, then these early Australians might be expected to show little physical similarity to Chinese and other Asians of the hundreds of thousands of years before this time, such as those at Zhoukoudian and Java, because the Australians would have migrated to Australia as much as 140,000 years after the replacement of the world's population began. If, as Klein suggests, however, the replacement occurred after 50,000, then these Australians may be a mix of early and later peoples, some of whom were closely related to Africans of this period.

Some anthropologists think that the east Asian fossil and archaeological record constitutes persuasive evidence for the rejection of the Total Replacement model. Pope, Wolpoff, Thorne,[73] and others see strong similarity between the early Australians and the Javanese, for example, and all of them as very distinct from Africans of the same age (i.e., circa 400,000 to 50,000 years ago). They focus on physical traits such as the "shovel" shape of the cross-sections of human incisors, which occurs in high frequency in Asian populations and much lower frequencies in Africans.[74] Frayer and his colleagues conclude that there is a very distinctive combination of facial and cranial features in Java, for example, and that this "unique combination of regional features . . . was stable for at least 700,000 years, while other characteristics continued evolving. The more recent Java remains have expanded brains that reached the modern range."[75] These patterns of anatomical continuity would be expected on the basis of the Multiregional Evolution/Continuity hypothesis.

Advocates of the Multiregional Evolution/Continuity hypothesis also see strong evidence of continuity in the physical forms of humans in northeast Asia, as well as gradual regional evolution here of modern human brain capacities. Crania from Zhoukoudian, Dali, Jinniushan, Yunxian, and fragmentary finds from elsewhere form the basic evidence here.

Advocates of the Total Replacement model disagree with these interpretations. Some have suggested that claims that early Asian humans show evolution toward "modern" *Homo sapiens sapiens* forms are based on a biased selection of only a few physical traits and inappropriate statistical manipulation of these data. They also stress the fragmentary and possibly biased record of fossils in Asia.

There is little evidence in the east Asian archaeological record of some obvious advantage in technology or other aspect of adaptation. From about 400,000 years ago onward, Asian stone tools show strong similarities, and some contrasts between Asian and African and European tools seem to go back far into prehistory. It is possible, of course, that invading Africans adopted the lithic technology of the groups they replaced, but this would seem unlikely.

In summary of the Asian evidence, scholars disagree entirely on the extent to which these data support the various hypotheses about human origins, and these debates turn on abstractions of statistical analyses of scarce and fragmentary human fossils. The stone tools of east Asia would seem to support the Multiregional Evolution/Continuity hypothesis in that east Asian forms seem to show similarity over hundreds of thousands of years as well as differences that distinguish them from those of other areas. But if replacement by Africans occurred in east Asia after 50,000 years ago, as Klein suggests, then the archaeological evidence becomes even more ambiguous. The few well-dated and excavated sites of this period show some minor indications of greater use of "style" in the form of pierced shells and other artifacts. That these changes represent an African invasion, however, is far from clear.

The Evidence from Western Asia and Europe   We know a great deal more about the prehistory of Europe and western Asia than of the rest of the world. One might optimistically think this fact would result in a much more uniform interpretation of this evidence, but in fact disagreements about the European and western Asian evidence are even more intense than those for Africa and east Asia.

About all scholars agree on is that: (1) there were humans living in Europe and western Asia by 500,000 years ago but they were not *Homo sapiens sapiens*; (2) a distinctive form of human, the "Neanderthals," who were different from us in important anatomical ways, lived in Europe, western Asia, and perhaps North Africa between about 100,000 and 40,000 years ago; and (3) by 30,000 years ago all the Neanderthals and other distinctive physical forms of humans, except ourselves, *Homo sapiens sapiens*, had disappeared.

To review this evidence requires discussion of a bewildering array of site names, fossil names, types of technologies, etc. To focus all these data and to make them coherent, one can consider again the kinds of evidence stipulated above as to be expected on the basis of the Total Replacement model. That is, do we see various kinds of evidence in the European fossil and archaeological record that Africans invaded western Asia and Europe at some point after about 200,000 years ago and drove the indigenous people in these areas into extinction by virtue of some advantage in intelligence, technology, etc.?

To set the stage for an examination of the evidence bearing on this question, we must go back to the beginning of human occupations in Europe and western Asia. As noted above, a few sites in the Middle East date, perhaps, to more than 500,000 years ago (e.g., 'Ubeidiya, in Israel), and some fragmentary finds of human bones and archaeological sites in Europe seem securely dated to before 500,000 years ago (see above). Who were the people who left these remains and are they related genetically to modern humans?

To begin with the physical types of hominids that made these transitions, Chris Stringer (and his colleagues) and Erik Trinkhaus have arranged most of the fossils between 500,000 and 30,000 into an order based on morphology.[76] Grade 1 hominids may be as old as 500,000 years, but dating these fossils has proved difficult in most cases. Some Grade 1 fossil specimens come from Europe. Trinkhaus notes that some of these have been classified as *Homo erectus* and others seem to have Neanderthal traits (see below), but as a group they seem to be consistent with a gradual change toward modern human forms (for example, increased size of the cranial vault and decreasing mean dimensions of molars).

In Europe these Grade 1 hominids are followed by a group that seems to fall between the grades, in that they are quite archaic in some characteristics but also resemble slightly the Neanderthals, who generally seem later in time than the Grade 1 group. A good example of these intermediate Grade 1-2 fossils is from Swanscombe, England, along the Thames River, not far from London. In 1935 workers in a cement plant uncovered a cranial bone from a gravel bank, and a year later another cranial fragment was found nearby that articulated perfectly with the first bone. Later, during excavations connected with preparations for the 1944 Allied invasion of France, another bone from the same skull was found just twenty-five meters from the site of the first find. It is very possible, incidentally, that more hominid bones were included in the gravel used to make concrete for floating docks during the D-Day operation.

In the same gravel layers that produced these bones, excavators recovered the bones of extinct forms of elephants, deer, rhinoceroses, and pigs which, together with subsequent chemical analysis and geological evidence, dated the Swanscombe fossils to an interglacial period about 225,000 years ago, when the abundance of horses, elephants, rhinoceroses, and other big-game species would have made England an ideal place for generalized hunting-and-gathering groups.[77] Nor is there any problem explaining how these hominids would have gotten there, since Britain and Ireland were physically joined to Europe by a land bridge at various times during the Pleistocene.

The Swanscombe cranial remains are probably those of a woman of twenty to twenty-five years of age, with a cranial capacity of about 1,325 cubic centimeters—well within the range of modern humans, but on the small side.[78] Hand-axes roughly similar to those of the Acheulian assemblages of France and Africa are among the most frequent tools in the level where the skull was found, but lower levels contain only flakes and choppers. Similar flakes and choppers have been found elsewhere in England and are commonly referred to as the Clactonian assemblage.[79] A wooden object that looks like the shaped end of a spear was found at Clacton and is the earliest wooden artifact recovered anywhere, dating to 400,000 to 200,000 years ago. Stone projectile points are not found at Swanscombe, Zhoukoudian, or any other site prior to about 150,000 years ago, and thus the wooden spear fragment—if that is what it was used for—may be a clue to how these Middle Pleistocene peoples managed to kill animals. If animals were trapped in bogs, they could have been killed by multiple stab wounds with wooden spears—although it could not have been pleasant work.

But there is the usual debate about hunting vs. scavenging: Lewis Binford's analyses of cut-marks and other features of the animal bones from Swanscombe led him to suggest that "the Swanscombe fauna represents hominid scavenging at the source of the carcass."[80]

The Swanscombe hominid is usually considered part of a biological group that includes a fossil from Steinheim, Germany. This cranium, dated to about 250,000 years ago, probably belonged to a young woman whose brain size and facial features place her between *Homo erectus* and ourselves. Unfortunately, no artifacts were found with the Steinheim skull, so we cannot compare the site with the material from southern England. Nonetheless, the physical differences between this individual and *Homo erectus* at least raise the possibility that the transition from *Homo erectus* to *Homo sapiens* was well underway by 300,000 to 250,000 years ago and was taking place in more than one part of western Europe.

Excavations in a cave site in the French Pyrenees unearthed a skull (the Arago skull) and two mandibles (Figure 4.9) dated to about 200,000 years ago that seemed to fill the gap between *Homo erectus* and the European Neanderthals.[81] The skull possesses some morphological characteristics of the east Asian *Homo erectus*, but lacks the incipient sagittal crest usually found in these populations. The large size of the teeth and mandible and the structure of the chin seem to foreshadow the features of the "classic" (western European) Neanderthal.

Late *Homo* remains have also been found at Bilzingsleben in eastern Germany, along with a somewhat atypical assemblage of very small tools with much larger implements, all quite different from the typical Acheulian assemblage. In fact, Svoboda

FIGURE 4.9 The Arago skull, from France. This approximately twenty-year-old man had more robust facial features than many Neanderthals and is probably intermediate between *Homo erectus* and *Homo sapiens*.

has argued that the many small tools found at Arago, Vértesszöllös, and Bilzingsleben developed out of adapting to cold, open landscapes and thus could be expected to be different from the tools used in more forested environments.[82]

In general, tool technology, diet, site locations, and average group size in Europe about 200,000 years ago do not seem much different from those of several hundred thousand years earlier, but clearly, population densities were increasing, and as people moved into more diverse niches there was an increasing variety in the stone tools associated with them.

Until recently these various early European *Homo sapiens* were viewed as representatives of the changes that eventuated in us, *Homo sapiens sapiens*, but recent evidence raises many questions about this interpretation. A key element in interpreting these archaic *Homo* fossils is the Neanderthals.

THE NEANDERTHALS

Nothing about the Neanderthals seems simple. Evidence suggests they lived between about 130,000 and 35,000 years ago, but their precise period in history is difficult to define. Most of them seemed to have lived in Europe and western Asia, some as far east as central Asia and in much of the Middle East, but some of their characteristic physical features seem to appear in fossil remains as far away as Africa and east Asia. The "Classic," or western, Neanderthals were different from us and from their contemporaries in Africa, east Asia, and Australia in various physical characteristics, but scholars disagree on the extent and significance of these differences. Some think the Neanderthals could speak with about as much fluency as we do, others think the Neanderthals did not have the mentality or vocal apparatus for normal human speech. Scholars disagree perhaps most heatedly about what "happened" to the Neanderthals: that is, are we descendants of the Neanderthals, or did they lose out in competition with our ancestors?

The fossil that gave this stage of human evolution its name was found in the Neander Valley in southwestern Germany in 1856, and because it belonged to the first pre-modern human identified, the Neanderthals received much of the initial hostility to the concept of human evolution (earlier Neanderthal finds were not recognized as such). From the beginning, anthropologists, clergy, and others held that the Neanderthals were an aberrant stage in human development, not directly related to our own—presumably superior—ancestors.

C. Loring Brace argued that the initial classification of Neanderthals as off the main line of our own evolution was rooted in the errors of nineteenth-century French paleontology.[83] The chief villain in Brace's history of Neanderthal studies is French paleontologist Marcellin Boule, who between 1911 and 1913 published studies that depicted the Neanderthals as bow-legged, slouching, simian-looking individuals who were neither very intelligent nor agile. He didn't actually state that Neanderthals couldn't walk and chew gum at the same time, or that they drooled incessantly, but Boule used the words "ape-like," "primitive," and "inferior" so frequently that neither he nor later scholars were anxious to claim Neanderthals as ancestors.

Before and after Boule's publications, however, some scholars suspected that the Neanderthals were the connecting link between *Homo erectus* and at least some populations of *Homo sapiens sapiens*. In 1957 a conference on the Neanderthal produced evidence that Neanderthal brain size on the average was larger than that of some modern human groups and that there were no grounds for concluding that their brains were structurally inferior or that they did not walk fully erect. In fact, it was suggested that "if he could be reincarnated and placed in a New York subway—provided that he were bathed, shaved, and dressed in modern clothing—it is doubtful he would attract any more attention than some of its other denizens."[84]

Yet there are differences between ourselves and the Neanderthals. The characteristics most frequently used to define them are: (1) a receding or virtually absent chin; (2) large cheekbones and prominent brow ridges curving over the eye orbits and connecting across the bridge of the nose; (3) prognathism (protruding lower face); (4) a strong masticatory apparatus, including larger front teeth than are found in most modern human populations; (5) short (average of perhaps 5 feet) but powerful stature, with thick and slightly curved long bones; and (6) a cranial capacity within the range of modern humans, though slightly larger on average for the classic "Western" type.

Erik Trinkhaus has shown how the shapes and sizes of Neanderthal teeth and heads vary in many obvious and also subtle ways from our own.[85] He interprets the projecting mid-face of the Neanderthals as a feature selected by natural selection in part "to facilitate the use of the anterior teeth as a vise."[86] Neanderthals would have had no problems with candied apples or corn on the cob, had they been available. They probably ate meat by the stuff-and-cut method common among contemporary Eskimos, stuffing their mouths and then cutting off the excess meat with a stone knife before chewing.

Based on their legs and lower bodies, Trinkhaus concluded that the overall impression of Neanderthal locomotor anatomy is "one of great strength, as with the upper limb, but also one adapted for endurance for prolonged locomotion over irregular terrain." Trinkhaus concludes that the anatomy of their legs "suggests that they spent a significant portion of their waking hours moving across the landscape . . . far more than did early modern humans."[87] The Neanderthals would have been a bit short to be good offensive football linemen, but they would have made superstar wrestlers or baseball catchers, given their tremendous arm strength (though their ability to grip the ball might have been less than ours).

The Neanderthals were adept stone toolmakers. Most of their tools belong to the Mousterian stone tool industry (named after the site of Le Moustier in southern France), which includes several distinctive stylistic and functional elements (Figure 4.10). The scores of Mousterian sites in the Dordogne region of southwestern France include cave sites, rock shelters, and "open-air" locations, and one of the largest and most complex Mousterian sites here is a cave in the Combe Grenal Valley, near the Dordogne River. Francois Bordes uncovered sixty-four superimposed occupational levels in this cave, spanning the period from about 85,000 to 45,000 years ago, with few long periods of abandonment. The lowest levels contained tools resembling the Acheulian tools found at Swanscombe, but all later levels had the classic Mousterian tools usually associated with Neanderthals. More than 19,000 Mousterian implements were collected and analyzed from this cave, and the tools from different levels con-

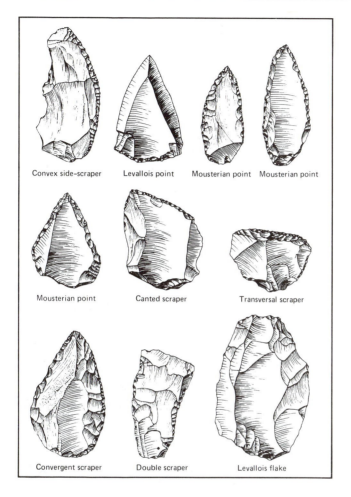

Convex side-scraper   Levallois point   Mousterian point   Mousterian point

Mousterian point   Canted scraper   Transversal scraper

Convergent scraper   Double scraper   Levallois flake

FIGURE 4.10   Some typical tool types of the Mousterian period. The Neanderthals made effective but not particularly elaborate stone tools for a variety of purposes.

trast sharply. Some levels contained many small flake-like pieces of stone, while others had concentrations of scores of "toothed" or "denticulated" tools. Moreover, analysis of the different levels revealed that certain types of tools tended to be spatially associated with a number of other types. That is, levels containing a relatively high number of projectile points would usually contain relatively large numbers of scrapers and flakes—but few denticulates.

This diversity of tools may seem relatively unimportant, but it was the focus of a long debate that involved issues fundamental to the development of the discipline of archaeology and to contemporary views of human origins. The specific case of the Mousterian tools became part of a larger question: How are we to measure and interpret variability in ancient artifacts? For the Mousterian tools, Francois Bordes spent years in excavation and analysis to establish a typology that has been the framework for much of the work done on this period. Bordes classified all Mousterian tools into four categories, based on the relative frequencies of certain types.[88] Bordes considered various explanations of the diversity of Neanderthal tools, such as that this variability reflected different time periods, climates, or seasons of the year. On the basis of the archaeological evidence, however, he rejected these possibilities and eventually concluded that the four different clusters of tools are the remains of four distinct cultural traditions, or "tribes," which developed certain kinds of tool manufacture and retained these distinctive expressions over the 30,000 years of the Mousterian period. Bordes's vision of the Mousterian was one in which different tribes of Neanderthals wandered much of the Old World for generation after generation, through tens of thousands of years, each group maintaining its unique styles of tool manufacture and meeting the others infrequently and usually with hostility.

This vision was questioned by Lewis and Sally Binford, who assumed that Mousterian tool variability was largely a reflection of the different tasks Neanderthals had to perform to meet successfully the demands of their environment.[89] They tried to test their interpretation by a statistical analysis of Mousterian tools from three widely separated sites: the Jabrud Rock Shelter near Damascus, Syria; Mugharet es-Shubbabiq Cave, in Israel; and an "open-air" station near Houpeville, France. Each site contained several different levels, representing different occupations; the total number for all three sites was sixteen. Lithics from each site were classified in terms of Bordes's system and statistically analyzed for evidence that these groups of tools were used for different economic activities, rather than simply representing stylistic traditions. Factor analysis was the statistical method used to determine which of the tool types were usually found in close proximity to one another in the various levels of the different sites. On this basis they defined several different "tool kits," whose presumed functions included tool preparation, wood-working, butchering, and various other tasks.

The Binfords' study stimulated interest in statistical analysis of archaeological data, and since that time many archaeologists have worked at developing statistical applications to archaeological data that would help create a truly scientific form of archaeology. But the exact nature of Neanderthal tool-making variability and subsistence has remained a matter of dispute. It seems highly likely that much of the variability in the tools is related to the specific functions they were used for, of course. But reconstructing these functions has involved many problems of interpretation. Even whether or not the Neanderthals were systematic hunters has been disputed. Binford concludes that regular hunting of mid- to large-size animals like deer and reindeer became an important part of human economies just prior to the appearance of *Homo sapiens sapiens*.[90]

Neanderthal Culture and Society   As if the slurs cast on Neanderthal intelligence and posture by early archaeologists were not enough, some anthropologists have questioned whether or not Neanderthals were able to produce the range of sounds necessary for normal human speech. P. Lieberman and E. Crelin reconstructed the vocal apparatus of Neanderthals using a computer simulation based on the measurement of a classic Neanderthal, and using the vocal tracts of chimpanzees and human infants for comparison, they concluded that western European Neanderthals would not have been able to make some vowels, such as *e*, and perhaps some labial and dental consonants, such as *b* and *d*.[91] Others doubt that the Neanderthals could speak at all. Frayer and Wolpoff[92] challenge the old idea that the size and shape of the hyoid bone and other Neanderthal anatomy are sufficiently different from that of modern humans to be used as evidence that the Neanderthals had any less linguistic ability than we do.

Archaeologists have long believed that, whatever their verbal fluency, the Neanderthals were at least human enough to bury their dead. Excavations at La Chapelle-aux-Saints, in France, revealed a Neanderthal corpse apparently laid out in a shallow trench, with a bison leg placed on his chest, and the trench filled in with bones, tools, and other debris—perhaps representing offerings of meat and implements. At La Ferrassie, France, a Neanderthal "cemetery" was found, where a man, a woman, two children, and two infants seem to have been buried. A flat stone slab was on the man's chest, the woman was in a flexed position, and, toward the back of the cave, the skull and skeleton of one of the children were buried in separate holes, about one meter apart. At Monte Cicero, in Italy, a Neanderthal skull—with a hole cut into the base—was placed in the middle of a circle of stones, but it is not at all certain that this skull is evidence of ritual cannibalism. At Teshik-Tash, in Siberia, a Neanderthal child was buried in a grave with goat skulls whose horns seemingly had been jabbed into the ground. At Shanidar Cave in Iraq, the soil near a Neanderthal's body contained massive quantities of flower pollen. Ralph Solecki, the excavator, and Arlette Leroi-Gourhan, the palynologist, concluded that the skeleton had been buried with garlands of flowers.

But in these and other cases the evidence is at least somewhat equivocal. Even in the best of circumstances, archaeological excavation is a messy, ambiguous business of judging the significance of faint changes in the texture and color of sediments, and the Neanderthal cave burials are notoriously difficult to excavate and interpret. Such caves have been homes not just to people but to hundreds of thousands of generations of cave bears, rodents, and other animals, and the natural processes of roof fall and sediment accumulation make for a confusing stratigraphic sequence. Thus, where one excavator may see a Neanderthal carefully buried in a pit with a rock slab placed on his chest, another may observe evidence of a Neanderthal who simply expired and was covered with rocks falling from the cave roof and by other debris. Thus some scholars see no evidence that any Neanderthals were intentionally buried, while others believe that the Neanderthals invested death with human-like emotion and ritual.[93] Richard Klein, for example, suggests that the Neanderthals did in fact bury their dead, but probably only as a matter of hygiene and without any or much ceremony.[94] Lawrence Straus concludes[95] that Neanderthal burial was a rare event, but he also makes the useful point that it is not at all clear than even *Homo sapiens sapiens* always buried their dead.

There is good evidence that Neanderthals were not insensitive to the plight of the handicapped. Some Neanderthals evidently suffered terribly from arthritis or had lost limbs and so could not have contributed much to the group's food supply. Yet, they must have been supported by the rest of their society. Despite these touching displays of societal concern, there is also some evidence that Neanderthals killed, butchered, and perhaps ate one another. At Krapina in Yugoslavia, excavations revealed twenty Neanderthals—men, women, and children—whose skulls and long bones had been smashed and split in suspicious ways. But Trinkhaus questions whether cannibalism was actually practiced.[96]

All Neanderthals were apparently hunters and gatherers, but they must have varied considerably throughout their range in the kinds of resources they exploited. The archaeological record is no doubt biased, because most Neanderthal sites found and excavated are those made evident by masses of animal bones associated with stone tools; the remains of plant foods and wooden tools, of course, do not preserve nearly so well and are not as easily found.

Neanderthal population densities appear to have been low, and it is likely that most Neanderthals lived with the same group of twenty-five or fifty people their whole lives, from time to time meeting other bands for mate exchanges. They were skilled hunters (Figure 4.11), locked into seasonal migrations with the animals they hunted, but in most habitats they probably foraged widely for eggs, birds, plants, and other small resources. They competed quite successfully with other predators for game (Figure 4.12), but must have occasionally lost out to the zoological carnival of horrors whose ranges they shared. Giant cave bears, saber-toothed cats, and wolves

FIGURE 4.11   Photo provided by John Yellen.

FIGURE 4.12 John Shea (1988) has shown that many pointed stone tools show the typical damage patterns of high speed impact, such as would be expected on spear tips. This fracture pattern is illustrated on this Levallois point from Hayonim Cave, Israel. Such evidence suggests that people in this area 50,000–100,000 years ago did considerable systematic big-game hunting.

occasionally "selected out" an unfortunate Neanderthal: "Some days you eat the bear, some days the bear eats you" was probably no empty cliché to them.

Trinkhaus[97] examined 40 nearly complete Neanderthal skeletons as well as bones from 166 other Neanderthals, from both Europe and the Middle East, and compared their estimated age at death to the age at death for a variety of other groups, including ethnographically observed groups like the Yanomamö hunter-gatherers of South America and the !Kung Bushmen of southern Africa, as well as archaeologically retrieved skeletons from North America, Japan, Mexico, and elsewhere. Noting all the biases and other problems in estimating time of death and other factors, Trinkhaus concluded that the Neanderthals experienced relatively high "young adult mortality"[98]—meaning that a higher percentage of Neanderthals died during their young adult years than did in these other groups. Trinkhaus suggests that these mortality patterns may be the result of various factors, including a relatively high level of adaptive stress. Almost all Neanderthals would have been required to have a high degree of mobility, except infants in arms.

Neanderthals and *Homo sapiens sapiens*   William Golding, in his novel *The Inheritors*, imagined a world of the past in which peaceful, egalitarian, vegetarian Neanderthals faced oblivion at the hands of villainous, meat-eating, beer-drinking *Homo sapiens sapiens*. This literary version of the Total Replacement model is studded with obvious symbolism intended to elevate this imaginary conflict into a statement about the human condition, but it is an interesting anthropological scenario as well, raising many questions. Throughout the ages, for example, humans have expressed a fine democratic and egalitarian spirit in few areas of life, but one of them—to some extent, at least—is in sexual congress: wherever different "races" have coexisted, they have immediately and continually interbred. Did the Neanderthals and other humans mate?

Such a question brings us back to the contrasting models of human origins presented in Figure 4.1. As these illustrations indicate, some scholars believe that no Neanderthal genes are represented in contemporary human populations, while others think that some or even a lot of Neanderthal genetic inheritance can be seen in contemporary European populations (Figure 4.13).

Who is right? We begin with the intriguing fact that the Neanderthals entirely "disappeared" as a physical type sometime after about 30,000 years ago. No Neanderthal bones have been found post-dating this time, and in some sites tool types widely believed to be associated with Neanderthals are overlain with levels containing tools different in style. The Neanderthals successfully lived over much of Europe and the Middle East for tens of thousands of years—why should they have vanished?

Two possible explanations for their disappearance are currently being considered seriously by anthropologists, and Michael Day summarizes these as follows.[99] The *Neanderthal Phase of Man* hypothesis places the Neanderthals between *Homo erectus* and modern humans as one of the direct ancestral forms of our line, and implies that people of European ancestry today are directly related genetically to the Neanderthals. Few hominid fossils from the period between 45,000 and 25,000 years ago in western Europe have been found, so we do not know much about what was happening to the physical form of these populations during this interval. C. L. Brace suggested that the improved efficiency of Mousterian tools greatly relaxed the selective pressures for a heavy masticatory apparatus, which is a primary difference between Neanderthal and modern skeletal material.[100] Most Neanderthal dentition shows evidence of extreme wear on the front teeth, so the process may have been only beginning in the early Mousterian period.

The major differences between Neanderthals and ourselves are in head and face shapes and sizes, but the Neanderthal skeleton, especially the limbs and hip bones, is also different in size and morphology from that of modern humans. The torsional strength of Neanderthal leg bones, for example, is about twice that of moderns.[101] Tools may have had a role in changing the selective pressures on the teeth, but how could tools or any other factor have altered the skeletal parts? At this point we simply don't know what selective forces might have caused such changes, or if they did. Some scholars, such as Fred Smith, maintain that the fossils from south and central European Neanderthals all exhibit morphological changes in the direction of modern hominids.[102]

The *PreNeanderthal* hypothesis suggests that "the Neanderthals arose from a Pre-Neanderthal stock that became progressively specialized for resisting cold, [and] underwent severe natural selection and restricted gene flow that led to 'classic' Neanderthal isolates."[103] According to this idea, the Neanderthals evolved their distinctive features as part of adapting to cold climates and had so little genetic connection to people living elsewhere in the world that they became distinctive. Eventually, however, they were absorbed or displaced by more modern-looking humans.

If the Neanderthals were entirely replaced by modern *Homo sapiens sapiens* moving out of Africa, it is possible that this extinction involved a *social* transformation, not just some slight difference in tool-making ability or other skill. Olga Soffer, for example, argues[104] that the Middle to Upper Paleolithic transition in Eurasia involved the appearance of modern human family structure and the division of labor by sex. She suggests that sites left by Neanderthals are small and do not show the clusters of distinct artifacts that we would expect if people in various age and sex groups were

FIGURE 4.13 One reconstruction of human origins. The split of the Neanderthals from the main human line remains controversial.

doing different tasks in an integrated extended family. She also notes that Neanderthal sites typically include mainly artifacts made in raw materials available locally, and she infers that they did not transport food over substantial distances. Perhaps most important, she sees no evidence of symbolic abilities, as might have been expressed in figures or other media. In contrast, Soffer suggests that modern *Homo sapiens sapiens* left sites that show substantial evidence of a society in which there was a clear division of labor by sex, and the kinds of clusterings of artifacts that reflect a functionally differentiated and integrated group. She suggests that groups of modern *Homo sapiens sapiens* in Europe moved in seasonal rhythms that were much more complex than those of the Neanderthals; transported raw materials, tools, and food in longer and more complex patterns of movement; expressed themselves symbolically to a much greater degree; and, in general, developed the sense of *kinship* that one finds as the basic organizing principle of all known hunter-forager groups. Soffer concludes that some of these differences between the Neanderthals and *Homo sapiens sapiens* are even evident in their bones: we would expect that as sexual division of labor developed, size and shape differences between males and females would be accentuated, because they would be facing somewhat different selective pressures; and Soffer considers both Neanderthal males and females to have been robustly built, under repeated stress, and to have suffered high rates of juvenile mortality, while *Homo sapiens sapiens* show more physical differences between the sexes and less stress and juvenile mortality.

These and other ideas about the relationship of Neanderthals to other early *Homo sapiens*, and the relationship of both to ourselves, still cannot be systematically and conclusively tested against the archaeological record because there are so many gaps and biases in this record. But recent discoveries have at least given a sounder empirical basis for some of these debates about the Neanderthals. A key site here is Qafzeh. Helene Valladas and her colleagues used thermoluminescence to date twenty burnt flint tools from Qafzeh, a cave near Nazareth, in Israel, in strata that contained the bones of a somewhat modern-looking *Homo sapiens*.[105] Other human remains have been found at Qafzeh and electron spin resonance dating was done on some of these.[106] Various scholars have concluded on the basis of this analysis that a primitive form of modern humans lived here 92,000 years ago, and perhaps earlier—but at least 30,000 years before Neanderthals inhabited this region. Valladas and her colleagues speculate that Neanderthals came into the Middle East about 60,000 years ago, perhaps migrating into the Mediterranean areas as glaciers expanded during the Pleistocene. Thus, if modern humans evolved in Africa long before they reached Qafzeh, as the DNA evidence might suggest, then the Qafzeh region might have been a contact area between Neanderthals and early modern humans—since the Neanderthals lived all over Europe 125,000 years ago.

The Qafzeh dates raise many questions. There is no molecular biological or genetic evidence that modern people originated in the Middle East, so it is presumed that any early modern *Homo sapiens sapiens* in this area would have descended from Africans or, much less likely, Europeans. As Erik Trinkhaus noted, if early modern humans reached the Middle East 92,000 years ago, they must have lived there in some relationship to the Neanderthals for tens of thousands of years, since Neanderthal remains in the Middle East dating to the period between 60,000 and 36,000 are well documented.[107]

The human remains from Qafzeh must be understood in the context of evidence from nearby sites, especially the cave sites of Skhul, Tabun, and Kebara. New dates from human remains at Skhul suggest some of the individuals may have lived there as early as 100,000 years ago, and other finds at Skhul and Tabun indicate repeated human occupations between about 60,000 and 40,000 years ago.

So, who were these people in Palestine between 100,000 and 40,000 years ago, and what do they have to do with us? Given the great disparity in time these fossils cover, the mixture of ages and sexes they include, and their fragmentary nature, it is not surprising that the genetic relationships of these people remains hotly debated. Some scholars see these people as a mixture of *Homo sapiens sapiens* and Neanderthals. Others group these fossils more closely to Neanderthals than to moderns but with some non-Neanderthal characteristics.

The point here is that advocates of the Total Replacement model see these remains as belonging to two different species, one (*Homo sapiens sapiens*) superior to the other (the Neanderthals) and in the process of replacing them, not mating with them. These scholars see "modern" elements in the crania of some of these hominids and very little overlap between these Palestinians and the Neanderthals in important elements of the post-cranial skeleton, such as the length of the pubis. But other scholars see these humans as belonging to the same general population and exhibiting anatomical variation that is "less, often considerably less, than normally found in a modern city."[108]

If the replacement of other humans by *Homo sapiens sapiens* occurred after 50,000 years ago, however, then the earliest "modern" *Homo sapiens* at Qafzeh could have been members of a population of archaic humans who were also replaced.

Given these ambiguities of interpretations of anatomy, what about the tools? Even the staunchest advocates of the original versions of the Total Replacement model have difficulty seeing an intrusive culture in the Palestinian artifacts. There seems to be great continuity in the kinds of tools made, the species of game hunted, and other aspects of culture.[109]

In some ways the eastern Mediterranean can be considered part of "Africa" during periods of the Pleistocene,[110] given its proximity and similarities of climate and ecology. We might expect, then, these kinds of ambiguities in interpretations of what happened in the eastern Mediterranean. But what about Europe?

Predictably, opinions vary. Some see the Neanderthals as an archaic form of human who made no significant contribution to ourselves; some believe that modern Europeans represent an admixture of African and Neanderthal genes;[111] and some see evidence in the Neanderthal fossil record of an evolution toward modern humans and believe that the Neanderthals became the modern humans of Europe through regional evolution and genic exchange with other populations outside Europe.[112]

The context of the debates about the validity of these various ideas goes back to what Harvey Bricker has called the "classical" model of the Upper Paleolithic.[113] This model had its origins when, in 1868, five very ancient-appearing human skeletons were found in a rock shelter during a road-widening project near Les Eyzies in southern France. The first Neanderthals had been discovered a few years before, and uneasy feelings about our descent from such barbaric-looking creatures had already begun to surface. But the bones from near Les Eyzies—named Cro-Magnon man after the rock shelter where they had been found—proved to be from individuals physically very much like modern Europeans. Here was an extremely ancient man, but of a race with which nineteenth-century Europeans could feel a strong sense of kinship and even pride. Average cranial capacity for these humans was over 1,500 cubic centimeters—larger than that of the Neanderthals and of that of the average reader of this book.[114] The discovery of these respectable ancestors stimulated great interest in prehistory, and amateur archaeologists soon began to pillage sites all over Europe.

French archaeologists initially defined the Upper Paleolithic into periods based on specific types of tools, such as "end-scrapers," "burins," and long blade-like tools, and various kinds of bone, antler, and ivory artifacts. Because these tools were not known in many areas, including Southeast Asia and sub-Saharan Africa, they concluded that these areas did not "have" an Upper Paleolithic, even suggesting that some of these areas were culturally "retarded." But subsequent research has shown a profusion of "Upper Paleolithic" technologies in many areas of the world, and recent archaeological discoveries have challenged the direct equation between types of stone tools and types of hominids. These equations between human types and stone tool types are important. Unlike the sequence of tools at, for example, Qafzeh (in Palestine) (Figure 4.14) and Zhoukoudian (in China), the European archaeological record *does* appear to show a relatively sudden change: at many sites levels of "Mousterian" tools dating to the period when Neanderthals were here do appear to be overlain with occupational debris containing substantially different stone tools and other remains that may or may not be the products of *Homo sapiens sapiens*.[115] But does this reflect replacement of one group by another?

Much of the debate on this topic has to do with debates about stone-tool technologies. The "Aurignacian" tool kit (Figure 4.15) has been found all over Europe and into the Middle East in sites dated to between about 40,000 to 30,000 years ago (some dates are outside this range).[116] To the specialist, these Aurignacian tools look completely different from the Mousterian tools traditionally associated with Neanderthals across this same area, Europe and the Middle East. Mousterian tools are primarily made of chert flakes, whereas Aurignacian tools include a lot of blades, bladelets, burins, and other distinctive tools. Often the people who made Mousterian tools and those who made the Aurignacian ones used the same sources of flint and they often hunted about the same range of animals, but these two stone-tool industries are made in very different ways and in radically different shapes. There is no evidence that the Mousterian tools were gradually developed into Aurignacian ones—in many sites Aurignacian assemblages lie directly on top of levels containing Mousterian tools. And only the very latest Aurignacian tools have been found with modern *Homo sapiens sapiens*, so we must keep open the possibility that the earliest Aurignacian may be associated with Neanderthals.

Recently, Straus's analysis of the results of intensely dating many Spanish Aurignacian sites with both radiocarbon and uranium-series dates, and comparing them with those from Europe and the Middle East, revealed that "[f]ew if any other European Aurignacian assemblages have been reliably shown to be as old as the Span-

FIGURE 4.14 Early *Homo sapiens* in Asia. Most of these sites are estimated to be between 100,000 and 50,000 years old.

ish ones."[117] "So what?" one might ask. The answer is that this pattern of dates may conflict with the idea that the Neanderthals were driven into extinction by people who radiated out of Africa and abruptly replaced Neanderthals by virtue of a superior technology—as might be represented by the Aurignacian tool kit. If that scenario were accurate, we would expect the Spanish Aurignacian sites to be the youngest, not the oldest, because presumably the modern *Homo sapiens sapiens* coming out of Africa arrived first in the Middle East, after which generations of their descendants and their descendants' descendants moved through eastern Europe, and only eventually into southwestern-most Europe, Spain. Alternatively, if people came out of Africa across the Straits of Gibraltar and arrived in Europe first in Spain, we would expect many Upper Paleolithic sites in southern Spain, and there are virtually none. As Straus notes, "[g]iven the present chronometric situation, it would be necessary for such a migration to have taken place virtually instantaneously to account for the Spanish dates. No possible migration patterns can be confidently reconstructed on the basis of the available chronometric dates for early Aurignacian sites."[118]

FIGURE 4.15 European toolkits, 35,000 – 11,000 years ago. The increasingly diversified economies of the late Pleistocene are reflected in increasingly diverse and sophisticated tools kits compared to earlier periods. (Not drawn to scale).

Another key site in these debates about the relationship of the Neanderthals to ourselves is in France at Saint-Cesaire. Human occupations here date to about 36,000 years ago—precisely the period when Neanderthals were disappearing from the archaeological record. The problem is that, while the tools found at this site appear to be Upper Paleolithic in their stylistic and functional attributes, the human body found with them appears to some scholars to be a Neanderthal. Some scholars have analyzed the anatomy of this fossil human and found it to be a "transitional" form that shows the evolution of the Neanderthals into modern humans. Other scholars conclude that it is a Neanderthal and cannot be "transitional" because fully modern humans are well-known elsewhere at this period.[119] As Trinkhaus notes:

> If the Chatelperronian industry was produced solely by Neanderthals and all the Aurignacian assemblages were the products of early modern humans . . . then there must have been temporal overlap of these two human groups in western Europe, given the contemporaneity and interstratification of Chatelperronian and early Aurignacian as-

semblages. . . . Even if a direct biological-industrial association cannot be assumed, it is still evident that Neanderthals were present in western Europe less than [35,000 years ago] and that early modern humans were present there by at least [30,000 years ago].[120]

The significance of this is that 5,000 years is a very short time for the physical changes observed between Neanderthals and modern humans to have occurred. The oldest artifacts associated with modern humans in Europe belong to the Aurignacian period. The lowest levels in which Aurignacian-style tools were found at Abric Romanî], in Spain, yielded radiocarbon dates of about 37,000 years ago, but uranium series dates put this site at about 40,000 years ago, and it shows an "abrupt" replacement of earlier levels containing Mousterian remains.[121]

But other anthropologists suggest that the Neanderthals were simply evolving into modern humans and that the association of Upper Paleolithic tools with the later forms of Neanderthals is exactly what one would expect if this regional evolution process took place, even if there continued to be gene flow into Europe from outside. Fred Smith, for example, sees clear signs of reduction over time in the size of the brow-ridges of Neanderthals at Krapina and Vindija in Yugoslavia, and at other central European sites.[122]

In looking at this problem of the disappearance of the Neanderthals as it applies to the archaeological record of Spain, Larry Straus[123] found difficulties in matching the archaeological record to the premise that modern humans radiating from Africa abruptly replaced Neanderthals in this area.

Some scholars have focused on stature and body proportions in debates about the relationship of Neanderthals to us. The European Cro-Magnon after 30,000 years ago appears to have, on average, much longer limbs than did the Neanderthals. Relatively long limbs are associated with adaptations to heat (as with the Dinka of East Africa today), whereas short limbs are associated with cold adaptation, such as in Eskimos and other north Asians. But it is difficult to make direct equations between stature and height, given that "culture," in the form of clothes, fire, etc., modify the direct effects of climate. Still, there are many puzzling bits of evidence. The tallest of the post-Neanderthal Pleistocene Europeans seem to appear just before 20,000 years ago, in the coldest period of the Pleistocene, when we might have expected natural selection to favor a shorter, stockier body type; and then later, in warmer periods, stature seems to have declined—again, the opposite of what we might expect.[124] Stature is so directly related to diet and other factors, however, that we should not expect to see a clear correlation between it and temperature in every case—except in the long term, and even then the relationship is likely to be modified by migrations, differences in technology and economy, etc.

The small sample sizes of post-cranial skeletons in Europe and Africa make systematic statistical comparison of stature and limb ratios difficult, and the evidence is made even more complex by the presumed great variations in nutrition and adaptations to micro-climates.

Models of Modern Human Origins: Summary   The most recent academic debates about models of modern human origins[125] reveal profoundly different conclusions, with scholars disputing everything from the size and shape of particular characteristics of specific fossil skulls to the nature of basic evolutionary processes.

It may be that these disputes are never resolved to everyone's satisfaction on the basis of evidence. In the face of these ambiguities, Francis Thackeray suggests we consider the probability that:

> All modern humans can trace their origin to descendants of *Homo erectus*, but both the ancestral populations of *H. erectus* and the descendant populations of *H. sapiens* have expanded and contracted in response to many climatic and habitat changes, with the result that the very concept of "origin" in the context of gene pools can never be precisely determined; continuity occurred in some areas, replacement occurred in other regions, but the net effect was a very high degree of morphological variability within the single species which we today refer to as *H. sapiens*.[126]

LIFE, ART, AND RITUAL IN THE UPPER PALEOLITHIC

Writing about art is like dancing about architecture.

Anonymous

In 1868, near the Spanish port of Santander, so the story goes, a hunter's dog fell into a crevice in some boulders, and in rescuing the animal the hunter moved some rocks, revealing the opening of a cave. The owner of the land on which the cave (known as Altamira) was located, a Spanish nobleman and amateur archaeologist, eventually began to excavate the cave floor. He found some stone artifacts, but, according to the story, was unaware of the paintings in the cave until his twelve-year-old daughter visited the site and glanced at the ceiling. In the glow of her lantern she saw beautiful visions of animals. The central painting is of a group of about twenty-five animals, mainly bison, with a few horses, deer, wolves, and boars. Roughly life-size, these paintings were done in rich browns, yellows, reds, and blacks, and the natural configuration of the cave ceiling had been used to emphasize the shape of the animals. The rounded haunch of a bison, for example, was painted over a natural bulge in the stone ceiling, creating a three-dimensional effect.[127]

Scholarly reception to the Altamira discoveries was almost uniformly negative. Some respected prehistorians even hinted that Don Marcelino, their discoverer, had hired an art student to fake these paintings, while another scholar dismissed them as simply the expression "of a mediocre student of the modern school." So abused by critics was the Don that eventually he padlocked the cave, and he died in 1888 without having seen his discoveries accepted as true Paleolithic expressions. Years later, when many more paintings and other art works had been discovered, Altamira's antiquity was finally acknowledged, and most of these paintings are now given dates between about 34,000 and 12,000 years ago. Analysis shows that the colors were produced by mixing natural mineral pigments, such as ocher and manganese dioxide, with a binder (blood, urine, vegetable juice, or something similar), and that they were either brushed on with an implement made of animal hair or applied by making a kind of crayon from the pigments and lubricant. Some painting may also have been done by using a pipe to blow the powdered pigments on a surface prepared with animal fat. Many of these paintings were executed in the dark recesses of caves, by light provided by lamps made of stone bowls filled with animal fat, with a wick made of lichens, grass, or juniper.[128]

During World War II, paintings on a scale comparable to those of Altamira were discovered at Lascaux Cave, in France. Researchers estimate that the Lascaux paintings date to about 15,000 B.C. but were done on many different occasions and perhaps over a much longer span. Many varieties of animals are depicted here, including some one hopes were imaginary. The animals are often painted as if they are in motion, and the general effect is very impressive (Figure 4.16). One of the many curious things about these and other Upper Paleolithic cave paintings is that while the animals are depicted in very real, very representational terms, the figures of humans are either simple stick drawings or else weird half-humans, half-animals.

Since the Altamira and Lascaux discoveries, rock carvings, paintings, and other Paleolithic representations have been found all over the world, and many scholars have tried to assess what these pictures and paintings mean (Figure 4.17). We must accept at the onset that we can never really know the thoughts of these long-dead Paleolithic artists. The same might be said of Vincent Van Gogh or any other artist,

FIGURE 4.16   Paleolithic cave art may have been drawn to increase the chances of success in hunting, or simply as an expression of aesthetic sensibility, but whatever its purpose, it is superb art.

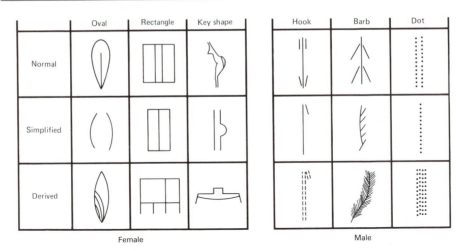

FIGURE 4.17   Many cave paintings include realistic depictions of sexual organs, and some scholars interpret some abstract cave paintings as stylized sexual representations. Leroi-Gourhan here illustrates three groups of symbols for each sex in normal, simplified, and derived forms.

of course, given that aesthetic expressions can never be fully, rationally comprehended, even by the artist. But neither Van Gogh's work nor Paleolithic art can be expected to be random with regard to theme, technique, or style. Art can be expected to tell us something about the artist. And in any case, there is something profoundly unsatisfying about analyses of ancient peoples based only on stone tools, hut foundations, and other techno-environmental residues. Most people, including archaeologists, wish to know the "minds" of ancient peoples, and in few ways do these seem so accessible as in their art.

People apply the term Paleolithic art to a great range of materials, including cave paintings, rock carvings, sculpted and carved animal bones, ivory statuettes, and baked clay objects. As Margaret Conkey noted,[129] one should probably not imagine that all these expressions were fundamentally aesthetic in nature, in the sense that we think of aesthetics as removed from economic function. An early interpretation of the great cave paintings was that they were expressions of sympathetic magic, done to ensure success in hunting and other activities. By picturing animals with spears stuck in them or caught in traps, Upper Paleolithic people may have thought they increased their chances of killing and trapping these animals. Many of the paintings are in small, hidden passages where working conditions were very cramped, suggesting that these pictures were not created for the pleasure of the general viewing public. Then again, many paintings are superimposed on one, two, or even more older ones, indicating perhaps that these efforts were ritual in nature, not simply artistic. And it may be significant that animals most likely to be feared in hunting, such as mammoths, are portrayed more frequently than less dangerous prey.[130] In fact, the most common themes of these Upper Paleolithic artists were food and sex, with food receiving most of the attention.

The disemboweled bulls, prancing deer, and other hunting scenes, plus the popularity of the penis and vulva motifs, suggest to some that these earliest of Spanish and French impressionists were men. But recently Elizabeth Fisher has argued that students of cave art have concealed the high frequency of female sex organs represented and thus the implication that many of the artists were probably women.[131] Line markings that some archaeologists have considered calendrical devices, Fisher thinks may be records of menstrual periods. It would not be surprising, however, if the many incisings and markings that one finds on Upper Paleolithic artifacts and in caves are in fact calendrical or astronomical in nature.[132] A Pleistocene hunting and gathering group surprised by the onset of winter or the seasonal unavailability of plants and animals would not only have been invincibly stupid, it would have been in deep trouble.

These economic interpretations of Paleolithic art were challenged by Andre Leroi-Gourhan, who plotted the relative frequencies of lions, mammoths, bison, reindeer, and other animals in caves with many such representations; he concluded that these paintings were invested with cosmological significance—reflecting in various ways the patterns in which Paleolithic peoples ordered their world.[133]

In recent years various alternative explanations of Paleolithic art have been suggested. Lewis-Williams and Dowson have argued that much of Paleolithic art was the product of people in "entopic," or altered, states of consciousness—either through drugs or meditation.[134] They note that ethnographic studies of contemporary hunter-gatherers show wide use of hallucinogens, trances, and such altered states to produce paintings and carvings. They also argue that it seems a feature of human neuroanatomy that images perceived in altered states of consciousness include both "real" representational forms and fantastic non-representational forms, and that people tend to project these images on walls and ceilings in their minds. Thus, "Tracing projected mental images with a finger in the sand or on the soft wall of a cave to experience them more fully would have 'fixed' them and would have been an initial step in the history of art. They were merely touching them and marking *what was already there.*"[135]

Others have argued that the florescence of Paleolithic art was a result of the maturing mentalities of our ancestors, as they replaced the less-intelligent Neanderthals.[136]

The study of Paleolithic visual imagery and art is a demonstration of a point made well by Hodder, that archaeology is not necessarily a neutral discipline in which analyses are scientific and culture-free.[137] Paleolithic art has often been a "Rorschach test," in the sense that modern-day observers have tried to read into it the mind and spirit of primitive humans, but they perhaps have learned more about their own psyches than about the primitives'. In any case, as Conkey notes, " 'paleolithic art' [is] an extremely diverse and abundant repertoire of material culture that cannot be accounted for by any inclusive umbrella except perhaps as 'cultural.' "[138]

Yet John Halverson argues that "*If,* as I suppose, Paleolithic art had no practical function, it may be the first cultural work of mankind to be freed from praxis and therefore belongs in the general category of play and in the specific category of play of the mind."[139]

If we compare western European art to that elsewhere in the world in the late Pleistocene, we see some sharp differences. There is an almost complete absence of two-dimensional figurative art in Asia at this time—most of it is three-dimensional, such as figurines.[140]

Randall White has summarized these many interpretations of not only the cave paintings but of other apparently aesthetically important objects in the transition from the Middle to the Upper Paleolithic and concluded that:

> It is likely that in this complex [amalgam] of technological innovation, increasingly strained human/land relationships, and the emergence of an internally and externally differentiated sociopolitical world is to be found the reason that material representation came to be valued by people of the Aurignacian and all of their descendants in the Upper Paleolithic and beyond.[141]

HUMAN COLONIZATION OF THE WORLD: C. 20,000 TO 10,000 YEARS AGO

> *One main factor in the upward trend of animal life has been the power of wandering.*
>
> Alfred North Whitehead

Unless the earth is truly different from every other known celestial body, any humans left on this lovely green-blue world in a few billion years will be converted to their component atoms—along with the pyramids of Egypt, the Great Wall of China, and all other human artifacts and natural features—and compressed to a density such that they will spend eternity as elements of a lightless, timeless "black hole."

Given our human history, however, we can anticipate that our descendants will have long since colonized other worlds when that fateful day comes. However tenuous our links to these distant successors may become, some portion of "us" may reverberate through space and time forever.

"In our beginning is our end," perhaps. For our ancestors have always moved, always wandered, always colonized. Generation after generation, our ancestors left Africa, probed Europe and Asia, settled the Americas, Australia, the farthest ends of the planet (Figure 4.18). Many of the readers of this book can expect to see human colonies on the moon and perhaps beyond in their lifetimes. And anyone with a computer and a bit of math can estimate how long it might take us to move on from there. Exponential functions are impressive aspects of our universe. In time a single mutated virus turns into uncountable billions and disperses throughout a system. We may not like the analogy, but we may "infect" the universe in the same way.

There are no certainties, of course. The Big Bang may be followed by the Big Crunch, and then who knows what assortment of atoms will persist, perhaps evolve?

All this may seem far from the sturdy human hunter-foragers of the past hundred thousand years, but we are linked to them by the long-term growth functions of which we are all a part.

In various chapters of this book the focus is a major question about a particular human development: Why did culture evolve, how did *Homo sapiens sapiens* emerge

FIGURE 4.18 After the end of the Pleistocene about 12,000 years ago, hunter-gatherers spread into almost all of the world's environments and adapted to local environments. These remains of East African (Somalia) burials date to between about 8100 and 5400 B.P. and are some of the earliest known African examples of burials with grave goods—in this case, skulls of the lesser kudu.

as the only remaining hominids? In this chapter, however, we simply consider the spread of our ancestors across the world. If we ask "why" they colonized the world, we are left with the "because it's there" kind of answer Sir Edmund Hillary gave when asked why he climbed Mt. Everest. Simple demographic models suggest that any population will colonize appropriate environments through growth and migration, and our own ancestors' travels seem adequately "explained" by such formulations. But it is also hard to deny a human "instinct" for travel, an inherent desire to see what's beyond the next hill or valley. Also, as we have noted in previous chapters, maintaining genetic variability through genic exchange confers great advantages in terms of long-term survival.

Scholars have long debated whether the "incest taboo" found in many cultures is biologically based or just a culturally developed psychological construct, but it seems clear that marriages between people related at the degree of first cousin or closer produce a horrific cost in genetically determined death and retardation. Natural selection has no way of "knowing" that migration and dispersal of any species, ourselves included, is "good," but from some perspectives it certainly is.

Thus, if there is in fact an instinctive human urge to travel, it would be "adaptive" in an evolutionary sense, for long-term evolutionary success comes with dispersal and variation. Our ancestors accomplished both: they penetrated almost all of the world before the end of the Pleistocene, and although they remained a single species, they developed great variety in their physical forms and cultural adaptations.

On the one hand, the superficial variations our ancestors acquired as they colonized the world are the most trivial in all of human evolution; on the other hand, these differences of skin color, facial features, and other characteristics, and the cultural differences that accompanied them, are of the greatest socioeconomic and political importance in today's world—for human variations are inextricably linked to the idea of "race." Despite the rejection of this concept by many scholars, the concept of "race" is likely to remain with us until gene flow is sufficient that obvious differences in physical appearance all but disappear—for many decades, if not centuries, in other words. Most anthropologists do not like the concept of "race" because, aside from the negative social problems associated with it, the characteristics used by most people to define race appear to be superficial, to be crude typologies imposed on a multi-dimensional underlying variability, and to be poorly correlated in some ways with underlying genetic relationships of various groups.[142] "Black" skin tones, for example, are shared by Australian Aborigines and west Africans—two groups of people whose degree of genetic relatedness may be much less than that between west Africans and Scandinavians. Physical features such as skin tones, degree of hair follicle "curl," nose shape and eyelid shape, etc., tend to fall on geographic clines—that is, they exhibit variation over space and through time that is continuous, not discrete. And often variations within groups ("polymorphism") is greater than that between groups ("polytypy").[143]

For good or ill, however, the migrations and radiations of our ancestors over the past 30,000 years have produced or continued group differences that remain an important part of today's cultural world.

In this chapter we surveyed the world at the end of the Pleistocene and into the current geological period, the "Holocene." Only time will tell whether or not our own era, the past 10,000 years, is just another short-term interglacial period, before the glaciers crunch their way down into our world again—or whether it's a period in which our own smog, pollution, and other filth so contaminate the world that the stately cycle of cold and warm will be disrupted for the long term.

LATE PLEISTOCENE CLIMATES AND GEOGRAPHY

If we were ever fortunate enough to find people of about 30,000 years ago well-preserved in some glacier, we would probably see few differences between them and us. Over much of the world human teeth have become smaller during the past 30,000 years and some subtle changes in other aspects of our form and physiology have occurred, but not much else about us physically is different from the people of 30,000 years ago. Human brain size was slightly larger for some of the people at that time, but it is unlikely that they were of a fundamentally different mentality.

By 30,000 years ago people were living in almost every part of the Old World, and in Australia; their arrival in the Americas was certainly before 12,000 years ago, but the evidence for earlier occupations (see below) is controversial.

Oscillating sea levels had some role in this dispersal, since in some periods land bridges allowed people to walk from Southeast Asia to many areas that are now islands, such as Java, Sumatra, and Borneo. Rising sea levels may also have forced people into migrations, even though the rates at which these levels rose were likely slow enough that no single individual had a personal sense of them. Thiel argues that people on islands in danger of being submerged by rising waters made the colonizing trips to Australia 50,000 or more years ago.[144] Elsewhere, people had to abandon many other low-lying areas, such as the shores of the eastern Mediterranean and the broad plains that now lie under the English Channel.

These climatic alterations and ensuing changes in geography and ecology can be thought of as giant engines, acting to mix and move human populations, offering adaptational challenges that elicited human ingenuity in various forms. But people were never simple passive victims of climatic and ecological happenstance: humans not only developed the technology to make a living in the vast span of the world, but also evolved the social systems that were an indispensable part of this adaptation.

Late Pleistocene Europeans

Between about 30,000 and 10,000 years ago, European climates began a long cooling trend with some periods of extreme cold, but for most of the period the summers were cool and the winters relatively mild. The rich European grasslands and mixed forest habitats supported great numbers of herbivores, including reindeer, deer, bison, wild ox, ibex, woolly rhinoceros, and mammoths. France seems to have been densely occupied during this period, particularly near the confluence of the Dordogne and Vezere rivers. This lovely part of the world is a well-watered, heavily forested limestone formation, honeycombed with caves and rock shelters, which offered excellent places to live. Mammoths, horses, and many other animals were hunted by these Upper Paleolithic peoples, but the reindeer was the staff of life: at many sites 99 percent of all the animal bones found belonged to reindeer; reindeer hides provided clothing and coverings for shelters; reindeer antlers were the hammers, or the "batons," used to produce the long elegant blades for which these people are justly famous; and reindeer bone was the raw material for fish gorges, needles, awls, and other important tools.

Reindeer travel long distances each year as they follow the grazing lands from one climatic zone to another. Thus, through the reindeer herds Upper Paleolithic peoples of southern France could exploit land they had never seen; the reindeer would browse their way to the far north each year and then return to southern France for the winter, at which time they could be harvested.

Average human group size may have been relatively large during the Upper Paleolithic in Europe, the Middle East, and other areas because of the requirements of hunting large gregarious mammals such as reindeer, bison, horses, and wild cattle. With some of these species, an efficient hunting technique is the drive, where many people work together to stampede a herd over a cliff or into a bog. Such mass slaughter also requires many people to process the carcasses, and a large group would also have been advantageous in these circumstances as a means of defending particularly favorable places along the animals' migration routes.

The overall population also increased in some parts of Europe—and probably much of Eurasia—during the last millennia of the Pleistocene. Several factors were probably important in this population growth. The stone tool technology of this period, with its indirect percussion and punch-blade techniques, was vastly more efficient than previous industries. Spear throwers, or atlatls, were also in common use—a very significant innovation considering the heavy reliance on big game, since an atlatl can increase the range of a short spear from about 60 meters, if thrown by hand, to about 150 meters. Eventually, the bow and arrow also added significantly to hunting effectiveness. Some of the earliest evidence of bows and arrows comes from the Stellmoor site, near Hamburg, Germany, where about a hundred wooden arrows dating to approximately 10,000 B.P. were recovered. But the bow-arrow combination was probably invented independently many times and perhaps long before 10,000 years ago.

Life in the Upper Paleolithic was somewhat more severe than one might imagine. From a sample of seventy-six Upper Paleolithic skeletons drawn from sites in Europe and Asia, Vallois found that less than half of these individuals had reached the age of twenty-one, that only 12 percent were over forty, and that not a single female had reached the age of thirty.[145] In fact, the distribution of ages and sexes represented by these skeletons was not significantly different from what one might expect from a comparable sample of Neanderthals.[146] But even worse, many skeletons evidenced rickets, malnutrition, and other diseases and deformities. Not content with nature's provisions for population control, Upper Paleolithic peoples seem also to have occasionally slaughtered each other. At the site of Sandalja II (12,000 B.P.), near Pula, Yugoslavia, for example, the skeletal remains of twenty-nine people were found in a smashed and splintered condition. Elsewhere, there is unmistakable evidence of wounds from arrows and spears.

By about 14,000 years ago, the people of western Europe had developed fish traps to harvest the countless salmon that migrated up the rivers there each year. This relatively late exploitation of fish in Europe has a parallel in prehistoric southeastern North America, where Native Americans lived for thousands of years subsisting primarily on deer, mussels, and a variety of plant foods, almost totally ignoring the myriad fish in nearby lakes and streams. If salmon were present in great numbers in European rivers during the Mousterian and early Upper Paleolithic, their exploitation may have been blocked by the terms of human adaptation to reindeer and other animals. Reindeer and other game would have been a more dependable resource for humans, in the sense that at least some of these animals would have been available year-round, while the salmon would have been sharply seasonal. Salmon runs, in fact, might have conflicted with the scheduling of reindeer hunting, and as a consequence these peoples may have been far from the river, exploiting different resources, at the time the salmon were most available. Perhaps even more important, the successful exploitation of salmon would have required technological readaptation on a major scale. Catching salmon one by one would not have been especially productive: their real utility probably came only after nets, fish weirs, drying racks, smoking racks, and other largely non-portable technology came into common use.

The slow growth of world-wide human population density through most of the Pleistocene would seem to suggest that Upper Paleolithic populations were not in any sense "driven" by population pressures to exploit new resources, such as reindeer and salmon. Rather, it seems the reverse: as people began to devise ways to exploit rich salmon streams, reindeer herds, and other resources, larger groups could be supported. And just a slight increase in fertility or the number of offspring who lived on the average to reproductive age would in the long run produce vastly greater population densities.

And it was not just in France and the ecologically richer parts of Europe that populations were growing in the late Pleistocene. Olga Soffer has documented, for example, the ingenuity of generations of peoples as they adapted to the harsh winters of the central Russian Plain.[147] One of the most amply documented Upper Paleolithic cultures in eastern Europe is the Kostenki-Bershevo culture centered in the Don River Valley, about 470 kilometers southeast of Moscow. About 25,000 to 11,000 years ago, the Kostenki-Bershevo area was an open grassland environment, with no rock shelters, caves, or other natural habitations, and with very little wood available for fires. People here left a variety of archaeological sites, including base camps, where pit houses were constructed by digging a pit a meter or so deep, ringing the excavation with mammoth bones or tusks, and then draping hides over these supports (Figure 4.19). The savage winters of Pleistocene Russia must have required constantly burning fires, and the great quantities of bone ash found at these sites indicate that these fires were often fed with mammoth bones in lieu of very scarce wood. Some excavated pit houses were relatively large, with many hearths, suggesting that several families may have passed the winter together. The people of Kostenki subsisted primarily through big-game hunting, mainly of mammoths or horses, with an occasional wild cow or reindeer. Numerous wolf and fox bones at these sites probably reflect the hunting of these animals for their fur for clothing. Like their Upper Paleolithic counterparts elsewhere, the Kostenki people manufactured a variety of decorative items, including "Venus" figurines (representations of women, usually with exaggerated secondary sexual characterists) (Figure 4.20).

Throughout much of central and eastern Europe, big-game hunting was the main subsistence basis for thousands of hunting and gathering bands, much as it had been for tens of thousands of years.[148] But the mammoth hunters of central and eastern Europe probably did not aggregate into relatively large groups, as the people in western Europe and the Middle East at this time are thought to have done. Mammoths probably were not as gregarious as reindeer, horses, or wild cattle, and their hunting may have required only a few men working together.

FIGURE 4.19 The reconstruction of a 27,000-year-old settlement at Dolni Vestonice illustrates how people used shelters to colonize the frigid plains of eastern Europe.

Late Pleistocene Asians

Until recently, few Upper Paleolithic sites were known in East Asia. Excavations at Zhoukoudian revealed levels dating to about 10,000 years ago containing approximately seven individuals—all of whom had been killed, but apparently not eaten. One individual had clearly died from an arrow or small spear wound to the skull, and another had been beaten about the head with a large stone. Elsewhere, two skulls have been retrieved from Wadjah, in central Java, but dating these has proved difficult.

Hundreds of late Pleistocene sites have been found in Japan. Dating these sites is difficult, but the classic European Upper Paleolithic blade and burin industries are well represented in Japan, particularly in the northern areas across from Siberia.

The earliest known stone tools from Southeast Asia may be those of the Sonvian assemblage from northern Vietnam, dating to about 23,000 B.P.,[149] but the Hoabinihian lithics of about 12,000 years ago are the earliest *widespread* Upper Paleolithic lithic industry in this area.

One of the most intriguing problems in Asian prehistory is the initial colonization of Australia. One has to imagine that people who were living in a world in which the Neanderthals still had 30,000 years of domination of Europe left somehow managed to float, sail, or swim to Australia. The geology seems to admit no other possibilities, because even with the most extreme estimates of the extent to which Pleistocene glaciers lowered world-wide sea levels, people could not have got to Australia except over some very deep water. Nor is swimming a realistic possibility. Probably thousands of coastal fisherfolk were washed out to sea and drowned in many millennia of typhoons and floods, before some fortunate castaways finally made it to Australia.

In any case, between 60,000 and 30,000 years ago, the ancestors of the Australian Aborigines somehow managed to cross at least a few kilometers of open ocean to reach Australia. And while it is possible that an occasional boat of fisherfolk was shipwrecked on the New Guinea-Australia coast, computer simulations that take into account normal fertility rates and the genetic diversity of modern populations suggest that more than just a boatload or two of colonists founded that area's present aboriginal population.[150] Two distinct groups of ancient people have been found there,[151] which scholars believe indicate colonization by two different groups, one a more robust type, by 50,000 years ago, the other, a more gracile people, before 20,000 years ago. Like their contemporaries in America, the late Pleistocene Australians lived at a time when many large and small animal species were becoming extinct, and their possible role in this extinction pattern remains a matter of controversy.

The Australian Aborigines offer a wonderful subject for meditations on the nature of humanity. Consider: these people lived in what may have been nearly com-

FIGURE 4.20 Cast of Venus figurine from Willendorf, Austria. Late Pleistocene peoples appear to have celebrated human fertility in much of their art.

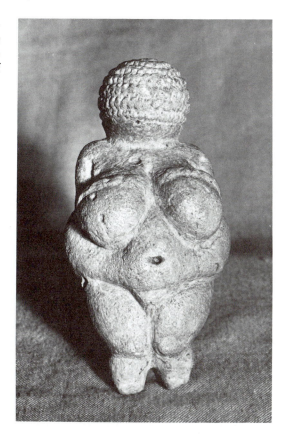

plete isolation for more than 40,000 years in an ecologically diverse continent, and when first encountered by Europeans in the 17th century, their technology hardly approached the sophistication of the Neanderthals: just simple stone tools and rudimentary wooden implements; and yet they evolved a kinship system and cosmology that most graduate students in anthropology have struggled to comprehend in all its complexity—and probably never do.

THE WORLD AT 30,000 YEARS AGO

Soon after 30,000 years ago the world was inhabited by only one human species, *Homo sapiens sapiens*—ourselves—and our ancestors had penetrated almost every environment of the Old World, and perhaps the New World as well (see Chapter 5). Across this great expanse people had developed a great diversity of tools, in stone, bone, and other materials, much of which has probably long since disappeared from the archaeological record. The evidence of fish hooks and barbed spear points suggests that many people had finally added fish to their diet—a seemingly obvious choice, but one that does not appear to have been made by many people until about 30,000 years ago and later. In many environments fish can greatly supplement other foods and thereby support much greater human populations with considerable reliability. Other technological advances, such as the atlatl, or throwing stick, probably also greatly extended the hunting prowess of many groups, and exploitation of plant foods was probably also rapidly improving in efficiency.

SUMMARY AND CONCLUSIONS

We began this chapter with humans of about 1.5 million years ago spread out along the warm margins of Africa and Asia, making a reasonable living with little more than crude stone tools, intellectual abilities far poorer than our own, and probably only the rudiments of human social organization. We end this chapter, in effect, with ourselves, in the form of our late Pleistocene relatives of just 30,000 years ago. As to what happened in this period of a million and a half years, we have a lot of data, but not enough to describe with certainty some of the most important evolutionary patterns and dynamics. Every year anthropologists meet in conferences around the world to discuss their research, and this year, like last year and every previous year, they will debate the origins of modern humans. Like this chapter, these debates will end with no real resolution. Some anthropologists are convinced that one or another of these models of human origins is accurate, but no one really knows. Even with a tenfold increase in finds of relevant human fossils, these debates would likely continue for years to come. If Richard Klein is correct,[152] for example, the origins of modern humans may have arisen directly from a single mutation, perhaps in a single individual, that allowed one group of East Africans to conceptualize time, space, and human possibilities in a way superior to that of all other humans. Such a mutation could have occurred and left no trace in fragmentary crania. If Frayer, Wolpoff, Thorne, Smith, and Pope—all advocates of multiregional continuity in human evolution—are correct, they apparently will need much additional data to convince their colleagues.

Yet, as noted above, it is not necessarily pointless to review evidence and arguments in unresolved debates. In these conflicting ideas about the nature and history of our origins we can see how "science" operates and we can get a sense of the significance of these intellectual problems. Currently, hardly a day passes without the announcement of some new breakthrough in identifying the genetic basis for some aspect of the human condition, from our personalities to our susceptibility to disease. To the extent that we are expressions of our genes, our history and fate, then, are in the selective forces of the past hundreds of thousands of years. These forces and these genetic patterns are, of course, the basic data in these debates about modern human origins.

Given the pace of genetic research, it is not impossible that we will eventually be able to recreate a Neanderthal, but until we do and then give him or her the SATs, we will not be able to resolve arguments conclusively about just who these people were, what they were capable of, and how they relate to us.

In searching for causes of the increasing brain size and other changes that took place between 400,000 and 30,000 years ago, we might note that rates of evolutionary change frequently seem to be higher along the margins of a species' range. This may have been the case with *Homo*, as bands of these hominids probed far into England, northern Europe, and perhaps northern Eurasia, and began to specialize in various forms of hunting, scavenging, and gathering. The Swanscombe and Steinheim individuals, with their nearly modern brain size, may be reflections of these developments along the northern periphery. Gene flow in most hunting and gathering societies is sufficiently high that these changes in brain size and facial architecture would probably have been quickly disseminated over a wide area. Michael Day suggests that the Swanscombe fossil, for example, can best be regarded as a female example of the transitional form between *Homo erectus* and *Homo sapiens* that was at the root of the evolution of European Neanderthals.[153]

But the "margins" of a cultural animal like early humans can be culturally and technologically—not just geographically—defined. As noted below, brain sizes may have increased most rapidly in Africa, not on the world's cold periphery. Brain tissue has a relatively high "cost": it consumes great amounts of energy and oxygen. Also, giving birth to large-brained offspring requires a pelvic bone structure that reduces maternal mobility. Since *Homo erectus* was obviously an efficient scavenger, hunter (at least of small game), forager, and toolmaker, perhaps the increased brain size was related to increasing emotional capacities rather than to improvements in the problem-solving abilities that were important in hunting or tool-making. Great advantages would accrue to a Pleistocene hunting-and-gathering group that could organize itself as part of a social network involving many different bands and hundreds of individuals, and perhaps the increasing brain size had to do with the selective advantage of being able to generalize emotions to scores of "kinsmen."

In any case, the great variability of cranial capacity among "normal" people today, and the fact that human brain size seems generally to have increased quite uniformly up to about 100,000 years ago, should warn against simplistic explanations of this phenomenon.

To explain the relatively slow rate of technological change between 2 million and 100,000 years ago, we must reflect on the fact that not only were our ancestors of this era less intelligent, there were also many fewer of them. Although technological innovation is not a simple product of the number of minds available to create new ideas, a strong relationship exists between population numbers and innovation in the simple hunting-gathering economies of the early and middle Pleistocene. Even as late as 500,000 years ago, there were probably only a million people in the entire world. Also, people of this era tended to live much shorter lives. Few survived past thirty years of age, and—although few adolescents of any age have believed it—people learn a great deal and retain considerable creativity past thirty.

Finally, if we look beyond the bones and stones and the practical analytical questions about our past, we might muse on the implications of the evidence presented here. It is worth noting that the facts and models about the dynamics of our ancestry recounted here and in chapter 3 all but killed a beautiful world- and life-view. The idea of "Nature, red in tooth and claw," as the means by which we emerged from our reptilian past has appalled people since the dark truth of our origins was first made prominent by Darwin. It is thus appropriate to end this chapter with an artful expression of this mortally wounded vision of the world and the cosmos by Alfred, Lord Tennyson, a contemporary of Darwin, and a man revolted by Darwin's ideas.

> Are God and Nature then at strife,
> That Nature lends such evil dreams?
> So careful of the type she seems,
> So careless of the single life;
>
> That I, considering everywhere
> Her secret meaning in her deeds,
> And finding that of fifty seeds
> She often brings but one to bear,
>
> I falter where I firmly trod,
> And falling with my weight of cares
> Upon the great world's altar-stairs
> That slope thro' darkness up to God,
>
> I stretch lame hands of faith, and grope,
> And gather dust and chaff, and call
> To what I feel is Lord of all,
> And faintly trust the larger hope.
>
> "So careful of the type?" but no.
> From scarpéd cliff and quarried stone
> She cries, "A thousand types are gone:
> I care for nothing: all shall go.

"Thou makest thine appeal to me:
I bring to life, I bring to death:
The spirit does but mean the breath:
I know no more." And he, shall he,

Man, her last work, who seem'd so fair,
Such splendid purpose in his eyes,
Who roll'd the psalm to wintry skies,
Who built him fanes of fruitless prayer,

Who trusted God was love indeed
And love Creation's final law—
Tho' Nature, red in tooth and claw
With ravine, shriek'd against his creed—

Who loved, who sufferd countless ills,
Who battled for the True, the Just,
Be blown about the desert dust,
Or seal'd within the iron hills?

No more? A monster then, a dream,
A discord. Dragons of the prime,
That tare each other in their slime,
Were mellow music match'd with him.
(From In Memoriam, 1850)

BIBLIOGRAPHY

Aiello, L. C. 1993. "The Fossil Evidence for Modern Human Origins in Africa: A Revised View." *American Anthropologist* 95:73–96.

Aiello, L. C., and R. I. M. Dunbar. 1993. "Neocortex Size, Group Size, and the Evolution of Language." *Current Anthropology* 34:184–92.

Ambrose, S. H. 1994. "Technological Change, Volcanic Winter, and Genetic Evidence for the Spread of Modern Humans from Africa." Presented at the Third Annual Meeting of the Paleoanthropology Society. Anaheim, CA, April, 19–20.

Arens, W. 1979. *The Man-Eating Myth.* New York: Oxford University Press.

Arsuaga, J-L., I. Martinez, A. Garcia, J-M. Carretero, and E. Carbonell. 1993. "Three New Human Skulls from the Sima de los Huesos Middle Pleistocene Site in Sierra de Atapuerca, Spain." *Nature* 362:534–37.

Arsuaga, J-L., J-M. Bermúdez de Casto, and E. Carbonell. 1994. "La Sierra de Atapuerca: Los Homínidos y sus actividades." *Revista de Arqueología* 15:12–25.

Asfaw, B., Y. Beyene, G. Suwa, R. C. Walter, T. D. White, G. WoldeGabriel, and T. Yemane. 1992. "The Earliest Acheulean from Konso-Gardula." *Nature* 360:732–35.

Baffier, D., and M. Julien. 1990. "L'Outillage en Os des Niveaux Châteloerroniens d'Arcy-sur-Cure (Yonne). In *Paléolithique Moyen Récent et Paléolithique Supérieur Ancien en Europe,* ed. C. Farizy. Mémoires du Musée de Préhistoire d'Ile de France 3, Nemours, pp. 329–34.

Bahn, P. G. 1994. "New Advances in the Field of Ice Age Art." In *Origins of Anatomically Modern Humans*, eds, M. H. Nitecki and V. Nitecki. New York: Plenum Press.

Bahn, P., and J. Vertus. 1988. *Images of the Ice Age*. New York: Viking Press.

Barfield, L. 1994. "The Iceman Reviewed." *Antiquity* 68(258):10–26.

Barnard, A. 1983. "Contemporary Hunter-Gatherers: Current Theoretical Issues in Ecology and Social Organization." *Annual Review of Anthropology* 12:193–214.

Bar-Yosef, O. 1975. "Archaeological Occurrences in the Middle Pleistocene of Israel." In *After the Australopithecines*, eds. K. W. Butzer and G. L. Isaac. The Hague: Mouton.

———. 1980. "Prehistory of the Levant." *Annual Review of Anthropology* 9:101–33.

———. 1994a. "The Lower Paleolithic of the Near East." *Journal of World Prehistory* 8:211–65.

———. 1994b. "The Contributions of Southwest Asia to the Study of Origin of Modern Humans." In *Origins of Anatomically Modern Humans*, eds. M, H. Nitecki and V. Nitecki. New York: Plenum Press.

Bar-Yosef, O., and N. Goren-Inbar. 1993. "The Lithic Assemblages of 'Ubeidiya: A Lower Paleolithic Site in the Jordan Valley." *Qedem* (Jerusalem) 45:1–266.

Bar-Yosef, O., and B. Vandermeersch. 1993. "Modern Humans in the Levant." *Scientific American* April:94–100.

Bar-Yosef, O., B. Vandermeersch, B. Arensburg, P. Goldberg, H. Laville, L. Meignen, Y. Rak, E. Tchernov, and A. Tillier. 1986. "New Data on the Origin of Modern Man in the Levant." *Current Anthropology* 27(1):63–65.

Bar-Yosef, O., M. Arnold, A. Belfer-Cohen, P. Goldberg, R. Housley, H. Laville, L. Meignen, N. Mercier, J. C. Vogel, and B. Vandermeersch. 1995. "The Dating of the Upper Paleolithic Layers in Kebara Cave, Mt. Carmel." *Journal of Archaeological Science* 22.

Bednarik, R. G. 1992. "Paleoart and Archaeological Myths." *Cambridge Archaeological Journal* 2:27–43.

Bellwood, P. 1986. *The Prehistory of the Indo-Malaysian Archipelago*. Orlando, FL: Academic Press.

———. 1987. "The Prehistory of Island Southeast Asia: A Multidisciplinary Review of Recent Research." *Journal of World Prehistory* 1(2):171–224.

Bender, M. 1983. "Comment on G. Krantz (*CA* 21:773–79)." *Current Anthropology* 24(1):113.

Berger, T. D., and E. Trinkhaus. 1995. "Patterns of Traumas among the Neandertals." *Journal of Archaeological Science* 22 (in press).

Binford, L. R. 1968. "Post-Pleistocene Adaptations." In *New Perspectives in Archeology*, eds. L. Binford and S. Binford. Chicago: Aldine.

———. 1981. *Bones: Ancient Men and Modern Myth*. New York: Academic Press.

———. 1982. "Comment on Rethinking the Middle/Upper Paleolithic Transition." *Current Anthropology* 23:177–81.

———. 1984. *Faunal Remains from Klasies River Mouth*. New York: Academic Press.

———. 1985. "Human Ancestors: Changing Views of Their Behavior." *Journal of Anthropological Archaeology* 4(4):292–327.

———. 1986. "Reply to J. F. Thackeray (Further Comment on Fauna from Klasies River Mouth," *Current Anthropology* 27(5):511–12)." *Current Anthropology* 27(1):57–62.

———. 1990. "Isolating the Transition to Cultural Adaptations: An Organizational Approach." In *Emergence of Modern Humans: Biocultural Adaptations in the Later Pleistocene*, ed. E. Trinkhaus. New York: Cambridge University Press.

Binford, L. R., and S. Binford. 1966. "A Preliminary Analysis of Functional Variability in the Mousterian of Levallois Facies." In *Recent Studies in Paleoanthropology* (*American Anthropologist* special publication), pp. 238–95.

Binford, L., and N. Stone. 1986. "Zhoukoudian: A Closer Look." *Current Anthropology* 27(5):453–75.

Bischoff, J. L., R. Julià, and R. Mora. 1988. "Uranium-Series Dating of the Mousterian Occupation at Abric Romani, Spain." *Nature* 332:668–70.

Bischoff, J. L., K. Ludwig, J. Francisco Garcia, E. Carbonell, M. Vaquero, T. W. Stafford, and A. J. T. Jull. 1994. "Dating of the Basal Aurignacian Sandwich at Abric Romani (Catalunya, Spain) by Radiocarbon and Uranium-series." *Journal of Archaeological Science* 21:541–51.

Boaz, N. T. 1982. "Comment on F. H. Smith 'Upper Pleistocene Hominid Evolution in South-Central Europe: A Review of the Evidence and Analysis of Trends.' " *Current Anthropology* 23(6):667–703.

Bordes, F. 1961a. *Typologie du paleolithique ancien et moyen.* Bordeaux: Publication de l'Institut de Prehistoire de l'Universite de Bordeaux.

———. 1961b. "Mousterian Cultures in France." *Science* 134:803–10.

———. 1968. *The Old Stone Age.* London: Weidenfeld & Nicholson.

———. 1972. *A Tale of Two Caves.* New York: Harper & Row.

———. 1978. "Typological Variability in the Mousterian Layers at Pech de l'Aze II and IV." *Journal of Anthropological Research* 34:181–93.

Bordes, F., and D. de Sonneville-Bordes. 1970. "The Significance of Variability in Paleolithic Assemblages." *World Archaeology* 2:61–73.

Boule, M. 1923. *Les Hommes Fossiles: Elements de Paleontologie Humaine,* 2nd Ed. Paris: Masson et Cie.

Boule, M. and H. Vallois. 1932. *Fossil Men.* London: Thames and Hudson.

Bowcock, A. M., A. Ruiz-Linares, J. Tomfohrde, E. Minch, K. R. Kidd, and L. L. Cavalli-Sforza. 1994. "High Resolution of Human Evolutionary Trees with Polymorphic Microsatellites." *Nature* 368:455–57.

Bowdler, J. M., R. Jones, and A. G. Thorne. 1970. "Pleistocene Human Remains from Australia: A Living Site and Human Cremation from Lake Mungo, Western New South Wales." *World Archaeology* 2:39–60.

Bower, B. 1988. "An Earlier Dawn for Modern Humans?" *Science News* 133:138.

Brace, C. L. 1964. "The Fate of the 'Classic' Neanderthals: A Consideration of Human Catastrophism." *Current Anthropology* 5:3.

———. 1967. *The Stages of Human Evolution: Human and Cultural Origins.* Englewood Cliffs, NJ: Prentice-Hall.

———. 1975. "Review of *Shanidar: The First Flower People,* by R. Solecki." *Natural History* 80:82–86.

Brace, C. L., D. P. Tracer, L. Allen Yaroch, J. Robb, K. Brandt, and A. Russel Nelson. 1993. "Clines and Clusters Versus 'Race': A Test in Ancient Egypt and the Care of a Death on the Nile." *Yearbook of Physical Anthropology* 36:1–31.

Bräuer, G. 1992. "Africa's Place in the Evolution of *Homo sapiens.*" In *Continuity or Replacement: Controversies in* Homo sapiens *Evolution,* eds. G. Bräuer and F. H. Smith. Rotterdam: A. A. Balkema.

Brennan, M. U. 1991. *Health and Disease in the Middle and Upper Paleolithic of Southwestern France: A Bioarchaeological Study,* Ph.D. Dissertation. New York University, New York.

Bricker, H. 1976. "Upper Paleolithic Archaeology." *Annual Review of Anthropology* 5:133–48.

Brooks, A. S., D. M. Helgren, J. S. Cramer, A. Franklin, W. Hornyak, J. M. Keating, R. G. Klein, W. J. Rink, H. P. Schwarcz, J. N. L. Smith, K. Stewart, N. E. Todd, J. Verniers, and J. E. Yellen. 1995. "Dating and Context of Three Middle Stone Age Sites with Bone Artifacts in the Upper Semliki Valley, Zaire." *Science* 268:548–52.

Brose, D., and M. Wolpoff. 1971. "Early Upper Paleolithic Man and Late Paleolithic Tools." *American Anthropologist* 73:1156.

Brothwell, D. 1961. "Upper Pleistocene Human Skull from Niah Caves, Sarawak." *Sarawak Museum Journal* 9:323.

Butzer, K. W., and G. L. Isaac, eds. 1975. *After the Australopithecines.* The Hague: Mouton.

Campbell, B. 1985. *Humankind Emerging,* 3rd Ed. Boston: Little, Brown.

Cann, R. L., Rickards, O., and J. K. Lum. 1995. "Mitochondrial DNA and Human Evolution: Our One Lucky Mother." In *Origins of Anatomically Modern Humans,* eds, M, H. Nitecki and V. Nitecki. New York: Plenum Press.

Cann, R. L., M. Stoneking, and A. C. Wilson. 1987. "Mitochondrial DNA and Human Evolution." *Nature* 325:31–36.

Carbonell, E., J. M. Bermudez de Castro, J. L. Arsuaga, J. C. Diez, A. Rosas, G. Cuenva-Bescos, R. Sala, M. Mosquera, and X. Rodríguez. 1995. "Lower Pleistocene Hominids and Artefacts from Atapuerca-TD6 (Spain)." *Science* 269:826–30.

Carlisle, R. C., and M. I. Siegel. 1974. "Some Problems in the Interpretation of Neanderthal Speech Capabilities. A Reply to Lieberman." *American Anthropologist* 76:319–22.

Cavalli-Sforza, L. L., P. Menozzi, and A. Piazza. 1994. *The History and Geography of Human Genes.* Princeton, NJ: Princeton University Press.

Chase, P. G. 1986. *The Hunters of Combe Grenal: Approaches to Middle Paleolithic Subsistence in Europe.* Oxford: BAR International Series 286.

Chase, P. G., and H. L. Dibble. 1987. "Middle Paleolithic Symbolism: A Review of Current Evidence and Interpretations." *Journal of Anthropological Archaeology* 6:263–96.

Chazan, M. 1995. "The Language Hypothesis for the Middle-to-Upper Paleolithic Transition: An Examination Based on a Multiregional Lithic Analysis." *Current Anthropology* 36(5):749–68.

———. 1992. "Scientific Archaeology and the Origins of Symbolism: A Reply to Bednarik." *Cambridge Archaelogical Journal* 2:43–51.

Clark, G. A., ed. 1991. *Perspectives on the Past: Theoretical Biases in Mediterranean Hunter-Gatherer Research.* Philadelphia: University of Pennsylvania Press.

———. 1992. "Continuity or Replacement? Putting Modern Human Origins in Evolutionary Context." In *The Middle Paleolithic*, eds. H. L. Dibble and P. A. Mellars. Philadelphia: University of Pennsylvania Museum.

Clark, G. A., and J. Lindly. 1991. "On Paradigmatic Biases and Paleolithic Research Traditions." *Current Anthropology* 32:577–87.

Combier, J. 1988. "Témoins Moustériens d'Activités Volontaires." In *De Néandertal à Cro-Magnon,* eds. J-B. Roy and A-S. LeClerc. Musée de Prehistoire d'Ile de France, Nemours, pp. 69–72.

Conkey, M. 1980. "The Identification of Prehistoric Hunter-Gatherer Aggregation Sites: The Case of Altamira." *Current Anthropology* 21:609–30.

———. 1987. "New Approaches in the Search for Meaning? A Review of Research in 'Paleolithic Art.' " *Journal of Field Archaeology* 14(4):413–30.

Conroy, 1990.

Coon, C. S. 1981. *Races: A Study of The Problems of Race Formation in Man.*

Davidson, I., and W. Noble. 1989. "The Archaeology of Perception: Traces of Depiction and Language." *Current Anthropology* 30:125–55.

Day, M. H. 1986. *Guide to Fossil Man*, 4th Ed. Chicago: University of Chicago Press.

De Beaune, S. A. 1987. "Paleolithic Lamps and Their Specialization: A Hypothesis." *Current Anthropology* 28(4):569–77.

de Vos, J., P. Sondaar, and C. Swisher. 1994. "Dating Hominid Sites in Indonesia." *Science* 266:1726–27.

Deacon, H. J. n.a. South African Archaeological Bulletin.

———. 1992. *The Origins of Modern People: The Evidence from Klasies River.*

Dubois, E. 1921. "The Proto-Australian Fossil Man of Wadjak, Java." *Proceedings: Koninklijke Nederlandse Akademie van Wetenschappen* 23:1013.

Dzaparidze, V., G. Bosinki, T. Bugianisvili, L. Gabunia, A. Justus, N. Kloptovskaja, E. Kvavadze, D. Lordkipanidze, G. Majsuradze, N. Megladze, M. Niodardze, E. Pavlenisvili, H-U. Schmincke, D. Sologasvili, D. Tusabramisvili, M. Tvalcrelidze, and A. Vekua. 1992. "Der Altpaläolithische Fundplatz Dmanisi in Georgien (Kaukasus)." *Jahrbuch des Römisch-Germanischen Zentralmuseums Mainz* 6:67–116.

Edey, M. A., and Editors of Time-Life. 1972. *The Missing Link.* New York: Time-Life.

Falk, D. 1975. "Comparative Anatomy of the Larynx in Man and the Chimpanzee: Implications for Language in Neanderthal." *American Journal of Physical Anthropology* 43:123–32.

Farb, P., and G. Armelagos. 1980. *Consuming Passions.* Boston: Houghton Mifflin.

Farizy, C. 1990. "The Transition from Middle to Upper Palaeolithic at Arcy-sur-Cure (Yonne, France): Technological, Economic and Social Aspects." In *The Emergence of Modern Humans*, ed. P. Mellars. Ithaca, NY: Cornell University Press.

———. 1994. "Behavioral and Cultural Changes at the Middle to Upper Paleolithic Transition in Western Europe." In *Origins of Anatomically Modern Humans*, eds. M. H. Nitecki and V. Nitecki. New York: Plenum Press.

Ferraro, G., W. Trevatham, and J. Levy. 1994. *Anthropology. An Applied Perspective*. St. Paul, MN: West Publishing Company.

Fisher, E. 1979. *Woman's Creation*. New York: McGraw-Hill.

Foley, R., ed. 1984. *Hominid Evolution and Community Ecology*. London: Academic.

———. 1987. "Hominid Species and Stone-tool Assemblages: How Are They Related?" *Antiquity* 61:380–92.

Frankel, D. 1991. Remains to be Seen: Archaeological Inisghts into Australian Prehistory. Melbourne: Longman Cheshire.

Frayer, D. W. 1981. "Body Size, Weapons Use, and Natural Selection in the European Upper Paleolithic and Mesolithic." *American Anthropologist* 83:57–73.

———. 1986. "Cranial Variation at Mladec and the Relationship between Mousterian and Upper Paleolithic Hominids." *Anthropos* 23:243–56.

Frayer, D. W., and M. H. Wolpoff. 1993. "Comment on 'Glottogenesis and Modern *Homo sapiens*' (R. G. Milo and D. Quiatt)." *Current Anthropology* 34(5):582–584.

Frayer, D. W., M. Wolpoff, A. G. Thorne, F. H. Smith, and G. G. Pope. 1993. "Theories of Modern Human Origins: The Paleontological Test." *American Anthropologist* 95:14–50.

———. 1994. "Getting It Straight." *American Anthropologist* 96:424–38.

Freeman, L. G. 1975. "Acheulian Sites and Stratigraphy in Iberia and the Maghreb." In *After the Australopithecines*, eds. K. W. Butzer and G. L. Isaac. The Hague: Mouton.

———. 1994. "Torralba and Amrbona: A Review of Discoveries." In *Integrative Paths to the Past: Paleoanthropological Advances in Honor of F. Clark Howell*, eds. R. S. Corruccini and R. L. Ciochon. Englewood Cliffs, NJ: Prentice-Hall.

Freeman, M. 1971. "A Social and Economic Analysis of Systematic Female Infanticide." *American Anthropologist* 73:1011–18.

Frolov, B. A. 1978–1979. "Numbers in Paleolithic Graphic Art and the Initial Stages of Development of Mathematics." *Soviet Anthropology and Archeology* 17:41–74.

Gabow, S. L. 1977. "Population Structure and the Rate of Hominid Brain Evolution." *Journal of Human Evolution* 6:643–65.

Gabunia, L., and A. Vekua. 1995. "A Plio-Pleistocene Hominid from Dmanisi, Georgia." *Nature* 373:509–12.

Gambier, D. 1989. "Fossil Hominids from the Early Upper Paleolithic (Auignacian) of France." In *The Human Revolution: Behavioral and Biological Perspectives on the Origins of Modern Humans*, eds. P. Mellars and C. B. Stringer. Edinburgh: Edinburgh University Press.

Gamble, C. 1986. *The Palaeolithic Settlement of Europe*. Cambridge, England: Cambridge University Press.

———. 1994. Gamble, C. 1994. *Timewalkers: The Prehistory of Global Colonization*. Cambridge, MA: Harvard University Press.

Gargett, R. H. 1989. "Grave Shortcomings: The Evidence for Neanderthal Burial." *Current Anthropology* 30(2):157–90.

Garn, S., and W. Block. 1970. "The Limited Nutritional Value of Cannibalism." *American Anthropologist* 72:106.

Gee, H. 1995. "New Hominid Remains found in Ethiopia." *Nature* 373:272.

Gisis, I., and O. Bar-Yosef. 1974. "New Excavations in Zuttiyeh Cave, Wadi Amud, Israel." *Paléorient* 2:175–80.

Goebel, T. 1995. "The Record of Human Occupation of the Russian Subarctic and Arctic." *Byrd Polar Research Center Miscellaneous Series* M-335:41–46.

Goren-Inbar, N., S. Belitsky, K. Verosub, E. Werker, M. Kislev, A. Heimann, I. Carmi, and A. Rosenfeld. 1992. "New Discoveries at the Middle Pleistocene Acheulian Site of Gesher Benot Ya"aqov, Israel." *Quarternary Research* 38:117–28.

Gould. S. J. 1980. *The Panda's Thumb*. New York: Norton.

———. 1989. *Wonderful Life*. New York: W.W. Norton.

Grine, F. E. 1988. "Evolutionary History of the "Robust" Australopithecines: A Summary and Historical Perspective." In *The Evolutionary History of the Robust Australopithecines*, ed. F. E. Grine. New York: Aldine de Gruyter.

Gron, O. 1987. "Seasonal Variation in Maglemosian Group Size and Structure." *Current Anthropology* 28(3):303–27.

Groves, C. P. 1989. *A Theory of Human and Primate Evolution.* Oxford: Clarendon Press.

———. 1992. "The Origin of Modern Humans." *Interdisciplinary Science Reviews* 19:23–34.

Halverson, J. 1987. "Art for Art's Sake in the Paleolithic." *Current Anthropology* 28(1):63–89.

Harpending, H. 1994. "Gene Frequencies, DNA Sequences, and Human Origins." *Perspectives in Biology and Medicine* 37:384–94.

Harrold, F. B. 1989. "Mousterian, Châtelperronian, and Early Aignacian in Western Europe: Continuity or Discontinuity." In *The Human Revolution: Behavioral and Biological Perspectives on the Origins of Modern Humans,* eds. P. Mellars and C. B. Stringer. Edinburgh: Edinburgh University Press.

Hayden, B. 1993. "The Cultural Capacities of the Neandertals: A Review and Re-Evaluation." *Journal of Human Evolution* 24:113–46.

Haynes, C. V. 1992. "Contributions of Radiocarbon Dating to the Geochronology of the Peopling of the New World." In *Radiocarbon After Four Decades,* eds. R. E. Taylor, A. Long, and R. S. Kra. New York: Springer-Verlag.

Herrnstein, R. J. and C. Murray. 1996. *The Bell Curve. Intelligence and Class Structure in American Life.* New York: Simon and Schuster.

Hodder, I. 1986. *Reading the Past: Current Approaches to Interpretation in Archaeology.* Cambridge, England: Cambridge University Press.

Hoffecker, J. G., W. R. Powers, and T. Goebel. 1993. "The Colonization of Beringia and the Peopling of the New World." *Science* 259:46–53.

Holloway, R. L., Jr. 1989. "Comment on 'On Depiction and Language.' " *Current Anthropology* 30(3):331–32.

Howell, F. C. 1961. "Isimila: A Paleolithic Site in Africa." *Scientific American* 205:118–31.

———. 1965. *Early Man.* New York: Time-Life.

———. 1966. "Observations on the Earlier Phases of the European Lower Paleolithic." *American Anthropologist* 68(2)(pt.2):88–201.

———. 1994. "A Chronostratigraphic and Taxonomic Framework of the Origin of Modern Humans." In *Origins of Anatomically Modern Humans,* eds., M. H. Nitecki and V. Nitecki. New York: Plenum Press.

Howells, W. W. 1975. "Neanderthal Man: Facts and Figures." In *Australopithecus Paleoanthropology: Morphology and Paleoecology,* ed. R. H. Tuttle. The Hague: Mouton.

Hublin, J-J. 1990. "Les Peuplements Paléolithiques de'Europe: Un Point de Vue Géographique." In *Paléolithique Moyen Récent et Paléolithique Supérieur Ancien en Europe,* ed. C. Farizy. Mémoires du Musée de Préhistoire d'Ile de France 3, Nemours, pp. 29–37.

Isaac, G. 1975. "Sorting Out the Muddle in the Middle—An Anthropologist's Post-Conference Appraisal." In *After the Australopithecines,* eds. K. W. Butzer and G. Isaac. The Hague: Mouton.

———. 1984. "The Archaeology of Human Origins: Studies of the Lower Palaeolithic in East Africa, 1971–1981." *Advances in World Archaeology* 3:1–89.

James, S. R. 1989. "Hominid Use of Fire in the Lower and Middle Pleistocene: A Review of the Evidence." *Current Anthropology* 30(1):1–26.

Jelinek, A. J. 1982a. "The Tabun Cave and Paleolithic Man in the Levant." *Science* 216:1369–75.

———. 1982b. "The Middle Palaeolithic in the Southern Levant, with Comments on the Appearance of Modern *Homo sapiens.*" In *The Transition from Lower to Middle Palaeolithic and Origin of Modern Man,* ed. A. Ronen. Oxford: BAR International Series 151.

———. 1994. "Hominids, Energy, Environment, and Behavior in the Late Pleistocene." In *Origins of Anatomically Modern Humans,* eds., M. H. Nitecki and V. Nitecki. New York: Plenum Press.

Jones, R. 1990. "From Kakadu to Kutikina: The Southern Continent at 18,000 Years Ago." In *The World at 18,000 BP: Low Latitudes,* eds. C. Gamble and O. Soffer. London: Unwin Hyman.

Jorgensen, G. 1977. "A Contribution of the Hypothesis of a Little More Fitness of Blood Group O." *Journal of Human Evolution* 6:741–44.

Kimble, W. H., D. C. Johanson, and Y. Rak. 1994. "The First Skull and Other New Discoveries of *Australopithecus afarensis* at Hadar, Ethiopia." *Nature* 368:449–51.

Klein, R. G. 1973. *Ice-Age Hunters of the Ukraine*. Chicago: University of Chicago Press.

———. 1978. "Stone Age Predation of Large African Bovids." *Journal of Archaeological Science* 5:195–217.

———. 1987. "Reconstructing How Early People Exploited Animals: Problems and Prospects." In *The Evolution of Human Hunting*, eds. M. H. Nitecki and D. V. Nitecki. New York: Plenum Press.

———. 1988. "The Causes of 'Robust' Australopithecine Extinction." In *The Evolutionary History of the Robust Australopithecines*, ed. F. E. Grine. New York: Aldine de Gruyter.

———. 1989. *The Human Career*. Chicago: University of Chicago Press.

———. 1994. "Southern Africa Before the Iron Age." In *Integrative Paths to the Past: Paleoanthropological Advances in Honor of F. Clark Howell*, eds. R. S. Corruccini and R. L. Ciochon. Englewood Cliffs, NJ: Prentice-Hall.

———. 1995. "Anatomy, Behavior, and Modern Human Origins." *Journal of World Prehistory* 9(2):167–98.

———. Personal communication.

Kuhn, S. L. 1989. "Projectile Weapons and Investment in Food Procurement Technology during the Middle Paleolithic (abstract)." *American Journal of Physical Anthropology* 78:257.

Kuzmin, Y. V. 1994. "Prehistoric Colonization of Northeastern Siberia and Migration to America: Radiocarbon Evidence." *Radiocarbon* 36:367–76.

Lahr, M. M. 1994. "The Multiregional Model of Modern Human Origins: A Reassessment of its Morphological Basis." *Journal of Human Evolution* 26:23–56.

Larichev, V., U. Khol'ushkin, and I. Laricheva. 1987. "Lower and Middle Paleolithic of Northern Asia: Achievements, Problems, and Perspectives." *Journal of World Prehistory* 1(4):415–64.

Laville, H., Rigaud J.-P., and J. Sackett. 1980. *Rock Shelters of the Perigord*. New York: Academic Press.

Leakey, L. S. 1951. *Olduvai Gorge, 1931–1951*. Cambridge, England: Cambridge University Press.

Leakey, M. D. 1975. "Cultural Patterns in the Olduvai Sequence." In *After the Australopithecines*, eds. K. W. Butzer and G. L. Isaac. The Hague: Mouton.

Leroi-Gourhan, A. 1965. *Treasures of Palaeolithic Art*. New York: Abrams.

———. 1968. "The Evolution of Paleolithic Art." *Scientific American* 209(2):58–74.

———. 1982. *The Dawn of European Art*. Cambridge, England: Cambridge University Press.

Leveque, F., A. M. Backer, and M. Guilband, eds. 1993. *Context of a Late Neandertal: Implications of Multidisciplinary Research for the Transition to Upper Paleolithic Adaptations at Saint-Cesaire, Charente-Maritime, France*. Madison, WI: Prehistory Press.

Leveque, F., and B. Vandermeersch. 1980. "Les Decouvertes de Restes Humains dans un Horizon Castelperronien de Saint-Cesaire (Charente-Maritime)." *Bulletin de la Societe Prehistorique Francaise* 77:35.

Lewin, R. 1987. "Debate over Emergence of Human Tooth Pattern." *Nature* 235:748–50.

Lewis-Williams, J. D., and T. A. Dowson. 1988. "The Signs of All Times: Entopic Phenomena in Upper Paleolithic Art." *Current Anthropology* 29(2):201–46.

Lieberman, D. E. 1995. "Testing Hypotheses about Recent Human Evolution from Skulls." *Current Anthropology* 36:159–97.

Lieberman, L., and F. L. C. Jackson. 1995. "Race and Three Models of Human Origin." *American Anthropologist* 97(2):231–42.

Lieberman, P. E. 1991. *Uniquely Human: The Evolution of Speech, Thought, and Selfless Behavior*. Cambridge, MA: Harvard University Press.

Lieberman, P. E., and E. S. Crelin. 1971. "On the Speech of Neanderthals." *Linguistic Inquiry* 2:203–22.

Lieberman, P. E., E. S. Crelin, and D. H. Klatt. 1972. "Phonetic Ability and Related Anatomy of the Newborn and Adult Human, Neanderthal Man, and the Chimpanzee." *American Anthropologist* 74:287.

Lindly, J. M., and G. A. Clark. 1990. "Symbolism and Modern Human Origins." *Current Anthropology* 31:233–40.

Littlefield, A., L. Lieberman, and L. T. Reynolds. 1982. "Redefining Race: The Potential Demise of a Concept in Physical Anthropology." *Current Anthropology* 23(6):641–55.

Lourandos, H. 1987. "Pleistocene Australia: Peopling a Continent." In *The Pleistocene Old World: Regional Perspectives*, ed. O. Soffer. New York: Plenum.

Lovejoy, O., and E. Trinkhaus. 1980. "Strength of Robusticity of the Neanderthal Tibia." *American Journal of Physical Anthropology* 53:465–70.

Luguet, G. 1930. *The Art and Religion of Fossil Man.* New Haven: Yale University Press.

Lumley, H. de. 1969a. "A Paleolithic Camp at Nice." *Scientific American* 225:42–59.

———. 1969b. *Le Paleolithique Inferieur et Moyen du Midi Mediterraneen dans son Cadre Geologique, Vol. 1: Ligurie Provence.* Paris: Editions du Centre National de La Recherche Scientifique.

———. 1971. *Le Paleolithique Inferieur et Moyen du Midi Mediterranean dans son Cadre Geologique, Vol. 2: Bas—Languedoc, Roussillon, Catalogue.* Paris: Editions du Centre National de la Recherche Scientifique.

———. 1975. "Cultural Evolution in France in Its Paleoecological Setting During the Middle Pleistocene." In *After the Australopithecines*, eds. K. W. Butzer and G. L. Isaac. The Hague: Mouton.

Lumley, H. de, and M. A. de Lumley. 1971. "Decouverte de restes humains anteneandertaliens dates du debut du Riss la Caune de l'Arago (Tautavel, Pyrenees-Orientales)." *Comptes Rendus de l'Academie des Sciences de Paris* 272:1739–42.

Lumley, M. A. de. 1973. *Anteneandertaliens et neandertaliens du Bassin Mediterraneen Occidental Europeen.* Etudes Quaternaires, Memoire n. 2. Universite de Provence.

———. 1975. "Ante-Neanderthals of Western Europe." In *Australopithecus Paleoanthropology: Morphology and Paleoecology*, ed. R. H. Tuttle. The Hague: Mouton.

McHenry, H. M. 1992. "How Big Were Early Hominids?" *Evolutionary Anthropology* 1:15–20.

———. 1994a. "Tempo and Mode in Human Evolution." *Proceedings of the National Academy of Sciences* 91:6780–86.

———. 1994b. "Behavioral Ecological Implications of Early Hominid Body Size." *Journal of Human Evolution* 27:77–87.

Marks, J. 1995. *Human Biodiversity: Genes, Race, and History.* Hawthorne, NY: Aldine de Gruyter.

Marshack, A. 1976. "Some Implications of the Paleolithic Symbolic Evidence for the Origins of Language." *Current Anthropology* 17:274–82.

———. 1984. "The Ecology and Brain of Two-Handed Bipedalism: An Analytic, Cognitive, and Evolutionary Assessment." In *Animal Cognition*, eds. H. Terrace, H. Roitblat, and T. Bever. Hillsdale, NJ: Lawrence Erlbaum.

———. 1991. "A Reply to Davidson on Mania and Mania." *Rock Art Research* 8:47–58.

Mellars, P. 1985. "The Ecological Basis of Social Complexity in the Upper Palaeolithic of Southwestern France. In *Prehistoric Hunter-Gatherers: The Emergence of Cultural Complexity*, eds. T. D. Price and J. Brown. Orlando, FL: Academic Press.

———. 1989. "Major Issues in the Emergence of Modern Humans." *Current Anthropology* 30:349–85.

———, ed. 1990. *The Emergence of Modern Humans.* Ithaca, NY: Cornell University Press.

———. 1992. "Cognitive Changes and the Emergence of Modern Humans in Europe." *Cambridge Archaeological Journal* 1:63–76.

———. 1993. "Archaeology and the Population-Dispersal Hypothesis of Modern Human Origins in Europe." In *The Origin of Modern Humans and the Impact of Chronometric Dating*, eds. M. J. Aitken, C. B. Stringer, and P. A. Mellars. Princeton, NJ: Princeton University Press.

Mellars, P., and C. Stringer, eds. 1989. *The Human Revolution*, Vol. 1. Princeton, NJ: Princeton University Press.

Mellars, P. A., H. M. Bricker, J. A. Gowlett, and E. E. M. Hedges. 1987. "Radiocarbon Accelerator Dating of French Upper Paleolithic Sites." *Current Anthropology* 28(1):128–33.

Melnick, D. J., and G. A. Hoelzer. 1993. "What Is mtDNA Good for in the Study of Primate Evolution?" *Evolutionary Anthropology* 2(1):2–10.

Meltzer, D. J. 1993. "Pleistocene Peopling of the Americas." *Evolutionary Anthropology* 1:157–69.

Mercier, N., and H. Valladas. 1994. "Thermoluminescence Dates for the Paleolithic Levant." In *Late Quaternary Chronology and Paleoclimates of the Eastern Mediterranean*, eds. O. Bar-Yosef and R. S. Kra. Tucson: Radiocarbon.

Milo, R. G., and D. Quiatt. 1994. "Language in the Middle and Late Stone Ages: Glottogenesis in Anatomically Modern *Homo sapiens*." In *Hominid Culture in Primate Perspective*, eds. D. Quiatt and J. Itani. Niwot, CO: University Press of Colorado.

Mountain, J. L., A. A. Lin, A. M. Bowcock, and L. L. Cavalli-Sforza. 1993. "Evolution of Modern Humans: Evidence from Nuclear DNA Polymorphisms." In *The Origin of Modern Humans and the Impact of Chronometric Dating*, eds. M. J. Aitken, C. B. Stringer, and P. A. Mellars. Princeton, NJ: Princeton University Press.

Nitecki, M. H., and D. V. Nitecki, eds. 1995. *Origins of Anatomically Modern Humans.* New York: Plenum Press.

O'Connell, J. F., K. Hawkes, and N. Blurton-Jones. 1988. "Hadza Scavenging: Implications for Plio/Pleistocene Hominid Subsistence." *Current Anthropology* 29:356–63.

O'Kelley, M. J. 1988. *Early Ireland.* Cambridge, England: Cambridge University Press.

Olsen, J. W., and S. Miller-Antonio. 1992. "The Paleolithic in Southern China." *Asian Perspectives* 31:129–60.

Palmqvist, P., J. Gibert, J. A. Pérez-Claros, and J. L. Santamaría. 1995. "Comparative Morphometric Study of a Human Phalanx from the Lower Pleistocene Site of Cueva Victoria (Murcia, Spain) By Means of Fourier Analysis, Shape Coordinates of Landmarks, Principal and Relative Warps." *Journal of Archaeological Science* 22.

Parés, J. M., and A. Pérez-Gonzalez. 1995. "Paleomagnetic Age for Hominid Fossils at Atapuerca Archaeological Site, Spain." *Science* 269:830–32.

Pfeiffer, J. E. 1978. *The Emergence of Man.* New York: Harper & Row.

———. 1986. "Cro-Magnons Were Really Us, Working Out Strategies for Survival." *Smithsonian* (October):74–85.

Phillips, J. L. 1991. "Refitting, Edge-Wear and Chaînes Opératoires: A Case Study from Sinai." In *25 Ans d'Études Technologiques en Préhistoire, Centre de Recherches Archéologiques due CNRS*, 25:305–17. Sophia Antipolis: Éditions APDCA-Juan-les-Pins.

Pilbeam, D. 1975. "Middle Pleistocene Hominids." In *After the Australopithecines*, eds. K. W. Butzer and G. L. Isaac. The Hague: Mouton.

Poirier, F. E. 1973. *Fossil Man.* St. Louis: Mosby.

Pope, G. G. 1984. "The Antiquity and Palaeoenvironment of the Asian Hominidae." In *The Evolution of the East Asian Environment*, ed. R.O.I. Whyte. Hong Kong: Center of Asian Studies, University of Hong Kong.

———. 1989. "Bamboo and Human Evolution." *Natural History* 10:(89):49–56.

Prideaux, T., and the Editors of Time-Life. 1973. *Cro-Magnon Man.* New York: Time-Life.

Protsch, R. 1982. Public Lecture. Seattle.

Renfrew, C. 1988. "Archaeology and Language." *Current Anthropology* 29(3):437–68.

Rice, P. C., and A. L. Paterson. 1985. "Cave Art and Bones: Exploring the Interrelationships." *American Anthropologist* 87(1):94–100.

Rigaud, J. P. 1982. "Le Paleolithique en Perigord: Les Donnes du Sud-Ouest Sarladais et Leur Implications." Ph.D. Dissertation. France: University of Bordeaux.

Rightmire, P. 1990. *The Evolution of* Homo erectus. Cambridge: Cambridge University Press.

———. 1992. "*Homo erectus:* Ancestor of Evolutionary Side Branch?" *Evolutionary Anthropology* 1:43–49.

Roberts, D. F. 1953. "Body Weight, Race and Climate." *American Journal of Physical Anthropology* NS 11:533–58.

Roberts, M. B., Stringer, C. B., and Parfitt, S. A. 1994. "A Hominid Tibia from Middle Pleistocene Sediments at Boxgrove, UK." *Nature* 369:311–312.

Roberts, R. G., R. Jones, N. A. Spooner, M. J. Head, A. S. Murray, and M. A. Smith. 1994. "The Human Colonisation of Australia: Optical Dates of 53,000 and 60,000 Years

Bracket Human Arrival at Deaf Adder Gorge, Northern Territory." *Quaternary Science Reviews* 13:575–86.

Roberts, R. G., et al. 1990. "Thermoluminsescence Dating of a 50,000-year-old Human Occupation Site in Northern Australia." *Nature* 345:153–156.

Roe, D. A. 1981. *The Lower and Middle Paleolithic Periods in Britain.* London: Routledge & Kegan Paul.

Roebroeks, W. 1994. "Updating the Earliest Occupation of Europe." *Current Anthropology* 35:301–305.

Ronen, A., ed. 1982. "The Transition from Lower to Middle Palaeolithic and Origin of Modern Man." BAR International Series 151.

Rushton, J. P. 1994. *Race, Evolution, and Behavior: A Life History Perspective.* New Brunswick, NJ: Transaction Publishers.

Schick, K. D., and D. Zhuan. 1993. "Early Paleolithic of China and Eastern Asia." *Evolutionary Anthropology* 2(1):22–35.

Schwarcz, H. P. 1994. "Chronology of Modern Humans in the Levant." In *Late Quaternary Chronology and Paleoclimates of the Eastern Mediterranean*, eds. O. Bar-Yosef and R. S. Kra. Tucson: Radiocarbon.

Serge, A., and A. Asconzi. 1984. "Italy's Earliest Middle Pleistocene Hominid Site." *Current Anthropology* 25(2):230–235.

Sevink, J., E. H. Hebeda, H. N. Priem, and R. H. Verschure. 1981. "A Note on the Approximately 730,000-year-old Mammal Fauna and Associated Human Activity Sites near Isernia, Central Italy." *Journal of Archaeological Science* 8:105–6.

Shapiro, H. 1974. *Peking Man.* New York: Simon and Schuster.

Shea, J. J. 1988. "Spear Points from the Middle Paleolithic of the Levant." *Journal of Field Archaeology* 15(4):441–56.

Sherry, S. T., A. R. Rogers, H. Harpending, H. Soodyall, T. Jenkins, and M. Stoneking. 1994. "Mismatch Distributions of mtDNA Reveal Recent Human Population Expansions." *Human Biology* 66:671–75.

Shipman, P. 1983. "Early Hominid Lifestyle: Hunting and Gathering or Foraging and Scavenging?" In *Animals and Archaeology: Hunters and Their Prey*, eds. J. Clutton-Brock and C. Grigson. Oxford, England: British Archaeological Reports.

Sieveking, A. 1979. *The Cave Artists.* London: Thames & Hudson.

Sigmon, B. A. and J. S. Cybulski, eds. 1981. *Homo Erectus Papers in Honor of Davidson Black.* Toronto: University of Toronto Press.

Singer, R., and J. Wymer. 1982. *The Middle Stone Age at Klasies River Mouth in South Africa.* Chicago: University of Chicago Press.

Singer, R., B. Gladfelter, and J. Wymer. 1993. *The Lower Paleolithic Site at Hoxne, England.* Chicago: University of Chicago Press.

Smith, F. H. 1982. "Upper Pleistocene Hominid Evolution in South-Central Europe: A Review of the Evidence and Analysis of Trends." *Current Anthropology* 23(6):667–703.

———. 1994. "Samples, Species, and Speculations in the Study of Modern Human Origins." In *Origins of Anatomically Modern Humans*, eds., M. H. Nitecki and V. Nitecki. New York: Plenum Press.

Smith, F. H., and G. C. Ranyard. 1981. "Evolution of the Supraorbital Region in Upper Pleistocene Fossil Hominids from South-central Europe." *American Journal of Physical Anthropology* 53:589–610.

Smith, F. H., J. F. Simek, and M. S. Hamill. 1989. "Geographic Variation in Supraorbital Torus Reduction During the Later Pleistocene (c. 80,000-15,000 BP)." In *The Human Revolution: Behavioural and Biological Perspectives on the Origins of Modern Humans*, eds. P. Mellars and C. B. Stringer. Edinburgh: Edinburgh University Press.

Smith, F. H., and F. Spencer, eds. 1984. *The Origins of Modern Humans.* New York: A. R. Liss.

So, J. K. 1980. "Human Biological Adaptation to Arctic and Subarctic Zones." *Annual Review of Anthropology* 9:63–82.

Soffer, O. 1985. *The Upper Paleolithic of the Central Russian Plain.* New York: Academic Press.

———. 1987. "Upper Palaeolithic Connubia, Refugia, and the Archaeological Record from

Eastern Europe." In *The Pleistocene Old World*, ed. O. Soffer, New York: Plenum Press.

———. 1990. "Before Beringia: Late Pleistocene Bio-social Transformations and the Colonization of Northern Eurasia." In *Chronostratigraphy of the Paleolithic in North, Central, East Asia and America*. Novosibirsk: Academy of Sciences of the USSR.

———. 1993. "Upper Palaeolityic Adaptations in Central and Eastern Europe and Man-Mammoth Interactions." In *From Kostenki to Clovis*, eds. O. Soffer and N. D. Praslov. New York: Plenum Press.

———. 1994. "Ancestral Lifeways in Eurasia—the Middle and Upper Paleolithic Records." In *Origins of Anatomically Modern Humans*, eds. M. H. Nitecki and D. V. Nitecki. New York: Plenum Press.

———, ed. 1987. *The Pleistocene Old World: Regional Perspectives*. New York: Plenum Press.

Soffer, O., and C. Gamble, eds. 1990. *The World in 18,000 B.P.* Edinburgh: Edinburgh University Press.

Soffer, O., and N. D. Praslov, ed. 1995. *From Kostenki to Clovis: Upper Paleolithic—Paleo-Indian Adaptations*. New York: Plenum Press.

Speth, J. D. 1990. "Seasonality, Resource Stress, and Food Sharing in So-Called 'Egalitarian' Foraging Societies." *Journal of Anthropological Archaeology* 9:148–88.

Spoor, F., B. Wood, and F. Zonneveld. 1994. "Implications of Early Hominid Labryinthine Morphology for Evolution of Human Bipedal Locomotion." *Nature* 369:645–48.

Stoneking, M. 1993. "DNA and Recent Human Evolution." *Evolutionary Anthropology* 2:60–73.

Straus, L. G. 1982. "Carnivores and Cave Sites in Cantabrian Spain." *Journal of Anthropological Research* 38:75–96.

———. 1993/1994. "Upper Paleolithic Origins and Radiocarbon Calibration: More New Evidence from Spain." *Evolutionary Anthropology* 2(6):195–98.

———. 1995. *Iberia before the Iberians: The Stone Age Prehistory of Cantabrian Spain*. Albuquerque: University of New Mexico Press.

Straus, W., and A. Cave. 1957. "Pathology and the Posture of Neanderthal Man." *Quarterly Review of Biology* 32:348.

Stringer, C. 1984. "Human Evolution and Biological Adaption in the Pleistocene." In *Human Evolution and Community Ecology*, ed. R. Foley. London: Academic Press.

Stringer, C., and P. Andrews. 1988. "Genetic and Fossil Evidence for the Origin of Modern Humans." *Science* 239:1263–68.

Stringer, C., and G. Bräuer. 1994. "Methods, Misreading, and Bias." *American Anthropologist* 96:416–424.

Stringer, C., and C. Gamble. 1993. *The Search for the Neanderthals*. London: Thames and Hudson.

Stringer, C. et al. 1979. "The Significance of the Fossil Hominid from Petralona, Greece." *Journal of Archaeological Science* 6:235–53.

———. 1984. "The Origin of Anatomically Modern Humans in Western Europe." In *The Origins of Modern Humans*, eds. F. Smith and F. Spencer. New York: A. R. Liss.

Susman, R. L. 1993. "Hominid Postcranial Remains from Swartkrans." In *Swartkrans: A Cave"s Chronicle of Early Man*, ed. C. K. Brain. Pretoria: Transvaal Museum Monograph 8, pp. 117–136.

———. 1994. "Fossil Evidence for Early Hominid Tool Use." *Science* 263:1570–73.

Svoboda, J. 1987. "Lithic Industries of the Arago, Vértesszöllös, and Bilzingsleben Hominids: Comparison and Evolutionary Interpretation." *Current Anthropology* 28(2):219–27.

Swedlund, A. 1974. "The Use of Ecological Hypotheses in Australopithecine Taxonomy." *American Anthropologist* 76:515–29.

Swisher, C., et al. 1994. "Age of the Earliest Known Hominids in Java, Indonesia." *Science* 263:1119–1121.

Taborin, Y. 1990. "Les Prémices de la Parure." In *Paléolithique Moyen Récent et Paléolithique Supérieur Ancien en Europe*, ed. C. Farizy. Mémoires du Musée de Préhistoire d'Ile de France 3, Nemours, pp. 335–44.

Tchernov, E. 1992. "Biochronology, Paleoecology, and Dispersal Events of Hominids in the

Southern Levant." In *The Evolution and Dispersal of Modern Humans in Asia*, eds. T. Akazawa, K. Aoki, and T. Kimura. Tokyo: Hokusen-sha.

———. 1994. "New Comments on the Biostratigraphy of the Middle and Upper Plesitocene of the Southern Levant." In *Late Quaternary Chronology and Paleoclimates of the Eastern Mediterranean*, eds. O. Bar-Yosef and R. S. Kra. Tucson: Radiocarbon.

Thackeray, A. I. 1992. "The Middle Stone Age South of the Limpopo River." *Journal of World Prehistory* 6:385–440.

Thackeray, J. F. 1986. "Further Comment on Fauna from Klasies River Mouth." *Current Anthropology* 27(5):511–12.

———. 1995. "Comment." *Current Anthropology* 36(2):185.

Thiel, B. 1987. "Early Settlement of the Philippines, Eastern Indonesia, and Australia-New Guinea: A New Hypothesis." *Current Anthropology* 28(2):236–41.

Thorne, A. 1980. "The Arrival of Man in Australia." In *The Cambridge Encyclopedia of Archaeology*. New York: Crown Publishers/Cambridge University Press.

Tierney, J., with L. Wright, and K. Springen. 1988. "The Search for Adam and Eve." *Newsweek*, January 11.

Tobias, P. V. 1991. *Olduvai Gorge, Vol. 4. The Skulls, Endocasts and Teeth of* Homo habilis. Cambridge: Cambridge University Press.

Tobias, P., and G. Von Koenigswald. 1964. "Comparison between the Olduvai Hominines and Those of Java and Some Implications for Phylogeny." *Nature* 204:515.

Toth, N., K. D. Schick, E. S. Savage-Rumbaugh, R. A. Sevick, and D. M. Rumbaugh. 1003. "*Pan* the Tool-Maker: Investigations into the Stone Tool-making and Tool-using Capabilities of a Bonobo (*Pan paniscus*)." *Journal of Archaeological Science* 20:81–91.

Trinkhaus, E. 1982. "Evolutionary Continuity among Archaic *Homo sapiens*." In *The Transition from Lower to Middle Palaeolithic and Origin of Modern Man*, ed. A. Ronen. Oxford: BAR International Series 151.

———. 1983. *The Shanidar Neanderthals.* New York: Academic Press.

———. 1986. "The Neanderthals and Modern Human Origins." *Annual Review of Anthropology* 15:193–218.

———. 1988. Quoted in B. Bower, "An Earlier Dawn for Modern Humans?" *Science News* 133:138.00

———. 1992. "Morphological Contrasts Between the Near Eastern Qafzeh-Skhul and Late Archaic Human Samples." In *The Evolution and Dispersal of Modern Humans in Asia*, eds. T. Akazawa, K. Aoki, and T. Kimura. Tokyo: Hokusen-sha.

———. 1993. "Femoral Neck-Shaft Angles of the Qafzeh-Slhul Early Modern Humans." *Journal of Human Evolution* 25:393–416.

———. 1995. "Neanderthal Mortality Patterns." *Journal of Archaeological Science* 22:121–42.

———. ed. 1983. *The Mousterian Legacy.* Oxford: British Archaeological Reports, International Series, No. 151.

Trinkhaus, E., and W. W. Howells. 1979. "The Neanderthals." *Scientific American* 241:118–33.

Trinkhaus, E., and P. Shipman. 1992. *The Neanderthals: Changing the Image of Mankind.* New York: Alfred A. Knopf.

———. 1993. "Neanderthals: Images of Ourselves." *Evolutionary Anthropology* 1(6):194–201.

Turner, A. 1992. "Large Carnivores and Earliest European Hominids: Changing Determinants of Resource Availability during the Lower and Middle Pleistocene." *Journal of Human Evolution* 22:109–26.

Valladas, H., J. L. Reyss, J. L. Joron, G. Valladas, O. Bar-Yosef, and B. Vandermeersch. 1988. "Thermoluminescence Dating of Mousterian 'Proto-Cro-Magnon' Remains from Israel and the Origin of Modern Man." *Nature* 331:614–16.

Vallois, H. 1961. "The Social Life of Early Man: The Evidence of the Skeletons." In *Social Life of Early Man*, ed. S. Washburn. Chicago: Aldine

Villa, P. 1983. *Terra Amata and the Middle Pleistocene Archaeological Record of Southern France.* Berkeley: U.C. Publications in Anthropology, Vol. 13, University of California Press.

———. 1991. "Middle Pleistocene Prehistory in Southwestern Europe: The State of Our Knowledge and Ignorance." *Journal of Anthropological Research* 47:193–217.

Walker, A. 1993. "The Origin of the Genus *Homo*." In *The Origin and Evolution of Humans and Humanness*, ed. D. T. Rasmussen. Boston: Jones and Bartlett.

Walker, A., and R. E. Leakey, eds. 1993. *The Nariokotome* Homo erectus *Skeleton*. Cambridge, MA: Harvard University Press.

Weidenreich, F. 1946. *Apes, Giants, and Man*. Chicago: University of Chicago Press.

White, J. P., and J. F. O'Connell. 1982. *A Prehistory of Australia, New Guinea and Sahul*. Sydney: Academic.

White, R. 1982. "Rethinking the Middle/Upper Paleolithic Transition." *Current Anthropology* 23:169–91.

———. 1986. *Dark Caves and Bright Visions*. New York: American Museum of Natural History.

———. 1989. "Production Complexity and Standardization in Early Aurignacian Bead and Pendant Manufacture." In *The Human Revolution: Behavioral and Biological Perspectives on the Origins of Modern Humans*, eds. P. Mellars and C. B. Stringer. Edinburgh: Edinburgh University Press.

———. 1992. "Beyond Art: Toward an Understanding of the Origins of Material Representation in Europe." *Annual Review of Anthropology* 21:537–64.

White, T. D. 1991. "The Question of Ritual Cannibalism at Grotta Guattari." *Current Anthropology* 32(2):103–38.

White, T. D., G. Suwa, W. K. Hart, R. C. Walter, G. Wolde, G. J. de Heinzelin, J. D. Clark, B. Asfaw, and E. Vrba. 1993. "New Discoveries of *Australopithecus* at Maka in Ethiopia." *Nature* 366:261–64.

White, T. D., G. Suwa, and B. Asfaw. 1994. "*Australopithecus ramidus*, a New Species of Early Hominid from Aramis, Ethiopia." *Nature* 371:306–12.

Windels, F. 1965. *The Lascaux Cave Paintings*. London: Faber and Faber.

Wobst, H. M. 1974a. "Boundary Conditions for Paleolithic Social Systems: A Simulation Approach." *American Antiquity* 39:147–78.

Wolpoff, M. 1968. "Climatic Influence on the Skeletal Nasal Aperture." *American Journal of Physical Anthropology* 29:405–23.

———. 1970. "The Evidence for Multiple Hominid Taxa at Swartkrans." *American Anthropologist* 72:56–57.

———. 1971. "Vértesszöllös and the Presapiens Theory." *American Journal of Physical Anthropology* 35:309.

———. 1988. Quoted in B. Bower, "An Earlier Dawn for Modern Humans?" *Science News* 133:138.

———. 1995. *Paleoanthropology*, 2nd ed. New York: McGraw Hill.

Wolpoff, M., Xinzhi Wu, and A. G. Thorne. 1984. "Modern *Homo sapiens* Origins: A General Theory of Hominid Evolution Involving the Fossil Evidence from East Asia." In *The Origins of Modern Humans: A World Survey of the Fossil Evidence*, eds. F. H. Smith and F. Spencer. New York: Alan R. Liss.

Wolpoff, M. H.. A. G. Thorne, F. H. Smith, D. W. Frayer, and G. G. Pope. 1994. "Multiregional Evolution: A World-Wide Source for Modern Human Populations." In *Origins of Anatomically Modern Humans*, eds., M. H. Nitecki and V. Nitecki. New York: Plenum Press.

Wood, B. A. 1991. *Koobi Fora Research Project, Vol. 4: Hominid Cranial Remains*. Oxford: Clarendon Press.

———. 1992. "Origin and Evolution of the Genus *Homo*." *Nature* 355:783–90.

———. 1993. "Early *Homo*: How Many Species?" In *Species, Species Concepts and Primate Evolution*, eds. W. H. Kimbel and L. B. Martin. New York: Plenum Press.

Wu Rukang and Jia Lampo. 1994. "China in the Period of *Homo habilis* and *Homo erectus*." *History of Humanity*, Vol. 1, ed. S. J. De Laet. London: Routledge.

Yellen, J. E., A. S. Brooks, E. Cornelissen, M. J. Mehlman, and K. Stewart. 1995. "A Middle Stone Age Worked Bone Industry from Katanda, Upper Semliki Valley, Zaire." *Science* 268:553–56.

Zubrow, E. 1989. "The Demographic Modeling of Neanderthal Extinction." In *The Human*

Revolution: Behavioural and Biological Perspectives on the Origins of Modern Humans, eds. P. Mellars and C. B. Stringer. Edinburgh: Edinburgh University Press.

NOTES

1. Gould, *Wonderful Life.*

2. See, for example, Frayer et al., "Theories of Modern Human Origins: The Paleontological Test," p. 17.

3. Ibid., p. 16.

4. Ibid., p. 17–18.

5. Aiello cites Bräuer, for example, "Africa's Place in the Evolution of *Homo sapiens.*"

6. Leakey, *Olduvai Gorge.*

7. Weidenreich, *Apes, Giants, and Man.*

8. See also Coon.

9. Howells (quoted in Frayer et al., "Theories of Modern Human Origins: The Paleontological Test," p. 15).

10. Frayer, Wolpoff, Thorne, Smith, and Pope, "Theories of Modern Human Origins: The Paleontological Test," p. 15.

11. See, for example, Lieberman and Jackson, "Race and Three Models of Human Origin," Table 1; also see Gamble, *Timewalkers: The Prehistory of Global Colonization..*

12. See Brace et al., "Clines and Clusters Versus 'Race': A Test in Ancient Egypt and the Case of a Death on the Nile."

13. Herrnstein and Murray, *The Bell Curve.*

14. Rushton, *Race, Evolution, and Behavior: A Life History Perspective.*

15. See, for example, book reviews of Rushton's *Race, Evolution, and Behavior: A Life History Perspective.*

16. Day, *Guide to Fossil Man,* p. 238.

17. Ibid., p. 409.

18. Klein, "Anatomy, Behavior, and Modern Human Origins."

19. Reviewed in Day, *Guide to Fossil Man,* pp. 177–178, for Olduvai Gorge.

20. Isaac, "The Archaeology of Human Origins," p. 60.

21. Pope, "Bamboo and Human Evolution."

22. Isaac, "Sorting Out the Muddle in the Middle—An Anthropologist's Post-Conference Appraisal," p. 504.

23. Shipman, "Early Hominid Lifestyle."

24. Binford, *Bones: Ancient Men and Modern Myth,* p. 294; idem., "Human Ancestors."

25. Roberts, "Body Weight, Race and Climate."

26. Jorgensen, "A Contribution of the Hypothesis of a Little More Fitness of Blood Group O."

27. Conroy, 1990.

28. Binford, "Human Ancestors: Changing Views of Their Behavior."

29. Bar-Yosef, "Archeological Occurrences in the Middle Pleistocene of Israel."

30. Klein, "Anatomy, Behavior, and Modern Human Origins."

31. Klein, ibid, p.178.

32. Carbonell's report as characterized here was taken from news reports; an article on these finds is in *Science*.

33. Sevink et al., "A Note on the Approximately 730,000-year-old Mammal Fauna and Associated Human Activity Sites near Isernia, Central Italy."

34. Wu Rukang and Jia Lampo, "China in the Period of *Homo habilis* and *Homo erectus*."

35. Ibid.

36. Binford and Stone, "Zhoukoudian: A Closer Look."

37. Arens, *The Man-Eating Myth*.

38. Garn and Block, "The Limited Nutritional Value of Cannibalism."

39. Shapiro, *Peking Man*.

40. Freeman, "Acheulian Sites and Stratigraphy in Iberia and the Maghreb," p. 664.

41. Ibid.

42. Ibid., p. 682, suggests large groups of hunters; but see Binford, "Human Ancestors," and James, "Hominid Use of Fire," for contrasting views; Shipman and Rose, "Evidence of Butchery and Hominid Activities at Torralba and Ambrona."

43. de Lumley, H., "A Paleolithic Camp at Nice"; Villa, *Terra Amata and the Middle Pleistocene Archaeological Record of Southern France*.

44. de Lumley, "A Paleolithic Camp at Nice."

45. Villa, *Terra Amata and the Middle Pleistocene Archaeological Record of Southern France*.

46. Klein, "Anatomy, Behavior, and Modern Human Origins."

47. Day, *Guide to Fossil Man*, p. 100.

48. Reviewed in Howell, "Observations on the Earlier Phases of the European Lower Paleolithic."

49. Tennyson was alluding to Goethe here.

50. Bender, "Comment on G. Krantz (*CA* 21:773–79)."

51. White, "Beyond Art: Toward an Understanding of the Origins of Material Representation in Europe," p. 560.

52. Klein, "Anatomy, Behavior, and Modern Human Origins."

53. White, "Rethinking the Middle/Upper Paleolithic Transition."

54. Lieberman, "Testing Hypotheses about Recent Human Evolution from Skulls."

55. Wobst, "Stylistic Behavior and Information Exchange."

56. White, "Rethinking the Middle/Upper Paleolithic Transition."

57. Ferraro et al., *Anthropology*, p. 129 presents a simplified description of this issue.

58. Aiello, "The Fossil Evidence for Modern Human Origins in Africa: A Revised View."

59. Melnick and Hoelzer, "What Is mtDNA Good for in the Study of Primate Evolution?" p. 9.

60. Frayer et al., "Theories of Modern Human Origins: The Paleontological Test."

61. Ibid, p. 39.

62. See, for example, Bräuer, "Africa's Place in the Evolution of *Homo sapiens*."

63. The following points of evidence are adapted from Frayer et al., "Theories of Modern Human Origins: The Paleontological Test," pp. 19–20.

64. Ibid.

65. Singer and Wymer, *The Middle Stone Age at Klasies River Mouth in South Africa.*

66. Ibid.

67. Frayer et al., "Theories of Modern Human Origins: The Paleontological Test."

68. Ibid., p. 36.

69. Deacon, "Southern Africa and Modern Human Origins"; Deacon and Schuurman, "The Origins of Modern People: The Evidence from Klasies River"; Bräuer, "Africa's Place in the Evolution of *Homo sapiens*."

70. Klein, "Anatomy, Behavior, and Modern Human Origins," p. 190.

71. Cited in news articles, in *Science*.

72. Frankel, *Remains to be Seen.*

73. Pope, "The Antiquity and Palaeoenvironment of the Asian Hominidae"; Wolpoff et al., "Modern *Homo sapiens* Origins: A General Theory of Hominid Evolution Involving the Fossil Evidence from East Asia"; Thorne, "The Arrival of Man in Australia."

74. See table 2 in Frayer et al., "Theories of Modern Human Origins: The Paleontological Test," for their argument that proponents of the Eve hypothesis have systematically misinterpreted the data from Africa with regard to shovelling.

75. Frayer et al., "Theories of Modern Human Origins: The Paleontological Test," p. 22.

76. Stringer et al., "The Significance of the Fossil Hominid from Petralona, Greece"; Trinkhaus, "Evolutionary Continuity among Archaic *Homo sapiens*."

77. Day, *Guide to Fossil Man*, p. 20.

78. Ibid., p. 22.

79. Roe, *The Lower and Middle Paleolithic Periods in Britain.*

80. Binford, "Human Ancestors," pp. 316–17.

81. de Lumley, "Ante-Neanderthals of Western Europe."

82. Svoboda, "Lithic Industries of the Arago, Vértesszöllös, and Bilzingsleben Hominids: Comparison and Evolutionary Interpretation."

83. Brace, "The Fate of the 'Classic' Neanderthals: A Consideration of Human Catastrophism."

84. Straus and Cave, "Pathology and the Posture of Neanderthal Man."

85. Trinkhaus, "The Neandertals and Modern Human Origins."

86. Ibid., p. 203.

87. Ibid., p. 205.

88. Bordes, *Typologie du Paleolithique ancien et moyen.*

89. Binford and Binford, "A Preliminary Analysis of Functional Variability in the Mousterian of Levallois Facies."

90. Binford, "Human Ancestors," p. 319.

91. Lieberman and Crelin, "On the Speech of Neanderthals."

92. Frayer and Wolpoff, "Comment on 'Glottogenesis and Modern *Homo sapiens.*' "

93. For a review of the evidence and dissenting comments on this topic, see Gargett, "Grave Shortcomings: The Evidence for Neanderthal Burial"; Chase and Dibble, "Middle Paleolithic Symbolism"; Brace, "Review of *Shanidar: The First Flower People,* by R. Solecki," p. 86.

94. Klein, "Anatomy, Behavior, and Modern Human Origins."

95. Straus, *Iberia before the Iberians: The Stone Age Prehistory of Cantabrian Spain.*

96. Trinkhaus, "The Neanderthals and Modern Human Origins."

97. Trinkhaus, "Neandertal Mortality Patterns."

98. Ibid., p. 121.

99. Day, *Guide to Fossil Man,* pp. 414–16.

100. Brace, *The Stages of Human Evolution: Human and Cultural Origins.* See also Smith and Ranyard, "Evolution of the Supraorbital Region in Upper Pleistocene Fossil Hominids from South-Central Europe."

101. Lovejoy and Trinkhaus, "Strength of Robusticity of the Neanderthal Tibia."

102. Smith, "Upper Pleistocene Hominid Evolution in South-Central Europe: A Review of the Evidence and Analysis of Trends."

103. Day, *Guide to Fossil Man,* p. 415. See also Trinkhaus and Howells, "The Neanderthals."

104. Soffer, "Ancestral Lifeways in Eurasia—the Middle and Upper Paleolithic Records."

105. Valladas et al., "Thermoluminescence Dating of Mousterian 'Proto-Cro-Magnon' Remains."

106. Schwarcz, "Chronology of Modern Humans in the Levant."

107. Trinkhaus, quoted in B. Bower, "An Earlier Dawn for Modern Humans?" p. 138.

108. Frayer et al., "Theories of Modern Human Origins: The Paleontological Test," p. 37.

109. Bar-Yosef, "Late Pleistocene Adaptations in the Levant"; Shea, "Spear Points from the Middle Paleolithic of the Levant"; summarized in Frayer et al., "Theories of Modern Human Origins: The Paleontological Test," p. 20.

110. Klein, "Anatomy, Behavior, and Modern Human Origins."

111. Bräuer, Gunter. "The Evolution of Modern Humans: A Comparison of the African and Non-African Evidence."

112. Frayer et al., "Theories of Modern Human Origins: The Paleontological Test."

113. Bricker, "Upper Paleolithic Archaeology."

114. Klein, personal communication.

115. Reviewed in Straus, "Upper Paleolithic Origins and Radiocarbon Calibration: More New Evidence from Spain."

116. Ibid., p. 197.

117. Ibid., p. 196.

118. Ibid.

119. Leveque and Vandermeersch, "Les Decouvertes de Restes Humains."

120. Trinkhaus, "The Neandertals and Modern Human Origins," p. 198.

121. Bischoff et al., "Dating of the Basal Aurignacian Sandwich at Abric Romani (Catalunya, Spain) by Radiocarbon and Uranium-series."

122. Smith, "Upper Pleistocene Hominid Evolution in South-Central Europe: A Review of the Evidence and Analysis of Trends."

123. Straus, "Upper Paleolithic Origins and Radiocarbon Calibration: More New Evidence from Spain."

124. Frayer et al., "Theories of Modern Human Origins: The Paleontological Test," p. 32.

125. See, for example, the discussion in *Current Anthropology* 36(2): 159–197.

126. Thackeray, *Current Anthropology* 36(2):185.

127. Prideaux et al., *Cro-Magnon Man*, pp. 93–94.

128. De Beaune, "Paleolithic Lamps and Their Specialization: A Hypothesis."

129. Conkey, "New Approaches in the Search for Meaning? A Review of Research in 'Paleolithic Art.' "

130. Rice and Paterson, "Cave Art and Bones: Exploring the Interrelationships," p. 98.

131. Fisher, *Woman's Creation*.

132. Marshack, "Some Implications of the Paleolithic Symbolic Evidence for the Origins of Language."

133. Leroi-Gourhan, "The Evolution of Paleolithic Art."

134. Lewis-Williams and Dowson, "The Signs of All Times: Entopic Phenomena in Upper Paleolithic Art."

135. Ibid., p. 215 (emphasis theirs).

136. See, for example, Pfeiffer, "Cro-magnons Were Really Us, Working Out Strategies for Survival."

137. Hodder, *Reading the Past*; also see Straus, *Iberia before the Iberians: The Stone Age Prehistory of Cantabrian Spain*.

138. Conkey, "New Approaches in the Search for Meaning? A Review of Research in 'Paleolithic Art,' " p. 422.

139. Halverson, "Art for Art's Sake in the Paleolithic," p. 71.

140. Bednarik, "Paleoart and Archaeological Myths."

141. White, "Beyond Art: Toward an Understanding of the Origins of Material Representation in Europe," p. 560.

142. Marks, *Human Biodiversity: Genes, Race, and History.*

143. Marks, *Human Biodiversity: Genes, Race, and History*; Brace et al., "Clines and Clusters Versus 'Race': A Test in Ancient Egypt and the Case of a Death on the Nile."

144. Thiel, "Early Settlement of the Philippines, Eastern Indonesia, and Australia-New Guinea: A New Hypothesis."

145. Vallois, "The Social Life of Early Man: The Evidence of the Skeletons."

146. Ibid.

147. Soffer, *The Upper Paleolithic of the Central Russian Plain.*

148. See, for example, Klein, *Ice-Age Hunters of the Ukraine*; Soffer, *The Upper Paleolithic of the Central Russian Plain.*

149. Bellwood, *The Prehistory of the Indo-Malaysian Archipelago*; Sonviian assemblage—Vietnam.

150. White and O'Connell, "Australian Prehistory: New Aspects of Antiquity."

151. Thorne, "The Arrival of Man in Australia."

152. Klein, "Anatomy, Behavior, and Modern Human Origins."

153. Day, *Guide to Fossil Man.*

5

THE FIRST AMERICANS

*At break of day the shore was thronged with people all
young . . . all of good stature, fine looking. . . . I was anxious
to learn whether they had any gold, as I noticed that some
of the natives had rings hanging from holes in their noses. . . .
I tried to get them to go for some, but they could not
understand they were to go.*

Christopher Columbus (13 October 1492)

Columbus and most "discoverers" of the New World were not surprised to find "Indians" there, because they thought they had landed in India, or perhaps Japan. But as soon as Europeans realized they were not in the Orient and became aware of the rich diversity of New World cultures, they began to struggle with the problem of the origin of the Native Americans. The Bible, the final authority for most Europeans of this era, was strangely silent on the very existence of this "second-earth," so Europeans began speculating on how the "Indians" could have reached the New World from the Garden of Eden, where they were assumed to have originated. Early explorers were greatly impressed by "similarities" between Egyptian and aboriginal American cultures, such as the great pyramids to be found in Egypt, Mexico, and the Mississippi Valley, and so some concluded that the Native Americans were descendants of Ham, one of Noah's sons, who was also thought to have been the father of the Egyptians.[1] Another popular idea was that the Native Americans were descendants of the "lost tribes of Israel," Jews who had been evicted from Palestine by the Romans.[2] The "lost tribes" idea eventually was incorporated into the doctrines of the Church of the Latter-Day Saints, whose *Book of Mormon* explains how the Native Americans were remnants of tribes of Israel that had come to the New World by ship hundreds of years before Columbus. Others believed that Native Americans were descendants of people who fled Atlantis or Mu—islands which some think were destroyed thousands of years ago by volcanic eruption.

But by 1590 a Spanish Jesuit, José de Acosta, had proposed that Native Americans had come from Asia, and by 1781 Thomas Jefferson could describe the peopling of the New World in terms most scholars today think are accurate:

Late discoveries of Captain Cook, coasting from Kamschatka to California, have proved that if the two continents of Asia and America be separated at all, it is only by a narrow

240

straight. So that from this side also, inhabitants may have passed into America; and the resemblance between the Indians of America and the eastern inhabitants of Asia, would induce us to conjecture, that the former are the descendants of the latter, or the latter of the former: excepting indeed the Eskimaux, who, from the same circumstances of resemblance, and from identity of language, must be derived from the Groenlanders, and these probably from some of the northern parts of the old continent.[3]

In their search for clues to the origins of Native Americans, Jefferson and others of his age were struck by the close physical resemblance the Native Americans had to Asian races with their dark brown eyes, black, coarse, straight hair, and, relative to Europeans, widely spaced cheekbones (Figure 5.1). But differences were also apparent: except for the Eskimos and Aleuts, most aboriginal Americans had less pronounced epicanthic folds (part of the eyelid) than those that distinguish east Asian populations, and many Native Americans had relatively more prominent noses than east Asians.

Europeans also noted that the New World included an impressive diversity of languages—in some cases people who lived relatively close to one another spoke mutually unintelligible languages—and that none of the languages of Native Americans

FIGURE 5.1   An early photograph of a Native American. Physical resemblances between Americans and Asian peoples reflect their common origins.

bore any obvious resemblance to Old World languages. Thus, it seemed certain that although the aboriginal Americans were probably descendants of Asian peoples, they must have lived in America for a long time for such physical and linguistic divergence to have occurred.

That people have lived in the New World for at least 12,000 years has been evident for a long time. In 1908 a cowboy riding along the edge of a gully in New Mexico, near the town of Folsom, discovered some "arrowheads" and animal bones protruding from a layer of soil about six meters beneath the surface of the plain. Eventually, in 1925, his finds came to the attention of J. D. Figgins, director of the Colorado Museum of Natural History, who began a long series of excavations at this site.[4] A primary find was a long, "fluted" (it had two long strips removed near the base and parallel to the length of the point) "projectile point" that was embedded in the ribs of a species of bison that had been extinct for about 10,000 years. Since most archaeologists and others were skeptical of the idea that humans had been in the New World that long, Figgins insisted on excavating the site with a committee of archaeologists on hand to watch his every move so that no one could claim the evidence had been faked.

In 1932 another important find was made, this time near the town of Clovis, New Mexico. Here, too, large blade tools were discovered in association with extinct animals. But at this site artifacts somewhat different from those at Folsom (Figure 5.2) were found in a layer beneath some "Folsom points." Analysis suggested a date of about 12,000 years ago for the earliest Clovis-style artifacts, and within a few years artifacts similar in size, shape, and style to the Clovis points were discovered at many different places in North America. Since then, stone points resembling Clovis arti-

Dalton   Clovis   Eden   Folsom

FIGURE 5.2   Some types of early American projectile points.

facts have been found in much of North and South America, from the Arctic to the tip of South America.

Disputes about early Americans thus focus on the question of whether or not anyone was here before the Clovis cultures in existence about 12,000 years ago.

Today, the view that the first Americans came from east Asia via a land route is generally accepted. Thus, the term "Native American" is something of a misnomer, for on the grand chronology of the human species, the time difference between the arrival of the very first humans in the New World and that of Columbus is relatively trivial. All Americans are immigrants, and even contemporary Native Americans would have a difficult time making a persuasive case for initial ownership of the Americas, for the evidence suggests that most living Native Americans are descendants of groups that came to the Americas thousands of years after the first immigrants, and perhaps even displaced them (see below).

INITIAL COLONIZATION OF THE AMERICAS

Analyses of the initial colonization of the Americas usually focus on four related questions: What Old World people were the ancestors of the first Americans? *When* did the first people enter the New World and colonize subarctic and temperate zones? What routes did they follow in colonizing North and South America? What kinds of technologies and economies did these initial waves of colonists have?

These questions may seem to be rather simple empirical problems, subjects of speculation studied on the basis of inadequate data about questions that may be intrinsically important but without much wider significance. Whether the first Americans arrived in the New World 30,000 years ago or 13,000 years ago would not seem to make much difference in the grand scheme of things.

But the colonization of the New World does have much greater significance than these simple questions might suggest. Most important is the fact that the subsequent history of these peoples in the New World was largely independent of influences from the Old World. Whenever they first arrived, New World peoples give us a comparative case—a long and rich cultural history that can be compared with that of the Old World. Moreover, the colonization of the New World involves one of the most complex issues in paleolithic archaeology, the nature and processes of human *adaptive radiation*. All animal species seem to radiate across the world "naturally" until they reach the limits of their adaptation. Some tropical species, such as the elephant, evolved cold-adapted subspecies that allowed it to penetrate into the far north of both the Old and New Worlds, but even these evolutionary adaptations could not produce an animal capable of supporting its huge bulk in the icy extremes of the poles. Evolutionary change seems to be most rapid along the limits of adaptations, but measuring the tempo of evolutionary change in extinct species is difficult.

Human patterns of migration and adaptive radiation are a complex blend of evolving physical characteristics and culture. Thus, the New World archaeological record provides us with an opportunity to study in detail a complex mosaic of human adaptations across a gigantic and highly varied landscape.

Why people came to the Americas has never been an issue. People, like other animal species, seem to penetrate their entire available range "naturally." The "budding-off" process described in the previous chapter is probably applicable to the colonization of the Americas. Ethnographic studies tell us that hunter-forager groups often increase to a certain size level until friction develops among some members of the group, or resources become too scarce, and then the social unit splits, with some members going off into new territory. The long winter nights of northern Asia doubtless offered ample opportunity to brood on what a jerk one's cousin was, or to muse on what Garden of Eden might lie over the horizon, and as a result of tens of thousands of years of group-fissioning, population growth, and small group social interactions, the world was populated.

There remains some doubt about *how* people first got to North America, because, as we saw in the previous chapter, people were certainly living in Australia long before 30,000 years ago, and there seems no way they could have reached there except by boat. But the evidence strongly suggests that the first Americans travelled there the old-fashioned way—they walked.

Any explanation of the colonization of the New World from Asia must consider the kinds of physical environments these colonists would have faced, and recent research has challenged many traditional ideas on this point (Figure 5.3).

Today, Eskimos using skin boats easily cross the ninety kilometers of open sea separating Siberia and America, and recently an American woman slathered herself with grease and actually swam from Alaska to Siberia. But such a sea crossing would not have been necessary during much of the Pleistocene. During periods of glacial advance within the last million years, enormous quantities of water were converted to ice, lowering the sea level sufficiently to expose a 1500- to 3000-kilometer-wide expanse of the floor of the Bering Sea. This land bridge—usually referred to as Beringia (Figure 5.4)—was probably available at least four times in the last 60,000 years.

The kinds of resources Beringia would have offered hunter-foragers would have depended on the period in which the migrants crossed. At various times, ocean currents created an ice-free, tundra-covered connection from eastern Siberia across the land bridge and into central Alaska. These conditions are reflected in the many non-Arctic-adapted animal species that crossed from Asia to America during the Pleistocene. Prior to 10,000 years ago, species of deer, bison, camels, bears, foxes, mammoths, moose, caribou, and even rodents crossed from Siberia into the New World. Going the other way—from America to Asia—were foxes, woodchucks, and, during the early Pleistocene, the ancestors of modern forms of horses, wolves, and other animals.[5] In some periods Beringia would not have been particularly rich—there is even the possibility of dust storms, so dry and barren was most of it.[6] But at other times, migrants on the land bridge in the brief but warm summers of some periods of the Pleistocene would have found musk-oxen and other large herbivores, along with fish, birds, and sea mammals along the shore.

Interior Alaska and Canada were relatively rich environments in the mid-Wisconsin interglacial, and at times humans may have had a *narrow but* clear ice-free run all the way to South America during this period. Pollen cores from easternmost Beringia suggest that from 30,000 to 14,000 years ago, the time when most archae-

FIGURE 5.3 Between 60,000 and 12,000 years ago, world climate warmed several times, opening routes between the Arctic and more southern latitudes of the New World. Two possible periods of colonization are during the Mid-Wisconsin Interglacial about 40,000 years ago, and after the Late Wisconsin Glaciation, about 18,000 years ago.

FIGURE 5.4 Several archaeological sites in Siberia may be of cultures ancestral to the first Americans.

ologists think the first Americans arrived,[7] the "landscape [of Beringia] consisted of relatively bare polar desert or fell-field tundra, a rocky terrain sparsely vegetated by herbs and dwarf shrubs. This suggests that the late Wisconsian environment in this part of Beringia was as harsh as the modern high Arctic."[8]

It used to be thought that southward migrations could have occurred only a few times, because it was assumed that for most of the Pleistocene the way would have been blocked by coalescing ice sheets (Figure 5.5). Even if these ice sheets did not completely bar the way south, most authorities thought that any narrow open corridor between them would have had too little food to support groups of hunters and gatherers—who require large territories to support even low population densities.

But some scholars now believe that the two or three major glaciers of North America reached their peaks at different times, formed more rapidly than previously thought, and were perhaps thinner than earlier estimates.[9] If so, even during the coldest periods of the late Pleistocene, about 22,000 to 18,000 years ago, North America would not have been so formidable a place for human colonization and migration as previously thought. The various expansions and contractions of the glaciers would have displaced people and animals, and, as Fladmark notes, in some cases people in southern Canada and the northern United States may even have been forced back toward Beringia as the glaciers expanded.[10]

The exact path the first Americans took is not known, but the most likely course would be along the coast of the land bridge, then into Alaska north of the Brooks

FIGURE 5.5 Some of the earliest known American sites. Most of these sites range from 20,000 to 10,000 years ago.

Range, up the Yukon River Valley, then into the Mackenzie River Valley, and from there southward, along the eastern slopes of the Rockies and on into the Dakotas and then further southward. Along the coast of the land bridge were probably abundant resources in the form of fish, birds, eggs, invertebrates, and many plant foods. If groups did come this way, it is unlikely that we shall ever be able to document their journey archaeologically, for the rising seas of the post-Pleistocene era have submerged the ancient shoreline. A Pacific Coast route is technically possible, but here again we have no evidence because such sites would lie deep beneath the current coastal seas.[11]

We might expect that if the immigrants crossed the land bridge primarily along the coast, then the groups migrating south would have retained some elements of the generalized hunting, fishing, and foraging economies required in the intertidal zone. If, on the other hand, they came across the middle of the land bridge, a greater reliance on big-game hunting would have been essential. Whatever their adaptation, the migrants were almost certainly not constantly on the move southward. The budding-off process described above is the usual one in cases when new species move into empty niches, and many thousands of years may have passed between the time the first human set foot on the land bridge and the year the first groups arrived in the mid-latitudes of North America.

North winds blowing off the northern glacial ice sheets made the climate of Pleistocene North America much different from today's climate. Much of Nevada and Utah was covered by Lake Bonneville, of which only a shrinking remnant (the Great Salt Lake) remains. Wyoming, Iowa, and other parts of the Great Plains were vast pine, spruce, and tamarack forests and lush open grasslands. To the south, the area between the Mississippi River and the Rockies was a verdant mosaic of grasslands, lakes, and birch and alder forests. In eastern North America huge expanses of coniferous forests stretched from the edge of the glacial ice sheets to the lower Ohio River Valley. The animals inhabiting this wilderness of 14,000 to 12,000 years ago closely approximate a modern hunter's vision of paradise. Giant moose, three meters and more in height, could be found in many of the wetter areas, along with *Castoroides*, a species of beaver as large as a modern bear (Figure 5.6). Along the woodland edges of the southeastern United States were large populations of giant ground sloths, ungainly creatures fully as tall as modern giraffes. In more open country were vast herds of straight-horned bison, caribou, musk-oxen, and mammoths—some four meters high at the shoulders. In the more forested areas of the east and south were the mammoth's cousin, the mastodon, a more solitary animal than the mammoth and apparently a browser rather than a grassland grazer. Amid all these large creatures were rabbits, armadillos, birds, camels, peccaries, and other animals. And the carnivores that such a movable feast attracted were equally impressive. Packs of dire wolves roamed most of the New World, as did panthers as large as modern lions and two species of saber-toothed cat, one about the size of a lion.[12] Thus, the first Americans were hardly entering an "empty niche," since these ferocious predators no doubt provided stiff competition for people trying to specialize in hunting. Central and South America were also rich game preserves during and just after the Pleistocene, but in the rain forests of the Amazon Basin, the great coniferous forests of the North American South and East, and a few other locations, so much energy was in the form of

FIGURE 5.6   Some large mammals of Pleistocene America. The scale preserves relative size.

inedible and unnutritious vegetation (cellulose) that there would have been few resources for primitive hunters and gatherers.

With this sense of the environments and resources that the New World offered, we can attempt to answer the questions posed above concerning the biological ancestry of the first Americans, the chronology and geography of their colonization, and the economic and technological basis of their colonization. To do this, we can appeal to several categories of evidence involving: (1) the physical anthropology of Native Americans and possible ancestral groups in the Old World; (2) the archaeological records both of the New World and of the areas in the Old World from which the colonists might have come; and (3) linguistic evidence—in the sense of those clues that indigenous New World languages can provide us about the cultural origins, cultural relationships, and migration patterns of the first Americans.

All scholars studying the problem of New World colonization use these same categories of evidence, but they disagree profoundly in their conclusions.[13]

PHYSICAL ANTHROPOLOGICAL EVIDENCE

By 100,000 years ago, Old World peoples seem to have had all the skills at making clothes, fire, and tools that would have been necessary for the trek to the New World. But intensive research has failed to turn up any New World human skeletons that cannot be fitted comfortably within our own species, *Homo sapiens sapiens*. And because the first *Homo sapiens sapiens* appear in the Middle East and Europe about 35,000 years ago, we might assume that the aboriginal Americans must have come over since then, but we do not know when the first *Homo sapiens sapiens* appeared in the east Asian areas—they may have been there long before they were in the Middle East or Europe.[14]

With regard to the Old World ancestors of Native Americans, the physical anthropological data strongly suggests that they were, of course, east Asians, and were almost certainly the Pleistocene peoples of the areas near Alaska. But questions remain about the earlier genetic ancestors of these east Asian people: Were they, for example, people from coastal areas west of Japan, perhaps, or were they north central Chinese, or were they western Asians who migrated east from northern Eurasia?

Many scholars have analyzed the teeth, skulls, and other physical features of early and current Native Americans in hopes of identifying their origins. It is uncertain when some east Asian populations developed epicanthic folds, small noses, and relatively flat facial profiles, but in view of the prominent noses of most Native Americans and their non-Mongolian eye shapes, it is apparent that these differences can be attributed to one or more possibilities: the Americans are only distantly related to these populations; they emigrated before the Asian populations developed their distinctive features; these different characteristics existed in different Asian populations, and that what we see in the contrasts of Amerind populations are the results of successive migrations by different human groups. We have very little evidence on which to estimate rates of evolutionary change in these superficial physical characteristics, and variations in them are thus difficult to interpret.[15]

C. Turner, in an analysis of teeth from various populations, produced the cluster-diagram presented in Figure 5.7. Teeth preserve well, have morphological characteristics that are under relatively simple genetic control, and seem to change relatively quickly under changing selective conditions. Figure 5.7 indicates the relative frequency in various groups of incisor "shoveling"—the degree to which the lingual surface of incisors is curled or ridged. On this trait alone, one would clearly see North Chinese ancestry for Native Americans.[16] Turner looked at many different features of teeth, including shoveling, and variations in the number of roots of premolars and molars. By comparing large samples of teeth on many different measurements, Turner concluded that: (1) New World groups are more like Asians than like Europeans; (2) all New World groups resemble each other more than they do most Old World populations; (3) dental variation is greater in North America than in South America; (4) there are three "clusters" of New World peoples.[17]

As Turner notes, these characteristics seem to make sense if there were three distinct migrations into the Americas, all from North China. It is very difficult, however, to estimate rates of change in these kinds of physical features, and thereby to estimate how long ago the migrations to the Americas began, but Turner's calcula-

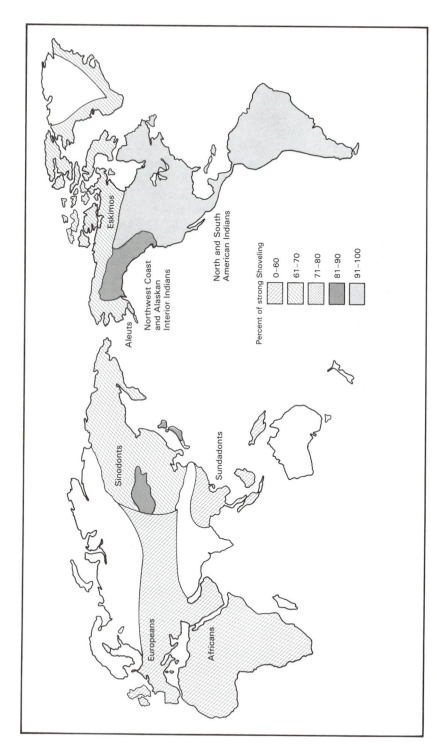

FIGURE 5.7 Variations in human teeth shapes reflect genetic ancestry. Incisor "shoveling"—the curved cross-sectional shape of incisors—occurs most frequently in northeast Asian and New World peoples and distinguishes them from the rest of the world. This evidence supports the view that the New World was colonized by three successive migrations from Asia.

tions estimate a date of about 12,000 years ago for the initial colonization of the New World, with two much later waves of colonizations.

These separate migrations also seem to be reflected in a study by Steele and Powell, who did a complex statistical analysis of measurements on the teeth, skulls, and skeletons of the earliest known Americans and compared them to various other populations. Their results indicate that the earliest Americans were different physically from more recent Native Americans and northern Asians, having longer and narrower braincases and shorter and narrower faces.[18]

Just as DNA has been used to estimate the divergences that mark the early hominid record (see chapters 3 and 4), so too the genetic diversity of Native Americans has been considered as evidence concerning when the New World was colonized and who colonized it. Analyses of DNA from both Siberians and Native Americans have led some scholars to conclude that the original colonization of the Americas occurred sometime between 34,000 and 17,000 years ago, but as always, these estimates are speculative and disputed.[19]

It is interesting to note that these various studies of Native American physical anthropology have some relevance for the problem of the origins of modern *Homo sapiens sapiens* (chapter 4). On the basis of their general dental morphology, Turner labeled north Asians and Americans as *sinodonts*, and the eastern and southern Asians as *sundadonts*, and he noted that both are very different from Europeans. As we noted in chapter 4, some scholars see traces of these sinodont and sundadont patterns in humans in Asia going back many hundreds of thousands of years, and on that basis they argue against the idea that we are all today descended from Africans who replaced all these very early Asian peoples.

LINGUISTIC EVIDENCE

Various scholars have tried to estimate the date and patterns of New World colonization by examining Native American languages. Just as the resemblances among English, Greek, Persian, and other languages point toward a common Indo-European original language, the Native American languages have been screened for signs of common origin. A recent controversial analysis of this problem is made by Joseph Greenberg, who argues that New World languages reflect three periods of colonization—the earliest, which is associated with Amerind, then a group of what are called Na-Dene speakers, and finally, at a later time, Eskimo-Aleut speakers.[20] Each of these three language groups probably originated from separate Old World language families, and there is some (controversial) evidence that all the world's languages can be traced to a single language family.[21] But like studies of teeth, estimates of the time of New World colonization on the basis of language changes must be considered quite speculative. Greenberg's three language groups appear to fit the archaeological and dental evidence for three periods of migrations rather well, but estimates of the rates at which languages diverge over time, as well as estimates of similarity between ancient languages on the basis of contemporary languages, are always speculative.

ARCHAEOLOGICAL EVIDENCE

One might think that good, solid archaeological data—bones and stones—would be a firmer basis for analyzing New World colonization, given the ambiguities in estimating rates of change in teeth, languages, etc. The truth, however, is that the archaeological record does not resolve these questions and disputes about the date, routes, and adaptations of the first Americans.

At this time there is no conclusive evidence that people were in the New World and south of Alaska *before* about 13,000 B.C. That they were there at that time or shortly thereafter is certain (insofar as science can ever be certain), since scores of sites have been dated by many different methods to between 13,000 and 10,000 B.C.

But the evidence for earlier occupations, although intriguing, is far from convincing. One might think that, since hundreds of Asian sites have been securely dated to before 13,000 B.C. while no American sites have thus far been dated to that time, then, as weak as negative evidence is, this would suggest that there are no American sites of comparably early age. But it is at least possible that people were in the New World long before 13,000 B.C. but simply left no traces that have been found yet. In the North American East, for example, exposed land surface in what would have been resource-rich areas of Tennessee, Alabama, and the Ohio Valley are extremely old, and artifacts found on them are difficult to date. Crude "pebble-tools" on these land surfaces could conceivably be the only surviving traces of very early occupations here. These pebble-tools show simplicity and extreme patination in comparison to other artifacts, and they resemble crude pebble-tools and other implements found in Peru that have been radiocarbon-dated (controversially) to between 19,600 and 14,150 B.C. Some have characterized the earliest New World cultures as the Pre-Projectile Point Stage.[22] The absence of projectile points and the simplicity of these early artifacts may mean that the earliest immigrants were not highly specialized big-game hunters, which suggests that they came over during the warmer periods of the Pleistocene as generalized hunters and gatherers. We cannot be certain, of course, because successful big-game hunters (like *Homo erectus*) used crude stone tools, but these pebble tools do not look as if they were specialized killing or butchering implements. Nor have they been found with butchered animal bones or in environmental circumstances suggesting specialized hunting.

Except for this pebble-tool complex, however, to a large degree arguments about the date of New World colonization come down to one's belief in specific radiocarbon dates. And although the radiocarbon dating method has been shown to be broadly accurate around the world (see chapter 2), any single radiocarbon date can be misleading because of any number of factors, ranging from natural contamination through oil seeps or coal deposits to incompetent laboratory technicians. When the first radiocarbon dates were produced on Egyptian materials, for example, Egyptologists rejected these "scientific" dates because they conflicted with a decidedly unscientific farrago of evidence from king-lists, artifact styles, etc. But the Egyptologists were right. Until archaeologists discovered that radiocarbon dates had to be corrected for past fluctuations in the amounts of radiocarbon in the atmosphere, these radiometric dates were off by centuries.

So we must regard individual New World dates with proper skepticism, and put our faith only in broad patterns.[23]

If individual radiocarbon dates are always somewhat suspect, the only other obvious basis on which to date New World colonization would seem to be a comparison of Old World artifact styles and sites and the earliest New World sites and implements. But when we try to do this, we find that similarities between North Asian and early American stone tools are very much in the eye of the beholder.

NORTH ASIA

We might expect to find a long trail of archaeological sites stretching from northeastern Siberia along the sea floor of the now-submerged land bridge into central Alaska, and then southward, between the ice caps. If these early immigrants were big-game hunters, we would expect many sites to be concentrations of animal bones, hearths, and flint tools appropriate for killing and preparing these animals. Alas, the gap between the real and ideal—so persistent in all archaeological research—is particularly great in this case. Some sites do fit this pattern, but the evidence is far from conclusive. First of all, adequate surveys of northeastern Siberia have never been completed. Aside from the rigors of the Arctic climate, the politics of doing surveys amid ICBM missile silos and radar stations have, until recently, deterred most Western scholars. Russian archaeologists,[24] nonetheless, have done excellent research in these areas, and now that Siberia is opening to Western scholars, collaborative research should clarify the cultural relationships of Pleistocene east Asian and North American cultures.

Present evidence suggests that before about 40,000 years ago, Siberia had extremely low population densities or was unsettled altogether—its great frigid interior swamps and forests may have barred human colonization, at least until huts had been developed. In any case, the earliest known sites in northeastern Siberia date to about 23,000 years ago and reflect a life focused on the hunting of mammoths and other large animals. Projectile points, scrapers, and burins—tool types associated with big-game hunters all over the Old World—are the most frequent implements at Siberian sites, such as Mal'ta, Afontova gora II, and other sites of this period. Stone tools from Mal'ta in deposits radiocarbon-dated to 14,750 years ago do not include Clovis-style points but seem to show at least similarities to early American assemblages—although there do not appear to be many large, finely crafted projectile points.[25] Haynes has even raised the possibility that Mal'ta represents an intermediate point in migrations of eastern European people across Siberia and into the New World—which he thinks is plausible because of the similarities between Clovis assemblages and late Pleistocene eastern European industries.[26]

N. Dikov's work on the shores of Lake Ushki offers at least some evidence about possible American ancestors. Dikov found the remains of what appears to be a large camp, in which people lived in hide or wood shelters. The center of one camp area was a deep burial pit in which the poorly preserved fragments of a body were found, along with about a thousand soft stone beads, some pendants of the same material, and some amber beads. The whole area of the burial was covered with red ocher, used probably to simulate blood or a living complexion on bodies.

Radiocarbon dating places the site about 14,300 to 13,600 years ago, but other dating methods and considerations of groundwater contamination have led Dikov to estimate the date as at least 1,500 to 2,000 years older than that. For purposes of linking this site to the Americas, it is significant that Dikov found stone points in the bifacial, leaf-shape form that resemble those from the North American Great Basin of about 13,000 to 11,000 years ago. Bifacial leaf-shape points have also been found at the Dyuktai Cave site on the Alden River in Siberia. These points probably date to about 15,000 years ago and also appear in Alaskan and western Canadian sites.

Dikov reviewed the evidence for other sites on the way to what would have been Beringia and concluded that nothing "challenges the conservative view that the significant population movements from Asia occurred after the peak of the last glaciation, which was some 18,000 years ago."[27]

NORTH AND SOUTH AMERICA

The evidence is also somewhat sketchy on the American side of the land bridge. The Alaskan and northern Canadian climates make surveys very difficult, and farther south the constant waxing and waning of the glacial ice sheets and the vast riverine systems that drained them have thoroughly chewed up much of the land along the Canadian corridor. No doubt many sites in these areas have long since been scoured away by ice or water.

Ironically, the site with perhaps the best claim to a pre-12,000 B.P. date in the Americas is among the farthest south, Monte Verde, in south central Chile (Figure 5.5). Here Tom Dillehay and his crew have excavated a camp site that has been radiocarbon-dated to about 13,000 years ago, and below the levels of that age are layers of tools and debris that may be much older, perhaps up to 33,000 years old.[28]

Monte Verde is particularly interesting because, unlike most other sites of this age, it is not a cave or rock shelter. It is an open-air site located in a cold, wet, forested area that was covered by a peat bog and thereby extremely well preserved. A piece of mastodon flesh was found intact, plus a human footprint, log foundations for huts, animal skins, numerous plant remains, and many other remains. Almost all the bones from the site were from seven mastodons, which appear to have been killed elsewhere and carried home in large segments. Scores of plants were eaten, and remains of some plants with medicinal properties were found in the camp debris. Trade with other groups was indicated by the presence of salt, bitumen, non-native plants, and other commodities. Dillehay estimates that thirty to fifty people lived at Monte Verde at one time, with an impressive degree of occupational specialization in woodworking, stone-tool manufacturing, and other skills.

Monte Verde, if it truly is as old as the radiocarbon dates suggest, is one of the most important sites in the New World. If people were here at 13,000 B.P., they must have been in the New World far earlier; if they lived in the almost sedentary communities that Monte Verde seems to represent, many models of hunting-foraging economies may not apply to much of the New World's earliest populations. And if the layers of the site dated by radiocarbon methods to 34,000 B.P. really are that old, then most of the debates about New World colonization have been beside the point.

The Monte Verde dates have received some support in the form of radiocarbon dates of hearths from sites near Pedra Furada, in eastern Brazil, where numerous stone tools and animal bones were found with charcoal in stratified layers that yielded a consistent series of twelve dates, from about 32,000 to 17,000 years ago.[29]

Some of the earliest dates for a New World site come from Pikimachay Cave in Peru, where archaeologist Richard MacNeish excavated crude stone tools and animal bones that have been radiocarbon-dated as early as 22,000 years ago.[30] The association between these stone tools and some forms of extinct animals is unmistakable in 12,000-year-old levels of the site, but some archaeologists doubt that its earliest levels represent human occupation, and all the early Peruvian dates seem at least somewhat equivocal.[31] The evidence for extensive penetration of most of South America by 11,000 B.P. is overwhelming, however, even in difficult environments like the interior of Brazil.[32]

One of the most controversial and potentially important early New World sites is Meadowcroft Rock Shelter, near Avella, Pennsylvania, where many layers of alluvial sediments were deposited by a tributary of the Ohio River. Interspersed in these alluvial sediments are many clear indications of human occupation, including prismatic flint blades, basketry, and hearths. Millennia of reoccupation left a sixteen-foot-thick "layercake" of tools, bones, baskets, and other debris. The question is, how far back does Meadowcroft's earliest occupation date? The site was excellently excavated, and there is no question about the provenience of the artifacts. A bit of charred basketry from near the bottom was radiocarbon-dated to 19,600 ± 2,400 and 19,150 ± 800 years B.P. Charcoal from a level beneath the basketry dates to as old as 37,000 years ago, but there were no associated artifacts. Unfortunately, there is some suggestion that the samples may have been contaminated by groundwater and that the site's stratigraphy has been misunderstood.[33] The kinds of bones found at the site also pose some problems, in that they do not seem to be from animals one would expect this close to the glaciers that would have pushed far down into the northeastern United States in the late Pleistocene.

The stone tools of Meadowcroft's earliest levels are similar to the typical Clovis assemblage of 12,000 years ago, but some blade sizes and types are different. Adovasio has compared the Meadowcroft lithics to those from other sites and suspects that they may represent a link between Old World tool industries and early North American cultures, such as the Clovis.[34]

But if the earlier dates for Meadowcroft are accepted, it means that people were in the continental United States before the last glacial advance, which implies that the ice sheets were in fact no barrier and that the scarcity of sites found is a matter of inadequate searching, low population densities, and the post-depositional destruction of sites.

If people entered the New World 30,000 or more years ago, it might seem surprising that more archaeological sites have not been found dating to this period; after all, hundreds of Old World sites date to this age. But population densities in Europe and other parts of the Old World had been slowly building for hundreds of thousands of years before people entered the New World. In addition, most European sites of this age are found in caves and rock shelters, and there are relatively few of these along the probable route into the New World. Alternatively, the first Americans may have worked out adaptations to cold climates that did not require caves. Indeed, their ancestors must have done this, because there are no caves along the Siberia-Beringia-Alaska route.

Another problem in locating early sites in eastern North America is that in much of the lower Mississippi area, alluviation has been so great that many such sites would be buried under tens of meters of soil. And in the rest of the South and East, where the glacial ice sheets never extended, the present land surface is millions of years old. Thus, soft-drink bottles and ancient artifacts can be found in virtually the same soil, because accumulation of soil over these areas has been so slow for millions of years. Additionally, bones and other datable materials do not preserve well under these humid, exposed conditions.

Still, there *are* suitable land surfaces in North America where pre-Clovis occupations could have been preserved, and none have been found that convince the many skeptics, so the debate will probably continue until—and if—more persuasive evidence is found. David Whitley and Ronald Dorn evaluated hypothetical migration and fertility rates for a population entering North America through Beringia and compared them with sites whose ages are accepted by nearly all archaeologists, and they conclude that "it is impossible to reconcile the Clovis-first hypothesis with empirical evidence accepted by its own advocates."[35]

Early American Economies   For many thousands of years after people reached mid-continental and southern latitudes in the New World, population densities were probably extremely light, and most bands no doubt stayed in the same general mixed forest and grassland environments their ancestors had adapted to in more northern areas. By about 12,000 years ago, however, they began to display greater diversity in subsistence strategies as they evolved adaptations to a greater range of environments.

Archaeologists think their reconstructions of these early American cultures may be somewhat inaccurate because of the nature of the archaeological record these cultures left. The easiest archaeological sites to find are those with large stone tools and the bones of large animals, and many early New World sites are of this type: dozens of stone tools intermixed with mammoth, bison, and other bones, often near streams or bogs where hunters ambushed these animals. But there may be many less obvious sites—those not yet found because they are not marked by masses of animal bones or impressive stone tools. In 1987, for example, a Clovis site in a Washington State apple orchard (the Ritchie Site) was found when holes were dug for new trees, and beautiful, exceptionally large stone points were unearthed. But if this had been an earlier site containing only crude pebble tools, it is highly improbable that it would ever have been recognized. In short, extreme biases are likely in our recognition of the early American archaeological record. Many archaeologists question, for example, even the presumption that the Clovis and Folsom peoples were mainly big-game hunters, although there is some evidence that groups along the tundra zone, in New York and Massachusetts, specialized in caribou.[36] Meltzer argues that in much of the southeast United States, the people who left the many fluted points in this area were generalized foragers who probably used many of the points as hafted knives, not as spear points.[37]

Similarly, several sites dating to about 11,000 B.C. have been found in Mexico, most of them comprised of debris from killing and butchering mammoths. The consistency with which mammoths are found in these sites may seem to reflect an economy specialized in hunting large animals, but most of the people of Mexico at this time were probably generalized hunters and gatherers, and only because of the great size and preservation of the mammoth bones do we find so many of these sites. As MacNeish noted, these early hunters probably killed one mammoth in a lifetime—and never stopped talking about it.

But there is no question that some people did kill and eat big animals. Alan Bryan described excavations at Taima-taima, in Venezuela, in which the skeleton of a young mastodon was found with a large stone point inside the pubic cavity, and cut-marks inside the rib cage suggested that some ancient hunter crawled into the animal's carcass to remove internal organs.[38] The mastodon's head was missing, and cut-marks showed where steaks had been removed from a foreleg. Leg bones of a larger mastodon had been used as a butcher's block to hack up the younger one. Near the skeleton and preserved by the site's wetness, a mass of vegetable matter whose sheared ends and compaction suggest that it was the mastodon's stomach contents was dated by the radiocarbon method to no later than 13,000 years ago.

Perhaps the most direct way to demonstrate hunting of large animals by early Americans is to find residues of animal tissue on the tools themselves, and in a few cases this is possible. At least one of the large fluted points at the Ritchie Site in eastern Washington State was found to have traces of blood on it—bovine blood, in fact, probably from a mammoth.

Other evidence of hunting comes from Arctic sites, such as Dry Creek, Trail Creek, and similar occupations, most of which date to between 11,000 and 8,000 years ago. These sites seem to be hunting camps in unglaciated areas and are marked by bifacial knives, tiny blades, and the bones of horses, bison, hares, ducks, and other animals. By this time, these Arctic hunters may have been pursuing a dying way of life, as the glaciers and the rich animal life they supported were slowly withdrawing.[39]

Shortly after 8000 B.C. at least some groups in the American West were undoubtedly specializing in hunting big game. They often practiced "jump hunting," in which many people cooperated to stampede bison herds or other animals over a precipice, killing them by the score. Where there were no convenient precipices, animals were driven into natural cul-de-sacs, where they could be easily killed. In sites reflecting these practices, archaeologists find the bones of hundreds of bison, many showing clear butchering marks. These hunters took cuts of meat from these animals in a way that showed a shrewd appreciation of their nutritional value.[40] By drying the meat, these hunters could accumulate large food reserves, and the skin, hide, and bones of the bison had many uses.

A good example of the varied nature of early American adaptations is the *Desert West*. The Desert West refers to the area between the Rocky Mountains and the Sierra Nevada and Cascade Mountain range, extending from Canada to southern Mexico.[41] About 12,000 years ago, when the glacial ice sheets were still a kilometer high along the northern border of the United States, some of the Desert West was probably cooler and wetter than it is today and had many large lakes and marshes. Then, between 12,000 and 10,000 years ago, the lakes shrank, rivers ceased to flow, and springs began to dry up.

The Desert West has less diverse flora and fauna than most other parts of North America, but for most of the last 10,000 years it has supported large populations of squirrels, rabbits, marmots, wood rats, peccaries, and other small animals, as well as localized herds of deer, bison, elk, and big-horn sheep. Sunflowers, pickleweed, yucca, piñon nuts, and other vegetable foods are available seasonally in most of this area. Resource diversity is particularly great as one moves up and down the hills and ridges of the Desert West: a single day's climb can take one from a desertic environment to Arctic-alpine environments in the uplands. An especially important element in the subsistence of prehistoric peoples of the Desert West was the lakes and marshes probably present here during much of the Pleistocene. Fish, waterfowl, invertebrates, marsh plants, and many other resources were exploited as soon as colonization began and have played an important part in determining human settlement here to the present. Generally, then, the Desert West offers archaeologists an opportunity to study the many ways prehistoric populations in this area have adapted their subsistence strategies, population densities, technologies, and seasonal movements to the nuances of a somewhat extreme physical environment.

If we accept the 30,000 to 15,000 year dates for other early sites in the Americas, we might suspect that bands were also in the Desert West at this time, but we have little evidence. The earliest reliably dated sites are all between 12,000 and 10,000 years old, although remains of earlier occupations will probably be found when the archaeology of the Desert West is better known. Many of the rock shelters and caves in the Desert West were submerged by lakes during the late Pleistocene, so most of the early sites may be "open-air" sites and thus difficult to find and date.

The first well-documented Desert West cultures are represented by lithic artifacts very like the Clovis points that appeared in the Great Plains about 12,000 years ago. These artifacts have been found at many locations in the Desert West, but almost all were surface finds, with no associated animal or plant remains that could tell us much about either the age or the economy of these cultures. Often associated with these points are stone artifacts usually interpreted as gravers, borers, and other types of projectile points.

From about 11,000 to 8,000 years ago, many of the Desert West peoples apparently organized their economies around the resources of lakes and marshes, while groups in more arid areas probably adopted a more generalized hunting-and-gathering strategy. Remains of pole-and-thatch huts have been found in some areas, but the size, location, and contents of most sites of this period suggest that for most of the year Desert West peoples lived in small bands and followed complex seasonal rounds, exploiting different resources as they became available.

Between 9,000 and 2,500 years ago these cultures worked out a marvelous array of subsistence technologies and strategies, and the aridity of the Desert West has preserved artifacts so well that we can reconstruct their way of life in considerable detail. Scraps of fur clothing have been found, as well as hide moccasins, woven sandals, wooden clubs, twined basketry, grinding stones, atlatl points, and many other items.

Analysis of the animal and plant remains from sites dated between 9,000 and 2,500 years ago reveals an extremely diverse diet. Rabbits, rats, and squirrels were trapped—probably with twined nets—and bison, antelopes, and mountain sheep were also occasionally taken. At sites near bodies of water, grebes, pelicans, herons, ducks, swans, geese, and even hawks and ravens appear to have been eaten. The number of grinding stones and digging sticks found in Desert West sites suggests that, as with most hunters and gatherers, much of the diet was supplied by plant foods. At Hogup Cave, in Utah, for example, human feces contain masses of pickleweed seeds, and the archaeological deposits are stained yellow by pickleweed chaff *quids*, the fossilized expectorated fibers of succulent plants, which have been found in such great quantities in so many Desert West sites that their numbers suggest these plants were a source of both food and water.

A human mummy found in Spirit Cave, Nevada, recently dated with the most advanced radiocarbon dating methods, was found to be a surprising 9400 years old.[42] This man was buried wearing moccasins and was wrapped in a shroud of neatly woven marsh plants. So expert was the weaving (a method known as "diamond plating") that it appears these people had already mastered the use of looms. This individual was about 5'2" tall and had suffered a fractured skull—and huge dental abscesses that would probably have been more painful than the headache he might have suffered, if he ever regained consciousness after his skull was fractured. He seems to be quite different physically and genetically from modern Native Americans: he has a long cranium and a small face, which looks more like Southeast Asian peoples than contemporary Native Americans.

The generalized hunting-and-gathering way of life persisted in the Desert West into the present century, except in a few favored areas where, beginning about 2,000 years ago, a horticultural way of life, based on domesticated maize, beans, and squash, was possible.

The earliest distinctive and widely distributed tool complex found in the North American East is distinguished by the presence of large stone projectile points. Most such points are between twelve and thirty centimeters long and occasionally have been "fluted." Formerly, many archaeologists thought these eastern points were imitations of the Folsom and Clovis points, but it is now evident that these larger points occur as early—and probably earlier—in the eastern woodlands as on the Plains and are more numerous in the East: Alabama alone, for example, has yielded more points than the entire western half of North America.[43]

The many millennia between the time the first Americans set foot in the eastern part of North America and the origins of maize-beans-squash agriculture in this area (chapter 15) saw people adapting to a variety of environments in many ingenious ways. The forests and other ecological zones of the North American East might seem to have been rich, but dense forests are relatively low in resources for hunter-foragers, and human population densities in the east probably remained low for many centuries. The rich stands of nut-bearing trees found all over the east and mid-west, however, offered a reliable resource that, when combined with berries, deer, squirrels, shellfish, fish, and many other foods, could form the basis for a secure life. Perhaps the best known example of these early American adaptations is reflected in the evidence from the Koster site, in the Illinois River Valley. First occupied at about 7500 B.C., people lived at this site many times, at least until about 2500 B.C. Over these millennia, the people who occupied the Koster site, like their contemporaries elsewhere in the North American East, changed in many ways. First, their numbers grew—slowly to be sure—but generation by generation there was a small rate of increase in population. Second, these people slowly improved their technologies, adding new varieties of stone tools, more permanent forms of housing made of clay, poles, and thatch, rare implements of copper for which they traded with neighboring groups, and various other tools. Third, they also became masters at mixing and matching the resources of their environments. The annual autumn nut harvests gave them a stable nutritious food base, which they complemented with a wide variety of game, fruits, plants, fish, shellfish, migratory water fowl, and other foods.[44]

Pleistocene Extinctions   The spread of human hunting and gathering societies over the New World after 12,000 years ago, at the end of the last glacial period, coincides with the extinction of many animal species, and by about 10,000 years ago, all or most of the mammoths, mastodons, long-horned bison, tapirs, horses, giant ground sloths, dire wolves, camels, and many other creatures had disappeared. Extinction is, of course, a natural evolutionary development and can be accounted for by known biological processes. But the number of animal species that became extinct in the New World and their apparently rapid rate of extinction has led some to conclude that human hunters forced many New World animals into extinction shortly after the Pleistocene.[45]

But people may have had little or nothing to do with these extinctions. In a sample of thirty-five early sites in North America, the animal bones found were mainly those of mammoths and bison—species that did in fact become extinct; but many of the other large animals that became extinct during this period are either not found at all in these sites or in very limited numbers. Perhaps even more significant, game species were not the only ones to die out. Donald Grayson has shown that numerous species of birds also became extinct at this time, and it is difficult to believe that people could have played any role in this.[46] Also, some "big-game" species such as the mastodon lived in the North American South and East while humans were there and are known to have died out shortly after the end of the Pleistocene, but their bones have rarely been found in association with evidence of human activities. Thus, it would seem that at least some larger animals became extinct without much human assistance. Finally, we might also note that there is no archaeological evidence that the hunting practices most likely to lead to animal extinctions, such as drives and jumps, were ever used during the period, some 10,000 to 8000 years ago, when most of the larger species became extinct.

Kelly and Todd present an alternative to the overkill model, arguing that the Clovis peoples were unlike most known hunter-foragers in that they may have had very little processing technology for food storage, relying instead on proficient hunting using high-quality flint bifacial tools, and shifting their range as they exhausted the resources of an area.[47] They suggest that the pattern of Pleistocene extinctions would have been similar even if people had never entered the New World.

If we rule out human hunting as the most important factor in these extinctions, what alternative explanation can we give? Many have been suggested, but none is really very satisfactory. Clearly, the immediate post-Pleistocene period was one of radical climate change, and no doubt this was of some importance. Of thirty-one genera of mammals that became extinct, however, only seven had entered the New World during the last 70,000 years; all the others had managed to adapt to the climatic changes of the previous interglacial periods, which were fully as dramatic as those after the last glacial retreat. Why did they become extinct after the last period?

Some have suggested that New World animals might have been decimated by diseases introduced from the Old World during one of the later intervals when the Bering land bridge route was open—a situation reminiscent of the frightful casualties inflicted on aboriginal Americans by smallpox, measles, and other diseases introduced by the Europeans. Such epidemics, however, usually do not cause species to become extinct: they decimate local populations over a large area but generally leave small pockets of resistant individuals who eventually reestablish the species.

As Grayson has pointed out, it is entirely possible that these Pleistocene extinctions were the results of climatic changes and human interactions of fairly subtle and presently unknown dimensions.[48]

By about 5000 B.C., the glaciers had retreated to the point that the flora and fauna of the eastern United States were very similar to what they are today—except where changed by human activity—and there was a broad cultural readaption to the changing environments.

Generally, the early Holocene in the Americas was a time of cultural specialization, as technologies, social systems, and subsistence systems were evolved to meet diverse and changing environments. The full length of the New World was inhabited shortly after 12,000 B.P., with sites radiocarbon dated to this early period now known all the way south into southern Argentina.[49]

Human population densities rose in many parts of the New World, and, as we will see in chapter 15, by 7,000 years ago some hunting and gathering societies were already in the process of domesticating plants and beginning the transition to the agricultural, complex cultures of late prehistoric America.

SUMMARY AND CONCLUSIONS

Despite the evidence for early sites, such as Monte Verde, most archaeologists still consider the actual date of the New World colonization to be undemonstrated. We know that people were here in substantial numbers by 12,000 years ago, and within a few thousand years they had occupied most of the more productive New World areas and were beginning to diversify culturally. It seems unlikely that the massive wave of extinctions of large animals after about 12,000 B.C. had much to do with human activities.

The initial colonization of the New World may seem to be an epochal development, but it was in fact just one aspect of the great radiation of the human species during the late Pleistocene. From Australia to South America to Siberia and the Arctic, people colonized the world and adapted to its many environments.

BIBLIOGRAPHY

Adovasio, J. M. 1993. "The Ones That Will Not Go Away: A Biased View of Pre-Clovis Occupation in the New World." In O. Soffer and N. D. Praslov, eds., *From Kostenki to Clovis: Upper Paleolithic Paleo-Indian Adaptations.* New York: Plenum Press.

Adovasio, J. M., and R. C. Carlisle. 1987. "The First Americans." *Natural History* 95(12):20–27.

Adovasio, J. M., J. Donahue, and R. Stuckenrath. 1990. "The Meadowcroft Rockshelter Radiocarbon Chronology, 1975–1990." *American Antiquity* 55(2):348–54.

Adovasio, J. M., J. Donahue, J. D. Gunn, and R. Stuckenrath. 1981. "The Meadowcroft Papers: A Response to Dincauze." *Quarterly Review of Archaeology* 2:14–15.

Aikens, C. M. 1978. "Archaeology of the Great Basin." *Annual Review of Anthropology* 7:71–87.

———. 1970. *Hogup Cave.* Salt Lake City: University of Utah Press.

Bada, J. L., and P. M. Helfman. 1975. "Amino Acid Racemization Dating of Fossil Bones." *World Archaeology* 7:160–73.

Bellwood, P. 1986. *The Prehistory of the Indo-Malaysian Archipelago.* Orlando, FL: Academic Press.

Berger, R. 1975. "Advances and Results in Radiocarbon Dating: Early Man in North America." *World Archaeology* 7:174–84.

Bettinger, R. L. 1977. "Aboriginal Human Ecology in Owens Valley: Prehistoric Change in the Great Basin." *American Antiquity* 42:3–17.

Brown, J., and J. Phillips, eds. 1983. *Late Archaic Hunter-Gatherers in the Midwest.* New York: Academic Press.

Bryan, A. 1987. "The First Americans." *Natural History* 96(6):6–11.

Chard, C. S. 1956. "The Oldest Sites of Northeast Siberia." *American Antiquity* 21:405–9.

———. 1960. "Routes to Bering Strait." *American Antiquity* 26:283–85.

Claiborne, R. and the Editors of Time-Life. 1973. *The First Americans.* New York: Time-Life.

Crawford, M. H. 1993. "DNA Variability and Human Evolution." *Evolutionary Anthropology* 2(4):115.

Cwyner, L. C., and J. C. Ritchie. 1980. "Arctic Step-Tundra: A Yukon Perspective." *Science* 208:1375–77.

DeJarnette, D. L. 1967. "Alabama Pebbletools: The Lively Complex." *Eastern States Archaeological Federation Bulletin 26.*

deTerra, H. 1949. "Early Man in Mexico." In *Tepexpan Man*, by H. deTerra, J. Romero, and T. D. Stewart. New York: Viking Fund Publications in Anthropology 11:11–86.

Dikov, N. N. 1977. *Monuments in Kamchatka, Chukotka, and the Upper Reaches of the Kolyma: Asia Joining America in Ancient Times.* Moscow: Nauka.

———. 1987. "On the Road to America." *Natural History* 97(1):12–15.

Dillehay, T. D. 1987. "By the Banks of the Chinchihuapi." *Natural History* 96(4):8–12.

Dincauze, D. 1981. "The Meadowcroft Papers." *The Quarterly Review of Archaeology* 2:3–4.

Dixon, E. J. 1995. *Quest for the Origins of the First Americans.* Albuquerque: University of New Mexico Press.

Dragoo, D. W. 1976. "Some Aspects of Eastern North American Prehistory: A Review 1975." *American Antiquity* 41:3–27.

Figgins, J. D. 1927. "The Antiquity of Man in America." *Natural History* 27:229–39.

Fladmark, K. 1986. *British Columbian Prehistory.* Chicago: University of Chicago Press.

———. 1987. "Getting One's Berings." *Natural History* 95(11):8–19.

Frison, G. C., M. Wilson, and D. J. Wilson. 1976. "Fossil Bison and Artifacts from an Early Altithermal Period Arroyo Trap in Wyoming." *American Antiquity* 41:28–57.

Frison, G. C., R. L. Andrews, J. M. Adovasio, R. C. Carlisle, and Robert Edgar. 1986. "A Late Paleoindian Animal Trapping Net from Northern Wyoming." *American Antiquity* 51(2):352–61.

Frison, G. C. and L. C. Todd, eds. 1987. *The Horner Site.* Orlando, FL: Academic Press.

Gowlett, J. A. J. 1987. "The Archaeology of Radiocarbon Accelerator Dating." *Journal of World Prehistory* 1(2):127–70.

Grayson, D. K. 1977. "Pleistocene Avifaunas and the Overkill Hypothesis." *Science* 195:691–93.

————. 1987. "Death by Natural Causes." *Natural History* 96(5):8–13.

————. 1991. "Late Pleistocene Mammalian Extinctions in North America: Taxonomy, Chronology, and Explanations." *Journal of World Prehistory* 5(3):193–231.

Greenberg, J. H., C. G. Turner II, and S. L. Zegura. 1986. "The Settlement of the Americas: A Comparison of the Linguistic, Dental, and Genetic Evidence." *Current Anthropology* 27(5):477–97.

Greenman, E. F. 1963. "The Upper Paleolithic in the New World," *Current Anthropology* 4:41–91.

Griffin, J. B. 1960. "Some Prehistoric Connections Between Siberia and America." *Science* 131:801–12.

————. 1967. "Eastern North American Archaeology: A Summary." *Science* 156:175–91.

Guidon, N. 1987. "Cliff Notes." *Natural History* 96(8):6–12.

Guthrie, R. D. 1980. "The First Americans? The Elusive Arctic Bone Culture." *The Quarterly Review of Archaeology* 1:2.

Haag, W. G. 1962. "The Bering Strait Land Bridge." *Scientific American* 206:112–23.

Hagelberg, E. 1993. "Ancient DNA Studies." *Evolutionary Anthropology* 2(6):199–207.

Harris M. 1977. *Cannibals and Kings: The Origins of Culture.* New York: Random House.

Hayden, B. 1981. "Research and Development in the Stone Age: Technological Transitions among Hunter-Gatherers." *Current Anthropology* 22:519–48.

Haynes, C. V., Jr. 1969. "The Earliest Americans." *Science* 166:709–15.

————. 1971. "Time, Environment, and Early Man." In "Papers from a Symposium on Early Man in North America, New Developments: 1960– 1970," ed. R. Shutler, Jr. *Arctic Anthropology* 8:3–14.

————. 1974. "Elephant Hunting in North America." *New World Prehistory: Readings from Scientific American*, eds. Ed. Zubrow et al. San Francisco: Freeman.

————. 1987. "Geofacts and Fancy." *Natural History* 97(2):4– 12.

Hopkins D. M., ed. 1967. *The Bering Land Bridge.* Stanford, CA: Stanford University Press.

Hopkins, D. M., J. V. Matthews, Jr., C. E. Schweger, and S. B. Young. 1982. *Paleoecology of Beringia.* New York: Academic Press.

Irving, W. N. 1985. "Context and Chronology of Early Man in the Americas." *Annual Review of Anthropology* 14:529–55.

————. 1987. "New Dates from Old Bones." *Natural* History 96(2):8–13.

Jaffe, A. J. 1992. *The First Immigrants from Asia: A Population History of the North American Indians.* New York: Plenum Press.

Jairazbhoy, R. A. 1974. *Old World Origins of American Civilization.* 2 vols. London: Rauman and Littlefield.

Jennings, J. D. 1964. "The Desert West." In *Prehistoric Man in the New World*, eds. J. D. Jennings and E. Norbeck. Chicago: University of Chicago Press.

————. 1974. *The Prehistory of North America*, 2nd ed. New York: McGraw-Hill.

Jennings, J. D. and E. Norbeck, eds. 1964. *Prehistoric Man in the New World.* Chicago: University of Chicago Press.

Kelly, R. L. and L. C. Todd. 1988. "Coming into the Country: Early Paleoindian Hunting and Mobility." *American Antiquity* 53(2):231–44.

Krieger, A. D. 1964. "Early Man in the New World." In *Prehistoric Man in the New World*, eds. J. D. Jennings and E. Norbeck. Chicago: University of Chicago Press.

Larichev, V., U. Khol'ushkin, and I. Laricheva. 1987. "Lower and Middle Paleolithic of Northern Asia: Achievements, Problems, and Perspectives." *Journal of World Prehistory* 1(4):415–64.

Larichev, V. et al. 1993. "The Upper Paleolithic of Northern Asia: Achievements. Problems, and Perspectives III: Northeastern Siberia and the Russian Far East." *Journal of World Prehistory* 6(4):441–76.

Lively, M. 1965. "The Lively Complex: Announcing a Pebble Tool Industry in Alabama." *Journal of Alabama Archaeology* 11:103–22.

Lyell, C. 1863. *Principles of Geology.* London: Murray.

MacNeish, R. S. 1971. "Early Man in the Andes." *Scientific American* 4:36–46.

————. 1978. *The Science of Archaeology?* North Scituate, MA: Duxbury Press.

MacNeish, R. S., ed. 1973. *Early Man in America*. San Francisco: Freeman.

Madsen, D. B., and M. S. Berry. 1975. "A Reassessment of Northeastern Great Basin Prehistory." *American Antiquity* 40:391–405.

Malouf, D. 1993. *Remembering Babylon*. New York: Pantheon Books.

Marks, J. 1995. *Human Biodiversity: Genes, Race, and History*. Hawthorne, NY: Aldine de Gruyter.

Martin, P. S. 1973. "The Discovery of America." *Science* 179:969–74.

Martin, P. S., and J. E. Guilday. 1967. "A Bestiary for Pleistocene Biologists." In *Pleistocene Extinctions: The Search for a Cause*, eds. P. S. Martin and H. E. Wright, Jr. New Haven: Yale University Press.

Martin, P. S., and R. Klein, eds. 1984. *Quarternary Extinctions: A Prehistoric Revolution*. Tucson: University of Arizona Press.

Martin, P. S., and H. E. Wright, Jr., eds. 1967. *Pleistocene Extinctions: The Search for a Cause*. New Haven: Yale University Press.

Mehringer, P., Jr. 1977. "Great Basin Late Quaternary Environments and Chronology." In *Models in Great Basin Prehistory: A Symposium*, ed. D. D. Fowler. *Desert Research Institute Publications in the Social Sciences* 12:113–68.

Meltzer D. J. 1988. "Late Pleistocene Human Adaptations in Eastern North America." *Journal of World* Prehistory 2(1):1–52.

Meltzer, D. J., and J. I. Mead. 1983. "The Timing of Late Pleistocene Mammalian Extinctions in North America." *Quaternary Research* 19:103–35.

Moismann, J. E., and P. S. Martin. 1975. "Simulating Overkill by Paleoindians." *American Scientist* 63:304–13.

Moratto, M. J. Foreword by F. A. Riddell. Contributions by D. A. Frederickson, C. Raven, and C. N. Warren. 1984. *California Archaeology*. New York: Academic Press.

Morlan, R.E., and J. Cinq-Mars. 1982. "Ancient Beringians: Human Occupation in the Late Pleistocene of Alaska and the Yukon Territory." In *Paleoecology of Beringia*, eds. D. M. Hopkins, et al. New York: Academic Press.

Mueller-Beck, H. J. 1966. "Paleo-Hunters in America: Origins and Diffusion." *Science* 152:1191–1210.

Orquera, L. A. 1987. "Advances in the Archaeology of the Pampa and Patagonia." *Journal of World Prehistory* 1(4):333–413.

Reeves, B. O. R. 1971. "On the Coalescence of the Laurentide and Cordilleran Ice Sheets in the Western Interior of North America." In *Aboriginal Man and Environments on the Plateau of Northwest America*, eds. A. Stryd and R. A. Smith. Calgary: University of Calgary Archaeological Association.

Ruhlen, M. 1987. "Voices from the Past." *Natural History* 96(3):6–10.

Schmitz, P. E. 1987. "Prehistoric Hunters and Gatherers of Brazil." *Journal of World Prehistory* 1(1):53–126.

Speth, J. 1987. "Les strategies alimentaires des chasseurs-cueilleurs." *La Recherche* 18(190):894–903.

Spielmann, K. A., M. J. Schoeninger, and K. Moore. 1990. "Plains-Pueblo Interdependence and Human Diet at Pecos Pueblo, New Mexico." *American Antiquity* 55(4):745–65.

Steele, D. G. and J. F. Powell. 1993. "Paleobiology of the First Americans." *Evolutionary Anthropology* 2(4):138–46.

Steponaitis, V. 1986. "Prehistoric Archaeology in the Southeastern United States 1970–1985." *Annual Review of Anthropology* 15:363–404.

Stewart, T. D. 1973. *The People of America*. New York: Scribner's.

Stone, A. C., and M. Stoneking. 1993. "Ancient DNA from a Pre-Columbian Amarind Population." *American Journal of Physical Anthropology* 92:463–71.

Struever, S. and F. A. Holton. 1979. *Koster: Americans in Search of Their Past*. New York: Anchor Press.

Tuohy, D. R. 1968. "Some Early Lithic Sites in Western Nevada." In *Early Man in Western North America*, ed. C. Irwin-Williams. Portales, NM: Eastern New Mexico University Press.

Turner, C. G., II. 1987. "Tell-tale Teeth." *Natural History* 96(1):6–10.

Vescelius, G. S. 1981. "Early and/or Not-so-Early Man in Peru: Guitarrero Cave Revisited." *Quarterly Review of Archaeology* 2:8–13, 19–20.

Warren, C., and A. Ranere. 1968. "Outside Danger Cave: A View of Early Man in the Great Basin." In *Early Man in Western North America*, ed. C. Irwin-Williams. Portales, NM: Eastern New Mexico University Press.

Webb, C. H. 1968. "The Extent and Content of Poverty Point Culture." *American Antiquity* 33:297–331.

Wheat, J. B. 1972. "The Olsen-Chubbuck Site: A Paleo-Indian Bison Kill." *Memoirs of the Society for American Archaeology*, no. 26, pt 2.

Whitley, D. S., and R. I. Dorn. 1993. "New Perspectives on the Clovis vs. Pre-Clovis Controversy." *American Antiquity* 58(4):626–47

Zegura, S. L. 1987. "Blood Test." *Natural History* 96(7):8–11.

NOTES

1. Stewart, *The People of America*, p. 60.

2. Film fans will remember this idea in *Cat Ballou*.

3. Quoted in Stewart, *The People of America*, p. 70; it should be noted that Jefferson thought it possible for reverse migration from the Americas into Asia and then back again.

4. Figgins, "The Antiquity of Man in America."

5. Haag, "The Bering Strait Land Bridge," p. 269.

6. Cwyner and Ritchie, "Arctic Step-Tundra: A Yukon Perspective"; also see Dixon, *Quest for the Origins of the First Americans*.

7. Dixon, *Quest for the Origins of the First Americans*.

8. Fladmark, "Getting One's Berings," p. 14.

9. Ibid.

10. Ibid, p. 16.

11. Fladmark, *British Columbian Prehistory*; idem., "Getting One's Berings."

12. Martin and Wright, *Pleistocene Extinctions: The Search for a Cause*, pp. 32–33.

13. Reviewed in Irving, "Context and Chronology of Early Man in the Americas."

14. Bellwood, *The Prehistory of the Indo-Malaysian Archipelago*.

15. Marks, *Human Biodiversity: Genes, Race, and History*.

16. Turner, "Tell-tale Teeth."

17. Turner, "Tell-tale Teeth"; Greenberg, Turner, and Zegura, "The Settlement of the Americas: A Comparison of the Linguistic, Dental, and Genetic Evidence," p. 484.

18. Steele and Powell, "Paleobiology of the First Americans."

19. Crawford, "DNA Variability and Human Evolution."

20. Greenberg, Turner, and Zegura, "The Settlement of the Americas: A Comparison of the Linguistic, Dental, and Genetic Evidence."

21. Ruhlen, "Voices from the Past."

22.. Krieger, "Early Man in the New World."

23. Gowlett, "The Archaeology of Radiocarbon Accelerator Dating."

24. See, for example, Larichev et al., "The Upper Paleolithic of Northern Asia: Achievements, Problems, and Perspectives III: Northeastern Siberia and the Russian Far East."

25. Haynes, "Geofacts and Fancy," p. 12.

26. Ibid.

27. Dikov, "On the Road to America," p. 15.

28. Dillehay, "By the Banks of the Chinchihuapi."

29. Guidon, "Cliff Notes."

30. MacNeish, *The Science of Archaeology?*, p. 203.

31. See, for example, Vescelius, "Early and/or Not-so-Early Man in Peru: Guitarrero Cave Revisited."

32. Schmitz, "Prehistoric Hunters and Gatherers of Brazil."

33. Dincauze, "The Meadowcroft Papers"; cf. Adovasio et al., "The Meadowcroft Papers: A Response to Dincauze."

34. Adovasio and Carlisle, "Pennsylvania Pioneers."

35. Whitley and Dorn, "New Perspectives on the Clovis vs. Pre-Clovis Controversy."

36. Meltzer, "Late Pleistocene Human Adaptations in Eastern North America."

37. Ibid., p. 43.

38. Bryan, "The First Americans."

39. Hopkins et al., *Paleoecology of Beringia*.

40. Speth, "Les strategies alimentaires des chasseurs-cueilleurs."

41. For surveys of Desert West archaeology, see Jennings, *The Prehistory of North America*, 2nd Ed.

42. This account is taken from C. Goldberg's newspaper article (*New York Times*, April 27, 1996), "Oldest Mummy 'Found' on Museum Shelf."

43. Dragoo, "Some Aspects of Eastern North American Prehistory: A Review 1975."

44. Struever and Holton, *Koster: Americans in Search of Their Past*.

45. Martin and Wright, *Pleistocene Extinctions*; Haynes, "Elephant Hunting in North America"; Moismann and Martin, "Simulating Overkill by Paleoindians"; Martin and Klein, *Quaternary Extinctions. A Prehistoric Revolution*.

46. Grayson, "Pleistocene Avifaunas and the Overkill Hypothesis."

47. Kelly and Todd, "Coming into the Country: Early Paleoindian Hunting and Mobility"; Whitley, and Dorn, "New Perspectives on the Clovis vs. Pre-Clovis Controversy," p. 642.

48. Grayson, "Death by Natural Causes."

49. Orquera, "Advances in the Archaeology of the Pampa and Patagonia."

6

THE ORIGINS OF AGRICULTURE

*The greatest events come to pass without any design; chance
makes blunders good. . . . The important events of the world
are not deliberately brought about: they occur.*

George C. Lichtenberg

An alien visitor to earth might understandably come to the conclusion that humans naturally and instinctively cultivate plants. For, he, she, or it would see that almost every human residence and community, from the meanest shack in the poorest country, to the verdant parks of the world's richest metropolises, are adorned with flowers and other cultivated plants, and it would become quickly obvious to this visitor that such "civilizations" as the earth had produced were largely the product of human abilities to extract energy from plants.

But the cultivation of plants has never been an instinctive part of the human repertoire; in fact, it is a comparatively recent human activity, practiced for far less than 1 percent of the time our genus has been on this planet. And it involved a radical alteration in the way people lived. The several million years separating the first tool-using hominids of Africa and the French cave artists of just 20,000 years ago encompassed a period of momentous change. Human brain size trebled, crude stone implements were replaced by an impressive array of specialized tools, and our ancestors were able to colonize most of the world. But in one important respect all Pleistocene societies, from the barely human hominids of two million years ago to the creative hunter-foragers of just 10,000 years ago, were alike: they made their living by gathering and hunting their food, not by producing it, in the sense that they did not "farm."

We can look back, perhaps even with a bit of pride, at the adaptability and durability of our ancient hunting-gathering forebears. They lived as hunter-gatherers for millions of years, in every kind of environment, from the polar ice cap to the jungles of the Amazon. To do this required, in many cases, profound knowledge of environments, a sophisticated yet still portable technology, and a demanding life on the move. As Robert Kelly noted, "[t]here are no Gardens of Eden on earth, no single

268

locales, that can provide for all human needs. Mobility . . . was the first means humans used to overcome this problem."[1]

Even today, a few hunter-gatherer societies persist on the margins of modern states. But the hunting-gathering way of life began to contract to fewer and fewer areas after the first farmers appeared. Just after 10,000 years ago, people in several widely separated areas of the world began to domesticate a few plant and animal species. At about the same time they built villages, began living in them year-round, and began to subsist mainly on plants they cultivated and animals they kept. In most environments these agricultural economies have been able to produce much greater amounts of food than hunting and gathering could, and do so much more reliably. Today, hunter-gatherers exist only in the Amazon Basin, the Arctic, and the few other places where hunting-gathering is still (or until recently was) more productive than agriculture, and even in these few areas hunter-gatherers depend in part on their neighbors' agricultural economies.

When we look at the history of this massive change in human lifeways around the world, two curious facts emerge: first, all of the largest and most complex civilizations throughout history have been based on the cultivation of one or more of just six plant genera—wheat, barley, millet, rice, maize, and potatoes; other plants, such as sorghum, rye, beans, yams, taro, and thousands more, have been critical to the survival of many peoples, and domesticated animals have also been important sources of calories and power, but the six plant genera listed above have been the main engines of "civilizations." Second, one of the particularly striking characteristics of the "agricultural revolution" is that, not only was it rapid and widespread, but it also happened independently in different parts of the world at about the same time. For millions of years our ancestors subsisted solely on the proceeds of hunting and gathering, yet within just a few thousand years, between about 10,000 and 3,500 years ago, people all over the world—without any apparent connection—began growing crops and establishing agricultural economies based on, for example, potatoes in the Andes, maize in Mexico, wheat in Southwest Asia, rice in China, and many other crops in many other places.

The fact that very few species provide most of the world's food, and that plants and animals were domesticated at about the same time at different places in the world, raises important questions. Is there something entirely special, for example, about these particular plants that they became the staples of people around the world, or do they represent chance associations between people and particular plant species at specific times? And why did people make the transition to a life based on these and other plants? Agriculture has had such tremendous importance in human affairs that one is tempted to the logical fallacy of assuming that the factors that first produced agricultural economies must be equally momentous. They may have been; at this point we do not know. Perhaps only slight changes in climate, population density, or technology set off the "agricultural revolution." We know approximately where and when the most important domesticates first appeared but, as we shall see, the reasons *why* they appeared where they did and when they did are still not fully understood. Almost all general explanations of agricultural origins, as we shall see, appeal to the same three basic factors: climate changes, rising population densities, and improving technologies. Yet combining these factors into a compelling explanation of all the world's agricultural origins remains difficult.

In this chapter we review some of the evidence of early domestication and farming and consider more abstract questions concerning why people become farmers after so many long years of hunting-foraging, why agriculture appeared in many different places in the world at about the same time, and how agricultural economies came to dominate the world.[2]

AGRICULTURE, DOMESTICATION, AND SEDENTARY COMMUNITIES

Discussions of agricultural origins involve many specialized terms, and some of these terms are rather vague and descriptive. The difference between a "crop" and a "weed," for example, is in a sense a cultural construct rather than a precise botanical concept. Luther Burbank, the pioneering American botanist, defined a weed as a plant whose uses to humanity simply had not yet been discovered. Geneticists Blumler and Byrne define a weed as "an uncultivated plant taxon that benefits from human impacts or "disturbance"";[3] but they note that it also has an economic definition in the sense of weeds as plants that reduce crop yields. Even the species names given to specific plants and animals, as well as cultural terms such as "farming" and "domesticated," are attempts to impose static categories on a dynamic and multidimensional underlying variability. The easy "opposites," too, of "hunter-forager"/"agriculturalist" and "wild"/"domesticated" camouflage underlying continuous variability.[4]

Thus, some precision in terminology is useful. The key concept in the notion of *agriculture* involves human efforts to modify the environments of plants and animals to increase their productivity and usefulness.[5] By weeding gardens, fashioning scarecrows, penning pigs, and a thousand other farming tasks, people over the millennia have sought to get more food out of their labors. But hunter-gatherers also modify the environments of plants and animals. Some of them, for example, set fires to open up habitats for certain plants and animals; others, simply by collecting and eating wild species, modify the environments of others and have an effect on these gene pools. Agriculture, however, usually involves systematic and purposeful modification of plant and animal environments with the goal of increasing productivity. This definition of agriculture, like that of domestication, is relative. At the one extreme are the simple efforts a group might make to suppress weeds near a stand of wild wheat; at the other are contemporary agri-businesses where crops are grown on precisely leveled fields and treated with pesticides and fertilizers, and where chickens live out unremarkable lives in cages until a computer determines that their ratio of food-consumption and growth has reached a critical—and fatal—value.

The term *cultivation* is often used in lieu of, or in combination with, the concept of agriculture. Blumler and Byrne define cultivation as the "growing of plants from seeds, bulbs, shoots, and so on."[6] They note that cultivated plants are not always domesticated, and that cultivation may have long preceded domestication in some cases.

The essence of *domestication* in many definitions is *mutualism*. David Rindos, for example, has defined domestication as a "coevolutionary process in which any given taxon diverges from an original gene pool and establishes a symbiotic protection and dispersal relationship with the animal feeding upon it."[7] When people domesticate plants and animals, they do so by active interference in the life cycles of these species in such a way that subsequent generations of these organisms are in more intimate association with, and often of more use to, people. By interfering in these life cycles, people have produced plants and animals that are less "fit," in some ways, than their undomesticated relatives: domesticated maize, for example, no longer has an effective natural mechanism for seed dispersal, because the seeds are all clustered on a cob that, without human intervention, usually remains tightly attached to the plant. Similarly, a variety of sheep in Southwest Asia has been selectively bred over the last several thousand years so that its tail is a five- to eight-pound mass of fat, making it necessary, it is said, for people to help some of these animals mate.

In general, humans have intruded in the natural cycles in that they have altered these plants' *dormancy* cycles, *dispersal mechanisms*, and physical and chemical *defenses* against the animals that eat them.[8] People have altered animal genera in ways usually directed at exaggerating characteristics that are useful to humans, such as meat, milk production, fleece, docility, traction power, and environmental tolerance.

But the kinds of mutualistic relationships we think of as domestication and agriculture are not unique to humans and their plant and animal food, nor do they depend on human intellect. David Rindos points out that African cultivator ants prepare special beds, generally of plant debris, cut-up leaves, flowers, and excrement, in special chambers in the ant nest. The ants are meticulous about growth conditions within the chamber; numerous ventilation passages are dug, and these are opened or closed to regulate both temperature and humidity. To construct the beds, the ants chew the substrate material to make a pulpy mass and deposit it in layers in the chamber. The bed is then planted with propagules from previously maintained beds. Constant care is given the beds. The ants remove alien fungi and add anal and salivary secretions, which apparently have a positive effect on the growth of the fungi. These cultivation activities encourage the production, by the fungus, of small whitish round bodies, the so-called kohlrabi structures. These structures are the principal food of the ant colony.[9]

One does not see tiny scarecrows or silos among these ants, but Rindos's point is well taken: in terms of their ecological relationship with the sustaining species, ants do not differ significantly from us. And if this is true, the import of his observation is obvious: what we consider the uniquely human activities of domestication and agriculture are in fact somewhat common ecological relationships that can be "fixed" by natural selection without regard to the intelligence or volition of the organism involved. In fact, "domestication" is to some extent a matter of perspective: if one looks at domestication from the cereals' point of view, for example, people have proved to be excellent devices for cereals to conquer the world. Wheat, which in its undomesticated forms was limited to small areas of the Middle East, has managed to extend its range from South America to central Russia, all by "domesticating" humans in such a way that they became dependent on it. As much as we are the creators of modern plant and animal hybrid domesticates, then, we are their creation; we are locked together in coevolutionary embrace. In these transitions to agriculture and sedentary life we see a subtle evolutionary dynamic in which people were physically changed as they physically changed the plants and animals on which they depended.[10] Agricultural economies allowed the evolution of epidemic diseases such as cholera that "selected out" untold millions of people with genetic susceptibilities to these diseases. Agricultural diets generally increase periodontal and dental diseases and relax selection for robust dentition, so that the spread of agriculture across the world has resulted in a gradual reduction in human teeth size and strength—and in dental health.

This issue of the importance of human intentions remains a major point of contention in studies of agricultural origins. We live in an age in which farmers are constantly and intentionally manipulating plants and animals in order to effect desired changes in them, so it is not surprising that some scholars think this same intentionality was a critical factor in agricultural origins.[11] People may have begun to domesticate many plant and animal genera not out of the desire or intention of making these plants more useful to people, but rather through making relatively minor and unintentional changes in the way they exploited them. Any plant or animal species regularly eaten or used by people will reflect this relationship in its genetic characteristics, and thus all through the Pleistocene hunters and gatherers had some effect on the genetic makeup of various plant and animal species. But the low population densities and mobile way of life of the period before about 10,000 years ago kept people from exploiting plant and animal populations with sufficient intensity to perpetuate the kinds of mutations represented by contemporary maize and fat-tailed sheep.

Domestication seems to have been in most cases a relatively long-term *process*, not something that an occasional genius invented. As discussed below, for example, it took several thousand years to change the wild ancestor of maize into something that looks like an ear of corn. And domestication has usually taken place as a long-term process in which the physical characteristics of plant and animal species change as these species' relationships to their human consumers change. Some scholars believe that domestication of wheat and other plants may have happened over only a few years, while others contend that it took centuries (Figure 6.1). And human intentions to domesticate plants and animals are neither archaeologically retrievable nor logically important to this notion of domestication. As Rindos points out: "People could not create the variation [in plants and animals] that would permit domestication, they could only select; and they could not have known how important the products of their selection would become."[12] According to this point of view, human intentions and goal-oriented behavior, while important, are not archaeologically retrievable and in most cases must be assumed to be constants: that is, there is no reason to believe that agriculture appeared in one place and not another because in the latter case people just did not successfully analyze the situation and solve the problems of adaptation. And at another level, what people *thought* they were doing in making the adaptations that led to domestication and agriculture does not matter; it is what they actually *did*, in the sense of eating this or that kind of food, moving from one area to another seasonally, etc., that is important. But other scholars disagree and see the origins of domesticates as processes in which human intentions "speeded-up" the process almost from the beginning.[13]

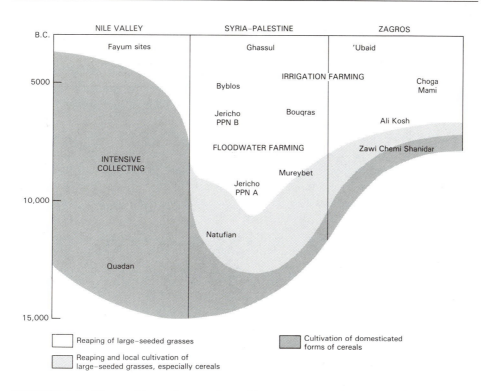

FIGURE 6.1   The world was forever changed by mutualistic relationships that evolved between people and large seeded grasses sometime before about 15,000 years ago. Agriculture was only the last stage of the evolution of these relationships, but the large and reliable harvests made possible by the domestication of wheat and barley were the basis on which ancient and modern civilizations evolved.

As noted above, another issue in studying the problem of agricultural origins is determining why people chose the particular genera they did to domesticate and cultivate. We will examine this question later in this chapter with regard to the economic equations in specific areas of the world where agriculture appeared independently, such as Southwest Asia. But whatever the importance of human intentionality in producing agricultural economies, it is important to recognize that human food and taste "preferences" seem to have played little role in agricultural origins. In fact, food preferences and other cultural aspects of the diverse human interactions with the foods they eat are a fascinating example of the blend of economic forces and ideologies that govern human actions. One must recognize, for example, that maggoty meat, fresh cow blood, rotted fish-heads, charred goat-intestines, tuna noodle casserole, sheep eyes, pot roasts simmered in packaged onion soup—all these are today savored with as much gusto as anything from the restaurants of Milan or Paris. Economic conditions usually are the major determinants of food preferences and of food production. The reason local supermarkets are currently offering special prices on New Zealand lamb and not Labrador retrievers has more to do with the economics of raising these animals (and the economic conditions of the ancient societies in which they were first domesticated) and with the accidents of cultural ideologies than with the foods' intrinsic tastes. There are few more convincing demonstrations that food preferences are primarily "styles" and cultural constructs, rather than reflections of the inherent subtleties and complexities of tastes and textures, than the crowds of people of all nations who queue for hamburgers at a McDonald's in Rome (near the Spanish Steps), less than 100 meters from the competitively-priced 37–item antipasto buffet at the Ristorante a la Rampa.

As we shall see below, a complex set of factors seems to have determined why specific genera became domesticated and cultivated while others did not. In terms of historical impact, one of the most important things about agriculture is that it produces not just great amounts of food, it supplies *reliable* and *predictable* amounts of food, and thereby allows population densities to rise and people in many areas of the world to live year round in the same place—in *sedentary communities.* Such communities probably first appeared in Southwest Asia as much as 1,000 years before agriculture or domesticated wheat or barley, while in Mesoamerica at least five plant species were in the process of domestication several thousand years before the first sedentary or agricultural communities appeared. But in both cases the transition to agriculture provided strong pressures for permanent residence in one particular place.

Sedentary life usually involves the construction of permanent structures. For a million years and more before agriculture, people built crude shelters and lived in caves, but in almost every case they moved to other camps for part of the year because they had to go to where their food was, and this changed continually as animals migrated, wild plants changed with the seasons, etc. In many areas of the world, people probably had to break up into seasonal groups and spend part of the year away from their kinfolk to thin their population density to a level that could be supported in the leanest seasons of the year. By 10,000 years ago, human societies were tied together by trade networks and, probably, by social bonds that extended beyond the group that lived together for most of the year. Traditionally, archaeologists have imagined the people of this period as egalitarian and organized only in simple forms of bands and tribes. But we don't really know if this was true. As we shall see in later chapters, wherever there is plentiful and reliable food and other resources, our ancestors have responded in one way, and one way only: they have social systems that exaggerate differences among themselves and among their social groups in access to wealth, power, and prestige.

During the past decade there has been a thorough rethinking of these concepts of sedentism and mobility.[14] Archaeologists now recognize that the idea of sedentism and mobility as two basic polar opposite human living arrangements is a distortion and over-simplification of the underlying complexity of adaptations. The archaeological record of people traditionally called "hunter-gatherers" and assumed to be mobile is now recognized as reflecting many different kinds of mobility. Bettinger and Baumhoff,[15] for example, envision mobility patterns for hunter-gatherer groups in the American West as a continuum from *travelers* to *processors.* Travelers are highly mobile and concentrate on high-return resources, such as big-game; processors are less mobile and focus on a diversity of resources, especially plant foods. They suggest that groups at different points along this continuum reflect great differences in other cultural elements, such as demographic structure (e.g., the prevalence of infanticide as a population control mechanism). Even the concept of sedentary society is a misleading typological construct. As Robert Kelly observed, "no society is sedentary, not even our own industrial one—people simply move in different ways."[16]

But when our ancestors began living year-round in the same villages, a complex set of relationships between people, plants, and animals was established that had never existed before. Village life has many effects on the human community. Compared to hunting-foraging societies, village communities usually have higher fertility rates, higher incidences of epidemic diseases, and a basic economic unit based on the family, not the group. Village life also allows the accumulation of material goods. There is a tremendous "inertia" in village agriculture, once it is established. In only a few environments can people move easily from agricultural to other kinds of economies, for the essence of agriculture is that one concentrates one's energies on a very limited number of species that are very reliable. In most agricultural economies, activities that conflict with agricultural production are soon abandoned. In Denmark, for example, analysis of human bone composition shows that in one area along the ocean shore, people before 4000 B.C. lived mainly on marine resources, but after that time they subsisted almost entirely on agricultural products, even though their villages were within a few hundred meters of the rich fish and other resources of the shore.[17]

As Brian Byrd notes, a lot of archaeological attention has been devoted to the initial transition from hunting-foraging to agriculture[18] but much less is known about the "social and economic mechanisms created to integrate and maintain larger populations in early sedentary villages."[19] The change to village life was a radical shift in the way people dealt with each other and the world, and it produced a completely new social fabric.

Here, too, it is probably a mistake to think of these first villagers in terms of consciously trying to identify all problems they encountered in making a living in this new setting and organizing themselves socially, or their developing a wide range of new behaviors to meet these new needs. People cannot always be considered entirely rational consumers who put together economies that are optimally efficient, and we cannot explain agricultural origins simply as the natural outcome of people who search through all the possibilities and put together the best economy based on their technology. But *everything* cultural is subjected to natural selection to some extent, and so we must consider agriculture to be the outcome, at least in part, of behaviors that "worked."

HYPOTHESES ABOUT THE ORIGINS OF DOMESTICATION, AGRICULTURE, AND SEDENTARY COMMUNITIES

> Cursed is the ground for thy sake,
> in sorrow shalt thou eat of it all the days of thy life,
> Thorns also and thistles shall it bring forth to thee
> In the sweat of thy face shalt thou eat bread.
> (*Genesis 3:17–18*)

To begin with, we can dismiss the idea that people domesticated plants and animals because someone came from outer space and taught them how to do it, or because someone in ancient Syria had a brilliant idea and it spread around the world, or because people simply got sick of chasing animals and wanted an easier way to live.

The roughly contemporary appearance of a vast variety of domesticates, from palm trees to potatoes, across the same approximate latitudes around the world, and the several millennia it took for hunting and gathering to give way to farming in most areas, make any of the above scenarios improbable. And, although there is great variability, hunters and gatherers tend to have more leisure time than primitive agriculturists—farming is hard work, as even the suburban gardener knows full well. Moreover, hunters-foragers do not seem to spend their time in continual efforts to improve their lot—or designing cathedrals or composing string quartets. Studies of these groups around the world show that they spend almost all of their spare time talking or sleeping—skills, as Sharp notes, that most of them have already thoroughly perfected.[20]

Even so, the idea that people became farmers because it was an easier way of life than hunting-foraging seems so plausible—particularly to most Westerners—that it is hard to discredit this myth.

The world-wide origins of agriculture constitute a complex *evolutionary* and historical event, and thus cannot be expected to be analyzable in mechanical terms: that is, evolutionary sequences are by definition inherently unpredictable in terms of their specifics. After all, no one could have predicted the evolution of tigers—or of us—from the world's fauna of 100 million years ago. Nothing that has a history in which natural selection has had an effect can be explained in mechanical deterministic terms like those of physics.

But the origins of agriculture tempt one to look at it in somewhat mechanical and deterministic terms because it happened independently, in several places in the Old and New Worlds alike, and at about the same time and in similar environments. Anyone considering the problem of agricultural origins has to be impressed by three major categories of evidence; first, we know that world climates changed greatly just before domestication and agriculture first appeared in the Old World; second, world population densities had also been increasing for hundreds of thousands of years before agricultural origins; third, human technology seems to have been improving in many ways over the whole history of our genus. Not surprisingly, climate change and population growth are included in most models of agricultural origins, and there is some suggestion in many hypotheses that the accumulation of knowledge about toolmaking was an important element in the transition to agriculture.

EARLY HYPOTHESES ABOUT AGRICULTURAL ORIGINS

Among the first hypotheses about agricultural origins was the so-called "Oasis Hypothesis," an idea associated with the Australian archaeologist V. Gordon Childe,[21] who attempted to explain the origins of agriculture in terms of the climate changes associated with the end of the Pleistocene some 10,000 years ago. Childe and other advocates of this idea suggested that as the world became warmer and drier, people, animals, and plants would be forced into close conjunction and human communities would be under stress to find new food sources, and out of this propinquity and need would arise animal domestication and then farming.[22]

Doubts about the accuracy of the Oasis Hypothesis appeared when it was demonstrated that the wild ancestors of wheat and barley did not grow in the areas where post-Pleistocene oases were thought to have been concentrated, and by evidence that deserts and oases had not formed in most of Southwest and Central Asia at the time domestication began. But more recently, various scholars have reassessed the evidence and find support for the general idea that post-Pleistocene changes in patterns of rainfall and other climatic factors did have a role in the origins of agriculture.[23]

Recent work in Egypt suggests that a change in rainfall patterns there also may have forced people out of oases and into the Nile Valley, where they may have become farmers of wheat and barley species that were first domesticated in Southwest Asia.[24]

But there were many periods of climatic alteration in the past hundreds of thousands of years in which agriculture did not appear, so either there was something distinctive, perhaps unique, about this last period of climate change, or else there must be some additional factors. Also, domestication and agriculture appeared in an extremely diverse range of environments, from cold valleys high in the Andes to the plains of southern Palestine to the humid lowlands of Southeast Asia. If climate change was such a powerful force for agricultural origins, how could it have affected such a diverse range of habitats to produce the same results? It is not impossible that the climate changes at the end of the last Pleistocene period were unique in subtle ways, influencing aspects of weather such as the difference between winter and summer maxima, the length of growing seasons, etc. Just because one observes that the average temperature change between, say, the late Pleistocene and today is a certain number of degrees, and that a similar difference has occurred at many times in the past, does not exclude the possibility that there were specific aspects of the climate changes at the end of this last Pleistocene period that go far to explain agricultural origins in some areas.[25] But again, domestication involved so many different environments and so many different species that it seems unlikely that climate change can be the main and most direct cause of this development as a world-wide phenomenon.

Another early idea about agricultural origins has been termed the "Natural Habitat Hypothesis." Harold Peake and Herbert Fleure suggested in 1926 that the first domesticates and agriculturalists would have appeared in the upper valley of the Euphrates River, because they knew that this is the "natural habitat" of wild species of wheat and barley. In the early 1950s Robert Braidwood of the University of Chicago organized a series of excavations to evaluate post-Pleistocene climatic changes and to look for early farming communities in northern Mesopotamia. His expeditions were among the first to include specialists in botany, geology, and zoology as well as archaeology, and this multidisciplinary approach has proven to be a highly successful research strategy.

Braidwood's excavations at Jarmo, in the hill country of northern Iraq, revealed an agricultural settlement dating to about 6500 B.C.—much earlier than had been found elsewhere.[26] About 6500 B.C. Jarmo was a settlement of a few dozen mud-walled huts inhabited by about 150 people who relied partly on wild plants and animals, such as snails, pistachios, and acorns, but who also seem to have been involved in herding domesticated goats and, perhaps, sheep. But Braidwood also found at Jarmo the remains of partially domesticated wheat in association with grinding stones, sickle blades, and storage pits. Braidwood suggested that the cumulative effects of generations of interaction between people, plants, and animals in these natural habitat zones led to agriculture.

Braidwood's research into agricultural origins was one of the few systematic investigations into this problem at the time, and he provided crucial evidence for the next stage of research on this problem—trying to understand the precise mechanisms by which agriculture appeared. Evidence that some of the earliest agricultural communities had appeared, not in the middle of the natural habitat, but on the margins or outside of it[27] raised the possibility that agriculture was not just a natural result of people exploiting wild stands of wheat and barley.

Also, a series of experiments was performed by botanist Jack Harlan in eastern Anatolia in 1966 in which, using a crude sickle made with flint blades set in a wooden handle, he was able to harvest wild emmer wheat at the rate of about 6.25 pounds per hour.[28] A family of four or five could probably have collected a year's supply of grain with only a few weeks' labor, and this would seem to suggest that the people who lived in the natural habitat of wheat and barley had perhaps the least incentive to domesticate and farm it, because they could collect more than enough from wild stands.

A particularly influential synthesis and extension of some of these early hypotheses about agricultural origins was Lewis Binford's "Edge-Zone Hypothesis," which although widely regarded as flawed and to some extent obsolete, is still important because most later models have been written in reaction to it. Binford assumed that prior to the first farmers, hunting and gathering bands were in equilibrium with their natural environment, using wild plants and animals but not altering them in ways we recognize as domestication.

What could have upset this ancient equilibrium? Binford argues that this was essentially a case where changes in the demographic structure of one region resulted in one group's impingement on the territory of another, upsetting the equilibrium and increasing the population density in some areas to the point that new ways of manipulating the natural environment to increase productivity would be favored. He notes that Southwest Asia is an ecological mosaic, with close juxtapositioning of very different climates and plant and animal communities, and suggests that late Pleistocene hunters and gatherers used budding-off as the primary mechanism for population-size control. This phenomenon, noted in many parts of the world, involves a group slowly increasing its size up to a certain number, at which point, because of squabbling or insufficient resources, the group splits, with half the people emigrating to another, usually adjacent, territory. Budding-off can also become the primary population-control mechanism if a new resource or subsistence technique—such as domestication and agriculture—opens a new niche.[29]

Given varying population growth rates, Binford maintains that budding-off would have certain consequences that could have led to domestication and agriculture:

> From the standpoint of the populations already in the recipient zone, the intrusion of immigrant groups would disturb the existing density equilibrium system and might

raise the population density to the level at which we would expect diminishing food resources. This situation would serve to increase markedly for the recipient groups the pressures favoring means for increased productivity. The intrusive group, on the other hand, would be forced to make adaptive adjustments to their new environment. . . . There would be strong selective pressures favoring the development of more efficient subsistence techniques by both groups.[30]

Thus, Binford is particularly concerned with describing situations that would select for, or reward, a cultural innovation like domestication or agriculture. Once the population-to-resources balance was disturbed, there was a premium on every resource, and domestication might have come about in a number of ways. Perhaps the immigrant groups, in an attempt to regain the resources of their former habitats, would have tried to introduce wild wheat and barley into these marginal, "edge" zones. This would have exposed these plants to different selective environments, and domestication might have occurred as people manipulated these plant communities in these new environments.

Binford's edge-zone hypothesis provoked much discussion and research, but it has some weaknesses. Most of the earliest agricultural communities in Southwest Asia, for example, have been found in areas like the Negev Desert, where it is difficult to imagine any form of "population pressure." In any case, in most instances of early domestication and agriculture, domesticates seem to represent only about 5 percent of the total diet for centuries after they begin to be domesticated—a slow process in which it's difficult to imagine much daily stress.[31]

On the other hand, aspects of the shift to cereals and other resources may help explain how agriculture—once it was in its initial stages—changed human demographic patterns. In hunting-gathering societies, fertility rates are suppressed significantly simply by maternal mobility: a pregnant woman's chances of spontaneous abortion go up considerably if she walks a lot and works heavily. Thus, those late Pleistocene groups that became less mobile, perhaps because they began to concentrate on salmon runs or wild cereal patches, might have experienced a rise in fertility rates. Also, a direct correlation exists between the amount of carbohydrates in the diet and fertility rates. Studies have shown that it is almost impossible for a woman to become pregnant until she has about 27,000 calories, or 20 to 25 percent of her body weight, stored as fat[32] (the author assumes no liability for the accuracy of this statistic). Nursing a child requires about 1,000 calories a day, and in many hunter-gatherer societies, the rigors of mobility and their high-protein diet can mean that nursing itself prevents sufficient fat build-up for a successful subsequent pregnancy for about three years. But with the change to a high-carbohydrate, cereal-based diet and restricted mobility of sedentary life, fertility rates may well have risen rapidly.[33]

CONTEMPORARY MODELS OF AGRICULTURAL ORIGINS

In a recent review of models of agricultural origins,[34] Blumler and Byrne compare these models on three questions: (1) Was domestication effected in these plants before or after cultivation? (2) Was the human selection for the desired traits conscious, unconscious, or both? (3) Was the domestication process rapid or slow?

Blumler and Byrne find all of these models inadequate or false. They argue that the mathematics of population genetics strongly suggest that it is difficult to construct plausible models that would permit even partial domestication in the wild or long before the initiation of cultivation.

Population growth, thus, has been an important element in most accounts of agricultural origins. Mark Cohen, for example, argues that: "the nearly simultaneous adoption of agricultural economies throughout the world could only be accounted for by assuming that hunting and gathering populations had saturated the world approximately 10,000 years ago and had exhausted all possible (or palatable) strategies for increasing their food supply within the constraints of the hunting-gathering life-style. The only possible reaction to further growth in population, worldwide, was to begin artificial augmentation of the food supply."[35]

Differences in the rate and timing of the adoption and spread of agriculture, Cohen suggests, may be found in local environmental variation, such as the mobility that resources of a given area require of a hunter-gatherer for their exploitation.[36]

A major problem in assessing any hypothesis based on ancient population densities is the difficulty of estimating changes in these densities with any precision using archaeological data. One has to locate all the relevant archaeological sites (of which many are certain to have been destroyed or not found), then estimate the numbers of people at each site, and then develop a chronology for these sites that is fine enough to reconstruct changes over fairly short periods of time. Consequently, most population estimates based on archaeological data must be considered extremely speculative; and the relationship between agriculture and demographic change remains complex and not well understood.

Some support for Cohen's arguments seems to exist in the paleopathological data from around the world. Agriculture allows more people to be fed, but compared to hunting-foraging in general, agriculture is associated with shorter life expectancies, higher disease rates (especially among infants), smaller body size, and chronic malnutrition.[37]

Marvin Harris has formulated an explanation of agricultural origins that resembles Cohen's in its stress on increasing human populations, declining worldwide availability of large game animals, and the competition among groups for survival.[38] In addition, Harris considers a fascinating topic—food taboos. In trying to explain food taboos he has illuminated some of the central problems of trying to understand human economic history. Consider, for example, the humble pig. Eventually Islam, Judaism, and some Hindu religions instituted complete bans on pork to the extent that, even today, riots flare in some parts of the world if pigs invade religious areas.

Pigs are one of the most efficient converters of garbage, animal wastes, and other materials discarded by farmers—better in many respects than goats, sheep, or cows. In preindustrial economies and today around the world in Europe, America, and China, the pig is used to convert grains that are not made into food or whisky into portable, storable food. So why should the sturdy farmers of the Middle East reject such a good food source after millennia in which the pig was a staple part of the diet?

This question has set up a conflict between people who believe that all such religious prohibitions, and almost every other aspect of cultural behavior, can be understood directly in terms of technological, ecological, and demographic variables, and those who think it is impossible to explain adequately such things as religious food prohibitions and general religious and social behavior in terms of the conditions of technology, ecology, and demography.

Harris dismisses the notion that this prohibition has anything to do with the common infection of pigs with trichinae, parasites that can kill people.[39] Recent studies have shown that pigs raised in hot climates seldom transmit this disease; moreover, Southwest Asian farmers ate cattle, sheep, and goats, which carry anthrax, brucellosis, and other diseases as dangerous or more so than anything pigs can transmit.

Instead, Harris explains prohibitions of pork in terms of the cost-benefit ratio of the animal in early subsistence agricultural systems. Pigs, unlike sheep, goats, and cattle, cannot subsist on husks, stalks, or other high-cellulose foods; their natural diet is tubers, roots, nuts, and fruits. Also, pigs are native to woodlands and swamps and do not tolerate direct sun and open country well. Thus, the clearing of land coincident with the spread of agriculture in Southwest Asia greatly reduced the habitat and natural foods available to pigs, and, increasingly, pigs had to be fed on grain, which brought them into competition with people; they also had to be provided with artificial shade and considerable water. Moreover, Harris points out that, in contrast to other domesticates, pigs cannot be milked, sheared, ridden, or used to pull a plow. In short, they lost their cost effectiveness relative to sheep, goats, and cattle, and their eventual proscription made excellent economic "sense."

And, as in all instances, it is not important that people ever recognize their motives in cases of such prohibitions: natural selection "fixes," or perpetuates, economically sound behaviors, regardless of what people think their motives are. Harris extends his argument to many other animals, in particular the sacred cow of India and the animals listed in the Old Testament. In every case he tries to show that when one considers the economic conditions in which these prohibitions arose, one can see that there was at least some minor overall advantage to be gained. Thus, he notes that the Old Testament forbids eating any insects other than locusts, which just happen to be the only ones that have much caloric value in relation to the cost of capturing them (and they are crop pests as well).

Against Harris and his supporters are many people who believe that Harris is propagating a bastardized version of a misconception of Marxian theory.[40] Sahlins, for example, points to the United States, where millions of cattle are slaughtered every year but where virtually every horse lives out its full life in relative luxury and, usually, enjoying considerable affection. Why, Sahlins asks, do Americans arbitrarily proscribe horsemeat and accept beef? Sahlins answers his own question, arguing that it is because every culture creates its own belief systems from its unique blend of economy, society, and ideology. The essential point, Sahlins says, "is that material rationality exists for men not as a fact of nature but as a construct of culture. . . . The natural conditions of viability (selective forces) comprise merely negative constraints, limits of functional possibilities, which remain indeterminate with respect to the generation of particular cultural forms."[41] Moreover, he says, one can never read directly from material circumstances to cultural order as from cause to effect. "It is not that these techno-environmental variables have no effect, rather that everything depends on the way these properties are culturally mediated—given meaningful organization by a mode of cultural organization."[42]

All this is rather far from the poor abandoned pigs of Southwest Asia, but the point is an important one. For if archaeologists must seek the causes of changes in the archaeological record (like the succession of pig bones by sheep and goat bones in the levels of a site) in the cultural mediation of "the mode of cultural organization," they will have to apply techniques of archaeological analysis currently not known or, possibly, not within the capacities of any other than a Divine Intellect.

Harris argues that one can show by examining the relative susceptibility to disease, dietary requirements, and other economic and historical factors that it makes economic "sense" to eat cattle and not horses in contemporary America. He does not insist all human behavior has such a delicate economic tuning or that there can be no whimsical aspects of culture. He says only that in the long run, if one is trying to understand something like these different uses of animals, one should look first at the economics of the situation.

Another general explanation of agricultural origins has been proposed by Brian Hayden. He begins with the assumption that ancient hunters and gatherers were, like most people, trying to maintain the reliability and stability with which they could get food.[43] He suggests that for the last several million years our ancestors diversified their "income" by eating a wide range of plant and animal species and developing digging sticks, hand-axes, nets, and all the other implements of pre-agricultural peoples. They also became in many areas sophisticated predators of large gregarious herbivores like deer.

Rather than a constant drive from population growth or "pressure" which forced these innovations and broadening of diets, Hayden envisions great stability in the population-to-resources balance. Unlike Cohen, he expects that if we had complete human skeletal evidence from the Pleistocene, we would see no more evidence of dietary stress in the late Pleistocene than in the early Pleistocene.[44]

But by the end of the Pleistocene 10,000 years ago, all the larger, more obvious animal species had been exploited, and people faced with the same kinds of cyclical food shortages that always had been humankind's lot could only turn to grasses, seeds, fish, and mice—in other words, the smaller, in some ways less desirable species. Hayden uses here a division of the animal world according to reproductive "strategy": "k"-selected species, like deer, are long-lived, tend to have long maturation periods, have only one or a few offspring each reproductive cycle, and are susceptible to over-exploitation; "r"-selected species, on the other hand, like grasses, which reproduce in incalculably large numbers, are genetically plastic, live only a year, are extremely resistant to over-exploitation, and quickly reestablish themselves after floods, fires, and droughts.

Switching to a diet of mainly "r"-selected species, Hayden argues, would have encouraged a sedentary way of life, stimulated the development of ground-stone tools, wooden implements, and other agricultural devices, stabilized the food supply, and lessened the need for group cooperation and common food storage. In Hayden's view, the rise of agriculture is just a "natural and logical extension of the trends" that led to the late Pleistocene refocusing of exploitation strategies from big-game animals to smaller animals and plants.

As for the timing and location of the first agricultural economies:

It is especially notable that domestication did not first occur where the environments were rich enough to support sedentary, hunting-gathering-based ranked societies, with wealth competition and primitive valuables, such as those found in California, the Northwest Coast, Florida, and Palestine. According to my model, even though these areas had the highest population densities, their resource bases would have been much more stable and they would have experienced resource stress relatively infrequently. Because sedentism, wealth competition, and ranking in rich environments did not result in domestication in these areas, it is reasonable to conclude that such developments were not sufficient, or perhaps even necessary, conditions for domestication. Instead, domestication can be more usefully linked to the same Paleolithic processes which gave rise to the Mesolithic and Archaic: the effort to increase resource reliability in areas of frequent stress.[45]

Hayden's model, as well as the others discussed in this chapter, are to some extent incomplete and untested. We must presume that more powerful explanations will be formulated as the theory of archaeology continues to develop and new evidence becomes available.

David Rindos's model (discussed earlier in this chapter) explains a great deal about what domestication and agriculture *are*. What remain to be explained are the timing and distribution of early agricultural communities.

Finally, with regard to theories of agricultural origins, it is at least plausible that more powerful explanations of this phenomena must somehow take into account social and ideological factors. As Barbara Bender[46] has noted, many groups around the world in the period just before agriculture appeared seem to be different from their predecessors in intriguing ways. They were trading more extensively and their burials and other artifacts seem to suggest a growing sense of ethnic identity and status differentiation. These may have stimulated intensified production and exchange in ways that affected the transition to agriculture. It is tempting to see these changes as *reflections* or results of the economic changes, but societies are integrated functional units in which change is not easily explained strictly in terms of clearly identifiable causes and effects.

In the rest of this chapter we examine in detail two cases of the transition to agriculture—Southwest Asia and Mesoamerica—and attempt to match this evidence to these and other ideas about agricultural origins.

EARLY DOMESTICATION AND AGRICULTURE: THE MESOLITHIC BACKGROUND

We must assume that, to some extent, the causes of agriculture are to be found in the thousands of years of hunting-gathering that immediately preceded the first agricultural societies. A critical interval may be the period between 15,000 and 8,000 years ago—a time of major climatic changes for much of the world. Climate changes cannot be a full and final explanation of the worldwide transition to agriculture, because over the past hundreds of thousands of years there have been many periods of climate change, but one important factor may have been the appearance of strongly seasonal rainfall patterns in various parts of the world in the period of transition between the Pleistocene and the Holocene.[47] Byrne argues that these seasonal patterns of rainfall would have encouraged the growth of annuals and other plants that eventually became domesticated, and thus encouraged a shift to intensification of plant-collecting by hunter-foragers.[48]

In Western Europe, population densities shifted as the herds of reindeer and horses that once supported many hunting bands moved northward with the retreating glaciers. Some people moved with them, but others worked out subsistence strategies stressing plants, smaller game, and fish. Salmon became especially important in Europe as traps, drying racks, and other tools were developed to make salmon exploitation a reliable way to make a living. In Southwest Asia, parts of Africa, and parts of the Americas, some late Pleistocene and early post-Pleistocene peoples began to eat more small game, fish, waterfowl, clams, wild cereals, and similar foods; elsewhere, big-game hunting specializations persisted. In North America, for example, some groups centered their lives around vast bison herds.[49]

Where a shift to smaller, more varied resources was made, technologies also changed. The bow and arrow and throwing stick replaced the stabbing spears, and new tools were developed to dig plants, trap wild fowl, and prepare and cook this broader diet (Figure 6.2). Small, simple, geometric stone tools predominated in many

FIGURE 6.2   After about 10,000 years ago, people all over Europe began to exploit a much greater diversity of plants and animals than did their Pleistocene predecessors. This shift is reflected in Mesolithic fishing and hunting equipment: (1) limpet hammer; (2) bone fish-spear with microlith barbs, southern Sweden; (3) barbed point in red deer antler, c. 7500 B.C., Star Carr, Yorkshire; (4) leister prongs of Eskimo fishermen (shows how the barbed point may have been used); (5) net-making needle (?) and (6) bone fish hook, Denmark; (7, 8) microliths or transverse arrowheads, one found in peat hafted in wood with sinew binding, Denmark; (9) core-ax with transversely sharpened edge, Sussex; (10) flake-axe, Denmark.

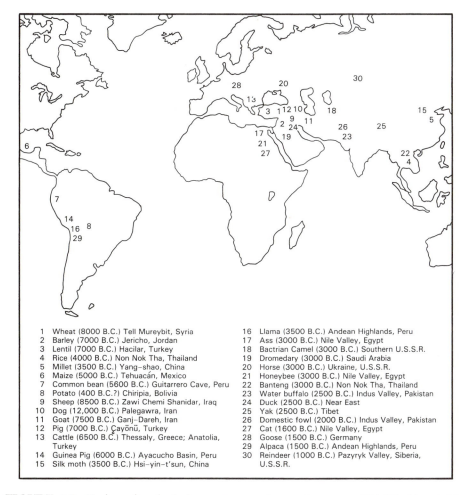

FIGURE 6.3 Early archaeological occurrences of some important Old World and New World domesticates. Domestication is a process, not an event, and these specific sites represent only some early occurrences of species domesticated over wide areas. Many other species have been domesticated.

areas. The world about 12,000 years ago was relatively diverse culturally, as some groups remained big-game hunters while others took up fishing, intensive foraging, and other pursuits. Thus, a great diversity of plants and animals was being exploited with varying intensities and technologies in a wide range of climates. Out of this vast mixture of peoples, plants, animals, and places the first domesticates and farmers appeared. (Figure 6.3).

But which of these groups became agriculturalists and why? Although all the people before about 10,000 years ago were hunter-gatherers, this term covers a wide range of economies.[50] Much of the variability in hunter-gatherer adaptations seems to be linked to *food storage*.[51] Alain Testart notes that some hunter-gatherers store large amounts of food, others do not, and that:

> storing hunter-gatherer societies exhibit three characteristics—sedentism, a high population density, and the development of socioeconomic inequalities—which have been considered typical of agricultural societies and possible only with an agricultural way of life. Furthermore, their economic cycle—massive harvest and intensive storage of a seasonal resource—is the same as that of societies based on the cultivation of cereals. The difference between storing hunter-gatherers and agriculturalists lies in whether the staple food species are wild or domesticated: this proves to be only a minor difference, since it does not affect the main aspects of society. Agriculturalists and storing hunter-gatherers together are neatly in opposition to non-storing hunter-gatherers. The conclusion to be drawn is that it is certainly not the presence of agriculture or its absence which is the relevant factor when dealing with such societies, but rather the presence or absence of an economy with intensive storage as its cornerstone.[52]

Thus, in looking for causes of agricultural economies, we must consider kinds of adaptations where storage is a potential factor. This relates directly to certain types of foods. Cereals store well, but many tubers do not. Sheep, pigs, barnyard fowl, and other animals can also be considered a form of food storage, since one simply feeds them excess or unwanted foods until the need arises to eat them.

In looking for the origins of agriculture, we can look for environments where food storage was an early and important option. It is probably also significant, as Kent Flannery notes, that the major seed crops that supported the first farmers and remain the basis of modern economies, including wheat, barley, millet, and rice, appear to have derived from wild ancestors that were "third-choice" foods: plants that were usually more difficult to gather and process than other wild plants and thus were probably first eaten in quantity because people had to do so, not because they wanted to.[53] On the other hand, most of these third-choice foods are easily storable, plentiful, easy to grow, and, as annuals, are genetically malleable—altering the selective forces on them each year can quickly change them genetically.

THE ORIGINS OF DOMESTICATION, AGRICULTURE, AND SEDENTARY COMMUNITIES IN SOUTHWEST ASIA

The best known and perhaps the world's first case of the origins of domestication and agriculture occurred in Southwest Asia, and involved peoples and environments ranging from Afghanistan to Greece over a time period of at least 14,000 years. From this region came domesticated sheep, goats, cattle, pigs, wheat, barley, and many other crops on which much of the world today depends.

The environment in which this transition took place is extremely complex. Millions of years ago movements of the earth's crust forced the Arabian Peninsula toward the stable Iranian Plateau, compressing the land in between so that it is pleated like the folds of an accordion. At the end of the Pleistocene, the uplands of the "Fertile Crescent" (Figure 6.4) supported large herds of wild sheep, goats, cattle, and pigs and, in many areas, dense stands of wild wheat and barley. In lower elevations and wetter regions, lakes and streams had abundant supplies of waterfowl and fish.

Between about 20,000 and 12,500 B.C., glaciers expanded over many areas of America and Eurasia, altering climates around the world. Because scholars have assumed that the transition to agriculture has its roots in this time period, the climatic changes of this era have been intensively studied.[54] Various models of climate changes and consequent vegetation changes have been proposed, but the evidence is far from clear. Generally, Southwest Asia was cooler and drier in this period, but other periods appear to have been cooler and wetter.[55] Within the span from 20,000 to 12,500 B.C. there were shorter cycles of climate change, periods of several thousand years in which the climates became relatively warmer or cooler, drier or wetter.[56] For most of this period, the sea coasts expanded as ocean levels fell. Forests covered coastal areas around the northern and eastern Mediterranean, but many higher areas of Southwest Asia were dry steppe or grasslands.

Then between about 13,000 and 8000 B.C., as the glaciers retreated, most of Southwest Asia became warmer. Between about 12,500 and 10,000 B.C. the eastern Mediterranean appears to have experienced a period of relatively high rainfall, but then between 10,000 and 8,000 B.C. there were periods of growing aridity.[57] The rising sea levels of these warmer periods would have submerged from ten to twenty kilometers of coastal plains around much of Southwest Asia, perhaps forcing people into new areas. The sea level rose a maximum of about 120 meters when the Pleistocene cold was greatest (about 18,000 B.P. to 10,000 B.P.), but the average annual rise would have been only seven to eight millimeters, so one should not imagine late Pleistocene hunter-foragers scurrying in front of unexpected floods.[58]

FIGURE 6.4 The "Fertile Crescent" and some important early pre-agricultural and agricultural sites.

It is against this backdrop of climatic change that we can examine the archaeological record to see how patterns of people-plant-animal interactions changed in ways that might explain agricultural origins in this period. Since there were many previous glacial fluctuations and climatic changes in this area that did not produce agriculture, these climatic variations are obviously not a complete explanation of agricultural origins; but it is not without significance for the timing and location of agricultural origins that they coincided with these environmental changes. Also, no two periods of climate change are exactly alike. Average changes in temperature and rainfall do not tell the whole story. Subtle changes in seasonality, maximum heat and cold, and other factors have complex impacts on ecologies, and it is difficult to sort these out for periods in the distant past. There may have been something special or unique about the climatic and ecological changes of 12,000 years ago that explains much about agricultural origins. Joy McCorriston and Frank Hole,[59] for example, argue that about 10,000 years ago, as the Pleistocene ended, the climates of the Jordan Valley and adjacent areas of the Middle East became much more arid and more sharply seasonal. They suggest that the climate changes of this period encouraged the growth and spread of annual species of cereals and legumes, and that because the summers were hyper-arid and there were few resources available, people began to store more of their food, which in turn required them to become more sedentary—to stay near their stored foods. They note that these climate changes resulted in the establishment of agriculture because at the time they occurred, people in this area had developed tools for processing wild cereals and had partially depleted their environments of some of the wild plants and animals that had sustained Pleistocene hunter-foragers here. The fact that domestication appeared independently in many different environments at many different times and involved scores of plant and animal species, however, suggests that climatic changes alone do not entirely explain the origins of agriculture.

SOUTHWEST ASIAN DOMESTICATES

To understand the origins of agriculture in Southwest Asia, we have to understand the domestication of wheat, barley, cattle, sheep, and goats, for these have been the primary food sources in this area from about 9,000 years ago to the present day. Lentils and other legumes may have been domesticated here earlier,[60] and pigs were more important than cattle, sheep, and goats in some areas and places, but in general it was wheat and barley and cattle, sheep, and goats that supported Southwest Asia's cultural evolution.

If you were a peasant agriculturalist forced to farm the wild ancestors of wheat and barley, you would have had a hard time. Wild wheat, for example, has many limitations as a food crop: its distribution is sharply limited by temperature, soil, and moisture. As a result, stands of these grains can be widely scattered and therefore difficult to harvest. Much greater efficiency could be attained if these plants could be adapted to a greater variety of temperature, soil, and moisture ranges—especially to the torrid summers of the lowlands, where the rivers offered the potential of irrigation agriculture.

Also, the rachis, the segment of the stalk to which the kernels of wheat or barley are attached, becomes extremely brittle as wild wheat ripens. This brittleness is essential to the successful propagation of these plants, because it allows the seeds to be separated from the plant and dispersed by the merest touch of an animal or simply the force of the wind. The head of the plant becomes brittle gradually, from top to bottom, and seed dispersal is spread over one to two weeks. Although this is advantageous for the plant because it prevents the seeds from sprouting in a dense mass of competing seedlings, it poses problems for the human collector. If the grain is gathered when quite ripe, the slightest contact will cause the rachis to fall off, so harvesting with a sickle is difficult—although holding the stalk over a basket and tapping it with a stick works. If, on the other hand, the grain is harvested before it is fully mature, excess moisture in the unripe kernels will cause them to rot in storage. A plant with a tougher rachis and on which the kernels ripen at about the same time would clearly be more useful to people.

Another problem with wild wheat is that the kernels are enclosed in very tough protective husks, called glumes. These protect the seeds from frost and dehydration, but primitive threshing often will not separate the seeds from the glumes, and the human digestive tract cannot break down their tough fibers. Thus a cereal with less tough and less developed glumes would be more digestible.

Also, each stalk of wild grain has only two rows of kernels. Domesticated varieties have six rows, rendering them much more productive as a food resource, and wild species had to change in this direction before it was profitable to invest energy in sowing, cultivating, and harvesting wheat and barley in many areas—particularly in those areas where natural conditions were not optimal for wild cereals.

To base your economy on wheat and barley would also require some specialized tools, for cutting, transporting, threshing, storing, milling, and baking. A full-time cereal farmer is best off living year round in a village or town because of the costs of moving large quantities of grain and because successful harvesting requires that collectors be near stands at very precise times. In contrast to many plants, wild grain can be collected only during the few days when the plants are ripening, and even then there is considerable competition from birds and other predators. Another consideration is that women and children in cereal-gathering societies could contribute a great deal to the food supply, whereas in many societies specializing in hunting, women and children have less direct economic return.

Given all these liabilities and required cultural adjustments, one might wonder why and how these cereals were domesticated. In fact, this seems to have been a relatively rapid process in Southwest Asia, occurring within a few thousand years (and perhaps much less [Figure 6.5]), in several native grasses, including wild barley (*Hordeum spontaneum*), wild einkorn (*Triticum boeoticum*), and wild emmer wheat (*Triticum dicoccum*), each with different habitats and characteristics.

At the same time these plants were being domesticated about 10,000 years ago, sheep, goats, pigs, and cattle were also being domesticated. In some areas, such as the southern Mesopotamian alluvial plain, permanent settlement was not possible until domesticated animals were available to supply the fats and proteins that were not readily obtainable from any other source. Domesticated animals also provided a way of converting highland grasses, weeds, shrubs, surplus grain stubble, and other plants

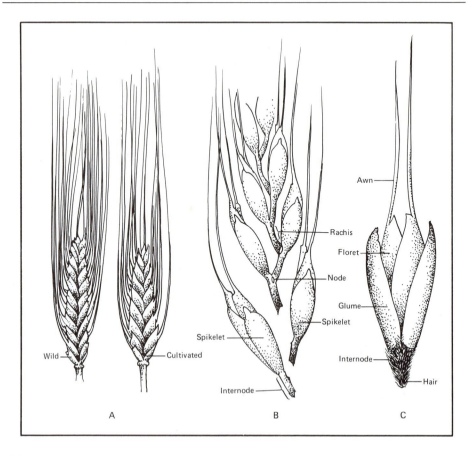

FIGURE 6.5 Domestication of wheat, one of the world's most important crops, involved both human manipulation and natural hybridization between related genera. Human intervention appears to have been aimed at producing free-threshing, nonshattering varieties. The simplest wheats are "diploid," meaning that they have two sets of seven chromosomes. Hybridization with related species produced tetraploid wheats, with six sets of chromosomes, which occur only in cultivated species of wheat. By mixing genetic material from various species, early farmers produced forms of wheat that could adapt to diverse habitats.

into storable, portable, high-quality foods and other usable products. Later, some animals, such as cattle, horses, and donkeys, provided draught and transport power.

Each of the economically most important animals domesticated in Southwest Asia involved somewhat different patterns of change. Cattle, for example, became smaller, perhaps as an adaptation to two factors: the problem of keeping cool in the torrid lowlands where most of the farms eventually were located, and the relatively poor diet that was available to cattle there in the leanest seasons. Sheep developed a thick multi-layered fleece that both protected them from intense temperatures and provided an important product—wool.

THE ARCHAEOLOGICAL RECORD OF PLANT AND ANIMAL DOMESTICATION IN SOUTHWEST ASIA

Archaeological sites throughout Southwest Asia during the late Upper Pleistocene, from about 20,000 to 16,000 B.C., are often concentrations of stone tools, ash, and the bones of large, hoofed mammals. Almost all the meat eaten by people came from just a few species of ungulates (hoofed mammals), mainly gazelles and wild cows. Based on the tools and other artifacts from Southwest Asian sites of this period, it appears that the basic social unit was a band of about fifteen or twenty people comprising several families who season after season moved through this area hunting animals and gathering plants.

To understand how these age-old patterns of human adaptation were displaced in just a few thousand years by farmers, we must look in detail at a variety of evidence. The best known archaeological record of this transition is that of the Levant, the area that extends from southeastern Anatolia into the Sinai Peninsula, and east into what is now western Syria and Jordan.

The Levantine cultures of between 18,000 and 15,000 years ago are called *Kebaran* (named, as so many ancient peoples are, after stone tools from a particular site), followed from about 15,000 to 12,500 B.P. by the *Geometric Kebaran* cultures, and from 12,500 to 10,000 years ago by the *Natufian* cultures.[61]

If the Kebaran peoples were doing something that inexorably led their remote descendants to become farmers, it is not obvious in their archaeological traces. Such traces are almost all small concentrations of bones and stone that reflect a people skilled principally in hunting deer and other large grazing animals.

In the Geometric Kebaran record, however, we get a few indications of economic changes that may be harbingers of agriculture. Some Kebaran sites, such as the Neve David site, on the western slopes of Mt. Carmel, seem to have been occupied for a time by a relatively large group, a "macroband." This site has the full range of ground-stone tools, and it contains two small stone structures, one in a circular form about two meters in diameter. A grave at the site holds a body interred with apparent ritual use of grinding stones.[62] Grinding stones are a key artifact in examining the transition to agriculture because they were indispensable tools for processing cereals and many other plant foods.

Early studies of Kebaran sites and those of later periods led several scholars to the conclusion that there was a "broad spectrum revolution" between 20,000 and 10,000 years ago, in which people in Southwest Asia and many other parts of the world began eating a broader range of foods,[63] including wild cereals. In addition to the wide range of plant and animal species found in some sites toward the end of this period, the variety and efficiency of tools used seems to have increased as these millennia passed. Not only do grinding stones appear in quantity, but also barbed spears and arrows, bows, knives made by setting obsidian and flint flakes into bone or wood, and other tools indicate a greater range of subsistence activities. Some animal species were exploited systematically for the first time, and the grinding stones, "sickles," and other new tools indicate that vegetable foods, including wild cereal grasses, may have been important parts of the diet. Minor local trade in obsidian and sea shells was carried on, and substantial huts appeared in some areas. Apparently, population densities were slowly increasing in some areas—although the archaeological evidence for this is not at all clear.[64]

But in some ways, the broad spectrum revolution and the agricultural revolution may together form an example of that "great tragedy of Science—the slaying of a beautiful hypothesis by an ugly fact," as Thomas Huxley put it. In a long and thorough review of the evidence from Southwest Asia, archaeologist Donald Henry came to two conclusions:

> First, the proposal of a gradual broadening of the economy leading to a more secure subsistence base, the emergence of sedentary communities, and a growth in population can be rejected. Such a trend is not indicated by the pre-Natufian subsistence evidence. Secondly, the emergence of large sedentary communities, as represented by the Natufian, can best be explained by the intensive exploitation of cereals and nuts. Specialization, as opposed to diversification, characterized the Natufian economy. Although small animal species did form a larger portion of the diet in Natufian times than earlier, these food sources furnished an exceedingly small, almost negligible, part of the overall diet. Instead the specialized hunting of gazelle and the intensive collection of cereals and nuts contributed the greatest part of the subsistence base.[65]

Naomi Miller also questions the occurrence of a "broad spectrum revolution," and on the basis of an interpretation of the evidence that may have great significance for understanding the whole history of Southwest Asian agricultural origins. Miller suggests that many of the remains of cereals found in archaeological sites in many areas of Southwest Asia may have come from cattle dung, which was burned as a fuel by ancient villagers. If so, then these plant remains indicate what these animals ate, not what people did.[66]

Some evidence of the specialized gazelle hunting that Henry mentions has been provided by Legge and Rowley-Conwy, who have shown that 11,000 years ago, in the Euphrates Valley in Syria, at the site of Tell Abu Hureya, people intensively hunted gazelles.[67] Of the 60,000 identifiable animal bones found at this site, about 80 percent are from gazelles—and from gazelles of all sizes and ages and both sexes. Near the site are the traces of stone enclosures, and Legge and Rowley-Conwy have concluded that for thousands of years the people of Tell Abu Hureya drove herds of gazelle into these enclosures and killed them all. Many of these enclosures have been found and it is possible that eventually the gazelle were driven so close to extinction that people turned to sheep and goats, and in the process domesticated them.

The Natufian Culture   In the archaeological record of the Natufian Period, from about 12,500 to 10,200 years ago, in the Levant, we see clear evidence of agricultural origins. The stone tools of the Natufians include many lunate (i.e., shaped like a segment of the moon) flakes of chert, but there is also something new: they used "sickle blades" that show a pattern of wear characteristic of cereal harvesting. Also, querns (hand mills), mortars, pestles, pounders, and other ground-stone tools occur in abundance at Natufian sites, and many such tools show signs of long, intensive use. There is also evidence that these heavy grinding stones were transported long distances, more than thirty kilometers in some cases,[68] and this is not something known to have been done by people of preceding periods. Fish hooks and gorges and net sinkers attest to the growing importance of fish in the diet in some areas. Stone vessels indicate an increased need for containers, but there is no evidence of Natufian clay working or pottery. Along with these sickle blades are many grinding stones, mainly mortars and pestles of limestone or basalt. Studies of attrition of the teeth of Natufians also strongly suggest that these people specialized to some extent in collecting cereals, and may have been cultivating them and in the process of domesticating them. But they were also still hunter-foragers, who intensively hunted gazelle and deer in more lush areas, and wild goats and equids in more arid zones.

The Natufians had a different settlement pattern from that of their predecessors. Some of their "base-camps" are far larger (over 1,000 square meters) than any of the earlier periods, and they may have lived in some of these camps for half the year or even more. In some of the camps people made foundations and other architectural elements out of limestone blocks. Trade in shell, obsidian, and other commodities seems to have been on the rise, and we suspect that exchange of perishables, such as skins, foodstuffs, and salt, was also increasing. With the increased importance of wild cereals in the diet, salt probably became for the first time a near necessity: people who eat a lot of meat get many essential salts from this diet, but diets based on cereals can be deficient in salts. Salt was probably also important as a food preservative in early villages.

As always, there is more to a major cultural change than simply a shift in economics. The Natufians made (and presumably wore) beads and pendants in many materials, including gemstones and marine shells that had to be imported, and it is possible this ornamentation reflects a growing sense of ethnic identity and perhaps some differences in personal and group status. Cleverly carved figurines of animals, women, and other subjects occur in many sites, and Natufian period cave paintings have been found in Anatolia, Syria, and Iran.[69] More than 400 Natufian burials have been found, most of them simple graves set in house floors. Grave goods are infrequent, but some burials indicate concern with the philosophical implications of death: at 'Ain Mallaha skeletons were buried with their heads wedged between two stones and their joints covered with large stones, "to ensure perhaps that the deceased would not rise from his grave."[70] In the late Natufian period, some Natufians began burying the body and head of selected people in different but prepared graves. As Belfer-Cohen notes, these burials may reflect an ancestor cult and a growing sense of community emotional ties and attachment to a particular place, and toward the end of the Natufian period people in this area were making a strict separation between living quarters and burial grounds.[71] Compared to the Pleistocene cultures of the Levant, there appears to have been considerable social change in the Natufian.

The question of *why* the Natufians differed in these and other ways from their predecessors, and why they made these first steps toward the farming way of life, remains unclear. There were climate changes, of course, and growing aridity and rising population densities may have forced them to intensify exploitation of cereals, which in turn might have stimulated the development of sickles and other tools and the permanent communities that make agriculture efficient. But precisely how these factors interacted with others is poorly understood.

The Southwest Asian Neolithic   The earliest farmers of the Middle East appear to have been simultaneously domesticating plants and animals, but animal domestication may have begun slightly earlier and been a longer process than that of cereals. Hillman and Davies,[72] for example, estimate that wheat and barley could have been domesticated in parts of the Middle East in 200 years or less.

So we begin with the animals. The dog[73] is no doubt the oldest animal domesticate in Southwest Asia, probably having been fully domesticated between 22,000 and 10,000 B.C. Hunters and gatherers the world over are known to have remarkably unsentimental ideas about pets, and we should probably see the early domestication of dogs as a result of a symbiotic, utilitarian relationship. Dogs probably served as watchdogs, assisted in the hunt, and were eaten as a starvation food.

But in economic terms, the most important domesticated animals in Southwest Asia are sheep and goats. From about 9000 B.C. to the present, most meat, milk, and hide products used in the region have come from these animals.

Detecting the process of animal domestication on the basis of archaeological data is a complex matter on which archaeologists disagree, but the concept of domestication in an archaeological sense usually involves three classes of evidence.[74] Just the presence of an animal species outside its natural range, such as the presence of highland species of sheep in lowland environments, may indicate herding. Second, in most animals, morphological changes occur as domestication progresses. In sheep and goats, the size and shape of horns are major factors in reproductive success, since the larger males fight with their horns to establish breeding hierarchies. As humans domesticated these animals, however, they relaxed selective pressures for large, strong horns (Figure 6.6), and the size and shape of horns changed (morphological changes can also occur at the microscopic level). A third indication of domestication may be evidence of abrupt increases in the number of some species relative to others, which cannot be accounted for by natural causes (for example, at many Southwest Asian sites the proportion of sheep and goat bones increased dramatically, relative to other animals, at about 8000 B.C.).

The first evidence of sheep domestication may be the presence of sheep bones in Neolithic (c. 9000 to 6000 B.C.) settlements in the Jordan Valley. These bones reflect no morphological changes in the direction of domestication, but since sheep and goats are not native to this area, their presence here probably reflects intentional introduction.

Ethnographic studies of modern pastoralists suggest that they typically sell or eat 50 percent or more of the animals born each year. Those animals sold or eaten are principally the males, since the females can be kept for reproduction and only a few males are required to service the breeding population. Once a male has reached two years of age, any further investment of food or time in him yields little additional return. Members of archaeological projects spending their first season in the Middle East are often surprised to find that they eat chicken almost every day, but almost never get lamb, even though the villages swarm with sheep. This is mainly because lamb and mutton are relatively expensive; in 1988 an adult sheep sufficiently healthy and well-formed to be slaughtered for an important religious holiday (which commemorates Abraham's sacrifice of a sheep instead of Isaac) cost the equivalent of between $40 and $60. Even before the distortions introduced by modern urban mar-

Type of Horn Core

Phase	Site	Zone	Cross section quadrilateral	Cross section lozenge-shaped	Medially flat, but untwisted	Medially concave, helical twist	Too young or too broken to diagnose
Bayat	TS	A$_1$				1	
Bayat	TS	A$_2$				1	
Bayat	TS	A$_3$			1	3	1
Mehmeh	TS	B$_1$			1		
Mehmeh	TS	B$_2$				1	1
Mehmeh	TS	B$_3$					1
Khazineh	TS	C$_1$					1
Khazineh	TS	C$_2$					
Khazineh	TS	C$_3$					3
Sabz	TS	D			2	1	6
Mohammad Jaffar	AK	A$_1$	4	1		1	7
Mohammad Jaffar	AK	A$_2$					8
Ali Kosh	AK	B$_1$		1	2		3
Ali Kosh	AK	B$_2$	11	7	8		27
Bus Mordeh	AK	C$_1$	2?	2			
Bus Mordeh	AK	C$_2$		2			7

Ca. 3700 B.C. (top) — Ca. 7500 B.C. (bottom)

FIGURE 6.6 The essence of archaeological interpretation is to discern patterns of change in the archaeological record over time. Here, the goat horn cores found at some sites in western Iran indicate that the shape of these horns was changing rapidly between 7500 B.C. and 3700 B.C. One explanation is that in the process of domestication the selective forces that kept these horns quadrilateral—and therefore relatively strong—were being relaxed, probably as a result of the domestication process. Farmers kept goats in herds and selectively bred them, and the strength of the horns apparently was no longer an important determinant of the reproductive success of these goats.

kets, the economic importance of sheep and goats was mainly in the milk, cheese, yo-gurt, and wool obtained from these animals. A well-kept animal can supply many times its own weight in nutritious, storable foods each year for several years, so only young males are regularly slaughtered for meat.

Evidence from two sites near Zawi Chemi Shanidar in Iraq indicates that simi-lar selective slaughtering may have been underway as early as 9000 B.C. Prior to 12,000 B.C., only about 20 percent of the animals killed and eaten at one of the sites were immature, but by 8650 B.C., 44 to 58 percent of the sheep and 25 to 43 percent of the goats eaten were immature when butchered.[75]

At Ganj Dareh, in the mountains of western Iran, there is evidence that by 7000 B.C. goats and cattle were being herded and domesticated, and there is much other evidence that all over Southwest Asia, sheep, goats, cattle, pigs, and other animal species were well into the process of being domesticated and integrated into a cereal-based farming way of life.

Naomi Miller has recently suggested that there are several generalizations that, despite considerable re-evaluation of established ideas about Southwest Asian agri-cultural origins, still seem to hold true:

> "1. Plant cultivation began in the Jordan Valley during the 9th millennium b.c. and spread along the hilly flanks/Zagros arc. . . .
> "2. Plant domestication followed permanent settled village life not just in the Natufian Levant but also in Anatolia and Iraq. . . .
> "3. Domestication of ungulates for meat probably began in the 9th millennium b.c. in the hilly-flanks/Zagros uplands and spread west. . . . New discoveries, however, sug-gest that the first such domesticate may have been pig. . . ."[76]

The evidence for Miller's generalizations comes mainly from Natufian peoples and their contemporaries. While some of the later Natufian peoples retained a mobile way of life, others established sedentary communities, such as at 'Ain Mallaha, near Lake Huleh, Israel, which between 9000 and 8000 B.C. comprised about fifty huts, most of them circular, semi-subterranean, rock-lined, and from 2.5 to 9.0 meters in diameter (Figure 6.7). Mortars and pestles litter the site and occur in most huts (Fig-ure 6.8), and storage pits were found both in individual huts and in the compound's interior. These people may have been simply collecting wild cereals instead of culti-vating them, but the pattern quickly changed. Some of the earliest evidence for do-mesticated grain cultivation in the Levant comes from the lower levels of Jericho (c. 8350 to 7350 B.C.), next to the springs in the center of this oasis. At some time dur-ing this period domestic forms of wheat and barley were cultivated in quantity here. Neither wild wheat nor barley appears to have been native to the arid wastelands that surround the site, so these grains were probably brought down from the uplands of the Jordan Valley and grown at Jericho, perhaps as wild species initially. No domes-tic animals were used in this period, but wild gazelles, goats, cattle, and boars were intensively hunted. Two thousand or more people probably lived at Jericho at any time between 8350 and 7350 B.C., and although the earlier communities were ap-parently un-walled, around 7350 B.C. the inhabitants built a massive stone wall, three meters thick, four meters high, and perhaps 700 meters in circumference. Asphalt,

FIGURE 6.7   Simplified plan of an early settlement at 'Ain Mallaha (Israel). Compounds of circular huts such as those at 'Ain Mallaha were widespread in Southwest Asia after about 8000 B.C., but by 6000 B.C. had been superseded largely by villages of rectangular huts.

sulfur, salt, and a little obsidian seem to have been traded, but in moderate quantities. The biblical references to the collapse of Jericho's walls may have to do with the earthquakes that frequently flattened the town in the past.

At the same time that agricultural economies were evolving in Palestine, specialized nomadic economies were also probably developing.[77] And people living on the flanks of the Zagros and Taurus mountains were making the transition to sedentary communities based on intensive plant collection. One of the earliest such communities was at Tell Mureybit, on the Euphrates River east of Aleppo, Syria. There, at about 8200 to 8000 B.C., people built circular stone huts, similar in almost every respect to the circular huts at 'Ain Mallaha. Charred wild einkorn seeds have been recovered from Tell Mureybit, as well as the remains of wild barley, lentils, bitter vetch, pistachios, toad rush, and possibly peas. Most of these plants can be found locally, but wild einkorn and barley are not native to this area and in fact can be found in natural stands no nearer than the Anatolian hills some 100 to 150 kilometers to the northwest.[78] The impracticality of moving large amounts of grain this distance suggests that Tell Mureybit may be one of the earliest agricultural settlements in Southwest Asia—that here and in adjacent areas intensive collectors first tried to plant, cultivate, and harvest their own fields of grain. Tell Mureybit is a deep site, and its many levels of construction, first of circular compounds of crude huts, then larger rectangular villages, suggest the success of this experiment.

FIGURE 6.8   Common implements for grinding and preparing grain in Iraq, between 7000 and 4000 B.C. The ceramic husking tray above was used to strip grain from chaff; the heavy stone quern and round pestle below were used to grind grain to flour.

Kent Flannery has noted that many contemporary African peoples also live in compounds of circular huts and that most such societies share several characteristics: (1) only one or two people are usually housed in each hut; (2) many of the huts are not residential, but are used for storage, kitchens, stables, and the like; (3) huts are often placed in a circle around a cleared space; (4) food space is usually open and shared by all occupants; and (5) perhaps most important, the social organization of the typical compound, like that of hunting-and-gathering groups, usually consists of six to eight males, each associated with from one to three women and their respective children, and includes a strong sexual division of labor.[79]

Flannery argues that settlements of adjacent rectangular buildings—which he calls villages—have advantages over settlements of circular buildings—which he calls compounds. The former are more easily enlarged because rooms can simply be added on, whereas increasing the number of circular residences rapidly increases the diameter of the settlement to an unwieldy size.

Villages are also more defensible than compounds for a number of reasons. But the primary difference is in their respective capacities for intensification of production. In compounds, storage facilities are open and shared, and the basic economic unit is the group; but in villages the basic unit is the family, which maintains its own storage of supplies and thus has greater incentives for intensification of production—the seeds, in other words of private enterprise and the first steps toward capitalist economies.[80]

If Flannery is correct, the transition that occurred between 9000 B.C. and 7000 B.C. from compounds of circular structures to villages of rectangular rooms is a reflection of changes in the social organization of the Greater Mesopotamian peoples, with the nuclear family gradually replacing the hunting-and-gathering group as the unit of economic production (Figure 6.7). And although the circular-building tradition continued for several thousand years in parts of Southwest Asia, it was eventually entirely supplanted by rectangular-unit villages.

These kinds of changes appear to be particularly clearly reflected at an early agricultural Levantine community, Beidha, in Jordan. Nine thousand years ago there was a farming community here, set amidst grasslands in adjacent valleys, with forests on the slopes above it. This community was occupied for hundreds of years, and, as Brian Byrd[81] notes, changes over time in the architecture of the village reflect fundamental changes in social organization, economy, and many other aspects of life. In the earliest phases, people lived in small semi-circular buildings with few interior features other than posts. The debris in these houses suggests that many activities of daily life (such as sleeping, tool-making, preparing and eating food, etc.) were done in the same interior spaces. Storage appears to have been communal, as the store-room is not associated with any particular house. Over time this village organization gave way to one in which people lived in larger rectangular buildings that were subdivided into areas where specialized activities were done. Some of the houses were two-story buildings, with the floors divided into what appear to be separate sleeping areas, tool-making rooms, storage rooms, etc. Also, in these later phases, large buildings were constructed that were centrally located and appear to have been public settings for special community activities, or ". . . formal venues for events that integrated the community as a whole."[82]

Soon after 8000 B.C., sedentary communities and domestic plants and animals had appeared at several places along the flanks of the Zagros. At Ali Kosh, situated on the arid steppe of western Iran, at about 7500 B.C., people hunted gazelles, onagers (wild asses), and pigs, fished in the Mehmeh River, collected shellfish, and snared wild fowl. They also collected vetch and other plants, and between 8000 and 6500 B.C. they began growing domestic, two-rowed, hulled barley and emmer wheat. These early farmers lived in crude clay huts furnished with reed mats, stone bowls, and a few other small household goods, but this settlement was neither rich nor impressive. Possibly the people came here only in the winter, since summers in the region are unearthly hot and the cooler mountains would have provided many plant and animal products. Wild wheat is not native to the Ali Kosh area, but wild barley is available within a few kilometers, and the people here may have been growing grains that had been domesticated elsewhere.[83]

Archaeologists used to think that the earliest communities of farmers in Southwest Asia and elsewhere remained egalitarian societies for centuries, perhaps millennia, after full-time farming became the subsistence base, but if we look at the early agricultural communities in Southwest Asia, we see very early signs of a changing social world. At Jericho, in Jordan, soon after 7000 B.C., the populace built a stone wall some 1.5 meters thick and more than 3.5 meters high around a complex of stone houses, even though the populace was still hunting and gathering wild resources to complement their primitive agriculture (Figure 6.9). If an essential element in cultural complexity is activity specialization to the point that large populations are socially and economically interdependent, Jericho was not a complex community; but the construction of the wall indicates that its people were beginning to direct their energies in a way quite different from that of most hunters and gatherers.

The disposal of the dead, usually an excellent reflection of changing cultural complexity, suggests that people at Jericho and perhaps elsewhere were not much different socially from their predecessors. Forty headless adult bodies were found buried beneath one room at Jericho, and further excavations revealed a cache of skulls that

FIGURE 6.9 An early Natufian house, situated on virgin soil at Tell as-Sultan, Jericho. The round shallow pits in the floor were probably storage pits, and the stone querns to the left were probably used for grinding cereals.

FIGURE 6.10 The people of Neolithic Jericho removed the skulls from some bodies and formed human features on them in plaster.

had been reconstructed with plaster, painted, and then decorated with "eyes" made from seashells (Figure 6.10). Whether these represent ancestor worship, war trophies, or some other ritual will probably never be known.

The importance of the bulldozer as an archaeological tool was demonstrated in the late 1970s, when one cut a roadway through a hill in Amman, Jordan, exposing a huge archaeological site. In 1982 archaeologists began excavating this site, now called 'Ain Ghazal ("spring of the gazelles"), one of the largest known Neolithic sites in the Middle East.[84] The first major period of occupation at 'Ain Ghazal began at about 7200 B.C., and it was probably occupied most or all of the time until about 5000 B.C. Covering approximately 30 acres, 'Ain Ghazal is about three times larger than Jericho, but it is unclear how much of the site was occupied at any one time. It probably had at one point at least several hundred inhabitants, who ate wheat, barley, lentils, sheep, and goats, and lived in mudbrick buildings of various sizes and shapes. For its early age, the community of 'Ain Ghazal has impressive art. Large plaster figures of people were found under house floors. Numerous figures of people and animals have been unearthed (Figure 6.11), and in one cache two clay figures of cattle had flint blades stuck into their heads, necks, and chests.

The diet of the early inhabitants of 'Ain Ghazal is impressive in its diversity. Goats were probably both hunted and herded, and pigs, gazelles, birds, and many other species were exploited, along with some wheat and barley, peas, lentils, and

FIGURE 6.11 Figurines from the early agricultural village of 'Ain Ghazal, Jordan.

many wild plants. But toward the end of its occupation, the people of 'Ain Ghazal seem to have fallen on hard times. Late in its history, it seems to have been occupied only seasonally by pastoral peoples.

By 6000 B.C. there is evidence of domestic sheep and goats at sites all over Southwest Asia and even into Greece and southern Europe, and it appears that once domestication was well advanced, the spread of sheep- and goat-raising was very rapid. Most farming villages have hedgerows, patches of weeds and thorny plants, clippings, and stubble that are perfectly acceptable to the rather undiscriminating sheep and goats; these animals, with their heavy fleece, are well protected against the sun and heat of the Middle East.

Domestic cattle were herded on the Anatolian Plateau (central Turkey) by about 5800 B.C. and were probably present in the Balkans by 6500 B.C. As with sheep and goats, cattle domestication seems to have been a widespread phenomenon, probably beginning sometime after 9000 B.C. and occurring in many areas from China to western Europe. Across this vast area, ancient farmers seem to have bred cattle for reduced size, increased docility and milk production, and increased tolerance of climatic conditions. An important step in the evolution of civilizations, as we will see in the next chapter, was the process by which cattle were adapted to the hot lowlands of the river valleys. The cattle found there today are thin, small animals that seem woefully scrawny by comparison to European cattle, but these Mesopotamia varieties are extraordinarily hardy. The late Shah of Iran tried to "improve" the cattle in the hot lowland of Iran by importing Dutch and Danish cows that were about four times the size of local varieties and produced vastly more milk and meat—until they strolled out into the hot plains (which we were surveying for archaeological remains), where most of them were felled by heat stroke. These European cattle had to be kept in air-conditioned barns to be productive, whereas the local varieties could do perfectly well on the hottest day, eating poor quality foods that would have killed the larger cattle.

Cattle were probably especially important to the first settlers on the southern Mesopotamian alluvial plain. During the dry, hot summers in this region, few reliable protein sources are available to primitive agriculturalists, and cow meat and milk apparently provided a crucial nutritional component. Oxen (castrated bulls) may also have been used to pull plows and carts. In many areas of Southwest Asia where rainfall is sufficient for cereal cultivation, plowing is essential because natural vegetation is thick. Later, the horse, donkey, and mule were also used as draught animals, and there is evidence of the use of domesticated horses in the Levant by at least the late fourth millennium B.C.[85]

Another important domesticated animal was the pig, whose bones have been recovered from sites all over Southwest Asia. By 6000 B.C. and even as late as 2700 B.C., pig bones represented 20 to 30 percent of all mammal remains at many large sites. As discussed below, however, sometime after about 2400 B.C., pork apparently was religiously proscribed in most Mesopotamian cities, as well as in Egypt and elsewhere in Southwest Asia.

By 6000 B.C. agricultural villages spread over much of Southwest Asia, most of them comprising just a few score mud huts, a few hundred people, and the same essential economic functions. From Greece to Afghanistan, these villages looked very much alike and, taken on the basis of their archaeological remains, they were not impressive in their material wealth. Even sites like Jericho and Çatal Hüyük (see chapter 8), which were larger than most and had relatively impressive art and architecture, were self-sufficient communities without many economic, political, or social ties outside their region. And the vast majority of these villagers were simple farmers without great aesthetic, religious, or social diversions.

As unremarkable as these villages were, however, their inhabitants were the first to focus their lives on agricultural products and to live in the sedentary communities that even today are the basic component of Middle Eastern settlement patterns. And as early as 6000 B.C., the processes that were to transmute these villages into states and empires were already underway.

OTHER OLD WORLD DOMESTICATES

The domesticates and allied agricultural economies developed in Southwest Asia proved so successful that within centuries of their appearance they had spread far outside the Fertile Crescent. By 7000 B.C. farmers at Argissa-Maghula in Greek Thessaly were subsisting on cultivated emmer wheat and barley as well as domestic cattle and pigs. Recent recalibration of carbon-14 dates for scores of early European sites reveals that the basic wheat-barley/cattle-pigs-sheep complex diffused at the rate of about a mile a year, reaching Bulgaria about 5500 B.C., southern Italy about 5000 B.C., and Britain and Scandinavia between 4000 and 3000 B.C.[86] To the east, domestic wheat and barley reached the Indus Valley by at least 5000 B.C. (and probably much earlier), and by the later first millennium B.C., domestic wheat was in cultivation in northeastern China.

The processes by which these domesticates and their associated agricultural techniques replaced hunting-and-gathering economies in much of the Old World are not well known but appear to have involved both the replacement of hunters and gatherers by agriculturalists and the conversion of hunters and gatherers to agricultural ways of life (see chapter 12).

The grasslands and forests of temperate Europe and Eurasia contrast sharply with the steppes and arid plains of the Fertile Crescent, and the spread of agriculture northward and eastward required new strains of plants and animals and different social and technological adaptations. Methods had to be developed to clear the dense northern forests, and in some areas the rich hunting, gathering, and fishing resources formed such a productive food base that there was considerable "resistance" to the introduction of agriculture. Despite its long-term productivity in most areas, primitive agriculture in even fertile areas of the world was probably marked by famine in seasons of bad harvests, and by heavy labor—compared to hunting-foraging—in the best of times.

Ammerman and Cavalli-Sforza formulated a "wave of advance" model for the spread of agricultural economies into Europe, postulating that the rate of spread could be predicted with some accuracy simply on the basis of the distance of any area from the centers of domestication in the Mediterranean world.[87] Their model is simple, elegant, and powerful, and the correlation of radiocarbon dates of agricultural evidence and human genetic evidence is impressive.[88] But their model is an oversimplification—as all models are. Graeme Barker interprets the evidence to show that the spread of agriculture into Europe was not as predictable and independent of local factors as the "wave of advance" model suggests.[89]

One interesting aspect of the spread of agriculture may have been the spread of Indo-European languages and culture. Colin Renfrew, in a highly controversial analysis,[90] has suggested that Indo-European languages and culture spread into Europe through Turkey and came with agriculture, which seems to have been established in much of Turkey at least 8,000 years ago. This would explain much about why most of the languages of South and northwest Asia appear to have been ancestral to almost all the native languages of Europe.

Egypt's initial transition to agriculture was based on introductions of wheat, barley, sheep, and goats from outside the Nile Valley, probably both from the Middle East and from North African desert and coastal areas.[91] In the Sudanese part of the Nile Valley, sorghum seems to have been the basis of initial agriculture—although the evidence for its use is scanty.[92]

Many herbs, fruits, and other plants were domesticated in India and Southeast Asia, but it was rice and millet that provided the majority of the food energy for the great Asian civilizations. Imprints from rice-grain husks have been found in potsherds from the site of Non Nok Tha in central Thailand in levels dating to between 6800 and 4000 B.C., but it is difficult to determine whether these represent domesticated rice. The use of the husks as tempering in ceramic manufacture may suggest domestication, but they may have been from collected wild species of rice. Bellwood identifies China's lower Yangtze drainage as a center of early rice cultivation, but he suspects that there were independent centers of domestication in India and, possibly, Thailand.[93]

Vegeculture of tubers and other crops probably has a long history in the moist lowlands of Asia. In vegeculture, plants are propagated not from seeds, but from cuttings taken from leaves, stems, or tubers of plants like manioc, yams, potatoes, and taro. Bellwood disputes the notion that vegeculture generally preceded cereal agriculture in much of tropical Southeast Asia, but root-crop cultivation may have been the earliest kind of farming in areas like New Guinea.[94]

One of the world's most important cereals—millet—was apparently domesticated and first cultivated on the great Yellow River flood plain in north China (Figure 6.3). The alluvial soils in this area are extremely fertile and sufficiently arid so that there was little vegetation to clear for agriculture in many areas. By about 4000 B.C. scores of villages existed in north China, most of them subsisting on millet and a few other domesticates and a considerable amount of hunted and gathered food. These villages usually contained about two or three hundred inhabitants, who lived in wattle-and-daub houses that looked very much like the circular houses and compounds marking the evolution of agricultural communities in Southwest Asia some 3,000 years earlier.

Another crop of considerable importance in north China was soybeans; several wild varieties are native to this area. The little evidence available suggests soybeans were in cultivation by at least 1600 B.C. Soybeans are a remarkably versatile and nutritious crop, and are also good "green manure," enriching the soils on which they grow through nitrogen fixation. The substitution of soybeans for milk and meat in early Chinese diets explains why many Asian populations never evolved the enzymes necessary to digest milk products, causing them to suffer intestinal upsets if they eat these foods. Similar intolerances are found in Africa and South America.

The establishment of agricultural economies in Japan had some similarities to the pattern in Europe. In both areas, rich northern forested environments supported dense populations of hunter-foragers, and, when agriculture came, it supplanted the ancient hunting-foraging economies at different rates in different areas—slowly in areas heavily dependent on marine resources, more quickly in others.[95]

AGRICULTURAL ORIGINS IN THE NEW WORLD

In the New World, the most important domesticates were maize, beans, squash, peppers, potatoes, turkey, guinea pigs (as a food source) and llamas (although some people would add to this list cacao, from which chocolate is derived). Like their Old World relatives, New World peoples complemented their staple domesticates with a wide range of other plants, including manioc, sunflowers, amaranth, gourds, and cotton, as well as "recreational" plants like coca (from which cocaine is derived) and tobacco.

But, for reasons not clearly understood, New World peoples did not domesticate any large draught animals suitable for plowing or riding, and this fact alone may explain much of the difference between the later cultural histories of the Old and New Worlds: plowing, even the simple, single blade of a wood plow, opens up many areas to agriculture that cannot be farmed otherwise. In the Old World, human and material transport was dependent from a very early time on domesticated donkeys and, later, horses, and both of these allowed warfare and trade to expand enormously. The llama of South America certainly was an important transport animal, but it does not compare to either donkeys or horses for transport or military uses. Also, no animals equivalent to the Old World pig or sheep were domesticated in the New World, perhaps because there were no suitable native species (although the Rocky Mountain sheep would seem to have possibilities).

MESOAMERICA AND CENTRAL AMERICA

There were two major centers of plant domestication in the New World, one in Mesoamerica, where maize, beans, squash, and sweet potatoes became the most important crops, and a second center in the Andean highlands, where potatoes and other root crops were grown and llamas were domesticated. But, as in the Old World, these processes of domestication and the transition to agriculture were long-term processes that occurred over a wide area, and involved many different peoples and species. And just as in the old world, we see the emergence of a very limited range of species as the primary crop plants. Native North Americans, for example, domesticated sunflowers and other plants, and some of these remain commercially important crops even today, but the efficiencies of the maize-beans-squash-potatoes group is such that it was the basis of life all over the New World when the European colonists first arrived.

The background of New World domestication, like that of the Old World, is many millennia of hunting, gathering, and foraging. Kent Flannery has suggested, for example, that the foods the aboriginal Mexican foragers relied on, such as maguey cactus, prickly pear, and rabbit, were species that could withstand intensive human consumption for many millennia without changing much in their physical characteristics as genera, and that because of the nature of these foragers' seasonal movements, they rarely exerted great pressure on these resources for any length of time.[96] For example, cactus-fruit collecting had to be done during a two- to three-week period, and during this time rabbits would not be hunted. This seasonal concentration on resources kept groups small and dispersed for most of the year, and one wonders why the Spanish found Mesoamerica (roughly from northern Mexico to southern Guatemala) to be a world of cities and farms instead of a domain of hunters and gatherers.

Despite effective mechanisms that maintained the hunting-and-gathering way of life for so long in Mesoamerica, sometime after 8000 B.C. these people—probably unintentionally—began to domesticate maize, beans, squash, peppers, and other plant species. Why and how this happened is not clear. Climate changes, increasing population densities, and other factors may have been involved, and recent ecological analyses suggest that in the beginning the shift to agriculture may have involved only a slight change in the way people in Mesoamerica hunted and foraged.[97]

Robert Reynolds's computer simulation[98] of dietary changes reflected in the archaeological record of Guilá Naquitz Cave, in Oaxaca, southern Mexico, between 8750 and 6670 B.C. suggests a subtle pattern of adaptations to the changing conditions in this period. People who lived here eventually focused on a particularly reliable and productive mix of plant and animal foods, one that Reynolds's simulation model linked to complex calculations about travel distances, seasonal availability, and many other factors. He concluded that cultivation here may have begun as a way to increase the density of certain plants and to mitigate the effects of wet-year/dry-year fluctuations, increasing human population densities, and other circumstances.

Eventually maize was domesticated out of millennia of such manipulations and cultural ecological contexts. Domesticated maize was the most important food through much of later Mesoamerican prehistory, and at present it is the only domesticated plant from this area whose evolutionary history we know in any detail. A few fragments of early forms of beans, squash, and peppers have been found, but not enough to reconstruct recent changes in their morphological characteristics. Occasionally there are claims that maize was either brought to or from the Old World at a very early date, usually based on ancient sculptures or other art,[99] but no trace of ancient corn plants has ever been found in the Old World.

Most of our evidence about early plant cultivation in Mesoamerica comes from dry caves in Tamaulipas, Tehuacán, and Oaxaca, so we must immediately suspect biases in preservation: there is little reason to believe that just because the earliest known maize comes from these sites, that these sites were the earliest places to domesticate maize. Also, as Gayle Fritz has noted,[100] there is some evidence that for many years scholars have greatly overestimated the age of maize domestication and agriculture in the New World. Scholars used to believe that maize domestication evolved out of the hunting-foraging groups who lived in this area between 10,000 and 5000 B.C. But more recent evidence and dates[101] raise the possibility that domestication and agriculture first appeared shortly before 3500 B.C. and evolved out of hunter-foragers who had become much less mobile than their ancestors, moving only a few times a year, if at all, and concentrating their efforts on the wild ancestors of plants they eventually domesticated.

Until about 1970 the most widely accepted view of maize domestication was advanced by a geneticist, Paul Mangelsdorf, who argued that domesticated maize evolved from a "wild maize," now extinct, with small cobs topped by small tassels. This would have been a "pod-corn"—that is, the individual kernels would have been enclosed in chaff rather than the cup-like fruit-case of domesticated varieties. Mangelsdorf explains the extinction of this wild maize as the result of two factors: overgrazing by European-introduced cattle and genetic "swamping" from continual hybridization with emerging species of domesticated maize.[102]

In the early 1960s, Richard MacNeish excavated several dry caves near Tehuacán, Mexico, and his findings clarified some aspects of Mesoamerican agricultural origins. Recent radiocarbon dating results suggest that the plant remains from different strata of Tehuacán were mixed, and thus the site might be less a record of early maize domestication than originally thought. The earliest maize cobs (four samples) are now dated to between 3500 and 3300 B.C.—much younger, as Gayle Fritz notes,[103] than the fifth and sixth millennium B.C. dates originally ascribed to these remains (Figure 6.12). Despite these revisions and new and interesting evidence from elsewhere, the Tehuacán sequence remains the best archaeological reflection of the sequences of changes in cultural behavior that were involved in the period of the origins of agriculture in Mesoamerica.[104] During the *Ajuereado* phase (c. 10,000–7000 B.C.[105]), peo-

FIGURE 6.12 The evolution of maize cob size at Tehuacán, from the smallest cob (*left*), which dates to about 3500 B.C. to the cob on the far right, an entirely modern variety dating to about B.C./A.D.

ple apparently lived in small mobile groups and exploited many wild plants. But they also depended heavily on hunting, exploiting wild horses, antelopes, and jack rabbits at first, and then shifting to deer and cottontail rabbits as post-Pleistocene climates and environments changed, supplementing these resources with gophers, rats, turtles, and birds. In the succeeding *El Riego* phase (c. 7000–5000 B.C.), people appear to have lived much the same nomadic life in bands, but the groups may have been somewhat bigger, and there is evidence that they were exploiting wild squash, chiles, avocados, and other plants that were later domesticated. In the *Coxcatlán* phase (5000–3400 B.C.) the size of the groups that made repeated and probably seasonal visits to Tehuacán seems to have grown significantly, and they exploited more plants and did less hunting. In the *Abeja* phase (c. 3400–2300 B.C.), MacNeish believes that the area was occupied by "central-based bands," people who lived for long periods, and perhaps most of the year, in large camps and relied heavily on cultivated plants. In succeeding periods these Tehuacános used pottery and began to subsist mainly on domesticated maize, beans, squash, and the other staples of Mesoamerica.

The Tehuacán botanical remains seemed to confirm Mangelsdorf's hypothesis: the earliest corn cobs found were very small, and the tassels did indeed emerge from the tops of the fruits. But the early maize found by MacNeish seemed to have many morphological similarities to another wild perennial grass common in the semi-arid, subtemperate regions of Mesoamerica, a grass called teosinte (*Zea mexicana*), and some botanists questioned Mangelsdorf's reconstruction, partially because the supposed placement of kernels on a cob such as wild and domesticated maize would seem a very inefficient mechanism for seed dispersal.

In 1972 plant geneticist George Beadle reasserted his argument of some decades previous: that there had never been a "wild maize," that domesticated corn instead was a descendant of teosinte.[106] Teosinte is a tall (up to two meters) annual grass found throughout the semi-arid and subtropical zones of Mexico and Guatemala, where it thrives in disturbed areas and rapidly invades open areas such as abandoned cornfields. Teosinte can be found growing in fields that also include wild beans and squash, sometimes with the beans twining around the teosinte stalk. Thus, the three staffs of life for Mesoamerica—maize, beans, and squash—are a "natural" association.[107] Teosinte plants look like maize, except for the seed structure, where instead of maize's heavy husk-covered cobs of many rows of kernels, teosinte has just two rows of six to twelve triangular kernels enclosed in a very hard covering. Although these seeds look quite different from maize kernels, Beadle was able to produce reasonably good popcorn and mock "Fritos" from teosinte kernels.

Chemical analyses of teosinte and maize and studies of their genetic characteristics seem to support Beadle's view of teosinte as the major ancestor of maize—although Mangelsdorf mounted a spirited counterattack.[108]

Domesticated maize shares several characteristics with teosinte. As Naomi Miller notes,[109] these include: (1) teosinte and maize frequently and freely hybridize under natural conditions; (2) they have the same chromosome number (10), and these chromosomes appear nearly identical in structure; (3) maize and teosinte look very much alike in anatomy and morphology; and (4) pollen from maize and teosinte are quite similar in size. She notes, however, that pinpointing where teosinte was transformed into maize, if this did indeed occur, has proven difficult. The type of teosinte that seems most closely related genetically to maize is the Chalco-type (*Zea Mexicana* ssp. *mexicana*), which is native to the Basin of Mexico (modern Mexico City and environs), but this may a result of hybridization.

If teosinte is the ancestor of domesticated maize, the primary changes in the domestication process were: (1) the development of a less brittle rachis, followed by the evolution of the cob; (2) the development of a soft fruit-case, so that the kernels could be shelled free of the cob; and (3) the evolution of larger cobs and more rows of kernels. A single gene—the so-called tunicate allele—controls to some extent both the brittleness of the rachis and the toughness of the fruit case, and thus these features could easily have been produced by direct selection of mutants with these characteristics. The third change, increased cob size, was very gradual and probably differed sharply from area to area. If the new dates for the Tehuacán maize remains are accurate (see above), maize cobs in this area were selected for larger and larger size in such a way that the average length grew from a little less than two centimeters in length to about thirteen centimeters in length between about 3500 B.C. and A.D. 1500.

As is discussed below, various explanations of agricultural origins involve the "dump-heap" hypothesis. Hunter-foragers who exploited plants would doubtless have discarded and scattered plant remains around their campsites, and over time and with intensive exploitation one can imagine a process of domestication occurring. When people harvest wild seeds they remove and consume some plants and leave others, thereby removing some plants and their genes from the gene pool and not others. But some seeds collected are usually lost in the process of threshing and other processing, and these can germinate on the dump heaps and other margins of a camp. Over time it is possible that people began to recognize that they could plant these seeds and began selecting for the most productive plants. But there is no strong evidence for a slow, gradual change over many centuries from teosinte to ears of maize, so, either we have not yet found the remains that would show this (always a possibility), or the transition must have been quite rapid.

Stephen J. Gould accepts Beadle's claim for the derivation of maize from teosinte, but he rejects Beadle's hypothesis of a slow process of gradual genetic change.[110] Gould notes that the Tehuacán maize cobs are smaller than modern varieties, but at least they are cobs, and we do not find intermediate stages between the teosinte "ears," which botanically are radically different from the maize ears. Also, as Gould notes, maize and teosinte are extremely similar genetically, and one would expect that a slow process of domestication toward maize would have resulted in some major genetic differences.

Instead Gould champions Hugh Iltis's hypotheses about maize domestication. Iltis's argument is a complex botanical and genetic scenario that cannot be examined in detail here, but its basic assumption is that there was a small genetic change in teosinte that produced what Iltis called a "catastrophic sexual transmutation."[111] Some minor genetic mutations could transmute male teosinte tassel spikes to female corn ears. This kind of change accords well with Gould's conception of evolution as a series of sudden changes, not the accumulation of gradual changes. But Iltis's scheme requires that people recognize the potential of the "hopeful monsters" a mutant teosinte plant would represent, for it is unlikely this mutant would be able to reproduce easily. In this case, human intentions are an important part of the overall equation of domestication.

While maize is an excellent food source, it is deficient in a number of important proteins and vitamins, and the evolution of agricultural economies in Mesoamerica derived considerable impetus from the domestication of other plant species, the most important of which were beans and squash. In fact, the evidence suggests that beans, squash, pumpkins, and other plants may have been cultivated before maize. Three species of beans (common beans, runner beans, and tepary beans) have wild ancestors in Mesoamerica, and changes in their morphological characteristics began to appear at about the same time as those of maize. Wild bean remains recovered in caves in Tamaulipas date to 7000 to 5500 B.C., and in Oaxaca from 8700 to 6700 B.C., but the earliest known domesticated beans did not make their appearance in these areas until between 4000 and 3000 B.C.

The domestication of beans seems to have involved: (1) increased seed permeability, so that the beans need not be soaked so long in water before being processed; (2) a change from a corkscrew-shaped, brittle pod that shatters easily to a straight, limp, non-shattering pod; and (3) in some cases, a shift from perennial to annual growth patterns.[112] The primary importance of beans is that they are rich in lysine, which maize is deficient in; thus the two are nutritionally complementary.

The domestication of squash and pumpkins, members of the genus *Cucurbita*, seems to have been aimed at improving the seeds (rather than the flesh) since wild cucurbita have flesh so bitter or thin that they have little food value. Squash and pumpkin seeds, on the other hand, like most large seeds, are veritable vitamin pills, as they include complex plant starches and other nutrients. Squash and pumpkin seeds, in fact, remain a favorite snack food, especially in less developed countries. The earliest cultivated squash seeds known are from Guilá Naquitz Cave, in Oaxaca and date to 8750–7840 B.C., and from caves in Tamaulipas and Levant from the same period.[113]

Like all other early farmers, the ancient Mesoamericans were domesticating a variety of other plants, only some of which were eventually developed into staple food sources. Chili peppers, avocados, foxtail grass, "goosefoot" (*Chenopodium*), various kinds of cactus, several root crops, and many other plants were combined in a reliable and highly productive agricultural economy.

The species of maize that eventually became the staple crop of North and South America seems to have been derived from species indigenous to central Mexico, perhaps the area around Mexico City, but the stimulus for the adoption and spread of the agricultural and village way of life may also have involved coastal areas. There, rich resources in the littoral/terrestrial interface may have provided sufficient food for non-agricultural but sedentary communities.[114] In time, these sedentary communities could have incorporated the new domesticated plants into their "pre-adapted" economies and social organizations, forming the first agricultural communities. From that point on, the superior productivity of village-based agriculture would have ensured its rapid spread over all the areas where these crops could be grown successfully. Currently we do not have sufficient data to evaluate this reconstruction rigorously, but recent evidence indicates it may be correct. Large mounds of shellfish remains, cracked rock, and stone tools have been found on both the Gulf and Pacific coasts of Mesoamerica, but few have been excavated or firmly dated. Many groups of people lived in the rich terrestrial/marine niches along Mexico's coasts after 3000 B.C., and some of them may have lived in villages and formed some maize and other crops, but the evidence for substantial farming and the spread of villages in Mexico is scanty until shortly after 2000 B.C.[115]

With regard to the question of *why* agriculture appeared in Mesoamerica when and where it did, we are left with the rather unsatisfactory models discussed earlier in this chapter. The sole single factors that seems to have affected most centers of agricultural origins, from China to Mesoamerica, are the changes in plant, animal, and human communities that resulted from the change in climates as the glaciers retreated at the end of the last Pleistocene period. If we then pose the standard challenge to the importance of these climate changes—specifically, that they happened many times previously in the Pleistocene without the same effects—this challenge may not be relevant to New World agricultura origins: if, as seems more and more likely, people were not even in the New World in substantial numbers in previous periods of Pleistocene climate changes, then this challenge to the climate-change hypothesis is not an issue; and, if they were in the New World earlier, we can only surmise that there was something unique about this last period of post-Pleistocene climate change or something different about the demography, technological capacities, or some other aspect of human communities 10,000 years ago, compared to earlier groups.

SOUTH AMERICA

How and when Mexican varieties of domesticated maize spread into Central and South America (Figure 6.13) are not well known. There are some interesting bits of evidence, however, that suggest maize may have been cultivated in Ecuador, Peru, Argentina, and Chile as early as 3000 B.C.,[116] and perhaps earlier.[117] By 3300 B.C. there were villages on the coast of Ecuador where people (the *Valdivia* culture) used pottery and may have cultivated plants, perhaps including maize. Pottery is not a perfect indicator of agriculture, but in nearly every part of the ancient world where people were making the transition to cultivation, they invented and used pottery early in this developmental sequence. Pottery has been found in numerous archaeological sites in Ecuador, Columbia, and Venezuela that date to between 3300 and 2100 B.C.,[118] but it apparently was not used in Peru—the center of later civilizations—until shortly after 2000 B.C.

Physical remains of crops would, of course, be better evidence for the spread of agriculture than pottery, but the botanical record of early South American cultivation is poorly known. Maize phytoliths (the microscopic hard remains of some plant cells) have been found at a few South American sites that date to before 4000 B.C., and there is evidence in the form of phytoliths and pollen for maize in several areas of South America between 4000 and 1500 B.C., but only at sites dated after about 900 B.C. are maize remains commonly found—often in coastal locations. Deborah Pearsall suggests that maize was introduced into South America before 5000 B.C. but did not become an important crop until after 1500 B.C.[119]

Maize was just one of the important food crops in Andean South America, and in some areas, potatoes, beans, and quinoa (pronounced "keen-wa") were the staffs

FIGURE 6.13   Some areas of early American domestication and agriculture. Other areas may be buried under coastal waters or undiscovered in dense coastal vegetation zones.

of life. There is some evidence that beans may have been domesticated before 8000 B.C., based on a few remains from Guitarrero Cave, and there are fairly secure finds of beans there dating to about 5700 B.C.,[120] but the evidence of the earliest stages of the domestication of beans and many other plants is scanty. The origins of potato domestication, too, are poorly preserved. Domesticated potatoes were found in sites in Peru's Casma Valley in occupations dating to 2250–1775 B.C.,[121] and there are traces of cultivation that may go back as early as about 4400 B.C.[122] This prolific plant, which today is grown in hundreds of varieties in Peru, may not store as well as cereals, but it can be grown in wet cold soils where cereals do not do well—as evidenced by its popularity in Ireland and northern Europe. The ancient South Americans developed a method of storing potatoes by freeze-drying them, and the potato is intrinsically very nutritious, and so this plant could provide the stability and reliability of production for South Americans that cereals did in many other places.

It is an interesting footnote to Peruvian plant domestication that quinoa is becoming increasingly popular in North America. The seeds of this plant can be milled into a flour that has one of the highest protein contents of any plant (but made a miserable chocolate chip cookie in one experiment), and health food enthusiasts are using this plant in growing numbers.

The role of animal domestication in early Peru is unclear, but llamas and guinea pigs were certainly domesticated in central Peru by 3500 B.C. As in Mexico, however, hunting continued to play an important role in many areas until quite late.[123]

The relationship of plants and animals, agriculture, and sedentary communities in northwestern South America in general suggests that domestication and sedentary communities may have preceded specialized agricultural economies in some areas by many centuries, particularly on the coast, where small sedentary communities of fishers, foragers, and part-time bean and squash cultivators were established before maize cultivation was of any importance (Figure 6.14).

Deborah Pearsall[124] has broken the South American "center" of agricultural origins into three complexes. The origins of the *Lowland Complex* are poorly understood because the remains of some of the most important early plants that may have been native to the tropical forests, such as manioc (*Manihot esculenta*) and sweet potatoes (*Ipomoea batatas*), do not preserve very well archaeologically. Maize eventually became a dominant crop in the lowlands, but it was preceded and eventually complemented by a wide range of other plant foods, ranging from flavoring foods (such as chili peppers) to squash to fruits (including avocado and, later, papaya and pineapple). Pearsall's *Mid-Elevation Complex*, which includes areas between about 1500 and 3000 meters of elevation, includes amaranths, peanuts, jicama, various beans, and other plants, including coca. Here, too, maize cultivation eventually relegated many of these crops to the status of supplemental foods, but the range of genera domesticated across the Andes and into the lowland coasts and forests underscores just how pervasive and eco-

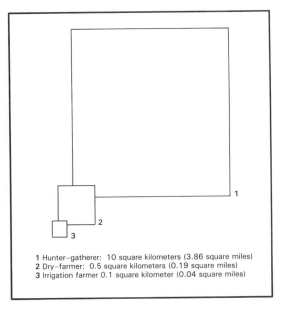

1 Hunter–gatherer: 10 square kilometers (3.86 square miles)
2 Dry–farmer: 0.5 square kilometers (0.19 square miles)
3 Irrigation farmer 0.1 square kilometer (0.04 square miles)

FIGURE 6.14 These three squares show the relative amount of land needed to feed individuals obtaining food in different ways.

logically diverse the domestication process was. Pearsall's *High-Elevation Complex* is found in areas over about 3000 meters of elevation. In this cold and agriculturally demanding zone, potatoes and various other tubers provided the dietary staple, in combination with meat from domesticated llamas and alpacas. Certainly other plants were cultivated, including quinoa and chenopods, but few traces of these and other plant remains have been found.

Christine Hastorf and Sissel Johannessen have studied changes in the use of maize as the political system of Andean South America changed between A.D. 500 and 1500, and they argue that people here used beer made from maize as a prestige item that the elites associated with imperial power and the theology of the state. People were brought together in communal feasts in which beer was consumed, and at these feasts the elites could reinforce their position: by providing beer in this context they could underscore the indebtedness of the peasantry to them and put the labor that the peasantry did for the elites in the context of the national religion and the highly stratified class system. Hastorf and Johannessen's study underscores an important point about food production and consumption: these can never be simply extracted from their cultural context and treated in isolation, as purely ecological and economic factors. Food production and consumption in all ancient states were tightly integrated into the national ideology and were used to reinforce this ideology and to manipulate socioeconomic and political roles and relationships.[125]

DOMESTICATION, AGRICULTURE, AND SEDENTARY COMMUNITIES: SUMMARY AND CONCLUSIONS

Generally, we have no evidence that people of the immediate post-Pleistocene era experienced recurrent periods of starvation, or that they "invented" domesticates and agriculture as a way of addressing their immediate food supply problems (Figure 6.15). Instead, the situation may well have been one in which, as population densities slowly rose, people gravitated into various niches where the exploitation of wild wheat and barley, teosinte, and other third-choice plants was marginally increased. Even if they were not forced into these areas by expanding population densities and were not under the dire threat of imminent starvation (so that they radically increased their consumption of these third-choice foods), the plasticity of some of these species was such that minimal changes in selective pressures might have quickly and directly rewarded this increased exploitation.

In this sort of reconstruction it does not seem likely that the timing of wheat and barley domestication, for example, was the result mainly of "lucky" mutations. All over the post-Pleistocene world so many diverse animal and plant species were domesticated that explaining them all in terms of "lucky" mutations would require coincidences of a highly unlikely nature. Nor was this a technological revolution: the first intensive cereal collectors required only minimal tools—implements certainly no more complex or imaginative than the fish traps and bows and arrows of the late Pleistocene.

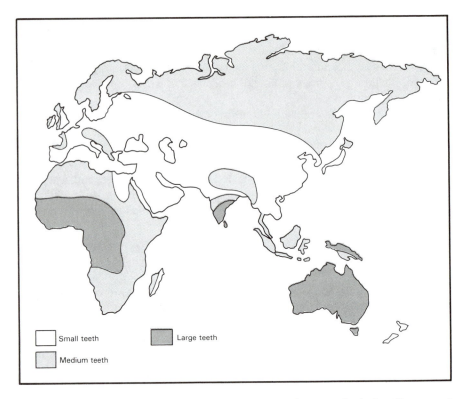

FIGURE 6.15   The distribution of tooth size among modern peoples before European influences affected this characteristic. The largest teeth occur among groups used to eating tough foods raw; the smallest teeth occur among groups that have had agriculture the longest.

Finally, for the individual with too few things to worry about, we might note that there is a certain danger in the fact that almost all the world's population now depends for most of its subsistence on only about twenty genera of plants. As hybrid strains are replacing local varieties at an ever-increasing rate, the chances for truly catastrophic mutations of new crop diseases are growing, particularly with expected worldwide changes in climate. The Irish potato famine was largely the result of a whole country becoming dependent on a single crop that was cloned from a small genetic population and therefore subject to almost complete destruction by disease. Eventually the world may be at the same risk. The transition to economies based on domesticated plants and animals thus is a process still in operation and one whose future direction is unclear.

Against this uncertain future seed "banks" have been established, such as the one at Washington State University, where seeds of more than 1,700 plant species are kept in special conditions against the day when their genetic resources might be useful. Every species is a unique and complex product of evolution, whose members are in a sense chemical factories able to synthesize the most complex compounds from only air, water, and soil. Not only food but medicines and many other products are mainly made from plant materials, and we have every reason to believe that the continuing destruction and extinction of plant communities in the Amazon Basin and elsewhere in the developing world will eventually be recognized as irremediable catastrophes. As we have noted previously, in the evolutionary game in which all of earth's life-forms participate, there is usually great advantage to the maintenance of genetic *variability*. We are so mutually interdependent with plants and animals that loss of variety in the non-human biological world will almost certainly come back to haunt us.

BIBLIOGRAPHY

Adams, R. E. W. 1977. *Prehistoric Mesoamerica*. Boston: Little, Brown.

Aitkens, C. M., K. M. Ames, and D. Sanger. 1986. "Affluent Collectors at the Edges of Eurasia and North America: Some Comparisons and Observations on the Evolution of Society among North Temperate Coastal Hunter-Gatherers." In *Prehistoric Hunter-Gatherers in Japan*, eds. T. Akazawa and C. M. Aikens. Tokyo: University of Tokyo Press.

Akazawa, T., and C. M. Aikens, eds. 1986. *Prehistoric Hunter-Gatherers in Japan*. Tokyo: University of Tokyo Press.

Ammerman, A. J., and L. L. Cavalli-Sforza. 1972. "A Population Model for the Diffusion of Early Farming in Europe." In *The Explanation of Culture Change: Models in Prehistory*, ed. C. Renfrew. London: Duckworth.

———. 1984. *The Neolithic Transition and the Genetics of Populations in Europe*. Princeton, NJ: Princeton University Press.

Anderson, E. N., Jr. 1986. "On the Social Context of Early Food Production." *Current Anthropology* 27(3):262–63.

Anderson-Gerfaud, P. C. 1990, "Experimental Cultivation and Harvest of Wild Cereals: Criteria for Interpreting Epipalaeolithic and Neolithic Artifacts Associated with Plant Exploitation." In *Préhistoires de L'Agriculture: Nouvelles Approches Experimentales et Ethnographiques*, ed. P. C. Anderson-Gerfaud. Valbonne: Monographies du Centre de Recherches Archéologiques.

Athens, J. S. 1977. "Theory Building and the Study of Evolutionary Process in Complex Societies." In *For Theory Building in Archaeology*, ed. L. R. Binford. New York: Academic Press.

Bar-Yosef, O. 1980. "Prehistory of the Levant." *Annual Review of Anthropology* 9:101–33.

———. 1991. "The Early Neolithic of the Levant: Recent Advances." *The Review of Archaeology* 12(2):1–18.

Bar-Yosef, O., and A. Belfer-Cohen. 1989. "The Origins of Sedentism and Farming Communities." *Journal of World Prehistory* 3:447–98.

Barker, G. 1985. *Prehistoric Farming in Europe*. Cambridge, England: Cambridge University Press.

Barnard, A. 1983. "Contemporary Hunter-Gatherers: Current Theoretical Issues in Ecology and Social Organization." *Annual Review of Anthropology* 12:193–214.

Beadle, G. W. 1972. "The Mystery of Maize." *Field Museum of Natural History Bulletin* 43:2–11.

———. 1980. "The Ancestry of Corn." *Scientific American* 242:112–19.

Belfer-Cohen, A. 1991. "The Natufian in the Levant." *Annual Review of Anthropology* 20:167–210.

Bellwood, P. 1986. *The Prehistory of the Indo-Malaysian Archipelago*. Orlando, FL: Academic Press.

Belyaev, D. K. 1969. "Domestication of Animals." *Science Journal* 5:47–52.

Bender, B. 1978. "Gatherer-Hunter to Farmer: A Social Perspective." *World Archaeology* 10:204–22.

———. 1985. "Emergent Tribal Formations in the American Midcontinent." *American Antiquity* 50(1):52–62.

Bettinger, R. L., and M. Baumhoff. 1982. "The Numic Spread: Great Basin Cultures in Competition." *American Antiquity* 47:485–503.

Binford, L. R. 1968. "Post-Pleistocene Adaptations." In *New Perspectives in Archaeology*, eds. S. R. Binford and L. R. Binford. Chicago: Aldine.

———. 1972. *An Archaeological Perspective*. New York: Seminar Press.

Blumler, M. A., and R. Byrne. 1991. "The Ecological Genetics of Domestication and the Origins of Agriculture." *Current Anthropology* 32(1):23–54.

Boserup, E. 1965. *The Conditions of Agricultural Growth*. Chicago: Aldine.

———. 1981. *Population and Technology*. Chicago: University of Chicago Press.

Braidwood, R. J. 1960. "The Agricultural Revolution." *Scientific American* 203:130–41.

———. 1973. "The Early Village in Southwestern Asia." *Journal of Near Eastern Studies* 32:34–39.

Braidwood, R. J. and L. S. Braidwood, eds. 1983. *Prehistoric Archaeology along the Zagros Flanks*. Chicago: The Oriental Institute.

Braidwood, R. J., H. Cambel, and P. J. Watson. 1969. "Prehistoric Investigations in Southeastern Turkey." *Science* 164:1275–76.

Brush, C. 1965. "Pox Pottery: Earliest Identified Mexican Ceramic." *Science* 149:194–95.

Butzer, K. W. 1971. "The Significance of Agricultural Dispersal into Europe and Northern Africa." In *Prehistoric Agriculture*, ed. S. Struever. Garden City, NY: Natural History Press.

———. 1976. *Early Hydraulic Civilization in Egypt*. Chicago: University of Chicago Press.

Byrd, B. F. 1989. "The Natufian: Settlement Variability and Economic Adaptations in the Levant at the End of the Pleistocene." *Journal of World Prehistory* 3:159–97.

———. 1994. "Public and Private, Domestic and Corporate: The Emergence of the Southwest Asian Village." *American Antiquity* 59(4):639–679.

Byrne, R. 1987. "Climatic Change and the Origins of Agriculture." In *Studies in the Neolithic and Urban Revolutions: The V. Gordon Childe Colloquium, Mexico, 1986*, ed. L. Manzanilla. British Archaeological Reports International Series 349.

Carneiro, R. 1970. "A Theory of the Origin of the State." *Science* 169:733–38.

Carneiro, R., and D. Hilse. 1966. "On Determining the Probable Rate of Population Growth During the Neolithic." *American Anthropologist* 68:177–81.

Caton-Thompson, G., and E. W. Gardner. 1934. *The Desert Fayum*. London: Royal Anthropological Institute.

Cauvin, J. 1972. "Nouvelles Fouilles Tell Mureybet (Syria) 1971–1972. Rapport Preliminaire." *Annales Archeologiques de Syrie* 22:105–15.

Cavalli-Sforza, L. L., and M. W. Feldman. 1981. *Cultural Transmission and Evolution: A Quantitative Approach*. Princeton, NJ: Princeton University Press.

Chang, K. C. 1976. *Early Chinese Civilization: Anthropological Perspectives*. Cambridge, MA: Harvard University Press.

Childe, V. 1952. *New Light on the Most Ancient East*, 4th Ed. London: Routledge & Kegan Paul.

Clark, J. G. D. 1952. *Prehistoric Europe: The Economic Basis*. London: Methuen.

———. 1980. *Mesolithic Prelude. The Paleolithic-Neolithic Transition in Old World Prehistory*. Edinburgh: Edinburgh University Press.

Clark, J. D., and S. A. Brandt, eds. 1984. *From Hunters to Farmers*. Berkeley: University of California Press.

Coe, M. D. 1960. "Archaeological Linkages with North and South America at La Victoria, Guatemala." *American Anthropologist* 62:363–93.

Cohen, N. M. 1977. *The Food Crisis in Prehistory*. New Haven and London: Yale University Press.

———. 1989. *Health and the Rise of Civilization*. New Haven: Yale University Press.

Cohen, N. M., and G. J. Armelagos. 1984. *Paleopathology at the Origins of Culture*. New York: Academic Press.

Connell, J. H. 1978. "Diversity in Tropical Rain Forests and Coral Reefs." *Science* 199:1302–10.

Cowan, C. W., and B. D. Smith. 1993. "New Perspectives on a Wild Gourd in Eastern North America." *Journal of Ethnobiology* 13:17–54.

Cowan, C. W., and P. J. Watson, eds. 1992. *The Origins of Agriculture: An International Perspective*. Washington, DC: Smithsonian Institution Press.

Crites, G. D. 1993. "Domesticated Sunflower in Fifth Millennium B.P. Temporal Context: New Evidence from Middle Tennessee." *American Antiquity* 58:146–48.

Davis, S., and F. R. Valla. 1978. "Evidence for Domestication of the Dog 12,000 Years Ago in the Natufian of Israel." *Nature* 276:608–10.

Dennell, R. C. 1973. "The Phylogenesis of *Triticum dicoccum*: A Consideration." *Economic Botany* 27:329–31.

———. 1983. *European Economic Prehistory: A New Approach*. New York: Academic Press.

Diener, P., and E. E. Robkin. 1978. "Ecology, Evolution, and the Search for Cultural Origins: The Question of Islamic Pig Prohibition." *Current Anthropology* 19:493–540.

Doebley, J. F. 1990. "Molecular Evidence and the Evolution of Maize." In *New Perspectives on the Origin and Evolution of New World Domesticated Plants. Economic Botany 44* (Supplement): 28–38. ed. P.K. Bretting.

Doebley, J. F., and H. H. Iltis. 1980. "Taxonomy of *Zea* [Gramineae]. I. A Subgeneric Classification with Key to Taxa." *American Journal of Botany* 67:982–93.

Dyson-Hudson, R., and N. Dyson-Hudson. 1980. "Nomadic Pastoralism." *Annual Review of Anthropology* 9:15–61.

Ekholm, G. F. 1964. "Transpacific Contacts." In *Prehistoric Man in the New World*, eds. J. D. Jennings and E. Norbeck. Chicago: University of Chicago Press.

Ellen, R. 1982. *Environment, Subsistence and System*. Cambridge, England: Cambridge University Press.

Feldman, M., and E. R. Sears. 1981. "The Wild Gene Resources of Wheat." *Scientific American* 244:102–13.

Fieldel, S. J. 1987. *Prehistory of the Americas*. Cambridge, England: Cambridge University Press.

Flannery, K. V. 1965. "The Ecology of Early Food Production in Mesopotamia." *Science* 147:1247–56.

———. 1968. "Archeological Systems Theory and Early Mesoamerica." In *Anthropological Archeology in the Americas*, ed. B. J. Meggers. Washington, DC: The Anthropological Society of Washington.

———. 1969. "Origins and Ecological Effects of Early Domestication in Animals." In *The Domestication and Exploitation of Plants and Animals*, eds. P. J. Ucko and G. W. Dimbleby. London: Duckworth.

———. 1971. "Origins and Ecological Effects of Early Domestication in Iran and the Near East." In *Prehistoric Agriculture*, ed. S. Struever. Garden City, NY: Natural History Press.

———. 1972. "The Origins of the Village as a Settlement Type in Mesoamerica and the Near East: A Comparative Study." In *Man, Settlement and Urbanism*, eds. P. J. Ucko, R. Tringham, and G. W. Dimbleby. London: Duckworth.

———. 1973. "The Origins of Agriculture." *Annual Review of Anthropology* 2:271–310.

Flannery, K. V., and M. D. Coe. 1968. "Social and Economic Systems in Formative Mesoamerica." In *New Perspectives in Archeology*, eds., S. R. Binford and L. R. Binford. Chicago: Aldine.

Friedman, J. 1974. "Marxism, Structuralism, and Vulgar Materialism." *Man* 9:444–69.

Frisch, R., and J. McArthur. 1974. "Menstrual Cycles: Fatness as a Determinant of Minimum Weight for Height Necessary for Their Maintenance or Onset." *Science* 185:949–51.

Frison, G. C. 1978. *Prehistoric Hunters on the High Plains*. New York: Academic Press.

Fritz, G. J. 1994. "Are the First American Farmers Getting Younger?" *Current Anthropology* 35(3):305–309.

Galinat, W. C. 1971. "The Origin of Maize." *Annual Review of Genetics* 5:447–78.

———. 1985. "The Missing Links Between Teosinte and Maize: A Review." *Maydica* 30:137–60.

Garrod, D. 1957. "The Natufian Culture. The Life and Economy of a Mesolithic People in the Near East." *Proceedings of the British Academy* 43:211–17.

Gebauer, A., and T. D. Price, eds. 1992. *Transitions to Agriculture in Prehistory*. Madison, WI: Prehistory Press.

Gould, S. J. 1985. *The Flamingo's Smile*. New York: W. W. Norton.

———. 1989. *Wonderful Life*. New York: W. W. Norton.

Gowlett, J. A. J. 1987. "The Archaeology of Radiocarbon Acclerator Dating." *Journal of World Prehistory* 1(2):127–70.

Gowlett, J. A. J., R. E. M. Hedges, I. A. Law, and C. Perry. 1987. "Radiocarbon Dates from the Oxford AMS System: Archaeometry Datelist 5." *Archaeometry* 29:125–55.

Grigson, C. 1993. "The Earliest Domestic Horses in the Levant." *Journal of Archaeological Science* 20(6):645–655.

Grun, P. 1990. "The Evolution of Cultivated Potatoes." In *New Perspectives on the Origin and Evolution of New World Domesticated Plants. Economic Botany 44* (Supplement): 28–38, ed. P. K. Bretting.

Haaland, R. 1987. *Socio-Economic Differentiation in Neolithic Sudan*. Oxford, England: British Archaeological Reports, International Series 350.

Halperin, R. 1980. "Ecology and Mode of Production: Seasonal Variation and the Division of Labor by Sex among Hunter-Gatherers." *Journal of Anthropological Research* 36:379–99.

Harlan, J. R. 1967. "A Wild Wheat Harvest in Turkey." *Archaeology* 20: 197–201.

———. 1986. "Plant Domestication: Diffuse Origins and Diffusion." In *The Origin and Domestication of Cultivated Plants*, ed. C. Barigozzi. Amsterdam, Netherlands: Elsevier.

———. 1989. "The Tropical African Cereals." In *Foraging and Farming: The Evolution of Plant Exploitation*, eds. D. R. Harris and G. C. Hillman. London: Unwin Hyman.

———. 1992. "Indigenous African Agriculture." In *The Origins of Agriculture: An International Perspective*, eds. C. Cowan and P. Watson. Washington, DC: Smithsonian Institution Press.

Harlan, J. and D. Zohary. 1966. "Distribution of Wild Wheats and Barley." *Science* 153:1074–80.

Harlan, J., J. M. J. De Wet, and A. B. L. Stemler, eds. 1976. *Origins of African Plant Domestication*. The Hague: Mouton.

Harner, M. 1970. "Population Pressure and the Social Evolution of Agriculturalists." *Southwestern Journal of Anthropology* 26:67–86.

Harpending, H., and H. Davis. 1976. "Some Implications for Hunter-Gatherer Ecology Derived from the Spatial Structure of Resources." *World Archaeology* 8:275–86.

Harris, D. R. 1986. "Plant and Animal Domestication and the Origins of Agriculture." In *Archaeological Results from Accelerator Dating*, eds. J. A. J. Gowlett and R. E. M. Hedges. Oxford Committee for Archaeology Monograph 11.

Harris, D., and G. Hillman, eds. 1989. *Farming and Foraging*. Oxford: Clarendon Press.

Harris, M. 1974. *Cows, Pigs, Wars, and Witches*. New York: Random House.

———. 1977. *Cannibals and Kings*. New York: Random House.

———. 1979. *Cultural Materialism*. New York: Random House.

Hassan, F. A. 1980. *Demographic Archaeology*. New York: Academic Press.

Hastorf, C. A. and S. Johannessen. 1993. "Pre-Hispanic Political Change and the Role of Maize in the Central Andes of Peru." *American Anthropologist* 95(1):115–137.

Hayden, B. 1981. "Research and Development in the Stone Age: Technological Transitions among Hunter-Gatherers." *Current Anthropology* 22:519–48.

———. 1990. "Nimrods, Piscators, Pluckers, and Planters: The Emergence of Food Production." *Journal of Anthropological Archaeology* 9:31–69.

Helback, H. 1964. "First Impressions of the Çatal Hüyük Plant Husbandry." *Anatolian Studies* 14:121–23.

———. 1969. "Plant Collecting, Dry-farming, and Irrigation Agriculture in Prehistoric Deh Luran." In *Prehistory and Human Ecology of the Deh Luran Plain*, eds. F. Hole, K. V. Flannery, and J. A. Neely. Ann Arbor: Memoirs of the Museum of Anthropology, University of Michigan, no. 1.

Henry, D. 1983. "Adaptive Evolution Within the Epipaleolithic of the Near East." In *Advances in World Archaeology, Vol. II*, eds. F. Wendorf and A. Close. New York: Academic Press.

———. 1989. *From Foraging to Agriculture: The Levant at the End of the Ice Age*. Philadelphia: University of Pennsylvania Press.

Higgs, E. S., and M. R. Jarman. 1969. "The Origins of Agriculture: A Reconsideration." *Antiquity* 43:31–41.

Hillman, G., and M. S. Davies. 1990. "Measured Domestication Rates in Wild Wheats and Barley Under Primitive Cultivation, and Their Archaeological Implications." *Journal of World Prehistory* 4:157–222.

Ho, P. 1969. "The Loess and the Origin of Chinese Agriculture." *American Historical Review* 75:1–36.

Hole, F. 1962. "Archeological Survey and Excavation in Iran, 1961." *Science* 137:524–26.

———. 1971. "Comment on 'Origins of Food Production in Southwestern Asia' by G. Wright." *Current Anthropology* 12:472–73.

———. 1984. "A Reassessment of the Neolithic Revolution." *Paléorient* 10:49–60.

Hole, F., K. V. Flannery, and J. A. Neely. 1969. *Prehistory and Human Ecology of the Deh Luran Plain*. Ann Arbor: Memoirs of the Museum of Anthropology, University of Michigan, no 1.

Iltis, H. 1983. "From Teosinte to Maize: The Catastrophic Sexual Mutation." *Science* 222:886–94.

———. 1987. "Maize Evolution and Agricultural Origins." In *Grass Systematics and Evolution*, eds. T. R. Soderstrom, K. W. Hilu, C. S. Campbell, and M. E. Barkworth. Washington, DC: Smithsonian Institution Press.

Johannessen, C. L. 1988. "Indian Maize in the Twelfth Century B.C." *Nature* 332:587.

Johnson, F., ed. 1972. *The Prehistory of the Tehuacan Valley*, Vol. 4. Austin: University of Texas Press.

Just, P. 1980. "Time and Leisure in the Elaboration of Culture." *Journal of Anthropological Research* 36:105–15.

Kaufman, D. 1986. "A Reconsideration of Adaptive Change in the Levantine Epipaleolithic." In *The End of the Paleolithic in the Old World*, ed. L. G. Straus. Oxford: British Archaeological Reports International Series 284.

Keene, A. S. 1981. "Optimal Foraging in a Nonmarginal Environment: A Model of Prehistoric Subsistence Strategies in Michigan." In *Hunter-Gatherer Foraging Strategies*, eds. B. Winterhalder and E. A. Smith. Chicago: University of Chicago Press.

Kelly, R. L. 1992. "Mobility/Sedentism: Concepts, Archaeological Measures, and Effects." *Annual Review of Anthropology* 21:43–66.

Kirkbride, D. 1968. "Beidha: Early Neolithic Village Life South of the Dead Sea." *Antiquity* 42:263–74.

Kirkby, A. 1973. *The Use of Land and Water Resources in the Past and Present Valley of Oaxaca, Mexico*. Memoirs of the Museum of Anthropology, University of Michigan, no. 5.

Kislev, M. E., and O. Bar-Yosef. 1988. "The Legumes: The Earliest Domesticated Plants in the Near East?" *Current Anthropology* 29(1):175–178.

Lange, F. W. 1971. "Marine Resources: A Viable Subsistence Alternative for the Prehistoric Lowland Maya." *American Antiquity* 73:619–39.

Lee, R. B. 1969. "!Kung Bushman Subsistence: An Input-Output Analysis." In *Environment and Cultural Behavior*, ed. A. P. Vayda. Garden City, NY: Natural History Press.

Legge, A. J., and P. A. Rowley-Conwy. 1987. "Gazelle Hunting in Stone Age Syria." *Scientific American* (August) 88–95.

Lippe, R. N., R. M. Bird, and D. M. Stemper. 1984. "Maize Recovered at La Ponga, an Early Ecuadorian Site." *American Antiquity* 49(1):118–24.

Lynch, T. F. 1980. *Guitarrero Cave: Early Man in the Andes*. New York: Academic Press.

———. 1983. "The South American Paleo-Indians." In *Ancient Native Americans*, ed. J. D. Jennings. San Francisco: Freeman.

McCorriston, J., and F. Hole. 1991. "The Ecology of Seasonal Stress and the Origins of Agriculture in the Near East." *American Anthropologist* 93:46–69.

MacNeish, R. S. 1964. "Ancient Mesoamerican Civilization." *Science* 143:531–37.

———. 1966. "Speculations about the Beginnings of Village Agriculture in Mesoamerica." *Actas y Memorials del 35a Congreso Internacional de Americanistas* 1:181–85.

———. 1971. "Early Man in the Andes." *Scientific American* 4:36–46.

———. 1983. "Mesoamerica." In *Early Man in the New World*, ed. R. Shutler, Jr. Beverly Hills, CA: Sage Publications.

———. gen. ed. 1970. *The Prehistory of the Tehuacan Valley: Chronology and Irrigation*, Vol. 4. Austin: University of Texas Press.

Mangelsdorf, P. 1974. *Corn: Its Origin, Evolution, and Improvement*. Cambridge, MA: Harvard University Press.

———. 1983. "The Mystery of Corn: New Perspectives." *Proceedings of the American Philosophical Society* 127(4):215–47.

Martin, P. S., and P. J. Mehringer, Jr. 1965. "Pleistocene Pollen Analysis and Biogeography of the Southwest." In *The Quaternary of the United States, Biogeography: Phytogeography and Palynology, part 2*, eds. H. E. Wright, Jr. and D. G. Frey. Princeton, NJ: Princeton University Press.

Matheny, R. T., and D. Gurr. 1983. "Variation in Prehistoric Agricultural Systems of the New World." *Annual Review of Anthropology* 12:79–103.

Meggers, B. 1975. "The Transpacific Origins of Mesoamerican Civilization: A Preliminary Review of the Evidence and Its Theoretical Implications." *American Anthropologist* 77:1–27.

Mellaart, J. 1966. *The Chalcolithic Early Bronze Ages of the Near East and Anatolia*. Beirut: Khayats.

———. 1975. *The Neolithic of the Near East*. London: Thames and Hudson.

Mellars, P. 1985. "The Ecological Basis of Social Complexity in the Upper Palaeolithic of Southwestern France." In *Prehistoric Hunter-Gatherers*, eds. T. D. Price and J. Brown. Orlando, FL: Academic Press.

Milisauskas, S. and J. Kruk. 1989. "Neolithic Economy in Central Europe." *Journal of World Prehistory* 2(3):403–46.

Miller, N. 1992. "The Origins of Plant Cultivation in the Near East." In *The Origins of Agriculture*, eds., C. W. Cowan and P. J. Watson. Washington, DC: Smithsonian Institution Press.

———. 1996. "Seed Eaters of the Ancient Near East: Human or Herbivore?" *Current Anthropology* 37(3):521–28.

Molleson, T. 1989. "Seed Preparation in the Neolithic: The Osteological Evidence." *Antiquity* 63(239):356–62.

Moore, A. M. T. 1979. "A Pre-Neolithic Farming Village on the Euphrates." *Scientific American* 241(2):62–70.

———. 1985. "The Development of Neolithic Societies in the Near East." *Advances in World Archaeology* 4:1–70.

———. 1989. "The Transition from Foraging to Farming in Southwest Asia: Present Problems and Future Direction." In *Foraging and Farming: The Evolution of Plant Exploitation*, eds. D. R. Harris and G. C. Hillman. London: Unwin Hyman.

Mortensen, P. 1972. "Seasonal Cacips and Early Villages in the Zagros." In *Man, Settlement and Urbanism*, eds. P. Ucko, R. Tringham, and G. W. Dimbleby. London: Duckworth.

Munchaev, R. M., and N. Y. Merpert. 1971. *New Studies of Early Agricultural Settlements in the Sinjar Valley*. VIII Congress International des Sciences Prehistoriques et Protohistoriques, Belgrade.

Olsen, S. 1985. *Origins of the Domestic Dog*. Tucson: University of Arizona Press.

Palerm, A., and E. Wolf. 1960. "Ecological Potential and Cultural Development in Mesoamerica." *Social Science Monographs* 3:1–38.

Pearsall, D. M. 1992. "The Origins of Plant Cultivation in South America." In *The Origins of*

Agriculture, eds., C. W. Cowan and P. J. Watson. Washington, DC: Smithsonian Institution Press.

Pearsall, D. M., and D. R. Piperno. 1990. "Antiquity of Maize Cultivation in Ecuador: Summary and Reevaluation of the Evidence." *American Antiquity* 55:324–37.

Perkins, D., Jr. 1973. "The Beginnings of Animal Domestication in the Near East." *American Journal of Archaeology* 77:279–82.

Perkins, D., Jr., and P. Daly. 1968. "A Hunter's Village in Neolithic Turkey." *Scientific American* 210:94–105.

Pianka, E. R. 1978. *Evolutionary Ecology*, 2nd Ed. New York: Harper & Row.

Plog, S. 1990. "Agriculture, Sedentism, and Environment in the Evolution of Political Systems." In *The Evolution of Political Systems: Sociopolitics in Small-Scale Sedentary Societies*. ed. S. Upham. New York: Cambridge University Press.

Price, T. D. 1985. "Foragers of Southern Scandinavia." In *Prehistoric Hunter-Gatherers*, eds. T. D. Price and J. Brown. New York: Academic Press.

———. 1987. "The Mesolithic of Western Europe." *Journal of World Prehistory* 1(3):225–305.

Price, T. D. and J. Brown, eds. 1985. *Prehistoric Hunter-Gatherers*. New York: Academic Press.

Price, T. D. and A. B. Gebauer, eds. 1995. *Last Hunters First Farmers*. Santa Fe, NM: School of American Research.

Pryor, F. L. 1986. "The Adoption of Agriculture: Some Theoretical and Empirical Evidence." *American Anthropologist* 88(4):879–97.

Pumpelly, R. 1908. *Explorations in Turkey, the Expedition of 1904: Prehistoric Civilization of Anau.* Vol. 1. Washington, DC: Publications of the Carnegie Institution, no. 73.

Redding, R. W. 1988. "A General Explanation of Subsistence Change: From Hunting and Gathering to Food Production." *Journal of Anthropological Archaeology* 7:59–97.

Reed, Charles, A., ed. 1977. *Origins of Agriculture*. The Hague: Mouton.

Reichel-Dolmatoff, G. 1965. *Columbia*. New York: Praeger, Ancient Peoples and Places Series, no. 44.

Renfrew, C. 1987. *Archaeology and Language*. London: Jonathan Cape.

Renfrew, C., J. E. Dixon, and J. R. Cann. 1966. "Obsidian and Early Cultural Contacts in the Near East." *Proceedings of the Prehistoric Society* 32:30–72.

Reynolds, R. G. 1986. "An Adaptive Computer Model for the Evolution of Plant Collecting and Early Agriculture in the Eastern Valley of Oaxaca." In *Guilá Naquitz: Archaic Foraging and Early Agriculture in Oaxaca, Mexico*, ed. K. Flannery. New York: Academic Press.

Rick, J. W. 1980. *Prehistoric Hunters of the High Andes*. New York: Academic Press.

Rindos, D. 1980. "Symbiosis, Instability, and the Origins and Spread of Agriculture: A New Model." *Current Anthropology* 21:751–72.

———. 1984. *The Origins of Agriculture: An Evolutionary Perspective*. New York: Academic Press.

———. 1989. "Darwinism and Its Role in the Explanation of Domestication." In *Foraging and Farming: The Evolution of Plant Exploitation*, eds. D. R. Harris and G. C. Hillman. London: Unwin Hyman.

Roosevelt, A. 1980. *Parmana. Prehistoric Maize and Manioc Subsistence along the Amazon and Orinoco*. New York: Academic Press.

Rosen, S. A. 1988. "Notes on the Origins of Pastoral Nomadism: A Case Study from the Negev and Sinai." *Current Anthropology* 29(3):498–506.

Rosenberg, M. 1990. "The Mother of Invention: Evolutionary Theory, Territoriality, and the Origins of Agriculture." *American Anthropologist* 92(2):498–506.

Rosenberg, M., and M. K. Davis. 1992. "Hallan Çemi Tepesi, An Early Aceramic Neolithic Site in Eastern Anatolia." *Anatolica* VXIII:1–18.

Rowly-Conwy, P. 1986. "Between Cave Painters and Crop Planters: Aspects of the Temperate European Mesolithic." In *Hunters in Transition*, ed. M. Zvelebil. Cambridge: Cambridge University Press.

Sahlins, M. 1968. "Notes on the Original Affluent Society." In *Man the Hunter*, eds. R. B. Lee and I. DeVore. Chicago: Aldine.

———. 1976. *Culture and Practical Reason*. Chicago: University of Chicago Press.

———. 1978. "Comment on A. H. Berger's *Structural and Eclectic Revisions of Marxist Strategy: A Cultural Materialist Critique*." Current Anthropology 17:298–300.

Sanders, W. T., and B. J. Price. 1968. *Mesoamerica: The Evolution of a Civilization*. New York: Random House.

Smith, B. D. 1994a. *The Emergence of Agriculture*. New York: Scientific American Library.

———. 1994b. "The Origins of Agriculture in the Americas." *Evolutionary Anthropology* 3(5):174–84.

Smith, P. E. L. 1967. "New Investigations in the Late Pleistocene Archaeology of the Kom Ombo Plain (Upper Egypt)." *Quaternaria* 9:141–52.

———. 1972. "Ganj Dareh Tepe." *Iran* 10:165–68.

———. 1976. "Early Food Productions in Northern Africa as Seen from Southwestern Asia." In *Origins of African Plant Domestication*, eds. J. R. Harlan, J. M. J. de Wet, and A. Stemler. The Hague: Mouton.

Solecki, R. L. 1981. "An Early Village Site at Zawi Chemi Shanidar." *Bibliotheca Mesopotamica*. Vol. 13.

Solecki, R. S. 1965. "Shanidar Cave, a Late Pleistocene Site in Northern Iraq." *VI International Congress on the Quaternary, Reports* 4:413–23.

Solecki, R. S., and R. L. Solecki. 1980. "Paleoecology of the Negev." *Quarterly Review of Archaeology* 1:8, 12.

Spuhler, J. 1985. "Anthropology, Evolution, and 'Scientific Creationism.'" *Annual Review of Anthropology* 14:103–33.

Stark, B., and B. Voorhies, eds. 1978. *Prehistoric Coastal Adaptations: The Economy and Ecology of Maritime Middle America*. New York: Academic Press.

Stothert, K. E 1985. "The Preceramic Las Vegas Culture of Coastal Ecuador." *American Antiquity* 50(3):613–37.

Struever, S., and F. A. Holton. 1979. *Koster: Americans in Search of Their Past*. New York: Anchor Press/Doubleday.

Tauber, H. 1981. "13C Evidence for Dietary Habits of Prehistoric Man in Denmark." *Nature* 292:332–33.

Testart, A. 1982. "The Significance of Food Storage among Hunter-Gatherers: Residence Patterns, Population Densities, and Social Inequalities." *Current Anthropology* 23(5):523–27.

Tringham, R. 1971. *Hunters, Fishers, and Farmers of Eastern Europe 6000–3000 B.C.* London: Hutchinson University Library.

Tringham, R., et al. 1980. "The Early Agricultural Site of Selevac, Yugoslavia." *Archaeology* 33(2):24–32.

Turnball, P. F., and C. A. Reed. 1974. "The Fauna from the Terminal Pleistocene of Palegawra Cave." *Fieldiana* (Chicago Field Museum of Natural History) 63.

Ugent, D., S. Pozorski, and T. Pozorski 1984. "New Evidence for Ancient Cultivation of *Canna edulis* in Peru." *Economic Botany* 38(4):417–32.

Unger-Hamilton, R. 1989. "The Epi-Palaeolithic Southern Levant and the Origins of Cultivation." *Current Anthropology* 30:88–103.

Upham, S., et al. 1987. "Evidence Concerning the Origin of Maize de Ocho." *American Anthropologist* 89(3):410–19.

Van Loon, M. 1968. "The Oriental Institute Excavations at Mureybit, Syria: Preliminary Report on the 1965 Campaign." *Journal of Near Eastern Studies* 27:265–90.

Van Zeist, W., and W. A. Casparie. 1968. "Wild Einkorn Wheat and Barley from Tell Mureybit in Northern Syria." *Acta Botanica Nederlandica* 17:44–53.

Van Zeist, W., and J. A. H. Bakker Heeres. 1986. "Archaeobotanical Studies in the Levant. Late Paleolitic Mureybit." *Palaeohistoria* 26:171–99.

Vavilov, N. I. 1949–50. "The Origin, Variation, Immunity, and Breeding of Cultivated Plants." *Chronica Botanica* 13.

Webster, G. S. 1986. "Optimization Theory and Pre-Columbian Hunting in the Tehuacan Valley." *Human Ecology* 14(4):415–35.

Wendorf, F., and A. E. Marks, eds. 1975. *Problems in Prehistory, North Africa and the Levant.* Dallas: SMU Press.

Wenke, R. J., J. E. Long, and P. E. Buck. 1988. "Epipaleolithic and Neolithic Subsistence and Settlement in the Fayyum Oasis of Egypt." *Journal of Field Archaeology* 15(1):29–51.

Western, C. 1971. "The Ecological Interpretation of Ancient Charcoals from Jericho." *Levant* 3:31–40.

Wills, W. T. 1992. "Plant Cultivation and the Evolution of Risk-Prone Economies in the Prehistoric American Southwest." In *Transitions to Agriculture in Prehistory*, eds. A. B. Gebauer and T. D. Price. Madison: Prehistory Press.

Winterhalder, B., and E. A. Smith, eds. 1981. *Hunter-Gatherer Foraging Strategies.* Chicago: University of Chicago Press.

Wright, G. 1971. "Origins of Food Production in Southwestern Asia: A Survey of Ideas." *Current Anthropology* 12:447–77.

Wright, H. E., Jr. 1968. "Natural Environment of Early Food Production North of Mesopotamia." *Science* 161:334–39.

———. 1976. "The Environmental Setting for Plant Domestication in the Near East." *Science* 194:385–89.

———. 1977. "Environmental Change and the Origin of Agriculture in the Old and New Worlds." In *Origins of Agriculture*, ed. C. A. Reed. The Hague: Mouton.

Wright, H. T. 1993. "Environmental Determinism in Near Eastern Prehistory." *Current Anthropology* 12:447–78.

Zevallos, M. C., W. C. Galinat, D. W. Lathrup, E. R. Leng, J. G. Marcos, and K. M. Klumpp. 1977. "The San Pablo Corn Kernel and Its Friends." *Science* 196:385–89.

Zohary, D. 1989. "Pulse Domestication and Cereal Domestication: How Different Are They?" *Economic Botany* 43:31–34.

Zohary, D., and M. Hopf. 1988. *Domestication of Plants in the Old World.* Oxford: Oxford University Press.

NOTES

1. Kelly, "Mobility/Sedentism: Concepts, Archaeological Measures, and Effects," p. 60.

2. For detailed recent reviews of agricultural origins around the world see Cowan and Watson, eds., *The Origins of Agriculture: An International Perspective.*

3. Blumler and Byrne, "The Ecological Genetics of Domestication and the Origins of Agriculture," p. 24.

4. Price, "The Mesolithic of Western Europe."

5. R. C. Dennell is among the first I know to use this definition.

6. Blumler and Byrne, "The Ecological Genetics of Domestication and the Origins of Agriculture," p. 24.

7. Rindos, *The Origins of Agriculture*, p. 143.

8. Blumler and Byrne, "The Ecological Genetics of Domestication and the Origins of Agriculture," p. 24.

9. Rindos, "Symbiosis, Instability, and the Origins and Spread of Agriculture: A New Model," p. 754.

10. Cohen and Armelagos, eds., *Paleopathology at the Origins of Agriculture.*

11. Blumler and Byrne, "The Ecological Genetics of Domestication and the Origins of Agriculture."

12. Rindos, *The Origins of Agriculture.*

13. Others, e.g., Blumler and Byrne, "The Ecological Genetics of Domestication and the Origins of Agriculture," disagree; Rosenberg, "The Mother of Invention: Evolutionary Theory, Territoriality, and the Origins of Agriculture."

14. Reviewed in Kelly, "Mobility/Sedentism: Concepts, Archaeological Measures, and Effects."

15. Bettinger and Baumhoff, "The Numic Spread: Great Basin Cultures in Competition."

16. Kelly, "Mobility/Sedentism: Concepts, Archaeological Measures, and Effects," p. 60.

17. Tauber, "13C Evidence for Dietary Habits. . . ."

18. Harris and Hillman, *Farming and Foraging.*

19. Byrd, "Public and Private, Domestic and Corporate: The Emergence of the Southwest Asian Village," p. 639.

20. See, e.g. Price and Gebauer, eds., *Last Hunters First Farmers;* Harris and Hillman, *Farming and Foraging.*

21. Childe, *New Light on the Most Ancient East.*

22. Pumpelly, *Explorations in Turkey, the Expedition of 1904: Prehistoric Civilization of Anau,* pp. 65–66; Childe, *New Light on the Most Ancient East.*

23. McCorriston and Hole, "The Ecology of Seasonal Stress and the Origins of Agriculture in the Near East."

24. See, for example, Hassan, *Demographic Archaeology.*

25. McCorriston and Hole, "The Ecology of Seasonal Stress and the Origins of Agriculture in the Near East."

26. Braidwood, "The Agriculture Revolution."

27. See Hole, Flannery, and Neely, *Prehistory and Human Ecology of the Deh Luran Plain;* see also Hole, "Comment on 'Origins of Food Production in Southwestern Asia' by G. Wright."

28. Harlan and Zohary, "Distribution of Wild Wheats and Barley."

29. Binford, "Post-Pleistocene Adaptations," p. 334.

30. Ibid., p. 331.

31. Anderson, "On the Social Context of Early Food Production."

32. See, for example, Frisch and McArthur, "Menstrual Cycles: Fatness as a Determinant of Minimum Weight for Height Necessary for Their Maintenance or Onset."

33. Harris, *Cannibals and Kings.*

34. Blumler and Byrne, "The Ecological Genetics of Domestication and the Origins of Agriculture," p. 34.

35. Cohen, *The Food Crisis in Prehistory,* p. 279.

36. Ibid.

37. Cohen and Armelagos, *Paleopathology at the Origins of Culture*.

38. Harris, *Cannibals and Kings*; Harris, *Cultural Materialism*.

39. Harris, *Cows, Pigs, Wars, and Witches*.

40. See, for example, Friedman, "Marxism, Structuralism, and Vulgar Materialism"; Sahlins, *Culture and Practical Reason*.

41. Sahlins, "Comment on A. H. Berger's *Structural and Eclectic Revisions of Marxist Strategy: A Cultural Materialist Critique*."

42. Ibid.

43. Hayden, "Research and Development in the Stone Age: Technological Transitions among Hunter-Gatherers."

44. Cohen, *The Food Crisis in Prehistory*.

45. Hayden, "Research and Development in the Stone Age: Technological Transitions among Hunter-Gatherers," p. 530.

46. Bender, "Emergent Tribal Formations in the American Midcontinent."

47. Byrne, "Climatic Change and the Origins of Agriculture."

48. Ibid.

49. Frison, *Prehistoric Hunters on the High Plains*.

50. Barnard, "Contemporary Hunter-Gatherers."

51. Ellen, *Environment, Subsistence and System*.

52. Testart, "The Significance of Food Storage among Hunter-Gatherers," p. 530.

53. Flannery, "The Origins of Agriculture," p. 307.

54. Reviewed in Byrd, "The Natufian: Settlement Variability and Economic Adaptations in the Levant at the End of the Pleistocene."

55. Bar-Yosef, "Prehistory of the Levant," p. 115; Moore, "The Transition from Foraging to Farming in Southwest Asia: Present Problems and Future Direction."

56. Henry, *From Foraging to Agriculture: The Levant at the End of the Ice Age*.

57. Byrd, "The Natufian: Settlement Variability and Economic Adaptations in the Levant at the End of the Pleistocene," p. 170; Wright, "The Environmental Setting for Plant Domestication in the Near East."

58. Spuhler, "Anthropology, Evolution, and 'Scientific Creationism,'" p. 115.

59. McCorriston and Hole, "The Ecology of Seasonal Stress and the Origins of Agriculture in the Near East."

60. Kislev and Bar-Yosef, "The Legumes: The Earliest Domesticated Plants in the Near East?"

61. For this discussion of early Southwest Asian domestication I have relied heavily on Donald O. Henry's *From Foraging to Agriculture. The Levant at the End of the Ice Age*.

62. Kaufman, "A Reconsideration of Adaptive Change in the Levantine Epipaleolithic."

63. Binford, "Post-Pleistocene Adaptations"; Flannery, "The Origins of Agriculture"; Hayden, "Research and Development in the Stone Age: Technological Transitions among Hunter-Gatherers."

64. Solecki and Solecki, "Paleoecology of the Negev."

65. Henry, *From Foraging to Agriculture: The Levant at the End of the Ice Age*, pp. 29–30.

66. Miller, "Seed Eaters of the Ancient Near East: Human or Herbivore?"

67. Legge and Rowley-Conwy, "Gazelle Hunting in Stone Age Syria."

68. Belfer-Cohen, "The Natufian in the Levant," p. 169.

69. Ibid., p. 171.

70. Mellaart, *The Neolithic of the Near East*, p. 50.

71. Belfer-Cohen; "The Natufian in the Levant."

72. Hillman and Davies, "Measured Domestication Rates in Wild Wheats and Barley Under Primitive Cultivation, and Their Archaeological Implications."

73. Olsen, *Origins of the Domestic Dog*.

74. Perkins and Daly, "A Hunter's Village in Neolithic Turkey."

75. Wright, Origins of Food Production in Southwestern Asia: A Survey of Ideas," p. 463; see also Solecki, "An Early Village Site at Zawi Chemi Shanidar."

76. Miller, "Seed Eaters of the Ancient Near East: Human or Herbivore?"

77. Rosen, "Notes on the Origins of Pastoral Nomadism: A Case Study from the Negev and Sinai," p. 504.

78. Mellaart, *The Neolithic of the Near East*, p. 46.

79. Flannery, "The Origins of the Village as a Settlement Type in Mesoamerica and the Near East: A Comparative Study."

80. Ibid., p. 48.

81. Byrd, "Public and Private, Domestic and Corporate; The Emergence of the Southwest Asian Village."

82. Ibid., p. 658.

83. Hole, "Comment on 'Origins of Food Production in Southwestern Asia' by G. Wright," p. 473.

84. Simmons et al., " 'Ain Ghazal: A Major Neolithic Settlement in Central Jordan."

85. Grigson, "The Earliest Domestic Horses in the Levant."

86. Ammerman and Cavilli-Sforza, "A Population Model for the Diffusion of Early Farming in Europe."

87. Ammerman and Cavalli-Sforza, *The Neolithic Transition and the Genetics of Populations in Europe*.

88. Ibid.

89. Barker, *Prehistoric Farming in Europe*; also see Price, T. "The Mesolithic of Western Europe."

90. Renfrew, *Archaeology and Language*.

91. Butzer, *Early Hydraulic Civilization in Egypt*; Wenke et al., "Epipaleolithic and Neolithic Subsistence and Settlement in the Fayyum Oasis of Egypt."

92. Haaland, *Socio-Economic Differentiation in Neolithic Sudan.*

93. Bellwood, *The Prehistory of the Indo-Malaysian Archipelago.*

94. Ibid.

95. Akazawa and Aikens, *Prehistoric Hunter-Gatherers in Japan.*

96. Flannery, "Archeological Systems Theory and Early Mesoamerica."

97. Webster, "Optimization Theory and Pre-Columbian Hunting in the Tehuacan Valley."

98. Reynolds, "An Adaptive Computer Model for the Evolution of Plant Collecting and Early Agriculture in the Eastern Valley of Oaxaca."

99. Johannessen, "Indian Maize in the Twelfth Century B.C."

100. Fritz, "Are the First American Farmers Getting Younger?"

101. Ibid.

102. Mangelsdorf, *Corn: Its Origin, Evolution, and Improvement.*

103. Fritz, "Are the First American Farmers Getting Younger?" p. 306.

104. See MacNeish, "Early Man in the Andes": Miller, *The Origins of Agriculture in Mesoamerica and Central America*, pp. 157–158.

105. All of these period dates are now somewhat suspect because of recent AMS dates on these materials (see Fritz, "Are the First American Farmers Getting Younger?"), but additional research will be required to determine if just the botanical remains are mixed or if other occupational debris are mixed as well.

106. Beadle, "The Mystery of Maize"; Beadle, "The Ancestry of Corn."

107. Flannery, "The Origins of Agriculture."

108. See, for example, Galinat, "The Origin of Maize"; but cf. Mangelsdorf, "The Mystery of Corn: New Perspectives."

109. Miller, *The Origins of Agriculture in Mesoamerica and Central America*, pp. 148–149.

110. Gould, *The Flamingo's Smile.*

111. Iltis, "From Teosinte to Maize: The Catastrophic Sexual Mutation."

112. Flannery, "The Origins of Agriculture," p. 300.

113. Miller, *The Origins of Agriculture in Mesoamerica and Central America*, p. 154.

114. Flannery and Coe, "Social and Economic Systems in Formative Mesoamerica"; Stark and Voorhies, *Prehistorical Coastal Adaptations: The Economy and Ecology of Maritime Middle America.*

115. Stark and Voorhies, *Prehistoric Coastal Adaptations: The Economy and Ecology of Maritime Middle America*; Fiedel, *Prehistory of the Americas*, pp. 160–84.

116. Lynch, "The South American Paleo-Indians."

117. Stothert, "The Preceramic Las Vegas Culture of Coastal Ecuador"; Lippi, Bird, and Stemper, "Maize Recovered at La Ponga, an Early Ecuadorian Site."

118. Reviewed in Pearsall, "The Origins of Plant Cultivation in South America"; also see Reichel-Dolmatoff, *Columbia*, Roosevelt, *Parmana. Prehistoric Maize and Manioc Subsistence along the Amazon and Orinoco.*

119. Pearsall, "The Origins of Plant Cultivation in South America," p. 192.

120. Lynch, *Guitarrero Cave: Early Man in the Andes.* Flannery, "The Origins of Agriculture," p. 303.

121. Ugent et al., "New Evidence for Ancient Cultivation of *Canna edulis* in Peru."

122. Reviewed in Pearsall, "The Origins of Plant Cultivation in South America," p. 190.

123. Rick, *Prehistoric Hunters of the High Andes.*

124. Pearsall, "The Origins of Plant Cultivation in South America."

125. Hastorf and Johannessen, "Maize and Politics in the Pre-Hispanic Andes."

7

THE EVOLUTION OF
COMPLEX SOCIETIES

*I should like to see, and this will be the last and most ardent of
my desires, I should like to see the last king strangled with the
guts of the last priest.*

J. Messelier (clause in a will, Paris, 1733)

Messelier's vengeful wish in his will was prompted by his feelings of exploitation as a citizen of France during the last period of its monarchy, when French society was ruled by oppressive kings and a venal clergy. Societies ruled and exploited by kings and priests have existed for thousands of years, and citizens of all civilizations have echoed Messelier's complaints. Throughout the world, inequalities in wealth, power, and prestige seem to have grown ever greater through history, both within societies and between different states.[1] In today's world billions of people subsist on a tiny fraction of the goods and services that the West, Japan, and a few other countries enjoy, and even within the richest states there are great inequalities.

Why have societies for thousands of years been organized in terms of social classes and economic inequalities? Are these inequities somehow the "natural" order of things? Will they ever disappear? What has determined who was rich and powerful and who was poor and weak throughout history?

To begin to answer such questions it is important to recognize that although exploitative political and religious elites have formed the very warp and woof of our concept of "civilization," they are just one of many elements in our sense of "civilization," or, in the terms of anthropology, "complex" society. Scholars, predictably, disagree on exactly what social or cultural "complexity," or a "civilization," or a "state," is, particularly when these terms are applied to the bones, stones, and bricks of the archaeological record. But when archaeologists speak of the development in the past of the first "complex" societies, most have in mind the kinds of changes we think happened first long ago in Mesopotamia, on the broad Tigris-Euphrates alluvial plains and adjacent hills of what is now Iraq. Based on well over a century of systematic archaeology, we know that if you were a member of an ordinary community here at about 6000 B.C., you would have lived in a village of a few hundred people, most of whom were your blood relatives. You and almost everyone else in your community would have worked in the fields to produce the grain held in common stores for large extended families and the community as a whole. And if you were an older adult male you would have made most of the decisions for you and your family about every aspect of your life. People much like you and communities very like yours would be found in all directions from your home, but your only contacts with them would have been minor trade in obsidian, flint, semi-precious stone, and a few other commodities, the exchange of young men and women in marriage, and—probably—the occasional fight. For all practical purposes, you and your fellow villagers were on your own in terms of religion, manufacturing tools, defense, and food production; probably you and every other adult in town would know most of the skills necessary for survival; and your extended family—and every other extended family—probably could muster all the technological and social skills necessary for survival.

But if you lived in this same area—perhaps the same town—3,000 years later, at about 3000 B.C., you would have led a very different life. You could have been a slave or a king, depending on accidents of birth. Unlike your ancestors, who were almost all full-time farmers, you may have been a fisherman, potter, weaver, priest, or some other specialist; but unless you were among the elite, many of the decisions you made about your job and your life would have been out of your hands—the prerogative of royal administrators. You would have been taxed and expected to fight with the army in any of the numerous wars and revolutions you would have seen in your lifetime. As a farmer or any other semi-skilled or skilled worker, you would have been dependent for your continued existence and way of life on people with skills you yourself did not possess, such as potters, warriors, herdsmen, scribes, doctors, metalsmiths, sailors, and priests. Instead of a village of a few hundred people, you might have lived in a city of thousands, perhaps tens of thousands; you would probably have been a fervent believer in the national religion, and you would probably have been acutely aware of your social class, whether high or low. In these and many other ways, your society would have been "complex," at least in comparison to the simple, cooperative, communistic peasants of your ancient ancestry.

In summary then, when anthropologists speak of sociocultural *complexity*, they are generally ranking particular societies on a single scale but on the basis of several primary variables. For any given society these variables include: (1) the degree of *differential access to wealth, power, and prestige*; (2) the extent to which differential access to wealth, power, and prestige are *inherited*, as opposed to earned; (3) the degree to which individuals in a community are *specialized* in their *occupations*, and the extent to which these different occupations are *integrated* and *organized* in the economy as a whole; and (4) the degree to which political power is *centralized* in a government.

The same kinds of changes in these variables that we have described above for Mesopotamia also happened—largely independently—in various other areas of the ancient world, in Egypt, the Indus Valley, China, Peru, Mesoamerica, and a few other places, and they happened in many other times and places in societies that were in contact with civilizations and by now the reader will not be at all surprised to learn that the question that has fascinated archaeologists for centuries is: Why? Why did simple agriculturalists give way to socially more complex forms in these specific areas, and not in other areas? Why did our ancestors not remain simple farmers, or revert to the ancient security of the hunting-foraging way of life? Why were these early civilizations so much alike in socioeconomic structures and political systems? More-over, why was this transition so rapid and pervasive? Although complex societies have existed for only the last five or six millennia, they have almost completely replaced the simpler cultural forms in which our ancestors had lived for a million years or more. Today, in the Amazon Valley, the Kalahari Desert, and a few other places, hunting-and-gathering groups still follow some of their ancient ways, but if current trends continue, soon there will be no groups left in the world that resemble our Pleistocene ancestors in society and economy.

To answer all these various questions about the evolution of complex societies, and to understand why today almost all people of the world live in them, we must appeal to a wide range of evidence. Since all largely independent cases of the evolution of cultural complexity happened before any written languages had been developed, much of this analysis must be based on archaeological data. But in many areas of the world written languages were used later in these developmental sequences and these provide fascinating information about the early civilizations.

The fact that complex societies, like agricultural economies, evolved independently in the Old and New Worlds gives us the opportunity for *comparative analyses*. As we shall see, ancient Egypt, for example, had a language completely incomprehensible to the Aztecs, worshipped Gods unknown to the Aztecs, and lived in a riverine ecological system unimaginable to the Aztecs. Egyptian and Aztec culture histories were unique, different, unconnected. But for a century, the idea of a science of history has been based on the idea that the ancient Egyptians and Aztecs were fundamentally alike—were members of the same class of political entities and could be analyzed in the same terms.

Perhaps the most famous general attempt to categorize all cultures and explain their similarities and differences is that by Karl Marx, but as we shall see in this chapter, there have been many others. Bruce Trigger, for example, compiled a comparative analysis of the ancient civilizations of Egypt, Mesopotamia, China, Mesoamerica, and South America, as well as the early Yoruba state—all chosen because they were class-based societies in which power was derived from control of agricultural production, and because there is relatively good archaeological, ethnographic, and textual data for each. In this context, Trigger has come to an interesting conclusion about the results of his many years of study of early civilizations:

> I expected to discover that, because of ecological constraints, the differences in economic systems [among early states] would be limited, and there would be more variation in sociopolitical organization, religious beliefs, and art styles. In fact, I have found that a wide variety of economic behavior was associated with early civilizations, the one constant being the production of surpluses that the upper classes appropriated through a tributary relationship. Yet I have been able to discover only one basic form of class hierarchy, two general forms of political organization, and a single basic religious paradigm . . . I have documented significant variation from one early civilization to another only in terms of art styles and cultural values.[2]

Trigger's perceptive conclusion expresses clearly the fundamental issues in analyses of ancient civilizations. He sees, for example, extremely little variation among them except in art styles and cultural values. Thus we must ask, why were they so similar? It seems reasonable to assume, as Trigger does, that there is such little variation in some elements in these early civilizations because of these elements' relative "efficiency,"[3] and great variations in other elements because they have little effect on the adaptiveness and competitive success of the social organism of which they are a part. If so, then one aspect of an archaeological analysis can be an examination of the specific factors that may have determined the adaptiveness and efficiency of these cultural elements, and changes in these variables over time and space. This kind of investigation does not require that one ignore the great extent to which the unique and specific values, ideas, and concepts of these ancient civilizations formed the structure of these cultures and, in a sense, determined their history. Trigger suggests that we must examine both the similarities and differences in ancient cultures and try to understand and explain them, using a variety of perspectives and methods (see below).

Today, however, the premise that a science of history can be developed on the basis of comparative analyses of cultures is under sustained attack.[4] Some scholars argue that the only similarities between, for example, Egypt and Mexico and others of their supposed class, such as the Sumerians, the Shang Chinese, and the Harappan of the Indus Valley, are simply the products of gross similarities in environments and technologies. They suggest that the more important focus of archaeological analysis should be the ways in which the people in these different cultures constructed different worlds and realities through the use of incommensurable cultural categories. Shanks and Tilley, for example, refer to the "sledge hammer of cross-cultural generalizations,"[5] implying that traditional methods of cross-cultural comparisons pulverize meaning and significance in history. Also, many scholars today are wary of the term "evolution" as applied to cultures. For some, "evolution" as applied to cultures implies that some cultures are "better," or more evolved than others. For others, the difference in systems of trait-transmission between biological entities (sexual and asexual reproduction) and cultural systems (e.g., learning) makes any sense of evolution inapplicable to cultures. But other scholars have found Darwinian evolution to be applicable to cultural changes, if one divorces this sense of evolution from biological concepts and focuses on trait-transmission, not any particular *method* of trait-transmission.[6]

We shall examine this issue in detail later in this chapter, and in the remaining chapters, because it is fundamental to all that follows: Do the similarities and differences exhibited by various extinct cultures offer the raw material for some kind of "scientific" analysis of history, or do they simply represent gross analogies among societies that were intrinsically incommensurate and that can only be analyzed in terms of their unique histories and characteristics?

Another difficult issue here involves the obvious problems of trying to analyze the ideologies of extinct human groups on the basis of their material archaeological record. Karl Marx is just one of many scholars who over the millennia have tried to explain the rise of civilization in terms of environments, technologies, economies, etc. But can we understand the course of history from this perspective? The rise of Islam, for example, might seem to be a case where a powerful ideology spurred people, who previously had lived in simple tribal groups, to conquer huge areas of Asia and Europe. Is the spread of Islam to be understood as a result of the appearance of this unique inexplicable ideology, or is the ideology just a reflection of powerful underlying historical and economic forces? Similarly, the ancient Egyptian state seems to be something that we can only understand in terms of its national *ideology:* as we shall see in chapter 9, all the temples, tombs, and pyramids of Egypt are reflections of their principle of "divine kingship." Ancient Egyptian civilization was to a certain extent a product of the rich Nile Valley environment, but it was also a sociopolitical construct, an idea. But how does one analyze the power of ideas from the archaeological record, especially since most of Egyptian civilization formed long before the written language began recording its development?

To take another example, based on inferences from the archaeological record, ancient texts, and ethnography, one of the fundamental things that apparently all early complex societies evolved was a *coercive sociopolitical elite*—that is, a class of people who took most of the society's power, prestige, and wealth. And they apparently did so without regularly resorting to armed robbery or direct confiscation by their personal militias. These societies evolved *ideologies* that sanctioned this confiscatory behavior and monopolization of power.[7] In ancient Egypt, for example, the pharaoh was considered a manifestation of God, and therefore duly entitled to monopolize political power and much of the country's wealth. Ancient Egyptians might have whined about taxes, but they rarely if ever managed a revolution to dispossess the elites (nor did the Victorian British or many other modern peoples, for that matter). But how are we to study the origins and dynamics of the evolution of these all-important belief systems? The earliest such societies all evolved elites and the accompanying ideology before they did written languages, so this is mainly a matter for archaeology. We have some traces of this evolution in such things as differences in the wealth of individual burials, but these only indicate (possibly) that coercive sociopolitical elites existed, not how they came about or the ideological basis of their status.

We may never know much in an objective fashion about the evolution of ideologies, but, as we shall see in this chapter, this has not kept archaeologists from rampant speculation on the matter.

Another issue in analyzing these early civilizations involves our assumptions about how similar they all were in terms of power relationships. It is important to recognize, that not every society in history can be placed at some point on a continuum between a simple band of hunter-foragers and the dimensions of complexity described above and applied to, for example, ancient Mesopotamia. The term "heterarchy" has been applied by Carol Crumley[8] to aspects of social relationships in early states, particularly those, like ancient Greece, for example, where economic control by elites and many other social interactions were not entirely set within the context of rigid, bureaucratic, hierarchical, administrative institutions. In such cases the activities and interests of the elites do not entirely correspond to the activities and interests of the state. She suggests that states can include social structures that are heterarchical in the sense that elements in these structures are either unranked relative to other elements or possess the potential for being ranked in a number of different ways. In such situations she suggests that power is not ranked, it is "counterpoised."

The concept of heterarchy is linked to ideas about dialectical social relationships that are beyond the scope of this book, but we must assume that the social relationships of ancient societies cannot be fit exactly and simply into traditional notions about dominance and hierarchy.

Before launching into a detailed analysis of the *evolution* of civilizations, it is important to note also that one must also analyze in this context the *collapse* of such civilizations. The cases of cultural evolution detailed in the following chapters repeatedly show that cultural evolution is not a continuous, cumulative, gradual change, in most places. "Fits and starts" better describes it. In Mesopotamia, the Indus Valley, and elsewhere, there is clear evidence of communities that seem on the verge of cultural complexity—either to die out without further development or to be overtaken by developments in some core area to which they have become the periphery. As B. Bronson noted:

> The leading characteristics of this model are complexity, factor feedback, and instability. A great many agencies—sedentariness, epidemiology, genetics, environmental structure, technologies of subsistence and non-subsistence, political evolution, economic development, warfare, the density and distribution in space of populations—are recognized as potential influences, without seriously contending that any necessarily have priority. . . . Change, driven by the sheer impossibility of keeping so many interacting factors out of disequilibrium, is a normal condition. What requires explaining is stability, not change.[9]

SOCIAL COMPLEXITY AND HUMAN VALUES

Before considering how societies evolved into different forms, it is worthwhile to muse on the fact that over the centuries people have had a very difficult time coming to terms with their perceptions of the relative virtues of types of societies. One of the oldest and commonest human errors has been to confuse cultural complexity and cultural worth. Already by 2500 B.C., a haughty citizen of a city-state in Iraq disparagingly described his nomadic neighbors as "[barbarians], who know no house or town, the boor of the mountains . . . who does not bend his knees [to cultivate the land] . . . who is not buried after his death."[10] Even in our own age, it is difficult to avoid the notions that civilizations have emerged because of the special gifts and vitality of their populaces, that simpler societies are incompletely developed, and that all the world's cultures are at various points along a gradient whose apex is the modern Western industrial community. This attitude was a great advantage in the age of European colonialism because it allowed the Europeans to treat other peoples as hardly human, and therefore undeserving of the full protection of laws and morality. Immanuel Kant said that the essence of immorality is to treat other people as objects, and in a way this is the Original Sin of cultural complexity. Europeans are routinely used as examples of colonialism, but it must be recognized that all cultures that have achieved dominance by virtue of time and circumstance have been equally colonialistic.

To classify, as archaeologists do, history's thousands of societies in terms of their inferred social stratification, size, and the complexity of information, matter, and energy exchanges, is a research tactic that has as its goal the elucidation of the processes that produced these forms of complexity; but we should not consider these measures as ultimate criteria. If we categorized human societies in terms of piety, social cohesiveness, "justice," or other abstract but important concepts, we would see an ordering of societies very different from the earlier discussion, concerned as it was with "cultural complexity."

Because of the nature of archaeological data, we must limit ourselves primarily to the artifacts of these extinct civilizations, the bones and stones and debris that have survived them. But it is worth reflecting on the tremendous impact the evolution of cultural complexity has had on the way people view themselves and the world. If recent band societies resemble Pleistocene band societies, most Pleistocene individuals were deeply embedded in social and family relationships and had a clear role in society. Marshall Sahlins observed that our hunting-and-gathering ancestors took the "Zen road to affluence": people living in complex sedentary communities seem to live in the eternal economic dilemma of unlimited wants and limited means, but simpler societies have adjusted to their limited means by having few wants.[11] Because they are frequently moving, hunters and gatherers cannot accumulate large quantities of material objects and therefore do not covet air conditioners and trash compactors, and they live in such small and scattered groups that social hierarchies are of little use or relevance. Ethnologist Richard Lee described how one Christmas he supplied a group of Kalahari Bushmen with a 1,200-pound ox for a great feast (Figure 7.1)—the ox represented far more meat than the group could eat.[12] Everyone in the group complained, however, about how scrawny the animal was and how poor his gift was. Lee realized eventually that the cool reception to his generosity was the Bushmen's way of maintaining an egalitarian spirit: any particularly valuable or productive act or service met the same response, because group dynamics worked best if no one could take great personal and public prestige from his accomplishments.

Hunter-gatherers of the recent and contemporary world are probably uncertain guides to what life was like during the millennia when all of our ancestors lived this way. But any romantic visions one might have of this ancient world may well be illusions. We might want to think of our ancestors as generous and sharing, and perhaps they were, but not necessarily. We will consider the example of the Yanomamö, and other groups exhibit similar affronts to what many consider politeness. Nicolas Peterson reports, for example, that one aboriginal Australian in the group he was studying said to him, "I want to owe you five dollars." Peterson labels this kind of behavior "demand sharing," in which exchange of resources is stripped of all pretense that people do it because they want to or feel generous.[13] Sharing is to everyone's advantage in some social organizations, particularly band societies, but there is no necessary reason that it has to be cloaked in an aura of generosity and altruism. We will never know how our Pleistocene forebears organized their patterns of sharing and cooperation, but they were probably not the "noble savages" that we sometimes imagine.

All forms of social organization, of course, have their human costs, as well as benefits. In complex societies, from ancient times to the present, people often have felt themselves to be minor replaceable cogs in a machine that operates mainly for the benefit of others. From some of the earliest written documents, those from

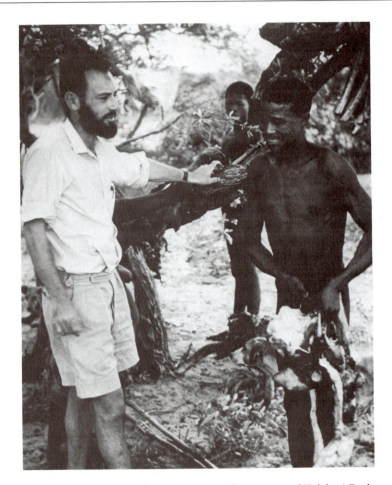

FIGURE 7.1 Richard Lee at a Christmas ox roast for a group of Kalahari Bushmen, southern Africa (see text for discussion of egalitarian principles of band organization demonstrated at this event).

Mesopotamia in the third millennium B.C., we hear the age-old complaints about poverty, taxes, oppressive rulers, governmental harassment, and other ills of cultural complexity. Little wonder that from these early records we also see the beginnings of Utopian movements, made up of those who yearn for a return to a hypothetical simpler place and time, when political, religious, and economic hierarchies did not exist, when all people were considered of equal worth, where all had an equal share, and where no one had power over anyone else.

Many of the perceived pathologies in modern societies are attributed to greed, but one must at least consider the premise that human selfishness and greed are "engines" that have propelled humanity to ever-more-complex socioeconomic and political forms. The Biblical sentiment that "the love of money is the root of all evil" is no doubt true, but the love of money also has had some beneficial side effects. Novelist John LeCarré explores this theme in one of his books[14] in the form of an argument between two characters, one who is sickened by the excesses of greed, waste, and inequity in capitalistic "pigs in clover" societies, and another character who defends the West on the premise that capitalism uses human greed and acquisitiveness to produce goods and services that, ultimately, enhance human life, dignity, and liberty.

As I write this in 1997 eastern Europe is in the midst of a painful transition, from centralized quasi-socialist systems to more capitalistic market-oriented economies— or at least that is the intention of the politicians and planners. The impetus for this change appears to be the simple fact that economies based on self-interest have been far more productive than other forms in terms of goods and services. The last great bastion of communism, China, too has found that it can sustain impressive growth rates by allowing individuals to profit from their own labor and initiative, with the result that barely twenty years after the Maoist Red Guards terrorized any individual not totally subservient to the idea of a pure theoretical communism, Chinese "millionaires" are emerging in ever-greater numbers.

Only the future will reveal if the great complexity and integration that seems to make societies highly productive and "efficient" can be achieved without the stimulus of individual and corporate competitiveness, and without socioeconomic inequalities.

CROSS-CULTURAL COMPARATIVE ANALYSES: THE CHARACTERISTICS AND VARIETIES OF SOCIOCULTURAL ORGANIZATION

Analyzing different kinds of societies and comparing them implies that one can put them into categories that have some analytical significance and then use their similarities and differences to focus on the determinants of cultural variation. Such studies are, for obvious reasons, almost exclusively the products of highly complex societies. And it is interesting to look in detail at the point of contact between two cultures in which one is studying the other, and, in a sense, *vice versa*.

When anthropologist Napoleon Chagnon[15] first visited the Yanomamö Indians, who live in the jungles of Venezuela and Brazil, he found a people who had had so little contact with the outside world that they had never seen a cow and had no idea that such an animal existed; their most complicated tools were crude clay pots and bows and arrows, and almost all of their food came from simple hunting and collecting.

Much about the Yanomamö repulsed or frightened Chagnon. The men usually had long streams of mucus hanging from their noses because they habitually blew powdered hallucinogenic plants up their nostrils, and they continually drooled as they chewed tobacco. Their villages and houses stank and vicious underfed dogs plagued him everywhere he walked. If he accepted the gift of some plantains or other native foods, the donor would demand payment in the form of a machete or some other expensive good. If he did not share his own food (largely oatmeal, canned sardines, and peanut butter), he was aggressively insulted, and the Yanomamö ceaselessly tried to separate him from his few possessions, saying things like "Give me an ax or I'll break into your hut when you are away visiting and steal one!"[16] If he gave into one demand, the threats and requests escalated. After months of this, Chagnon noted that "Privacy is one of Western culture's greatest achievements."[17] He himself had little: to escape the constant begging he occasionally locked himself into his hut for hours on end. He found that the Yanomamö existed in a constant state of warfare and general aggression. Wife-beating was common, war was unceasing, and abortion was frequent (often accomplished by a pregnant woman asking a friend to jump on her stomach). Baby girls, considered very mixed blessings in this militaristic culture, were often strangled at birth or simply thrown headfirst against a tree and left to die.[18]

Yet Chagnon found that the Yanomamö have a rich mythology, abstract and even witty folk tales, and a complex kinship system. They believe in a spirit world in which the dead exist, and living people regularly eat small amounts of the powdered ash of cremated relatives in hopes that this will help them visit their relatives after their own death.

Among the many questions one may ask about the Yanomamö is one of central importance to this chapter, and that is: What, if anything, do the Yanomamö tell us about our hunter-forager ancestors? The Yanomamö are just one of the many hundreds of hunter-forager groups that anthropologists have studied,[19] and many are radically different from the Yanomamö, in every respect except the hunting-foraging basis of their economy. Collectively, what do these groups tell us about our past?

The basic issues here are the concepts of "cross-cultural comparisons" and "ethnographic analogy." To what extent can we extrapolate from recent and present societies to the past? Archaeologists have been heavily influenced in their conceptions of ancient cultural complexity by ethnographers who have studied not just hunter-foragers, but other people who live in social organizations and with economies that may resemble those of our extinct ancestors.

TRADITIONAL SOCIOCULTURAL TYPOLOGIES

Although the ethnographic categories formulated by anthropologists such as Elman Service and Morton Fried were devised principally to classify the diversity of extant and recent cultures, their ideas have been widely applied by archaeologists to prehistoric societies. The use of ethnographic data to categorize ancient societies that exist only as rubble and discarded artifacts can, of course, be misleading, particularly since "it . . . seems possible that every hunter-gatherer or tribal society in the world was influenced to some degree by contact with technologically more advanced societies prior to ethnographic study."[20]

In some ways social typologies and taxonomies are a hindrance to good archaeological analysis because they inexactly lump together societies on the basis of unstated and sometimes irrelevant criteria.[21] But almost all archaeologists continue to think of the archaeological record in terms of three or four basic *types* of societies. These types are abstractions that may fit precisely no particular case, especially with regard to extinct societies, but they are convenient summaries of the kinds of social differences archaeologists think were involved in the evolution of complex societies.

EGALITARIAN SOCIETIES: BANDS AND TRIBES

As we noted in chapters 3 and 4, the archaeological evidence is undeniable that for the first three million years of our history as a genus, we lived in what anthropologists generally—if inexactly—call *band* societies. The Yanomamö described above are typical of band societies, but there is great variation[22] in these societies, and all have been influenced to some extent by industrial cultures. Eskimos who use snowmobiles to hunt bears and Kalahari Bushmen who steal their neighbors' cows, for example, are often seen as distorted remnants of band societies, because when first described by explorers and anthropologists, they exhibited far fewer signs of "contamination" by industrial societies.

Archaeologists have developed a sense of what a "band" society is mainly by distilling and combining ethnographic studies of societies in many different parts of the world. The Copper Eskimo, African Pygmies, Kalahari Bushmen, and Australian Aborigines are usually cited as examples of this social form. In contemporary and recent band societies, the most salient characteristic seems to be that there are only minor differences among members of the group in terms of prestige; in these societies no one has any greater claims to material resources than anyone else. In most of these societies, older males who are good providers gain the most respect, but they have little or no power to coerce other band members. This lack of social differentiation is tied to their economy: band members spend most of their lives in groups of fifteen to forty people, moving often as they exploit wild plants and animals. Julian Steward concluded that most, perhaps all, bands were patrilineal and patrilocal—that is, people reckoned their descent primarily through their father and newlyweds lived with the husband's band.[23] Whether or not this is true is still a major issue in ethnography, and many ethnologists think that band societies can be extremely flexible in where newlyweds live, for example, based on available resources and other factors.[24] In any case, this is the kind of thing archaeologists can never be sure about when applying the model of a band society to a scatter of stones and bones. The division of labor in bands is generally along basic age and sex lines, and the economic structure is a sort of practical communism: money is not used, and exchange usually takes place between people who consider themselves friends or relatives. This gift-giving is usually done very casually, and relationships are frequently cemented by offers of reciprocal hospitality.

In the context of the topic of this chapter, the origins of cultural complexity, one of the most important things about bands is that they appear to be largely *functionally redundant*. That is, these individual bands are very much alike in their social organization and economy, and each individual is able to do almost everything needed for the group to survive and reproduce itself. Each band contains, in the form of its members' skills, all of the expertise it needs to function and persist. As we shall see, it is the change from this kind of functional redundancy to functional *interdependence* that seems to be at the heart of the origins of complex societies.

And, in any case, the question remains: How similar are (or were) these ethnographically described groups to our hunter-forager ancestors—whose lives constitute 99 percent of our human past?

Tribe is the rather ambiguous term that anthropologists have used to label social groupings that are larger than band societies but generally not particularly complex in terms of economy, social hierarchies, law, etc. People living in tribes are often subsistence farmers, such as the Pueblo Indian maize farmers of the American Southwest or New Guinea yam cultivators. Tribes often have a nominal leader—usually male—who acts to redistribute food and perform a few minor ceremonial activities, but, as in band societies, he has no privileged access to wealth or power. He leads only by example and serves at the pleasure of the tribe. Exchange in such societies is still usually accomplished through reciprocal trading within a kinship structure. Typically, tribal societies are larger, more territorial, have more elaborate ceremonialism and kinship systems, and make more distinctions in terms of prestige than band societies.[25]

In many cases, tribes may have been transitional forms, appearing where farmers were in the transition to more complex forms of social organization, and in some cases tribal societies may have been direct outgrowths of the influences of or contacts with state societies.[26]

RANKED SOCIETIES: CHIEFDOMS

Timothy Earle defines *chiefdoms* as "regionally organized societies with a centralized decision-making hierarchy coordinating activities among several village communities."[27] For many authorities, "chiefdoms" are different from bands and tribes both in degree and in kind. Chiefdoms are based on the concept of "rank," or hereditary inequality: in a chiefdom, if you are the first son of a chief, chances are you will become chief no matter how unsuitable you may be; and if you are able but born a "commoner," your options in life will be narrowly circumscribed.

These differences in prestige usually correlate with preferential access to wealth; chiefs and their families can claim the best farmlands or fishing places as well as more food and more exotic and expensive items than "commoners." They are often regarded as divine and typically marry within noble families. The economies of these societies typically show a greater degree of specialization and diversification than those of tribes or bands. Craftsmen exist, but they are usually also farmers, and there is no permanent class of artisans as there is in states. Chiefdoms are much larger than tribes, often involving thousands of people. Examples of chiefdoms include the pre-contact Nootka of British Columbia and early Hawaiian societies.

Earle stresses the ideological bases of chiefdoms. He notes that chiefs typically create sacred places, such as pyramids; they also use symbols of individual power and position in burial cults, and their mortuary symbolism often includes expressions of military might. To some extent, recent archaeological research on chiefdoms has focused on the political and ideological activities of chiefs, rather than just the simple deterministic factors of agriculture and economy that permit the evolution of chiefdoms.[28] In fact, the current literature on chiefdoms clearly mirrors a major conceptual trend in contemporary archaeology: traditional analyses of chiefdoms have concentrated on the functionalist and adaptive aspects of these societies, such as how chiefs may have been responsive to the problem of redistributing resources in rapidly growing societies; but contemporary approaches[29] stress the varieties of ways in which chiefs gain and maintain control.

The archaeology of chiefdoms is a particularly valuable endeavor, as Dick Drennan points out, because in some cases they seem to have been a transitional phase leading to states, and elsewhere they were "terminal," in the sense that the indigenous developmental factors seem to have produced chiefdoms but not states. Drennan defends the use of the concept of chiefdoms on various grounds. He notes that "Their story is, in one respect, the story of the emergence of substantial inequality, but it has a number of other aspects as well, such as spatial and demographic scale, centralization, economic specialization, exchange, supralocal political organization. . . . Very broadly speaking, these aspects are known to be correlated with each other.[30]

STRATIFIED SOCIETIES: STATES

What a *state* is depends to some extent on what an analyst sees as the causal factors in producing cultural complexity. The term "stratified" refers to the division of the society into hierarchically arranged strata of socioeconomic classes and political elites. Generally, states are assumed to have centralized governments composed of political and religious elites who exercise economic and political control. In addition to being larger in population and territory than other societal forms, states are characterized by having full-time craftsmen and other specialists, whose products are distributed in part through an integrated national economy. The state codifies and enforces laws, drafts soldiers, levies taxes, and exacts tribute. States have powerful economic structures, often centered on market systems, and they have a diversity of settlement sizes, such as villages, towns, and sometimes cities.

Wright and Johnson, for example, define the state in terms of a political polity that has at least three levels in the decision-making hierarchy, such as village headmen, provincial governor, and national leader.[31]

Early states formed essentially independently in at least six areas of the ancient world: Mesopotamia, Egypt, the Indus Valley, China, Mesoamerica, and Peru; ethnographic and historical accounts of state formation include cases in Africa, Madagascar, and various other places.

Scholars use the same term, "state," to refer both to ancient Egypt and to the United States, for example, despite their gross differences in complexity. Yet in a sense the differences between ancient Egypt and the modern United States are matters of degree. The level of occupational specialization in the contemporary United States is much greater than in ancient Egypt, of course, but it is mainly an elaboration of the same basic economic principle. Some scholars, however, use the term "preindustrial state" to distinguish ancient states from those of the industrial era.

Many of the early states seem to have been involved in competitive relationships with other, adjacent states, and for long periods this apparently limited their size and power. Eventually, however, in all the early centers of state formation these competitive relationships broke down and one state was able to increase its size and influence drastically—usually so rapidly that it had few competitors. In fact, its ultimate size seems to have been limited only by the level of its communications technology and its administrative efficiency.

States—or "empires," as they are sometimes called—of this type first appeared in Mesopotamia toward the end of the second millennium B.C. and within a thousand years thereafter in Egypt, the Indus Valley, and China. The Inka state of Peru and the Aztec state of Mexico also seem to have achieved imperial dimensions just before the arrival of the Europeans, in the sixteenth century A.D.

CONTEMPORARY APPROACHES TO SOCIOCULTURAL TYPOLOGY

Rather than think of the archaeological record primarily in terms of bands, tribes, chiefdoms, and states, it is probably more accurate to see the record as a great continuum of variability, reflecting the unique flexibility that humans bring to any situation. We can be certain the australopithecines had no academic conferences on mathematics or international labor federations, and no great ancient state was founded principally on caribou hunting. But most other generalizations about these social typologies are likely to be imprecise.

The important point here is that simple categories such as "bands," "tribes," "chiefdoms," and "states" are static descriptive types that are not of much use in analyzing the origins and functions of the phenomena these labels loosely describe. Labeling ancient Egypt a "state," for example, based on the inferred appearance of characteristics such as centralized government or a class-structured society, is more a description than an analysis. To many scholars such typologies are inexact, atheoretical categorizations of a continuous and multidimensional underlying variability. McGuire argues that such "an approach inevitably degenerates into taxonomic arguments: What is a simple society? What is a state?"[32]

Some of these issues are illustrated in Figure 7.2, which makes evident the problems of typologies: How do we decide where to draw a boundary line that defines a "state" in such a pattern of continuous variability? This graph reveals the critical problem with archaeological analyses of cultural variability: there is no powerful theory that tells us what the proper units of analysis are and what principles explain their functions. Compare this situation to biology: Darwinian theory and modern genetics give biology a powerful explanatory theory that reveals much about the history and operations of the biological universe. Darwinian theory and modern genetics tell the researcher what units to use (genes, cells, populations, etc.) and explain change over time and space in the biological universe. Archaeology has no comparable theories and thus has no comparably effective units or principles of analysis. Some scholars argue that because archaeology deals with people (even if they are dead) and unique cultures (even if they are extinct), it will never be possible to have comparably powerful theories. Others argue that we already have the beginnings of powerful theories—a position discussed below in terms of Marxism and Cultural Evolutionary theory.

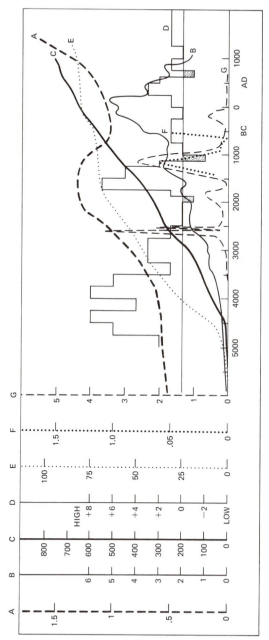

FIGURE 7.2 A major theoretical problem in modern archaeology is how to study the causes and effects of cultural changes on the basis of archaeological data. In this chart, a sample of variables from ancient Egypt has been plotted on comparative scales. One might look for intervals where many important variables changed significantly (such as between 3000 and 2500 B.C. here) to try to explain the origins of complex societies in Egypt. But the archaeological data are meager, correlation does not prove causal connection, and the shape of these plots will depend on how the data are statistically transformed. The variables here are (**A**) coefficient of rank-size distribution of settlement size, (**B**) population in millions, (**C**) population density per square kilometer, (**D**) lake volumes and stream discharge in east Africa, (**E**) percentage of domesticated animals in total faunal assemblage (estimated from reports on excavated materials), (**F**) price of farmland per unit (in silver), (**G**) monumental architecture in cubic meters of worked stone. Many other variables could be plotted (e.g., average transport distance of craft items).

In the face of these ambiguities, many archaeologists have resorted to trying to break down typologies as exemplified by the "bands," "tribes," "chiefdoms," and "states" paradigm, and to examine the underlying variability in selected aspects of societies. Numerous archaeologists, for example, have focused on the concepts of *specialization* and *exchange*. Cathy Costin, for example, has developed[33] a complex categorization of how societies produce and distribute goods and services. Similarly, Elizabeth Brumfiel and Timothy Earle break down the concept of occupational specialization into at least four dimensions: (1) specialists can be *independent* or *attached*, in the sense that a potter, for example, can supply pots for an unspecified, changing market, perhaps just for members of his or her own village, or for the larger region; or the potter can be attached to a particular patron, and make ceramics only for a given noble family or governing institution; (2) specialists differ in the *nature of their products*, in that they can produce *subsistence* items, such as grain; *wealth*, such as ritual feather headdresses or gold bracelets; or *services*, such as military duty or religious ceremonies; (3) specialists differ in the *intensity of production*, in that they could be part-time hunters, who contribute an occasional deer to the village economy, or full-time weavers, who do little else but produce textiles for trade; (4) specialists also differ in the *scale* of production, in the sense that in some economies a large group of people, or a village, or even a region may specialize in something, such as salt production, while in other cases, one or two people may produce a particular good or service.[34] Brumfiel and Earle also note that there are many different kinds of exchange: between an elite and its supporting citizenry, among different elites, and in the wide variety of political and social arrangements in which subsistence goods and non-subsistence "wealth" can be circulated within and among communities, regions, and larger political entities.

Another aspect of contemporary rethinking of typologies of ancient societies has to do with the notion of the "collapse" of civilizations. Many scholars over the centuries have thought of civilizations almost as if these societies were organisms, with a birth, life-span, and death, or collapse. And there certainly are some examples in the past of cultures that appear to have quickly and pervasively lost some of their unique, fundamental cultural expressions, such as the Maya civilization of Mesoamerica (see chapter 13). But in most cases the collapse of civilizations seems to involve not a collapse and mass extinction of people and their cultural ideas, but rather adaptation, sometimes in the form of a process—to use Mark Kenoyer's terms[35]—of *decentralization* and *localization*, in which political authorities lose their ability to control people and economies. These periods of decentralization can in fact involve periods of population growth, rather than decline, and in many cases decentralization was followed by a larger, more politically potent polity in the same area. We will return to this point in later chapters.

THE ARCHAEOLOGY OF COMPLEX SOCIETIES

Archaeologists regularly talk about the band societies of the Middle Pleistocene and the early chiefdoms of prehistoric Mesopotamia, but we do not have these societies trapped in amber; we have only their artifacts, and we use the words "bands," "tribes," and "states" to describe them only with some license. To deal with this problem, archaeologists typically equate these terms with specific categories of physical evidence.

At the heart of many conceptions of cultural complexity is the idea of changing forms and levels of matter, energy, and information exchange. Each person and each society exists because it is able to divert energy from the natural world, through food sources and technology, and some of these changes are selective advantages. The greater the amount of energy a culture can capture and efficiently utilize, the better its competitive chances. And we can measure this in part by measuring such variables as population density and agricultural and commodity productivity.

Leslie White's equation of cultural evolution, with the amount of energy captured per person per year, has been widely criticized, but it remains of interest.[36] The fundamental data of archaeology are usually the stones and pots and other implements with which people converted energy to their purposes—the very appliances of energy use, in other words, that White stressed. And every early state left a record of its economic basis in the form of such things as irrigation canals, stone tools, and agricultural fields. Yet in essence every ancient state was also an *idea*. The Egyptians viewed their state and culture metaphorically as a living organism, an organism of which they were all a part, from the pharaoh himself to the lowliest slave.

All other early states had a similar intellectual foundation—an ideology that embraced the people and elements of the state. For all early states, the process of analyzing them archaeologically requires that the material remains of these cultures be interpreted in the context of their ideologies.

ARCHITECTURE

Perhaps the most obvious differences between the archaeological record of the Pleistocene and that of the last five or six millennia is the presence in the latter period of massive amounts of residential and public architecture. All early states built palaces and tombs; hunter-gatherers occasionally built permanent structures but rarely on the same scale as agriculturalists.

The appearance of substantial houses and other forms of *residential* architecture is mainly a reflection of economic productivity: if a group produces or gathers sufficient resources within a small enough area, it can become sedentary, and in most climates shelter from rain, sun, heat, cold, and other elements is worth the cost and effort required to build it.

Soon after permanent communities appeared in both the Old and New Worlds, the architecture of these settlements began to reflect changing levels of cultural and social complexity. Whereas the first houses in all communities were probably built very much alike and had the same contents, later communities incorporated residences that varied considerably in expense of construction and furnishing. Ethnographic evidence leaves little doubt that this architectural variability reflects economic, social, and political differentiation within the community, but the essential point is that, relative to earlier societies, there was a change in patterns of investment of societal energy and resources.

Similarly, once residential architectural variability appeared in many of these early communities, "monumental" architecture also appeared. Pyramids, earthen or brick platforms, "temples," "palaces," and other constructions protrude from the ruins of ancient settlements from North China to the high mountain valleys of Peru. Here, too, the important thing is that the ability and incentive to make these investments are radically different from the capacities of Pleistocene bands, in that they imply the ability of some members of the society to control and organize others.

MORTUARY EVIDENCE

For much of its early history archaeology was almost synonymous with grave-robbing. Its early practitioners were primarily concerned with finding ancient burials so that they could loot the beautiful goods that people so often have lavished on their departed.

Objects carefully enclosed in burials are often much better preserved than those found in houses or tool-making sites. Also, death for our ancestors, as for ourselves, was invested with more ritual than any other cultural aspect. In many burials we have, so to speak, the crystallization of complex religious and social forces, as well as reflections of social status. It is in their great *variability* that mortuary customs are so informative: corpses can be buried, burned, ritually exposed, or entombed; they can be laid out flat, on their sides, or flexed; they can be oriented to the cardinal points of the compass or to a geographical feature; they can be placed in earth, in caves, in crypts, in trees, or on refuse heaps. Burial contents can range from nothing to enormous quantities of jewelry and furnishings and scores of sacrificed human attendants and animals.

It is a fundamental archaeological assumption that a correlation exists between the level of social complexity of a people and the way they treat their dead.[37] Ethnographic studies show that the correlation between subsistence strategy, social organization, and mortuary practices is strong: bands and tribes differed comparatively little in mortuary practices, while sedentary agriculturalists varied their practices according to a wide range of age, sex, and status distinctions.[38] These correlations are strong but not perfect: in some cultures, including our own, some of the most important and wealthiest people are cremated and leave no material record of their passing, their status, or their wealth.

The presence of juveniles buried with rich grave goods has been given considerable importance in defining the cultural complexity of ancient societies, because such burials are considered indications of ascribed status: we assume that young individuals could not have earned these goods on their own. Similarly, some ancient cemeteries have three or four distinct classes of burials. Some types are well constructed of stone, have rich grave goods, and are centrally located, while others are simple graves with little in them except the corpse. And it is a reasonable inference that these divisions correspond to different economic and social classes.[39]

FUNCTIONAL DIFFERENTIATION AND INTEGRATION

In chapter 15 we will see that the aboriginal Americans who built the huge mounds that dot the eastern North American river valleys had great trade systems, intensive maize agriculture, thousands of inhabitants, and a mortuary cult that involved human sacrifice and great expenditures of wealth on dead leaders—yet most archaeologists do not consider that these societies constituted "states," because these Native Americans were almost all full-time maize farmers, with only a few specialists: in religion, hunting, warfare, and other areas. In some definitions of cultural complexity, the essential component is the division of a community into functionally interdependent entities of such complexity that no small group of people can maintain all that community's activities. This is important because it produces a situation in which societies survive or die out as *societies*, as groups; in contrast, among hunter-gatherers the focus of selection is usually the *individual*, or at most the twelve or fifteen people with whom each individual spends most of the year. In other words, the unit of "selection" changes with cultural complexity. Contemporary North Americans, for example, are extremely interdependent, in the sense that we are all reliant for our continued existence as both physical individuals and social organizations on the 3 or 4 percent of the population that produces nearly all our food.

To translate this sense of functional interdependence into archaeological terms, we must look for concentrations and distributions of artifacts indicating a certain level of activity specialization. In early agricultural villages, each house and each group of houses had approximately the same contents in terms of numbers and types of ceramics, stone tools, figurines, and garbage. But in later, more complex societies we find concentrations of artifacts that clearly represent such things as pottery or stone-tool manufacturing workshops, indicating that people specialized in these activities. Again, we infer that they were specialized, but the significant point archaeologically is that certain classes of artifacts are found in places, volumes, and diversities far different from what would be produced by, say, a hunting-and-gathering group. Certain differences will also be evident if we compare the contents of settlements. Some settlements might specialize in salt-making, or barley agriculture, or pottery manufacture. This variability in the artifacts found within discrete but contemporary sites is a key element in our identification of cultural complexity.

SETTLEMENT PATTERNS

In addition to measuring social complexity by looking at objects excavated at specific sites, we can also look at how settlements are distributed spatially. First, we can examine variability in settlement size and configuration. Early Southwest Asian agricultural villages were almost all approximately the same size, but settlements there several thousand years later were of many different sizes, ranging from a few hundred square meters to several square kilometers. Similarly, the basic shape of the settlements changed; some were apparently fortified rectangular compounds, while others were just five or six mudbrick houses. Thus, any archaeological analysis of cultural complexity will involve measuring the variability in site size and shape in a large sample of contemporary sites.

Second, we can look at the placement of settlements relative to the environment and to each other. A major part of the cost of exploiting any resource is the distance it must be transported. This applies equally to the deer hunted by Paleolithic bands and the irrigated rice of ancient China. It also applies to the cost of making decisions about resource production, movement, and storage. With primitive communications systems, for example, an official in one settlement cannot make many timely decisions about the agriculture or craft production of thirty or forty other settlements many kilometers away, because the cost of gathering the relevant information and accurately and rapidly acting on it is too high: he would need teams of observers and relay runners.

As a consequence, some arrangements of settlements are more common than others under certain conditions, and we can tell something about the relationships between settlements by analyzing their respective locations. On a relatively broad agricultural plain, towns and villages that exchange goods and services tend to be placed so as to form a pattern of interlocking hexagons (Figure 7.3), because this arrange-

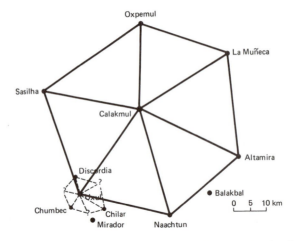

FIGURE 7.3   One of the initial archaeological signs of changing levels of complexity in regional economic and political systems is the appearance of settlement patterns in which settlements are arranged spatially in recognizable patterns. The *Central Place* model suggests that on a flat plain where all resources are uniformly distributed, the settlements will be arranged in different patterns depending on the strength of marketing, transport, administrative, and other factors. No perfectly uniformly endowed plains exist, of course, but actual maps of archaeological settlements can be matched against the theoretical ideal and similarities noted to these ideal models. The hexagonal areas surrounding the settlements in the above models are produced by assuming that on a featureless plain each settlement would have a circular area around it, the inhabitants of which would go to the center for goods and services. But since a plain packed with such circular "demand zones" would leave some areas outside these circles, the theoretical model assumes that the circles are slightly overlapped and that the overlapping areas are bisected. The resulting figures are hexagons. Modern settlement maps as well as archaeological site maps for a given area often roughly approximate the variations of hexagonal distributions illustrated above. Here some of the major settlements of the Maya in lowland Mexico were spaced in an hexagonal arrangement.

ment is especially efficient if there is a high level of movement of goods and people among the various settlements.[40] In our discussion of archaeological evidence relevant to the origins of cultural complexity, we will see several instances where ancient settlements are arranged in a hexagonal pattern or some other form. Here too it is relatively unimportant whether or not the distribution of ancient settlements corresponds exactly to the patterns observed among present ones. What is important is that we know a major change in settlement patterning has occurred over time. Paleolithic hunters and gatherers and early agriculturalists lived in locations determined largely by the availability of material resources. But later, in some areas of the ancient world, settlements began to be located with less regard for natural resources and more concern for trade routes, political frontiers, and administrative networks. Again, these changes occurred in settlements that were also building monumental structures, achieving denser population concentrations, and evolving some or all of the other elements of cultural complexity.

For these reasons, archaeological settlement pattern analyses have provided significant insights into the nature of ancient social, political, and economic changes.[41]

One of the continuing debates in archaeology is the relationship of *urbanism* and state societies. Some civilizations, such as those in Mesopotamia, seemed to have been formed out of cities, while others, such as Egypt, remained largely non-urban for much of their history. Trigger evaluates the attempts to place examples of the pre-industrial city on a single continuum and concludes that, while we can identify key variables that link these examples, the variables combine "to shape an indefinite number of trajectories or paths of pre-industrial urban development, any one of which may be associated with a particular civilization."[42] He identifies three variables of particular importance:

> (1) The degree of economic complexity of the society in which the city is found, as measured in terms of the degree of division of labour in craft production, the increasing number of people divorced from food production . . . , and the increasingly large areas and numbers of people that are effectively linked by routine economic interaction . . . ; (2) the different strategies by which urban dwellers obtain food from their hinterland . . . ; (3) The political context within which cities occur.[43]

It may seem as if the elements of cultural complexity we have sketched here are mainly found in the urban centers and ceremonial centers of early states, but this is not so. In Egypt, for example, the remains of tiny provincial villages appear to reflect a simple agrarian life, undisturbed by the events and forces emanating from the center of the Egyptian state; but a closer look at the remains of these provincial communities reveals many reflections of the state as a whole. Artifact styles are those of every other community in the state, inscribed clay commodity sealings bespeak a commercial connection to the royal court, and trade items reflect standardization and integration into the national and international economy. Similar patterns are observed in most early states.[44]

To summarize archaeological approaches to determining cultural complexity, we have several specific lines of evidence: we can look for changes in architecture, technology, mortuary complexes, and settlement size and location; and we can attempt to link these changes to different levels and forms of energy and information usage and overall thermodynamic capture.

Most of the rest of this book is a summary of how different cultures in various parts of the world made the transition to complexity, and this summary is based on these forms of evidence of evolving complexity. But before considering the specifics, let us look first at the general problem of explaining these evolutionary patterns. As in the case of the origins of cultural behavior itself and the appearance of agricultural economies, we would like some kind of theoretical constructs that will help tie all these separate early states together as members of a class and then will account for the time and location of their appearance.

EXPLAINING THE EVOLUTION OF CIVILIZATIONS: THE SEARCH FOR CAUSES

The earliest scholars believed the rise of cities and states and other elements of evolving cultural complexity required no explanation, because they assumed these developments to be mainly or entirely the work of the gods. The scholars of the Enlightenment and subsequent centuries usually explained the origins of cultural complexity in evolutionary terms. Drawing a parallel with the biological world, Europeans felt that competition between human societies was inevitable, and that to a large extent they had already "won."

Darwin thought that:

> civilized nations are everywhere supplanting barbarous nations, excepting where the climate opposes a deadly barrier; and they succeed mainly, though not exclusively, through their arts, which are the products of the intellect. It is, therefore, highly probable that with mankind the intellectual facilities have been gradually perfected through natural selection.[45]

John Locke saw the cultures of North America as exemplifying a moral and philosophical lesson:

> There cannot be a clearer demonstration of [European cultural superiority] than . . . [the] several nations of the Americans . . . , who are rich in land and poor in all the comforts of life; whom nature having furnished as liberally as any other people, with the materials of plenty, i.e. a fruitful soil, apt to produce in abundance, what might serve for food, raiment, and delight; yet for want of improving it by labor, have not one hundredth part of the conveniences we enjoy; and a king of a large and fruitful territory there, feeds, lodges, and is clad worse than a day-labourer in England.[46]

Even in the early part of this century, many scholars believed that the cultural evolution of the whole world was to some extent a result of the rise of the West. The ancient states of China, India, and even the Americas were thought to have been prodded to higher achievements by contact with the European/Middle Eastern core areas. Thor Heyerdahl's expeditions, for example, perpetuate this notion that all civilizations are derived from a Middle Eastern, or at least Old World, source.

The coincidence of the village farming way of life with the rise of cultural complexity represented to some scholars a sufficient explanation of the evolution of cultural complexity. People then finally had enough leisure time and sedentary habits, it was argued, to develop architecture, art, writing, cities, and the rest of "civilization." The problems with this explanation are apparent even with a superficial examination. Many agricultural groups apparently never developed into "states," while at least one early complex culture (in Peru) may have evolved without a primary agricultural economy. In any case, many hunters and gatherers have more leisure time than primitive agriculturalists.

TECHNO-ECOLOGICAL HYPOTHESES ABOUT THE ORIGINS OF CIVILIZATIONS

For many analysts of early civilizations, the search for an explanation of how these cultures evolved in highly similar yet distinctive ways logically should begin with a consideration of these similarities and differences. What, in other words, did these early civilizations share in the way of, for example, climate, ecology, demographics, or any other factors, that might explain why it was Mesopotamia, Egypt, the Indus Valley, China, Mesoamerica, and Andean South America that gave rise to the first great states and civilizations, and not Australia, Polynesia, Scandinavia, California, Japan, or Scotland?

If you knew nothing about the archaeology of early complex cultures and began to compare them, chances are you would be struck by the same facts that so forcefully impressed Julian Steward, V. G. Childe, and other early scholars who studied the problem of cultural complexity origins: most of these cultures developed in similar physical environments and were based on similar economies.[47] The earliest states and empires arose for the most part in arid or semi-arid environments where crops like wheat and barley could be grown without having to turn over thick grasslands or fight back lots of competing vegetation, and where agricultural production could be easily intensified, either by canals, terracing, building up fields in lake beds, or some other method.

Thus, you might look for one or two key factors that had operated in each of these early societies to *cause* civilization in a rather mechanical fashion, in which these civilizations were the outcome of the proper mix of population growth, agricultural intensification, trade, and the peculiarities of the human mind.

In some ways it is easy to imagine societies becoming more complex once the first elements of complexity are in place. A powerful chief, for example, could become a national king, if he were successful in battle and conquered a large, exploitable hinterland like the Mesopotamian Alluvium. And once a city had organized its production and distribution of pottery and grain, it seems an easy step to extend these administrative institutions to fish, beer, plows, and tax revenues; and once the first royal tombs filled with grave gifts are constructed, the building of great mortuary pyramids seems a fairly simple extension of the basic idea.

But what could produce the first irrevocable breaks with the strong traditions of practical communism and social equality of the first agricultural communities?

To begin with the most obvious factor, as noted above, even though intensive agriculture is the foundation of almost all early complex cultures, it is not a sufficient explanation in and of itself. Therefore most attempts to understand the origins of complexity try to link specific agricultural patterns with other factors. Anthropologist J. Athens notes that agriculture is an effort to maintain an artificial ecosystem, and in some climates, such as arid or temperate environments, the plowing, irrigating, and other efforts needed to maintain agricultural ecosystems are so great that it is doubtful that "the more intense forms of agricultural production would be developed or become adopted unless there was a compelling reason to do so."[48] Athens maintains (as does Ester Boserup)[49] that the only reason sufficient to account for the enormous efforts required to maintain agricultural systems would be an imbalance between the population and available food supply.

In both arid and temperate environments, annual agricultural production can vary greatly because of crop disease, weather, and other factors, and there is some incentive to try to stabilize production in these areas by intensive weeding, land leveling, augmenting the irrigation system, and other tasks that require a great deal of labor. In arid, semi-arid, and temperate regions, the growing season is often sharply restricted by the weather, and thus "cultivation . . . does not permit cycling of plantings in such a way as to equalize the labor requirement throughout the year."[50] Each spring, for example, many different activities might have to be performed to avoid poor harvests, and under these conditions, according to Athens, there is a strong selection for certain kinds of cultural complexity. Increasing the territorial size of the cultural system would help meet crises brought on by a flood or some other disaster striking a single village; individuals and villages might also become specialized in trades and crafts to make production more efficient; and, perhaps most important, it would be advantageous to have a hierarchical administrative organization, so that work and production could be closely and efficiently administered.

Many explanations of the evolution of complex societies combine certain forms of agricultural intensification with *population growth*. But what causes human population growth? The immediate cause of population growth is well-known, but the more important question is: What are the causes and effects of the gradual rise in population densities and total population that all early civilizations experienced? George Cowgill remarked that many analysts of cultural evolution have assumed that a pervasive and powerful factor in human history has been the strong tendency of human populations to increase up to the point where serious shortages of important resources are in the offing; and that experience or anticipation of such shortages has been a major factor, or even the dominant factor, in stimulating intensification of agricultural production and other technical and social innovations. In extreme versions, the entire history of complex societies and civilizations is seen as hardly more than the outcome of measures that began as ways of coping with problems posed by relentless human fertility—what might be called the "strictly from hunger" point of view of developmental processes.[51]

It is easy to see the attractiveness of these ideas, for if one examines history, a strong positive statistical correlation between population growth and cultural complexity is evident. The relationship between human population growth and cultural complexity may not be one of direct cause and effect, however, for correlation does not necessarily demonstrate causation. Moreover, even if the relationship is in some sense causal, it may be that the evolution of cultural complexity leads to rising population densities, rather than the reverse. Empirically, too, there seem to be some problems with the idea that human population growth somehow caused the evolution of cultural complexity. All societies have evolved mechanisms like migration, abortion, infanticide, marriage rules, and contraceptive techniques to control population growth, and thus we might expect people faced with stresses because of overpopulation to impose population controls, rather than "invent" cultural complexity.[52]

It is worth noting that the greatest recent falls in fertility rates come not as the result of food shortages or technical advances in contraception, but as correlates of increasing educational levels for women, greater social mobility, increasing urbanization, the expanding role of women in the work force—in sum, the lessening of women's dependence on husbands and children for support.

The actual causal mechanisms by which these factors are translated into reduced fertility are not clear, however. In any case, there is no evidence human populations have ever increased at anything approaching the biologically feasible rate. If the world's population 5,570 years ago were only one thousand people and their annual rate of increase since then were four per thousand people—a relatively moderate growth rate—the world's present population would be between seven and eight trillion. Obviously, human populations in the past have been under fairly stringent natural and cultural controls, and if we are to link population growth to increasing cultural complexity, we must specify additional factors or principles in causal "models" of how these variables were related.

It should be stressed, however, that most of the following "models" of cultural evolution are relatively simple, and many current scholars consider them incomplete or flawed as explanations of early complexity.

Irrigation Agriculture and the Evolution of Cultural Complexity   Perhaps the most obvious common denominator of ancient complex societies was extensive irrigation systems. Even today aerial photographs of Mesopotamia, Peru, and most other areas of early state formation clearly show the massive remnants of these ancient structures, and similar constructions were built by early "chiefdoms" in such places as Hawaii and southwestern North America. This led some scholars to conclude that the construction and operation of extensive irrigation systems were at the heart of the origins of complex societies. A particularly influential proponent of this view was Karl Wittfogel, whose *Oriental Despotism* is a detailed excursion into comparative history and sociological analysis.[53]

Wittfogel notes that the limiting factors on agriculture are soil conditions, temperature, and the availability of water. Of these, water is the most easily manipulated, but its weight and physical characteristics impose limitations on this manipulation. To divert water to agricultural fields requires canal systems, dams, and drainage constructions that can only be built efficiently with organized mass labor; and, once built, irrigation systems require continued enormous investments of labor and resources to operate, clean, and maintain them. In addition, these systems necessitate complex administration and communication, because crucial decisions have to be made about construction and repairs, water allocation, and crop harvesting and storage. Thus, a complex irrigation system under ancient conditions required cooperation and centralized hierarchical decision-making institutions.

Irrigation systems also have the intrinsic capacity to create another element in the process of the evolution of complex societies: wealth and status differentials. Fields closer to main rivers are better drained and more easily irrigated, and possess a higher natural fertility; thus control of such lands would create immediate wealth differentials. Correspondingly, wealth and status would most likely accrue to the elites of the decision-making hierarchies. Wittfogel concludes that irrigation-based agriculture has many other effects on a society. It encourages the development of writing and calendrical systems, so that records can be kept of periods of annual flooding, agricultural production statistics, the amounts of products in storage, and the allocation of water. Construction of roads, palaces, and temples would also be encouraged, because the mobilization of labor for the canal works could be generalized to these other endeavors very easily, and roads would contribute to the movement of agricultural produce and to the communication required for efficient operation of the systems. The construction of temples and palaces would also serve to reinforce the position of the hierarchy. The creation of standing armies and defensive works would also likely follow, because irrigation systems are extremely valuable but not very portable, and they are easily damaged by neglect or intentional destruction.

Wittfogel's hydraulic hypothesis still has some currency, but there seem to be logical and empirical problems with his ideas as a general model of the origins of cultural complexity. Simple societies in several parts of the world have been observed operating extensive irrigation works with no perceptible despotic administrative systems or rapid increases in social complexity.[54] More damaging to Wittfogel's hypothesis is the scarcity of archaeological evidence of complex irrigation systems dating to before, or to the same time as, the appearance of monumental architecture, urbanism, and other reflections of increasing cultural complexity, in Southwest Asia and perhaps other areas where complex societies appeared independently and early.

Nonetheless, the difficulties of dating irrigation canals, inadequate archaeological samples, and other deficiencies of evidence are such that we cannot conclude that irrigation was unimportant in virtually any case of early cultural complexity.

Warfare, Population Growth, and Environmental Circumscription   "War is the father of all things," said Heraclitus, and, given its frequency in human affairs, we should not be surprised that many scholars see warfare as a natural adjunct of population growth in driving cultural evolution. In the film *The Third Man*, Orson Welles—justifying his profiteering in postwar Vienna to Joseph Cotton—says, "in Italy for thirty years under the Borgias they had warfare, terror, murder, bloodshed, but they produced Michelangelo, Leonardo da Vinci, and the Renaissance. In Switzerland, they had brotherly love, they had five hundred years of democracy and peace. And what did that produce? The cuckoo-clock."

Welles's character was stating what for many is an uncomfortable truth: human competition seems to be a powerful engine of cultural evolution. No early state—not Mexico, or China, or Sumer, or Peru—was without a background level of organized violence that occasionally erupted into great wars spanning decades.

Why should this be so? Why doesn't "natural selection" favor those cultures that develop institutions to resolve conflicts? Why doesn't cultural selection seem to give the edge to communities that pool their resources to build irrigation canals, establish universities, and work for world peace?

Desmond Morris, Richard Ardrey, and other scholars say it is because we have a propensity for competition or violence woven deeply into our chromosomes. But most scholars do not believe that warfare is genetic, they consider it simply a cultural behavior that is elicited by environmental and cultural conditions.

Anthropologist Robert Carneiro argues that warfare was the primary mechanism for the evolution of social complexity in ancient Peru, Mesopotamia, Egypt, Rome, northern Europe, central Africa, Polynesia, Mesoamerica, Colombia, and elsewhere. He believes, however, that:

> warfare cannot be the only factor. After all, wars have been fought in many parts of the world where the state never emerged. Thus while warfare may be a necessary condition for the rise of the state, it is not a sufficient one. Or, to put it another way, while we can identify war as the mechanism of state formation, we need also to specify the conditions under which it gave rise to the state.[55]

Carneiro sees two such conditions as essential to the formation of complex societies in concert with warfare: population growth and environmental circumscription. He notes that human population densities have been increasing in many areas for millennia, but that only in certain environmental zones can population growth join with warfare to produce highly complex early civilizations. These environmental zones are exceptionally fertile areas "circumscribed," or surrounded, by areas of lesser productivity such as deserts, mountains, or oceans. As an example, Carneiro points to the coast of Peru, where approximately seventy-eight rivers run from the Andes to the ocean through an eighty-kilometer stretch of some of the driest deserts on earth. Here, he says, are fertile, easily irrigated strips of land along the rivers, but in any direction one soon encounters desert, mountains, or the ocean. Similar conditions, he asserts, prevailed in Mesopotamia, Egypt, and the other centers of early civilizations.

Again using Peru as an example, Carneiro suggests that shortly after the appearance of the village farming way of life, these fertile riverine areas were sparsely occupied by small autonomous villages. He assumes that in such conditions populations grew and, as these populations increased, villages tended to divide because of internal conflicts and pressure on agricultural lands. Some of the inhabitants would then establish a new community some distance away. Such movements were easily accomplished in this early period because there was no shortage of land and little investment in terracing or irrigation systems. As a consequence, the number of villages increased faster than village size, and all communities remained essentially the same in political and social organization.

Eventually, however, given this constant population growth and the proliferation of villages, all the land that could be irrigated and exploited easily became occupied, and the expanding population rapidly began to outrun the available food supplies. Since they could not move into the sea or deserts or easily colonize the mountains, early Peruvian farmers chose agricultural intensification. They built terraces and irrigation canals and tried to keep pace with their population growth rates, but they were caught in the classic Malthusian dilemma: food supplies can be increased, but not nearly as quickly as population increases. At this point, Carneiro concludes, people turned to warfare as the only alternative. The village under the most stress would attack the weakest adjacent village, and the victor would expropriate the land and harvests of the loser. The conquered people not killed in the fighting could not simply move away and reestablish their villages, and they could not emigrate to the highlands because their whole culture was based on the village farming way of life. They were either taken back to the victors' village, where they became slaves or artisans, or they were left as serfs who were taxed so heavily that they had to reduce their own consumption and intensify their production still further.

These developments encouraged the formation of an institutionalized bureaucracy to administer the taxes and slaves, and the establishment of the bureaucracy in turn intensified wealth and status differentials, as the most successful military leaders were given the administrative posts. In addition, the defeated peoples came to constitute a lower class, and thus the stratification of society increased as the level of warfare rose. Carneiro believes that warfare continued in Peru until all of each river valley was under the control of one integrated authority, a development he terms a state. Subsequently, again because of the never-ending pressure of population, these states contended with each other until a whole series of river valleys was controlled by a single dominant center.

Carneiro uses ancient Peru as an example of this developmental pattern, but he argues that it applies almost point-for-point to the other major centers of early development.

Carneiro's ideas are diagrammed in Figure 7.4, where it can be seen that the whole structure rests on two "causal" factors: (1) the assumption that constant population growth among early village agriculturalists would inexorably demand increases in food production; and (2) the assumption that warfare is the most likely response to these conditions.

Since many primitive societies had remarkably precise control of their population-to-resources balance, population growth cannot be regarded as automatic. There is no demonstrated and inevitable reason why these populations could not have maintained their size below the stress level rather than resorting to agricultural intensification or warfare. Thus, to strengthen Carneiro's hypotheses we must stipulate other factors that encouraged or allowed these presumed growth rates.

In a reconsideration of Carneiro's model, David Webster maintains that warfare's principal importance in the evolution of the first states was the role it played in breaking down the kinship ties that organized early chiefdoms.[56] He notes that chiefdoms apparently are kept from evolving into states partially because the chief's power and prestige are tied to his role as a redistributive head, and if the chief begins to hoard wealth or exploit people, he begins to lose the support of his kinsmen and deputy

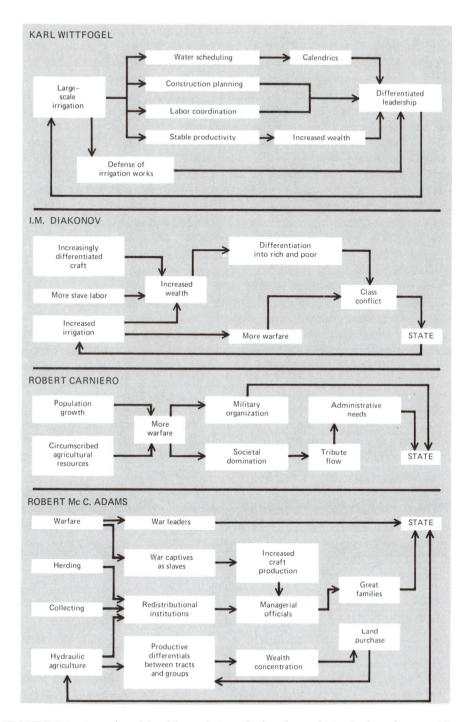

FIGURE 7.4 Several models of the evolution of cultural complexity. In these diagrams Henry Wright (1977) has depicted the most important hypothetical cause-and-effect relationships in several models of the origins of states and urbanism.

rulers. Webster proposes that warfare produces a potent environment for the evolutionary change to state-level societies by rendering ineffective many of the internal constraints that keep chiefdoms in a stable sociopolitical status. Continued warfare between chiefdoms would place great adaptive value on a stable military leadership, thereby dampening the constant petty squabbles between rival rulers. A chief who is successful in warfare can also claim more wealth in the form of booty than he could on the basis of his redistribution of his own society's production.

It is difficult to test archaeologically the many hypotheses that Carneiro's model has stimulated. Analyzing the possible interrelationship of, for example, population growth, warfare, and cultural change would require that we find evidence of conflict and demonstrate that it is linked to pressures exerted on resources by increasing population densities. If Carneiro is correct, complex societies appeared only after a long period of population growth in circumscribed environments; and monumental architecture, irrigation systems, urbanism, land terracing, and other aspects of "civilization" emerged only at population density peaks and were associated in time and space with defensive constructions, mass burials, burned settlements, concentrations of weapons, and other evidences of conflict.

Carneiro's ideas have stimulated much research[57] and seem to have broad applicability to various cultures.[58] But in contemporary archaeology there is a widespread sense that the key points of analysis in understanding the origins of early states must be at a socioeconomic and political level, not just demographics, physical environments, and the assumption of warfare.

Marxist and Materialist Explanations of Early Cultural Complexity   For much of this century, Marxist social scientists had few doubts about the proper explanation of the origins of civilization. Friedrich Engels's remarks at Karl Marx's grave expressed this certainty: "As Darwin discovered the law of evolution in organic nature so Marx discovered the law of evolution in human history."[59]

Despite the collapse of Marxist states all over the world, and despite the interweaving of Marx's economic analysis with dubious political polemic, there is no denying the tremendous influence Marx's contributions have had on the analysis of social systems.

Almost any attempt to sum up Marx's theories about the origins of cultural complexity and the dynamics of history necessarily involves great oversimplification and arguable interpretations. Marx's famous statement of his basic ideas is worth quoting at length and studying carefully because it is still one of the most astute and revolutionary observations on the nature of cultural evolutionary history:

> In the social production of their subsistence men enter into determined and necessary relations with each other which are independent of their wills—production-relations which correspond to a definite stage of development of their material productive forces. The sum total of these production-relations forms the economic structure of society, the real basis, upon which a juridical and political superstructure arises, and to which definite forms of social consciousness correspond. The mode of production of material subsistence conditions the social, political and spiritual life-process in general. It is not the consciousness of men which determines their existence but on the contrary it

is their social existence that determines their consciousness. At a certain stage of their development, the material productive forces of society come in conflict with the existing production relations, or what is merely a juridical expression for the same thing, the property relations within which they operated before. From being forms of development of the productive forces, these relations turn into fetters upon their development. Then comes an epoch of social revolution. With the change in the economic foundation the whole immense superstructure is slowly or rapidly transformed. In studying such a transformation one must always distinguish between the material transformation in the economic conditions essential to production—which can be established with the precision of the natural science—and the juridical, political, religious, artistic, or philosophic, in short ideological forms, in which men become conscious of this conflict and fight it out. As little as one judges what an individual is by what he thinks of himself, so little can one judge such an epoch of transformation by its consciousness; one must rather explain this consciousness by the contradictions in the material life, the conflict at hand between the social forces of production and the relations in which production is carried on.[60]

Marx continues:

No social formation ever perishes before all the productive forces for which there is room in it have been developed; and new, higher relations of production never appear before the material conditions of their existence have matured in the womb of the old society itself. . . . In broad outline Asiatic, ancient, feudal, and modern bourgeois modes of production can be designated as progressive epochs in the economic formation of society. The bourgeois relations of production are the last antagonistic form of the social process of production. . . . This social form brings, therefore, the prehistory of human society to a close.[61]

What all this means in terms of the whole history of complex societies is the point of enough books to fill a large library, and Marx's basic premises are being constantly reinterpreted. Still, many accept as valid the basic tenets of Marxian analyses of history, and there is certainly great power to some of his ideas.[62]

Marx himself, however, had very little to say specifically about the origins of complex societies. His primary attention was given to detailing the problems of capitalism and the dynamics of the transition from feudalism to capitalist societies. Much more attention was paid to the problem by later followers of Marx, particularly Engels and Lenin, and, recently, V. V. Streuve and I. Diakonov.[63]

Until the origins of agriculture, these scholars suggest, all societies were classless, all goods were shared, no one really owned anything, and all were treated equally. But gradually, after the achievement of domestication and the agricultural way of life, some people managed to control more than their fair share of the land, which is of course the basic source of wealth in an agricultural community. By controlling land, these elites were able to enslave others and force these people to work the land for them. In time the ruling classes developed the state, the laws, and the church to justify, protect, and perpetuate their economic and political privileges. The state is then seen as an exploitative mechanism created by the elites to control and oppress the workers. Marx promulgated a "labor theory of value," according to which capitalists steal much of the value that a worker produces, by paying the worker only a fraction of the value his labor confers on goods and produce and appropriating the rest.

According to Marxian theory, every economic system based on the division of society into socioeconomic classes and on exploitation carries within itself the seeds of its own destruction, because generally the means of producing wealth constantly improve, technologically and otherwise, and at a certain stage outgrow the social system constructed on them. Thus, slave societies would eventually give way to feudal societies and, eventually, communist societies will replace capitalist societies.

I. Diakonov has been the most prominent modern but traditional Marxist archaeologist. His model of early Mesopotamian state formation (Figure 7.4) rests on the assumption that if wealth differentials can arise, they will, and that once these differentials exist, antagonism between socioeconomic classes will follow and eventually the state will form to promote and protect the vested interests of the ruling class.[64]

Economists and others have challenged many of Marx's ideas, but evidence from early Mesopotamian and Egyptian societies does support some aspects of the Marxian reconstruction: wealth differentials developed early and were impressive, and slavery existed, as did communal labor pools, warfare, irrigation systems, trade networks, and other elements integral to the Marxian scheme. But that is not to say that this scheme is correct or complete. Much of it was constructed on the basis of evidence from early documents, and some forms of the Mesopotamian state evolved several hundred years prior to writing; thus the textual evidence is most likely of only limited relevance to the origins of social complexity. More important, it is very difficult to test the Marxian reconstruction with archaeological data. Without written records, we cannot conclusively demonstrate class conflict or slavery, and many of the crucial elements of the Marxian paradigm, such as the labor theory of value and the contradictions between economies and their social correlates, seem utterly beyond the reach of archaeological research per se. Zagarell uses documents from Mesopotamia, however, to show that by the time the first extensive texts were written, some correspondences do exist between Marxian ideas and what we know from these texts about property, the rights of women, etc.[65]

Other scholars have focused on the importance of trade in a Marxian context. Kipp and Schortman, for example, argue that an important factor in some cases of early state formation was the destabilizing effects markets in luxury goods had on early chiefdoms. In chiefdoms personal relationships between elites and the populace are important, but, as market economies evolved, chiefs and other elites had an increasingly difficult time trying to control these markets: "When leadership is undermined by a market blind to everything except profits, policies of systematic impoverishment are as essential to leaders as armies. Economic exploitation joins tyranny, and so states are born."[66]

Marvin Harris has tried to combine some of Marx's ideas with those of Wittfogel, Carneiro, and others to formulate a model that, although many reject it, at least has the advantages of being stipulated and partially testable with the archaeological data.[67]

Harris attributes the slower rate of the agricultural revolution in the New World to the lack of a large domesticable animal, thus the basic conditions from which societies in the New and Old Worlds were transformed into complex societies were somewhat different. But in both areas he thinks warfare was a common and early so-lution to the requirements of life as low-density cultivators. Warfare, he says, affects the demography of early cultivators in various ways. With its extreme valuation of and emphasis on males, warfare promotes female infanticide and nutritional neglect of young girls, thereby suppressing population growth rates; fights between members of villages and among villages foster the dispersal of villages, as people move away and create no-man's lands between them (which preserves ecological systems and hunting opportunities).

But the big step in Harris's view is the rise of chiefdoms, which he ties to the ap-pearance of "big men," particularly influential older men whose advice and guidance the community seeks. Village big men act as the "nodes" of three important institu-tional complexes: they intensify production, carry out redistribution of harvest sur-pluses and trade goods, and use their prestige and position to lead the way in fight-ing or trading with neighboring villages.

Harris says that simple

chiefdoms come into being with the first intensifier-redistributor-warrior complexes. The more production is intensified, the more there is to redistribute and to trade, the larger the population, the more intense the warfare, the more complex and powerful the chiefly sector. Other things being equal, all such systems tend to move from sym-metric forms of redistribution (in which the primary producers get back everything they produce) to asymmetric forms (in which the redistributor gets more of what is produced for longer and longer periods). Eventually the retained portion of the har-vest surplus provides the chief with the material means for coercing his followers into further intensification.[68]

If all this is a standard developmental trajectory, why did chiefdoms never appear among the Eskimo, while they appeared in Melanesia but stabilized at that level of development, and while they quickly became interregional states in Mesopotamia and many other areas?

Harris turns to basic factors of demography, economy, environment, and tech-nology to answer this question. He suggests that for chiefdoms to appear and then to become states and empires, the appropriate "energy gates" had to be available: yams and tubers are poor energy gates because they do not store well and have no clearly defined harvest period, so a big man or chief cannot easily shut off the flow of proteins and calories produced by the farmers; but grains store well and have de-fined periods of harvest, so a chief with command of community grain stores ab-solutely controls the lives of his associates.

Harris notes that the "paleotechnic infrastructures most amenable to intensifica-tion, redistribution, and expansion of managerial functions were those based on the grain and ruminant (e.g., cattle) complexes of the Near and Middle East, southern Europe, northern China, and northern India."[69]

Harris thinks that most advanced chiefdoms did not evolve directly into states, because they were based on incipient social stratification and other characteristics that made them relatively unstable and prone to factional disputes, revolts, and frequent migrations by people seeking to leave the sphere of influence of an exploitative chief.

Thus he expects the first "pristine" states to arise in areas of sharp ecotones, where there is good potential for intensifying agriculture, but where away from the agricultural lands the environment is such that a family would suffer a sharp drop in standard of living if they moved away.[70]

Drawing on the work of Robert Carneiro (see above), Harris identifies the sharply circumscribed farmlands of Egypt, Mesopotamia, northern India, the Yellow River Basin, central highland Mexico, the Peruvian coast, and the Andes highlands as areas where pristine states could be expected.[71] And once pristine states form in an area, their expansionist tendencies and economic impact act as a "single gigantic amplifier," as the whole region is caught in cycles of agricultural intensification, population growth, warfare, etc.

Harris explains the difference between early states principally in terms of their environments. The collapse of the Maya state in lowland central America he links to the limits on agricultural intensification in an area of relatively poor soil and prolonged drought. To explain Egypt, Peru, Mexico, and other cultural centers, he relies heavily on Karl Wittfogel's ideas about "oriental despotism" (see above). In those areas where a single river was the source of much of the agricultural wealth, highly stratified, centralized despotic states would emerge because of the needs for control, administration, and repair of irrigation works, and the ability of a single monarch to control such systems. But rainfall "agriculture leads to dispersed, multicentered forms of production. Hence it is doubtful that any pristine state ever developed on a rainfall base. Most rainfall states were probably secondary formations brought into existence to take advantage of the opportunity for trade and plunder created by the expansion of hydraulic empires."[72] Harris links the rise of feudalism and capitalism in the West to the fact that rainfall agriculture is not as easily controlled as the produce of a single great river system, such as in Egypt.

Harris's version of Marxist analysis is rejected by many as being too "vulgar" and "mechanical," in that it focuses on demographic and ecological variables and appeals to these as the primary explanations of differences and similarities in early states.

Contemporary Approaches to the Explanation of the Evolution of Civilizations

> *It is better to know some of the*
> *questions than all of the answers.*
>
> James Thurber (1894–1961)

Attempts by Childe, Wittfogel, Harris,[73] and others to formulate general models of cultural evolution, on the basis of correlations between techno-environmental and demographic variables and social and political patterns and processes, stimulated a great deal of creative research, and there is still much of value about these ideas (especially, I think, in the case of Carneiro[74]). But many contemporary scholars[75] argue that identifying correlations between these variables, patterns, and processes does not and cannot "explain" all the important aspects of the evolution of ancient civilizations. With the growing appreciation of the limits of techno-ecological analyses and traditional Marxist approaches, contemporary archaeologists have gone in many different directions in their approaches to the problem of the origins of civilizations.

Contemporary Marxist Perspectives   Many contemporary archaeologists continue to draw inspiration from Marx and his theoretical successors. Friedman and Rowlands,[76] for example, have interpreted Marx in such a way that the focus of the analysis is the social relations of production that economies embody, rather than just the blunt forces of technology, environment, and agriculture. Their study defies easy translation and summary, but contains at least the following elements. Friedman and Rowlands assert that we must "reconstruct the structures of reproduction of particular social forms," which they define as the "social structures that dominate the process of production and circulation and which therefore constitute the socially determined form by which populations reproduce themselves as economic entities."[77]

Although Friedman and Rowlands's complex approach includes much of interest, it involves various problems. The primary one is that so much of it seems untestable with the archaeological record. Testability with archaeological data cannot, of course, be taken as the ultimate criterion of social theory, but archaeologists must try to measure the "fit" of their ideas against the reality of the bones and stones they excavate. In Friedman and Rowlands's approach, as in so many Marxist and Structuralist endeavors, causation is expressed in terms of dominances and constraints. Friedman and Rowlands say that the physical environment, technology, and general economic forces impose a system of constraints that make certain kinds of things unlikely to evolve (like a drive-through bank set up and frequented by hunter-gatherers); but, working in the opposite direction, the relations of production dominate the entire functioning of the system, determining its characteristics and developmental pattern. To find "relations of production" archaeologically, however, and then to demonstrate how they were the causes of other cultural phenomena, is difficult. In Friedman and Rowlands's approach, something like an organized system of ancestor worship can—in a given society and instance—be the *result* of a complex of economic factors, and in another society and time organized ancestor worship can be a *cause* of economic behavior.

In general, many contemporary Marxist archaeologists are bound together by several basic ideas. One of these involves the rejection of "functionalist" ideas about adaptation. We might conclude, for example, that all early civilizations were rigidly stratified by socioeconomic classes because, in the absence of modern communications technology, an industrial base, and other means of economic production and social integration like those of contemporary societies, ancient civilizations could only organize themselves and function efficiently if their citizens were born into classes that automatically determined what occupational speciality they would perform and what access to wealth, power, and prestige they would have. Many Marxists reject this kind of functionalism and adaptationism on various grounds but particularly because such interpretations are descriptions, not explanations, and because they tend to emphasize the stability of these adaptations—and in so doing, justify them to some extent. Most forms of Marxism are about the necessity and social desirability of radical social change arising out of social conflict and inequities. It is not surprising, thus, that they see any attempt to interpret the appearance of such phenomena as social classses, legal systems, administrative bureaucracies, etc. as adaptive responses to problems societies faced as interpretations that obscure the conflicts and contradictions that are the true forces behind social changes. But contemporary Marxist critiques of traditional archaeology go much deeper than this. Marxists reject the notion that people in any society are just passive players whose actions and ideas are entirely the result of external forces. They focus on the social relationships that are the nexus of interactions among individuals and groups.

Marxism continues to have a strong influence on contemporary archaeology, although Marx himself might not recognize, or might reject, many contemporary applications of his ideas to the archaeological record. A continuing issue for Marxist archaeologists is the testability of their ideas in terms of the material remains of the archaeological record. In the absence of a written language, how are we to know if, for example, overt or institutionalized class conflict, or the subordination of women, or other social behaviors and concepts were part of the origins of the first states in the northern Andes—or anywhere else? If one rejects the notion that the archaeological record offers the possibility of a scientific and empirical test of the validity of *any* theory of history, however, as some archaeologists do, then the apparent difficulties of relating Marxian ideas to the material record of the past disappear.

The details of contemporary Marxist approaches are beyond the scope of this book, but the interested reader is referred to the bibliography of this chapter for additional sources on this topic.

Cultural Evolution   The term "cultural evolution" is heavily encrusted with past misuse and inappropriate applications, and for many scholars it immediately suggests that the analysis will be based on a false analogy with biology, will invoke sterile social typologies, will rearrange all human history in a sequence leading to the apex of Western civilization, and will apply capitalist and colonialist misperceptions to the analysis of history.

S. Gould summed up this view as follows: "Cultural evolution is not even a good analogue for biological evolution because it proceeds so much more rapidly and, especially, because it works by amalgamation and coalesence across lineages—the very topology precluded on the Darwinian tree of continuous divergence."[78]

The kind of evolutionary theory that some archaeologists now are applying to cultures, however, is different from the Spencerian form of traditional neo-evolutionism that was, in fact, guilty of many of these sins. Evolutionary theory basically concerns the transmission of traits through time and space, and there is no necessary linkage with biology. As Robert Dunnell has observed, what matters in evolutionary theory is not so much how a characteristic is transmitted—whether by genes or culture—as it is the mechanisms by which traits are perpetuated in an individual.[79] Thus, whether a person gets eye color through genetic inheritance or gets religious beliefs through parental instruction is irrelevant in the sense that both traits have been transmitted. Nonetheless, the objects that comprise the archaeological record do not reproduce in the same way that people do, and thus the rules of genetics cannot be applied; also, whereas change in the biological world is through the relatively slow processes of genetic mutation, drift, selection, and so on (see chapter 3), cultural changes can be conveyed quickly and pervasively from one group to another (as in the spread of agriculture). Ammerman and Cavalli-Sforza offer a relatively simple illustration of this in the form of their evolutionary model of the spread of agriculture across prehistoric Europe using evolutionary ideas as discussed in chapter 6.[80]

One issue in evolutionary models of cultural complexity involves the *scale* of selection. In the biological universe, the transmission of traits takes place at the level of the individual. The individual genes of the plant or animal do or do not get perpetuated, not the species as a whole. Therefore, the most productive point at which to analyze a given evolutionary problem is the transmission of traits from individual to individual. But in cultural situations, many individual traits, specifically behavioral ones, are the products of instruction by the complete community of parents, teachers, and friends. And people act in corporate groups in ways that make these the functional units of the society. For example, in the next chapter we will see that religions appeared early in all great civilizations and that these formed effective ways to get people to act in concert for the corporate good—such as in fighting wars, clearing irrigation canals, and building pyramids. To summarize, in the production and transmission of cultural characteristics, cultural selection can act on groups as well as individuals.

So, to apply evolutionary theory to archaeological data will require analyzing a great diversity of concepts of trait transmission.

Figure 7.2, a speculative reconstruction of change in selected variables in Egypt during its period of state-formation, is an attempt to illustrate some of these questions. This graph shows that had we enough data, we could try to find a point in time where intersecting patterns of rapid change occurred, which would suggest that in seeking the explanation of this cultural history we might concentrate our attention on that period. It also illustrates that not all variables—once adjusted for increasing population size—are significant in cultural evolution.

Many ambiguities and complexities are associated with applying evolutionary ideas to culture. To take a simple example, we assume that much of the human physiology is the product of long-term selection. Aging, for example, seems to make evolutionary sense, in that the life-span of a human being is probably the result of complex selection for organisms that can live long enough to reach reproductive age in a condition where they will make effective parents—that is, they know how to feed and secure their offspring. It is not clear that radically longer human life-spans would be "good" in some abstract sense. Change is essential to evolutionary sequences: each new generation offers new chances at evolution. Social evolution, and sometimes generation life-spans seem to explain much about evolutionary sequences, such as why perennial cereals were rapidly domesticated, whereas oak trees were not. Change in social forms, too, is the raw material of evolutionary sequences.

Even if we had the data to establish very accurately the kinds of variability hypothesized in Figure 7.2, however, we would not have explained the evolutionary history of ancient Egypt. These graphs serve only to draw our interest to the time, place, and variables that may be most important in the developmental pattern we are trying to understand.

The supposed "unification" of the Nile Delta and Valley cultures at about 3200 B.C. provides a useful example here. This pivotal event in Egyptian history apparently involved a process in which the cultural repertoire of the Valley cultures—in terms of artifact styles, political ideology, etc.—was imposed upon, or integrated into, or largely replaced, those of the Delta cultures.

How are we to understand such a process of trait-transmission? And, at a higher level, how are we to understand similar processes in other early civilizations? Consider again Trigger's conclusion, quoted earlier, concerning the extremely limited variations in what he observed in early states in their most important elements. In trying to account for this lack of variation, Trigger appeals to the apparent "efficiency" that these basic social and political forms must have conferred on their individual cultures. If we accept that supposition, the analytical problem then becomes one of understanding and measuring the relative efficiency of various mechanisms of social forms and phenomena—and the kinds of selection that operate on variability, and how that variability is generated in the first place. If evolutionary theory has any application to the analysis of ancient and modern cultures, it would seem to be precisely with regard to these questions of cultural change.

Another example of evolutionary change in the Egyptian archaeological record involves "waste." A distinguishing characteristic of early civilizations in Egypt, Mesopotamia, Mexico, Europe, and other areas is that each of them invested vast amounts of resources in pyramids, tombs, or other monumental constructions. Why should such elaborately "wasteful" structures appear in these rather primitive and fragile state economies? And why should they appear at the same point in the developmental trajectory of these states?

White, Dunnell, and others,[81] for example, have attempted to explain variations in the rate of monumental architecture construction and its geographic distribution in terms of factors of functional efficiency. The importance of pyramids and other monumental buildings in Egypt, Mesopotamia, Mexico, the North American southeast, and elsewhere, for example, has been interpreted in terms of their role in validating religious and political hierarchies, providing an impressive focus for the state apparatus, retarding unstable rates of population growth and economic expansion through "waste," and maintaining important local and foreign exchange networks. Dunnell[82] has drawn a parallel between Egyptian pyramid construction and many other examples of changes in the relative investment in "waste" of various cultures. In the late Paleolithic-Mesolithic transition, for example, highly crafted stone points, cave paintings, etc., seem to disappear and are replaced by a "drab" but functionally more complex technology. Both this transition and the decline of pyramid building, he suggests, may be linked to changes in carrying capacity. That is, the abundance of luxury goods, such as gold bowls, pyramids, or even spear points, tends to increase during the formative stages of adaptations, whether agricultural or not, because the production of these goods suppresses unstable rates of growth; luxury goods diminish in importance in these systems, however, once the adaptation has reached a new level of stability, through improved agricultural and craft production, more efficient governmental administration, or other factors.

Most early complex societies, for example, underwent a transition in which labor-intensive, highly decorated pottery was replaced by mass-produced forms of much less aesthetic appeal. Various scholars have seen cultural collapse and dissolution in such changes, but as Trigger notes, this replacement does "not indicate a decline in cultural or aesthetic standards. Instead it suggests that pottery no longer served as a medium of artistic expression."[83] In fact, the appearance of these mass-produced forms of pottery seems to be a prime indicator of increasing complexity in the institutions administering and controlling craft production. G. Johnson, R. McC. Adams,[84] and others have concluded that the rapid development of Southwest Asian states occurred during the period when the beautiful painted wares of the early fourth millennium were largely replaced by the unimpressive, mass-produced beveled rim bowl. Egyptian pottery seems to have made a parallel transition in the Early Dynastic and Old Kingdom periods, when various low-fired wares including "bread molds" were the dominant ceramic types.

Several factors may explain these dramatic changes in pottery manufacture. The individual and corporate social groups identified by regional pottery styles, for example, are, in a sense, dangerous expressions of individualism and group distinctiveness that detract from the unity of the larger state, and it is possible that these states suppressed some expressions of group identity not derived from the state structures. The greater efficiency, too, of producing massive quantities of cheap and nearly identical pottery vessels would be best realized in a state organization.

Other explanations of these changes in pottery decoration could be offered. But the important point here is that we need to construct the proper analytical units and make the necessary measurements of variability, if evolutionary theory is to be usefully applied to these changes in pottery decoration, to variations in investments in monumental architecture, and to many other changes evident in the Egyptian archaeological record.

Moreover, the formulation of a powerful evolutionary theory will require that we avoid the naive "functionalism" of early versions of cultural evolutionism: i.e., evolutionary theory must supply some explanation for cultural change other than that a given cultural characteristic made a positive contribution to a culture's efficiency of adaptation.

Many scholars have explored these issues.[85] The development of evolutionary theory as applied to archaeological data remains, however, at a relatively primitive level. Major questions remain about how one can use concepts such as "scale of selection" in cultural analyses. One interesting current trend in these forms of evolutionary analyses involves non-linear systems analyses and the "emergent" properties of complex systems. The recent book *Complexity*[86] popularizes research done by physicists, biologists, anthropologists, and others on the processes whereby simple systems grow in complexity in an apparently Lamarckian way—able to direct the generation of variety that is then selected. Lansing and Kremer[87] have published one of the first applications of these ideas to an anthropological problem, the evolution of Balinese economic systems.

Post-Processual Approaches to the Origins of Civilizations   As noted earlier, Shanks and Tilley, for example, refer to the "sledge hammer of cross-cultural generalizations"[88] that pulverizes meaning and significance in history. They suggest that such analyses are not only misguided, they result from conscious or unconscious attempts to further the cause of Western imperialism.[89] In contrast to materialist deterministic models, Giddens[90] and many others have emphasized the power of sociopolitical factors over economic factors as determinants of the character and histories of pre-industrial class-based societies. "Post-Processualists" and "Post-Modernists," in general, argue that "positivist" scientific epistemologies are fundamentally inappropriate for understanding the past.[91]

Critiques of the methodology of comparative studies have come from a wide variety of sources. Philip Kohl, for example, himself an advocate of a form of materialist theory, suggests that: "[l]inear models of class and state formation, which decontextualize social and historical processes, make meaningful comparative studies impossible."[92] Even some traditional Marxists[93] now emphasize how different cultures construct unique and—at some levels—incommensurable social forms and histories.

And it is not just the post-processualists and post-modernists who have challenged the validity of traditional anthropological comparative studies. Contemporary thought in evolutionary theory, as applied to both cultural and biological systems, emphasizes the uniqueness and essential unpredictability of evolutionary trajectories.[94]

If even evolutionists conclude that evolutionary sequences are unpredictable and unique, what is the importance of comparative analyses as applied to, for example, Old Kingdom Egypt and the Inka state?

Holistic and Synthetic Approaches   A "holistic" perspective, to use Bruce Trigger's term, is a multifaceted one in which any and every form of inquiry that seems to expand one's knowledge of the past is used. Trigger, for example, compiled a comparative analysis of the ancient civilizations of Egypt, Mesopotamia, China, Mesoamerica, and South America, as well as the early Yoruba state -—all chosen because they were class-based societies in which power was derived from control of agricultural production, and because there is relatively good archaeological, ethnographic, and textual data for each.

As noted above, Trigger found that a wide variety of economic behavior was associated with early civilizations, but that in every single one there was production of surpluses that the upper classes appropriated through a tributary relationship. He found only one basic form of class hierarchy, two general forms of political organization, and a single basic religious paradigm, and he was able to document significant variation from one early civilization to another only in terms of art styles and cultural values.[95]

Trigger argues[96] that the future of analyses of the origins of civilizations must include combining all our ideas, perspectives, and methods in a way that examines all the factors that "constrain" human behavior, in the present and the past. He notes that these constraints can be ecological, such as the great river valleys that were the homes of many of the first great civilizations and which directly determined the kinds of agriculture and settlement patterns that could be effective in this kind of environment, but he notes that these constraining and shaping factors can also be ideologies and cultural traditions.

Trigger dismisses the simplistic materialist determinism of, for example, Wittfogel,[97] and acknowledges the research importance of the unique aspects of early states. But in his concluding essay, he writes:

> [my] findings indicate that practical reason plays a greater role in shaping cultural change than many postprocessual archaeologists and postmodernist anthropologists are prepared to admit. This encourages me to accord greater importance to an evolution-

ist analysis and less importance to a cultural particularist one than I would have done when I began my study. A particularlist approach is necessary to understand many aspects of early civilizations. But it is clearly a mistake to ignore, or even to underestimate, the importance of evolutionism, as those who would privilege cultural reason would have us do.[98]

Trigger's contrast of the concepts of "practical reason" and "cultural reason" derives from Sahlins.[99] Sahlins argues that "material rationality exists for men not as a fact of nature but as a construct of culture. . . . The natural conditions of viability (selective forces) comprise merely negative constraints, limits of functional possibilities, which remain indeterminate with respect to the generation of particular cultural forms."[100] Moreover, he says, one can never read directly from material circumstances to cultural order as from cause to effect. "It is not that these techno-environmental variables have no effect, rather that everything depends on the way these properties are culturally mediated—given meaningful organization by a mode of cultural organization."[101]

As quoted above, Trigger's comparative analysis of early civilizations led him to a somewhat different conclusion than Sahlins. Trigger acknowledges the power and primacy of cultures to construct their own realities, but he also sees extremely limited worldwide variation in some of the core structures and processes of early civilizations.[102]

Trigger ascribes the lack of variation he observed in some of these elements to their relative "efficiency,"[103] and the great variations he observed in other elements to the fact that they have little effect on the adaptiveness and competitive success of the social organism of which they are a part. One can, therefore, usefully study what factors contribute to the "efficiency" of these rather invariant elements of early civilizations, perhaps from the "evolutionist" perspective Trigger suggests. But the baroque variability of "art styles and cultural values" provides ample material for particularistic studies that need not appeal to cross-cultural and comparative analyses for intellectual justification.

Trigger thus provides a justification and rationale for a wide variety of theoretical perspectives in archaeology, embracing both particularist studies and cross-cultural comparative analyses aimed at understanding the selective forces that so greatly constrained variation in some elements of these early civilizations.

Moreover, even in those elements that seem relatively invariant in early civilizations, there is considerable interesting variety in specific expression. Trigger suggests that many archaeologists have assumed "that aspects of civilizations that were shaped most directly by the constraints of environment and technology would display the greatest degree of cross-cultural uniformity."[104] He notes, however, that this is not the case. Metal working, for example, was a core industry in Mesopotamia, where it was used to produce tools as well as ornaments, whereas in Egypt it was used to make weapons but not often to make agricultural tools, and in the New World it was used exclusively to produce ornaments. Also, metallurgy seems to appear late in the formative sequence of these civilizations, but it seems to have appeared much earlier in the case of the Yoruba.

There may well be good functional reasons for these patterns (e.g., the scarcity of stone for implements such as hoes in Mesopotamia), but cultural constructs may be equally determinative even in such basic technologies as metallurgy.

Similarly, Trigger[105] sees no obvious correlation between variations among these civilizations in kinship systems and family organization, and in other environmental settings or political structures. In his chapter on the economic foundations of early states, Trigger compares these polities on the basis of agriculture, land ownership, taxation, authority, the army, and other factors, and he finds great variability but within the context of an overall similarity.

In his chapter on religion, Trigger states he initially assumed that, given the flexibility of the human intellect, religious behavior would vary much more greatly in early civilizations than economic behavior, but he concluded that this was not the case. He identifies strong recurrent patterns in many religious systems. Kings, for example, tend to trace their descent to strangers, probably in order to minimize their kinship obligations to the people they dominate. He suggests that all early civilizations had religious systems based on establishing social relationships with unseen forces in the natural world in order to manipulate it.[106] The early civilizations Trigger surveys are all ones, he notes, that existed prior to the appearance of "transcendent religions"—those that make strict distinctions between the social, the natural, and the supernatural.

Some of the commonalities in ideology that Trigger finds in early civilizations seem obviously understandable in functional terms. Most placed their own civilization in the center of a world that had four quarters corresponding to the cardinal directions; political competition was cast in terms of religious struggles; and the universe was once—or regularly—threatened with extinction and could only be saved by the intercession of gods, who had to be placated by human activities and earthly wealth.

In his concluding chapter, or "Postscript," Trigger examines the intellectual history of comparative studies in the light of his own analyses. He argues that two major ideas have impeded progress in comparative studies: Karl Wittfogel's concept of "oriental despotism"; and Karl Polyani's[107] denial of profit-motivated exchange in early civilizations. He then argues for the continued importance of a materialist research strategy—but coupled with a recognition of the importance and validity of particularistic studies and the power of ideology to construct sociocultural realities. He says, for example, that

> Far from undermining my faith in a materialist analysis of human behavior, the discovery that early civilizations with differing economic and sociopolitical systems had evolved a fundamentally similar set of religious beliefs confirms this faith. Religious beliefs are linked, both in general and also in specific terms, to the central economic institutions of early civilizations—the tributary relationship.[108]

In summary, Trigger's basic goal and strategy is to use many different ideas and techniques to analyze early civilizations—not in a simplistic positivist sense but, still, in a sense that does not admit the possibility that any "reading" of the record of the past is equally valid, equally "true." He stresses that cultural differences are as important in this context as are cultural similarities, and he admits particularistic studies as useful adjuncts in a synthetic approach to the past. But his basic goal is to understand why these similarities and differences appeared, and he invokes materialist and evolutionist ideas in this regard.

All explanations of cultural complexity focus on the similarities and differences that the various forms of cultural evolution exhibit. But what is the significance of these similarities and differences?

Stephen Jay Gould, in his book *Wonderful Life*,[109] emphasizes how every evolutionary sequence is unique; and the state of uniqueness, like that of pregnancy, permits no qualifications or degrees. But if every sequence is unique, what is the significance of the similarities of cultural systems unconnected by genetics or history? The Aztecs and the Egyptians—who knew nothing of each other and lived thousands of years separated in time—did many of the same things, from building pyramids to establishing state religions; but what is the significance of these similarities? Scholarly opinion, of course, remains divided on this point.

Brumfiel and Earle have categorized some of the variability they see in early civilizations in terms of three "models": (1) *commercial development models*, in which increasing occupational specialization and exchange are seen as the "natural" outgrowth of economic growth; (2) *adaptationist models*, in which political leaders are assumed to have intervened directly in the economy, to redistribute goods, for example, or to manage irrigation systems; and (3) *political models*, in which local rulers intervene in economies but, unlike their role in adaptationist models, these leaders are assumed to be the primary beneficiaries of their efforts.[110] Brumfiel and Earle propose that "political elites consciously and strategically employ specialization and exchange to create and maintain social inequity, strengthen political coalitions, and fund new institutions of control, often in the face of substantial opposition from those whose well-being is reduced by such actions."[111]

It is worth noting here that most of these many kinds of explanations of cultural complexity are *functional arguments*. The basic idea of a functionalist explanation was introduced above in the context of contemporary Marxist perspectives on archaeology. Functional arguments attempt to explain the origins of something (e.g., the human heart) in terms of the functions it performs (e.g., blood circulation). To the question, "Why do people have hearts?" the answer that some device is needed to circulate blood is an explanation of sorts, but it does not explain why some other kind of life-support system did not evolve, nor does it explain the evolutionary history of the heart or the selective pressures that shaped this history.

Similarly, to assert that complex societies developed because a leader was needed to coordinate irrigation and redistribute agricultural production is a functional explanation, and does not explain why the society did not remain egalitarian, or develop a capitalist economic system, or go off in some other developmental direction.

Yet functional explanations seem to work so well for certain phenomena. The national religious cults that all early states developed, for example, seem so transparently a device for social control. Montaigne said that "Man is certainly stark mad. He cannot make a worm, and yet he will be making gods by the dozen." But for an early state few things are as useful as gods in whom everyone believes. Then one can despise and kill (and take possession of the property of) all non-believers, foreign and domestic, without qualms; one is willing to sacrifice oneself in battles, or participate in pyramid building, or accept a social hierarchy, simply because the gods have so decreed. And the best part is that one does all these things without much cost to the state—people fight in wars, work for the common good, or accept life as a disenfranchised slave often on the premise that in the afterlife things will be greatly improved.

Thus, functionalist arguments have the strong heuristic value of suggesting hypotheses about a specific development and indicating crucial variable relationships. Marxist and other scholars see such functionalist interpretations as adequate *descriptions*, perhaps, but not *explanations*, which must involve, in their opinion, an analysis of the social relations out of which arise social changes.

SUMMARY AND CONCLUSIONS

In the rest of this book we will review numerous cases of the evolution of civilizations, but in all these analyses of cultural and social complexity, archaeologists must come to terms with a fundamental problem: most of the origins and development of ancient societies cannot be fully explained on the basis of the archaeologically retrievable facts of climate, technology, economy, and demography. Cultural evolution instead must be analyzed at some level above these basic conditions—at the higher level of the social, economic, and political relationships of peoples and social entities. But how do we get at these higher-level interactions through the data and methods of archaeology? Some archaeologists have concluded that we cannot do so in any scientific way, and thus archaeology cannot be a science; others argue that only the principles of evolutionary theory will help us understand these patterns of cultural change, but that we can never get at the specifics of the changes in social relations at the heart of the origins of civilizations; still other archaeologists believe that we can make inferences about these kinds of social changes and in various ways incorporate them in a holistic discipline of archaeological analysis.

The following chapters of this book, thus, should be seen as more of a *description* of the problems of analyzing the evolution of civilizations than an *explanation* of these evolutionary processes, for we are still very far from any powerful comprehensive explanation of them—and there is little agreement about how we might analyse these processes or even about the usefulness of trying to analyze them. If that summary sounds somewhat nilhilistic, it is well to recall that there is much about the pyramids of Egypt, the first written texts of Mesopotamian civilization, the glory that was Greece and the grandeur that was Rome, etc., that is interesting and rewarding to consider, even if we can't ultimately and utterly explain their origins.

BIBLIOGRAPHY

Adams, R. N. 1981. "Natural Selection, Energetics, and Cultural Materialism." *Current Anthropology* 22:603–24.
———. 1988. *The Eighth Day*. Austin: University of Texas Press.

Adams, R. McC. 1966. *The Evolution of Urban Society*. Chicago: Aldine.

⸻. 1981. *Heartland of Cities*. Chicago: Aldine.

Alexander, R. D. 1975. "The Search for a General Theory of Behavior." *Behavioral Science* 220:77–100.

⸻. 1979. "Evolution and Culture." In *Evolutionary Biology and Human Social Behavior: An Anthropological Perspective*, eds. N. Chagnon and W. Irons. North Scituate, MA: Duxbury Press.

⸻. 1987. *The Biology of Moral Systems*. Hawthorne, NY: Aldine de Gruyter.

Algaze, G. 1989. "The Uruk Expansion." *Current Anthropology* 30(5):571–608.

Ammerman, A. J. and L. L. Cavalli-Sforza. 1973. "A Population Model for the Diffusion of Early Farming in Europe." In *The Explanation of Culture Change*, ed. C. Renfrew. Pittsburgh, PA: University of Pittsburgh Press.

Appadurai, A., ed. 1986. *The Social Life of Things*. Cambridge: Cambridge University Press.

Athens, J. S. 1977. "Theory Building and the Study of Evolutionary Process in Complex Societies." In *For Theory Building in Archaeology*, ed. L. S. Binford.. New York: Academic Press.

Audouze, F. 1987. "Des modèles et des faits: Les modèles de A. Leroi-Gourhan et de L. Binford confrontés aux résultats récents." *Bulletin Societe Préhistorique Française* 84:343–52.

Aveni, A. F., ed. 1988. *World Archaeoastronomy*. Cambridge: Cambridge University Press.

Bahn, P. G., and J. Vertut. 1988. *Images of the Ice Age*. New York: Facts on File.

Bar-Yosef, O. 1987. "Late Pleistocene Adaptations in the Levant." In *The Pleistocene Old World: Regional Perspectives*. ed. O. Soffer. New York: Plenum Press.

Bard, K. 1994. *From Farmers to Pharaohs*. Monographs in Mediterranean Archaeology 2. Sheffield, England: Sheffield Academic Press.

Barnard, A. 1983. "Contemporary Hunter-Gatherers: Current Theoretical Issues in Ecology and Social Organization." *Annual Review of Anthropology* 12:193–214.

Bartel, B. 1982. "A Historical Review of Ethnological and Archaeological Analyses of Mortuary Practice." *Journal of Anthropological Archaeology* 1(1):32–58.

Bass, G. F. 1987. "Splendors of the Bronze Age." *National Geographic*, 693–732.

Bass, G. F., C. Pulak, D. Collon, and J. Weinstein. 1989. "The Bronze Age Shipwreck at Ulu Burun: 1986 Campaign." *American Journal of Archaeology* 13(4):271–79.

Beck, L. A., ed. 1995. *Regional Approaches to Mortuary Analysis*. New York: Plenum Press.

Bender, B. 1985. "Emergent Tribal Formations in the American Midcontinent." *American Antiquity* 50(1):52–62.

Berlinski, D. 1976. *On Systems Analysis*. Cambridge, MA: MIT Press.

Bernal, M. 1987. *The Afroasiatic Roots of Classical Civilization*. New Brunswick, NJ: Rutgers University Press.

Berry, B. 1967. *Geography of Market Centers and Retail Distribution*. Englewood Cliffs, NJ: Prentice-Hall.

Bettinger, R. I. 1991. *Hunter-Gatherers: Archaeological and Evolutionary Theory*. New York: Plenum Press.

Betzig, L. L. 1986. *Despotism and Differential Reproduction: A Darwinian View of History*. Hawthorne, NY: Aldine de Gruyter.

Binford, L. R. 1971. "Mortuary Practices: Their Study and Their Potential." In *Approaches to the Social Dimensions of Mortuary Practices*, ed. J. A. Brown. Memoirs of the Society for American Archaeology 25:6–29.

Blanton, R. E. 1995. *Houses and Households: A Comparative Study*. New York: Plenum Press.

Boserup, E. 1965. *The Conditions of Agricultural Growth*. Chicago: Aldine.

Boyd, R., and P. J. Richerson. 1985. *Culture and the Evolutionary Process*. Chicago: University of Chicago Press.

Braun, D. P. 1986. "Midwestern Hopewellian Exchange and Supralocal Interaction." In *Peer Polity Interaction and Socio-Political Change*, eds. C. Renfrew and J. F. Cherry. Cambridge: Cambridge University Press.

Bronson, B. 1980. "South-east Asia: Civilizations of the Tropical Forest." *Cambridge Encyclopedia of Archaeology*.

Brumfiel, E. M., and T. K. Earle, eds. 1987. *Specialization, Exchange, and Complex Societies.* Cambridge, England: Cambridge University Press.

———. 1987. "Specialization, Exchange, and Complex Societies: An Introduction." In *Specialization, Exchange, and Complex Societies*, eds. E. M. Brumfiel and T. K. Earle. Cambridge, England: Cambridge University Press.

Buck. R. C. 1956. "On the Logic of General Behavior Systems Theory." In *The Foundations of Science and the Concept of Psychology and Psychoanalysis*, eds. H. Feigl and M. Scriven. Minnesota Studies in the Philosophy of Science 1:223–28. Minneapolis: University of Minnesota Press.

Camp, J. M. 1986. *The Athenian Agora.* New York: Thames & Hudson.

Carniero, R. 1970. "A Theory of the Origin of the State." *Science* 169:733–38.

Carr, C., and J. E. Neitzel, eds. 1995. *Style, Society, and Person: Archaeological and Ethnological Perspectives.* New York: Plenum Press.

Cavalli-Sforza, L. L., and M. W. Feldman. 1981. *Cultural Transmission and Evolution. A Quantitative Approach.* Princeton, NJ: Princeton University Press.

Chagnon, N. *Yanomamö: The Fierce People.* New York: Holt, Rinehart and Winston.

Childe, V. G. 1934. *New Light on the Most Ancient East.* London: Kegan Paul.

———. 1936. *Man Makes Himself.* London: Kegan Paul.

Clark, J. G. D. 1986. *Symbols of Excellence: Precious Materials as Expressions of Status.* Cambridge: Cambridge University Press.

Cohen, G. A. 1978. *Karl Marx's Theory of History: A Defense.* Princeton, NJ: Princeton University Press.

Cohen, R. 1981. "Evolutionary Epistemology and Human Values." *Current Anthropology* 22:201–18.

Cook, B. F. 1987. *Greek Inscriptions.* London: British Museum Publications.

Costin, C. L. 1991. "Craft Specialization: Issues in Defining, Documenting, and Explaining the Organization of Production." *In Archaeological Method and Theory, Vol. 3*, ed. M. B. Schiffer. Tucson: University of Arizona Press.

———. 1996. "Ceramic Production and Distribution." In *Empire and Domestic Economy: Transformation in Household Economics of Xauxa Soceity Under the Inkas*, eds. T. D'Altroy and C. Hastorf. Washington, DC: Smithsonian Institution Press.

Costin, C. L. and T. Earle. 1989. "Status Distinction and Legitimation of Power as Reflected in Changing Patterns of Consumption in Late Prehispanic Peru." *American Antiquity* 54(4):691–714.

Cowgill, G. 1975. "On the Causes and Consequences of Ancient and Modern Population Changes." *American Anthropologist* 77:505–25.

Crumley, C. L. 1979. "Three Locational Models. An Epistemological Assessment for Anthropology and Archaeology." In *Advances in Archaeological Method and Theory, Vol. 2*, ed. M. B. Schiffer. New York: Academic Press.

———. 1992. "A Dialectical Critique of Hierarchy." In *Power Relations and State Formation*, eds. T. Patterson and C. Gailey. Salem, WI: Sheffield Publishing Company.

Crumley, C. L., and W. H. Marquardt, eds. 1987. *Regional Dynamics: Burgundian Landscapes in Historical Perspective.* Orlando, FL: Academic Press.

Darwin, C. 1871. *The Descent of Man and Selection in Relation to Sex.* New York: Appleton.

Demarest, A. A. and G. W. Conrad, eds. 1992. *Ideology and Pre-columbian Civilizations.* Santa Fe, NM: School of American Research.

Diakonov, I., ed. 1969. *Ancient Mesopotamia.* Moscow: Nauka.

———. 1991. *Early Antiquity.* Chicago: University of Chicago Press.

Drennan, R. D. 1995. "Chiefdoms in Northern South America." *Journal of World Prehistory* 9(3):301–40.

Drennan, R. D., and C. A. Uribe, eds. 1987. *Chiefdoms in the Americas.* Lanham, MD: University Press of America.

Dunnell, R. C. 1971. *Systematics in Prehistory.* New York: Free Press.

———. 1978. "Style and Function: A Fundamental Dichotomy." *American Antiquity* 43:192–202.

———. 1980. "Evolutionary Theory and Archaeology." In *Advances in Archaeological Method and Theory*, Vol. 3, ed. M. B. Schiffer. New York: Academic Press.

———. 1982. "Science, Social Science, and Common Sense: The Agonizing Dilemma of Modern Archaeology." *Journal of Anthropological Research* 38:1–25.

———. 1987. "Methodological Issues in Americanist Artifact Classification." In M.B. Schiffer (ed.), *Advances in Archaeological Method and Theory*, 149–27. New York: Academic Press.

———. Personal communication.

Dunnell, R. C., and R. J. Wenke. 1980. "An Evolutionary Model of the Development of Complex Societies." Paper presented at the Annual Meeting of the American Association for the Advancement of Science, San Francisco.

Durham, W. H. 1990. "Advances in Evolutionary Culture Theory." *Annual Review of Anthropology* 19:187–242.

Earle, T. K. 1987. "Chiefdoms in Archaeological and Ethnohistorical Perspective." *Annual Review of Anthropology* 16:279–308.

———., ed. 1991. *Chiefdoms: Power, Economy, Ideology*. Cambridge, England: Cambridge University Press.

Earle, T. and R.W. Preucel. 1987. Processual Archaeology and the Radical Critique. *Current Anthropology* 28(4): 501–38.

Eisenstadt, S. N. 1963. *The Political System of Empires*. New York: Free Press of Glencoe.

Ember, C. R. 1975. "Residential Variation among Hunter-Gatherers." *Behavioral Science Research* 10:199–227.

d'Errico, F. 1989. "Paleolithic Lunar Calendars: A Case of Wishful Thinking?" *Current Anthropology* 30:117–18, 491–500.

Evans, S. "Settlement Models in Archaeology." *Journal of Anthropological Archaeology* 1:275–304.

Flannery, K. V. 1972. "The Cultural Evolution of Civilizations." *Annual Review of Ecology and Systematics* 3:399–426.

———. 1973. "Archeology with a Capital S." In *Research and Theory in Current Archeology*, ed. C. L. Redman. New York: Wiley.

Fried, M. H. 1960. "On the Evolution of Social Stratification and the State." In *Culture in History*, ed. S. Diamond. New York: Columbia University Press.

———. 1967. *The Evolution of Political Society*. New York: Random House.

Friedman, J., and M. J. Rowlands. 1977. *The Evolution of Social Systems*. Pittsburgh: University of Pittsburgh Press.

Gamble, C. 1986. *The Palaeolithic Settlement of Europe*. Cambridge: Cambridge University Press.

Gellner, E., ed. 1980. *Soviet and Western Anthropology*. London: Duckworth.

Getz-Preziosi, P. 1987. *Early Sculptors of the Cyclades*. Ann Arbor: University of Michigan Press.

Giddens, A. 1981. *A Contemporary Critique of Historical Materialism, Vol 1. Power, Property and the State*. London: Macmillan.

———. 1985. *A Contemporary Critique of Historical Materialism, Vol 2. The Nation-State and Violence*. Cambridge: Polity Press.

Gould, S.J. 1989. *Wonderful Life*. New York: W.W. Norton.

———. 1987. *An Urchin in the Storm*. New York: W.W. Norton

Graber, R. B. 1994. *A Scientific Model of Social and Cultural Evolution*. Lanham, MD: University Press of America.

Harris, M. 1968. *The Rise of Anthropological Theory*. New York: Crowell.

———. 1977. *Cannibals and Kings*. New York: Random House.

———. 1979. *Cultural Materialism: The Struggle for a Science of Culture*. New York: Vintage Press.

Harris, M., and E. B. Ross. 1990. *Death, Sex and Fertility: Population Regulation in Preindustrial and Developing Societies*. Irvington, NY: Columbia University Press.

Hassan, F. 1988. "The Predynastic of Egypt." *Journal of World Prehistory* 2(2): 135–85.

Hastorf, C. A. and S. Johannessen. 1993. "Pre-Hispanic Political Change and the Role of Maize in the Central Andes of Peru." *American Anthropologist* 95(1):115–137.

Henry, D. O. 1989. *From Foraging to Agriculture*. Philadelphia: University of Pennsylvania Press.

Hill, J. N. 1977. *Explanation of Prehistoric Change.* Albuquerque: University of New Mexico Press.

Hill, K., and A. M. Hurtado. 1995. *Aché Life History: The Ecology and Demography of a Foraging People.* Hawthorne, NY: Aldine de Gruyter.

Hodder, I. 1986. *Reading the Past: Current Approaches to Interpretation in Archaeology.* Cambridge: England: Cambridge University Press.

Johnson, G. A. 1977. "Aspects of Regional Analysis in Archaeology." *Annual Review of Anthropology* 6:479–508.

———. 1980. "Rank-size Convexity and System Integration: A View from Archaeology." *Economic Geography* 56:234–47.

———. 1982. "Organizational Structure Scalar Stress." In *Theory and Explanation in Archaeology.* New York: Academic Press.

———. 1981. "Monitoring Complex System Integration and Boundary Phenomena with Settlement Size Data." In *Archaeological Approaches to Complexity*, ed. S. E. van der Leeuw. Amsterdam: University of Amsterdam.

———. 1987. "The Changing Organization in Uruk Administration on the Susiana Plain." In F. Hole (ed.), *The Archaeology of Western Iran.* Washington, DC: Smithsonian Institution Press.

Kemp, B. J. 1989. *Ancient Egypt: Anatomy of a Civilization.* London and New York: Routledge.

Kenoyer, J. M. 1991. "The Indus Valley Tradition of Pakistan and Western India." *Journal of World Prehistory* 5(4):331–85.

Kipp, R. S., and E. M. Schortman. 1989. "The Political Impact of Trade in Chiefdoms." *American Anthropologist* 91(2):370–85.

Kirch, P. V. 1988. "Circumscription Theory and Sociopolitical Evolution in Polynesia." *American Behavioral Scientist* 31(4):416–27.

———. 1990. "The Evolution of Sociopolitical Complexity in Prehistoric Hawaii: An Assessment of the Archaeological Evidence." *Journal of World Prehistory* 4(3):311–346.

Kohl, P. L. 1987. "The Use and Abuse of World Systems Theory." *Advances in Archaeological Method and Theory*, Vol. 11, ed. M. B. Schiffer. New York: Academic Press.

Lansing, J. S. and J. N. Kremer. 1993. "Emergent Properties of Balinese Water Temple Networks." *American Anthropologist* 95(1):97–114.

LeCarré, J. 1974. *Tinker, Tailor, Soldier, Spy.* New York: Knopf.

Lee, R. E. 1969. "!Kung Bushmen Subsistence: An Input-Output Analysis." In *Environment and Cultural Behavior*, ed. A. P. Vayda. Garden City, NY: Natural History Press.

Legros, D. 1977. "Chance, Necessity and Mode of Production: A Marxist Critique of Cultural Evolutionism." *American Anthropologist* 79:26–41.

Lewarch, D. E. 1977. "Locational Models and the Archaeological Study of Complex Societies: A Dilemma in Data Requirements and Research Design." Paper presented at the 76th Annual Meeting of the American Anthropological Association, Houston, Texas.

Locke, J. 1980 (orig. A.D. 1690). *Second Treatise on Government.* Indianapolis: Hackett.

Lumsden, C. J. and E. O. Wilson. 1981. *Genes, Mind, and Culture.* Cambridge, MA: Harvard University Press.

McCorriston, J., and F. Hole. 1991. "The Ecology of Seasonal Stress and the Origins of Agriculture in the Near East." *American Anthropologist* 93:46–69.

McGuire, R. H. 1992. A Marxist Archeology. San Diego: Academic Press.

McGuire, R. H., and R. Paynter, eds. 1991. *The Archaeology of Inequality.* Cambridge, MA: Basil Blackwell.

McGuire, R. H. and M. B. Schiffer. 1983. "A Theory of Architectural Design." *Journal of Anthropological Archaeology* 2:277–303.

Madsen, T. 1982. "Settlement Systems of Early Agricultural Societies in East Jutland, Denmark: A Regional Study of Change." *Journal of Anthropological Archaeology* 1:197–236.

Mann, M. 1986. *The Sources of Social Power I: A History of Power from the Beginning to AD 1760.* Cambridge: Cambridge University Press.

Marx, K. 1932. (orig. 1859). *Capital and Other Writings.* New York: The Modern Library.

———. 1973 (original manuscript 1857–1858). *Grundrisse: Foundations of the Critique of Political Economy*. New York: Vintage Press.

Marx, K., and F. Engels. 1970. *Selected Works*, in 3 Vols. Moscow: Progress Publishers.

May, D. A., and D. M. Heer. 1968. "Son Survivorship, Motivation and Family Size in India: A Computer Simulation." *Population Studies* 22:199–210.

Miller, D. 1985. "Ideology and the Harappan Civilization." *Journal of Anthropological Archaeology* 4(1):34–71.

Mithen, S. 1990. *Thoughtful Foragers: A Study of Prehistoric Decision Making*. Cambridge: Cambridge University Press.

Moore, A. T. 1985. "The Development of Neolithic Societies in the Near East." *Archaeology*. 4:1–70.

de Montmollin, O. 1989. *The Archaeology of Political Structure: Settlement Analysis in a Classic Maya Polity*. Cambridge: Cambridge University Press.

Neiman, F. D. 1995. "Stylistic Variation in Evolutionary Perspective: Inferences from Decorative Diversity and Interassemblage Distance in Illinois Woodland Ceramic Assemblages." *American Antiquity* 60(1): 7–36.

O'Shea, J. M. 1984. *Mortuary Variability—An Archaeological Investigation*. New York: Academic Press.

Patterson, T. C., and C. W. Gailey, eds. 1987. *Power Relations and State Formation*. Washington, DC: American Anthropological Association.

Peebles, C. S. 1971. "Moundville and Surrounding Sites: Some Structural Considerations of Mortuary Practices, II." In *Approaches to the Social Dimensions of Mortuary Practices*, ed. J. A. Brown. Society for American Archaeology Memoir no. 25.

———. 1987. "Moundville from 1000–1500 AD." In *Chiefdoms in the Americas*, eds. R. D. Drennan and C. A. Uribe. Lanham MD: University Press of America.

Peterson, N. 1993. "Demand Sharing: Reciprocity and the Pressure for Generosity Among Foragers." *American Anthropologist* 95(4):860–874.

Polyani, K., C. M. Arensberg, and H. W. Pearson. 1957. *Trade and Market in the Early Empires*. Glencoe: Free Press.

Price, T. D., and J. A. Brown, eds. 1985. *Prehistoric Hunter-Gatherers: The Emergence of Cultural Complexity*. Orlando, FL: Academic Press.

Price, T. D., and G. M. Feinman, eds. 1995. *Foundations of Social Inequality*. New York: Plenum Press.

Redman, C. L. 1978. *The Rise of Civilization*. San Francisco: Freeman.

Renfrew, C. 1972. *The Emergence of Civilization*. London: Methuen.

———. 1986. "Varna and the Emergence of Wealth in Prehistoric Europe." In *The Social Life of Things*, ed. A. Appaudrai. Cambridge: Cambridge University Press.

———. 1987. *Archaeology and Language*. London: Jonathan Cape.

Renfrew, C., and J. F. Cherry, eds. 1986. *Peer Polity Interaction and Socio-political Change*. Cambridge: Cambridge University Press.

Rindos, D. 1984. *The Origins of Agriculture*. New York: Academic Press.

Roberts, N. 1989. *The Holocene: An Environmental History*. Oxford: Blackwell.

Robins, G. 1986. *Egyptian Painting and Relief*. Aylesbury: Shire.

Rothschild, N. A. 1979. "Mortuary Behavior and Social Organization at Indian Knoll and Dickson Mounds." *American Antiquity* 44(4):658–75.

Roux, G. 1964. *Ancient Iraq*. Baltimore: Penguin.

Sabloff, J. A. 1989. *The Cities of Ancient Mexico*. London and New York: Thames & Hudson.

Sahlins, M. 1968. "Notes on the Original Affluent Society." In *Man the Hunter*, eds. R. Lee and I. DeVore. Chicago: Aldine.

———. 1976. *Culture and Practical Reason*. Chicago: University of Chicago Press.

———. 1978. "Comment on A. H. Berger's 'Structural and Eclectic Revisions of Marxist Strategy. A Cultural Materialist Critique.'" *Current Anthropology* 17:298–300.

Salmon, M. H., and W. C. Salmon. 1979. "Alternative Models of Scientific Explanation." *American Anthropologist* 81:61–74.

Sanders, W. T., and B. J. Price. 1968. *Mesoamerica*. New York: Random House.

Saunders, N. 1989. *People of the Jaguar*. London: Souvenir Press.

Schacht, R. M. 1988. "Circumscription Theory." *American Behavioral Scientist* 31(4):438–48.

Schele, L., and M. E. Miller. 1986. *The Blood of Kings: Dynasty and Ritual in Maya Art*. Fort Worth: Kimbell Art Museum.

Schwartz, G. M., and S. E. Falconer, eds. 1994. *Archaeological Views from the Countryside: Village Communities in Early Complex Societies*. Washington, DC: Smithsonian Institution Press.

Service, E. 1962. *Primitive Social Organization*. New York: Random House.

———. 1975. *Origins of the State and Civilization*. New York: Norton.

Shanks, M., and C. Tilley. 1987a. *Re-Constructing Archaeology*. Cambridge, England: Cambridge University Press.

———. 1987b. *Social Theory and Archaeology*. Oxford: Polity Press.

———. 1989. "Archaeology into the 1990s." *Norwegian Archaeological Review* 22(1):1–12.

Shennan, S. J. 1987. "Trends in the Study of Later European Prehistory." *Annual Review of Anthropology* 16:365–82.

———. 1988. *Quantifying Archaeology*. Edinburgh: Edinburgh University Press.

Smith, M. E. 1977. "State Systems of Settlement: Response to Crumley." *American Anthropologist* 79:903–6.

Spooner, B., ed. 1972. *Population Growth: Anthropological Implications*. Cambridge, MA: MIT Press.

Stein, G. J., and M. J. Blackman. 1993. "The Organizational Context of Specialized Craft Production in Early Mesopotamian States." *Research in Economic Anthropology* 14:29–59.

Steward, J. 1936. "The Economic and Social Basis of Primitive Bands." In *Essays in Anthropology in Honor of Alfred Louis Kroeber*. Berkeley: University of California Press.

———. 1949. "Cultural Causality and Law: A Trial Formulation of the Development of Early Civilizations." *American Anthropologist* 51:1–27.

Streuve, V. V. 1969. "The Problem of the Genesis, Development and Disintegration of the Slave Societies in the Ancient Orient," trans. I. Levit. In *Ancient Mesopotamia*, ed. I. M. Diakonov. Moscow: Nauka.

Tainter, J. A. 1987. *The Collapse of Complex Societies*. Cambridge, England: Cambridge University Press.

Teltser, P. A. 1995, ed. *Evolutionary Archaeology: Methodological Issues*. Tucson: University of Arizona Press.

Testart, A. 1982. "The Significance of Food Storage among Hunter-gatherers: Residence Patterns, Population Densities, and Social Inequalities." *Current Anthropology* 23(5):523–37.

Torrence, R. 1986. *Production and Exchange of Stone Tools: Prehistoric Obsidian in the Aegean*. Cambridge: Cambridge University Press.

Trigger, B. 1972. "Determinants of Urban Growth in Pre-Industrial Societies." In *Man, Settlement and Urbanism*, eds. P. J. Ucko, R. Tringham, and G. W. Dimbleby. London: Duckworth.

———. 1983. "The Rise of Egyptian Civilization." In *Ancient Egypt: A Social History*, eds. B. Trigger, B. J. Kemp, D. O'Connor, and A. B. Lloyd. Cambridge, England: Cambridge University Press.

———. 1984. "Archaeology at the Crossroads: What's New?" *Annual Review of Anthropology* 13:275–300.

———. 1985. "The Evolution of Pre-industrial Cities: A Multilinear Perspective." *Melanges offerts à Jean Vercoutter*. Paris: Editions Recherce sur les Civilisations.

———. 1989. *History of Archaeological Thought*. Cambridge: Cambridge University Press.

———. 1991. "Distinguished Lecture in Archaeology: Constraint and Freedom." *American Anthropologist* 93(3):551–69.

———. 1993. *Early Civilizations: Ancient Egypt in Context*. Cairo: American University in Cairo Press.

Valentin, B. 1989. "Nature et Fonctions des Foyers de'Habitation No. 1 à Pincevent." *Nature et Fonction des Foyers Préhistoriques.* Actes du Colloque de Nemours 1987. Mémoires du Musée de Préhistoire de l'Ile de France 2:209–19.

Waldrop, M. M. 1992. *Complexity.* Touchstone, New York.

Wallerstein, I. 1974. *The Modern World System.* New York: Academic Press.

Webb, M. 1975. "The Flag Follows Trade: An Essay on the Necessary Integration of Military and Commercial Factors in State Formation." In *Ancient Civilization and Trade*, eds. J. Sabloff and C. C. Lamberg-Karlovsky. Albuquerque: University of New Mexico Press.

Webster, D. 1975. "Warfare and the Evolution of the State: A Reconsideration." *American Antiquity* 40:471–75.

Weiss, R. M. 1976. "Demographic Theory and Anthropological Inference." *Annual Review of Anthropology* 5:351–81.

Wenke, R. J. 1981. "Explaining the Evolution of Cultural Complexity: A Review." In *Advances in Archaeological Method and Theory*, Vol. 4, ed. M. B. Schiffer. New York: Academic Press.

White, L. 1949. *The Science of Culture.* New York: Grove Press.

Wittfogel, K. A. 1957. *Oriental Despotism: A Comparative Study of Total Power.* New Haven: Yale University Press.

Wolf, E. R. 1966. *Peasants.* Englewood Cliffs, NJ: Prentice-Hall.

Woodburn, J. 1982. "Egalitarian Societies." *Man* (NS) 17:432–51.

Woodbury, R. B. 1961. "A Reappraisal of Hohokam Irrigation." *American Anthropologist* 63(3):550–60.

Wright, H. 1977. "Recent Research on the Origin of the State." *Annual Review of Anthropology* 6:379–97.

Wright, H., and G. A. Johnson. 1975. "Population, Exchange, and Early State Formation in Southwestern Iran." *American Anthropologist* 77:267–89.

Yellen, J. E. 1976. "Settlement Patterns of the !Kung: An Archaeological Perspective." In *Kalahari Hunter-Gatherers: Studies of the !Kung San and Their Neighbors*, eds. R. Lee and I. DeVore. Cambridge, MA: Harvard University Press.

Yoffee, N. 1979. "The Decline and Rise of Mesopotamian Civilization: An Ethnoarchaeological Perspective on the Evolution of Social Complexity." *American Antiquity* 44:5–35.

Yoffee, N., and G. Cowgill, eds. 1988. *The Collapse of Ancient States and Empires.* Tucson: University of Arizona Press.

Yoffee, N., and A. Sherratt, eds. 1993. *Archaeological Theory: Who Sets the Agenda?* Cambridge: Cambridge University Press.

Zagarell, A. 1986. "Trade, Women, Class, and Society in Ancient Western Asia." *Current Anthropology* 27(5):415–30.

NOTES

1. This topic is reviewed in the various articles in Price and Feinman, eds., *Foundations of Social Inequality.*

2. Trigger, *Early Civilizations: Ancient Egypt in Context*, p. 110.

3. Ibid., p. 110.

4. See, for example, Shanks and Tilley, *Re-Constructing Archaeology.*

5. Shanks and Tilley, *Re-Constructing Archaeology*, p. 95.

6. See, for example, Graber, *A Scientific Model of Social and Cultural Evolution*; Neiman, "Stylistic Variation in Evolutionary Perspective: Inferences from Decorative Diversity and Interassemblage Distance in Illinois Woodland Ceramic Assemblages"; Dunnell, "Science, Social Science, and Common Sense: The Agonizing Dilemma of Modern Archaeology."

7. See, for example, Demarest and Conrad, eds., *Ideology and Pre-columbian Civilizations*.

8. Crumley, "A Dialectical Critique of Hierarchy."

9. Bronson, "South-east Asia: Civilizations of the Tropical Forest," p. 262.

10. Roux, *Ancient Iraq*, p. 161.

11. Sahlins, "Notes on the Original Affluent Society."

12. Lee, "!Kung Bushmen Subsistence."

13. Peterson, "Demand Sharing: Reciprocity and the Pressure for Generosity Among Foragers."

14. LeCarré, *Tinker, Tailor, Soldier, Spy*.

15. Anyone interested in anthropology should read Chagnon's *Yanomamö: The Fierce People*, on which this following description is based. Also see Hill and Hurtado, *Aché Life History: The Ecology and Demography of a Foraging People*.

16. Chagnon, *Yanomamö: The Fierce People*, p. 8

17. Ibid.

18. Ibid., p. 75.

19. See also Hill and Hurtado, *Aché Life History: The Ecology and Demography of a Foraging People*.

20. Trigger, "Archaeology at the Crossroads: What's New?" p. 287.

21. Wenke, "Explaining the Evolution of Cultural Complexity: A Review."

22. Recently other typologies have been developed based on food storage and other characteristics.

23. Steward, "The Economic and Social Basis of Primitive Bands."

24. Barnard, "Contemporary Hunter-Gatherers: Current Theoretical Issues in Ecology and Social Organization," pp. 195–7; Ember, "Residential Variation among Hunter-Gatherers."

25. Flannery, "The Cultural Evolution of Civilizations."

26. Service, *Origins of the State and Civilization*.

27. Earle, "Chiefdoms in Archaeological and Ethnohistorical Perspective," p. 288.

28. Ibid.

29. See, for example, Earle, ed., *Chiefdoms: Power, Economy, Ideology*.

30. Drennan, "Chiefdoms in Northern South America." also see Drennan and Uribe, *Chiefdoms in the Americas*.

31. Wright and Johnson, "Population, Exchange, and Early State Formation in Southwestern Iran."

32. McGuire, *A Marxist Archeology* (also see Rindos, *The Origins of Agriculture*; Yoffee, "The Decline and Rise of Mesopotamian Civilization: An Ethnoarchaeological Perspective on the Evolution of Social Complexity"; Wenke, "Explaining the Evolution of Cultural Complexity: A Review"; cf. Wright, "Recent Research on the Origin of the State").

33. Costin, "Craft Specialization: Issues in Defining, Documenting, and Explaining the Organization of Production."

34. Brumfiel and Earle, "Specialization, Exchange, and Complex Societies: An Introduction," p. 5.

35. Kenoyer, "The Indus Valley Tradition of Pakistan and Western India."

36. White, *The Science of Culture*.

37. Binford, "Mortuary Practices: Their Study and Their Potential"; Rothschild, "Mortuary Behavior and Social Organization at Indian Knoll and Dickson Mounds"; also see Beck, ed., *Regional Approaches to Mortuary Analysis*.

38. See also O'Shea, *Mortuary Variability—An Archaeological Investigation*; Peebles, "Moundville and Surrounding Sites"; Bartel, "A Historical Review of Ethnological and Archaeological Analyses of Mortuary Practice."

39. O'Shea, *Mortuary Variability—An Archaeological Investigation*.

40. Berry, *Geography of Market Centers and Retail Distribution*.

41. Johnson, "Aspects of Regional Analysis in Archaeology"; Johnson, "Monitoring Complex System Integration and Boundary Phenomena with Settlement Size Data"; Evans, "Settlement Models in Archaeology"; Crumley and Marquardt, *Regional Dynamics*; Madsen, "Settlement Systems of Early Agricultural Societies in East Jutland, Denmark."

42. Trigger, "The Evolution of Pre-industrial Cities: A Multilinear Perspective," p. 343.

43. Trigger, "The Evolution of Pre-industrial Cities: A Multilinear Perspective," pp. 344-45.

44. See, for example, Schwartz and Falconer, eds., *Archaeological Views from the Countryside: Village Communities in Early Complex Societies*.

45. Darwin, *The Descent of Man and Selection in Relation to Sex*, p. 154.

46. John Locke, *Second Treatise on Government*, section 41.

47. See, for example, Steward, "Cultural Causality and Law: A Trial Formulation of the Development of Early Civilizations."

48. Athens, "Theory Building and the Study of Evolutionary Process in Complex Societies," p. 375.

49. Boserup, *The Conditions of Agricultural Growth*.

50. Athens, "Theory Building and the Study of Evolutionary Process in Complex Societies," p. 366.

51. Cowgill, "On the Causes and Consequences of Ancient and Modern Population Changes," p. 505.

52. Harris and Ross, *Death, Sex and Fertility: Population Regulation in Preindustrial and Developing Societies*.

53. Wittfogel, *Oriental Despotism*.

54. Woodbury, "A Reappraisal of Hohokam Irrigation."

55. Carniero, "A Theory of the Origin of the State," p. 734.

56. Webster, "Warfare and the Evolution of the State: A Reconsideration."

57. Schacht, "Circumscription Theory."

58. Kirch, "Circumscription Theory and Sociopolitical Evolution in Polynesia."

59. Quoted in Harris, *The Rise of Anthropological Theory*, p. 217.

60. Marx, *Capital and Other Writings*, pp. 10–11.

61. Quoted in Cohen, *Karl Marx's Theory of History: A Defense*, pp. viii-ix.

62. See, for example, G. A. Cohen's excellent *Karl Marx's Theory of History: A Defense*.

63. See, for example, Streuve, "The Problem of the Genesis, Development and Disintegration of the Slave Societies in the Ancient Orient"; or Diakonov, *Early Antiquity*.

64. Diakanov, *Ancient Mesopotamia*.

65. Zagarell, "Trade, Women, Class, and Society in Ancient Western Asia."

66. For example, Kipp and Schortman, "The Political Impact of Trade in Chiefdoms."

67. Harris, *Cannibals and Kings*; idem., *Cultural Materialism*.

68. Harris, *Cultural Materialism*, p. 92.

69. Ibid., p. 94.

70. Webster, "Warfare and the Evolution of the State: A Reconsideration"; Webb, "The Flag Follows Trade."

71. See Carniero, "A Theory of the Origin of the State."

72. Harris, *Cultural Materialism*, p. 105.

73. Childe, *New Light on the Most Ancient East*; Wittfogel, *Oriental Despotism: A Comparative Study of Total Power*; Harris, *Cultural Materialism*.

74. See Carneiro, "A Theory of the Origin of the State."

75. For example, Hassan, "The Predynastic of Egypt," p. 166; Trigger, "The Rise of Egyptian Civilization"; Bard, *From Farmers to Pharaohs*; Kohl, "The Use and Abuse of World Systems Theory."

76. Friedman and Rowlands, *The Evolution of Social Systems*; also see Patterson and Gailey, *Power Relations and State Formation*.

77. Friedman and Rowlands, *The Evolution of Social Systems*.

78. *An Urchin in the Storm*, pp. 33–34

79. Dunnell, "Evolutionary Theory and Archaeology."

80. Ammerman and Cavalli-Sforza, " A Population Model for the Diffusion of Early Farming in Europe."

81. White, *The Science of Culture*; Dunnell, *Systematics in Prehistory*.

82. Dunnell, personal communication.

83. Trigger, "The Rise of Egyptian Civilization," p. 64.

84. Johnson, "The changing organization in Uruk administration on the Susiana Plain"; R. McC. Adams, *Heartland of Cities*.

85. See, for example, Dunnell, ""Science, Social Science, and Common Sense: The Agonizing Dilemma of Modern Archaeology"; Rindos, *The Origins of Agriculture*; Lumsden and

Wilson, *Genes, Mind, and Culture*; Boyd and Richerson, *Culture and the Evolutionary Process*; Wenke, "Explaining the Evolution of Cultural Complexity: A Review"; Ammerman and Cavalli-Sforza, "A Population Model for the Diffusion of Early Farming in Europe"; Kirch, "The Evolution of Sociopolitical Complexity in Prehistoric Hawaii: An Assessment of the Archaeological Evidence"; R. N. Adams, "Natural Selection, Energetics, and Cultural Materialism"; Cavalli-Sforza and Feldman, *Cultural Transmission and Evolution. A Quantitative Approach*; Neiman, "Stylistic Variation in Evolutionary Perspective: Inferences from Decorative Diversity and Interassemblage Distance in Illinois Woodland Ceramic Assemblages"; Teltser, *Evolutionary Archaeology.*

86. Waldrop, *Complexity.*

87. Lansing and Kremer, "Emergent Properties of Balinese Water Temple Networks."

88. Shanks and Tilley, *Re-Constructing Archaeology*, p. 95a.

89. See, for example, Shanks and Tilley, "Archaeology into the 1990s."

90. Giddens, *A Contemporary Critique of Historical Materialism, Vol 1. Power, Property and the State.*

91. See, for example, Shanks and Tilley, *Re-Constructing Archaeology, Social Theory and Archaeology*, "Archaeology into the 1990s"; Hodder, *Reading the Past.*

92. Kohl, "The Use and Abuse of World Systems Theory," pp. 10–11.

93. See, for example, Diakonov, ed., *Early Antiquity.*

94. See, for example, Gould, *Wonderful Life.*

95. Trigger, *Early Civilizations: Ancient Egypt in Context*, p. 110.

96. Ibid., p. 563.

97. Wittfogel, *Oriental Despotism.*

98. Trigger, *Early Civilizations: Ancient Egypt in Context*, p. 112.

99. Sahlins, *Culture and Practical Reason.*

100. Sahlins, "Comment on A. H. Berger's 'Structural and Eclectic Revisions of Marxist Strategy. A Cultural Materialist Critique,'" pp. 298–299.

101. Ibid., p. 299.

102. Trigger, *Early Civilizations: Ancient Egypt in Context*, p. 110.

103. Ibid., p. 110.

104. Ibid., p. 8.

105. Ibid., p. 37.

106. Ibid.

107. Polyani, et al., *Trade and Market in the Early Empires.*

108. Trigger, *Early Civilizations: Ancient Egypt in Context*, p. 110.

109. Gould, *Wonderful Life.*

110. Brumfiel and Earle, "Specialization, Exchange, and Complex Societies: An Introduction."

111. Ibid., p. 3.

8

THE ORIGINS OF
COMPLEX SOCIETIES
IN SOUTHWEST ASIA

And Babylon, the glory of kingdoms, the beauty
of the Chaldees excellency, shall be as when God
overthrew Sodom and Gomorrah.
It shall never be inhabited, neither shall it be dwelt in from generation to
generation: neither shall the Arabian pitch tent there; neither shall the
shepherds make their fold there.
But wild beasts of the desert shall lie there; and
their houses shall be full of doleful creatures; and
owls shall dwell there, and satyrs shall dance there.
And the wild beasts of the islands cry in their desolate houses, and dragons
in their pleasant places: and her time is near to come, and her days shall
not be prolonged.

Isaiah 13:19–22

Isaiah did not predict the American bombs that landed near Babylon during
the 1990 Gulf War, but the rest of his dire vision of Babylon's future was fairly
accurate: for thousands of years, Babylon—once the brightest star in a galaxy
of brilliant ancient cities—was little more than a great rubbish heap. Current efforts to restore part of the city are luring a few tourists and ending the site's isolation.

Five thousand years ago, however, when many of the world's people were dirt-
poor illiterate farmers or hunters and gatherers, and when the peoples of the New
World were still many centuries from village life, Babylon and its surroundings were
a cosmopolitan world of cities, libraries, schools, international trade, roads, taxes, temples, and many of the other elements we identify with civilization. Indeed, much of
the world's population today is still living the *urban* way of life that first evolved in
these ancient Southwest Asian cities.

386

Southwest Asian cultural history is so rich, so ancient, that even short journeys here take one through dense histories (Figure 8.1). Before recent wars it was possible to drive from the eastern outskirts of Babylon, near Baghdad, Iraq—the heartland of the oldest cities in the world—north and east to Susa, one of the world's first true metropolises, where the Bible says Daniel and Esther once lived, then north through the area of some of the world's first farms, along the margins of the Zagros Mountains in Iran and Syria, and the foothills of the Taurus Mountains in Turkey. North from Syria through Turkey one crosses the same terrain that Xenophon tells us ancient Greek soldiers traversed as—homesick for Greece—they fought their way to the Black Sea to ships to take them home.[1] South from Turkey through Syria and along the Mediterranean coast one follows a route very close to that taken by European crusaders a millennium later, to effect the fateful collision of Christianity and Islam.

Amidst the ruins of these millennia of civilization, scholars have tried to sort out much about the human condition. This, after all, was the homeland of several of the world's great religions and the place where writing, cities, metallurgy, and many other aspects of civilization first appeared. And all the obvious questions apply: Why here? Why in forms so strikingly similar to later developments in China, Egypt, Mesoamerica, and elsewhere?

FIGURE 8.1   Southwest Asia. The world's first complex societies evolved in the alluvial plains of the Tigris and Euphrates Rivers and their tributaries, but they had their origins in these early agricultural communities.

THE ECOLOGICAL SETTING

Two ecological elements are particularly important to analyses of Southwest Asian cultural history: first is the great diversity and reliability of agriculture in this area, and second is the impressive diversity of its cultures and its openness to regional and international cultural influences. As Nicholas Postgate observes:

> Egypt, physically constrained within the narrow strip of the Nile Valley and isolated from western Asia, retained its highly idiosyncratic identity with little infusion from elsewhere, and did not export its language or script or other artistic forms, except up-stream to Nubia. Mesopotamia was open along both flanks to intrusion from the desert and mountain, and its cuneiform script was exported across thousands of miles.[2]

The first states and cities appeared in a relatively small area of southern Iraq and Iran, but the factors that produced them involved most of the Fertile Crescent and the surrounding lowlands it encompasses, or "Greater Mesopotamia," as it is known (Figure 8.1).

The lower elevations of the great arc of mountains of the Fertile Crescent were the natural habitats of wild wheat, barley, sheep, and goats. In ancient times this area was covered with vast grasslands and oak and pistachio forests, and, even as late as the nineteenth century, sheep grazing these verdant uplands were brought to lowland markets with their wool stained scarlet by wildflowers in their range. Today the forests are almost entirely gone, and the whole area is severely overgrazed.

From the very beginnings of life on the alluvial lowlands, people there fought and traded for the gold, silver, copper, stone, wheat, sheep, and goats of the mountain areas. Today there is still no better way to integrate the highlands and lowlands economically than this same ancient pattern in which nomads and herders take sheep and goats to these highlands in the lush summer months, using the animals to convert mountain vegetation into milk, meat, and hides, which can then be exchanged for lowland products.

Below the high ridges of the Zagros and Taurus mountains, the foothills and rolling plains of the piedmont saw some of the world's earliest agricultural villages. Ancient Neolithic farms are found here almost every place rainfall is sufficient to grow wheat and barley with reasonable reliability.

Coming down from the piedmont, one finds north and northwest of Baghdad the dry, undulating northern Mesopotamian Plains. The Tigris and Euphrates have cut deeply into the land surface, so that irrigation here requires sophisticated damming and canalization. But with irrigation, the high productivity of this area made these northern plains the "breadbasket" of some of the greatest empires of antiquity.

For the very first cities, however, the heartland is the lower alluvial plains of Mesopotamia. Historian Arnold Toynbee argued that civilizations first evolved in physical circumstances that challenged the inhabitants to overcome severe problems of climate and resources, and he was thinking in part about southern Mesopotamia. Nothing in this region appears to account for its pivotal role in human history. The unprepossessing hot plains have no usable stone or metal, few trees, and a climate whose extremes of heat and humidity have been a main topic of conversation for generations of archaeologists.

But most early civilizations are the "gift" of some great river system, and this is particularly true of Mesopotamian cultures (in fact, "Mesopotamia" means "between the rivers" in Greek). The Tigris and Euphrates rivers created the alluvial plain with annual deposits of flood-borne fertile silt and clay, and they provide the irrigation water that makes agriculture possible here. The swamps and wetlands formed by the rivers support a variety of usable wild plants, such as flax for textiles and rushes for basketry, but in addition to these plants and water for irrigation, the major gift of the rivers is fish. The scrub forests along the rivers cannot support many game animals, and thus fish—and later, domestic cattle—furnished the protein indispensable to survival on the alluvial plain. Vegetarianism was not an option for ancient agriculturalists here, because the blend of vegetable proteins necessary to substitute for animal protein was not always available. Fish fill this lack admirably, however, and many clues point to their importance for the early inhabitants: "altars" in buildings dating to the fifth millennium B.C. have been found covered with layer upon layer of fish bones. Mesopotamia's rivers also provided a vital transportation artery. None of these rivers was as navigable as the Nile, for example, but with the proper boats one could move goods, armies, etc. from ports along the Turkish and Syrian foothills, south through the heart of Mesopotamia.

From May to October, the average daily high temperature is over 40°C (104°F), and hot winds dry the soil to the depth of a meter and darken the sky with choking clouds of dust. Anyone who has spent a summer in Mesopotamia understands why several Middle Eastern religions have envisioned heaven's primary recreation to be sitting by shaded streams in cool palm groves, eating fruit, in complaisant company. But the fiery summers are balanced by temperate, lovely, warm autumns, winters, and springs; and with adequate irrigation, the Mesopotamian alluvial plain richly rewards those who farm it, so that throughout history this region has been celebrated for its melons, oranges, pomegranates, dates, wheat, barley, olives, lentils, onions, and other crops.

Part of Mesopotamia's rich agricultural heartland is enclosed in large deserts, from Syria far into the Arabian peninsula. Nomads and pastoralists eventually occupied some of these areas, and trade routes crossed them, but even in our own age some of these desert areas are only sparsely inhabited.

As noted in chapter 4, Southwest Asia in the Pleistocene can be thought of as an extension of Africa, in terms of its climates, flora, and fauna, and even as late as a few thousand years ago African animals such as ostriches, cheetahs, lions, and hartebeest were common in large areas of Southwest Asia.

The climates and physical geography of Southwest Asia have been much the same for the past nine thousand years, with some variations. At times tectonic movements have raised or lowered Mesopotamia, and these movements, in combination with fluctuations in the water level of the Persian Gulf and the deposition of massive amounts of alluvial silts and clays in some areas, have made it difficult to determine where the coastline was during the past 10,000 years. Some areas, for example, that were farmed a millennium ago are now underwater, and it is possible that some important parts of the ancient archaeological record are under the Gulf, too. Human alterations of river courses, deforestation, and climate changes have so greatly altered the landscape (and probably even microclimates) that we may never have an entirely clear picture of what Southwest Asia was like as a natural landscape when its first civilizations began forming.[3]

FUNDAMENTALS OF THE SOUTHWEST ASIAN ARCHAEOLOGICAL RECORD

Southwest Asian peoples have lived in villages for nine millennia, and there is hardly a square meter there that does not contain a few sherds, stone tools, bones, or old irrigation canal banks. Nevertheless, the most common unit of analysis in Southwest Asian archaeology is still the "site," which usually takes the form of a mound, referred to as a *tell* (Arabic) or *teppeh* (Persian). These tells are a result of the construction and continual reconstruction of villages or towns on the same spot (Figure 8.2). For thousands of years, people here have used mudbricks as their basic building material, and their settlements have taken the form of closely packed, small, rectangular structures. Although ideally suited to the climate and resources of the area, such buildings become so dilapidated after fifty or a hundred years that it is easier to rebuild than to repair them, and because there are incentives to rebuild on the same spot (less land is lost to cultivation and higher elevation gives better drainage and protection against floods and attack), settlements become mound-shaped as they are constantly reconstructed on the debris of the previous ones.

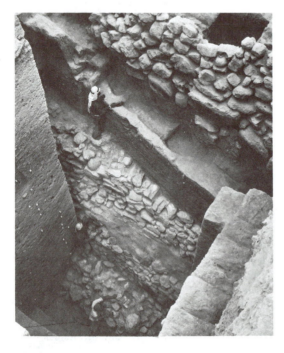

FIGURE 8.2 Millennia of rebuilding at Jericho formed many superimposed layers containing stone walls.

Hundreds of thousands of such mounds dot the Southwest Asian landscape, some of them rising fifty meters or more above plain level, while others—occupied for only a few decades or so—are only imperceptibly higher than the surrounding plains. The mounds are littered with stone tools, bones, broken pottery, broken clay bricks, collapsed walls, eroding ovens and pottery kilns, and corroding metal. Burrowing animals, well and terrace construction, and erosion often mix the layers of these mounds so that usually one finds the remnants of every phase of a site's occupation on its surface. This allows archaeologists to estimate a site's periods of occupation simply by inspecting the surface artifacts. At some sites bones and floral remains are well preserved, but at other sites, such as those in areas with a high level of salty groundwater, even ceramics do not preserve well.

Besides mounds, the most obvious archaeological features of Southwest Asia are irrigation canals. Seven millennia of irrigation agriculture have resulted in a landscape criss-crossed with canals, and it is not unusual to find abandoned irrigation canals several thousand years old with banks still two or three meters high. Aerial photographs are particularly useful in charting these ancient waterworks.

Because of the time and expense of archaeological excavation and the destruction of sites, far less than five percent of all sites dating from 8000 to 2350 B.C., for example, have been, or will ever be, properly excavated, and thus our interpretations must be tempered with some tentativeness. On the other hand, the rich archaeological remains provide an opportunity to use sampling procedures and to test hypotheses; and by using aerial reconnaissance, surface surveys, and regional analyses, archaeologists can determine when and for how long unexcavated sites were occupied. In the case of Mesopotamia, a generation of archaeologists has followed Robert McC. Adams in performing regional surveys.[4] In many of these surveys, archaeologists have used aerial photographs and maps to locate ancient sites, and then made maps of these individual sites and collected ceramics from them to infer their cultural histories. But Southwest Asia's archaeological record is so vast that many hundreds of thousands of ancient towns and villages will probably never be excavated —and many hundreds of thousands more have already been destroyed by agricultural expansion and industrialization.

THE NEOLITHIC ORIGINS OF SOUTHWEST ASIAN CIVILIZATION (C. 7000–6000 B.C.)

When we left the first farmers of Southwest Asia in chapter 6, they were living in thousands of small villages, from Afghanistan to western Turkey, occupying in small numbers those areas with sufficient rainfall to support wheat and barley without extensive irrigation. In most areas the simple village farming way of life continued largely unchanged into the last few millennia B.C., but in other areas changes were underway by 7000 B.C.

We saw in chapter 6 that soon after 7000 B.C. people at Jericho, in Jordan, for example, began building stone walls and other buildings that indicate that they were beginning to direct their energies in a way quite different from that of most hunters and gatherers. Also, the apparent ancestor cult at Jericho, in which human skulls were plastered with clay and fitted with eyes made from seashells, and the clay figures of people and animals at sites such as 'Ain Ghazal, in Jordan, suggests a changing social context of village life.

Some of the most dramatic evidence of these social changes has been found in Turkey, at Çatal Hüyük (pronounced rather like Chatal Huooyook). James Mellaart, who excavated much of this site, suggested that

> It may be said without undue exaggeration that Anatolia, long regarded as the bar-barous fringe to the fertile crescent, has now been established as the most advanced center of neolithic culture in the Near East. The neolithic civilization revealed at Çatal Hüyük shines like a supernova among the rather dim galaxies of contemporary peas-ant culture.[5]

Çatal Hüyük may not merit all the superlatives its excavators have showered on it, but it is one of the most interesting sites in Southwest Asia. Located in south central Anatolia (Turkey) and first occupied at about 6250 B.C., Çatal Hüyük was probably inhabited continuously until its abandonment at about 5400 B.C. During some of this time it may have extended over thirteen hectares and had a population of about 4,000 to 6,000—several times larger than any other known site in this period.

A great fire swept through Çatal Hüyük in the middle of its history, nicely pre-serving the earliest levels, but unfortunately only less than a hectare of the site was excavated before the project was ended by political disputes and other problems.

Nestled against the first ranges of the Taurus Mountains, Çatal Hüyük controls access to a critical resource: the obsidian sources at the Hasan Dag volcano. Because each obsidian source is chemically distinctive, we can track the great quantities of ob-sidian from the Çatal Hüyük area that were distributed throughout Anatolia, the Lev-ant, and Cyprus (Figure 8.3) after 7000 B.C. Beautiful obsidian artifacts were found in Çatal Hüyük itself, but so far no obsidian storage or workshop areas have been discovered in the small fraction of the site that has been excavated.

Most of the 158 structures uncovered at Çatal Hüyük are not very different from their contemporaries elsewhere in Southwest Asia: each is built of shaped mud and composed of rectangular rooms with plastered walls and floors, and most houses are about twenty-five meters square, one story high, and abut one another, except where occasionally separated by an open courtyard. Inside most rooms are two raised plat-forms, probably for sleeping, and an occasional rectangular bench. Unlike any other community of this period and area, access to the rooms of Çatal Hüyük was only by ladder through the roof—there are no front doors—and the close packing of struc-tures is such that much of the movement among the houses must have been on the roofs. The roof access may reflect a need for defense, for once the inhabitants had pulled up the ladders on the outside walls, the settlement would have been difficult to attack. Other Southwest Asian sites had walls at this time, but most settlements were small unfortified hamlets.

The forty or so shrines at Çatal Hüyük have essentially the same floor plan as the other structures, but their walls are richly decorated with paintings, reliefs, and engravings expressing many naturalistic themes, most concentrating on the two fa-vorites of ancient art—fertility and death. Vultures are portrayed ripping apart head-

FIGURE 8.3   The circulation of obsidian throughout Southwest Asia was an important economic process that may have contributed to the evolution of political and economic institutions.

less human corpses, women give birth to bulls and ride leopards, and other symbols such as breasts, vultures, bulls, and rams abound. Some of the rooms have intricate arrangements of cattle skulls and horns (Figure 8.4). Walls were plastered and then painted, and periodically the walls were replastered and new designs were painted or engraved on them. One wall was plastered and painted forty times. These shrines do not seem to have required the expenditure of vast amounts of labor and resources for essentially noneconomic purposes, as did the monumental constructions of later periods. Nor do they enclose radically different amounts of expensive goods, indicating great wealth disparities. Little about them, in fact, conflicts with the interpretation that they were kinship-cult centers in a simple ranked society.

Such a conclusion would be strengthened if we found only minor variability in mortuary practices, and indeed this seems to be the case. Many corpses appear to have been taken outside the settlement and exposed to the vultures and the elements until the flesh was gone, after which the bones were interred in the house floors. Men, women, and children were buried in much the same way, either in baskets or simply in holes. Most of the graves contained no goods, but some women and children were accompanied by shell and stone necklaces, armlets and anklets, and, occasionally, obsidian mirrors and bone cosmetic implements. Some men were buried with mace heads, flint daggers, obsidian projectile points, clay seals, and other items.

In one complex of rooms, the so-called Vulture Shrine, six individuals were buried in the floor with significantly richer grave goods than were found in the residential

FIGURE 8.4   These reconstructions of "cult-centers" at Çatal Hüyük show the importance of the cattle motif. All early complex societies evolved rituals and religions that functioned as organizing and controlling institutions.

burials.[6] However, we do not find any infants at Çatal Hüyük buried with disproportionately rich or numerous grave goods, nor is there any significant variation in construction expense of the graves themselves; there are no stone coffins, tombs, or the like.

The people of Çatal Hüyük subsisted on the typical late Neolithic combination of agriculture, hunting, and gathering. Emmer, another kind of wheat known as "einkorn," barley, pea vetch, and other crops were grown in quantity, but with simple techniques. Domestic cattle supplied meat, hides, milk, and perhaps traction: even simple cattle-drawn wood plows that do no more than scratch the surface greatly increase agricultural productivity by suppressing weeds and increasing soil permeability. We do not know when the first plows were used in the Middle East, but the domestication of cattle probably did not precede the development of the plow by more than a millennium or two.

Trade at Çatal Hüyük was considerable, but mainly in small quantities of exotic items. Shells from the Mediterranean (160 kilometers distant) and Syrian flint were found here, perhaps taken in trade for obsidian artifacts (Figure 8.3). But there is no evidence of voluminous trade in agricultural products, or even in large amounts of obsidian, and there are no obvious workshops for goods, no stores of obsidian, no complex technologies.

Settlements dating to between 7500 and 6000 B.C. have also been found else-where in Anatolia, but all are very simple, undifferentiated farming communities with little discernible public architecture, intense occupational specialization, or elaborate mortuary practices.

Jarmo, in Iraqi Kurdistan, is an example of the drab peasant culture that Mellaart invidiously compared to Çatal Hüyük. Jarmo was first settled sometime before 6750 B.C. and was occupied intermittently to 5000 B.C., and thus it overlaps with Çatal Hüyük for perhaps as much as 1000 years. But unlike Çatal Hüyük, Jarmo was prob-ably home to no more than 200 people, and for most of its existence it consisted of only about twenty small mud houses. Burials at Jarmo are quite uniform, as are the contents of the houses. There is not nearly the diversity of aesthetic expression found at Çatal Hüyük in wall paintings, finely worked obsidian, or the like; there are just a few clay figurines of pregnant women and animals. Jarmo has no fortified walls or large, nonresidential buildings, and the technology seems to have been mainly de-voted to the processing of plant foods. Perhaps the most significant difference be-tween the two sites is that Çatal Hüyük controlled a localized and important resource (obsidian), whereas Jarmo did not.

Elsewhere in the Zagros, northern Mesopotamia, and the Iranian Plateau, most communities established between 8000 and 6000 B.C. were also farming villages, with little public architecture, elaborate mortuary cults, or occupational specialization.

Charles Redman has pointed out that

> Çatal Hüyük exemplifies those communities that may have made many of the crucial advances leading to civilization, but for one reason or another did not become urban societies. In some ways, the town of Çatal Hüyük and its inhabitants should be con-sidered a premature flash of brilliance and complexity that was a thousand years be-fore its time.[7]

The various excavations at Jericho, Çatal Hüyük, Jarmo, and other sites provide a picture of the kinds of communities that immediately preceded civilization in South-west Asia, but we still lack many elements of this picture. In a rightly ordered world, the combined international archaeology faculties and their students—funded by the United Nations—would begin surveys in western Anatolia and work their way east into Afghanistan and south into Iraq, mapping and excavating sites along the way. In-stead, our evidence for the world's first socially complex societies is gathered mainly from fewer than a hundred well-excavated settlements and perhaps twenty or thirty regional site surveys in this huge area.

FIGURE 8.5 Halafian and Samarran (bottom two vessels) pottery styles spread over large areas of sixth millennium B.C. Mesopotamia.

INITIAL CULTURAL COMPLEXITY
(C. 6000–4000 B.C.)

An early indication of social change in Southwest Asia is evident in the distribution of pottery styles. As with agriculture, the invention of pottery seems to have occurred independently in many areas of Southwest Asia, where clay had been used for centuries for figurines and storage pits. The multiple origins and rapid spread of pottery after about 6500 B.C. no doubt reflect the increasing importance of containers in these agricultural economies—probably for carrying water and for storing, cooking, and serving food.

Soon after ceramic vessels came into general use in Southwest Asia, the first sophisticated pottery styles appeared, and by about 5500 B.C. two distinctive styles, the Samarran and the Halafian, had achieved wide distribution (Figures 8.5 and 8.6)[8] Samarran pottery tends to be simpler in shape than the Halafian and is painted in matte colors, whereas the Halafian colors are glossy. Halafian and Samarran ceramics are important beyond their aesthetics: they are the first complex styles of artifacts to be so widely distributed. These highly stylized ceramics were first made with a tournette, a wooden slab affixed to a peg that could be set in a hole in the ground that acted as a pivot around which the slab could be turned by hand. Simple as this sounds, it was a major advance over simply hand-molding a pot; the tournette allowed

FIGURE 8.6 Distribution of Samarran and Halafian pottery. One of the first steps in the evolution of complex societies seems to be a rapid expansion of an art style over a large area.

the potter to turn the pot to shape and paint it.[9] So intricate and delicate are the Halafian and Samarran designs that one might assume that specialists produced them. But Frank Hole cautions us not to underestimate the skill of villagers— Persian carpets being just one example of an extraordinarily complex and beautiful product made by simple villagers.[10] And despite the wide geographical distribution of the Halafian and Samarran designs, there is little evidence that ceramic production was centrally organized and administered. Exactly what kinds of social changes the spread of these styles may reflect remains obscure. Their distributions tend to overlap a great deal and there is no convincing proof that they belong to different time periods or social groups.[11] Yet people of the Halafian era transported decorated pottery over distances of almost 1000 kilometers, and it is difficult to believe that this was a simple utilitarian and cost-effective adaptation to the growing need for containers in agricultural economies. Pottery is heavy, breaks easily, and can be made from local materials in nearly every part of Southwest Asia, so why transport it in massive quantities? The expanding zones of distribution of Halafian and other decorated ceramics would seem to make the most sense as expressions of a growing sense of social status and political allegiance. At some point in every ancient civilization, elites were able to begin appropriating elaborate and exotic goods and use them to indicate their status and power. Perhaps these early pottery styles are early indications of this process of the emergence of elites.

The distribution of Halafian and Samarran ceramics coincides with the extension of cultivation to the arid areas of Mesopotamia, and this involved what may have been the world's first systematic artificial irrigation systems. At sites such as Choga Mami, in the areas just east of Baghdad, for example, people used irrigation canals to grow cereals, linseed (for oil), and other crops. Another significant site of this period is Tell as-Sawwan, located in north central Iraq at the juncture of the northern arid steppe country and the alluvial plains.[12]

Preliminary excavations indicate that from 6000 to 5000 B.C. Tell as-Sawwan was home to a few hundred people, most of whom were engaged in simple irrigation farming of wheat, barley, and linseed. They also kept domestic goats, sheep, and cattle, hunted onagers, antelopes, and other animals, and gathered fish and mussels from the Tigris, which ran close to the site.

In most ways, this settlement resembled other early agricultural villages: granaries, kilns, ovens, and small mudbrick houses were arranged around open courtyards. In addition, a large ditch or moat was constructed around the site by cutting into the natural conglomerate rock on which the site was located. The discovery of many hardened clay balls (sling missiles) in the ditch led its excavators to conclude it was a defensive structure, reminiscent of the fortifications at Jericho.

The residential architecture of Tell as-Sawwan contrasts somewhat with that of other settlements of the period, consisting mainly of huts with stone foundations and the more common rectangular clay structures, although there is still little variability in building size or apparent construction cost.

At least 128 burials at Tell as-Sawwan date to approximately 5500 B.C., and they contain one of the richest assortments of grave goods for this period of any site known in Southwest Asia. Of the classifiable skeletons, fifty-five were infants, sixteen were adolescents, and thirteen were adults. The graves differ little in orientation, location, or construction. Most bodies were placed in a contracted position, facing west, in simple shallow oval pits dug into house floors. Most graves had at least one craft item, mainly carved alabaster, beads in exotic stones, or pottery. Although most rooms had many burials (one had up to twenty-three), one room contained only an adult male's burial, whose relatively rich grave goods may reflect emerging status ascription. But the Tell as-Sawwan burials do not seem to reflect *inherited* status and wealth. As noted in chapter 7, attempts to draw conclusions about the social systems of extinct societies from examination of burial characteristics is somewhat speculative, but there does seem to be a period in all early civilizations where burials begin to reflect inherited status. An infant buried with massive amounts of wealth that he or she could not possibly have earned personally may reflect nothing more than a wealthy and caring family, but in all known early civilizations wealth and status eventually became largely inherited aspects of everyone's life. Although there are some signs of differences of wealth and status at Tell es-Sawwan, there is nothing to indicate this wealth and status was inherited.

Tell as-Sawwan is just one of many sites of this period, and soon after Halafian, Samarran, and other pottery styles spread through the highlands, the developmental focus shifted to the Mesopotamian alluvial plain.

The few sites on the alluvial plain that may antedate 5500 B.C. are poorly known—most are probably covered by much larger and later sites. The earliest known sites on the alluvial plain are near the estuary of the Persian Gulf, and there is some evidence that with the end of the Pleistocene, the Gulf shoreline moved inland as much as 180 kilometers.[13] Thus, the key settlements in the transition to life on the alluvial plain—and the origins of cultural complexity here—may now be under sea water. Between about 5500 and 3500 B.C. Mesopotamian climates were comparatively humid, with a change to cooler and drier conditions after about 3500 B.C. Subtle changes in climate like this might have had major effects on the settlement history of the area, because the zones in which dry-field rainfall-based grain cultivation was possible may have shifted. Also, changes in sea levels at this time may have meant that lands that previously were flooded were opened to settlement.[14]

Frank Hole has argued that

> economic necessity, caused by environmental shocks that were induced by climatic changes, resulted in major dislocations of local [Mesopotamian] populations as early as the second half of the sixth millennium [B.C.], and continued into the fourth, during which there was a qualitative reorientation of society around urban places. These natural events resulted first in the loss of sites and decline of population. Except at a few favorable locations, these conditions discouraged nucleation. However, with the steady flow of dislocated people who could provide labor, larger and more dependable agricultural systems could be built. The first urban-sized places may have been composed of disparate populations who developed an organic interdependence as they filled many . . . ecological and economic niches.[15]

If Hole is correct, then the rise of cities and civilizations was based on ecological factors, and once these developments were underway, very complex patterns of socio-economic changes would have developed. Subsistence in most parts of the alluvial plain is more complex than in the highlands, requiring many timely decisions in which floods must be anticipated and controlled, land irrigated and drained, and cattle pastured, tended, and milked. Fishing adds to this complexity because it is seasonal to some extent and requires coordination to be maximally effective. Even obtaining sufficient stone for simple agricultural implements necessitates considerable organization here, for such stone often had to be obtained in the mountains, far from lowland settlements.

If Ali Kosh in Iranian Mesopotamia is typical, the movement onto the alluvial plain required a very generalized diet, in which many small plant seeds eventually were discarded in favor of the wheat-barley-lentil group augmented by sheep-goat-cattle proteins.[16] There is some evidence that the cuisine centered on a variant of the one-pot approach, a stone or clay vessel filled with water, cereals, and other plants, and bits of whatever animals were about. Like the spartan meals of ancient Sparta (described as consisting of two courses, the first a kind of porridge, and a second, which was a kind of porridge), the diets of these Mesopotamian villagers probably relied on blending as many plant and animal nutrients as possible in soups and stews. Breakfasts may have been rather uninspiring, but perhaps these early farmers subsisted on something quite like their modern descendants, and ate porridge, bread, cheese, and dates.

THE 'UBAID PERIOD (C. 6000–3700 B.C.)

In the ancient Sumerian account of the creation of the universe, the city of Eridu was the first to have emerged from the primeval sea that covered the world before humans. Eridu is in fact one of the earliest known settlements on the southern Mesopotamian alluvial plain, having been established at about 4750 B.C. But by about 5700 B.C., there were small communities of farmers living on the southern Mesopotamian alluvium. These earliest southern communities belong to the 'Ubaid Period, named after a small town of this period, and are associated with a particular and distinctive style of ceramics. These people may be identified with their styles of pottery, but they did something much more important than make ceramics: they were the first to establish a productive economy on the basis of a traditional Mesopotamian farming strategy, based on cereals (in this case, barley) and various vegetables and fruits (particularly dates) in combination with the milk and meat of cattle, sheep, and goats. Living in communities that ranged in size from fewer than fifty to a few thousand, the 'Ubaid peoples did small-time irrigation of crops, traded for a few products, and in general were able to produce the base materials out of which the alchemy of cultures produces civilization, namely economic *surpluses*. Anthropologists have long argued about the applicability of the term surplus to premonetary economies, such as that of the 'Ubaid farmers, but the most important point is that, once established, the agricultural economy of the alluvial lowlands could be intensified in such a way that ever greater populations could be supported and massive amounts of materials and energy could be devoted to pyramid building, warfare, and ever more diversified occupational specialization, from kings to foot-soldiers, from scribes to potters.

Debates continue as to the ethnic origins of the 'Ubaid people—they may have been Iranians who migrated to the river valleys as domesticated wheat, barley, sheep, and goats became adapted to these environments, and as changes in climates and river regimes made the alluvium more suitable for simple farming.[17]

If we look at the 'Ubaid archaeological record for the first signs of these fundamental changes, we see only a few indirect reflections. One of the earliest known 'Ubaid sites is at Tell al-Quelli, near Larsa, which dates to at least 5300 B.C., and recent excavations deep into the great site of Uruk suggest that occupations of the earliest 'Ubaid sites are probably deeply buried at many major sites. A major temple dating to after 4000 B.C. at Uruk was found to have been built on the exact same site as a temple of the 'Ubaid period, indicating a great continuity of religious traditions.[18] At Eridu, the earliest known structure is thought to have been a temple. Archaeologists have been accused of bestowing this term on virtually any structure large enough to stand upright in, but the earliest building at Eridu is very similar to others known through texts and other evidence to have been temples. A single small room (3.5 by 4.5 meters) with an altar faces the entrance, and a pedestal is in the center; in these specifics the building is nearly identical to the temples of later periods. The ceramics found here resemble those of Halaf and Samarra, but few other artifacts were discovered. These temples may reflect a low level of social complexity, and some of the larger 'Ubaid communities included some fairly impressive mudbrick buildings, but for the most part the people of the 'Ubaid period appear to have been small-time farmers; no clear evidence has been found indicating differential access to wealth, power, or prestige, and their economy seems only marginally more diversified and integrated than that of the first Southwest Asian farmers a millennium earlier.

But by 4500 B.C. some signs of cultural changes toward complexity appeared in a large region of the lower alluvial plain, in the foothills of the Zagros, and in some of the larger valleys in the Zagros. Henry Wright notes that in these areas

> There were large centers with populations of 1,000 to 3,000, which dominated networks of smaller settlements. Excavation on some of these larger centers revealed central platforms, supporting ritual buildings, segregated elite residences with large storage structures, and indications of socially segregated cemeteries.[19]

As Wright notes, there is evidence that there had been a *previous* period in which larger centers had emerged, but here too, as in the case described above for Çatal Hüyük, we see no uniform gradual pattern of increasing complexity. The whole history of early complexity, in fact, seems to be a messy boom-or-bust cycle, with only a very general long-term overall trend toward complexity.

In addition to the central Mesopotamian plains in Iraq, the Susiana Plain (Figure 8.7) in southwestern Iran was also a major developmental center for early complexity—probably because one could do both rainfall agriculture and irrigation farming here, and because trade routes from the Gulf to the Iranian plateau ran across the Susiana. By about 4500 B.C.—perhaps much earlier—several large centers may have dominated surrounding areas economically and politically. The people of this era made beautiful hand-painted pottery in such large quantities and with such great

FIGURE 8.7   The first socially complex societies were concentrated in areas of Mesopotamia where rivers allowed great agricultural productivity.

similarity that, even given the virtuosity of peasant artisans, some occupational specialization may be reflected.[20]

In summarizing this and other evidence from the Susiana, Gregory Johnson observed that

> In sharp contrast to the pervasive smaller villages of the [earlier] periods, Choga Mish on the Susiana Plain covered an area of some fifteen hectares by 4300 B.C. Most architecture consisted of residences and associated ceramic kilns. The community also contained at least one monumental building, perhaps more. This ten-by-fifteen-meter structure had walls of between one and two meters thick and contained several interior rooms. One of these was stacked with storage jars, while another was apparently used in working flint. A substantial mud-brick platform stood nearby. This period in Susiana and elsewhere saw the introduction of formalized closure of containers using clay sealings that carried the impression of a decorated seal. This practice is ordinarily associated with problems of security in materials storage or shipment.[21]

Johnson goes on to note that the high degree of similarity in ceramics across the plain indicates that not everyone was making these—that their production might already have been somewhat centralized. All this evidence, he says,

Strikes me as indicative of a hierarchically organized social system with some degree of influence over labor and resource allocation. The fact that the known major architecture at Choga Mish was destroyed by fire and the community abandoned . . . suggests that elite influence over the population in general was less than elites might have wished.[22]

Frank Hole's interpretation of Susiana culture history differs somewhat from Johnson's.[23] He suspects that even toward the end of the fifth millennium B.C., the Susiana was loosely tied together by small-scale trade and a regional religious cult, centered at Susa, in which priests and people were in a voluntary mutually supportive relationship dedicated to the continued success of agriculture.[24]

To the west of the Susiana, in central Mesopotamia, the later 'Ubaid Period (after about c. 4500 B.C.) saw the gradual settlement of the plain by villagers. By 4350 B.C. the 'Ubaid culture was quite uniform over most of the alluvial plain: all the settlements seem to have been located on reliable water courses and almost all were less than ten hectares in size (most of them only one or two).

The spread of the 'Ubaid culture is remarkable for many reasons, particularly its great extent. 'Ubaid-style ceramics are found far into central Turkey, to the southwest in the Arabian Plateau, and in highland Iran—an area much greater than that encompassed within the Halafian and Samarran stylistic zones. The potter's wheel was probably invented by the end of the 'Ubaid Period, when the pivoted working surface, or tournette, was altered by setting the wheel's axle in bearings and weighting the wheel in such a way that high speeds could be produced. This allowed delicate vessels to be made, and painted decorations like bands could be easily applied simply by holding a paint brush steady against a rotating ceramic vessel.[25]

Virtually every 'Ubaid settlement had a large nonresidential building, probably a temple, built of mudbrick on platforms of clay or imported stone. Access typically was by a flight of stairs, to a room about ten meters in length, with a broad platform at one end and a table or small altar at the other. Smaller rooms were built on both sides of the main room, and ladders in these would sometimes give access to a second story. The exteriors of the buildings were often decorated with projections and recesses, where light and shadows created pleasing effects. In later periods, mosaics of colored ceramic cones and bitumen were used as decorations. At Eridu, seventeen such temples were found superimposed, giving the later ones considerable elevation. Such structures are found all over Greater Mesopotamia soon after their appearance on the southern alluvial plain.

Until about 5000 B.C., settlements seem to have been located primarily with regard to the availability of resources and the land's agricultural potential, not on the basis of political and economic relationships. People tend to organize their territories in patterns reflecting changing social and economic conditions; thus when the movement of people and goods between settlements becomes important, and the area is agricultural and relatively flat, these settlements often are quite regularly spaced, as is evident in both the Warka area and the Susiana Plain.

By 4000 B.C., the number of small settlements had increased dramatically in many areas, and there was increasing variability in their arrangement and composition.

EARLY STATES: THE URUK PERIOD AND
JEMDET NASR PERIODS (C. 3600–3000 B.C.)

The Uruk period is regarded as the era of primary state formation in Southwest Asia. Cultural forces and processes probably in operation for thousands of years culminated in this interval in the appearance of the complete checklist of civilization: cities, warfare, writing, social hierarchies, advanced arts and crafts, and other elements.

Steven Falconer and Stephen Savage have argued[26] that the wave of urbanism that swept across Greater Mesopotamia in the third and fourth millennia B.C. arose out of many different factors, and that the process of urbanization was different from place to place. This is perhaps the best way to interpret this phenomenon—a multifaceted response to different factors and environments.

The central Mesopotamian alluvial plain and the Susiana Plain offer our earliest and best known examples of the changes that occurred in Greater Mesopotamia in the Uruk Period. As many as 10,000 people may have lived in the city of Uruk by 3800 B.C., and around the town were many smaller villages and towns whose sizes and distribution suggest they may not have been tightly integrated into Uruk's political and economic systems[27] (Figure 8.8). Then, at about 3000 B.C., the city of Uruk apparently grew rapidly to about 50,000 people, who lived behind substantial defensive walls. There is also evidence of widespread simultaneous abandonment of almost all the rural settlements surrounding Uruk—leaving little doubt, Robert McC. Adams suggests, that the growth of the city was a result of the immigration or forcible transference of the population from the hinterlands into the city.[28]

Archaeologists who have excavated Uruk settlements usually have found themselves ankle deep in the remains of millions of bevel-rimmed bowls, surely one of the ugliest ceramic types ever made outside a kindergarten, but also one of the most significant. Gregory Johnson has shown that various measurements of these bowls change over time, so that the Late, Middle, and Early Uruk periods can be defined in part by changes in their form.[29] Hans Nissen has also argued that these bowls probably were ration bowls and were used to pay workers in grain for their labors.[30] Most have a capacity that corresponds to what a laborer's daily ration was asserted to be in ancient texts, and the symbol for to eat in early Mesopotamian writing seems to be that of a person eating from a bevel-rimmed bowl. Others have suggested that these bowls were used to bake bread. These bowls were mass produced, probably by simply molding, and they represent one of the first craft items for which the government organized some aspects of the production and distribution system. But these simple features of mass production and, perhaps, government administration of commodity production and distribution were fateful steps in the evolution of states. To most modern people, few things are more natural than governmental forms of organization and control, but our ancestors lived as farmers for many centuries without government in this sense; these first few steps in the direction of government in Mesopotamia were a long, slow process in these initial stages; later, the process of ancient state formation was largely one in which the government increasingly intruded on socioeconomic and political life.

In a sense, the rise of Mesopotamian states is the rise of urbanism. As the centuries of the fourth millennium B.C. passed, towns that had once been home to hun-

FIGURE 8.8 In simple societies the location of settlements with respect to each other is dictated mainly by ecological factors like water availability. But as societies become more complex, political and economic relationships begin to influence where settlements are located and how large they become. In Gregory Johnson's reconstruction (1975) of exchange networks among late Uruk Period (c. 3200 B.C.) settlements in southern Iraq, the spatial arrangement of the settlements with respect to one another is quite regular (the wall cones were used to decorate administrative centers, and their distribution here may indicate lines of political authority).

dreds became cities of thousands of inhabitants. Urbanism does not just increase the size of communities, however: a key element of Mesopotamian urbanism was that proportionately greater numbers of people lived in larger settlements, and the people in these settlements became increasingly specialized in their occupations. All of these people—kings, priests, scribes, farmers, soldiers, slaves, etc.—became functionally integrated in the sense that they all depended on each other to perpetuate the community, and all derived benefits from the greater efficiency of functional differentiation and integration. Toward the end of the 'Ubaid period, almost all major settlements were fortified, and documents written much later, at about 2600 B.C., speak at length of conflict between the people of Ur, Uruk, Umma, and the other city-states. In subsequent chapters, we will see that the initial stimulus for urbanization in other parts of the world also seems to be related to defensive needs: Egypt, which was protected from hostile outside forces by the deserts and the sea, developed urban societies only comparatively late; while in the Indus Valley, which was much more of a crossroads for nomadic and other groups, urbanism was present almost from the very first. In this context, Adams argues that early Mesopotamian urbanization may have been imposed on a rural populace by a small, politically conscious superstratum that was motivated principally by military and economic interests.[31]

Because of defensive considerations and the cost of transporting labor and products, agricultural land nearest the urban areas would have been most intensively exploited, and this may have stimulated the construction of large irrigation systems. Another important possible effect of urbanism is that it might have created—and to some extent have been created by—the large nomadic populations thought to have been present in Southwest Asia as early as 6000 B.C. Most of these people were probably similar to the present-day Bakhtiari of western Iran, who herd sheep and goats in the uplands during much of the year but come down to the lowlands in the winter to sell their animals wool, meat, and milk products and to buy craft items, food, and other products. The relationships between these upland nomadic and lowland sedentary groups are varied and complex.[32] Historically, when central governments have weakened in Southwest Asia, some marginal cultivators revert to nomadic pastoralism in times of war or poor harvests, while other pastoralists become laborers or marginal farmers if they lose too many sheep. One of the effects of urbanism suggested by the archaeological record—the depopulation of the countryside—may have given nomads a new niche. By working the mountain areas and highlands for most of the year, the nomads could have come down and exploited the marginal areas between urban centers—peacefully most of the time, but other times with hostility—and then traded with the townspeople.

The sequence of Uruk culture history on the Susiana Plain parallels in many ways developments on the central alluvium. Gregory Johnson and Henry Wright have analyzed Susiana cultural history by focusing on the evolution of administrative institutions.[33] They have been principally concerned with the origins of the state, which they define as a society with at least three levels of hierarchically arranged, specialized administrators. For example, in a simple agricultural village, many of the decisions about what crops to plant, how much of the harvest is to be stored, who gets what share of the land, who marries whom, and so forth are made by individuals. Some of those decisions—particularly those that directly affect the whole community—are made by a village headman. We might say that this individual represents the first level of the decision-making hierarchy—he directs the activities of others who do the work. A second level of administrative hierarchy would exist if there were people who coordinate the activities of these village headmen and correct or approve their decisions—perhaps government agents charged with taxing and administering local affairs. Such agents would be under a third administrative level, and additional levels may exist above this.

In addition to suggesting that the ancient Mesopotamian state can be defined as a society with at least three such levels of specialized administrators, Wright and Johnson contend that the effectiveness of such societies and their dominance over other societal forms are tied to their ability to store and process information and make correct decisions at specific points within the control hierarchy.

Wright and Johnson examined several areas where the first Mesopotamian states developed, looking for evidence of this change. One type of evidence was the actual administrative documents themselves. In most of Mesopotamia at this time, the administration of people and goods was facilitated by using pieces of inscribed stone to impress clay with signs of authorization. These stones were usually either in the form of stamps, used like the rubber stamps of today, or cylinders that were rolled across the clay to make an impression, and they varied in size and in the complexity of the symbols incised on them. Fortunately, the clay impressed with these seals and the seals themselves are often preserved in archaeological sites, and they can be used to infer the levels of administration in these extinct societies. The impressed clay can be divided into two classes. *Commodity sealings* were used to certify the contents of a container such as a vessel, basket, bale, or storeroom. They were made by placing a lump of clay over a knot that had to be untied to gain access to the container, so that unauthorized entry could be detected. Discarded commodity sealings indicate the receipt of stored or redistributed goods. Other seals are termed *message sealings* and convey or store facts about goods or people. Some are plain counters whose shape indicates a numerical unit, while others (bullae) are small spheroidal jackets that were once wrapped around sets of counters, and still others are flat, rectangular tablets stamped with numerical symbols. Writing, as we know it, did not exist until after the state—as defined by Wright and Johnson—emerged, but these stamps and seals obviously conveyed a great deal of information. Clay tokens have also been found in about ten geometric shapes at many early Mesopotamian sites, and Denise Schmandt-Besserat argues that these tokens, which were usually enclosed in clay envelopes, represented such commodities as pots of grain, numbers of animals, and areas of land, and are the direct precursors of later written scripts.[34]

Wright and Johnson used commodity and message sealings found at sites on the Susiana to reconstruct some aspects of the production, transport, and administration of goods. They concluded that they could determine when the change was made from one- and two-level decision-making institutions to the three levels that define the state.

Wright and Johnson also analyzed the locational arrangement of the settlements in southwestern Iran and found that after about 3600 B.C. there were trends toward more regular spacing of settlements and the emergence of distinctive site size groupings—both consistent with the change from a two-level to a three-level control hierarchy. This pattern of developing settlement arrangements, which correlate with changes in the technology of administration, is apparently not unique to southwestern Iran.

> The transition seems to occur in several adjacent regions in Iraq between [2700 B.C. and 3250 B.C.] around the ancient centers of Nippur, Nineveh, and Uruk. . . . Thus rather than one case of state emergence, there was a series of emergences of individual states in a network of politics.[35]

Johnson concludes that although a state society formed on the Susiana by about 3500 B.C., by 3200 B.C.

> Conflict broke out between elites of Susa . . . [and] Choga Mish. These apparently found their source in an attempt of Choga Mish to sever its dependent relationship with longer established elites in western Susiana. Scenes of violence appeared on cylinder seals, many villages and small centers were abandoned, and a no-man's land separated the contending parties east and west. Settled population declined rapidly, a process that would continue into the third millennium.[36]

Wright and Johnson suggest that decisions involving problems posed by drought, overpopulation, conflict, or some other single factor could probably be handled by a two-level hierarchy—something on the order of a chiefdom, perhaps—but a combination of problems would require additional decision-making capacity. They suspect that one important factor in early Southwest Asian state formation may have been the economic interactions between nomadic pastoralists and lowland farmers, probably in the form of the exchange of cheese, rugs, meat, minerals, and other highland resources for pottery, grain, and other lowland commodities. Economic models suggest that fluctuating demand for certain craft products in relatively simple economies often stimulates the centralization of workshops and economic administration, and Wright and Johnson suggest that in prehistoric Mesopotamia the economic demands of nomads on lowland economies may have fluctuated sufficiently to produce a similar effect, with the eventual emergence of a three-level hierarchy.

Johnson has applied various concepts from what is known as hierarchy theory and the so-called rank-size rule to the Susiana data.[37] Hierarchy theory is essentially a search for explanations of how everything, from molecular structures to world governments, seems to involve hierarchical orderings. The assumption here is that there are principles common to all these forms of hierarchies and that the processes by which hierarchies change and appear can be mathematically analyzed.

The rank-size rule is an empirical observation that many settlement patterns are similar in terms of the relative sizes of their component settlements. Thus, in any region, state, or country, the distribution of people can be expected to be somewhere between the extreme distributions in which either everyone lives in one settlement or the populace is divided into settlements of exactly equal population size. A rank-size plot is produced by ranking each settlement in terms of its population, assigning the number one to the largest, two to the second largest, and so on, and then graphing the actual population of each settlement against the rank of that settlement on a full logarithmic scale. Geographers have noted that for many developing countries, such as Egypt, the rank-size plot will be a *primate* one. For example, Cairo is much larger than any other settlement and forms such a large proportion of the total Egyptian population that a rank-size plot of Egypt is sharply concave, in contrast to a linear distribution in which the second-ranked city is only slightly smaller than the largest, the third is slightly smaller than the second, and so on. It is sufficient here to note that major shifts in the political and economic organization of an area are usually reflected in its rank-size plot. To use Egypt as an example again, the great growth of Cairo's population to over fourteen million people recently has correlated with the growing power of the national government and the rapidly industrializing economy. Prior to 1965, a much greater percentage of Egyptians lived in smaller towns and villages than do now.

The archaeological applications of this are obvious. If we know when a site was occupied and how big it was, we can then estimate population sizes, construct rank-size plots, and perhaps detect when great political and economic changes were taking place. The application of this idea to various areas of Mesopotamia yields mixed results. Clearly there were different rank-size patterns at different times, which might signal the origins of state-level societies.[38] This would not *explain* their appearance, but it would help identify them. But it is difficult to estimate the populations of sites in different time periods with precision. Also, no one really knows what the different kinds of rank-size plots mean. They are essentially empirical generalizations without any theory to explain them.

Nonetheless, a fundamental problem of archaeology is to define and interpret patterns in the distribution of artifacts through space and time, and these rank-size plots at least have the virtue of showing us some possible patterns.

Various other archaeologists have proposed alternative models of how the Uruk states formed. Guillermo Algaze,[39] for example, has argued that this development was essentially a process in which the peoples of the resource-deficient Mesopotamian lowlands expanded their state through trade and warfare in order to incorporate resource-rich areas on the periphery and to establish secure trade routes extending far beyond the Uruk heartland. We see, for example, communities in which Uruk styles of architecture and ceramics were used in western Iran, north into Syria, and even as far away as the Nile Delta.

In evaluating the many models of the development of the Uruk and Jemdet Nasr periods, Susan Pollock notes that these models present these ancient people as rather passive elements in these developments and tend to focus on the adaptations large groups made over time and large areas. She suggests that archaeological analyses should attempt to make our appreciation of the Uruk peoples more human and that "archaeological analyses . . . must also highlight internal conflicts generated from acts of daily social life, as well as those deriving from major sociocultural transformations."[40] In making these and other points, Pollock joins numerous other contemporary archaeologists in trying to see the peoples of the Uruk Period—and of all other cultures and eras—as individuals, real, live people.

Warka: An Uruk City State   The ancient settlement of Uruk (known as Warka in Arabic and Erech in the Bible), located in the heart of the southern alluvial plain, is one of the oldest cities in the world and may have been the center of one of the earliest states.

The residential architecture of Uruk reflects a diversity of occupational, economic, and social classes. All the buildings were mudbrick, but some were larger, better built, and more elaborately decorated. Many of the people lived in small rectangular buildings along narrow winding streets through which ran both above- and below-ground drainage canals. Apparently, houses were one story high for the poor and two stories tall for the wealthier, but both types were similar. Built of mudbrick and whitewashed, they represent an ideal architectural adaptation to the climate. Similar houses today are comfortable and attractive, with their whitewashed walls contrasting effectively with beautiful dyed rugs and textiles.

By the middle of the fourth millennium B.C., the population of Uruk included specialists in scores of arts and crafts. Potters, using molds and mass-production techniques, turned out enormous quantities of pottery. In earlier periods great numbers of beautifully painted vessels were made at most larger settlements, but by the middle and late fourth millennium, pottery manufacture had become a centralized, administered activity at Uruk and many other settlements. Other specialists included stonecutters, metalsmiths, bricklayers, farmers, fishermen, shepherds, and sailors. Writing did not come into general use in Mesopotamia until the first half of the third millennium B.C., but at Uruk and other sites, in levels dating from the fifth millennium onward, archaeologists frequently find stamp and cylinder seals, which were used to impress clay sealings for containers, bales of commodities, and documents. Some of these seals convey in picture form the economic specialization of the community. Boats, domestic animals, grain, deities, and many other motifs are portrayed.

By the late fourth millennium B.C., Uruk was already an impressive settlement of perhaps 10,000 people and several large temples. Between about 3200 and 3100 B.C., the "White Temple" at Uruk was built on a ziggurat (a stepped tower of successively receding stories) some twelve meters above ground level. Constructed of whitewashed mudbrick and decorated with elaborate recesses, columns, and buttresses, it must have been an impressive sight—especially to peasants coming into the city on market days. Inside the temple were tables and altars, all arranged according to the same ritual plan evident at Eridu some 2,500 years earlier.

The temple architecture and ziggurats of Mesopotamian antiquity raise an important point. As we will see in surveying other early complex cultures around the world, one of the most consistent signs of evolving cultural complexity is the diversion of enormous amounts of energy and materials into pyramids, ziggurats, palaces, platforms, and other huge constructions. Why would people who could just as easily—and certainly more profitably—build irrigation canals, terrace slopes, weave wool, or do other productive tasks instead "waste" their labors on these mammoth construction projects?

The answer to this question may lie precisely in the fact that these constructions are, in a limited sense, "wasteful." They may, for example, have helped prevent high and unstable rates of population growth, perhaps by deflecting investments in food production. As Leslie White suggested: "It would appear that the ruling class was frequently confronted with the problems of over-production and the threat of technological unemployment or a surplus of population among the lower classes. Their great public works programs, the wholesale disposition of wealth in mortuary customs, etc., enabled them to solve both these problems with one stroke."[41] Similarly, Robert Dunnell[42] has drawn a parallel between Egyptian pyramid construction and many other examples of changes in the relative investment in "waste" of various cultures. In the late Paleolithic-Mesolithic transition, for example, highly crafted stone points, cave paintings, etc., seem to disappear and are replaced by a "drab" but functionally more complex technology. Both this transition and the decline of pyramid building, he suggests, may be linked to changes in carrying capacity. That is, peaks in the abundance of luxury goods, such as gold bowls, pyramids, or even spear points, tend to increase in use during the formative stages of adaptations, whether agricultural or not, because they suppress unstable rates of growth. But they then diminish in importance in these systems once the adaptation has reached a new level of stability through improved agricultural and craft production, more efficient governmental administration, or other factors.

Similarly, most early complex societies, for example, underwent a transition in which labor-intensive, highly decorated pottery was replaced by mass-produced forms of much less aesthetic appeal. Various scholars have seen cultural collapse and dissolution in such changes, but as Trigger notes, such changes do "not indicate a decline in cultural or aesthetic standards. Instead it suggests that pottery no longer served as a medium of artistic expression ."[43] In fact, the appearance of these mass-produced forms of pottery seems to be a prime indicator of increasing complexity in the institutions administering and controlling craft production. G. Johnson,[44] R. McC. Adams,[45] and others have concluded that the rapid development of Southwest Asian states occurred during the period when the beautiful painted wares of the early fourth millennium were largely replaced by the unimpressive, mass-produced beveled rim bowl. Egyptian pottery seems to have made a parallel transition in the Early Dynastic and Old Kingdom periods, when various low-fired wares including "bread molds" were the dominant ceramic types.

Several factors may have contributed to these dramatic changes in pottery manufacture. The individual and corporate social groups identified by regional pottery styles, for example, are, in a sense, dangerous to the unity of the larger state: we can see in our own world many examples of the fragility of states in which ethnic differences are great, from Bosnia to Rwanda to Israel. The elites of most states try to divide their country into provincial administrative units but suppress any tendency for provincial identities that might eventuate in attempts at secession. The greater efficiency, too, of producing massive quantities of cheap and nearly identical pottery vessels would be best realized in a state organization.

Just as important, monumental construction programs could reinforce social and political hierarchies. Frankfort speculates that

The huge building, raised to establish a bond with the power on which the city depended, proclaimed not only the ineffable majesty of the gods but also the might of the community which had been capable of such an effort. The great temples were witnesses to piety, but also objects of civic pride. Built to ensure divine protection for the city, they also enhanced the significance of citizenship. Outlasting the generation of their builders, they were true monuments of the cities' greatness.[46]

Toward the end of the fourth millennium B.C., the Mesopotamian alluvium and adjacent regions were the heartland of a developed sociopolitical and economic organization that most would call a civilization. Writing had been developed, great temples soared up from the centers of large cities, and the economy was both productive and complexly interdependent. Also, the Uruk polity spread far beyond the central alluvial plain. At Habuba Kabira South, in Syria, a large later Uruk settlement is so similar to the great Uruk cities to the south in styles of ceramics and architecture that it may well have been built by people who came directly from the south to found this city.[47]

As noted above, this expansion and intensification of the Uruk sphere of cultural interaction undoubtedly involved extension of commercial links between and within communities, but there was probably a strong element of conflict as well.

THE EARLY DYNASTIC PERIOD (C. 3000–2350 B.C.)

To the modern urbanite, it may seem inappropriate to label as a "state" a collection of twelve or fourteen cities with a combined population of perhaps 100,000 and an area of only a few thousand square kilometers, but, as someone once observed, it is the small states, like fifth century B.C. Athens, Renaissance Florence, and Elizabethan England, that have put posterity most in their debt. To this list can be added Early Dynastic Sumer.

Sumerian Civilization   Approximately thirteen city-states made up Sumerian "civilization" between about 3000 and 2350 B.C. Through most of their history, these city-states were politically autonomous, but they belonged to the same cultural tradition, and by 3000 B.C. they had collectively developed many of the classical elements of Southwest Asian civilization, including ziggurats, brick platforms, the potter's wheel, wheeled carts, metal-working, sailboats, and writing.

The fact that the Sumerian language was essentially unlike those of the contemporary but less-developed Semitic cultures that surrounded the Sumerians has led some to place Sumerian origins in Turkey, Bahrain, or even outer space. The Sumerians, of course, thought of themselves as a distinct and superior culture, and their myths speak of origins in some distant land; but we will probably never determine their ethnic origins, and in a sense this is an unimportant question. The achievements of cultures cannot be explained in terms of the special characteristics and mental gifts of the people of these cultures: people are constants in the equations of cultural evolution, and it is their circumstances and position in place and time that determine their cultural "achievements."

Sumerian Writing   We have a detailed picture of life in these Sumerian city-states, because shortly before 3000 B.C. they began to develop a written language. What we know about the Sumerian language is derived from the thousands of clay tablets on which they wrote (Figure 8.9). Their script is known as cuneiform, from the Latin for wedge-shaped, a reference to the fact that Sumerian was written by impressing wet clay with the end of a reed, leaving wedge-shaped marks. When baked, these clay

FIGURE 8.9   A cuneiform text on clay.

tablets essentially become ceramic and thus can survive in even wet sediments for thousands of years.

The earliest known written documents may be clay tablets and sealings from early occupations at Uruk (c. 3400 B.C.). These documents include signs for carpenter, donkey, boat, copper, and many other things, totaling fifteen hundred symbols in all (Figure 8.10). Some signs seem to mean to buy, while others refer to *en*, the title of a lord, and to *unken*, which may have been a people's assembly.[48] The hierarchical nature of Mesopotamian society by the end of the Uruk Period is vividly illustrated by one of the oldest documents known, the "Standard Professions List," which gives the titles of officials and names of professions, all arranged according to what is apparently a composite sense of power and prestige.[49]

The ability of this cumbersome writing to convey abstract concepts or the spoken language was initially quite limited, but in the centuries after 2900 B.C. the Sumerians improved it. Phoneticization, by which some signs came to represent distinct words and syllables of the spoken language, was a most important development. Thus, the sign of an arrow came to mean both arrow and the Sumerian word for life, the connecting link being that the spoken word for both was *ti*.[50] Eventually, much of spoken Sumerian was represented by written symbols, and the pictographic elements slowly lost their representational character as the scribes stylized them and reduced the number of directions in which the stylus had to move to write them.[51] Unique

EARLIEST PICTOGRAPHS (3000 B.C.)	DENOTATION OF PICTOGRAPHS	PICTOGRAPHS IN ROTATED POSITION	CUNEIFORM SIGNS CA. 1900 B.C.	BASIC LOGOGRAPHIC VALUES		ADDITIONAL LOGOGRAPHIC VALUES		SYLLABARY (PHONETIC VALUES)
				READING	MEANING	READING	MEANING	
	HEAD AND BODY OF A MAN			LÚ	MAN			
	HEAD WITH MOUTH INDICATED			KA	MOUTH	KIRI₃ ZÚ GÙ DUG₄ INIM	NOSE TEETH VOICE TO SPEAK WORD	KA ZÚ
	BOWL OF FOOD			NINDA	FOOD, BREAD	NÍG GAR	THING TO PLACE	
	MOUTH + FOOD			KÚ	TO EAT	ŠAGAR	HUNGER	
	STREAM OF WATER			A	WATER	DURU₅	MOIST	A
	MOUTH + WATER			NAG	TO DRINK	EMMEN	THIRST	
	FISH			KUA	FISH			KU₆ HA
	BIRD			MUŠEN	BIRD			HU PAG
	HEAD OF AN ASS			ANŠE	ASS			
	EAR OF BARLEY			ŠE	BARLEY			ŠE

FIGURE 8.10 The evolution of Sumerian writing. Fourth millennium B.C. tablets were inscribed vertically with pictographs, but in the early third millennium, the direction of the writing and the pictographs were rotated to the horizontal. In succeeding millennia the symbols were stylized and given phonetic meanings.

signs were developed for most Sumerian vowels and syllables, but the language was never reduced to an alphabetic system where every distinct sound is represented by a unique sign. Instead, it remained a welter of signs that represented pictographs of concrete objects, signs that represented syllables of speech, and signs that represented ideas. This made reading the script a complicated process, requiring the memorization of hundreds of different characters. One sign, for example, which ultimately derived from a pictograph representing a mountain, acquired a total of ten possible phonetic values and four ideographic values as well.[52] At first the reader had to infer the exact meaning of the word by considering its context, but eventually the Sumerians devised a system of determinatives—signs placed before or after a word to indicate the general category to which the word belonged, such as birds, male proper nouns, or deities.

Over the centuries the Sumerians' successors reduced the complexity of the written language, but even as late as about 1900 B.C., it had between six and seven hundred unique elements. At this stage it was similar to Chinese and a few other modern languages, which faithfully represent the spoken language and are adequate for most purposes, but which, compared to alphabetic systems, are very cumbersome. It is difficult to construct typewriters or computers for languages with hundreds of unique elements, and even minimal literacy in such languages is the product of long and arduous training. (To become literate in modern Chinese, for example, one must memorize several thousand characters.) Most Semitic languages were—and still are—written without the short vowels, but this is no barrier to effective communication if one is accstmd t rdng th scrpt.

The first truly alphabetic written languages appear to have developed about the middle of the second millennium B.C. among Semitic-speaking peoples in Palestine and northern Syria. In the tenth or ninth centuries B.C., the Greeks adapted the Syrian or Phoenician variant of these early alphabets to their own language, reducing the number of signs to fewer than twenty-five and making several major refinements in the process. The Greek alphabet became the basis for all modern European writing systems, including the Cyrillic alphabet of eastern Europe.

The role of writing in early Mesopotamian societies seems largely economic. Simple pictographs and the spoken language cannot efficiently meet the requirements of a society that has surpluses to be stored and redistributed, water to be allocated, land rights to be assigned and adjudicated, ritual prayers to be said, and all the other tasks we find in complex cultures. In fact, only the Inka of Peru managed to develop states and empires without a written language, but they had a fairly efficient substitute in the form of a vast bureaucracy and the *quipu*, a system of knotted strings in which the length of strings and placement of knots was used as a device to assist the memory of the recordkeeper.

The economic element in ancient Mesopotamian scripts is evident in their mathematical notations. Georges Ifrah notes that the Sumerians used a counting system with a base of 60, instead of the base-10 system we have.[53] It is difficult for most people to accept that there is nothing inherently necessary about a base-10 numbering system. But modern computers employ a base-2 system, for example, using just 1s and 0s to represent all numbers. We probably use a base-10 system because we have 10 fingers—there are many base-20 systems that probably reflect our 20 fingers and toes. Whatever base is used, people usually have given a unique name to *each* of the numbers, so a base-2 system is the simplest and a base-60 system is rather unwieldy. Mathematicians have often proposed that we scrap our base-10 system and use something more convenient, like a base-12 system, where numbers would have a large number of divisors, or a base-11 system, which, as a prime number, would eliminate the ambiguities of a quantity like "0.36," which can reduce to 36/100, 18/50, 9/25, etc.[54] The Sumerians got around the problem of having to learn and use a unique name for each number between zero and 60 by giving a name to each multiple of 10 lower than or equal to 60. They may have developed a base-60 system because six times 60 is close to the number of days in the year, but the origins of the numbering system probably go far back beyond the first written evidences we have of it. As H. W. F. Saggs notes, the ancient Sumerians and their successors used their mathematical systems not only for economic accounting but also for land surveying, calendrical calculations, and astronomical science.[55] By about 1800 B.C. the people of Mesopotamia (1) had calculated the square root of 2 to a value correct to 1 in two million; (2) had formulated massive tables of reciprocals of sexagesimal numbers; (3) knew how to calculate the length of a hypotenuse from the lengths of the sides of right-angled triangles (1200 years before Pythagoras); (4) could calculate cube roots; and (5) knew some algebraic operations.[56]

The way of life described by the Sumerian texts, and by texts of other Southwest Asian cultures of the third millennium B.C., is still recognizable to anyone who has traveled in these areas. Sheep, goats, and cattle are tabulated, taxed, and exchanged; children are shepherded to school—as always, much against their will; a council of elders meets to consider grievances against the inhabitants of an adjoining town; and Sumerian proverbs express ideas recognizable in many societies:

> Upon my escaping from the wild ox,
> The wild cow confronted me.
> When a poor man dies,
> do not try to revive him.[57]

But when they turn to mythological and eschatological themes, the ancient Mesopotamians are less accessible—perhaps even a bit bizarre—by our standards, as in this section of the myth of the revival of the goddess Inanna:

> Go to the underworld.
> Enter the door like flies.
> Ereshkigal, the Queen of the Underworld, is moaning
> With the cries of a woman about to give birth.
> No linen is spread over her body.
> Her breasts are uncovered.
> Her hair swirls about her head like leeks.
>
> When she cries, "Oh! Oh! My inside!"
> Cry also, "Oh! Oh! Your Inside!"
> When she cries, "Oh! Oh! My outside!"
> Cry also, "Oh! Oh! Your outside!"
> The queen will be pleased.
> She will offer you a gift.
> Ask her only for the corpse that hangs from the hook on the wall.
> One of you will sprinkle the food of life on it.
> The other will sprinkle the water of life.
> Inanna will arise.[58]

Western philosophy and theology are deeply influenced by the philosophies first propounded in ancient Greece, philosophies very different from those of ancient

Sumer. Thus, most Westerners see the world in terms of beginnings and ends, causes and effects, and the importance and "will" of the individual. We cannot completely reconstruct Sumerian philosophy on the basis of fragmentary texts, but it seems evident that the Sumerians saw a much more static and magical world than we do. Although their technology and complex organizations demonstrate that they were shrewd, rational people, there seems to have been little emphasis on or analysis of human motivation or the physical world. They viewed the earth as a flat disk under a vaulted heaven and believed that various gods guided history according to well-laid-out plans and that the world continues without end and with little change. Each god was in charge of something—the movements of the planets, irrigation, or brick-making, for example—and each was immortal and inflexible. As with humans, the deities were hierarchically arranged in power and authority and were given to power struggles and many vices.

Like most people, the Sumerians thought that the gods had a special interest in them. Just as the back of every American dollar bill has the assertion that "annuit coeptis" ("[God] has favored our undertaking"), almost every official Sumerian pronouncement and inscription invoked the favor of the gods who, it was assumed, favored the city's fortunes.

One way in which Sumerian religion and ideology has influenced modern cultures is in its influence on Judeo-Christian religious traditions. The biblical account of the Noachian flood, for example, is clearly related to Sumerian stories that predated the Old Testament by thousands of years. Finegan has identified some of the similarities:[59]

Babylonian Cuneiform	*Genesis*
1. The gods decide to make a flood	1. The Lord decides to destroy wicked mankind
2. The God Ea warns Artarhasis to build a ship	2. The Lord warns Noah to build an ark
3. Artarhasis is to take his family and animals aboard	3. Noah is to take his family and animals aboard
4. The flood turns mankind into clay	4. The flood destroys all flesh
5. The ship grounds on Mount Nisir	5. The ark comes to rest on the Ararat Mountains
6. Artarhasis learns when the waters have subsided by sending out a dove, a swallow, and a raven	6. Noah learns when the waters have subsided by sending out a dove, a swallow, and a raven
7. He offers sacrifice to the gods	7. He offers sacrifice to the Lord
8. The gods smell the sweet savor	8. The Lord smells the pleasing odor
9. The god Enlil blesses Artarhasis and his wife	9. God blesses Noah and his sons

In 1929 S. Langdon, excavating the Sumerian city of Kish, and Sir L. Woolley, excavating at Ur, both announced that they had found thick levels of clean sand that they presumed were evidence of the biblical flood. Some members of these expeditions are even said to have sold vials of sand labeled "Samples from the Great Flood."

But Spuhler notes that many layers thought to be flood deposits are really sand dunes produced by winds, while others are ordinary river deposits.[60] In any case, radiocarbon dates for levels thought to be of the biblical flood range from 4500 B.C. to 2700 B.C., and the absence of sand strata at many other nearby sites, and the evidence of life as usual all over Mesopotamia at this time, rule out fairly conclusively any scientific evidence for the biblical flood—except in the opinion of the people who keep climbing Mount Ararat looking for pieces of the ark. Popular press reports of a Russian pilot who saw the outline of a boat far above the tree line on this mountain have fueled several expeditions to recover the ark, but so far only a few questionable bits of wood have been found. Only the drearily unimaginative archaeologist would be impressed by the fact that all the samples of wood were radiocarbon dated to about 3,500 years ago—a time for which there is no evidence that the rest of the world was flooded.[61]

Sumerian Institutions and Economy   Tantalizing clues in documents suggest that many Sumerian city-states had a public assembly in which, perhaps, people formulated policy and made decisions through consensus and even a form of simple democracy.[62] Cities appear to have been divided into something like modern "wards," but we really do not know the organizing principles. There is some evidence[63] that people were organized in clans, and kinship ties probably remained the connective tissue of Sumerian civilization through most of its history. Yet one of the things that all states do is complement kinship ties with links among and within socioeconomic classes in order to provide effective methods of getting people to operate in useful corporate groups (e.g., serving in military units tied together by kinship and place of origin, as in units in the American Civil War). In the long run, state societies seem to wear away at kinship ties, replacing them with socioeconomic class ties and other kinds of corporate groups.

The Sumerian extended family appears to have been a strong and durable unit, protected by laws governing rights of inheritance, recompense for injuries, etc. As Nicholas Postgate notes, women were reasonably well treated both by law and custom in Sumerian society, but there seems little doubt that this was a strongly patriarchal culture, as evidenced by divorce law:

> If a wife rejects her husband and says "You are not my husband", they shall cast her into the river. If a husband says to his wife "You are not my wife", he shall pay 1/2 mina of silver."[64]

In Sumer, wheat, barley, vegetables, and dates were the major crops, while cattle raising and fishing were of almost equal importance. Cattle were raised for draft power, hides, and milk and meat. Fish was a staple, as were mutton, goat, and pork. It is interesting in view of their later status as a taboo food in much of the Middle East that pigs were a common sight on Sumerian farms, prized for their fat and grease (although rarely if ever depicted in art, except in figures and ceramics[65]).

Out of each measure of wheat or barley harvested, the Mesopotamian farmer probably fed about 16 percent to his animals, reserved about 10 percent for the next year's sowing, lost about 25 percent in storage, and ate the rest.[66] If ethnographic studies are to be believed, in the absence of modern transport, people did not cultivate fields much more than four kilometers from their houses. At any given time, much of the land around a village in ancient times would have been fallow, while other land would have been unirrigatable or of marginal productivity. Adams estimates that for subsistence each person would need about one hectare of barley and wheat fields, along with at least some pastures and orchards.[67]

One of the less desirable "firsts" of Sumerian civilization was probably in the field of epidemic diseases. Just as there are certain disastrous things a hunter and gatherer can do (e.g., to presume on too slight evidence that a cave bear is not at home), one of the worst things a villager can do is contaminate drinking water with sewage, and this is hard to avoid in a primitive town. Typhoid, cholera, and many other diseases require certain levels of population density to evolve, to maintain a reservoir of infected individuals, and to perpetuate themselves. These levels were probably reached for the first time in Sumer. Once people started digging wells and irrigation canals in areas with many people and animals, disease and epidemics quickly followed.

Few economies in history or prehistory have been as organized as the Sumerian. Tablet after tablet records endless lists of commodities produced, stored, and allotted. Ration lists, work forces, guild members—all are recorded in numbing detail. Even the city's snake-charmers were organized.

The state and church controlled economic matters through much of Mesopotamian history, but individual merchants and capitalist elements also seem to have been significant fairly early on. This is important for the Marxian scholar because once you have individual wealth and capital, the possibilities for class conflict and the rest of the Marxian paradigm exist. Although Sumerian society was organized on the basis of kinship, people also belonged to and acted through occupational and social classes. In the event of war, for example, members of different "guilds," such as silversmiths or potters, would be under the command of their "guild president." One of the major trends in the evolution of complex societies generally was the change from a kinship-based society to one based on divisions along occupational, social, and economic class lines, and by 3000 B.C. there is evidence that this trend was developing in Mesopotamian societies. Even so, kinship ties have been powerful social forces throughout the history of Southwest Asia. At the pinnacle of Sumerian society was a god-king, assumed to be a descendant of the gods who was also in contact with the gods. Beneath him was a leisure class of nobles. There was also a class of wealthy businessmen who lived in the larger, better houses of the city; of lesser wealth and prestige were the many artisans and farmers, including smiths, leather-workers, fishermen, bricklayers, weavers, and potters. Scribes apparently held fairly important positions, and literacy was an admired accomplishment. At the bottom of society were the slaves, often war captives or dispossessed farmers.

Money, as we know it, did not exist in ancient Sumer; most exchange was "in kind," the trading of products for other products. Local and long-distance trade was voluminous, however, and ships sailed up the rivers from the gulf carrying shell, carnelian, lapis lazuli, silver, gold, onyx, alabaster, textiles, and food and other produce.

One of the most spectacular differences between Sumerian societies after 3000 B.C. and their predecessors is in mortuary practices. At the end of the 'Ubaid period (3800 B.C.), graves varied little, even at the largest settlements; but after 3000 B.C. a radical shift occurred. The famous death pit at Ur is an impressive display of wealth and pomp (Figure 8.11). Excavating here in 1927–1928, Sir Leonard Woolley came upon five bodies lying side by side, each with a copper dagger and other items.[68] Beneath them was a layer of matting on which he encountered the bodies of ten women, lying in two rows, each richly ornamented with gold, lapis lazuli, and carnelian jewelry. Nearby was a gold- and jewel-encrusted harp, across which were the bones of the gold-crowned harpist. The bodies were lying on a ramp, and as the excavators continued down the platform they encountered a heavily jeweled chariot, complete with the remains of oxen and grooms. Then the investigators began unearthing masses of gold, silver, stone, and copper vessels, as well as additional human bodies, weapons, and other items. Nearby, another set of six male skeletons equipped with copper knives and helmets was found, as well as the remains of two four-wheeled wooden wagons—also decorated with harnesses of gold and silver and accompanied by the skeletons of grooms and drivers. Other arrangements of human skeletons, harps, wagons, and model boats appeared as the excavations continued. At the end of the tomb was a wooden bier containing the remains of the queen. The entire upper part of her body was hidden by a mass of beads of gold, silver, lapis lazuli, carnelian, agate, and chalcedony. Her headdress and other furnishings were lavishly ornamented with gold, silver, and precious jewels. Liberally strewn about the chamber were human bodies, jewelry, vessels of precious metals, silver figurines, silver tables, cosmetics, seashell ornaments, and a number of other treasures.

All together some sixteen "royal" burials were found at Ur, all of them distinguished from the myriad common graves by the fact that each was not merely a coffin but rather a structure of stone, or stone and mudbrick, and by the inclusion of human sacrifices—up to eighty in one case. At least three categories of burials seemed evident, ranging from the sixteen royal graves to less elaborate but still richly furnished graves in which the common people were presumably placed.

As brilliant as Sumerian civilization was, one must realize that it was just one of the states of this era (Figure 8.12). In the southwestern highlands of Iran, for example, between 3300 and 2800 B.C. a great "Proto-Elamite" trading state arose, perhaps on the basis of its ability to dominate trade over the rich routes between Mesopotamia and the Iranian Plateau.[69]

SOUTHWEST ASIA AFTER 2350 B.C.

For centuries after 3000 B.C., the Sumerian city-states engaged in almost constant warfare, with first one and then another gaining temporary ascendancy. With the rise to power of Sargon of Akkad at about 2350 B.C., however, the political fabric of ancient Southwest Asia was forever changed. Sargon and his several immediate successors used the city of Akkad as a military base from which they mounted spectacularly successful attacks in all directions. Akkadian historical documents recount thirty-four battles fought by Sargon against the southern city-states, during which he moved

FIGURE 8.11 Crushed skull of a female attendant in the death pit at Ur (above). Note the gold jewelry and precious stones. This Sumerian model of a goat and a tree (below) is made of wood, lapis, and gold, and is about 51 cm high. It was found at Ur and dates to about 2600 B.C.

FIGURE 8.12   Gypsum statuettes of an aged couple, residents at about 2500 B.C. of Nippur, one of the largest cities in southern Mesopotamia during this period.

down the alluvial plain, capturing many kings, smashing city walls, and finally "cleansing his weapons in the sea." Sargon appointed Akkadians to administrative posts in the conquered city-states and then began expanding his other frontiers, invading Syria, Lebanon, and western Iran.

After 2250 B.C. quarrels arose among rival claimants to the Akkadian throne, and the state fragmented under the onslaught of peoples moving in from the highlands on its margins. This "dark age" lasted until about 2100 B.C., when one or more Sumerian kings were able to evict the invaders and reestablish political control over much of the southern alluvial plain under what is known as the Ur III dynasty. One ruler, Ur-Nammu, based at the ancient city of Ur, aggressively extended his influence into much of the area formally encompassed by the Akkadians. Great volumes of obsidian, lapis lazuli, and copper are thought to have passed into central Mesopotamia from as far away as Afghanistan, Anatolia, and even Cyprus. Legal texts of the late third millenium describe in detail problems of land use, irrigation rights, compensation for bodily injury, penalties for adultery, and many other elements of daily life.

Despite its apparent stability, the Ur III political system of the late third millenium was constantly under pressure from internal political rivalries, as well as from the incursions of semi-nomads and rival groups along the state's frontiers. The coup de grace was administered at about 2004 B.C. with the invasion from western Iran of the Elamites, who led the king of Ur away in captivity.

From about 2000 to 1800 B.C., Greater Mesopotamia was politically fragmented as kings at Isin, Larsa, Susa, and elsewhere established contending states.[70] Eventually, the ancient city of Babylon became the most powerful political entity, and by 1792 B.C. Hammurabi established the Babylonian Empire, based mainly on the southern alluvial plain. The many documents of his reign that have survived reflect a skillful politician adept at bureaucratic, military, and political uses of power: his famous law code, although harsh by modern standards, reflects efficient administration. Both Hammurabi and his successors encountered opposition from southern city-states and from a rival state in Assyria, to the north. As always, the nomads and other peoples on the empire's periphery—in this case the Kassites and Hurrians—made inroads as soon as the central government weakened, and eventually they overran much of the Babylonian Empire.

After about 1600 B.C., the political history of Southwest Asia becomes extremely complicated, with frequent political realignments and, ultimately, the gradual development and extension of imperial power (Figure 8.13). Assyrians, Elamites, Achaemenids, and other cultural groups established empires, and eventually the political and military scale became distinctly internal as empires centered in Egypt, Anatolia, and Iran met and, more often than not, came into conflict (Figure 8.14).

THE ORIGINS OF CULTURAL COMPLEXITY IN SOUTHWEST ASIA: SUMMARY AND CONCLUSIONS

It is possible that some archaeologist will, while sweating over a Mesopotamian mud-brick building foundation one day, discover a library of cuneiform tablets that record in great detail a history of the origins of the Mesopotamian state, complete with population statistics, war casualties, changes in the weather, average fertility rates, and a demographic analysis of the whole critical two millennia of state origins.

In fact, recent discoveries from Syria, dated to the late third millennium B.C., of previously unknown archives of thousands of texts do provide some information of

FIGURE 8.13   The extent of the Assyrian and Persian (Achaemenid) empires.

FIGURE 8.14 At about 500 B.C. the capital of the Achaemenid empire was Persepolis, in central Iran. This grand stairway ascends to the Palace, and along it are reliefs that illustrate real life processions to pay homage to the king. Some of these sculpted figures carry flowers and other gifts for the ruler.

this kind. But for the most part, only archaeological data can provide evidence of the long-term and broad-scale factors that form the framework of Southwest Asian cultural history. We have some sense of such factors as the rates of population growth, evolution of trade networks, changing settlement patterns, etc. (Figure 8.15), but excavations are slow and expensive, and political problems continue to hinder research.

With the information now available, however, the evolution of complex societies in Mesopotamia seems to have been the result of multiple factors, operating in complex patterns that differed from place to place (Figure 8.16). The alluvial plain has the potential to produce tremendous quantities of food, more than is required in most years to sustain millions of people and their domestic animals. Such surpluses do not necessarily create great differences in wealth, but they certainly allow the formation of rich and poor social classes, and it seems to be a pattern that wherever one finds economic systems that produce great surpluses, one also discovers elaborate social hierarchies of administrators to organize, store, distribute, and exploit these surpluses.

What factors stimulate the production of surpluses and thus create the conditions for the establishment of social classes and administrative hierarchies? Our review of the evidence from Southwest Asia suggests that irrigation cannot be said to be the "primary cause" of early Southwest Asian cultural complexity. Occupational specialization, monumental architecture, changes in settlement spacing and size hierarchies, architectural variability, mortuary stratification—in short, the whole range of physical evidence of cultural complexity—appear before evidence of significant extension of irrigation systems. This is true for both the heartland of Sumer and for the Susiana Plain in southwestern Iran—the two areas for which we have the best archaeological data. In much of Southwest Asia, in fact, increased investments in irrigation systems appear to be the result of urbanism, not its cause.[71]

For large cities to form and persist, the areas surrounding them must be particularly productive, because it was not feasible for these ancient city dwellers to farm

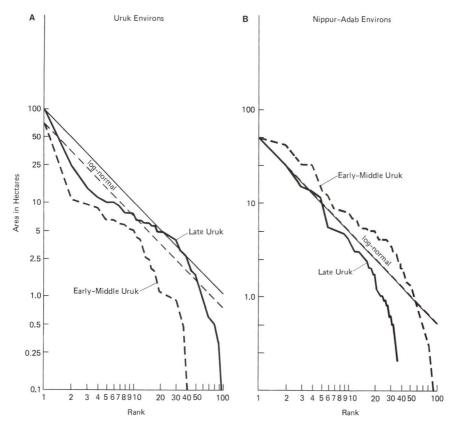

FIGURE 8.15 Settlement rank-size plots produced by Robert McC. Adams (1981) for two areas of Mesopotamia during the early Middle Uruk period (c. 3400 B.C.) and the Late Uruk period (c. 3200 B.C.), the periods when the first "states" were appearing in this part of Mesopotamia. Rank-size plots like these are formed by ranking the settlements from largest to smallest and then plotting a settlement's rank against its size on a log-log scale. Geographers have found that different shapes of such plots correlate with certain kinds of economic and political situations. The "flat-top"plot of the Early Uruk in the Nippur-Adab region (**B**) often is associated with very loose economic integration, whereas a log-normal distribution (the dotted lines in the graphs) is associated with considerable political and economic integration. The fact that both the plots for the Late Uruk period—when the first developed complex societies here were in operation—changed over time in the same direction from markedly different original plots, may reflect the growing economic and political interdependence of settlements in the late Uruk "state."

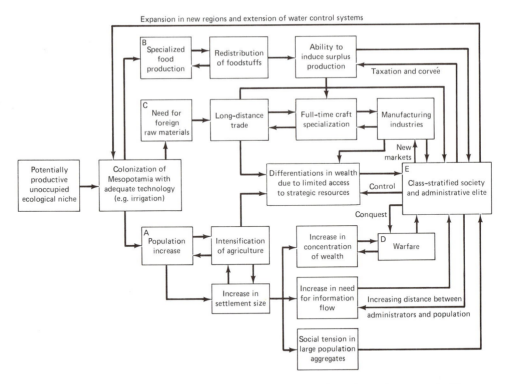

FIGURE 8.16 A model (by C. Redman [1978]) illustrating hypothetical cause-and-effect relationships among variables that led to the formation of class-structured "states" in Mesopotamia.

areas more than five or ten kilometers from the city. Irrigation was absolutely necessary for any sedentary existence on the alluvial plain, but if the spread, integration, and construction of irrigation systems were the mechanisms whereby complex societies first evolved and developed, we would expect to see a direct and positive correlation between the size and complexity of irrigation systems and the complexity of cultures based on them.

Instead, we find that 'Ubaid, Uruk, and Early Dynastic settlements subsisted on the produce of fields that could be irrigated by relatively simple, autonomous canal works. Only many centuries after the appearance of the first complex societies were complex, integrated irrigation systems in place.

Some scholars have tried to explain the origins of cultural complexity in Southwest Asia and elsewhere as mainly the result of human population growth. The persistence of this view must be seen in large part as a result of the fact that if one graphs the approximate population of Greater Mesopotamia from about 8000 B.C. to about 3000 B.C against evidence of activity specialization, monumental architecture, agricultural productivity, and other indications of cultural complexity, then an impressively close correlation is apparent. Also, it is difficult not to be impressed by the evidence that warfare was a potent factor in Mesopotamian cultural evolution. Great brick walls ring cities and villages alike in some periods, and there are caches of weapons, chariots, documents, and representational art to tell us that warfare formed the very weft and warp of Mesopotamian history. Nor is this sustained level of warfare merely a historical curiosity: if some adult male citizen in ancient Mesopotamia of almost any century were transported through time to our own age, the thing he would find most familiar, perhaps, is the battle that raged through the 1980s between Iran and Iraq, or the 1990 Gulf War. Armies have met here in this same general area in almost every century for more than 5,000 years.

If we apply the principles of evolutionary biology, warfare is simply an expression of competition, which is common to all life forms. To give it a name, however, is not to explain it, nor is the importance of warfare in *initial* Mesopotamian cultural complexity manifestly evident. One might expect that with the cheapness of clay construction, there would be many more walled settlements in the early civilizations if warfare were a frequent curse. The walling of towns does occur very soon after the emergence of urbanism, and warfare may have played a significant role in the major increases of cultural complexity that followed the earliest "states," but extensive circumvallation of sites is common on the southern alluvial plain mainly after about 2900 B.C.—some centuries after the appearance of other evidence of cultural complexity. After 2900 B.C. the historical records leave no doubt that warfare was almost continuous throughout Southwest Asia. But can population growth and warfare be shown to have been antecedent conditions to the rise of Mesopotamian states? In Iranian Mesopotamia, on the Susiana Plain, Wright and Johnson conclude that

> The available data show there was a period of population decline prior to state formation. States emerged perhaps during a period of unsettled conditions as population climbed back toward its former level. As Carneiro suggested, warfare may have a role in state formation, but in this case, increasing population in a circumscribed area cannot be the sole or direct cause of such warfare. If the hypothesis that population increase was the primary cause of state formation were correct, the state should have emerged in Susiana times [before 4000 B.C.] because population in that period seems to have been as high as in early Uruk times [3700 B.C.].[72]

The Susiana Plain, however, is an area where rainfall agriculture is possible, and there are some questions about the reliability of Wright and Johnson's population estimates.[73] What about the southern Mesopotamian alluvial plain, the Sumerian heartland? Robert McC. Adams concludes that

> Possibly the attainment of some minimal population level was necessary to set the process [for urbanization] into motion. But such evidence as there is suggests that appreciable population increases generally followed, rather than preceded, the core processes of the Urban Revolution. Particularly in Mesopotamia, where the sedentary village pattern seems to have been stabilized for several millennia between the establishment of effective food production and the "take-off" into urbanism, it may be noted that there is simply no evidence for gradual population increases that might have helped to precipitate the Urban Revolution.[74]

Adams here is principally concerned with the phenomenon of urbanism rather than complex societies in general, but his "Urban Revolution" includes many of the essential transitions we have defined as the basis for the evolution of complex societies. What about agricultural intensification? In Carneiro's scheme this is a direct result of population pressure; thus we should find evidence of increasingly intensive irrigation and of farming of marginal lands just before, and along with, the evolution of cultural complexity. But major investments in irrigation and land reclamation seem to have occurred after the emergence of urbanism and other evidences of cultural complexity. In addition, as Adams notes, urbanization appears to have involved the widespread abandonment of large areas of formerly intensively farmed lands. Furthermore, there is no evidence that any of the areas of early state formation ever approached their agricultural limits; that is, with only minor investments in additional irrigation systems, they could have enormously increased the numbers of people who could be supported, yet the population size remained quite stable. In short, agricultural intensification seems to have been more a result than a cause of the emergence of complex societies.

Adams nonetheless attributes considerable importance to environment and agriculture in the evolution of Southwest Asian civilization:

> In the largest sense, Mesopotamian cities can be viewed as an adaptation to [the] perennial problem of periodic, unpredictable shortages. They provided concentration points for the storage of surpluses, necessarily soon walled to assure their defensibility. The initial distribution of smaller communities around them suggests primarily localized exploitation of land, with much of the producing population being persuaded or compelled to take up residence within individual walled centers rather than remaining in villages closer to their fields. Tending to contradict a narrowly determinist view of urban genesis as merely the formation of walled storage depots, the drawing together of significantly larger settlements than had existed previously not only created an essentially new basis for cultural and organizational growth but could hardly have been brought about without the development of powerful new means for unifying what originally were socially and culturally heterogeneous groups.[75]

Adams argues "that the primary basis for [political-economic] organization was religious allegiance to deities or cults identified with particular localities, political superordination resting ultimately on the possibility of military coercion, or a fluid mixture of both."[76] Charles Redman concluded that

> City-states were the pervasive political units that were only temporarily unified into larger national states. The causes for these periods of unification and centralized authority are diverse, but economic factors seem to be a recurrent theme. Lowland Mesopotamia is devoid of some of the most basic raw materials. . . . The importance of these goods may have been crucial in the emergence of urbanism in Mesopotamia. . . . Two major forces were called upon to forge nation-states out of the heterogeneous Mesopotamian cities: militarism and complex administration. These two factors were the primary unifying elements, although in different proportions, in all Mesopotamian state governments and in subsequent ones.[77]

So, as with other areas of early civilization, when we examine the basic factors of environment, ecology, technology, demography, and agriculture, we see strong correlations between these factors and the shape and history of Southwest Asian history. Yet, these correlations do not constitute a powerful explanation or comprehensive understanding of Southwest Asian cultures. At a fundamental level these civilizations were a set of ideas and social relations. The ideology that legitimized the strict hierarchies of power, prestige, and wealth, and the social relationships among the many peoples in these hierarchies are a crucial focus of analysis in trying to understand why Southwest Asian civilizations evolved and how they functioned. Ancient texts, in combination with other archaeological data, help us understand much about these social relationships, but there is much we still do not understand.

BIBLIOGRAPHY

Abu es-Soof, B. 1968. "Tell Es-Sawwan: Excavations of the Fourth Season (Spring 1967) Interim Report." *Sumer* 24:3–16.

Adams, R. McC. 1955. "Developmental Stages in Ancient Mesopotamia." In *Irrigation Civilizations. A Comparative Study*, ed. J. H. Steward. Washington, DC: Pan-American Union, Social Science Monographs.

———. 1965. *Land Behind Baghdad*. Chicago: University of Chicago Press.

———. 1966. *The Evolution of Urban Society: Early Mesopotamia and Prehispanic Mexico*. Chicago: Aldine.

———. 1972. "Patterns of Urbanization in Early Southern Mesopotamia." In *Man, Settlement and Urbanism*, eds. P. G. Ucko, R. Tringham, and G. Dimbleby. London: Duckworth.

———. 1975. "The Mesopotamian Social Landscape: A View from the Frontier." In *Reconstructing Complex Societies*. Supplement to the Bulletin of the American Schools of Oriental Research, No. 20.

———. 1981. *Heartland of Cities*. Chicago: Aldine.

Adams, R. McC. and H. Nissen. 1972. *The Uruk Countryside*. Chicago: University of Chicago Press.

Akkermans, P. P. M. G. 1989. "Tradition and Social Change in Northern Mesopotamia during the Later Fifth and Fourth Millenium B.C." In *Upon This Foundation— The Ubaid Reconsidered*, eds. E. F. Henrickson and I. Thuesen. Copenhagen: Museum Tusculanum Press.

Alden, J. R. 1982. "Trade and Politics in Proto-Elamite Iran." *Current Anthropology* 23(6):613–40.

Algaze, G. 1989a. "A New Frontier: First Results of the Tigris-Euphrates Archaeological Reconnaissance Project, 1988." *Journal of Near Eastern* Studies 48:241–81.

———. 1989b. "The Uruk Expansion, Cross-cultural Exchange in Early Mesopotamian Civilization." *Current Anthropology* 30(5):571–608.

———. 1993. *The Uruk World System*. Chicago: University of Chicago Press.

Algaze, G., M. E. Evins, M. L. Ingraham, L. Marfoe, and K. A. Yener. 1990. *Town and Country in Southeastern Anatolia*. Vol. 2: *The Stratigraphic Sequence at Kurban Höyük*. Oriental Institute Publications 110. Chicago: Oriental Institute.

Algaze, G., R. Breuninger, C. Lightfoot, and M. Rosenberg. 1991. "The Tigris-Euphrates Archaeological Reconnaissance Project: A Preliminary Report on the 1989–1990 Seasons." *Anatolica* 17:175–240.

Areshian, G. E. 1990. "Further Thoughts on the Uruk Expansion." *Current Anthropology* 31:396–98.

Athens, J. S. 1977. "Theory Building and the Study of Evolutionary Process in Complex Societies." In *For Theory Building in Archaeology*, ed. L. R. Binford. New York: Academic Press.

Ball, W., D. Tucker, and T. J. Wilkinson. 1989. "The Tell Al-Hawa Project: Archaeological Investigations in the North Jazira, 1986–87." *Iraq* 41:1–66.

Bar-Yosef, O. 1980. "Prehistory of the Levant." *Annual Review of Anthropology* 9:101–33.

Behm-Blancke, M. R. 1989. "Mosaiksifte am oberen Euphrat—Wandschmuck aus Uruk- Zeit." *Istanbuler Mitteilungen* 39:73–83.

Boehmer, R. M. 1991. "Uruk 1980–1990: A Progress Report." *Antiquity* 65:465–78.

Breniquet, C. 1989. "Les origines de la culture d'Obeid en Mésopotamie du nord." In *Upon This Foundation—The Ubaid Reconsidered*, eds. E. F. Henrickson and I. Thuesen. Copenhagen: Museum Tusculanum Press.

Byrd, B.F. 1989. "The Natufian: Settlement Variability and Economic Adaptation in the Levant at the End of the Pleistocene." *Journal of World Prehistory* 3(2): 159–98.

———. 1994. "Public and Private, Domestic and Corporate: The Emergence of the Southwest Asian Village." *American Antiquity* 59(4): 639–666.

Chase-Dunn, C., and T. D. Hall. 1991. "Conceptualizing Core/Periphery Hierarchies for Comparative Study." In *Core/Periphery Relations in Pre-capitalist Worlds*, eds. C. Chase-Dunn and T. D. Hall. Boulder, CO: Westview Press.

Childe, V. G. 1952. *New Light on the Most Ancient East*, 4th Ed. London: Routledge and Kegan Paul.

Cowgill, G. 1975. "On Causes and Consequences of Ancient and Modern Population Changes." *American Anthropologist* 77:505–25.

Crawford, H. 1991. *Sumer and the Sumerians*. Cambridge: Cambridge University Press.

Cribb, R. 1991. *Nomads in Archaeology*. Cambridge: Cambridge University Press.

Crumley, C. L. 1979. "Three Locational Models: An Epistemological Assessment for Anthropology and Archaeology." In *Advances in Archaeological Method and Theory*, Vol. 2, ed. M. B. Schiffer. New York: Academic Press.

Diakonoff, I. M., ed. 1969. *Ancient Mesopotamia*. Moscow: Nauka.

Diringer, D. 1962. *Writings*. New York: Praeger.

Dunnell, R. Personal communication.

Evins, M. A. 1989. "The Late Chalcolithic/Uruk Period in the Karababa Casin, Southeastern Turkey." In "Out of the Heartland: The Evolution of Complexity in Peripheral Mesopotamia during the Uruk Period, Workshop Summary," ed. M. Rothman. *Paléorient* 14:270–71.

Falconer, S. E., and S. H. Savage. 1995. "Early Urbanization in Mesopotamia and the Southern Levant."

———. 1995. "Heartlands and Hinterlands: Alternative Trajectories of Early Urbanization in Mesopotamia and the Southern Levant." *American Antiquity* 60(1):37–58.

Finegan, J. 1964. *Handbook of Biblical Chronology: Principles of Time Reckoning in the Ancient World and Problems of Chronology in the Bible*. Princeton: Princeton University Press.

Flannery, K. V. 1972. "The Cultural Evolution of Civilizations." *Annual Review of Ecology and Systematics* 3:399–426.

Frankfort, H. 1956. *The Birth of Civilization in the Near East*. Garden City, NY: Doubleday.

Friedman, J. and M. J. Rowlands. 1977. *The Evolution of Social Systems*. Pittsburgh: University of Pittsburgh Press.

Gelb, I. J. 1952. *A Study of Writing: The Foundations of Grammatology*. Chicago: University of Chicago Press.

———. 1969. "On the Alleged Temple and State Economics in Ancient Mesopotamia." *Estratto da studi in onore di Edouard Vtoltera* 4:139–54.

Gibson, M. 1972. "Population Shift and the Rise of Mesopotamian Civilization." In *The Explanation of Cultural Change: Models in Prehistory*, ed. C. Renfrew. London: Duckworth.

Goldstein, P. S. 1989. "The Tiwanaco Occupation of Moquegua." In *Ecology, Settlement, and History in the Osmore Drainage, Peru*, eds. D. S. Rice, C. Stanish, and P. R. Scarr. Oxford: British Archaeological Review, International Series 545.

Hamblin, D. J., et al. 1973. *The First Cities*. New York: Time-Life.

Higham, C. 1989. *The Archaeology of Mainland Southeast Asia.* Cambridge: Cambridge University Press.

Hole, F. 1977. "Pastoral Nomadism in Western Iran." In *Explorations in Ethnoarcheology*, ed. R. A. Gould. Albuquerque: University of New Mexico Press.

———. 1978. "The Prehistory of Herding: Some Suggestions from Ethnography." *Colloques International du CNRS*, no. 580.

———. 1987. "Settlement and Society in the Village Period." In *The Archaeology of Western Iran*, ed. F. Hole. Washington, DC: Smithsonian Institution Press.

———. 1994. "Environmental Instabilities and Urban Origins." In *Chiefdoms and Early States in the Near East: The Organizational Dynamics of Complexity. Monographs in World Archaeology* 18:121–151.

Hole, F., K. V. Flannery, and J. A. Neely. 1969. *Prehistory and Human Ecology of the Deh Luran Plain.* Memoirs of the Museum of Anthropology, University of Michigan, no. 1.

Hout, J-L. 1979, "Ubaidian Villages of Lower Mesopotamia." In *Upon This Foundation—The Ubaid Reconsidered*, eds. E. F. Henrickson and I. Thuesen. Copenhagen: Museum Tusculanum Press.

Ibrahim, M., J. A. Sauer, and K. Yassine. 1976. "The East Jordan Valley Survey, 1975." *Bulletin of the School of Oriental Research* 22:42–64.

Ifrah, G. 1985. *From One to Zero.* Trans. L. Bair. New York: Viking Penguin.

Jacobsen, T., and R. Adams. 1958. "Salt and Silt in Mesopotamian Agriculture." *Science* 128:1251–58.

Jawad, A. J. 1965. *The Advent of the Era of Townships of Northern Mesopotamia.* Leiden: Brill.

Johnson, G. A. 1973. *Local Exchange and Early State Development in Southwestern Iran.* Museum of Anthropology, Anthropological Papers, University of Michigan, no. 51. Ann Arbor.

———. 1975a. "Locational Analysis and the Investigation of Uruk Local Exchange Systems." In *Ancient Civilization and Trade*, eds. J. Sabloff and C. Lamberg-Karlovsky. Albuquerque: University of New Mexico Press.

———. 1975b. "Early State Organization in Southwestern Iran: Preliminary Field Report." *Proceedings of the 4th Annual Symposium on Archaeological Research in Iran.* Teheran.

———. 1977. "Aspects of Regional Analysis in Archaeology." *Annual Review of Anthropology* 6:479–508.

———. 1981. "Monitoring Complex System Integration and Boundary Phenomena with Settlement Size Data." In *Archaeological Approaches to the Study of Complexity*, ed. S. E. van der Leeuw. Amsterdam: University of Amsterdam.

———. 1982. "Organizational Structure Scalar Stress." In *Theory and Explanation in Archaeology.* New York: Academic Press.

———. 1987a. "The Changing Organization in Uruk Administration on the Susiana Plain." In *The Archaeology of Western Iran*, ed. F. Hole. Washington, DC: Smithsonian Institution Press.

———. 1987b. "Nine Thousand Years of Social Change in Western Iran." In *The Archaeology of Western Iran*, ed. F. Hole. Washington, DC: Smithsonian Institution Press.

Just, P. 1980. "Time and Leisure in the Elaboration of Culture." *Journal of Anthropological Research* 36:105–15.

Kantor, H. J. 1992. "The Relative Chronology of Egypt and Its Foreign Correlations before the First Intermediate Period." In *Chronologies in Old World Archaeology*, 3d ed., ed. R. Ehrich. Chicago: University of Chicago Press.

Kipp, R. S., and E. M. Schortman. 1989. "The Political Impact of Trade in Chiefdoms." *American Anthropologist* 91:370–85.

Kramer, S. N. 1959. *History Begins at Sumer.* Garden City, NY: Doubleday.

Larsen, C. E. 1975. "The Mesopotamian Delta Region: A Reconsideration of Lees and Falcon." *Journal of the American Oriental Society* 95:43–57.

Larsen, C. E. and G. Evans. 1978. "The Holocene History of the Tigris-Euphrates-Karun Delta." In *The Environmental History of the Near and Middle East Since the Last Ice Age*, ed. W. C. Brice. London: Academic Press.

Lees, S. H. and D. G. Bates. 1974. "The Origins of Specialized Nomadic Pastoralism: A Systematic Model." *American Antiquity* 30:187–93.

Loding, D. 1976. *Ur Excavations: Economic Texts from the Third Dynasty*. Philadelphia: Publication of the Joint Expedition of the British Museum and the University Museum, University of Pennsylvania.

Maisels, C. K. 1993a. *The Emergence of Civilization: From Hunting and Gathering to Agriculture, Cities and the State in the Near East*. New York: Routledge.

———. 1993b. *The Near East: Archaeology in the "Cradle of Civilization."* New York: Routledge.

Mallowan, Sir M. E. L. 1965. *Early Mesopotamia and Iran*. London: Thames and Hudson.

Margueron, J-Cl. 1992. "Le bois dans l'architecture." *Bulletin on Sumerian Agriculture* 6:79–96.

Melikishvili, G. A. 1978. "Some Aspects of the Question of the Socioeconomic Structure of Ancient Near Eastern Societies." *Soviet Anthropology and Archaeology* 7:25–72.

Mellaart, J. 1965. *Earliest Civilizations of the Near East*. London: Thames and Hudson.

———. 1975. *The Neolithic of the Near East*. London: Thames and Hudson.

Mellink, M. 1989. "Archaeology in Asia Minor, Samsat." *American Journal of Archaeology* 93:114.

Mitchell, W. 1973. "The Hydraulic Hypothesis: A Reappraisal." *Current Anthropology* 4:532–34.

Nissen, H. 1972. "The City Wall of Uruk." In *The Explanation of Cultural Change: Models in Prehistory*, ed. C. Renfrew. London: Duckworth.

———. 1988. *The Early History of the Ancient Near East, 9000–2000 B.C.* Chicago: University of Chicago Press.

Nutzel, W. 1976. "The Climatic Changes of Mesopotamia and Bordering Areas." *Sumer* 32.

Oates, J. 1980. "The Emergence of Cities in the Near East." *The Cambridge Encyclopedia of Archaeology*. New York: Crown Publishers/Cambridge University Press.

Oppenheim, A. L. 1964. *Ancient Mesopotamia: Portrait of a Dead Civilization*. Chicago: University of Chicago Press.

Oren, E. 1989. "Early Bronze Age Settlement in Northern Sinai: A Model for Egypto-Canaanite Interconnections." In *L'urbanization de la Palestine à l'âge du Bronze Ancien*, ed. P. de Miroschedji. Oxford: British Archaeological Review, International Series 527.

Palmieri, A. 1989. "Storage and Dsitribution at Arslantepe-Malatya in the Late Uruk Period." In *Anatolia and the Ancient Near East: Studies in Honor of Tahsin Özgüç*, eds. K. Emre et al. Anakara: Türk Tarih Kurumu.

Pattee, H. H. 1973. *Hierarchy Theory: The Challenge of Complex Systems*. New York: Braziller.

Pollock, S. 1983. "Style and Information: An Analysis of Susiana Ceramics." *Journal of Anthropological Archaeology* 2(4):354–90.

———. 1992. "Bureaucrats and Managers, Peasants and Pastoralists, Imperialists and Traders: Research on the Uruk and Jemdet Nasr Periods in Mesopotamia." *Journal of World Prehistory* 6(3):297–336.

Postgate, N. 1994. *Early Mesopotamia: Economy and Society at the Dawn of History*. New York: Routledge.

Redman, C. L. 1978. *The Rise of Civilization*. San Francisco: W. H. Freeman.

Reimer, S. 1989. "Tell Qraya on the Middle Eurphrates." In "Out of the Heartland: The Evolution of Complexity in Peripheral Mesopotamia during the Uruk Period, Workshop Summary," ed. M. Rothman. *Paléorient* 15:273.

Renfrew, C. 1975. *The Emergence of Civilization*. London: Methuen.

———, ed. 1972. *The Explanation of Cultural Change: Models in Prehistory*. London: Duckworth.

Roux, G. 1976. *Ancient Iraq*. Baltimore: Penguin.

Sabloff, J. and C. C. Lamberg-Karlovsky, eds. 1975. *Ancient Civilization and Trade*. Albuquerque: University of New Mexico Press.

Saggs, H. W. F. 1989. *Civilization Before Greece and Rome*. New Haven: Yale University Press.

Scammell, G. V. 1989. *The First Imperial Age*. London: Unwin Hyman.

Schacht, R. 1987. "Early Historic Cultures." In *The Archaeology of Western Iran*, ed. F. Hole. Washington, DC: Smithsonian Institution Press.

Schmandt-Besserat, D. 1981. "Decipherment of the Earliest Tablets." *Science* 211:283–84.

Service, E. R. 1962. *Primitive Social Organization*. New York: Random House.

———. 1975. *Origins of the State and Civilization*. New York: Norton.

Simmons, A. H., I. Kohler-Rollefson, G. O. Rollefson, R. Mandel, and Z. Kafafi. 1988. "'Ain Ghazal: A Major Neolithic Settlement in Central Jordan." *Science* 240:35–39.

Smith, P. E. L., and T. C. Young, Jr. 1972. "The Evolution of Early Agriculture and Culture in Greater Mesopotamia. A Trial Model." In *Population Growth: Anthropological Implications*, ed. B. Spooner. Cambridge, MA: MIT Press.

Soylemez, M., and C. S. Lightfoot. 1991. "The Tigris-Euphrates Archaeological Reconnaissance Project Numismatic Notes." In *Recent Turkish Coin Hoards and Numismatic Studies*, ed. C. Lightfoot. Oxford: Oxbow Books.

Spooner, B., ed. 1972. *Population Growth, Anthropological Implications*. Cambridge, MA: MIT Press.

Spuhler, J. 1985. "Anthropology, Evolution, and 'Scientific Creationism.' " *Annual Review of Anthropology* 14:103–33.

Stager, L. 1992. "The Periodization of Palestine from Neolithic to Early Bronze Times." In *Chronologies in Old World Archaeology*, 3d ed., ed. R. Ehrich. Chicago: University of Chicago Press.

Stein, G. J., and M. J. Blackman. 1993. "The Organizational Context of Specialized Craft Production in Early Mesopotamian States." *Research in Economic Anthropology* 14:29–59.

Steward, J. H. 1949. "Cultural Causality and Law: A Trial Formulation of the Development of Early Civilizations." *American Anthropologist* 51:1–27.

Taylor, R. E., and R. Berger. 1980. "The Date of Noah's Ark." *Antiquity* 54:35–36.

Tosi, M. 1972. "The Early Urban Revolution and Settlement Pattern in the Indo-European Borderland." In *The Explanation of Cultural Change: Models in Prehistory*, ed. C. Renfrew. London: Duckworth.

———. 1984. "The Notion of Craft Specialization and Its Representation in the Archaeological Record of Early States in the Turanian Basin." In *Marxist Perspectives in Archaeology*, ed. M. Spriggs. Cambridge: Cambridge University Press.

Trigger, B. 1983. "The Rise of Egyptian Civilization." In *Ancient Egypt: A Social History*, eds. B. Trigger, B.J. Kemp, D. O'Connor, and A.B. Lloyd. Cambridge: Cambridge University Press.

Ucko, P., R. Tringham, and G. Dimbleby, eds. 1972. *Man, Settlement and Urbanism*. London: Duckworth.

Wattanmaker, P. 1990. "On the Uruk Expansion." *Current Anthropology* 31:67–68.

Wattanmaker, P., and G. Stein. 1989. "Leilan 1987 Survey: Uruk Summary." In "Out of the Heartland: The Evolution of Complexity in Peripheral Mesopotamia during the Uruk Period, Workshop Summary," ed. M. Rothman. *Paléorient* 15:273.

Webb, M. 1975. "The Flag Follows Trade: An Essay on the Necessary Integration of Military and Commercial Factors in State Formation." In *Ancient Civilization and Trade*, eds. J. Sabloff and C. C. Lamberg-Karlovsky. Albuquerque: University of New Mexico Press.

Weiss, H. 1977. "Periodization, Population, and Early State Formation in Khuzestan." In *Mountains and Lowlands: Essays in the Archaeology of Greater Mesopotamia*, eds. L. D. Levine and T. C. Young, Jr. Malibu: Undena.

Weiss, H., ed. 1986. *The Origins of Cities in Dry-farming Syria and Mesopotamia in the Third Millennium B.C.* Guildford, CT: Four Quarters Publishers.

Wenke, R. J. 1975–76. "Imperial Investments and Agricultural Developments in Parthian and Sasanian Khuzestan: 150 B.C. to A.D. 640." *Mesopotamia* 10–11:31–217.

———. 1981. "Explaining the Evolution of Cultural Complexity. A Review." In *Advances in Archaeological Method and Theory*, Vol. 4, ed. M. B. Schiffer. New York: Academic Press.

———. 1987. "Western Iran in the Partho-Sasanian Period: The Imperial Transformation." In *The Archaeology of Western Iran*, ed. F. Hole. Washington, DC: Smithsonian Institution Press.

———. 1989. "Egypt, Origins of Complex Societies." *Annual Review of Anthropology* 18:129–55.

White, L. 1949. *The Science of Culture*. New York: Grove Press.

Wilkinson, T. J. 1990a. *Town and Country in Early Southeastern Anatolia*. Vol. 1: *Settlement and*

Land Use in the Lower Karababa Basin. Oriental Institute Publications 109. Chicago: Oriental Institute.

———. 1990b. "The Development of Settlement in the North Jazira Region between the Seventh and First Millennia B.C." *Iraq* 52:49–62.

Willcox, G. H. 1992. "Timber and Trees." *Bulletin on Sumerian Agriculture* 6:1–31.

Wittfogel, K. A. 1957. *Oriental Despotism: A Comparative Study of Total Power.* New Haven: Yale University Press.

Wolkstein, D., and S. N. Kramer. 1983. *Inanna, Queen of Heaven and Earth.* New York: Harper & Row.

Woolley, Sir L. 1965. *Excavations at Ur.* New York: Crowell.

Wright, H. T. 1969. *The Administration of Rural Production in an Early Mesopotamian Town.* Ann Arbor: Museum of Anthropology, Anthropological Papers, University of Michigan, n. 38.

———. 1977. "Recent Research on the Origin of the State." *Annual Review of Anthropology* 6:379–97.

———. 1986. "The Evolution of Civilizations." In *American Archaeology. Past and Future*, eds. D. Meltzer, D. Fowler, and J. Sabloff. Washington, DC: Smithsonian Institution Press.

———. 1987. "The Susiana Hinterlands During the Era of Primary State Formation." In *The Archaeology of Western Iran*, ed. F. Hole. Washington, DC: Smithsonian Institution Press.

Wright, H. T., and G. A. Johnson. 1975. "Population, Exchange, and Early State Formation in Southwestern Iran." *American Anthropologist* 77:267–89.

Yasin, W. 1970. "Excavation at Tell Es-Sawwan, 1969 (6th Season)." *Sumer* 26:4–11.

Yener, A. K., H. Ozbal, A. Minzoni-Deroche, and B. Alsoy. 1989. "Bokardag: Archaeo-metallurgy Surveys in the Taurus Mountains, Turkey." *National Geographic Research* 5:477–94.

Yener, A. K., E. V. Sayre, E. C. Joel, H. Ozbal, et al. 1991. "Stable Lead Isotope Studies of Central Taurus Ore Sources and Related Artifacts from Eastern Mediterranean Chalcolithic and Bronze Age Sites." *Journal of Archaeological Science* 18:541–77.

Young, C. T., Jr. 1972. "Population Densities and Early Mesopotamian Origins." In *Man, Settlement and Urbanism*, eds. P. J. Ucko, R. Tringham, and G. W. Dimbleby. London: Duckworth.

Young, C. T., Jr., P. E. L. Smith, and P. Mortensen, eds. 1983. *The Hilly Flanks and Beyond: Essays on the Prehistory of Southwestern Asia.* Chicago: Studies in Ancient Oriental Civilization, No. 36, University of Chicago.

Zagarell, A. 1986. "Trade, Women, Class, and Society in Ancient Western Asia." *Current Anthropology* 27(5):415–30.

NOTES

1. Xenephon, *Anabasis.*

2. Postgate, *Early Mesopotamia: Economy and Society at the Dawn of History*, p. xxi

3. Reviewed in Postgate, *Early Mesopotamia: Economy and Society at the Dawn of History.*

4. See, for example, Adams, *Land Behind Baghdad*, or Adams and Nissen, *The Uruk Countryside.*

5. Mellaart, *Earliest Civilizations of the Near East*, p. 77.

6. Mellaart, *The Neolithic of the Near East*, pp. 101–5.

7. Redman, *The Rise of Civilization*, p. 187.

8. Information is just coming out now about excavations of sites of this period by Soviet ex-cavators.

9. Mellaart, *Earliest Civilizations of the Near East*, p. 77.

10. Hole, "Settlement and Society in the Village Period," p. 95, citing Childe, *New Light on the Most Ancient East*, p. 111.

11. Nissen, *The Early History of the Ancient Near East, 9000–2000 B.C.*, p. 57.

12. Abu es-Soof, "Tell Es-Sawwan: Excavations of the Fourth Season (Spring 1967) Interim Report"; Yasin, "Excavation at Tell Es-Sawwan, 1969 (6th Season)."

13. Larsen and Evans, "The Holocene History of the Tigris-Euphrates-Karun Delta."

14. Nutzel, "The Climatic Changes of Mesopotamia and Bordering Areas."

15. Hole, "Environmental Instabilities and Urban Origins," p. 140.

16. Hole, Flannery, and Neely, *Prehistory and Human Ecology of the Deh Luran Plain*.

17. Nissen, *The Early History of the Ancient Near East, 9000–2000 B.C.*

18. Postgate, *Early Mesopotamia: Economy and Society at the Dawn of History*, p. 24.

19. Wright, "The Evolution of Civilizations."

20. Cf. Hole, "Settlement and Society in the Village Period," p. 95.

21. Johnson, "Nine Thousand Years of Social Change in Western Iran," p. 284.

22. Ibid., p. 285.

23. Hole, "Settlement and Society in the Village Period."

24. Ibid., p. 96.

25. Nissen, *The Early History of the Ancient Near East, 9000–2000 B.C.*, pp. 47–48.

26. Falconer and Savage, "Early Urbanization in Mesopotamia and the Southern Levant."

27. Adams, "Patterns of Urbanization in Early Southern Mesopotamia."

28. Ibid., p. 739.

29. Johnson, *Local Exchange and Early State Development in Southwestern Iran*; Johnson, "Organizational Structure Scalar Stress."

30. Nissen, *The Early History of the Ancient Near East, 9000–2000 B.C.*, pp. 84–85.

31. Adams, "Patterns of Urbanization in Early Southern Mesopotamia," p. 743.

32. Cribb, *Nomads in Archaeology*.

33. Johnson, *Local Exchange and Early State Development in Southwestern Iran*; Johnson, "The Changing Organization in Uruk Administration on the Susiana Plain"; Wright, "The Evolution of Civilizations"; Wright, "The Susiana Hinterlands During the Era of Primary State Formation"; Wright and Johnson, "Population, Exchange, and Early State Formation in Southwestern Iran."

34. Schmandt-Besserat, "Decipherment of the Earliest Tablets."

35. Wright and Johnson, "Population, Exchange, and Early State Formation in Southwestern Iran," pp. 273–74.

36. Johnson, "Nine Thousand Years of Social Change in Western Iran," p. 287.

37. Johnson, "Aspects of Regional Analysis in Archaeology"; Johnson, "Organizational Structure Scalar Stress." For a description of hierarchy theory, see Pattee, *Hierarchy Theory: The Challenge of Complex Systems.*

38. Crumley, "Three Locational Models: An Epistemological Assessment for Anthropology and Archaeology."

39. Algaze, "The Uruk Expansion"; also see Algaze, *The Uruk World System.*

40. Pollock, "Bureaucrats and Managers, Peasants and Pastoralists, Imperialists and Traders: Research on the Uruk and Jemdet Nasr Periods in Mesopotamia," p. 330.

41. White, *The Science of Culture,* p. 383.

42. Personal communication.

43. Trigger, "The Rise of Egyptian Civilization," p. 64.

44. Johnson, "The Changing Organization in Uruk Administration on the Susiona Plain."

45. Adams, *The Evolution of Urban Society: Early Mesopotamia and Prehispanic Mexico,* and *Heartland of Cities.*

46. Frankfort, *The Birth of Civilization in the Near East,* pp. 56–58.

47. Nissen, *The Early History of the Ancient Near East, 9000–2000 B.C.,* pp. 120–21.

48. Oates, "The Emergence of Cities in the Near East."

49. Nissen, *The Early History of the Ancient Near East, 9000–2000 B.C.,* p. 81.

50. Diringer, *Writings.*

51. Nissen, *The Early History of the Ancient Near East, 9000–2000 B.C.,* p. 136.

52. Ibid., p. 40.

53. Ifrah, *From One to Zero.*

54. Ibid., p. 35.

55. Saggs, *Civilization Before Greece and Rome.*

56. Ibid., pp. 225–27.

57. Hamblin et al., *The First Cities,* pp. 103–4.

58. Wolkstein and Kramer, *Inanna, Queen of Heaven and Earth.*

59. Finegan, *Handbook of Biblical Chronology: Principles of Time Reckoning in the Ancient World and Problems of Chronology in the Bible,* pp. 42–43; quoted in Spuhler, "Anthropology, Evolution, and 'Scientific Creationism,'" p. 116.

60. Spuhler, "Anthropology, Evolution, and 'Scientific Creationism.'"

61. Taylor and Berger, "The Date of Noah's Ark."

62. See Postgate, *Early Mesopotamia: Economy and Society at the Dawn of History,* for an excellent review of Sumerian civilization.

63. Ibid., pp. 82–83.

64. Ibid., p. 105.

65. Ibid., p. 166.

66. Adams, *Heartland of Cities*.

67. Ibid., p. 87.

68. Woolley, *Excavations at Ur*.

69. Alden, "Trade and Politics in Proto-Elamite Iran."

70. Schacht, "Early Historic Cultures."

71. Adams, "Patterns of Urbanization in Early Southern Mesopotamia."

72. Wright and Johnson, "Population, Exchange, and Early State Formation in Southwestern Iran," p. 276.

73. Weiss, "Periodization, Population, and Early State Formation in Khuzestan."

74. Adams, *Heartland of Cities*, p. 252–54.

75. Ibid., p. 244.

76. Ibid., p. 78.

77. Redman, *The Rise of Civilization*, p. 319.

9

THE ORIGINS OF COMPLEX
SOCIETIES IN EGYPT

Concerning Egypt I shall extend my remarks to a great length,
because there is no country that possesses so many wonders,
nor any that has such a number of works that defy description.

Herodotus (c. 440 B.C.)

Ancient Egyptian civilization may have come into full flower a century or two later than Mesopotamian cultures and, perhaps, somewhat under their influence, but Egypt's cultural evolution was largely an independent process so distinctive and brilliant that ancient Egypt remains perhaps the most widely renowned of all ancient civilizations.

Egypt's similarities to other early civilizations are obvious: Egypt is yet another variation on an ancient theme, a developmental pattern in which farmers succeeded the hunter-forager-gatherers who had roamed northeast Africa for millennia, and then within a few centuries produced state-level governments, writing, monumental architecture, and the other aspects of "civilization," including a spiral of, first, civil wars, and later, centuries of ever-wider spheres of international warfare (Figure 9.1). In these and other developmental similarities Egypt is just one of a general class of phenomena—pre-industrial states (chapter 7).

Yet the similarities among ancient civilizations should not blind us to the unique genius of each. Egypt was a distinctive civilization whose excellence in arts, letters, and science can only be dimly glimpsed in its artifacts that lie in museum cases all over the world.

Ancient Egypt's most important contributions to the comparative analyses of early civilizations may derive from its variations on the themes evident in other early civilizations. Egypt, for example, was one of the most politically centralized of early states, yet it also seems to have been the least urban; the complexity of its governmental bureaucracy was extraordinary, with rank upon rank of viziers, governors, and other officials, but the vast majority of people seem to have lived in largely self-sufficient villages and towns; and though its political cycles were closely related to a single environmental factor (Nile flood levels), within these environmental limits Egypt's sociopolitical evolution was a baroque interweaving of factors, personalities, and events.

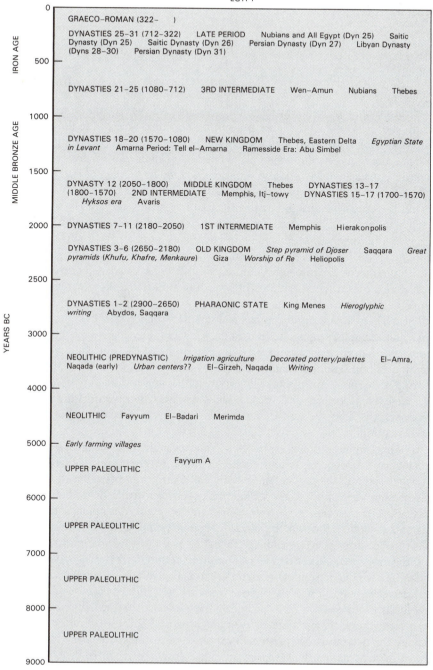

EGYPT

GRAECO–ROMAN (322–   )

DYNASTIES 25–31 (712–322)   LATE PERIOD   Nubians and All Egypt (Dyn 25)   Saitic
Dynasty (Dyn 25)   Saitic Dynasty (Dyn 26)   Persian Dynasty (Dyn 27)   Libyan Dynasty
(Dyns 28–30)   Persian Dynasty (Dyn 31)

DYNASTIES 21–25 (1080–712)   3RD INTERMEDIATE   Wen–Amun   Nubians   Thebes

DYNASTIES 18–20 (1570–1080)   NEW KINGDOM   Thebes, Eastern Delta   *Egyptian State
in Levant*   Amarna Period: Tell el–Amarna   Ramesside Era: Abu Simbel

DYNASTY 12 (2050–1800)   MIDDLE KINGDOM   Thebes   DYNASTIES 13–17
(1800–1570)   2ND INTERMEDIATE   Memphis, Itj–towy   DYNASTIES 15–17 (1700–1570)
    Hyksos era   Avaris

DYNASTIES 7–11 (2180–2050)   1ST INTERMEDIATE   Memphis   Hierakonpolis

DYNASTIES 3–6 (2650–2180)   OLD KINGDOM   *Step pyramid of Djoser*   Saqqara   *Great
pyramids (Khufu, Khafre, Menkaure)*   Giza   *Worship of Re*   Heliopolis

DYNASTIES 1–2 (2900–2650)   PHARAONIC STATE   King Menes   *Hieroglyphic
writing*   Abydos, Saqqara

NEOLITHIC (PREDYNASTIC)   *Irrigation agriculture*   *Decorated pottery/palettes*   El–Amra,
Naqada (early)   *Urban centers??*   El–Girzeh, Naqada   *Writing*

NEOLITHIC   Fayyum   El–Badari   Merimda

Early farming villages

Fayyum A

UPPER PALEOLITHIC

UPPER PALEOLITHIC

UPPER PALEOLITHIC

UPPER PALEOLITHIC

FIGURE 9.1   A cultural chronology of ancient Egypt.

THE ECOLOGICAL SETTING

Egypt . . . is an acquired country, the gift of the [Nile].

Herodotus (c. 440 B.C.)

Egypt is, indeed, in Herodotus's much-repeated phrase, the gift of the Nile, and the Nile in turn is the gift of rainstorms in the mountains of eastern and central Africa. The "White Nile" flows out of the lakes and springs of central Africa, and flows northward, where it is joined at Khartoum, in the Sudan, by the "Blue Nile," which is fed by summer monsoonal rains in the Ethiopian savannas and highlands.[1] Further north in the Sudan, the Atbara River, which also drains the Ethiopian highlands, joins the Nile.

The White Nile's volume does not vary much from season to season or year to year, but the Blue Nile and the Atbara fluctuate with the sharply seasonal rainstorms in their watersheds. Thus, until this century, when huge dams were built in southern Egypt, the torrential spring rains in east Africa annually sent silt-choked floods pulsing down the Nile Valley, depositing along the way a rich layer of fertile silts and clays. Along the river's course this natural alluviation has produced one of the world's richest agricultural niches, which with even the simplest tools supports as many as 450 people per square kilometer.

The Nile itself was an enormous source of food and other resources. The Nile perch,[2] for example, was a favorite food of ancient Egyptians before they became farmers and then throughout the pharaonic period as well. This fish lived in the ancient Nile in huge numbers and it is often found in warm shallow water—where it can easily be harpooned. It regularly grows to 75 kilograms in weight, and one specimen caught in Lake Nasser in recent times was over two meters long and weighed 175 kilograms.[3] The Nile also teemed with wildfowl—a favorite food throughout Egyptian antiquity.

Although highly productive, the Nile Valley is really only an extremely elongated oasis (Figure 9.2) where agricultural lands are sharply circumscribed in most regions by rocky deserts. From the Sudanese border to Cairo, the cultivable strip along both banks of the river is only a few kilometers wide in most places, and so sharp is the demarcation that, as the cliché has it, one can stand with one foot on the red desert sands and the other foot on the black, irrigated croplands. The ancient Egyptians called their country *Kemet*, or "black land," after the life-giving dark silts that produced the crops that sustained them. The surrounding deserts they called *Deshret*, or "red land." This distinction between desert and croplands is so marked because Egypt does not get enough precipitation to sustain any agriculture based on rainfall alone. The Nile is a single river through most of the land of Egypt, but north of Cairo it divides into several main branches, creating a delta of flat, well-watered, fertile land. Although the origins of Egyptian civilization were in the south, near Hierakonpolis, in later Egyptian history the Delta was the agricultural heartland of the country, famed for its wines, wheat, fruit, garden crops, and huge herds of cattle pastured there. As Egypt's political and cultural focus increasingly turned toward Syro-Palestine, the Delta also became a more important staging ground for armies and a crossroads of overland and maritime trade routes.

FIGURE 9.2 Some major Egyptian sites. Egypt's desert and mountain frontiers protected it for many centuries against outside influences, but already by 3000 B.C. its trade and military contacts extended into Palestine, Nubia, and the Mediterranean world.

The ancient Egyptians appreciated the basic geographic dichotomy of the Valley and Delta and thought of their country as composed of two different geographical units: from the Nubian border to the border of the Delta was *ta-shema*, the "land of the *shema* reed"; north of that, the Delta, was *ta-mehu*, the "land of the papyrus plant." Today most archaeologists refer to this division as that between "Upper Egypt" in the south and "Lower Egypt" in the north, the "Upper" and "Lower" reflecting the gradient of the Nile.

Thanks to the Nile, ancient Egyptians could traverse the length of their country in just a week or so of pleasant sailing, providing a rapid, reliable channel for the movement of goods, people, and information. The Egyptians did not use the wheel—either for vehicles, pottery manufacture, or other uses—until quite late, many centuries after it was a mainstay of Asian technology, probably because wheeled vehicles did not have much use in a country where the Nile provides such easy transport and where there is limited advantage to moving products among communities in an ecosystem that is quite similar over its entire length. Egypt's ecological similarity over most of its area and the Nile's efficiency as a transport and communications artery were key factors in the highly centralized governments that developed in later Egyptian antiquity, and it is not surprising that in the southern reaches of the Nile, where five cataracts (steep rapids) constitute impassable barriers to navigation, the power of the Egyptian government often weakened.

Although there have been major fluctuations in the annual volume of the Nile—for example, catastrophically low water levels in some of the years between 2250 and 1950 B.C.—the Nile floodplain has existed in essentially its present form since about 3800 B.C. In ancient times, however, the Mediterranean coastline was farther inland (Figure 9.2) because the Delta had not sunk nearly as far as it has now under the weight of accumulated silt. The gradient, periodicity, and other attributes of the Nile are such that complex irrigation systems using dams and long feeder canals up river became important only fairly late in Egypt's history. For the most part the Nile forms small flood basins that a few villages could manage successfully.[4] One simply waited for the spring floods to recede, leaving behind their rich sediments, and then scattered seeds on the ground, herded pigs or sheep over the cropland to trample the seeds into the ground, weeded and hoed the crops as they needed it, and then waited for the bountiful harvest. And while the Egyptians faced a lot of competition for grain ripening in fields, especially from birds and rodents, they had the friendly help of cats, which they "domesticated" (and vice versa), and most harvests were bountiful.

The annual floods were usually visible in southern Egypt, near the Nubian border, by late May, and the river rose quickly thereafter, until the beginning of September, when it began a long slow recession to its lowest level the next May. The Egyptian annual calendar was based on this flood cycle, dividing the year into three periods of four months each. The period of flooding, from July to October, was called *akhet*, which may have meant "inundation." Most of the crops were planted between November and February, a season called *peret*, or "time of emergence," in the sense that the farmland emerged as the floods receded. The harvest season, or *shemu*, was from March to June.

By ancient standards, Egypt was a rich country. The Israelites, wandering in the Sinai deserts, bemoaned the rich meals they had enjoyed while living in Egypt:

[A]nd the children of Israel . . . wept again and said, who shall give us flesh to eat? We remember the fish, which we did eat in Egypt for nought; the cucumbers, and the melons, and the leeks and the onions and the garlic.[5]

But if the spring floods were too high, then water stayed on the lands too long and crops could not be sown in time to harvest them before the summer heat destroyed them; if the floods were too low, not enough sediment and water were available for good harvests. Ancient Egyptians used tripods to dip water from the river to irrigate crops, and in some cases they trapped water behind dams during low flood years, so that they could use it later for irrigation; but in the long run—and with sensible storing of grains—the Nile Valley was rich enough to support high population densities.

EARLY EGYPTIAN AGRICULTURE

The Nile Valley and Delta are among the richest agricultural niches in the world, and thus the farming way of life may seem to be the "natural" state of human habitation there, but in fact farming came to Egypt only relatively late. For many millennia before farming appeared in Egypt, people lived there simply by hunting, fishing, and gathering the area's rich profusion of indigenous plants and animals. Today the Nile Valley looks like a rather poor place to try to make a living as a hunter-forager, because the narrow Nile floodplain runs through one of the driest deserts on earth, the Sahara; but before about 10,000 years ago rainfall made the deserts bloom for many millennia. In this Pleistocene Epoch the Nile itself teemed with fish and wildfowl, and areas that are now deserts along the Nile were for long periods rich grasslands that supported wild cows, gazelles, and many other large animals which, in turn, supported ancient Egyptian hunter-foragers.

This centuries-old way of life began to fade away about 10,000 years ago. As the great ice sheets in temperate latitudes shrank, the African rainfall patterns shifted, and the deserts replaced grasslands across much of North Africa. And as these deserts expanded, almost all human life in Egypt was concentrated in the Nile Valley and Delta. People in Egypt appear to have been in the process of domesticating cattle and other plant and animal species just as the Pleistocene was ending and the deserts were beginning to close around the Nile, about 10,000 years ago (perhaps earlier). But only at about 7,500 years ago did some of them become full-time farmers and make the transition to village life and an economy based mainly on the foods that eventually were to serve as the staples of pharaonic Egypt —emmer wheat, barley, sheep, goats, cattle, and pigs.

How did this transition to agriculture occur in Egypt? Egypt provides an interesting case to study this question because it involves both the processes by which people transmuted "wild" species into the ordinary domesticates of the village farm, and also how these people came to adopt Southwest Asian domesticates.

With the end of the last ice age at about 8000 B.C., the Nile Valley and its adjacent deserts took on much of the form and climate that they have today. The way of life just after 8000 B.C., at least as we know it from excavations in the southwestern

Egyptian desert, the Fayyum Oasis, and elsewhere, was apparently a slow seasonal round of hunting the desert margins for wild cattle, gazelle, birds, and many other animals, and exploiting the Nile for fish, fowl, and other animals and plants.

There is some suggestion of intensified plant use at late Pleistocene northeast African sites in areas like Kom Ombo and Wadi Kubbaniyya, in the form of mortars, sickle blades, and other implements, but the adaptation appears to have been a mobile one, based on small groups pursuing a diversified hunting-foraging economy.[6] Sometime after about 10,000 years ago, Egyptians appear to have been domesticating several varieties of local grasses,[7] and they also apparently were in the process of domesticating cattle, and then later some other animals, such as the mongoose (ichneumon), gazelle, oryx, addax, ibex, and hyena—none of which ever became completely domesticated or extensively used as farm or food animals.

The earliest evidence of forms of subsistence, settlement, and technology that differed significantly from those of the late Pleistocene in northeast Africa comes from the desert areas of Bir Kiseiba and Nabta in southwest Egypt (Figure 9.2). On the basis of evidence from this area, Wendorf, Schild, and Close note that both "cattle and pottery seem to have been known in the Sahara as early as anywhere else in the world."[8] Moreover, they observe that the people of about 6200–5900 B.C. lived in communities in which:

> The houses and pits indicate long term or, at least, recurrent settlement. At the very least, they must have been occupied for most of the year, and it seems likely that the Nile no longer played an important role in the settlement system, suggesting that a different kind of exploitation was now being employed in the desert. Instead of sites representing small family units or task-groups, there are now medium-sized villages, composed of perhaps as many as 14 family units . . . where there was at least sufficient social control to determine the arrangement of the community.[9]

We really do not know what these early hunter-foragers of the Egyptian deserts based their diets on—there are numerous ground stone tools but few plant remains from these sites.[10] They may have been cattle herders,[11] but the evidence is not entirely conclusive.[12]

Compared to the glories of pharaonic civilization, these tiny communities described by Wendorf, Schild, and Close might seem of negligible importance and interest, but they demonstrate again the great breadth and pervasiveness of the changes that swept the world after the end of the last Pleistocene era. As we saw in chapter 6, for reasons not altogether clear people around the world after about 10,000 years ago began to interact with plants and animals in ways that led in many cases to domestication and agriculture; and in this same period of transition people all over the world appear to have begun living in larger communities, in which they spent much or all of the year. Not every group around the world changed in these ways, and hunting-foraging in the traditional ways continued throughout most of the world. But when we place these early Egyptian communities in the context of similar changes in Anatolia, Mesoamerica, northern China, and many other places, this pattern of worldwide change appears revolutionary.

These early Egyptian communities also illustrate the nature of cultural evolutionary processes: cultural change and transformation is a fitful process of dead-ends, failures, extinctions, and only occasionally the kinds of slight changes that result in long-term revolutionary cultural transformation. For example, apparently these early Egyptian communities did not make the transition to a fully agricultural, sedentary way of life in these arid zones. Fekri Hassan and others have argued that eventually climate changes induced people to abandon areas that were slowly turning into deserts and migrate into the richer Nile Valley.[13] Had these climatic changes not forced people out of what are now the deserts of Egypt, perhaps they would have evolved their own agricultural communities on the basis of local grasses, cattle, and other resources—but we will never know: evolutionary processes are not predictable and only reveal a "pattern" when viewed backward in time.

Sometime between 6000 and 5000 B.C., domesticated wheat, barley, sheep, goats, and cattle were introduced from outside Egypt and became the basis for the evolution of Egyptian civilization. Whether these domesticates were introduced for the first time in this millennium or were just successfully farmed for the first time is unknown, as are their ultimate origins. The most likely source of the domestic wheat, barley, sheep, and goats that formed the staples of the Egyptian diet is Syro-Palestine and other areas of Southwest Asia, where they had already been in agricultural use for 2,000 years.

Our most systematic evidence about these early agriculturalists is from the Fayyum Oasis. British archaeologist Gertrude Caton-Thompson conducted excellent excavations along the lake's north shore in the 1930s, Fred Wendorf and Romauld Schild's work there in the 1970s greatly augmented Caton-Thompson's findings, and additional work has been done by other scholars.[14]

Agriculture has such great inertia because once people begin making and using large grinding stones, big grain storage silos, sickles, and all the rest of the primitive farmer's tool kit, there is a strong incentive not to move. Also, cereal grains ripen over a short interval, and a farmer who is out hunting the week they ripen can expect to come back to a field stripped bare by rodents and birds.

Thus it is puzzling that the ancient peoples of the Fayyum left no traces of houses or prolonged occupation (Figure 9.2). Caton-Thompson found complete sickles in silos full of wheat and barley in Fayyum sites dating to about 5000 B.C., but people here seem to have combined some minor cereal farming with the ancient hunting-foraging ways. Partly for this reason, some scholars see a resistance to the spread of agriculture in Egypt because of the richness of the lake and river environments. But by 4000 B.C. agriculture had spread over much of Egypt, including the southern areas that had taken a few tentative steps toward agriculture in the late Pleistocene. Some people still depended on fish and wild plants for much of their food, while others were already heavily dependent on the wheat-barley, sheep-goat-cattle-pig combination that underlies so much of Middle Eastern cultural evolution.

THE PREDYNASTIC PERIOD (C. 4000–3000 B.C.)

One of the most impressive and puzzling things about ancient Egypt is the apparent rapidity and comprehensiveness with which hundreds of unconnected and functionally similar villages were transmuted into an organized social, economic, and political unity—the first Egyptian state. This transmutation began at about 4000 B.C. in the south and rapidly spread to the north, encompassing most of Egypt by 3000 B.C.

The rise of the Egyptian "state" after c. 3100 B.C. is really just a bold reconstruction of what we infer happened. These inferences are based on: (1) the spread over much of Egypt of pottery and architectural styles that suggest close, continuing contacts among people over large areas of the country; (2) the investment of massive amounts of labor and resources in tombs and monumental buildings in such a way as to imply an unequal distribution of wealth, power, and prestige; and (3) some equivocal signs, like the Narmer Palette (Figure 9.3), that seem to indicate a potentate in the process of exercising kingly authority.

The evolution of Egyptian civilization began in the south, in Upper Egypt. In 1894 Sir Flinders Petrie excavated more than 2,000 graves at the site of Naqada, just north of Luxor, and defined the Predynastic cultural sequence. These graves were filled with pottery in different styles, as well as slate palettes, beautiful flint tools, jewelry made of bone and other materials, untold beads, figurines, and other riches. These graves and other Predynastic sites reveal a society quickly changing in the direction

FIGURE 9.3 The Narmer Palette, a thin sheet of stone engraved with symbols that may reflect the political unification of Egypt. King Narmer is shown wearing different crowns on the different sides of the palette, possibly symbolizing the political unification of the Delta and Nile Valley, under the representation of the hawk-headed god Horus. Scenes of battle and what appears to be a beheading suggest a military unification of the country.

of the class-stratified, religious unity that we know from documents of less than a thousand years later.[15]

The largest and most complex cluster of Predynastic settlements in Egypt are those at Hierakonpolis, the "City of the Hawk," where excavations have gone on for almost a century (until recently under the direction of the late Michael Hoffman).[16]

The Predynastic people of Hierakonpolis lived in rectangular, semi-subterranean houses of mudbrick and thatch, they apparently worshipped in small, perhaps wooden shrines, they made and distributed regionally several kinds of pottery, some of it very beautiful. They also hunted, herded, fished, and farmed the by now traditional array of Egyptian plants and animals, and they buried their dead in rock and mudbrick tombs of a size and content to reflect the social power and prestige of the individual. The famed Narmer Palette (Figure 9.3), which traditionally has been interpreted as commemorating the unification of the Nile Valley and Delta into a national state, was found at Hierakonpolis, which may indicate that this city was an early capital of Egypt. But many scholars doubt that the Narmer Palette was a unique record of the first unification of Egypt.[17]

Elsewhere in southern Egypt, excavations by Fekri Hassan at Naqada (Figure 9.2) suggest that by the middle of fourth millennium B.C. this site was a large town that already was fully dependent on agriculture. Naqada and Hierakonpolis may have been by far the largest communities in all of southern Egypt at this time, with much smaller communities scattered down the valley.

In the north, beginning at about 3650 B.C. there were at least some large and comparatively wealthy communities, such as those at Ma'adi and El-Omari, both of which are just south of what is now Cairo. Stone tools, pottery, and other artifacts show that the people of Ma'adi exchanged products with Palestine, and they may have been part of a large trade network that integrated commodities from the Levant, the Nile Valley, and even the deserts and oases. The bones of donkeys have been found at Ma'adi, and one can imagine these people sending caravans off across the desert to Palestine, while their boats plied the Nile River trade. Burials at El-Omari included some apparently wealthy and perhaps powerful people who were buried in straw mats and along with large stores of pots, stone tools, and other goods.

Other Predynastic communities have been found in northern Egypt, most of them dating to just before 3000 B.C. At Minshat Abu Omar, hundreds of graves have been found containing the distinctive pottery, alabaster jars, slate palettes, and other riches of the late Predynastic. Recent excavations at Buto, in the northwestern Delta, have revealed clay cones identical to those used to decorate temples in the Uruk state centered in Mesopotamia at about 3200 B.C. Buto may have been one of the most important ports on maritime trade routes over which vast quantities of timber, oil, wine, minerals, pottery, and other commodities passed.[18]

THE ARCHAIC, OLD KINGDOM, AND FIRST INTERMEDIATE PERIODS (C. 3000–2040 B.C.)

Despite the apparent extent of commercial relationships in Predynastic Egypt, the ceramics of northern and southern Egypt remained quite different in style until about

3100 B.C. As we noted in chapter 8 with regard to Southwest Asia, and as we will see in later chapters, one apparently unfailing sign of increasing cultural complexity in ancient societies was a growing uniformity over larger and larger areas of styles of pottery. In fact, around the world, these increases in the area of distribution of certain styles and their growing uniformity correlate precisely with the appearance of other elements of complexity, such as more complex settlement patterns, monumental architecture, agricultural intensification, mortuary cults, etc. Thus, we might suspect that in Egypt the same pattern would hold, and there is evidence that it did. The distinctive styles of pottery from northern sites like Ma'adi, Buto, and various other sites in the Delta[19] appear to have been quickly and completely replaced by the styles of southern Egypt.

If this pattern of change does reflect the unification of Egypt, we may wonder how it was actually accomplished. As noted above, traditional sources suggest that Menes (also known as Narmer), a minor official from Upper Egypt, rose to power and conquered Lower Egypt at about 3100 B.C., and that he and his successors established a theocratic political system over the entire navigable length of the Egyptian Nile. Menes is recorded as having built a capital at Memphis (near modern Cairo), diverting the stream of the Nile to create a strategic position at the junction of Upper and Lower Egypt. His next several successors were also powerful kings, but there is some evidence of internal dissension at about 2900 B.C. Later, peace appears to have been restored, and major construction projects were undertaken in the centuries before 2700 B.C. We know from tombs and other archaeological evidence that already by the early Old Kingdom (c. 2700 B.C.), Egypt was a complexly organized nation-state, with monumental architecture, a multi-tiered economy, and a centralized and hierarchically arranged bureaucracy.

Fekri Hassan has shown that the evolution of complex societies in Predynastic Egypt was a long, involved process, in which climate changes, warfare, evolving agricultural efficiency, and the development of religions and political institutions were all subtly interrelated. He stresses that no simple ecological model can account for these changes, and that Egypt is not likely to have been unified by any single battle or ruler.[20]

And while the Predynastic period saw the first complex Egyptian societies, in trade patterns, occupational specialization, and settlement patterns, the Archaic and Old Kingdom periods were the great formative era of Egyptian civilization, the time when Upper and Lower Egypt were first united politically and Egyptian forms of writing, architecture, administration, and ideology emerged.

By 2700 B.C. the economic sphere was already quite complex, involving long-distance trade to Syria and beyond and considerable local exchange of craft goods and foodstuffs; but most Egyptians of the Old Kingdom period continued to live in unwalled, largely self-sufficient villages. Apart from Memphis there were few towns or cities, which may have contributed to the political integration of the country, since there were no urban power centers to resist incorporation.[21] Large areas of the middle Nile Valley were only sparsely settled, and population growth was quite slow, with little competition for agricultural land or irrigation water (although many new settlements appear to have been established in the Delta). Apparently, the slow population growth during the Old Kingdom (Butzer estimates an annual rate of 0.8 per

1,000 people) eventually did begin to exert some pressure on available resources toward the end of the period, since large game almost disappeared from the Alluvium and contemporary documents describe a shift away from pastoralism to a greater reliance on grain agriculture.[22]

The middle of the third millennium B.C. was for Egypt a marvelous age in which many of the greatest pyramids and palaces were built, an integrated royal bureaucracy was formed, and arts and crafts were brilliantly executed (Figures 9.4 and 9.5). Because of the relatively comprehensive documents from this period, we know many of its political and social details.[23] Economic exchange was apparently controlled almost entirely through the king; there were no "merchants"—in the capitalistic sense at least—until centuries after the end of the Old Kingdom. Craftsmen, scribes, peasants, and everyone else were required to perform some services in the name of the king and were liable for military and civil conscription, but there is a clear contrast

FIGURE 9.4 Ancient Egyptian art exudes a timeless beauty.

FIGURE 9.5 Lifelike funerary portrait masks such as this one, from the Fayyum, are a highlight in the history of mortuary art.

here with the partially capitalistic, multi-tiered, highly differentiated economic system characteristic of the later Mesopotamian states.

What Old Kingdom Egypt was like outside the main centers is less well known. Recent excavations and surveys have shown that the Old Kingdom Delta was densely occupied.[24] Many Delta settlements were probably "pious donations," the granting of tax exemptions to certain communities whose revenues were used to support mortuary cults at Giza and elsewhere. Pharaoh Wahkare' Khety III (2070–2040 B.C.), in his instructions to his son, Merykare, forcefully recommended building towns as a means to counteract political fragmentation and inefficient organization, especially in the eastern Delta, which, he lamented, was being subdivided into rival provinces and cities.[25] Old Kingdom Egypt had complex commercial and political relationships to Southwest Asian cultures, and since most of the sea and land routes to these areas were through the Delta, the Delta's importance increased. In fact, by about 2400 B.C.

the majority of Egypt's population probably lived north of Saqqara, and the seat of government power remained at Memphis, in the north, through much of Egypt's ancient history. Old Kingdom towns at Hierakonpolis and other southern cities remained important, however. Also, the Old Kingdom fort at Elephantine, near Aswan, guarded the southern approaches to the Kingdom.

Some characteristics distinguish Old Kingdom Egypt from Mesopotamia and other early complex societies. For example, there seem to have been no standing armies during most of the Old Kingdom and no economically significant slavery. In some ways the economic system—although highly administered—was a simple redistributive, almost chiefdom-like system, quite different from that of early Mesopotamian states.

PYRAMIDS

Djoser, the second king of the Third Dynasty, who reigned from about 2630 to 2611 B.C., was able to organize Egypt's people and economy to the extent that he, or his grand vizier, Imhotep, could arrange construction of the great step pyramid at Saqqara as his tomb. The actual crypt was built inside the pyramid, whose six levels rose over 60 meters and were surrounded by large buildings and a stone wall more than 9 meters wide with a perimeter of more than 1.6 kilometers. The pyramid complex at Saqqara was the world's first large-scale stone building and remains, despite much deterioration and the looting of its limestone facing, one of the most beautiful. It truly must have been an impressive sight, forty-five centuries ago, with its crisp white limestone facing contrasting with the cobalt blue sky, green palm groves, and desert sands.

Djoser's successors, particularly those of the Fourth Dynasty (c. 2575–2465 B.C.)—the beginning of the Old Kingdom Period—also built massive pyramids and experimented with designs and constructions until the "perfect" pyramid form was achieved by King Khufu—as exemplified by the pyramids at Giza (Figure 9.6). It is not just the massive size of this and other pyramids of this era that is so impressive, but also the complex engineering, the deft execution of stone sculpture, and the precise planning such projects would have required.

So much has been said and imagined about the pyramids, yet we can hope to know so little. The minds that designed them and invested them with meaning are these many centuries gone to dust, and not a single ancient Egyptian text of the period when they were built describes how they were constructed or why.

Cairo sprawls out and around the pyramids today in such clamorous ubiquity that the only way to see the pyramids in a manner anything like that of the ancient Egyptian is to come in from the west, in the early morning, in the quiet of the desert. The pyramids were all located on the west bank of the Nile, an equation no doubt with death and the setting sun. All are situated on the limestone outcrop near the river, to facilitate the transfer of innumerable blocks of limestone and alabaster, some of which had to be shipped down the Nile and then transported up the bank to the construction area.

Exactly how the blocks were quarried and transported remains unknown, but we have some clues. Quarrying probably involved a combination of hammering with hard

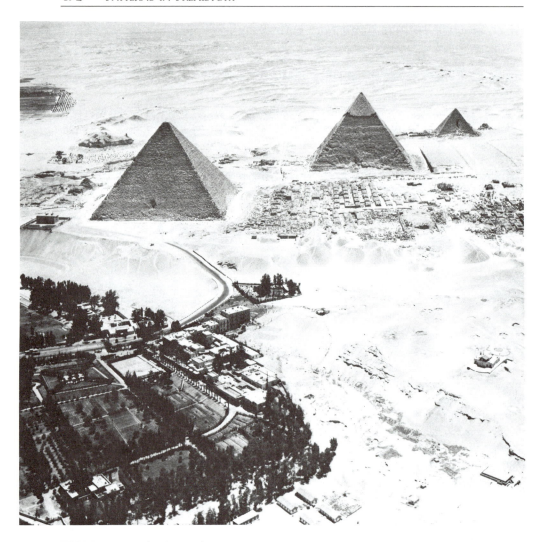

FIGURE 9.6 The Pyramids at Giza are the focal points in a vast mortuary complex of tombs and temples. But outside these mortuary centers Egypt was primarily a rural, agricultural society, with few cities.

stones, chopping with copper adzes, and fracturing by heating the rock with fires and then splashing cold water on it. Mark Lehner has thoroughly analyzed evidence relating to the surveying and construction methods used to build the pyramids, and he has evaluated the various possible combinations of ramps, rollers, and so on against the physical remains.[26] The Great Pyramid of Giza required the quarrying, transport, preparation, and laying of about 2,300,000 stone blocks, each with an average weight of 2.5 tons, and an estimated labor force equivalent to about 84,000 people employed for eighty days a year for twenty years. We do not know how these people were mobilized and administered, but many think the construction was done by the peasantry during the flood seasons, when little agricultural activity was required. The administration, feeding, direction, and planning required to control such a work force, which included many highly trained craftsmen as well as laborers, would obviously argue a high degree of political and bureaucratic centralization. The king was apparently able to call on all the resources of the country, and direct them and the people to virtually any end, and at times the entire national economy was probably focused on these projects. The monarch's absolute control is directly reflected in the texts and in the mortuary complexes of the various levels of high-ranking administrators who served him, many of whose tombs are laid out around the king's, reflecting his control over them even into eternity.

With the construction techniques available to Old Kingdom craftsmen, a pyramid is the only architectural form that could support its own weight when built to the scale that the Old Kingdom pyramids were. But we also have to account for the dimensions and angles used. Engineering considerations obviously constrained the Egyptians to build the pyramids at angles such that stone blocks could be raised to each new level and that the whole could sustain its own weight. But I. E. S. Edwards suggested that this angle (about 52 degrees) parallels that of the slant of light on winter afternoons[27] in Egypt, and he says the texts hint that the pharaohs ascended into heaven by walking up the rays of light.[28] The pyramids thus would be a first step to the pharaoh's union with the sun god and eternity.

Limited as they were by the lack of electronic survey equipment and precisely engineered tools, we cannot expect Egyptian craftsmen to have been up to modern construction standards. The north corner of the Great Pyramid at Giza, for example, is almost a whole inch higher than the south corner.

Some of the most impressive features associated with the pyramids were the "solar boats," which are thought to have been buried at the time of the pharaoh's death, to facilitate his sailing into eternity. These boats were disassembled and buried in stone pits near the pyramids, and in the 1960s and 1970s, when one was excavated and reconstructed, the wood, ropes, and other components were found to be almost perfectly preserved by the dark and aridity of the boat pits. In 1987 scientists introduced a camera through an airlock into another boat pit, in the hopes that the atmosphere would be unchanged since the time of burial, but the camera showed dung beetles walking around somewhat decayed segments of the boat.

Mark Lehner has argued that the placement of the various elements of the Giza monuments in relation to the geology of the area indicates that the Sphinx, the three main Giza pyramids, and various temples are part of a single unified design, in which the different strata of limestone on the Giza Plateau were carefully used to produce this magnificent ceremonial center.[29]

The pyramids continue to fascinate most people who see them, and numerous ideas have been suggested about what the pyramids meant to the ancient Egyptians and how they were constructed. On hot summer nights some tourists continue experiments to determine if the pyramids retard aging, heighten sexual potency, cure diseases, or in other ways give off powerful emanations.

EGYPTIAN TEMPLES

The Egyptians built thousands of temples, some of which still stand as classics of architectural accomplishment, such as the Temple of Queen Hatshepsut at Deir el-Bahri.

In our own world architecture seems a somewhat chaotic art form and discipline, with the highest adulation often reserved for those who break free from tradition and introduce new forms that express an aesthetic sense but also function well. "Form follows function" and "less is more" are principles that have guided some great architects of the modern world, but new materials and methods allow them a freedom to experiment that was utterly unknown in the ancient world.

Egyptian architects, too, evolved forms and developed new aesthetic expressions, but there was a canon of architectural principles for many buildings that did not permit innovation in certain fundamental aspects. In Ancient Egypt there was no sense of "art for the sake of art," in the sense of a free-form expression of whim and whimsy. Egyptian architects did not, for example, use gigantic stone replicas of papyrus plants as columns for temples because of simple personal aesthetic preference. Everything had a purpose. Egyptian architecture was made to "work" in a profound sense.

The traditional plan of Egyptian temples was based on the belief that the temple was not a place of meditation, as a modern church might be said to be, but, instead, a home of a god. Egyptian temples were static realizations in stone of the creation of the universe and are to be seen as replicas of the universe at this moment of creation. Thus, the temples were aligned on an east-west axis, so that each morning the rising sun, the god Ra, would shine through the double pylon gate, representing two mountains, and penetrate the westernmost chamber of the temple, to illuminate the statue of the god. The temple itself was subdivided into different chambers, so that a person entering would only *gradually* pass through toward the god, reflecting a step-by-step process of purification in preparation for approaching the god. As Nicholas Grimal explains:

> The approach consisted of a gradual movement from light to shadow, achieving total darkness in the holy of holies where the god dwelt. At the same time the ground slowly rose, achieving its highest point under the naos [large carved stone cubicles], which was thus located on the primeval mound emerging from Nun, the lake of chaos. Out of this aqueous environment rose the stems of the papyrus columns, their architraves holding up the sky, which was usually represented on the ceiling. In order to achieve this effect, the temple had to consist of at least three elements: a courtyard, a colonnade, and a pylon entrance.[30]

In this movement from light to dark, low to high, profane to sacred, ancient Egyptian worshippers expressed many elements of their view of the world and the significance of their lives.

THE INTELLECTUAL FOUNDATIONS OF THE ANCIENT EGYPTIAN STATE

Wilson notes that the written language of Old Kingdom Egypt had no words for "government" or "state" as impersonal terms, conceived apart from the pharaoh; the

Egyptian "theory of government was that the king was everywhere and did everything. . . . The fiction of direct delegation of duty and of a direct report to the king was impossible to maintain in practice; but in the theory of government it was no fiction, it was a working reality."[31]

Thus, the Egyptians viewed their state and culture metaphorically as a living organism, an organism of which they were all a part, from the pharaoh himself to the lowliest slave.

A key concern to the Egyptian theory of government was "divine kingship."[32] The ancient Egyptians viewed their state as a complex blend of human and divine elements that was created and sustained by the interactions of people and gods, particularly through the agency of the pharaoh. The divinity of the pharaoh was a complex idea, however. Various scholars[33] have suggested that the position of pharaoh, his "job," in a sense, was regarded as divine but that the person of the pharaoh was not considered divine. For example, a statue of Khephren, for whom the second pyramid at Giza was constructed, shows the god Horus protecting him by spreading his wings over Khephren. And usually the pharaoh is pictured as confronting the gods, not as one of them. The pharaoh's responsibility was the "containment of unrule"—in other words, he had to ensure domestic tranquillity and prosperity. To that end he participated in many religious rituals.

Shortly after 2495 B.C. there was a change in dynasties as well as in the religious and political texture of the Old Kingdom. The worship of the sun god, Ra, emerged as the dominant religion, and the nobility and provincial authorities began to encroach on the king's authority.

THE FIRST INTERMEDIATE PERIOD (C. 2134–2040 B.C.): BREAKUP OR TRANSFORMATION?

In a sense the end of the first cycle of dynastic Egypt appears to have occurred between about 2134 and 2040 B.C., when the Old Kingdom state seems to have experienced a short period of disruption and change. Kemp suggests that in Upper Egypt the control of local affairs by the pharaoh's overseer was gradually diluted during the late Old Kingdom, culminating in the appearance of provincial governors, or *nomarchs*.[34] Scholars differ on the extent of fluctuations of royal power during the Fourth and Fifth Dynasties. Trigger raises the possibility that a slow but continuous expansion and elaboration of society and economy in the Old Kingdom may have been accompanied by growing complexity and power of provincial administrative institutions.[35] The apparent emergence of powerful *nomarchs* in the Sixth Dynasty may reflect a reduction of pharaonic power, but the pharaohs of this period were still able to send expeditions to Nubia and Palestine and to exert considerable internal control as well.[36]

The political breakdown of Egypt toward the end of the Old Kingdom may have been in part a result of dramatic climatic changes. Rainfall decreased in much of Egypt after about 2900 B.C., and Butzer notes that decreasing rainfall would have reduced the resources and numbers of desert nomads as well as eliminated much of the seasonal pastoral movements into the deserts.[37]

The concept of societal "collapse," a dominant theme in many analyses of Egypt, Mesopotamia, China, and other early states,[38] has some application to Egypt, but the periodic partial disintegrations of Egyptian polities seem to have been quite different. When its central government weakened, there was a reversion to greater autonomy for the provinces for brief periods. Even during the three "intermediate periods" that are taken as major divisions of Egypt's culture history, the level of disruption may have been less than originally estimated.[39] There was always a base level of expansion-collapse cycles as a result of variations in the Nile's annual flow. Various texts describe social disruptions that may be associated with flood-level fluctuations, but the Egyptian state evolved effective mechanisms to cope with these problems.

To some extent, Egypt's "intermediate periods" may have been periods of reorganization rather than of collapse. For example, the great decline in pyramid construction that marked the end of the Old Kingdom and the beginning of the First Intermediate Period does not necessarily reflect catastrophe; in fact, there is evidence that any economic dislocations in these periods were short-lived and relatively minor.[40]

THE MIDDLE KINGDOM AND SECOND INTERMEDIATE PERIODS (2040–1550 B.C.)

Reconstructing the sociopolitical changes of the Middle Kingdom (c. 2080–1640 B.C.)—Egypt's "Classical" period—is a complex matter. In general, the history of the Middle Kingdom contains the same cycles of expansion and collapse that can be seen in all the great ancient empires. Periods of well-regulated trade, prosperity, and brilliance in art, architecture, and literature were punctuated by periods of revolution, poverty, and political fragmentation. The Middle Kingdom originated in the great civil unrest of the twenty-first century B.C., when, according to a contemporary account:

> [Grain] has perished everywhere. . . . People are stripped of clothing, perfume, and oil. . . . Everyone says, "There is no more." . . . Strangers have come into Egypt everywhere. . . . Men do not sail to Byblos today: What shall we do for fine wood? Princes and pious men everywhere as far as the land of Crete are embalmed with the resins of Lebanon, but now we have no supplies. . . . The dead are thrown in the river. . . . Laughter has perished. Grief walks the land.[41]

In the face of this turmoil, successive rulers sought to increase national integration while directing defense and trade along increasingly active frontiers.[42] The Eleventh Dynasty pharaoh Nebhepetre' Mentuhotpe (c. 2061–2010 B.C.) and his immediate successors of the Eleventh Dynasty reunified the country. He and his successors of the Eleventh and Twelfth Dynasties reorganized the country with considerable energy, undertaking expeditions into Nubia, Libya, and Syria, reopening trade routes to the Red Sea, and commencing again the construction of monumental buildings. The capital was reestablished near Memphis, from which both Upper and Lower

Egypt could be ruled effectively, trade routes were extended, fortresses were built along the country's frontiers, and the tradition of co-regency was established, in which sons were made co-rulers toward the end of their fathers' reigns, thereby eliminating some of the bloody battles for succession that had plagued previous dynasties.

There were also advances in Egyptian art and architecture during this period. Many literary classics were composed, and the cult of Osiris completed its replacement of the colder, sterner religion of Ra and gave the common people some hope of the afterlife that in the past had been restricted to royalty.

From about 1786 to about 1720 B.C., various kings managed to remain in general control of most of Egypt, but gradually people from, it appears, Syro-Palestine, who were collectively referred to as the Hyksos, began to infiltrate the Delta, and they eventually appear to have been absorbed into the lower levels of Egyptian society. Gradually the power of these Asiatic peoples increased. At about 1640 B.C. they captured Memphis, and the Hyksos king adopted the trappings of Egyptian royalty. Artifacts made in the Hyksos manner have been found all along the Nile Valley and as far south as Karnak, but it is not clear how directly they were able to control most of the population. The skull of a ruler of southern Egypt, Seqenenre' Ta'o II (c. ruled at about 1600 B.C.) bears the imprint of a western Asiatic-type battle ax,[43] and there are other evidences of frequent conflict between Egyptians and Asiatics along the eastern Delta border.

THE NEW KINGDOM AND THIRD INTERMEDIATE PERIODS (1550–712 B.C.)

The hated Asiatics were largely expelled from Egypt by Pharaoh Ahmose I (c. 1550–1525 B.C.), who ushered in a new age of political unity. The major cities of the New Kingdom were Memphis, near what is now Cairo, and Thebes, at Luxor. Ahmose, a native of Thebes, expelled the Hyksos from the Delta, and after several battles drove them beyond the eastern frontier. He even captured the rich city of Sharuhen, in Palestine, and he and his successors reformed the bureaucracy, modeling it after that of the Middle Kingdom. He and his immediate successors also undertook massive building projects to restore and expand cult complexes at Abydos, Deir el-Bahari, and other major southern towns.

By the mid-fifteenth century B.C. Egypt probably had a population of many millions of people, whose governmental institutions, religion, language, economy, and most other aspects of life were probably remarkably like those of their ancestors during all of the preceding 2,000 years.[44] This great weight of tradition must be considered when analyzing Egyptian history. Time and time again Egypt would fragment under revolt and invasion, but the ancient order would always persist and reform.

New Kingdom documents, such as the Wilbour Papyrus, describe a highly stratified society, with a king and elite who could draw freely on the country's wealth (Figure 9.7), and under them provincial nobles, who inherited their titles and wealth, lesser bureaucrats, priests, military officers, wealthy farmers, craftsmen, soldiers, and tenant-farmers, with peasants supporting the whole structure (Figure 9.8).[45]

FIGURE 9.7 Mummy of Queen Tiye—her lovely hair still largely intact—who died about 1350 B.C. The position of the left hand is typical of Egyptian royalty.

One of the greatest New Kingdom rulers, Thutmosis III, reigned for fifty-four years (1479–1425 B.C.), and his mummified body suggests that he died still looking quite young for his many years and accomplishments.[46] Thutmosis III established Egypt's Asiatic empire with his conquest of much of the eastern Mediterranean coastal areas. Even powerful Assyria paid material tribute to the Egyptian Empire, as did the Babylonians and the Hittites. His surprise attack on Megiddo in Palestine and his amphibious operation against the Mitanni, a powerful northern Mesopotamian kingdom, established Egypt as a world power. By about 1450 B.C. Egypt had commercial contacts on a large scale, exchanging products with Phoenicia, Crete, the Aegean Islands, and its traditional African trading partners. Military pacification programs were extended far into Nubia, and vast quantities of Nubian gold and building stone were shipped to the Nile Valley.

One of the most famous New Kingdom monarchs was Akhenaten (ruled 1353–1335 B.C.), who introduced a semi-monotheistic religion and tried to eradicate vestiges of older polytheistic cults. He built marvelous temples to Aten, the new god, and constructed a new capital at Tell el-Amarna in central Egypt, complete with magnificent religious and administrative buildings.

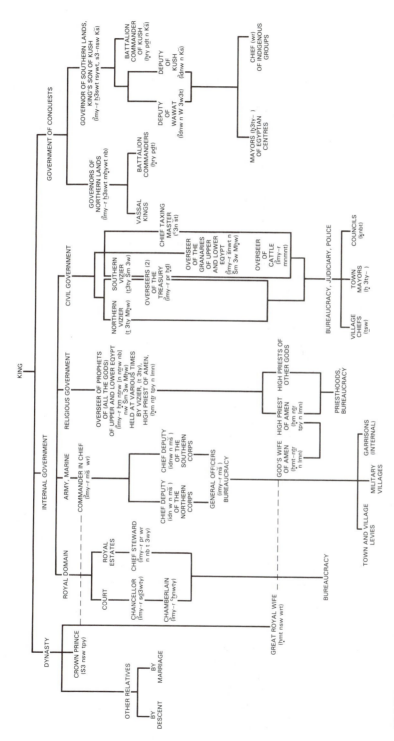

FIGURE 9.8 The bureaucratic organization of Egypt in the New Kingdom Period. This reconstruction by David O'Connor (1983) shows the numerous officials who organized most aspects of Egyptian society.

459

Akhenaten's physical appearance suggests he may have been a hermaphrodite, and some suspect that he had physical problems that produced some mental instabilities, but he was a reasonably effective civil and military leader.

> Akhenaten started off with certain disadvantages. From statues and portraits medical historians have diagnosed tuberculosis, hyperpituaritism, hypogonadism, and acromegaly. . . . Nor was his emotional life any healthier. His first wife appears to have been his mother, Tiy . . . they had one daughter. Then he married his maternal cousin, Nefretiti, and fathered three more daughters. His third and fourth wives were not blood relatives, and there was one son of each marriage, the second of whom was to rule as the boy pharaoh Tutankhamun. Akhenaten's fifth and last marriage was to the third of his own daughters by Nefretiti. . . .[47]

Soon after Akhenaten's death, the old religions were reestablished by Smenkhare and the famous Tutankhamun. Akhenaten's mummy was probably intentionally destroyed by bitter opponents of his attacks on the old religious traditions of Egypt.[48] The "Boy King," Tutankhamun, reigned as a teenager from about 1333 to 1323 B.C., and powerful members of his court tried to reestablish the power of the central court by reviving the state religion in the classical traditions of the cult of Amun.

When Howard Carter, whose work was funded by a British nobleman, Lord Carnarvon, discovered Tutankhamun's undisturbed tomb in 1922, his find captured the world's attention as no other archaeological discovery has. Lord Carnarvon's death from an infected mosquito bite in 1923 and other bad luck (to which we can add Howard Carter's favorite donkey, who was bitten on the lip by a cobra and died within three hours),[49] inspired the notion of the "Curse of the Pharaohs" and made Lord Carnarvon's son so disenchanted with things Egyptian that he had some of his father's antiquities sealed away in the family castle. In 1988, with the help of a seventy-five-year-old butler, these antiquities were rediscovered, but the most important finds from this tomb had long since been distributed among various museums, principally Cairo's Egyptian Museum.

Between about 1327 B.C. and the accession of Ramesses II (ruled 1290–1224 B.C.), Egypt's fortunes varied, with periods of foreign invasion and some internal breakdowns of the social order. And from Ramesses II on, "[c]ontraction, not expansion, characterized the foreign policy while the disintegration of government became evident."[50] Even in an era of megalomaniacs, Ramesses II is impressive. While invading Palestine, he allowed himself and his army to be ambushed by Hittites. He barely salvaged himself by a strategic retreat, and then proceeded to cover almost every available flat stone surface in Egypt (and much papyri) with heroic accounts of his mighty victory. Ramesses II and his successors were also plagued by court intrigues, probably some assassination attempts, various economic problems, and threats along the frontiers. Some scholars think that it may have been Ramesses II, or his successor, Mer-ne-Ptah, who refused to let the Israelites leave, as related in the biblical Exodus story, but few scholars consider this story to have much—if any—historical basis.[51] There is little if any reliable evidence of major changes in the archaeological record of Palestine at the time the Exodus story is supposed to have occurred, nor are there any evident traces in Sinai, where presumably the million or more Israelites would have wandered. The eastern Delta was a strongly fortified military area at the time the Exodus is supposed to have occurred, and the area of Palestine which they were recorded in the Bible to have invaded was already largely controlled by the Egyptians, so it is difficult to imagine how the Exodus story could have occurred as recorded. Also, the pyramids were built thousands of years before the Israelites arrived in Egypt—or were recognized as a distinct people, and it may be that the building projects described in the Bible as their work were small mudbrick complexes in the eastern Delta.

In any case, the Exodus story is a classic example of the collision of myth and the positivistic view of history. As discussed in chapter 1, all history is interpretation, and the phrase "what actually happened" is to some scholars meaningless.

At about 1000 B.C., Egypt lost military control of Nubia, and the breakup of its Asiatic empire brought it into confrontation with the Israel of David and Solomon. The Egyptians captured a city on the border of Israel and agreed to peace with the marriage of the pharaoh's daughter to Solomon. But five years after Solomon's death Seshonk I invaded Israel, plundered Jerusalem, and reestablished Egypt's control.

During the first millennium B.C., Egypt had various periods of resurgence when various kings reasserted Egyptian influence in Palestine and Africa, and as late as 715 B.C. Shako conquered the Delta and forged a unified country once again. But continued military pressures from Kush and the disintegration of national political and economic systems ate away at the country's structure and stability, and at about 525 B.C. Cambyses, a Persian king, conquered Egypt and reduced it to a vassal kingdom, proclaiming himself pharaoh. In 332 B.C., Alexander the Great marched into Egypt, evicted the Persians, and built the city of Alexandria. Later, the Romans, Arabs, and British would complete the conquest of Egypt, submerging almost entirely this distinctive civilization that was for so many years the light of the ancient world (Figure 9.9). Not until A.D. 1952 was Egypt again ruled by Egyptians.

ANCIENT EGYPTIAN ART AND THOUGHT

As we noted in chapter 1, some archaeologists now argue that the archaeological record can only really be interpreted if we shift our attention away from the simplicities of technology, environment, and economy, to the ideas, concepts, and world-views of ancient peoples. Unlike many areas, in Egypt it is in some ways possible to do this, because of its rich and early literature. Through most of antiquity, Egyptians believed that their society and life in general had been established by the gods, and that they and all their social, political, and economic relationships were part of a divinely designed, immutable world order. To some extent, the Egyptian past makes sense only when viewed in that way.

Certain themes are deeply embedded in ancient Egyptian culture. For one thing, Egyptians seem to have been a "God-intoxicated" people, "half in love with easeful death." Herodotus wrote that they were the most "religious" people he had encountered, given to incessant and elaborate religious rituals and an enormous priestly bureaucracy. Their concern with death, and the vast energies and richness they invested

FIGURE 9.9   Members of a 1920s-era Chicago Cubs baseball team play a road game.

in preparing for it, are manifestly evident, but it is also a testament to a people so passionately alive that they tried everything to perpetuate life into death.

Mummification was an attempt to preserve the body for use in the afterlife, when it would be revived and rehabilitated. Burial in the arid desert sands must have been the first form of mummification, but chemical methods were already developed by the Old Kingdom period. After death, the corpse was placed on a board and washed. The brain was removed by a hooked wire passed through the nose, an incision was made in the abdomen, and all the internal organs except the kidneys and heart were removed. A Greek of the third century A.D. reported that the stomach was then placed in a box and offered to the sun god, with the incantation, "If I have sinned in eating or drinking what was unlawful, the fault was not mine, but of this" (showing the box containing the stomach).

The heart was left in, so that on the final day it could be weighed against a feather, to see if its accumulated sins would tip the balance against eternal life. After the internal organs had been removed, the abdomen and chest cavity were washed in palm wine, and the viscera were placed in a container of natron (hydrated sodium carbonate) for forty days. The liver, lungs, stomach, and intestines were then placed separately in four "canopic" jars, to be guarded over by four different deities. The body was then stuffed with sand, sawdust, linen, or straw and covered with dry natron crystals to desiccate it for another forty days. Then it was washed once more and rubbed with wine, spices, and oils. The cheeks were sometimes restored to life-like dimensions with rag stuffing, the incised abdomen was sewn up, and the hair and complexion were touched up with paint. The entire body was protected with a coating of resin, wrapped in linen bandages (up to 324 square meters of linen could be used), placed in a coffin or tomb, and carried across to the west bank of the Nile for interment. At the close of ceremonies, the priest would incant: "You live again, you revive always, you have become young again, you are young again, and forever. . . ." It must have been a great comfort to the ancient Egyptians to hear these words and see the extensive care given the dead.

Egyptian deities were conceived of as very human in their behavior, even to the extent that they could be intimidated. Egyptians recited prayers in which they ticked off the services rendered a god, demanding payment in the form of the prayer answered.

For the Westerner, the physical world is a rather neutral place, where a lightning bolt or virus may strike one down, but on the basis of chance, without malevolence. Rocks are rocks, the dark is peopled only by morbid human projections, and death is inevitable, final, complete. For the ancient Egyptian, however, the world teemed with unseen but animate, conscious forces; malignant spirits were everywhere, as were forces for good; and, with sufficient effort, some of the inconveniences of being dead could be mitigated.

Ancient Egyptians seem to have had a monophysitic perspective in that everything in the universe was thought to have been derived from one substance and to be an expression of that substance. The god Amun, for example, might reside in a stone statue, but also in a well-formed ram or a duck, or in all three at the same time. Nor were these considered just different representations; rather, "the image was the god for all working purposes."[52] The symbolic, mythical element seemed to pervade even quite practical areas, such as medicine. One remedy for schistosomiasis (a disease characterized by bloody urine) was to shape some cake dough like a penis, then wrap it in meat, recite an incantation, and feed it to a cat.[53]

In all this supernatural and symbolic content, we should not lose sight of the practical, canny Egyptian. These were not people paralyzed by the Infinite: they built houses, boats, and beautiful buildings, and they enjoyed themselves in a world of color, play, and physical pleasures that still seems attractive and alive, even when viewed only in fragmentary 4,000-year-old paintings on tomb walls. When contemporary tourists see Egyptian wall paintings they are often surprised at the riot of colors—even the great temple columns of Karnak were brightly colored. This seems strange to many because we see beauty in the monochrome simplicity of Egyptian stone reliefs and buildings. But it helps to understand their art if one experiences firsthand the qualities of Egyptian natural light, the sun rolling up redly over the horizon, illuminating the blues and greens of river, sky, and vegetation with a vividness possible only in the thin arid air of the Sahara, with the limestone of the pyramids and temples absorbing and transforming the light into weights and colors and dimensions and textures that constantly change.

To our own, essentially Greek, minds, the Egyptians seem to have been unable to distinguish between things and representations of things. J. Wilson argues that the Egyptians saw no difference between supplying a dead king with real loaves of bread, wooden models of bread, or loaves painted on the walls; it was not the actual thing that mattered, it was the idea.[54] The physical man needed physical bread, but in the spirit world, "spiritual" bread was appropriate.[55]

Similarly, Egyptian art challenges Western notions about aesthetics. For the Egyptians, art was mainly functional and had a purpose— it was done so that people and things could live forever. Wall frescoes, statues, and drawings were all done not just to record an image, but "to create and maintain a perfect world in which the good life . . . could continue to flourish without opposition from the bad."[56] Therefore, decay and imperfection are seldom shown in Egyptian art—people and objects are shown in ideal condition, since they are meant to be part of an ideal afterlife. And given this purpose, people and objects, whether loaves of bread, geese, gardens, or boxes, should be depicted in their most easily recognizable forms and positions, and not necessarily from a single point of view or in perspective.

The ethical basis of Egyptian society was a composite sense of order, fairness, and justice, all expressed in the concept of *maat*, which is usually translated as "justice," "truth," or "right-dealing." It is interesting that English really has no single word equivalent to the sense of *maat*, or to the Greek concept of "virtue," which has a little of the same sense of *maat*. For the Egyptian, *maat* was recognizing the order of the world and universe and the necessity of doing the right thing, which usually meant following religious and civil laws and customs. Justice tempered with mercy, giving to the widow and the orphan but encouraging self-reliance and planning, doing one's share—all these and more were part of *maat*. One could demand justice and respect as a moral right, based on *maat*.

EGYPTIAN WRITING AND LITERATURE

One of the many mysteries of Egypt is the origin of its written language, or hieroglyphs ("sacred carvings") (Figure 9.10). These were first used shortly before 3100

EGYPTIAN SCRIPTS (Alphabet)

Hieroglyphic sign	Meaning	Transcription	Sound value	New Kingdom Hieratic	Demotic	Coptic
	vulture	ꜣ	glottal stop			omitted or ЄI
	flowering reed	i	I			ЄI or Є
	forearm & hand	ꜥ	ayin			omitted
	quail chick	w	W			OY
	foot	b	B			Π or Β
	stool	p	P			Π or Β
	horned viper	f	F			Ϥ
	owl	m	M			M
	water	n	N			N
	mouth	r	R			ρ or λ [Є]
	reed shelter	h	H			8
	twisted flax	ḥ	slightly guttural			8 or omitted
	placenta (?)	ḫ	H as in "loch"			8 or ϭ
	animal's belly	ẖ	slightly softer than h			8
	door bolt	s, z	S			c
	folded cloth	s, ś	S			c
	pool	š	SH			ϣ
	hill	ḳ	Q			K, ϭ
	basket w. handle	k	K			K, ϭ
	jar stand	g	G			ϭ
	loaf	t	T			T, θ
	tethering rope	ṯ	TJ			Ϫ, T
	hand	d	D			T
	snake	ḏ	DJ			Ϫ

EGYPTIAN ROYAL TITULARY

Horus Name (srḫ)	Nebty Name (nbty)	Golden Horus Name (Ḥr nbw)	Prenomen (ny-sw bit)	Nomen (sꜣ Rꜥ)

FIGURE 9.10 The hieroglyphic signs in early Egyptian writing were representations of common objects, but they eventually acquired phonetic meaning—sound values—that allowed Egyptians to express their entire spoken language in writing. In later periods the signs were stylized and simplified to facilitate writing. The names of royalty were written in ovals—cartouches—and each ruler used several different names.

B.C. and continued in use until about A.D. 1100 (and are still used today by the crafty forgers in modern Cairo's tourist traps). Elements of the spoken ancient Egyptian are still used in the liturgy of the Coptic Christian church. But hieroglyphic writing first appeared in such a developed form that we cannot see the full transition from what was probably pictographic writing first expressed on papyrus. Some scholars think writing was introduced from Mesopotamia, where it may have been in use some centuries before it appeared in Egypt, but there are great differences between the characters and materials used.

Ancient Egyptian was a mixture of signs and symbols, some of them expressing sounds in the spoken language, others indicating to the reader how a written character with several possible meanings was to be read in that specific context (Figure 9.11). It was not used as a truly alphabetic system, but virtually everything in the spoken language could be efficiently conveyed in the written language.

To a much greater degree than in modern English, hieroglyphs were written in a manner that expressed both contemporary aesthetic styles and the subject matter. Thus, we get simple, grave characters in early religious writings and more overblown, showy characters in later military texts. The beautifully simple hieroglyphic characters were complemented very early on by a *hieratic* script, which was much more abstract and cursive and thus could be written easily on papyrus with a reed pen and ink.

Various scholars had tried to decipher ancient Egyptian writing in the eighteenth century and had guessed correctly about the sound values and meaning of some of the characters, but they were also wrong about most of the characters. One key to the eventual decipherment of the language was the discovery of the Rosetta Stone, which had been found by Napoleon's soldiers in 1799 in the northern Delta. We now know that its text is an unimportant tribute to the Pharaoh Ptolemy V, written at about 196 B.C., but it is significant because the same text was written in Greek as well as in two forms of ancient Egyptian, hieroglyphic and demotic—a cursive form of handwriting that was easier to write on papyrus than the hieroglyphic script. The English scholar Thomas Young, for example, recognized the names of Ptolemy, Cleopatra, and Berenice—in parts of the Rosetta Stone inscriptions.

It was Jean-François Champollion, however, to whom we are most indebted for the decipherment of ancient Egyptian. Champollion was born in France in 1790, and by the age of sixteen he was fluent in Latin, Greek, Coptic, and at least five other languages; and from boyhood his physical features were such that eventually he was nicknamed "The Egyptian." To enter a Parisian school he was asked to write a paper on the subject of his choice, and he wrote on *Egypt under the Pharaohs* with such obvious intelligence that he was immediately asked to join the faculty.

A key to Champollion's success in deciphering Egyptian script was his extensive knowledge of the many ancient Egyptian texts, and a major breakthrough was when he

> became the first man in fourteen centuries to recognize the dual principle behind the Egyptian hieroglyphic script. . . . The name Ramses illustrates most clearly the dual principle: Ra means "sun" in Coptic, and in the cartouche [the name of the king written in an oval] Champollion recognised the sun-disk, clearly representing the sense or idea "sun", with the sound-value *ra* in Egyptian. The sign at the end of the cartouche was used to write the letter *s* in the name Ptolemy (Greek form in full Ptolemaios) on the Rosetta Stone, and so Champollion could read *ra-?-s-s*; he was then able to guess that the middle sign should read *m*, and he had the name Ramses, which he could explain from his knowledge of Coptic as "Ra-mise" or "Ra is the one who gives birth to him".[57]

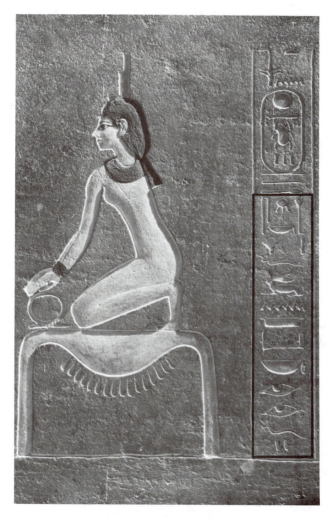

FIGURE 9.11   Reading hieroglyphic writing required recognizing symbols that convey sound values, symbols that are determinatives—which clarify meanings in ambiguous contexts, and symbols that are grammatical markers. The inscription outlined above is on the sarcophagus of Amenhotep II (died c. 1412 B.C.) and reads "Illumine his face, open his eyes."

By extending these principles to other names and inscriptions, and by using the work of previous scholars, Champollion eventually became the first person in centuries to be able to read an Egyptian text. He made mistakes, and later scholars greatly extended his work (and this work continues), but after Champollion the meaning of many ancient Egyptian texts could be understood.

The ancient written Egyptian language was different from ancient Mesopotamian scripts in a significant structural element. Sumerian nouns and verbs did not vary in their written forms depending on grammatical context, so that the word for mouth (*ka*), for example, was always the same, whether it was the subject, direct object, or some other grammatical element; but in ancient Egyptian the first letter in the word for mouth, *r*, was followed by a different vowel, depending on the grammatical position of the word.[58] As H. W. F. Saggs notes, an important consequence of this is that the ancient Egyptians "already had an alphabet within their grasp." Ancient Egyptians could have written all or most of their spoken language with just twenty-four signs. Saggs points out, however, that the Egyptians never simplified their written language to this alphabetic format—probably, as he says, because it would have been against the interest of the scribes who had mastered the difficult and more cumbersome syllabic forms to use a system anyone could have mastered in just a few months—a reaction similar to that of print unions throughout history.[59]

Since hieroglyphs give us only consonantal sound values (and not vowels), we will never know what ancient Egyptian really "sounded" like precisely, although no cat lover would have any problem with the fact that the ancient Egyptian word for cat was written with the sound values "MIW."

Egyptian literature took many forms. Dedicatory inscriptions recording the activities and histories of the kings and priests predominate, but there are also many poems, songs, financial records, letters, medical texts, astronomical accounts, etc. As ancient and strange as pharaonic culture may seem, there are many signs that these were very human people and would be recognizable to us in many ways.

The theme of one love poem of the New Kingdom, for example, is the timeless lament of a young man prostrated by the adolescent passions that poetry celebrates in all cultures. He proclaims that the absence of the object of his desires (where she's gone we don't know) has so sickened him that doctors and priests are helpless. But if his girlfriend could only visit!

> Why, that girl's better than any prescription,
> more to me than the Pharmacopoeia—
> My own secret Hathor Home Remedy?—
> Her slipping into my room from the road!
> (have *her* examine me, *then* watch my energy!)
> And just let her look me full in the eye,
> every bit of my body is back in its prime.
> At the sound of her voice my heart leaps to her tune,
> And then when I kiss her, feel her length breast to thigh,
> Love's evil spirits fly clean from my system—
> God, what a girl, what a woman!
> And that bitch has been gone for a week![60]

Aside from the pyramids and the Sphinx, perhaps the most glorious expression of ancient Egyptian culture is its many temples. The ancient Egyptians considered these temples to be an actual physical house of the God, not merely a place for meditation. If properly run, if the proper rites were performed, the temple was a "machine"[61] that delivered benefits to humans by keeping the cosmos in order. If properly operated, the image of the god, placed in the inner sanctum, became suffused with the power of the god, and thus the temple truly became the house of the god.

Temples varied greatly in architecture, but most were intended as a replica of the universe at the moment of creation. As Nicholas Grimal explains:

> The approach consisted of a gradual movement from light to shadow, achieving total darkness in the holy of holies where the god dwelt. At the same time the ground slowly rose, achieving its highest point under the naos [large carved stone cubicles], which was thus located on the primeval mound emerging from Nun, the lake of chaos. Out of this aqueous environment rose the stems of the papyrus columns, their architraves holding up the sky, which was usually represented on the ceiling. In order to achieve this effect, the temple had to consist of at least three elements: a courtyard, a colonnade, and a pylon entrance.[62]

Most temples are oriented from east to west, like the path of the sun, so that the sun could illuminate a statue of god in the innermost sanctuary at specific times.

WHO WERE THE ANCIENT EGYPTIANS?

Victory has a thousand fathers; defeat is an orphan.

(Chinese proverb)

This chapter is mainly a review of ancient Egyptian cultural history, but the ancient Egyptians offer an opportunity to consider some larger issues about such difficult topics as cultural "achievement," "race," and the nature of historical interpretation. History is not only kind to "winners," most of history is written by them; also, most people like to be associated with cultural "achievements": thus, it is not surprising that, as with the Sumerians (chapter 8), many people have tried to claim the ancient Egyptians as their physical or intellectual ancestors.

The great Egyptologist Sir Flinders Petrie, for example, concluded that the glories of ancient Egypt were the result of a "dynastic race" of invaders from Syro-Palestine. In contrast, some, primarily African-American, scholars argue that "ancient Egypt was part of the Negro world."[63]

Beyond disputes about the physical identity and genetic affinities of the ancient Egyptians, there is the question of their contributions to Western civilization. The traditional academic view is that the origins of Western civilization are mainly in the classical Greek world, with some influences from Southwest Asia, but few if any from Egypt.[64] But the historian M. Bernal has argued that Western scholars have had anti-Jewish, anti-Arab, and anti-Black African biases that resulted in their intentionally ignoring the contributions of Egypt and Africa to Greek and Western civilization. Few scholars give much credence to Bernal's claims, but in this politically sensitive era they have achieved a level of debate far beyond their rather esoteric academic subject.

Most contemporary social scientists assume that cultural "achievement," however that elusive quality is defined, has no demonstrated causal connection to "race," how-

ever that even more elusive quality is defined. As was discussed in chapter 4, most biological scientists reject the term "race" as imprecise and misleading. Patterns of evolutionary variability in people seem best understood in terms of *clines*, or gradients
of variation through time and space that are not easily and discretely compartmentalized. Skin color, for example, varies greatly if one examines people on a
cline from Sweden to South Africa, and these variations are only crudely described
as "black" and "white." Also, some of the traits commonly used to identify "race,"
such as skin tone, eyelid shape, nose and lip shape, etc., also show immense variation along gradients through time and space, and often independently: that is,
southern Indians, West Africans, some Pacific Islanders, and others share a relatively dark skin pigmentation but differ greatly in nose and lip shape, hair texture,
and other features.

With regard to the ancient Egyptians, various studies strongly suggest that
they were a distinctive people early in the pharaonic period, but with much of the
same variations of physical characteristics that one sees in modern Egypt. The
most recent comprehensive analysis of ancient Egyptian physical anthropology
was done by Brace and his colleagues.[65] They measured hundreds of ancient
Egyptian bodies and estimated the genetic affinities of the ancient Egyptians to
other groups, and they concluded that the characteristic suite of physical features
of ancient Egyptians has been relatively the same since the Pleistocene, and that
ancient Egyptians were most closely related genetically to circum-Mediterranean
peoples and Europeans, less so to sub-Saharan Africans. Nothing about this inferred genetic family tree should be particularly surprising. The vast Sahara desert
impeded gene flow from central Africa, except along the Nile, whereas the northern Nile Valley has been open to Mediterranean peoples from prehistoric times.
In ancient Egypt as now, the population showed the results of this blending of
peoples.

On the other hand, there is little support in these data or others[66] for the invasion of a Southwest Asian "dynastic race," as Sir Flinders Petrie and others supposed.

If sufficient DNA can be extracted from ancient Egyptians, the question of their
genetic and ethnic affinities will be even more securely established. Work in this area
is in its early stages, and if expected improvements in methodology occur, we may
eventually have conclusive evidence on this point.

The ancient Egyptians, of course, considered themselves different from all other
peoples and superior to them. They disparaged all other peoples, particularly those
with whom they had the most interactions, such as the "Asiatics" of Syro-Palestine
and the Nubians beyond their southern border.

Their artistic representations of their neighbors are demeaning, and they clearly
show that the ancient Egyptians considered themselves physically different from Nubians and other sub-Saharan Africans in facial features and skin tones, and from "Asiatics" as well. Egyptian men were painted a darker color than women to underscore
gender differences, misleading some to conclude that most ancient Egyptians were
very dark in skin tone; but there is no evidence that they were much different in this
regard from modern Egyptians, with a wide range from the very light Mediterranean
types to sub-Saharan African tones.

THE ORIGINS OF COMPLEX SOCIETIES IN EGYPT: CONCLUSIONS

Many simplistic notions about the origins of cultural complexity have foundered on the evidence from Egypt. Population growth, for example, may have produced fairly dense concentrations of people in favorable agricultural areas, but the long-term pattern of population growth was probably one of very slow increase through most of antiquity. Karl Wittfogel's notion of large-scale irrigation as a powerful impetus to empire (chapter 7) may have some application to Egypt, for irrigation no doubt was important early on, and some of the first Egyptian stone engravings apparently show royalty in the process of opening irrigation canals.[67] But irrigation in ancient Egypt was primarily through the passive blessings of the Nile flood, and such irrigation works as were constructed seem to have been small, local installations that did not require a lot of people or "paperwork" to run them. Similarly, the Egyptians were fond of murals showing their kings defeating hordes of foreigners, and people in the competing areas of pre-state Egypt may well have been given to bloody civil wars. But the location of settlements, the lack of walled towns and forts, and the art and literature do not support the notion that the critical factor in Egyptian state origins was Menes or someone else strapping on his sword, massing his troops, and marching to the Mediterranean, leaving a unified political state in his wake. Warfare was part of state formation processes, but probably as a mechanism, not a primary cause.

Nor is there much solace for the orthodox Marxian searching for the power of class conflict to produce states. Many scholars can and do see Egypt as an example of the validity of Marxian theory, but Egyptian literature and iconography seem to exhibit more mutually supportive bonds of kinship and religion than naked class struggle.

The pressure of nomads and others on the Egyptian periphery seems to have been a factor occasionally, but there is not much of a parallel here with the situation in ancient Mesopotamia or in China, where nomad-farmer relationships were a central theme in imperial developments.

A comparison of Mesopotamian and Egyptian settlement patterns underscores that urbanization is just one strategy, not an indispensable condition of cultural complexity. Whereas the people of Mesopotamia early and dramatically aggregated into fortified towns and cities, from which they conducted agricultural, industrial, religious, and administrative operations, the Egyptians did not even have a permanent capital until late in the second millennium, when Thebes emerged as a center—although recent excavations reveal a greater degree of urbanization than was previously thought to have existed. The comparatively slow development of Egyptian urbanism probably had many causes, including: (1) the absence of any powerful foreign peoples on Egyptian borders, and thus relatively little need for large walled defensive cities; (2) the uniformity of the environment all along the Nile, so that there was little to be gained from large-volume, inter-regional exchange of food or craft products; and (3) the pronounced political centralization, which inhibited development of secular, economic differentiation.

When the largest pyramids and other structures were built, population growth rates were slow, there was apparently little pressure on the country's resources, and large areas of uninhabited but fertile land existed. If we view these pyramids as mechanisms to mobilize and train a large work force, we must ask why such a work force would be an advantage, because when the first pyramids were built there were few large irrigation works and little demand for a standing army. If we view the vast expenditures of wealth in the funerary complexes as a means of "balancing" the economy by taking out of circulation inordinate amounts of gold, silver, or craft items, there is some difficulty in explaining why this would have been necessary in a society whose economic system and long-distance trade were strictly controlled by the monarchy and where there were few large markets and almost no free enterprise or capitalism of any kind.

FIGURE 9.12 This late second millennium B.C. Egyptian sculpture of a noble woman has the vibrant, sensual quality typical of some later periods but in great contrast to archaic forms.

In conclusion, it has proven remarkably difficult to prise apart the many causes and effects that make up Egyptian cultural history, but we are beginning to understand at least some aspects of this history. And, like other early civilizations, there is much about Egypt that is interesting and rewarding at a level beyond that of the mechanics of its history (Figure 9.12).

BIBLIOGRAPHY

Adams, R. McC. 1981. *Heartland of Cities*. Chicago: University of Chicago Press.

Adams, R. N. 1981. "Natural Selection, Energetics, and Cultural Materialism." *Current Anthropology* 22(6):603–24.

Aldred, C. 1961. *The Egyptians*. New York: Praeger.

Allen, R. O., H. Hamroush, and D. J. Stanley. 1993. "Impact of the Environment on Egyptian Civilization before the Pharaohs." *Analytical Chemistry* 65(1):36–43.

Anderson, W. 1992. "Badarian Burials: Evidence of Social Inequality in Middle Egypt during the Predynastic Era." *Journal of the American Research Center in Egypt* xxix:51–66.

Angel, J. L. 1972. "Biological Relations of Egyptians and Eastern Mediterranean Populations during Pre-dynastic and Dynastic Times." *Journal of Human Evolution* 1:307-13.

Asante, M. K. 1990. *Kemet, Afrocentricity, and Knowledge*. Trenton, NJ: Africa World Press.

Atzler, M. 1971-72. "Randglossen zur Ägyptischen Vorgeschichte." *Jaarbericht Ex Oriente Lux* 22:228-46.

Badawy, A. 1967. "The Civic Sense of the Pharaoh and Urban Development in Ancient Egypt." *Journal of the American Research Center in Egypt* 6:103–9.

Baer, K. 1960. *Rank and Title in the Old Kingdom*. Chicago: University of Chicago Press.

Baines, J. 1990. "Restricted Knowledge, Hierarchy, Decorum: Modern Perceptions and Ancient Institutions." *Journal of the American Research Center in Egypt* xxvii:1-23.

Bakr, M. 1988. "The New Excavations at Ezbet el-Tell, Kufur Nigm: The First Season (1984)." In *The Archaeology of the Nile Delta: Problems and Priorities*, ed. E. C. M. van den Brink. Amsterdam: Netherlands Foundation for Archaeological Research in Egypt.

Bard, K. A. 1987. "The Geography of Excavated Predynastic Sites and the Rise of Complex Society." *Journal of the American Research Center in Egypt* 24:81-93.

———. 1992. "Toward an Interpretation of the Role of Ideology in the Evolution of Complex Society in Egypt." *Journal of Anthropological Archaeology* II:1-24.

———. 1994. *From Farmers to Pharaohs*. Sheffield, England: Sheffield Academic Press.

Bard, K. A., and R. L. Carneiro. 1989. "Patterns of Predynastic Settlement Location, Social Evolution, and the Circumscription Theory." *Societes Urbaines en Egypte et au Soudan, Cahiers de Recherches de l'Institut de Papyrologie et d'Egyptologie de Lille* 11:15-23.

Bernal, M. 1987. *Black Athena: The Afroasiatic Roots of Classical Civilization*, Vol. 1: *The Fabrication of Ancient Greece*. New Brunswick, NJ: Rutgers University Press.

Bietak, M. 1979. "The Present State of Egyptian Archaeology." *Journal of Egyptian Archaeology* 65:156–60.

Bokonyi, S. 1985. "The Animal Remains of Maadi, Egypt: A Preliminary Report." In *Studi di Paletnologia in Onore di S. M. Puglisi*. Rome: Universita di Roma "La Sapienza."

Bourriau, J. 1981. *Umm el-Ga'ab: Pottery from the Nile Valley before the Arab Conquest*. Cambridge: Fitzwilliam Museum.

Boyd, R., and P. J. Richerson. 1985. *Culture and the Evolutionary Process*. Chicago: University of Chicago Press.

Brace, C. L., D. P. Tracer, L. A. Yaroch, J. Robb, K. Brandt, and A. R. Nelson. 1993. "Clines and Clusters Versus 'Race': A Test in Ancient Egypt and the Case of a Death on the Nile." *Yearbook of Physical Anthropology* 36:1–31.

Brewer, D. J. 1991. "Temperature in Predynastic Egypt Inferred from the Remains of the Nile Perch." *World Archaeology* 22(3):288-303.

Brewer, D. J., and R. Friedman. 1989. *Fish and Fishing in Ancient Egypt*. Warminster: Aris & Phillips.

Brewer, D. J., and R. J. Wenke. 1992. "Transitional Late Predynastic-Early Dynastic Occupations at Mendes: A Preliminary Report." In *The Nile Delta in Transition: 4th-3rd Millennium BC, Proceedings of the Seminar held in Cairo, 21 - 24 October, 1990,* ed. E. C. M. van den Brink. The Netherlands Institute of Archaeology and Arabic Studies.

Brothwell, D. R., and B. A. Chiarelli, eds. 1973. *Population Biology of the Ancient Egyptians*. London: Academic Press.

Butzer, K. W. 1976. *Early Hydraulic Civilization in Egypt*. Chicago: University of Chicago Press.

———. 1978. "Perspectives on Irrigation Civilization in Egypt." In *Immortal Egypt*, ed. D. Schmandt-Beserat. Malibu, CA: Undena.

———. 1980. "Pleistocene History of the Nile Valley in Egypt and Lower Nubia." In *The Sahara and the Nile*, eds. M. Williams and H. Faure. Rotterdam: Balkema.

———. 1984. "Long-Term Nile Flood Variation and Political Discontinuities in Pharaonic Egypt." In *From Hunters to Farmers*, eds. J. D. Clark and S. A. Brandt. Berkeley: University of California Press.

Butzer, K. W., G. Isaac, J. L. Richardson, and C. K. Washbourn-Ramau. 1972. "Radiocarbon Dating of East African Lake Levels." *Science* 175:1069–76.

Caneva, I., M. Frangipane, and A. Palmieri. 1987. "Predynastic Egypt: New Data from Maadi." *The African Archaeological Review* 5:105-14.

———. 1989. "Recent Excavations at Maadi (Egypt)." In *Late Prehistory of the Nile Basin*, eds. L. Krzyzaniak and M. Kobusiewicz. Poznan: Polish Academy of Sciences.

Cavalli-Sforza, L., and M. Feldman. 1981. *Cultural Transmission and Evolution*. Princeton, NJ: Princeton University Press.

Childe, V. G. 1934. *New Light on the Most Ancient East*. London: Routledge & Kegan Paul.

———. 1936. *Man Makes Himself*. London: Routledge & Kegan Paul.

Clark, J. D. 1971. "A Re-Examination of the Evidence for Agricultural Origins in the Nile Valley." *Proceedings of the Prehistoric Society* 37(2).

———. 1976. "Prehistoric Populations and Resources Favoring Plant Domestication in Africa." In *Origins of African Plant Domestication*, eds. J. R. Harlan et al. The Hague: Mouton.

Close, A. E., ed. 1987. *Prehistory of Arid North Africa. Essays in Honor of Fred Wendorf*. Dallas: Southern Methodist University Press.

Coutellier, V., and D. J. Stanley. 1987. "Late Quaternary Stratigraphy and Paleogeography of the Eastern Nile Delta, Egypt." *Marine Geology* 77:257-75.

Crumley, C. L. 1987. "A Dialectical Critique of Hierarchy." In *Power Relations and State Formation*, eds. T. C. Patterson and C. W. Gailey. Washington, DC: American Anthropological Association.

Cruz-Uribe, E. 1985. *Saite and Persian Demotic Cattle Documents*. Chico, CA: Scholars Press.

Davis, W. 1989. *The Canonical Tradition in Ancient Egyptian Art*. Cambridge, England: Cambridge University Press.

———. 1992. *Masking the Blow*. Berkeley: University of California Press.

Decker, W. (trans. A. Guttmann). 1992. *Sports and Games of Ancient Egypt*. New Haven: Yale University Press.

Derrida, J. 1976. *Of Grammatology*. Baltimore: Johns Hopkins University Press.

Diop, C. A. 1974. *The African Origin of Civilization: Myth or Reality*. New York: L. Hill.

Dunnell, R. 1980. "Evolutionary Theory and Archaeology." In *Advances in Archaeological Method and Theory* 3, ed. M. B. Schiffer. New York: Academic Press.

———. 1992. "Is a Scientific Archaeology Possible?" In *Metaarchaeology*, ed. L. Embre. The Netherlands: Kluver.

———. 1994. Personal communication.

Edwards, I. E. S. 1961. *The Pyramids of Egypt*. London: Parrish.

Eiwanger, J. 1987. "Die Archaologie der spaten Vorgeschichte: Bestand und Perspektiven." In

Problems and Priorities in Egyptian Archaeology, eds. J. Assmann, G. Burkard, and V. Davies. London: Routledge & Kegan Paul.

Fairservis, W. 1972. "Preliminary Report on the First Two Seasons at Hierakonpolis." *Journal of the American Research Center in Egypt* 9:7–27, 67–99.

———. 1991. "A Revised View of the *Na'rmr* Palette." *Journal of the American Research Center in Egypt* XXVIII:1–20.

Farooq, M. 1973. "Historical Development." In *Epidemiology and Control of Schistosomiasis (Bilharziasis)*, ed. N. Ansari. Baltimore: University Park Press.

Fattovich, R. 1979. "Trends in the Study of Predynastic Social Structure." *First International Congress of Egyptology, Cairo, Actes* (Berlin): 17-39.

Foster, J. L. (Illustrator, Translator); Davies, Nina M. (Illustrator). 1992. *Love Songs of the New Kingdom* (Reprint ed.). Austin: University of Texas Press.

Foucault, M. 1986. *The Foucault Reader*, ed. P. Rabinow. Harmondsworth: Penguin.

Frank, A. G. 1993. "Bronze Age World System Cycles." *Current Anthropology* 34(4):383-430.

Frankfort, H. 1956. *The Birth of Civilization in the Near East*. Garden City, NY: Doubleday.

Frankfort, H., J. Wilson, and T. Jacobsen. 1949. *Before Philosophy*. Baltimore: Penguin.

Friedman, J., and M. J. Rowlands. 1977. *The Evolution of Social Systems*. Pittsburgh: University of Pittsburgh Press.

Gautier, A. 1984. "Archaeozoology of the Bir Kiseiba Region, Eastern Sahara." In *Cattle-Keepers of the Eastern Sahara. The Neolithic of Bir Kiseiba*, ed. A. E. Close. New Delhi: Pauls Press, pp. 49–72.

———. 1987. "Prehistoric Men and Cattle in North Africa: A Dearth of Data and a Surfeit of Models." In *Prehistory of Arid North Africa*, ed. A. E. Close. Dallas: Southern Methodist University.

Ghoneim, W. 1977. "Die Okonomische Bedeutung des Rindes im Alten Agypten." *Lexikon der Agyptologie* 5:259.

Goedicke, H. 1967. *Konigliche Dokumente aus dem alten Reich*. Wiesbaden: Harrasowitz.

Gould, S. J. 1989. *Wonderful Life*. New York: W. W. Norton.

Grimal, N. 1991. *A History of Ancient Egypt* (trans. I. Shaw). Cambridge, MA: Blackwell.

Haaland, R. 1987. *Socio-Economic Differentiation in the Neolithic Sudan*. Oxford, England: British Archaeological Reports International Series 350.

Haas, H., J. Devine, R. J. Wenke, M. E. Lehner, W. Wolfli, G. Bonani. 1987. "Radiocarbon Chronology and the Historical Calendar in Egypt." In *Chronologies in the Near East*, eds. O. Avrenche, J. Evin, and P. Hours. *British Archaeological Reports* 379:585–606.

Haas, J. 1982. *The Evolution of the Prehistoric State*. New York: Columbia University Press.

Hadidi, N. 1980. "Vegetation of the Nubian Desert (Nabta Region)." In *Prehistory of the Eastern Sahara*, eds. F. Wendorf and R. Schild. New York: Academic Press.

Hamilton, E. 1930. *The Greek Way*. New York: Norton.

Harlan, J. R. 1982. "The Origins of Indigenous African Agriculture." In *The Cambridge History of Africa*, Vol. 1, ed. J. D. Clark. Cambridge, England: Cambridge University Press.

Harlan, J. R., J. M. de Wet, and A. B. Stemler, eds. 1976. *Origins of African Plant Domestication*. The Hague: Mouton.

Harris, J. E., and K. R. Weeks. 1973. *X-Raying the Pharaohs*. New York: Scribner's.

Hassan, F. 1986. "Desert Environment and Origins of Agriculture in Egypt." *Norwegian Archaeological Review* 19:63–76.

———. 1988. "The Predynastic of Egypt." *Journal of World Prehistory* 2(2):135-85.

———. 1992. "Primeval Goddess to Divine King. The Mythogenesis of Power in the Early Egyptian State." In *The Followers of Horus: Studies Dedicated to Michael Allen Hoffman*, eds. R. Friedman and B. Adams. Oxford: Oxbow.

———. 1993. "Town and Village in Ancient Egypt: Ecology, Society, and Urbanization." In *The Archaeology of Africa*, eds. T. Shaw, P. Sinclair, B. Andah, and A. Okpoko. London: Routledge & Kegan Paul.

Hassan, F. A., and S. W. Robinson. 1987. "High-Precision Radiocarbon Chronometry of Ancient Egypt and Comparisons with Nubia, Palestine and Mesopotamia." *Antiquity* 61(231):119-35.

Helck, W. 1971. *Die Beziehungen Agyptens su Vorderasien im 3. und 2. Jahrtausend v. Chr.* Wiesbaden: Harrasowitz.

———. 1974. *Die altagyptische Gaue.* Weisbaden: Harrassowitz.

———. 1975. *Wirtschaftsgeschichte des alten Agyptens im 3. und 2. Jahrtausend vor Chr.* Leiden-Koln: Brill.

Herodotus (trans. A. D. Godley). 1972. *Books I and II.* London: Loeb Classical Library.

Hess, R. 1993. *Amarna Personal Names.* ASOR Diss Series 9, Eisenbrauns.

Hoffman, M. 1980. *Egypt Before the Pharaohs: The Prehistoric Foundations of Egyptian Civilization.* New York: Knopf.

———. 1982. *The Predynastic of Hierakonpolis—An Interim Report.* Egyptian Studies Association, Publication no. 1. Cairo: Cairo University Herbarium and the authors.

———. 1989. "A Stratified Predynastic Sequence from Hierakonpolis (Upper Egypt)." In *Late Prehistory of the Nile Basin and the Sahara*, eds. L. Krzyzaniak and M. Kobusiewicz. Poznan: Muzeum Archeologicznew Poznaniu.

Hoffman, M. A., H. A. Hamroush, and R. O. Allen. 1986. "A Model of Urban Development for the Hierakonpolis Region from Predynastic through Old Kingdom Times." *Journal of the American Research Center in Egypt* 23:175-87.

Hoffmeier, J. K. 1994. "The Structure of Joshua 1–11 and the Annals of Thutmoses III," in *Faith, Tradition and History.* Winona Lake: Eisenbrauns.

Jacquet-Gordon, H. 1962. *Les Noms des Domaines Funeraires sous l'Ancien Empire Egyptien.* Cairo: Institut Francais d'Archeologie Orientale.

Janssen, J. J. 1978. "The Early State in Egypt." In *The Early State*, ed. H. J. M. Claessen and P. Skalnik. The Hague: Mouton.

Janssen, R., and J. Janssen. 1989. *Egyptian Household Animals.* Aylesbury, England: Shire.

Jeffreys, D. G. 1985. *The Survey of Memphis I.* London: The Egypt Exploration Fund.

ben-Jochannan, Y. B. 1972. *Cultural Genocide in the Black and African Studies Curriculum.* New York: ECA Associates.

Joffee, A. 1991. "Early Bronze I and the Evolution of Social Complexity in the Southern Levant." *Journal of Mediterranean Archaeology* 4(1):3-58.

———. n.d. "Parallelisms and Divergences in a Third Millennium Periphery: The Case of the Northern and Southern Levant." Manuscript on file with the author.

Johnson, A. L., and N. C. Lovell. 1994. "Biological Differentiation at Predynastic Naqada, Egypt: An Analysis of Dental Morphological Traits." *American Journal of Physical Anthropology* 93:427–33.

Johnson, G. A. 1977. "Aspects of Regional Analysis in Archaeology." *Annual Review of Anthropology* 6:479-508.

———. 1982. "Organizational Structure and Scalar Stress." In *Theory and Explanation in Archaeology*, eds. C. Renfrew, M. J. Rowlands, and B. A. Seagraves. New York: Academic Press.

Kaiser, W. 1964. "Einige Bermerkungen zur agyptische Fruhzeit." *Zeitschrift agyptische Sprache Altertumskunde* 91:86-125.

———. 1985. "Zur Sudausdehnung der vorgeschichtlichen Deltakulturen und zur fruhen Entwicklung Oberagyptens." *Mitteilungen des Deutschen Archaologischen Instituts Abteilung Kairo* 41:61-87.

Kanawati, N. 1977. *The Egyptian Administration in the Old Kingdom: Evidence on Its Economic Decline.* London: Warminster, Aris & Phillips.

Kaster, J., trans. and ed. 1968. *Wings of the Falcon.* New York: Holt.

Kees, H. 1961. *Ancient Egypt: A Cultural Topography.* Chicago: University of Chicago Press.

Kemp, B. J. 1977. "The Early Development of Towns in Egypt." *Antiquity* 51:185–200.

———. 1982. "Old Kingdom, Middle Kingdom and Second Intermediate Period in Egypt." In *The Cambridge History of Africa*, Vol. 1, ed. J. D. Clark. Cambridge, England: Cambridge University Press.

———. 1983. "Old Kingdom, Middle Kingdom and Second Intermediate Period c. 2686-1552 B.C." In *Ancient Egypt: A Social History*, eds. B. Trigger, B. J. Kemp, D. O'Connor, and A. Lloyd. Cambridge, England: Cambridge University Press.

————. 1993. *Ancient Egypt: Anatomy of a Civilization*. New York: Routledge.

Kitchen, K. A. 1989. "The Rise and Fall of Covenant, Law, and Treaty." TynBul 40.

————. 1995. "The Patriarchal Age-Myth or History?" BAR 21 (2)

Kitto, H. D. F. 1951. *The Greeks*. Harmondsworth: Pelican.

Knapp, A. B. 1988. *The History and Culture of Ancient Western Asia and Egypt*. Chicago: Dorsey.

Kroeper, K. 1988. "The Excavations of the Munich East-Delta Expedition in Minshat Abu Omar." In *The Archaeology of the Nile Delta: Problems and Priorities*, ed. E. C. M. van den Brink. Amsterdam: Foundation for Archaeological Research in Egypt.

————. 1989. "Settlement in the Nile Delta to the End of the Old Kingdom." Doctoral dissertation. Warsaw: Uniwersytet Warszawski Wydzial Historcyczny.

————. 1990. "Tell Ibrahim Awad North-eastern Delta." *Bulletin de Liaison* 14:6-8.

Kroeper, K., and D. Wildung. 1985. *Minshat Abu Omar*. Munich: Staatliche Agyptischer Kunst.

Kromer, K. 1978. "Siedlungsfunde aus dem fruhen Alten Reich in Giseh." *Denkschriften, Oesterreichische Akademie der Wissenschaften, Philosophisch-historische Klasse* 136:1-130.

Krzyzaniak, L. 1977. *Early Farming Cultures on the Lower Nile: The Predynastic Period in Egypt*. Warsaw: Polish Academy of Sciences.

————. 1988. "Research on the Location of the Predynastic Settlement at Minshat Abu Omar." Paper presented at the Fifth International Congress of Egyptology, Cairo.

Krzyzaniak, L., and M. Kobusiewicz, eds. In press. *Late Prehistory of the Nile Basin and Sahara*. Poznan: Poznan Archaeological Museum.

Lehner, M. 1983. "Some Observations on the Layout of the Khufu and Khafre Pyramids." *Journal of the American Research Center in Egypt* 20:7–29.

————. 1985. *The Pyramid Tomb of Hetep-heres and the Satellite Pyramid of Khufu*. Mainz am Rhein: Philipp von Zabern.

Leprohon, R. Personal communication.

Levy, T. E. 1993a. "Production and Social Change in the Southern Levant." In *Spatial Boundaries and Social Dynamics: Case Studies from Agrarian Societies*, eds. A. F. C. Holl and Thomas E. Levy. Ann Arbor: International Monographs in Prehistory.

————. 1993b. "Regional Interaction in the Southern Levant." Paper presented at the Annual Meeting of the Society for American Archaeology, St. Louis.

Lovell, N. 1990. "Biosocial Consequences of the Development of Complex Societies in the Nile Valley and Delta." Proposal to the Social Sciences and Humanities Research Council of Canada. Manuscript on file with the author, Seattle, WA.

Lewontin, R. C. 1979. "Sociobiology as an Adaptationist Program." *Behavioral Science* 24:5-14.

Lubell, D., P. Sheppard, and M. Jackes. 1984. "Continuity in the Epipaleolithic of Northern Africa with Emphasis on the Maghreb." *Advances in World Archaeology* 3:143–68.

Maisels, C. K. 1990. *The Emergence of Civilization*. London: Routledge & Kegan Paul.

Marx, K. 1932 [1852]. *Capital and Other Writings*. New York: Modern Library.

Millet, N. B. 1990. "The Narmer Macehead and Related Objects." *Journal of the American Research Center in Egypt* 27:53-59.

Mills, A. 1984. "Research in the Dakhleh Oasis." In *Origin and Early Development of Food-Producing Cultures in North-Eastern Africa*, eds. L. Krzyzaniak and M. Kobusiewicz. Poznan: Poznan Archaeological Museum.

Moens, M., and W. Wetterstrom. 1989. "The Agricultural Economy of an Old Kingdom Town in Egypt's West Delta: Insights from the Plant Remains." *Journal of Near Eastern Studies* 3:159–73.

Morenz, S. (trans. A. E. Keep). 1973. *Egyptian Religion*. Ithaca, NY: Cornell University Press.

O'Connor, D. 1983. "New Kingdom and Third Intermediate Period, 1552–664 B.C." In *Ancient Egypt. A Social History*, eds. B. Trigger, B. Kemp, D. O'Connor, and A. Lloyd. Cambridge, England: Cambridge University Press.

————. 1987. "The Old Kingdom Town at Buhen." Paper presented at the Annual Meeting of the American Research Center in Egypt.

————. 1989. "New Funerary Enclosures (*talbezirke*) of the Early Dynastic Period at Abydos." *Journal of the American Research Center in Egypt* 26:51-86.

O'Connor, D., and D. Silverman, eds. 1994. *Ancient Egyptian Kingship*. New York: E. J. Brill.

Oren, E. D. 1989. "Early Bronze Age Settlement in Northern Sinai: A Model for Egypto-Canaanite Interconnections." In *Proceedings of The Colloque d'Emmaus, British Archaeological Reports* (527I):389–405.

Patterson, T. C., and C. W. Gailey, eds. 1987. *Power Relations and State Formation*. Washington, DC: American Anthropological Association.

Paynter, R. 1989. "The Archaeology of Equality and Inequality." *Annual Review of Anthropology* 18:369-99.

Petrie, W. M. F. 1900. "The Royal Tombs of the First Dynasty, Part 1." *Egypt Exploration Fund Memoir* 18. London.

Pollock, S. 1992. "Bureaucrats and Managers: Peasants and Pastoralists, Imperialists and Traders: Research on the Uruk and Jemdet Nasr Periods in Mesopotamia." *Journal of World Prehistory* 6(3):297-336.

Porten, B., and A. Yardeni. 1993. *Textbook of Aramaic Documents from Ancient Egypt*, (2 vols.). Jerusalem: The Hebrew University; Winona Lake: Eisenbrauns.

Posener-Krieger, P. 1976. *Les Archives du Temple Funeraire de Neferirkare-kaki*. 2 vols. Cairo: Institut Francais d'Archeologie Orientale du Caire.

Posnansky, M., and R. McIntosh. 1976. "New Radiocarbon Dates for Northern and Western Africa." *Journal of African History* 17:161–95.

Postgate, N. 1993. *Early Mesopotamia: Economy and Society at the Dawn of History*. London: Kegan Paul.

Preucel, R. W., ed. 1992. "Processual and Postprocessual Archaeologies." *Center for Archaeological Investigations, Occasional Paper* 10. Carbondale, IL.

Quirke, S. 1990. *The Administration of Egypt in the Late Middle Kingdom: The Hieratic Documents*. New Malden: Sia.

———. 1992. *Ancient Egyptian Religion*. London: British Museum Press.

Quirke, S., and J. Spencer, eds. 1992. *The British Museum Book of Ancient Egypt*. New York: Thames & Hudson.

Redding, R. W. 1992. "Egyptian Old Kingdom Patterns of Animal Use and the Value of Faunal Data in Modeling Socioeconomic Systems." *Paleorient* 18(2):99-107.

Redford, D. B. 1986. "Egypt and Western Asia in the Old Kingdom." *Journal of the American Research Center in Egypt* 23:125-43.

———. 1989. "Prolegomena to Archaeological Investigations of Mendes." Manuscript on file with the author, Seattle, WA.

———. 1992. *Egypt, Canaan, and Israel in Ancient Times*. Princeton, NJ: Princeton University Press.

Reeves, C. 1992. *Egyptian Medicine*. Buckinghamshire, England: Shire.

Reeves, N. 1990. *The Complete Tutankhamun*. New York: Thames and Hudson.

Reeves, N., and J. H. Taylor. 1992. *Howard Carter before Tutankhamun*. London: British Museum Press.

Renfrew, C. 1989. "Comments on Archaeology into the 1990s." *Norwegian Archaeological Review* 22(1):33-41.

Rice, M. 1990. *Egypt's Making: The Origins of Ancient Egypt*. London: Routledge & Kegan Paul.

Rindos, D. 1984. *The Origins of Agriculture*. New York: Academic Press.

Rizkana, I., and J. Seeher. 1984. "New Light on the Relation of Maadi to the Upper Egyptian Cultural Sequence." *Mitteilungen des Deutchen Archaologischen Instituts Abteilung Kairo* 40:237–52.

Saggs, H. W. 1991. *Civilization before Greece and Rome*. Yale University Press.

Sanders, W. T., and D. L. Nichols. 1988. "The Valley of Oaxaca and Ecological Theory." *Current Anthropology* 29:33-80.

Seidlmayer, S. 1987. "Wirtschaftliche und gesellschaftliche Entwicklung im Ubergang vom Alten zum Mittleren Reich: Ein Beitrag zur Archaologie der Graberfelder der Region Qau-Matmar in der Ersten Zwischenzeit." In *Problems and Priorities in Egyptian Archaeology*, eds. J. Assman, G. Burkhard, and V. Davies. London: Routledge & Kegan Paul.

Service, E. 1975. *Origins of the State and Civilization*. New York: Norton.

Shafer, B. E., ed. 1991. *Religion in Ancient Egypt: Gods, Myths, and Personal Practice*. Ithaca, NY: Cornell University Press.

Shanks, M., and C. Tilley. 1987a. *Social Theory and Archaeology*. Oxford: Polity Press.

———. 1987b. *Reconstructing Archaeology*. Cambridge, England: Cambridge University Press.

———. 1989. "Archaeology into the 1990s." *Norwegian Archaeological Review* 22(1):1-12.

Shaw, I. 1991. *Egyptian Warfare and Weapons*. Aylesbury: Shire

Sjoberg, G. 1960. *The Preindustrial City*. New York: The Free Press.

Smith, H. S., and D. G. Jeffreys. 1986. "A Survey of Memphis, Egypt." *Antiquity* LX:88-95.

Spencer, A. J. 1982. *Death in Ancient Egypt*. Harmondsworth: Penguin.

Strudwick, N. 1985. *The Administration of Egypt in the Old Kingdom: The Highest Titles and Their Holders*. London: KPI.

Tannahill, R. 1982. *Sex in History*. Briarcliff Manor, NY: Scarborough Books.

Teeter, E. 1993. Personal communication.

Trigger, B. G. 1979. "Egyptology and Anthropology." In *Egyptology and the Social Sciences*, ed. K. Weeks. Cairo: American University in Cairo Press.

———. 1982a. "The Rise of Civilization in Egypt." In *The Cambridge History of Africa*, Vol. 1, ed. J. D. Clark. Cambridge, England: Cambridge University Press.

———. 1982b. "Archaeological Analysis and Theories of Causality." *Culture* 2(2):31-42.

———. 1983a. "The Rise of Egyptian Civilization." In *Ancient Egypt: A Social History*, eds. B. Trigger, B. J. Kemp, D. O'Connor, and A. B. Lloyd. Cambridge, England: Cambridge University Press.

———. 1983b. "Archaeology at the Cross-roads: What's New?" *Annual Review of Anthropology* 13:275-300.

———. 1984. "The Mainlines of Socioeconomic Development in Dynastic Egypt to the End of the Old Kingdom." In *Origin and Early Development of Food-Producing Cultures in North-Eastern Africa*, eds. L. Krzyzaniak and M. Kobusiewicz. Poznan: Poznan Archaeological Museum.

———. 1985. "The Evolution of Pre-industrial Cities: A Multilinear Perspective." *Melanges offerts Jean Vercoutter*. Paris: Editions Recherce sur les Civilisations.

———. 1989. "Comments on Archaeology into the 1990s." *Norwegian Archaeological Review* 22(1):28-31.

———. 1990. "Monumental Architecture: A Thermodynamic Explanation of Symbolic Behavior." *World Archaeology* 22:119-31.

Uphill, E. P. 1988. *Egyptian Towns and Cities*. Aylesbury, England: Shire.

Van den Brink, E.,ed. 1988. *The Archaeology of the Nile Delta: Problems and Priorities*. Amsterdam: Amsterdam Foundation for Archaeological Research in Egypt.

Vinogradov, I. V. 1982. "The Predynastic Period and the Early and the Old Kingdoms in Egypt." In *Early Antiquity*, ed. I. M. Diakonoff. Chicago: University of Chicago Press.

Von der Way, T. 1987. "Tell el-Fara'in - Buto, 2 Bericht mit einem Beitrag von Klaus Schmidt zu den lithischen Kleinfunden." *Mitteilungen des Deutschen Archaologischen Instituts Abteilung Kairo* 3:241-50.

———. 1988. "Investigations Concerning the Early Periods in the Northern Delta of Egypt." In *The Archaeology of the Nile Delta: Problems and Priorities*, ed. E. C. M. van den Brink. Amsterdam: Netherlands Foundation for Archaeological Research in Egypt.

———. 1992. "Indications of Architecture with Niches at Buto." In *The Followers of Horus: Studies Dedicated to Michael Allen Hoffman*, eds. R. Friedman and B. Adams. Oxford: Oxbow.

Waldrop, M. M. 1992. *Complexity*. New York: Touchstone.

Watson, R. A. 1990. "Ozymandias, King of Kings: Postprocessual Radical Archaeology as Critique." *American Antiquity* 55(4):673-89.

Wendorf, F. 1968. *The Prehistory of Nubia*. 2 vols. and atlas. Dallas: Fort Bergwin Research Center and Southern Methodist University Press.

———. 1976. "The Use of Ground Grain during the Late Paleolithic of the Lower Nile Valley, Egypt." In *Origins of African Plant Domestication*, eds. J. R. Harlan et al. The Hague: Mouton.

Wendorf, F., R. Said, and R. Schild. 1970. "Egyptian Prehistory: Some New Concepts." *Science* 169:1161.

Wendorf, F., and R. Schild. 1975. "The Paleolithic of the Lower Nile Valley." In *Problems in Prehistory: North Africa and the Levant*, eds. F. Wendorf and A. Marks. Dallas: Southern Methodist University Press.

———. 1980. *Prehistory of the Eastern Sahara*. New York: Academic Press.

———. 1980. *Loaves and Fishes: The Prehistory of Wadi Kubbaniyya*, ed. A. E. Close. New Delhi: Pauls Press.

———. 1984. *Cattle-Keepers of the Eastern Sahara. The Neolithic of Bir Kiseiba*. New Delhi: Pauls Press.

———. 1989. *The Prehistory of Wadi Kubbaniya*, Vols. 2 and 3. Dallas: Southern Methodist University Press.

Wenke, R. J. 1981. "Explaining the Evolution of Cultural Complexity: A Review." In *Advances in Archaeological Method and Theory*, ed. M. B. Schiffer. New York: Academic Press.

———. 1986. "Old Kingdom Community Organization in the Western Egyptian Delta." *Norwegian Archaeological Review* 19(1):15-33.

———. 1989a. "Egypt: Origins of Complex Societies." *Annual Review of Anthropology* 18:129-55.

———. 1989b. "Comments on Archaeology into the 1990s." *Norwegian Archaeological Review* 22(1):31-33.

———. 1991. "The Evolution of Early Egyptian Civilization: Issues and Evidence." *Journal of World Prehistory* 5(3):279–329.

Wenke, R. J. and D. J. Brewer. 1996. "The Archaic—Old Kingdom Delta: The Evidence from Mendes and Kom el-Hisn." In *House and Palace in Egypt*, ed. M. Bietak. Vienna: Austrian Archaeological Institute.

Wenke, R., J. Long, and P. Buck. 1988. "Epipaleolithic and Neolithic Settlement in the Fayyum Oasis of Egypt." *Journal of Field Archaeology* 15(1):29–51.

Wenke, R. J., R. Redding, P. Buck, H. A. Hamroush, M. Kobusiewicz, and K. Kroeper. 1988. "Kom el-Hisn: Excavations of an Old Kingdom West Delta Community." *Journal of the American Research Center in Egypt* xxv:5–34.

White, L. 1949. *The Science of Culture*. New York: Grove Press.

Wilson, H. n.d. *Egyptian Food and Drink*. Princes Risborough, England.

Wilson, J. A. 1946. "Egypt: The Nature of the Universe." In *Before Philosophy*, eds. H. A. Frankfort et al. Baltimore: Penguin.

———. 1951. *The Culture of Ancient Egypt*. Chicago: University of Chicago Press.

———. 1960. "Civilizations without Cities." In *City Invincible*, eds. C. H. Kraeling and R. McC. Adams. Chicago: University of Chicago Press.

Wittfogel, K. A. 1957. *Oriental Despotism: A Comparative Study of Total Power*. New Haven: Yale University Press.

Wright, H. T. 1977. "Recent Research on the Origin of the State." *Annual Review of Anthropology* 6:379-98.

———. 1986. "The Evolution of Civilizations." In *American Archaeology, Past and Future*, eds. D. J. Meltzer, D. D. Fowler, and J. A. Sabloff. Washington, DC: Smithsonian Institution Press.

Wright, H. T., and G. A. Johnson. 1975. "Population, Exchange, and Early State Formation in Southwestern Iran." *American Anthropologist* 77:267–89.

Yoffee, N. 1979. "The Decline and Rise of Mesopotamian Civilization: An Ethnoarchaeological Perspective on the Evolution of Social Complexity." *American Antiquity* 44:5-35.

Yoffee, N., and G. Cowgill, eds. 1988. *The Collapse of Ancient States and Empires*. Tucson: University of Arizona Press.

Younger, K.L. 1990. *Ancient Conquest Accounts: A Study in Ancient Near Eastern and Biblical History Writing*. JSOT Supp 98, JSOT Press.

NOTES

1. The film *Mountains of the Moon* is an entertaining story of the search for the origins of the Nile.

2. *Lates niloticus.*

3. Brewer and Friedman, *Fish and Fishing in Ancient Egypt*, p. 74.

4. Butzer, "Long-term Nile Flood Variation."

5. *The Bible*, Numbers 11:4–6.

6. Wendorf and Schild, *Cattle-Keepers of the Eastern Sahara. The Neolithic of Bir Kiseiba*; Wendorf and Schild, *Loaves and Fishes: The Prehistory of Wadi Kubbaniya*, Vols. 2 and 3; Close, *Prehistory of Arid North Africa: Essays in Honor of Fred Wendorf*; Lubell, Sheppard, and Jackes, "Continuity in the Epipaleolithic of Northern Africa with Emphasis on the Maghreb."

7. *Aristida, Eragrostis, Panicum, and* Echinocloa.

8. Wendorf and Schild, *Cattle-Keepers of the Eastern Sahara: The Neolithic of Bir Kiseiba*, p. 428.

9. Ibid., p. 425.

10. Hadidi, "Vegetation of the Nubian Desert (Nabta Region)," p. 347.

11. Gautier, "Archaeozoology of the Bir Kiseiba Region, Eastern Sahara," p. 70.

12. Gautier, "Prehistoric Men and Cattle in North Africa."

13. Hassan, "Desert Environment and Origins of Agriculture in Egypt"; Hassan, "The Predynastic of Egypt."

14. Reviewed in Wenke, Long, and Buck, "Epipaleolithic and Neolithic Settlement in the Fayyum Oasis of Egypt."

15. Hassan, "The Predynastic of Egypt." Also see Bard, *From Farmers to Pharaohs.*

16. Hoffman, *Egypt before the Pharaohs*; Hoffman, *The Predynastic of Hierakonpolis—An Interim Report*; Hoffman et al., "A Model of Urban Development for the Hierakonpolis Region from Predynastic through Old Kingdom Times."

17. Reviewed in Wenke, "The Evolution of Early Egyptian Civilization: Issues and Evidence."

18. von der Way, "Investigations Concerning the Early Periods in the Northern Delta of Egypt"; van den Brink, ed. *The Archaeology of the Nile Delta: Problems and Priorities.*

19. See van den Brink, ed., *The Archaeology of the Nile Delta: Problems and Priorities;* Wenke, "The Evolution of Early Egyptian Civilizations: Issues and Evidence."

20. Hassan, "The Predynastic of Egypt."

21. Service, *Origins of the State and Civilization*, p. 228.

22. Butzer, *Early Hydraulic Civilization in Egypt.*

23. Trigger, "The Rise of Civilization in Egypt."

24. Wenke et al., "Kom el-Hisn: Excavations of an Old Kingdom West Delta Community."

25. Badawy, "The Civic Sense of the Pharaoh and Urban Development in Ancient Egypt," p. 105.

26. Lehner, "Some Observations on the Layout of the Khufu and Khafre Pyramids."

27. See Emily Dickinson's "There's a certain slant of light..." for a lovely meditation on this light and, of course, death.

28. Edwards, *The Pyramids of Egypt.*

29. Lehner, "Some Observations on the Layout of the Khufu and Khafre Pyramids."

30. Grimal, *A History of Ancient Egypt*, pp. 264–65.

31. Wilson, *The Culture of Ancient Egypt*, p. 79. See also Kemp, "Old Kingdom, Middle Kingdom and Second Intermediate Period c. 2686–1552 B.C."; Trigger, "Egyptology and Anthropology," pp. 32–50.

32. See O'Connor and Silverman, eds., *Ancient Egyptian Kingship.*

33. Ibid.; R. Leprohon, personal communication.

34. Kemp, "Old Kingdom, Middle Kingdom and Second Intermediate Period c. 2686–1552 B.C.," p. 108.

35. Trigger, "The Mainlines of Socioeconomic Development in Dynastic Egypt to the End of the Old Kingdom," p. 107. See also Kanawati, *The Egyptian Administration in the Old Kingdom. Evidence on its Economic Decline*, pp. 69–77; Goedicke, *Konigliche Dokumente aus dem Alten Reich.*

36. Butzer, "Pleistocene History of the Nile Valley in Egypt and Lower Nubia," p. 278; Kemp, "Old Kingdom, Middle Kingdom and Second Intermediate Period c. 2686–1552 B.C.," p. 113.

37. Butzer, *Early Hydraulic Civilization in Egypt*, pp. 26–27.

38. Yoffee, "The Decline and Rise of Mesopotamian Civilization: An Ethnoarchaeological Perspective on the Evolution of Social Complexity"; Yoffee and Cowgill, *The Collapse of Ancient States and Empires.*

39. Strudwick, *The Administration of Egypt in the Old Kingdom: The Highest Titles and Their Holders.*

40. Ibid.

41. Aldred, *The Egyptians*, p. 102.

42. Kemp, "Old Kingdom, Middle Kingdom and Second Intermediate Period c. 2686–1552 B.C."

43. Quirke and Spencer, *The British Museum Book of Ancient Egypt*, p. 40.

44. O'Connor, "New Kingdom and Third Intermediate Period, 1552–664 B.C.," p. 190.

45. Ibid., pp. 194–195.

46. Ibid., p. 219.

47. Tannahill, *Sex in History*, pp. 77–78.

48. O'Connor, "New Kingdom and Third Intermediate Period, 1552–664 B.C.," p. 222.

49. Carter's donkey was named San Toy, and reportedly would wander through the excavation camp until she found Carter and then "bray with delight." Reeves and Taylor, *Howard Carter before Tutankhamun*, p. 60.

50. O'Connor, "New Kingdom and Third Intermediate Period, 1552–664 B.C.," p. 222.

51. This issue remains contentious. See Hess, *Amarna Personal Names*; Younger, *Ancient Conquest Accounts: A Study in Ancient Near Eastern and Biblical History Writing*; Kitchen, "The Rise and Fall of Covenant, Law, and Treaty"; Kitchen, "The Patriarchal Age-Myth or History?"; Hoffmeier, "The Structure of Joshua 1–11 and the Annals of Thutmoses III."

52. Wilson, "Egypt: The Nature of the Universe," p. 73.

53. Farooq, "Historical Development," p. 2.

54. Wilson, "Egypt: The Nature of the Universe," p. 72.

55. Ibid.

56. Quirke and Spencer, *The British Museum Book of Ancient Egypt*, p. 150.

57. Quirke and Spencer, *The British Museum Book of Ancient Egypt*, p. 129.

58. Saggs, *Civilization before Greece and Rome*, pp. 73–74.

59. Ibid.

60. Translation by John Foster, *Love Songs of the New Kingdom*, pp. 58, 61.

61. See Quirke and Spencer, p. 74, pp. 160–165.

62. Grimal, *A History of Ancient Egypt*, pp. 264–65.

63. Diop, *The African Origin of Civilization: Myth or Reality*; also see Asante, *Kemet, Afrocentricity, and Knowledge*.

64. See Frankfort, *The Birth of Civilization in the Near East*; Hamilton, *The Greek Way*; Kitto, *The Greeks*.

65. Brace et al., "Clines and Clusters Versus 'Race': A Test in Ancient Egypt and the Case of a Death on the Nile."

66. See, for example, Johnson and Lovell, "Biological Differentiation at Predynastic Naqada, Egypt: An Analysis of Dental Morphological Traits."

67. Wittfogel, *Oriental Despotism: A Comparative Study of Total Power*; Hoffman, *Egypt before the Pharaohs: The Prehistoric Foundations of Egyptian Civilization*, p. 315.

10

THE EVOLUTION OF
COMPLEX SOCIETIES IN
THE INDUS VALLEY

*Enough has been said to show that India confronts
Egypt and Babylonia in the third millennium [B.C.]
with a thoroughly individual, and independent
civilization of her own, technically the peer of the
rest. And plainly it is deeply rooted in India soil.*

V. Gordon Childe[1]

ncient texts seem to bring the people of the past to life much more vividly
than do their bricks, bones, and pots, and thus it is particularly frustrating
that the written language of the first great civilization of South Asia, the
Harappan State (c. 2600–2000 B.C.) (Figure 10.1), continues to defy decipherment.

This is a pity, because the Harappan civilization is highly intriguing. Since the
discovery of its archaeological remains early in the twentieth century, the Harappan
civilization that flourished in the Indus Valley, in what is now Pakistan and India, in
the third millennium B.C., has been unfairly considered a sort of poor relation to the
great states and empires that graced the Mesopotamian alluvial plain and the Nile
Valley. Not only did the Indus Valley cultures mature many centuries later than those
in Egypt and Southwest Asia, they also neglected to leave much in the way of the
pyramids, tombs, and palaces so prized by archaeologists. Nor was the Harappan a
particularly long-lived civilization; it appeared and disappeared within the space of
about five centuries (Figure 10.2). Perhaps the most important factor in the relative
neglect of Harappan culture by scholars is that until its first great cities were discovered in the first half of the twentieth century (primarily by Sir John Marshall), no
one had any idea of its existence. Scholars knew that Alexander the Great had raided
the northwestern part of the Indus Valley in 326 B.C., but they had no idea that 2,000
years earlier a great civilization had flourished and died in this area. As Gregory Possehl noted,[2] we "do not know what these people called themselves or their cities . . .
We have no king lists, no internal chronology . . . no historical account of commerce,
production . . . no historical record of the internal social organization."

FIGURE 10.1 The heartland of the Harappan civilization is the Indus Valley. The larger cities are shown as squares in this map, the smaller communities as dots. Thousands of other communities are probably buried under the alluvium.

But based on its archaeological record, we know that the Harappan culture is yet another example of the appearance of a pre-industrial "state," whose major evolutionary dynamics now appear to have been primarily self-contained, with only minor aspects that were the results of outside influences. In fact, the Indus Valley cultures are of great interest for the study of the origins of cultural complexity for several reasons: (1) Harappan civilization may have appeared very rapidly, with a highly urbanized society developing out of a rather simple one in perhaps as little as 100–150 years[3]—although others dispute this view;[4] (2) they constructed massive cities with perhaps the most advanced sense of town planning and provision of city services (e.g., a municipal water and sewage system) in the ancient world until the advent of the Romans; (3) their area of cultural and political influence and control extended over almost 1.3 million square kilometers—considerably more territory than any other Old World civilization of this period; (4) Harappan culture over this large area appears very homogenous, compared to Mesopotamia; and (5) the Indus cities seem to have a very equitable distribution of wealth—even a degree of primitive socialism, perhaps—in an era when other comparable civilizations were highly stratified groupings of a few extraordinarily wealthy and powerful nobles and priests supported by tens of thousands of peasants.

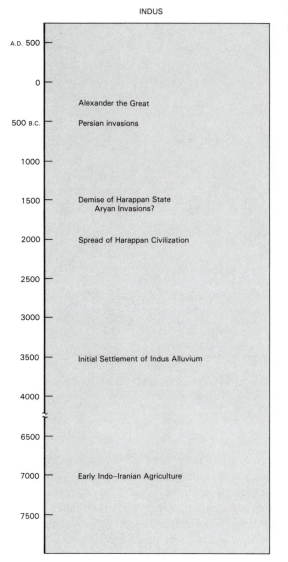

INDUS

FIGURE 10.2 A simplified chronology of South Asian prehistory.

A.D. 500

0

500 B.C. — Alexander the Great

Persian invasions

1000

1500 — Demise of Harappan State
Aryan Invasions?

2000 — Spread of Harappan Civilization

2500

3000

3500 — Initial Settlement of Indus Alluvium

4000

6500

7000 — Early Indo-Iranian Agriculture

7500

It is not an uncommon archaeological irony that the Indus civilization, so interesting in various ways, is one of the most archaeologically inaccessible. Some critical phases of its archaeological record are buried beneath meters of alluvium and beneath the water table. Along with the pleasures of sloshing through mud against a background whine of pumps, the archaeologist working on early complex societies in the Indus must be prepared for the collapse of huge walls of debris as he or she cuts down through the alluvium to the earliest levels. For this and other reasons, our knowledge of Harappan civilization is in some ways less than that of Egypt and Mesopotamia. One effect of this has been that interpretations of Harappan civilization have suffered the effects of "received wisdom": in the absence of adequate data, characterizations of Harappan civilizations made in the 1950s and before have been repeated and recycled long past the time they have been shown to be inaccurate. Thus, as Jim Shaffer notes, Stuart Piggot's characterization in 1950 of the Harappan civilization as rigidly stratified, centralized, and authoritarian, has been "repeated in nearly every synthesis on the culture to date,"[5] despite evidence that challenges these characterizations.[6]

THE ECOLOGICAL SETTING

> *Aristobulus . . . says that when he was sent upon a certain*
> *mission [to Pakistan and India] he saw a country of more than*
> *a thousand cities, together with villages, that had been deserted*
> *because [a great river] had abandoned its proper bed.*
>
> Strabo (c. 63 B.C.–24 A.D.)[7]

Millions of years ago, movements of the earth's crust forced the Indian subcontinent against the main Eurasian land mass with such pressure that the land in between was squeezed upward, creating the Himalayan Mountains. Every spring, melting snow in these mountains sends floods down the rivers that cross the lowlands to the sea. Of these rivers, the Indus and its flood plain form a large segment of the area between the borders of present-day Pakistan and India (Figure 10.1).

So little rain falls on this plain during the average year that reliable agriculture is possible only through irrigation from the river. Thus Indus civilization, the first urban society to form in this area, is, like those in all other "pristine" cases except Mexico, the gift of large rivers. Indus Valley cultures are really the products of two rivers, the Indus and the Ghaggar-Hakra, which is now extinct. In ancient times these two rivers ran roughly parallel to each other, creating a vast alluvial plain with great potential for farming and herding. The Ghaggar-Hakra was the legendary Saraswati River mentioned in later Sanskrit texts—and it may have been the river that had supported the settlements that Aristobulus saw abandoned, as quoted above. According to the archaeologist M. Mughal,[8] the Ghaggar-Hakra supported many communities, including two cities that were as large as the two largest known Indus Valley cities, Mohenjo-daro and Harappa.

Compared to the Nile, the Indus River, and probably the Ghaggar-Hakra River as well, were relatively unpredictable, with great annual fluctuations in their volume and course. Frequently, the rivers flowed across the countryside in devastating floods. Centuries of this flooding have left the Indus floodplain a maze of old river channels and great deposits of silt, all smoothed down by the action of wind and water. The great fertility of these soils is complemented by the arid, hot climate, which, like that of Egypt and Mesopotamia, supports several crops a year and a great diversity of plant species. But unlike Egypt, for example, rainfall in the Indus Valley after about 2400 B.C.—spanning the period of both Harappa's rise and fall as a civilization—was sufficient for some dry-land farming and stock-raising, and thus the people of the Indus were not totally dependent upon their rivers.

Because the Indus River is navigable over much of its length, ships could sail between Harappan cities with goods and, presumably, transport the bureaucrats sent by the central government to collect taxes and administer the provinces.

Like those of ancient Mesopotamia, the ancient cultures and polities of the Indus Valley must be seen as the products of a wide sphere of long-term cultural interactions of people far beyond the river plain itself. To the west of the hot Indus plains the arid foothills and mountains of Pakistan, Afghanistan, and Iran sharply limit the extension of agriculture, but they also provide valuable minerals, metals, animal products, and other goods, and are the homelands of pastoral and nomadic peoples who exerted great influence on lowland civilizations. Because the Himalayas to the north posed a formidable barrier to transport, the diffusion of new ideas, objects, and peoples into and out of the Indus Valley was mainly along routes through these western borderlands, or along the thin coastal strip on the Arabian Sea. The Great Indian Desert to the east of the Indus Valley reduced contacts with the rest of the subcontinent. As a result, the Indus Valley was, like Egypt and Peru, an area of rich agricultural lands sharply bounded by highlands, desert, and ocean.

THE NEOLITHIC BACKGROUND TO SOUTH ASIAN CULTURAL COMPLEXITY

One of the primary archaeological discoveries of the past decade in South Asia is that the village farming way of life, which was once thought to have been a rather recent development in this area, actually has deep and extensive roots.[9] The ancestors of the people who built the Indus civilizations spent thousands of years as small-time farmers and herders in the highlands above the Indus; most of the plain was perhaps only lightly occupied during these centuries. Domesticated wheat and the remains of domesticated sheep and goats have been found in levels dating to about 7000 B.C. in several sites in Afghanistan and Baluchistan, and the evidence suggests that thereafter the agricultural and pastoral ways of life spread gradually, from west to east, throughout highland areas where rainfall and streams provided sufficient water.

The Neolithic background to Harappan Civilization has been clarified by recent work at several sites, including Kili Ghul Mohammad in the Quetta Valley, Baluchistan; Ghar-i-Mar and Aq Kupruk II in Afghanistan; and especially at Mehrgarh, on the Kachi Plain, in Pakistan.

Mehrgarh was first occupied shortly after 7000 B.C. by people who lived in simple, multi-roomed mudbrick buildings and seem to have subsisted on a blend of cereal farming and hunting. This community is the first known example in the Indus area of the basic domesticated plants, animals, agricultural technologies, and the village form of community organization, all appearing together as a functioning entity—a form of economy and society that would be the basic building block of all the civilizations that followed in this part of Asia. Around the world, pottery is usually found at locales where economies were based on domesticated cereals since pottery is so useful in making the soups, stews, and porridges (and beer) that take maximum advantage of cereals. But like the earliest Neolithic peoples of Southwest Asia, the people of early Mehrgarh did not use pottery to store their domesticated wheat and barley. Archaeologists have found fireplaces in these buildings, so the people of Mehrgarh may have mainly used these cereals for bread. They also hunted extensively. Most of the bones from the earliest levels of Mehrgarh are from gazelle, deer, antelope, wild water buffalo, wild sheep and goat, wild cattle, wild pig, and even elephant.

Soon after about 5500 B.C., however, the people of Mehrgarh had begun to specialize mainly on sheep, goat, and cattle, which Richard Meadow, a faunal analyst, thinks is an indication that these animals were being kept and in the process of domestication. He notes that some evidence from Mehrgarh indicates that they were using domesticated hump-backed cattle ("zebu"), and he suggests that the keeping and herding of zebu (*Bos indicus*) appeared on the eastern margins of the Middle East as early as non-humped cattle (*Box taurus*) were kept and herded in the western areas of the Middle East.[10] Moreover, beginning at about 5500 B.C. the people of Mehrgarh began to use a crude but serviceable kind of pottery. They also used copper tools and imported turquoise and lapis lazuli from Iran and Afghanistan and marine shell from the Arabian Gulf area—and they used some of these exotic items in the form of beads to decorate the corpses of their deceased.

As the farming way of life spread over South Asia, people seem to have domesticated other animals, such as the pig, water buffalo, and the distinctive hump-backed cattle still found all over this area. And like their neighbors in Southwest Asia, they complemented wheat and barley with many other crops, including peas, lentils, and other legumes, which people all over the world discovered could provide the vegetable proteins so often needed in the uncertain circumstances of primitive agriculture.

Like other early agriculturalists around the world, the early farming peoples of southern Asia solved the problem of clothing by domesticating a plant for fiber, specifically, cotton. Just as linen and wool were the staple textiles in Egypt and Mesopotamia, respectively, cotton became the primary source of cloth for South Asia—as it did in Peru and elsewhere. Textiles are by no means the invention only of agriculturalists, however: various hunter-foragers around the world wove natural plant fibers into clothing. The growing populations of early farming cultures, however, and the need for seasonally adaptable and cheap clothing seems to have resulted in the domestication of a plant that could be grown intensively and easily converted to textiles. Cotton was probably domesticated in several areas of southern Asia between about 7000 and 5000 B.C., but the evidence of precisely when and where this occurred is unclear.

As humble as these beginnings of South Asian civilization might seem, they clearly involve the same elements that we have already seen in Egypt and Mesopotamia. By about 7000 B.C. people from all over this area, though just a few thousand years removed from their hunter-forager ancestors, were experimenting with various economic strategies. Within a few thousand years these people had achieved a reliable, productive blend of economic activities that particularly suited their circumstances. They all solved the same basic problems of living. They found that cattle, pigs, sheep, and goats were a particularly productive mix of large domesticated animals, that wheat and barley could form the core of their food-production, that ceramic containers were ideal food-processing and storage vessels, that textiles could be made from a diversity of plants and animals, and that mudbrick buildings and permanent villages made effective residences.

All of these developments may seem natural, almost inevitable, but they were not. We should not imagine that these people—from North Africa to India—fine-tuned their economies from generation to generation until they all converged on essentially the same solutions to these problems of living. People experimented with various aspects of these economies to solve personal needs, and some solutions proved better than others. The process for making durable pottery, for example, may well have been independently "invented" scores, perhaps hundreds, of times in South and West Asia and North Africa. Textile production, too, was probably independently "invented" many times.

One gets the sense that necessity really was the mother of invention in many of these developments. Pottery's uses are probably most obvious. Primitive farmers in general had to find a way to water their plants effectively, store the grain, boil it, and serve it, and although animal skins, wooden bowls, and other containers can meet some of these uses, only pottery is cheap, durable, available everywhere, and reasonably effective at meeting all these needs. Textiles, too, offer obvious advantages over animal skins and other possible sources for clothing, bags, ropes, nets, etc. To make clothing out of animal skins, which we have reason to believe were the primary source of clothing for almost all hunter-foragers, one must truly "cut one's coat to fit one's cloth," as the old maxim has it. But cotton, linen, or wool textiles can be mass-produced in variable sizes and textures in relatively cheap and reliable fashion, as opposed to the exigencies of antelope or tiger hunting. Moreover, although people could certainly have worn clothing of leather and other forms of animal skin in the hot river valleys of the Nile, the Indus, the Tigris-Euphrates, etc., life must have been much more comfortable in the linens, cottons, and thin wools that these people eventually wore.

THE NEOLITHIC–URBAN TRANSITION

Harappan civilization, like those of the Nile Valley and Mesopotamia, seems so much a creation of its specific environment that it is easy to lose sight of the wider ecological and cultural contexts in which it was set. Harappan civilization, in particular, can be seen as a direct product of the village farming tradition that spread all over the uplands of Iran, Afghanistan, and Pakistan after 5000 B.C.[11]

At this time, many settlements in the highlands west of the Indus were probably based on simple wheat farming supplemented by sheep and goat raising and some hunting and gathering. These farmers made pottery and used a few copper tools, but the sites of some villages are so insubstantial that they suggest a relatively mobile population and perhaps only seasonal occupation.[12] Slowly, however, these villages grew and farming became the way of life over an ever-larger area. To the south and east, too, Neolithic cultures were forming. Rice may well have been cultivated on the Ganges Plain by 4500 B.C.; indeed, all over South Asia at this time people made intensive use of many cereals, although most of these never became staples like wheat and rice.[13] In a sense, it is as if all of these farming traditions coalesced on the Indus flood plain. Boosted by the great agricultural productivity of this area and its easy riverine transport, these village-farming adaptations were subsequently transformed into an urban civilization.

THE FORMATIVE PERIOD OF HARAPPAN CULTURE

Like the origins of farming itself, the cultural transformation of a simple agricultural society into a state might appear in retrospect to be an automatic and inevitable outcome of a favorable mix of agricultural economies and particularly productive conditions for farming, but this is not the case. The Indus Valley civilizations seem another classic demonstration of the discontinuous nature of cultural evolution. Rather than a smooth building process wherein Neolithic villages added the components of civilization trait by trait, we see in the Indus area the same pattern evident in Mesopotamia, where initial moves toward complexity stalled and disappeared, while areas that were once on the periphery became the core developmental regions.

As Kenoyer notes,[14] early interpretations of Indus civilizations tended to imagine these people as coming from a single ethnic group and using their own language, but the evidence suggests that the Indus civilizations—like those of Mesopotamia—were built of mosaics of ethnic groups, languages, and adaptations.

Harappan civilization was much like Mesopotamia in its pattern of core-periphery relationships, and very much unlike Egypt, for example. Egypt was sheltered by poor harbors on the north, steep rapids in the south, and largely unpopulated deserts on the east and west; thus, the idea of a "core" and a "periphery" is not really applicable, except in the sense of the differences between the central government and provincial authorities and towns. In Mesopotamia, in contrast, hundreds of distinctive cultures and economies flourished in the area from Anatolia to highland Iran and the Persian Gulf, although states centered in Mesopotamia repeatedly dominated these other cultures.[15]

Daniel Miller sees a similar pattern of core-periphery relationships between the edge of the highlands bordering the Indus Plain and the Plain itself. He notes that by 4000 B.C. communities all over what is now Pakistan traded in marine shells, lapis lazuli, and other goods, had a degree of overall planning evident in the architecture, and produced pottery in regional styles that may reflect competitive political entities.[16]

Unfortunately, the first critical steps toward complexity, in the form of growing differences in the size and socioeconomic and political power of some communities is difficult to document with settlement pattern data[17] and other evidence[18] (Figure 10.3).

Miller observes that several regions on the Indus Plain and in eastern Iran at this time were "moving toward a greater degree of social complexity and urbanization,"[19] although eventually the Indus Plain became the developmental center. And although much of the mature Harappan civilization can be found in these developments of the fifth and fourth millennia B.C., the cultural changes that occurred as part of the Harappan civilization after about 2600 B.C. seem to have an indigenous and in some ways revolutionary character.[20] As Possehl has noted,[21] the emergence of Harappan civi-

FIGURE 10.3   Some elements of the "Citadel" at Mohenjo-daro are evident in this photograph (the large circular Buddhist shrine in the background was built many centuries after Mohenjo-daro was abandoned).

lization seems to have involved great continuity over thousands of years in such things as the production and use of items for basic subsistence, local trade, and personal decoration (such as chert knives, clay female figurines, and copper rings), but also considerable discontinuity in cultural trends: these discontinuities appear most pronounced in such things as degree of urbanism, social stratification, and occupational specialization.

These discontinuities—relatively abrupt changes in core aspects of these societies between about 3200 and 2600 B.C.—have been archaeologically exposed at only a few sites (e.g., Amri, Nausharo, and Harappa), but there are many other sites that date to this period. Possehl[22] lists 463 sites of this period and notes that they do not seem to vary greatly in size (and therefore, by inference, in population). Most are about five hectares in area, although there are a few much larger communities in the twenty-two- to thirty-hectare range. As we noted in chapter 8, one of the things archaeologists look at to infer changes in the sociopolitical nature of a society is the degree of diversity in the population size of the communities in a particular polity. States tend to have a wide range of communities of different sizes, ranging from large cities to many tiny villages. But communities in areas that are not politically and economically integrated and administered tend to be about the same size. In the Indus area the sites that date to the mature Harappan period (after about 2600 B.C.) include three relatively huge communities (c. eighty to eighty-five hectares). These cities—Mohenjo-daro, Harappa, and Ganwariwala—are evenly spaced, as we would expect on the basis of locational theory of state-level settlement patterns (see chapter 7), but there are also clusters of sites in other size categories. Whether or not these corresponded to the traditional sense of terms like "capital," "regional capital," "provincial center," "town," "village," "hamlet," etc., is unclear. There may have been only two general size groups, big cities and smaller towns and villages,[23] but overall, the population in the region appears to have more than tripled between about 3200 and 2600 B.C. In addition, more remote areas, such as the Kuli complex in Baluchistan, were brought into the Harappan cultural sphere. Between 3000 and 2400 B.C., settlements appeared at Kot Diji, Harappa, Kalibangan, and elsewhere, perhaps founded by people moving in from the western highlands. The few excavated settlements of this period reveal simple mudbrick houses in small villages scattered in areas where no extensive irrigation would have been necessary. Some villages were walled, though there was certainly no shortage of land or pressure on other resources at this time. These various lowland settlements prior to 2600 B.C. show some stylistic uniformity and a great deal of economic and architectural similarity, but they appear to have been economically and politically independent and self-sufficient, and reflect none of the rigid planning typical of later settlements here.

When we look at the changes in the composition of these communities during this same period of settlement pattern changes (i.e., between 3200 B.C. and 2600 B.C.), we see some interesting developments. As noted in chapter 7, in every one of the world's early civilizations there was a gradual elaboration of "public," often monumental, architecture, in the form of pyramids, forts, temples, plazas, warehouses, municipal waterworks, etc. Given this, it is not surprising that until about 2600 B.C. few of the communities found in the Harappan area have much evident public architecture. A few possible defensive walls at Kot Diji and a few other sites have been found, but as Possehl notes, only three of the 463 known pre-urban sites of this formative period have walls around the community. Nor is there much evidence of social stratification, as would be indicated by elaborate tombs, expensively constructed residences, etc. But after 2600 B.C. the major Harappan cities are marked by large buildings, such as "citadels" and "warehouses," and by differences in residential structures that probably correlate with wealth and status.

If we look for factors in the evolution of Harappan civilization, we find the usual correlates of early civilizations: an ecological setting that permitted relatively high agricultural productivity with simple technology; a riverine system that facilitated transport and command/control mechanisms; and a highly varied mix of cultures and natural resources concentrated in a relatively small area by natural terrain features. But the Harappan civilization may be one of the few cases where foreign trade was a powerful stimulus to the development of this culture and many of its forms. Harappan communities extracted minerals, metals, animal products, and many other commodities from the surrounding foothills and mountains, and circulated these not only through local and regional trade, but also with Mesopotamian states via the sea lanes of the Persian Gulf. The cities of Harappa, Mohenjo-daro, and Lothal, for example, seem to be evenly spaced and optimally placed to exploit specific resources found in the areas around them; they may have been "central places" (chapter 7) in a commercial network of integrated local, regional, and foreign trade.[24] Mesopotamian texts suggest that states in this area regularly received commodities from far to the east, as well as from Magan and Meluhha, two ports whose location is not certain but which may have been in the Indus Valley. Gold, silver, copper, carnelian, lapis lazuli, ivory, oils, and many other commodities probably flowed west from the Indus to Mesopotamian towns, most of which were located far from natural sources of these exotic goods. But the Mesopotamians could reciprocate with cereals, leather, wool, and other products of their prolific agricultural system. The details of such trading patterns are poorly preserved in the archaeological record because the foodstuffs would have been consumed, leaving no traces (not even pollen), while the exotics, such as gold and precious stones, were fungible wealth: they could change hands hundreds of times and be converted to many different kinds of wealth, obscuring their original point of production and entry into the initial exchange network.

In the contemporary world there are great "economies of scale" and other advantages to international trade that are directly economic in impact. If individual nations concentrate on what they do best economically and exchange products in an integrated network, great advantages accrue to all—at least according to classical economic theory. Modern Japan and Singapore have few resources, but they have concentrated on highly efficient production of goods for export. In today's world, oil from the Persian Gulf, fruit from Central America, metals from Africa, financial services from the United Kingdom, and tens of thousands of other goods and services lock most of the world's people into interdependent economies that offer at least some benefits to all, despite the exploitative labor they stimulate and the destruction of rain forests and other environments that they cause directly.

But trade in the ancient world was not entirely the same thing. If the only transport available is pack animals and primitive sailing ships, there is little advantage to shipping dates from the Indus Valley to the Tigris-Euphrates Valley. Nor does it make much sense to move pottery from Egyptian kilns to Mohenjo-daro. The pattern of trade we infer between Harappan and Mesopotamian civilizations included some useful functional items, but much was in the form of exotics such as gold, whose most direct use was in reinforcing and elaborating the social distinctions between elites and commoners. One cannot consider these exotics to be functionally worthless on this account, however, because class-stratification seems to have been a basic functional element in constructing the competitive expansionist societies that all early states were.

Trade may have been an important stimulus to the rise of Harappan civilization, but Harappan civilization seems to have "taken off" at a time when there is some evidence (in the form of burned buildings) of regional warfare.[25]

HARAPPAN CIVILIZATION

The appearance of large cities shortly after 2600 B.C., and the associated spread of a distinctive constellation of artifacts and architectural styles over much of the Indus

Valley, marked the emergence of Harappan civilization. This political system survived only about five hundred years, but managed to integrate much of the Indus Plain in a political and cultural unit.

More than eight hundred "mature Harappan" sites are known, and these are spread over an area that at 1.25 million square kilometers is larger than the first Egyptian state and the total area of Sumer, Akkad, and Assyria.[26]

Miller notes that Harappan civilization is not really a strictly riverine civilization, for Harappan settlements are found in many ecological zones, and only after the main Harappan developments were well underway did settlements begin to cluster along the river. Most research on Indus sites has been devoted to the largest settlements, especially Mohenjo-daro, Harappa, Chanhu-daro, Pathiani Kot, Judeirjo-daro, Kalibangan, and Lothal. Doubtless many smaller Harappan settlements are buried beneath silt or have been washed away by floods.

The largest Harappan settlement, Mohenjo-daro (Figure 10.3), covers at least 2.5 square kilometers and may have had 40,000 inhabitants. M. Jansen has argued that Mohenjo-daro was not so regularly constructed as archaeologists once thought, and that only the central "platform mound" area (about 100 hectares)[27] of the city was planned—although there were many more hectares of suburban unplanned residential areas around the main city center. Compared to the jumbled anarchy of most Mesopotamian city plans, however, Mohenjo-daro was quite orderly.[28] M. A. Fentress has questioned the overall similarity of Mohenjo-daro and Harappa, but here too, by Mesopotamian standards, these settlements are quite similar.[29] Miller, in fact, notes that even tiny Harappan hamlets seemed to try to emulate the grid pattern and other designs of the major Harappan metropolises.[30]

Mohenjo-daro was bisected by a north-south street some nine meters wide that was flanked by drainage ditches. Public toilets and sewers and bathrooms in houses were connected to the main sewage lines. Most residences were made of fired brick, comprising several rooms arranged around an open courtyard, and the majority appear to have had private showers and toilets drained by municipal sewage systems. Some houses were two stories high and larger and more elaborate than others, but the overall impression is one of uniformity. In fact, A. Sarcina found that almost all houses at Mohenjo-daro were of two basic patterns: those having a courtyard at one corner that was flanked by rooms on two sides, or those with a courtyard in the center and rooms on three sides.[31] Also, almost all the houses were of the same approximate size and construction: 77 percent of the buildings seem to have been ordinary houses, while the rest were small shops and businesses distributed throughout the living areas.[32] If gross differences in wealth divided the inhabitants, these inequities are not reflected in residential architecture, at least not to the extent that they were in Mesopotamia.

At Mohenjo-daro and some other large sites, such as Harappa, the carefully arranged residential areas were flanked on the west by a large raised mound with a wall around it. This mound (sometimes called a "citadel" or "Mound of the Great Bath") is about 150 meters to the north of the area of settlement known as the "Lower Town." These residential areas appear to have been adjacent to areas that were devoid of any settlement and perhaps were regularly flooded by a branch of the river. It has even been suggested that this flooding may have been deliberate, to create a pool of water for bathing, fishing, or some other activity.

One of the most interesting structures on the high mound itself is the "Great Bath," a swimming-pool-like building about 12 by 7 meters and 2.5 meters in depth with a sunken enclosure, constructed of baked brick and lined with bitumen. Flanking the pool are what appear to have been dressing rooms, carefully staggered to give maximum privacy.[33] The Great Bath may have figured in some religious activities, but it contained no obvious icons or other religious elements and may have been mainly just a public bathing facility.

Adjacent to the bath are various mudbrick platforms and rooms, variously—and imaginatively—interpreted as granaries, assembly halls, and garrisons, but there is little evidence with which to infer their functions. Overall, the Mound of the Great Bath was about 450 meters long and 90 meters wide at its maximum extent—representing a major investment of labor and materials. Thus, while there is nothing at Mohenjo-daro or any other Indus city to compare with the Egyptian pyramids or the White Temple at Uruk, the Indus city dwellers nonetheless diverted considerable energy and resources to building projects. The major difference seems to have been that, in contrast to the largely ceremonial public architecture in Mesopotamia and Egypt, the Indus Valley constructions provided some return in the way of administrative buildings, better defenses, and more storage space.

There is at least a possibility that Harappan civilization was "cut off" in the midst of its development by invasion, flood, interrupted trade routes, or some other factor, and that more "wasteful" monumental architecture might eventually have appeared in the Indus cities had they been allowed to develop for a longer period. The absence of easily accessible building stone may also account for the comparatively utilitarian and drab Harappan monumental architecture.

The thousands of people who lived at Mohenjo-daro included many craftsmen, such as goldsmiths, potters, weavers, brick masons, architects, and many other specialists, and streets were lined with stores and shops. Cereals—particularly barley, but also wheat—were the basis of the economy, supplemented by dates, melons, sesame, peas, mustard, and other crops. Cattle, sheep, goats, pigs, and domestic fowl were the major animal foods, and buffaloes, camels, asses, dogs, and cats were also kept. A few elephant bones have even been found. The horse apparently was rarely used until the very end of the Harappan period.

Most of the larger Harappan settlements were similar to Mohenjo-daro in architecture and economy, but the site of Lothal, although only about 250 to 300 meters in size, shows an impressive complexity for a relatively small settlement.[34] A large tank, which the excavator, S. R. Rao, and others have interpreted as a dock,[35] may not be[36]—its function is unclear. There was a factory for making beads from carnelian, crystal, jasper, and other stones, and facilities for making ornaments out of bronze, elephant tusks, and many other commodities. Possehl sees in Lothal's precise layout and concentrations of exotic commodities an entrepôt, a frontier settlement of entrepreneurs who were processing raw materials from the hinterlands and sending products on to the great Harappan cities. He also notes that Harappan urbanites and hunter-gatherers probably not only co-existed, they were probably continually trading products, with such things as copper knives, pottery, and steatite beads from Harappan communities, while hunter-gatherers supplied stone, meat, beeswax, wood, charcoal, string, rope, reeds, etc.[37]

We know little about the smaller Harappan settlements. The few that have been examined seem to have brick walls around a district within the site, perhaps in imitation of the citadels at the larger cities, and the basic arts and crafts and subsistence practices also appear to have been patterned after those of the larger cities.

Relatively few Harappan cemeteries have been found, but the bodies so far excavated were buried with far fewer evidences of social differentiation than in Mesopotamia and Egypt.[38]

Harappan settlements, with their precisely administered character, would seem to be excellent subjects for the systematic analysis of settlement patterns. Such an analysis might help archaeologists discern the economic and political forces that dictated where people lived, but generally, archaeologists have not competed with each other for a chance to do systematic surveys on the intensely hot, heavily populated Indus Plain.

Scholars have debated whether Harappan civilization was a "chiefdom," "state," or an "empire." As is discussed at length in chapter 7, such debates are usually unresolvable because few people agree on what these political types are, and what kinds of archaeological evidence reflect them. Even if we discard these political typologies and concentrate on things we can measure archaeologically, such as the size of the area over which we find similar artifact styles, or differences in the sizes of communities that existed at the same time, or the existence of a script, standardized system of weights and measures, etc., the evidence from Harappa remains ambiguous. What we do know of Indus settlement patterns suggests at least four different size categories (see chapter 7), comparable to, for example, those of Mesopotamia in the third millennium B.C.. If we consider three or more administrative levels to be evidence of state-level political organization, then the Harappan civilization was certainly a state. In fact, the Harappan population at the beginning of the second millennium B.C. probably totaled at least 200,000 people, and the tightly organized fabric of their lives suggests perhaps an empire-like political system, but we may never know how complex the socioeconomic and political institutions of this culture were.

THE INDUS SCRIPT AND WEIGHTS AND MEASURES

The similarity of Harappan cities, towns, and villages probably reflects a nation in which various settlements were in regular and diverse communication with each other. Clay and metal models of wheeled carts and river boats are the only artifacts remaining of a transportation system that once probably moved large quantities of flint tools, pots, and other artifacts, some mass-produced at a few locations. The considerable degree of occupational specialization evident in these artifacts suggests intensive local trade, but there is a strong possibility that this was a kind of administered, non-capitalistic redistribution, rather than a free-enterprise or peasant marketing system. One possible key to the Harappan economic system is the hundreds of Harappan stamps and seals (Figure 10.4) that have been found; these may have been used to denote ownership or make records of transactions. The apparently ritual scenes depicted in so many of these might argue against this interpretation, but the question will remain unresolved as long as the Harappan script is undeciphered.

FIGURE 10.4   Harappan seals were inscribed with many different symbols in complex arrangements, suggesting a form of written language, but this language has not yet been deciphered.

Much of Harappan writing is in the form of inscriptions on these stamp seals. Many other documents could have been written on palm leaves or some other long-since decayed medium. The estimated number of unique symbols is between 350 and 425, which means that the writing is almost certainly not alphabetic: alphabetic languages use one symbol for each unique sound in the spoken language, and no known language has more than about fifty alphabetic characters. Since the Indus script contains about four hundred unique characters, it is probably made up of symbols indicating syllables in the spoken language, plus some determinatives and other marks to aid interpretation.

Parpola[39] used a computer analysis to try to find a language that fit the apparent structure of the Indus script, but he concluded that it is not related to any known writing system. One of the Indus languages may have been Dravidian, from southern India, but no links have been conclusively demonstrated. Various scholars have suggested that the ancient Indus language was part of a group that extended from the

Elamite-speakers of Iran into northern India, and that the Indus script represents this language family—not Dravidian itself.

If other early scripts are any guide, the majority of these Indus documents and those that presumably have been lost may have had to do with such mundane matters as Farmer A selling eighteen cows to Farmer B and paying the appropriate taxes; others may include a ritual prayer or blessing on the ruler, followed by some record of events and transactions of ordinary daily life. Computers now hum away, trying to find patterns of co-occurrence among the four hundred Indus symbols, and some day we may have a clear sense of what they mean. But the texts are so few and the characters so stylized that it will not be easy to decipher them.

The most common form[40] of Indus writing was on intaglio seals (i.e., an engraving on stone or some other hard material so that when clay or some soft material is impressed with it the engraved elements appear in shallow relief). Impressions of seals have been found on pottery, lumps of wet clay, and other materials. The script also appears as graffiti, scratched or painted on clay surfaces. Examination of these reveals that the script was often written from right to left, and from top to bottom, but in some longer inscriptions the lines are *boustrophedonic*, meaning that the lines alternated (i.e., first line from right to left, second line from left to right, and so on). Most inscriptions are short, containing just five or six signs—far fewer elements than most Egyptian or Mesopotamia documents.

Archaeologists have tried to correlate the locations where these seals were found with some notions of their use, but they seem to be distributed throughout the communities in which they were used. George Dales and Mark Kenoyer[41] have recently suggested that the spatial distribution of the seals may suggest that the people who used them were restricted to certain areas, such as along main streets and access routes.

Unlike Mesopotamian writing, there is no evidence that Harappan writing evolved out of the gradual elaboration of a simpler system. This writing seems to have appeared rapidly and in full form—something like the ancient written Egyptian language. This might suggest that the idea of writing was introduced from western Asian cultures and adapted to local styles, but there are no clear similarities between the Indus script and others. Also, as with ancient written Egyptian, we don't know whether the "suddenness" of the appearance of the Indus script is not simply a result of archaeological biases: early forms of these languages may have been written on materials that did not preserve, or on materials that have not been found in sufficient numbers to trace the origins of these languages.

The writing system was complemented by a standardized system of weights and measures. Small, precisely cut pieces of chert in both binary and decimal arrangements were used as counterweights in balances, and several measuring sticks marked off in units of about 33.5 centimeters have been found; apparently this unit was the common measurement of length, much like the English "foot," for many of the buildings are precisely constructed to this scale.[42]

The writing, seals, and weights suggest substantial interregional—perhaps international—trade, and we have some reports of Harappan colonies as far away as Afghanistan and Oman.[43] But Miller claims that: "It can, however, by now be asserted that there is a remarkable lack of evidence for external trade in Harappan material."[44] Harappan peoples may have traded principally in raw materials rather than the finished goods that would allow identification of trade patterns, but the overall evidence of foreign trade is slight when compared with Mesopotamia at the same period of development.

The Harappan art and religious architecture so far discovered seem less varied, complex, and beautiful than that of the same period in Mesopotamia, but they have a certain affecting quality (Figure 10.5). The most popular art was in the form of terra cotta figurines, the majority of which were standing females, heavily adorned with jewelry. For reasons that will probably forever remain unclear, the Harappan people simply did not produce large amounts of "art" in the form of sculpture, figurines, paintings, or even bodily adornment—or at least few such things have been preserved into our own time (Figure 10.6).

THE DECLINE OF HARAPPAN CIVILIZATION

As we have noted, most civilizations do not die the same way that biological organisms do. Civilizations are transmuted by time and circumstance so that they change, but usually complexes of their constituent elements live on for millennia in languages, art, and other forms.

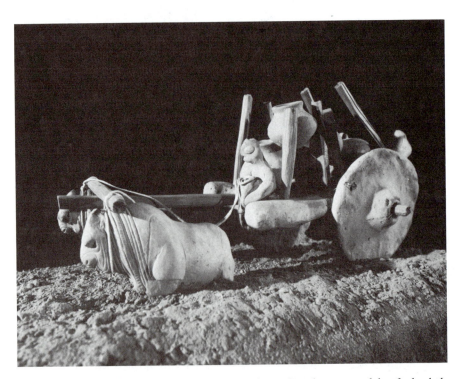

FIGURE 10.5   This Harappan toy cart is one of the earliest known models of wheeled vehicles.

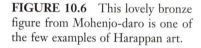

FIGURE 10.6 This lovely bronze figure from Mohenjo-daro is one of the few examples of Harappan art.

The Harappan civilization is part of the cultural stream that connects even the present-day inhabitants of the Indus to their long and complex ancestry, but archaeologists have long wondered if the Indus might really be that rare civilization that, rather than being transformed, was obliterated, perhaps by flood, drought, invasion, or some other calamity. The principal archaeological evidences relating to the demise of Harappan civilization are: (1) the increasing heterogeneity of pottery and other artifact styles within the same area that in earlier centuries had been so uniform stylistically; (2) the "degradation" of art and architecture toward the end of the Harappan period—which has led some imaginative scholars to suppose that the Harappans had lost their sense of central unity and purpose; and (3) the discovery of about a score of human skeletons "sprawled" in the streets and buildings of Mohenjo-daro (Figure 10.7), thought by some to be perhaps the aftermath of an invasion.

Hydrologist Robert Raikes suggests that Harappan civilization was terminated by destruction of their fields and settlements as a result of floods brought on by major shifts of the earth's crust near the mouth of the Indus River.[45] Raikes notes the lack of settlements in the area near the mouth of the river and points out that the fossil beaches are many miles inland from the present coast. This is what one would expect if the river's route to the sea were blocked by an uplift of land near the mouth,

FIGURE 10.7 These skeletons found lying in a public area of Mohenjo-daro were interpreted by some as evidence of an invasion, but there is little proof of this.

since water would have been backed up into a large lake that eventually could have inundated the Harappan area.

Alternatively, Possehl notes that several strains of domesticated African millet were introduced to South Asia at about the time of the Harappan decline. He suggests that these domesticates were better suited to areas south of the Harappan homeland, and that populations might have thus shifted to those areas.[46]

B. K. Thapar[47] sees the demise of Harappa in a destructive combination of several factors, including: (1) tectonic movements that made the Indus and other rivers in this area prone to shifting courses and flooding at destructive levels; (2) wholesale destruction of forests and over-grazing in the Himalayan foothills that led to erosion and subsequent changes in stream courses as these channels built up their beds with silt; (3) tectonic movements and marine regressions that stranded major ports several kilometers inland and lowered the water table in many areas.

A more romantic suggestion is that the Harappan civilization was destroyed by repeated invasions of semi-nomadic peoples coming out of Central Asia and Iran. The *Rig Veda*, the oldest surviving Vedic Sanskrit text, describes the conquest of the dark-skinned natives of the Indus Plain by lighter-skinned Aryan invaders, and the Harappans have traditionally been associated with the former. The translation of Sanskrit literature, first accomplished in the sixteenth century, revealed major similarities between Sanskrit, Greek, and European and Central Asian language families. These similarities were eventually traced to origins in the Caucasus Mountains of southern Russia and adjacent areas and associated with tall, long-headed, fierce peoples collectively referred to as Aryans or Indo-Europeans. Shortly after 1900 B.C., these peoples apparently invaded and influenced the cultures of India, Central Asia, Western Asia, and Europe. How they were able to do this is one of the great unresolved questions of history.

Bronze weapons and other artifacts traditionally associated with the Indo-Europeans have been found in the upper levels of some Harappan sites, and some scholars have identified these with the invaders referred to in the *Rig Veda*. It is difficult to substantiate these invasions, and many now believe that such invasions would have been at most only a minor part of the Harappan collapse. Kennedy specifically rejects the notion that the bodies Sir Mortimer Wheeler found at Mohenjo-daro were massacred.[48]

The "invasion" of largely pastoral peoples into agricultural areas in the Harappan case and in similar circumstances elsewhere probably was more a gradual infiltration than a brutal massive invasion of the sort so often led by Yul Brynner and his colleagues in cinematographic histories. Overall, there may have been a gradual shift of power away from the Harappan heartland to peripheral groups in the south and east, where the evolutionary potential may have been higher because of the emergence there of rice or millet agriculture. Political and cultural influence may well have gravitated to those areas outside the primarily wheat-growing regions of the Harappan sphere of influence.[49] Colin Renfrew has challenged the old notion of Indo-European invaders who sacked the Indus civilizations, and suspects that the people of the Indus Plain were already Indo-European speakers.[50] Rather than a violent spread of Indo-European storm-troopers, there may well have been a spread of the Indo-European *languages*, along with elements of crops and agriculture.

The end of Harappan civilization was probably a result of many factors. Continued pressure from peripheral groups, the altering courses of the Indus River and the drying up of other rivers as their courses and sources changed, droughts, floods, earthquakes—all may have contributed to the gradual abandonment of Harappan centers.

After the Harappan downfall, many diverse cultures appeared throughout India and Pakistan, ranging from hunters and gatherers to highly sophisticated urban-based civilizations. The centers of power and influence gradually shifted from the Indus Valley to the great Ganges River Valley where, after about 1100 B.C., large cities were built and state-level political systems were formed. Many Harappan elements appeared in these later societies, including aspects of metallurgy, architecture, pottery styles, and agriculture.

THE INDUS VALLEY CIVILIZATION: CONCLUSIONS

Scholars dispute general interpretations of the Indus culture history. Some stress the ecological, demographic, and technological bases of life on the Indus Plain,[51] while others emphasize sociopolitical factors.[52]

It is difficult to see an obvious equation between the simple ecological circumstances of life on the ancient Indus Plain and the differences that distinguish Harappan settlements from those in Mesopotamia or Egypt. The planning and execution of Harappan settlements bespeak a powerful centralized authority, perhaps rivaling that of ancient Egypt, but there is no evidence in Harappa of the great tombs, palaces, and pyramids that accompanied theocratic states in Egypt and elsewhere.[53]

Because of its brevity, lack of monumental architecture, and absence of obvious wealth differential and militarism, some people have argued that the Harappan civilization was not a true state, merely a chiefdom.[54] But as Jacobson notes, recent discoveries cast doubt on this interpretation.[55] Settlement pattern studies show considerable variation in the sizes of communities and rates of population growth that are consistent with changes to state-level societies.[56] The Harappan civilization also featured a form of writing which, even if not developed, conveyed a great deal of administrative and economic information, and recent excavations show a degree of military fortification and economic stratification not previously suspected.

Shaffer concludes that in some ways the analytical models applied to Mesopotamia and other early states are not really applicable to Harappan culture.[57] He notes, for example, that compared to Mesopotamia, the Harappan culture did not seem to exhibit the same degree of cyclical rise and fall of state governments, and that in the Indus Valley, a technologically advanced, urban, literate culture was achieved without the usually associated social organization based on hereditary elites, centralized political government (states, empires), and warfare.[58]

Kenoyer suggests

> that the Indus state was composed of several competing classes of elites who maintained different levels of control over the vast region of the Indus and Ghaggar-Hakra Valley. Instead of one social group with absolute control, the rulers or dominant members in the various cities would have included merchants, ritual specialists, and individuals who controlled resources. . . . These groups may have had different means of control, but they shared a common ideology and economic system. . . . This ideology would have been shared by occupational specialists and service communities, who appear to have been organized in loosely stratified groups.[59]

Long-distance trade, particularly the flow of goods from the Indus Valley to Mesopotamia, has frequently been suggested as a key factor in the development—and decline—of Harappan civilization. Harappan seals and seal impressions have been found in limited quantities in Mesopotamia and along the Persian Gulf, and there clearly was some commerce between these areas, perhaps by way of ships sailing along the coast and caravans traversing the Iranian Plateau. Exactly which commodities would have been shipped from the Indus Valley westward is unknown, although steatite and a few kinds of semi-precious stones and other minerals would have been likely trade items. Commerce appears to have been very one-sided, however, with little going from Southwest Asia to the Indus area, and this has suggested to some that Harappan civilization may have been established and maintained mainly by Mesopotamian or Iranian states. Indeed, some Mesopotamian elements exist in the Indus cultures—carved stone boxes, dice, faience, wheeled vehicles, shaft-hole axes, religious art motifs, and the "ram-style" sculptural motif. But taken as a whole, long-distance trade seems to have had little importance in the evolution of cultural complexity in the Indus Valley. The volume of product exchange was very low and mainly in luxury items, and the movement of goods appears to have been accomplished through intermediaries in the Iranian Plateau, rather than through deliberate and directly administered trade between Harappans and Mesopotamians.

As in the case of Egypt and Mesopotamia, rates of population growth in the Indus Valley appear to have been slow, and there is no evidence of pressure on the agricultural systems until long after the Harappan civilization had collapsed.

In summarizing Harappan civilization, Daniel Miller suggests that the city plans and other architecture are designed as an order "that opposes both the natural environment and the human"; and that in religious practices, burials, and other artifacts, the Harappan culture "represents a standardization of and around the mundane." Miller looks for the explanation of the Harappan culture within its own ideology, an ideology he links to later, historical cultures in this area, and in which personal differences are suppressed. He links the end of the Harappan civilization to "a contradiction between its refusal to acknowledge or represent change and its actual history which could only finally manifest itself with the revolutionary overthrow of the entire state."[60]

So in the case of the Indus civilizations we again see the divergence in modern archaeological interpretation. For some, the ecological, technological, and demographic factors are primary, and interpretations are limited quite closely to aspects of administration, class differences, trade, and other aspects of the society that can be related directly to artifacts. But Miller and others consider such analyses to be limited, and they stress, instead, the ideological elements that determine a society. In turn, some archaeologists consider Miller's attempts to use inferences about the importance of the "mundane" in the minds of the Harappan peoples to be ultimately speculative and untestable.

BIBLIOGRAPHY

Adams, R. McC. 1979. "The Natural History of Urbanism." In *Ancient Cities of the Indus*, ed. G. L. Possehl. New Delhi: Vikas Publishing House.

Agrawal, D. P. 1971. *The Copper Bronze Age in India*. New Delhi: Manoharlal.

———. 1982. *The Archaeology of India*. Guildford: Curzon Press.

———. 1984. "Metal Technology of the Harappans." In *Frontiers of the Indus Civilization*, eds. B. B. Lal and S. P. Gupta. New Delhi: Books and Books.

Agrawal, D. P., and S. D. Kusumgar. 1974. *Prehistoric Chronology and Radiocarbon Dating in India*. New Delhi: Manoharlal.

Allchin, F. R. 1960. *Piklihal Excavations*. Hyderabad, India: Government of Andhra Pradesh.

———. 1961. *Utnur Excavations*. Hyderabad, India: Government of Andhra Pradesh.

———. 1963. *Neolithic Cattle-keepers of South India*. Cambridge: Cambridge University Press.

———. 1968. "Early Domesticated Animals in India and Pakistan." In *Man, Settlement and Urbanism*, eds. P. J. Ucko, R. Tringham, and G. W. Dimbleby. London: Duckworth.

———. 1969. "Early Cultivated Plants in India and Pakistan." In *The Domestication and Explanation of Plants and Animals*, eds. P. J. Ucko and G. W. Dimbleby. London: Duckworth.

———. 1974. "India from the Late Stone Age to the Decline of Indus Civilization." *Encyclopaedia Britannica* 9:336–48.

———. 1989. "City and State Formation in Early Historic South Asia." *South Asian Studies* 5:1–16.

Allchin, B., and F. R. Allchin. 1968. *The Birth of Indian Civilization*. Baltimore: Penguin.

———. 1983. *The Rise of Civilization in India and Pakistan*. Cambridge: Cambridge University Press.

Allchin, F. R., and D. K. Chakrabarti, eds. 1979. *A Source Book of Indian Archaeology*, Vol 1. New Delhi: Munshirman Maroliarlal.

Bhan, K. K. 1989. "Late Harappan Settlements of Western India, With Specific Reference to Gujarat." In *Old Problems and New Perspectives in the Archaeology of South Asia*, ed. J. M. Kenoyer. Madison: Wisconsin Archaeological Reports, Vol. 2.

Bisht, R. S. 1984. "Structural Remains and Town Planning of Banawali." In *Frontiers of the Indus Civilization*, eds. B. B. Lal and S. P. Gupta. New Delhi: Books and Books.

Buchanan, B. "A Dated Seal Impression Connecting Babylonia and Ancient India." In *Ancient Cities of the Indus*, ed. G. L. Possehl. New Delhi: Vikas Publishing House.

Chakrabarti, D. K. 1984. "Origins of the Indus Civilization: Theories and Problems." In *Frontiers of the Indus Civilization*, eds. B. B. Lal and S. P. Gupta. New Delhi: Indian Archaeological Society.

Childe, V. G. 1953. *New Light on the Most Ancient East*. New York: Praeger.

———. 1979. "The Urban Revolution." In *Ancient Cities of the Indus*, ed. G. L. Possehl. New Delhi: Vikas Publishing House.

Cornwall, P. B. 1979. "On the Location of Dilmun." In *Ancient Cities of the Indus*, ed. G. L. Possehl. New Delhi: Vikas Publishing House.

Cunningham, A. 1979. "Harappa." In *Ancient Cities of the Indus*, ed. G. L. Possehl. New Delhi: Vikas Publishing House.

Dales, G. F. 1964. "The Mythical Massacre at Mohenjo Daro." *Expedition* 6(3):36–43.

———. 1965. "New Investigations at Mohenjo Daro." *Archaeology* 18(2):145–50.

———. 1966a. "Recent Trends in the Pre- and Protohistoric Archaeology of South Asia." *Proceedings of the American Philosophical Society* 110:130–39.

———. 1966b. "The Decline of the Harappans." *Scientific American* 214(5):93–100.

———. 1968. "Of Dice and Men." *Journal of the American Oriental Society* 88(1):14–23.

———. 1973. "Archaeological and Radiocarbon Chronologies for Protohistoric South Asia." In *South Asian Archaeology*, ed. N. Hammond. Park Ridge: Noyes Press.

———. 1979. "The Balakot Project: Summary of Four Years Excavations in Pakistan." In *South Asian Archaeology 1977*, ed., M. Taddei. Naples: Istituto Universitario Orientale.

Dales, G. F., and J. M. Kenoyer. 1990. "Excavation at Harappa—1988." *Pakistan Archaeology* 24:68–176.

Durante, S. 1979. "Marine Shells from Balakot, Shahr-i Sokhta and Tepe Yahya: Their Significance for Trade and Technology in Ancient Indo-Iran." In *South Asian Archaeology 1977*, ed. M. Taddei. Naples: Istituto Universitario Orientale.

During-Caspers, E. L. C. 1984. "Sumerian Trading Communities Residing in Harappan Society." In *Frontiers of the Indus Civilization*, eds. B. B. Lal and S. P. Gupta. New Delhi: Books and Books.

Dyson, R. H. 1982. "Paradigm Changes in the Study of the Indus Civilization." In *Harappan Civilization: A Contemporary Perspective*, ed. G. L. Possehl. New Delhi: AIIS.

Fairservis, W. A., Jr. 1956. "Excavations in the Quetta Valley, West Pakistan." *Anthropological Papers of the American Museum of Natural History* 45(2).

———. 1961. "The Harappan Civilization: New Evidence and More Theory." *Novitates* 2055:1–35.

———. 1967. "The Origin, Character and Decline of an Early Civilization." *Novitates* 2302:1–48.

———. 1975. *The Roots of Ancient India*, 2nd ed. Revised. Chicago: University of Chicago Press.

———. 1984. "Archaeology in Blauchistan and the Harappan Problem." In *Frontiers of the Indus Civilization*, eds. B. B. Lal and S. P. Gupta. New Delhi: Books and Books.

Fairservis, W. A., and F. C. Southworth. 1989. "Linguistic Archaeology and the Indus Valley Culture." In *Old Problems and New Perspectives in the Archaeology of South Asia*, ed. J. M. Kenoyer. Madison: Wisconsin Archaeological Reports, Vol. 2.

Fentress, M. A. 1976. *Resource Access, Exchange Systems and Regional Interaction in the Indus Valley: An Investigation of Archaeological Variability at Harappa and Mohenjodaro*. Ann Arbor: University Microfilms.

————. 1979. "Indus Charms and Urns, a Look at the Religious Diversity at Harappa and Mohenjodaro." *Man and Environment* 3:9–104.

————. 1985. "Water Resources and Double Cropping in Harappan Food Production." In *Recent Advances in Indo-Pacific Prehistory*, eds. V. N. Misra and P. Bellwood. New Delhi: Oxford and IBH.

Flam, L. 1991. "Excavations at Ghazi Shah, Sindh, Pakistan." In *Harappan Civilization: A Contemporary Perspective*, 2nd Ed., ed. G. L. Possehl. New Delhi: Oxford and IBH.

Flannery, K. V. 1979. "The Cultural Evolution of Civilizations." In *Ancient Cities of the Indus*, ed. G. L. Possehl. New Delhi: Vikas Publishing House.

Frankfort, H.-P., and M.-H. Pottier. 1978. "Sondage Preliminaire sur l'Establissement Protohistorique Harapeen et Post-Harapeen de Shortugai." *Ars Asiatique* 34:29–86.

Gadd, C. J. 1979. "Seals of Ancient Indian Style Found at Ur." In *Ancient Cities of the Indus*, ed. G. L. Possehl. New Delhi: Vikas Publishing House.

Gadd, C. J., and S. Smith. 1979. "The New Links Between Indian and Babylonian Civilization." In *Ancient Cities of the Indus*, ed. G. L. Possehl. New Delhi: Vikas Publishing House.

Gupta, S. P. 1978. *Archaeology of Soviet Central Asia and the Indian Borderlands*, Vol. 1. New Delhi: B. R. Publishing Co.

Ikawa-Smith, F., ed. 1978. *Early Paleolithic in South and East Asia*. The Hague: Mouton.

Jacobson, J. 1979. "Recent Developments in South Asian Prehistory and Protohistory." *Annual Review of Anthropology* 8:467–502.

Jansen, M. 1979. "Architectural Problems of the Harappa Culture." In *South Asian Archaeology 1977*, ed. M. Taddei. Naples: Istituto Universitario Orientale.

————. 1981. "Settlement Patterns in the Harappa Culture." In *South Asian Archaeology 1979*, ed. H. Hartel. Berlin: Dietrich Reimer.

————. 1987. "Mohenjo-Daro—Stadt am Indus." In *Vergessen Städt am Indus*, eds. M. Jansen and G. Urban. Mainz am Rhein: Phillip von Zabern.

Jarrige, J. F. 1981. "Economy and Society in the Early Chalcolithic/Bronze Age of Baluchistan." In *South Asian Archaeology 1979*. Berlin: Dietrich Reiner.

————. 1984. "Chronology of the Early Period of the Greater Indus as Seen from Mehrgarh, Pakistan." In *South Asian Archaeology 1981*, ed. B. Allchin. Cambridge: Cambridge University Press.

Jarrige, J. F., and M. Lechevaleier. 1979. "Excavations at Mehrgarh, Baluchistan: Their Significance in the Prehistorical Context of the Indo-Pakistan Borderlands." In *South Asian Archaeology 1977*, ed. M. Taddei. Naples: Istituto Universitario Orientale.

Jarrige, J. F., and R. H. Meadow. 1980. "The Antecedents of Civilization in the Indus Valley." *Scientific American* 243(2):122–33.

Johnson, G. A. 1973. *Local Exchange and Early State Development in Southwestern Iran*. Museum of Anthropology, Anthropological Papers, University of Michigan, no. 51. Ann Arbor.

Joshi, J. P., and M. Bala. 1981. "Manda: A Harappan Site in Jammu and Kashmir." In *Harappan Civilization: A Contemporary Perspective*, ed. G. L. Possehl. New Delhi: Oxford and IBH.

Kelly, D. H. and B. Wells. 1995. "Recent Progress in Understanding the Indus Script." *The Review of Archaeology* 16(1):15–23.

Kennedy, K. 1982. "Skulls, Aryans and Flowing Drains: The Interface of Archaeology and Skeletal Biology in the Study of the Harappan Civilisation." In *Harappan Civilization*, ed. G. Possehl. Warminster, England: Aris & Phillips.

————. 1984. "Trauma and Disease in the Ancient Harappans." In *Frontiers of the Indus Civilization*, eds. B. B. Lal and S. P. Gupta. New Delhi: Books and Books.

Kennedy, K., and G. L. Possehl, eds. 1976. *Ecological Backgrounds of South Asian Prehistory.* South Asia Occasional Papers and Theses, no. 4.

Kenoyer, J. M. 1991. "The Indus Valley Tradition of Pakistan and Western India." *Journal of World Prehistory* 5(4):331–85.

Kohl, P. L. 1979. "The 'World Economy' of West Asia in the Third Millennium B.C." In *South Asian Archaeology 1977*, ed., M. Taddei. Naples: Istituto Universitario Orientale.

————. 1987. "State Formation: Useful Concept or Idée Fixe?" In *Power Relations and State Formation*, eds. T. C. Patterson and C. W. Gailey. Washington, DC: American Anthropological Association.

Kramer, S. N. 1964. "The Indus Civilization and Dilmun: The Sumerian Paradise Land." *Expedition* 6(3):44–52.

Lamberg-Karlovsky, C. C. 1967. "Archaeology and Metallurgical Technology in Prehistoric Afghanistan, India and Pakistan." *American Anthropologist* 69:145–62.

————. 1975. "Third Millennium Modes of Exchange and Modes of Production." In *Ancient Civilization and Trade*, eds. J. Sabloff and C. C. Lamberg-Karlovsky. Albuquerque: University of New Mexico Press and the School of American Research.

————. 1979. "Trade Mechanisms in Indus-Mesopotamian Interrelations." In *Ancient Cities of the Indus*, ed. G. L. Possehl. New Delhi: Vikas Publishing House.

Lambrick, H. T. 1967. "The Indus Flood Plain and the 'Indus' Civilization." *Geographical Journal* 133(4):483–95.

————. 1979. "Stratigraphy at Mohenjo Daro." In *Ancient Cities of the Indus*, ed. G. L. Possehl. New Delhi: Vikas Publishing House.

Leshnik, L. S. 1968. "The Harappan 'Port' at Lothal: Another View." *American Anthropologist* 70:911–22.

McEvedy, C. 1967. *The Penguin Atlas of Ancient History*. Harmondsworth: Penguin.

Mackay, E. J. H. 1979. "Further Links Between Ancient Sind, Sumer and Elsewhere." In *Ancient Cities of the Indus*, ed. G. L. Possehl. New Delhi: Vikas Publishing House.

Mahadevan, I. 1979. "Study of the Indus Script through Bi-lingual Parallels." In *Ancient Cities of the Indus*, ed. G. L. Possehl. New Delhi: Vikas Publishing House.

Mallory, J. P. 1988. *In Search of the Indo-Europeans*. New York: Thames and Hudson.

Marshall, J. 1979a. "First Light on a Long-Forgotten Civilization." In *Ancient Cities of the Indus*, ed. G. L. Possehl. New Delhi: Vikas Publishing House.

————. 1979b. "Harappa and Mohenjo Daro." In *Ancient Cities of the Indus*, ed. G. L. Possehl. New Delhi: Vikas Publishing House.

Meadow, R. H. 1984. "Animal Domestication in the Middle East: A View from the Eastern Margin." In *Animals and Archaeology*, eds. J. Clutton-Brock and C. Grigson. Vol. 3. Oxford: British Archaeological Reports, S-202.

————. 1993. *Harappan Civilization: A Recent Perspective*, 2nd ed., ed. G. Possehl. New Delhi: Oxford and IBH Publishing.

Miller, D. 1985. "Ideology and the Indus Civilization." *Journal of Anthropological Archaeology* 4(1):34–71.

Mughal, M. R. 1970. "The Early Harappan Period in the Greater Indus Valley and Northern Baluchistan." Doctoral dissertation, University of Pennsylvania.

————. 1972. "Present State of Research on the Indus Valley Civilization." In *Proceedings of the International Symposium on Mohenjo Daro*. Karachi: National Book Foundation.

————. 1974. "New Evidence of the Early Harappan Culture from Jalilpur, Pakistan." *Archaeology* 27:106–13.

————. 1990. "Further Evidence of the Early Harappan Culture in the Greater Indus Valley: 1971–90." *South Asian Studies* 6:175–200.

Oppenheim, A. L. 1979. "The Seafaring Merchants of Ur." In *Ancient Cities of the Indus*, ed. G. L. Possehl. New Delhi: Vikas Publishing House.

Pande, B. M. 1973. "Inscribed Copper Tablets from Mohenjo Daro: A Preliminary Analysis."

In *Radiocarbon and Indian Archaeology*, ed. D. P. Agrawal and A. Ghosh. Bombay: Tata Institute of Fundamental Research.

Parpola, A. 1986. "The Indus Script: A Challenging Puzzle." *World Archaeology* 17(3):399–419.

———. 1994. *Deciphering the Indus Script*. Cambridge: Cambridge University Press.

Perrtula, T. 1977. "Between the Indus and Euphrates: The Comparison of the Evolution of Complex Societies." Seattle: Mimeographed.

Pfeiffer, J. E. 1977. *The Emergence of Society*. New York: McGraw-Hill.

Piggott, S. 1950. *Prehistoric India*. London: Pelican.

Possehl, G. L. 1974. "Variation and Change in the Indus Civilization." Doctoral dissertation, University of Chicago.

———. 1976. "Lothal: A Gateway Settlement of the Harappan Civilization." In *Ecological Backgrounds of South Asian Prehistory*, eds. A. P. Kennedy and G. L. Possehl. *South Asia Occasional Papers and Theses* 4:118–31.

———. 1977. "The End of a State and the Continuity of a Tradition in Proto-Historic India." In *Realm and Region in Traditional India*, ed. R. Fox. Durham: Duke University Program in South Asian Studies.

———, ed. 1979. *Ancient Cities of the Indus*. New Delhi: Vikas Publishing House Pvt Ltd.

———. 1980. "African Millets in South Asian Prehistory." Mimeographed.

———, ed. 1982. *Harappan Civilization*. Warminster (U.K.): Aris & Phillips.

———. 1990a. *Radiocarbon Dates for South Asian Archaeology* (Manuscript). Philadelphia: University of Pennsylvania, University Museum.

———. 1990b. "Revolution in the Urban Revolution: The Emergence of Indus Urbanism." *Annual Review of Anthropology* 19:261–82.

———. 1992. "The Harappan Civilizations in Gujarat: The Sorath and Sindhi Harappans." *The Eastern Anthropologist* 45(No. 1 & 2): 117–54.

———, ed. 1993. *Harappan Civilization: A Recent Perspective*, 2nd ed. New Delhi: Oxford and IBH Publishing.

Possehl, G. L., and M. H. Raval. 1989. *Harappan Civilization and Rojdi*. New Delhi: Oxford and IBH and AIIS.

Raikes, R. L. 1964. "The End of the Ancient Cities of the Indus." *American Anthropologist* 66(2):284–99.

———. 1965. "The Mohenjo-Daro Floods." *Antiquity* 39:196–203.

Raikes, R. L., and R. H. Dyson, Jr. 1961. "The Prehistoric Climate of Baluchistan and the Indus Valley." *American Anthropologist* 63(2):265–81.

Ralph, E. K., H. N. Michael, and M. Han. 1979. "Radiocarbon Dates and Reality." In *Ancient Cities of the Indus*, ed. G. L. Possehl. New Delhi: Vikas Publishing House.

Ramaswamy, C. 1968. "Monsoon over the Indus Valley During the Harappan Period." *Nature* 217(5129):628–29.

Rao, S. R. 1968. "Contacts Between Lothal and Susa." *Proceedings of the Twenty-sixth International Congress of Orientalists*, Vol. II, pp. 35–37.

———. 1973. *Lothal and the Indus Civilization*. Bombay: Asia House.

———. 1979. "A 'Persian Gulf' Seal from Lothal." In *Ancient Cities of the Indus*, ed. G. L. Possehl. New Delhi: Vikas Publishing House.

Ratnagar, S. 1981. *Encounters, The Westerly Trade of the Harappan Civilization*. Delhi: Oxford University Press.

Redfield, R. 1979. "Civilizations as Things Thought About." In *Ancient Cities of the Indus*, ed. G. L. Possehl. New Delhi: Vikas Publishing House.

Renfrew, C. 1988. "Archaeology and Language." *Current Anthropology* 29(3)437–68.

Saggs, H. W. F. 1989. *Civilization Before Greece and Rome*. New Haven: Yale University Press.

Sankalia, H. 1974. *The Prehistory and Protohistory of India and Pakistan*. Pune, India: Deccan College.

———. 1979. "The 'Cemetery H' Culture." In *Ancient Cities of the Indus*, ed. G. L. Possehl. New Delhi: Vikas Publishing House.

Sarcina, A. 1979a. "The Private House at Mohenjodaro." In *South Asian Archaeology 1977*, ed. M. Taddei. Naples: Istituto Universitario Orientale.

————. 1979b. "A Statistical Assessment of House Patterns at Mohenjodaro." *Mesopotamia* 13/14:155–99.

Sayce, A. H. 1979. "Remarkable Discoveries in India." In *Ancient Cities of the Indus*, ed. G. L. Possehl. New Delhi: Vikas Publishing House.

Service, E. 1975. *Origins of the State and Civilization.* New York: Norton.

Shaffer, J. G. 1978. *Prehistoric Baluchistan.* Delhi: B. R. Publishers.

————. 1982. "Harappan Culture: A Reconsideration." In *Harappan Civilization*, ed. G. L. Possehl. New Delhi: Oxford and IBH.

————. 1984. "The Indo-Aryan Invasions: Cultural Myth and Archaeological Reality." In *The People of South Asia*, ed. J. R. Lukacs. New York: Plenum Press.

————. 1988. "One Hump or Two: The Impact of the Camel on Harappan Society." In *Orientalia Iosephi Tucci Memoriae Dicata*, eds. G. Gnoli and L. Lanciotti. Rome: IsMEO.

————. 1991. "The Indus Valley, Baluchistan and Helmand Traditions: Neolithic Through Bronze Age." In *Chronologies in Old World Archaeology*, 3rd Ed., ed. R. Ehrich. Chicago: University of Chicago Press.

Singh, G. 1979. "The Indus Valley Culture." In *Ancient Cities of the Indus*, ed. G. L. Possehl. New Delhi: Vikas Publishing House.

Stein, G. J., and P. Wattenmaker. 1990. "Settlement Trends and the Emergence of Social Complexity in the Leilan Region of the Habur Plains (Syria) From the Fourth to the Third Millennium B.C." In *The Origins of North Mesopotamian Civilization: Ninevite 5 Chronology, Economy, Society*, ed. H. Weiss. New Haven: Yale University Press.

Thapar, B. K. 1975. "Kalibangan: A Harappan Metropolis beyond the Indus Valley." *Expedition* 17(2):19–32.

————. 1993.

Tosi, M. 1984. "The Notion of Craft Specialisation and Its Representation in the Archaeological Record of Early States in the Turanian Basin." In *Marxist Perspectives in Archaeology*, ed. M. Spriggs. Cambridge: Cambridge University Press.

Trigger, B. 1972. "Determinants of Urban Growth in Pre-Industrial Societies." In *Man, Settlement and Urbanism*, eds. P. J. Ucko, R. Tringham, and G. W. Dimbleby. London: Duckworth.

Van Lohnizen-de Leeuw, J. E., and J. M. M. Ubagns, eds. 1974. *South Asian Archaeology.* Leiden, Netherlands: Brill.

Vishnu-Mittre. 1977. "Discussion on Local and Introduced Crops." In *The Early History of Agriculture: A Joint Symposium of the Royal Society and the British Academy*, organized by J. Hutchinson. London: Oxford University Press.

Wheatley, P. 1972. "The Concept of Urbanism." In *Man, Settlement and Urbanism*, eds. P. J. Ucko, R. Tringham, and G. W. Dimbleby. London: Duckworth.

Wheeler, Sir M. 1966. *Civilizations of the Indus Valley and Beyond.* New York: McGraw-Hill.

————. 1968. *The Indus Civilization*, 3rd ed. Supplementary volume to *The Cambridge History of India.* Cambridge: Cambridge University Press.

————. 1979. "Harappan Chronology and the Rig Veda." In *Ancient Cities of the Indus*, ed. G. L. Possehl. New Delhi: Vikas Publishing House.

Wheeler, R. E. M. 1950. *Five Thousand Years of Pakistan.* London: Royal India and Pakistan Society.

Wolpert, S. A. 1977. *A New History of India.* London: Oxford University Press.

Wright, H. T. 1986. "The Evolution of Civilizations." In *American Archaeology Past and Future*, eds. D. J. Meltzer, D. D. Fowler, and J. A. Sabloff. Washington, DC: Smithsonian Institution Press.

Wright, H. T., and S. Pollock. 1985. "Regional Socio-economic Organization in Southern Mesopotamia: The Middle and Late Fifth Millennium B.C." In *La Mesopotamie: Pre- et Protohistoire*, ed. J.-L. Huot. Paris: C.N.R.S.

Wright, R. P. 1989. "The Indus Valley and Mesopotamian Civilizations: A Comparative View of Ceramic Technology." In *Old Problems and New Perspectives in the Archaeology of South Asia*, ed. J. M. Kenoyer. Madison: Wisconsin Archaeological Reports, Vol. 2.

Yoffee, N. 1988. "The Collapse of Ancient Mesopotamian States and Civilization." In *The Col-*

lapse of Ancient States and Civilization, eds. N. Yoffee and G. L. Cowgill. Tucson: University of Arizona Press.

Yule, P. 1982. *Lothal*. Munich: C. H. Beck.

Zide, A. R. K. 1979. "A Brief Survey of Work to Date on the Indus Script." In *Ancient Cities of the Indus*, ed. G. L. Possehl. New Delhi: Vikas Publishing.

NOTES

1. Childe, *New Light on the Most Ancient East*, p. 183; cited by Possehl, "Revolution in the Urban Revolution: The Emergence of Indus Urbanism," p. 267.

2. Possehl, "Revolution in the Urban Revolution: The Emergence of Indus Urbanism," p. 262.

3. Ibid, p. 261.

4. Kenoyer, "The Indus Valley Tradition of Pakistan and Western India."

5. Shaffer, "Harappan Culture: A Reconsideration."

6. Also see Possehl, "Revolution in the Urban Revolution: The Emergence of Indus Urbanism."

7. Strabo and many other Greek historians wrote about the eastern lands Alexander had conquered, but few of them appear to have seen them in person, and thus their accounts were based on travelers' accounts and second-hand knowledge.

8. Mughal, "Further Evidence of the Early Harappan Culture in the Greater Indus Valley: 1971–90."

9. Possehl, "Revolution in the Urban Revolution: The Emergence of Indus Urbanism," p. 261.

10. Meadow, *Harappan Civilization: A Recent Perspective*, p. 311.

11. Fairservis, "The Origin, Character and Decline of an Early Civilization."

12. Allchin, "India from the Late Stone Age to the Decline of Indus Civilization," p. 337.

13. Vishnu-Mittre, "Discussion on Local and Introduced Crops."

14. Kenoyer, "The Indus Valley Tradition of Pakistan and Western India," p. 332.

15. Miller, "Ideology and the Indus Civilization," p. 38.

16. Ibid., p. 39; Jarrige and Lechevaleier, "Excavations at Mehrgarh, Baluchistan: Their Significance in the Prehistorical Context of the Indo-Pakistan Borderlands"; Gupta, *Archaeology of Soviet Central Asia and the Indian Borderlands*; Durante, "Marine Shells from Balakot, Shahr-i Sokhta and Tepe Yahya"; Fairservis, *The Roots of Ancient India*.

17. Wright, "The Evolution of Civilizations."

18. Ibid., p. 337. In comparing the Indus Valley and Mesopotamia, Wright concludes that by the late fifth and early fourth millennia B.C. some areas of the Indus Plain had settlements of such different sizes that we may suspect that they reflect hierarchically organized societies.

19. Miller, "Ideology and the Indus Civilization," p. 40.

20. Mughal, "The Early Harappan Period in the Greater Indus Valley and Northern Baluchistan."

21. Possehl, "Revolution in the Urban Revolution: The Emergence of Indus Urbanism," p. 270.

22. Ibid, p. 270.

23. Ibid, p. 271.

24. Possehl, ed., *Harappan Civilization: A Recent Perspective*.

25. Wright, "The Evolution of Civilizations," p. 340.

26. Jansen, "Settlement Patterns in the Harappa Culture," p. 252; Agrawal, *The Archaeology of India*, p. 135; Miller, "Ideology and the Harappan Civilization," p. 40.

27. Jansen, "Settlement Patterns in the Harappa Culture."

28. Shaffer, "Harappan Culture: A Reconsideration."

29. Fentress, *Resource Access, Exchange Systems and Regional Interaction in the Indus Valley*, pp. 136–37.

30. Miller, "Ideology and the Harappan Civilization."

31. Sarcina, "The Private House at Mohenjodaro"; Sarcina, "A Statistical Assessment of House Patterns at Mohenjodaro."

32. Miller, "Ideology and the Harappan Civilization," p. 48; Sarcina, "The Private House at Mohenjodaro"; Sarcina, "A Statistical Assessment of House Patterns at Mohenjodaro."

33. Fairservis, *The Roots of Ancient India*, pp. 246–47.

34. Possehl, "The End of a State and the Continuity of a Tradition in Proto-Historic India."

35. Rao, *Lothal and the Indus Civilization*.

36. Possehl, "The End of a State and the Continuity of a Tradition in Proto-Historic India."

37. Ibid. For Possehl's analysis of the interactions between Harappans and hunter-foragers, see his "The Harappan Civilizations in Gujarat: The Sorath and Sindhi Harappans," especially pp. 125–126.

38. Miller, "Ideology and the Harappan Civilization," pp. 56–57; but also see Fentress, "Indus Charms and Urns, a Look at the Religious Diversity at Harappa and Mohenjodaro."

39. Parpola, "The Indus Script: A Challenging Puzzle." I am indebted to Gregory Possehl (personal communication) for references and a summary of current interpretations for this paragraph on the language affiliation of the Indus script.

40. The following description of Indus writing is taken mainly from Kenoyer, "The Indus Valley Tradition of Pakistan and Western India." Also see Kelly and Wells, "Recent Progress in Understanding the Indus Script."

41. Dales and Kenoyer, "Excavation at Harappa—1988"; Kenoyer, "The Indus Valley Tradition of Pakistan and Western India."

42. Allchin, "India from the Late Stone Age to the Decline of Indus Civilization."

43. Frankfort and Pottier, "Sondage Preliminaire sur l'Establissement Protohistorique Harapeen et Post-Harapeen de Shortugai"; Miller, "Ideology and the Harappan Civilization," p. 54.

44. Miller, "Ideology and the Harappan Civilization," p. 55.

45. Raikes, "The Mohenjo-Daro Floods."

46. Possehl, "African Millets in South Asian Prehistory."

47. Thapar, "Kalibangan: A Harappan Metropolis Beyond the Indus Valley."

48. Kennedy, "Skulls, Aryans and Flowing Drains: The Interface of Archaeology and Skeletal Biology in the Study of the Harappan Civilisation."

49. Fairservis, *The Roots of Ancient India*, p. 311.

50. Renfrew, "Archaeology and Language."

51. Shaffer, *Prehistoric Baluchistan*; Possehl, "African Millets in South Asian Prehistory."

52. Miller, "Ideology and the Indus Civilization."

53. Service, *Origins of the State and Civilization*, p. 246.

54. Ibid.

55. Jacobson, "Recent Developments in South Asian Prehistory and Protohistory."

56. Johnson, *Local Exchange and Early State Development in Southwestern Iran.*

57. Shaffer, "Harappan Culture: A Reconsideration."

58. Ibid., p. 49; Miller, "Ideology and the Indus Civilization."

59. Kenoyer, "The Indus Valley Tradition of Pakistan and Western India," p. 369.

60. Miller, "Ideology and the Indus Civilization," p. 64.

11

THE EVOLUTION OF COMPLEX
SOCIETIES IN CHINA

Let the past serve the present.

Mao Zedong

A t about 1800 B.C., just a century or so after Hammurabi had established a great empire in Southwest Asia, the people of North China began a period of development that was to take them from simple agricultural tribes to one of the most brilliant and complex civilizations of antiquity (Figure 11.1). But because scientific archaeology in China is only a few decades old and has been interrupted by wars and revolution, we still see only the broad outlines of these developments.

Like ancient Egypt, China was, superficially at least, intensely self-absorbed and inward-looking, and it saw itself as the center of the world whose periphery was populated by vicious barbarians. But China has a far larger and more varied physical landscape than Egypt—or Mesopotamia, for that matter—and this and other factors made its civilization a rich amalgam of many ethnic groups and a diversity of cultures.

Mesopotamia, Egypt, and Europe gave the world many great technological inventions, but China's and east Asia's contributions include such fundamental advances as the magnetic compass, gunpowder, printing, paper, paddle-wheel propulsion, and many other inventions.[1] But "technology" is more than invention, it is also development and application. The Chinese used gunpowder mainly for fireworks, for example, but the Europeans quickly saw other interesting potential uses for it. China, like other ancient civilizations, provides an object lesson in a rather brutal historical dynamic: China was once among the largest, most powerful, and most innovative civilizations in the world, but it too was eventually dominated by the rise of the West and exploited for centuries. As the twentieth century ends, however, there are indications that the world's center of power is shifting back toward China. The world has become so interconnected politically and economically that the kinds of massive imbalances of power of nations that marked the nineteen and early twentieth centuries may never occur again, but China's enormous population, strong national sense of identity and culture, and rich natural resources may support a great expansion of its economy and power in the next century.

514

CHINA

AD 618 — Tang dynasty unifies China; empire based on Chang'an, world's largest city (1 million inhabitants)

AD 220 — Collapse of Han dynasty; China divided into three independent states

AD 150 — Buddhism reaches China

AD 105 — Paper comes into use in China

50 BC — Chinese silk traded to Romans

108 BC — Chinese take control of Korea, establishing military outposts

119 BC — Chinese iron industry becomes state monopoly

206 BC — Accession of the Han dynasty

210 BC — Emperor Shih Huang-ti interred in vast mausoleum with terracotta army

— Shih Huang-ti, first Ch'in emperor, builds the Great Wall

221 BC — Unification of China by the Ch'in dynasty.

350 BC — Crossbow invented

403 BC — Warring States Period; finds of bronze and iron weapons and city defenses

500 BC — Beginning of coinage

550 BC — First significant iron production

770 BC — Beginning of Eastern Chou

1027 BC — Chou dynasty replaces the Shang

1400 BC — First written inscriptions, on oracle bones and bronze ritual vessels

— Urban settlements

1800 BC — Emergence of Shang civilization in northeast China

— Production of wheel-thrown pottery

2500 BC — Emergence of walled settlements in Longshan

— First bronze artifacts

2700 BC — Evidence of silk weaving

3000 BC — Finds of possible ploughshares in Hangzhou area

FIGURE 11.1 A cultural chronology of ancient China.

THE ECOLOGICAL SETTING

Modern China incorporates an area slightly larger than the contemporary United States. Within this territory are vastly different environments, ranging from the Himalayas to the Pacific shore, and people from many of these areas came to play some role in shaping Chinese civilization. K.C. Chang—whose work and writings provide much of what is known about China in the West—defined three ecological zones as crucial areas in the evolution of ancient Chinese civilization: the Huanghe (formerly transliterated, under the Wade-Giles system, as "Hwang Ho") valley; the southern deciduous zone; and the northern forests and steppes.[2] He also notes that for some thousands of years after the end of the Pleistocene at about 12,000 years ago, China's climate was somewhat warmer and moister than it is today, and much of the country was probably heavily forested, from the temperate forests of the north to the jungles in the south. Chang observes that because of China's mountainous nature and heavy post-Pleistocene vegetative cover, people were probably restricted to the river valleys at first, since these would have been the richest sources of food and would have offered the most open land for farming. Developments in these three ecological zones eventually overlapped, and in later periods of antiquity the vast populations of nomads on the northern and western frontiers of China greatly influenced the character of Chinese civilization.

Wheat and barley supplied much of the energy that ran Mesopotamian and Egyptian societies, but in China rice and millet were in many instances as important as wheat or barley. North China's developmental leadership was closely tied to its agricultural potential. Pleistocene winds blowing off the Gobi Desert covered parts of North China with a layer of loess (a fine grain sediment) that reached a depth of several hundred meters. The Huanghe (or "Yellow River"—from the color given it by the loess it carries) cuts through these loess plains, frequently changing its course, and through flooding and draining it has created a rich agricultural zone of lakes, marshes, and alluvial fields. Loess is the agricultural soil *par excellence:* it is organically rich, requires little plowing, and retains near the surface much of the sparse rain that falls on North China. Moreover, it can yield large crops with little fertilization, even under intensive cultivation. The southern alluvial plains, with their hot, humid climate, eventually became the great rice heartlands.

Early farmers around the world converged in finding, through domestication and agriculture, four key ingredients to the village-farming way of life: they all found (1) a source for textiles, (2) a productive, high carbohydrate, main crop plant, (3) an edible oil for cooking, and (4) a reliable source of animal protein. The initial northern Chinese solutions to these problems were hemp for textiles, millet for a main crop plant, rapeseed and soybeans for edible oils, and pigs for meat. But east Asia—including Japan, Southeast Asia, Korea, and other areas peripheral to the mainland—domesticated an impressive range of other plants, perhaps more than any other area of the world. Wheat, barley, and perhaps other plants may have been introduced from western Asia, but east Asian domesticates and/or early cultivars include apricot, peach, pear, persimmon, and plum trees; soybeans, mung beans, peas, and other legumes; buckwheat, various kinds of millet, barley, and rice; safflower, rape, and other producers of edible oils; chinese cabbage, radishes, and other vegetables; and a variety of special-purpose plants such as the lacquer tree (lacquer), hops (flavoring agent), hemp (fibers and drugs), and the bottle gourd (containers).

EARLY FARMERS (C. 7000 B.C.–5000 B.C.)

K. C. Chang[3] suggested that one of the most significant discoveries in the prehistoric archaeology of North China in recent years is the discovery in eastern Shensi Province and other areas of microlithic stone tools dating perhaps (the dating is uncertain) to about 13,000 years ago. These finds are important because little is known about the people of China as the Pleistocene ended or about their descendants, whose hunting-foraging culture gave way to the first farmers. The distinctive artifact styles of these stone tools and other finds indicate that a large population of pre-agricultural peoples were widely distributed over much of China about 10,000 years ago. Most of these people were hunter-gatherers, with some groups specializing in fishing near the coasts and large lakes.

Although there are gaps in the archaeological record in the centuries just after these microlithic industries were in use, during the past decade many sites have been found that appear to have been the earliest Chinese farming communities. These villages date to between about 6500 and 5000 B.C. and have been grouped into regional clusters (Figure 11.2). Known as the Cishan, Peiligang, and Dadiwan cultures,[4] these settlements were located along the lower terraces of the western highlands, in the valleys of the Wei, Huanghe, and a few other rivers. This warm, moderately rainy area has great agricultural potential, especially in the alluvial plains, the loess plateau,

FIGURE 11.2 The earliest Neolithic cultures of China appeared in several distinct regions, shown here in darker shading, with the approximate boundaries of their artifact style distributions shown in lighter shading.

and the hilly lands of the Shangdong peninsula. Early farmers in this area took advantage of these zones by staking their subsistence on several highly reliable and stable resources. Probably the most important food source was millet, a cereal grass (both foxtail millet [*Setaria italica*] and broomcorn millet [*Panicum miliaceum*]) that produces a very nutritious grain. Nutritionally as rich as wheat, millet is also quick-maturing and drought-resistant—making it admirably suited to North China—and its stems can be used for food, fuel, and fodder. Stone sickle blades, grinding stones, and other tools indicate that much farming was devoted to millet, which they complemented with vegetables, an edible vegetable oil (in the form of rapeseed [*Brassica*]), and meat from domesticated pigs and chickens. They also collected walnuts, hazelnuts, and other wild plant foods, and hunted deer. Like many other peoples around the world, their first domesticate was probably the dog, skeletons of which have been found at various sites. These early farmers lived mainly in small (two to three meters in diameter) subterranean houses. They already knew how to make pottery at this time, and used an impressive diversity of ground-stone grinders, bone needles, and many other implements of stone, bone, and wood.

The earliest agricultural sites in South China are only a bit later than those in the north, but our knowledge of them is much less advanced. Several caves in China and Thailand have deeply buried remains from this period, and some of these early levels contain cord-marked pottery and what may be the remains of domesticated plants.

REGIONAL NEOLITHIC DEVELOPMENTS IN NORTH CHINA (5000–3000 B.C.)

The largest and best-known early agricultural Chinese communities are those of the Yangshao culture (Figure 11.2). The Yangshao covered the same approximate area as did the earlier P'ei-li-kang culture, and the similarities between these two indicate cultural continuity. Most of the Yangshao settlements were distributed along the banks of the Huanghe and other river systems in central China. Bones of most of the larger animals native to this part of China, from rabbits to rhinos, have been found in Yangshao settlements, but millet probably provided most of the calories, while sorghum and a few other crops were also cultivated. Like their counterparts in the forests of temperate Europe, early Chinese farmers probably cleared land for farming by slashing down vegetation with stone axes and then burning it off when it had dried.[5]

And like other early cultivators they took full advantage of game animals, wild plants, and fishing—as evidenced by the hundreds of hooks, fish gorges, and net weights found. Pigs, domestic fowl, and later cattle, sheep, and goats, were favored sources of meat.

In a real sense, the first ancestors of the civilization we know imprecisely as "China" were probably the sturdy peasants of the Yangshao period (radiocarbon-dated to c. 5100–3900 B.C.[6]), who lived in villages like Bampo (formerly "Pan-p'o"). Wearing rough clothes made of hemp, bunkered down in houses with floors dug several feet below ground (Figure 11.3) to shield themselves from winter snows and summer

FIGURE 11.3 This reconstruction of a Neolithic house at Bampo (Pan-p'o-ts'un) illustrates how early Chinese farmers protected themselves against the harsh north China winters by living in pit- houses.

heat, the people of Bampo followed the familiar agricultural cycle of China. Millet was the staple, pigs and ducks recycled wastes into the basic meats of what was even then perhaps a world-class cuisine, and cattle, sheep, and goats contributed their all in the form of meat, milk, draft power, leather, and wool. The few hundred people at Bampo, like most of their neighbors, were probably self-sufficient in everything that really mattered except marriageable women.

Another Yangshao village that has been extensively excavated is Jiangzhai, in Shaanxi Province.[7] Over an area of about 50,000 square meters the people here built a neatly organized community that was surrounded by a defensive moat and was arranged in five complexes, each with a large house surrounded by ten to twenty smaller ones. Most of the houses were semi-subterranean with wood superstructures. Like other early farmers, the people of Jiangzhai buried their dead with household objects, which suggests a belief in a life after death that was something like their life in this world. Children were buried in ceramic urns—an ancient practice that still continues in parts of Asia.

Yangshao villages seem to have been abandoned and reoccupied periodically—probably because these people practiced slash-and-burn farming, wearing out the soil in the area around their community, then relocating the village, and eventually returning to the abandoned areas when the fertility was renewed by re-growth of vegetation.

Already by the time of Bampo the Chinese aesthetic sense is evident in the designs and color of pottery, jade carvings, and other artifacts. Stylized fish and animals grace some of the burnished pottery, and some pots were marked with symbols that may be early expressions of written Chinese. Around the houses were many deep pits, presumably for storing millet and other commodities. No doubt most villagers were full-time agriculturalists, but some engaged in silkworm cultivation, pottery manufacture, jade carving, and leather and textile production.

Bampo has been converted into an impressive museum, and more than two hundred of the original inhabitants of this community are still there, their skeletons protruding from house floors and pits. Most of the site has been enclosed in a building, with some of the most important houses and artifacts left in place. At some Yangshao sites the bodies of people seem to have been re-buried in groups. K. C. Chang notes that at Yuan-chun-miao, fifty-seven graves were arranged "in six north-south rows, the earliest being the first and fourth rows, the latest the third and sixth rows. . . . This layout and chronological order have led to the reasonable speculation that the cemetery was divided into two moieties, reflecting the two-clan composition of the village."[8]

In the middle of Bampo was a distinctive building, much larger than the typical house and of different construction. To the Chinese excavators, this building seems most likely to have been a communal meeting hall; but one might also suspect that a bit of capitalistic inequality had infected the Yangshao culture, and that this was the house of a "big man" or chief.[9] However, there are no evident signs of varying status in other artifacts at the site.

More than a hundred Neolithic sites (c. 5000 to 3000 B.C.) have been found in the Lake T'ai-hu area, southeast of Nanking. Rice cultivation provided the main staple, but the range of animals hunted was impressive, including boars, elephants, alligators, deer, and many other species. One example of an early southern Neolithic community is at Hemudu, in northern Zhejiang Province, where excavations in 1973 through 1978 revealed a 7,000-year-old village of wooden houses built on piles along the shore of a small lake. The preservation of objects at this site is spectacular. Excavators found bone hoes, wooden shuttles for weaving, ivory carvings, and many plant and animal remains, including rice, bottle gourds, water chestnuts, domesticated water buffalo, pigs, dogs, and wild animals such as tigers, elephants, and rhinoceroses.

The extension of pottery styles over much of North China during the period between 5000 and 3000 B.C. is probably the clearest early sign that by this time people were developing the integrated economic and political institutions on which the later Chinese states were constructed.

EARLY COMPLEX CHINESE SOCIETIES (3000–2000 B.C.)

In the early third millennium B.C., the people of North and central China—at least on the basis of our limited archaeological evidence—seem the very picture of egalitarian, peaceful villagers; but by the beginning of the second millennium B.C., signs of social rank and violence are everywhere.

Chinese legend relates that the first Chinese emperor was Huang Di, a northern Chinese warlord who is reputed to have established a dynasty in 2698 B.C. Whatever

the validity of this legend, the archaeological record indicates rapidly increasing social complexity after c. 2400 B.C., with the emergence of the Longshan and related
cultures (Figure 11.4). Longshan cultures, like the Yangshao, are defined on the basis of similar styles of artifacts—in the Longshan case by highly burnished, wheel-
made, thin-walled black pottery in many different vessel forms; these pots are found,
with minor stylistic variations, from the southeastern coast of China to the northern
provinces. Very early Longshan pottery and other diagnostic artifacts are found over
most of the old Yangshao heartland. And while Yangshao communities in some places
seem to have given rise almost directly to Longshan communities, the linkages between these periods and peoples are still quite obscure.[10]

As with the Yangshao, the Longshan peoples lived mainly in villages made up of
pit houses arranged around a central "long house," and virtually every Longshan adult
male was probably still a millet farmer who supplemented the family fortunes with
hunting, collecting, and part-time craft production of pottery, jade, or another commodity. But Longshan villages were, on the average, significantly larger than those
of the Yangshao period, and were likely occupied for longer periods of time.

Like their counterparts in other early civilizations, ancient Chinese farmers eventually made a momentous transition: instead of the slash-and-burn agriculture practiced in the Yangshao period, shifting fields from year to year, they began in Longshan times to cultivate the same fields each year. The costs of doing this are high:
one has to use animal manure, clovers, and discarded plants to renew fertility, or else
irrigation water must be led to the fields through canals to replenish soil fertility. In

FIGURE 11.4   Archaeological sites of the Longshan and related cultures.

some places, of course, in China as in Egypt, the annual floods renew soil fertility, but in all ancient civilizations a point was eventually reached where intensification of agriculture was required to sustain life. Longshan agriculture, although still based on millet and a few domesticated animals, seems to have been more intensive than that of the Yangshao. Domestic poultry, sheep, and cattle became more important, and there is evidence of the increasing significance of rice agriculture in some southern areas.

There are also signs of change in social organization. Compared with Yangshao graves, Longshan burials seem to differ between those of richer and those of poorer people, at least as reflected in the pots, metal implements, and other items buried with these people. Longshan pottery and jade ornaments are so technologically sophisticated and beautiful that they suggest the existence of at least some semi-specialized craftsmen.

Based on an analysis of pig skulls in burials at several Neolithic sites, Seung-Og Kim has argued[11] that pigs were used as important status and wealth markers. Pigs were supremely adapted to Neolithic Chinese agriculture. Evidence suggests that pigs were even kept in household latrine areas and subsisted in part on human waste products—an early indication of the extraordinary practicality of Chinese cuisine and their ability to convert materials from every stage of the food chain into appealing foods. Kim found that the Chinese Neolithic graves with the most wealth in the form of ivory and jade ornaments, pottery, and other goods also, on average, had more pig skulls and carved pig tusks in them. Kim suggests that these interred pig bones reflect a society in which the great economic value of the pig as the most important domestic animal (in terms of its popularity as a food) was complexly linked to the social context of ritual, wealth, and political prestige. He hypothesizes that pigs could be used as a form of exchangeable wealth, and that some individuals could have risen in wealth and prestige by using pigs to acquire exotic prestige goods such as jade and turtle shell through long-distance trade. As Kim notes, ethnographic studies of Melanesian and other societies show that pigs often are viewed as a form of wealth, and that pig slaughtering and meat distribution are important parts of the competition for power, wealth, and prestige in these "big-man" or tribal societies. Kim argues that between about 4000 and 2000 B.C. the elites in many Chinese communities used pigs as "concentratable and productive internal wealth in order to establish political authority."[12]

Longshan people sought knowledge through *scapulimancy*, the art of writing signs on bones, applying heat to the bone to crack it, and then interpreting the pattern of cracking to foretell the future. Archaeologist K. C. Chang interprets the appearance of this art in Longshan times as a reflection of the rise of at least a semi-professional class of shamans—an interpretation made credible by the fact that the character meaning "book" already appears on these bones and may signify the existence of specialized scribes.

Chang also notes that the first traces of town walls—which became a standard feature of later communities—are found at the Longshan site of Ch'eng-tzu-yai. It was built with the "stamped-earth" technique, in which layer after layer of fine loess silts and clays were stamped by workers into a compact wall. The wall at Ch'eng-tzu-yai has now largely deteriorated, but from its traces the excavators estimate it was six meters high and nine meters wide at the top.

Longshan and related communities were probably still largely self-sufficient and independent. Settlement patterns of this period are poorly known, but there is little evidence of population aggregation or regular spacing of settlements according to economic or administrative principles. Nonetheless, the transition to life in permanent villages and established agricultural fields was made over much of North China in the Longshan period, from the western highlands into the northern Manchurian highlands and well into southern China.

K. C. Chang has summarized the overall developments of China in the third millennium B.C. in terms of eight features that, taken together, indicate evolving cultural interaction and complexity: (1) the beginnings of copper metallurgy; (2) the widespread use of sophisticated potter's wheels and presumably the emergence of a specialized class of potters; (3) the stamped-earth walls found at some sites, and their implication of the need for civil defense; (4) burials of bodies in wells, mass graves, and other conditions that suggest warfare; (5) the use of animal and other motifs in artworks in ways that indicate emerging status differences; (6) decorated jade masks and other objects that suggest an emerging ritual system practiced over a large part of the country; (7) the widespread use of scapulimancy, also suggesting ritual interaction over a large area; and (8) signs of social ranking and wealth differences in burials.[13]

We can easily draw parallels here with Egypt, Mesopotamia, and the Indus Valley: the Chinese use of jade, scapulimancy, and so forth are distinctive in their specifics, but the general pattern is one of emerging and evolving class-consciousness, functional specialization, and administrative complexity.[14]

EARLY SHANG CIVILIZATION (C. 1800–1650 B.C.)

After about 2000 B.C., large towns and cities began to replace or emerge from the tens of thousands of villages that marked earlier, simpler times. During the second millennium B.C. China really became "China," in the sense that this period marked the first widespread use of the distinctively Chinese forms of writing, architecture, art, and ideology. Also during this period all the correlates of cultural complexity, such as monumental architecture, large population concentrations, occupational specialization, written records, gross differences in wealth, power, and prestige, and large public-works projects, appeared in full measure.

Legends and early texts suggest that the first Shang kings established seven or more capital cities in the central area of the Huanghe River basin. One of the earliest sites of this transitional period to complexity is Erh-li-t'ou (Yen-shih) (Figure 11.5). Here lies a vast complex of ruins, scattered over an area about 1.5 by 2.5 kilometers, and extending to a depth of 3 meters in some places.

Among the most impressive features at Erh-li-t'ou are the foundations of two buildings that some have called "palaces": one is 108 by 100 meters and is associated with a large earthen platform. In one area of its foundation was a group of burials, including one person who seems to have been buried with his hands bound. The other, smaller palace was drained with a system of pottery pipes and associated with a large earthen tomb—long since plundered of most of its wealth. The richness of Erh-li-t'ou's jade, bronze, pottery, and other artifacts, the indications of human sac-

FIGURE 11.5 K. C. Chang's (1986) reconstructions of (**A**) major Erh-li-t'ou Culture sites and traditional Hsia Dynasty capitals; (**B**) traditional Shang Dynasty capitals.

rifice, and the large buildings all suggest a level of emerging cultural complexity greater than that of previous periods. Other sites of the same age as Erh-li-t'ou have been found, and these together may represent the transitional period between the late Neolithic and the indisputable cultural complexity of the later Shang period.

MIDDLE SHANG PHASE (C. 1650–1400 B.C.)

The Middle Shang phase (or Erh-li-kang phase) is best documented archaeologically at the cluster of settlements largely buried under the modern city of Zhengzhou (formerly "Chengchou"). The central area of Erh-li-kang phase settlement was a roughly rectangular arrangement of buildings extending about 3.4 square kilometers, much of which was enclosed by a pounded-earth wall some 36 meters wide at the base and 9.1 meters in height—as estimated from the segments still remaining.[15] The central area of the site is thought to have been the residence and ceremonial center of the ruling elite, and around it were thousands of pit houses, animal pens, shops, storage pits, and other features that make it clear that many of the people of Shang China lived lives radically different from those of Neolithic times. Hundreds of skilled, full-time craftsmen probably resided at Zhengzhou. In one area thousands of pieces of animal and human bone were recovered, much of it already fashioned into fish hooks, awls, axes, and hairpins. In another area were more than a dozen pottery kilns, each surrounded by masses of broken and over-fired pottery.

But the Zhengzhou craftsmen really displayed their skill in working bronze. Large areas were given over to workshops for casting fish hooks, axes, projectile points, and various ornaments. A kind of mass production was achieved by using multiple molds, made by impressing a clay slab with the forms of six arrowheads, with each impression connected by a thin furrow to a central channel. A second clay mold was placed over the first, the two bound together, and then molten bronze was poured in. After cooling, the individual points could be sawed off from the central stem.

In Western societies especially, there is a tendency to think of cultural change as often being driven by technological change. The invention of the locomotive, for example, radically altered nineteenth-century Western society. When we look at ancient China, there is a temptation to see a culture shaped and formed by the invention of bronze-working and iron-working. Bronze-working seems to have been an indigenous development in Shang civilization, probably made possible by the high-temperature kilns first used to fire pottery. The requisite copper and tin could be found within several hundred kilometers of the Shang homeland, and various processes using clay models and the lost-wax process were known. The first great diffusion of Shang culture, which probably marked both the rise of national consciousness and the ramifying of political and economic networks that underlay the emergence of Shang civilization, was also marked by the spread of bronze artifacts.

But the use of bronze seems to have been mainly a stylistic phenomenon rather than a great technological advance. Though lovely to look at, the myriad bronze Shang vessels offer few culinary advantages over ceramics, and there is no evidence that bronze weapons revolutionized Shang-period warfare. And for clearing forests—

an important part of the Shang expansion—stone axes and hoes would probably have worked at least as well as bronze tools, which were, in any case, a luxury item.

Bronze-making may have been invented at different times by different people. Already by 4500 B.C. people in Southeast Asia, at sites like Ban Chiang, in Thailand, were using cast-bronze spearheads and ornaments.[16] We know relatively little about these early Southeast Asian bronze-using cultures, but it seems likely that their precocious use of bronze was a result of the proximity of copper and tin deposits. Their evolution to cultural complexity followed that of the north in all essential elements and occurred much later.

Both archaeological evidence and ancient documents written after the Shang period indicate that Shang society was headed by a king, who ruled through a hierarchically arranged nobility. Commoners were conscripted for public works and military service; there were highly organized and incessant military campaigns; and many settlements were apparently integrated into an organized inter-village system of commerce.[17] It has not been determined if there were large-scale irrigation systems, but at Zhengzhou at least a canal system was in use, perhaps to carry water to the settlement or else to remove drainage water or sewage from the complex.[18]

The great mass of Shang people, however, probably lived much as their ancestors had, in villages of pit houses located along river systems, subsisting on the same kinds of crops and agricultural technology as people of previous millennia.

LATE SHANG CIVILIZATION (C. 1400–1110 B.C.)

The last and most brilliant phase of Shang civilization, the Yin phase, seems to have begun about 1384 B.C., when the Shang king P'an-keng is reported to have moved his capital to the city of Angang (formerly "An-yang"), in Hunan Province.

Excavations at Angang and contemporary sites in this area have been conducted intermittently since the 1920s, but the publication of this research is far from complete. Scores of sites within an area of about twenty-four square kilometers have been tested, and the evidence suggests that the complex at Angang includes a large ceremonial and administrative center surrounded by smaller dependent hamlets and craft centers.[19] True to tradition, most peasants still lived in small pit houses—not very different from those of 2,000 years earlier. Scattered throughout the settlement were granaries, pottery kilns, storage pits, bone and bronze workshops, animal pens, ditches, and other familiar features of ancient Chinese life.

No city wall has been found at Angang, but monumental buildings were constructed. The largest of these was about sixty meters long, rectangular in form, with large stone and bronze column bases, and founded on a large platform of compacted earth. There were at least fifty-three structures of this type (though somewhat smaller) in one group at Angang, arranged in three main clusters. Although not lavish in construction, these buildings were surrounded by scores of human and animal sacrificial burials, as well as many pits containing royal records written on oracle bones and numerous small structures thought to be for service personnel.[20] Near the cluster of buildings a cemetery held eleven large graves, replete with lavish, expensive burial goods and many human sacrificial burials—the whole complex surrounded by 1,200 smaller, much less lavish burials.

Elsewhere, a complex of ceremonial buildings at Hsiao-T'un was dedicated with what appears to have been the sacrifice of 852 people, 15 horses, 10 oxen, 18 sheep, 35 dogs, and 5 fully equipped chariots and charioteers.[21] A recent bumper sticker declared "If I can't take it with me, I ain't going"—a sentiment probably very agreeable to Shang rulers. Tomb after tomb was stocked with everything from chariots to rice. Like the early Mesopotamian peoples, the Chinese probably believed that burying a ruler's wives, servants, guards, and other staff with him would provide him with full services in the afterlife. The Shang may also have employed that most efficient of all incentives to a devoted domestic staff—the ritual murder of a king's staff on the occasion of his own death. Unlike feudal European nobility, few Shang nobles probably feared poisoning by members of their households. In some Shang tombs bodies were found decapitated or dismembered, and some of them had been bound before they died. How others of these people were killed—if they were—before burial is not clear, but their orderly arrangement in these and other tombs would be certain to arouse the suspicions of a coroner.

The Shang ceremonial and administrative structures are perhaps not as impressive in size or cost as the ziggurats and temples of Mesopotamia, but the level of occupational specialization, the immense wealth of the burials, and the intensity of organization of the agricultural and economic systems remind one of the Mesopotamian city-states of the late fourth millennium B.C.

Little urbanism and only a thin distribution of bronze-working and a few other Shang cultural traits appear in most of non-Shang China at this time, and most of these non-Shang cultures were probably still at a predominantly Neolithic level of development.

Late in the Shang period (about 1200 B.C.), the written language had evolved (perhaps quite rapidly) to the point that texts from this period give us a detailed portrait of Shang life. Over 3,000 phonetic, ideographic, and pictographic characters were in use (of which about 1,200 have been identified), and more than 160,000 inscribed shells (of which only some have been translated) and numerous inscriptions in bronze or stone date to this period.[22]

According to the texts, the late Shang rulers held sway over a territory extending from the Pacific shore to Shensi Province in the west, and from the Yangtze River in the south to southern Hupeh in the north. At the apex of Shang society was the king, who ruled directly on many affairs of state and was assisted by a complex hierarchy of nobles possessing considerable local autonomy in their respective territories. These lords were charged with defending the homeland, supplying men for armies and public-works projects, and collecting and contributing state taxes. Toward the end of the Shang period, many nobles apparently achieved almost feudal status and were virtually independent in their own domains. But the king was still considered to have superior supernatural powers and to be the pivot of all ritual procedures. The kingdom was viewed in the traditional Chinese fashion, with itself as the center of the universe but ringed by non-Shang "barbarians," whom the Shang kings manipulated through force and diplomacy.[23]

On occasion, royal armies of up to about 30,000 men were conscripted and led by the nobles against insurgent "barbarians" and neighboring principalities. The basis of the army was the horse-drawn chariot, supported by infantrymen armed with powerful laminated wood and bone bows and bronze-tipped arrows, and equipped with small knives and/or halberds, which were large knives or axes mounted on the end of a wood shaft about six feet long. Royal records indicate that military campaigns often incurred and inflicted frightful casualties. No doubt many hundreds of thousands of people died in ferocious wars of which history no longer has any record. Staggering quantities of plunder were often taken, along with thousands of prisoners, most of whom were apparently sacrificed or enslaved.[24]

The agricultural system seems to have been essentially the same as previously, with millet, wheat, rice, and vegetables the major crops, cattle, sheep, pigs, and poultry the main livestock, and water buffalo the only "new" domestic animal. The proportions of these crops and animals may have shifted somewhat, with wheat and rice expanding their range at the expense of millet, but the evidence for this is questionable. There is little record of large irrigation systems anywhere in the Shang domain, and hunting and gathering still supplied a substantial part of the diet. The mammalian faunal remains from Angang include massive quantities of boar, deer, bear, and other hunted animals, including a few elephants, rhinoceroses, leopards, and even part of a whale.[25] Apparently intra-village trade in foodstuffs was voluminous.

Local occupational specialization was considerable. Many villages lacked one or more of the more important handicraft workshops, suggesting that products were exchanged among these settlements.[26] The discovery of large caches of agricultural implements (3,500 stone sickles, new and used, in a single pit at one site, for example) may indicate a degree of centralized management of both agriculture and craft production.[27] The Shang even had a type of money, in the form of strings of cowrie shells.

Toward the end of the Shang period, there were many walled towns and villages in North and central China, and, compared to earlier periods, a much greater proportion of the populace lived in these semi-urban settings. But if we compare the settlement size distribution of late Shang China—or rather what we estimate it to have been—with that of Mesopotamia or Mesoamerica at a comparable level of development, it is clear that Shang China was a much less urbanized society. There were no settlements the size of Ur or Teotihuacán.

We cannot know the minds of the Shang Chinese in any detailed sense, but their artifacts give us clues as to what they thought of the world. Like many ancient peoples, they seem to have sought a basic symmetry in all things. All temples and tombs were oblong or square and oriented to the four cardinal directions. Bronzes were always symmetrical, and even the messages inscribed on turtle shells for divinations were repeated on the right and left sides. The world was conceived of as square, the wind as blowing from four quarters, and four groups of foreigners were thought to live on China's borders. Throughout their art, architecture, and literature, elements appear two by two, four by four, and in other intricate but symmetrical arrangements.

The texts and inscriptions tell us that the Shang nobles felt in constant and clear communication with their ancestors, whom they consulted through oracles about the best actions to take in multitudes of situations.

EARLY IMPERIAL CHINA (1100 B.C.–A.D. 220)

The early phases of Chinese civilization are often called the "Three Dynasties"—the Erh-li-t'ou/Hsia being the first, the Shang the second, and the Zhou (formerly known as "Chou") the third. Yet these three dynasties overlapped somewhat, and as K. C. Chang notes, the developmental pattern was one of "Early Shang, interacting with Erh-li-t'ou, and proto-Zhou, interacting with Shang."[28]

Chang goes on to quote a poem dating to the Zhou Dynasty that ascribes the dynasty's origins to divine will:

> August is God on high;
> Looking down, he is majestic;
> He inspected and regarded the [states of] the four quarters,
> He sought tranquillity for the people.
> These two kingdoms [of Hisa and Shang],
> Their government had failed;
> Throughout those states of the four [quarters] he investigated and
> estimated;
> God on high brought it to a settlement;
> Hating their extravagance,
> He looked about and turned his gaze to the West,
> And there he gave an abode.[29]

The "West" of this lyric, chosen by God, was the Zhou state. Had we the means to see it in all its splendor, ancient imperial China under the Zhou and later states may well have appeared to us as the most complex and colorful civilization of all antiquity. After 1100 B.C., the Zhou empire (Figure 11.6) and its successors arranged much of China in a feudal system that led to the growth of cities, great cycles of peace followed by warfare, and minutely differentiated administrative hierarchies.[30] Again and again particular families of nobles or commoners would rise to power, make war on their neighbors, extend their kingdoms, and then collapse under the onslaught of competing warlords. Through it all, exquisite bronzes, porcelains, pots, and jewelry were made and lavished on the rich; untold thousands of people were sacrificed to be buried with their rulers; and millions lived and died in the eternal agricultural cycle of rural China (Figure 11.7).

By 500 B.C. iron-working became widespread, and iron agricultural tools were in common use. Iron weapons, mass burials, and military annals tell of a savage form of warfare, not at all like the depersonalized modern combat of tanks, missiles, and automatic weapons. Men in armor fought at close quarters with swords and knives on battlefields swarming with chariots, cavalry, and bowmen.

At about the time iron was introduced, Confucius (551–479 B.C.) lived and taught and, together with the spread of Buddhism in the third century A.D., moved much of Chinese thought beyond the reach of the foreigner.

Amid the panoply of arts, crafts, and religion, the prosaic elements of agriculture were also changing. After 500 B.C. great irrigation works were brought into use, allowing the intensive cultivation of wet-rice species as well as many other crops. This

FIGURE 11.6   From the original Shang-period state, China evolved into true empires during the Zhou and Han Dynasties, whose extents are indicated here.

in turn supported the tremendous population densities of China. Along with the introduction of the ox-drawn plow and the evolution of precise crop-rotation practices, Chinese agriculture underwrote the impressive cultural elaborations we associate with the Qin (221 to 207 B.C.) and Han (202 B.C. to A.D. 120) dynasties.

The great richness and opulence of the Qin Dynasty is lavishly displayed in the Museum of Qin Shi Huang, in Shaanxi Province. In a project worthy of Egyptian pharaohs, the emperor Qin Shi Huang drafted 700,000 people to build a huge mausoleum and palace complex. The work lasted for thirty-nine years, and when it was finished it was full of rare and beautiful objects. Historical records of the time say that the complex was lighted with lamps fueled by the fat of giant salamanders. In 206 B.C. the whole complex was burned in a popular revolt. When archaeologists excavated they found 56.25 square kilometers of buildings and features, including "tombs of immolated slaves, table pits, stone material processing workshops, tombs of criminals, pits for the execution of slaves, pits of life-size terra cotta warriors and horses, and pits of bronze chariots and horses."[31] The site so far has revealed thousands of life-size statues of warriors and horses, all rendered in exquisite detail.

One of the world's first imperial censuses was conducted in China in A.D. 1 to 2 and tallied 57,700,000 people, at least 10 percent of whom lived in rectangular wooden buildings in towns with populations of up to about 250,000. Coins circulated, schools flourished, and a rich store of literature was created.

Through it all, along the northern and western frontiers, the nomadic horsemen and herders of Asia pressed on the periphery of successive empires. The Great Wall, built about 100 B.C., was meant to keep the nomad out and the farmer in, but it was probably not too successful. Throughout Chinese history there was a constant interchange between sedentary and nomadic cultures.

Westerners tend to think of China as a static civilization with ancient and fixed forms. But from the long-term perspective, it has been a varied, ineffably complex cultural pageant.

THE ORIGINS OF CULTURAL COMPLEXITY IN NORTH CHINA: SUMMARY AND CONCLUSIONS

If we look at Chinese civilization for the standard markers of early civilizations, as described in chapter 7, they are all evident: (1) an initial spread of regional styles of ceramics and artifacts reflecting increasing intensity and scope of cultural interactions among Neolithic farmers; then (2) the appearance of burials indicating inherited

FIGURE 11.7   Some bodies in Chinese tombs were so well preserved that autopsies can reveal causes of death. Here a Chinese radiologist X-rays Lady Dai, a Han Dynasty noblewoman who died in 141 B.C. of a heart attack.

wealth, power, and prestige (Figure 11.8); (3) the gradual development of towns and cities, often ringed with defensive walls, in which administrative bureaucracies and craft-production facilities were concentrated; (4) a rising level of regional and national warfare; (5) an elaboration over time in monumental architecture, writing, and other arts and crafts, and the development of a national religion and ideology; and (6) throughout the whole sequence, an overall increase in the population density, technological production, and size of competing nation-states.

Chinese civilization also offers some contrasts to other civilizations. Compared to Mesopotamia, for example, early Chinese societies were less urban than the Sumerian peoples, although in later Chinese history the country became heavily urbanized. Many hypotheses have been suggested for why people aggregate in settlements of different sizes under different conditions. Unfortunately, the archaeological evidence from China during the critical periods is not sufficiently complete to evaluate the several possibilities. Some have thought that warfare was important in determining the settlement size distribution in ancient China, and in fact warfare did have a profound influence on Chinese developments. But warfare, too, seems to be simply another—and somewhat variable—expression of more fundamental changes going on within societies as their complexity and differentiation increase.

One factor of continual importance in all Chinese developments was the great spread of the nomadic and semi-nomadic peoples who lived on the borders of the agricultural heartland. Some of the earliest documents attesting to the rise of the Chinese state, for example, imply that the Zhou Empire was initiated by the movement of the warlord Tai Wang to the central Shaanxi Province under pressure from his nomadic neighbors.[32] And Owen Lattimore's comprehensive history of relationships between nomad and farmer in China illustrated the crucial role of this relationship in the formation of all later Chinese empires.[33]

FIGURE 11.8 Like their contemporaries in Egypt and Mesopotamia, early Chinese complex societies expended enormous amounts of wealth in mortuary cults. This Chinese princess of the late second millennium B.C. was entombed in a suit made of 2000 jade tiles tied together with gold wire.

Chinese civilization also appears to have placed women in positions of power to a much greater degree than some other civilizations. In all known ancient civilizations women of elite and royal families had special status and prerogatives, but in ancient China women were important bureaucrats, served as royal envoys, and in at least one instance commanded an army.[34]

K. C. Chang suggests that Chinese civilization was extraordinarily absorbed with *shamanism*—the connection to another world, a world of the gods and magical powers, through priests. Chang also offers this condensed hypothesis about Chinese cultural evolution: "the wealth that produced the civilization was itself the product of concentrated political power, and the acquisition of power was accomplished through the accumulation of wealth."[35] Chang suggests that Chinese civilization operated on a profoundly religious basis, with kings, nobles, and commoners arranged in a layered universe, under a pantheon of gods, with communication between the physical and spirit worlds channeled through priests. Hence the abiding concern with divining the will of the gods through oracles—the king himself was credited with oracular powers. And, as Chang notes, technology has a reduced importance in such a fundamentally religious and abstract cosmology, which may explain even some of the contemporary differences between East and West.

China eventually became locked in the same cyclical pattern of expansion and collapse we documented in other ancient civilizations. Indeed, the apparent cyclicity of Chinese history has been the basis for many general models of cultural complexity, ranging from Marx to Marvin Harris.[36] In these ancient empires it is as if some internal limiting factors exist that restrain growth past a certain point, at least until certain evolutionary conditions are present. Perhaps these were primarily technological limits in these early empires. Without modern means of information collection, storage, retrieval, and dissemination, political systems have very definite limits in terms of the numbers of people, projects, and provinces they can successfully integrate.

BIBLIOGRAPHY

An, Zhimin. 1994. "China during the Neolithic." In *History of Humanity, Vol. 1: Prehistory and the Beginnings of Civilization*, ed. S. J. De Laet. New York: Routledge.

Anonymous (trans. Du YouIiang [sic]). 1982. *Neolithic Site at Bampo Near Xian*. Guide to the Banpo Museum, printing data written in Chinese.

Barnard, N. 1961. *Bronze Casting and Bronze Alloys in Ancient China*. Canberra: Australian National University.

———. 1972. "The First Radiocarbon Dates from China." *Monograph on Far Eastern History 8*. Canberra: School of Pacific Studies, Australian National University.

Barnes, G. L. 1990. *Bibliographic Reviews of Far Eastern Archaeology 1990: Hoabhinian, Jomon, Yayoi*. Oxford, England: Oxbow Books.

———. 1993. *China, Korea, and Japan*. London and New York: Thames and Hudson.

Bayard, D. 1979. "The Chronology of Prehistoric Metallurgy in North-East Thailand: Silabhumi or Samrddhabhumil." In *Early South-East Asia*, eds. R. B. Smith and W. Watson. London: Oxford University Press.

———. 1986. "Agriculture, Metallurgy, and State Formation in Southeast Asia." *Current Anthropology* 25(1)L 103–5.

Bellwood, P. 1986. *The Prehistory of the Indo-Malaysian Archipelago*. Sydney: Academic Press.

Chang, K. C. 1970. "The Beginning of Agriculture in the Far East." *Antiquity* 44:175–85.

———. 1976. *Early Chinese Civilization: Anthropological Perspectives.* Cambridge, MA: Harvard University Press.

———. 1977. *The Archaeology of Ancient China,* 3rd ed. New Haven: Yale University Press.

———. 1980. *Shang Civilization.* New Haven, CT: Yale University Press.

———. 1981. "In Search of China's Beginnings: New Light on an Old Civilization." *American Scientist* 69:148–58.

Chang, S. 1963. "The Historical Trend of Chinese Urbanization." *Annals of the Association of American Geographers* 53:109–43.

Chang, T. 1957. *Archaeological Studies in Szechwan.* Cambridge, England: Cambridge University Press.

———. 1963. *Archaeology in China, Vol. 3: Chou China.* Cambridge: Heffer.

De, Zhou Shi. 1987. "Classical Chinese Contributions to Shipbuilding." *Endeavour* NS. 11(1):2–4.

Harris, M. 1977. *Cannibals and Kings.* New York: Random House.

Higham, C. 1989. *The Archaeology of Mainland Southeast Asia.* Cambridge, England: Cambridge University Press.

Kim, S. O. 1994. "Burials, Pigs, and Political Prestige in Neolithic China." *Current Anthropology* 35(2): 119–42.

Lattimore, O. 1951. *Inner Asian Frontiers of China.* Boston: Beacon Press.

Li, C. 1957. *The Beginnings of Chinese Civilization.* Seattle: University of Washington Press.

Meacham, W. 1977. "Continuity and Local Evolution in the Neolithic of South China: A Non-Nuclear Approach." *Current Anthropology* 18:419–40.

Nelson, S. M., ed. 1995. *The Archaeology of Northeast China: Beyond the Great Wall.* New York: Routledge.

Olsen, S, J. 1987. "The Practice of Archaeology in China Today." *Antiquity* 61(232):282–90.

Service, E. 1975. *Origins of the State and Civilization.* New York: Norton.

Skinner, G. W. 1964. "Marketing and Social Structure in Rural China." *Journal of Asian Studies* 24:3–43.

Stover, L. E. 1974. *The Cultural Ecology of Chinese Civilization.* New York: Pica Press.

Toynbee, A., ed. 1973. *Half the World.* New York: Holt.

Triestman, J. 1972. *The Prehistory of China.* Garden City, NY: Natural History Press.

Trigger, B. G. 1993. *Early Civilizations: Ancient Egypt in Context.* Cairo: American University in Cairo Press.

Watson, W. 1960. *Archaeology in China.* London: Parrish.

———. 1971. *Cultural Frontiers in Ancient East Asia.* Edinburgh: Edinburgh University Press.

———. 1974. *Ancient China.* Greenwich, CT: New York Graphic Society.

Wheatley, P. 1971. *The Pivot of the Four Quarters.* Chicago: Aldine de Gruyter.

Wittfogel, K. A. 1957. *Oriental Despotism: A Comparative Study of Total Power.* New Haven: Yale University Press.

Wu, Z. 1985. "The Museum of Qin Shi Huang." *Museum* 147:140–47.

NOTES

1. De, "Classical Chinese Contributions to Shipbuilding."

2. Chang, *The Archaeology of Ancient China,* pp. 95–99.

3. Chang,"In Search of China's Beginnings."

4. An, "China during the Neolithic."

5. Triestman, *The Prehistory of China.*

6. An, "China during the Neolithic," p. 484.

7. Ibid.

8. Chang, "In Search of China's Beginnings: New Light on an Old Civilization," pp. 152–53.

9. Watson, *Ancient China*.

10. The following discussion of early complex Chinese societies is taken mainly from Chang, *The Archaeology of Ancient China*.

11. Kim Seung-Og, "Burials, Pigs, and Political Prestige in Neolithic China."

12. Ibid., p. 120.

13. See Chang, *The Archaeology of Ancient China*, for a review of the archaeological record of these cultural elements.

14. In addition to Chang, *The Archaeology of Ancient China*, see also Triestman, *The Prehistory of China*.

15. Chang, *The Archaeology of Ancient China*, pp. 286–94.

16. Bayard, "The Chronology of Prehistoric Metallurgy in North-East Thailand: Silabhumi or Samrddhabhumil."

17. Chang, *Early Chinese Civilization: Anthropological Perspectives*.

18. Wheatley, *The Pivot of the Four Quarters*.

19. Ibid.

20. Chang, *Early Chinese Civilization: Anthropological Perspectives*, p. 10.

21. Wheatley, *The Pivot of the Four Quarters*, p. 93.

22. Chang, *Early Chinese Civilization: Anthropological Perspectives*, p. 48.

23. Wheatley, *The Pivot of the Four Quarters*.

24. Ibid., p. 63.

25. Ibid.

26. Chang, *The Archaeology of Ancient China*, pp. 138–39.

27. Wheatley, *The Pivot of the Four Quarters*, p. 76.

28. Chang, "In Search of China's Beginnings: New Light on an Old Civilization," p. 156.

29. Ibid.

30. Wu Zilin, "The Museum of Qin Shi Huang," p. 141.

31. Chang, "In Search of China's Beginnings: New Light on an Old Civilization."

32. Lattimore, *Inner Asian Frontiers of China*.

33. Ibid.

34. Trigger, *Early Civilizations: Ancient Egypt in Context*, p. 37.

35. Chang, *The Archaeology of Ancient China*, p. 414.

36. See, for example, Harris, *Cannibals and Kings*.

12

LATER STATES AND EMPIRES OF THE OLD WORLD

*The day may come when, contemplating a world given back
to the primeval forest, a human survivor will have no means
of even guessing how much intelligence Man once imposed
upon the forms of the earth, when he set up the stones of
Florence in the billowing expanse of the Tuscan olive-groves.
No trace will be left then of the palaces that saw Michelangelo
pass by, nursing his grievances against Raphael; and nothing
of the little Paris cafes where Renoir once sat beside Cezanne,
Van Gogh beside Gauguin. Solitude, vicegerent of Eternity,
vanquishes men's dreams no less than armies, and men
have known this ever since they came into being and
realized that they must die.*

Andre Malraux

To imply that the ancient glories of Greece, Ghana, Germany, Thailand, and other areas were "later" states and empires, or "secondary" in some sense, compared to the "primary" states of, for example, Mesopotamia and Mexico, is to imply, perhaps, an inappropriate sense of a hierarchy of importance. In many ways these later states and empires were largely independent developments—creations primarily of their own environments, peoples, and unique histories, even if they incorporated elements from earlier civilizations. Interactions among the world's many different cultures, moreover, have gradually increased in the past two millennia, with the balance of power and wealth frequently shifting from place to place and time to time.

But ancient cultures of temperate Europe, Sub-Saharan Africa, Southeast Asia, and many other areas were, in fact, influenced by the first civilizations, and to some extent were derivatives of them. And while European cultures, for example, eventually came to dominate the civilizations of Egypt, China, and Mesopotamia, they did so partly on the basis of the forms of agriculture and technology invented by these earlier civilizations.

It is beyond the scope of this book to review these later states and empires in great detail,[1] and they are described briefly here mainly to illustrate the diversity of

536

ancient cultures and the extent to which after about 3000 B.C. the Old World became a mosaic of evolving cultures, none of which developed in isolation. From the last few millennia B.C. onward, Old World history is a dizzyingly complex tapestry in which to separate individual strands and even patterns is difficult. The reader may also wish to consider anew the Biblical prophecy that "the last shall be first," a sentiment repeatedly demonstrated in Old World culture history, where "peripheral" political systems often rose to imperial power.

Old World prehistory after about 4000 B.C. is in a sense an account of the division of the world into fewer and fewer great empires, and the slow economic intermeshing of Europe, Asia, and Africa. At about 2700 B.C. a citizen of Memphis, the capital of the Egypt state, and a hunter-forager working the north coast of France probably had no impact on each other's lives, not even as the end points of trading networks in the most exotic of commodities. But by about A.D. 200, northern France and Egypt were provinces in the Roman Empire, and French veterans of Roman armies were sometimes paid their pensions in the form of farms in Egypt. That process of a growing interconnection occurred all over Europe, Asia, and Africa, but it was greatly modified by environments, transport routes, and specific historic events. Ships plying the Mediterranean coast linked millions of people in Asia, Europe, and Africa, but the Sahara desert cut much of Africa off from this intense interaction; the mountains of central and western Europe had a similar effect for a time, as did the deserts, tundra, and other barriers to the east.

Today, however, nearly the whole world is interconnected and everywhere there are indications of a worldwide homogenization of cultures: Eskimos drive snowmobiles, Chinese drink American soft drinks, and a financial tremor in the money markets of, say, Singapore reverberates powerfully through the world's economies.[2] The rapid growth of the Internet and worldwide communications systems now links peoples in what can be considered a new form of organism, whose nervous system transcends distances and cultural differences. Although our world today seems very different from the world of, say, 5,000 years ago, what we see today is a continuation of the same basic trends that were evident by 3000 B.C., when ships were beginning to sail the Mediterranean and farming was being extended into Europe, Asia, and Africa.

THE AEGEAN AND WESTERN ANATOLIA

Anatolian sites such as Çatal Hüyük (chapter 8) were part of the first appearances of social complexity in Southwest Asia, but when the evolutionary focus moved to Mesopotamia, Anatolia became somewhat peripheral to the great states and empires of the Tigris-Euphrates Alluvium. As we saw in chapter 8, from their very beginnings the great civilizations of Mesopotamia and Egypt exploited the richness of the Aegean world, but by about 3000 B.C. indigenous cultures in the Aegean region began to evolve into powerful complex societies in their own right.

The "wine dark sea" of which Homer rhapsodized is the lovely expanse of the Aegean between Greece and Anatolia that encloses Lemnos, Lesbos, and hundreds of other islands. These islands and much of the mainlands of Asia and Europe that border on the Aegean and the Mediterranean seas are relatively arid, but they became very productive farmlands and also were an abundant source of metals, woods, and other materials.

Domesticated wheat, barley, sheep, goats, grapes, olives, and other crops were established all over the Mediterranean by 5000 B.C., and by 3000 B.C. great volumes of commodities were flowing throughout the eastern Mediterranean world. By about 2700 B.C. Troy, Poliochni on the island of Lemnos, and other communities were already cities, with impressive stone buildings, efficient roads, and a diversified economy that included specialized and lucrative production of objects in gold, tin, and other metals.

These metals were, in a sense, not economically indispensable to the economies of the Aegean world of this age. Some bronze tools and weapons were no doubt useful, but much of this trade seems to have been in luxury goods without direct economic utility—gold figurines, for example. But a lot of the other products were basic staples and commodities. Probably the greatest volumes of trade were in commodities long since consumed and therefore archaeologically invisible, such as the millions of gallons of wine no doubt shipped all over the Mediterranean. In any case, it is really not quite accurate to think of golden figurines as economically useless: status, and the pursuit and social reinforcement of status, were primary economic stimuli all over the ancient world.

By about 2500 B.C., the Aegean islands, including Crete, and the Anatolian and Greek mainlands were dotted with hundreds of towns and villages. And while gold was a central element in trade among these communities, painted pottery, obsidian bowls, marble statues and figurines, dyed textiles, and hundreds of other products were not only widely traded, but also important as mortuary goods in the rich tombs here that indicate societies already stratified into the rich and the poor, the powerful and the weak. Hissarlik, the "Troy" of the Classical world, a city at 2300 B.C., with fortress walls and many larger stone buildings, is probably a good example of a typical large and powerful community of this era.

No area of the world has contributed more to world civilization than the Mediterranean Basin, especially in the form of Greek science, arts, and letters. But throughout the history of this region it also seems to have been the most fractious, with at least a 5000 year history of warfare and resistance to political unification. Some of the communities of later third millennium B.C. seem to have been redistributive centers for the towns and villages around them, but for the most part this was an era of hundreds of small and competitive cities.

At about 2200 B.C. many communities on the Greek mainland and some of the islands appear to have been burned at about the same time, and when they were rebuilt some of the styles of architecture and pottery seem quite different from the earlier periods. Contemporary archaeologists are suspicious of explanations of major cultural changes that appeal to single factors such as climate changes and invasions, but the whole course of history in the Mediterranean world may well have been transformed by the invasion at about this time of Indo-European peoples—perhaps proto-Greek speakers, whose descendants ultimately would dominate this part of the world.

Crete seems not to have been affected much by these mainland developments, and eventually Crete came to dominate much of the Aegean world. People have lived on Crete in farming villages since at least 6000 B.C., and in succeeding millennia they combined a productive agricultural economy with a thriving maritime trade. By about 1900 B.C. the many small towns and villages on Crete seem to have become linked increasingly into a state-level political, economic, and religious system. This general pattern of change is similar to that of all the other early civilizations: monumental architecture, increasingly interdependent economies, rising population densities, and everywhere the signs of rank, wealth, and power. The settlement at Knossos included a large palace that probably functioned as a production center for many commodities, such as pottery, goldwork, and lovely vessels in serpentine and other hard stones. A writing system, known as Linear A, was developed, probably as a way to manage this complex economy.

The culture of Crete of the second millennium B.C. is generally known as the Minoan civilization, and throughout this era the wealth and power of Crete seems to have increased. Minoan goods are found all over the Aegean and the Greek and Anatolian mainlands, and as far away as the Levant and Egypt. Knossos probably had a population of 10,000 people just in the central areas of the settlement. Great palaces and rich tombs are the most obvious signs of the character of this society, but it was all based on a thriving economy. The warehouses at Knossos held hundreds of huge pottery storage vessels with enough capacity to hold tens of thousands of gallons of wine and olive oil.[3]

About 1700 B.C. an earthquake destroyed the palace at Knossos, but the community was rebuilt and became even more prosperous and powerful. In 1500 B.C. a volcano erupted on the island of Thera, just 70 miles away, and probably destroyed some Minoan towns on Crete.

Toward the end of the second millennium B.C., Minoan culture and power was supplanted over most of the Aegean world by Mycenaean civilization. The origins of Mycenaean culture seem to have been on the Argos plain on the Greek mainland. The stone fortress at Mycenae (Figure 12.1) appears to have been the center of a warrior kingdom, based on an extensive trade network. The rich shaft-graves found at Mycenae reflect a luxurious yet violent society, caught up in competition for economic and political dominance of not only the mainland but the Aegean islands and western Anatolia as well.

Scholars will never be able to resolve how much of Homer's *Iliad* and *Odyssey* is fiction and how much fact, but these epics probably reflect much of the character of late Mycenaean civilization.

At about the same time the Mycenaean culture was flourishing in the Aegean region, the Hittites, an Indo-European people, had established a large rich state in central and eastern Anatolia. The Hittites eventually became a major player in the complex political and economic competition between Egypt and Assyria.

In the early first millennium B.C., the eastern Mediterranean world entered a period of complex political and economic interaction. Greek city-states continued their millennia-old traditions of combat, the Phoenicians of the Levant established a rich trading empire that reached as far west as Spain, and the Etruscans of Italy began to lay the political and economic foundations of what would become the Roman Empire.

FIGURE 12.1   Heinrich and Sophia Schliemann seated to the right of the legendary Lion Gate at Mycenae in 1876.

TEMPERATE EUROPE

Until about the seventh millennium B.C., "Barbarian Europe"—the great forests, grasslands, and mountain ranges beyond the Aegean Sea and extending north to Britain, Scandinavia, and Russia—was inhabited only by hunters and foragers. In succeeding millennia, Europeans developed complex forms of subsistence and adaptation, and a rich cultural repertoire of technology and social systems, but throughout prehistory and well into the early centuries of the first millennium A.D., European cultures were not the equal of those of Egypt, Mesopotamia, China, and other areas in most of the characteristics of cultural "complexity" (see chapter 7).

One of the great questions of comparative history is why for thousands of years much of the creativity of the world was centered in Mesopotamia, China, the Indus, and the Mediterranean, and then, after the middle of the second millennium A.D., the cultural center of the world seemed to shift so decisively to western Europe. Europeans seem to have incorporated many cultural elements of older, foreign cultures and then developed them in unique ways in an environment very different from that of these older civilizations. Karl Marx and others have argued that one key element in the eventual dominance of Western Europe was that its societies were based on rainfall agriculture, instead of the large riverine-canal systems of the older civilizations of Egypt, Mesopotamia, and China. Central governments can control every aspect of life, if their citizens are inextricably tied to an irrigation system fed by a great river through canal systems controlled by the government. In Western Europe, however, a central government could try to conquer smaller polities but it could not control the rainfall that was the indispensable element in farming the rich lands of temperate Europe. Marx used this environmental fact to explain much of the transition to feudalism and capitalism that made Western Europeans masters of so much of the world.

Yet the economic and political history of the Old World cannot be easily or simply explained. Steven Shennan notes that many early scholars, especially V. Gordon Childe and the Marxists, saw history as a case in which "the Olympic torch of development was passed from East to West."[4] During the past two decades, research has suggested that many innovations were, in fact, independently invented in Europe, and in general there has been a critical reevaluation of the notion that to understand European prehistory one should look first and always at Mediterranean civilizations.[5]

TEMPERATE EUROPE: EARLY AGRICULTURE

As discussed in chapter 6, the rough distinction between "farmers" and "hunter-foragers" obscures great variations within and between these abstract socioeconomic types. But debates about the origins of European agriculture have often been thought of in these terms. Between about 6000 and 2000 B.C. hunting-foraging economies in most of temperate Europe were replaced by agricultural economies based on cereals that had first been domesticated in the Middle East and, perhaps, introduced into Europe, including einkorn wheat, barley, and rye; these crops were complemented by sheep and cattle—which also may have been introduced as domesticates from the Middle East. As Robin Dennell notes, the only major cereal crop domesticated in Europe was probably oats, which did not become economically important until late in prehistory.[6]

As with most such long-term, widespread, and radical processes of culture change, archaeologists have tended to focus on the *mechanisms* of these cultural changes. One traditional model offered to explain these mechanisms is that farmers from southern Europe and the Middle East colonized temperate Europe over several millennia and displaced hunter-foragers. As Marek Zvelebil and Paul Dolukhanov have noted,[7] this view focuses almost entirely on the circumstances and the processes of colonization, but largely ignores the response of the hunter-foragers who were presumably displaced. Other more recent models for the agricultural transition in Europe posit a greater role for the indigenous hunter-foragers. Robin Dennell[8] suggests that the climate changes in Europe after the end of the ice-ages favored the growth of grasses such as einkorn and barley, and Europeans may have begun exploiting them in ways that led to domestication and cereal agriculture—a largely indigenous development, in other words, that may have involved some introduced plants and animals from Southwest Asia, but was not simply the transplanting of Asians or their agricultural systems into Europe. Emmer wheat, bread wheat, sheep, and other crops and animals, nonetheless, seem certainly to have been domesticated in Southwest Asia and then introduced to Europe.

Unfortunately, the archaeological evidence with which to evaluate some of these contrasting ideas, especially the archaeology of postglacial hunter-foragers of Mesolithic Europe, is just beginning to be treated systematically.[9] The European Mesolithic is defined in terms of a shift in stone tool types, especially the replacement of larger tanged stone points by much smaller geometric ones—which may reflect primarily the introduction and improving efficiency of bows and arrows.[10] As Douglas Price has noted, this transition may have been mainly the result of different raw materials available as the glaciers retreated and of the evolution of tool-making skills, rather than profound social or cultural changes.[11] He also points out that we have lost much of the Mesolithic archaeological record because sea levels in northern Europe did not reach current levels until about 6000 B.C.

Among the earliest evidence for cereal farming comes from Argissa-Maghula in Greece, where people were cultivating emmer wheat and barley and raising cattle, sheep, and pigs by 6000 B.C.—and probably earlier.

On the Mediterranean fringes of European farming communities, agricultural villages were established on a reliable, productive mixture primarily of cereals, olives, and grapes in combination with sheep and goats. The processes by which domesticates and farming spread from the Middle East and Mediterranean areas into the great temperate forests of northern Europe remain one of the most interesting and intensively researched subjects in contemporary archaeology. Bogucki's analysis of agricultural origins in the northern European Plain, particularly in the region of Poland, for example, suggests that for centuries Mesolithic foragers and primitive agriculturalists were increasingly symbiotic in their economies, and that the first agriculturalists, the Funnel Beaker People, involved the "selective incorporation of cultigens and domestic animals into an essentially Mesolithic way of life."[12] He also suggests that the great stone monuments and tombs that eventually appeared all over Europe were in fact territorial markers, which became important considerations as agriculture spread.

There are great environmental differences between the semiarid Mediterranean zone and the wetter, cooler regions of Britain, the Low Countries, northern Germany, and southern Scandinavia. A prehistoric farmer in southern Italy needed only a few hand tools to farm successfully, but a peasant in northern Germany required capital-intensive equipment, such as the horse-drawn mouldboard plow. As Graeme Barker has observed,

The object of Mediterranean plowing has always been to conserve the moisture content of the soil by scuffling the surface, whereas in northern Europe heavy equipment is needed to break up the thick mass of roots in order to release the soil nutrients from the lower depths. . . . The analysis of the early history of agriculture in particular, and of the productive economy in general, in the two areas has been characterized by a definite sense of entrepreneurial risk takers in the Mediterranean contrasting with their honest but stolid contemporaries in the north, rather like the familiar contrast between the respective football teams of southern and northern European countries today.[13]

The rate and pattern of agriculture's spread across Europe raise some interesting questions. To a certain extent, this spread can be assumed to be determined by the blunt forces of environment, technology, and demography. The genetic composition of cereals sets a strict limit to the rate at which species adapt to different environments, and without artificial fertilizers the yields of crops—and therefore human population densities—are narrowly constrained. But when we look at the problem of how small-time European farmers eventually produced complex societies here, we can begin to see how complexly interrelated are four dimensions of these ancient societies: climate-environment, farming technology, human population fluctuations, and sociopolitical institutions.[14] By 6000 B.C., a Mediterranean complement of domestic grains, cows, and sheep—and the technology to exploit them—had moved up the Danube into central Europe. People lived in small clusters of wooden huts, often with their animals, and farmed narrow plots near rivers and streams. Some of the spread of this form of agricultural settlement in Europe is marked after about 5300 B.C. by pottery decorated with incised, linear patterns—the Bandkeramik style. The Bandkeramik peoples and their agricultural way of life appear first along the Danube in central Europe, and by shortly after 5000 B.C. had settled as far north as southern Holland. These sturdy farmers lived in small homesteads composed of timber-and-thatch houses, and subsisted on barley, einkorn, wheat, cattle, sheep, goats, and a variety of other crops and animals. Unlike that of the semiarid plains of the Middle East and the Mediterranean littoral, however, the agricultural way of life in Europe proper required clearing thick forests and grasslands, at first by cutting down the trees, later by plowing.

Alasdair Whittle has reviewed the evidence for the variations in the location and composition of Neolithic European sites and has shown that the distribution of loess and alluvium and the forces of trade and social stratification produce considerable variations in the density and sizes of settlements across the European Plain.[15] Marek Zvelebil and Peter Rowley-Conwy[16] have argued that the transition to agriculture in much of Europe involved a continuum of social and economic changes in which, at first, hunter-foragers and farmers encountered each other and traded a few products but were largely independent of each other; over time, however, hunter-foragers and farmers began to compete directly, as farmers moved into areas that had been exploited by hunter-foragers; eventually, the superior economic resources of farmers probably enabled them to displace hunter-foragers in the most productive areas—although crop failures and other disasters probably forced farmers to rely on hunting and foraging to survive on many occasions.

After about 5000 B.C., as populations grew and farmers adapted their crops and technologies to the diverse European environments, larger communities formed, some with apparent fortifications of earthworks and enclosure walls of timber. Some people were buried in large communal graves, marked by earthen mounds and megaliths (large stone monuments).

By 3000 B.C. agricultural villages were to be found from Great Britain far into eastern Russia. There were hundreds of local resource specializations, but most of these settlements subsisted mainly on domesticated cereals and cattle. Copper axes and ornaments were widely distributed, especially in central Europe and the Balkans.

Colin Renfrew has recently proposed that the spread of farming across Europe between 6000 and 3000 B.C. was associated with the replacement of local languages by Indo-European languages (Figure 12.2).[17] Population densities were heaviest in the central European areas where rivers supplied broad alluvial fields, but after 3000 B.C. villages appeared in light to heavy densities over almost every area where the environment permitted stock-raising and cereal agriculture. The areas where this kind

FIGURE 12.2   The spread of Celtic languages toward the end of the first millennium B.C. and some of the trade routes that connected temperate Europe to Mediterranean civilizations.

of subsistence was possible were greatly expanded by the introduction (perhaps from the Middle East) of the animal-drawn plow. In the absence of an arid climate or alluvial soils, it is difficult for the agriculturalist to compete with wild vegetation and renew the fertility of the soil. But the plow gave these early European farmers a way to expose the soil for seeding, and it contributed to weed control and soil fertility by plowing under vegetation (although the deep plowing of modern times was a later invention). Susan Gregg has devised a complex computer model that simulates the kinds of economic interactions that hunter-foragers and Neolithic agriculturalists may have established. She suggests that long-term, stable economic relationships may have developed between foragers and immigrant farmers, as these farmers colonized more and more of temperate Europe.[18]

Once most Europeans became agriculturalists, the stage was set for the evolution of complex forms of social organization. Some of the factors that transformed Europe were local, others international.

Some of the earliest signs of social change in temperate Europe are, predictably, in southern Europe, on the fringes of the Mediterranean world. For example, the Varna cemetery near the Black Sea coast of Bulgaria, dating to about 4000 B.C., contained massive hoards of golden and copper tools, suggesting not only great differences in economic classes in this society, but also the existence of a metallurgical industry of considerable sophistication.[19] Varna may well have flourished on the basis of a Black Sea trade.

Because they are so common and preserve well, metal and ceramic objects have been used as the defining characteristics of European peoples before the Romans. The "Battle Ax People," for example, is the general term for people who lived between about 3500 and 2300 B.C., whose copper and stone axes are found all over temperate Europe, mainly in graves, along with their distinctive cord-marked pottery. These people seem to have originated in central and eastern Europe, and they may have begun using the domestic horse and wheeled carts as early as 3000 B.C. As usual, it is difficult to determine if people in eastern Europe physically migrated westward *en masse*, or if their art styles and economic impact spread across Europe much in advance of any actual population movements. If Indo-European languages originated in the Caucasus Mountains, then the spread of the Battle Ax peoples may well have been one in which people moved rapidly westward, displacing or intermarrying with the natives.

Another spread of artifact styles involved the "Beaker Culture," named after the distinctive pottery they produced. The Beaker Culture was evident in much of western and central Europe just after 3000 B.C., and eventually the Battle Ax and Beaker cultures seem to have coalesced.

In talking about these cultures we must remember, of course, that nearly all the people of this era were simple agriculturalists, with a few families living together in tiny hamlets. Most would have lived out their lives in small houses and farms. Houses were simple structures of logs, clay, and thatch.

Another indication of the social changes that accompanied the spread of farming in Western Europe are megaliths. By about 4500 B.C.—1500 years and more before the Egyptians began to build large stone buildings—farmers in Spain were using large stones weighing many tons to build tombs, and over the next several millennia people all over Western Europe built large megalithic tombs. These tombs were often composed of several interior rooms with stone walls, with large blocking stones covering entrances to the complex and to its various compartments. These tombs were usually communal, with numerous corpses in them, and there is some evidence that the dead were exposed to the elements for a time and then their bones were entombed. Many tombs were covered by earth and thus formed long "barrow" mounds.

Tombs were not the only megalithic structures in Europe. Huge stones were raised in complex designs in areas of France, for example. Stonehenge (Figure 12.3), in England, is the most famous example of the circular arrangements of European megaliths.

Like the pyramids of Egypt, the megalithic structures of Europe have elicited many speculations about the societies and ideologies of which they were a part, but we will never know the motives of the people who built these monuments. Their spatial arrangements in some cases suggest that they were positioned to mark boundaries of some kind. Stonehenge and similar arrangements were probably ritual centers, and some, perhaps, were used for astronomical observations and calculations. The long "barrow" mounds that enclose megalithic tombs may have been evocations of the long houses in which these early farmers lived[20]—and thus perhaps were a reflection of the ties of community and kinship that united these people in life and death. Like the Egyptians, these monuments no doubt reinforced social hierarchies of power and ideology and maintained the connections between generations past, present, and future.[21]

FIGURE 12.3 Stonehenge began as a series of ritual excavations about 2700 B.C. and was greatly elaborated between 2000 and 1000 B.C. The arranged stones probably had astronomical significance. Stonehenge is just one example of thousands of stone monuments built in this period in western Europe.

In the end, however, we are left mainly with speculations about motives and ideas. A somewhat different question is, aside from what the people who built these monuments thought about them, why did these structures appear when they did and where they did? As noted in chapter 9, with regard to the Egyptian pyramids, these colossal stone monuments around the world (similar forms are considered in later chapters in Mexico, Peru, and North America) seem to appear at times of particular stress and rapid change. In North America, for example, as Robert C. Dunnell[22] has noted great communal tombs not unlike the megalithic tombs of Europe appeared in the Ohio and Mississippi river valleys just at the time when maize-beans-squash-based agriculture was being established in these areas, and these monuments seem to appear on the edges of the area where that agricultural adaptation was effective.[23] Perhaps these great "wastes" of energy and resources stabilized these societies by reducing population growth and economic expansion. Viewed from this perspective, what the ancient Europeans actually thought about these monuments is not just unknowable, it is not particularly important: what is important is that these monuments had profound socioeconomic impact on these societies. The prehistoric natives of Mississippi and of England may have had vastly different ideas about the significance of their monuments—yet each built them at similar points in their cultural evolutionary history.

The organization and planning required to build monuments like Stonehenge probably reflect a society with at least incipient rank, class, and occupational specialization, and all through the last few millennia B.C. expanding trade between Europe and the Mediterranean and Aegean regions would have provided some stimulus to cultural change.

Lewthwaite used the term "Mafia model" to describe views of the emergence of complex societies in Europe in which "the motor for social change is the ambition of certain individuals to dominate and control their fellow human beings, an ambition that can be realized in certain ecological . . . circumstances."[24]

From burials not only of bodies but also of hoards of precious metals and artifacts, we can speculate that warrior tribes contended all across Europe in the late second millennium B.C., with their fortunes rising and falling to some extent with their success in maintaining trading links with the Mediterranean and Aegean societies. Baltic amber, salt, metal tools, and hundreds of other products flowed along these ancient trade routes.

Until about 1000 B.C. the secret of iron-making was a monopoly of the Hittite state in Anatolia, but after this time knowledge of the technique spread north and west into Europe. Iron is a much more utilitarian metal than bronze or gold: iron tools could make a major difference in efficiencies of plows, hoes, awls, knives, swords, arrowheads, and a thousand other products.

One early European iron-working culture, the Hallstatt, is reflected in the distinctive artifacts of this tradition from the Low Countries after about 700 B.C. The Hallstatt and La Tene cultures of first-millennium B.C. Europe flourished in a period of rapid population expansion, migrations of various ethnic groups, reformation of trade routes along lines dictated by Mediterranean cultures, and other major social changes.

With the expansion of Roman power between 200 B.C. and well into the first millennium A.D., the character of Europe was forever changed, becoming a hybrid mix of Greek, Middle Eastern, and native elements.

AFRICA

Africa is so rich in gold, silver, iron, jewels, ivory, palm oil, and other resources, that one might expect it to have been a center of initial origins of cultural complexity, as it was for the first three million years of our genus. But Africa has formidable barriers that afflict the agriculturalist more than the hunter-gatherer.[25] The enormous Sahara Desert, expanding and contracting with Pleistocene and Post-Pleistocene climatic changes, has almost always isolated most of Africa from the critical mass of Middle Eastern and Mediterranean cultures. And even in the more humid Sub-Saharan regions the dense vegetation, poor soils, and unpredictable rainfall make large-scale intensive agriculture unproductive for the primitive cultivator. Nor do the great rivers, like the Niger, have the regular regimes, large semiarid alluvial plains, or latitude that make the Nile, Tigris and Euphrates, and Yellow river valleys so productive. To make matters worse, Africa has a veritable horror show of diseases, including a tsetse fly-borne cattle illness that barred pastoralists from many areas, and malaria, which recurrently wiped out human populations in the more tropical areas.

Given these and other ecological problems, early African societies are an object lesson in human inventiveness and adaptability in the face of an extreme environment.

Archaeologists used to think that Sub-Saharan Africa was a cultural backwater—a veritable "cultural museum"—in the Pleistocene, but recent research indicates that an advanced stone-tool technology, pottery, and animal domestication were indigenous developments here, and many areas have deep and varied culture histories.[26]

In Ghana, for example, as Ann Stahl notes, there is a long culture history that does not fit easily into a "progressive evolutionary model."[27] About the size of Great Britain, Ghana includes not only the dense humid jungles many people associate with equatorial Africa, but also drier uplands, savannas, forests, and lakes.

Sub-Saharan Africa of the last few millennia B.C. was probably a rich blend of hunting, foraging, fishing, and agricultural societies, with extensive trade networks in gold, salt, and foodstuffs. We know comparatively little about the earliest phases of these societies because of the problems of preservation and inadequate archaeological research—although the intensity of research is increasing.[28] It seems that everywhere that competent surveys are undertaken, the development of African civilization is revealed. Surveys in the mid-1980s in Equatorial Guinea and Gabon, for example, revealed Neolithic Bantu villages already well-acquainted with iron-smelting by the mid-first-millennium B.C.[29]

The character of all these cultures was changed radically, however, by the introduction (beginning about 500 B.C.) of an iron-working technology. In an extensive review of the origin of iron-working in west Africa, McIntosh and McIntosh conclude that the evidence for an independent indigenous origin there is "exceedingly slim at present."[30] Iron artifacts were used extensively there from the end of the first millennium B.C.

Complex societies quickly followed the introduction of iron in west Africa, and first-millennium B.C. tombs in Nigeria and Senegal reflect great differences in wealth. At Igbo-Ukwu in Nigeria, one burial chamber contained cast-bronze objects and thousands of glass and carnelian beads.[31] Arab accounts of these societies in the eighth through the eleventh centuries A.D. describe complex empires, with armies, kings, and massive craft industries.[32] Many scholars have concluded that it was Arab commerce that stimulated west African cultural complexity, but McIntosh and McIntosh conclude that the spread of Arab goods and culture "reflects the grafting of Arab commerce onto a preexisting infrastructure of Saharan and Sub-Saharan networks. Such an explanation implies that earlier phases of development at Igbo-Ukwa were characterized by indigenous processes of trade expansion and increasing social stratification."[33]

The first five centuries A.D. saw the rapid spread over much of Africa of agriculturalists using iron tools and weapons and subsisting in part on indigenous domesticates like sorghum and squash, and on domestic cattle and other animals (Figure 12.4). Only in a few arid wastelands were these agriculturalists unsuccessful in displacing the stone-age hunters who were the heirs of the millions-of-years-old tradition of African hunting-foraging. Formerly, it was widely accepted that there was a great migration of Bantu-speaking peoples who changed Sub-Saharan societies, but Hall has effectively challenged the notion of a great southward spread of Bantu farmers.[34]

In contrast to the earlier-held view that the first African states were "contact-states," created by the economic and political "touch" of the established North African and Egyptian states, it now seems more reasonable to see Sub-Saharan indigenous states as products of their own cultural matrix. The rapid population growth associated with the introduction of agriculture to these areas, the rising spiral of trade in gold, copper, salt, and slaves, and the sporadic influences of distant Mediterranean and Asian empires probably all combined to produce the rich second-millennium A.D. African chiefdoms and states. Archaeologists are just beginning to unravel the history of these complex cultures, and it is beyond the scope of this book to review them in detail. Most seem to have been marked by some public buildings and were composed of a ruler and an upper class who organized and taxed a complex economic system comprised of farmers, herders, miners, ironworkers, traders, and religious leaders. Cemeteries often show great variations of wealth and, presumably, social status.

By the sixteenth century, much of west Africa was divided among several states, all locked into trade networks that ultimately fed hundreds of products to the empires of the Mediterranean world and Asia.

After the sixteenth century, Africa fell increasingly under the control of non-Africans, and only in the last fifty years have most Africans retrieved their autonomy. They were held in thrall for so long by outsiders because of their inferior economic position, but also because European-introduced diseases killed many people, and because of slavery: the African slave trade was organized and profited from by Africans well before the sixteenth century; some have estimated that nearly as many African slaves were shipped north into the Middle Eastern and Mediterranean areas as were eventually carried to the New World.

FIGURE 12.4   In the first millennium A.D. trade routes in various commodities connected west African kingdoms with each other and with coastal traders from the Middle East, Europe, and the Mediterranean.

THE EURASIAN PERIPHERY

Nomadic pastoralists ranged from the eastern shores of the Black Sea to the Gobi Desert and eventually came to represent a major force in European and Asian developments. Domestic horses and camels were in use by the mid-second millennium B.C. in much of this area, and with the addition of two-wheeled carts, the development of a diet based on milk products rather than meat, and the emergence of an aggressive chiefdom-like command structure, Eurasian nomads terrorized Europe and sacked China time and time again.

Japan's cultural isolation during many periods of its history offer scholars something like the experimental control that laboratory scientists in other disciplines can exert. That is, Japan's rich history was influenced by China at various critical points, but it has always been so distinctive and self-contained that on some levels it can be understood only in its own terms. But in Japan, too, the familiar developmental stages of ancient cultural complexity were followed. The initial spread of pottery styles was followed by monumental architecture and vast wealth differentials, culminating in the development of one of the most rigid and complex social hierarchies the world has ever seen.

One of the many remarkable things about ancient Japan was the early date at which hunter-foragers began living in permanent communities. Melvin Aikens and Takeru Akazawa note that by 11,000 B.C. Japanese of the Jomon culture were using pottery—the earliest known extensive ceramics industry in the world—and living for all or most of the year in communities of pit-houses, subsisting on a rich and varied diet of deer, bear, whale, salmon and many other fish, seabirds, shellfish in abundance, and numerous kinds of berries, nuts, and other plants.[35] The rather minimalist modern Japanese diet centered on rice, kelp, and raw fish was a very late development, a product of massive population growth and an extraordinarily intensive agricultural system. As in other areas of the world, after the end of the Pleistocene Japanese hunter-foragers began exploiting some species of plants with enough intensity to begin changing these plant species genetically. There is some evidence that by 5000 B.C. rice, barley, buckwheat, and millet were being intensively exploited in some areas of Japan. But not until the first millennium B.C. did rice agriculture supplant the ancient foraging-collecting economy in Japan. Rice agriculture seems to have spread in a very intricate pattern, at different rates and in different ways, based on the ecological differences in the various areas of Japan. Rice agriculture spread most quickly into those zones that offered poorer and less stable wild resources—another example, in other words, of the close cost-benefit calculations cultural evolution seems to make.

Analyses of skeletons of early Japanese show that there was continued mixing with Korean and Chinese peoples, but Japan began to develop a very distinctive national culture in the last few millennia B.C.

To those familiar with its culture, Japan—like ancient Athens and many other early civilizations—is an object lesson showing that the blunt analytical tools of archaeology, with their fixation on economy, environment, and architecture, can reveal very little of the most fascinating aspects of these societies.

In Southeast Asia, not only do we not know many of the most crucial links in the culture history (in part because of poor climatic conditions for archaeological preservation), but what we do know flagrantly contradicts our most comforting archaeological expectations. As Bronson notes, recent Southeast Asian culture history contains such disconcerting paradoxes as cannibals and collecting groups with alphabets of their own (the Batak of Sumatra and the Tagbanwa of Palawan), hunter-gatherers with the ability to make excellent steel (some Punan groups in Borneo), and even (as in nineteenth-century northern Vietnam) complex and populous states without settlements that can readily be called cities.[36] At least some of these developments, however, are the direct result of outside contacts and, generally, only northern Vietnam can be said to have the usual hallmarks of cultural complexity before about 100 B.C. The great monuments of Thailand, Cambodia, and Vietnam are all products of the late first and second millennia A.D. and are intertwined with Chinese and Indian history. Charles Higham has argued persuasively, however, that although India was a powerful force in, for example, the origins of complex societies in Southeast Asia, many important developments were the result of local factors.[37]

One of the most interesting aspects of the rise of states and cities in Thailand, for example, is the extent to which these developments seem to have been tied to trade. People who lived mainly on wet-rice agriculture and practiced both iron- and metal-working had settled in the Non Chai area of northeastern Thailand by the first millennium B.C. Bronze ornaments, salt, salted and fermented fish, marine shells, and many other commodities were probably traded in great volumes in the lower Mekong Valley, in association with chiefdoms or small states.[38]

COLONIZATION OF THE WESTERN PACIFIC ISLANDS

By definition, archaeology can never be a truly experimental science. But the distribution of societies across the great arch of the southern Pacific (Figure 12.5) is as close as we might hope to get to having an archaeological laboratory. Island by island, people colonized this part of the world, and the subtle variations of local climates and different times of colonization have produced a varied cultural landscape that is, in the cliché, a giant cultural laboratory.[39]

These areas have great significance for a truly evolutionary analysis of the past. In Polynesia, for example, during the last three millennia peoples spread out from island to island, and the development of their languages, adaptations, and physical types reflects the workings of basic evolutionary mechanisms.[40] Patrick Kirch has argued that, in some ways, the evolution of complex societies in Hawaii, Tonga, and other areas of Polynesia agrees well with the "circumscription hypothesis" of Robert Carneiro (see chapter 7).

Scholars have long wondered how ancient peoples sailed across the tropical Pacific from west to east, when the prevailing winds and ocean currents move from east to west. Various simulation model have been considered,[41] and different colonizing rates and processes are possible. Finney reports a voyage during 1986–1988 of the *Hokule'a*, a 19-meter double-hull canoe under the command of Hawaiian navigator, Nainoa Thompson.[42] By exploiting occasional spells in which the prevailing winds shifted, the canoe was sailed from American Samoa east to Tahiti, along the track the ancient settlers of these islands might have traveled.

We shall never know the motives of the peoples who settled, island by island, the great expanse between Easter Island and the South Asian mainland. Some no doubt were driven off course by storms and reached island refuges after long and desperate struggles. Others may have fled their homelands after losing wars or communal disputes; still others, perhaps, intentionally and bravely set off on voyages of discovery.

As always in human colonization, the timing and nature of the colonization depended on the evolution of technologies and cultural adaptations that could provide sufficient food. Colonization of Pleistocene Western Europe, for example, probably occurred only after early humans had developed the skills to make a living through hunting and gathering in that vast frigid expanse north of the Alps. The resources of

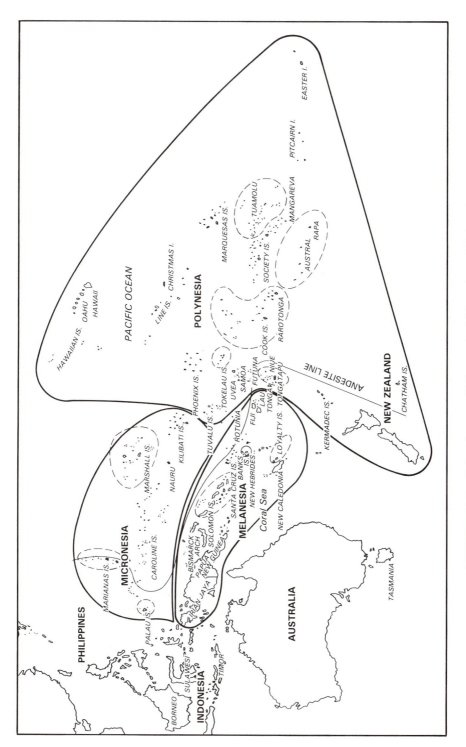

FIGURE 12.5 Cultural areas of Micronesia, Melanesia, and Polynesia.

the Pacific Islands were very different, in that even islands with rich resources of animals and plants tended to be small enough that hunting and foraging of wild plants and animals would not support many people. The key to colonization of these islands was in the form of several domesticated plants and animals that together provided a stable source of food. Domesticated pigs and chickens were primary meat sources, along with fish and birds, but the mainstays of the diet were cultivated tubers. One of the most important of these is taro, a perennial tropical plant with large, starchy, tuberous roots. Lowland taro roots generally are prepared by heating them to destroy the chemicals that give them a bitter taste, then grinding and fermenting them into an edible paste called poi (very much an acquired taste for most non-islanders). Taro species native to dry lands produce corms that are eaten like potatoes in Japan, China, the West Indies, and elsewhere.

Another Pacific Island staple is breadfruit, the globular fruit of the breadfruit tree. The breadfruit tree grows to heights of 18 meters (60 feet) or more. The yellow-green fruit is up to 30 centimeters (12 inches) in diameter, and its starchy pulp can be cooked in various ways to supply a good source of carbohydrates.

Among the most important foods of the Pacific are yams, the tuberous roots of several species of vines. Yams are grown and eaten much like potatoes and have a similar role as a dietary staple and source of vitamins and carbohydrates. Yams look something like sweet potatoes but the two are not even distantly related. The yams available in North American markets represent only some of the varieties found in the Pacific. Some species of Pacific yams produce tubers weighing up to an impressive 45 kilograms (100 pounds). These tubers have brown or black skin and white, purple, or red flesh. Like potatoes, yams are usually propagated by planting the crowns of the large tuberous roots or small whole tubers. The climbing vines of yam plants are supported on stakes or trellises to maximize yields.[43]

Founder groups from mainland Southeast Asia made the sea-crossing to Australia and New Guinea about 38,000 years ago, based on recent evidence, and hunter-gatherers across Southeast Asia gradually evolved somewhat different physical characteristics.[44]

From about 3000 B.C. onward, there seems to have been a continuous expansion into much of Southeast Asia of farmers whose physical and cultural origins were in subtropical mainland Asia:[45] The reasons for the expansion of these people probably can be related to the high demographic densities and territorial demands of an agricultural life-style, together with superior transport technology (i.e., sailing canoes). This expansion reached its limits in Polynesia during the first millennium A.D.[46]

One of the most interesting patterns in the colonization of the Pacific is the spread of the "Lapita Cultural Complex." The people associated with this culture made a particularly elaborately decorated pottery that has come to define them, in a sense. Lapita pottery appears at about 1500 B.C. in the Bismarck Archipelago (Figure 12.6), an island group in the southwest Pacific that includes part of Papua New Guinea, New Britain, New Ireland, the Admiralty Islands, and other islands to the east of Australia. These hot, humid, volcanic islands form the core of "Melanesia" (from the Greek for "black islands") and are homes to an impressive variety of peoples, languages, and cultures. Many of the people seem to be the descendants of negroid and Australoid peoples; some groups show cultural affiliations with Polynesia and Micronesia.

FIGURE 12.6   Photo provided by Patrick Kirch.

Lapita pottery occurs over an area more than 5000 miles (8100 kilometers) long, encompassing hundreds of islands, and this spread of a pottery style poses the same kinds of questions we have seen elsewhere: Does this spread of a particular artifact style represent people who migrated and carried with them their pottery and the rest of their culture? Or were indigenous peoples incorporated into a growing exchange network in which they eventually came to use pottery in Lapita styles, as well as obsidian and other commodities traded among these many islands? In previous chapters the notion of "progress," at least in the sense of the notion of people constantly seeking to improve their standards of living, has been questioned, and there is no evidence of a grand design to Lapita expansion. But islands, like all varied environments, have the potential for economic expansion through the exchange of commodities. If the costs of extracting or producing goods and transporting them and exchanging them with neighbors are less than their value in these exchanges, everyone—producers and consumers alike—is richer than if they consumed only the resources they themselves produce. And it is not only food and other utilitarian objects that have value. In the Pacific as in every other human society of our recent past, people used objects as status markers and ceremonial items. In the Pacific shells, pearls, and other commodities were circulated and used in ways that seem to have defined, facilitated, and maintained exchange networks and social hierarchies.

New Zealand appears to have been first settled, by colonists from Polynesia, between about A.D. 1000 and 1200.[47] The two large islands that constitute New Zealand have temperate climates, and some of the plant food staples of areas to the north, such as coconuts, did not grow in New Zealand. Yams, taro, sweet potatoes, and other Polynesian foods could be grown in the warmer areas of New Zealand, and the islands were rich in foods that could be hunted and gathered, including fish and moa birds. Moas were flightless land birds that ranged from about 1 to perhaps 3 meters (3 to 10 feet) in height. The largest of these huge birds probably weighed over 250 kilograms (550 pounds)—a great food source for the successful hunter—and when the Maoris colonized New Zealand they systematically hunted these birds and appear to have overexploited them to the point that, in combination with other factors, the moa became extinct by the eighteenth century (or perhaps later). As we saw in chapter 5, with the extinction of many North American species of large animals, sorting out the exact factors that cause extinctions is difficult, but there is no doubt that the Maoris intensively exploited moas.

Maori culture became extremely militaristic, with repeated warfare—here, too, not unlike the Aztecs and Maya of the New World. And like New World cultures, the Maori were decimated by European diseases.

One of the most interesting examples of the evolution of sociopolitical complexity is Hawaii. Hawaii was probably settled in the late first millennium B.C., by settlers from the Marquesas Islands and perhaps other areas of eastern Polynesia. Eighteenth- and nineteenth-century ethnographic accounts provide a detailed account of a highly stratified society with inherited power, prestige, and wealth, a diversified economy, complex trade relationships, monumental architecture, and many other elements associated with complex societies. The many different ideas about how the ancient Hawaiians developed these cultural complexities reflect theoretical trends in archaeology in general.[48] Some scholars see population growth and various cultural ecological factors as primary factors in Hawaii's cultural evolution, others appeal to sociopolitical factors. Hawaii's remoteness and its superb ethnographic record make it a virtual laboratory for analyzing the evolution of cultural complexity to the level of "tribes" and "chiefdoms."

CONCLUSIONS

The cultures on the periphery of the Old World, from northern Scandinavia to Hawaii, repeat the common fact that most aspects of cultural complexity are the partial products of technology and agricultural productivity. Reindeer herders in Lapland and the yam farmers and pig herders of Oceania represent gradients of cultural complexity, but nowhere in these marginal areas do we find the towns, the libraries, the many-leveled hierarchical arrangements of functional interdependence, or the regional political powers that mark states and empires.

BIBLIOGRAPHY

No attempt is made here to provide a comprehensive bibliography for the many secondary states and empires of the ancient world.

Aikens, C. M., K. M. Ames, and D. Sanger. 1986. "Affluent Collectors at the Edges of Eurasia and North America: Some Comparisons and Observations on the Evolution of Society among North-Temperate Coastal Hunter-Gatherers." In *Prehistoric Hunter-Gatherers in Japan*, eds. T. Akazawa and C. M. Aikens. Tokyo: University of Tokyo Press.

Aikens, C. M., and T. Higuchi. 1981. *Prehistory of Japan*. New York: Academic Press.

Akazawa, T. 1982. "Cultural Change in Prehistoric Japan." *Advances in World Archaeology* 1:151–212.

Akazawa, T., and C. M. Aikens, eds. 1986. *Prehistoric Hunter-Gatherers in Japan*. Tokyo: University Museum, University of Tokyo, Bulletin No. 27.

Anderson, A. 1987. "Recent Developments in Japanese Prehistory: A Review." *American Antiquity* 61(232):270–81.

———. 1992.

Barber, R. L. N. 1988. *The Cyclades in the Bronze Age*. Iowa City: University of Iowa Press.

Barker, G. 1985. *Prehistoric Farming in Europe*. Cambridge, England: Cambridge University Press.

Barker, G., and C. Gamble. 1985. "Beyond Domestication: A Strategy for Investigating the Process and Consequence of Social Complexity." In *Beyond Domestication in Prehistoric Europe*, eds. G. Barker and C. Gamble. New York: Academic Press.

Barker, G., and C. Gamble, eds. 1985. *Beyond Domestication in Prehistoric Europe*. New York: Academic Press.

Bellwood, P. 1986. *The Prehistory of the Indo-Malaysian Archipelago*. Sydney, Australia: Academic Press.

———. 1987. *The Polynesians*. London: Thames and Hudson.

———. 1987. "The Prehistory of Island Southeast Asia: A Multidisciplinary Review of Recent Research." *Journal of World Prehistory* 1(2):171–224.

Bellwood, P., and J. Koon. 1989. "Lapita Colonists Leave Boats Unburned." *Antiquity* 63 (240):613–22.

Bintliff, J., ed. 1984. *European Social Evolution*. Bradford, England: Bradford University Press.

Bogucki, P. 1987. "The Establishment of Agrarian Communities on the North European Plain." *Current Anthropology* 28(1):1–24.

———. 1988. *Forest Farmers and Stockherders*. Cambridge, England: Cambridge University Press.

Bronson, B. 1980. "South-east Asia: Civilizations of the Tropical Forest." *Cambridge Encyclopedia of Archaeology*, pp. 262–66. New York: Crown Publishers/Cambridge University Press.

Castleden, R. 1993. *Minoans: Life in Bronze Age Crete*. New York: Routledge.

———. 1994. *The Making of Stonehenge*. New York: Routledge.

Champion, T. G., et al. 1984. *Prehistoric Europe*. New York: Academic Press.

Charoenwongsa, P., and D. Bayard. 1983. "Non Chai: New Dates on Metalworking and Trade from Northeastern Thailand." *Current Anthropology* 24(4):521–23.

Childe, V. G. 1958. *The Prehistory of European Society*. Baltimore: Penguin.

Clist, B. 1987. "Early Bantu Settlements in West Central Africa: A Review of Recent Research." *Current Anthropology* 28(3):380–82.

Coles, J. M., and A. F. Harding. 1979. *The Bronze Age in Europe*. London: Methuen.

Collis, J. 1984. *The European Iron Age*. London: Batsford.

Connah, G. 1987. *African Civilizations*. Cambridge, England: Cambridge University Press.

Davidson, J. 1985. "New Zealand Prehistory." *Advances in World Archaeology* 4:239–292.

Dennell, R. C. 1983. *European Economic Prehistory: A New Approach*. New York: Academic Press.

————. 1992. "The Origins of Crop Agriculture in Europe." In *The Origins of Agriculture*, eds. C. W. Cowan and P. J. Watson. Washington, DC: Smithsonian Institution Press.

Dickinson, O. 1994. *The Aegean Bronze Age.* Cambridge, England: Cambridge University Press.

Ekholm, K. 1981. "On the Structure and Dynamics of Global Systems." In *The Anthropology of Pre-Capitalist Societies*, eds. J. Kahn and J. Lobera. London: Macmillan.

Fagan, B. 1995. *People of the Earth*, 8th ed. New York: HarperCollins College Publishers.

Finney, B. 1988. "Voyaging Against the Direction of the Trades: A Report of an Experimental Canoe Voyage from Samoa to Tahiti." *American Anthropologist* 90(2):401–5.

Fischer, A., P. V. Hansen, and P. Rasmussen. 1984. "Macro and Micro Wear Traces on Lithic Projectile Points." *Journal of Danish Archaeology* 3:19–46.

Fitzhugh, W. 1975. *Prehistoric Maritime Adaptations of the Circumpolar Zone*. The Hague: Mouton.

Gilman, A. 1981. "The Development of Social Stratification in Bronze Age Europe." *Current Anthropology* 22:1–8.

Green, M. 1993. *Symbol and Image in Celtic Religious Art*. New York: Routledge.

Gregg, S. A. 1988. *Foragers and Farmers*. Chicago: University of Chicago Press.

Grigg, D. B. 1982. *The Dynamics of Agricultural Change*. London: Hutchinson.

Hagelberg, E. 1993. "Ancient DNA Studies." *Evolutionary Anthropology* 2(6):199–207.

Hagelberg E., S. Quevedo, D. Turbon, and J. B. Clegg. 1994. "DNA from Ancient Easter Islanders." *Nature* 369:25–26.

Hall, M. 1987. *The Changing Past: Farmers, Kings, and Traders in Southern Africa, 200–1860*. Cape Town, South Africa: David Phillip.

Harding, A. F. 1984. *The Mycenaeans and Europe*. New York: Academic Press.

Harlan, J., J. DeWet, and A. Stemler, eds. 1976. *Origins of African Plant Domestication*. The Hague: Mouton.

Higham, C. 1988. *The Archaeology of Mainland Southeast Asia*. Cambridge, England: Cambridge University Press.

Hodder, I. 1990. *The Domestication of Europe*. Oxford: Blackwell.

Hood, S. 1973. *The Minoans*. London: Thames & Hudson.

Irwin, G. 1992. *The Prehistoric Exploration and Colonisation of the Pacific*. Cambridge, England: Cambridge University Press.

Isager, S., and J. E. Sydsgaard, eds. 1995. *Ancient Greek Agriculture: An Introduction*. New York: Routledge.

Kinnes, . 1982. "Les Fouaillages and Megalithic Origins." *Antiquity* 56:24–30.

Kirch, P. V. 1984. *The Evolution of Polynesian Kingdoms*. Cambridge, England: Cambridge University Press.

Kirch, P. V., ed. 1986. *Island Societies*. Cambridge, England: Cambridge University Press.

————. 1988. "Circumscription Theory and Sociopolitical Evolution in Polynesia." *American Behavioral Scientist* 31(4):416–27.

————. 1990. "The Evolution of Sociopolitical Complexity in Prehistoric Hawaii: An Assessment of the Archaeological Evidence." *Journal of World Prehistory* 4(3):311–345.

Kirch, P. V., and R. C. Green. 1987. "History, Phylogeny, and Evolution in Polynesia." *Current Anthropology* 28(4):431–56.

Kirch, P. V., and T. L. Hunt. 1988. *Archaeology of the Lapita Cultural Complex: A Critical Review*. Seattle: Burke Museum.

Lewis, D. 1972. *We the Navigators*. Honolulu: University of Hawaii Press.

Lewthwaite, J. 1981. "Comment on A. Gilman, 'The Development of Social Stratification in Bronze Age Europe.'" *Current Anthropology* 22:14.

McIntosh, S. K., and R. J. McIntosh. 1983. "Current Directions in West African Prehistory." *Annual Review of Anthropology* 12:215–58.

McIntosh, S. K., and R. J. McIntosh. 1988. "From Stone to Metal: New Perspectives on the Later Prehistory of West Africa." *Journal of World Prehistory* 2(1):89–133.

Milisauskas, S. 1978. *European Prehistory*. New York: Academic Press.

Nishida, M. 1983. "The Emergence of Food Production in Neolithic Japan." *Journal of Anthropological Archaeology* 2(4):305–22.

Nygaard, S. E. 1989. "The Stone Age of Northern Scandinavia: A Review." *Journal of World Prehistory* 3(1):71–116.

Pawley, A., ed. 1991. *Man and a Half.* Auckland, New Zealand: Polynesian Society, Memoir 48.

Pfeiffer, J. E. 1977. *The Emergence of Society.* New York: McGraw-Hill.

Price, T. D. 1986. "The Earlier Stone Age of Northern Europe." In *The End of the Paleolithic in the Old World*, ed. L. G. Straus. Oxford: B.A.R. International Series 284.

———. 1987. "The Mesolithic of Western Europe." *Journal of World Prehistory* 1(3):225–305.

Renfrew, C. 1973. *Before Civilization.* New York: Alfred A. Knopf.

Renfrew, C. 1988. "Archaeology and Language." *Current Anthropology* 29(3):437–68.

Rowlands, M., M. Larsen, and K. Kristiansen, eds. 1987. *Center and Periphery in the Ancient World.* Cambridge, England: Cambridge University Press.

Rowley-Conwy, P., M. Zvelebil, and H. P. Blankholm. 1987. *Mesolithic Northwest Europe: Recent Trends.* Sheffield, England: John R. Collis.

Shennan, S. J. 1987. "Trends in the Study of Later European Prehistory." *Annual Review of Anthropology* 16:365–82.

Stahl, A. 1994. "Innovation, Diffusion, and Culture Contact: The Holocene Archaeology of Ghana." *Journal of World Prehistory* 8(1):51–112.

Straus, L. G. 1986. "The End of the Paleolithic in Cantabrian Spain and Gascony." In *The End of the Paleolithic in the Old World*, ed. L. G. Straus. Oxford: B.A.R. International Series 284.

Terrell, J. 1986. *Prehistory in the Pacific Islands.* New York: Cambridge University Press.

Trump, D. 1980. *The Prehistory of the Mediterranean.* New Haven: Yale University Press.

Weisler M. 1990. "Sources and Sourcing of Volcanic Glass in Hawaii: Implications for Exchange Studies." *Archaeology in Oceania* 25:16–23.

Weissleder, W. 1978. *The Nomadic Alternative: Models and Models of Interaction in the African-Asian Deserts and Steppes.* The Hague: Mouton.

Wemick, R., and the Editors of Time-Life. 1973. *The Monument Builders.* Alexandria, VA: Time-Life.

Whittle, A. 1987. "Neolithic Settlement Patterns in Temperate Europe." *Journal of World Prehistory* 1(1):5–52.

Zvelebil, M., ed. 1986. *Hunters in Transition.* Cambridge, England: Cambridge University Press.

Zvelebil, M., and P. Rowley-Conwy. 1984. "Transition to Farming in Northern Europe: A Hunter-Gatherer Perspective." *Norwegian Archaeological Review* 17:104–28.

Zvelebil, M., and P. Dolukhanov. 1991. "Transition to Farming in Eastern and Northern Europe." *Journal of World Prehistory* 5(3):233–278.

NOTES

1. See Fagan, *People of the Earth*, for more detailed coverage of these later states and empires.

2. In 1995, for example, a financial broker in Singapore trading in the Japanese stock market bankrupted a British bank, which was then bought by a Dutch concern.

3. Pfeiffer, *The Emergence of Society*, p. 282.

4. Shennan, "Trends in the Study of Later European Prehistory"; see also Childe, *The Prehistory of European Society*.

5. See, e.g., Harding, *The Mycenaeans and Europe*.

6. Dennell, "The Origins of Crop Agriculture in Europe," p. 91.

7. Zvelebil and Dolukhanov, "Transition to Farming in Eastern and Northern Europe."

8. Dennell, *European Economic Prehistory: A New Approach*.

9. See, e.g., Rowley-Conwy et al., *Mesolithic Northwest Europe: Recent Trends*; Price, "The Mesolithic of Western Europe"; Nygaard, "The Stone Age of Northern Scandinavia: A Review."

10. Fischer, Hansen, and Rasmussen, "Macro and Micro Wear Traces on Lithic Projectile Points."

11. Price, "The Earlier Stone Age of Northern Europe," p. 3.

12. Bogucki, "The Establishment of Agrarian Communities on the North European Plain," p. 11.

13. Barker and Gamble, *Beyond Domestication in Prehistoric Europe*, p. 9.

14. Grigg, *The Dynamics of Agricultural Change*; Barker and Gamble, *Beyond Domestication in Prehistoric Europe*, p. 22.

15. Whittle, "Neolithic Settlement Patterns in Temperate Europe."

16. Zvelebil and Rowley-Conwy, "Transition to Farming in Northern Europe: A Hunter-Gatherer Perspective"; see also Zvelebil, *Hunters in Transition*.

17. Renfrew, "Archaeology and Language."

18. Gregg, *Foragers and Farmers*.

19. Renfrew, "Archaeology and Language."

20. Hodder, *The Domestication of Europe*.

21. Renfew, *Before Civilization*.

22. Personal communication

23. Also see Kinnes, "Les Fouaillages and Megalithic Origins."

24. Lewthwaite, "Comment on A. Gilman, 'The Development of Social Stratification in Bronze Age Europe.' "

25. Harlan et al., *Origins of African Plant Domestication*.

26. Reviewed in McIntosh and McIntosh, "Current Directions in West African Prehistory."

27. Stahl, "Innovation, Diffusion, and Culture Contact: The Holocene Archaeology of Ghana," p. 51.

28. Stahl, "Innovation, Diffusion, and Culture Contact: The Holocene Archaeology of Ghana."

29. Clist, "Early Bantu Settlements in West Central Africa: A Review of Recent Research."

30. McIntosh and McIntosh, "From Stone to Metal: New Perspectives on the Later Prehistory of West Africa," p. 106.

31. Ibid., p. 110.

32. Ibid.

33. Ibid., p. 120.

34. Hall, *The Changing Past: Farmers, Kings, and Traders in Southern Africa, 200–1860*.

35. Akazawa and Aikens, *Prehistoric Hunter-Gatherers in Japan*; Aitkens, Ames, and Sanger, "Affluent Collectors at the Edges of Eurasia and North America"; Nishida, "The Emergence of Food Production in Neolithic Japan."

36. Bronson, "South-east Asia: Civilizations of the Tropical Forest," p. 262.

37. Higham, *The Archaeology of Mainland Southeast Asia.*

38. Charoenwongsa and Bayard, "Non Chai: New Dates on Metalworking and Trade from Northeastern Thailand."

39. See Pawley, *Man and a Half.*

40. Kirch and Green, "History, Phylogeny, and Evolution in Polynesia"; Kirch and Hunt, *Archaeology of the Lapita Cultural Complex: A Critical Review.*

41. Reviewed in Terrell, *Prehistory in the Pacific Islands.*

42. Finney, "Voyaging Against the Direction of the Trades: A Report of an Experimental Canoe Voyage from Samoa to Tahiti."

43. These descriptions of Pacific Islands and crops are based on entries in the Grolier Electronic Publishing.

44. Bellwood, "The Prehistory of Island Southeast Asia: A Multidisciplinary Review of Recent Research."

45. Ibid.

46. Ibid., p. 191.

47. Anderson, 1992

48. Reviewed in Kirch, "The Evolution of Sociopolitical Complexity in Prehistoric Hawaii: An Assessment of the Archaeological Evidence."

13

THE EVOLUTION OF COMPLEX SOCIETIES IN MESOAMERICA

*During the morning we arrived at a broad causeway and
continued our march towards Iztapalapa, and when we saw
so many cities and villages in the water and other great towns
on dry land and that straight and level causeway going
towards Mexico, we were amazed and said it was like the
enchantments they tell of in the legend of Amadis, on account
of the great towers . . . and buildings rising from the water,
all built of masonry. And, some of our soldiers asked
whether the things we saw were not a dream.*

Bernal Diaz del Castillo[1]

In Easter week of 1519, the Spanish *conquistador* Hernan Cortez landed on the coast of Veracruz, Mexico, and began a military campaign that would end in the crushing defeat of the indigenous Aztec civilization. For tens of thousands of years before Cortez's arrival, the peoples of the Old and New Worlds had had so little contact that they were physically different, spoke entirely different languages, and had no idea that the others even existed. But here is the curious thing: when Cortez traveled the road from Veracruz to the Aztec capital near Mexico City, he passed through cities, towns, villages, markets, and irrigated fields; he saw slavery, poverty, potentates, farmers, soldiers, temples, massive pyramids, roads, boats, pottery, gold jewelry, and textiles; in short, he encountered a world whose almost every aspect he could understand in terms of his own experience as an urban Spaniard of the sixteenth century.

There were, of course, many dissimilarities between the Spanish and Aztec peoples. The Aztecs had no ocean-going ships or advanced metallurgy, for example. And the ideological differences between the Aztecs and their European conquerors were particularly profound. The Spanish, despite their imperialism and murderous ferocity in warfare, viewed the Aztecs' preoccupations with death and human sacrifice with abhorrence, and the Aztecs found many aspects of Roman Catholic Christianity both evil and incomprehensible.

Yet despite profound differences in their respective morals and ideas, the Spanish and the Aztecs were fundamentally alike in cultural respects: they lived in hierarchically organized, class-structured, expansionist empires in which state religions provided much of the context of life, while intensive agriculture and highly specialized and integrated systems of craft production formed the economic basis of their civilizations.

Spanish military superiority, coupled with the diseases they introduced, effectively ended the indigenous developments of Mesoamerican civilizations, and it is interesting to speculate about what the Europeans would have found in the Americas if they had come a few centuries later—would there have been a great Pan-American empire to rival that of Spain? Or is it possible that in, say about A.D. 1850, people living on the coast of England (or France or Spain) might have awakened to the sight of Aztec warships in their harbors? The latter scenario is unlikely because New World peoples did not develop two technologies fundamental to the powerful imperialism of Old World societies—iron in the form of tools and weapons, and large domesticated animals capable of providing traction and transport (although New World peoples used metals in ornaments and had domesticated some beasts of burden, mainly the llama, in South America).

In any case, scholars have assumed for centuries that the rise of agricultural and complex societies in the New World offered them a "Second Earth," a comparative case, and that by examining these cultural developments in two somewhat different environments and times, the causes of these forms of cultural evolution might be more clearly revealed. Despite contemporary reassessment of that premise,[2] the early Mesoamerican states, in combination and comparison with the Inka of the Andes, Sumerian Mesopotamia, Old Kingdom Egypt, and other early polities, all illustrate that, whatever the factors are that produced these societies, they operated similarly around the world and at different times. Beyond these fundamental similarities of early civilizations, their unique arts and ideologies provide ample material for particularistic studies that need not appeal to cross-cultural and comparative analyses for intellectual justification. In this regard, the early states of Mesoamerica (Figure 13.1) are some of the most fascinating in the world.

In previous chapters (see, for example, chapter 7) we have considered the problem of ethics, moral relativism, and history: a central issue here is the political consequences of interpretations of different cultures and their histories. The European conquerors of the New World, for example, pointed to the prevalence of warfare, human sacrifice, and ritual murder as evidence that the New World peoples were barbarians who could only benefit from the imposition of Western "civilization." In this chapter and in chapters 14 and 15 the evidence for these New World practices is reviewed, and to some this may seem to perpetuate the stigmatization of New World peoples. But the fact is that warfare, human sacrifice, and ritual murder, as well as every other kind of gross exploitation of people, were common elements of cultures all over the world, from China to England. The point of discussing the evidence here is not to titillate the morbidly-inclined reader; it is to confront the problem of the origins of ideologies and the nature of their transformations—and to emphasize how cultures can make any behavior, no matter how reprehensible in our own view, into virtues that facilitate the workings of their political systems.

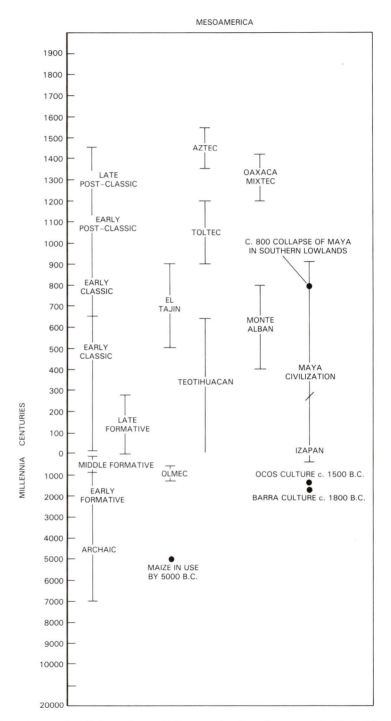

FIGURE 13.1 A cultural chronology of Mesoamerica. People were probably in Mesoamerica before 10,000 B.C. but the evidence is controversial.

THE ECOLOGICAL SETTING

As in other areas of early civilization, the first complex societies did not appear in just one area of Mexico and then gradually expand to occupy Mesoamerica; instead, there were several developmental centers, including the South Gulf Coast, the Valley of Mexico, the Valley of Oaxaca, and the Maya lowlands and highlands (Figure 13.2). Eventually some of these regions coalesced into larger political polities, but only after centuries of competition, cooperation, expansion, and collapse.

In each of these Mesoamerican areas, cultural evolution was much influenced by three general ecological conditions: (1) the millions of years of mountain-building volcanic activity that left Mesoamerica a still-trembling land of towering mountains and circumscribed valleys, and which in many areas compressed extremely different flora, fauna, and climates into close proximity, thereby rewarding inter-regional exchange, even though it made transport and communication difficult; (2) the absence of any domesticable animal suitable for providing milk, transport, or draft power; and (3) the relative scarcity of large rivers with extensive alluvial plains in warm latitudes: unlike, Egypt, Mesopotamia, the Indus Valley, North China, and Andean South America, for example, Mesoamerica has few large, navigable rivers in the semi-arid environments where primitive agriculture is highly productive.

FIGURE 13.2 The geography of Mesoamerica. The darker shading identifies developmental centers of early cultural complexity.

All civilizations can be understood to a limited extent purely in thermodynamic terms. From the food that keeps our bodies at proper metabolic temperature to the draft animals, engines, or nuclear reactors that propel our vehicles, the connection between energy and culture is close and causal. And, as in all early civilizations, in ancient Mesoamerica a few plant and animal species were, in effect, the power base of cultural evolution. Not just any domesticated plants and animals would do: there had to be a reliable, voluminous carbohydrate source and nutritionally complementary plants and animals. In Mesoamerica these foods were, principally, maize, beans, and squash, augmented by protein from rabbits, deer, dogs, and in some places, fish and shellfish.[3] These rather plain foodstuffs were enlivened in antiquity by the use of cacao (from which chocolate is derived), incendiary peppers, numerous herbs and spices, and several natural hallucinogens. And like all ancient farmers, they used the magic of fermentation to improve the food products of various high-sugar plants— cactus being the principal source of alcohol in Mesoamerica.

THE ARCHAEOLOGICAL RECORD OF EARLY COMPLEX MESOAMERICAN SOCIETIES (C. 1600 B.C.–A.D. 1524)

As we saw in chapter 6, between 9,000 and 4,000 years ago most of Mexico was inhabited mainly by hunter-foragers who lived in small bands that moved with the seasons to exploit cactus fruits, deer herds, nuts, and the hundreds of other plant and animal species in their range, depending on the season. Since these bands were small in size and never stayed in one place for a sufficient period of time to have much long-term effect on the plant and animal populations on which they subsisted, the hunter-foragers' overall impact on their environment was low. A few groups along the margins of the lake in the Valley of Mexico may have been sedentary villagers, as were some groups along the coasts, and their role in the domestication of plants and animals and the eventual spread of agriculture is unclear.[4] Kirkby suggests that by about 4,000 years ago, maize cob size was large enough that people over large areas of the Mexican highlands could subsist mainly on maize.[5] Grinding corn and making tortillas out of it may not seem to be a great technological leap forward from hunting-foraging, but maize, along with beans, squash, and a variety of other plants, provided the reliable and productive source of food required for people to be able to live in one place permanently.

The recent re-dating of some of the supposedly earliest domesticated maize in Mesoamerica to about 3500 B.C. raises the possibility, as Gayle Fritz notes,[6] that initial agriculture evolved out of intensified foraging by groups of people who were relatively sedentary, perhaps living all or most of the year in one or a few places, and that they were perhaps even in the process of developing social differences that increased the intensity of their foraging. However maize was domesticated, and by whom, maize appears to have reached sufficient productivity to permit the village-farming way of life soon after about 2000 B.C., and agricultural communities appeared at about this time in many different areas.

From the hot, wet Guatemalan lowlands to the arid Tehuacán Valley, the earliest villages were quite similar in size and contents.[7] Almost all houses (Figure 13.3) were built using the wattle-and-daub method—sticks, branches, and cane were woven in-and-out between vertical wall poles, then covered with a mud plaster, which was dried by the hot sun. Houses, which were seldom larger than four by six meters, featured thatched roofs and tamped clay floors on which fine sand was scattered.

Most of the earliest farming communities were tiny hamlets, villages of ten to twelve houses that were home to about fifty to sixty people, but some communities were larger. Most houses that have been excavated have yielded the same remains, mainly grinding stones, storage pits, pieces of large ceramic storage jars, bones of cottontail rabbits, carbonized maize fragments, and broken pieces of ceramic charcoal braziers.[8] In addition, ovens, middens, and graves are very common. While the proportion of plant and animal foods varied somewhat, all villages probably grew maize, beans, squash, peppers, and some other crops, and hunted deer and rabbits. Each village, or each extended family, may have had a specialist who did pressure flaking of stone, leather-working, or a similar craft, and individual villages may have concentrated on specialties like salt production, feather-weaving, shell-working, grinding stone manufacture, and the like.

FIGURE 13.3 Mexico's first agriculturalists lived in wattle-and-daub houses much like these contemporary homes in Morelos, Mexico. The people in this village speak Nahuatl, which is derived from the language of the Aztecs.

As in Mesopotamia, China, and elsewhere, the background to the origins of complex society in Mesoamerica was a great scatter of relatively simple agricultural villages in which the mechanics of producing a reliable, expandable food supply had been mastered. Many areas of Mesoamerica contributed to the overall rise of the first Mesoamerican states, but four areas appear to have been particularly important: the South Gulf Coast, the Valley of Mexico, the Valley of Oaxaca, and the Maya lowlands.

EARLY COMPLEX SOCIETIES ON THE SOUTH GULF COAST (C. 1500 B.C.–400 B.C.)

An early and radical break with the simple village farming tradition of Mesoamerica occurred in the sweltering lowlands of the South Gulf Coast. Here, beginning at about 1000 B.C., people built massive clay pyramids and platforms, lived in small-town groups of hundreds or even thousands, intensively farmed a variety of ecological zones, and produced what is one of the world's most valued examples of stone sculpture.

These people are known to us as the Olmec, a name derived from an ancient American word for rubber—doubtless a reference to the rubber trees that grow in this area—but a name they themselves probably did not use.

Some scholars have considered the possibility that the Olmec culture was the *cultura madre* (mother culture) of all later complex societies in Mesoamerica, and that they were directly responsible for transforming their neighbors by military, political, religious, or economic means into complex societies. Other scholars, however, have argued convincingly that the Olmec represent only one of several largely independent cases of the evolution of social complexity in Mesoamerica. As we have seen in other areas of the world, civilizations seem not to have developed, in general, because of the behavior of a particular group or the actions of a few particularly gifted individuals: civilizations all appear to be the products of broad regional and long-term historical processes that manifest themselves differently at different places and times.

The Olmec heartland is a coastal strip approximately 350 kilometers in length, extending inland about 100 kilometers. It was created by the alluviation of several rivers that run to the sea from the highlands. Except for a few areas, the region is thickly forested. Torrential rains fall during the summer, but the area is dry in the winter, which permits swidden, or slash-and-burn agriculture, as it is sometimes called. Swidden agriculture involves cutting down all the vegetation in a particular area and then waiting for the dry season so that the cut vegetation can be burned. Nutrients are thus returned to the soil—an important contribution since manure and artificial fertilizers were not available (unlike the peasants of Mesopotamia, the Olmec had no manure-producing cattle to graze on and replenish fields). After burning, the land is sown, and the crops germinate and come to maturity in the rainy season. After one or two years of exploitation, however, the land must be left fallow, sometimes for twenty years or more. If the cycle is accelerated, productivity falls rapidly. Until recent times, in the flat lowlands of the Olmec Heartland as much as 70 to 90 percent of the land was fallow at any one time.[9]

Maize, beans, and squash were agricultural staples in early formative times, supplemented by hunting and fishing and collecting wild plant foods. In coastal areas, mussels and other rich marine resources could also be collected. And while much of Olmec agriculture may have been swidden-based, very productive farming was possible on the river levees. Some river levees near the coast are annually inundated with water-borne silt of such fertility that it was possible to raise two crops a year using swidden techniques. Indeed, the precocity of the Olmec in developing one of the first complex Mesoamerican cultures was probably tied directly to the great agricultural potential and rich floral and faunal resources of these riverine environments. The economic basis of Olmec culture is still relatively poorly known. Although plant remains do not preserve well in the South Gulf Coast, we know that most of the people were maize farmers. They ate some peccary and deer, but fish and domestic dogs provided most of their protein. Human bones found at San Lorenzo with obvious burning and butchering marks suggest cannibalism, undertaken for either ritual or more secular motives. Although the remains of a species of marine toad (*Bufo marinus*) with hallucinogenic qualities have been found here, archaeologists believe that these represent later intrusions into the middens these people left behind. Obsidian, imported in large volumes from the Mexican highlands to the west, was used for arrowheads, knives, and many other tools.

After many years of research, we finally have substantial data about the early formative cultures of the South Gulf Coast, although we will probably never know with great precision the population densities in the countryside in many periods because the tiny hamlets they apparently lived in are covered by vegetation and easily missed in archaeological surveys.[10]

As a result, we know the Olmec primarily from their larger ceremonial centers, and on this basis they are an impressive culture. On the San Lorenzo plateau in southern Veracruz, for example, people had been living since about 1500 B.C., exploiting its good soil and natural springs. Then, sometime after about 1250 B.C., the inhabitants of this area began moving tons of earth and clay in baskets to level the plateau's upper surface over an area some 600 by 100 meters. At first, perhaps, they were simply trying to raise the elevation of their residential areas above the flood levels of the seasonally-inundated plains on which they lived. Within a century or two, however, they began to build pyramids and ceremonial platforms adorned with monumental stone sculptures and other impressive monuments.[11]

San Lorenzo actually is a group of sites within about a five kilometer area, a complex that reached its peak between about 1150 and 900 B.C., when several thousand people probably lived there; but after about 900 B.C. construction of monuments ceased and population densities appear to have declined.

San Lorenzo's florescence was followed by that of another Olmec site, La Venta, located on a small island in a coastal swamp near the Tonal River. At this location the Olmec constructed a series of mounds, platforms, courts, and pyramids covering more than five square kilometers. Much of this has been destroyed by looters and an oil well/processing installation, but excavations have revealed a large portion of this site's plan. Dominating the area is a pyramid of clay, 128 by 73 meters at the base and 33.5 meters high. Two long, low mounds extend out to the north from the pyramid, with a circular mound between them. All these mounds are oriented eight degrees west of true north.

A particularly striking remnant of Olmec culture at both San Lorenzo and La Venta are the Olmec "heads" and other monumental sculptures. The most impressive artworks at La Venta are four "Olmec heads," some of which are over eight feet tall. They often depict a human head with a stern, not to say sneering, facial expression, and usually are shown wearing a "helmet." Presumably these sculptures are of Olmec rulers, but we will probably never know for certain. Since the Olmec had no metal tools, we assume they worked with grinding and pecking stone implements, and it is difficult to believe that these sculptures were made by anyone other than skilled specialists. Major Olmec sites often also included other monumental stone carvings, such as those of free-standing figures of kneeling men and carved stelae and "altars," all carefully executed from massive basalt blocks. On some of them are engraved fantastic mythical creatures representing hybrids of snakes, jaguars, and humans. The basalt for these carvings was imported from eighty kilometers or more away, probably by being floated down rivers on rafts. Some of the heads weigh more than twenty tons, so scores of people must have been involved in quarrying, transporting, carving, and then erecting the stone blocks in monumental compositions.

The Olmec also decorated their ceremonial complexes with many other kinds of expensive and exotic goods, such as the "pavements" at La Venta. To form these mosaic-like pavements, hundreds of serpentine (a green hard stone) blocks about the size of small construction bricks were laid out in a traditional Olmec design—a jaguar mask—and then carefully buried.

Unfortunately, the acidic, damp soils of the Olmec region do not preserve bones well, and we have only meager knowledge of Olmec burial practices. At La Venta a tomb in a large mound near the central pyramid was elaborately constructed of basalt columns, and on its limestone floor two juveniles were laid out in fabric bundles heavily coated with red paint. Buried with the bodies were jade figurines, beads, a shell ornament, a stingray spine, and a few other items, and these burials may reflect inherited wealth and prestige. Other types of evidence relating to social complexity, such as residential architecture and settlement patterns, are not well represented at La Venta. And while there is little residential debris there (except for pottery and a few clay figurines), scholars now believe that the people who built La Venta did live there permanently.[12]

Other Olmec ceremonial centers were built at Laguna de los Cerros and elsewhere (Figures 13.4, 13.5, and 13.6), and between about 900 B.C. and 400 B.C. Olmec culture reached its peak on the South Gulf Coast. It is possible to have large buildings and other trappings of social complexity on the basis of a very simple economic system, but between 900 and 400 B.C. the Olmec also had an intensive and productive agricultural system. In addition, they traded jade, iron ore, obsidian, bitumen, magnetite mirrors, shark teeth, stingray spines, perhaps cacao and pottery, and many other goods in complex patterns between the Olmec heartland and highland Mexico and as far south as Guatemala.

As we have seen in other civilizations, a key element in the development of most of them was some formative *idea*, some set of religious or philosophical ideology that people over a large area adopted and expressed in ways that linked them in complex

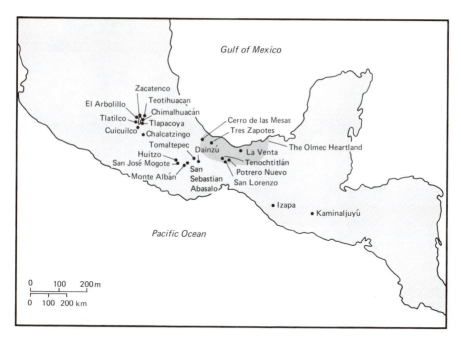

FIGURE 13.4 Centers of initial cultural complexity in first millennium B.C. Mesoamerica.

FIGURE 13.5 The Olmec complex at La Venta included a 30-meter-high pyramid and several other lower mounds.

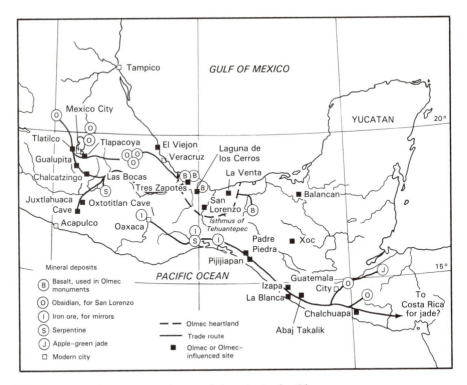

FIGURE 13.6   Major sites and mineral deposits in the Olmec area.

interrelationships. The core ideology of the Olmec is hard to discern and decipher, however. Judging from their art style, the Olmec seem to have believed that at some distant time in the past a woman mated with a jaguar and gave issue to a line of half-human/half-feline monsters, or "were-jaguars." These were portrayed in pottery, stone, and other media in a highly stylized way, usually as fat infants of no discernible sexuality (Figure 13.7). Their snarling mouths, toothless gums, and cleft heads give them a strikingly bizarre quality that some scholars have explained as an imitation of a birth defect of the neural tubes, or as the deformities one would expect of a mating between a human and a jaguar.[13]

   "Olmec" ceramic and sculptural designs have also been found far outside the borders of the South Gulf Coast. Some bas-relief rock carvings at Las Victorias in highland El Salvador strongly resemble those at La Venta, and similar sculptures have been discovered in the highlands of Guerrero and Morelos in western Mexico. At Chalcatzingo, in Morelos, cliff sculptures include a standard Olmec motif of a human (probably male) seated in what may have been meant as the mouth of a cave or a steaming monster (Figure 13.8). Olmec styles of pottery, worked stone, jade, and other artifacts have also been found at several sites in the Valley of Oaxaca, at Tlatilco and Tlapacoya near Mexico City, in Guatemala, and elsewhere in Mesoamerica.

The later Olmec and their immediate successors may have formulated some of the ideology that formed the basis of the Maya (see below), but the evidence is controversial. In 1902 a small jadeite figure of a person with what appears to be the bill of a duck was found at San Andres Tuxtla. On it were engraved some glyphs that appeared to be a date, but without the signs that would allow it to be converted to our calendar, and other glyphs, some of which resembled those of later Maya writing but many others that did not. Scholars disputed the significance of this figure for many years, and in 1986 another find helped clarify its significance. This was the La Mojarra Stela 1, found in southern Veracruz, where writing was found that appeared to be the same script as that of the Tuxtla duck-billed figurine. John Justeson and Terrence Kaufman[14] have argued that these inscriptions are in the Zoquean language, which is only distantly (if at all) related to the language of the later Maya, and consists of separate glyphs for each combination of the eleven consonants and six vowels of Zoquean (thus, sixty-six possible consonant-vowel combinations). What is particularly important, however, is that this Epi-Olmec script contains logograms that are semantically equivalent to very similar-looking Maya glyphs[15] and that the Olmec were using essentially the same calendar. These Epi-Olmec inscriptions refer to the accession of various rulers, to what seems to be a war between brothers-in-law, and to other dynastic and calendrical matters.

FIGURE 13.7 These Olmec ceramic "baby" figurines were distributed over a large region of central Mesoamerica.

FIGURE 13.8 Relief 1, Chalcatzingo, Morelos. One interpretation of this Olmec motif is that it is a ruler within a cave or a stylized monster's mouth, which gives off steam or smoke, while raindrops fall from above.

Whether or not the Olmec can be credited with the origins of Maya ideology, the Olmec were far different from their hunter-forager ancestors, and if we match them against the checklist of monumental architecture, burials of juveniles with wealth, voluminous craft production and trade, writing, etc., the Olmec were clearly a complex society. Their relatively low population densities and small population numbers in centers is probably a direct result of the constraints of their agricultural methods, although we may have an inaccurate sense of their agriculture, which may have been more intensive than many scholars think.

La Venta appears to have been intentionally destroyed soon after about 400 B.C., or at least we might infer this from the fact that some of its greatest stone monuments were intentionally defaced. Like the Maya, the history of the Olmec appears to have been one in which small centers of power and prestige, such as San Lorenzo and La Venta, alternately became dominant. And while the people of these centers probably shared core cultural elements, ranging from language to theology, it is not certain that they ever formed a united, integrated political unit over the entire Olmec region.

EARLY COMPLEX SOCIETIES IN THE VALLEY OF MEXICO (C. 1100 B.C.–600 B.C.)

The Valley of Mexico is a large basin with no external drainage that is rimmed on three sides by high mountain walls cut by only a few passes; even in the north where there are no mountains, the valley is delimited by a series of low hills. The valley has often been considered a "natural" analytical unit, bounded as it is by such impressive natural barriers, but archaeological research has revealed that almost from their arrival here the people of this area interacted with cultures far beyond the valley itself.[16]

Much of the Valley of Mexico lies beyond the temperature limits of maize agriculture, but until the last four hundred years, a large lake covered the low central portion of the valley, providing rich resources in the form of fish, fowl, turtles, algae, and reeds.

There is not a single navigable stream or river in the whole Valley of Mexico today, and agriculture in most places in the Valley would have depended on rainfall and small streams.[17] Rainfall is sharply seasonal and varies considerably from north to south. Today, as in the past, the upper slopes of the Valley of Mexico provide many wood products, and in earlier times the slopes supported large deer herds that were an important part of the prehistoric and early historic diet.

Modern urbanization in the Valley of Mexico has probably destroyed many of the earliest villages and towns there. What we do know suggests that by about 1000 B.C. there were small villages and hamlets in several areas of the Valley. Only a few larger sites have been found, such as Tlatilco and Cuicuilco.[18] We know little about Cuicuilco, since later volcanic eruptions have covered large areas of the site with lava. Recent radiocarbon dating of this site suggests that it had been abandoned long before the volcanic eruption that buried it took place, and that it was already in decline by about A.D. 150.[19] The decline may have been a result of population loss to Teotihuacán (see below), but the site remains heavily obscured by lava and is difficult to excavate.

Tlatilco has been largely destroyed by looters and the activities connected with a modern brick factory built on the site. How much of the occupation there dates to the period between 1100 B.C. and 800 B.C. will probably never be known.

The Valley's apparent two-tiered site size hierarchy, with a few large towns like Tlatilco and Cuicuilco and many small villages, suggests a simple, perhaps tribal, organization, and the distribution of settlements does not point to any political or social spacing. Settlements seem to be located principally around the edge of the great lake, although a few small villages have also been found in highland areas where the soil is particularly rich and deep. Differences in settlement size seem to be a result of local variations in agricultural potential.

Nor is there much evidence of complex architecture at these settlements. A few small mounds and platforms may date to before 800 B.C., but none is on the scale of the pyramids, platforms, and other structures found later on the South Gulf Coast and in the Maya areas. No evidence of elaborate residential structures or monumental sculptures has been found.

The cemetery at Tlatilco provides little evidence that the occupants of the Valley of Mexico were living in complex cultures. Burial goods include pottery, shell ornaments, obsidian tools, figurines, bone tools, and jade and serpentine objects. Some women seem to have been buried with more numerous and more expensive objects than other people in the cemetery, perhaps even with sacrificed men and children. But there is no evidence of lavish mortuary cults.

From about 800 B.C. to about 500 B.C., the population density of the Valley of Mexico increased considerably. At least ten sites were larger than fifty hectares (each inhabited by about 1,000 people), and one, Cuicuilco, probably had a population of about 2,500. All the larger sites are located along the lake margin, while scattered small hamlets have been found in the highlands. The larger settlements along the lake are fairly evenly spaced at eight- to ten-kilometer intervals, and they all used similar styles of pottery, suggesting some degree of social or political integration, but probably at a low level.

EARLY STATES IN THE VALLEY OF MEXICO (C. 600 B.C.–A.D. 900)

As discussed in chapter 7, applying a static concept such as "state" to complex multidimensional cultural changes involves many difficulties, but as an informal descriptive term the notion of "state" implies a society based in part on socioeconomic classes, a centralized, hierarchically arranged bureaucratic structure, and the economic and functional integration of many settlements over a comparatively large area. Cuicuilco, with its early stone monuments, intensified agricultural system, and other developments, may be Mesoamerica's first state in the sense described below, but it is clear that other areas of Mesoamerica, especially the Valley of Oaxaca, were undergoing roughly contemporaneous and similar processes of state-formation.

Thanks to the hard work of William Sanders, Jeffrey Parsons, George Cowgill, Rene Millon, and many others in the Valley of Mexico, we can now reconstruct over 4,000 years of settlement history and other evidence related to the process of state-formation here.[20] Elizabeth Brumfiel, for example, attempted to test the hypothesis that "population pressure" was an important factor in cultural evolution in the Valley of Mexico between 500 B.C. and A.D. 1—the important interval just before the florescence of Teotihuacán.[21] She did this by estimating the agricultural productivity and the potential for intensification of each settlement known for this period. Her argument is complex and mathematical, but one of her conclusions is quite simple: an important factor in the growth of smaller towns and villages was the imposition of tribute by elites in the largest communities. She found little convincing evidence of "population pressure" at the critical period—although, as usual in archaeology, the data are not conclusive.[22]

Several other analyses of these Valley of Mexico settlement patterns have been set in mathematical geographical terms,[23] and the results have stimulated a great deal of discussion about Mesoamerican cultural history and the applicability of these kinds of analytical techniques. The settlement pattern data we have here come from archaeological surveys where the procedure was to collect a sample of pottery from each site and then estimate the site size, periods of occupation, and distinctive architectural features. The limitations of such data have been intensively reviewed by Tolstoy and others, but this information is by far the most useful and systematic archaeological evidence in Mesoamerica.[24] As such, it has been used for the application of several kinds of quantitative analyses.

For the period between about 500 B.C. and 200 B.C., there is persuasive evidence of changing cultural complexity in the Valley of Mexico. The population of the valley grew substantially in this period, and in most of Mesoamerica as well,[25] and people were now living in larger settlements. Cuicuilco may have had as many as 7,500 people at this time—an unmanageable size without considerable social organization and control. Many other settlements of eighty to one hundred hectares existed, intermediate and small settlements also increased in number, and there are some early signs of irrigation agriculture. Small "temple" platforms of stone and clay, some three to four meters high, appeared in several areas, and Cuicuilco and other sites had large stone structures. Cuicuilco had the largest early pyramid structure in central Mexico, an anticipation of the great stone pyramids at Teotihuacán (see below).

As we saw in the case of Mesopotamia (chapter 8) and Egypt (chapter 9), early polities that were developing centralized political authority, class-based social organizations, and other elements of social complexity often seemed to begin building massive ceremonial structures very early in this evolutionary process. That so many people around the world chose the pyramid form has nothing to do with instinctive human aesthetics or the mystical power of pyramids, and everything to do with the simple engineering reality that people with primitive tools who try to build a monumental structure capable of bearing its own weight can only construct a few basic shapes. Of these, the pyramid is the easiest to build in terms of raising materials to the top of the structure and the amount of materials and labor needed. As discussed in previous chapters, monumental structures are functionally efficient in early complex societies, despite their apparent "waste" of resources and labor, because they legitimize and focus the religious and social hierarchies of which they are an expression, and they may also act to dampen unstable rates of population growth and economic expansion.

Before 200 B.C. the Teotihuacán area of the Valley of Mexico had been relatively unimportant culturally, but it has large areas suitable for irrigated agriculture and possesses large springs capable of supplying irrigation systems. Obsidian is also available nearby, and the area is thought to have supported large stands of maguey cactus, used for its fiber and to make *pulque* (a kind of beer), as well as edible nopal cactus, a plant species that is home to an insect that can be rendered into a red dye highly prized in pre-Hispanic Mexico. Moreover, Teotihuacán stands along a natural trade route to eastern Mesoamerica—an important advantage given the difficult terrain of this region.

Between about 500 B.C. and 150 B.C., Teotihuacán supported a few small villages with a combined population of at most 3,000, but between 150 B.C. and 1 B.C. the population growth rate exceeded that of any other period, and a city extending some six to eight square kilometers formed and reached about one-third its eventual max-imum size.[26] Between about A.D. 1 and A.D. 150 Teotihuacán's growth rate was still high but had slowed; the average population during this period was probably between 60,000 and 80,000,[27] and rose to between 100,000 and 200,000 by A.D. 500.

During this time work was completed on the massive Pyramids of the Sun and the Moon (Figure 13.9) and on at least twenty other important temple complexes.[28] The Pyramid of the Sun is 198 meters long on each side of its base—as large an area as the great pyramid of Khufu in Egypt—and rises 64 meters (half the height of the Khufu pyramid). The pyramid seems to have been built over an earlier, smaller struc-ture made of sun-dried bricks and is filled with an additional one million cubic me-ters of earth, stone, and rubble. In volume, this probably equaled two million cubic meters of uncompressed fill, which would have required the excavation, transport, and shaping of the soil in an area 1.4 kilometers square to a depth of 1 meter—a con-siderable effort by any standards. The Pyramid of the Moon is somewhat smaller (150

FIGURE 13.9 The Pyramid of the Sun (upper left) and the Pyramid of the Moon (from which this photograph was taken) were the ceremonial center of Teotihuacan. At times the city probably had a population of more than 100,000, and there were hundreds of workshops and houses.

meters at the base, 45 meters high), but of greater architectural sophistication, with a series of inset trapezoidal platforms. Pottery fragments in the fill of these pyramids indicate that the pyramids were constructed by using material from earlier occupations near the city. Considering the size of these structures, it is little wonder that the later Aztecs believed that the pyramids had been constructed by giants and that some of the gods were buried beneath them.

By about A.D. 100 Teotihuacán had hundreds of workshops, with perhaps as much as 25 percent of its population employed as craft specialists, making products in obsidian, ceramics, precious stones, slate, basalt, seashells, feathers, basketry, leather, and other materials. Massive public constructions were underway, considerable variability existed in mortuary complexes and residential architecture, and the settlement patterns in the surrounding areas were heavily influenced by the city.

The rest of the city is perhaps even more significant in terms of its evidence of cultural complexity. It was laid out in quadrants, formed by the Street of the Dead intersected by streets running east to west. Some of the quadrants were more densely occupied than others, and very different architectural styles and artifacts were found in various zones of the city. Along the main north-south street were elaborate residences, presumably for societal elites, as well as large and small temple complexes. Many of the more impressive buildings were built on platforms and often faced inward on patios and courtyards. Most buildings were one story high. In some temple complexes the walls were decorated with beautiful murals depicting religious themes, warfare, imaginary animals, and scenes from daily life.

The basic residential unit of Teotihuacán appears to have been large, walled, often windowless compounds made of adobe bricks and chunks of volcanic rock. Many such compounds measured fifty meters or more on a side and internally were divided into many rooms, porticoes, patios, and passageways. In some, open patios let in sun and air and drained the compounds through underground stone troughs. Many walls were decorated with frescoes of jaguars, coyotes, trees, gods, and people in naturalistic settings.

Some residential complexes at Teotihuacán were found to have concentrations of artifacts characteristic of distant areas of Mesoamerica. The Oaxaca Barrio, for example, included ceramics, funeral urns, burials, and other elements indistinguishable from the artifacts used in Oaxaca—over 400 kilometers to the south—and very much in contrast to the distinctive artifacts of the Teotihuacán natives. These foreign "barrios" appear to have remained culturally distinct and intact for at least several centuries and may have been trade entrepôts or ethnic "ghettos," but no persuasive explanation for these features has been made.

The city's people apparently ate large quantities of nopal and other kinds of cactus, as well as maize, beans, squash, and a variety of other domesticated and nondomesticated plants and animals. Deborah Nichols has shown how extensive was the irrigation system that supported the intensive agriculture that fed Teotihuacán's tens of thousands of people.[29] Even at Teotihuacán's peak, however, there was considerable hunting, as evidenced by the fact that about 80 percent of the animal remains found were deer bones.

Rebecca Storey analyzed sixty-seven bodies from burials in one of the poorer compounds at Teotihuacán and found that, as it did for their fellow early city dwellers in Rome and elsewhere, living in early pre-industrial cities shortened life: half the people died before about fifteen years of age, and only a very few lived past the age of thirty.[30]

By the time Teotihuacán reached its maximum size, it had apparently depopulated much of the rest of the Valley of Mexico: only one other major settlement appears in the Valley at about A.D. 500, and it is but a small fraction of the size of Teotihuacán. In fact, the abandonment of rural sites correlates so closely with Teotihuacán's growth that it appears likely that populations were either drawn or coerced directly into the city; overall population growth in the Valley of Mexico at this time (A.D. 100 to A.D. 600) was probably very minor and absorbed by Teotihuacán.[31] By A.D. 500 Teotihuacán-style ceramic vases were placed in the richly furnished burials of apparently high-status individuals on the Gulf Coast, in Oaxaca, and elsewhere.

Teotihuacán so dominated the Valley of Mexico that some have wondered if its power extended far beyond the valley itself. It seems unlikely that the few hundred thousand people at Teotihuacán were able to extend military control over the millions of people living in the rest of Mesoamerica: fighting a military campaign in the rough terrain of these distant areas would have been suicidal. More likely, the Teotihuacános were tied to the many other areas through trade networks. The city has no major defensive fortifications, but it does have what appear to be large market areas, and the ecological diversity of Mesoamerica would have put a high premium on large-volume trade in basic agricultural and technological commodities. By circulating these many products, people would have had a much higher standard of living and much greater protection against food shortages.

Sometime before A.D. 600, Teotihuacán's size and influence began to decline. As the city shrank in population, new centers and settlements appeared throughout the Valley of Mexico, particularly on its edges. Significantly, after A.D. 600 Teotihuacán styles in pottery, architecture, and other artifacts disappeared from the rest of Mesoamerica. It is as if a complicated exchange network had been beheaded, and local cultures began developing their own distinct traditions.

Archaeologist George Cowgill has argued that Teotihuacán stopped growing in size and power after A.D. 600 because it had reached the limits of productivity of its sustaining area: there are only a few thousand hectares of land near Teotihuacán suitable for canal irrigation, and once the city's population reached about 100,000, much of the food would have had to have come from riskier, less productive forms of agriculture and from collecting and hunting wild plants and animals.[32]

Various factors appear to have diminished Teotihuacán's population growth and influence after A.D. 600.[33] Teotihuacán may have been eclipsed by other political systems based on more productive agricultural and economic resources: there is some evidence that at least part of its sphere of influence was encroached on by emerging states in the Maya areas. Even closer to home, political systems centered at Tula, Xochicalco, and elsewhere in the Valley of Mexico may have begun to block Teotihuacán's access to needed raw materials and foodstuffs.

There is some evidence that Teotihuacán was burned down at about A.D. 650, perhaps intentionally, and its population dispersed to the countryside. Whatever malignant conjunction of wars, fires, droughts, and other factors that destroyed it, Teotihuacán was one of the first great states of the New World.

EARLY COMPLEX SOCIETIES IN OAXACA[34]
(C. 1500 B.C.–500 B.C.)

In the Olmec area the basis of cultural evolution was the productivity of the coastal zone and river alluvium, while in the Valley of Mexico it was the lake shore and adjacent areas, but in the Valley of Oaxaca, cultural evolution seems to have been based on the diversity of ecological zones and the presence of some small river valleys. On the valley floor are large, fertile, flat alluvial areas with a water table sufficiently high for irrigation to be easily accomplished. Grading up into the mountains, the piedmont areas are less fertile than the alluvium, but they can be productively farmed by diverting water from the perennial streams that run toward the valley floor. The higher mountains are cooler and wetter than the other zones and are still covered with pine and oak trees. Frost is not nearly the limiting factor on agriculture it is in the Valley of Mexico, although it can be a significant determinant of productivity. Since formative times, irrigation by means of canals and wells has been an important aspect of agriculture in Oaxaca.

Some of the most important resources of Oaxaca were the native iron ores, including magnetite, ilmenite, and hematite. Small pieces of these materials were polished and used as mirrors and ornaments, which were then traded widely over Mesoamerica and used as marks of status.

Shortly after 1400 B.C., the most productive areas of the piedmont and the alluvium in the Valley of Oaxaca were occupied by small villages composed of perhaps fifty people living in tiny wattle-and-daub structures. The first significant deviation from this pattern of egalitarian farmers occurred sometime between 1350 B.C. and 1150 B.C., when the inhabitants of at least one site (San José Mogote) at different times built several "public buildings" of earth and adobe construction.[35] Although these structures average only 5.4 by 4.4 meters each, they are interpreted as public buildings because the floors were carefully covered with a distinctive white lime plaster and swept clean, in contrast to the average house of this period, the floors of which were usually stamped clay and sand and covered with household debris.

Other evidence suggests that these buildings at San José Mogote may have been intended for special functions: they were repaired and reused over longer periods of time than the obviously residential structures; at least one of them had an "altar" or step against one wall; and they are oriented eight degrees west of true north, about the same as the major monumental constructions at La Venta, in the Olmec Heartland, which suggests that the strong Mesoamerican tradition of imputing magic to place and arrangement (see below) was already in force.

Most of the other formative villages in Oaxaca lack such public structures, although one, Tomaltepec, was found to have a large prepared mudbrick platform.[36] In the floor of this structure was a storage pit, considerably larger than any of the others at the site, containing relatively large quantities of obsidian, ornamental seashell, and deer and rabbit bones.[37] Between 1400 and 1000 B.C., overlapping in time with the construction of this platform, a large cemetery was created at Tomaltepec. Eighty burials containing a total of about 100 individuals were found at the cemetery, and most of these burials had almost the same goods, mainly ceramics and a few other small items. In four of the burials, small quantities of obsidian, magnetite, and jade were found, but these differences in grave goods seem fairly small in view of the overall similarity. And, interestingly, no juveniles or infants were buried here; all the bodies were of adults, suggesting that this society had not yet achieved significant social stratification.

Analysis of trade items in the valley between 1400 B.C. and 1000 B.C. also reinforces this impression of low-level community organization. A few items, such as obsidian, were traded, but in small amounts, and the trade was probably organized through individual households.[38]

But archaeological evidence suggests that major changes were in process in the cultural organization of Oaxacan society between about 1400 B.C. and 1100 B.C. More crafts were apparently performed at San José Mogote than at other settlements in the valley at this time. Debris from working obsidian, jade, magnetite, shell, and other substances has been found here in concentrations proportionately greater than at other sites. There was a major increase in the volume of "exotic" traded materials in Oaxaca at this time also, perhaps in response to increasing social stratification: these materials seem to have been used most frequently to make ornaments that reflect differences in social rank.

As is discussed below, in the context of the Maya, a widespread religious practice in Mesoamerica was ritual self-mutilation to produce blood—often in the form of cutting one's tongue or (for men) penis with obsidian blades or stingray spines. This practice is thought to have been a way of materializing the gods and invoking their powers, and the presence of these materials at San José Magote may reflect this practice. The spread of common elements of ideology over Mesoamerica also seems reflected in other ways. There are clear resemblances between Olmec figurines and ones of comparable age from Oaxaca, for example, and some pottery with Olmec motifs reminiscent of the South Gulf Coast has been found in Oaxaca. Certainly, magnetite and obsidian were moved in substantial volumes between Oaxaca and the South Gulf Coast between 1100 B.C. and 850 B.C.

Kent Flannery and Joyce Marcus have challenged[39] the notion that "Olmec" motifs on early Oaxaca pottery support the contention that somehow the South Gulf Coast cultures stimulated cultural developments in Oaxaca. They note that Oaxaca seems to have been more influenced by cultures in the Valley of Mexico than the South Gulf Coast, and that Oaxaca society was, in any case, among the earliest in Mesoamerica to develop public architecture and other evidence of increasing cultural complexity.

After about 850 B.C., variation in settlement size in Oaxaca increased; by 550 B.C., San José Mogote, for example, grew to fifteen times the size of the next largest community. Many settlements excavated have public architecture, and their distribution seems to mirror the growing importance of social and political factors in determining site location.

It seems unlikely that cultural evolution in either Oaxaca or the Valley of Mexico was directly instigated by the Olmec through military imposition, economic exploitation, or slavish imitation.[40] The wide distribution of Olmec styles of ceramics, figurines, and sculpture and the construction in Oaxaca and elsewhere of public buildings with astronomical orientations similar to those of the Olmec buildings seem to reflect inter-regional trade networks and perhaps the circulation of important people, but the archaeological evidence does not support the idea of unified political and military control of these three regions.[41]

EARLY STATES IN THE VALLEY OF OAXACA (C. 500 B.C.–200 B.C.)

The rise of early states in Oaxaca paralleled that in the Valley of Mexico in many ways. Many years of intensive survey, for example, have shown that the settlement patterns changed from one in which small villages predominated to one in which villages proliferated in number but were also complemented by larger towns and villages.[42]

Richard Blanton notes that shortly after about 500 B.C., Oaxaca experienced at least the following transformations: (1) population density increased at a more rapid rate than in any previous period; (2) agricultural intensification in the form of canal irrigation became important; (3) pottery manufacture became specialized and perhaps was part of the Valley's first market system; and (4) the settlement at Monte Albán, on a high plateau in the center of the Valley, grew to become a major regional center.[43] Blanton has argued that the capital at Monte Albán was founded in an unpopulated area between various important settlements as an expression of a new confederation between people who previously may have been linked by rather low-level social and economic ties.[44]

Blanton and his colleagues estimate that Monte Albán grew from an unoccupied, waterless mountain top to a great religious and political complex of 5,000 people in fewer than 200 years.[45] To accomplish this rate of increase, they suggest, people would have had to move up from settlements in the valley to their new home on the plateau, and agriculture in the valley and piedmont would have had to be intensified to support the town.

By 200 B.C. the population of Monte Albán reached about 17,000—a great city, by ancient standards. Agriculture was intensified around Monte Albán as well, and rural population densities soared. Craft specialization in pottery and other commodities was sharpened, and the location and products of kilns indicate some degree of regional administrative control, although Blanton concludes that Monte Albán itself remained mainly a ceremonial center with few economic functions.[46]

One of the main plaza buildings at Monte Albán contains a gallery of carved stone reliefs whose main theme seems to be the commemoration of military conquests. Scores of bodies are depicted with open mouths, closed eyes, and blood streaming from them in flowery patterns.[47] These depictions have many parallels in themes around the ancient world, such as in the Egyptian "Narmer Palette" (chapter 9).

In succeeding centuries, population densities and settlement patterns varied considerably, but the investments in monumental architecture, the hierarchical arrangements of towns in terms of the distribution of goods and services, and other markers of cultural complexity persisted and became more elaborate. Thus, by 200 B.C. or shortly thereafter, a state, by almost any definition, appears to have been operating in Oaxaca.

It may be overstating the case to say that by 200 B.C. we have also moved from prehistory to history in Mesoamerica, but the engraved signs and symbols at Oaxaca and elsewhere in Mexico seem to be well on the way to the development of a true writing system.

Although the rough outlines of Oaxacan cultural history have been established, scholars argue about what forces determined this history. Sanders and Nichols stressed the importance of irrigation agriculture and population growth as factors in the valley's florescence.[48] Kowalewski and Feinstein, in a lengthy assessment of the development of economic systems in Oaxaca, conclude that much of this "economic variation was largely determined by the changing functions and degrees of chiefly or state power."[49] They reconstruct a situation in which the power and predilections of elites changed, and with them the permeability of the borders of Oaxacan political systems.[50]

THE MAYA

*In Mexico the gods ruled, the priests interpreted and
interposed, and the people obeyed. In Spain, the priests ruled,
the king interpreted and interposed, and the gods obeyed.
A nuance in an ideological difference is a wide chasm.*

Richard Condon

At about the same time the civilization of Teotihuacán was developing in the Valley of Mexico, Maya civilization was emerging in southern Mexico, Guatemala, Belize, and Honduras.

Early Maya civilization may have been influenced to some minor degree by Teotihuacán, but it was largely its own creation. The Maya devised a complex writing system, built temples and palaces that are spectacularly beautiful monumental constructions, and they are thought to have organized vast areas and many peoples in a series of independent states. The Maya have traditionally been considered a civilization without cities, but Maya centers such as Tikal and Dzibilchaltun had thousands, perhaps tens of thousands, of people in permanent residence[51]—although these settlements never attained the population or physical size of Teotihuacán, and they had less diversity in residential architecture and perhaps less occupational specialization than existed in Teotihuacán or Oaxaca at a comparable time.

It is difficult to fault archaeologists who spend most of their time excavating the spectacular Maya ceremonial centers instead of surveying the snake-infested jungles for the rural settlements that supported these centers, but the result is that we still know comparatively little about regional economic and demographic aspects of the Maya. Much valuable work has recently been done,[52] however, and the general picture is much clearer than previously.[53]

Much of the Maya homeland is hot, semitropical forest, but large areas are highlands created by a string of snow-capped volcanoes that extend from southeastern Chiapas toward lower Central America. In the highlands volcanic ash and millennia of wind and water erosion have created a rich thick layer of soil spread over a convoluted landscape of ravines, ridges, and valleys. Hard seasonal rains make this a fairly productive agricultural zone.

The tropical lowlands at the steamy heart of Maya civilization cover the Petén and the Yucatan Peninsula, a massive limestone shelf lifted out of the seas over millions of years by tectonic movements. The land is rugged toward the southern part of the Petén, but most of the peninsula is flat. There are few rivers or lakes because the porous limestone quickly drains away surface water.

The lowland climate is hot and humid for most of the year, but drought can be a severe problem because the rainfall is seasonal and localized. In early spring a period of drought sets in, and the agricultural cycle slows. Trees are burned to open fields for crops, and the land dries. In May and June the rains begin, and the lowland landscape is transformed into a riot of life as plants green and animals multiply.

Recent research has revealed large irrigation systems in some Maya areas and, during at least some periods, permanent field agriculture with annual cropping, which was probably very important economically in the lowlands. In much of the Maya area, the fields used for maize, beans, squash, tomato, and pepper cultivation must be fallow for four to eight years after about three years of production. But even with this restriction, the Maya homeland was sufficiently productive that some estimates of the land's carrying capacity on the basis of traditional swidden agriculture indicate that they were capable of supporting up to sixty to eighty people per square kilometer.[54]

Studies of contemporary Maya cultivators have been summarized by Matheny and Gurr, and when all the evidence of canals, raised fields, botanical remains from sites, and other data are considered, it is clear that permanent-field, intensified agriculture, not swidden agriculture, must be seen as the basis for Maya civilization.[55] Most peasant cultivators use animals, whether wild or domestic, to convert brush and hedgerow vegetation into usable form, and the small Yucatec deer—which was intensively hunted—apparently filled this role in the Maya lowlands, along with domestic dogs, rabbits, and wildfowl. The Maya were sophisticated farmers who blended field cultivation with a form of tropical-forest management in which they were able to use foods from both in a complementary, productive, and highly stable way.[56] Dennis Puleston suggested that the nuts of the ramón tree were an especially important food in this system, but archaeological research has turned up little evidence that these nuts were an important part of the diet—except perhaps as a starvation food.[57] Since the Maya clearly were masters at exploiting the many plants and animals of their forest environment, this brings into question most ideas about the "collapse" of Maya civilization, which rest on the assumption that the Maya over-stressed their environments.

Maya Ideology In Karl Marx's somewhat self-contradictory and ambivalent view, state religions were seen almost as by-products of state economies. He saw religions as ideologies that evolved as a way of legitimizing state authority and of controlling the masses after the real causes of state-formation—changes in the economic and technological base of the society—had produced the socioeconomic classes and governmental structures of states.

The case of the Maya, however, is one of many in history where one might argue for the primacy of the *idea* of the state. The great agricultural productivity of the Maya area was, of course, the base of Maya civilization and not only provided its energy but shaped its culture. But little about Maya civilization seems understandable apart from their ideas of the divinity of kings and the nature of the cosmos.

It is a truism, a cliché, that we can really never fully enter into the ideology of another culture, whether that cultural ideology be the "dream time" of the Australian aborigines, the Marxist-Confucian ethos of modern China, or the spirit world of the ancient Maya. And, unfortunately, much of a culture makes little "sense" unless one can share the cultural perspective from which it derived. This is particularly true of the Maya, whose beautiful monuments and intricate written language derive from a world and life view that is in so many ways fundamentally different from our own. So, we can only *try* to see the world and time through the perspective of other cultures—try to get some sense of the fundamental ideas that bound people together in time and place and community.

More than many people, the Maya seemed to bear the burden of history in that they were, as Linda Schele and David Friedel note, "preoccupied with demonstrating historical action as the inevitable result of cosmic and ancestral necessities."[58]

For the Maya, the world manifested itself in two complementary dimensions—one in which they lived out their lives, the other (the Otherworld) in which gods, ancestors, and other supernatural beings existed—that were inextricably locked together.[59] The Maya apparently saw their dimension as three layered domains, "the starry arch of heaven, the stony Middleworld of earth made to flower and bear fruit by the blood of kings, and the dark waters of the Underground below."[60] The Maya believed that these three regions were interrelated, that shamans and others, for example, could penetrate the Underground world via ecstatic trances. Above all, in the sky, was a great crocodilian monster who "made the rains when it shed its blood in supernatural counterpoint to the royal sacrifices on the earth below."[61] The human world was envisioned as floating in a primordial sea, and was sometimes represented as the back of a caiman (a crocodile-like animal) or a turtle. These various interrelated worlds and planes of existence, including the earth, were imbued by the gods with a sacredness that was especially concentrated at special points, such as caves and mountains. As Schele and Freidel note:

> The principal pattern of power points had been established by the gods when the cosmos was created. Within this matrix of sacred landscapes, human beings built communities that merged with the god-generated patterns and created a second human-made matrix of power points. These two systems were perceived to be complementary, not separate. . . . [The] world of human beings was connected to the Otherworld along the *wacah chan* ["six sky," or "raised up sky"—a tree-like axis whose base was in the watery underworld and whose top was in the highest heavens of the Otherworld] which ran through the center of existence. This axis was not located in any one earthly place, but could be materialized through ritual at any point in the natural and human-made landscape. Most important, it was materialized in the person of the king, who brought it into existence as he stood enthralled in ecstatic visions atop his pyramid-mountain."[62]

Through proper ritual, the Maya believed that the power points on the earthly plane, whether they be places, people, or objects, could be intensified and become charged with accumulated energy. Kings, for example, rebuilt temples on the same spot time after time, thereby compounding the sacred power within them.

"Blood-letting" was a "focus ritual of Maya life."[63] The Maya believed that beings of the Otherworld could be materialized through the ritual shedding of blood. Men are shown in inscriptions using obsidian blades and other implements to pierce their tongues or penises, and women are shown piercing their tongues. Through blood-letting one could, in a sense, give "birth" to a god or ancestor, enabling it to materialize in physical form on the earthly plane of existence. Ritual blood-letting apparently was practiced not just by elites and priests but even by lowly peasant farmers in remote villages.

Like many other cultures, the Maya rationalized and justified the great inequities of wealth, power, and prestige in their society by setting these inequities in a divine context. The king and his relatives *deserved* their wealth and power because the king was the pinnacle of the population and it was through him that contact could be made with the sacred, the Otherworld. Every Maya, from highest to lowest, benefited from the king's intercession with the divine world, and they all shared in the material wealth that the king provided the community through successful performance of his powers.[64]

Like most early states, the Maya appear to have been strongly patriarchal—if the sex of people commemorated in royal inscriptions accurately reflects this society. But Maya royalty included women of high status. As Joyce Marcus notes,[65] an inscribed stela records an occasion in which a royal woman from Calakmul improved the prestige of a particular lineage at El Perú by marrying the local ruler, who was socially beneath her.

To the modern mind, the entire Maya world and life view may seem bizarre and to represent a patent misunderstanding of how the cosmos operates. But by means of their ideology, the Maya in a sense invented a civilization. In terms of their technology the Maya never advanced much past that of any Neolithic farming culture, but as Schele and Freidel observed, "They invented ideas that harnessed social energy. . . . They invented political symbols that transformed and coordinated such age-old institutions as the extended family, the village, the shaman, and the patriarch into the stuff of civilized life."[66]

Thus Maya civilization was as much an idea as a physical manifestation in towns and villages, farms and monuments. The beginnings of Maya ideology and its physical manifestations go back deep into the Mesoamerican past.[67]

A few traces of evidence about the predecessors of the Maya—or perhaps their genetic ancestors—have been found in what are termed *Archaic* sites, such as at Coha in Belize. The hunter-foragers who lived here, probably shortly before about 1000 B.C., seem very similar to Archaic hunters elsewhere in the Americas, but they were supplanted by farmers who apparently lived at low population densities from about 1000 B.C. onwards, subsisting on slash-and-burn farming. Another early Maya agricultural community was at Cuello, in Belize, where between about 1200 B.C. and 900 B.C.[68] a small hamlet of people farmed maize and used pottery—in other words, formed the kind of village community that was the basic socioeconomic building block of all later Maya culture. As David Pendergast observed, the differences between these Archaic period occupations, which show no or few traces of Maya culture, and the "full-blown" Maya forms evident in ceramic designs, house architecture, etc., in the early occupations at Cuello constitute a "monumental gap in both time and in cultural evolution between early occupation and the first known Maya remains."[69]

By 800 B.C. agricultural hamlets were scattered all over the lowlands and parts of the highlands of the Maya world. If these villages were anything like the contemporary Maya villages that look very much like them, these people lived in small, egalitarian groups, and communicated with other villages only by means of hand-to-hand trade in basic foodstuffs and tools, marriage exchange, and a few other sociopolitical links. Fleas may have plagued them,[70] and seasonal droughts probably occasionally starved them, but extended families in small villages remained the primary social fabric of the Maya areas for many millennia.

Thus, for the earliest Maya, as with the many other cultures we have considered in this book, we come back to some basic and difficult questions. Why and how did kings, priests, writing, pyramid-building, and all the other facets of ancient civilization arise out of these unprepossessing communities of farmers? For most Westerners it is difficult to rid one's mind of the assumption that "civilization" is the "natural" outcome of agricultural life and that complex societies will somehow develop out of societal competition, individual strivings, the accumulation of technological advances, and other factors in all environments (except for those in areas such as the Arctic, where there simply are not enough people and not enough food and wealth to be expropriated). But archaeology shows us many examples of cultures that did not automatically progress to "civilizations," even in environments where it would seem technically possible for them to have done so (e.g., aboriginal Australia).

The early agricultural economy of the Maya shows that it had the potential for at least one of the major common denominators of all ancient civilizations: agricultural production of sufficient quantity and diversity that it could be intensified, administered, and expropriated.

The Preclassic Maya (1000 B.C.–A.D. 300)   One direct stimulus to the development of Maya civilization appears to have been the migration of people from the periphery of the Maya areas into the core areas of the lowlands and highlands between about 1000 B.C. and A.D. 600. Archaeological time scales are usually coarse-grained enough that we cannot easily discriminate rapid population growth from migrations, but, as in Mesopotamia, it appears as if there was something happening in these core Maya areas that drew people into them.

William Rathje argued that a major stimulus to Maya development was trade in obsidian, stone, and salt.[71] Others have argued that there probably was no need to trade for these commodities in most of the Maya area.[72]

The discovery that the Maya had intensive permanent-field agriculture with canals, reservoirs, and moats has led some to conclude that irrigation agriculture was a powerful stimulus of Maya developments;[73] some Maya canals are an impressive 1.6 kilometers in length, 30 meters in width, and 3 meters deep. We do not know how many such irrigation systems remain undiscovered in the tropical forests of the Maya lowlands, and thus cannot estimate how important they may have been in the evolution of Maya cultural complexity, or even what the water carried by the canals was used for. Matheny proposed that they were used for drinking water, irrigation water for small garden plots, and as a source of mud for renewing soil fertility, and Marvin Harris suggested that irrigation to grow two crops a year may have also been part of the motivation for these projects.[74]

Another critical stimulus to the development of Maya civilization was the evolution of the central elements of Maya ideology, although we will probably never fully understand when and where this occurred. One element may have been the growing Maya belief that dead ancestors could be conduits for power from the Otherworld and that their relationship to the dead extended beyond just their immediate families. All early states appear to have made a transition wherein people began thinking of themselves as belonging to entities that extended far beyond the immediate family. The first suggestions we have that these changes were underway are found in burial practices: like ancient Chinese, Mesopotamians, and many others, the early Maya farmers buried their closest relatives under their house floors, perhaps to retain in some remote way the intimacy of family connections to house and home, and to lay claim forever to the land of their ancestors. At about 600 B.C., however, some Maya, such as those at K'axob,[75] began burying their dead in the core of large stone and earth platforms—which themselves are an architectural reflection of important changes occurring in these formerly simple small villages.

Some of the first great stone Maya buildings, such as pyramids and platforms, appeared in the Maya area just after about 800 B.C. (at the site of Komchen, for example). For the Maya as for many other ancient civilizations, monumental architecture appears as one of the first signs of the transformation of the society. Between 600 B.C. and 400 B.C. people at Nakbe[76] and other sites built lovely stone and masonry buildings on huge platforms and depicted gods and ancestors on building façades, stelae, masks, and other objects. If the people of Nakbe and other Preclassic Maya communities were already enmeshed in the formal Maya theology that we know from the later Maya, they probably regarded these buildings as important points from which to tap into the power of the cosmos and amplified their sacredness by building and rebuilding these impressive complexes.

The largest Preclassic Maya community was El Mirador, in the jungles of the Guatemalan part of the Petén—an area so remote that even though the site had been sighted from an airplane in the 1930s, its inaccessibility prevented exact location and excavation until the 1970s. El Mirador is remarkable for its early dates, its massive size, and its anticipation of many core elements of later Classic Maya culture—including pyramid complexes, stucco mask representations of Maya gods, and Maya writing. Some of the earliest examples of Maya writing have been found here in the form of an inscribed pot sherd and inscribed symbols on stone sculpture.

Richard Hansen and Donald Forsyth have also found here some of the earliest Maya ceremonial complexes yet reported,[77] including several pyramidal mounds eighteen to twenty-eight meters high which appear to date to between 600 B.C. and 300 B.C. Between about 150 B.C. and A.D. 50 the people of El Mirador built hundreds of large stone constructions, including buildings, pyramids, plazas, and causeways. The

"Tigre" complex, for example, includes a pyramid that rises more than fifty meters above the jungle floor, set amidst a temple and other buildings.

Most of these buildings were coated with a white plaster and then painted deep red.[78] To modern aesthetics the great stone buildings of the Maya, the Greeks, Egyptians, and others have an elegant and simple beauty in their natural light stone colors, but ancient peoples undoubtedly had different aesthetic preferences, and they probably also painted their buildings in primary colors for cultic and ideological reasons, and not primarily, if at all, because of aesthetic preferences.

Cerros Shortly before about 50 B.C. at Cerros, where the New River, which runs through the eastern part of the Yucatán Peninsula, empties into Chetumal Bay, the Maya established a small community of farmers, fishermen, and traders. At this time Cerros was unremarkable, just one of the hundreds of others like it in the Petén. But within the space of two generations, perhaps forty or fifty years, the people of Cerros experienced a revolution: "The Coming of Kings." As Linda Schele and David Freidel note, this transition appears to have been so rapid that many individuals probably personally experienced the transition from life in a simple village to one in which they became citizens of a large ceremonial city, living amid great stone temples, plazas, and other monuments, and initiated into the full ideology of the Maya world and life view.[79] We will never know exactly what happened to effect this transformation at Cerros, but the archaeological evidence suggests that this was a conscious reformulation of a community: they apparently broke their pottery, jade ornaments, and other objects into small bits and scattered them over their simple houses, buried flowers and other talismanic objects in the rubble, and then proceeded to build a new, vastly larger community around and over the remains of their abandoned village. They began by building a temple at the water's edge (edges in the natural world were places of power in the Maya view[80]) and then proceeded to build a large complex of temples, plazas, pyramids, stairways, causeways, and other monuments—all laid out on the axis that connected this world to the other planes of reality (see above). Decorating many of these structures were stucco representations of the gods. Artisans made these by applying wet plaster to a wall and modeling the plaster, as well as some appliqué pieces, into extremely complex designs. Few if any of these designs were actual texts, but they can be read and they portray complex Maya religious ideas. On one temple, for example, representations of the Jaguar Sun God on a south-facing wall would, when lighted by the sun, present the sun "rising" on the east side of the wall and "setting" on the west side as the sun made its daily trek across the sky. Based on later texts at other sites, we can get a sense of what the Maya were trying to express here, but the profundities of this ideology will never be entirely understood.

Despite all its beauty and magic, Cerros declined and all but disappeared as a community after only a few generations of glory—another example of a fundamental rhythm of Maya political history, in which small communities all over their world were rapidly transformed into great gleaming ceremonial settlements, home to tens of thousands of people, only to fade and die in a relatively short time. Where many of the greatest Old World cities, such as Memphis in Egypt and Warka in Mesopotamia, counted their histories of dominance in millennia, most Mesoamerica centers ruled their particular worlds for only 400 to 600 years at most.

The Classic Maya (A.D. 300–A.D. 900)   As we have seen in the case of the Harappan (Indus Valley) and Halafian (Mesopotamian) ceramics, the spread of a distinctive, uniform artifact style over large areas often precedes rapid and fundamental cultural change. By about A.D. 1, a distinctively styled pottery was in use over the entire 250,000 square kilometers of the Maya lowlands, and pyramids, platforms, and other large public buildings were being constructed at Yaxun, Dzibilchaltun, Uaxactún, and elsewhere. Between A.D. 300 and A.D. 900, Maya civilization reached its climax as hundreds of beautiful pyramids, temples, and other buildings were completed, and painting and sculpture flourished.

The first part of this period corresponds to the florescence of Teotihuacán, and some see the Maya as developing principally under Teotihuacán's stimulus.[81] Trade between the Maya area and Teotihuacán probably occurred, but much of Maya development was autonomous and distinctive. After A.D. 600, when Teotihuacán rapidly began to lose influence and population, the Maya began a three-hundred-year period of intense development. Hundreds of temple complexes were constructed and beautiful stone sculptures executed—many dated and inscribed.

But despite these material indications of their brilliant achievements, the Maya peoples themselves seem to have lived much as their ancestors had. They still had not aggregated in cities, and although thousands of people must have cooperated to construct these great complexes, most still lived in small undifferentiated rural hamlets. Stephen Houston has used archaeological evidence and interpretations of Maya writing to estimate that most Maya polities were organized within areas of seventy kilometers diameter or less—with most of the settlements within a day's walk of the major center.[82] These dispersed agricultural hamlets were grouped around small ceremonial centers that included a small temple pyramid and a few other stone constructions. Several districts of small ceremonial centers were congregated around the major ceremonial centers of Tikal, Uaxactún, Palenque, Uxmal, and other sites. By this time much of southern Mesoamerica featured beautiful, gleaming, white limestone pyramids and temples that were surrounded by marvelously executed stone sculptures and decorated with wall paintings.

Most centers also had ball courts made of stucco-faced rock. We know little about how the ball game was played.[83] Apparently the objective of the game, played by two opposing teams, was to try to get a rubber ball through a goal, probably not by throwing or batting it, but by using knees, elbows, or torso. The ball apparently could not be held in the hands when it was in play. As played by the Mesoamericans, this game was not a sport: the ball may have represented the sun, and the court and play were imbued with ritual and cosmological imagery. Losing players were sometimes executed. A relief panel from a ball court at El Tajín, in Veracruz, Mexico, shows the captain of the losing team being stretched out over a sacrificial stone while the victor drives a knife into his chest.[84] Maya representations of this ball game show a ball that, if the proportions are correct, would be larger than a basketball, but the Maya may have simply been exaggerating these representations to focus attention on the ball.

John Fox has argued that these ball courts were imbued with great and complex ideological and social significance, and that they were the focus of feasts, competitions, and other rituals that provided "strategic settings for the negotiations of power relations. These rituals centered on the redistribution of food and wealth and the symbolic renewal of agricultural fertility;" and he concludes that these ball courts, as places with "supernatural associations, served as [stages] for rituals in which political conflict was mapped onto and resolved through cosmological drama."[85]

The kingdom of Copán,[86] one of the many Maya centers that flourished from about A.D. 600 to A.D. 800, was located in the southeastern highlands of the Maya world, far (about seventy kilometers) from other Maya centers and (at about 600 m elevation)—one of the highest major Maya communities. It was probably a world unto itself in many ways. Peasant farmers settled this rich valley after 1100 B.C., and in succeeding centuries their population grew and they began to show signs of social stratification in the wealth of burials and individual residences. Between about 300 B.C. and A.D. 150, however, Copán, for no obvious reasons, seems to have been radically depopulated. But by about A.D. 200, population was again on the rise and construction had started on some of the city's great monuments, including the "acropolis," a complex of buildings about 160 meters on a side. Again, there are no obvious reasons for this florescence. Three later kings recorded December 18, A.D. 159 as a critical date in the history of the community, but we do not know what actually happened on this date. In the centuries between about A.D. 600 and A.D. 800, most of the people of Copán (which probably featured a population of about 25,000–30,000 at its peak) lived in an oasis-like forty-kilometer stretch of fertile river valley hemmed in by largely unpopulated mountains. At the heart of this area was a royal compound of plazas, temples, palaces, and other buildings.

Although Copán was perhaps a largely self-contained community, it participated in the greater Maya world in various ways. According to one inscription, the mother of Yax Pac, one of the city's rulers, was from a royal family in the Maya center of Palenque, which was about 400 kilometers to the northwest. But wars of conquest and political conflicts seem to have been a more frequent form of contact with the outside world. The ruler of Copán between A.D. 628 and A.D. 695 was Smoke-Imix-God K, who brought Copán to its greatest glory. He placed five stelae as boundary markers to define the core sacred territory of Copán, and dominated the nearest neighboring Maya center, at Quiriguá. His successor, 18-Rabbit, created a cosmopolitan community through migrations of non-Maya peoples from what is now the central region of Honduras, and by commissioning many beautiful works in sculpture and architecture.

The French king Louis XIV said: "Every time I appoint someone to a position, I make one ungrateful person and a hundred with a grievance." The unfortunate 18-Rabbit would no doubt have agreed with that sentiment. Just as Copán was entering a period of great artistic florescence and expansion of political power, 18-Rabbit was captured in battle and sacrificed at Quiriguá, on May 3, A.D. 738, by Cauac-Sky—whom 18-Rabbit himself had installed as lord of Quiriguá.[87]

The decline of Copán is yet another example of what seems to be a basic pattern in many early civilizations—a decline that seems to have had some basic economic causes, but which probably seemed to be the result of war, conflict, and the loss of the favor of the gods to the people who lived during the period of collapse. The massive expansion of Copán's monumental architecture quickly covered some of the best farm lands in the central river valley, and as farmers tried to extend their fields up the slopes of encroaching mountains they would have seen productivity fall and erosion increase. Sculptures and inscriptions on an altar dedicated to the last king of Copán were begun but never finished. And as Schele and Freidel note:

> The people simply walked away. Within two centuries of the demise of the last king of Copán, 90 percent of the population in the Copán Valley was gone. They left a land so ravaged that only in this century have people returned to build the population back to the levels it knew in the time of Yax-Pac [who died May 6, A.D. 820].[88]

Tikal and Uaxactún[89]   Tikal and Uaxactún, two great Classic Maya communities, provide in their individual elements and the history of their relationship to each other both an illustration of all the essential elements of Maya civilization and also an object lesson regarding the political history of early states in many parts of the world.

Tikal and Uaxactún are located about forty miles south of El Mirador in the hot lowland jungles of the Petén, and much of their destiny was determined by the fact that they were built only about twelve miles apart: much of the social interactions of the ancient world were determined by the distance a person could walk in a day or so—distances that linked cultures in conflict and cooperation—and Tikal and Uaxactún were less than a day's walk for both traders and soldiers. In the end, it was the soldiers whose efforts shaped most of the history of these communities.

Tikal originated at about 600 B.C. in the form of a small farming village set on a small hill in the middle of a swamp. Simple peasants these people may have been, but in one of the burials of this period a severed human head was placed next to the corpse of a man—perhaps an anticipation of the ritual decapitation of later Maya court rituals. Over succeeding centuries the people of Tikal built one of the greatest ceremonial centers of the New World. Temple I at Tikal, built about A.D. 700, captures much of the architectural brilliance of the Maya. In previous centuries the people of Tikal had covered the original village with a massive complex of temples, plazas, causeways—all the standard elements of Maya ceremonial centers, but realized in particularly beautiful form. Well-preserved tombs at Tikal included the bodies of kings and elites and rich offerings of pottery, food, stingray spines, and other goods. One of the richest tombs, Burial 85, contained a headless and thighless body wrapped in a cinnebar-impregnated bundle along with a marine shell and a stingray spine—common tools in ritual bloodletting. Schele and Friedel suggest that the Maya may have kept some of the bones of dead kings as relics and talismans; they also note that the bodies of kings and elites show that they were larger and more robust than the commoners of this community.[90]

Computer simulations have been used to suggest that as many as 77,000 people may have lived in Tikal's immediate environs at its peak,[91] and probably 300,000 or more people lived in the entire 965 square miles that this center dominated.

Uaxactún's florescence generally paralleled that of Tikal, and by about A.D. 320 they were both the centers of large, powerful kingdoms. Then an extraordinary Tikal king named Great-Jaguar-Paw ascended the throne, and on January 16, A.D. 378, he conquered Uaxactún and installed a warrior from Tikal named Smoking-Frog as ruler. These names may sound somewhat comic to the modern ear, but there was nothing comical about these people or their wars of conquest. As Schele and Freidel note, before the ascension of Great-Jaguar-Paw, Maya warfare had a personal, almost formal quality: the Maya fought not to kill their enemies but to capture them, usually in hand-to-hand combat, so that the captured ruler and nobles could be carried back to the victorious city to be tortured and sacrificed in public rituals. But Great-Jaguar-Paw fought a war not of stylized, formalized combat aimed at taking captives for sacrifice for personal glory. Instead, he fought a war of conquest when he attacked Uaxactún:

> This was war on an entirely different scale, played by rules never before heard of and for stakes far higher than reputations or lives of individuals. In this new warfare of death and conquest, the winner would gain the kingdom of the loser.[92]

Great-Jaguar-Paw and his warriors not only physically killed the Uaxactún elites, they killed this community spiritually, cutting off the people from the guidance and protection of their ancestors and gods.

Tikal and Uaxactún were two of the most prominent Classic Maya communities, but there were many others of interest. Some of the greatest of all known Maya frescoes are at Bonampak, dating to the end of the eighth century A.D. Here, in several rooms of murals, the paintings tell a story of warfare, torturing of prisoners of war, and celebration. The carefully drawn murals, which depict mutilated bodies, marching bands, richly dressed figures, and men with weapons, convey an extraordinarily vivid sense of militarism, royalty, and religion. Mary Ellen Miller has argued that these scenes are in part a depiction of raids to take prisoners. Unfortunately, these murals have been obscured by seepage through the composite limestone, so that they are only clearly visible when they are splashed with water or kerosene.[93]

Themes of military triumph, the torture of captives, and the power of the ruling classes were also commonly depicted in bas-relief sculpture throughout the Classic period—even in the Valley of Oaxaca and the peripheral areas of the Maya sphere of influence. Individuals of presumably higher status were juxtaposed in stone carvings with persons of lower status, and differences of dress, bearing, and position sharpened the contrast. In some cases, representations of prisoners were carved into the facings of stone steps, so that they were trod on by the nobility—a not too subtle visual pun.[94]

Maya Political Organization   Scholars have advanced several different competing ideas about the political organization of the Maya. Joyce Marcus,[95] for example, has suggested that the various Maya centers constituted a political hierarchy, with some royal families at particular centers being more powerful and prestigious than others, but with these various dynasties linked through marriage alliances and other ties. Stephen Houston, however, challenges this view, suggesting that the "Maya Lowlands may have consisted not only of centralized polities, with control some 30 km in any direction, but of 'buffer zones' in which smaller polities switched allegiance at will while remaining essentially independent. . . . Yet other areas may have been politically 'neutral' centers of pilgrimage."[96]

Edward Schortman and Patricia Urban[97] have argued that the "core-periphery" relationships among the Late Classic Maya were perhaps more complex than has traditionally been thought. They examined the relationship of Maya communities on the periphery of the central Maya lowlands to centers such as Copán and Quirigua, and concluded that these relationships varied depending on whether one considers politics, economy, or ideology. They suggest that despite the signs of great military domination by the most powerful communities in the central Maya area, no community could dominate to the extent that there was severe inter-regional exploitation in all dimensions of these relationships.

These and other views of how the Maya were organized politically raise fundamental questions about the nature of human societies in general. From the perspective of our own world and time we can look back and see the cultures of the world inexorably being linked closer and closer and ever more intensively. The United Nations, the European Common Market, and other political and commercial organizations now affect the flow of goods and ideas in even the most distant corners of the world. But this long-term evolutionary pattern has been a fitful one, with frequent reversals and great variations through time and space. And it is not clear that increasing complexity in these forms of organization is necessary or even "good." The various foreign conquests of the ancient Greek city-states, for example, are traditionally attributed to the Greeks' apparent inability to forge durable commercial, military, and political ties and unite against their aggressors, but this lack of unity did not seem to cripple these cultures intellectually—quite the opposite, in fact, when we consider their cultural contributions.

Basic geography certainly seems to explain part of the differences in level of political organization that we see in the ancient world. The Maya, like the Greeks, did not have the easy transport and communication channel that the Nile provided the ancient Egyptians, for example. And the Maya did not have the domestic horses and donkeys that allowed Middle Eastern societies to move goods, people, and information across a complex and vast social landscape. As discussed in chapter 7, ancient civilizations are in essence *ideas*: Maya ideology appears to have linked the many different centers that constituted this civilization, but there is little evidence that this ideological unity ever culminated in political or economic integration that extended beyond small regions.

Maya Writing   Maya writing is in many ways a more impressive achievement than their pyramids and temples. Fortunately, we have many Classic Maya texts in the form of inscriptions on stone and pottery, written in the same writing system as the "books" that followed 1,000 years later. These books consist of long strips of bark paper covered with a layer of plaster and folded like screens. Only a few of these "books" survive, but three are quite long and informative: the Dresden, Madrid, and Paris codices.

The sixteenth-century Spanish cleric Bishop Landa thought Maya writing (Figure 13.10) at first to be entirely alphabetic. Scholars quickly realized, however, that Maya writing was to be read in double columns, from left to right and from top to bottom, and by the turn of the last century Maya glyphs had been identified for the "zero" and "twenty" signs, the cardinal points of the compass, the basic colors, Venus, the months of the year, and the "Long Count," the system of reckoning by which the Maya figured how many years had elapsed since the beginning of their time.

cu-tz(u)
"turkey"

[bu] -lu-c(u)
"eleven"

tzu-l(u)
"dog"

cu-ch(u)
"burden"

chu-ca-h(a)
"to capture"

chi-kin-il
"West"

hu-ch(i)
"vulture"

ku-k(u)
"quetzal"

mu-t(i)
"omen"

mu-an-il
"Muan" (month)

m(o)-o-o
"macaw"

FIGURE 13.10 Some Mayan glyphs and the phonetic values assigned to them by Y. V. Knorosov. Research in the last two decades has shown that ancient Maya writing is a finely nuanced, beautiful orthography that probably records the entire spoken language of these people.

Unlike the case with Egyptian hieroglyphs and Mesopotamian cuneiform, Maya writing had to be deciphered without the aid of "parallel scripts"—that is, the expression of the same text in two different languages, one of which is known.[98] As noted in chapter 8, *phoneticization* is a key step in the evolution of a written language, for once the elemental sounds of the spoken language are represented by abstract characters, the complete language can be written. The Russian linguist Yuri Knorosov was the first to demonstrate that Maya writing was indeed a phonetic system, and since his initial translations, many inscriptions have been almost entirely translated.[99] Building on the work of Tatiana Proskouriakoff, Henrich Berlin, and Yuri Knorosov, a new generation of Mayanists has made great progress: David Stuart, Peter Mathews, Steve Houston, Karl Taube, James Fox, John Juteson, and Michael Coe are just some of the scholars of the past two decades whose combined efforts have shown that ancient Maya writing is a finely nuanced, beautiful orthography that probably records the entire spoken language of these people.[100]

Maya script is somewhat similar to Egyptian hieroglyphs (chapter 9) in that it includes a mixture of signs, some representing whole words or ideas, others expressing syllables, sounds, and determinatives that clarify meanings.

In the Middle East the first writings are almost unrelievedly economic, but in Mesoamerica the surviving documents are primarily calendrical and historical, recording, for example, when a temple was begun, when a king defeated a rival, and what lands were under the control of the state. About the dull details of maize and men, they seemed much less concerned.[101] Recently, however, the inscriptions on hundreds of ceramics have been translated, and they do provide a great deal of economic information. Michael Coe, Steve Houston, and others[102] have shown that these texts recorded such information as the class of vessels a particular pot belonged to, its methods of adornment, the contents (e.g., chocolate or flavored maize gruel[103]), and occasionally the person who made or owned the vessel and its contents. As Houston also notes, the inscribed dates for the birth, accession, death, and other primary events in the lives of elites offer at least a speculative basis for estimating basic anthropological data about life spans. Justifying the fulsomeness of inscriptions on headstones and mortuary monuments, Samuel Johnson said, "In lapidary inscriptions a man is not upon oath," and it may be that there is a fictional element in the life-histories recorded for elite Maya. But the inscriptions fit rather well with some anthropological data that indicate that the Maya rarely lived past fifty-five to sixty-five years.[104]

The Maya were sophisticated mathematicians. They used a base-twenty system in which they expressed the quantity thirty-nine, for example, as nineteen numbers after twenty, and the value sixty as three twenties.[105] They discovered the concept of zero and used a place-value notation system that allowed them to express numbers beyond 100,000,000. They had no way to express fractions in mathematical notation, but they computed the length of the solar year to 365.242000 days, compared to our own Gregorian calendar figure of 365.242500 days (the true value is approximately 365.242198 days). The Maya used two calendars. One was the familiar solar calendar in which a year equaled 365 days, but whereas we intercalate an extra day every four years to compensate for the year being actually 364.25 days long, the Maya blithely ignored this and let the seasons creep around the calendar. And in contrast to our system of twelve months of from twenty-eight to thirty-one days, the Maya had eighteen named months of twenty days each, with five days, which were considered highly unlucky, added to the end.

The second calendar (which may have been formulated by predecessors of the Maya) involved a 260–day year, composed by intermeshing the sequence of numbers from one to thirteen with twenty named days (Figure 13.11). These two calendars ran parallel, and thus every particular day in the 260–day calendar also had a posi-

FIGURE 13.11   One of the Maya calendars was calculated from the correlation of the numbers from one to thirteen and twenty named days.

tion in the solar calendar. The calendars' permutations are such that each named day would not reappear in the same position for 18,980 days, or fifty-two of our solar years. Every day on the Maya calendar had its omens, and activities were rigorously scheduled in accordance with their astrological significance.

In some of the later adaptations of the Maya calendar, it appears that people were named after the day on which they were born and could not marry if they shared a numerical coefficient (e.g., Mr. "8 deer" could not marry Ms. "8 flower").[106] The Maya were thoroughly attuned to these calendrical cycles and used them to schedule many aspects of daily live and ritual. The Maya's "zero day," from which they counted time (and which they perhaps believed was the date on which the world was created) was August 13, 3114 B.C. Contrary to some speculations, the Maya apparently did not believe the world will end on December 24, A.D. 2011, but this date does mark the point at which the Long Count will return to the symmetry of its beginning. Pacal, king of Palenque, predicted in one of his inscriptions that the eightieth Calendar Round of his accession will be celebrated on October 15, A.D. 4772 —a man who took the long view, indeed.[107]

The Postclassic Maya (c. A.D. 900–A.D. 1517)   For decades scholars have debated the "collapse" of Maya civilization. It is in part a Western view of the world to see periods of rise and collapse in nations' histories and to search for causes. But the collapse of states, ancient and modern, never seems easily explained, and this is especially true of the Maya.

"Collapse" in the sense of what happened to the Maya has many meanings, since hundreds of thousands of people who spoke Mayan and were the direct genetic descendants of the classic first millennium A.D. Maya were there to greet the first Europeans on their arrival in the sixteenth century. And as Andrews and others have noted, the "collapse" of the Maya may be more apparent than real. A decline in temple construction and in the production of lavish goods does not necessarily mean societal collapse. As we noted in the discussion of changes in Egypt and elsewhere in the ancient world, declines in certain kinds of "waste" seem to be more indicative of a changing economic basis and administrative structure than the destruction of a culture. Had the Spanish not arrived when they did, the people of the Maya areas might have been reformulated by time and circumstance into a larger, more powerful, nation-state.

But Classic Maya culture did change—it lost many of its most important elements, and many formerly great communities were abandoned. One of the last kings of the Maya, Can-Ek, ruler of Itzá, met Cortés as he and his expedition crossed the Petén in A.D. 1525. But Maya culture was in decline long before that. As Anthony Andrews notes:

> In the eighth and ninth centuries the Maya area was a densely populated mosaic of large and small city-states ruled by regal and ritual dynasties who oversaw the great achievements of what we now call Classic Maya Civilization. These polities were also crossing the threshold of their demographic and ecological limits, which when coupled with managerial shortcomings, warfare, and the breakdown of political structure, led to a spectacular process of societal collapse. Cities throughout the southern lowlands

were abandoned—some quickly . . . . Small populations survived in pockets . . . but for the most part they had severed their ties with the Classic past.[108]

Until about A.D. 910, the Maya usually accompanied any new monumental building with a stone stela engraved with the date of its construction, and thus we know that while many buildings were completed during the eighth and ninth centuries A.D., by A.D. 889 only three sites were under construction, and by about A.D. 900, construction seems to have ended for good. On the basis of ceramics and other information, we know that depopulation of the countryside and centers apparently followed quickly.

We know from inscriptions at Palenque, Dos Pilas, and other sites that the ninth century A.D. was a time of intense warfare and conquest, but there were also sporadic attempts to reestablish control and build communities in the ancient traditions. But the last king to erect a "tree-stone," a traditional royal inscription to celebrate the end of a calendrical cycle, did so on January 20, A.D. 909, and after that the Maya traditions in the southern lowlands contracted and all but disappeared in the next few centuries.

But in the northern lowlands the ninth and tenth centuries A.D. were a time of great expansion. Cities such as Chichén Itzá established empires that transcended in size and power those of the Classic period. Despite these periods of regional florescence and empire, however, Maya writing fell out of use, and with it, perhaps, the central ideology of the Maya world—the complex ideas about the universe and human affairs that melded these people into a culture and inspired them to build their civilization.

Shortly after A.D. 900 the Toltecs, a people whose culture was centered at Tula in the Valley of Mexico, apparently established feudal control over some areas of the Maya lowlands—an event that set off many years of internal dissension and local revolt. During this time various centers were built and some major population concentrations developed, but in terms of population density, construction projects, art styles, inscribed stelae, settlement patterns, and mortuary complexes, the power and glory of Maya culture began to fade.

Many factors have been suggested as causes of the collapse, and also the development, of Maya civilization, and new interpretations sporadically appear. Not surprisingly, many involve the ecology of the Maya homeland, which seems at first glance to be a major barrier to cultural evolution.

A traditional archaeological approach to explaining the development of something is to imagine a set of problems to which the development is a solution. We might ask, given the Maya environment, under what conditions would it have been advantageous to organize into larger political and social units? Perhaps the answer lies in the necessity of local exchange to meet the threat of drought, disease, or disturbance. Rainfall is quite variable within the Maya area, and many other factors can adversely affect each community's agricultural system. Because the communities were all so similar in the crops they grew and their techniques for growing them, a major drought, such as happens in this area every eight to ten years, could result in the starvation of many people in hundreds of hamlets. But this could be avoided if many villages established exchange networks that spread the risks. Each year earthquakes, droughts, disease, floods, warfare, or some other combination of calamities might wipe out some sectors of the subsistence system, but if a village belonged to an organization that included many hamlets, it could get help or give help, depending on its fortunes. Because of the inability to intensify agricultural production drastically in any one area, cities were, of course, out of the question. Similarly, population-control regulators were very important, hence the monumental construction projects in this most unlikely of places.

Whatever was at the root of the Maya cultural evolution, the collapse of this culture poses equally interesting questions. Warfare seems to have increased toward the end of the Maya period, and we might ask why it became more prevalent then and why the Maya were unable to fight off its effects at this time, after so many centuries of successful dealings among themselves and with their neighbors. No appreciable land shortages or overpopulation seem to have occurred, nor is there much evidence of foreign military pressures on these people.

We have argued that the evolution of Maya society could probably be tied to the necessity of spreading the "risk" of life in this area by integrating many different settlements under a centralized authority. But by the same token, such an integrated system might eventually have encountered a series of catastrophes and internal problems that were spaced so closely together and in such a sequence that their effects could not be successfully fought off. "Murphy's Law" stipulates that if anything can go wrong, it will. This is especially true for cultural systems spanning millennia. Earthquakes, disease, warfare, drought, crop disease—all have certain periodicities, and unfavorable conjunctions must necessarily arise if the system is sufficiently long-lived.

It is also possible that Maya civilization collapsed in bloody civil wars and class conflicts. As Lowe points out, coups d'etat are not exactly rare in Central America, and there have been some interesting mathematical analyses of the rate and direction of the Maya contraction that are not at variance with the ideas of a proletarian revolution.[109]

But the rather weak data we have from the Maya areas can be made to fit many different hypotheses about the source and kind of cultural changes involved. Many more years of patient research, especially through archaeological surveys of remote jungle lowland sites, will be required to reach any comprehensive understanding of the determinants of Maya cultural history.[110]

POST-CLASSIC MESOAMERICA (A.D. 900–A.D. 1524)

As Maya political power in the lowlands was beginning to wane, much of highland Puebla, Mexico, and Hildago was apportioned among several competing power centers. One group, the Toltecs, began to dominate the Valley of Mexico after about A.D. 900. According to Aztec legends (the Aztecs claimed descent from the Toltecs), the Toltecs came to central Mexico from northwestern Mexico. The desert plateaus of northwestern Mexico were for many millennia the home of the "Chichimeca," groups of nomadic hunter-foragers, and it is possible that some of these people migrated south and did, in fact, join with (or displace) local cultures to produce the

Toltec culture. One of the major centers of the Toltec polity was at Tula, just north of the Valley of Mexico. Shortly after about A.D. 900, the Toltec built two stone pyramids and a ball-court at Tula. On one of the pyramids they placed a temple dedicated to the Serpent god, Quetzalcóatl. On top of the pyramid (which is just over ten meters high) they placed stone statues of warriors, which are about 4.6 meters high, as supports for a temple, and these figures continue to dominate the site. The base of the pyramid is decorated with reliefs of prowling jaguars and coyotes and eagles eating hearts.[111]

The Toltecs established trade and military outposts in many areas of northern and western Mexico, and exported metal, gemstones, and other commodities as far north as Arizona and New Mexico. To the south, the Toltecs influenced and interacted with Chichén Itzá, a large Maya community of the northern lowlands that persisted after most of the other centers in the southern lowlands had been abandoned. The exact relationship between the Toltecs and the people of Chichén Itzá is unclear, however. The Toltecs may have dominated Chichén Itzá, or there may have been a fusion of the two cultures.

Chichén Itzá represents a major break in Maya cultural traditions. As Anthony Andrews notes, the community featured changes "in almost every aspect of Maya life, from household economics to large-scale shifts in the social, economic, and political structures of Maya society."[112] Toltec influences on Chichén Itzá may have contributed to these changes, in which the efficient political apparatus of Chichén Itzá allowed it to create one of the largest cities in Prehispanic Mesoamerica and to dominate most of the northern Maya lowlands and significantly influence most of the rest of the Maya world.[113]

Eventually, Toltec power weakened. Under the onslaught of the invading Chichimec from the north, the Toltecs broke up into many smaller, competitive groups. Tula itself was almost entirely destroyed by invaders at about A.D. 1156. Succeeding centuries saw the rise of various other cultural traditions in central Mexico, such as the Tarascan state.[114] Chichén Itzá also went into a period of decline, to be replaced by a loose confederation of provinces, called the "League of Mayapán," and the island of Cozumel, on Yucatan's east coast, which was a major trading center between A.D. 1250 and the arrival of the Spanish in A.D. 1519.[115] But by the time of the arrival of the Spanish, the community at Mayapán had been abandoned and the Maya areas were a welter of small chiefdoms at war with one another.[116]

One of the last tribes to invade central Mexico from the north and west was the Aztecs. Aztec histories and legends, as recorded by the Spanish, tell of their arrival in the Valley of Mexico as rag-tag foragers and primitive agriculturalists who at first were forced by the established residents of the valley to live in the swamps around the lake, subsisting on flies, snakes, and vermin. According to legend, rival political groups in the valley enlisted the Aztecs in their campaigns but avoided other contacts with them because of the Aztecs' predilections for human sacrifice and other barbarisms. At war with various groups, the Aztecs were forced to take refuge on islands in the lake where, according to legend, they built their first city, Tenochtitlán (Figure 13.12). In time Tenochtitlán grew to become a massive complex of pyramids, courts, and other buildings (now largely buried beneath the streets of Mexico City).

FIGURE 13.12   The most important Aztec cities were built around the lake that used to cover part of the Valley of Mexico. The lake margins were intensively farmed, and boats conveyed great quantities of food and craft products among these cities.

As allies of the Tepanec kingdom of Atzcapotzalco, the Aztecs conquered many of the surrounding cities, and at about A.D. 1427 they turned on their erstwhile allies and through savage warfare brought most of central Mexico under their control. Military expeditions conquered peoples all the way to the Guatemalan border, and garrison towns were established from the Pacific Coast to the Gulf of Mexico.

Although the Aztecs are usually associated with militarism, they also created an impressive civil and commercial administration. Between about A.D. 1300 and A.D. 1520 they drained large areas of the Valley of Mexico, transforming them into productive agricultural plots. Michael Smith has argued that the Valley of Mexico settlement pattern during Aztec times was a hierarchically-arranged marketing system of products with intense local specialization in goods and services.[117] Many commodities, including salt, reeds, fish, stone, cloth, various crops, ceramics, gold, and wood were exchanged among hundreds of communities (Figure 13.13). In fact, the improbable location of Tenochtitlán—on an island in the middle of the lake—is probably best understood in terms of its central role in these redistributive networks.[118] In A.D. 1519 Tenochtitlán is estimated to have had about 200,000 to 300,000 inhabitants, five times the population of London at that period, and there were many other

FIGURE 13.13 A Mexican tribute list (from the Codex Mendoza) describing the tribute paid to the government by towns in Guerrero Province. Among the commodities described are uniforms, shields, jade, gourds, sage, and amaranth.

large cities within the Aztec domain.[119] Many cities had broad avenues, causeways, temples, pyramids, and other large buildings, often interspersed with gardens, courtyards, and large markets.

It is estimated that between one and two million people lived in the Valley of Mexico in late Aztec times.[120] The lake provided great and reliable quantities of food in the form of fish, waterfowl, and salamanders. In the southern areas of the valley's lake system, maize, beans, squash, tomatoes, and other crops were grown on *chinampas*, long rectangular plots of ground created out of the lake bed by piling up layers of aquatic weeds, mud, human feces, garbage, and other materials. According to ancient documents, the Aztecs initially made the chinampas by braiding grass and reeds into thick mats that could float, and thus they were able to float entire fields from one place to another—an agricultural system unparalleled in the ancient world.[121] The Aztecs and their successors planted trees, including the *ahejote* (a kind of willow), that eventually anchored most plots. Farmers who still cultivate chinampas water the plots until they are the consistency of pudding and then use a rake to grid them into squares about an inch on a side. Seeds are placed in each square and covered with organic material to provide a greenhouse effect, and once the seedlings are at the proper size they are transplanted to other fields. As many as four crops per year can be grown on these exceptionally fertile plots of land.

The Aztecs were organized into a highly stratified class system headed by a divine king. Beneath the king were the nobles, the *pillitin*, all of whom belonged to the royal house, while the great mass of the populace were commoners who were organized in large clans, called *calpulli* ("big house"). The *calpulli* were the basic units of Aztec society. Each was composed of several lineages, totaling several hundred people, one of whom was designated the *calpule*, or leader. Members of a *calpulli* usually lived in the same village or ward, fought together as a unit if drafted for war, held and worked land in common, paid taxes as a unit, and worshipped at the shrine maintained by the *calpulli*. The leaders of the *calpulli* were the direct link between the imperial government and the people. There was also a class of professional merchants called *pochteca*.

The *calpulli* differed from one another in social rank. There was some social mobility for individuals—usually by virtue of extraordinary service to the state in warfare, trade, or religion. At the bottom of the social scale were the landless peasants and slaves, who worked the fields, performed other menial tasks, and were sacrificed in enormous numbers to various gods.

The Aztecs believed that the present world was just one in a succession of creations by the gods, and that constant effort was required to forestall the extinction of the sun and the utter disappearance of humanity. Human blood was an essential part of the ritual (Figure 13.14) whereby the end of the world was postponed, and each time a human heart was ripped from a sacrificed person, another small step was taken toward prolonging the daily rebirth of the sun.[122] At times long lines of sacrificial victims snaked down the steps of the major pyramid mounds, on the top of which priests spent hour after hour engaged in the bloody process of heart removal. After the heart and blood had been offered to the gods, the body was thrown down the steps of the pyramid and subsequently flayed and then, perhaps, eaten. Other victims slated for sacrifice were pitted in gladiatorial contests, or beheaded, or drowned, or

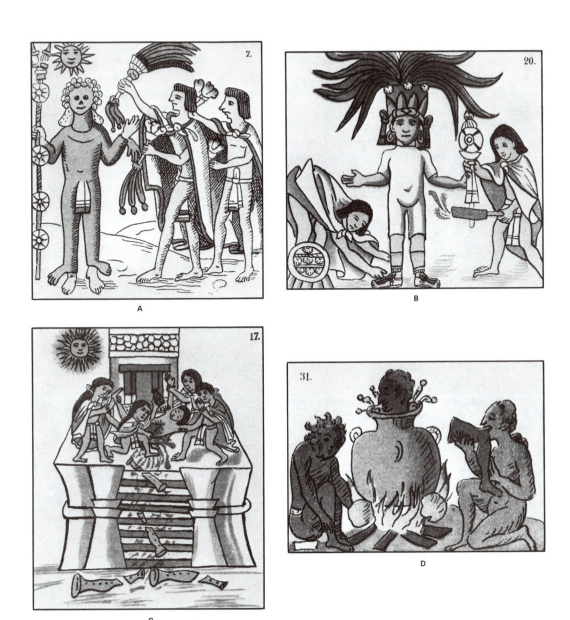

FIGURE 13.14 These early drawings (from the Codex Florentino) describe the sequence of ritual human sacrifice. (**A**) The priest is dressed in the skin of a sacrificed person; another person (**B**) was given a shield, mirror, and other ritual items and played the part of the god Tezcatlipoca; the individual was then sacrificed (**C**) and eaten (**D**).

cast into fires. The Spanish conquistadors may have exaggerated the numbers of peo-ple sacrificed, but it seems inescapable that the Aztecs annually killed many tens of thousands and perhaps hundreds of thousands of people. This slaughter was accepted by the common people; in fact, it seems to have been widely supported. All war cap-tives knew their fate, and it was an act of honor to accept a sacrificial death. In ad-dition, young men were selected each year to lead a life of luxury in which they were surrounded by complaisant young women and feasted on the best of food, realizing full well that at the end of the year they would be sacrificed. In addition, parents throughout the land turned over infants and children to government officials for use in annual sacrificial rites. One sixteenth-century (apparently) eye-witness account of the ritual execution of a woman who played the role of the goddess Uixtociuatl gives us a sense of what these rites may have been like:

> And after they had slain the captives, only [then] Uixtociuatl ['s impersonator] followed; she came only at the last. They came to the end and finished only with her.
> And when this was done, thereupon they laid her down upon the offering stone. They stretched her out upon her back. . . . They laid hold of her; they pulled and stretched out her arms and legs, bending [up] her breast greatly, bending down her head taut, toward the earth. And they bore down upon her neck with the tightly pressed snout of a sword fish, barbed, spiny, spined on either side.
> And the slayer stood there; he stood up. Thereupon he cut open her breast.
> And when he opened her breast, the blood gushed up high; it welled up far as it poured forth, as it boiled up.
> And when this was done, then he raised her heart as an offering [to the god] and placed it in the green jar, which was called the green stone jar.
> And as this was done, loudly were the trumpets blown. And when it was over, then they lowered the body and the heart of [the likeness of] Uixtociuatl, covered by a pre-cious mantle.[123]

Many of the sacrificial victims, as well as soldiers who died in battle, people struck by lightning, and mothers who died in childbirth, were thought to spend eternity in various paradises, cosseted with the pleasures of this world and the next.

With its emphasis on death, blood, and cosmic cataclysm, it is little wonder that Aztec theology struck the Spanish as somewhat heterodox (Figure 13.15). Even an-thropologists, renowned for their cultural relativism, are impressed with the violence of Aztec religion. But human sacrifice is an old and recurrent theme in the evolution of complex cultures: in Mesopotamia, China, North America, and most other places, examples of warfare and slaughter can be found which equaled that of the Aztecs in form, if not in intensity. Also, as noted at the beginning of this chapter, the Euro-peans probably exaggerated the violence of Mesoamerican life, for the Europeans had a political agenda well-served by depicting the Native Americans as savages.

But human sacrifice and blood-letting *were* important elements in Mesoamerican cultures, and it is an interesting anthropological problem to explain why these acts, so repugnant to the modern mind, became so celebrated by the ancients of Mesoamer-ica, China, Mesopotamia, and elsewhere. It is not difficult to posit "functional" ex-planations that are plausible, if largely untestable. Michael Harner, for example, has argued that the key to Aztec sacrifice is the contribution the cannibalism of sacrifi-

FIGURE 13.15 The supreme Aztec divinity was Tezcatlipoca, whose skull is modeled here in jade and crystal.

cial victims made to the Aztec diet.[124] Mesoamerica lacks any large domesticated animals that could have been effectively integrated with Aztec agricultural strategies, and this animal protein and fat deficiency may have been compensated for by cannibalism. But the Mesoamerican diet is generally a rich one, with a nutritionally adequate basis of maize, beans, squash, fish, frogs, birds, deer, dogs, and other animals. This diet was sufficient to have supported long-term population growth and the needs of hundreds of thousands of people who lived around what is now Mexico City. There is little doubt that the Aztecs engaged in cannibalism, since several sixteenth-century Europeans described it as it happened, but we have insufficient evidence with which to evaluate Harner's thesis.

In previous chapters we have considered the idea that "waste," whether in the form of pyramids or human sacrifice, serves an important function in the rapidly expanding and unstable political systems of early civilizations. As noted in chapter 7, for example, Robert Dunnell has suggested that these forms of waste retard population growth and help to stabilize rates of economic expansion, but then tend to die out for a time once a major advance in "carrying capacity" is achieved through the development of agriculture, better central government administration, etc.

These kinds of explanations, however, clash to some extent with other perspectives that tend to see cultures and ideologies as determinatives of cultures, not just reflections of economic factors. Certainly Aztec human sacrifices were a direct means by which elites monopolized and wielded power.

Despite their death cults, the Aztecs in everyday life were a colorful and in some ways engaging people. The Spanish remarked on their love of flowers and natural beauty, and their poetry contains many references to the joys of the natural world. The Spanish were amazed to find that Aztecs bathed their entire bodies most days— a level of personal cleanliness that would have struck even most eighteenth- and nine-teenth-century Europeans as bizarre and unhealthy.

Dress for men and women often consisted of a loincloth and a woven cloak, and brightly colored cotton fabrics were used for ornamentation. In the countryside women often went about naked to the waist, but middle- and upper-class urban women wore decorated blouses.[125]

The diet of the Aztecs centered on maize, beans, squash, and tomatoes, although the wealthier people could eat various fruits, nuts, meats, and other exotic foods. The relatively unvaried diet was enlivened with peyote and other natural hallucinogens, and by tobacco and *pulque*, a cactus-derived alcoholic drink with impressive powers to revive the weary.

THE SPANISH CONQUEST

> The captain Alonso Lopez de Avila . . . captured during the war . . . a young Indian woman of lovely and gracious appearance. She had promised her husband, fearful lest they should kill him in the war, not to have relations with any other man but him, and so no persuasion was sufficient to prevent her from taking her own life to avoid being defiled by another man; and because of this they had her thrown to the dogs.[126]

The melancholy history of the conquest of Mesoamerica by Spanish adventurers in the early sixteenth century was recorded in detail by the Spanish themselves. Accounts on both sides of this meeting of worlds provide a fascinating look at the clash of cultures.[127]

In A.D. 1519 Cortez left Cuba with a sizable force of ships, men, armaments, and horses and sailed to the coast of Veracruz. With the advantage of horses, cannons, war dogs, and an extraordinary esprit de corps, Cortez and his men were able to march directly into the Aztec capital at Tenochtitlán, where they were at first welcomed by the Aztec king, Moctezuma, who was under the delusion that the Spanish were gods returning to their ancestral homeland. He could hardly have been more wrong. Within a short time, the Spanish had kidnapped and jailed him and were forming alliances with local non-Aztec peoples, who were only too happy to help the Spanish displace the Aztecs. Moctezuma and many of his people were eventually killed in a fierce battle at Tenochtitlán, after which Aztec resistance stiffened; but within a few years the Spanish had captured most of the Aztec heartland. In 1524 they hanged the last Aztec king, and thereafter Spanish domination of Mexico was rapid. When the Spanish first arrived, the population of the heartland of the Aztec empire was probably more than a million; 150 years later it probably held fewer than 70,000 people—the survivors of war, disease, slavery, and the other plagues of this epic clash of cultures.

SUMMARY AND CONCLUSIONS

As in all the other cases of early cultural complexity we have considered, it is clear that simple aspects of economy, ecology, and demography explain much of what happened in the New World. The Olmec, Teotihuacán, Oaxacan, Maya, Aztec, and other Mesoamerican societies appeared where they did and not in Newfoundland or Nebraska because of the exceptional productivity of the South Gulf Coast, Oaxaca, and other areas of Mesoamerica, given a simple farming technology and the maize-beans-squash complex.

We see in Mesoamerica, too, the stimulus to development provided by irrigation agriculture, environmental circumscription, inter-regional exchange, and other factors.

But once we get beyond this simple ecological level of analysis, we encounter a welter of variability in sociopolitical forms, economic histories, settlement patterns, and the other elaborations in these complex societies. In the absence of sufficient written documents, it is difficult to apply Marxian or other sociopolitical models to Mesoamerica. So we are left with a case of cultural evolution that is so striking a parallel to what happened in, for example, Mesopotamia, that we must consider both areas examples of a single developmental pattern. But efforts to discern the intrinsic combinations of causes in any of these early complex cultural sequences remain a largely unrealized goal of archaeology.

From a non-scientific point of view, in some ways the most interesting thing about early Mesoamerican societies is the psychological contrast they make with ourselves. We may be sure that the average Olmec town of 500 B.C. had a full range of human personality types and an agricultural existence that we can all imagine. But in their cosmologies and world and life views, ancient Mesoamericans were profoundly different from the Spanish who first met them. Indeed, their views were probably profoundly different from those of any of the other Western European traditions.

BIBLIOGRAPHY

Adams, R. E. W. 1977. *Prehistoric Mesoamerica*. Boston: Little, Brown.

Adams, R. E., W. E. Brown, Jr., and T. P. Culbert. 1981. "Radar Mapping, Archaeology, and Ancient Mayan Land Use." *Science* 213:1457–63.

Alden, J. R. 1979. "A Reconstruction of the Toltec Period Political Units in the Valley of Mexico." In *Transformations: Mathematical Approaches to Culture Change*, eds. C. Renfrew and K. L. Cooke. New York: Academic Press.

Algaze, G. 1989. "The Uruk Expansion." *Current Anthropology* 30(5):571–608.

Anderson, A. O., and C. Dibble, eds. 1978. *The Florentine Codex*. Salt Lake City: University of Utah Press.

Andrews, E. W., and N. Hammond. 1990. "Redefinition of the Swasey Phase at Cuello, Belize." *American Antiquity* 55(3):570–84.

Andrews, A. P. 1993. "Late Postclassic Lowland Maya Archaeology." *Journal of World Prehistory* 7(1):35–70.

Armillas, P. 1971. "Gardens on Swamps." *Science* 174:653–61.

Arnold, J. E., and A. Ford. 1980. "A Statistical Examination of Settlement Patterns at Tikal, Guatemala." *American Antiquity* 45:713–26.

Ashmore, W., ed. 1981. *Lowland Maya Settlement Patterns*. Albuquerque: University of New Mexico Press.

Berlo, J. C., ed. 1992. *Art, Ideology and the City of Teotihuacan: A Symposium at Dumbarton Oaks, 8th and 9th October 1988*. Washington, DC: Dumbarton Oaks.

Berrin, K., and Pasztory, R., eds. 1994. *Teotihacan*. London: Thames and Hudson.

Blanton, R. E. 1972. "Prehistoric Adaptation in the Ixtapalapa Region, Mexico." *Science* 175:1317–26.

———. 1976. "The Origins of Monte Albán." In *Cultural Change and Continuity*, ed. C. E. Cleland. New York: Academic Press.

———. 1978. *Monte Albán: Settlement Patterns at the Ancient Zapotec Capital*. New York: Academic Press.

———. 1980. "Cultural Ecology Reconsidered." *American Antiquity* 45:145–51.

———. 1983. "Advances in the Study of Cultural Evolution in Prehispanic Highland Mesoamerica." In *Advances in World Archaeology*, Vol. 2, eds. F. Wendorf and A. E. Close. New York: Academic Press.

Blanton, R. E., S. A. Kowalewski, G. Feinman, and J. Appel. 1981. *Ancient Mesoamerica, A Comparison of Change in Three Regions*. Cambridge: Cambridge University Press.

Bove, F. J. 1981. "Trend Surface Analysis and the Lowland Classic Maya Collapse." *American Antiquity* 46:93–112.

Brumfiel, E. 1976. "Regional Growth in the Eastern Valley of Mexico: A Test of the 'Population Pressures' Hypothesis." In *The Early Mesoamerican Village*, ed. K. V. Flannery. New York: Academic Press.

———. 1983. "Aztec State Making: Ecology, Structure, and the Origin of the State." *American Anthropologist* 85(2): 261–84.

Brush, C. F. 1969. "A Contribution to the Archaeology of Coastal Guerrero, Mexico." Doctoral dissertation. Columbia University, New York.

Chippendale, C., N. Hammond, and J. Sabloff. 1988. "The Archaeology of Maya Decipherment." *Antiquity* 62(234):119–22.

Clancy F. S., and P. D. Harrison, eds. 1995. *Vision and Revision in Maya Studies*. Albuquerque: University of New Mexico Press.

Clendinnen, I. 1991. *The Aztecs: An Interpretation*. Cambridge: Cambridge University Press.

Coe, M. D. 1965a. *The Jaguar's Children: Pre-Classic Central Mexico*. New York: Museum of Primitive Art.

———. 1965b. "The Olmec Style and Its Distribution." *Handbook of Middle American Indians* 3:739–75.

———. 1968a. *America's First Civilization: Discovering the Olmec*. New York: American Heritage.

———. 1968b. "San Lorenzo and the Olmec Civilization." In *Dumbarton Oaks Conference on the Olmec*, ed. E. P. Benson. Washington, DC: Dumbarton Oaks.

———. 1970. "The Archaeological Sequence at San Lorenzo Tenochtitlán, Veracruz, Mexico." *Contributions of the University of California Archaeological Research Facility*, n. 8, pp. 21–34.

———. 1984. *Mexico*. New York: Thames and Hudson.

———. 1992. *Breaking the Maya Code*. London and New York: Thames and Hudson.

———. 1993. *The Maya*, 5th ed. London and New York: Thames and Hudson.

———. 1994. *Mexico*, 4th ed. New York: Thames and Hudson.

Coe, M., and R. Diehl. 1980. *The Land of the Olmec: The People of the River*, Vol. 2. Austin: University of Texas Press.

Coe, M., D. Snow, and E. Benson. 1986. *Atlas of Ancient America*. New York: Facts on File.

Coe, W., and W. A. Haviland. 1982. *Introduction to the Archaeology of Tikal, Guatemala*. Philadelphia: University Museum, University of Pennsylvania.

Coggins, C. 1985. *The Sacred Cenote of Sacrifice*. Austin: University of Texas Press.

Collier, G. A., R. I. Rosaldo, J. D. Wirth. eds. 1982. *The Inca and Aztec State*. New York: Academic Press.

Conrad, G. W., and A. A. Demarest. 1984. *Religion and Empire: The Dynamics of Aztec and Inca Expansionism*. Cambridge: Cambridge University Press.

Cook, S. 1946. "Human Sacrifice and Warfare as Factors in the Demography of Precolonial Mexico." *Human Biology* 18:81–102.

Cordova, C., A. L. M. del Pozzo, and J. L. Camacho. 1994. "Palaeolandforms and Volcanic Impact on the Environment of Prehistoric Cuicuilco, Southern Mexico City." *Journal of Archaeological Science* 21: 585–96.

Cowgill, G. 1974. "Quantitative Studies of Urbanization at Teotihuacán." In *Mesoamerican Archaeology: New Approaches*, ed. N. Hammond. Austin: University of Texas Press, pp. 363–96.

Cowgill, U. 1962. "An Agricultural Study of the Southern Maya Lowlands." *American Anthropologist* 64:273–86.

———. 1971. "Some Comments on Manihot Subsistence and the Ancient Maya." *Southwest Journal of Anthropology* 27:51–63.

Culbert, T. P. 1973. *The Classic Maya Collapse*. Albuquerque: University of New Mexico Press.

———. 1988. "Political History and the Decipherment of Maya Glyphs." *Antiquity* 62(234):135–52.

Culbert, T. P., and D. S. Rice, eds. 1995. *Precolumbian Population History in the Maya Lowlands*. Albuquerque: University of New Mexico Press.

Demarest, A., and G. W. Conrad, eds. 1992. *Ideology and Pre-Columbian Civilizations*. Santa Fe, NM: School of American Research Press.

DePalma, A. 1993. "Mexico City Restoring Area Tilled by Aztecs," *New York Times*, Sept. 14, 1993, p. B7.

Diaz del Castillo, B. 1928. *The Discovery and Conquest of Mexico*. London: Routledge.

Dickson, D. B. 1981. "Further Simulations of Ancient Agriculture and Population at Tikal, Guatemala." *American Antiquity* 46:922–26.

Doty, D. C. 1979. "A New Mayan Long Count-Gregorian Conversion Computer Program." *American Antiquity* 44:780–83.

Drennan, R. D. 1976. "Religion and Social Evolution in Formative Mesoamerica." In *The Early Mesoamerican Village*, ed. K. V. Flannery. New York: Academic Press.

Earle, T. 1976. "A Nearest-Neighbor Analysis of Two Formative Settlement Systems." In *The Early Mesoamerica Village*, ed. K. V. Flannery. New York: Academic Press.

Fash, W. L. 1991. *Scribes, Warriors and Kings: The City of Copan and the Ancient Maya*. New York: Thames and Hudson.

———. 1988. "A New Look at Maya Statecraft From Copan, Honduras." *Antiquity* 62(234):157–69.

Ferdon, E. M. 1959. "Agriculture Potential and the Development of Cultures." *Southwestern Journal of Anthropology* 15:1–19.

Fiedel, S. J. 1992. *Prehistory of the Americas*. Cambridge: Cambridge University Press.

Flannery, K. V. 1968. "The Olmec and the Valley of Oaxaca: A Model for Inter-Regional Interaction in Formative Times." In *Dumbarton Oaks Conference on the Olmec*, ed. E. P. Benson. Washington, DC: Dumbarton Oaks.

———. 1976a. "The Early Mesoamerican House." In *The Early Mesoamerican Village*, ed. K. V. Flannery. New York: Academic Press.

———. 1976b. "Evolution of Complex Settlement Systems." In *The Early Mesoamerican Village*, ed. K. V. Flannery. New York: Academic Press.

———. 1976c. "Linear Stream Patterns and Riverside Settlement Rules." In *The Early Mesoamerican Village*, ed. K. V. Flannery. New York: Academic Press.

———. 1976d. "Contextual Analysis of Ritual Paraphernalia from Formative Oaxaca." In *The Early Mesoamerican Village*, ed. K. V. Flannery. New York: Academic Press.

Flannery, K. V., ed. 1982. *Maya Subsistence: Studies in Memory of Dennis E. Puleston*. New York: Academic Press.

Flannery, K. V., and J. Marcus. 1994. *Early Formative Pottery of the Valley of Oaxaca, Mexico* (with a technical ceramic analysis by W. O. Payne). Memoirs of the Museum of Anthropology 27. Ann Arbor: University of Michigan Press.

Flannery, K. V., J. Marcus, and S. A. Kowalewski. 1981. "The Preceramic and Formative of the Valley of Oaxaca." *Supplement to the Handbook of Middle American Indians.* Austin: University of Texas Press, pp. 48–93.

Flannery, K. V., and M. C. Winter. 1976. "Analyzing Household Activities." In *The Early Mesoamerican Village,* ed. K. V. Flannery. New York: Academic Press.

Folan, W. J., E. R. Kintz, and L. A. Fletcher. 1983. *Coba: A Classic Maya Metropolis.* New York: Academic Press.

Fox, J. W. 1987. *Maya Postclassic State Formation.* Cambridge: Cambridge University Press.

Fox, J. G. 1996. "Playing with Power: Ballcourts and Political Ritual in Southern Mesoamerica." *Current Anthropology* 37(3):483–509.

Freidel, D. A., and J. A. Sabloff. 1984. *Cozumel: Late Maya Settlement Patterns.* New York: Academic Press.

Fritz, G. J. 1994. "Are the First American Farmers Getting Younger?" *Current Anthropology* 35(3):305–309.

Fry, R., ed. 1980. *Models and Methods in Regional Exchange.* SAA Papers no. 1. Washington.

Fry, R., and S. Cox. 1974. "The Structure of Ceramic Exchange at Tikal, Guatemala." *World Archaeology* 6:209–25.

Graham, I. 1988. "Homeless Hieroglyphs." *Antiquity* 62(234):122–26.

Grennes-Ravits, R., and G. Coleman. 1976. "The Quintessential Role of Olmec in the Central Highlands of Mexico." *American Antiquity* 41:196–205.

Grove, D. C. 1968. "The Pre-Classic Olmec in Central Mexico: Site Distribution and Inferences." In *Dumbarton Oaks Conference on the Olmec,* ed. E. P. Benson. Dumbarton Oaks, Washington, DC: Dumbarton Oaks.

———. 1992 . "Ideology and Evolution at the Pre-State Level." In *Ideology and Pre-Columbian Civilizations,* eds, A. Demarest and G. W. Conrad. Santa Fe, NM: School of American Research Press.

Grove, D. C., ed. 1987. *Ancient Chalcatzingo.* Austin: University of Texas Press.

Hammond, N. 1991. "Introduction." In *Classic Maya Political History,* ed. P. T. Culbert. Cambridge and Santa Fe (NM): Cambridge University Press and the School of American Research.

———. 1995. *Ancient Mayan Civilization.* New Brunswick, NJ: Rutgers.

Harner, M. 1977. "The Ecological Basis for Aztec Sacrifice." *American Ethnologist* 4:117–35.

Harris, M. 1977. *Cannibals and Kings: The Origins of Cultures.* New York: Random House.

Hodge, M. 1991. "Land and Lordship. The Politics of Aztec Provincial Administration in the Valley of Mexico." In *Land and Politics in the Valley of Mexico: A Two-Thousand Year Perspective,* ed. H. R. Harvey. Albuquerque, NM: University of New Mexico Press.

———. 1995. "Polities Composing the Aztec Empire's Core." In *Economies and Polities in the Aztec Realm,* eds. M. E. Smith and M. G. Hodge. Albany, NY: State University of New York.

Houston, S. D. 1988. "The Phonetic Decipherment of Mayan Glyphs." *Antiquity* 62(234):126–35.

———. 1989. "Archaeology and Maya Writing." *Journal of World Prehistory* 3(1):1–32.

———. 1989. *Maya Glyphs.* Berkeley: University of California Press.

Hunt, R. C., and E. Hunt. 1976. "Canal Irrigation and Local Social Organization." *Current Anthropology* 17:389–411.

Ifrah, G. 1985. *From One to Zero.* Trans. L. Bair. New York: Viking Penguin.

Joyce, R. A. 1986. "Terminal Classic Interaction on the Southeastern Maya Periphery." *American Antiquity* 1986: 313–29.

Justeson, J. S., and T. Kaufman. 1993. "A Decipherment of Epi-Olmec Hieroglyphic Writing." *Science* 259:1665–1796.

Kelley, D. H. 1981. *Mayan Culture History as Process.* Ithaca, NY: Cornell University Press.

———. 1993. "The Decipherment of Epi-Olmec Script as Zoquean by Justeson and Kaufman." *The Review of Archaeology* 14(1):29–32.

Kirkby, A. 1973. *The Use of Land and Water Resources in the Past and Present Valley of Oaxaca, Mexico.* Ann Arbor: Memoirs of the Museum of Anthropology, University of Michigan, no. 5.

Knorozov, Y. 1982. *Maya Hieroglyphic Codices.* Trans. by S. D. Cole. Austin: University of Texas Press.

Kowalewski, S.A. 1990. "The Evolution of Complexity in the Valley of Oaxaca." *Annual Review of Anthropology* 19:39–58.

Kowalewski, S. A., and L. Feinstein. 1983. "The Economic Systems of Ancient Oaxaca: A Regional Perspective." *Current Anthropology* 24(4):413–41.

Kurtz, D. V. 1987. "The Economics of Urbanization and State Formation at Teotihuacán." *Current Anthropology* 28(3):329–53.

Landa, D. de. 1975. *The Maya Account of Affairs of Yucatan.* Chicago: J. O'Hara.

Lees, S. H. 1973. *Sociopolitical Aspects of Canal Irrigation in the Valley of Oaxaca.* Ann Arbor: Memoir of the Museum of Anthropology, University of Michigan, no. 6.

Lounsbury, F. G. 1991. "Distinguished Lecture: Recent Work in the Decipherment of Palenque's Hieroglyphic Inscriptions." *American Anthropologist* 93(4):809–25.

Lowe, J. W. G. 1982. "On Mathematical Models of the Classic Maya Collapse: The Class Conflict Hypothesis Reexamined." *American Antiquity* 47:643–52.

McAnany, P. 1994. *Living with the Ancestors: Kinship and Kingship in Ancient Maya Society.* Austin: University of Texas Press.

MacNeish, R. S. 1962. *Second Annual Report of the Tehuacan Archaeological-Botanical Project.* Andover, MA: R. S. Peabody Foundation for Archaeology.

———. 1964. "Ancient Mesoamerican Civilization." *Science* 143:531–37.

Marcus, J. 1973. "Territorial Organization of the Lowland Classic Maya." *Science* 180:911–16.

———. 1974. "The Iconography of Power Among the Classic Maya." *World Archaeology* 6:83–94.

———. 1976a. "The Size of the Early Mesoamerican Village." In *The Early Mesoamerican Village,* ed. K. V. Flannery. New York: Academic Press.

———. 1976b. "The Origins of Mesoamerican Writing." *Annual Review of Anthropology* 5:35–68.

———. 1976c. "The Iconography of Militarism at Monte Albán and Neighboring Sites in the Valley of Oaxaca." In *The Origins of Religious Art and Iconography in Preclassic Mesoamerica,* ed. H. B. Nicholson. Los Angeles: Latin American Center, U.C.L.A.

———. 1993. *Mesoamerican Writing Systems: Propaganda, Myth, and History in Four Ancient Civilizations.* Princeton, NJ: Princeton University Press.

Matheny, R. T. 1976. "Maya Lowland Hydraulic Systems." Science 193:639–46.

———. 1986. "Early States in the Maya Lowlands during the Late Preclassic Period: Edzná and El Mirador." In *City-States of the Maya,* ed. E. P. Benson. Denver: Rocky Mountain Institute for Pre-Columbian Studies, pp. 1–44.

Matheny, R. T., and D. L. Gurr. 1983. "Variation in Prehistoric Agricultural Systems of the New World." *Annual Review of Anthropology* 12:79–103.

Meggers, B. J. 1954. "Environmental Limitation in the Development of Culture." *American Anthropologist* 56.

Miller, M. E. 1986. *The Murals of Bonampak.* Princeton: Princeton University Press.

Miller, M., and K. Taube. 1993. *The Gods and Symbols of Ancient Mexico and the Maya.* London and New York: Thames and Hudson.

Millon, R. 1974. "The Study of Urbanism at Teotihuacán, Mexico." In *Mesoamerican Archaeology: New Approaches,* ed. N. Hammond. Austin: University of Texas Press.

Millon, R., R. B. Drewitt, and G. L. Cowgill. 1973. *Urbanization at Teotihuacán, Mexico,* Vol. 1, Parts 1 and 2. Austin: University of Texas Press.

Moctezuma, E. M. 1988. *The Great Temple of the Aztecs.* New York: Thames and Hudson.

Murdy, C. N. 1981. "Congenital Deformities and the Olmec Were-Jaguar Motif." *American Antiquity* 46:861–69.

Nations, J. D. 1980. "The Evolutionary Potential of Lacondon Maya Sustained-Yield Tropical Forest Agriculture." *Journal of Anthropological Research* 36:1–30.

Nichols, D. L. 1982. "A Middle Formative Irrigation System Near Santa Clara Coatitlan in the Basin of Mexico." *American Antiquity* 47:133–44.

————. 1988. "Infrared Aerial Photography and Prehispanic Irrigation at Teotihuacán: The Tlajinga Canals." *Journal of Field Archaeology* 15:17–27.

————. 1995. "The Organization of Provincial Craft Production and the Aztec City-States of Otumba." In *Economies and Polities in the Aztec Realm*, eds, M. Hodge and M. Smith, Albany, NY: Institute for Mesoamerican Studies, State University of New York.

Niederberger, C. 1979. "Early Sedentary Economy in the Basin of Mexico." *Science* 203:131–46.

O'Brien, M. J., J. A. Ferguson, T. D. Holland, and D. E. Lewarch. 1989. "On Interpretive Competition in the Absence of Appropriate Data: Monte Albán Revisited." *Current Anthropology* 30(2):191–99.

O'Brien, M. J., R. D. Mason, D. E. Lewarch, and J. A. Neely. 1982. *A Late Formative Irrigation Settlement Below Monte Albán.* Austin: University of Texas Press.

Offner, J. A. 1981. "On the Inapplicability of 'Oriental Despotism' and the 'Asiatic Mode of Production' to the Aztecs of Texcoco." *American Antiquity* 46:43–61.

Palerm, A., and E. Wolf. 1957. "Ecological Potential and Cultural Development in Mesoamerica." In *Studies in Human Ecology* 3:1–38.

Parsons, J. R. 1968. "Teotihuacán, Mexico, and Its Impact on Regional Demography." *Science* 162:872–77.

————. 1971. *Prehistoric Settlement Patterns in the Texcoco Region, Mexico.* Ann Arbor: Memoir of the Museum of Anthropology, University of Michigan, no. 3.

————. 1974. "The Development of a Prehistoric Complex Society: A Regional Perspective from the Valley of Mexico." *Journal of Field Archaeology* 1:81–108.

Peebles, C. S. 1988. "From Art to Algebra in Maya Studies." *Antiquity* 62(234):170–72.

Pelzer, R. J. 1945. *Pioneer Settlement in the Asiatic Tropics.* Special Publications, no. 29. New York: American Geographical Society.

Pendergast, D. M. 1993. "Late Postclassic Maya Archaeology." *Journal of World Prehistory* 7(1):35–70.

Pires-Ferreira, J. W. 1975. *Formative Mesoamerican Exchange Networks with Special Reference to the Valley of Oaxaca.* Ann Arbor: Memoirs of the Museum of Anthropology, University of Michigan, no. 7.

Pollard, H. P. 1980. "Central Places and Cities: A Consideration of the Protohistoric Tarascan State." *American Antiquity* 45:677–97.

Porter, M. N. 1953. *Tlatilco and the Pre-Classic Cultures of the New World.* New York: Viking Fund Publications in Anthropology, no. 19.

Puleston, D. E. and O. S. Puleston. 1971. "An Ecological Approach to the Origins of Maya Civilization." *Archaeology* 24:330–36.

Pyne, N. M. 1976. "The Fire-Serpent and Were-Jaguar in Formative Oaxaca: A Contingency Table Analysis." In *The Early Mesoamerican Village*, ed. K. V. Flannery. New York: Academic Press.

Rathje, W. L. 1971. "The Origin and Development of Lowland Classic Maya Civilization." *American Antiquity* 36:275–85.

————. 1973. "Classic Maya Development and Denouement: A Research Design." In *The Classic Maya Collapse*, ed. T. P. Culbert. Albuquerque: University of New Mexico Press.

Reilly, K. 1991. "Olmec Iconographic Influences on the Symbols of Maya Rulership: An Examination of Possible Sources." In *Sixth Palenque Round Table, 1986*, ed. V. M. Fields. Norman: University of Oklahoma Press, pp. 151–74.

Robertson, R. A., and D. A. Freidel, eds. 1988. *Archaeology at Cerros, Belize, Central America. Volume I: An Interim Report.* Dallas: Southern Methodist University Press.

Rust, W. and R. Sharer. 1988. "New Settlement Data from La Venta." *Science* 242:102–4.

Sabloff, J. A. 1989. *The Cities of Ancient Mexico.* New York: Thames and Hudson.

————. 1990. *The New Archaeology and the Ancient Maya.* New York: Scientific American Library.

Sabloff, J. A., and D. A. Freidel. 1984. *Cozumel: Late Maya Settlement Patterns.* New York: Academic Press.

Sahagun, F. B. de. 1976. *A History of Ancient Mexico.* Trans. F. R. Bandelier. Glorieta NM: Rio Grande Press.

Sahlins, M. 1968. "Notes on the Original Affluent Society." In *Man the Hunter*, eds. R. B. Lee and I. DeVore. Chicago: Aldine de Gruyter.

Sanders, W. T. 1973. "The Cultural Ecology of the Lowland Maya: A Re-Evaluation." In *The Classic Maya Collapse*, ed. T. P. Culbert. Albuquerque: University of New Mexico Press.

Sanders, W. T., and D. L. Nichols. 1988. "Ecological Theory and Cultural Evolution in the Valley of Oaxaca." *Current Anthropology* 29(1):33–80.

Sanders, W. T., J. R. Parsons, and M. H. Logan. 1976. "Summary and Conclusions." In *The Valley of Mexico*, ed. E. Wolf. Albuquerque: University of New Mexico Press.

Sanders, W. T., J. R. Parsons, and R. S. Santley. 1979. *The Basin of Mexico: Ecological Processes in the Evolution of a Civilization*. New York: Academic Press.

Sanders, W. T., and B. Price. 1968. *Mesoamerica: the Evolution of a Civilization*. New York: Random House.

Sanders, W. T., and D. Webster. 1978. "Unilinealism, Multilinealism, and the Evolution of Complex Societies." In *Social Archaeology*, eds. C. L. Redman, et al. New York: Academic Press, pp. 249–302.

Saunders, N. 1989. *People of the Jaguar*. London: Souvenir Press.

Schele, L., and D. Freidel. 1990. *A Forest of Kings*. New York: Morrow.

Schele, L., D. Freidel, and J. Parker. *Maya Cosmos*. New York: Morrow.

Schele, L., and E. Miller. 1986. *The Blood of Kings*. Austin: University of Texas Press.

Schortman, E. M. and P. A. Urban. 1994. "Core and Periphery in Southeastern Mesoamerica." *Current Anthropology* 35(4):401–30.

Sempowski, M. L., and M. W. Spence. 1995. *Mortuary Practices and Skeletal Remains at Teotihuacán*, ed. R. Millon. Salt Lake City: University of Utah Press.

Sharer, R. 1989. "Olmec Studies: A Status Report." In *Regional Perspectives on the Olmec*, eds. R. Sharer and D. Grove. Cambridge: Cambridge University Press, pp. 3–7.

Sharer, R., and D. Grove, eds. 1989. *Regional Perspectives on the Olmec*. Cambridge: Cambridge University Press.

Sheets, P. D., ed. 1983. *Archeology and Volcanism in Central America*. Austin: University of Texas Press.

Siemens, A. H., and D. E. Puleston. 1972. "Ridged Fields and Associated Features in Southern Campeche: New Perspectives on the Lowland Maya." *American Antiquity* 37:228–39.

Sisson, E. B. 1970. "Settlement Patterns and Land Use in the Northwestern Chontalpa, Tabasco, Mexico: A Progress Report." *Ceramica de Cultura Maya* 6:41–54.

Sjoberg, G. 1965. "The Origin and Evolution of Cities." *Scientific American* 213(3):54–63.

Smith, M. 1979. "The Aztec Marketing System and Settlement Pattern in the Valley of Mexico: A Central Place Analysis." *American Antiquity* 44:10–24.

Soustelle, J. 1961. *Daily Life of the Aztecs*. Trans. P. O'Brian. Stanford: Stanford University Press.

Stark, B., L. Heller, F. W. Nelson, R. Bishop, D. M. Pearsall, D. S. Whitley, and H. Wells. 1985. "El Balsamo Residential Investigations: A Pilot Project and Research Issues." *American Anthropologist* 87(1):100–11.

Steponaitis, V. P. 1981. "Settlement Hierarchies and Political Complexity in Non-market Societies: The Formative Period in the Valley of Mexico." *American Anthropologist* 83:320–63.

Storey, R. 1985. "An Estimate of Mortality in a Pre-Columbian Urban Population." *American Anthropologist* 87(3):519–35.

———. 1992. *Life and Death in the Ancient City of Teotihuacán*. Birmingham: University of Alabama Press.

Thomas, P. M. 1981. *Prehistoric Maya Settlement Patterns at Becan, Campeche, Mexico*. New Orleans: Middle American Research Institute, Tulane University.

Todorov, T. 1984. *The Conquest of America*. Trans. R. Howard. New York: Harper & Row.

Tolstoy, P. 1981. "Advances in the Basin of Mexico, pt. 1." *The Quarterly Review of Archaeology* 2:33–34,36.

Tolstoy, P., and A. Guinette. 1965. "Le Placement de Tlatilco dans le Cadre du Pre-Classique du Basin de Mexico." *Journal de la Societe des Americanistes* (Paris) 54:47–91.

Tolstoy, P., and L. Paradis. 1970. "Early and Middle Preclassic Culture in the Basin of Mexico." *Science* 167:344–51.

Townsend, R. F. 1992. *The Aztecs.* London and New York: Thames and Hudson.

Trigger, B. G. 1993. *Early Civilizations: Ancient Egypt in Context.* Cairo: American University in Cairo Press.

Turner, B. L. 1974. "Prehistoric Intensive Agriculture in the Maya Lowlands." *Science* 185:118–24.

Turner, B. L., and P. D. Harrison, eds. 1978. *Prehispanic Maya Agriculture.*

———. 1984. *Pulltrouser Swamp: Ancient Maya Habitat, Agriculture, and Settlement in Northern Belize.* Austin: University of Texas Press.

Urban, P. A., and E. M. Schortman, eds. 1986. *The Southeast Maya Periphery.* Austin: University of Texas Press.

Weaver, M. P. 1991. *The Aztecs, Maya, and Their Predecessors,* 3d ed. New York: Academic Press.

Webster, D. 1988. "Copan as a Classic Maya Center." In *The Southeast Classic Maya Zone,* eds. E. Boone and G. Willey. Washington, DC: Dumbarton Oaks.

Webster, D. 1992. "Maya Elites: The Perspective from Copan." In *Mesoamerican Elites,* eds. D. Chase and A. Chase. Norman: University of Oklahoma Press.

Webster, D., and N. Gonlin. 1988. "Household Remains of the Humblest Maya." *Journal of Field Archaeology* 15(2):169–90.

Whalen, M. E. 1974. "Community Development and Integration During the Formative Period in the Valley of Oaxaca, Mexico." Paper read at the Annual Meeting of the American Anthropological Association, Mexico City.

———. 1976. "Zoning Within an Early Formative Community in the Valley of Oaxaca." In *The Early Mesoamerican Valley,* ed. K. V. Flannery. New York: Academic Press.

———. 1981. *Excavations at Santo Domingo Tomaltepec: Evolution of a Formative Community in the Valley of Oaxaca, Mexico.* Ann Arbor: Museum of Anthropology, University of Michigan, no. 12.

Wilcox, V. L. and D. R. Scarborough, eds. 1993. *The Mesoamerican Ballgame.* Tucson: University of Arizona Press.

Wilk, R. R., and W. Ashmore, eds. 1987. *House and Household in the Mesoamerican Antiquity* 62(237):703–07.

Winter, M. 1972. "Tierras Largas: A Formative Community in the Valley of Oaxaca, Mexico." Doctoral thesis, University of Arizona.

———. 1976. "The Archaeological Household Cluster in the Valley of Oaxaca." In *The Early Mesoamerican Village,* ed. K. V. Flannery. New York: Academic Press.

Wolf, E. 1959. *Sons of the Shaking Earth.* Chicago: University of Chicago Press.

Wolf, E., ed. 1976. *The Valley of Mexico.* Albuquerque: University of New Mexico Press.

NOTES

1. Bernal Diaz del Castillo, *The Discovery and Conquest of Mexico,* pp. 190–191.

2. Reviewed in Trigger, *Early Civilizations: Ancient Egypt in Context.*

3. Harner, "The Ecological Basis for Aztec Sacrifice."

4. Niederberger, "Early Sedentary Economy in the Basin of Mexico."

5. Kirkby, *The Use of Land and Water Resources in the Past and Present Valley of Oaxaca, Mexico.*

6. Fritz, "Are the First American Farmers Getting Younger?"

7. Flannery, "The Early Mesoamerican House," p. 13–15.

8. Flannery and Winter, "Analyzing Household Activities," p. 36.

9. Pelzer, *Pioneer Settlement in the Asiatic Tropics*.

10. Sisson, "Settlement Patterns and Land Use in the Northwestern Chontalpa, Tabasco, Mexico: A Progress Report."

11. Coe and Diehl, *The Land of the Olmec: The People of the River*.

12. Rust and Sharer, "New Settlement Data from La Venta."

13. Murdy, "Congenital Deformities and the Olmec Were-Jaguar Motif."

14. Justeson and Kaufman, "A Decipherment of Epi-Olmec Hieroglyphic Writing."

15. Kelley, "The Decipherment of Epi-Olmec Script as Zoquean by Justeson and Kaufman," p. 31.

16. Sanders, Parsons, and Santley, *The Basin of Mexico: Ecological Processes in the Evolution of a Civilization*.

17. Nichols, "A Middle Formative Irrigation System Near Santa Clara Coatitlan in the Basin of Mexico."

18. Parsons, "The Development of a Prehistoric Complex Society: A Regional Perspective from the Valley of Mexico," p. 91.

19. Cordova et al., "Palaeolandforms and Volcanic Impact on the Environment of Prehistoric Cuicuilco, Southern Mexico City," p. 593.

20. See, for example, the works of William Sanders (Sanders, Parsons, and Santley, *The Basin of Mexico: Ecological Processes in the Evolution of a Civilization*), Jeffrey Parsons (Parsons, *Prehistoric Settlement Patterns in the Texcoco Region, Mexico*; idem., "The Development of a Prehistoric Complex Society: A Regional Perspective from the Valley of Mexico"), and Richard Blanton (Blanton, "Prehistoric Adaptation in the Ixtapalapa Region, Mexico"); O'Brien et al., "On Interpretive Competition in the Absence of Appropriate Data."

21. Brumfiel, "Regional Growth in the Eastern Valley of Mexico: A Test of the 'Population Pressures' Hypothesis."

22. Ibid. See Tolstoy, "Advances in the Basin of Mexico, pt. 1."

23. Alden, "A Reconstruction of the Toltec Period Political Units in the Valley of Mexico."

24. Tolstoy, "Advances in the Basin of Mexico, pt. 1."

25. Grove, "Ideology and Evolution at the Pre-State Level."

26. Cowgill, "Quantitative Studies of Urbanization at Teotihuacán."

27. Ibid.

28. Millon, "The Study of Urbanism at Teotihuacán, Mexico," p. 42.

29. Nichols, "Infrared Aerial Photography and Prehispanic Irrigation at Teotihuacán."

30. Storey, "An Estimate of Mortality in a Pre-Columbian Urban Population."

31. Parsons, "The Development of a Prehistoric Complex Society: A Regional Perspective from the Valley of Mexico."

32. Cowgill, "Quantitative Studies of Urbanization at Teotihuacán."

33. Kurtz, "The Economics of Urbanization and State Formation at Teotihuacán"; Blanton, "Advances in the Study of Cultural Evolution in Prehispanic Highland Mesoamerica."

34. This section relies heavily on Kowalewski's review article, "The Evolution of Complexity in the Valley of Oaxaca."

35. Flannery, "Contextual Analysis of Ritual Paraphernalia from Formative Oaxaca," p. 335; Flannery and Marcus, "Evolution of Public Building in Formative Oaxaca," in *Cultural Change and Continuity.*

36. Whalen, "Zoning Within an Early Formative Community in the Valley of Oaxaca."

37. Whalen, *Excavations at Santo Domingo Tomaltepec: Evolution of a Formative Community in the Valley of Oaxaca, Mexico.*

38. Winter, "The Archaeological Household Cluster in the Valley of Oaxaca."

39. Flannery and Marcus, *Early Formative Pottery of the Valley of Oaxaca, Mexico.*

40. Despite some evidence to the contrary (Coe, "The Olmec Style and Its Distribution").

41. Blanton et al., *Ancient Mesoamerica, A Comparison of Change in Three Regions*, pp. 180–83; Flannery, "The Olmec and the Valley of Oaxaca: A Model for Inter-Regional Interaction in Formative Times"; Grennes-Ravits and Coleman, "The Quintessential Role of Olmec in the Central Highlands of Mexico"; Flannery, Marcus, and Kowalewski, "The Preceramic and Formative of the Valley of Oaxaca."

42. Kowalewski, "The Evolution of Complexity in the Valley of Oaxaca," p. 44.

43. Blanton, "Advances in the Study of Cultural Evolution in Prehispanic Highland Mesoamerica," pp. 261–62; Blanton et al., *Ancient Mesoamerica, A Comparison of Change in Three Regions*, p. 67.

44. Blanton, "Cultural Ecology Reconsidered."

45. Blanton et al., *Ancient Mesoamerica, A Comparison of Change in Three Regions.*

46. Ibid. See also Blanton, "Advances in the Study of Cultural Evolution in Prehispanic Highland Mesoamerica," p. 2.

47. Marcus, "The Iconography of Militarism at Monte Albán and Neighboring Sites in the Valley of Oaxaca."

48. Sanders and Nichols, "Ecological Theory and Cultural Evolution in the Valley of Oaxaca."

49. Kowalewski and Feinstein, "The Economic Systems of Ancient Oaxaca: A Regional Perspective," p. 425.

50. See *Current Anthropology* 29(1):52–80 for a discussion of this point.

51. Culbert and Rice, *Precolumbian Population History in the Maya Lowlands.*

52. Siemens and Puleston, "Ridged Fields and Associated Features in Southern Campeche: New Perspectives on the Lowland Maya"; Coe and Diehl, *The Land of the Olmec: The People of the River;* Turner and Harrison, *Prehispanic Maya Agriculture.* Reviewed in Matheny and Gurr, "Variation in Prehistoric Agricultural Systems of the New World"; Cowgill, "An Agricultural Study of the Southern Maya Lowlands"; Flannery, *Maya Subsistence. Studies in Memory of Dennis E. Puleston;* Ashmore, *Lowland Maya Settlement Patterns.* In recent years we have seen greatly increased research on the smaller Maya sites, such as Cerros, in Belize. See Robertson and Freidel, *Archaeology at Cerros, Belize, Central America: Volume I: An Interim Report.*

53. See, for example, Clancey and Harrison, eds., *Vision and Revision in Maya Studies.*

54. Cowgill, "An Agricultural Study of the Southern Maya Lowlands."

55. Matheny and Gurr, "Variation in Prehistoric Agricultural Systems of the New World"; Turner and Harrison, *Pulltrouser Swamp: Ancient Maya Habitat, Agriculture, and Settlement in Northern Belize.*

56. Coe and Diehl, *The Land of the Olmec.*

57. Marcus, *Mesoamerican Writing Systems: Propaganda, Myth, and History in Four Ancient Civilizations*, p. 693.

58. Schele and Freidel, *A Forest of Kings*, p. 66.

59. Ibid., p. 65.

60. Ibid., p. 66.

61. Ibid.

62. Ibid., p. 67–68.

63. Ibid., p. 70

64. Ibid. p. 98

65. Marcus, *Mesoamerican Writing Systems.*

66. Schele and Freidel, *A Forest of Kings*, p. 97.

67. See Andrews, "Early Ceramic History of the Lowland Maya," and Schele and Freidel, *A Forest of Kings.*

68. The early dates for this site have recently been revaluated; see Pendergast, "Late Postclassic Maya Archaeology"; also Hammond, "Introduction."

69. Pendergast, "Late Postclassic Maya Archaeology."

70. Schele and Freidel, *A Forest of Kings*, p. 43.

71. Rathje, "Classic Maya Development and Denouement: A Research Design."

72. Fry, *Models and Methods in Regional Exchange.*

73. Matheny, "Maya Lowland Hydraulic Systems."

74. Ibid.; Harris, *Cannibals and Kings: The Origins of Cultures*, p. 91.

75. McAnany, *Living with the Ancestors: Kinship and Kingship in Ancient Maya Society.*

76. Coe, *The Maya.*

77. Cited as "personal communication, 1989" in Schele and Freidel, *A Forest of Kings*, p. 422.

78. Matheny, "Early States in the Maya Lowlands during the Late Preclassic Period: Edzná and El Mirador"; Coe, *Breaking the Maya Code*, p. 63.

79. Schele and Freidel, *A Forest of Kings*, p. 103.

80. Ibid., p. 102

81. Sanders and Price, *Mesoamerica: The Evolution of a Civilization.*

82. Houston, "Archaeology and Maya Writing," p. 26.

83. Wilcox and Scarborough, eds., *The Mesoamerican Ballgame.*

84. This scene is well-illustrated in Coe, Snow, and Benson, *Atlas of Ancient America*, pp. 108–109.

85. Fox, "Playing with Power: Ballcourts and Political Ritual in Southern Mesoamerica."

86. The following description is primarily from Fash, *Scribes, Warriors and Kings: The City of Copan and the Ancient Maya*.

87. Schele and Freidel, *A Forest of Kings*, p. 317.

88. Ibid., p. 345.

89. The following discussion is based largely on Schele and Freidel, *A Forest of Kings*.

90. Ibid., p. 135.

91. Dickson, "Further Simulations of Ancient Agriculture and Population at Tikal, Guatemala."

92. Schele and Freidel, *A Forest of Kings*, p. 145.

93. Miller, *The Murals of Bonampak*.

94. Marcus, "The Iconography of Power Among the Classic Maya," p. 92.

95. Marcus, "The Origins of Mesoamerican Writing."

96. Houston, "Archaeology and Maya Writing," p. 26.

97. Schortman and Urban, "Core and Periphery in Southeastern Mesoamerica."

98. Chippendale, Hammond, and Sabloff, "The Archaeology of Maya Decipherment."

99. Knorozov, *Maya Hieroglyphic Codices*.

100. Reviewed in Coe, *Breaking the Maya Code*.

101. See Houston, *Maya Glyphs*.

102. Reviewed in Houston, "Archaeology and Maya Writing."

103. Ibid., p. 13.

104. Reviewed in Houston, "Archaeology and Maya Writing."

105. Ifrah, *From One to Zero*, p. 404.

106. Marcus, "The Origins of Mesoamerican Writing."

107. Schele and Freidel, *A Forest of Kings*, p. 82.

108. Andrews, "Late Postclassic Lowland Maya Archaeology," p. 54.

109. Lowe, "On Mathematical Models of the Classic Maya Collapse: The Class Conflict Hypothesis Reexamined"; see also Bove, "Trend Surface Analysis and the Lowland Classic Maya Collapse."

110. Webster and Gonlin, "Household Remains of the Humblest Maya."

111. Tula is well illustrated in *The Atlas of Ancient America*, Coe, Snow, and Benson eds., pp. 134–135.

112. Andrews, "Late Postclassic Lowland Maya Archaeology," p. 54.

113. Coggins, *The Sacred Cenote of Sacrifice*.

114. Pollard, "Central Places and Cities: A Consideration of the Protohistoric Tarascan State."

115. Freidel and Sabloff, *Cozumel: Late Maya Settlement Patterns*.

116. Andrews, "Late Postclassic Lowland Maya Archaeology," p. 55.

117. Smith, "The Aztec Marketing System and Settlement Patten in the Valley of Mexico: A Central Place Analysis."

118. Parsons, "The Development of a Prehistoric Complex Society: A Regional Perspective from the Valley of Mexico," p. 107.

119. Coe, *Mexico*, p. 151.

120. Parsons, "The Development of a Prehistoric Complex Society: A Regional Perspective from the Valley of Mexico."

121. Some of this description is taken from DePalma, "Mexico City Restoring Area Tilled by Aztecs."

122. Soustelle, *Daily Life of the Aztecs*, p. 97.

123. Quoted in Harris, *Cannibals and Kings*, p. 101.

124. Harner, "The Ecological Basis for Aztec Sacrifice."

125. Soustelle, *Daily Life of the Aztecs*, p. 135.

126. Diego de Landa, *Relacion de las Cosas de Yucatan*, p. 32 (quoted in Todorov, *The Conquest of America*).

127. Todorov, *The Conquest of America*; Collier, Rosaldo, and Wirth, *The Inca and Aztec State*.

14

THE EVOLUTION OF COMPLEX SOCIETIES IN ANDEAN SOUTH AMERICA

*In the lands assigned to Religion and to the Crown, the Inka
kept overseers and administrators who took care in supervising
their cultivation, harvesting the products and putting them in
storehouses. The labor of sowing and cultivating these lands
and harvesting their products formed a large part of the tribute
which the taxpayer paid to the king. . . . The people assembled
to cultivate them in the following way. If the Inka himself . . .
or some other high official happened to be present he started
the work with a golden [spade] . . . and following his example,
all did the same. However the Inka soon stopped working, and
after him the other officials and nobles stopped also and sat
down with the king to their banquets and festivals which were
especially notable on such days.
The common people remained at work . . . each man put into
his section his children and wives and all the people of his
house to help him. In this way, the man who had the most
workers finished his suyu first, and he was considered a rich
man; the poor man was he who had no one to help him in his
work and had to work that much longer. . . .*

Father Bernabe Cobo (c. A.D. 1639)[1]

Father Cobo's observations remind us of a point reviewed in detail in chapter 7
and other previous chapters: ancient civilizations varied greatly in many respects, but one of the fundamental ways in which they were all profoundly similar is that each and every one evolved social institutions that not only permitted the
pervasive exploitation of the many by the few, but also made that exploitation into a
religious and civil virtue. Few "artifacts" demonstrate this "exploitation" more vividly
than the well-preserved corpse of a young Inka girl whose body was found frozen in
the high Andes several years ago—and which was on display at the Smithsonian Institution in Washington, D.C. in 1996. This young girl was dressed in beautifully

woven cotton clothes, and there is compelling evidence that she was dressed in ceremonial fashion and then, perhaps, drugged, after which she was killed by a blow to her head that smashed her skull. Perhaps this was a ritual sacrifice to some deity associated with the mountains—we simply will never know—but this girl and many similar finds in ancient civilizations around the world exemplify behavior that we think of as exploitation, but which the girl and her culture probably saw as necessary and virtuous acts of faith that kept the cosmos in order.

When European explorers reached Peru and the other countries of Andean South America, they found a civilization that was very strange to them in many ways, including ritual human sacrifice, but they recognized immediately that the Inka, just like the Europeans themselves, were organized in a rigidly stratified class society under a supreme monarch. The Europeans no doubt recognized also that the Inka Empire could be conquered most easily by decapitating it —that is, by killing its head, the Inka King; as is described below, this is exactly what they did.

As with other New World political systems, one has to wonder how it would all have turned out had the Spanish not beheaded this civilization in the sixteenth century through murder, warfare, and the spread of European diseases. The Spanish themselves did not know about the origins of smallpox and other diseases that so terribly afflicted aboriginal Americans, but their imposition of slavery and intentional destruction of South American civilizations (see below) seem particularly barbaric in retrospect, even in the context of the bloody sixteenth and seventeenth centuries.

Andean South American civilizations paralleled other early complex cultures in their intensive farming systems, massive pyramids and temples, large cities, powerful armies, and hierarchies of wealth, power, and prestige (Figure 14.1). But they were different from other early civilizations in interesting ways. The Inka Empire, for example, was the only one of the six "primary" (see chapter 7) ancient civilizations that did not develop a written language, despite the fact that it was the largest political system ever to evolve in the pre-Columbian New World. The Inka and some of their predecessors compensated to some extent for the lack of a written language by building a massive system of roads that linked people to the central government and to each other. Neither the Inka nor any other New World people, however, ever developed the wheeled chariots, wagons, and other vehicles that were a major reason why Old World civilizations were able to dominate the world for centuries.

THE ECOLOGICAL SETTING

> Ecological complementarity was a major human achievement, forged by Andean civilizations to handle a multiple environment, vast populations, and hence high productivity. It helps us understand the unique place of the Andean achievement in the repertory of human histories; it may even point to future possibilities.
>
> *John Murra*[2]

Like most other complex societies that developed independently, Andean South American civilization was possible because of—indeed, to an extent it can be defined as—the economic integration of the resources from highly varied physical environ-

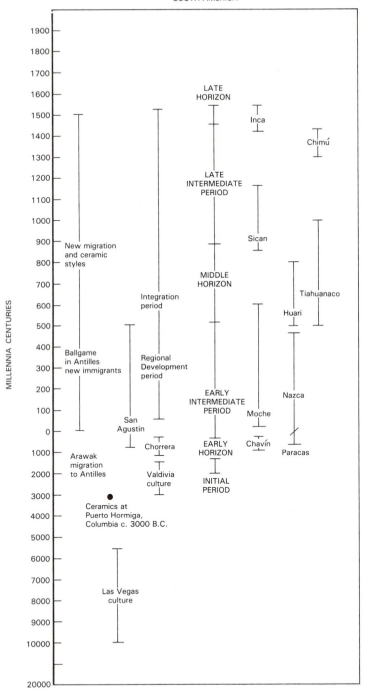

FIGURE 14.1 A cultural chronology of South America. People probably were in South America before 10,000 B.C. but the evidence is controversial.

ments.[3] Ancient Egypt (chapter 9) is something of an exception to this pattern, in that its resources were quite similar over the length of the Nile Valley and Delta, but in Andean South America there were great economic advantages to integrating the different natural resources of highlands and lowlands, ocean and farm. The Andes rise so sharply from the Pacific that only a thin strip of land, less than about sixty kilometers at its widest point, separates the mountains from the sea. And because the Andes shield the coast from the rain-bearing air currents crossing the continent from the Atlantic, most of this coastal strip is one of the world's driest deserts, a region where rain falls only once or twice every five years. In a few places winter fogs along the coast keep skies overcast and in most years this phenomenon provides enough moisture through condensation to support vegetation zones (called *lomas*). But most of the coastal strip is utterly dry, and when the wind blows, dunes can quickly cover houses and choke irrigation canals.

This desert is habitable only because of the fifty or so small rivers that flow down from the mountains, across the plain, and into the sea. Most contain water during only part of the year, but the larger, permanent ones support forests and shrubs and their attendant wildlife, and in some areas the rivers keep the water table sufficiently high so that cultivation is possible without irrigation. Near the mouths of the rivers are fish, freshwater shrimp, and other resources, and in some valleys, rivers have created broad alluvial plains of potentially rich farmlands. The coast has extraordinarily rich concentrations of fish, birds, birds' eggs, sea mammals, mollusks, crustaceans, kelp, and other plant foods. Human life along the coast is tied directly to these rivers and streams because they provide the only drinking water.

These rich marine resources are produced by a fascinating interplay of wind and ocean currents in which winds drive water north along the coast while the earth's rotation from east to west pushes the water westward, creating an upwelling of water from the ocean floor. Carried with these deep waters are tremendous concentrations of phosphates and other nutrients that support countless billions of microscopic plants, and these form the basis of a complex food chain comprising anchovies and other small fish that eat the plants; larger fish, birds, and sea mammals that eat the anchovies; and, ultimately, people, who exploit many links in the chain.

Occasionally, shifts in wind and water change the water temperatures and the plants die, cutting off the base of the food chain. When this happens, rotting plant and animal life fill the air with clouds of hydrogen sulfide that can blacken ships and houses.[4] Several years may pass before the fertility of the sea is restored. The frequency in prehistory of *el Niño* (a reference to the Christ child), as this disturbance is called, is unknown, but it has occurred somewhat regularly in historical times, and recently it has been recurring about once every two to seven years and usually lasts about a year. By late 1995 this area had been experiencing *el Niño* continuously for nearly four years, which seems exceptionally long. Assuming approximately the same conditions in ancient times, *el Niño* may have been a limiting factor on human population densities in coastal Andean South America.

In the mountains are lush valleys, large basins, and high grassy plateaus (called *punas*). Hunters and gatherers here were succeeded after 1800 B.C. by farmers of potatoes, maize, quinoa, and other crops, and by herders of llama and alpaca (domesticated New World camels).

The eastern slopes of the Andes, the *montaña*, are wet and heavily forested, and the combination of steep slopes and intense rain apparently limited exploitation by prehistoric peoples. East of the Andes is the Amazon Basin, a tropical rain forest from which rubber, feathers, and other products were harvested and brought into early Andean South American economic systems, but which was never directly controlled by Andean peoples. The earliest known pottery in the New World dates to between 6000 B.C. and 5000 B.C. and comes from the lower Amazon Basin, in Brazil, where it was apparently made by hunter-foragers who specialized in shellfishing.[5] But ceramics were independently invented many times in the New World, and the extent to which these tropical cultures may have influenced those of the Andean regions remains unclear.

EARLY HUNTERS AND GATHERERS

A few South American sites have been dated (controversially) to 20,000 to 15,000 years ago, but not until about 10,000 years ago is there substantial evidence of people in the mountains and coasts of Andean South America. John Rick has surveyed large areas of these uplands, and in caves and rock shelters he has found projectile points, scrapers, knife blades, and other traces of these early Peruvians: they ate a lot of deer, guanaco, and vicuna (an animal related to the llama, both of which are New World forms of camels), and in some cases were perhaps even able to live year round in small areas.[6] In the beginning they also hunted giant ground sloths and a few other animals that became extinct about 10,000 years ago.

Some of these people were probably "transhumant," meaning that they moved up and down the mountains to exploit various resources as they came in season. Many people made these seasonal moves once alpacas and llamas were domesticated, because these animals require constant tending and frequent moves to new pasturages, and these animals made it possible for them to exploit the different environments at different times of year. The "thin" air, intense cold, blizzards, and thick fogs of the highlands make movement difficult, and over millennia of adapting to these conditions, natural selection has produced Andean peoples with extraordinary cardiovascular systems. Genetics and life-long exposure to the strains of life at high altitudes have produced people who can work hard in air extremely low in oxygen, while others unadapted to this environment can hardly function.

We may never know if coastal Andean South America was occupied before or at the same early date as the mountains, because long stretches of what were beaches and inland areas before 3000 B.C. have been flooded by rising sea levels.[7] In areas that escaped flooding there is evidence of communities as early as 10,000 years ago, so some scholars suspect that coastal populations may have been substantial at an early date.[8]

THE AGRICULTURAL BASIS OF
ANDEAN CIVILIZATION

As was discussed in chapter 6, maize phytoliths (the microscopic hard remains of some plant cells) and pollen have been found at a few South American sites that date to between 4500 B.C. and 1500 B.C. In reviewing the evidence, though, Deborah Pearsall concluded that maize may have been introduced into South America before 5000 B.C., but probably did not become an important crop until after 1500 B.C.[9]

Maize was just one of the important food crops in Andean South America, and in some areas potatoes, beans, and quinoa (pronounced something like "keen-wa") were the staffs of life. Quinoa seeds can be milled into a flour that has one of the highest protein contents of any plant, and this plant was grown in many Andean regions. Domesticated potatoes were found in sites in Peru's Casma Valley in occupations dating around 2250 B.C. to 1775 B.C.,[10] and there are traces of cultivation that may go back as early as about 4400 B.C.[11] This prolific plant is well-suited to wet, cold soils where cereals do not do well, and the ancient South Americans partially solved a major problem of any agricultural system based on tubers—specifically, that tubers do not store well for long periods. Andean mountain peoples, however, developed a method of storing potatoes by freeze-drying them.

The domestication of cotton between about 4000 B.C. and 1200 B.C. provided a relatively cheap source of textiles, and cotton textiles were complemented by a highly developed weaving craft in which reeds and other grasses were woven into sandals, clothes, and many other products. Ancient Andean cotton textiles are a lovely fusion of form and function. Many ancient Andean textiles of various periods have survived because human corpses were frequently wrapped in them and buried in the coastal deserts, which desiccated and preserved both the textiles and the bodies. Using mineral and plant-derived dyes, ancient Andeans decorated many of their textiles with a wide variety of motifs, including geometric figures and stylized people and animals.

The role of animal domestication in early Peru is unclear, but llamas and guinea pigs were certainly domesticated in central Peru by 3500 B.C. As in Mexico, however, hunting continued to play an important role in many areas until quite late.[12] Evidence from several highland sites suggests that by about 4000 B.C. guinea pigs had been domesticated—if they were not domesticated by this time, then these Andean peoples were formidable hunters of these rodents, for guinea pig bones are thickly spread through many layers of occupational refuse. Guinea pigs do so well in captivity, are so prolific and easy to feed, and are so suitable in terms of size for the modern diet, that one wonders why international food conglomerates have not yet renamed and successfully marketed them.

THE FIRST COMPLEX SOCIETIES IN ANDEAN SOUTH AMERICA (C. 3000 B.C.–800 B.C.)

The formative period of Andean South American civilization can be thought of in terms of two periods, the Late Preceramic Period (c. 3000 B.C.–1800 B.C.)[13] and the Initial Period (c. 1800 B.C.–800 B.C.).

Like their archaeological colleagues working on early civilizations in other parts of the world, archaeologists in Peru have tried to identify when ancient Peruvian societies first made those fateful transitions in the direction of cultural complexity— complexity in the sense of the evolution of the kind of society represented by the Inka, with its bureaucratic hierarchies, class divisions, monumental architecture, economic differentiation and integration, expansionistic militarism, and elaboration of arts, crafts, and ideology.

As we have seen in other chapters, every early civilization around the world solved similar problems of nutrition and adaptation. Each found a reliable and productive plant to provide carbohydrates (rice, wheat, potatoes, maize, etc.), a legume to provide high-quality vegetable proteins (beans, peas, vetch, etc.), an animal protein source (usually a blend of hunting, fishing, and herding), and a textile to provide clothing (wool, linen, cotton, etc.). Not every society that evolved these adaptations became a great civilization (e.g., Polynesian societies based on tubers, pigs, and bark cloth), but all that did converged in their solutions to essentially the same problems of adaptation.

Peru offers an interesting possible variation on this theme because its sea coasts offer such a prolific source of food, in the form of many species of birds, shellfish, and fish—particularly schooling fish, such as anchovies. Even without farming, or with some minimal gardening, these coasts may have proffered enough reliable food to support many people—people who could live for all or much of the year in the same communities.

In the 1970s archaeologist Michael Moseley suggested that the initial stage of the rise of Andean societies was based on people who lived in villages and began to evolve some simple social stratifications on the basis of a fishing and foraging economy along the marine coasts rather than agriculture—at least at first. At one level this suggestion might not seem particularly radical. We know that all that is required for sedentary communities and the first appearances of complex societies is a highly productive and reliable blend of animal and plant foods, and it is not important whether these foods are agricultural (chapter 6) or not. Native Americans on the Northwest coast of North America managed to live in non-agricultural sedentary communities that were stratified by wealth and an elementary sense of class, for example, as did many others, including the hunter-foragers of Southwest Asia, whose descendants became the denizens of the great Sumerian and Babylonian empires (chapter 8).

But the Andes case would perhaps be the only known example in which a great civilization's first stages were based on intensive fishing and maritime foraging. Also, the Inka Empire managed to tie together a great diversity of upland and lowland environments in an economy that was fundamentally agricultural when the Spanish encountered it, so it is interesting to see what role maritime resources played in the overall cultural evolution of this area, both before agriculture became the dominant source of food and afterward.

We know that by at least 6000 B.C. quite a few people lived on the Pacific coast, probably moving between the river valleys, the *lomas* (fog-oases), and the coast.[14] For several millennia thereafter, these societies seemed to change little as they adapted to this rich complex of environments. Anyone who has had the good fortune to live at the interface between sea, plains, and mountains, where oysters, clams, and fish can be combined with the wealth of terrestrial foods, can appreciate the stability and diversity of such economies, and the Andean coast is among the richest such zones in the world.

Excavations at Paloma,[15] on the coast of the Chilca Valley, sixty-five kilometers south of Lima, illustrate some aspects of life in such regions. Paloma was located about 3.5 kilometers from the ocean and 7.5 kilometers from the Chilca River, on the edge of the *lomas* zone, where fogs supported some vegetation. Beginning about 8,000 years ago, people were living there in reed huts, probably already putting together a varied economy of plant collecting, hunting, and foraging. But shortly before 3000 B.C., some people apparently moved from the *lomas* in order to concentrate on the interface of coast and river valley, and small, dispersed settlements began to appear in these zones.[16] By about 2500 B.C., many small sedentary communities had appeared along the Andean coast. In some cases, the diet of these communities seems to have been based mainly on marine resources, with wild or domestic plants of only secondary importance,[17] but there was great variability from site to site.

At Alto Salaverry,[18] which was occupied from about 2500 B.C. to 1800 B.C., people cultivated and subsisted mainly on plants, but a lot of the calories in their diet came from sharks, bonito, mussels, and many other types of marine foods. In several communities of this period, skeletons show a pattern of bone growth in the inner ear that is common among people who spend a lot of time diving in cold water.[19]

At Chilca, the primary meat source appears to have been sea lions, but mussels, other invertebrates, and a variety of collected plants were also important. At other sites the remains of sharks, rays, cormorants, gulls, pelicans, and other animals attest to the importance of the resources of the coastal shallows, as does the presence of fish hooks, nets, and lines. No boats have been found at any of these sites, but the kinds of fish and invertebrates usually eaten along the coast are easily taken with simple nets.

By about 2000 B.C., numerous communities dotted the Andean coastline, many of them on river deltas and bays. Most of these seem to have been quite simple foraging-based communities, and few had more than several hundred inhabitants. At Chilca, examination of the burials of thirty adults and twenty-two children and adolescents indicated only minor differences in grave goods or positioning of the corpses. Some people were interned with spindles and spindlewhorls, others with fish hooks and lines, still others with cotton and weaving tools or a pointed stick and spatula kit that may have been used in shellfish gathering.

Once the Andean coast was fairly thickly settled, people here, like those in Egypt, Mesopotamia, China, and other early developmental centers, began building monumental architecture. It is absurd to think that people generally have some innate desire to build big stone buildings, but in Andean South America, too, no sooner had people devised economies of some reasonable reliability and richness than they began "wasting" massive amounts of their wealth in temples, tombs, and pyramids.

As was discussed in chapter 7 and other earlier chapters, the appearance of monumental architecture was one of the earliest signs of social transformations of cultures around the world. Andean South American civilization also followed this pattern. In the second millennium B.C., people in dozens of communities along the coast began to build impressive stone buildings and complexes of plazas, sunken pits, courts, truncated pyramids, and other large and formally arranged architecture.

A principal example of this development is El Paraíso, on the banks of the Rio Chillón, about two kilometers inland from the sea. This site is dominated by a large "temple" complex consisting of a central large structure flanked by two protruding wings, with the whole complex enclosing a large patio. The site has eight or nine distinct structural units, and the two largest complexes were built on artificial mounds more than 250 meters in length and fifty meters in width, rising to a height of over five meters. It has been estimated that there are over fifty hectares of such constructions here.[20] One complex of rooms, over 450 meters long, is among the largest buildings ever constructed in ancient Andean South America.[21]

There is much variability in early Andean South American monumental architecture, but there are also regularities that suggest that the builders of these structures shared a complex ideology and aesthetic. In previous chapters we have noted that early civilizations seem to have been built around a core of fundamental beliefs that integrated peoples over large areas and motivated them to work in concert within and between communities. Traces of this ideology seem to be expressed at El Paraíso. As Jeffrey Quilter noted,[22] the principal mounds at both El Paraíso and another coastal site, Piedra Parada,[23] are oriented to north 25 degrees east. This orients the sites

> toward the NE and SW maxima of the Milky Way, and the axis perpendicular to this orientation is directed to the rising of the sun at the Summer Solstice (December) in the east and the setting of the sun at the Winter Solstice (June), as calculated for the years ca. [1450 B.C.].[24] . . . This suggests that the astrocosmological concepts known to have been important for the Inka were established in Preceramic times."[25]

Other complexes of this period have different orientations, but most of them have a formal, almost stylized use of specific architectural elements and arrangements. Ancient Peruvians used the interplay of rectilinear arrangements with circular or rounded elements, as well as the placement of sunken courts, terraces, and other constructions at different levels of elevation. These arrangements may have been intended, like those of Egyptian temples, to take the individual who enters the complex through a progression of "sacred" spaces.[26] At El Paraíso, Huaca Florida, and other sites, people built complexes in a "U" pattern, in which people presumably entered the open part of the "U"-shaped complex of platforms and buildings and then proceeded through interior forecourts, sunken courts, and other structures.

The outer stone walls of El Paraíso were faced with clay and then painted; like the ancient Egyptians, Maya, Greeks, and others, the people of El Paraíso painted their monumental buildings in primary colors.

The significance of El Paraíso is difficult to assess. Most of the occupational refuse at the site has been destroyed by centuries of plowing. The paucity of residential remains at the site suggests it may have been mainly a ceremonial center (Moseley[27] estimates its population at 1,500 to 3,000 people), but it is difficult to determine how much of the site was occupied at a single time or how long it took to build the whole complex.[28]

Of the other early monumental buildings along the coast in the Preceramic period, most seem to have had a clear ritual purpose. Their alignment with mountain peaks, small inner rooms, internal burials, and other characteristics suggest ritual purposes, although like other early ceremonial structures around the world, they probably were centers for economic exchange and administration. Religion and economy, as we have noted, are inextricably intertwined throughout human history.

Richard Burger and Lucy Salazar-Burger have suggested[29] that much of the architecture of Andean South America between about 1900 B.C. and 1000 B.C. expresses a common religious ideology, the *Kotosh Religious Tradition* (named after the site of Kotosh). We will never know precisely what this religion comprised, but an important element appears to have been ritual fires. In many sites ceremonial hearths were constructed below the floor level of a chamber. Quilter notes[30] that El Paraíso's sunken pit, a rectangle about 4.5 × 4.25 meters, shows evidence of considerable burning. Benches around these pits are common in constructions of this period, and Quilter suggests that in ritual use ten to twelve adults sat around these ritual fires and offered marine shells, meat, quartz, or other goods in sacrifices—perhaps while under the influence of coca or alcohol.

People in the Andean highlands also built monumental structures. At Kotosh, at about the 1,800-meter level on the eastern slopes of the Andes, a large temple complex may have been begun before 1800 B.C. The earliest structure was built on a stone-faced platform some eight meters high. At least ten superimposed building levels were found at Kotosh, and the intensity of occupation and large scale of these constructions probably reflect the emergence of a chiefdom.

The earliest of these "temples" may even have been erected by non-agriculturalists.[31] Most of the later constructions appear to have been the work of maize farmers who relied heavily on domesticated animals, but the paucity of habitation refuse near these massive stone constructions may indicate that they were largely ceremonial, perhaps acting as focal points of trade and social exchange between widely spaced agricultural groups.[32]

THE MARITIME FOUNDATIONS OF ANDEAN SOUTH AMERICAN CIVILIZATION?

As noted above, Michael Moseley has argued that early Andean South American complex societies, as represented by El Paraíso and similar sites, were initially based on an essentially non-agricultural economy.[33] If so, this would be interesting but would not alter our basic understanding of cultural complexity, for what is important in cultural evolution at this stage is the overall productivity of an environment rather than the specific ways in which it is productive.

David Wilson[34] and others have challenged the notion of a non-agricultural basis for these early complex societies on the Peruvian coast,[35] but, unfortunately, the amount of materials excavated still does not allow a resolution of this question. Also, some of the cultivated plants—such as beans, tree fruits (e.g., guava), potatoes, and other tubers—that were available at this time and found at some sites do not preserve well in the archaeological record. Traces of maize have been found at a few sites, but it does not appear to have been important along the coast until after 1000 B.C.

Quilter and Stocker show that at most times during the Preceramic period, marine resources potentially could have supported large sedentary communities along the Andean South American coast, but they note that a key question here is the *reliability* of marine resources.[36] With *el Niño* as a periodic threat, maize agriculture may have represented a more stable (if somewhat more boring) resource than the riches of the sea. Maize, especially if grown with irrigation canals carrying reliable spring runoff waters from the melting snows of the Andes, would have the advantages of great reliability, productivity, and storability—at least compared to oysters and anchovies.

But as Quilter and Stocker point out, fish can be dried or converted to a paste that has at least some shelf life. People who know anchovies only from the oversalted horrors on pizzas may underestimate the appeal and nutritive potential of this staple of Andean South American life. This fish was served fresh, dried, or as a kind of paste that, as every cook knows, is a marvelous addition to many tomato-based sauces. And anchovies are only one of many species of fish available in great numbers on the Peruvian coast. Sea mammals, too, can be rendered into storable oil, and they provided a reliable source of meat in ancient times.

The evidence from Paloma (see above) indicates almost total reliance on marine animal products rather than hunted or domesticated animals,[37] and the site shows little evidence of an agricultural economy, but we still have far too little data to resolve this debate.

Sheila and Thomas Pozorski's history of the Casma Valley, located on the north central coast, between 2500 B.C. and 200 B.C., suggests that the coastal areas developed complex societies earlier than the highlands. Their history also suggests, however, that both highlands and coastal areas were to some extent linked culturally, and that they changed in the same direction.[38] Quilter and Stocker also argue that the highlands and lowlands were interrelated culturally in a complex fashion during the Preceramic Period.[39] Potatoes, cereals, fish, and many other remains were probably traded in substantial quantities, and in addition, a similarity in the style of shell ornaments and other artifacts suggests "a common ideological system that was shared by populations from the Pacific shore to the tropical forest, and that accompanied economic interactions."[40]

These various subsistence and technological changes were paralleled by changes in the distribution of settlements, as many of the fishing communities along the coast were slowly abandoned, and people moved inland to take up agriculture. The distribution of settlements in the inland valleys and the botanical remains found at these sites suggest that simple irrigation canals were being constructed from about 1800 B.C. to 1200 B.C. to grow squash, legumes, beans, sweet and white potatoes, and peanuts.[41] The transition to inland settlement and an agricultural economy required major social and technological changes in the form of technology for irrigation, ground preparation, harvesting, and storage, as well as organized, coordinated labor groups.[42] At Huaca Florida, for example, a site located about eight miles inland from El Paraíso, a large monumental complex of stone and adobe buildings was built about 1700 B.C.[43] The economic basis of this community probably involved a great deal of inter-regional trade, but it also directly depended on irrigation agriculture (crops raised probably included cotton, beans, and squash).

As these various sites indicate, cultural evolution rests not on any particular form of economy—all that is required is sufficient and reliable production. The shift inland from coastal communities, and the change from intense exploitation of marine resources to irrigation farming, probably was a result of the somewhat greater reliability and productivity of farming—especially once these communities could still get marine resources via trade with coastal communities.

In summary of the Initial Period, we see clear evidences of important social changes in these monumental complexes in the highlands and along the coast, but it seems likely that these communities remained relatively simply organized compared to the cultures that followed them. When we look at mortuary practices, for example, the small amount of very sketchy evidence we have shows a certain formalization of burial practices and some elaboration of them, but there's no clear evidence of massive disparities in wealth, power, or prestige. At the site of Asia, for example, forty-nine funeral bundles were recovered in which bodies and a few utilitarian goods were wrapped in reed mats and placed below the floor of a rectangular compound.[44] Differences in these burials may indicate some status differences, and there are a few "trophy heads" and headless bodies in this group that may indicate raiding or warfare, but overall the burial practices until about 900 B.C. suggest a society that is somewhat non-egalitarian, perhaps, but is not organized on the basis of class.

More important, insofar as the scanty evidence indicates, while these people traded products and evolved common ideologies, these communities were not functionally integrated to any great extent. Several small communities probably came together to build El Paraíso, but there is little evidence of functional specialization within and among communities.

THE EARLY HORIZON PERIOD (C. 800 B.C.–A.D. 1)

It is a fallacy of historical analysis to assume that increasing complexity is a natural, inherent quality in human societies. The idea of "progress" is so much a part of Western culture that it sometimes blinds people to the fits and starts of cultural evolution.

Yet Andean South American civilization is another example of a trend we have noted in many other places in the world. In Andean South America, too, many millennia of domesticating plants and developing an agricultural system culminated in the rapid evolution of ancient states and empires. "Explosive" is a somewhat incongruous term when applied to cultural changes that happened over centuries, but in retrospect the cultural transformation of Andean South America in the first millennium B.C. seems so pervasive and rapid that use of the term is not a great exaggeration.

The monumental constructions at El Paraíso and other sites presage the cultural changes underway in this period, and there are many other signs that the Andean world was changing after about 1000 B.C. As we saw in the cases of Egypt, Mesoamerica, and elsewhere, "art" was not just a minor peripheral part of the rise of ancient civilizations: art was an integral part of this process. In all early states, the cities, rank-wealth hierarchies, and functionally interdependent economies that arose were presaged by the spread of an art style that was usually expressed mostly directly in pottery.

Peru was no exception to this pattern. After about 900 B.C., people living at Chavín de Huántar (Figure 14.2) and other sites in the highlands of northern Andean South America began to use the same styles of decoration in their pottery, architecture, and

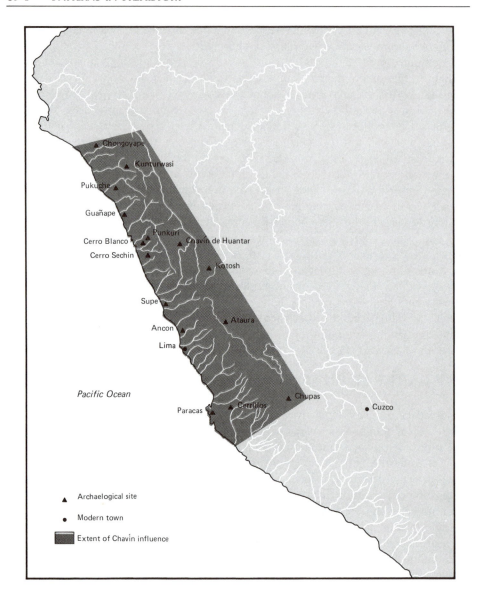

FIGURE 14.2   As in other early civilizations, initial cultural complexity in Andean South America was prefaced by the rapid spread of particular styles of pottery and other artifacts. Chavín-style artifacts have been found throughout the area indicated here.

other artifacts. Over succeeding centuries, tens of thousands of people over a great area participated in the Chavín Horizon, as this complex of stylistic elements is called.

The main motifs of Chavín art include fantastic depictions of hybrid combinations of people and jaguars, as well as snakes, bats, fish, crabs, and crocodile-like figures. In its fusion of tropical forest elements, such as snakes, jaguars, and caiman,

Chavín art may reflect earlier cultural influences from the forests east of the Andes, but the "story" of Andean South American civilizations is that of integrating different zones—coasts, mountains, and lowland forests. The spread of Chavín styles is probably a harbinger of the functional integration of these areas in later periods. In some areas these motifs spread at about the same time as apparent increases in product exchange, activity specialization, population densities, and investments in monumental buildings, but the general tenor of the Chavín diffusion is reminiscent of the initial spread of Olmec art in Mesoamerica—a relatively simple extension of aesthetic and perhaps religious traditions in the absence of elaborate political hierarchies or economic elites.

Chavín de Huántar, the site after which the art style is named (though it is probably not the earliest or even most important Chavín settlement), was occupied for all or most of the period between about 850 B.C. and 200 B.C.[45] It boasts a ceremonial complex composed of two low platform mounds, a massive terraced platform, and a sunken court, forty-eight meters on a side and paved with stone. This complex is arranged in the "U"-form (discussed above) that was established some centuries earlier at El Paraíso. Interior support for the *Castillo*, a central part of the monumental complex at El Paraíso, is provided by adobe walls that have been skillfully combined with cut stone beams, and many interior rooms appear to have been decorated with painted designs. Some rooms apparently served as repositories for offerings, since hundreds of finely crafted ceramic pots were found there, as well as masses of llama, guinea pig, and fish bones and seashells imported from distant coasts.[46]

By the fourth century B.C. as many as 3,000 people may have lived in and around the monumental complex at Chavín de Huántar—by no means the number traditionally associated with a "state," but still a large number of people, and there was probably some significant craft-specialization. Gold was the medium of the finest art in the Chavín era, as craftsmen cut, embossed, annealed, cast, and welded it into ear spools, nose ornaments, plaques, crowns, and face coverings for corpses. Copper and silver were also extensively used for making ornaments, and weaving became a fine art as well.

The central religious symbols of Chavín were widely distributed over the northern and central coasts, and Chavín-style ceramics and architecture are found even in small villages.

The Chavín cult, like other such early religions, was probably an effective means of stimulating people to act in coordinated ways. After all, the expenses of large buildings and the "furs and feathers" of office are cheap compared to their power in directing the population toward specific economic and political goals. The Amazonian animals typical of Chavín designs and the distribution of these designs suggest that the center at Chavín de Huántar may have been an intermediate point on routes connecting the coasts with the exotic, rich world of the interior Amazon. Llama herders from the mountains, maize farmers from the valleys, fishermen, artisans, and other specialists may have derived from the Chavín cult the kinds of administration and political support and integration that set the stage for the evolution of state societies.

There is some evidence in the form of fortresses, however, that the Chavín period may have been more violent than originally thought: redistribution centers and a unified religious iconography do not necessarily mean an era of ecumenism and peace.[47]

THE EARLY INTERMEDIATE PERIOD (A.D. 1–A.D. 600): EARLY STATES

In the first millennium A.D., Andean South American societies were transformed from relatively simple, small political units that we might call chiefdoms into much larger and more populous militaristic cultures that we can legitimately term states.[48] Within this period the population of Andean South America rose from a few hundred thousand to approximately four or five million, large cities appeared in scores of places, armies conquered thousands of square kilometers, irrigation systems brought rich harvests to the desert and mountains, and the ceramic, architectural, metallurgical, and textile arts reached such heights that archaeologists have traditionally referred to this period as the "Classic" Period.[49]

This transformation seems to have arisen out of the disintegration of the Chavín cult at about 200 B.C., which was followed by the emergence of as many as fifteen different centers of regional development. Ceremonial centers can be found in many places in the southern Andean South American highlands at this time, as well as in the Nazca Valley and other coastal regions. Some of these were sizable towns, such as Tambo Viejo in the Acari Valley (Nazca area), which contains hundreds of rectangular rooms, most of which seem to have been residences. But the Nazca state probably remained a mix of villages and towns.[50] Also numerous along the northern coast were great fortresses of terraced adobe platforms with room complexes and defensive peripheral walls.

Two of the best known examples of Early Intermediate Period cultures are the Moche and the Nazca. The Moche culture was concentrated in about a 400-kilometer coastal strip that extended about 50 kilometers inland, thanks to an elaborate irrigation system that at its peak probably supported more than 50,000 people. By 200 B.C. the community at Cerro Arena, for example, contained hundreds of houses and public buildings that extended over an area of about a square mile. The economic basis of this and other communities was an irrigation system in which mud canals were built high in the hills, diverting water through kilometers of canals that snaked along the mountainside and down to the valleys. Because the Moche worked only with mud, the construction of these canal systems had to be done with great precision; if the water flowed too slowly, silt would accumulate so rapidly as to make the canal a vast waste of effort, while if it flowed too quickly, the whole system could be eroded. Cleaning the wind-blown sand from these systems probably required the annual orchestration of thousands of laborers.

In chapter 7 the premise that irrigation systems like these are primary *determinants* of cultural evolution was discussed and, for the most part, rejected. Often in prehistory, great irrigation systems seem more the products of states than their immediate cause. But in the case of the Moche Valley and many other examples, irrigation agriculture and cultural evolution are perhaps better viewed as closely interrelated, with an increase in the complexity of administrative and economic systems going step by step with increases in the complexity of irrigation systems.

We know much about life in Andean South America during this period because the people recorded their activities in great detail in ceramics, sculpture, paintings, and tapestries. Pottery vessels depict people hunting deer with spears and clubs, fishermen putting to sea in small canoes, blowgun hunters taking aim at birds, weavers working under the direction of a foreman, and many people engaging in war, human sacrifice, and violence. People are also shown being carried on sedan chairs, seated on thrones, receiving tribute, and presiding at executions.

One of the most spectacular archaeological discoveries of the past decade was the Moche royal burial complex at Sipán, about 420 miles northwest of Lima. These burials are particularly important because, unlike most known Moche sites, they had not been looted (the tomb was rescued and protected from local thieves by a Peruvian archaeologist) and also because they express many elements of Moche culture. By now the reader, having surveyed Egypt, Mesopotamia, Mesoamerica, and other early civilizations in previous chapters, will not be surprised to learn that ancient Moche culture was based on massive inequalities in wealth, power, and prestige, that warfare was glorified and celebrated with the ritual executions of captives, that loving skill and precious materials were lavished on making beautiful objects—many of which were buried with dead elites—and that the entire society comprised an expansionistic and militaristic state.

The Sipán burials that reflect these aspects of Moche culture were found in the interior of a large mudbrick pyramid. In one burial a man identified by archaeologist Christopher Donnan[51] as a "warrior-priest" was found lying on his back in a wooden coffin. He was wearing gold nose and ear ornaments, turquoise bead bracelets, and copper sandals, and surrounded by other exotic goods, including spears, war clubs, shields, atlatl darts, sea shells, feather ornaments, lovely cotton fabrics, hundreds of pots, a dog, two llamas, and other goods. This man was also buried with what one might consider the most valuable of all commodities, three young women and two men. As we have seen in other ancient cultures, many of these societies were based on ideologies that sanctioned these sacrifices and probably promised the participants an eternal and joyful afterlife. Although we will never know for certain what was going on in the minds of these non-literate peoples, it seems a reasonable speculation that the Moche believed that by supplying this man with a few female and male attendants, food, tools, and some personal ornaments, they were assuring him of a reasonably comfortable eternity.

Depictions on Moche pots provide a "text," of sorts, for hundreds of them show similar scenes, apparently recording rituals in which warrior-priests slit the throats of war-captives, distributed the blood to be drunk, and then dismembered the bodies.

Among the other ideological expressions in ceramics of this period are the frank depictions of sexual practices. While every conceivable sexual variation is amply illustrated, oral sex is a predominant theme. Pots representing sexual themes in the most explicit terms may have been used in ordinary daily life, and to drink from them is to perform, symbolically at least, acts still considered illegal in some states in the USA. If the sexual practices depicted in pottery are in any way a reflection of the proclivities of the people—and reports of the Spanish and the Inka suggest this was the case—then the Moche may have devised a very efficient system of birth control.[52] For although there are few depictions of homosexuality (most involve lesbian relationships), procreative acts of sexual intercourse are much less celebrated than nonprocreative acts in this pottery.

If Moche pottery is an accurate reflection of daily life, men hunted, farmed, fished, and fought in wars, while women cooked food and performed other basic domestic services. Based on pottery representations and later ethnographic accounts, women also produced all or most of a primary kind of wealth in the form of textiles. Ethnographic evidence from the time of European contact to the present suggests that nearly all women wove textiles, and even the most elaborate fabrics may have been produced by peasant women working individually in villages.

The overall archaeological record of the Moche reveals the central patterns of all early complex societies. The evidence of warfare, for example, in ceramic depictions is supported by settlement patterns: every well-surveyed coastal valley has been found to have fortresses and fortified settlements dating to this period, and weapons are common in these sites, particularly along the southern coast. Trophy heads and mummified corpses showing signs of violence are frequently found in cemeteries.

Occupational specialization was still at a rather simple level, but skilled craftsmen must have been full-time specialists to be able to produce the intricate objects in gold, silver, copper, and many other commodities found here.

The economic productivity of the Moche, their class-based society, and their ideology were also expressed in monumental architecture. At various places in the Moche Valley they built large clay platforms, ramps, temples, pyramids, and other constructions. One Moche pyramid, Huaca del Sol, was 340 by 160 meters at the base, stood 40 meters high, and comprised an estimated 140 million mudbricks.

In the Nazca Valley people created huge figures on the desert floor by turning over patinated stones. Interpretations of these patterns have ranged from the absurd (Erich von Daniken suggests they were beacons for ancient astronauts) to the economic (make-work projects to keep idle peasants employed in the off-season).

The capital of Moche seems to have been flooded following an earthquake that changed the course of the Moche River between A.D. 400 and A.D. 500.[53]

In general, the Moche and other small states of this period appear to have been caught up in spirals of warfare, but they were also linked by trade mechanisms. Like other early states around the world, they seem to have expanded and contracted as the fortunes of war changed and as differences in the agricultural potential of various regions took effect.

THE MIDDLE HORIZON PERIOD (C. A.D. 600–A.D. 1000): COMPETING STATES

At about A.D. 600, the many rival "states" of Andean South America began to give way to several larger competing political systems, one centered at Wari in the Manteco Basin, another at Tiwanaku, at the southern end of Lake Titicaca, and a third in the Moche-Chimú area. In these and perhaps other areas, wars of conquest brought large territories under the control of centralized, hierarchically-organized governments and lessened regional isolation.[54]

Tiwanaku is one of the first and largest "states" to be based in large part on potatoes, which were intensively cultivated with other crops on raised fields reclaimed from the lake marshes. The people of Tiwanaku also herded vast numbers of llamas—invaluable beasts of burden in this high country of thin air, and where in the classic Andean tradition the resources of highlands and lowlands could best be exploited via voluminous trade.

The people of Tiwanaku included master stonecarvers, who produced monumental gates, statues, and other buildings that are some of the most impressive in all Andean South America.

Wari existed as a political system for only a century or two, but at its high point it carried out political and economic activities over most of the coast and highlands between Cajamarca in the north and Sicuani in the south. The evidence for the Wari "empire" comes mainly from the distribution of specific art styles and religious symbols over a wide area of the central highlands. Significantly, these motifs show up most frequently in the burials of individuals whose associated mortuary goods appeared to reflect particularly high status. The city of Wari expanded to an impressive ten square kilometers, making it one of the largest residential sites in the ancient New World.

It is probably significant that some of ancient Peru's major roadways may have been constructed during this period, for such roads would have been very important in facilitating the exchange of goods and services over an area as large as the one apparently administered from Wari.

Wari and Tiwanaku may have been fierce enemies or dual capitals of a single political polity—the evidence is not clear. The world-wide pattern of early states is one in which ever-larger polities compete with each other, with many expansions and contractions, but with a long-term increase in the size of the polities and the scale of the conflict. Wari, Tiwanaku, and other early states probably reflect this evolutionary paradigm.

THE LATE INTERMEDIATE PERIOD (C. A.D. 1000–A.D. 1476): EARLY EMPIRES

With the collapse of the Wari and Tiwanaku political systems between A.D. 800 and A.D. 1000, at least seven different areas in Andean South America became power centers, the best known and most developed of which was the Chimú state centered in the Moche Valley on the northern coast. A major center of the Chimú political system was the beautiful city of Chan-Chan, a planned settlement covering nearly eleven square kilometers—one of the largest pre-Columbian cities in the New World. It was divided into ten rectangular sectors, each containing houses, terraces, reservoirs, parks, roads, and public buildings. By the time Chan-Chan was built, Andean societies were rigidly stratified: Fiedel notes that in one area of Chan-Chan the skeletons of between two hundred and three hundred young women were found, "probably members of the royal harem, [who] were sacrificed either at the time of the deceased ruler's funeral or at later commemorative ceremonies."[55]

Goldworking, silverworking, ceramics, weaving, and sculpture were all highly developed crafts. Chimú society seems to have been rigidly stratified according to wealth and prestige, and the extension of political and economic control appears to have been based on a highly efficient army.[56]

Perhaps the most significant development in Andean South America during this period (A.D. 1000–A.D. 1476) was the multiplication of urban centers. Much of southern Peru remained largely rural, but in the northern half of the country some of the greatest cities of the pre-conquest period were built.[57]

THE LATE HORIZON (C. A.D. 1476–A.D. 1532): THE IMPERIAL TRANSFORMATION

The largest and most highly integrated ancient political system ever to appear in the New World evolved in Andean South America within the space of only eighty-seven years. Centered in the Cuzco Valley, the Inka Empire (more properly known as the Empire of Tahuantinsuyu ["world of the four quarters"]) eventually stretched from Colombia to central Chile and from the Pacific to the eastern jungles, tying together under the administration of a single royal lineage many diverse regional economic and political systems. At its height, as many as six million people may have been living under Inka rule in one of the most intricately ordered societies of all time.[58] Like Egypt, the Inka polity was a "hegemonic-territorial" state, to use Terence D'Altroy's term,[59] with its population spread rather thinly over a large area but with effective government control over most aspects of life.

Native and Spanish accounts say that the Inka began their rise to power out of the dissolution of the many small competing Andean South American states of the thirteenth and fourteenth centuries A.D. The people of Cuzco were attacked by a rival state at about A.D. 1435 and managed to prevail. Succeeding monarchs at Cuzco added new provinces to the empire by conquest, treaty, and simple annexation. The Inkas' oral histories—recorded by the Spanish—speak of military campaigns in which Inka kings smashed the rival power of Chan-Chan in the 1460s, put down large-scale revolts in the 1470s, and greatly expanded the empire in the 1480s.[60]

The economic basis of the Inka Empire (Figure 14.3) was a highly integrated system of fishing, herding, and farming. Rivers were channeled through stone-lined canals, while lowland irrigation systems, which had existed for thousands of years, were extended and brought under a centralized authority. Llamas and alpacas were raised for wool, while dogs, muscovy ducks, and guinea pigs provided most of the meat. But the staple foods were maize, beans, potatoes, quinoa, oca, and peppers.

The food storage methods used by the Inka were very important in establishing imperial food reserves. Potatoes were alternately dried and frozen to produce a black, pulpy product called *chuño*, meat was turned into jerky, and grain was brewed into *chica*, a nutritious beer. Archaeologists familiar with this combination say it is not as bad as it sounds.

FIGURE 14.3 The Inka road system connected almost every settlement to two main north-south routes and facilitated voluminous transports of goods and effective administration.

Christine Hastorf and Sissel Johannessen have studied changes in the use of maize as the political system of Andean South America changed between A.D. 500 and 1500, particularly among the Inka. The Inka and their immediate predecessors converted maize into beer and then defined this beer as a prestige item and associated it with imperial power and the theology of the Inka state. People were brought together in communal feasts in which beer was consumed, and at these feasts the elites could reinforce their position: by providing beer in this context they could underscore the indebtedness of the peasantry to them and put the labor that the peasantry did for the elites in the context of the national religion and the highly stratified class system.[61]

The people of the empire were organized in a complex way according to a decimal system in which there were administrators for every unit of taxpayer from 10 to 10,000. Most people were members of large kin groups, called *ayllu*; marriages were between members of the same *ayllu*. The *ayllu* were usually economically self-sufficient units that held land in common, and their members were bound together by complex patterns of reciprocal obligations, such as requiring members to work in each other's place when one was absent and to support widows and the infirm. Farmers worked a certain amount of time on state-owned plots, while craftsmen and specialists such as runners, weavers, and goldsmiths contributed according to their particular talents.

Records of taxes, transactions, and census figures were kept with the aid of the *quipu*, a set of strings tied into knots at different levels (Figure 14.4) according to a decimal notation system that was used by a special hereditary class of accountants to memorize the information.[62] A writing system of the type used in early Mesopotamia would no doubt have conveyed more religious and philosophical information, but for simple information storage and retrieval, the *quipu* appears to have been an adequate substitute for writing, when complemented by the enormous Inka bureaucracy.[63]

Gold, fabrics, and other luxury goods were collected from around the empire for distribution among the elites. Women, too, were treated as commodities. Government agents visited each village periodically and took selected girls of about age ten

FIGURE 14.4 The Inka never developed a written language, but administrators used the *quipu*, a set of knotted strings, to keep records.

back to provincial capitals where they were taught spinning, weaving, and cooking. They were then apportioned out as wives for the emperor and the nobles.

The Inka Empire both created and was created by its system of roads.[64] Most villages were largely self-sufficient, but the flow of goods and information and, most important, armies required to create the empire were dependent on the road system, comprising an overall network of about 40,000 kilometers of paved roads. Road beds were excavated through hillsides, swamps were crossed by drained causeways, walls were built along roadways to protect the traveler from the fierce gales of the uplands, and wide rivers and ravines were crossed by suspension bridges made of woven vines hung from stone towers. All along the roads were storehouses and administrative outposts, and runners stationed about a kilometer apart were reputed to carry messages over distances as great as 2,400 kilometers in just five days.[65]

Although they were master builders, most Inka lived in rural villages, not great metropolises. Typical Inka residential units were rectangular walled houses of stone or adobe, subdivided into smaller units. Most public constructions were in the form of palaces, temples, granaries, fortresses, barracks, and highway stations. The skill used in these constructions is amazing, considering the simple tools employed. The Inka cut stones into huge blocks simply by chipping and abrading them with harder stones, and they then fitted them together (without the use of mortar) so precisely that, as the cliché goes, a knifeblade could not be inserted between them.

The cultural order and social structure of the Inka were expressed not only in its public monuments, but even in its domestic architecture. Susan Niles has catalogued how, in one particular case, the buildings constituting the fifteenth-century estate of a noble family were arranged to reflect the rigid class hierarchy of the Inka polity.[66]

The capital city of Cuzco was an orderly arrangement of houses, monumental buildings, and streets, well-provided with a municipal water and drainage system. The great temple of Qori Kancha here had exterior walls measuring sixty-eight by fifty-nine meters and a semi-circular annex that rose to a height of more than thirty-four meters. A gold frieze about a meter wide ran along the exterior wall, and the entranceway was heavily sheathed in gold plate. Many other structures at the capital were lavishly decorated with gold and silver.

The comparatively great internal security of the empire made it unnecessary to defend most settlements, except with occasional hilltop forts. The heart of the Inka army was the common foot soldier, who was armed with club, mace, battle ax, or lance. Slings, bolas, and spear throwers were used prior to the main attack, but brutal hand-to-hand combat usually decided the issue. One successful tactical innovation of the Inka was the practice of holding back a large body of troops who were thrown in at a critical juncture—a simple tactic similar in a way to Napoleon's successful use of reserves.

THE EUROPEAN CONQUEST

Archaeological research in some areas of Andean South America was interrupted in the 1980s and early 1990s by peasant revolutions and armed conflict between the government and rebels. The colonial history of Andean South America explains a lot about the origins of these conflicts.

After sporadic, occasionally hostile contacts with the Inka people in the A.D. 1520s, the Spanish under Francisco Pizarro set out toward the provincial capital at Cajamarca, the residence of Atahualpa, the Inka king. Why the Spanish were never intercepted and massacred remains a mystery, but warfare between rival claimants to the Inka throne at this time was probably a factor. In any case, the Andean South Americans soon had cause to regret their diffidence. Pizarro and his men entered the city on 15 November 1532, and found it to be a massive, fortified center, but, surprisingly, nearly deserted. After establishing himself in a fortress with a couple of cannons and his few score soldiers, Pizarro elected to wait until the Inka king made an effort to visit him. Eventually the emperor came, borne on a litter and preceded by thousands of soldiers, attendants, and subjects. The first Spaniard to approach the king was the chaplain who, as part of Pizarro's contract with the king of Spain and the Pope, was charged with spreading the Christian faith. The chaplain immediately began to harangue the king, through an interpreter, about the creation of the world, the fall of Adam and Eve, the Virgin Birth, the establishment of the papacy, and other dogma, culminating his speech with the announcement that the Pope had given the Inka Empire to King Charles of Spain.

Not surprisingly, the Inka king took exception to parts of the chaplain's speech. He wanted to know how the Pope could give away something that was not his, and how it had happened that the god of the Christians had died, since the Inka deity, the Sun, was immortal.[67] When Atahualpa asked how the chaplain knew all these things, he was handed a breviary. The king looked briefly and no doubt uncomprehendingly inside, and then threw it away. At this point the Spanish attacked, and then the inexplicable happened: instead of killing the Spanish, the Inka fled, dropping their weapons and killing themselves in their panicked flight, and the Spanish were able to dispatch hundreds and capture the king with little trouble. They remained fortressed in Cajamarca for some months, detaining the king, who tried to win his release by offering to fill a room (supposed to have been 6.5 by 4.5 meters in size) with gold. The Spanish, meanwhile, took masses of gold and silver in raids, most of it in the form of exquisitely wrought figures, which they melted into ingots.

Rumors of insurrections in the countryside convinced the Spanish to execute the Inka king. They did so, but considered themselves enlightened for giving him the option of being garroted rather than burned at the stake—a reward to the king for allowing himself to be baptized. Atahualpa's death and the ensuing factionalism among rival claimants to the throne, as well as the devastation brought on by introduced diseases and the horror wrought on the populace through warfare and the destruction of the irrigation system, proved crippling. The population of Andean South America is thought to have dropped from over six million to fewer than two million within a few decades of the conquest.

THE ORIGINS OF COMPLEX CULTURES IN ANDEAN SOUTH AMERICA: CONCLUSIONS

The reader by now will not be surprised to learn that most scholars interpret the rise of civilization in Andean South America to be the result of a multiplicity of factors.

Robert Carneiro's hypotheses linking warfare, population growth, and environmental circumscription (chapter 7) to the rise of states seems particularly applicable to Andean South America. There are some suggestions that warfare was in fact an important "stress" that stimulated some kinds of complexity (though perhaps not in the manner suggested by Carneiro).[68] But sustained warfare seems to have been more of an important factor well *after* the appearance of such things as monumental buildings, the coordination of regional economies, craft specialization, and the rise of great religious traditions.

How, then, are we to account for Andean South American complex societies? Obviously, the rich maritime and agricultural resources were essential ingredients in this development. In only a few areas of the world is it possible to produce and gather enough food to run complex cultures on the basis of primitive technologies, and Andean South America is one of these regions.

An important "negative" element in the evolution of Andean South America appears to have been the fact that, unlike ancient China, Egypt, Mesopotamia, or the Indus Valley, Andean South America was geographically isolated from other highly complex political systems. Evolving Old World civilizations soon came into contact with one another, and their political, economic, and social interchanges appear to have transformed each of them to some degree. But, except for Mesoamerica—which was very distant and cut off by ocean and jungle—Andean South America evolved alone.

The absence of a domesticable draft animal also was a limit on Andean South American development. Llamas compensated for this to a degree, but they cannot compare with the transport or plowing abilities of horses, mules, or oxen. It is difficult to judge the effects the presence of a domesticable draft animal in Andean South America would have had, but it may be significant that almost all agricultural areas of Andean South America today are plowed.

Nor is it easy to weigh the effect on Andean South American developments of the scarcity of accessible iron ore. In the Old World, iron-working seems to have been intimately associated with the expansion of great empires, and, had it been available, it might also have changed the character of later Andean South American developments.

Thus, in summary of Andean South American prehistory, we see that cultural developments there paralleled those in other centers of independent complex society formation in most important details, including the initial spread of a religious cult, the presence of a highly productive economy, the widespread occurrence of monumental architecture, and the gradual emergence of highly stratified, economically integrated state and imperial political systems.

BIBLIOGRAPHY

Alva, W., and C. Donnan. 1993. *Royal Tombs of Sipán*. Los Angeles: Fowler Museum of Cultural History, UCLA.

Ascher, M., and R. Ascher. 1982. *Code of the Quipu: A Study in Media, Mathematics, and Culture*. Ann Arbor: University of Michigan Press.

Bauer, B. S. 1992. *The Development of the Inca State*. Norman, OK: University of Oklahoma Press.

Benfer, R. A. 1982. "The Lomas Site of Paloma (5000 to 7500 B.P.), Chilca Valley, Peru." In *Andean Archaeology*, ed. R. Matos. New York: Academic Press, pp. 27–54.

———. 1984. "The Challenges and Rewards of Sedentism: The Preceramic Village of Paloma, Peru." In *Paleopathology and the Origin of Agriculture*, eds. M. N. Cohen and G. J. Armelagos. New York: Academic Press.

Benson, E. P., ed. 1971. *Dumbarton Oaks Conference on Chavín*. Washington, DC: Dumbarton Oaks Research Library and Collection.

Browman, D. L. 1974. "Pastoral Nomadism in the Andes." *Current Anthropology* 15:188–96.

———. 1975. "Trade Patterns in the Central Highlands of Peru in the First Millennium B.C." *World Archaeology* 6:322–30.

Burger, R. L. 1985. "Concluding Remarks: Early Peruvian Civilization and Its Relation to the Chavin Horizon." In *Early Ceremonial Architecture in the Andes*, ed. C. B. Donnan. Washington, DC: Dumbarton Oaks.

———. 1992. *Chavin and the Origins of the Andean Civilization*. London and New York: Thames and Hudson.

Burger, R. L., and L. Salazar-Burger, 1980. "Ritual and Religion at Huaricoto." *Archaeology* 33:26–33:26–32.

———. 1985. "The Early Ceremonial Center of Huaricoto." In *Early Ceremonial Architecture in the Andes*, ed. C. B. Donnan. Washington, DC: Dumbarton Oaks.

———. 1986. "Early Organizational Diversity in the Peruvian Highland: Huaricoto and Kotosh." In *Andean Archaeology, Papers in Memory of Clifford Evans, Monograph 27*, eds. M. R. Matos, S. A. Turpin, and H. H. Eling, Jr. Los Angeles: Institute of Archaeology, University of California.

———. 1990. "The Chronology and Function of Cardal's Public Architecture." Paper presented at the 18th Annual Midwest Conference on Andean and Amazonian Archaeology and Ethnohistory, February 24. Chicago: University of Chicago.

Burger, R. L., and N. Van Der Merwe. 1990. "Maize and the Origin of Highland Chavin Civilization: An Isotopic Perspective." *American Anthropologist* 92(1):85–95.

Bushnell, G. H. S. 1963. *Peru*. Rev. ed. New York: Praeger.

Carneiro, R. 1970. "A Theory of the Origin of the State." *Science* 169:733–38.

Cobo, Bernabe. 1990 (original c. A.D. 1639). *Inca Religion and Customs* (translated and edited by Roland Hamilton). Austin: University of Texas Press.

Coe, M., D. Snow, and E. Benson. 1986. *Atlas of Ancient America*. New York: Facts on File.

Collier, G. A., R. I. Rosaldo, and J. D. Wirth, eds. 1982. *The Inka and Aztec States, 1400–1800*. New York: Academic Press.

Conrad, G. W. 1981. "Cultural Materialism, Split Inheritance, and the Expansion of Ancient Peruvian Empires." *American Antiquity* 46:3–26.

D'Altroy, T. N. 1992. *Provincial Power in the Inka Empire*. Washington, DC: Smithsonian Institution Press.

Dillehay, T. D. 1990. "Mapuche Ceremonial Landscapes, Social Recruitment and Resource Rights." *Journal of World Archaeology* 22(2):223–41.

Dillehay, T. D., P. Netherly, and J. Rossen. 1989. "Early Preceramic Public and Residential Sites on the Forested Slope of the Western Andes, Northern Peru." *American Antiquity* 54(4):733–58.

Donnan, C. B. 1973. *Moche Occupation of the Santa Valley, Peru*. University of California Publications in Anthropology, no. 8. Berkeley: University of California.

———. 1976. *Moche Art and Iconography*. Los Angeles: U.C.L.A. Latin American Center Publications.

———. 1990. "Master Works Reveal a Pre-Inca World." *National Geographic Magazine* 177(6):34–49.

Donnan, C. B., ed. 1985. *Early Ceremonial Architecture in the Andes*. Washington, DC: Dumbarton Oaks.

Engel, F. 1957. "Early Sites on the Peruvian Coast." *Southwestern Journal of Anthropology* 13:54–68.

Engl, L., and T. Engl. 1969. *Twilight of Ancient Peru.* Trans. A. Jaffe. New York: McGraw-Hill.

Feldman, R. A. 1980. *Aspero, Peru: Architecture, Subsistence Economy, and Other Artifacts of a Preceramic Maritime Chiefdom.* Ph.D. Dissertation, Department of Anthropology, Harvard University.

———. 1985. "Preceramic Corporate Architecture: Evidence for the Development of Nonegalitarian Social Systems in Peru." In *Early Ceremonial Architecture in the Andes,* ed. C. B. Donnan. Washington, DC: Dumbarton Oaks.

Fiedel, S. J. 1987. *Prehistory of the Americas.* Cambridge: Cambridge University Press.

Flannery, K. V. 1973. "The Origins of Agriculture." *Annual Review of Anthropology* 2:271–310.

Greider, T. 1978. *The Art and Archaeology of Pashash.* Austin: University of Texas Press.

Gross, D. R. 1975. "Protein Capture and Cultural Development in the Amazon Basin." *American Anthropologist* 77:526–49.

Haas, J. 1987. "The Exercise of Power in Early Andean State Development." In *The Origins and Development of the Andean State,* eds. J. Haas, S. Pozorski, and T. Pozorski. New York: Cambridge University Press.

Haas, J., S. Pozorski, and T. Pozorski, eds. 1987. *The Origins and Development of the Andean State.* New York: Cambridge University Press.

Hastorf, C. A. and S. Johannessen. 1993. "Pre-Hispanic Political Change and the Role of Maize in the Central Andes of Peru." *American Anthropologist* 95(1):115–137.

Haopes, J. 1994. "Ford Revisited: A Critical Review of the Chronology and Relationships of the Earliest Ceramic Complexes in the New World, 6000–1500 B.C." *Journal of World Prehistory* 8(1):1–50.

Hyslop, J. 1984. *The Inka Road System.* New York: Academic Press.

Idyll, C. P. 1973. "The Anchovy Crisis." *Scientific American* 228:22–29.

Izumi, S. 1971. "Development of the Formative Culture in the Ceja de Montaña of the Central Andes." In *Dumbarton Oaks Conference on Chavin,* ed. E. P. Benson. Washington, DC: Dumbarton Oaks.

Japanese Scientific Expedition to Nuclear America. 1979. *Excavations at La Pampa in the North Highlands of Peru, 1975.* Tokyo: University of Tokyo Press.

Jones, G. D., and R. R. Kautz, eds. 1981. *The Transition to Statehood in the New World.* Cambridge: Cambridge University Press.

Kaplan, L., T. Lynch, and E. E. Smith, Jr. 1973. "Early Cultivated Beans (*Phaseolus vulgaris*) from an Intermontane Peruvian Valley." *Science* 179:76–77.

Keatinge, R. W. 1974. "Chimú Rural Administration Centers in the Moche Valley, Peru." *World Archaeology* 6:66–82.

———. 1988. *Peruvian Prehistory: An Overview of Pre-Inka and Inka Society.* New York: Cambridge University Press.

Lanning, E. P. 1967. *Peru Before the Inkas.* Englewood Cliffs, NJ: Prentice-Hall.

Lathrap, D. W. 1968. "Relationships Between Mesoamerica and the Andean Areas." In *Handbook of Middle American Indians.* Vol. 4. Austin: University of Texas Press.

———. 1973. "The Antiquity and Importance of Long-Distance Trade Relationships in the Moist Tropics of Pre-Columbian South America." *World Archaeology* 5:170–86.

———. 1985. "Jaws: The Control of Power in the Early Buclear American Ceremonial Center." In *Early Ceremonial Architecture in the Andes,* ed. C. Donnan. Washington, DC: Dumbarton Oaks, pp. 241–68.

Lumbreras, L. G. 1974. *The Peoples and Cultures of Ancient Peru.* Trans. B. J. Meggers. Washington, DC: Smithsonian Institution Press.

Lynch, T., ed. 1980. *Guitarrero Cave: Early Man in the Andes.* New York: Academic Press.

———. 1991. "Lack of Evidence for Glacial-Age Settlement of South America: Reply to Dillehay and Collins and to Bruhn and Bryan." *American Antiquity* 5(20):348–55.

MacNeish, R. 1971. "Early Man in the Andes." *Scientific American* 4:36–46.

MacNeish, R. S., R. K. Vierra, A. Nelken-Terner, R. Lurie, and A. G. Cook. 1983. *Prehistory of the Ayacucho Basin, Peru, Volume IV: The Preceramic Way of Life.* Ann Arbor: University of Michigan Press.

Masuda, S., I. Shimada, and C. Morris, eds. 1985. *Andean Ecology and Civilization.* Tokyo: University of Tokyo Press.

Morris, C. 1985. "From Principles of Ecological Complementarity to the Organization and Administration of Tawantinsuyu." In *Andean Ecology and Civilization*, eds. S. Masuda, I. Shimada, and C. Morris. Tokyo: University of Tokyo Press.

Moseley, M. E. 1972. "Subsistence and Demography: An Example of Interaction from Prehistoric Peru." *Southwestern Journal of Anthropology* 28:25–49.

———. 1975. *The Maritime Foundations of Andean Civilization.* Menlo Park, CA: Cummings.

———. 1983a. "The Evolution of Andean Civilization." In *Ancient Native Americans*, ed. J. D. Jennings. San Francisco: Freeman.

———. 1983b. "Central Andean Civilization." In *Ancient Native Americans*, ed. J. D. Jennings. San Francisco: W. H. Freeman.

———. 1985. "The Exploration and Explanation of Early Monumental Architecture in the Andes." In *Early Ceremonial Architecture in the Andes*, ed. C. Donnan. Washington, DC: Dumbarton Oaks, pp. 28–58.

———. 1992. *The Incas and their Ancestors.* London and New York: Thames and Hudson.

Moseley, M. E., and K. C. Day, eds. 1982. *Chan Chan: Andean Desert City.* Albuquerque: University of New Mexico Press.

Murra, J. 1958. "On Inka Political Structure." In *Systems of Political Control and Bureaucracy in Human Society*, ed. V. F. Ray. Seattle: University of Washington Press.

———. 1965. "Herds and Herders in the Inka State." In *Man, Culture and Animals.* Washington, DC: American Association for the Advancement of Science.

———. 1985. "The Limits and Limitations of the 'Vertical Archipelago' in the Andes." In *Andean Ecology and Civilization*, eds. S. Masuda, I. Shimada, and C. Morris. Tokyo: University of Tokyo Press.

Murra, J., and C. Morris. 1976. "Dynastic Oral Tradition, Administrative Records, and Archaeology in the Andes." *World Archaeology* 7:269–79.

Niles, S. A. 1988. *Callachaca.* Iowa City: University of Iowa Press.

Ortloff, C. R., M. E. Moseley, and R. A. Feldman. 1982. "Hydraulic Engineering Aspects of the Chimú/Chicama-Moche Intervalley Canal." *American Antiquity* 47:572–95.

Parsons, J. 1968. "An Estimate of Size and Population for Middle Horizon Tiahuanaco, Bolivia." *American Antiquity* 33:243–45.

———. 1977. Personal communication.

Parsons, J., and N. Psuty. 1975. "Sunken Fields and Prehispanic Subsistence on the Peruvian Coast." *American Antiquity* 40:259–82.

Parsons, M. 1970. "Preceramic Subsistence on the Peruvian Coast." *American Antiquity* 35:292–303.

Patterson, T. C. 1966. "Early Cultural Remains on the Central Coast of Peru." *Nawpa Pacha* 4:145–55.

———. 1971a. "Chavín: An Interpretation of Its Spread and Influence." In *Dumbarton Oaks Conference on Chavín*, ed. E. Benson. Washington, DC: Dumbarton Oaks.

———. 1971b. "Central Peru: Its Population and Economy." *Archaeology* 24:316–21.

———. 1983. "The Historical Development of a Coastal Andean Social formation in Central Peru, 6000 to 500 B.C." In *Investigations of the Andean Past, Papers from the First Annual Northeast Conference on Andean Archaeology and Ethnohistory*, ed. D. H. Sandweiss. Ithaca, NY: Cornell University Latin Studies Program.

———. 1985. "The Huaca La Florida, Rimac Valley, Peru." In *Ceremonial Architecture in the Andes*, ed. C. B. Donnan. Washington, DC: Dumbarton Oaks.

———. 1992. *The Inca Empire.* London: Berg.

Patterson, T. C., and E. P. Lanning. 1964. "Changing Settlement Patterns on the Central Peruvian Coast." *Nawpa Pacha* 2:113–23.

Patterson, T. C., and M. E. Moseley. 1968. "Late Preceramic and Early Ceramic Cultures of the Central Coast of Peru." *Nawpa Pacha* 6:115–33.

Pearsall, D. M. 1992. "The Origins of Plant Cultivation in South American." In *The Origins of Agriculture. An International Perspective*, eds. C. W. Cowan and P. J. Watson. Washington: Smithsonian Institution Press.

Pearsall, D. M., and D. R. Piperno. 1990. "Antiquity of Maize Cultivation in Ecuador: Summary and Reevaluation of the Evidence." *American Antiquity* 55(2):324–37.

Pickersgill, B. 1969. "The Archaeological Record of Chile Peppers (*Capsicum spp.*) and the Sequence of Plant Domestication in Peru." *American Antiquity* 34:54–61.

Pickersgill, B., and A. Bunting. 1969. "Cultivated Plants and the Kon-Tiki Theory." *Nature* 222:225–27.

Pozorski, S. 1987. "Theocracy vs. Militarism: The Significance of the Casma Valley in Understanding Early State Formation." In *The Origins and Development of the Andean State*, eds. J. Haas, S. Pozorski, and T. Pozorski. New York: Cambridge University Press.

Pozorski, T. 1987. "Changing Priorities Within the Chimu State: The Role of Irrigation Agriculture." In *The Origins and Development of the Andean State*, eds. J. Haas, S. Pozorski, and T. Pozorski. New York: Cambridge University Press.

Pozorski, S., and T. Pozorski. 1979. "Alto Salaverry: A Peruvian Coastal Preceramic Site." *Annals of the Carnegie Museum of Natural History* 49:337–75.

———. 1986. "Recent Excavations at Pampa de las Llamas-Moxeke, A Complex Initial Period Site in Peru." *Journal of Field Archaeology* 13(4):381–401.

———. 1987. "Chavín, the Early Horizon, and the Initial Period." In *The Origins and Development of the Andean State*, eds. J. Haas, S. Pozorski, and T. Pozorski. New York: Cambridge University Press.

———. 1988. *Early Settlement and Subsistence in the Casma Valley, Peru*. Iowa City: University of Iowa Press.

———. 1990. "Huaynun, a Late Cotton Paraceramic Site on the North Coast of Peru." *Journal of Field Archaeology* 17(1):17–26.

Prescott, W. H. 1908. *History of the Conquest of Peru*. London and New York: Everyman's Library.

———. 1989. *Life and Death at Paloma: Society and Mortuary Practices in Preceramic Peruvian Village*. Iowa City: University of Iowa Press.

Protzen, J.-P. 1986. "Inca Stonemasonry." *Scientific American* 254(2):94–105.

Proulx, D. 1985. "An Analysis of the Early Cultural Sequence in the Nepeña Valley, Peru." *Research Report of Department of Anthropology, University of Massachusetts, Amherst*, no. 25.

Quilter, J. 1985. "Architecture and Chronology at El Paraíso, Peru." *Journal of Field Archaeology* 12(3):274–98.

———. 1991a. "Late Preceramic Peru." *Journal of World Prehistory* 5(4):387–438.

———. 1991b. "Problems with the Late Preceramic of Peru." *American Anthropologist* 93(2):450–54.

Quilter, J., and T. Stocker. 1983. "Subsistence Economies and the Origins of Andean Complex Societies." *American Anthropologist* 85(3):545–62.

Ramenovsky, A. 1987. *Vectors of Death*. Albuquerque: University of New Mexico Press.

Raymond, J. S. 1981a. "Subsistence Economics and the Origins of Andean Complex Societies" *American Anthropologist* 46(4):806–21.

———. 1981b. "The Maritime Foundations of Andean Civilization: A Reconsideration of the Evidence." *American Antiquity* 46:806–20.

Reitz, E. J. 1988. "Faunal Remains from Paloma, an Archaic Site in Peru." *American Anthropologist* 90(2):310–22.

Richardson, J. B., III. 1981. "Maritime Adaptations on the Peruvian Coast: A Critique and Future Directions." Paper Presented at the 47th Annual Meeting of the Society for American Archaeology, San Diego, California.

Rick, J. W. 1980. *Prehistoric Hunters of the High Andes*. New York: Academic Press.

Rowe, J. H. 1946. "Inka Culture at the Time of the Spanish Conquest." *Bureau of American Ethnology Bulletin* 143:183–331.

————. 1967. "Form and Meaning in Chavín Art." In *Peruvian Archaeology: Selected Readings.* Palo Alto: Peek Publishers.

Schreiber, K. J. 1987. "Conquest and Consolidation: A Comparison of the Wari and Inka Occupation of a Highland Peruvian Valley." *American Antiquity* 52(2):266–84.

Scott, R. J. 1981. "The Maritime Foundations of Andean Civilization: A Reconsideration." *American Antiquity* 46:806–21.

Shady, R., and A. Ruiz. 1979. "Evidence for Interregional Relationships During the Middle Horizon on the North-Central Coast of Peru." *American Antiquity* 44:670–84.

Silverman, H. 1988. "Cahuachi: Non-Urban Cultural Complexity on the South Coast of Peru." *Journal of Field Archaeology* 15(4):403–30.

Ugent, D., S. Pozorski, and T. Pozorski 1984. "New Evidence for Ancient Cultivation of *Canna edulis* in Peru." *Economic Botany* 38(4):417–32.

Vescelius, G. 1981. "Early and/or Not-so-Early Man in Peru: Guitarrero Cave Revisited." *Quarterly Review of Archaeology* 2:8–13.

Von Hagen, V. W. 1952. "America's Oldest Roads." *Scientific American* 187:17–21.

————. 1965. *The Desert Kingdoms of Peru.* London: Weidenfeld and Nicolson.

Willey, G. R. 1962. "The Early Great Art Styles and the Rise of Pre-Columbian Civilizations." *American Anthropologist* 64:1–14.

————. 1971. *South America.* Vol. 2, *An Introduction to American Archaeology.* Englewood Cliffs, NJ: Prentice-Hall.

Wilson, D. J. 1981. "Of Maize and Men: A Critique of the Maritime Hypothesis of State Origins on the Coast of Peru." *American Anthropologist* 83:93–114.

————. 1983. "The Origins and Development of Complex Prehispanic Society in the Lower Santa Valley, Peru: Implications for Theories of State Origins." *Journal of Anthropological Archaeology* 2:209–76.

Wing, E. S. 1977. "Animal Domestication in the Andes." In *Origins of Agriculture*, ed. C. A. Reed. The Hague: Mouton Publishers.

NOTES

1. Father Cobo's description here is from various sections of his *Inca Religion and Customs*.

2. Murra, "Andean Ecology and Civilization," p. 11, in Masuda et al. *Andean Ecology and Civilization.*

3. Masuda et al., eds., *Andean Ecology and Civilization.*

4. Idyll, "The Anchovy Crisis."

5. Hoopes, "Earliest Ceramic Complexes in the New World," p. 41.

6. Rick, *Prehistoric Hunters of the High Andes.*

7. Richardson, "Maritime Adaptations on the Peruvian Coast: A Critique and Future Directions," pp. 140–45.

8. Quilter and Stocker, "Subsistence Economies and the Origins of Andean Complex Societies," p. 547.

9. Pearsall, "The Origins of Plant Cultivation in South American," p. 192.

10. Ugent et al., "New Evidence for Ancient Cultivation of *Canna edulis* in Peru."

11. Reviewed in Pearsall, "The Origins of Plant Cultivation in South American," p. 190

12. Rick, *Prehistoric Hunters of the High Andes.*

13. See Quilter, "Late Preceramic Peru," p. 387, for a discussion of these dates.

14. Patterson, "Central Peru: Its Population and Economy."

15. Benfer, "The Challenges and Rewards of Sedentism: The Preceramic Village of Paloma, Peru"; Reitz, "Faunal Remains from Paloma, an Archaic Site in Peru."

16. Quilter and Stocker, "Subsistence Economies and the Origins of Andean Complex Societies," p. 545.

17. Parsons, "Preceramic Subsistence on the Peruvian Coast," p. 297.

18. Pozorski and Pozorski, "Alto Salaverry: A Peruvian Coastal Preceramic Site."

19. Benfer, "The Challenges and Rewards of Sedentism."

20. Engl and Engl, *Twilight of Ancient Peru.*

21. Lanning, *Peru Before the Inkas*, p. 71.

22. Quilter, "Late Preceramic Peru," p. 417.

23. Quilter, "Late Preceramic Peru," citing Feldman, *Aspero, Peru: Architecture, Subsistence Economy, and Other Artifacts of a Preceramic Maritime Chiefdom*, p. 89.

24. Quilter, "Late Preceramic Peru," citing Urton personal communication, 1991.

25. Quilter, "Late Preceramic Peru."

26. Moseley, "The Exploration and Explanation of Early Monumental Architecture in the Andes."

27. Moseley, *The Maritime Foundations of Andean Civilization.*

28. Quilter and Stocker, "Subsistence Economies and the Origins of Andean Complex Societies," p. 554.

29. Richard Burger and Lucy Salazar-Burger, "Ritual and Religion at Huaricoto," and "The Early Ceremonial Center of Huaricoto."

30. Quilter, "Late Preceramic Peru," p. 420–21.

31. Lumbreras, *The Peoples and Cultures of Ancient Peru*, p. 47.

32. Moseley, "The Evolution of Andean Civilization."

33. Moseley, *The Maritime Foundations of Andean Civilization.*

34. Wilson, "Of Maize and Men: A Critique of the Maritime Hypothesis of State Origins on the Coast of Peru."

35. See also Scott, "The Maritime Foundations of Andean Civilization: A Reconsideration."

36. Quilter and Stocker, "Subsistence Economies and the Origins of Andean Complex Societies."

37. Reitz, "Faunal Remains from Paloma, an Archaic Site in Peru."

38. Pozorski and Pozorski, *Early Settlement and Subsistence in the Casma Valley, Peru.*

39. Quilter and Stocker, "Subsistence Economies and the Origins of Andean Complex Societies."

40. Ibid., p. 555, citing Lathrap, "The Antiquity and Importance of Long-Distance Trade Relationships in the Moist Tropics of Pre-Columbian South America."

41. Moseley, *The Maritime Foundations of Andean Civilization*, p. 105.

42. Ibid., p. 106.

43. Patterson, "The Huaca La Florida, Rimac Valley, Peru."

44. Quilter, "Late Preceramic Peru," p. 414.

45. Burger, *Chavin and the Origins of the Andean Civilization.*

46. Lumbreras, *The Peoples and Cultures of Ancient Peru*, p. 62.

47. Greider, *The Art and Archaeology of Pashash.*

48. Reviewed in Keatinge, *Peruvian Prehistory;* also see Haas, Pozorski, and Pozorski, *The Origins and Development of The Andean State;* Fiedel, *Prehistory of the Americas;* Donnan, ed., *Early Ceremonial Architecture in the Andes.*

49. Lanning, *Peru Before the Inkas*, pp. 114–15.

50. Silverman, "Cahuachi: Non-Urban Cultural Complexity on the South Coast of Peru."

51. Donnan, "Master Works Reveal a Pre-Inca World."

52. Donnan, *Moche Art and Iconography.*

53. Moseley, "The Evolution of Andean Civilization."

54. Lanning, *Peru Before the Inkas*, p. 127.

55. Fiedel, *Prehistory of the Americas*, p. 333.

56. Keatinge, "Chimú Rural Administration Centers in the Moche Valley, Peru," p. 79.

57. Moseley and Day, *Chan Chan: Andean Desert City.*

58. Collier, Rosaldo, and Wirth, eds. *The Inka and Aztec States, 1400–1800.*

59. D'Altroy, *Provincial Power in the Inka Empire.*

60. Lanning, *Peru Before the Inkas*, pp. 159–60.

61. Hastorf and Johannessen, "Maize and Politics in the Pre-Hispanic Andes."

62. Lanning, *Peru Before the Inkas*, p. 166–67.

63. Ascher and Ascher, *Code of the Quipu: A Study in Media, Mathematics, and Culture.*

64. Hyslop, *The Inka Road System.*

65. Von Hagen, "America's Oldest Roads."

66. Niles, *Callachaca.*

67. Engl and Engl, *Twilight of Ancient Peru*, p. 119.

68. Carneiro, "A Theory of the Origin of the State"; see also Wilson, "The Origins and Development of Complex Prehispanic Society in the Lower Santa Valley, Peru."

15

EARLY CULTURAL COMPLEXITY
IN NORTH AMERICA

*You must explain to the natives of [North America] that
there is only one God in heaven, and the emperor on
earth to rule and govern it, whose subjects they must
all become and they must serve.*

Instructions of the Viceroy to
Fray Marcos de Ninza (A.D. 1538)

A s Europeans invaded North America in the sixteenth and seventeenth centuries, they encountered what looked to them like the relics of ancient civilizations: hundreds of large earthen mounds, some nearly as large as the
Egyptian pyramids, dominated the Ohio and Mississippi River valleys; and in Arizona, Colorado, and New Mexico large, neatly planned, but abandoned towns that
had obviously once been inhabited by thousands were found along the major rivers
and even in the arid highlands (Figure 15.1).

The Europeans of this age were, like the citizens of all world powers, highly ethnocentric, so it is not surprising that they assumed that these impressive works had
been constructed by their own ancestors—the Celts, Romans, or perhaps the Vikings;
they simply could not believe that the ancestors of the poor and "degenerate" Native
Americans they saw about them might have had something to do with these great
monuments. Some Europeans even blamed the Native Americans for massacring what
the Europeans believed to be an ancient and extinct "superior" American race—the
ultimate in adding insult to injury, given the Native Americans' eventual fate.

The truth, of course, is that these mounds and abandoned settlements had indeed been built by Native Americans many centuries before the Europeans arrived,
and we now know that these ancient Americans had a rich culture history going back
more than 10,000 years in the New World.

Some of the people of "Pre-Columbian" North America were influenced by contact with the complex cultures of ancient Mesoamerica, and it is also true that, according to some criteria, aboriginal American cultures never reached the level of complexity attained in "independent" ancient centers of cultural evolution, such as
Mesoamerica and Mesopotamia. But the native North Americans did develop some

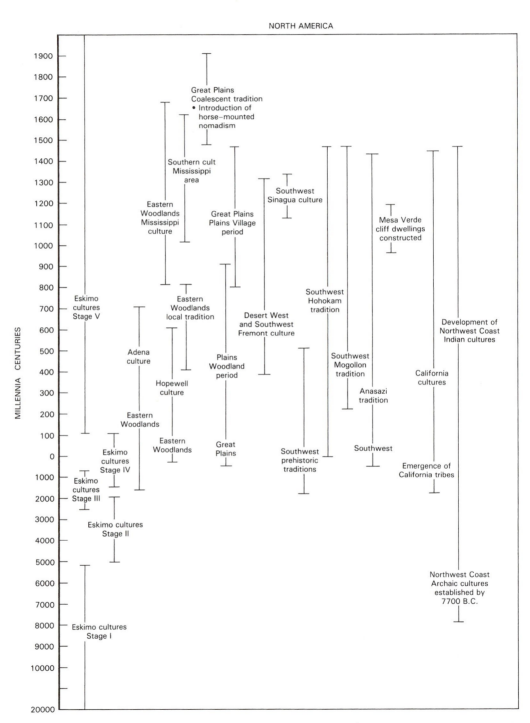

FIGURE 15.1 A cultural chronology of North America.

aspects of cultural complexity, and they did so largely independently. Moreover, the ecological and cultural reasons North American cultures did not exactly parallel those of Mexico or Peru provide some insights into all of these cultures.

For more than a century archaeologists have been systematically digging North American sites, from Alaska to southern Texas, and we should know more about developments here than virtually anywhere else in the world, given the high ratio of archaeologists per square kilometer. But, unfortunately, early American archaeologists also yielded to the temptations of excavating mainly rich tombs and large towns, resulting in a very biased view of the American past. And because of decades of turning ancient Native American cultural resources into parking lots and hamburger stands, and because of the looting that continues today, so much of the archaeological record of North America has been destroyed that much of the American past will forever remain a mystery.

The old, sometimes pejorative myths about "Indians" are now giving way in some circles to new ones stressing the social harmony, ecological purity, and superior metaphysics of ancient Native Americans. As with all cultures, there is much to admire about ancient North Americans, but the evidence suggests that for much of their antiquity, aboriginal Americans were like prehistoric peoples in every other part of the world—harried small-time foragers or farmers, worrying about this year's drought and next year's deluge, shifting their crops from year to year as they exhausted the soil and timber of one place after another, and as enmeshed in slavery, exploitation, and warfare as any ancient Chinese, Egyptian, or European.

The term "Native American" is gradually replacing the wildly imprecise "Indian" of bygone years, but it is well to remember that all Americans are immigrants, and rather recent ones at that. The people who colonized the New World and became "Native Americans" were, in fact, northern Asians who came in at least three periods of colonization (chapter 5)—the first of many waves of immigration to the New World.

THE NORTH AMERICAN EAST

THE ECOLOGICAL SETTING

The most complex ancient cultures in North America evolved in the great river valleys of the North American East, especially the Mississippi and Ohio Rivers and the lands they drain (Figure 15.2).

We saw in chapter 5 that about 12,000 years ago the huge glacial ice sheets that once covered much of eastern North America retreated into Canada, and the distribution of plant and animal species in this region became similar to that of the recent past. Between about 8000 and 6500 B.C., the annual temperature of much of the North American East was probably 2.5 degrees Celsius cooler than at present, and after that time aboriginal Americans were probably directly affected by a number of climate fluctuations, such as the Hypsithermal (c. 4000 B.C.), when climates seem to have been cooler and moister.[1] Subtle shifts of climate and effective rainfall may have had important effects on the distribution of nut-bearing trees, which were a very important food source, and also on the size and stability of rivers and

Extent of Hopewellian complexes

Adena–Hopewell heartland

• Hopewell

◆ Adena

CHERT   Source of raw material for trade

L. Superior

COPPER

SILVER

L. Huron

L. Michigan

L. Ontario

TREMPEALEAU HOPEWELLIAN

GOODALL HOPEWELLIAN

NEW YORK HOPEWELLIAN

GALENA

HAVANA HOPEWELLIAN

OHIO HOPEWELL

CHERT

KANSAS CITY HOPEWELLIAN

CHERT

CHERT

CRAB ORCHARD HOPEWELLIAN

COOPER HOPEWELLIAN

ARMSTRONG HOPEWELLIAN

MICA CRYSTAL CHLORITE

MILLER HOPEWELLIAN

ATLANTIC OCEAN

MARKSVILLE HOPEWELLIAN

PORTER HOPEWELLIAN

POTTERY

WHELK ALLIGATOR TULIP SHELL OLIVE SHELL

SHARK BARRACUDA TURTLE SHELL

GULF OF MEXICO

lakes—rich environments around which early Americans often built their hunting-foraging economies.

Temperate eastern North America is a rich niche for hunter-foragers, but its abundant agricultural potential can only be realized with an industrial technology. The American Southwest and West also include some very rich areas, but none of these areas has the same agricultural potential—given primitive technologies—as that, for example, of the Nile Valley or Mesopotamia. The modern United States' agricultural economy is so productive that it is somewhat surprising just how poor a place it was for pre-industrial subsistence farmers. First, most of it is far from the equator and therefore has less solar radiation and fewer frost-free days, and thus lower absolute agricultural potential, than more southern environments—such as the ones in the Middle East and Mesoamerica, for example, where the world's earliest farmers appeared. Second, those areas of North America that are today the fertile fields of Iowa, Missouri, and other areas of the Plains and Middle West were for the most part unavailable to the Native American farmer, because they lacked the plows and draft animals that can rip through thick grasses and other vegetation to reveal these fertile soils and the other machines that are needed to suppress the competition to crops from weeds. Third, much of the area between the Atlantic Coast and the western reaches of the Mississippi River drainage were thickly forested and relatively cool, "closed-canopy climax forests," which could be exploited for nuts and a few other resources but were in most areas an unprepossessing place for the maize-beans-squash farming that became the basis for Native American cultivation in North America. Fourth, the areas of California and other parts of the West that are today food suppliers to the world were far too arid for anything but basic subsistence agriculture until modern irrigation systems were installed.

AGRICULTURAL ORIGINS: THE LATE ARCHAIC PERIOD (C. 5000–800 B.C.)

Untangling the processes by which many Native Americans became farmers is difficult. In a recent survey of early agriculture in the North American East, Gayle Fritz noted[2] that people in eastern North America domesticated plants through different mechanisms and processes. She notes, for example, that sunflowers appear to have been domesticated in the East but from an ancestral strain that was introduced from the American West; that tobacco may have been domesticated through processes unlike any of the food plants because its main use was ritual and social; and that other plants, such as maize and beans, were introduced at a comparatively late date from

---

FIGURE 15.2 Adena-Hopewell and related cultures. The Adena culture was centered in Ohio, but Adena trade networks reached as far away as New York. Adena culture appears to have peaked at about 100 B.C. and was waning by A.D. 400. By about 100 B.C. Adena cultures in Ohio were being replaced by Hopewell cultures and for the next nine centuries the Hopewell cultures spread over much of the East.

the South but then underwent additional domestication and adaptation in place. Some domesticates, including strains of maize, tobacco, beans, and chenopods, may have been introduced into eastern North America at different times and from several different regions, including the Caribbean islands, Mesoamerica, and South America.[3]

One might consider maize and beans to be the most important domesticated plants in North America because they were the basis of the largest and most complex cultures in this area. But maize was a late introduction and only became an important source of food over most of eastern North America after about A.D. 1000. Maize pollen found in sediments of Lake Shelby in coastal Alabama seems securely dated to about 1500 B.C., but it is not clear that this plant was an important food resource at this time. One of the earliest and securely dated samples of maize in eastern North America is a collection of carbonized maize kernels found at the Icehouse Bottom site in eastern Tennessee and directly dated by radiocarbon methods to about A.D. 75; but until well into the first millennium A.D. maize remained a minor source of food.

Rather, it was the oil- and starch-rich seeds of a variety of plants that formed the basis of initial agriculture in eastern North America. Among the primary domesticated plants were goosefoot (*Chenopodium*), sumpweed (*Iva annua*), sunflowers (*Helianthus annus*), wild gourds (*Cucurbita*), maygrass (*Phalaris*), little barley (*Hordeum pusillum*), knotweed (*Polygonum erectum*), and other plants. The initial processes of agricultural origins occurred many millennia ago: as we saw in chapter 5, by 5000 B.C. people had colonized most of North America and had begun to differ considerably in the kinds of resources and technologies on which they based their economies. Until late in the first millennium B.C., hunting and foraging continued to be the way of life for most people, but through these many millennia after the Ice Age, the overall trend was toward increasing numbers of sedentary communities that specialized first in hunting and intensive plant collecting and later in maize and bean agriculture.

Richard Yerkes calls the last three millennia B.C. the "Transitional Period" because of the spectrum of cultural changes that slowly but fundamentally set the stage for the elaboration of American cultures in the last centuries before European colonization.[4] He notes that during this three-thousand-year period people in the American East increased exploitation of the river valleys in which their descendants would eventually establish agricultural villages, and that they also were the first to domesticate native plants, such as squash, gourds, goosefoot, sunflowers, and tobacco. People also increased the kinds and volumes of goods they exchanged. Bruce Smith has shown how, beginning about 3000 B.C., people in some parts of the East developed a way of life in which they migrated between summer and winter base camps, to take advantage of different resources as they changed with the seasons.[5]

The productive patches of maize, beans, and squash that eventually allowed Native Americans to live in great numbers all over North America were only the last, most productive stages of a long, slow shift—away from simple plant collecting and hunting and toward an ever-growing reliance on fewer and fewer kinds of plants. Long before maize reached temperate North America, people there had specialized in exploiting several kinds of plants in early forms of agriculture. So, the questions about North American agriculture are the same as those we asked about other areas. Why did agricultural economies appear when and where they did, through what processes, and with what results? And what was the long-term relationship between local domesticates and those introduced from elsewhere?

As in all other areas of early agriculture, climatic changes cannot be disregarded. Complex climatic changes between about 5000 and 2000 B.C., for example, changed the flow characteristics of streams and rivers across the eastern woodlands so that backwater swamps and lakes created by obstructions in river channels greatly expanded the abundance and accessibility of shellfish and other aquatic resources; and they also produced greater and more varied "disturbed" habitats—areas of the floodplain where floodwaters disturbed vegetation—which offered ecological niches for "pioneer" plants such as goosefoot, sumpweed, sunflowers, marsh elder (*Sambucus*), wild gourds, and other plants.[6] Native Americans exploited these plants throughout the period between 5000 and 2000 B.C., and they may have initiated domestication and done some minor agriculture (see chapter 6 for a discussion of these terms). They could have encouraged the growth of hickory trees, for example, by "girdling" (cutting through the bark and growth layers) other species of trees in stands of hickory, and they could have burned off other areas to encourage the growth of chenopods, sunflowers, and other edible plants.[7]

Perhaps the earliest domesticates found in the North American woodlands are gourds and squash. Charred squash rinds from west central Illinois have been dated to 5000 and 4000 B.C.,[8] and some from Missouri, Tennessee, and Kentucky have been dated to at least 2500 B.C. Species of this genera may have been introduced from Mexico or locally domesticated—or both. They were probably used as containers and for seeds, and occasionally eaten directly, and we may suppose that their use goes back many millennia before we have archaeological evidence of them. There is also a problem in distinguishing between species of gourds based on their few traces in the archaeological record.[9]

The first clear evidences of changes in the direction of domestication and agriculture in North America appear in the period between about 2050 and 1050 B.C. The primary evidence is in the form of changes in the morphology of the seeds of sunflowers, goosefoot, and other disturbed-habitat plants. As we saw in chapter 6, one of the ways in which people all over the world domesticated plants was to increase their usefulness by increasing seed size and number (for example, from two-row to six-row barley) and by altering the dormancy cycle of plants. When sunflowers, goosefoot, and other plants germinated in the spring, they would have faced tremendous competition, because these plants release many seeds in a small area. In such conditions, plants that are the earliest to sprout and are larger and more vigorous than others would be at an advantage. One key to early sprouting is the thickness of the seed coat, the *testa*. As Bruce Smith notes,[10] the average testa thickness on goosefoot seeds shows marked decline over a large area of the eastern woodlands after about 2500 years ago, based on specimens retrieved from cave sites and other occupations in Illinois, Arkansas, Kentucky, and adjacent areas. Other changes indicative of domestication appeared at about this same time in a variety of plants, but, as Smith notes, "there is little evidence that this process of domestication occurred within a framework of deliberate human selection, or that these domesticated plant species initially contributed substantially"[11] to the diet of people in the second millennium B.C.

Nonetheless, various scholars have tried to explain how the transition to initial agriculture might have occurred. Michael O'Brien has developed a "Coevolutionary" model to account for the transition to agriculture in one area, near the Illinois/Missouri border.[12] Based on David Rindos's work on plant domestication,[13] O'Brien suggests that the consistent but low-intensity use of sunflower seeds, goosefoot, marsh elder, and other native annuals during the period up to about 300 B.C. created a relationship between these plants and people that resulted in a form of domestication and agriculture. He argues that initial exploitation of these plants would not have been of great significance in the overall economy, but the costs of exploiting them were very low, since they did not conflict with other activities and one could carry these seeds as a minor food without too much effort. But then he says, "by 200 B.C. the interaction between human groups and their resource base had reached the point that sedentism became a viable option."[14] He notes that the risks of concentrating on these plants were considerable, in the way of droughts and floods. But they also had potential for supporting increased population densities.

Many of the seeds of native North American domesticates could be eaten simply by drying and cracking them, but they also appear to have been staples in processed foods (Figure 15.3). David Braun has shown that during the Middle and Late Woodland periods people began to make more and more pottery in ways that seem particularly designed to cook starchy seeds, such as those of goosefoot.[15] Such pottery has to withstand high heat and sudden temperature changes, and all over the world people making these kinds of pots invented the same globular shapes and kinds of tempering and wall thicknesses that facilitate the long, slow simmering of seeds and other foods in liquids. Stews and soups are not the most exciting foods in most cuisines (Szechuan and French Mediterranean excepted), but they are extraordinarily nutritious—and, more than that, they make excellent foods out of things that normally people cannot profit from much, such as dry goosefoot seeds and a picked-over rabbit skeleton: the best way to increase the nutrition of these annuals is to boil them, which "may increase palatability as well"[16] (it couldn't hurt, in this case). Simply by devising ways to slow-cook the abundant seeds in their environments, Native Americans seem to have enlarged their food resources to the point that a less mobile, less risky way of life was possible for more and more people. The pervasive effects of the shift to an economy based in part on starchy seeds have been documented over much of the North American East.[17]

Some have speculated that the techniques for making ceramic vessels were introduced into North America from Mexico, but it is more likely that pottery was independently invented in eastern North America at least once, and probably several times, as containers became increasingly important in plant collection and preparation.

The collection and domestication of these various plant species seem always and everywhere to have been combined with relentless hunting, fishing, and nut gathering, and there is little evidence that agriculture was being practiced at this time. That is, little energy was invested in modifying the environments of sunflowers and these other plants through hoeing, watering, or weeding. Melvin Fowler noted that most of the native plants apparently domesticated in the East are species that prefer open, disturbed areas, such as would have been provided by the refuse piles that must have

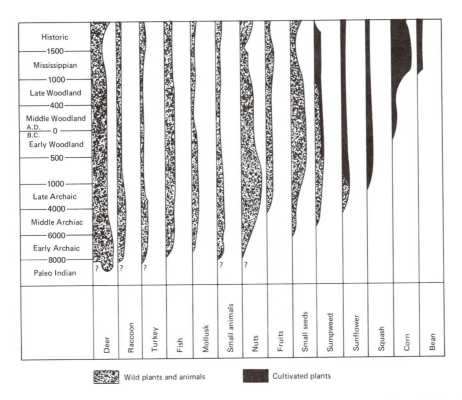

FIGURE 15.3 In the prehistoric American Middle West the transition to the agricultural way of life was a process in which native crops and wild plant foods were replaced by maize, beans, and squash (the thickness of the shaded and black areas reflects relative importance of the different resources).

become increasingly available as hunters and gatherers cluttered the landscape with snail and clam shells, fish bones, and other debris.[18] When and to what extent the kind of natural association between these plants and human disturbances was converted into farming, in the sense of people planting and caring for these crops, will probably always be difficult to measure.

Early Cultural Complexity in the North American East Like other hunter-foragers around the world, the people of the North American East began to show signs of increasing social differentiation as they intensified their exploitation of plants and as they became less mobile and spent more time in particular places.[19] One of the earliest signs of these changes is in burials. Beginning at about 2000 B.C., people all over the East began burying their dead with exotic items, such as copper, marine shells, and ground-stone jewelry—often covering the corpse with red ocher, a mineral pigment.[20] Yerkes suggests that these "individuals would go to their graves with the exotic materials that they had accumulated, but it is unlikely that they were able to pass their achieved status on to their descendants."[21] As we noted in chapter 4, even the Neanderthals of 100,000 years ago seem to have had at least some slight sense of death as a transition to another plane of existence, so it is not surprising that some burials in the North American East after 2000 B.C. contain exotic commodities, and that cremation was practiced in some areas. But, as in many other areas of the world, this early sense of ceremonialism was transmuted over time into elaborate mortuary cults in which social differentiations and other signs of increasing complexity are evident.

One of the earliest and most dramatic indications that American cultures were becoming more complex than those of the previous millennia is the Poverty Point culture of the lower Mississippi Delta. This culture is named after the Poverty Point site in Louisiana (Figure 15.4), where large earthworks were constructed sometime between 1200 and 600 B.C. The six nested ranks of earthen mounds at Poverty Point average about 25 meters wide and 3 meters high and are set about 40 meters apart. Near them stands an artificial mound more than 20 meters high and more than 200 meters across.[22] It is estimated that more than three million man-hours of labor were required to build this complex, with hundreds, perhaps thousands of people hauling dirt in baskets in an organized, planned effort. If each basket contained a cubic foot

FIGURE 15.4   One of the most impressive Archaic sites in North America is the complex of earthworks at Poverty Point, Louisiana. Between about 1500 and 700 B.C. hunter-gathering peoples in this area built six nested octagons of piled earth. The outer octagon is about 1300 meters in diameter. Part of this complex was later eroded away by a river. A small mound near these earthworks and other occupations produced many beautiful artifacts, as well as thousands of fired clay balls that were apparently heated and then dropped into containers to boil foods.

of dirt, about 1,236,007 loads would have been required.[23] Burials suggest that this complex was a mortuary cult, but its overall significance is difficult to assess. Some of the Poverty Point people were skilled artisans who made vessels out of steatite and sandstone, pipes out of clay and stone, and axes, adzes, saws, and weights from hard kinds of stone—importing these raw materials, in some cases, from sources more than 600 miles away. In fact, trade in exotic commodities and the production of craft goods from them may be the reason for Poverty Point's prominence, since it is located at the confluence of six major rivers. Some scholars have suggested that these people were in contact with the Olmec of Mesoamerica (chapter 13), but there is no indication of Olmec designs in Poverty Point pottery or other artifacts. Like any other large earthworks, those of Poverty Point offer points for astronomical observation: a person standing on the large mound at Poverty Point can see the vernal and autumnal equinoxes on a line across the center of the mound, looking east.[24] But, as with Stonehenge, any large monument offers a great array of possible observation points, and it is not difficult to find some astronomical regularity that may or may not have been the object of constructing that particular observation point.

As we have seen elsewhere in the ancient world, at sites such as Jericho, agriculture is not a prerequisite for substantial architecture—all that is required is sufficient productivity. The Poverty Point people may have practiced some limited agriculture with native plants, but it was probably a rich blend of hunting and foraging that supported these mound-builders.

In any case, the people of Poverty Point did what people at a similar level of cultural organization around the world did: they built monumental architecture, they expanded and intensified regional trade in exotic commodities (and probably subsistence ones as well) and apparently used these to mark differences in social status and other social and ethnic identification, and then, again like these other cultures, their culture began to decline in importance as that of other cultures began to increase. The Poverty Point culture began to contract at about 650 B.C. and went into decline as other areas to the northeast became more powerful.

After about 800 B.C. North America east of the Mississippi Valley became a mosaic of varying adaptations, with the use of ceramics and an economy based, perhaps, somewhat on local and imported domesticated plants, but still primarily on an archaic mix of hunted and collected resources.[25]

EVOLVING CULTURAL COMPLEXITY: THE EARLY, MIDDLE, AND LATE WOODLAND PERIODS (C. 800 B.C.–A.D. 800)

Between about 800 B.C. and A.D. 800, population densities in many parts of eastern North America increased sharply, thousands of gigantic earthworks were constructed, inter-regional trade expanded, and large villages were built. This era of change, usually referred to as the Woodland Period, is associated with two major cultural traditions: the *Adena* (centered in southern Ohio, and extending into Indiana, Kentucky, Pennsylvania, and West Virginia), and the *Hopewell* (centered in southern Ohio but extending widely over much of eastern North America). These cultures overlapped in time, with the Adena somewhat earlier than the Hopewell in some areas. Both are defined on the basis of styles of pottery, engraved stone tablets, textiles, and worked bone and copper.

The Adena Culture   Adena mound-building and artifact styles seem concentrated in the interval between about 500 B.C. and A.D. 700, and the richness of some of these sites, in the burial goods found in the mounds as well as the scale of the mounds themselves (Figure 15.5), originally led some scholars to suppose that these people already lived in chiefdoms, built on the sweat and labor of exploited farmers.

But the Adena seem to have been still mainly hunter-forager peoples who moved seasonally. Maize may have been cultivated on a small scale, but it was probably not very important.[26] And as impressive as the mounds are, they could easily have been built by small groups adding a layer or two each year, without much supervision,[27] perhaps as bodies were interred in layers that covered earlier burials.

Many of the mounds were mortuary centers in which one or more corpses were placed in log tombs or clay pits in communal burials, sometimes with beautiful stone tools and other goods, and then covered with earth. If the relative richness of these burials accurately reflects social differentiation in Adena society, then there were elites who could command in death special treatment in the form of log tombs, ocher and graphite decorations of their bodies, and expensive grave goods in copper, stone, and shell. Lower-status individuals appear to have been cremated with little ritual. These

FIGURE 15.5   Great Serpent Mound, an Adena construction near Cincinnati, Ohio.

mounds may have been ceremonial sites or centers for the exchange of goods, but they also could have served as territorial markers.[28]

Stone tobacco pipes are found in some Adena sites, and smoking probably played an important role in rituals. The native strains of tobacco were much more powerful than modern strains and could have produced narcotic effects much more powerful than modern cigarettes.[29]

It is unfortunate that so many Adena sites were destroyed by modern constructions, and also that archaeologists excavated scores of mounds but almost no ordinary Adena settlements. Those few settlements that have been excavated suggest simple, somewhat temporary structures, probably made by setting series of posts in the ground and covering them with hides or wood—the "wigwam."[30]

The Hopewell Culture   The Hopewell culture dominated parts of the Middle West from about 200 B.C. to A.D. 750. The Ohio Hopewell was centered in southern Ohio, and the Havana Hopewell dominated the central and lower Illinois River Valley, but Hopewell religious traditions were practiced as far north as Wisconsin, south into Louisiana, and east into New York.

While grave goods are not usually profuse in Adena mounds, Hopewell tombs often contain finely worked copper, pipestone, mica, obsidian, meteoric iron, shell, tortoise shell, shark and alligator teeth, bear teeth, ceramics, and other commodities; there is also evidence of the ultimate grave good—sacrificed humans. Hopewell settlements and mounds increased in size and number in the centuries before about A.D. 400, and major earthworks were often built near the burial mounds.

These burials may reflect something about the dead person's rank and status within the community—though burials are an uncertain guide to the actual prestige and power relationships of any community. Joseph Tainter carried out a statistical analysis of more than 500 Hopewell burials and concluded that there were six discrete levels of status within the Hopewell community, corresponding to six different forms of burial, ranging from simple holes in the ground to massive mounds in which the corpse was accompanied by the finest goods.[31] In some Adena and Hopewell mounds, infants and juveniles were found buried with great ceremony and rich goods, suggesting the inheritance of rank and prestige and the control of the society's resources by a limited number of its people.

To understand these mound complexes we need to place them in the context of a local economy—and about this we know comparatively little. Because many later Hopewell buildings and earthworks were precisely planned and relatively expensive to construct, we must suspect that at least some people had become specialized labor-organizers and engineers of sorts, perhaps even constituting a privileged social group. But one of the many puzzling things about these mound complexes is that in many areas they do not seem to have any associated domestic houses. Some archaeologists assumed that any society capable of building such impressive works must certainly have been composed of sedentary agriculturalists, but Hopewell peoples for the most part probably hunted and gathered essentially the same plant and animal species as did their ancestors, with deer, ducks, small mammals, fish, snails, mussels, pigweed, lambsquarter, sunflowers, and nuts providing much of their nutrition.

Outside the Adena and Hopewell spheres of influence, the Archaic subsistence and settlement systems appear to have remained essentially unchanged,[32] but this may have been the era in which the bow and arrow replaced the spear and atlatl over much of North America. George Odell studied thousands of stone tools from the Illinois Valley, looking for the kinds of damage to stone edges that projectile points typically sustain. He concluded that archaeologists have often looked at the wrong stone tools in trying to reconstruct ancient hunting: numerous stone tools besides obvious projectile points show evidence of high-energy impact typical of use as arrowheads; in fact, many of the lithics that show high-energy impact damage are crude-looking pieces archaeologists have often called "retouched flakes."[33] The use of such projectile points seems to have increased dramatically after about 4,000 years ago, and by the first few centuries A.D. the bow and arrow may have added enough extra production to some economies that significantly higher population densities were possible.

In any case, the Hopewell heartland was in no sense so poor that hunters and gatherers were desperately trying to become full-time maize farmers. Estimates of resources around the Hopewell settlement at Scoville, in the lower Illinois Valley, indicate that "within a half-hour's walk . . . there would annually be from 182,000 to 426,000 bushels of nuts and 48,000 to 484,000 bushels of acorns, 100 to 840 deer, 10,000 to 20,000 squirrels, and 200 turkeys. Not computed were seeds, fruits, smaller animals, fish, mussels, and migratory birds (6 million mallards were estimated to be in the Illinois River Valley in 1955)."[34] Given these abundant resources, it is not surprising that maize agriculture apparently appeared first in poorer, more marginal environments and displaced hunting and gathering in the lushest environments only much later.

Hopewell peoples traded extensively in exotic commodities, such as obsidian and grizzly bear teeth from Montana, silver from Ontario, copper from northern Michigan, and shark teeth and many marine shells and products from the Gulf Coast. By the first few centuries A.D., people all over eastern North America were participants in a great trading network, and by "consuming" these goods by lavishing them on the dead and burying them deeply in mound-tombs, the demand for these treasures was kept high and the trading system in constant operation.

Although the conspicuous consumption of the Hopewell era, with its great mounds, rich burials, and wide variety of arts and crafts, indicates that Archaic egalitarian social structures were changing, these societies seem to have been less complexly organized than, for example, Mesoamerican cities like Teotihuacán.[35] Most of the Hopewell and Adena communities were small sedentary groups of hunter-collectors who built the burial mounds and ceremonial complexes for reasons that may fundamentally have had to do with distributing resources. Whereas Archaic hunters and gatherers met their needs by following seasonal rounds and exploiting a diversity of resources, Hopewell communities probably accomplished the same thing by exchanging products among themselves. Like the Adena mounds, however, these constructions could have also been territorial markers.

But we know comparatively little about daily life for the mass of the Hopewell or Adena peoples. The few houses excavated seem to be rectangular or ovoid constructions supported on posts and covered with bark or mats. Most people apparently lived in small hamlets composed of a few such houses and a few storage pits and garbage dumps. Some people were obviously specialists in flint working and a few other arts and crafts, and some of these communities may have been organized around a "big-man" and his favored lineage. But at the Murphy site, in Licking County, Ohio—one of the few Hopewell sites that has been excavated and analyzed for evidence of functional specialization—William Dancey and Paul Hooge found little evidence of complex economic or social organization. This site was occupied in the first few centuries A.D., probably intermittently or annually during the summer and fall.[36] Dancey and Hooge carefully examined hundreds of stone tools for patterns of wear, and found that most of them were simply chipped from a core, used for a short time, and then pitched in the garbage. They found no evidence of craft-specialization or farming, although these people did use pottery.

The Late Woodland Period   After about A.D. 400 there is some evidence of a decline in mound-building and other changes in settlement patterns that used to be considered evidence of a Hopewellian "collapse." But it is not at all certain that there was, in fact, a collapse, at least in the sense of disintegrating economic relationships and declining productivity and population densities.

Richard Yerkes has reviewed studies by David Braun and others that suggest that although the people who lived toward the end of the Hopewell era, indeed, seem to have invested comparatively little effort in rich burials, pottery decoration, and trade of exotic goods, these cultural changes may be reflections of evolving—not disintegrating—cultural complexity.[37] At this time populations seem to have increased and people began producing more of their food through cultivation of native plants. People seem to have moved into most of the major river valleys and established small settlements, perhaps in small nuclear family groups. As we have seen elsewhere, monumental architecture may be a response to stress and a device to control societal growth, rather than just an expression of societal wealth and extravagance.

THE MISSISSIPPIAN CULTURE (A.D. 800-1650)

From about A.D. 600 to about 1650, the agricultural way of life spread over much of eastern North America, and in the North American East the Mississippian culture appeared—the high point of cultural evolution in aboriginal North America, particularly in terms of geographical extent of influence, ceremonialism, public works, technology, population density, and social stratification.[38]

Stoltman has listed some characteristics that define Mississippian culture, including: (1) intensive maize-beans-squash agriculture; (2) apparent complex social organization—perhaps with chiefs and elites who could expropriate great amounts of societal wealth and power; (3) a theocratic social organization, with elites having both religious and political power; (4) towns in which one hundred or, in some cases, one thousand or more people lived year-round, often behind fortifications; (5) monumental architecture, including mounds and tombs; (6) some occupational specialization in farming, trading, ritual, and administration; (7) mortuary cults involving certain patterns of burying the dead with "status goods" under earthen mounds; (8)

distinctive pottery in shell-tempered wares, sometimes in the form of animals, and often beautifully incised, polished, or in other ways decorated; (9) use of the bow and arrow, with distinctive small, triangular stone arrowheads; and (10) certain kinds of houses, built by digging wall trenches and then using clay and thatch to form rooms.[39]

The florescence of Mississippian culture may have been linked with the continuing domestication and improvement of maize. The sensitivity of maize to daylight duration and temperature is vividly demonstrated each summer along the northern fringe of its present range—such as in Seattle, where except in the warmest summers few maize varieties can be coaxed into production. But in more suitable environments, maize is a prolific source of food. Maize probably first became an agricultural staple in North America only in those southern zones where there are at least 200 frost-free days a year, but during the Mississippian era newer strains appeared that could be farmed productively with just 120 frost-free days. And so adaptable is the plant that it was a staple as far north as Ontario, Canada, by the time the Europeans arrived in the sixteenth century. Primitive strains of maize had such small cobs when first introduced from Mexico that considerable selective breeding was required before it was worthwhile to do all the work of clearing land, weeding, and harvesting necessary for successful maize agriculture here. But, as noted in chapter 6, once domesticated beans were combined with maize in North American fields, thereby supplying the critical amino acids lacking in maize, people could live in dense concentrations all over the North American East. The spread of maize farming has been detected by analyzing carbon isotope concentrations in the skeletons of ancient Native Americans. Maize contains relatively high amounts of ^{13}C, so people who eat maize also have high concentrations of this isotope. Several studies have shown that in Missouri, Arkansas, and other areas, skeletons of people who lived before about A.D. 1000 tend to have little ^{13}C, but beginning at about A.D. 900 to A.D. 1000, this isotope is found in radically higher concentrations.[40]

But to identify maize agriculture as an economic foundation of the Mississippian culture does not explain its emergence: here, too, as in every other case of early complex societies considered in this book, we must consider how elite groups manage to appropriate a society's resources and manage to perpetuate their domination. And for the Mississippian culture, as for other complex societies, there are many well-worn and largely unsatisfactory ideas about how this happened, ranging from the presumed economic benefits that would be provided by a "redistributor-chief" who could facilitate the circulation of goods, to the effects of increasing occupational specialization.[41]

Artifacts and mounds of the Mississippian type first appeared in the lower Mississippi Valley, but they soon spread into the Tennessee River drainage and by A.D. 800 to A.D. 900 occurred over much of the Ohio and Missouri river valleys. Between A.D. 900 and A.D. 1600, large towns with impressive ceremonial centers were built from Florida to northern Illinois, and from Ohio to eastern Oklahoma, but the heartland of this culture was in the central Mississippi Valley.

The largest prehistoric settlement north of Mexico was Cahokia, in East St. Louis, Illinois. Beginning at about A.D. 600 the people of Cahokia began building mounds and other features, and by about A.D. 1250 there were over 100 mounds within the 13 square kilometers of the site. Monk's Mound, an earthen pyramid in the center of Cahokia, is over 30 meters high, 241 by 316 meters at the base, and covers an area of more than 6.5 hectares (Figure 15.6). Thirty to forty thousand people are estimated to have lived in the environs of Cahokia at about A.D. 1200 in several large towns, a few smaller towns, and more than forty villages; no doubt people living within a large surrounding area had some contact with Cahokia.[42]

The beginnings of a class-based society in which elites could control community wealth is evident at Cahokia. One adult male was buried with 20,000 shell beads, 800 arrowheads, and sheets of mica and copper. In addition, there were many burials, including 4 mutilated men and 118 women, many of whom appear to have been ritually strangled; we can only surmise that, like their Chinese, Mesopotamian, Mesoamerican, and other counterparts, these ritual killings and entombments were attempts to provide elites in death with the same personal services they enjoyed in this life.

Some elite groups were permanent residents of Cahokia, but most of the people who built and sustained this center were probably maize farmers who lived in surrounding hamlets and who supplemented their farm incomes with hunting and gathering.

The mounds and burials at Cahokia and other sites are impressive monuments to status and power, but like other early complex societies, Mississippian society expressed these social dynamics in many ways. Timothy Pauketat and Thomas Emer-

FIGURE 15.6   This reconstruction of Cahokia shows the palisade that enclosed the center of the site and some of the seventeen other major structures that existed at about A.D. 1200. The base of Monk's Mound, the largest pyramid, is larger than the Great Pyramid at Giza, Egypt.

son, for example, have argued that a particular kind of Mississippian pottery, called Ramey Incised (which is incised with figures of eyes, fish, arrows, abstract objects, and various designs), served to legitimize and communicate a chief's authority:

> [These] pots were imbued with symbolism of order, hierarchy, and religiosity. . . . In the context of the rites of intensification, like the Green Corn ceremony, the Ramey Incised jar would have been a vehicle not only for the "redistribution" of comestibles, but also for the diffusion of elite ideas. Even the rudimentary actions of commoners, using Ramey Incised pots (after they had been ceremonially distributed from the administrative center[s]) may have provided a living metaphor of the role of elites—the source of the pots—as mediators of cosmic forces.[43]

Archaeologists have long debated the kind of sociopolitical entity that Cahokia represents. Some think Cahokia was a highly centralized, densely populated polity that can be thought of as a "chiefdom" (see chapter 7), perhaps even an embryonic state. Others think it was much less complex. George Milner, for example, suggests it was a "comparatively decentralized, geographically and socially segmented, less populous, and more dynamic cultural system."[44]

Cahokia is an impressive site, but it was probably not functionally similar to Teotihuacán or similar cities in prehistoric complex societies, at least in the degree of occupational specialization or the volumes and diversity of products produced, the class-stratification of the society, or the overall productivity of the economy.

At another great Mississippian site—Moundville, Alabama—a central earthen mound was the focus of a settlement in which elaborate burials, fortifications, and other structures were found. Christopher Peebles's statistical analysis of the grave goods unearthed with these burials suggests a society with considerable internal ranking.[45] Moundville had a complex history, and one gets the impression that here was a society with the potential to become a true urban metropolis, the center of a state.[46] Here too, however, the straight ecological arguments are quite convincing as to why this never happened: in a temperate forested environment, with an economy based on extensive cultivation of maize and a few other plants and on considerable hunting and foraging, there was not the stimuli of irrigation agriculture, interactions with nomads, and the other features of life present in early agricultural Mesopotamia, Egypt, or China. The environment simply does not permit or allow agricultural intensification on the scale possible in the tropical Olmec river basins, the Nile Valley, and other areas of advanced complexity.

Outside the great ceremonial centers, Mississippian villages were dispersed settlements of a few score wattle-and-daub structures, supported by internal wooden beams, with floors of packed earth.[47] The highest Mississippian population densities were along the rich river bottoms where it was possible to combine maize and bean farming with waterfowl exploitation.[48] In some areas the river annually renewed the fertility of the soil through alluviation, and permanent field agriculture was possible. Without plows or an advanced technology, the Native Americans in many areas relied on a form of swidden cultivation in which they burned off the vegetation on rich, well-drained alluvial plains, then planted maize and a few other crops, invested some effort in weeding and cultivation during the growing season, and then harvested and stored as much maize as they could. After one or two seasons a given plot of swidden land would lose its fertility, and the areas of cultivation—and perhaps the whole village—would have to be shifted elsewhere.

Where maize was most productive the people probably planted two crops a year in the richest lands, with beans planted next to the maize and encouraged to grow up its stalks. Beans, squash, sunflowers, and other crops were interspersed among the maize fields. The Mississippians were more gardeners than farmers compared to, for example, the wheat farmers of Southwest Asia. There is little evidence that Mississippian peoples ever did much in the way of flood control or irrigation, but they certainly used hoes and intensive weeding to boost crop yields. The Pilgrims' report that Native Americans put a fish in each hill of maize seeds has been disputed, but this too would have increased yields.

Our view of Mississippian life comes from both archaeological and ethnological sources, as Mississippian communities were still extant when the Europeans arrived in the sixteenth century. Initial accounts of the aboriginal Americans by Europeans must be viewed with suspicion, because there is every reason to believe that European diseases sped quickly through aboriginal populations—far faster in fact than the spread of the Europeans. Moreover, it was to the advantage of the Europeans to portray Native Americans as savages who could be legitimately displaced and to suggest that they had a moral duty to subdue and instruct these savages in the mores of civilized life. Some major diseases were introduced by the Europeans, but it now appears that mycobacterial diseases (possibly tuberculosis) were present in prehistoric Peru, and there is some evidence that apparently high incidences of tuberculosis in Native Americans "may have been the result of enforced changes in ecological and environmental factors rather than of exposure to a new infectious disease."[49] These early colonists described intensely stratified societies where the elites were able to draw almost without limit on the resources of the communities.

Warfare among competing Mississippian chiefdoms may have been frequent and brutal, particularly as the best lands were overexploited and fertility began to fall.[50]

Ethnographic accounts of Mississippian communities as they existed in the sixteenth and seventeenth centuries—long after the culmination of Mississippian culture—describe an intensely class-conscious society in which nobles and warriors alternately exploited and abused the "stinkards," commoners and slaves who made up most of these societies. The upper classes were slavishly obeyed and respected. They frequently married the lower classes, but the aristocrat could divorce or kill the lower-ranking spouse, given even minor cause. In A.D. 1720 the French explorer Le Page du Pratz witnessed the funeral of "Great Sun," a ruler of the Natchez Mississippian people. On the occasion of his death, Great Sun's wives, servants, and relatives were drugged and then clubbed to death and buried with him.[51]

Many late Mississippian and later period mounds and burials contain ornaments, pottery, and other artifacts decorated with motifs almost identical to some Mesoamerican motifs, including plumed serpents, eagles, jaguars, and warriors carrying trophy heads, as well as the fifty-two-year calendar round. Collectively, they are taken as evidence of a southern (Mesoamerican) religious cult. Opinions differ on their significance in terms of contacts with Mesoamerica; some consider them evidence of quite direct and sustained contacts, while others see them as minor borrowings with little more than an accidental connection to Mesoamerican cultures. The southern cult, as well as the Adena and Hopewell mortuary ceremonialism, likely achieved importance in North America only after cultural complexity in the north had reached a stage where these elements "made sense" for northern societies.

After A.D. 1000, Mississippian "colonists" began to emigrate from the cultural heartland, and some groups may have founded quasi-military enclaves in Alabama, Missouri, and elsewhere. Conceivably, these daughter communities were sent with the express purpose of extending Mississippian influence over other cultural groups, but the evidence for this is scanty.[52]

The spectacular Mississippian sites dominate the North American archaeological record, but all over the North American East there were divergent cultural traditions, many of them interacting economically, but also remaining distinctive in essential ways, from language to social organization. To the northeast, the Iroquois peoples adapted maize-beans-squash farming to the colder uplands of New York State, New England, and southeastern Canada. Their shifting pattern of swidden agriculture seems to have created land shortages and recurrent warfare, forcing people to live in well-fortified villages. To the west, marginal cultivators lived in the richer river valleys of Nebraska, South Dakota, and the other north-central states, with bison-hunting groups on the grasslands, where maize agriculture could not be practiced until the introduction by Europeans of deep-bottom plows. The horse-mounted nomadic hunters who range through thousands of Hollywood epics have some basis in reality, but only after the Europeans reintroduced the horse in America. Most of the desert regions of the west were thinly settled by hunter-foragers until European colonization, but rich and sedentary communities were established along the Pacific Northwest Coast and areas of California, where marine and terrestrial resources were so naturally productive that low-level complex societies could be sustained by simple fishing-foraging-hunting.

In contrast to most other ancient cultures, there is little question about the immediate cause of the decline of Mississippian culture. These people had no natural immunities to measles, smallpox, and cholera, and the densely settled Mississippian areas provided an ideal medium for the rapid spread of these highly contagious diseases.[53] Le Page du Pratz, who lived with the Natchez from 1718 to 1734, found that even "minor" diseases were devastating:

> Two distempers, that are not very fatal in other parts of the world, make dreadful ravages among them; I mean small-pox and a cold, which baffle all the arts of their physicians, who in other respects are very skillful. When a nation is attacked by the small-pox, it quickly makes great havock; for as a whole family is crowded into a small hut, which has no communications with the external air, but a door about two feet wide and four feet high, the distemper, if it seizes one, is quickly communicated to all. The aged die in consequence of their advanced years, and the bad quality of their food; and the young, if they are not strictly watched, destroy themselves, from an abhorrence of the blotches on their skin. . . . Colds, which are very common in winter, likewise destroy great numbers of the natives. In that season they keep fires in their huts day and night; and as there is no other opening but the door, the air within the hut is kept excessively warm without any free circulation; so that when they have occasion to go out, the cold seizes them, and the consequences of it are almost always fatal.[54]

Ann Ramenofsky has analyzed the archaeological evidence from several regions of the North American East and found that in each area there are significantly fewer settlements that date to the decades *just prior* to European invasion of these areas, which suggests that epidemic European diseases spread rapidly inland from the first physical encounters between most Native Americans and Europeans.[55] Native Americans died by the hundreds of thousands from diseases introduced by people they never saw.

Within a few decades of European contact in the sixteenth century, the once highly integrated and proud Mississippian people, and other cultures as well, were a much-reduced and poverty-stricken group, living amid thousands of abandoned settlements and eroding mounds attesting to their former greatness.

In summary of cultural developments in the North American East, we see the familiar script of cultural evolution. From a hunting-and-gathering base, specialized hunting and minor plant exploitation gradually gave way to intricate hunting-foraging economies in which fishing, nut collecting, shellfishing, and other activities were added to the subsistence repertoire according to what was probably a largely unrecognized but very precise "cost-benefit" analysis; then, after centuries of manipulation and selection, maize-based agriculture displaced less-productive economies in many areas, with consequent increasing population densities and the establishment of large sedentary communities. Once food production reached certain levels, the familiar harbingers of increasing cultural complexity, such as the spread of religious and stylistic traditions, monumental architecture, mortuary cults, and increasingly diverse and interdependent arts and crafts, also appeared (Figure 15.7). Social and religious hierarchies emerged as "efficient" ways to make the decisions necessary for the perpetuation of these increasingly complex economies, and the institutionalization of prestige and privilege may have arisen as an effective way of reducing competition between these populations and of maximizing administrative efficiency.

In these essentials, little differentiates the sequence of cultural evolution in North America from that in Mesoamerica, except that, given the available domesticates and technology, most of eastern North America had less agricultural potential than Mesoamerica, causing these northern cultures to stabilize at a much lower level of complexity. Had the Europeans not invaded and introduced their diseases, true state-level societies might well have evolved from the remnants of the Mississippian climax, but only if food production could have been increased drastically through technological, agricultural, or administrative innovations.

PREHISTORIC AGRICULTURALISTS IN THE NORTH AMERICAN WEST

The dramatic mountains, crystal skies, and primary colors of the Southwest make it an attractive place to live—especially if one has access to a municipal water system and a modern market and transport system. But from the perspective of a hunter and gatherer or subsistence farmer, most of the Southwest is not a lush environment: there are few large rivers or streams, and the combination of low rainfall and high

FIGURE 15.7   A sixteenth-century illustration by Jacques le Moyne of the burial of a Florida Indian chief. Arrows have been driven into the ground around the grave, and the chief's houses (upper left) are being ceremonially burned.

elevation renders much of the Southwest a land of searing summers and bitterly cold winters.

In some prehistoric periods the Southwest was wetter than it is today, but for most of the last ten thousand years the Southwest has usually been at least as hot and dry as it is today, and there were short periods of extreme drought.

As a consequence, although people have lived here for at least ten thousand years, and although they eventually adopted maize-based agriculture, aggregated into large towns, and evolved some occupational and administrative specialization, they never produced class-structured, hierarchically organized, economically differentiated societies. Periodic food shortages stimulated the development of small-scale cooperation among groups, but neither the economic inducements nor basic productivity were there to make such elaborate cultural forms necessary or possible.[56]

Yet the archaeological record of the American Southwest is an extraordinary cultural resource. Its proximity to major universities and excellent aridity-related preservation has meant that the archaeology of this region is among the best known in the world. Many important methodological advances in archaeology have developed in part out of research in the Southwest, including tree-ring dating, regional statistically-based sampling designs, analyses of site formation processes, and paleobotanical and paleoenvironmental research. Contemporary Native Americans living in the Southwest are in some cases direct descendants, both physically and culturally, of ancient groups, and thus the archaeology of the Southwest can be related to a well-studied ethnographic record.[57] Also, the fact that early Southwest cultures developed political and economic systems that, while less "complex" than those of, for example, Maya Mesoamerica, had sufficient complexity to offer an opportunity to study the kinds of cultural changes that in more productive environments are obscured archaeologically by the great states and empires that followed.[58] Moreover, there are some clear indications of cultural contacts between Southwest cultures and those of Mesoamerica, providing a "test case" in a sense for varying ideas about the nature of cultural contacts between more- and less-powerful groups in the ancient world.[59] And as Steadman Upham has shown, the American West provides an example of one of the enduring themes of human history, the relationship of nomads and agriculturalists. For, as people in some areas became farmers, they developed complex economic and social relationships with the many groups around them that continued to pursue the ancient hunting-foraging way of life.[60]

In any case, the Southwest archaeological record is one of considerable beauty. Southwestern ceramics, for example, are extraordinary both for their elegance and their reflection of sociopolitical and mythological themes.[61]

As we saw in chapter 6, people have been in the Southwest for at least twelve thousand years, and up to about A.D. 1, people here worked out a marvelous array of arid-land adaptations based on hunting and foraging. Foragers of the Cochise culture, heirs to a tradition thousands of years old of desert plant collecting, may have been exploiting maize for a long time. The apparent presence of maize pollen in samples dated to about 2000 B.C. suggests that this plant may have been exploited for some millennia before it became the staple food crop,[62] but the earliest evidence for substantial use of maize comes from Sheep Rock Shelter, Bat Cave, and several other sites and seems to cluster around 1000 B.C. Domesticated varieties of beans and squash also appear in the archaeological record at about this time, but the diet was still probably based on a broad range of other plants and animals. Even today Native Americans in the Southwest still hunt deer, rabbits, and other animals, and augment their farm produce with high-calorie nuts, berries, and seeds.

The earliest maize variety used in the Southwest was the Chapalote variant found much earlier at Tehuacán, and thus there was a long time lag before it was in significant use in the Southwest. It used to be thought that early varieties of maize had to be adapted to local Southwest environments, but as Paul Minnis notes, the recent recovery of Archaic maize from the deserts around Tucson does not support this idea. He suggests that the modern maize variety morphologically closest to Archaic maize, Chapalote, was well-adapted to high and low environments and could be grown under many conditions.[63] In any case, the people of the Southwest adapted maize to their world and combined it with beans, squash, and a wide variety of other resources in an economy with sufficient productivity to permit the village-farming way of life and the beginnings of cultural elaboration that we have seen in many other areas of the world.

THE HOHOKAM CULTURE

The Hohokam peoples, who flourished in the Salt and Gila River valleys (Arizona) between about A.D. 500 and A.D. 1200 (arguments about these dates remain)[64] seem to represent the confluence of Archaic hunting-and-gathering traditions and Mesoamerican cultures (Figure 15.8). Some archaeologists (e.g., Haury)[65] have concluded that the Hohokam were not just local peoples whose culture was transformed by contacts with the high civilizations of Mexico; on the basis of late Hohokam styles of architecture, construction, ceramics, turquoise ornaments, and other artifacts, they conclude that Hohokam styles are so similar to Mesoamerican examples that they can only be the result of an immigration of Mexican people who transplanted their way of life directly to the Hohokam area, where previously there had been only hunters and gatherers. But the Hohokam probably represent more a fusion of Mexican cultural traditions, via trade routes, and indigenous peoples than a large migration.[66] From the initial entrance of people into the New World until the present, one can find many examples of migration and colonization. Early agricultural systems in most parts of the world appear to have been highly unstable and probably had a great advantage from gradual developments in place: few groups of early farmers could have successfully taken up their worldly goods and hiked many miles in search of a new land.

One of the most interesting aspects of the Hohokam is their agricultural system. Their homeland is set in some of the driest deserts of North America, where summer temperatures have impressed even archaeological veterans of the Middle East. Beginning at about 300 B.C., the Hohokam channeled water from the Salt and Gila rivers to irrigate their gardens of maize and other crops. Modern buildings have erased much of the Hohokam irrigation system, but two canals near Phoenix were over sixteen kilometers long, several meters wide, and about sixty centimeters deep when first constructed. Tightly woven grass mats were probably used as gates to open and close canal segments, and earthen dams on the rivers in some places diverted water through canals for more than fifty kilometers across the desert floor, with many small branches serving individual fields.

In the recent past, Southwestern Native American irrigation systems, as well as comparable agricultural systems elsewhere in the world, have been operated by a few thousand people in relatively simple tribal organizations in which no coercion, permanent authorities, or police agencies were necessary, and this might well have been the case among the Hohokam.

Although the largest irrigation systems were apparently built sometime after A.D. 800, by about A.D. 300 there were already indications of minor increases in the complexity of Hohokam cultures. Some low platform mounds, about twenty-nine meters long, twenty-three meters wide, and three meters high, were built at the Snaketown site, and here and elsewhere people built large sunken ball courts like those found in Mesoamerica. The Hohokam ball courts were east-west oriented oval depressions about sixty meters long, with 4.5- to 6-meter-high sloping earth embankments on a side. Apparently the objective of the game, played by two opposing teams, was to try to get a rubber ball (several of which have been found in the Southwest) through a goal, probably not by throwing or batting it, but by using knees, elbows, or torso.

FIGURE 15.8 Major cultural traditions of the North American Southwest. These cultures are shown at their maximum extent, which they did not reach simultaneously.

The ball apparently could not be held in the hands when it was in play. As played by the Mesoamericans, this activity was not a sport: the ball may have represented the sun, and the court and play were imbued with ritual and cosmological imagery. Losing players were sometimes executed (see chapter 13).

The Southwestern ball courts were probably not stops on the northern road trips of the Mexican major leagues, but they do indicate very close southern affinities, as do the platform mounds. And between A.D. 900 and A.D. 1200, many other Mesoamerican elements were imported, including cotton textiles, certain ceramic motifs, pyrite mirrors, effigy vessels, cast copper bells, ear plugs, etched shell ornaments, and even parrots and macaws—probably imported from the south and kept and prized for their feathers.

Generally, however, there is little evidence in subsistence practices, settlements, or mortuary ceremonies of evolving rank and wealth differences. Most of the Hohokam lived in small square pit houses roofed with clay and grass domes supported by a wooden pole framework. Early dwellings appear large enough for several families, but single-family residences became more popular in later periods.

Hohokam settlement patterns are not well known. There are few indications of a master plan in village layouts or of economic specialization of villages. Most villages probably repeated all the economic activities of other villages, except that some favored locations allowed a greater reliance on maize, beans, squash, and other crops. Nonetheless, many atlatl dart points and arrowheads have been found at each Hohokam site, and botanical remains indicate that almost every community supplemented its diet with wild mustard, amaranths, chenopods, cactus fruits, mesquite, screwbeans, and other wild products.[67]

Artifacts in the Hohokam style have been found over a wide area, and various scholars have tried to determine whether these artifact distributions represent migrations, or trading expeditions, or the spread of regular trade networks, perhaps with associated political and social ties.[68]

THE MOGOLLON

The Mogollon peoples (pronounced something like "Mug-ee-yone"), who also were heirs to the Archaic desert foraging cultures of the last several millennia B.C., lived mainly in the mountains of east central Arizona and west central New Mexico. Sedentary villages and ceramics of the Mogollon type may have already been established by the last few centuries B.C., but the distinctive Mogollon red-and-brown pottery is securely dated to about the third century A.D., at which time villages of about fifteen pit houses each were scattered along ridges, bluffs, and terraces. Like their contemporaries in much of the Americas, they relied on the maize-beans-squash complex, supplemented by many wild plants and game. Mogollon burials of this period were often simple inhumations in house floors, accompanied by a few pottery vessels, turquoise ornaments, and stone tools typical of unstratified societies.

At the important Mogollon site of Swarts Ruins, in the Mimbres Valley, New Mexico, river boulders set in adobe were used to construct a large complex of conjoined rectangular rooms, access to which was apparently possible only through the roof, since there were no exterior doors. Inside walls were plastered with mud, and doorways led from one room to another. Storage bins, shelves, fireplaces, and benches constituted the essential furnishings. Corpses were frequently interred in the floors of abandoned rooms, in occupied rooms, or within the village compound; most burials were very simple.

The Mogollon built no pyramids, ball courts, or major irrigation systems, but they did produce an extraordinarily beautiful array of ceramics. Their "Mimbres" ceramic forms, decorated with vivid figures of frogs, insects, fish, deer, and other animal life painted against black backgrounds, are particularly notable. Stephen Jett and Peter Moyle have shown that many of the fish species illustrated on Mimbres pottery are marine species that could be found no closer to the Mimbres area than 1,500 kilometers southwest, in the Gulf of California.[69] The beauty of Mogollon pottery has resulted in widespread looting, a sickening destruction of yet another Native American culture.

Mogollon settlement patterns show some evidence of minor emerging social ranking. Mogollon villages seem to be of two types: a small cluster of fewer than five pit houses, without any large ceremonial kivas, and larger collections of one hundred or more pit houses associated with "great kivas." The largest pit houses in these communities tend to have the greatest amount of storage space, larger numbers of exotic trade items, and evidence of greater consumption of agricultural products. Lightfoot and Feinman interpret this evidence and other data to mean that a "suprahousehold" decision-making organization had developed among the Mogollon, perhaps as a result of competition among rival political leaders.[70] But it is hard to link changing distributions of artifacts like these to the fairly subtle social changes that would have been involved in the rise of suprahousehold administrative positions. In any case, there is little about the Mogollon to suggest profound social changes in the direction of complexity. Natural limitations on agricultural intensification seem to have restricted the complexity of social and political organization here.[71]

One of the major settlement pattern transitions in Southwestern cultural history occurred during the first millennium A.D., when people gradually, generation by generation, stopped living in relatively small villages of semi-subterranean pit houses and began building their communities in the "pueblo" style of blocks of contiguous aboveground rooms.

For the archaeologist, of course, such a change is immediately seen in adaptive terms: What conditions would induce this sort of long-term, regional change? In a consideration of this question from the perspective of Mogollon settlements in western Texas, Michael Whalen notes that the change is associated with an increase in regional population densities, the appearance of larger community size, a growing reliance on plant cultivation as the main subsistence source, and an increasingly elaborate ceremonialism, as expressed in the design and contents of structures.[72]

Whalen suggests that as populations grew, climates fluctuated, and settlements spread into different microenvironments, people tried to maintain their traditional way of life by extending agriculture into the margins of basins where water was more available. The greater productivity of these basin margins fostered certain kinds of economic agricultural specialization in which the community rather than the family was the basic social and economic unit. McGuire and Schiffer show that the transition from pit houses was the outcome of a long period of experimentation.[73]

Fred Plog analyzed the history of the Colorado Plateau for the period between A.D. 400 and about A.D. 1540 and concluded that at various times people in this area formed "alliances" in which there was fairly intensive trade, some emergent social ranking and stratification, and the formation of administrative and trade centers.[74] He distinguishes these Colorado Plateau systems from the more complex societies of Mesoamerica and elsewhere, noting that the Colorado Plateau societies never intensified agricultural production to the level that typically supported more complex societies, nor did they ever seem to include full-time craftsmen working in administered centralized workshops. The small steps the Southwesterners made in these directions, Plog concluded, arose out of the need to address imbalances between population densities and resources, but these changes were always strictly limited by the relatively great environmental diversity and generally low agricultural potential of the region.

Some Mogollon sites, such as the Casas Grandes sites in northern Mexico, have what appear to be Mogollon-style artifacts along with Mesoamerican items, such as ball courts, platform mounds, and jewelry in turquoise and shell. Here, too, scholars disagree as to whether such sites represent the direct intervention of Mesoamerican traders in Southwestern economies or a more peripheral, indirect kind of relationship. They also disagree about how complex these societies would have been.

Mogollon cultural traditions and population densities appear to have declined rapidly by A.D. 1300, perhaps as droughts contracted the areas in which they could survive, or as a result of invasion or absorption by neighboring Anasazi groups.

THE ANASAZI

Like the Mogollon and Hohokam, the Anasazi developed out of desert-foraging cultures, and their earliest pre-pottery representatives are widely known as the Basketmaker cultures. It is not entirely certain how mobile early Anasazi groups were, but by the first few centuries A.D. they were apparently living in many sedentary settlements located on old river terraces and mesa tops or in river valleys in the high plateau country of the central Southwest.[75] The earliest houses were circular structures of wattle and daub set on log bases, or semi-subterranean houses. These early Anasazi did not use pottery and, although they ate maize, beans, and squash, they invested little labor in cultivating these crops, relying instead on wild foods, such as roots, bulbs, grass seeds, nuts, acorns, berries, cactus fruits, sunflowers, deer, rabbits, antelopes, and wild sheep.

After about A.D. 400, the Anasazi began to use pottery and to build large pit houses, most of which were circular or rectangular, from 3 to 7.5 meters in diameter, and covered by log and mud roofs supported on center posts. Interior walls were plastered with mud or faced with stone, access was through a descending passageway, and fireplaces and benches were standard furnishings. At some sites, large ceremonial pit houses, or kivas, were built. After about A.D. 700, above-ground masonry houses were erected in some Anasazi communities, but the pit house and kiva combination continued to be the basic village type until the end of the thirteenth century A.D.

Defensive considerations, greater exploitation of more productive strains of maize, and climatic changes beginning about A.D. 700 may have spurred the Anasazi into constructing the "cliff cities" for which they are famous.[76] Pollen and geological studies suggest that summer rainfall, in the form of torrential storms, increased after A.D. 700, while winter rainfall decreased, and the resulting changes in water tables and stream flows may have forced the Anasazi to congregate around larger, permanently flowing rivers.[77] Hillsides were terraced to control erosion, and diversion canals and dams were constructed to control and store as much of the vital summer rainwater as possible. On Chapin Mesa, for example, in the Mesa Verde area, the older agricultural fields were extended by an elaborate checkdam system that added eight or twelve hectares of cultivable land.

In some areas erosion forced frequent settlement relocations, and some communities met the changing agricultural conditions by scattering into small family groups; but the prevailing response was to aggregate into large towns along the major rivers. By about 1100 A.D., prosperous enclaves were established at Mesa Verde, Chaco Canyon, Canyon de Chelly, and elsewhere, and in some ways these communities represent the high point of Southwestern culture. There were twelve large towns along Chaco Canyon, of which Pueblo Bonito was the largest, with over eight hundred rooms and perhaps twelve hundred people (Figure 15.9). In addition to these large, multi-story pueblos, there were many single-story and apparently unplanned villages—an architectural contrast that has led some scholars to infer that two different ethnic or cultural traditions were united to form this variant of Anasazi culture. Vivian[78] has shown that the Chaco Canyon was part of a large organized system that

FIGURE 15.9   Reconstruction of Pueblo Bonito, as it may have appeared at about A.D. 1050.

included a unified irrigation system and about 600 kilometers of roads which linked scores of small communities and facilitated trade in ceramics, turquoise, food, and other commodities. Two styles of architecture reflect two different kinds of social organization, one being a dual, or "moiety" system, in which a tribe is divided into two complementary groups, the other being a clan, or lineage-based system. The emergence of this regional culture appears to have occurred rather quickly, and it eventually lost much of the apparent organization and integration—the age-old pattern, in other words, of cultural evolution. All of the traditional explanations have been invoked to explain this rise and collapse, such as the emergence of managerial elites, climatic factors, etc.[79]

By about A.D. 1150, most of the known cliff cities in the Four Corners area had been established, all of very similar construction. Settlements grew by simple accretion: more rooms were added as needed. The remote location of the cliff towns may have had to do with defensive considerations, although the identity of any possible enemies is unknown (Figure 15.10).

As beautiful as many late Anasazi settlements were, they do not appear to have been the work of a highly complex society. The buildings, while superbly adapted to their environment, are quite crudely constructed. There may have been minor occupational specialization in ceramic manufacture, weaving, and turquoise carving, but most if not all of the people were subsistence farmers. Nor is any evidence of differential rank expressed in domestic architecture or in grave goods. Even the irrigation system, while intricate and efficient, was probably administered through simple kinship systems.

Shortly before A.D. 1300, many once-prosperous Anasazi communities began to be abandoned, and when the Spanish arrived in the sixteenth century, they found the descendants of the Anasazi living along the Rio Grande in small villages, each a largely autonomous political and economic unit.

In the first and early second millennia A.D., the Fremont culture, which was defined by distinctive artifact styles, appeared on the periphery of the Anasazi world, in what is now Utah. The Colorado River area was home to the Patayan, another peripheral group.

SUMMARY AND CONCLUSIONS

> *Illegal aliens have always been a problem in the*
> *United States. Ask any Indian.*
>
> Robert Orben

The New World was truly a "second earth," where long millennia of indigenous cultural development produced a rich spectrum of peoples and cultures unaffected by contact with European and Asian peoples. In some ways it is less than satisfying to conclude that the temperate latitudes of North America never produced states and empires because of the simple absence of draft animals, developed metallurgy, extensive warm arid alluvial plains, and a few other techno-environmental factors—but

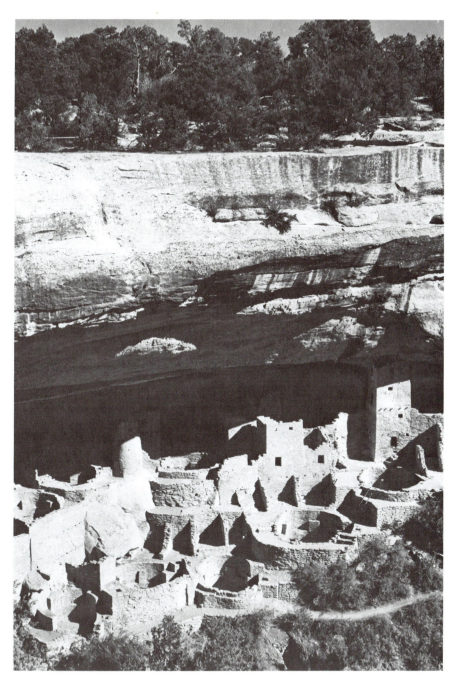

FIGURE 15.10 Cliff Palace, Mesa Verde, Colorado, is one of the most impressive settlements built under massive cliffs in the American Southwest.

this conclusion seems inescapable. From the perspective of the present, the violent collision between Old and New World cultures also seems an inevitable outcome of the competition dynamic of evolutionary processes and the demographic, techno-environmental, and other conditions of both areas. But to rank Old and New World cultures in this sense of an evolutionary scale is only a useful research device; it should not obscure the great richness of the ancient cultures of both areas.

BIBLIOGRAPHY

Anderson, D. G., and G. T. Hanson. 1988. "Early Archaic Settlement in the Southeastern United States: A Case Study from the Savannah River Valley." *American Antiquity* 53(2):262–86.

Asch, D. L., and N. B. Asch. 1985. "Prehistoric Plant Cultivation in West-Central Illinois." In *Prehistoric Food Production in North America*, ed., R. I. Ford, University of Michigan Museum of Anthropology, Anthropological Papers 75.

Baby, R., and S. Langlois. 1977. "Prehistoric Agriculture: A Study of House Types in the Ohio Valley." *Ohio Historical Society Echoes* 16(2):1–5.

Baugh, T. G., and J. E. Ericson. 1995. *Prehistoric Exchange Systems in North America*. New York: Plenum Press.

Braun, D. P. 1983. "Pots as Tools." In *Archaeological Hammers and Theories*, eds. A. Keene and J. Moore. New York: Academic Press.

———. 1987. "Comment on M. J. O'Brien, 'Sedentism, Population Growth, and Resource Selection in the Woodland Midwest: A Review of Coevolutionary Developments.' " *Current Anthropology* 28(2):189–90.

———. 1988. "The Social and Technological Roots of 'Late Woodland.' " In *Interpretations of Culture Change in Eastern Woodlands During the Late Woodland Period*, ed. R. W. Yerkes. Department of Anthropology, Ohio State University, Occasional Papers in Anthropology 3:17–38.

Braun, D. P., and S. Plog. 1982. "Evolution of 'Tribal' Social Networks: Theory and Prehistoric North American Evidence." *American Antiquity* 47:504–25.

Brose, D. S., and N. Greber, eds. 1979. *Hopewell Archaeology: The Chillicothe Conference*. Kent, OH: The Kent State University Press.

Brown, J. A. 1977. "Current Directions in Midwestern Archaeology." *Annual Review of Anthropology* 6:161–79.

———. 1985. "Long-term Trends to Sedentism and the Emergence of Complexity in the American Midwest." In *Prehistoric Hunter-Gatherers: The Emergence of Cultural Complexity*, eds. T. D. Price and J. A. Brown. Orlando, FL: Academic Press.

Broyles, B. J. 1971. *Second Preliminary Report: The St. Albans Site, Kanawha County, West Virginia*. West Virginia Geological and Economic Survey Report, Archaeological Investigation 3.

Bullen, R. P. 1971. "The Beginnings of Pottery in Eastern United States as Seen from Florida." *Eastern States Archaeological Federation Bulletin*, 30:10–11.

Bush, D. E. 1975. "A Ceramic Analysis of the Late Adena Buckmeyer Site, Perry County, Ohio." *Michigan Archaeologist* 21:9–23.

Caldwell, J. 1958. *Trend and Tradition in the Prehistory of the Eastern United States*. Menasha, WI: Memorial Series of the American Anthropological Association 88.

———. 1971. "Eastern North America." In *Prehistoric Agriculture*, ed. S. Struever. Garden City, NY: Natural History Press.

Clark, G. A., M. A. Kelley, J. M. Grange, and M. C. Hill. 1987. "The Evolution of Mycobacterial Disease in Human Populations." *Current Anthropology* 28(1): 45–62.

Cleland, C. E. 1966. *The Prehistoric Animal Ecology and Ethnozoology of the Upper Great Lakes Region.* Ann Arbor: Museum of Anthropology, Anthropological Papers, University of Michigan, no. 29.

Coe, M., D. Snow, and E. Benson. 1986. *Atlas of Ancient America.* New York: Facts on File.

Cordell, L. S. 1984. *Prehistory of the Southwest.* New York: Academic Press.

———. 1984. "Southwestern Archaeology." *Annual Review of Anthropology* 13:301–32.

Cordell, L. S., and G. J. Gumerman, eds. 1989. *Dynamics of Southwest Prehistory.* Washington, DC: Smithsonian Institution Press.

Cordell, L. S., and F. Plog. 1979. "Escaping the Confines of Normative Thought—A Reevaluation of Puebloan Prehistory." *American Antiquity* 44:405–29.

Cressman, L. S. 1977. *Prehistory of the Far West.* Salt Lake City: University of Utah Press.

Crown, P. L. 1990. "The Hohokam of the American Southwest." *Journal of World Prehistory* 4(2):223–55.

———. 1995. *Ceramics and Ideology: Salado Polychrome Pottery.* Albuquerque: University of New Mexico Press.

Crown, P. L. and J.W. Judge. 1991. *Chaco and Hohokam: Regional Systems in the American Southwest.* Santa Fe, NM: School of American Research.

DeJarnette, D. L. 1967. "Alabama Pebble Tools: The Lively Complex." *Eastern States Archaeological Federation Bulletin*, no. 26.

Dickson, D. B. 1975. "Settlement Pattern Stability and Change in the Middle Northern Rio Grande Region, New Mexico: A Test of Some Hypotheses." *American Antiquity* 40:159–71.

———. 1981. "The Yanomamo of the Mississippi Valley? Some Reflections on Larson . . . Gibson . . . and Mississippi Period Warfare in the Southeastern United States." *American Antiquity* 46:909–16.

Doyel, D. E. 1986. "A Short History of Hohokam Research." In *Emil W. Haury's Prehistory of the American Southwest*, eds. J. J. Reid and D. E. Doyel. Tucson: University of Arizona Press.

Dragoo, D. W. 1963. "Mounds for the Dead." *Annals of Carnegie Museum* 37:1–315.

———. 1976. "Some Aspects of Eastern North American Prehistory: A Review." *American Antiquity* 41:3–27.

Dunnell, R. C. 1967. "The Prehistory of Fishtrap, Kentucky: Archaeological Interpretation in Marginal Areas." Unpublished doctoral dissertation, Yale University.

Ericson, J. E., and T. G. Baugh, eds. 1995. *The American Southwest and Mesoamerica.* New York: Plenum Press.

Fagan, B. M. 1995. *Ancient North America*, 2nd ed. New York: Thames and Hudson.

Farnsworth, K. B. 1973. *An Archaeological Survey of the Macoupin Valley.* Springfield: Illinois State Museum, Reports of Investigations, no 26.

Farnsworth, K. B., and T. E. Emerson, eds. 1986. *Early Woodland Archaeology.* Kampsville Seminars in Archaeology, No. 2. Kampsville, IL: Kampsville Archeological Center, Center for American Archeology.

Fiedel, S. J. 1992. *Prehistory of the Americas*, 2nd ed. Cambridge: Cambridge University Press.

Ford, R. I. 1974. "Northeastern Archeology Past and Future Directions." *Annual Review of Anthropology* 3:385–414.

———. 1981. "Gardening and Farming before A.D. 1000: Patterns of Prehistoric Cultivation North of Mexico." *Journal of Ethnobiology* 1(1):6–27.

Fowler, M. L. 1969. *Explorations into Cahokia Archaeology.* Illinois Archaeological Survey Bulletin 7.

———. 1971. "Agriculture and Village Settlement in the North American East: The Central Mississippi Valley Area, a Case History." In *Prehistoric Agriculture*, ed. S. Struever. Garden City, NY: Natural History Press.

———. 1975. "A Pre-Columbian Urban Center on the Mississippi." *Scientific American* 233(2):93–101.

Fritz, G. 1990. "Multiple Ways to Farming in Precontact Eastern North America." *Journal of World Prehistory* 4(4): 387–436.

Glassow, M. A. 1980. *Prehistoric Agricultural Development in the Northern Southwest: A Study in Changing Patterns of Land Use.* Socorro, NM: Ballena Press.

Griffin, J. B. 1967. "Eastern North American Archaeology: A Summary." *Science* 156:175–91.

Gumerman, G. J., ed. 1988. *The Anasazi in a Changing Environment.* Cambridge: Cambridge University Press.

Haury, E. W. 1976. *The Hohokam Desert Farmers and Craftsmen.* Tucson: University of Arizona Press.

Hill, J. N. 1966. "A Prehistoric Community in Eastern Arizona." *Southwestern Journal of Anthropology* 22:9–30.

———. 1970. *Broken K Pueblo: Prehistoric Social Organization in the American Southwest.* Tucson: University of Arizona Press.

Hines, P. 1977. "On Social Organization in the Middle Mississippian—States or Chiefdoms?" *Current Anthropology* 18:337–38.

Houart, G. L. 1971. *Koster—A Stratified Archaic Site in the Illinois Valley.* Springfield: Illinois State Museum Reports of Investigations, no. 22.

Hunter-Anderson, R. L. 1981. "Comments on Cordell and Plog's 'Escaping the Confines of Normative Thought.' " *American Antiquity* 46:194–97.

———. 1986. *Prehistoric Adaptation in the American South-West.* Cambridge: Cambridge University Press.

Irwin-Williams, C. 1968. "The Reconstruction of Archaic Culture History in the Southwestern United States." In *Archaic Prehistory in the Western United States,* ed. C. Irwin-Williams. Portales, NM: Eastern New Mexico University Contributions in Anthropology.

Jennings, J. D. 1974. *Prehistory of North America,* 2nd ed. New York: McGraw-Hill.

Jett, S. C., and P. B. Moyle. 1986. "The Exotic Origins of Fishes Depicted on Prehistoric Mimbres Pottery from New Mexico." *American Antiquity* 51(4):688–720.

Keegan, W. F., ed. 1987. *Emergent Horticultural Economies of the Eastern Woodlands.* Occasional Paper No. 7. Carbondale, IL: Center for Archaeological Investigations, Southern Illinois University.

Le Page du Pratz, A. S. n.a. *Histoire de la Louisiane.*

Lightfoot, R. G., and G. M. Feinman. 1982. "Social Differentiation and Leadership Development in Early Pithouse Villages in the Mogollon Region of the American Southwest." *American Antiquity* 47:64–81.

Longacre, W. A. 1975. "Population Dynamics at the Grasshopper Pueblo, Arizona." In *Population Studies in Archaeology and Biological Anthropology: A Symposium,* ed. A. C. Swedlund. *American Antiquity* 40:71–74, memoir 30.

Lynott, M. J., T. W. Boutton, J. E. Price, D. E. Nelson. 1986. "Stable Carbon Isotopic Evidence for Maize Agriculture in Southeast Missouri and Northeast Arkansas." *American Antiquity* 51(1):51–65.

McGuire, R. H. 1992. *Death, Society, and Ideology in a Hohokam Community.* Boulder, CO: Westview Press.

McGuire, R. H., and M. B. Schiffer. 1982. *Hohokam and Patayan: Prehistory of Southwestern Arizona.* New York: Academic Press.

McGuire, R. H., and M. B. Schiffer. 1983. "A Theory of Architectural Design." *Journal of Anthropological Archaeology* 2:277–303.

Madsen, D. B. 1979. "The Fremont and the Sevier: Defining Prehistoric Agriculturalists North of the Anasazi." *American Antiquity* 44:711–22.

Madsen, D., and D. Rhode, eds. 1995. *Across the West: Human Population Movement and the Expansion of the Numa.* Salt Lake City: University of Utah Press.

Marquardt, W. H. 1985. "Complexity and Scale in the Study of Fisher-Gatherer-Hunters: An Example from the Eastern United States." In *Prehistoric Hunter-Gatherers: The Emergence of Cultural Complexity,* eds. T. D. Price and J. A. Brown. Orlando, FL: Academic Press.

Mathien, F. J., and R. H. McGuire, eds. 1986. *Ripples in the Chichimec Sea: New Considerations of Southwestern-Mesoamerican Interactions.* Carbondale, IL: Southern Illinois University Press.

Milanich, J. T., and C. H. Fairbanks. 1987. *Florida Archaeology*. New York: Academic Press.

Milner, G. 1990. "The Late Prehistoric Cahokia Cultural System of the Mississippi River Valley: Foundations, Florescence, and Fragmentation." *Journal of World Prehistory* 4(1):1–44.

Minnis, P. E. 1985. *Social Adaptation to Food Stress*. Chicago: University of Chicago Press.

———. 1992. "Earliest Plant Cultivation in the Desert Borderlands of North America." *The Origins of Agriculture*, eds. C. W. Cowan and P. J. Watson. Washington, DC: Smithsonian Institution Press.

Moratto, M. J. 1984. *California Archaeology*. Foreword by F. A. Riddell. Contributions by D. A. Frederickson, C. Raven, and C. N. Warren. New York: Academic Press.

Morse, D. F., and P. A. Morse. 1983. *Archaeology of the Central Mississippi Valley*. New York: Academic Press.

Muller, J. 1986. *Archaeology of the Lower Ohio River Valley*. New York: Academic Press.

Murphy, J. L. 1975. *An Archaeological History of the Hocking Valley*. Athens: Ohio University Press.

O'Brien, M. J. 1987. "Sedentism, Population Growth, and Resource Selection in the Woodland Midwest: A Review of Coevolutionary Developments." *Current Anthropology* 28(2):177–97.

Odell, G., ed. 1996. *Stone Tools. Theoretical Insights into Prehistory*. New York: Plenum Press.

Ortiz, A. 1979. "Southwest." *Handbook of North American Indians*. Vol. 9. Washington, DC: Smithsonian Institution Press.

Pauketat, T., and T. Emerson. 1991. "The Ideology of Authority and the Power of the Pot." *American Anthropologist* 93(4):919–41.

Peebles, C. S. 1977. "Moundville and Surroundings Sites: Some Structural Considerations of Mortuary Practices, II." In *Approaches to the Social Dimensions of Mortuary Practices*, ed. J. A. Brown. Society for American Archaeology Memoir, no. 25.

Pfeiffer, J. E. 1977. *The Emergence of Society*. New York: McGraw-Hill.

Phillips, J., and J. Brown, eds. 1983. *Archaic Hunter-Gatherers in the Midwest*. Orlando, FL: Academic Press.

Plog, F. 1983. "Political and Economic Alliances on the Colorado Plateaus, A.D. 400 to 1450." In *Advances in World Archaeology*, Vol. 2. eds. F. Wendorf and A. E. Close. New York: Academic Press.

Porter, J. W. 1969. *The Mitchell Site and Prehistoric Exchange Systems at Cahokia: A.D. 1000–300*. Illinois Archaeological Survey Bulletin, no. 7.

Powell, S.1983. *Mobility and Adaptation: The Anasazi of Black Mesa, Arizona*. Carbondale: Southern Illinois University Press.

Price, T. D., and G. M. Feinman, eds. 1995. *Foundations of Social Inequality*. New York: Plenum Press.

Prufer, O. H. 1964. "The Hopewell Cult." *Scientific American* 211:90–102.

———. 1965. "The McGraw Site: A Study in Hopewellian Dynamics." Cleveland Museum of Natural History Scientific Publications, n.s. 4(1).

Ramenofsky, A. F. 1987. *Vectors of Death: The Archaeology of European Contact*. Albuquerque: University of New Mexico Press.

Redman, C. L. 1993. *People of the Tonto Rim: Archaeological Discovery in Prehistoric Arizona*. Washington, DC: Smithsonian Institution Press.

Reid, J. J., and D. E. Doyel, eds. 1986. *Emil W. Haury's Prehistory of the American Southwest*. Tucson: University of Arizona Press.

Rice, G. E. 1975. "A Systemic Explanation of a Change in Mogollon Settlement Patterns." Unpublished doctoral dissertation, University of Washington.

Riley, T. J., R. Edging, and J. Rossen. 1990. "Cultigens in Prehistoric Eastern North America." *Current Anthropology* 31(5):525–41.

Rindos, D. 1984. *The Origins of Agriculture: An Evolutionary Perspective*. New York: Academic Press.

Ritchie, W. A. 1969. *The Archaeology of New York State*, 2nd ed. Garden City, NY: Natural History Press.

Rothschild, N. A. 1979. "Mortuary Behavior and Social Organization at Indian Knoll and Dickson Mounds." *American Antiquity* 44:658–75.

Schiffer, M. B. 1982. "Hohokam Chronology: An Essay on History and Method." In *Hohokam and Patayan Prehistory of Southwestern Arizona*, R. H. McGuire and M. B. Schiffer, eds. New York: Academic Press.

Schiffer, M., and J. Skibo. 1987. "Theory and Experiment in the Study of Technological Change." *Current Anthropology* 28(5):595–623.

Schoenwetter, J. 1962. "Pollen Analysis of Eighteen Archaeological Sites in Arizona and New Mexico." In *Prehistory of Eastern Arizona*, eds. P. S. Martin et al. [Fieldiana]: *Anthropology* 53:168–209.

Simmons, A. H. 1986. "New Evidence for the Early Use of Cultigens in the American Southwest." *American Antiquity* 51(1):73–89.

Smith, B. 1974. "Middle Mississippi Exploitation of Animal Populations—A Predictive Model." *American Antiquity* 39:274–91.

———. 1985. "The Role of *Chenopodium* as a Domesticate in the Pre-Maize Garden System of the Eastern United States." *Southeastern Archaeology* 4:51–72.

———. 1986. "The Archaeology of the Southeastern United States: From Dalton to de Soto, 10,500–500 B.P." *Advances in World Archaeology* 5:1–92.

Smith, B. D., ed. 1990. *The Mississippian Emergence*. Washington, DC: Smithsonian Institution Press.

———. 1992. *The Rivers of Change: Essays on Early Agriculture in Eastern North America*. Washington, DC: Smithsonian Institution Press.

Spielmann, K. A., M. J. Schoeninger, and K. Moore. 1990. "Plains-Pueblo Interdependence and Human Diet at Pecos Pueblo, New Mexico." *American Antiquity* 55(4):745–65.

Steponaitis, V. P. 1983. *Ceramics, Chronology, and Community Patterns: An Archaeological Study at Moundville*. New York: Academic Press.

Stewart, T. D. 1973. *The People of America*. New York: Scribner's.

Stoltman, J. B. 1983. "Ancient Peoples of the Upper Mississippi River Valley." In *Historic Lifestyles of the Upper Mississippi River Valley*, ed. J. Wozniak. New York: University Press of America.

———. 1986. *Prehistoric Mound Builders of the Mississippi Valley*. Davenport, IA: Putnam Museum.

Struever, S., and G. L. Houart. 1972. "Analysis of the Hopewell Interaction Sphere." In *Social Exchange and Interaction*. Ann Arbor: University of Michigan, Museum of Anthropology, Anthropological Papers, no. 46.

Struever, S., and K. D. Vickery. 1973. "The Beginnings of Cultivation in the Midwest-Riverine Area of the United States." *American Anthropologist* 75:1197–1220.

Tainter, J. 1975. "Social Inference and Mortuary Practices: An Experiment in Numerical Classification." *World Archaeology* 7:1–15.

Tuck, J. A. 1971. "An Archaic Cemetery at Port au Choix, Newfoundland." *American Antiquity* 36:343–58.

Upham, S. 1988. "Archaeological Visibility and the Underclass of Southwestern Prehistory." *American Antiquity* 53(2):245–61.

———. 1994. "Nomads of the Desert West: A Shifting Continuum in Prehistory." *Journal of World Prehistory* 8(2):113–68.

Upham, S., K. G. Lightfoot, and G. M. Feinman. 1981. "Explaining Socially Determined Ceramic Distributions in the Prehistoric Southwest." *American Antiquity* 46:822–36.

Utah Museum of Natural History. 1995. *Treading in the Past: Sandals of the Anasazi*. Salt Lake City: University of Utah Press.

Vivian, G. 1990. *The Chacoan Prehistory of the San Juan Basin*.

Vogel, J. C., and N. J. Van Der Merwe. 1977. "Isotopic Evidence for Early Maize Cultivation in New York State." *American Antiquity* 42:238–42.

Washburn, D. R. 1975. "The American Southwest." In *North America*, eds. S. Gorenstein et al. New York: St. Martin's Press.

Watson, P. J. 1974. *Archeology of the Mammoth Cave Area*. New York: Academic Press.

Whalen, M. 1981. "Cultural-Ecological Aspects of the Pithouse-to-Pueblo Transition in a Portion of the Southwest." *American Antiquity* 46:75–91.

Willey, G. R. 1966. *An Introduction to American Archaeology, Vol. 1: North and Middle America.* Englewood Cliffs, NJ: Prentice-Hall.

Wills, W. H., and R. D. Leonard, eds. 1995. *The Ancient Southwestern Community: Models and Methods for the Study of Prehistoric Social Organization.* Albuquerque: University of New Mexico Press.

Woosley, A. I., and J. C. Ravesloot, eds. 1995. *Culture and Contact: Charles C. DiPeso's Gran Chichimeca.* Albuquerque: University of New Mexico Press.

Yarnell, R. A. 1965. "Early Woodland Plant Remains and the Question of Cultivation." *The Florida Archaeologist* 18:78–81.

Yerkes, R. W. 1988. "The Woodland and Mississippian Traditions in the Prehistory of Midwestern North America." *Journal of World Prehistory* 2(3):307–58.

NOTES

1. Yerkes, "The Woodland and Mississippian Traditions in the Prehistory of Midwestern North America," pp. 311–12.

2. Fritz, "Multiple Ways to Farming in Precontact Eastern North America."

3. Riley, Edging, and Rossen, "Cultigens in Prehistoric North America."

4. Yerkes, "The Woodland and Mississippian Traditions in the Prehistory of Midwestern North America."

5. Smith, "Middle Mississippi Exploitation of Animal Populations"; Smith, "The Role of *Chenopodium* as a Domesticate in the Pre-Maize Garden System of the Eastern United States," p. 32.

6. Smith, *The Rivers of Change: Essays on Early Agriculture in Eastern North America*, pp. 102–106.

7. Smith, *The Rivers of Change: Essays on Early Agriculture in Eastern North America*, p. 106.

8. Asch and Asch, "Prehistoric Plant Cultivation in West-Central Illinois."

9. Fritz, "Multiple Ways to Farming in Precontact Eastern North America," p. 399.

10. Smith, *The Rivers of Change: Essays on Early Agriculture in Eastern North America*, p. 107

11. Ibid.

12. O'Brien, "Sedentism, Population Growth, and Resource Selection in the Woodland Midwest: A Review of Coevolutionary Developments."

13. Rindos, *The Origins of Agriculture.*

14. O'Brien, "Sedentism, Population Growth, and Resource Selection in the Woodland Midwest: A Review of Coevolutionary Developments," p. 186; also see Keegan, ed., *Emergent Horticultural Economies of the Eastern Woodlands.*

15. Braun, "Pots as Tools," and "Comment on M. J. O'Brien, 'Sedentism, Population Growth, and Resource Selection in the Woodland Midwest: A Review of Coevolutionary Developments.' "

16. Braun, "Comment on M. J. O'Brien, 'Sedentism, Population Growth, and Resource Selection in the Woodland Midwest: A Review of Coevolutionary Developments,' " p. 189.

17. Braun and Plog, "Evolution of 'Tribal' Social Networks: Theory and Prehistoric North American Evidence."

18. Fowler, "Agriculture and Village Settlement in the North American East: The Central Mississippi Valley Area, a Case History."

19. Price, and Feinman, eds., *Foundations of Social Inequality*.

20. Stoltman, *Prehistoric Mound Builders of the Mississippi Valley*; Marquardt, "Complexity and Scale in the Study of Fisher-Gatherer-Hunters"; Rothschild, "Mortuary Behavior and Social Organization at Indian Knoll and Dickson Mounds."

21. Yerkes, "The Woodland and Mississippian Traditions in the Prehistory of Midwestern North America," p. 315.

22. Fiedel, *Prehistory of the Americas*, p. 111

23. Fagan, *Ancient North America*, p. 331.

24. Ibid.

25. Farnsworth and Emerson, *Early Woodland Archaeology*; Morse and Morse, *Archaeology of the Central Mississippi Valley*.

26. Murphy, *An Archaeological History of the Hocking Valley*, pp. 161–63; Yerkes, "The Woodland and Mississippian Traditions in the Prehistory of Midwestern North America," p. 317.

27. Yerkes, "The Woodland and Mississippian Traditions in the Prehistory of Midwestern North America," p. 317.

28. Brown, "Long-term Trends to Sedentism and the Emergence of Complexity in the American Midwest," p. 219.

29. Coe, Snow, and Benson, *Atlas of Ancient America*, p. 50.

30. Bush, "A Ceramic Analysis of the Late Adena Buckmeyer Site"; Baby and Langlois, "Prehistoric Agriculture," p. 3.

31. Tainter, "Social Inference and Mortuary Practices: An Experiment in Numerical Classification."

32. Dragoo, "Some Aspects of Eastern North American Prehistory: A Review," pp. 18–19.

33. Odell, *Stone Tools*.

34. Jennings, *Prehistory of North America*, p. 232.

35. Brose and Greber, *Hopewell Archaeology: The Chillicothe Conference*.

36. Yerkes, "The Woodland and Mississippian Traditions in the Prehistory of Midwestern North America," p. 323.

37. Braun, "The Social and Technological Roots of 'Late Woodland.'"

38. For recent and varied considerations of Mississippian America, see Smith, ed., *The Mississippian Emergence*.

39. Stoltman, "Ancient Peoples of the Upper Mississippi River Valley," pp. 232–33.

40. Lynott et al., "Stable Carbon Isotopic Evidence for Maize Agriculture in Southeast Missouri and Northeast Arkansas."

41. Reviewed by Brown, Kerber, and Winters, in Smith, *The Mississippian Emergence*.

42. Porter, *The Mitchell Site and Prehistoric Exchange Systems at Cahokia: A.D. 1000–300*. See also Yerkes, "The Woodland and Mississippian Traditions in the Prehistory of Midwestern North America."

43. Pauketat and Emerson, "The Ideology of Authority and the Power of the Pot," p. 935.

44. Milner, "The Late Prehistoric Cahokia Cultural System of the Mississippi River Valley: Foundations, Florescence, and Fragmentation," p. 2; also Smith "The Archaeology of the Southeastern United States: From Dalton to de Soto, 10,500–500 B.P."

45. Peebles, "Moundville and Surrounding Sites."

46. Steponaitis, *Ceramics, Chronology, and Community Patterns: An Archaeological Study at Moundville*.

47. Jennings, *Prehistory of North America*, p. 256.

48. Smith, "Middle Mississippi Exploitation of Animal Populations—A Predictive Model."

49. Clark et al., "The Evolution of Mycobacterial Disease in Human Populations."

50. Dickson, "The Yanomamo of the Mississippi Valley? Some Reflections on Larson . . . Gibson . . . and Mississippi Period Warfare in the Southeastern United States."

51. Fagan, *Ancient North America*, p. 338.

52. Yerkes, "The Woodland and Mississippian Traditions in the Prehistory of Midwestern North America," p. 346.

53. Stewart, *The People of America*.

54. Le Page du Pratz.

55. Ramenofsky, *Vectors of Death*.

56. Minnis, *Social Adaptation to Food Stress*.

57. See, for example, Redman, *People of the Tonto Rim: Archaeological Discovery in Prehistoric Arizona*.

58. For example, Cordell and Gumerman, eds., *Dynamics of Southwest Prehistory*; Wills and Leonard, eds., *The Ancient Southwestern Community: Models and Methods for the Study of Prehistoric Social Organization*.

59. Woosley and Ravesloot, *Culture and Contact*.

60. Upham, "Nomads of the Desert West."

61. Crown, *Ceramics and Ideology: Salado Polychrome Pottery*.

62. Cordell, *Prehistory of the Southwest*; Simmons, "New Evidence for the Early Use of Cultigens in the American Southwest."

63. Minnis, "Earliest Plant Cultivation in the Desert Borderlands of North America," pp. 128–29.

64. See, e.g., Schiffer, "Hohokam Chronology."

65. Haury, *The Hohokam Desert Farmers and Craftsmen*.

66. Crown, "The Hohokam of the American Southwest"; Crown and Judge, *Chaco and Hohokam: Regional Systems in the American Southwest*.

67. Washburn, "The American Southwest," p. 124.

68. Reviewed in Cordell, *Prehistory of the Southwest.*

69. Jett and Moyle, "The Exotic Origins of Fishes Depicted on Prehistoric Mimbres Pottery from New Mexico."

70. Lightfoot and Feinman, "Social Differentiation and Leadership Development in Early Pithouse Villages in the Mogollon Region of the American Southwest," p. 81.

71. Minnis, *Social Adaptation to Food Stress.*

72. Whalen, "Cultural-Ecological Aspects of the Pithouse-to-Pueblo Transition in a Portion of the Southwest."

73. McGuire and Schiffer, "A Theory of Architectural Design."

74. Plog, "Political and Economic Alliances on the Colorado Plateaus, A.D. 400 to 1450."

75. Powell, *Mobility and Adaptation: The Anasazi of Black Mesa, Arizona.*

76. Dickson, "Settlement Pattern Stability and Change in the Middle Northern Rio Grande Region, New Mexico: A Test of Some Hypotheses."

77. Washburn, "The American Southwest," p. 114; but see Rice, "A Systematic Explanation of a Change in Mogollon Settlement Patterns."

78. Vivian, *The Chacoan Prehistory of the San Juan Basin.*

79. Reviewed in Vivian, *The Chacoan Prehistory of the San Juan Basin.*

16

PREHISTORY IN PERSPECTIVE

. . . what's past is prologue.

Shakespeare[1]

Having been led from the three-million-year-old hominid footprints of Laetoli through the sixteenth century A.D. European invasion of the Americas,
the reader is invited to return to the questions posed in the first chapter:
Does the world's archaeological record tell us why history has turned out as it has
and what the human future likely will be? Does the human past appear to have some
"meaning" that transcends the sum of the individual lives of the billions of people
who have comprised humanity? What does the past mean? Or, more precisely, how
are we to understand the past? Who owns the past, in the sense of who gathers evidence about it and interprets it?

These are, of course, the questions of the ages, and by now the reader will not
expect a clear, complete, ultimate answer from archaeology or this book.

Although it is perhaps a bad pedagogical tactic to raise important questions, review the evidence, and then conclude with "we're not really sure," most contemporary archaeologists find themselves in this position. We have a general sense of some
of the potentially important causes of various ancient cultural changes, but there is
no single, powerful, comprehensive explanation of the past. Thus, rather than demonstrating the power and accuracy of any specific models of culture and history, we have
simply explored the limitations and potentials of some of the more obvious explanations of the past. Moreover, as we have seen, the very possibility of a unified, objective, "scientific" understanding or explanation of the past has been rejected by some
archaeologists and questioned by most.

One of the earliest casualties of our review here was the Enlightenment and
nineteenth-century view of mechanical cultural evolutionism, with its belief in the
gradual improvement of people and their societies, generation after generation, as
we "progressed" from rude, murderous savagery to the better, brighter world of industry, liberalism, and democracy. The Victorian proponents of cultural evolutionism—who number among their ranks some of the greatest intellects of all time—
can be forgiven, perhaps, for this belief in progress, because they lived in an age of
marvelous change and an enormous expansion of human knowledge. Just Darwin's
insights alone revolutionized the way people viewed the world, themselves, and the

past. It is not surprising that the idea of a science of history had its greatest appeal to people of the late nineteenth century, for throughout their lives they saw "progress" in almost every kind of human endeavor. Consider, for example, the changes in both technology and dominant ideologies witnessed by someone like Oliver Wendell Holmes, Jr. (1841–1935), the great American jurist: Holmes wrote his senior thesis at Harvard in the quiet provincial America of the decade before Abraham Lincoln's election to the presidency, he then served in the Civil War (in many ways the first "modern" war), and in later life broadcast on the radio during Franklin Roosevelt's presidency. Holmes and others of his generation saw a world transformed by science and technology in a way that no other generation has experienced.

But, as Simone Weil said: "The great mistake of the nineteenth century was to assume that by walking straight on one mounted into the air." Two of the nineteenth century's greatest proponents of progressive evolution, Herbert Spencer and Karl Marx, today lie across from each other in death, both literally and figuratively. Their graves are on opposites sides of a gravel path in London's Highgate Cemetery. Unlike poor Herbert Spencer, Karl Marx is still remembered with red roses on his grave, but in time he will probably join Spencer in being more cited than read, and increasingly unregarded.

Yet it is difficult to discard entirely the notion of history as describing a "progressive" trajectory, leading to ourselves, and this idea is embedded in many cultures.[2] Our review of the archaeological records reveals, however, that instead of a smooth rising curve of social, physical, technological, and moral evolution, our past has been a series of fitful cycles, where social forms and technologies have reached their limits of growth and then failed, to be replaced by new social forms and technologies, more complex in some ways than their predecessors, but neither permanent nor "better" in any evident moral or philosophical sense. Clearly, there is nothing in the archaeological record to indicate that we are on a straight path to an earthly paradise. Today, two-thirds of the world's population are "involuntary vegetarians,"[3] whose diet, morbidity and mortality rates, and general standard of living compare poorly with those of most Pleistocene hunting and gathering bands; and even in the most industrialized countries, the vast majority labors longer for sustenance than did many of the people of prehistory. Moreover, the misery, poverty, wars, ethnic hatreds, and generic atrocities of our current world make it difficult for one to argue that the past shows some kind of human "moral evolution" that cannot be explained, ultimately, in terms of self-interest and Darwinian mechanics.[4]

But this lack of "progress" in the Victorian sense should not be taken as a complete indictment of the general notion of history as reflecting long-term directional change, which we can consider a form of "evolution"—and which provides the basic subject matter of archaeology. Despite repeated local reversals and long plateaus, for example, the past three million years can be seen as a patterned directional change in many aspects of humanity, from average brain-size to the complexity of cultures, as measured by changes in the size, differentiation, and interdependence of social, political, and economic systems—and by such basic dynamics as the ability to divert energy to human use, and the degree of economic interdependence of all the world's people.

Perhaps nowhere in the human past is there more convincing evidence of powerful general determinants of cultural evolution operating similarly but independently than in the appearance of early civilizations. Bruce Trigger's assessment of this situation (discussed in chapter 7) bears repeating:

> I expected to discover that, because of ecological constraints, the differences in economic systems [among early states] would be limited, and there would be more variation in sociopolitical organization, religious beliefs, and art styles. In fact, I have found that a wide variety of economic behavior was associated with early civilizations, the one constant being the production of surpluses that the upper classes appropriated through a tributary relationship. Yet I have been able to discover only one basic form of class hierarchy, two general forms of political organization, and a single basic religious paradigm. . . . I have documented significant variation from one early civilization to another only in terms of art styles and cultural values.[5]

Clearly, the world's archaeological record cannot be understood accurately as the reflection simply of the vagaries of human intentions or of unrelated and random cultural constructs. We have identified many patterns and parallels. Cross-cutting cultural developments all over the world are the same essential expressions of religion, warfare, population growth, emerging social stratification, and evolving economic productivity.

But when we try to break apart the *causal* processes that produced the past, we encounter complexity and great uncertainty. To take as an example something basic and apparently "simple," we have seen that human population growth has been correlated with almost every cultural transformation, from initial tool use to the appearance of industrial empires. This relationship may even be thought of as possibly causal: the rate of technological change might be linked simply to the number of minds available to solve problems and produce innovations. But this is clearly an incomplete explanation of our past. Time and time again the archaeological record discloses that the relationship between population growth and cultural change is neither consistent nor direct, and it remains for archaeologists to demonstrate the direct causal connections—if there are any—between the world's increasing population size and the specific, crucial transformations of prehistory and history.

This inability even to understand the impact of basic demographic factors on cultural change does not auger well for a deterministic science of culture and history, for basic demography would seem to be potentially the most easily understood aspect of change over time in the human past, compared to changes in technology, society, and ideology.

To consider another example of the complexity of unraveling the causal patterns of the past, the recurrent nature of human interspecies violence—from the cannibalism of some of our early hominid ancestors to World War II—clearly suggests that conflict is an evolutionary mechanism of considerable power; conflict must do something for societies, or it would be difficult to explain its depressing ubiquity in human affairs. But here, too, the actual mechanisms in most past societies whereby conflict interacted with other variables to produce cultural change are unknown.

In general, there appears to be nothing inevitable or even predictable about the specifics of ancient cultural change. It is the nature of evolutionary patterns that they only appear to have a direction when one looks backward. Ivy Compton-Burnett observed that "real life seems to have no plots," and in the same sense, evolutionary histories have no plots, except in retrospect. The first hunter-gatherers who made wild wheat part of their diet, for example, could have had no inkling their activities would eventually lead to vast stretches of North America being devoted to highly mechanized cultivation of distant genetic descendants of those wild Southwest Asian cereals; nor could those Neolithic foragers have *intentionally* generated the variability needed by evolutionary processes to produce agricultural economies—the random genetic variations that provided the basis for more productive, more reliable, more harvestable wheat.

We can look back and discern many similar evolutionary sequences in the past— the rise in human ability to divert energy to their own uses, for example, as exemplified in the changes between the first cloven rock and the appearance of industrial capitalism. To identify a long span of connections that link these developments, however, is not the same as *explaining* history, of course. No general theory of explaining our long evolutionary history has won universal acceptance. Most archaeologists employ a vaguely evolutionary perspective: they assume that cultural innovations are constantly arising in human societies, and that some of these innovations confer an adaptive advantage and are "fixed" within cultural systems and perpetuated until they too are outmoded and replaced. Many archaeologists also adopt a rather "vulgar" materialist determinism in that they assume that cultural forms and dynamics are to some extent constrained and shaped by technological, environmental, and economic variables. Great cities like Babylon could not have arisen in pre-industrial Alaska, and there seems to be no great mystery that the first productive agricultural economies appeared in fertile, easily farmed river valleys close to the natural habitat of the wild ancestors of domesticated plants. Such contrasting cultural forms as the social egalitarianism of hunters and gatherers in the Pleistocene and the rigid social stratification of emerging states are generally understood in part as results of their respective economic bases. Nonetheless, many contemporary archaeologists see such links between primary economics and environments and socioeconomic and political systems as only the starting points of analysis. Most now recognize that even if they are able to demonstrate a strong correlation in time and space between, say, population growth, warfare, and urbanism, they will still not have explained in a powerful way any of these factors or their relationships to each other.

In the face of these analytical ambiguities, many contemporary archaeologists have become profoundly *sociological* and *behavioral* in their theoretical approach, in the sense that they have focused on the ways people and societies have culturally constructed the specifics of their socioeconomic and political systems and ideologies. In previous chapters we have reviewed many attempts to analyze and interpret the social structures, dynamics, and ideologies of extinct societies. A great variety of sociological and political theories have been developed to explain how different cultures used the same organizational mechanisms to produce the worldwide and historical patterns we see in power relations, ethnicity, gender relationships, social reproduction, etc.

In contrast to these approaches, as we noted in previous chapters, other scholars have argued that it is not possible to formulate a true science of the behavior of extinct peoples, and that the long chains of inference that must be constructed to link the existing archaeological remains with such concepts as "class conflict" and "political domination" cannot be measured in the archaeological record and treated scientifically. Robert Dunnell argues that archaeology can never be a science of *behavior*, because behavior does not exist—artifacts exist; and because any science must deal with phenomena, a scientific archaeology must deal with artifacts, not with inferred behavior. Yet such a science of artifacts cannot be like physics, Dunnell has argued, because the artifactual record is primarily one created by evolutionary processes, in contrast to the uniform timeless laws that govern the physical universe.

Dunnell and numerous other scholars[6] are investigating applications of Darwinian evolutionary theory to history and humanity, and recent advances in such related fields as "complexity theory" and "chaos theory," and in studies of artificial intelligence, may eventually have great impact on the theory of archaeology. One interesting current trend in these forms of evolutionary analyses involves nonlinear systems analyses and the "emergent properties" of complex systems.[7] The recent book *Complexity*[8] relates research done by physicists, biologists, anthropologists, and others on simple systems that grow in complexity by processes that are not clearly understood. The most vivid example is that of biological organisms, such as ourselves, in which somehow there is a complete set of information in our genes such that as we are formed from the division of a single cell, subsequent cells are formed into skin, hair, bones, blood, and all the other tissues and organs that comprise us. We cannot draw an accurate and direct analogy between the formation of a human being and the evolution of an ancient state, but in each of these systems there is a growing complexity that seems in some sense inherent in the simpler earlier stages of these processes of evolution—a "Lamarckian" sense of evolution, in other words, instead of simply a Darwinian one.

But, as we have noted (chapter 1), attempts to make archaeology into a Darwinian or positivist science of any kind have been dismissed by other archaeologists, who reject the entire notion that "science" has any application to the explanation of the past—arguing that archaeology can never be a neutral, value-free, empirical science of artifacts. As discussed in chapter 1, the "post-processualists"[9] and others have argued that, just as one cannot assign a definitive single meaning to a text, one cannot make an empirically verifiable and definitive interpretation of the archaeological record. We create the past, they argue, and our interpretations of the past are limited by, and arise out of, our own cultural context. As discussed in chapter 1 and elsewhere, some contemporary archaeologists believe that there is no one "past," rather there is a continuing dialectical process in which each person confronts the past and comes to a unique understanding of it.

The general perspective taken in this book—a "holistic" approach, to use Bruce Trigger's phrase (chapter 1), or "cognitive processualism," to use Colin Renfrew and John Bintliff's term[10] (chapter 1)—may seem like a sensible moderate course. In this kind of archaeology one can use any analytical techniques that seem to increase understanding of the past, and one need not shrink from non-scientific interpretations of ancient ideologies on the one hand, or abandon scientific rigor in evaluating evidence and competing hypotheses on the other. But to many post-processualists, positivist science has *no* place in archaeology beyond technical applications (for example, radiocarbon dating), and to Darwinian evolutionists and other scientifically inclined archaeologists, the non-scientific interpretations of ancient ideologies and "meanings" may be a form of personal expression or art, but it is not scientific analysis.

These theoretical debates will no doubt continue for many years to come. In the meantime most archaeologists will do what they have always done, whatever their theoretical perspective, and that is to study the remains of the past—struggling to understand what they meant to the people of the past as well as what they mean to the archaeologist.

Bill Nye described Wagner's music as "better than it sounds," and in a way archaeology is like this: its limitations are obvious, but its achievements are also obvious: we understand human antiquity today to an extent unimaginable just a century ago. There is no need to review in detail the archaeological information we have considered in earlier chapters about early hominid taxonomy, Paleolithic technologies, the origins of domestication and agriculture, the rise of cultural complexity, and the many other prehistoric transformations that only a century ago were not even recognized, let alone analyzed and understood as they are today. The larger question, however, is: What is the significance of this knowledge? And on that question archaeologists profoundly disagree with one another.

LESSONS OF PREHISTORY?

> To think of time—of all that retrospection,
> To think of to-day, and the ages continued henceforward.
> Have you guess'd you yourself would not continue?
> Have you dreaded these earth-beetles?
> Is to-day nothing? is the beginningless past nothing?
> If the future is nothing they are just as surely nothing.
> *Walt Whitman*[11]

It would be gratifying if we could extract from our review of world prehistory some important predictions about the future of humankind, but, as we have noted, archaeology should not be considered a predictive science. It is not that we cannot look at the past and extrapolate trends we see into the future, it is that there is no *necessity* to these trends: evolutionary histories are what happened, not what had to happen or what has to happen, and they are unique.

This is especially true when we consider the long-range future, particularly now that humanity has instruments with which to terminate all life on this planet. But even should we survive as a species for millions of future generations, the virtuosity of culture as an adaptive device makes extrapolation into the far future an act of either ignorance or hubris. None of the human ancestors who strolled through Olduvai Gorge some Sunday morning two million years ago could have had even the dimmest vision of the gaudy technology and kaleidoscopic social and political forms of twentieth-century civilization, and this civilization was not a necessary outcome of our Olduvai forebears.

But, is there *any* sense in which Shakespeare's phrase, "what's past is prologue," is true? Shakespeare's point is less obvious than it might seem. *Of course* what's past is prologue, in the sense that everything in life comes *after* something, but Shakespeare was asserting that the past sets the stage for the future in the same way that the prologue of a play introduces the *dramatis personae*, the characters who are the instruments of the playwright's themes and plot dynamics.

So, we now consider whether or not, and to what extent, if any, the human past is really a prologue in the sense that it sets the stage and reveals the character and dynamics of what is to come.

No student of the past can overlook the persistent, powerful trends that tie the present—and perhaps the future—to the past. These trends extend beyond the simple cumulative increases in world population density and the technology of energy capture. The increasing functional differentiation and integration of the world's economies and societies can be seen in any food market, any airport. It may seem like a tenuous link between the development of, say, the Levallois technique (chapter 4), which made stone tool-making more efficient 150,000 years ago and allowed human radiation into more demanding environments, and today's rapidly mutating and invading Internet world electronic information system, but they are both part of an increasing "complexity" of human society and adaptation.

Nor are these changes just technological. In chapter 1 the Darwinian revolution in world- and life-views was discussed, but there is no reason to suspect that any ideology will be the final, definitive perspective for all humanity. Consider, for example, religion. I will let those with more confidence in their omniscience than myself pronounce on the ultimate nature of human religiosity; it is always sobering to recollect that neither the study of world prehistory nor any other art or science has much to offer in the way of a reason why we are out here, on a small planet in an incomprehensibly infinite universe, and to all evidence very much alone. Nonetheless, taken solely on the level of its effects on other aspects of culture, religion appears to operate principally as a highly adaptable, thermodynamically efficient mechanism of social control. We have in the archaeological and historical record an irrefutable demonstration that there is no act so repellent—be it sacrificing thousands of one's own countrymen to the gods or incinerating hundreds of thousands of one's "enemies"— that it cannot be made not only acceptable, but entirely virtuous within the context of religious systems. The exploitation of the many by the few to build massive pyramids, the complete catalogue of sexual "perversions," the avoidance of this or that food—all have been incorporated into state religions with no more difficulty than Christian faith, hope, and charity.

The recent wars in Bosnia, central Africa, Algeria, and elsewhere illustrate that, despite the apparent decline of formal theistic religions in some parts of the industrialized world, the power of ideology to set societies into conflict has not changed. These conflicts may stem in part from long-term underlying economic forces, but no observer of modern politics can help but be profoundly impressed by the awesome power of *ideas* about history and ethnicity to stimulate both genocide against one's perceived enemies and identification with one's kin (e.g., Rwanda, 1995–96).

The competitive advantage, as always, will lie with cultures that evolve belief systems that motivate people in specific, "efficient" directions, as is well illustrated in centuries past by the link between capitalism and Calvinism, and irrigation agriculture and the Sumerian pantheon. Marx thought organized religion would disappear with the advent of democracy and social equality, and only the future will tell if he was right; but even if secularism eventually embraces the world, an ideology of humanism that is very much like a religion is likely to take its place.

The late-twentieth-century societies of the West are almost obsessed with social and economic inequalities, and it would be significant if the study of world prehistory had anything to tell us about the future of differences in class, gender, and ethnicity. But the lessons of the archaeological record concerning the origins and significance of social and economic inequalities are not as clear as they might seem at first glance. It is inescapable that there has never been an economically powerful, sociopolitically complex society—especially the supposedly "classless" societies of Marxist Russia and China—that was not also stratified into groups having differential access to wealth, power, and prestige. It remains to be demonstrated, however, that cultural functional complexity and integration are inextricably linked to social stratification. It would appear that in the past the complexity of managing an economy based on agriculture, and later agriculture in combination with fossil fuels, could work effectively only through administrative and social hierarchies and class-structured societies. These social and cultural forms allowed great stability and predictability because peoples' functional roles in society and their contributions and consumption of goods and services were largely determined by the class into which they were born. But if in future centuries population densities are stabilized and perhaps reduced, if control of energy and food sources is decentralized and the production of material wealth made highly automated, it would seem at least possible that human societies will someday approximate the "social justice" of the late Pleistocene.

Perhaps the archaeological record's bleakest implication concerning our short-term future has to do with that ambiguous concept, "the quality of life." We have already noted that today most of the world's people have a diet and standard of living in many ways inferior to that of Pleistocene hunters and gatherers, and although medical technology, solar power, and contraceptives may change this by bringing the Western industrial standard of living to all parts of the world, this is by no means a certainty. Even given sufficient energy and rapid industrialization, fundamental questions remain about the short-term prospects for the quality of life on this planet. In the wealthiest countries today the abundance of luxury goods seems to convey a sense of ease and fulfillment, but modern economies work only because the vast majority of the population are coerced or induced to spend most of their lives at hard labor. And it is not only the poorer, laboring class whose quality of life is questionable. It has been observed that a citizen of Athens in the fifth century B.C. would consider today's professionals—physicians, politicians, professors, and football players alike—to be in the main incomplete, undeveloped people whose "success" has required them to devote so much of their lives to their specialty that they are grotesquely incompetent at the oratorical, conversational, athletic, philosophical, agricultural, and aesthetic skills that the ancient Greeks, for example, would insist on as necessary components of a "whole" person.

The past often takes on a rosy, romantic coloring from the perspective of the complexities and frustrations of the present, and we cannot ignore the illiteracy, warfare, and gross social exploitation that appear to be the very warp and woof of every ancient complex society, including ancient Athens. But many people feel that modern social and economic systems, whether they be capitalistic or socialistic, do not provide optimal environments for the balanced, liberal, personal development of the majority. Charles Darwin wrote: "Life in the crowded conditions of cities has many unattractive features, but in the long run these may be overcome, not so much by altering them, but simply by changing the human race into liking them."

Gloomy ruminations of this sort have a way of showing up in succeeding centuries as quaint quotations demonstrating the curious myopia of past generations, and I devoutly hope it will be so in this case. But despite the many advantages of modern technology, the long-term trend seems inexorably in the direction of greater specialization and compartmentalization of people, with consequent increasing alienation and frustration. How pleasant a society may be to live in has depressingly little to do with that society's evolutionary potential. As Jean-Paul Sartre complained, "Everything has been figured out except how to live."

It is one thing to chart apparent evolutionary trends in the human past and try to extrapolate from them to the future, but it is quite another to try to effect change in these trends. Social reformers in general might find the lessons of the archaeological record somewhat bleak. Complex societies are by definition complex systems, and the strong parallels in social forms that have evolved over the world in the past ten thousand years suggest, perhaps, that human social systems may not be easily changed for the better by altering selected variables, even with the best of intentions and enormous resources.

THE FUTURE OF ARCHAEOLOGY

When I was a boy of fourteen, my father was so ignorant I could hardly stand to have the old man around. But when I got to be twenty-one, I was astonished at how much the old man had learned in seven years.

Mark Twain

The energy produced by the breaking down of the atom is a very poor kind of thing. Anyone who expects a source of power from the transformation of these atoms is talking moonshine.

Ernest Rutherford (1871–1937), physicist, after he had split the atom for the first time[12]

History teaches us that it is often a fundamental mistake to extrapolate immediate experience and situations far into the future. Contemporary archaeology and the historical disciplines are in such a state of flux and ideological rivalry that we may have no sense of what these fields of inquiry will be like in a century or two.

In any case, the archaeological record is disappearing at such a rapid rate that the future of field archaeology on the problems of prehistory is very much in doubt. The worldwide wave of industrialism—the major destroyer of archaeological materials—seems destined to expand at ever-increasing speed.

Dismal as the loss of the archaeological record is, it may be that the major progress in archaeology in the next several generations will come not so much from the discovery of new bones and stones, but rather from a reconsideration of theoretical and methodological approaches and a re-analysis of existing data. We have recounted in this book the prospects of current analytical approaches, and these and other perspectives are likely to increase considerably our knowledge about our past. Does this mean that the general problem of, for example, the origins of cultural complexity will someday be as precisely solved as the formulae for making plastics? Probably not. These are very different kinds of questions with different criteria for solution. Yet, the history of science is replete with examples in which a seemingly impossible problem was not only solved but made routine: the general problems of prehistory we have discussed here may well fall into this category, to be solved in succeeding centuries in terms and with techniques which we now only dimly perceive. After all, people of only a few centuries ago no doubt would be astounded not only by our science and lush technology, but also by our knowledge of prehistory and the dynamics of culture.

BIBLIOGRAPHY

Alexander, R. D. 1987. *The Biology of Moral Systems*. Hawthorne, NY: Aldine de Gruyter.

Bintliff, J. 1986. "Archaeology at the Interface: An Historical Perspective." In *Archaeology at the Interface*, eds. J. L. Bintliff and C. F. Gaffney. Oxford: BAR International Series 300.

———. 1993. "Why Indiana Jones Is Smarter Than the Post-Processualists." *Norwegian Archaeological Review* 26(2):91–100.

Dunnell, R. C. 1982. "Science, Social Science, and Common Sense: The Agonizing Dilemma of Modern Archaeology." *Journal of Anthropological Research* 38:1–25.

———. 1992. "Is a Scientific Archaeology Possible?" In *Metaarchaeology*, ed. L. Embre, pp. 73–97. The Netherlands: Kluver.

Durham, W. H. 1990. "Advances in Evolutionary Culture Theory." *Annual Review of Anthropology* 19:187–242.

Gamble, C. 1994. *Timewalkers: The Prehistory of Global Colonization*. Cambridge, MA: Harvard University Press.

Harris, M. 1977. *Cannibals and Kings: The Origins of Cultures*. New York: Random House.

Hern, W. M. 1993. "Is Human Culture Carcinogenic for Uncontrolled Population Growth and Ecological Destruction?" *Bioscience* 43(11):768–73.

Hodder, I. Shanks, M., Alexandri, A., Buchli, V., Carman, J., Last, J., and Lucas, G. 1995. *Interpreting Archaeology: Finding Meaning in the Past*. New York: Routledge.

Lansing, J. S. and J. N. Kremer. 1993. "Emergent Properties of Balinese Water Temple Networks." *American Anthropologist* 95(1):97–114.

Neiman, F. D. 1995. "Stylistic Variation in Evolutionary Perspective: Inferences from Decorative Diversity and Interassemblage Distance in Illinois Woodland Ceramic Assemblages." *American Antiquity* 60(1): 7–36.

Pile, S. 1979. *The Book of Heroic Failure.* London: Macdonald Futura Publishers.

Shanks, M., et al. 1995. *Interpreting Archaeology: Finding Meaning in the Past.* New York: Routledge.

Trigger, B. 1991. "Distinguished Lecture in Archaeology: Constraint and Freedom." *American Anthropologist* 93(3):551–69.

———. 1993. *Early Civilizations: Ancient Egypt in Context.* Cairo: American University in Cairo Press.

Waldrop, M. M. 1992. *Complexity.* New York: Touchstone.

NOTES

1. Shakespeare, *The Tempest*, act II, scene I.

2. Gamble, *Timewalkers: The Prehistory of Global Colonization.*

3. Harris, *Cannibals and Kings*, p. x.

4. Durham, "Advances in Evolutionary Culture Theory."

5. Trigger, *Early Civilizations: Ancient Egypt in Context*, p. 110.

6. See, for example, Dunnell, "Science, Social Science, and Common Sense: The Agonizing Dilemma of Modern Archaeology," and "Is a Scientific Archaeology Possible?"; also see Neiman, "Stylistic Variation in Evolutionary Perspective: Inferences from Decorative Diversity and Interassemblage Distance in Illinois Woodland Ceramic Assemblages."

7. Lansing and Kremer ("Emergent Properties of Balinese Water Temple Networks"), for example, have published one of the first applications of these ideas to an anthropological problem, the evolution of Balinese economic systems.

8. Waldrop, *Complexity.*

9. See, for example, Shanks et al., *Interpreting Archaeology: Finding Meaning in the Past.*

10. See, for example, Bintliff, "Archaeology at the Interface," and "Why Indiana Jones Is Smarter than the Post-Processualists."

11. From Whitman's "To Think of Time."

12. Quoted by Pile, *The Book of Heroic Failure*, p. 216

ART CREDITS

INDEX

Note: Page numbers in **bold** refer to illustrations and captions.